T0180493

Lecture Notes in Computer Science   10635

Commenced Publication in 1973
Founding and Former Series Editors:
Gerhard Goos, Juris Hartmanis, and Jan van Leeuwen

More information about this series at http://www.springer.com/series/7407

Derong Liu · Shengli Xie
Yuanqing Li · Dongbin Zhao
El-Sayed M. El-Alfy (Eds.)

Neural
Information Processing

24th International Conference, ICONIP 2017
Guangzhou, China, November 14–18, 2017
Proceedings, Part II

 Springer

Editors
Derong Liu
Guangdong University of Technology
Guangzhou
China

Shengli Xie
Guangdong University of Technology
Guangzhou
China

Yuanqing Li
South China University of Technology
Guangzhou
China

Dongbin Zhao
Institute of Automation
Chinese Academy of Sciences
Beijing
China

El-Sayed M. El-Alfy
King Fahd University of Petroleum
  and Minerals
Dhahran
Saudi Arabia

ISSN 0302-9743   ISSN 1611-3349 (electronic)
Lecture Notes in Computer Science
ISBN 978-3-319-70095-3   ISBN 978-3-319-70096-0 (eBook)
https://doi.org/10.1007/978-3-319-70096-0

Library of Congress Control Number: 2017957558

LNCS Sublibrary: SL1 – Theoretical Computer Science and General Issues

Printed on acid-free paper

This Springer imprint is published by Springer Nature
The registered company is Springer International Publishing AG
The registered company address is: Gewerbestrasse 11, 6330 Cham, Switzerland

Preface

ICONIP 2017 – the 24th International Conference on Neural Information Processing – was held in Guangzhou, China, continuing the ICONIP conference series, which started in 1994 in Seoul, South Korea. Over the past 24 years, ICONIP has been held in Australia, China, India, Japan, Korea, Malaysia, New Zealand, Qatar, Singapore, Thailand, and Turkey. ICONIP has now become a well-established, popular and high-quality conference series on neural information processing in the region and around the world. With the growing popularity of neural networks in recent years, we have witnessed an increase in the number of submissions and in the quality of papers. Guangzhou, Romanized as Canton in the past, is the capital and largest city of southern China's Guangdong Province. It is also one of the five National Central Cities at the core of the Pearl River Delta. It is a key national transportation hub and trading port. November is the best month in the year to visit Guangzhou with comfortable weather. All participants of ICONIP 2017 had a technically rewarding experience as well as a memorable stay in this great city.

A neural network is an information processing structure inspired by biological nervous systems, such as the brain. It consists of a large number of highly interconnected processing elements, called neurons. It has the capability of learning from example. The field of neural networks has evolved rapidly in recent years. It has become a fusion of a number of research areas in engineering, computer science, mathematics, artificial intelligence, operations research, systems theory, biology, and neuroscience. Neural networks have been widely applied for control, optimization, pattern recognition, image processing, signal processing, etc.

ICONIP 2017 aimed to provide a high-level international forum for scientists, researchers, educators, industrial professionals, and students worldwide to present state-of-the-art research results, address new challenges, and discuss trends in neural information processing and applications. ICONIP 2017 invited scholars in all areas of neural network theory and applications, computational neuroscience, machine learning, and others.

The conference received 856 submissions from 3,255 authors in 56 countries and regions across all six continents. Based on rigorous reviews by the Program Committee members and reviewers, 563 high-quality papers were selected for publication in the conference proceedings. We would like to express our sincere gratitude to all the reviewers for the time and effort they generously gave to the conference. We are very grateful to the Institute of Automation of the Chinese Academy of Sciences, Guangdong University of Technology, South China University of Technology, Springer's *Lecture Notes in Computer Science* (LNCS), IEEE/CAA *Journal of Automatica Sinica* (JAS), and the Asia Pacific Neural Network Society (APNNS) for their financial support. We would also like to thank the publisher, Springer, for their cooperation in publishing the proceedings in the prestigious LNCS series and for sponsoring the best paper awards at ICONIP 2017.

September 2017   Derong Liu
                                                                                      Shengli Xie
                                                                                     Yuanqing Li
                                                                                    Dongbin Zhao
                                                                                El-Sayed M. El-Alfy

ICONIP 2017 Organization

Asia **P**acific **N**eural **N**etwork **S**ociety

General Chair

Derong Liu   Chinese Academy of Sciences and Guangdong University of Technology, China

Advisory Committee

Sabri Arik	Istanbul University, Turkey
Tamer Basar	University of Illinois, USA
Dimitri Bertsekas	Massachusetts Institute of Technology, USA
Jonathan Chan	King Mongkut's University of Technology, Thailand
C.L. Philip Chen	The University of Macau, SAR China
Kenji Doya	Okinawa Institute of Science and Technology, Japan
Minyue Fu	The University of Newcastle, Australia
Tom Gedeon	Australian National University, Australia
Akira Hirose	The University of Tokyo, Japan
Zeng-Guang Hou	Chinese Academy of Sciences, China
Nikola Kasabov	Auckland University of Technology, New Zealand
Irwin King	Chinese University of Hong Kong, SAR China
Robert Kozma	University of Memphis, USA
Soo-Young Lee	Korea Advanced Institute of Science and Technology, South Korea
Frank L. Lewis	University of Texas at Arlington, USA
Chu Kiong Loo	University of Malaya, Malaysia
Baoliang Lu	Shanghai Jiao Tong University, China
Seiichi Ozawa	Kobe University, Japan
Marios Polycarpou	University of Cyprus, Cyprus
Danil Prokhorov	Toyota Technical Center, USA
DeLiang Wang	The Ohio State University, USA
Jun Wang	City University of Hong Kong, SAR China
Jin Xu	Peking University, China
Gary G. Yen	Oklahoma State University, USA
Paul J. Werbos	Retired from the National Science Foundation, USA

Program Chairs

Shengli Xie	Guangdong University of Technology, China
Yuanqing Li	South China University of Technology, China
Dongbin Zhao	Chinese Academy of Sciences, China
El-Sayed M. El-Alfy	King Fahd University of Petroleum and Minerals, Saudi Arabia

Program Co-chairs

Shukai Duan	Southwest University, China
Kazushi Ikeda	Nara Institute of Science and Technology, Japan
Weng Kin Lai	Tunku Abdul Rahman University College, Malaysia
Shiliang Sun	East China Normal University, China
Qinglai Wei	Chinese Academy of Sciences, China
Wei Xing Zheng	University of Western Sydney, Australia

Regional Chairs

Cesare Alippi	Politecnico di Milano, Italy
Tingwen Huang	Texas A&M University at Qatar, Qatar
Dianhui Wang	La Trobe University, Australia

Invited Session Chairs

Wei He	University of Science and Technology Beijing, China
Dianwei Qian	North China Electric Power University, China
Manuel Roveri	Politecnico di Milano, Italy
Dong Yue	Nanjing University of Posts and Telecommunications, China

Poster Session Chairs

Sung Bae Cho	Yonsei University, South Korea
Ping Guo	Beijing Normal University, China
Yifei Pu	Sichuan University, China
Bin Xu	Northwestern Polytechnical University, China
Zhigang Zeng	Huazhong University of Science and Technology, China

Tutorial and Workshop Chairs

Long Cheng	Chinese Academy of Sciences, China
Kaizhu Huang	Xi'an Jiaotong-Liverpool University, China
Amir Hussain	University of Stirling, UK

James Kwok	Hong Kong University of Science and Technology, SAR China
Huajin Tang	Sichuan University, China

Panel Discussion Chairs

Lei Guo	Beihang University, China
Hongyi Li	Bohai University, China
Hye Young Park	Kyungpook National University, South Korea
Lipo Wang	Nanyang Technological University, Singapore

Award Committee Chairs

Haibo He	University of Rhode Island, USA
Zhong-Ping Jiang	New York University, USA
Minho Lee	Kyungpook National University, South Korea
Andrew Leung	City University of Hong Kong, SAR China
Tieshan Li	Dalian Maritime University, China
Lidan Wang	Southwest University, China
Jun Zhang	South China University of Technology, China

Publicity Chairs

Jun Fu	Northeastern University, China
Min Han	Dalian University of Technology, China
Yanjun Liu	Liaoning University of Technology, China
Stefano Squartini	Università Politecnica delle Marche, Italy
Kay Chen Tan	National University of Singapore, Singapore
Kevin Wong	Murdoch University, Australia
Simon X. Yang	University of Guelph, Canada

Local Arrangements Chair

Renquan Lu	Guangdong University of Technology, China

Publication Chairs

Ding Wang	Chinese Academy of Sciences, China
Jian Wang	China University of Petroleum, China

Finance Chair

Xinping Guan	Shanghai Jiao Tong University, China

Registration Chair

Qinmin Yang   Zhejiang University, China

Conference Secretariat

Biao Luo   Chinese Academy of Sciences, China
Bo Zhao   Chinese Academy of Sciences, China

Contents

Brain-Computer Interface

Computational Finance

Deep Learning

Tree-Structure CNN for Automated Theorem Proving

Kebin Peng[✉] and Dianfu Ma

School of Computer Science and Engineering, Beihang University, Colleage Road,
Haidian District. 37, Beijing 100191, China
kebinpeng@gmail.com, madf@act.buaa.edu.cn

Abstract. The most difficult and heavy work of Automated Theorem
Proving (ATP) is that people should search in millions of intermediate
steps to finish proof. In this paper, we present a novel neural network,
which can effectively help people to finish this work. Specifically, we
design a tree-structure CNN, involving bidirectional LSTM. We compare our model with other neural network models and make experiments
on HOLStep dataset, which is a machine learning dataset for Higher-
order logic theorem proving. Being compared to previous approaches,
our model improves accuracy significantly, reaching 90% accuracy on
the test set.

1 Introduction

Automated theorem proving (ATP) is a subfield of automated reasoning and
mathematical logic. The goal of the ATP is proving that conjecture is a logical
consequence of axioms and hypotheses. The traditional way of ATP is using
first order language such as Isabelle [13], HOL [18] to build axioms and make
reasoning. For example, [15] gives a form that made by premises-conclusion
pairs. [17] introduces a way that could give procedures and intermediate steps.
Nevertheless, in ATP, the whole process is strongly depended on researcher's
experience because people need to predicting whether a statement is useful in
the proof of a given conjecture (we call this process: premise selection). And
there are dozens of thousands of statement. All the thing that computer can do
is helping people to complete the logical inference. Meanwhile, although formal
proof requires couples of person-years, which is highly time-consuming, the result
is not well: the formal proof still cannot prove complex system [10].

In recent years, machine learning becomes a popular technology to solve ATP
problems [2,4]. Such as [11], provides a method that using machine learning to
build a ATP system. In [5], the author provides us a dataset named: HolStep.
This dataset is a machine learning dataset for ATP. At the same time [5] demonstrate state-of-the-art performance on HolStep, reaching 85% accuracy. But there
is no generalizability of the results. Because this model ignores the most basic
feature of ATP: recursion.

So in this paper, we are going to join recursion with Convolutional neural network, helping people deciding intermediate steps. We introduce the elementary

© Springer International Publishing AG 2017
D. Liu et al. (Eds.): ICONIP 2017, Part II, LNCS 10635, pp. 3–12, 2017.
https://doi.org/10.1007/978-3-319-70096-0_1

character—subgoal, main goal and recursion—into CNN and propose a novel neural network called Tree-structure CNN. The experimental results show that recursion is a effective way to tackle the formal proof, especially for the premise selection. Specifically, we change the traditional linear structure of CNN into Tree-structure in order to cope with recursion. In our evaluation, we run experiments in HolStep and compare our approach with four other models. The experimental results demonstrate that our model yields significant accuracy improvements compare to [5], reaching 90% accuracy on the HolStep.

The rest of this paper is organized as follows. In the Sect. 2, we will review related work. In the Sect. 3 we introduce ATP and the basic feature–recursive. This feature is the most important motivation of our paper. Our model and motivation is in Sect. 4. Experimental and results are shown in Sects. 5 and 6. At last, Discussion is in Sect. 7.

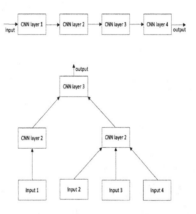

Fig. 1. Top traditional linear CNN structure. **Bottom** a tree-structure CNN with five leaf notes

2   Related Work

The combining machine learning and ATP is focused on two aspects: premise selection and strategy selection. The basic theorem proving task is premise selection. Given a number of proven facts and a conjecture to be proved, the problem that selecting the most possible facts to finish a successful proof is called premise selection [2], The task is crucial for the efficiency of the state-of-the-art automatic techniques [3]. In [9], The authors implement the SInE classifier to solve the large scale theory reasoning.

The subsequent theorem proving task is strategic selection. Strategy selection means that people use the premise to finish the proof according to a precise order. In modern ATP, for instance Vampire [11] or E [16], it includes language that can description the strategy and allow a user to specify the ordering.

At last, the machine learning method provides an effective way to help people for choosing the inference steps. In paper [1], the author raises a learning-based premise selection method that in a 50% improvement on the benchmark over the SInE, a state-of-the-art system. In paper [6] the author successfully applies it into higher-order logic proving.

3   Task Description

In a computer or mathematics system. There are some properties we think they are right. We call them axioms. For example, $rev[\ ] = [\ ]$. rev represents reverse operator for a list. $[\ ]$ is an empty list. $rev[\ ] = [\ ]$ means that reversing an empty list equal to list itself. For properties that we do not know or want to verify, such as $rev(rev\ xs) = xs$ (xs is a nonempty list), we call it conjecture. $rev(rev\ xs) = xs$ means that if we reverse a list twice, we get the original list. If we could use axioms to prove a conjecture, we call conjecture: premises. Our job is choosing a premise from a set of the premises. Because human have to specify intermediate steps in dozens of thousands of theorems, this is time-consuming work that could take a couple of years [10]. So in this paper, we give attention to the task that whether a premise is helpful to the final result. Apparently, the model of our paper is a binary conditioned classification model: If the premise is helpful for the final conclusion, it is belonging to the positive class. Otherwise belong to the negative class.

At first, we will give an example to explain what is the main goal and subgoal, the basic and important feature of formal proof. For instance, there is a list xs. We wish to prove that reverse the list twice is equal to the list itself. If we represent it formally, we could get the following equation:

$$rev(rec\ xs) = xs \tag{1}$$

rev is the action of reverse. xs is the list. This is our main goal. We seek to prove it. Firstly we are needed to prove a basic situation: an empty list. This is one of the subgoals. We can formally write it like this:

$$rev(rev[\ ]) = [\ ]. \tag{2}$$

Second, we need to prove another subgoal

$$rev(reclist) = list => rev(rev(a\#list)) = a\#list. \tag{3}$$

$a\#list$ means that take the first element from the list, for another word, take the head of the list. To prove the first subgoal, we need an axiom:

$$rev[\ ] = [\ ]. \tag{4}$$

To prove the second subgoal, we need a premise:

$$rev(xs\&ys) = (rev\ ys)\&(rev\ xs). \tag{5}$$

The symbol & means an operator, for example: #. This premise is helpful to our result, so it belong to the positive class. From this example, we can see that every time we choose a premise and make inference, we will get some new subgoals. To proof those new subgoals, we need more premises. This is a recursively process. Also, because recursion feature, the sequence of proof is important. For example, if we try to prove the second subgoal $rev(rev(a\#list)) = a\#list$. The proof would not have succeeded.

From this example, we can conclude that if we want CNN to deal with this task, CNN must has ability to deal with recursively process. Only in this way can we get a good result. Meanwhile, we know that tree-structure is a good way to deal with recursive, so we are going to design a tree-structure CNN.

4   Network Structure and Motivation

4.1   Motivation

The basic characteristic of ATP is that the proof process is a recursive process as Fig. 1 show (The bottom one). Bottom one of Fig. 1 is a tree. Every node in this tree is a goal that needs to be proofed in ATP. Specially, the root of the tree is the main goal. The leaf node of the tree is the subgoal. Proof process is searching the tree in deep first search sequence. According to this feature, we have two motivations: Firstly, we change the linear CNN structure into tree-structure. Secondly, we combine the CNN with LSTM (not show in Fig. 1). For the first motivation, we think traditional linear structure of CNN, as Fig. 1 show, could not be able to deal with the recursion very well. We therefore design a tree-structure CNN as same as the proof process. We use two CNN layers to handle the two input part, conjecture block and dependency (axiom) block, separately. Then we join those two layer's output together, as the joint note in Fig. 1. To proof the subgoal, we still need the dependency (axiom) block. So we put the dependency (axiom) block into CNN layer again. The conjecture block and dependency (axiom) block will be specifically narrated in Sect. 6.

For the second motivation, we combine LSTM with tree-structure CNN because the order is very important to ATP. There is an order relationship between the main goal and subgoals. If it is disordered, the proof process of ATP will fail. That is, the final goal cannot be proved. Due to the ability for processing order sequence, LSTM is a natural choice for our model.

The key of our model is a Tree-structure CNN, as showed in Fig. 1. Based on this hierarchical model. We can track the obvious feature of formal proof: Subgoal. Subgoal is a very common and important feature of formal proof, which we present in Sect. 4. The core idea of our model is the recursion. We try to use tree-structure to represent recursive process of ATP. In our model, recursion equal to tree-structure.

4.2   Network Structure

We are inspired by [2,5] and our model are based on the deep convolutional neural network too. Our model has two input: dependency (axiom) block and conjecture block. Our model includes one output: 0 imply that the dependency (axiom) block has no or negative relationship with the conjecture block. 1 imply that the dependency (axiom) block has a positive relationship with the conjecture block. We describe the format of input in Sect. 6 specifically.

The first layer should be word embedding layer. Word embedding layer will convert the dependency (axiom) block and conjecture block into an 256-dimensional vector. This layer has been implemented by an open source framework keras and we can use it's API directly. The specific principles are mentioned in [12]. This step is not a vital step in our model because we do not have to understand the process of word embedding. We only need the result of word embedding. Then we deal with vectors by CNN layer and maxpooling layer. The difference between our model and [2] is: We think the output of every CNN layer is the subgoal of ATP, so we try to merge the output of every CNN into a whole. After that, we use bidirectional LSTM to deal with the conjecture and LSTM deal with the dependency (axiom). At last, we choose the binary cross entropy function as loss function. We also utilize L2 regularization to prevent the overfitting. The whole structure is indicated exactly in Fig. 3.

Our key idea of this work is to enable the neural network to learn the recursive feature of ATP. In order to complete this goal, we use the tree-structure CNN. The tree-structure CNN is different from all previous works in an important aspect: previous approaches do not explicitly incorporate this recursive feature of ATP into model. So those models will generalize poorly, whereas our model incorporates recursion and will achieve perfect generalization.

5   Experiments

This dataset is made by google [2,5], which is well-suited for machine learning that are highly relevant for ATP. There are 2013046 training examples and 196030 testing examples in total. The dataset together with the description of the used format is available from: http://cl-informatik.uibk.ac.at/cek/holstep/.

The input of this data set and labeled of data is as follow: Each input file consists of a conjecture block, a number of dependency (axiom) blocks, and a number of training/testing example blocks. The conjecture block starts with an 'N' and consists of 3 lines:

N ⟨name of conjecture⟩
C ⟨text representation of the conjecture⟩
T ⟨tokenization of the conjecture⟩

Each dependency (axiom) block starts with a 'D' and consists of 3 lines:

D ⟨name of dependency (axiom)⟩
A ⟨text representation of the dependency (axiom)⟩
T ⟨tokenization of the conjecture⟩

Each training/testing example starts with the symbol + or −. where + means useful in the final proof and − not useful and consists of 2 lines:

+ ⟨text representation of the intermediate step⟩
T ⟨tokenization of the intermediate step⟩

Our model is implemented in tensorflow and keras. Each model was trained on a Nvidia 1070GTX. The complete evaluation on HolStep dataset is given in Tables 1 and 2, we run experiments on all five models in HolStep and compare our result with four other results:

1D CNN+LSTM and 1D CNN. This model is purposed by [2,5]. It is a simple but available model.

2-layer CNN+LSTM [8]. The difference between 1D CNN+LSTM and 2-layer CNN+LSTM is that there is only one input to 1D CNN+LSTM. In 2-layer CNN+LSTM, there are two input:statements and conjecture. The structure of this model is show as Fig. 2.

VGG-16. VGG-16 was purposed by Oxford Visual Geometry Group. It won the champion of ImageNet 2014. In this paper, we try to find whether this model could be used to deal with the natural language problem [14].

ResNet. ResNet is a residual learning framework to ease the training of networks that are substantially deeper than those used previously. It explicitly reformulate the layers as learning.

Residual functions with reference to the layer inputs, instead of learning unreferenced functions [7]. **Tree-structure CNN+BILSTM**. Our model tree-structure CNN and we change LSTM to bidirectional LSTM as Fig. 3 shown.

The first model only has one input: dependency (axiom) blocks. The second model includes two input: dependency (axiom) blocks and conjecture blocks. The structure of the first model is show as Fig. 2.

6   Results

At first, we compare the traditional classify approach with our model. Traditional classify approaches include: SVM, KNN, Logistic Regression. Experimental results are presented in Tables 1 and 2 (the model with * is ours). Our model yields 90% accuracy in training dataset. This shows that tree-structure CNN could deal with the recursive process well. Additionally, our model yields 85% accuracy in test dataset, 5% lower that train dataset. This difference is due to (1) lacking of training data and overfitting. (2) The dependent relationship between conjecture block and dependency (axiom) blocks is too complex. Meanwhile, SVM, KNN, Logistic Regression also do not have a good result. That is because traditional way could not deal with the recursive information. They just can measure the similarity of geometric space, such as Euclid Space.

Second, we compare other CNN models with our model. The result is showed in the Tables 3 and 4. From the Tables 3 and 4, we can conclude that the CNN models are better that traditional approach. However, the VGG-16 and ResNet (50 layers), which perform very well in ImageNet contest, do not get a satisfactory result in this dataset. This result means that there may not be generality between CV models and NLP models because the basic feature of the picture and ATP are different. So we still need to choose a suitable way for a specific task.

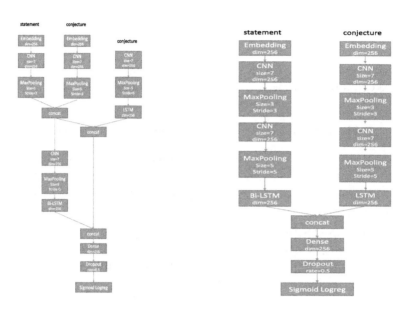

Fig. 2. Left shows the construction of our neural network. We try to involve all the output of every CNN layers into a whole. And we apply bidirection LSTM to deal with the last result. **Right** show the show the construction of [2]

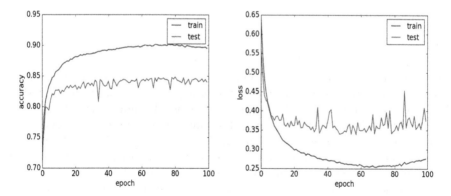

Fig. 3. Left shows the relationship between epoch and the accuracy. **Right** shows the relationship between the epoch and lost

Table 1. Train dataset.

Model	Accuracy
KNN	70.1%
SVM	72.5%
Logistic regression	63.2%
Tree-CNN+BILSTM*	90%

Table 2. Test dataset.

Model	Accuracy
KNN	68.8%
SVM	69.1%
Logistic regression	60.7%
Tree-CNN+BILSTM*	85%

Table 3. Train dataset.

Model	Accuracy
VGG-16	56.3%
ResNet(50 layers)	67.4%
CNN	81.6%
1D CNN+LSTM	82.4%
2-layer CNN+LSTM	85%
Tree-CNN+BILSTM*	90%

Table 4. Test dataset.

Model	Accuracy
VGG-16	54.7%
ResNet(50 layers)	61.2%
CNN	80.5%
1D CNN+LSTM	79.6%
2-layer CNN+LSTM	82.1%
Tree-CNN+BILSTM*	85%

For the 1D CNN+LSTM model and 2-layer CNN+LSTM model, the accuracy of the train set and test set are analogous. It shows that for those models, the dataset are enough. Nonetheless, for Tree-structure CNN+BILSTM, the dataset is not sufficient. Tree-structure CNN+BILSTM are more complicated than 1D CNN+LSTM and 2-layer CNN+LSTM. So our model could learn the feature more well. We need, however, more data to train.

7   Discussion

In this paper, we propose a deep learning model that can predict the usefulness of a statement to the final result. Our work could improve ATP techniques and save time for a formal proof. Our model has a significant generalization ability because our model can capture the basic characteristic: recursion. Also, the process of ATP is an orderly sequence. So we use the bidirectional LSTM and the experimental results show our model reaching 90% accuracy, 5% higher than [5]. But there are still some problems. The first one is we need more datasets to prove our model's generalization ability. Unfortunately, there are few datasets in this area. So one of our future works is making more datasets of ATP. The second problem is that although tree-structure CNN can improve the accuracy, it is a simple model that only cocaine several nodes. But the ATP always includes a huge number of subgoals. So when the ATP is too complicated, our model may not work well. At the same time, if we add more nodes into our model, the train will become highly time consuming. Also, more node may not improve the accuracy significantly. The third problem is that even if we improve the accuracy in 5%, there is still a big space left. So in the future, we are about revise the structure of LSTM. Changing the linear structure into tree-structure in the future. We hope this revision could improve the accuracy.

At last, we note that there is an interesting example in our experiment. The example is shown in the Fig. 4.

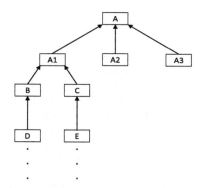

Fig. 4. Shows the proof relationship between main goal and subgoal. A → B means we need A to proof B. The suspension points means that more axioms are needed to proof D and E

The Fig. 4 clearly shows the proof relationship between subgoal and main goal. A is the main goal of our proof. If we want to proof A, we need A1, A2, and A3. So A1, A2, A3 have a positive relationship with the main goal. It is easy to know that all the leaf node in this tree are all have a positive relationship with the main goal. However, we find that in our experimental result. Our model classifies a leaf node in seven layer of this tree into a negative relationship (The seven layer is not shown in Fig. 4). Oppositely, SVM gives our the correct answer. From this example, we could get a conclusions: ATP is very complex. It contain many axioms and the relationship between them is also complex. So, we need to combine the traditional way with CNN. Only CNN or SVM may not be successful.

References

1. Alama, J., Heskes, T., Kühlwein, D., Tsivtsivadze, E., Urban, J.: Premise selection for mathematics by corpus analysis and kernel methods. J. Autom. Reasoning **52**(2), 191–213 (2014)
2. Alemi, A.A., Chollet, F., Irving, G., Szegedy, C., Urban, J.: DeepMath-deep sequence models for premise selection. arXiv preprint arXiv:1606.04442 (2016)
3. Aspinall, D., Kaliszyk, C.: What's in a theorem name? In: Blanchette, J.C., Merz, S. (eds.) ITP 2016. LNCS, vol. 9807, pp. 459–465. Springer, Cham (2016). doi:10.1007/978-3-319-43144-4_28

4. Autexier, S., Hutter, D.: Structure formation in large theories. In: Kerber, M., Carette, J., Kaliszyk, C., Rabe, F., Sorge, V. (eds.) CICM 2015. LNCS, vol. 9150, pp. 155–170. Springer, Cham (2015). doi:10.1007/978-3-319-20615-8_10
5. Cezary, K., Franois, C., Christian, S.: HolStep: machine learning dataset for higher-order logic theorem proving. ICLR (2016)
6. Färber, M., Brown, C.: Internal guidance for satallax. arXiv preprint arXiv:1605.09293 (2016)
7. He, K., Zhang, X., Ren, S., Sun, J.: Deep residual learning for image recognition. arXiv preprint arXiv:1512.03385 (2015)
8. Hochreiter, S., Schmidhuber, J.: Long short-term memory. Neural Comput. **9**(8), 1735–1780 (1997)
9. Hoder, K., Voronkov, A.: Sine Qua non for large theory reasoning. In: Bjørner, N., Sofronie-Stokkermans, V. (eds.) CADE 2011. LNCS, vol. 6803, pp. 299–314. Springer, Heidelberg (2011). doi:10.1007/978-3-642-22438-6_23
10. Klein, G., Elphinstone, K., Heiser, G., Andronick, J., Cock, D., Derrin, P., Elkaduwe, D., Engelhardt, K., Kolanski, R., Norrish, M., et al.: seL4: Formal verification of an OS kernel. In: Proceedings of the ACM SIGOPS 22nd Symposium on Operating Systems Principles, pp. 207–220. ACM (2009)
11. Kovács, L., Voronkov, A.: First-order theorem proving and VAMPIRE. In: Sharygina, N., Veith, H. (eds.) CAV 2013. LNCS, vol. 8044, pp. 1–35. Springer, Heidelberg (2013). doi:10.1007/978-3-642-39799-8_1
12. Mikolov, T., Sutskever, I., Chen, K., Corrado, G.S., Dean, J.: Distributed representations of words and phrases and their compositionality. In: Advances in Neural Information Processing Systems, pp. 3111–3119 (2013)
13. Nipkow, T., Paulson, L.C., Wenzel, M.: Isabelle/HOL: A Proof Assistant for Higher-Order Logic, vol. 2283. Springer, Heidelberg (2002)
14. Simonyan, K., Zisserman, A.: Very deep convolutional networks for large-scale image recognition. arXiv preprint arXiv:1409.1556 (2014)
15. Sutcliffe, G.: The TPTP problem library and associated infrastructure. J. Autom. Reasoning **43**(4), 337 (2009)
16. Voronkov, A.: Logic for Programming, Artificial Intelligence, and Reasoning. Springer, Heidelberg (2010)
17. Wenzel, M.: Isar — a generic interpretative approach to readable formal proof documents. In: Bertot, Y., Dowek, G., Théry, L., Hirschowitz, A., Paulin, C. (eds.) TPHOLs 1999. LNCS, vol. 1690, pp. 167–183. Springer, Heidelberg (1999). doi:10.1007/3-540-48256-3_12
18. Wiedijk, F.: The Seventeen Provers of the World. Lecture Notes in Computer Science, vol. 3600. Springer, Heidelberg (2006)

Training Deep Autoencoder via VLC-Genetic Algorithm

Qazi Sami Ullah Khan$^{(\boxtimes)}$, Jianwu Li, and Shuyang Zhao

Beijing Key Laboratory of Intelligent Information Technology,
School of Computer Science and Technology, Beijing Institute of Technology,
Beijing, China
qazisamiullah170@yahoo.com

Abstract. Recently, both supervised and unsupervised deep learning techniques have accomplished notable results in various fields. However neural networks with back-propagation are liable to trapping at local minima. Genetic algorithms have been popular as a class of optimization techniques which are good at exploring a large and complex space in an intelligent way to find values close to the global optimum.

In this paper, a variable length chromosome genetic algorithm assisted deep autoencoder is proposed. Firstly, the training of autoencoder is done with the help of variable length chromosome genetic algorithm. Secondly, a classifier is used for the classification of encoded data and compare the classification accuracy with other state-of-the-art methods. The experimental results show that the proposed method achieves competitive results and produce sparser networks.

Keywords: Neural networks · Genetic algorithm · Variable length chromosome · Deep autoencoder

1 Introduction

Neural network researchers had wanted for eras to train deep multi-layer neural networks [1,2], which is inspired by the architectural depth of the human brain but before 2006 no successful attempts were reported. Positive experimental results were reported by researchers with usually one or two hidden layers but training deeper networks repeatedly returned poorer results. Hinton et al. introduced Deep Belief Networks [3], with an unsupervised learning algorithm Restricted Boltzmann Machine (RBM) [4] that greedily trains one layer at a time. Later, autoencoders based algorithms were proposed [5,6], actually taking advantage of the same principle using of unsupervised learning to train of middle layer at each level [7]. More recently, other algorithms for deep learning were proposed using neither autoencoder nor RBMs but using the same principle [8,9].

Since 2006, deep learning have been applied on various tasks such as dimensionality reduction [10], classification [5,11,12], modeling textures [13], collaborative filtering [14], regression [15], object segmentation [16], natural language processing [8,17] and information retrieval [18,19].

© Springer International Publishing AG 2017
D. Liu et al. (Eds.): ICONIP 2017, Part II, LNCS 10635, pp. 13–22, 2017.
https://doi.org/10.1007/978-3-319-70096-0_2

In this paper we describe a variable length chromosome genetic algorithm (VLC-GA) for training deep autoencoder. We use VLC-GA for training deep autoencoder that not only succeeds in its task but outperforms backpropagation (the standard training algorithm) and another approach in [20] on MNIST handwritten digits dataset [21].

The rest of paper is organized as follow: In Sect. 2, related work is briefly reviewed. In Sect. 3, the proposed method is explained. In Sect. 4, experiments are presented. The contributions of this paper are concluded in Sect. 5.

2   Related Work

Neural networks (NNs) and genetic algorithms both have the ability to solve complex problem. The idea of combination of neural networks and genetic algorithms came up first in the late 80s, which is inspired from the nature. In real life, a successful person not only depends on his knowledge and expertise, which he gained through experience (the neural network training), but also depends on his inborn inheritance (set by the genetic algorithm) [22].

Since 1980, genetic algorithms have been effectively used for training neural networks. Genetic algorithms have been used as a replacement for the backpropagation algorithm, or in combination with backpropagation to increase the entire performance of the neural network [23]. A large number of problems have been examined by using various Genetic Algorithm Neural Networks (GANN) techniques, such as classification [24], face recognition [25], color recipe prediction [26], animates [27], etc.

In 2014, Omid E. David and Iddo Greental used a GA-assisted approach for training deep autoencoder which improved the performance of deep autoencoder and produced a sparser neural network [20]. In [28], Montana, David J., and Lawrence Davis used a different genetic algorithm for training feed forward networks which is not only prospers in its job but surpassed the standard training algorithm backpropagation on different datasets. In regards of genetic algorithm they showed a real world application of genetic algorithm to a big and difficult problem. They also show that adding domain specific information to genetic algorithm improves its performance. Philipp and Koehn [26] in their thesis, survey how genetic algorithms can be used to enhance the network topology, learning rate and initial weight of neural networks. They also inspect how various encoding strategies influence the combination of GANN. Besides this, many researchers used variable length genetic algorithm instead of constant length genetic algorithm for different problems [20, 29–32].

3   Methodology

3.1   Deep Autoencoder

An autoencoder, also called auto-associator or diabolo, network is an artificial neural network. Autoencoder were first introduced in 1980s by Hinton and Parallel Distributing Processing (PDP) group by using input data as a teacher to solve the problem of backpropagation without mentor [33]. Autoencoder is used for unsupervised learning that sets the target values to be equal to its inputs, i.e. the number of neurons at the input and output layers is equal, and the optimization goal for output neuron i is set to $x_i = \hat{x}_i$. Between input and output layers one or more hidden layers are used. Generally the number of neurons in hidden layer is less compared to input or output layers, thus making a bottleneck.

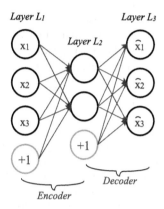

Fig. 1. Basic structure of autoencoder.

Architecturally, feedforward is the simplest form of an autoencoder. An autoencoder comprises of two parts encoder and decoder. As shown in Fig. 1, encoder consists of layer L_1 and L_2 while decoder consists of layer L_2 and L_3. The layer L_1 is input layer, L_2 is a hidden layer consisting of two neurons and each neuron represents by a function:

$$a(x) = f(Wx + b) \tag{1}$$

where W, b are weight matrix and bias vector respectively and $f(\cdot)$ is an activation function that can be sigmoid, hyperbolic, sine, gaussian function etc. And L_3 is the output layer that represents by a function $h(x) \approx x$:

$$h(a) = f'(W'a + b') \tag{2}$$

where $f'(\cdot)$, W' and b' of decoder may differ from encoder depending upon the design of autoencoder. Training of autoencoder is accomplished by reducing the reconstruction error (such as squared error):

$$E(x, \hat{x}) = \|x - \hat{x}\|^2 = \|x - f'(W'f(Wx + b) + b')\|^2 \tag{3}$$

A deep autoencoder consists of several layers of autoencoders such that the outputs of each layer are bound to the inputs of the next layer [19]. A greedy layer-wise procedure is used for obtaining good parameters for deep autoencoder.

3.2   Backpropagation Learning

Backpropagation is a technique of training artificial neural networks used in combination with an optimization method such as gradient descent. The algorithm has two main phases, propagation and weight update. The input data is transmitted forward layer by layer from the input layer to the output layer. Using a cost function, the desired output is compared to the output of network. At the output layer, for every neuron an error value is calculated. Starting from the output, the error values are then transmitted towards back and every single neuron takes its associated error value which shows its part in the original output. Later backpropagation uses these error values to compute the gradient of the cost function with respect to the weights in the network.

3.3   The Proposed Method

In this paper we propose a VLC-GA assisted approach which improves the performance of an autoencoder, and produce a sparser network. The autoencoder is trained with tied weights. We store various sets of weights W for a layer. That is, in our GA population each chromosome is one set of weights for an autoencoder. In this paper, the term of weights and chromosomes are used interchangeably. For creation of variable length chromosome, the chromosome size is multiplied with a variable v. This variable shows the maximum percent variation of the chromosome. For example if v is 20% and chromosome size is 392000, then the maximum variation in chromosome can be 78400 by choosing a number randomly between 0 and 78400. The same method is applied for the whole population of chromosome. The generation of variable length chromosome is also shown in Algorithm 1. While training the data, for each chromosome (which represents the weights of an autoencoder) the root mean squared error (RMSE) is calculated of training dataset m. The fitness of each chromosome is defined by a fitness function [20] as:

$$fitness(i) = {}^1\!/ \sqrt{\frac{\sum_{i=1}^{m}(x_i - \hat{x}_i)^2}{m}} \tag{4}$$

After calculating the fitness of all chromosomes, the least fit chromosomes are removed from the population and update the remaining chromosomes using backpropagation. After removing the least fit chromosomes, we used Roulette selection method for the selection of parent chromosomes from the rest population and then use uniform crossover method to create offspring. The offspring is mutated from the best chromosomes using specified mutation probability. The mutation process is described in Algorithm 2. The whole process (Algorithm 3) is run for a specific number of iterations and returns the best chromosomes. The same process applied on all layers and stacked all the layers to make a deep autoencoder.

To classify the compressed dimensional feature vector, softmax regression is used. As we are concerned in multi-class classification so it takes k different values instead of two (as in binary classification) and the equation becomes:

Algorithm 1. Creation of Variable Length Chromosome

1: $chromosomeSize \leftarrow input * hiddenNodes$
2: $variation \leftarrow \nu * chromosomeSize$
3: **for** $i = 1$ to $populationSize$ **do**
4:     $r_1 = randi([1 \; variation])$
5:     **for** $j = 1$ to r_1 **do**
6:         $r_2 = randi([1 \; chromosomeSize])$
7:         $chromosome_i(j, r_2) = 0$
8:     **end for**
9: **end for**

$$h_\theta(x)^i = \frac{1}{\sum_{j=1}^{k} e^{\theta_j^T x^{(i)}}} \begin{bmatrix} e^{\theta_1^T x^{(i)}} \\ e^{\theta_2^T x^{(i)}} \\ \vdots \\ e^{\theta_k^T x^{(i)}} \end{bmatrix} \tag{5}$$

Here θ_1, θ_2, $\cdots$, θ_k are the parameters of model and $\sum_{j=1}^{k} e_j^T x^{(i)}$ normalizes the distribution, so that it sums to one. After training all the layers of deep autoencoder, the encoded data and labels pass to softmax layer to train it with supervised fashion.

As backpropagation method are accountable for trapping at local minima. Our proposed method supports backpropagation in this regards, by decreasing the possibility of trapping at local minima. Moreover making the chromosomes (weights) variable produce sparser network (few active weights).

Algorithm 2. Mutation of Offspring

1: $mutationRate = mutationProb * chromosomeSize$
2: **for** $i = 1$ to $mutationRate$ **do**
3:     $r = randi([1 \; chromosomeSize])$
4:     $offspring(i \; r) = bestChromosome([i \; r])$
5: **end for**

---

4   Experiments

4.1   Data

In order to access the performance of the proposed approach, MNIST handwritten digits dataset [21] is used in all experiments of all methods. Each sample in the dataset is a $28 * 28$ image having a grey scale value between 0–255. Moreover each sample holds a target classification label between 0–9, which is used in supervised classification. The training dataset contains 60,000 samples and testing dataset contains 10,000 samples.

Algorithm 3. Training of Layer l_i

1: *initialize population of real values chromosomes.*
2: *convert chromosomes to variable length.*
3: *epoch* = 1
4: **while** (*epoch* >= *MaxEpoch*) **do**
5:     *calculation of fitness of chromosomes.*
6:     *removing of least fit chromosomes.*
7:     *using backpropagation to update the best chromosomes.*
8:     *selection of parents chromosomes to produce an offspring.*
9:     *mutation of offspring.*
10:     *epoch* = *epoch* + 1
11: **end while**
12: *return best chromosome (weights).*

4.2   Setup

MATLAB R2015a is used for the realization of code. In all experiments we used a deep neural network (autoencoder) of five layers. Initially the biases b_i^l are set to zero and weights W_{ij}^l are set to random numbers generated uniformly from the interval $\{-\sqrt{\frac{6}{(n_{in}+n_{hu}+1)}}, \sqrt{\frac{6}{(n_{in}+n_{hu}+1)}}\}$, where n_{in} is the number of inputs to the layer and n_{hu} is the number of neurons (units) in the layer. The first layer is the input layer consists of 784 units (neurons), followed by four hidden layers consisting of 500, 250, 100 and 50 units. Each layer is trained independently. First we train $784 - 500$ layer and used the output of that layer as input for the next $500 - 250$ layer. Secondly we train $500 - 250$ layer and used its output for the next layer input. Using the same manner we train the remaining layers ($250 - 100$ and $100 - 50$). We used sigmoid function (6) for activation of neuron.

$$f(z) = \frac{1}{1 + e^{-1}} \tag{6}$$

For VLC-GA implementation we used a population of 8 chromosomes. In each generation the 3 least fit chromosomes are substituted by the remaining 5 chromosomes offspring. We used a uniform crossover method and mutation probability of 0.01. For classification of the data we attach softmax regression classifier at the end of last layer and trained it for 100 generations. The parameters setup for all methods are summarized in the Table 1.

4.3   Results

To compare the performance of the proposed method with other methods we did the following experiments. In all experiments we set learning rate α and weight decay parameter λ to 0.5 and 0.003 respectively. Each result is the average of 10 experiments.

Table 1. Comparison of parameters used in all methods

Parameters	Proposed method	Method in [20]	AE using BP
Deep layers	5	5	5
Learning rate	0.5	0.5	0.5
Weight decay	0.003	0.003	0.003
Population size	8	10	-
Chromosome type	Variable	Constant	-
Selection method	Roulette wheel	Uniformly	-
Least fit chromosomes	3	5	-
Mutation	From best chromosome	Randomly	-
Crossover	Uniform	Uniform	-

Experiment-1. In this experiment we change the percentage of v to 10%, 20%, 30% and 40% in the process of generation of variable length chromosomes and then check its effect on classification accuracy. We used training dataset and testing dataset of 1,000 and 10,000 samples respectively. And train each layer for 1,000 generations. The result of this experiment is shown in the Fig. 2-left. We got best accuracy at $v = 20\%$ so we used the same value of v in all experiments.

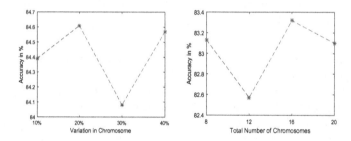

Fig. 2. Left-Classification accuracy of proposed method on different population size. **Right-**Classification accuracy of proposed method on different population size.

Experiment-2. In this experiment we used a population of 8, 12, 16 and 20 chromosomes in training of our method and check its effect on classification accuracy. This experiment is performed on 1,000 generations using subset of MNIST dataset. The subset created randomly by choosing 1,000 samples from training data. The result is shown in Fig. 2-right. As the number of chromosome increases the processing time also increases but there is no bigger change in classification accuracy that's why we used a population having less number of chromosomes (i.e. 8 chromosomes) in our experiments.

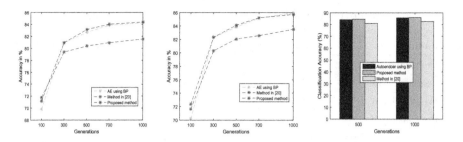

Fig. 3. Left-Comparison of classification accuracy of testing data using small training dataset. **Middle-**Comparison of classification accuracy of training data using small training dataset. **Right-**Comparison of classification accuracy of testing data using big training dataset.

Experiment-3. In this experiment we used small subset of MNIST dataset by randomly selecting 1,000 samples from training dataset. We train each method for 100, 300, 500, 700 and 1000 generations and then apply the classifier on the encoded data. The comparison of the classification accuracy of the testing dataset is shown in Fig. 3-left and the comparison of the classification accuracy of the training dataset is shown in Fig. 3-middle. On testing dataset our proposed method performs well on 300, 500, 700 and 1,000 generations but on 100 generations method in [20] perform better. On training dataset our method performs well on all generations expect 1,000 on which autoencoder using backpropagation method perform better.

Experiment-4. In this experiment we used the complete MNIST dataset (i.e. training dataset of 60,000 samples and the testing dataset of 10,000 samples). Firstly we train each method for 500 generations and compare the classification accuracy. Secondly we train each method for 1,000 generations and compare the classification accuracy. As shown in Fig. 3-right, on testing dataset our proposed method performs better than the other methods on both generations.

5   Conclusion

In this paper we presented a variable length chromosome genetic algorithm assisted deep autoencoder. We used roulette wheel selection method for the selection of parent chromosomes from the population. And the offspring are mutated from best parent chromosome. We used fewer chromosomes as compare to method in [20], this increase the processing speed of our method. According to results, our method improves the performance and produce sparser networks as compare to other methods. Though our implementation used an autoencoder, the same technique is applied to other forms of deep learning such as RBM, Convolutional Neural Networks (CNNs) etc. In future we will compare our work with more methods.

Acknowledgments. This work was supported by the National Natural Science Foundation of China (No. 61271374).

References

1. Bengio, Y., LeCun, Y., et al.: Scaling learning algorithms towards AI. Large-scale Kernel Mach. **34**, 1–41 (2007)
2. Utgoff Hinton, G.E., Osindero, S., Teh, Y.-W.: Many-layered learning. Neural Comput. **14**, 2497–2529 (2002). MIT Press
3. Hinton, G.E., Osindero, S., Teh, Y.-W.: A fast learning algorithm for deep belief nets. Neural Comput. **18**, 1527–1554 (2006). MIT Press
4. Freund, Y., Haussler, D.: Unsupervised learning of distributions of binary vectors using two layer networks, Computer Research Laboratory, University of California, Santa Cruz (1994)
5. Bengio, Y., Lamblin, P., Dan, P., et al.: Greedy layer-wise training of deep networks. In: Advances in Neural Information Processing Systems, vol. 19, p. 153. MIT Press (2007)
6. Ranzato, M., Poultney, C., Chopra, S., et al.: Efficient learning of sparse representations with an energy-based model. In: Proceedings of NIPS (2007)
7. Bengio, Y., et al.: Learning deep architectures for AI. In: Foundations and Trends in Machine Learning, vol. 2, pp. 1–127. Now Publishers, Inc. (2009)
8. Weston, J., Ratle, F., Mobahi, H., Collobert, R.: Deep learning via semi-supervised embedding. In: Montavon, G., Orr, G.B., Müller, K.-R. (eds.) Neural Networks: Tricks of the Trade. LNCS, vol. 7700, pp. 639–655. Springer, Heidelberg (2012). doi:10.1007/978-3-642-35289-8_34
9. Mobahi, H., Collobert, R., Weston, J.: Deep learning from temporal coherence in video. In: Proceedings of the 26th Annual International Conference on Machine Learning, pp. 737–744. ACM (2009)
10. Hinton, G.E., Salakhutdinov, R.R.: Reducing the dimensionality of data with neural networks, vol. 313, pp. 504–507. American Association for the Advancement of Science (2006)
11. Vincent, P., Larochelle, H., Bengio, Y., et al.: Extracting and composing robust features with denoising autoencoders. In: Proceedings of the 25th International Conference on Machine Learning, pp. 1096–1103. ACM (2008)
12. Ahmed, A., Yu, K., Xu, W., Gong, Y., Xing, E.: Training hierarchical feedforward visual recognition models using transfer learning from pseudo-tasks. In: Forsyth, D., Torr, P., Zisserman, A. (eds.) ECCV 2008. LNCS, vol. 5304, pp. 69–82. Springer, Heidelberg (2008). doi:10.1007/978-3-540-88690-7_6
13. Osindero, S., Hinton, G.E.: Modeling image patches with a directed hierarchy of Markov random fields. In: Advances in Neural Information Processing Systems, pp. 1121–1128 (2008)
14. Salakhutdinov, R., Mnih, A., Hinton, G.: Restricted Boltzmann machines for collaborative filtering. In: Proceedings of the 24th International Conference on Machine Learning, pp. 791–798. ACM (2007)
15. Hinton, G.E., Salakhutdinov, R.R.: Using deep belief nets to learn covariance kernels for Gaussian processes. In: Advances in Neural Information Processing Systems, pp. 1249–1256 (2008)
16. Levner, I.: Data Driven Object Segmentation. Citeseer (2009)
17. Mnih, A., Hinton, G.E.: A scalable hierarchical distributed language model. In: Advances in Neural Information Processing Systems, pp. 1081–1088 (2009)

18. Collobert, R., Weston, J.: A unified architecture for natural language processing: deep neural networks with multitask learning. In: Proceedings of the 25th International Conference on Machine Learning, pp. 160–167. ACM (2008)

19. Ranzato, M.A., Szummer, M.: Semi-supervised learning of compact document representations with deep networks. In: Proceedings of the 25th International Conference on Machine Learning, pp. 792–799. ACM (2008)

20. David, O.E., Greental, I.: Genetic algorithms for evolving deep neural networks. In: Proceedings of the Companion Publication of the 2014 Annual Conference on Genetic and Evolutionary Computation, pp. 1451–1452. ACM (2014)

21. LeCun, Y., Bottou, L., Bengio, Y., et al.: Gradient-based learning applied to document recognition. Proc. IEEE **86**, 2278–2324 (1998). IEEE

22. David, S.J., Whitley, D., Eshelman, L.J.: Combinations of genetic algorithms and neural networks: a survey of the state of the art. In: Combinations of Genetic Algorithms and Neural Networks, pp. 1–37. IEEE (1992)

23. Golberg, D.E.: Genetic Algorithms in Search, Optimization, and Machine Learning. Addison-Wesley, Boston (1989)

24. Koehn, P.: Combining Genetic Algorithms and Neural Networks: The Encoding Problem. Citeseer (1994)

25. Schiffmann, W., Joost, M., Werner, R.: Application of genetic algorithms to the construction of topologies for multilayer perceptrons. In: Albrecht, R.F., Reeves, C.R., Steele, N.C. (eds.) Artificial Neural Nets and Genetic Algorithms, pp. 675–682. Springer, Wien (1993). doi:10.1007/978-3-7091-7533-0_98

26. Hancock, P.J.B., Smith, L.S.: Gannet: genetic design of a neural net for face recognition. In: Schwefel, H.-P., Männer, R. (eds.) PPSN 1990. LNCS, vol. 496, pp. 292–296. Springer, Heidelberg (1991). doi:10.1007/BFb0029766

27. Bishop, J.M., Bushnell, M.J., Usher, A., et al.: Genetic optimisation of neural network architectures for colour recipe prediction. In: Albrecht, R.F., Reeves, C.R., Steele, N.C. (eds.) Artificial Neural Nets and Genetic Algorithms, pp. 719–725. Springer, Wien (1993). doi:10.1007/978-3-7091-7533-0_104

28. Montana, D.J., Davis, L.: Training feedforward neural networks using genetic algorithms. In: IJCAI 1989, vol. 89, pp. 762–767 (1989)

29. Zhang, M., Deng, Y., Chang, D.: A novel genetic clustering algorithm with variable-length chromosome representation. In: Proceedings of the Companion Publication of the 2014 Annual Conference on Genetic and Evolutionary Computation, pp. 1483–1484. ACM (2014)

30. Yahya, A.A., Osman, A., Ramli, A.R., et al.: Feature selection for high dimensional data: an evolutionary filter approach. Citeseer (2011)

31. Salakhutdinov, R., Hinton, G.: Semantic hashing. Int. J. Approximate Reasoning **50**, 969–978 (2009). Elsevier

32. Brie, A.H., Morignot, P.: Genetic planning using variable length chromosomes. In: ICAPS 2005, pp. 320–329 (2005)

33. Baldi, P.: Autoencoders, unsupervised learning, and deep architectures. In: ICML Unsupervised and Transfer Learning, vol. 27, p. 1 (2012)

Training Very Deep Networks via Residual Learning with Stochastic Input Shortcut Connections

Oyebade K. Oyedotun$^{(\boxtimes)}$, Abd El Rahman Shabayek, Djamila Aouada,
and Björn Ottersten

Interdisciplinary Centre for Security, Reliability and Trust (SnT),
University of Luxembourg, 1855 Luxembourg City, Luxembourg
{oyebade.oyedotun,abdelrahman.shabayek,djamila.aouada,
bjorn.ottersten}@uni.lu
http://wwwen.uni.lu/snt

Abstract. Many works have posited the benefit of depth in deep networks. However, one of the problems encountered in the training of very deep networks is feature reuse; that is, features are 'diluted' as they are forward propagated through the model. Hence, later network layers receive less informative signals about the input data, consequently making training less effective. In this work, we address the problem of feature reuse by taking inspiration from an earlier work which employed residual learning for alleviating the problem of feature reuse. We propose a modification of residual learning for training very deep networks to realize improved generalization performance; for this, we allow stochastic shortcut connections of identity mappings from the input to hidden layers. We perform extensive experiments using the USPS and MNIST datasets. On the USPS dataset, we achieve an error rate of 2.69% without employing any form of data augmentation (or manipulation). On the MNIST dataset, we reach a comparable state-of-the-art error rate of 0.52%. Particularly, these results are achieved without employing any explicit regularization technique.

Keywords: Deep neural networks · Residual learning · Dropout · Optimization

1 Introduction

Neural networks have been extremely useful for learning complex tasks such as gesture recognition [1] and banknote recognition [2]. More recently, as against shallow networks with one layer of feature abstraction, there has been massive interest in deep networks which compose many layers of features abstractions. There are many earlier works [3,4] which established that given a sufficiently large number of hidden units, a shallow network is a universal function approximator. Interestingly, many works addressing the benefit of depth in neural

© Springer International Publishing AG 2017
D. Liu et al. (Eds.): ICONIP 2017, Part II, LNCS 10635, pp. 23–33, 2017.
https://doi.org/10.1007/978-3-319-70096-0_3

networks have also emerged. For example, using the concept of sum-product networks, Delalleau and Bengio [5] posited that deep networks can efficiently represent some family of functions with lesser number of hidden units as compared to shallow networks. In addition, Mhaskar et al. [6] provided proofs in their work that deep networks are capable of operating with lower Vapnik-Chervonenkis (VC) dimensions. Bianchini and Scarselli [7] employing some architectural constraints, derived upper and lower bounds for some shallow and deep architectures; they concluded that using the same resources (computation units), deep networks are capable of representing more complex functions than shallow networks. In practice, the success of deep networks have corroborated the position that deep networks have a better representational capability as compared to shallow networks; many state-of-the-art results on benchmarking datasets are currently held by deep networks [8–10].

In recent times, the aforementioned theoretical proofs, practical results and new works [11,12] now suggest that employing *even deeper* networks could be quite promising for learning even *more complex or highly varying functions*. However, it has been observed that the training of models beyond some few layers results in optimization difficulty [13,14]. In this work, for the sake of clear terms, we refer to models with 2–10 hidden layers as 'deep networks', models with more than 10 hidden layers as 'very deep networks' and use the term 'deep architecture' to refer interchangeably to a deep network or very deep network. We consider the effective training of very deep networks; that is, simultaneously overcoming optimization problems associated with model depth increase and more importantly improving generalization performance. We take inspiration from an earlier work which employed residual learning for training very deep networks [14]. However, training very deep models with millions of parameters come with the price of over-fitting. On one hand, various explicit regularization schemes such as L^1-norm, L^2-norm and max-norm can be employed for alleviating this problem. On the other hand, a more appealing approach is to explore some form of implicit regularization such as reducing the co-adaptation of model units on one another for feature learning (or activations) [19] and encouraging stochasticity during optimization [8]. In this work, we advance in this direction with some modifications on the form of residual learning that we propose for implicitly improving model regularization by *emphasizing stochasticity* during training. Our contribution is that we propose to modify residual learning for training very deep networks where we allow shortcut connections of identity mappings from the input to the hidden layers; such shortcut connections are stochastically removed during training. Particularly, the proposed training scheme is shown to improve the implicit regularization of very deep networks as compared to the conventional residual learning. We employ our proposed approach for performing extensive experiments using the USPS and MNIST datasets; results obtained are quite promising and competitive with respect to state-of-the-art results.

The rest of this paper is organized as follows. Section 2 discusses related works.

Section 3 serves as background and introduction of residual learning. Section 4 gives the description of the proposed model. Section 5 contains experiments, results and discussion on benchmark datasets. In Sect. 6, we conclude the work with our key findings.

2   Related Work

The optimization difficulty observed in training very deep networks can be attributed to the fact that input features get diluted from the input layer through the many compositional hidden layers to the output layer; this is evident in that each layer in the model performs some transformation on the input received from the preceding layer. The several transformations with model depth may make features not reusable. Here, one can conjecture that the signals (data features) which reach the output layer for error computation may be significantly less informative for effective weights update (or correction). Many works have provided interesting approaches for alleviating the problem of training deep architectures. In [15,16], carefully guided initializations were considered for specific activation functions; these initializations were found useful for improving model optimization and the rates of convergence. In another interesting work [17], batch normalization was proposed for tackling the problem of internal covariate shift which arises from non-zero mean hidden activations. Nevertheless, the problem of training (optimizing) very deep networks commonly arises when the number of hidden layers exceeds 10; see Fig. 1. For example, Srivastava et al. [13] employed *transform* gates for routing data through very deep networks; they refer to their model as a *highway network*. The concept is that the transform gates are either closed or open. When the transform gates are closed, input data are routed through the hidden layers without transformations; in fact, each hidden layer essentially copies the features from the preceding layer. However, when the transform gates are open, the hidden layers perform the conventional features transformations using layer weights, biases and activation functions. Inasmuch as the highway network was shown to allow for the optimization of very deep networks and improving classification accuracies on benchmark datasets, it comes with a price of learning additional model parameters for the transform gates. Another work, He et al. [14] has addressed the problem of feature reuse by using residual learning for alleviating the dilution (or attenuation) of features during forward propagation through very deep networks; they refer to their model as a *ResNet*. The ResNet was also shown to alleviate optimization difficulty in training very deep networks. In [33], identity shortcut connections were used for bypassing a subset of layers to facilitate training very deep networks.

3   Background: Very Deep Models and Residual Learning

3.1   Motivation

We emphasize the problem of training very deep networks using the USPS dataset. Figure 1-left shows the performance of plain deep architectures with

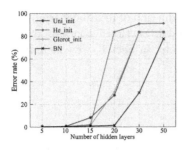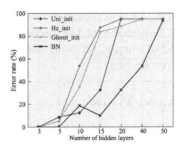

Fig. 1. Performance of deep architectures with depth. Left: Train error on USPS dataset. Right: Train error on COIL-20 dataset. It is seen that optimization becomes more difficult with depth

a different number of hidden layers. Particularly, it will be seen that the performance of the models significantly dips from over 10 hidden layers. We further emphasize this problem by going beyond the typical uniform initialization (i.e. Unit_init in Fig. 1) scheme for neural network models; we employ other initialization and training techniques which have been proposed for more effective training of deep models; these techniques include Glorot [15] initialization, He [16] initialization and batch normalization [17] which are shown as Glorot_init, He_init and BN in Fig. 1.

In addition, we investigate this problem using the COIL-20 dataset[1] which composes 1,440 samples of different objects of 20 classes. The concepts which we follow in using the COIL-20 dataset as sanity check are in two folds: (1) it is a small dataset, hence it is expected that deep architectures would easily overfit such training data (2) the dataset is of much higher dimensionality. Obviously, this training scenario can be seen as an extreme one which *indeed* favours deep models with enormous parameters for overfitting the training data. This follows directly from the concept of model complexity and curse of dimensionality with high dimensional input data as against the number of training data points. However, our experimental results do not support the overfitting intuition; instead, the difficulty of model optimization is observed when the number of hidden layers is increased beyond 10; see Fig. 1-right. It will be seen that for both USPS and COIL-20 datasets, training with batch normalization improved model optimization with depth increase. Nevertheless, model optimization remains a problem with depth increase. However, residual learning [14] has been employed in recent times for successfully training very deep networks. The idea is to scheme model training such that stacks of hidden layers learn residual mapping functions rather than the conventional transformation functions.

---

[1] http://www.cad.zju.edu.cn/home/dengcai/Data/MLData.html.

3.2 Residual Learning: ResNet

In this subsection, we briefly discuss residual learning as a building block for the model that we propose in this paper. In [14], residual learning was achieved by employing shortcut connections from preceding hidden layers to the higher ones. Given an input $H(x)^{l-1}$ (in block form), from layer $l-1$ feeding into a stack of specified number of hidden layers with output $H(x)^l$; in the conventional training scheme, the stack of hidden layers learns a mapping function of the form

$$H(x)^l = F^l(H(x)^{l-1}), \tag{1}$$

where the residual learning proposed in [14] uses shortcut connections such that the stack of hidden layers learns a mapping function of the form

$$H(x)^l = F^l(H(x)^{l-1}) + H(x)^{l-1}, \tag{2}$$

where $H(x)^{l-1}$ is the shortcut connection. The actual transformation function learned by the stack of hidden layers can be written as follows

$$F^l(H(x)^{l-1}) = H(x)^l - H(x)^{l-1}, \tag{3}$$

where $1 \leq l \leq L$ and $H(x)^0$ is the input data, x; L is the depth of the network. This training setup was found very effective in training very deep networks, achieving state-of-the-art results on some benchmarking datasets [14]. In a following work [18], dropping out the shortcut connections from preceding hidden layers was experimented with; however, convergence problems and unpromising results were reported.

4   Proposed Model

For improving the training of very deep models, we take inspiration from residual learning. Our proposed model incorporates some simple modifications to further improve on optimization and generalization capability as compared to the conventional ResNet. We refer to the proposed model as stochastic residual network (*S-ResNet*). The proposed training scheme is described below:

(i) There are identity shortcut connections of identity mappings from the input to hidden layers of the model; this is in addition to the shortcut connections from preceding hidden layers to the higher ones as seen in the conventional ResNets.

(ii) The identity shortcut connections from the input to the hidden layers are stochastically removed during training. Here, hidden layer units do not always have access to the untransformed input data provided via shortcut connections.

(iii) At test time, all the shortcut connections are present. The shortcut connections are not parameterized and therefore do not require rescaling at test time as in [8, 33].

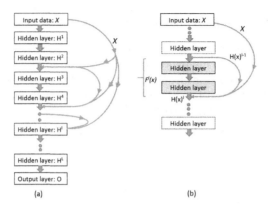

Fig. 2. (a) Proposed model with shortcut connections from the input to hidden layers (b) Closer view of the proposed residual learning with a hypothetical stack of two hidden layers

The proposed scheme for training very deep models is shown in Fig. 2(a); conventional shortcut connections from preceding hidden layers, with shortcut connections from the input to the different hidden layers are shown. For the modification that we propose in this work, the transformed output of a stack of hidden layers denoted, l, with shortcut connection from the preceding stack of hidden layers, $H(x)^{l-1}$, and shortcut connection from the input x can be written as follows

$$H(x)^l = F^l(H(x)^{l-1}) + H(x)^{l-1} + x. \tag{4}$$

where $1 \leq l \leq L \mid x = 0$ for $l = 1 \ \therefore \ \exists \ H(x)^0 = x$; $H(x)^l$, $F^l(H(x)^{l-1})$, $H(x)^{l-1}$ and x are of the same dimension. In this work, every stack of residual learning block composes two hidden layers. For a clearer conception of our proposed model, a single residual learning block of two hidden layers is shown in Fig. 2(b). From Fig. 2(b), assume that the underlying target function to be learned by a hypothetical residual learning block is $F^l(H(x)^{l-1})$, then using the aforementioned constraints on l, it learns a residual function of the form

$$F^l(H(x)^{l-1}) = H(x)^l - H(x)^{l-1} - x. \tag{5}$$

For dropout of shortcut connections from the input layer to the stack of hidden layers l, we can write

$$F^l(H(x)^{l-1}) = H(x)^l - H(x)^{l-1} - D * x, \tag{6}$$

where $D \in \{0, 1\}$ and $D \sim Bernoulli(p_s)$ determines that x (shortcut connection from input) is connected to the stack of hidden layers l with probability p_s; that is, $P(D = 1) = p_s$ and $P(D = 0) = 1 - p_s$ for $0 \leq p_s \leq 1$; and $*$ defines an operator that performs the shortcut connection, given the value of D. The conventional dropout probability for hidden units is denoted p_h.

5   Experiments and Discussion

For demonstrating the effectiveness of our proposed model, we train very deep networks and observe their optimization characteristics over various training settings using the USPS and MNIST datasets. The USPS dataset[2] composes handwritten digits 0–9 (10 classes) of 7,291 training and 2,007 testing samples; while the MNIST dataset[3] composes handwritten digits 0–9 of 60,000 training and 10,000 testing samples. For the USPS dataset, we use 2×2 convolutional filters, 2×2 max pooling windows and 2 fully connected layers of 300 ReLUs. For the MNIST dataset, we use 3×3 convolutional filters, 2×2 max pooling windows and 2 fully connected layers of 500 ReLUs. For both datasets, models have output layers of 10 softmax units. Our best model, 54-hidden layer S-ResNet, composes 50 convolution layers, 2 max pooling layers and 2 fully connected layers; we apply batch normalization only in the fully connected layers.

Figure 3-left shows the performance of our proposed model (S-ResNet) on the USPS dataset with different number of hidden layers at a dropout probability of $p_s = 0.8$ for the input shortcut connections to the hidden layers; for the conventional dropout of hidden units, a dropout probability of $(p_h = 0.6)$ is used. It will be seen that with 54-hidden layers, our model achieves a state-of-the-art performance; that is, an error rate of 2.69%, surpassing the conventional ResNet (baseline model). In addition, Fig. 3-right shows the performance of the best proposed model (54 hidden layer S-ResNet) with different dropout probabilities for input shortcut connections to the hidden layers. Table 1 shows the error rates obtained on the test data for the USPS dataset along with the state-of-the-arts results. We observe that the models with asterisk (i.e. $*$) employed some form of data augmentation (or manipulation). For example, [26,27] extended the training dataset with 2,400 machine-printed digits; while [28] employed virtual data in addition to the original training data. However, our proposed model employs no such data augmentation tricks. The result obtained with our proposed model, 54-hiddden layer S-ResNet, surpasses many works which did not employ any form of data augmentation.

We repeat similar experiments on the MNIST dataset. Figure 4-left shows the error rates of the S-ResNets and the conventional ResNets with different number of hidden layers. It is observed that the S-ResNets are better regularized as compared to the ResNets for all the different model depths. Particularly, with 54 hidden layers, the S-ResNet achieved a result competitive with the state-of-the-art results; we reach an error rate of 0.52%. Figure 4-right shows the error rates of the 54-hidden layer S-ResNet with different dropout probabilities for the input shortcut connections to the hidden layers. In Table 2, we report the obtained error rates for our experiments, along with the best results reported in recent works. Also, for the MNIST dataset, we found that dropping out input shortcut connections to the hidden layers with a probability of 0.8 yielded the best result as given in Table 2. For both datasets, the S-ResNets employed no explicit

---

[2] http://www.cad.zju.edu.cn/home/dengcai/Data/MLData.html.
[3] http://yann.lecun.com/exdb/mnist/.

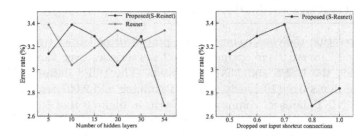

Fig. 3. Performance of deep architectures with depth on the USPS dataset. Left: Test error rate with depth. Right: Test error rate for different dropout probabilities of input shortcut connections

Table 1. Error rate (%) on the USPS dataset

Models	Test error (%)
Invariant vector supports [20]	3.00
Neural network (LetNet) [21]	4.20
Sparse Large Margin Classifiers (SLMC) [22]	4.90
Incrementally Built Dictionary Learning (IBDL-C) [23]	3.99
Neural network + boosting [21]	*2.60
Tangent distance [24]	*2.50
Human performance [24]	2.50
Kernel density + virtual data [25]	*2.40
Kernel density + virtual data + classifier combination [25]	*2.20
Nearest neighbour [25]	5.60
Baseline: Residual network (ResNet) - 54 hidden layers	3.34
Proposed model (S-ResNet) - 20 hidden layers	3.04
Proposed model (S-ResNet) - 54 hidden layers	**2.69**

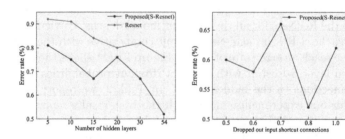

Fig. 4. Performance of deep architectures with depth on the MNIST dataset. Left: Test error rate with depth. Right: Test error rate for different dropout probabilities of input shortcut connections

Table 2. Error rate (%) on the MNIST dataset

Models	Test error (%)
Highway Net-16 [13]	0.57
Highway Net-32 [13]	0.45
Supervised Sparse Coding + linear SVM [26]	0.84
Deep Fried Convet [27]	0.71
PCANet [28]	0.62
Network in Network (NIN) [29]	0.45
Deeply Supervised Network (DSN) [30]	0.39
ConvNet + L-BFGS [31]	0.69
Neural network + adversarial examples [32]	0.78
Neural network ensemble + DropConnect [8]	0.52
Baseline: Residual network (Resnet) - 54 hidden layers	0.76
Proposed model (S-Resnet) - 15 hidden layers	0.64
Proposed model (S-Resnet) - 54 hidden layers	**0.52**

regularization technique for improving generalization capability; we relied on the implicit regularization of the models via dropout of input shortcut connections and hidden units for the S-ResNet, and dropout of hidden units only for ResNet. It is interesting to note that the proposed model do not suffer from convergence problem as reported in an earlier work which experimented with a similar training scheme [18]. In addition, the experimental results given in Tables 1 and 2 suggest that the proposed training scheme improves the implicit regularization of very deep networks; that is, lower test errors are achieved for the S-ResNets as compared to the ResNets. We conjecture that the simple modification employed for the proposed model helps to reduce the reliance of model units in one layer over others for feature learning. We observe that [8] also reported an error rate of 0.21%, however [8] employed some form of data augmentation using an ensemble of 5 neural networks; without data augmentation, they obtained a test error rate of 0.52%. Conversely, we employ no data augmentation and model ensemble.

6   Conclusion

Very deep networks suffer optimization problems even in situations that indeed favour over-fitting. Furthermore, assuming that we are able to optimize very deep networks, over-fitting is almost always inevitable due to large model capacity. We address the aforementioned problems by taking inspiration from residual learning. Our proposed model, stochastic residual network (*S-ResNet*), employs stochastic shortcut connections from the input to the hidden layers for essentially improving the implicit regularization of very deep models. Experimental results on benchmark datasets validate that the proposed approach improved implicit regularization on very deep networks as compared to the conventional residual learning.

Acknowledgments. This work was funded by the National Research Fund (FNR), Luxembourg, under the project reference R-AGR-0424-05-D/Björn Ottersten.

References

1. Oyedotun, O.K., Khashman, A.: Deep learning in vision-based static hand gesture recognition. Neural Comput. Appl. **27**(3), 1–11 (2016)
2. Oyedotun, O.K., Khashman, A.: Banknote recognition: investigating processing and cognition framework using competitive neural network. Cogn. Neurodyn. **11**(1), 67–79 (2017)
3. Hornik, K.: Approximation capabilities of multilayer feedforward networks. Neural Netw. **4**(2), 251–257 (1991)
4. Funahashi, K.I.: On the approximate realization of continuous mappings by neural networks. Neural Netw. **2**(3), 183–192 (1989)
5. Delalleau, O., Bengio, Y.: Shallow vs. deep sum-product networks. In: Advances in Neural Information Processing Systems, pp. 666–674 (2011)
6. Mhaskar, H., Liao, Q., Poggio, T.: Learning functions: When is deep better than shallow. arXiv preprint (2016). arXiv:1603.00988
7. Bianchini, M., Scarselli, F.: On the complexity of neural network classifiers: a comparison between shallow and deep architectures. IEEE Trans. Neural Netw. Learn. Syst. **25**(8), 1553–1565 (2014)
8. Wan, L., Zeiler, M., Zhang, S., Cun, Y.L., Fergus, R.: Regularization of neural networks using dropconnect. In: Proceedings of the 30th International Conference on Machine Learning (ICML-2013), pp. 1058–1066 (2013)
9. Graham, B.: Fractional max-pooling. arXiv preprint (2014). arXiv:1412.6071
10. Clevert, D.A., Unterthiner, T., Hochreiter, S.: Fast and accurate deep network learning by exponential linear units (ELUs), arXiv preprint, arXiv:1511.07289 (2015)
11. Simonyan, K., Zisserman, A.: Very deep convolutional networks for large-scale image recognition, arXiv preprint, arXiv:1409.1556 (2014)
12. Szegedy, C., Liu, W., Jia, Y., Sermanet, P., Reed, S., Anguelov, D., et al.: Going deeper with convolutions. In: Proceedings of the IEEE Conference on Computer Vision and Pattern Recognition, pp. 1–9 (2015)
13. Srivastava, R.K., Greff, K., Schmidhuber, J.: Training very deep networks. In: Advances in Neural Information Processing Systems, pp. 2377–2385 (2015)
14. He, K., Zhang, X., Ren, S., Sun, J.: Deep residual learning for image recognition. In: Proceedings of the IEEE Conference on Computer Vision and Pattern Recognition, pp. 770–778 (2016)
15. He, K., Zhang, X., Ren, S., Sun, J.: Delving deep into rectifiers: surpassing human-level performance on imagenet classification. In: Proceedings of the IEEE International Conference on Computer Vision, pp. 1026–1034 (2015)
16. Glorot, X., Bengio, Y.: Understanding the difficulty of training deep feedforward neural networks. AISTATS **9**, 249–256 (2010)
17. Ioffe, S., Szegedy, C.: Batch normalization: accelerating deep network training by reducing internal covariate shift, arXiv preprint, arXiv:1502.03167 (2015)

18. He, K., Zhang, X., Ren, S., Sun, J.: Identity mappings in deep residual networks. In: European Conference on Computer Vision, pp. 630–645 (2016)
19. Srivastava, N., Hinton, G., Krizhevsky, A., Sutskever, I., Salakhutdinov, R.: Dropout: a simple way to prevent neural networks from overfitting. J. Mach. Learn. Res. **15**(1), 1929–1958 (2014)
20. Schlkopf, B., Simard, P., Smola, A., Vapnik, V.: Prior knowledge in support vector Kernels. In: Proceedings of the 10th International Conference on Neural Information Processing Systems, pp. 640–646 (1997)
21. Simard, P.Y., LeCun, Y.A., Denker, J.S., Victorri, B.: Transformation invariance in pattern recognition – tangent distance and tangent propagation. In: Montavon, G., Orr, G.B., Müller, K.-R. (eds.) Neural Networks: Tricks of the Trade. LNCS, vol. 7700, pp. 235–269. Springer, Heidelberg (2012). doi:10.1007/978-3-642-35289-8_17
22. Wu, M., Schlkopf, B., Bakir, G.: Building sparse large margin classifiers. In: Proceedings of the 22nd International Conference on Machine Learning, pp. 996–1003 (2005)
23. Trottier, L., Chaib-draa, B., Giguère, P.: Incrementally built dictionary learning for sparse representation. In: Arik, S., Huang, T., Lai, W.K., Liu, Q. (eds.) ICONIP 2015. LNCS, vol. 9489, pp. 117–126. Springer, Cham (2015). doi:10.1007/978-3-319-26532-2_14
24. Simard, P., LeCun, Y., Denker, J.S.: Efficient pattern recognition using a new transformation distance. In: Advances in Neural Information Processing Systems, pp. 50–58 (1993)
25. Keysers, D., Dahmen, J., Theiner, T., Ney, H.: Experiments with an extended tangent distance. In: 15th International Conference on Pattern Recognition, Proceedings, vol. 2, pp. 38–42 (2000)
26. Yang, J., Yu, K., Huang, T.: Supervised translation-invariant sparse coding. In: IEEE Conference on Computer Vision and Pattern Recognition (CVPR), pp. 3517–3524 (2010)
27. Yang, Z., Moczulski, M., Denil, M., de Freitas, N., Smola, A., Song, L., Wang, Z.: Deep fried convnets. In: Proceedings of the IEEE International Conference on Computer Vision, pp. 1476–1483 (2015)
28. Chan, T.H., Jia, K., Gao, S., Lu, J., Zeng, Z., Ma, Y.: Pcanet: a simple deep learning baseline for image classification? IEEE Trans. Image Process. **24**(12), 5017–5032 (2015)
29. Lin, M., Chen, Q., Yan, S.: Network in network. In: International Conference on Learning Representations, abs/1312.4400 (2014)
30. Lee, C.Y., Xie, S., Gallagher, P., Zhang, Z., Tu, Z.: Deeply-supervised nets. In: Artificial Intelligence and Statistics, pp. 562–570 (2015)
31. Ngiam, J., Coates, A., Lahiri, A., Prochnow, B., Le, Q.V., Ng, A.Y.: On optimization methods for deep learning. In: Proceedings of the 28th International Conference on Machine Learning (ICML-2011), pp. 265–272 (2011)
32. Goodfellow, I.J., Shlens, J., Szegedy, C.: Explaining and harnessing adversarial examples. In: International Conference on Learning Representations, arXiv preprint, arXiv:1412.6572 (2015)
33. Huang, G., Sun, Y., Liu, Z., Sedra, D., Weinberger, K.Q.: Deep networks with stochastic depth. In: European Conference on Computer Vision, pp. 646–661 (2016)

Knowledge Memory Based LSTM Model for Answer Selection

Weijie An[1], Qin Chen[1], Yan Yang[1(✉)], and Liang He[1,2]

[1] Department of Computer Science and Technology, East China Normal University,
Shanghai 200241, China
{wjan,qchen}@ica.stc.sh.cn, {yanyang,lhe}@cs.ecnu.edu.cn
[2] Shanghai Engineering Research Center of Intelligent Service Robot,
Shanghai, China

Abstract. Recurrent neural networks (RNN) have shown great success in answer selection task in recent years. Although the attention mechanism has been widely used to enhance the information interaction between questions and answers, knowledge is still the gap between their representations. In this paper, we propose a knowledge memory based RNN model, which incorporates the knowledge learned from the data sets into the question representations. Experiments on two benchmark data sets show the great advantages of our proposed model over that without the knowledge memory. Furthermore, our model outperforms most of the recent progress in question answering.

Keywords: Knowledge memory · Answer selection · Deep learning

1 Introduction

Answer selection is a key subtask of open domain question answering. Given a question and a set of candidate answers, the goal is to find the most relevant answer sentence. Most traditional methods are based on information retrieval models or classification according to the lexical features such as word co-occurrence and syntactic tree edit distance [1–3]. In recent years, the recurrent neural networks (RNN) have attracted more attention, which represent the question and answer sentence in a continuous semantic space. Then, the similarity between the question and answer is calculated according to the representations.

To capture the salient information for question answering, various attention mechanisms have been proposed to obtain the attentive representations of questions and/or answers. Though the attention based RNN models have been proved to be effective for question answering [4,5], they mainly focus on the information of the current sentence and can not well capture additional knowledge that is useful for answer selections. For example, for the question: *where did the mayflower land?*, if we focus on the attentive word *mayflower*, we may pay more attention to the information that *mayflower is a ship which transported the English Pilgrims* in the answer sentence. However, it is still difficult to answer this question.

© Springer International Publishing AG 2017
D. Liu et al. (Eds.): ICONIP 2017, Part II, LNCS 10635, pp. 34–42, 2017.
https://doi.org/10.1007/978-3-319-70096-0_4

But once we have the knowledge that *"English Pilgrims were transported to New Land"*, it is easier to find the correct answer that contain the place *New Land*. Therefore, it is necessary to incorporate more knowledge for question answering.

Noting the knowledge gap between question and answer representations, a memory network architecture was proposed, which stored a specific knowledge base or the passage information in a memory for question representation [6] and answer inference [7]. However, in the answer selection task, it is difficult to find a suitable knowledge base due to the various types of questions issued by users. Moreover, the large-scale text corpus can not be directly stored due to the limited memory size in practice.

In this paper, we propose a knowledge memory based Bidirectional Long-Short-Term-Memory (**KM-BiLSTM**) model to enhance the question representations within the RNN framework. First, motivated by the findings that the word embeddings trained on the data set contain a certain amount of knowledge [8], we initialize the knowledge memory with the embeddings of the keywords selected from the data sets (i.e., knowledge embeddings), and update them automatically during the training process. Then, the knowledge weights specific to a question are calculated by measuring the similarity between the preliminary question representation obtained by BiLSTM and the knowledge embeddings stored in the memory. After that, we integrate the weighted summation of the knowledge embeddings with the question to obtain the knowledge-aware question representations. Finally, the similarities between the question and answer representations are measured for answer selections. We conduct experiments on two public benchmark datasets, namely TREC-QA and WikiQA. The results show that our proposed **KM-BiLSTM** model outperforms most of the recent answer selection models.

The main contributions of our work are as follows: (1) we propose a knowledge memory based BiLSTM model, which incorporates a knowledge memory into the RNN framework to obtain the knowledge-aware question representations; (2) we explore the effectiveness of the data set based knowledge to enhance the performance of answer selections, which does not rely on the external data source; (3) the experimental results have verified the effectiveness of our proposed model, and also provide a promising avenue to make full use of the data set based knowledge for other tasks.

The rest of this paper is organized as follows. Section 2 introduces the related work in question answering. Our proposed approach is demonstrated in Sect. 3, followed by the experimental setup and results analysis in Sect. 4. Finally, we conclude our work and present some ideas for future research in Sect. 5.

2   Related Work

Answer Selection task is defined as follows: Given a question and a set of candidate answers, the goal is to find the most relevant answer sentence. Previous work usually focused on employing feature engineering, linguistic tools, or external resources. For example, [1] used the WordNet to obtain the semantic features.

[3] utilized the syntactical trees to measure the similarity between questions and answers. [2] tried to fulfill the matching using minimal edit sequences between their dependency parse trees. [9] automated the extraction of discriminative tree-edit features over parsing trees.

Recently, the deep neural networks have attracted more attention due to the good performance in answer selections. To model the sentence with variable length, the Recurrent Neural Networks (RNN) have been widely used. [10] proposed the long short-term memory (LSTM) based RNN model, which helped alleviate the vanish of the gradient during the long distance transmission. Specifically, given an input sequence $\mathbf{x} = \{\mathbf{x}_1, \mathbf{x}_2, ..., \mathbf{x}_n\}$, the LSTM cell updates the hidden vector $\mathbf{h}(t)$ at each time step. LSTM controls the information flow through the cell with these gate operations. In general, the output of the last hidden unit can be regarded as the representation of the whole sentence.

In order to capture the salient information in a sentence, various attention mechanisms have been proposed [4,5]. However, these methods only focus on the information in the current sentences, which neglect the knowledge in the whole data sets. Noting the importance of the knowledge for reading comprehensions, [7] proposed a key-value memory network to store the information of the knowledge base or the passage itselft. However, it is usually difficult to find a suitable knowledge base for the answer selection task due to the various questions issued by users. Moreover, the large-scale text corpus can not be stored due to the limit of the memory size in practice. In this paper, we propose a knowledge memory based LSTM model for answer selections, where the knowledge is learned from the internal data set and utilized for knowledge-aware question representations.

3   Approach

3.1   Architecture of KM-BiLSTM

Figure 1 shows the architecture of our proposed KM-BiLSTM model. Specifically, we adopt the BiLSTM model to obtain the preliminary representations of the question and answer (donated as $\mathbf{q}$ and $\mathbf{R}_a$ respectively), which has shown good performance for answer selections [4,11]. To bridge the knowledge gap between questions and answers, we present a knowledge memory to obtain the knowledge-aware question representations. In particular, we first initialize the knowledge memory with the knowledge embeddings. Then, the similarities between the preliminary question representation ($\mathbf{q}$) and the knowledge embeddings are calculated as the knowledge weights specific to a question. After that, the weighted sum of the knowledge embeddings are integrated with $\mathbf{q}$ to obtain the new question representation ($\mathbf{R}_q$). Finally, the similarity between questions and answers are calculated by the Manhattan distance with L1 norm as shown in Eq. 1, which performs slightly better than the other alternatives such as cosine similarity as indicated in [12].

$$sim(\mathbf{R}_q, \mathbf{R}_a) = exp(-||\mathbf{R}_q - \mathbf{R}_a||_1) \tag{1}$$

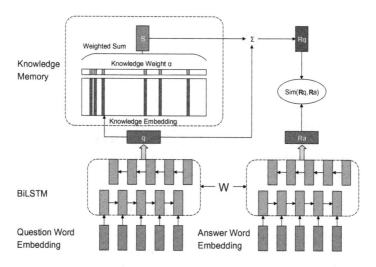

Fig. 1. Architecture of KM-BiLSTM

3.2 Knowledge Embedding

The word embeddings [8] have been widely used in many NLP and IR tasks [13,14] for their effectiveness. In general, the semantically related words usually have similar representations in the hidden space. For example, *"English Pilgrims were transported to New Land"*, *"Pilgrims"* and *"New Land"* are very close in the hidden space, because they have the relation *"were transported to"*. To some extent, the word embeddings imply much valuable knowledge, which can be utilized to enhance question representations by our assumption. Therefore, we adopt the word embeddings as the knowledge and present a memory for knowledge storage within the RNN framework.

Since not all words are equally important, we only select the informative keywords from the data set and use their embeddings as the knowledge, which makes a good balance between the performance and cost for our introduced knowledge memory. Various methods can be applied for keyword selection. In this paper, we treat each question or answer as a document, and adopt the widely used IDF metric for keyword selections. Specifically, the weight for each word is calculated by the following formula:

$$\mathbf{W}_{w_i} = log\frac{|D|}{|\{j : w_i \in d_j\}|} \qquad (2)$$

where D is the question and answer document set, $|D|$ is the number of documents, w_i is a word in the data set, and $|\{j : w_i \in d_j\}|$ denotes the number of documents contain the word w_i. We first initialize the knowledge memory with the embeddings of the top K informative keywords according to their IDF values. In order to obtain more accurate knowledge from the data set, the knowledge memory will be updated during the training process within the RNN framework.

3.3   Knowledge-Aware Question Representation

To obtain the knowledge specific to a question, we first calculate the weight of each knowledge embedding associated with a question as follows:

$$\alpha_j = \frac{exp(e(\mathbf{k}_j, \mathbf{q}))}{\sum_{k=1}^{l} exp(e(\mathbf{k}_k, \mathbf{q}))} \tag{3}$$

where k_j is the jth knowledge embedding in the knowledge memory, q is the preliminary question representation obtained by BiLSTM, l donates the knowledge memory size, and $e(\cdot)$ is a score function which measures the importance of each knowledge embedding for a given question.

More formally, the score function is defined as:

$$e(\mathbf{k}_j, \mathbf{q}) = \mathbf{v}^T tanh(\mathbf{W}_H \mathbf{k}_j + \mathbf{W}_Q \mathbf{q} + \mathbf{b}) \tag{4}$$

where $\mathbf{W}_H$ and $\mathbf{W}_Q$ are matrices, $\mathbf{b}$ is a bias vector, $tanh$ is the hyperbolic tangent function, $\mathbf{v}$ is a global vector and $\mathbf{v}^T$ denotes its transpose. $\mathbf{W}_H$, $\mathbf{W}_Q$, $\mathbf{b}$ and $\mathbf{v}$ are all parameters.

With the calculated knowledge weights, the knowledge specific to a question can be obtained by the weighted sum of all the knowledge embeddings:

$$\mathbf{s} = \sum_{j=1}^{l} \alpha_j \mathbf{k}_j. \tag{5}$$

Finally, we integrate the preliminary question representation with the specific knowledge to obtain the knowledge-aware question representation:

$$\mathbf{R}_q = \mathbf{q} + \mathbf{s} \tag{6}$$

4   Experiment

4.1   Experimental Setup

Datasets and Evaluation Metrics. We adopt two public answer selection data sets for evaluation: WikiQA and TREC-QA. WikiQA [15] is an open domain question-answering data set in which all answers are collected from the Wikipedia. TREC-QA was created by Wang et al. [3] based on the Text REtrieval Conference (TREC) QA track (8-13) data. Each dataset is split into 3 parts, i.e., train, dev and test, and the statistics are presented in Table 1. To evaluate the model performance, we adopt the mean average precision (MAP) and mean reciprocal rank (MRR), which are the primary metrics used in QA [4,11].

Parameter Settings. The pre-trained word embeddings released from the GloVe project[1] are utilized in our model. The parameters in BiLSTM are shared between questions and answers, which has been shown to be effective to improve the performance [11]. The hidden states size is turned to 50 and the knowledge memory size is set to 1000. We train our model using a batch size of 512. And in experiments we choose the top K (K = 1000) informative words for the knowledge memory initialization.

---

[1] http://nlp.stanford.edu/projects/glove/.

Table 1. Statistics of the datasets. We remove all the questions with no right or wrong answers. "Avg QL" and "Avg AL" denote the average length of questions and answers.

Dataset	# of questions (train/dev/test)	Avg QL (train/dev/test)	Avg AL (train/dev/test)
TREC-QA	1162/65/68	7.57/8.00/8.63	23.21/24.9/25.61
WikiQA	873/126/243	7.16/7.23/7.26	25.29/24.59/24.59

4.2 Effect of the Knowledge Memory

Table 2 shows the performance of the classical BiLSTM model and our proposed KM-BiLSTM model in TREC-QA and WikiQA. The last line denotes the improved rate of our model over BiLSTM. We observe that our proposed knowledge memory based model consistently outperforms that without knowledge memory. In particular, we achieve a maximum improvement of 6.63% in terms of MRR. This indicates that our proposed model is more effective for answer selections, by incorporating the specific knowledge into question representations. Moreover, we find that the improvements of MRR are higher than that of MAP, which shows the superiority of our proposed model in finding the first correct answer with the obtained knowledge-ware question representations.

Table 2. Performance of BiLSTM and KM-BiLSTM

Model	TREC-QA		WikiQA	
	MAP	MRR	MAP	MRR
BiLSTM	0.7032	0.7908	0.6904	0.7015
KM-BiLSTM	**0.7344**	**0.8432**	**0.7129**	**0.7269**
Improvement	(+4.43%)	(+6.63%)	(+3.26%)	(+3.62%)

4.3 Performance Comparisons

To further investigate the effectiveness of our proposed KM-BiLSTM model, we make a comparison with the recent work in answer selections. The results are shown in Tables 3 and 4. For TREC-QA, we use the models which are considered as the strong baselines in recent studies for comparisons: (1) A combination of the stack BiLSTM and BM25 model [11]; (2) RNN models with inner attention [4]; (3) A convolutional neural network (CNN) based architecture which used both the hidden features and the statistical features for ranking [16] and (4) A learning-to-rank method which leveraged the word alignment features as well as some lexical features for ranking [17]. As to WikiQA, in addition to the method [4] as mentioned above, we make a comparison with other three strong baselines: (1) A bigram CNN model with average pooling [15]; (2) A CNN model

Table 3. Performance on TREC-QA.

System	MAP	MRR
Wang and Nyberg 2015 [11]	0.7134	0.7913
Severyn and Moschitti 2015 [16]	0.7459	0.8078
Wang and Ittycheriah 2015 [17]	0.7460	0.8200
Wang et al. 2016 [4]	0.7369	0.8208
KM-BiLSTM	0.7344	**0.8432**

Table 4. Performance on Wiki-QA.

System	MAP	MRR
Yang et al. 2015 [15]	0.6520	0.6652
Yin et al. 2015 [5]	0.6921	0.7108
Alexander et al. 2016 [7]	0.7069	0.7265
Wang et al. 2016 [4]	**0.7341**	**0.7418**
KM-BiLSTM	0.7129	0.7269

which used an interactive attention matrix for the attentive representations of questions and answers [5] and (3) A key-value memory network which stored the knowledge base and passage information for question representations [7].

From Tables 3 and 4, we observe that our proposed model outperforms most of the recent work in answer selections. In particular, we achieve the best performance on TREC-QA and the second best on WikiQA in terms of the MRR metric. Regarding to MAP, our model is also comparable to if not better than most of the strong baselines. All these findings indicate the effectiveness of our knowledge memory, which helps bridge the gap between question and answer representations via the data set based knowledge. It is also worth noting that our model does not rely on additional features or interactions between questions and answers, which makes our model more efficiency.

4.4 Case Study

In order to better understand our proposed model, we provide an example to show why our dataset based knowledge memory is more effective for the answer selection task.

As shown in Table 5, for the question *"where did the persian war take place"*, it is required to find a place, and we observe that top 2 attentive words associate with the question are location names, such as *ecuador* and *ayburn*. In particular, these two words contain the information that associate with the key word *"Eurymedon"* in the right answer, which provides more useful information (knowledge) for answering the question. Therefore, we integrate the information of the knowledge embeddings into our model, which enhances the question representations to find more relevant answers.

Table 5. Effectiveness of Knowledge Memory

Question	Attentive word(top 5)	Answer
Where did the persian war take place	ecuador, ayburn, valentine, inmates, mustard	At the Battle of the Eurymedon in 466 BC, the League won a double victory that finally secured freedom for the cities of Ionia.

5   Conclusion

In this paper, we propose a knowledge memory based LSTM model for answer selections. With our knowledge memory, the knowledge specific to a question can be automatically learned from the data sets, which provides valuable information to answer questions. Experiments on TREC-QA and WikiQA have shown the effectiveness of our proposed model, especially in terms of the MRR metric which measures the performance in finding the first right answer. Furthermore, our model is comparable to if not better than the state-of-the-art approaches in answer selections. In the future, we will continue investigating the effectiveness of our data set based knowledge memory for other tasks such as information retrieval.

Acknowledgments. This work was supported by Xiaoi Research, Shanghai Municipal Commission of Economy and information Under Grant Project (No. 201602024) and the Natural Science Foundation of Shanghai (No. 172R1444900).

References

1. Yih, W.T., Chang, M.W., Meek, C., Pastusiak, A.: Question answering using enhanced lexical semantic models. In: Proceedings of the 51st Annual Meeting of the Association for Computational Linguistics (vol. 1: Long Papers), pp. 1744–1753. Association for Computational Linguistics, Sofia (2013)
2. Heilman, M., Smith, N.A.: Tree edit models for recognizing textual entailments, paraphrases, and answers to questions. In: Human Language Technologies: The 2010 Annual Conference of the North American Chapter of the Association for Computational Linguistics, pp. 1011–1019. Association for Computational Linguistics, Los Angeles (2010)
3. Wang, M., Smith, N.A., Mitamura, T.: What is the jeopardy model? a quasi-synchronous grammar for QA. In: Proceedings of the 2007 Joint Conference on Empirical Methods in Natural Language Processing and Computational Natural Language Learning (EMNLP-CoNLL), pp. 22–32. Association for Computational Linguistics, Prague (2007)
4. Wang, B., Liu, K., Zhao, J.: Inner attention based recurrent neural networks for answer selection. In: Proceedings of the 54th Annual Meeting of the Association for Computational Linguistics (vol. 1: Long Papers). pp. 1288–1297. Association for Computational Linguistics, Berlin (2016)
5. Yin, W., Schütze, H., Xiang, B., Zhou, B.: ABCNN: Attention-based convolutional neural network for modeling sentence pairs. arXiv preprint arXiv:1512.05193 (2015)
6. Sukhbaatar, S., Szlam, A., Weston, J., Fergus, R.: End-to-end memory networks. In: Advances in Neural Information Processing Systems, vol. 28, pp. 2440–2448. Curran Associates, Inc. (2015)
7. Miller, A., Fisch, A., Dodge, J., Karimi, A.H., Bordes, A., Weston, J.: Key-value memory networks for directly reading documents. In: Proceedings of the 2016 Conference on Empirical Methods in Natural Language Processing, pp. 1400–1409. Association for Computational Linguistics, Austin (2016)
8. Mikolov, T., Sutskever, I., Chen, K., Corrado, G.S., Dean, J.: Distributed representations of words and phrases and their compositionality. In: Advances in Neural Information Processing Systems, pp. 3111–3119 (2013)

9. Severyn, A., Moschitti, A.: Automatic feature engineering for answer selection and extraction. In: Proceedings of the 2013 Conference on Empirical Methods in Natural Language Processing, pp. 458–467. Association for Computational Linguistics, Seattle (2013)

10. Hochreiter, S., Schmidhuber, J.: Long short-term memory. Neural Comput. **9**(8), 1735–1780 (1997)

11. Wang, D., Nyberg, E.: A long short-term memory model for answer sentence selection in question answering. In: Proceedings of the 53rd Annual Meeting of the Association for Computational Linguistics and the 7th International Joint Conference on Natural Language Processing (vol. 2: Short Papers), pp. 707–712. Association for Computational Linguistics, Beijing (2015)

12. Mueller, J., Thyagarajan, A.: Siamese recurrent architectures for learning sentence similarity. In: AAAI, pp. 2786–2792 (2016)

13. Hu, Q., Pei, Y., Chen, Q., He, L.: SG++: word representation with sentiment and negation for twitter sentiment classification. In: Proceedings of the 39th ACM SIGIR, pp. 997–1000 (2016)

14. Grbovic, M., Djuric, N., Radosavljevic, V., Silvestri, F., Bhamidipati, N.: Context- and content-aware embeddings for query rewriting in sponsored search. In: Proceedings of the 38th ACM SIGIR, pp. 383–392 (2015)

15. Yang, Y., Yih, W.T., Meek, C.: Wikiqa: a challenge dataset for open-domain question answering. In: Proceedings of the 2015 Conference on Empirical Methods in Natural Language Processing, pp. 2013–2018 (2015)

16. Severyn, A., Moschitti, A.: Learning to rank short text pairs with convolutional deep neural networks. In: Proceedings of the 38th International ACM SIGIR Conference on Research and Development in Information Retrieval, pp. 373–382. ACM (2015)

17. Wang, Z., Ittycheriah, A.: FAQ-based question answering via word alignment. arXiv preprint arXiv:1507.02628 (2015)

Breast Cancer Malignancy Prediction Using Incremental Combination of Multiple Recurrent Neural Networks

Dehua Chen$^{(\boxtimes)}$, Guangjun Qian, Cheng Shi, and Qiao Pan

Department of Computer Science, Donghua University, Shanghai, China
chendehua@dhu.edu.cn, guangjunqian@126.com

Abstract. Breast cancer is the most common cancer among women worldwide. An early detection of malignant of breast cancer, followed by proper treatment, can great improve the survival rate of patients. Recently, the deep learning based malignancy prediction models for breast cancer have been proposed. However, these models are usually trained with single type of clinical text, which are still not effective enough to predict breast cancer malignancy. In this paper, we follow the deep incremental learning framework and propose a prediction model of breast cancer malignancy by incremental combination of multiple recurrent neural networks. Specially, the model first uses multiple recurrent neural networks (RNNs) for generating features from the multi-types of clinical text including B-ultrasound, X-rays, Computed Tomography (CT), and Nuclear Magnetic Resonance Imaging (MRI), and then combines the generated features in an incremental way. Finally, we add one more recurrent neural network layer for classifying benign and malignant of breast cancer based on combined generated features.

Keywords: Breast cancer · Text classification · Deep learning · Recurrent neural networks

1 Introduction

Breast cancer has become one of the susceptible diseases in women, seriously affected to the normal life of women. There is no doubt that breast cancer has developed into a worldwide problem. Breast cancer contains four types of examinations, which is B-ultrasound, X-ray, Computed Tomography (CT) and Nuclear Magnetic Resonance Imaging (MRI).

The prediction of benign and malignant of breast cancer is a text classification problem because each description of clinical report is text. There are many models can be successfully used in the text classification, such as support vector machines (SVMs) [1], decision trees, Bayes classifiers and so on. But it may have a poor performance on skewed data and sparse data. Deep learning has a huge development in recent years, such as recurrent neural network (RNN). But using a single RNN is usually trained with one clinical report, and it is not effective enough to predict breast cancer malignancy. Therefore, precise breast cancer prediction still remains a challenging problem.

© Springer International Publishing AG 2017
D. Liu et al. (Eds.): ICONIP 2017, Part II, LNCS 10635, pp. 43–52, 2017.
https://doi.org/10.1007/978-3-319-70096-0_5

To address this problem, we propose a categorization model for breast cancer prediction, called incremental recurrent neural network (IRNN). IRNN has multiple attribute RNNs which is used for feature construction [2] and one classification RNN. Each clinical report can be used as an input for attribute RNN. The features of the extraction increase as the inspection report increases. Therefore, the model includes B-ultrasound-RNN, X-ray-RNN, CT-RNN, and MRI-RNN. The description text can be converted into real-value vectors through word embedding. It is effective to concatenate the description word sequence for ambiguity. Each attribute RNN can generate some features based on word sequence and it will combine together as the input to classification RNN. The last layer of this model is an output layer. A cost function is defined for updating the weight of the model, the errors can be propagated through the classification RNN to the attribute RNNs.

2 Related Work

There are many ways to predict malignant of breast cancer, such as Artificial Neural Networks (ANNs) [3] and machine learning methods. Marcano [4] proposed a model which is consists of an input layer with nine neurons, four hidden neurons with sigmoid function as the activation function and an output layer. A multilayer perceptron which uses retro propagation of error algorithm is proposed by Guo and Nandi [5] for breast cancer classification, and it is used on WDBC dataset. Murat [6], constructs a network, it contains nine input neurons, one hidden layer with eleven hidden neurons and the last layer is an output layer which has a linear function. Zribi and Boujelbene [7], uses the neural networks with an incremental learning algorithm in breast cancer diagnosis. It is beginning with one neuron on its hidden layer. In the process of learning, compared with the previous step, the improvement of the error is not as good as the given threshold, then a new neuron will be added to the hidden layer. Only the weights of the last neuron will be fixed when the learning process is started again. The learning process will stop when the network error reaches the given threshold or the new neuron does not reduce the error compared with the previous process. In addition to artificial neural networks, there are some research use traditional machine learning algorithms. Xiu-feng Yang, uses Principal Component Analysis (PCA) [8] and SVMs based on multiple kernels for breast cancer diagnosis. First, PCA is used to transform high dimensional data into lower dimensional, and then, the SVM with multiple kernels is used to classify the lower dimensional data.

3 Clinical Data in Breast Cancer Diagnosis

3.1 Four Types of Diagnostic Data

There are mainly four different types of clinical examinations including B-ultrasound, X-rays, CT or MRI. In general, each examination outputs a textual report describing the status of the breast cancer in detail. Such as Bilateral gland echo increased, enhanced, less uniform distribution, gland surface is still light the whole, which is described by

B-ultrasound report. Obviously, such textual description of each examination is an important type of data source for determining the malignant grade of breast cancer.

3.2 Metadata Definition

A patient can be used as a metadata. Each metadata contains four attributes, B-ultrasound description, X-rays description, CT description and MRI description. And the label of each metadata is benign or malignant breast cancer abstracted from pathology report. Formally, a patient consists of its label y and an attribute vector x represented with a collection of four attributes:

$$P = \{x, y\} = \{x^{(1)}, x^{(2)}, x^{(3)}, x^{(4)}, y\} \tag{1}$$

Table 1 gives a detailed description of the metadata. The i-th metadata attribute of a patient is defined as the sequence of textual words as follows:

$$x^{(i)} = \{x_1^{(i)} x_2^{(i)} \ldots x_n^{(i)}\} \tag{2}$$

Table 1. Description of metadata attributes.

Var	Attribute	Value
$x^{(1)}$	B-ultrasound	Text
$x^{(2)}$	X-rays	Text
$x^{(3)}$	CT	Text
$x^{(4)}$	MRI	Text
y	Label	Nominal

4 Our Proposed Model

4.1 Deep Incremental Prediction Networks

Incremental recurrent neural network (IRNN) is an end-to-end deep learning model for classifying of benign and malignant of breast cancer. IRNN consists of multiple RNNs. Four RNNs are used for feature extraction, and the other is used to classify the extracted features. Text description data are converted into real-valued vectors and then as the input of attribute RNNs.

Firstly, we transfer the text data into real-value vectors by word embedding. The generated features can represent the different semantics of the word sequence. Each RNN receives an attribute as an input, and thus IRNN contains m RNNs when metadata consists of m attributes. Each RNN output one vector and then will be combined with precious one, which is as the input to classification RNN. The output layer can tell whether the patient is benign or malignant (Fig. 1).

IRNN can be the same as the traditional neural network with the formula to define. Let $_m^A h_t^{(n)}$ and $^C h_t^{(n)}$ denote the n-th layer at time t of the m-th RNN which is used to

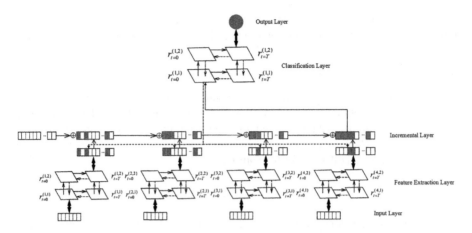

Fig. 1. The figure shows the structure of IRNN, it is consist of multiple RNNs, including input layer, feature extraction layer, classification layer and output layer.

extract features and the n-th layer at time t of the RNN which is used to classify the generated features. A and C mean attribute and classification. As previously described, $_m^A W^{kn}$ and $^C W^{kn}$ denote the weight matrix between the k-th and the n-th layers of the m-th RNN and the classification RNN. $_m^A h_t^{(n)}$ is defined as a function and its parameters is related with the hidden layer vector at t–1, $_m^A h_{t-1}^{(n)}$, and the hidden layer vector of (n–1)-th layer at time t, $_m^A h_t^{(n-1)}$:

$$_m^A h_t^{(n)} = {}_m^A f^{(n)} \left({}_m^A W^{(n-1)n A}_m h_t^{(n-1)} + {}_m^A W^{nn A}_m h_{t-1}^n + {}_m^A b^{(n)} \right) \tag{3}$$

$$_m^A h_t^{(1)} = {}_m^A f^{(1)} \left({}_m^A W^{x1 A}_m x + {}_m^A W^{11 A}_m h_{t-1}^{(1)} + {}_m^A b^{(1)} \right) \tag{4}$$

where $^R f^{(n)}$ and $^R b^{(n)}$ denote the activation function which is nonlinear and the bias vector of the $^R h_t^{(n)}$. The length of x and the length of vocabulary are equal. Each RNN which is used to generate features output one vector and then will be concatenated one vector d, which is as the input to classification RNN.

$$d = {}_1^R h_{l_1}^{(n)} \circ \cdots \circ {}_m^R h_{l_m}^{(n)} \tag{5}$$

where l_i denotes the length of the word sequence of the i-th attribute. The classification RNN is defined as follows:

$$^C h_t^{(n)} = {}^C f^{(n)} \left({}^C W^{(n-1)n C} h_t^{(n-1)} + {}^C W^{nn C} h_{t-1}^n + {}^C b^{(n)} \right) \tag{6}$$

$$^C h_t^1 = {}^C f^{(1)} \left({}^C W^{x1} x + {}^C W^{11 C} h_{t-1}^1 + {}^C b^{(1)} \right) \tag{7}$$

The activation function of each RNN we used is hyperbolic tangent function. It has a better performance than sigmoid function or others [9]. And we use a sigmoid function as the activation function in the output layer, it can output 0 or 1 which is corresponding to benign or malignant.

4.2 Learning Process

We define a binary-crossentropy function as our objective function, and it will be minimized by the training process. Figure 2 shows the learning flow of IRNN.

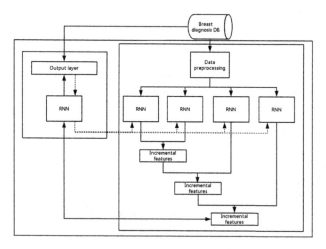

Fig. 2. The figure shows the learning flow of IRNN, solid and dashed lines denote the flows of data and errors during the learning process.

Formally, the objection function is defined as follows:

$$E = \sum_{i=1}^{m} -y_i \log(h_\theta(x)) - (1 - y_i) \log(1 - h_\theta(x)) \tag{8}$$

where y_i can only take two values, 0 or 1. The errors can propagate from the output layer into classification RNN and attribute-RNNs, the weights of the hidden layers are updated as follows:

$$w_i = w_i - \eta \frac{\partial E}{\partial w_i} \tag{9}$$

$$\delta_i = \begin{cases} (y_i^{(n)} - \hat{y}_i^{(n)})(1 - \tanh^2(net_i)), \text{if } i \in o \\ (\sum_{j \in J} \delta_j w_{ij})(1 - \tanh^2(net_i)), \text{if } i \in h \end{cases} \tag{10}$$

where $y_i^{(n)}$ and $\hat{y}_i^{(n)}$ denote the actual value and estimated value, o and h denote the node of an output and an inner hidden layer. The learning rate is η and the value of i-th node is net_i. The error of back propagation is propagated to each attribute-RNN, all the weights are updated by backpropagation through time (BPTT) [10] (Fig. 3).

Algorithm 1: Learning of IRNN

N_{it}: The number of iteration

D^{tr}/D^{te}: Training dataset/test dataset

M: The number of attribute RNNs

V: The vector after the combination

V_m: The vector generated by the m-th attribute RNN

E: The error of classification

$^{A}E_m$: The error of m-th attribute RNN

S: The number of separated minibatch datasets

$^{A}\theta_m^i / {}^{C}\theta^i$: The parameters of m-th attribute RNN and the classification RNN at i-th iteration

$({}^{A}\theta_1^0 ,..., {}^{A}\theta_M^0 , {}^{C}\theta^0) \leftarrow$Initialize (M)

for $i = 1$ **to** N_{it}

for $j=1$ **to** S

  $D^{tr} \leftarrow$GetMiniBatch(D)

  for $m = 1$ **to** M

    $V_m \leftarrow$ATTRIBUTE_RNN$(D^{tr}, {}^{A}\theta_m^{i-1})$; $V \leftarrow$Combine(V, V_m)

  endfor

  $E \leftarrow$CLASSIFICATION_RNN$(V, {}^{C}\theta^{i-1})$

  $({}^{C}\theta^i , {}^{A}E) \leftarrow$CLASSIFICATION_RNN_ BACKWARD$(E, {}^{C}\theta^{i-1})$

  for $m = 1$ **to** M

    $^{A}E_m =$Separate$({}^{A}E ,m)$

    $^{A}\theta_m^i =$ATTRIBUTE_RNN_BACKWARD$({}^{A}E_m , {}^{A}\theta_m^{i-1})$

  endfor

endfor

EvaluateModel$(D^{te}, {}^{A}\theta_1^0 ,..., {}^{A}\theta_M^0 , {}^{C}\theta^0)$

endfor

Fig. 3. The figure shows the algorithm of learning IRNN, including the variable definitions and the implementation process.

5   Experimental Results

5.1   Data and Parameters Setup

We evaluated the IRNN model on a data set which contains 3960 patients. Each patient have one or more diagnostic descriptions of B-ultrasound, CT, MRI and X-rays. The data are divided into training sets, validation sets and test sets, and their proportions are

7/10, 1/10, and 2/10. In the preprocessing, we ignore some unrelated symbols, including period, parenthesis and quotation.

5.2   Performance Evaluation

We use accuracy and F1 score to evaluate the model in our study. The value of F1 score is calculated from the precision and recall rate. It is defined as follows:

$$F1 = \frac{2 * P * R}{P + R} \tag{11}$$

where P and R denote the precision and the recall rate, respectively.

We compare our method to one RNN-based method and one SVM approach. The first is a model uses one RNN to classify according to one diagnostic description in B-ultrasound, CT, MRI and X-rays. In this setting, there is only one diagnostic text as the input of the model, and then the RNN will classify it. We have experimented with the four diagnostic data separately. The second is a traditional machine learning method, SVM. SVM also takes the word vector as input. In addition, a patient may check many times on B-ultrasound, CT, MRI or X-rays. Therefore, we also considered the impact of the number of times on the experimental results. The number of check times of most patients is twice, so we only consider twice.

5.3   Classification Performance

Table 2 shows the accuracy and the F1 score of IRNN compared to the single RNN and the traditional machine learning method, SVM. For Twice- IRNN, we have eight attribute RNNs for feature extraction, the first four attribute RNNs are used to extract the feature of the first four diagnostic descriptions and the remaining four are used for the second four diagnostic descriptions. According to the experimental results, more check times can significantly improve the accuracy and F1 score. Long short-term memories (LSTMs) [11] is a special type of RNN, it is suitable for handling and predicting very important events in the time series of intervals and delays. Therefore, LSTM has a better performance in our experiment according to the experimental results. We can also find that single RNN is better than SVM and combine with four kind of inspection data can improve the performance of classification.

Figure 4 shows the learning cures of our methods, including Once-IRNN, Once-ILSTM, Twice- IRNN and Twice-ILSTM. With the increase of the number of iterations, both the accuracy and the F1 score are increasing.

We investigate the effect of different parameters on model results, including the accuracy, F1 score and training time. In our study, we mainly focus on the effect of word-embedding vector size and the number of hidden layers.

Figure 5 shows the effects of different word-embedding vector size on experimental performance. We can find that larger word-embedding vector size provides better performance. Smaller word-embedding vector size can result in lower accuracy and F1 value because it is difficult to distinguish categories.

Table 2. Performance comparison of different methods.

Method	Accuracy	F1
B-ultrasound(SVM)	0.6573	0.6429
CT(SVM)	0.7257	0.4408
MRI(SVM)	0.4483	0.3217
X-rays(SVM)	0.4744	0.2195
B-ultrasound(Single-RNN)	0.7853	0.6242
CT(Single-RNN)	0.7373	0.4524
MRI(Single-RNN)	0.6363	0.3201
X-rays(Single-RNN)	0.6868	0.3160
B-ultrasound(Single-LSTM)	0.8017	0.6232
CT(Single-LSTM)	0.7563	0.4994
MRI(Single-LSTM)	0.7512	0.4901
X-rays(Single-LSTM)	0.7323	0.4373
Once-IRNN	0.8358	0.7239
Once-ILSTM	0.8522	0.7751
Twice- IRNN	0.8611	0.7873
Twice- ILSTM	0.8712	0.8153

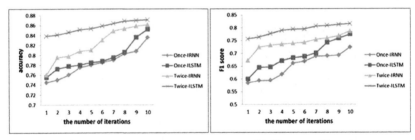

(a) Accuracy of learning curve   (b) F1 score of learning curve

Fig. 4. The figures show the learning curve of different models, including accuracy and F1.

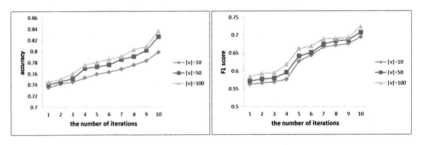

(a) The accuracy of different vector size   (b) The F1 score different vector size

Fig. 5. The figures show the accuracy and F1 score of Once-IRNN of different word vector size.

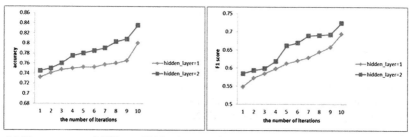

(a) The accuracy of different hidden layer   (b) The F1 score different hidden layer

Fig. 6. The figures show the accuracy and F1 score of Once-IRNN of different hidden layer.

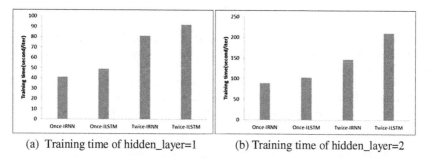

(a) Training time of hidden_layer=1   (b) Training time of hidden_layer=2

Fig. 7. The figures show the training time of different layers of different models, including hidden_layer = 1 and hidden_layer = 2.

Figure 6 shows the effects of different hidden layer numbers on the accuracy and F1 score. As shown we can find that more number of hidden layers provides better performance.

As shown in Fig. 7, the more of hidden layers, the longer training time will spend.

6 Conclusion

Breast cancer prediction is an important and challenging issue in medical field. We proposed an incremental recurrent neural network (IRNN) to classify benign and malignant of breast cancer. The proposed model consists of multiple attribute RNNs and a classification RNN. The classification errors are propagated back through the classification RNN to the attributes RNNs to update the weights. Each RNN receives an attribute as an input, and thus IRNN contains m RNNs when metadata consists of m attributes. This method can avoid the unclear semantics by combining attributes text, and it can keep the accuracy from being too low which is caused by too long word sequence length. Each RNN output one vector and then will be concatenated one vector, which is as the input to classification RNN. The output layer can tell whether the patient is benign or malignant. According to the experimental results, more check times and use LSTM provide better performance. Moreover, we will make the proposed model useful for other disease prediction.

Acknowledgements. This work was supported by the Shanghai Innovation Action Project of Science and Technology (15511106900), the Science and Technology Development Foundation of Shanghai (16JC1400802), the Special Fund of Shanghai Economic and Trade Commission Software and Integrated Circuit Industry Development (No. 160623), and the Shanghai Specific Fund Project for Information Development (XX-XXFZ-01-14-6349).

References

1. Lee, L.H., Wan, C.H., Rajkumar, R., Lee, L.: An enhanced support vector machine classification framework by using euclidean distance function for text document categorization. Appl. Intell. **37**(1), 80–99 (2012)
2. Mikolov, T., Kombrink, S., Burget, L., Černocký, J., Khudanpur, S.: Extensions of recurrent neural network language model. In: IEEE International Conference on Acoustics, Speech and Signal Processing, vol. 125, pp. 5528–5531 (2011)
3. Dayhoff, J.E., Deleo, J.M.: Artificial neural networks. Cancer **91**(S8), 1615–1635 (2001)
4. Marcano-Cedeño, A., Quintanilla-Domínguez, J., Andina, D.: WBCD breast cancer database classification applying artificial metaplasticity neural network. Expert Syst. Appl. **38**(8), 9573–9579 (2011)
5. Guo, H., Nandi, A.K.: Breast cancer diagnosis using genetic programming generated feature. In: 2005 IEEE Workshop on Machine Learning for Signal Processing, vol. 39, pp. 215–220 (2005)
6. Karabatak, M., Ince, M.C.: An expert system for detection of breast cancer based on association rules and neural network. Expert Syst. Appl. **36**(2), 3465–3469 (2009)
7. Zribi, M.: The neural networks with an incremental learning algorithm approach for mass classification in breast cancer. Int. J. Biomed. Data Min. **5**(1) (2016)
8. Jolliffe, I.T.: Principal component analysis: a beginner's guide — II. Pitfalls, myths and extensions. Weather **48**(8), 246–253 (1993)
9. Jozefowicz, R., Zaremba, W., Sutskever, I.: An empirical exploration of recurrent network architectures. In: Proceedings of the 32nd International Conference on Machine Learning (ICML-15), pp. 2342–2350 (2015)
10. Werbos, P.J.: Backpropagation through time: what it does and how to do it. Proc. IEEE **78** (10), 1550–1560 (1990)
11. Graves, A., Schmidhuber, J.: Framewise phoneme classification with bidirectional lstm and other neural network architectures. Neural Netw. **18**(5–6), 602–610 (2005)

TinyPoseNet: A Fast and Compact Deep Network for Robust Head Pose Estimation

Shanru Li[1], Liping Wang[2], Shuang Yang[3,4], Yuanquan Wang[5],
and Chongwen Wang[1(✉)]

[1] School of Software, Beijing Institute of Technology, Beijing 100081, China
shanru_li@163.com, wcwzzw@bit.edu.cn
[2] Purple Bull Funds, Beijing 100024, China
wlp@purplebull.cn
[3] Key Lab of Intelligent Information Processing of Chinese Academy
of Sciences(CAS), Institute of Computing Technology, CAS, Beijing 100190, China
shuang.yang@ict.ac.cn
[4] University of Chinese Academy of Sciences, Beijing 100049, China
[5] Hebei University of Technology, Tianjin 300401, China
wangyuanquan@scse.hebut.edu.cn

Abstract. As an inherent attribute of human, head pose plays an important role in many tasks. In this paper, we formulate head pose estimation in different directions as a multi-task regression problem, and propose a fast, compact and robust head pose estimation model, named TinyPoseNet. Specifically, we combine the tasks of head pose estimation in different directions into one joint learning task and design the whole model based on the principle of "being deeper" and "being thinner" to obtain a tiny model with specially designed types and particular small numbers of filters. We perform thorough experiments on 3 types of test sets and compare our method with others from several different aspects, including the accuracy, the speed, the compactness and so on. In addition, we introduce large angle data in Multi-PIE to verify the ability of dealing with large-scale pose in practice. All the experiments demonstrate the advantages of the proposed model.

Keywords: Head pose estimation · Deep learning · Data augmentation

1 Introduction

The research of face recognition has made great progress in the past few years [1,2]. However, about 75% of the face images in practice are not in frontal view [3], but with various head poses, which makes it much challenge for robust face recognition. As a basic attribute of the human head, head pose also plays an important role for many other tasks, such as expression recognition, driver fatigue detection, face anti-spoofing, human action analysis and so on. However, due to the difficulties caused by geometrical deformation, backlight illumination, foreground occlusion and many other factors in practice, the head pose estimation in multiple directions has been always a difficult problem.

© Springer International Publishing AG 2017
D. Liu et al. (Eds.): ICONIP 2017, Part II, LNCS 10635, pp. 53–63, 2017.
https://doi.org/10.1007/978-3-319-70096-0_6

As illustrated in Fig. 1, the head pose can usually be represented in the following manner. Considering the nose as the origin, the horizontal direction as the x axis, the vertical direction as the y axis, and the direction perpendicular to x and y axes as z axis, the angles rotated clockwise around x, y, and z axes are defined as the offset angle of the head in the Pitch, Yaw, Roll directions respectively. With the aid of machine learning technologies, head pose estimation has achieved great progress recently [4,5], mainly due to the emergence of big data in the related area and the powerful ability of deep neural networks to learn from big data. In this paper, we propose a new fast, compact and robust head pose estimation model based on the popular deep neural networks. Moreover, we have achieved several appealing results in many different aspects, including the speed, the model complexity, the robustness to large angles and so on.

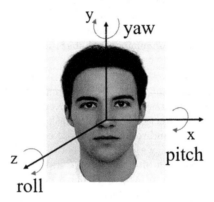

Fig. 1. Head pose representation.

2   Related Work

Head pose estimation has always been a popular topic and received more and more attention in recent years. According to the input information, we divide these methods into three classes: geometric methods, 2D image feature based methods, and RGB-D image based methods.

Firstly, Geometric pose estimation methods take the positions of facial key points as a priori to estimate the turned angles of head. For example, [6] proposed to learn the head pose representation based on labelled graphs and determine the head pose by geometric shape change; [7] proposed to use both subspace analysis and topography method for head pose estimation, and had a remarkably good performance. However, the facial key points are not always fully visible in practice, especially in the case of large turned angles of head, which makes this kind of methods not robust enough in practical applications.

Secondly, many approaches based on 2D images have obtained successful results for head pose estimation. They divide the range of head pose into a number of different intervals and perform head pose estimation as a regression or classification task. With the development of deep learning techniques in recent years, several end-to-end head pose estimation methods [8,9] have achieved excellent performance based on the pixels directly, but most of them suffer from a heavy computational complexity, which makes them cost too much when used in practice.

Thirdly, the methods based on RGB-D image introduce depth information to perform head pose estimation. Recently, a multimodal CNN [10] was proposed to estimate gaze direction by a regression approach for the RGB-D images. In summary, the Depth information is robust to light and occlusions, but always requires specific input devices.

In this paper, we propose a new fast, compact and robust deep model to perform head pose estimation in an end-to-end manner. The main contributions are summarized as follows.

(1) We propose a new fast and compact deep network model, named Tiny-PoseNet, to estimate the head pose in several different angles with a high accuracy. The TinyPoseNet is designed with particular small numbers and specially designed types of filters, such as particular number of 1×1 convolution filters, which produces a model with only 5 convolutional layers in the end. Then we introduce 3 fully-connected layers and put the output nodes through a sigmoid function to learn the actual pose data distribution.

(2) To further improve the ability of our model for large angles in practice, we perform a special 3D data augmentation to the training data, which is proved to be robust for several different angles.

(3) Besides the above special design for head pose estimation in model architecture, we have also obtained several appealing results: (a) The model is able to process one image of size 80×80 within only 2.1 ms in 3.5G Hz CPU; (b) The mean absolute error in three dimensions is only 1.89° in the UmdFaces dataset; (c) The final model is as small as 1.88 M. All these results are much encouraging and exciting for actual applications.

3   Method

In this section, we will present the details of the proposed TinyPoseNet. Head pose estimation often acts as a necessary pre-processing step or an important auxiliary module in face related tasks. This special characteristic makes the task of head pose estimation always require both high speed and small calculation with high accuracy. In order to achieve this goal, we compress the network structure to "be thinner" and to "be deeper" as much as possible by designing special types with 1×1 convolution operations and particular small numbers of filters with proper head pose loss functions. We also take the tasks of head pose estimation in different directions as a multi-label regression task to combine them into a joint learning task. Specifically, we add two 1×1 convolutional layers to learn the discriminative semantic features to compensate the performance loss resulted by compressing the network structure.

3.1 Architectures of TinyPoseNet

A good representation is crucial for good performance of head pose estimation. Inspired by VIPLFaceNet [11] which has obtained successful results in both computational efficiency and effectiveness for face recognition, we design a new fast, compact, and robust model for head pose estimation. We show the model architectures of our TinyPoseNet in Table 1, together with the architectures of AlexNet [12] and VIPLFaceNet. We keep each convolution filter to a proper size, and stack an appropriate small number of convolutional layers to reduce its computation and forward time without performance reduction. Meanwhile, we adjust the fully-connection layers to further improve its speed and minimize the model by initializing the parameters and drop out unnecessary nodes.

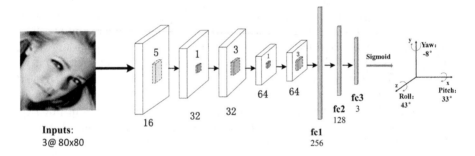

Fig. 2. Our TinyPoseNet.

As shown in Fig. 2, to simplify the calculation of head pose estimation for practice, we propose our tiny pose estimation model with only 8 layers. Different from pruning, trained quantization and Huffman coding in [13], we reduce the storage requirement of neural networks by designing a light weight network for the head pose estimation task. To be specific, we focus on two points including the model compactness and its speed to design our model.

Firstly, to make the model as fast as possible, we follow the idea of [14] and [15] by adding two 1×1 convolutional layers to increase the depth and so keep the rich distributed representations but with small calculation complexity. And then we remove the dropout [16] layer from the original VIPLFaceNet network to prevent overfitting caused by carrying quite sparse parameters.

Secondly, to improve the robustness of our model to large angles, we introduce a sigmoid non-linear function for the final output to ease the long tailed phenomenon in practice where most of the head poses are concentrated within $\pm 45°$ and there are only few poses in other angles. In addition, we formulate head pose estimation in different directions as a multi-task regression problem to get a satisfying result in all the three directions.

Thirdly, to reduce the model size and make it efficient for practical use, we reduce the parameters substantially stored in fully-connected layers, which leads the model size reduced from 216 MB to 1.88 MB and without explicit loss of accuracy. In addition, we remove the unnecessary output nodes for the much easier task, the head pose estimation, which also guarantees the generalization ability toward situations in the wild.

Table 1. The model architectures of AlexNet, VIPLFaceNet and TinyPoseNet.

AlexNet	VIPLFaceNet	TinyPoseNet
Conv1: 96x11x11, S:4, Pad: 0	Conv1: 48x9x9, S:4, Pad:0	Conv1: 16x5x5, S:2, Pad:2
LRN	-	-
Pool1: 3x3, S:2	Pool1: 3x3,S:2	Pool1: 3x3,S:2
Conv2: 256x5x5, G:2, S:1, Pad:2	Conv2: 128x3x3,S:1, Pad:1	Conv2: 32x1x1,S:1, Pad:0
LRN	-	-
-	Conv3: 128x3x3,S:1, Pad:1	Conv3: 32x3x3,S:1, Pad:1
Pool2: 3x3,S:2	Pool2: 3x3,S:2	Pool2: 3x3,S:2
Conv3: 384x3x3, S:1, Pad:1	Conv4: 256x3x3,S:1, Pad:1	Conv4: 64x1x1,S:1, Pad:0
Conv4: 384x3x3, G:2, S:1, Pad:1	Conv5: 192x3x3,S:1, Pad:1	Conv5: 64x3x3,S:1, Pad:1
-	Conv6: 192x3x3,S:1, Pad:1	-
Conv5: 256x3x3, G:2, S:1, Pad:1	Conv7: 128x3x3,S:1, Pad:1	-
Pool3: 3x3,S:2	Pool3: 3x3,S:2	Pool3: 3x3,S:2
FC1: 4096	FC1: 4096	FC1: 256
Dropout1: dropout_ratio:0.5	Dropout1: dropout_ratio:0.5	-
FC2: 4096	FC2: 2048	FC2: 128
Dropout2: dropout_ratio:0.5	Dropout2: dropout_ratio:0.5	-
FC3: 10575	FC3: 10575	FC3: 3
-	-	Sigmoid

3.2   Loss Function

To further ensure the performance for the head estimation task, we formulate the pose angle estimation as a multi-task regression problem. Specifically, we add a sigmoid function in Eq. (1) after the final output layer before the loss function and normalize the angle x to $[0, 1]$ on each dimensional output layer. Another reason is that the sigmoid function just ease the long tailed phenomenon that most of the head poses are concentrated within $45°$ and few large poses.

$$S(x) = 1 \ / \ (1 + e^{-x}) \tag{1}$$

During the training process of the network, small angles within $[-15°, 15°]$ are converted to values near 0.5 by the numerical transformation; the closer of the angle values to 90°, the closer of the transformed values to 1. After this process, small angles could reach a larger slope and large angles could be gently distributed, which makes the output of the network covering a large range and so keep in line with the true distribution of real head pose data.

After the normalization process, we design a multi-task loss to jointly estimate the angles in Pitch, Yaw, and Roll directions. To be specific, we compute the loss in each directions and combine them together by aggregation as follows:

$$E(W) = \frac{1}{2N} \sum_{n=1}^{N} \|\hat{y}_n - y_n\|_2^2 ,$$ (2)

where we define $\hat{y}$ as the output of the network, N as the number of samples in one batch, and $y_n \in [0, 1]$ as the ground truth of the normalized pose label. In the implementation process, the output $y_n \in [0, 1]$ will be transformed into angles between $[-90°, 90°]$ by the following linear function:

$$F(y) = \hat{y}_n \times 180 - 90$$ (3)

4 Experiments and Analysis

4.1 Data Set

The proposed TinyPoseNet is evaluated on the public datasets Multi-PIE [17], CAS-PEAL [18] and UMDFaces [19] for the head pose estimation. In the Multi-PIE face database, subjects were imaged under 15 view points and 19 illumination conditions while displaying a range of facial expressions. In the CAS-PEAL face database, each subject is captured by 9 cameras spaced equally in a horizontal semicircular shelf, asked to look up and down. In view of UMDFaces, the pose angle changes in a row. It includes 367,920 face photos, 8,501 different characters including national stars, people in different age, different races and so on. Considering the continuity of the head pose, the richness of the sample, and the authenticity of the images, we select UMDFaces dataset as the main train set. Subject to the discontinuity of the data distribution, these jobs such as [20] and [21] learned on Multi-PIE dataset are not well applied to the actual scene.

4.2 Data Augmentation

In the UMDFaces dataset, the ratio of large-angle images is less than 5% and there is almost no photo in the direction of Yaw with angles more than 65°. In the meanwhile, the maximum angle in the Pitch direction can only reach ±30°. It shows a serious data distribution imbalance and long tailed phenomenon, which is adverse for the model to be used in practice.

Therefore, to tackle the actual large head pose in practice, we augment the data based on 3D transformations. As shown in Fig. 3, we perform the augmentation as follows: (1) Select the large angle image ($\pm30°$, $\pm45°$, $\pm60°$, $\pm75°$, $\pm90°$) in the Yaw direction in the Multi-PIE dataset, which results 3700 photos at random in each direction. (2) We select the character of the UMDFaces dataset with $0°$ in the Pitch direction, together with the 68 feature points of the face to model the 3D image [22], and generate the images in the Pitch direction at $\pm30°$, $\pm35°$, $\pm40°$, and $\pm45°$ respectively to augment the data set. After this process, we increase about 3000 face images in each direction. Eventually we obtain a challenging dataset with several different large angles and rename it Mix-UMDFaces.

Fig. 3. The schematic diagram of 3D data augmentation.

4.3   Experiments and Analysis

The data used in our experiments are UMDFaces dataset Mix-UMDFaces dataset and the large angle data in UMDFaces test dataset. The large angle data in UMDFaces means the data whose absolute angle value is larger than $35°$ in the Yaw direction or is larger than $15°$ in the Pitch direction. We shuffled the data and selected the first 10 percent images for testing and the rest for training. For implementation, we use SGD with a mini-batch size of 128. The learning rate starts from 0.02, and the models are trained for up to 200 K iterations. We use a weight decay of 0.0002 and a momentum of 0.9.

We evaluate our method on 3 types of test sets, including UMDFaces dataset, Mix-UMDFaces dataset, and the large angle data in UMDFaces. We perform comparison from several different aspects, including the comparison of model architecture with both simple networks and complex networks, the comparison of speed and compactness, the comparison of performance for large angle head pose data and so on. All the experimental results demonstrate the advantages of our model on both speed and accuracy for head pose estimation.

Comparison of the Accuracy for Large Angle Data. As shown in Table 2, we compare the performance of the models with and without fine-tuning, and evaluate the TinyPoseNet models on large angle images. The head pose estimation results are represented by the mean absolute error value in each dimension.

Firstly, we train our model on UMDFaces and Mix-UMDFaces respectively and get satisfactory results in the previous lists of the experiments shown on sub-table(a) of Table 2. This results show clearly that the TinyPoseNet is much robust for the head pose estimation.

Table 2. The performance of TinyPoseNet models.

(a) The comparison between the TinyPoseNet models, trained on UMDFaces and Mix-UMDFaces, without fine-tuning and fine-tuned by pre-trained model on three directions.

(b) Contrast of the performance on the large angle manges dataset between the models trained by Umd-Faces and Mix-UmdFaces.

	UMDFaces		Mix-UMDFaces	
	Initial	*Fine-tuned*	*Initial*	*Fine-tuned*
Yaw	2.296°	2.275°	2.225°	2.210°
Pitch	2.118°	2.100°	2.137°	2.110°
Roll	1.256°	1.260°	1.258°	1.269°

	Large Angle Images	
	UmdFaces	*Mix-UmdFaces*
Yaw	4.250°	2.667°
Pitch	2.856°	2.070°
Roll	2.036°	1.280°

Then, we fine-tune our TinyPoseNet by the model which is pre-trained for face recognition on the WebFaces [23] database. By comparing the results between the initial model and the model with fine-tuning, we found that no obvious improvement results by fine-tuning which indicate the model is trained enough for the task of the head pose estimation.

Thirdly, we compare the performances on handling large angle data of the model pre-trained only on the UMDFaces dataset and Mix-UMDFaces dataset respectively. As shown in Table 2, the loss in the Yaw direction is reduced by 50% after the data augmentation and the mean loss is reduced to 72% of the original in the Pitch direction. Especially in the direction of Roll, the effect has been significantly improved.

Comparison of the Model Size with Other Models. We compare with models including both simple networks, like LeNet [24], and complex networks, like ResNet [25] on the UMDFaces database in Table 3. The results are represented by the mean absolute error value in each dimension, including the size of model. We can find that the TinyPoseNet model is significantly better than the same size of the LeNet model, and also better than both AlexNet and ResNet18 models whose size are much bigger than the TinyPoseNet model. Compare with the VIPLFaceNet model, the size of TinyPoseNet model is just one of its fifty-eight without reducing performance significantly.

Comparison of the Speed with Other Models. The time consumed of each Image by each network is shown in Table 3. Among the networks performing below 2° in the Mean value, TinyPoseNet is the only network running <10ms.

Table 3. The comparisons of effectiveness, speed and compactness with other methods.

	Yaw	Pitch	Roll	Mean	Time	Size
ResNet	2.370°	2.120°	1.469°	1.986°	89.16ms	42.70M
LeNet	4.581°	4.067°	2.485°	3.711°	0.48ms	1.63M
AlexNet	2.311°	2.116°	1.312°	1.913°	28.75ms	216.98M
VIPLFaceNet	2.075°	1.919°	1.117°	1.704°	15.85ms	109.85M
TinyPoseNet	2.296°	2.118°	1.256°	1.890°	2.142ms	1.88M

It is worth mentioning that, the time consumed of TinyPoseNet is 7 times lower than that of VIPLFaceNet. Meanwhile the maximum error is only 0.24° between VIPLFaceNet and TinyPoseNet in the directions of Yaw Pitch and Roll.

5   Conclusion

Head pose is a basic attribute of human head and also a key point for human action analysis and attention analysis. In this paper, we focus on the design of our model with low computation and high robustness for the head pose estimation. The main work of this paper can be summarized as follows: (1) Aiming at the problem of head pose estimation, we propose a pose estimation model with a much small computation and so a good performance simultaneously. (2) Compared with the traditional models, experimental results show the advantages of our model on both speed and accuracy for head pose estimation. As shown in the experiments, the model is more robust for large angle head pose data and so is much more suitable in practice. The method proposed in this paper can be used for fast head attitude estimation in several application scenarios, and is also able to defence face recognition system against video attack. In the future, we will try to further improve the performance of the model for head pose estimation and try to employ GAN to obtain a more smooth distribution of virtual samples.

References

1. Simonyan, K., Zisserman, A.: Very deep convolutional networks for large-scale image recognition. arXiv preprint arXiv:1409.1556 (2014)
2. Zeiler, M.D., Fergus, R.: Visualizing and understanding convolutional networks. In: Fleet, D., Pajdla, T., Schiele, B., Tuytelaars, T. (eds.) ECCV 2014. LNCS, vol. 8689, pp. 818–833. Springer, Cham (2014). doi:10.1007/978-3-319-10590-1_53
3. Kuchinsky, A., Pering, C., Creech, M.L., Freeze, D., Serra, B., Gwizdka, J.: Fotofile: a consumer multimedia organization and retrieval system. In: Proceedings of the SIGCHI conference on Human Factors in Computing Systems, pp. 496–503. ACM (1999)
4. Drouard, V., Ba, S., Evangelidis, G., Deleforge, A., Horaud, R.: Head pose estimation via probabilistic high-dimensional regression. In: IEEE International Conference on Image Processing (ICIP) 2015, pp. 4624–4628. IEEE (2015)

5. Wang, C., Song, X.: Robust head pose estimation via supervised manifold learning. Neural Networks **53**, 15–25 (2014)
6. Krüger, N., Pötzsch, M., von der Malsburg, C.: Determination of face position and pose with a learned representation based on labelled graphs. Image Vis. Comput. **15**(8), 665–673 (1997)
7. Wu, J., Trivedi, M.M.: A two-stage head pose estimation framework and evaluation. Pattern Recogn. **41**(3), 1138–1158 (2008)
8. Ahn, B., Park, J., Kweon, I.S.: Real-time head orientation from a monocular camera using deep neural network. In: Cremers, D., Reid, I., Saito, H., Yang, M.-H. (eds.) ACCV 2014. LNCS, vol. 9005, pp. 82–96. Springer, Cham (2015). doi:10.1007/978-3-319-16811-1_6
9. Yan, Y., Ricci, E., Subramanian, R., Liu, G., Lanz, O., Sebe, N.: A multi-task learning framework for head pose estimation under target motion. IEEE Trans. Pattern Anal. Mach. Intell. **38**(6), 1070–1083 (2016)
10. Mukherjee, S.S., Robertson, N.M.: Deep head pose: gaze-direction estimation in multimodal video. IEEE Trans. Multimedia **17**(11), 2094–2107 (2015)
11. Liu, X., Kan, M., Wu, W., Shan, S., Chen, X.: Viplfacenet: an open source deep face recognition sdk. arXiv preprint arXiv:1609.03892 (2016)
12. Krizhevsky, A., Sutskever, I., Hinton, G.E.: Imagenet classification with deep convolutional neural networks. In: Advances in Neural Information Processing Systems, pp. 1097–1105 (2012)
13. Han, S., Mao, H., Dally, W.J.: Deep compression: Compressing deep neural networks with pruning, trained quantization and huffman coding. arXiv preprint arXiv:1510.00149 (2015)
14. Lin, M., Chen, Q., Yan, S.: Network in network. Computer Science (2014)
15. Szegedy, C., Liu, W., Jia, Y., Sermanet, P., Reed, S., Anguelov, D., Erhan, D., Vanhoucke, V., Rabinovich, A.: Going deeper with convolutions. In: Proceedings of the IEEE Conference on Computer Vision and Pattern Recognition, pp. 1–9 (2015)
16. Srivastava, N., Hinton, G., Krizhevsky, A., Sutskever, I., Salakhutdinov, R.: Dropout: a simple way to prevent neural networks from overfitting. J. Mach. Learn. Res. **15**(1), 1929–1958 (2014)
17. Gross, R., Matthews, I., Cohn, J., Kanade, T., Baker, S.: Multi-pie. Image Vis. Comput. **28**(5), 807–813 (2010)
18. Gao, W., Cao, B., Shan, S., Chen, X., Zhou, D., Zhang, X., Zhao, D.: The cas-peal large-scale chinese face database and baseline evaluations. IEEE Trans. Syst. Man Cybern. Part A Syst. Hum. **38**(1), 149–161 (2008)
19. Bansal, A., Nanduri, A., Castillo, C., Ranjan, R., Chellappa, R.: Umdfaces: An annotated face dataset for training deep networks. arXiv preprint arXiv:1611.01484 (2016)
20. Davis, L.S., Gonzalez, J., Haj, M.A.: On partial least squares in head pose estimation: How to simultaneously deal with misalignment. In: IEEE Conference on Computer Vision and Pattern Recognition, pp. 2602–2609 (2012)
21. Heo, J., Savvides, M.: Face recognition across pose using view based active appearance models (vbaams) on cmu multi-pie dataset. In: International Conference on Computer Vision Systems, pp. 527–535 (2008)
22. Zhu, X., Lei, Z., Yan, J., Yi, D., Li, S.Z.: High-fidelity pose and expression normalization for face recognition in the wild. In: Proceedings of the IEEE Conference on Computer Vision and Pattern Recognition, pp. 787–796 (2015)
23. Yi, D., Lei, Z., Liao, S., Li, S.: Learning face representation from scratch. arXiv preprint arXiv:1411.7923 (2014)

24. Szegedy, C., Liu, W., Jia, Y., Sermanet, P., Reed, S., Anguelov, D., Erhan, D., Vanhoucke, V., Rabinovich, A.: Going deeper with convolutions. arXiv preprint arXiv:1409.4842 (2014)
25. He, K., Zhang, X., Ren, S., Sun, J.: Deep residual learning for image recognition. arXiv preprint arXiv:1512.03385 (2015)

Two-Stage Temporal Multimodal Learning for Speaker and Speech Recognition

Qianli Ma[1,2]($\boxtimes$), Lifeng Shen[1], Ruishi Su[1], and Jieyu Chen[3]

[1] School of Computer Science and Engineering,
South China University of Technology, Guangzhou 510006, China
qianlima@scut.edu.cn, scuterlifeng@foxmail.com
[2] Guangdong Key Laboratory of Big Data Analysis and Processing,
Guangzhou 510006, China
[3] Linguistic Department, University of California, San Diego, CA 92093, USA
jic387@ucsd.edu

Abstract. Temporal information prevails in multimodal sequence data, such as video data and speech signals. In this paper, we propose a two-stage learning to model the temporal information in multimodal sequences. At the first learning stage, static representative features are extracted from each modality at every time step. Then joint representations across various modalities are effectively learned within a joint fusion layer. The second one is to transfer the static features into corresponding dynamical features by jointly learning the temporal information and dependencies between different time steps with a Long Short-Term Memory (LSTM). Compared with previous multimodal methods, the proposed model is efficient in learning temporal joint representations. Evaluated on Big Bang Theory speaker recognition dataset and AVLetters speech recognition dataset, our model proves to outperform other methods.

Keywords: Temporal multimodal learning · Speaker recognition · Speech recognition

1 Introduction

In most cases, both visual and audio information plays a vital role in understanding a given circumstance by computers. For example, by employing facial information can we deal with speaker recognition to some extent. However, it would fail if real-world data had illumination variations or blurring information. Also, audio information alone is not sufficient for speech recognition either, because speech signals often contain noises. Thus, researchers tend to take both visual and audio information into account to reduce recognition errors, which has been verified by previous research [8, 10, 12].

In recent years, a number of approaches have been proposed to fuse audio and visual in-formation for better recognition. Recurrent Temporal Multimodal RBM (RTMRBM) [6] added joint layers on the top of Multimodal RBMs

© Springer International Publishing AG 2017
D. Liu et al. (Eds.): ICONIP 2017, Part II, LNCS 10635, pp. 64–72, 2017.
https://doi.org/10.1007/978-3-319-70096-0_7

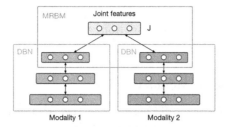

Fig. 1. Structure of Multimodal Deep Belief Network (MDBN)

(MRBMs) [13], which connects the sequence of MRBMs to learn temporal joint representation. RTMRBM attempted to model the overall joint distribution of the entire multimodal time series directly. Since its learning at each time step relies on the joint distribution of the whole time frames, it will significantly increase the training cost of the model. Most recently, Jimmy Ren [11] built the Multimodal Long Short-term Memory (Multimodal LSTM), and tried to explicitly model the long-term dependencies in a single modal both within the same modality and across modalities. To this end, multimodal LSTM duplicated the internal nodes but kept the parameters shared for each modality. However, different modalities will, more often than not, provide various information, and it is hard to extract all important information from various modalities with just one same set of weights.

In this paper, we propose a two-stage learning to model the temporal information in multimodal sequences. At the first learning stage, static representative features are extracted from each modality at each time step by a Deep Belief Network (DBN) [3]. Then joint representations across various modalities are effectively learned within a Multimodal Restricted Boltzmann Machine (MRBM). The second stage is to transfer static features into corresponding dynamical features by jointly learning the temporal information by a LSTM. Since there is no need of distribution estimation of the whole temporal data, our method will noticeably decrease the training cost at Stage I. Furthermore, our experimental results show that it is more efficient to learn temporal information and dependencies in high-level abstract features than in low-level ones. Our model achieves a better performance on Big Bang Theory dataset (speaker recognition), and AVLetters dataset (speech recognition) than other methods.

2   Background

2.1   Multimodal Deep Belief Network

Multimodal Deep Belief Network (MDBN) [13] is a generative model, which employs a Multimodal Restricted Boltzmann Machine (MRBM) [13] to extract joint multimodal features from the top layer of Deep Belief Network (DBN) [3].

For each modality, MDBN establishes a DBN to extract specific abstract features, and learn joint representations from specific features with a MRBM, as illustrated in Fig. 1.

2.2 Long Short-Term Memory

Long Short Term Memory (LSTM) [4] is a recurrent neural network (RNN) and is well-suited to learn sequence data. LSTM units are often implemented in "block" with several "gates" to control the flow of information into or out of their memory.

3 The Proposed Model

The schema of two-stage temporal multimodal learning (TS-TML) is illustrated in Fig. 2. Instead of directly modeling the overall joint distribution of the whole time frames, we only extract and fuse static features by a MDBN without taking into account temporal dependencies at Stage I. Following Stage I, we will obtain the high-level common abstract concept features of multiple modalities. At Stage II, we transfer static features into corresponding dynamical features by jointly learning the temporal in-formation with a LSTM.

Compared with previous multimodal methods, our two-stage learning yields two main benefits: One is that it will dramatically decrease the training cost at Stage I because there is no need of distribution estimation of the whole temporal sequences, which stands as a striking contrast to RTMRBM. The other one is that it is more efficient to learn temporal information and dependencies in high-level abstract features than in low-level ones from scratch.

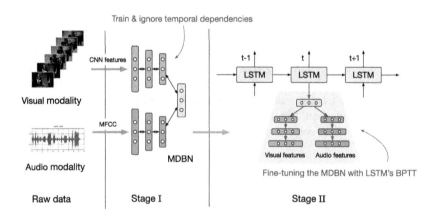

Fig. 2. Two-Stage Temporal Multimodal Learning (TS-TML)

3.1   Stage I

At Stage I, we employ a MDBN to extract static features from each modality and fuse them into common features J on the top of the MDBN, where $J \in \mathbb{R}^{N_{joint}}$, N_{joint} is the dimension of the common feature layer. Given a MDBN in Fig. 1, it joins two branches corresponding to two modalities (modal 1 and modal 2). Every two adjacent layers of the MDBN can be viewed as an RBM. The training of RBM depends on this inference and learning process. Firstly, we defined the joint distribution of adjacent layers. Let $v \in \mathbb{R}^{n_0}$ be the inputs of one modality, $h^1 \in \mathbb{R}^{n_1}$ denote the 1st hidden layer states and $h^2 \in \mathbb{R}^{n_2}$ denote the 2nd hidden layer states, and then we can formulate their joint distributions of RBM as follows:

$$P_\Theta(v, h^1) = \frac{1}{Z(\theta)} exp(\sum_{i=1}^{n_0} \sum_{j=1}^{n_1} \omega_{ij} v_i h_j^1 + \sum_{i=1}^{n_0} v_i \alpha_i + \sum_{j=1}^{n_1} h_j^1 \beta_j) \quad (1)$$

$$P_\Theta(h^1, h^2) = \frac{exp(\sum_{i=1}^{n_1} \sum_{j=1}^{n_2} \omega_{ij} h_j^2 h_i^1 + \sum_{i=1}^{n_1} h_i^1 \beta_i + \sum_{j=1}^{n_2} h_j^2 \gamma_j)}{Z(\theta)} \quad (2)$$

Similarly, the joint distribution between two modalities hidden states (h_1^2, h_2^2) and the joint hidden states J can be defined as:

$$P_\Theta(h_1^2, h_2^2, J) = \frac{exp((h_1^2)^T W_1 J + (h_2^2)^T W_2 J + (h_1^2)^T \gamma_1 + (h_2^2)^T \gamma_2 + J^T \sigma)}{Z(\theta)} \quad (3)$$

where h_1^2 denotes 2nd hidden layer states of modal 1 and h_2^2 denotes 2nd hidden layer states of modal 2, J denotes joint hidden units states on the top of two 2nd hidden layers, α, β, γ, σ are the bias of the input, the 1st hidden layer, the 2nd hidden layer, and the joint hidden units, respectively. W_1 and W_2 are the weights between the 2nd hidden layers corresponding to two modals and the joint hidden layer. $Z(\Theta)$ is the partition function.

Having obtained the formulation of joint distributions, we can train DBN layer by layer with Contrastive Divergence algorithm (CD-k) [3]:

Step1: Given visible layer's input $v \in \mathbb{R}^{n_v}$, sample hidden layer's value $h \in \mathbb{R}^{n_h}$ from the conditional distribution:

$$P(h_i = 1|v) = \frac{e^{-E(v,h)}}{\sum_v e^{-E(v,h)}} = \sigma(\sum_{j=0}^{n_v} \omega_{ij} v_j + c_i) \quad (4)$$

Step 2: Reconstruct visible layer's value v' with the sampled hidden layer state h:

$$P(v_j' = 1|h) = \frac{e^{-E(v',h)}}{\sum_h e^{-E(v',h)}} = \sigma(\sum_{i=0}^{n_h} \omega_{ij} h_i + b_i) \quad (5)$$

Repeating Step 1 and Step 2 for k times, we will obtain the last visible layer's value v^k. Then we use the data distribution and the model distribution to compute the gradients of parameters, such as the gradients of weights be formulated by

$$\frac{\partial L(\theta)}{\partial \omega_{ij}} = \sum_v P(h_j = 1|v)v_i - \sum_{i=1} P(h_j = 1|v_i^k)v_i^k \tag{6}$$

3.2 Stage II

After the MDBN being pre-trained at stage I, we can feed joint features J into the top LSTM at each time step. At this stage, we aim to employ the temporal modeling capacity of LSTM to adjust the learned joint features J and build a temporal dependencies in its joint feature spaces. At each time step, we output a predicted label for the current frame. And the entire sequence classification performance will be averaged over all time steps. The training loss is formulated by

$$E = \frac{1}{N} \sum_n^N \sum_k^K y_{nk} \log(O_{nk}) \tag{7}$$

where n denotes the n-th frame ($n = 1, 2, \ldots, N$), $y \in \mathbb{R}^k$ is one-hot vector and denotes groundtruth label. O_{nk} is the output at k-th unit at the time n. According to this average category loss, we adopt the back propagation through time (BPTT) algorithm to train the whole system, which includes the fine-tuning of the MDBN. In summary, we present our learning processes in Algorithm 1.

Algorithm 1. Two-Stage Temporal Multimodal Learning.

Require:
   Number of modal, M;
   Depth of DBN, L ($L = 3$ in Fig. 1);
   Length of multimodal sequences, N;
   Label sequences, y;
1: **for** modal m :$1 \rightarrow M$ **do**
2:     **for** i : $1 \rightarrow L - 1$ do: **do**
3:         Train the weights between h_i and h_{i+1} as a RBM with CD-k;
4:     **end for;**
5: **end for.**
6: Fix all pre-trained weights for each modal.
7: Obtain the L-th hidden states in each modal and learn a joint layer in a MRBM as the top of MDBN, which has the same training process as RBM.
8: Obtain N-length static joint representations for given multimodal sequences.
9: Input joint representation sequences and train LSTM, which includes fine-tuning the MDBN at each time.

Fig. 3. Speaker recognition on BBT data. From first line to second line, they are two speakers identified by our method: Shelton and Lenord, respectively.

Table 1. The speaker recognition accuracy (%) on Big Bang Theory dataset.

Models	Size of sliding windows					
	0.5	1.0	1.5	2.0	2.5	3.0
MLR (2013) [2]	-	-	-	-	77.8	-
MRF (2012) [14]	-	-	-	-	80.8	-
Multimodal CNN (2015) [7]	74.93	77.24	79.35	82.12	82.8	83.42
Multimodal LSTM (2016) [11]	86.59	89.00	90.45	90.84	91.1	91.38
Ours TS-TML	**98.01**	**98.22**	**98.45**	**98.56**	**99.20**	**99.30**

4 Experiments

4.1 Speaker Recognition

This task is to identify a person who is currently talking in a continuous multi-character conversation scene video and identify the person's identity through the person's facial features and vocal characteristics. We choose the Big Bang Theory (BBT) dataset as our experimental data. Due to illumination variations and blurring information of human face images, speaker recognition from BBT is a very challenging task.

We first use the face detection algorithm to locate faces in each video frame. These frames are manually annotated by five classes: Shelton, Lenord, Howard, Raj and Penny. Consequently, we have 310,000 consecutive hand-labeled frames of these five characters. For the audio data, we extract each character's speech in the video, and combine them into one audio file, and label them according to corresponding characters in image sequences. We use the first 6 episodes from the second season for training, and the first 6 episodes from the first season for testing.

We first pre-train a Caffenet with BBT dataset, and extract image features with this Caffenet. As for the audio data, we use the 20-millisecond-sliding-window-10-millisecond-step MFCCs [9] feature to preprocess them. Each sequence length is 49.

We set up 6 different sliding windows with 0.5 s, 1.0 s, 1.5 s, 2.0 s, 2.5 s, and 3.0 s, respectively. The results compared with the other models are shown in Table 1.

From Table 1, we can see that our model achieves a far better performance than other multimodal methods. In various sliding windows, our method improves 7.74%–11.42% accuracies. It proves that learning temporal information in high-level abstract features is more efficient than leaning it in low-level ones. In addition, with the increasing size of a time window, the accuracy of multimodal methods improves as well, indicating that more information will help to improve the performance of multimodal learning.

To present our results visually, we demonstrate a few frames obtained by our method in Fig. 3. Our method can identify the two main characters in BBT with audiovisual features in various scenarios.

Finally, we compare our method with our baseline models and LSTM which only employ visual or audio data. The results are listed in Table 2. It is noteworthy that, our temporal multimodal method outperforms the single modality one, which is also consistent with previous multimodal methods' results [6,13].

Table 2. Accuracy (%) of single modality and multimodal methods.

Models	Visual	Audio	Audio-visual
LSTM	88.27	46.4	-
Ours (single modality)	90.1	51	-
Ours TS-TML	-	-	**98.01**

Table 3. The average accuracy (%) of speech recognition on AVLetters.

Models	Acc.
MDAE (2015) [5]	62.90
CRBM (2014) [1]	64.8
RTMRBM (2016) [6]	66.04
Ours TS-TML	**66.51**

4.2 Speech Recognition

This task is to recognize what a certain person is speaking, given the lip motion and dubbing in a video clip.

We choose the AVLetters dataset with 780 short video clips. In each video there is a person reading letters from A to Z. There are 10 individuals, and each one reads the 26 letters for three times. The size of lip images in all frames is 60×80. The dataset also provides MFCC features of the audio data. We take the first two as a training set, and the last one as a testing set. Our experiment is speaker-dependent. To match the visual and audio frames' length, we input one image frame with four audio frames simultaneously into our model.

Our method is compared with the Multimodal Deep Auto Encoder (MDAE) [5], Conditional Restricted Boltzmann Machine (CRBM) [1], RTMRBM [6] on AVLet-ters dataset, and the results are shown in Table 3.

From Table 3, we can see that our method outperforms other multimodal models on this speech recognition task. Compared with non-temporal model MDAE and single temporal modality model CRBM, our method has a much better performance. Furthermore, instead of directly modeling the overall joint distribution of the whole video and audio frames as RTMRBM did, we only extract and fuse static features of each video and audio frame without considering temporal dependencies at Stage I and learn the temporal information at Stage II. The results show that our two-stage learning strategy has a better performance than RTMRBM. It demonstrates that learning temporal information and dependencies in high-level abstract features is more efficient than learning them in low-level ones from scratch.

4.3 Discussions of Computational Complexity

All our experiments are conducted on machine with an Intel Core i5-6500, 3.20-GHz CPU 32-GB RAM and a GeForce GTX 980-Ti 6G. Take AVLetters for example, there are 20800 multimodal data in total (dim of video frame: 4096, dim of audio: 104). We spent about 32s/epoch to pretrain the MDBN, 10s/epoch to train the LSTM and fine-tune our whole system. From these observations, we find that learning static joint features costs most of runtime, which depends on the complexity of MDBN. Compared with the strategy of learning joint distribution over the whole multimodal sequences, our learning method adopts the idea of transferring from static features to dynamic ones in two stages, which largely reduces the training cost of estimation the joint distribution.

5   Conclusion

We have proposed a two-stage learning to model the temporal information in multi-modal sequences. Instead of directly modeling the overall joint distribution of the whole time frames, our method merely extracts and fuses static features of each frame without considering temporal dependencies at Stage I, while it learns the temporal information at Stage II. These two stages make it easier to train the model and decrease the training cost. Our experimental results show that the proposed method performs better than single modality methods, non-temporal multimodal networks, as well as other temporal multimodal methods in the tasks of speaker and speech recognition.

Acknowledgment. This work is supported by the National Natural Science Foundation of China (Grant No. 61502174, 61402181), the Natural Science Foundation of Guangdong Province (Grant No. S2012010009961, 2015A030313215), the Science and Technology Planning Project of Guangdong Province (Grant No. 2016A040403046), the Guangzhou Science and Technology Planning Project (Grant No. 201704030051, 2014J4100006), the Opening Project of Guangdong Province Key Laboratory of Big Data Analysis and Processing (Grant No. 2017014), and the Fundamental Research Funds for the Central Universities (Grant No. D2153950).

References

1. Amer, M.R., Siddiquie, B., Khan, S., Divakaran, A., Sawhney, H.: Multimodal fusion using dynamic hybrid models. In: IEEE Winter Conference on Applications of Computer Vision, pp. 556–563, March 2014
2. Bauml, M., Tapaswi, M., Stiefelhagen, R.: Semi-supervised learning with constraints for person identification in multimedia data. In: The IEEE Conference on Computer Vision and Pattern Recognition (CVPR), June 2013
3. Hinton, G.E., Osindero, S., Teh, Y.W.: A fast learning algorithm for deep belief nets. Neural Comput. **18**(7), 1527–1554 (2006)
4. Hochreiter, S., Schmidhuber, J.: Long short-term memory. Neural Comput. **9**(8), 1735–1780 (1997)
5. Hong, C., Yu, J., Wan, J., Tao, D., Wang, M.: Multimodal deep autoencoder for human pose recovery. IEEE Trans. Image Process. **24**(12), 5659–5670 (2015)
6. Hu, D., Li, X., Lu, X.: Temporal multimodal learning in audiovisual speech recognition. In: The IEEE Conference on Computer Vision and Pattern Recognition (CVPR), June 2016
7. Hu, Y., Ren, J.S., Dai, J., Yuan, C., Xu, L., Wang, W.: Deep multimodal speaker naming. In: Proceedings of the 23rd ACM International Conference on Multimedia, MM 2015, NY, USA, pp. 1107–1110 (2015). doi:10.1145/2733373.2806293
8. Huang, J., Kingsbury, B.: Audio-visual deep learning for noise robust speech recognition. In: IEEE International Conference on Acoustics, Speech and Signal Processing, pp. 7596–7599 (2013)
9. Jamil, M., Rahman, G.R.S.: Speaker identification using Mel frequency cepstral coefficients (2004)
10. Ngiam, J., Khosla, A., Kim, M., Nam, J., Lee, H., Ng, A.Y.: Multimodal deep learning. In: International Conference on Machine Learning, ICML 2011, Bellevue, Washington, USA, June 28–July 2, pp. 689–696 (2011)
11. Ren, J., Hu, Y., Tai, Y.W., Wang, C., Xu, L., Sun, W., Yan, Q.: Look, listen and learn – a multimodal LSTM for speaker identification. In: Proceedings of the Thirtieth AAAI Conference on Artificial Intelligence, AAAI 2016, pp. 3581–3587. AAAI Press (2016)
12. Sohn, K., Shang, W., Lee, H.: Improved multimodal deep learning with variation of information. In: International Conference on Neural Information Processing Systems, pp. 2141–2149 (2014)
13. Srivastava, N., Salakhutdinov, R.: Multimodal learning with deep boltzmann machines. J. Mach. Learn. Res. **15**, 2949–2980 (2014). http://jmlr.org/papers/v15/srivastava14b.html
14. Stiefelhagen, R.: "Knock! knock! who is it?" probabilistic person identification in TV-series. In: Proceedings of the 2012 IEEE Conference on Computer Vision and Pattern Recognition (CVPR), CVPR 2012, pp. 2658–2665 (2012). http://dl.acm.org/citation.cfm?id=2354409.2354974

SLICE: Structural and Label Information Combined Embedding for Networks

Yiqi Chen and Tieyun Qian[(✉)]

State Key Laboratory of Software Engineering, Wuhan University,
No. 16 Luojiashan Road, Hubei 430072, Wuhan, China
{yiqic16,qty}@whu.edu.cn

Abstract. This paper studies the problem of learning representations for network. Existing approaches embed vertices into a low dimensional continuous space which encodes local or global network structures. While these methods show improvements over traditional representations on node classification tasks, they ignore label information until the learnt embeddings are used for training classifier. That is, the process of representation learning is separated from the labels and lacks such information.

In this paper, we propose a novel method which learns the embeddings for vertices under the supervision of labels. Motivated by the idea of label propagation, our approach extends the traditional label propagation to the deep neural network field. The embedding of a node could contain the structural and label information by broadcasting the label information during the training process. We conduct extensive experiments on two real network datasets. Results demonstrate that our approach outperforms both the state-of-the-art graph embedding and label propagation approaches by a large margin.

Keywords: Representation learning · Node classification · Label propagation · Deep neural network

1 Introduction

Information networks, such as social networks, publication networks, are becoming pervasive nowadays. Node classification tasks like recommendation or targeted advertising are very common in real network. Since many nodes are not so active and lack of information, researches may mainly depend on the link information to classify the nodes. What's more, the sparsity of network makes it difficult to get a good semantic relationship between nodes. Thus it has long been a fundamental task to embed the sparse network into a low-dimensional dense space with graph representation learning techniques.

It is hard for traditional methods like locally linear embedding (LLE) [14] or Laplacian EigenMap [4] to scale to real social networks since they rely on the solving of leading eigenvectors which are computationally expensive. Recently, a number of distributed network representations have been proposed.

© Springer International Publishing AG 2017
D. Liu et al. (Eds.): ICONIP 2017, Part II, LNCS 10635, pp. 73–81, 2017.
https://doi.org/10.1007/978-3-319-70096-0_8

Typically methods include DeepWalk [13] which combines skip-gram with random walk, LINE [15] which exploits the first-order and second-order proximity to preserve the local and global structures better, and Node2Vec [8] which optimizes DeepWalk with a flexible sampling strategy by carefully combining the breadth-first search and depth-first search. These network representation methods show improvements over a number of traditional approaches like Graph Factorization [1], Spectral Clustering [18], Modularity [16], EdgeCluster [17], IsoMap [3], and weighted-vote Relational Neighbor [10]. While the above three network representation methods show improvements over traditional techniques, they are all designed for a general purpose rather than the node classification, thus not make full use of the label information.

Another branch is based on graph convolutional theory. Methods like SGCNN [6], GCN [9] are proposed. They could be effective at node classification task, but need other original features(e.g. bag of words) for each node. However, we want to focus on the labeled graph without other information because features like text may be missing sometimes. Also, we have tried use the embeddings generated by deepwalk to replace the features, but the result is not that good. So we give up using these methods as baselines.

Label propagation [19, 21, 22] has been shown an effective technique to enhance the classification performance by utilizing the correlation between labels of linked objects. A more recent work OMNI-Prop [20] propagates labels on the graph by assigning each node with the prior belief and updating it using the evidence from its neighbor. OMNI-Prop could tackle arbitrary label correlations and get better performance than classic label propagation approaches. However, OMNI-Prop only takes the neighbor information as a bridge to introduce propagation and neglects the network structure information.

In this paper, we investigate the problem of learning representation for node classification. Our goal is to leverage the label information for enhancing the performance of classification. To this end, we train the node representation and classifier alternately to combine the label information. By incorporating graph embedding into the framework, we can better model the complex network structure than traditional label propagation. Our method also outperforms graph embedding approaches due to the integration of label information. In addition, our approach benefits from the connection between direct neighbors, thus avoiding the time-consuming sampling techniques used in graph embedding methods like Node2Vec [8]. Extensive experiments demonstrate that our proposed method achieves improvements over the graph embedding and label propagation baselines.

2   The Proposed SLICE Model

This section we introduce our SLICE (Structural and Label Information Combined Embedding) model.

2.1 Label as Constraint

In a traditional label propagation model, label information is transferred to one's neighbors through the adjacent matrix. However, label propagation only saves each node's label probability during the training, which is different from our embedding target. To solve this problem, we add label information as constraints as follows. Given a graph $G(V, E, L)$, for each undirected edge (u, v), we assume the unlabeled node v should have the same label as node u. To meet this assumption, we apply the cross entropy loss to measure the difference between the label of v and that of u.

$$J_{la(u,v)} = -\frac{1}{D_u} \sum_{j \in l_u} y_u \log h_{\theta_j}(x_v) + (1 - y_u) \log(1 - h_{\theta_j}(x_v)), \qquad (1)$$

where D_u is the degree of node u, y_u is u's true label, x_v is the embedding for node v, θ_j denotes the parameters for class j, and h is the sigmoid function defined as:

$$h_{\theta_j}(x) = \sigma(\theta_j * x) \qquad (2)$$

$$\sigma(x) = \frac{1}{1 + e^{-x}} \qquad (3)$$

From Eq. 1, we can see that x_v conveys the neighbor u's label information, which can be calculated as:

$$x_v \leftarrow x_v - \frac{\alpha}{D_u}(h_{\theta_j}(x_v) - y_u)\theta_j \qquad (4)$$

Note that we use $1/D_u$ as the multiplication weight for the following two reasons. First, different nodes contribute differently to their neighbors. Second, the large degree nodes may bring noises into the network and have neighbors with diverse labels, and hence it is intuitive to decay their effect on other nodes.

2.2 Incorporating Classifier Objective into Training

We use logistic regression to classify the nodes as baseline methods do after the embedding process. For each node u, the objective function can be defined as follows.

$$J_{lr(u)} = -\sum_{j \in l_u} y_u \log h_{\theta_j}(x_u) + (1 - y_u) \log(1 - h_{\theta_j}(x_u)) \qquad (5)$$

However, since training classifier in our model is a part of our embedding process, we can jointly update the parameters of classifier and node embedding at the same time. This is different from the separate classifiers in baselines which get features as input and update its parameters to reduce the prediction error. Our goal is to combine the classifier into the embedding process and bring the label information into the training process. Hence we update the parameters using the stochastic gradient descent (SGD) [5] as:

$$\theta_j \leftarrow \theta_j - \alpha(h_{\theta_j}(x_u) - y_u)x_u \qquad (6)$$

$$x_u \leftarrow x_u - \alpha(h_{\theta_j}(x_u) - y_u)\theta_j \qquad (7)$$

2.3   SLICE Model

We now present our SLICE model based on the above defined objective function. We use skip-gram [11] with negative sampling [12] to capture the basic structural information. In the original skip-gram, a window is sliding from the beginning to the end of the sentence to access the context of each word (node in graph). That signifies the center word which is related to multi-hop words. To be in consistent with the OMNI-Prop [20] baseline which only uses undirected edge (u, v), our structural context of each node will only contain its neighbors. In this way, we can avoid the time-consuming sampling procedure used in graph embedding methods. The structural objective function will be defined as follows.

$$J_{st(u,v)} = -(\log \sigma(\widetilde{x}_u, x_v) + \sum_{u'}(\log(1 - \sigma(\widetilde{x}_{u'}, x_v)))) \tag{8}$$

u' means the negative samples and $\widetilde{x}_{u'}$ is the parameter vector of negative samplings. Finally, for a graph $G = (V, E, L)$, we combine the three parts together and add the L2 regularization as follows.

$$
\begin{aligned}
J_{all} &= J_{emb} + J_{classifier} \\
&= \sum_{cen \in V, ctx \in N(cen)} (J_{st(cen,ctx)} + J_{la(cen,ctx)} + J_{reg}) + \sum_{cen \in V} (J_{lr(cen)} + J_{lrreg}),
\end{aligned}
\tag{9}
$$

where $N(cen)$ denotes the cen's neighbors. We jointly optimize the objective function J_{emb} and $J_{classifier}$ and keep the classifier parameters invariant while optimizing the J_{emb}. When the training process finish, we use the learnt classifier to predict the label probability of rest nodes.

The essential of our SLICE model is that we replace the propagation process between unlabeled nodes with structural information. Let us illustrate this using a typical label propagation. We first get an adjacent matrix A as an affinity matrix W and initialize labels $\hat{Y}^{(0)} \leftarrow (y_1, \cdots, y_{|L|}, 0, 0, \cdots, 0)$. Then we do iteration over:

$$1. \hat{Y}^{(t+1)} \leftarrow D^{-1}W\hat{Y}^{(t)}$$

$$2. \hat{Y}^{(t+1)} \leftarrow Y_l$$

until convergence. The difference between our model and propagation methods lies in that our approach would not transfer label information between unlabeled nodes directly. In contrast, label propagation methods make use of the unlabeled nodes and broadcast the labels to their neighbors. This to some extent may get good results due to the homophily property of graph. But, it is more possible for such a method to accumulate the propagation error at the same time. Thus we choose not to use such propagation between unlabeled nodes directly, but only model their structural similarity. The label information will be imported during the embedding process indirectly. Figure 1 presents an illustrative example.

In Fig. 1, circle nodes represent the unlabeled nodes. triangle and rectangle nodes represent nodes of different classes. For a typical label propagation

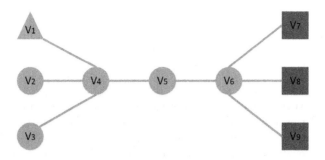

Fig. 1. A toy example of information network

method, nodes v_1, v_2, v_4 will be classified to rectangle class with about 0.7 confidence. That can be caused by the propagation along the path of $v_1 \rightarrow v_4$, $v_4 \rightarrow v_2, v_4 \rightarrow v_3$, in which label information between unlabeled nodes takes effect. Our approach is different. According to the structural information, v_5 is similar to v_7, v_8, v_9 because they all belong to the neighbors of v_6. With label information, v_6 would learn to be more close to rectangle class. Then v_4 would be more neutral due to its relation between v_1(triangle class) and v_6 (more likely to be rectangle class). Since label information will not propagate between unlabeled nodes $(v_4, v_5), (v_4, v_2), (v_4, v_3)$ directly, the label probability of v_2, v_3 will be around 0.5. In this way, we can avoid making a partial judgement if we meet such condition: v_1 is a noisy node and v_2, v_3 belongs to rectangle class. This also implies that our approach prefer adapting to the context when there does not have enough label information, rather than judging nodes with high confidence by label propagation.

3   Experimental Evaluation

In this section, we first provide an overview of the datasets in our experiment. We then introduce the baselines and experimental settings. Finally we report and analyze the experimental results.

3.1   Experimental Setup

Datasets. We conduct experiments on two well known and publicly available datasets. One is DBLP [2] dataset including approximately 16000 scientific publications chosen from the DBLP database including three categories: "Database", "Machine Learning", and "Theory". The nodes are papers and links are co-authorship information between documents. The other is BlogCatalog [17] which is a network of social relations among the authors of the bloggers. There are 39 classes (labels) representing the topic categories provided by the authors. It's a multi-label multi-class dataset on which DeepWalk [13] and Node2Vec [8] conduct experiments.

Baselines. We conduct extensive experiments to compare our methods with four state-of-the-art baselines. Three of them are graph embedding approaches: DeepWalk [13], LINE [15], and Node2Vec [8]. The remaining one is a latest label propagation OMNI-Prop [20] method.

Settings. We train a one *vs.* rest logistic regression classifier implemented by Liblinear [7] for each class as Node2Vec [8] did and select the class with maximum scores as the label. We take representations of vertices as features to train classifiers, and evaluate classification performance using 10-fold cross-validation with different training ratios. Since the samples in our dataset may have multiple labels, we deal with the stratified cross-validation problem like this: if one sample is chosen as a test data point in one class, then it will not appear in training data as the negative samples for other classes.

For a fair comparison with the relevant baselines, we treat the graphs as undirected graph and use the typical settings in DeepWalk [13] and Node2Vec [8]. Specifically, we set the dimension $d = 128$ and the number of walks $nw = 10$, walk length $wl = 80$, window size $ws = 10$, the number of negative samples $ns = 5$ and learning rate $\alpha = 0.025$ on all datasets. Since the embedding methods are similar, we would set updated node pairs to be approximately same magnitude for fair comparison. For DeepWalk and Node2Vec, the updated node pairs would be about $|V| * ws * 2 * wl * nw$ (with subsampling $ss = 10^{-3}$ to remove part of node pairs), thus we set samples $= 10$ million for LINE [15] using 1st+2nd proximity and iterate our methods for 100 times. For OMNI-Prop [20], we set $\lambda = 1.0$ as the default value.

3.2 Results

We report the average micro-F_1 and macro-F_1 as the evaluation metrics. The scores in bold represent the highest performance among all methods.

Comparison Results on DBLP. We first report classification results on DBLP dataset in Tabel 1. It is clear that the performance of SLICE trained with only 10% of the training data has already outperforms the embedding baselines (DeepWalk, Node2Vec, LINE) when they are provided with 90% of the training samples. This strongly demonstrates that our approach benefits a lot from label information even if there are only a small fraction of labeled nodes. Also, it is clear that OMNI-Prop performs well on this dataset and our approach really takes advantage of the idea of label propagation. The performance of SLICE becomes much more attractive with more training data and show great improvements over OMNI-Prop. We can attribute this to the combination of structural information learning from embedding methods and label information drawing from label propagation constraint. In other words, the label constraint could modify the network embedding and bias it to be more suitable for node classification tasks.

Table 1. Average macro-F_1 and micro-F_1 score on DBLP

macroF$_1$(%)	10	20	30	40	50	60	70	80	90
SLICE	81.73	**83.92**	**85.23**	**85.93**	**86.33**	**87.28**	**87.61**	**88.03**	**88.50**
DeepWalk	79.39	80.47	80.74	80.67	80.60	80.51	80.77	80.84	80.94
LINE	73.44	74.27	74.39	74.44	74.73	74.98	74.96	74.94	75.07
Node2Vec	79.93	80.34	80.58	80.82	80.85	81.09	80.92	80.86	80.89
OMNI-Prop	**82.11**	83.40	84.15	84.74	85.05	85.28	85.49	85.55	85.81
microF$_1$(%)	10	20	30	40	50	60	70	80	90
SLICE	82.29	**84.36**	**85.63**	**86.33**	**86.73**	**87.65**	**87.97**	**88.38**	**88.82**
DeepWalk	80.17	81.10	81.36	81.32	81.26	81.16	81.39	81.48	81.56
LINE	74.60	75.36	75.46	75.50	75.74	75.91	75.93	75.90	76.03
Node2Vec	80.61	80.94	81.21	81.41	81.48	81.71	81.53	81.49	81.54
OMNI-Prop	**82.33**	83.64	84.42	85.01	85.33	85.55	85.76	85.82	86.08

Table 2. Average macro-F_1 and micro-F_1 score on BlogCatalog

macroF$_1$(%)	10	20	30	40	50	60	70	80	90
SLICE	**23.08**	**24.91**	**26.00**	**26.64**	**27.22**	**27.34**	**27.70**	**27.63**	**27.78**
DeepWalk	18.64	20.28	21.07	21.64	22.08	22.17	22.46	22.72	23.25
LINE	15.67	17.35	18.67	18.89	19.51	19.94	20.46	20.53	21.02
Node2Vec	19.70	21.69	23.00	23.21	23.83	24.06	24.47	25.30	25.57
OMNI-Prop	4.46	5.59	6.78	7.89	8.52	9.12	9.42	10.00	10.49
microF$_1$(%)	10	20	30	40	50	60	70	80	90
SLICE	**36.58**	**38.00**	**38.89**	**39.24**	**39.94**	**40.46**	**40.73**	**40.75**	**40.92**
DeepWalk	34.56	35.58	36.25	36.54	37.00	37.22	37.40	37.56	37.67
LINE	32.38	33.59	34.47	34.83	35.14	35.35	35.74	35.81	36.09
Node2Vec	35.06	36.15	37.13	37.37	37.78	38.10	38.50	38.78	38.88
OMNI-Prop	19.51	21.39	23.21	24.86	25.55	26.31	26.80	27.49	28.14

Comparison Results on BlogCatalog. We now list classification results on BlogCatalog in Table 2.

We can see that SLICE consistently outperforms all other baselines. On this dataset, it is obvious that OMNI-Prop does not perform well. The reason could be that BlogCatalog is a multi-label multi-class dataset and has more categories than DBLP. Label propagation based method could not deal well with such situation and structural information plays an important role. However, even if label information is not propagated well among neighbors, with structural information and classifiers' help, our approach could still perform well instead of falling sharply. That is to say, the combination of the three parts in the objective is effective and complementary to some extent.

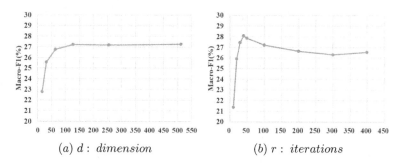

(a) d : dimension   (b) r : iterations

Fig. 2. Parameter sensitivity study on BlogCatalog

3.3   Sensitivity

Since our SLICE model does not use complex sampling techniques, we investigate
the common parameters including the embedding dimension d, iterations r. For
the learning rate η, we just set it to the default value 0.025, as the baselines
do. We conduct the experiment on the BlogCatalog dataset using a 50–50 split
between training and test data as Node2Vec [8] does. Except for the parameter
being tested, we use the default values for all other parameters. We report the
macro-F1 score as a function of d, r, in Fig. 2.

We observe from Fig. 2(a) that the curve of performance rises with the
increase of dimension and becomes stable later. Figure 2(b) shows that our approach converges at about 40 iteration and drops a little when the iteration is
large. That is reasonable since the noises in the label propagation process will
increase. This finding is consistent with that for OMNI-Prop approach on Blog-
Catalog.

4   Conclusion

We have introduced the SLICE approach which incorporates the label information into the embedding process. In particular, we jointly train the classifier and
use its parameters to help propagate the label information without using specialized sampling techniques. We conduct extensive experiments on real world
datasets and results demonstrate that our approach takes advantages of both
the embedding methods and label propagation based methods. In the future, we
plan to investigate how the improved embeddings can be used to other tasks like
link prediction.

Acknowledgments. The work described in this paper has been supported in part by
the NSFC projects (61572376), and the 111 project (B07037).

References

1. Ahmed, A., Shervashidze, N., Narayanamurthy, S., Josifovski, V., Smola, A.J.: Distributed large-scale natural graph factorization. In: Proceedings of WWW, pp. 37–48 (2013)
2. Angelova, R., Weikum, G.: Graph-based text classification: learn from your neighbors. In: Proceedings of SIGIR, pp. 485–492 (2006)
3. Balasubramanian, M., Schwartz, E.L.: The isomap algorithm and topological stability. Science **295**(5552), 7 (2002)
4. Belkin, M., Niyogi, P.: Laplacian eigenmaps and spectral techniques for embedding and clustering. In: Proceedings of NIPS: Natural and Synthetic, pp. 585–591 (2001)
5. Bottou, L.: Stochastic gradient learning in neural networks. In: Neuro-Nîmes (1991)
6. Defferrard, M., Bresson, X., Vandergheynst, P.: Convolutional neural networks on graphs with fast localized spectral filtering. In: Proceedings of NIPS, pp. 3837–3845 (2016)
7. Fan, R.E., Chang, K.W., Hsieh, C.J., Wang, X.R., Lin, C.J.: Liblinear: a library for large linear classification. J. Mach. Learn. Res. **9**, 1871–1874 (2008)
8. Grover, A., Leskovec, J.: node2vec: scalable feature learning for networks. In: Proceedings of ACM SIGKDD, pp. 855–864 (2016)
9. Kipf, T.N., Welling, M.: Semi-supervised classification with graph convolutional networks (2016). arXiv preprint: arXiv:1609.02907
10. Macskassy, S.A., Provost, F.: A simple relational classier. In: Proceedings of the Second Workshop on Multi-Relational Data Mining (MRDM) at KDD-2003, pp. 64–76 (2003)
11. Mikolov, T., Chen, K., Corrado, G., Dean, J.: Efficient estimation of word representations in vector space. CoRR abs/1301.3781 (2013)
12. Mikolov, T., Sutskever, I., Chen, K., Corrado, G., Dean., J.: Distributed representations of words and phrases and their compositionality. In: Proceedings of NIPS, pp. 3111–3119 (2013)
13. Perozzi, B., Al-Rfou, R., Skiena., S.: Deepwalk: online learning of social representations. In: Proceedings of ACM SIGKDD, pp. 701–710 (2014)
14. Roweis, S.T., Saul, L.K.: Nonlinear dimensionality reduction by locally linear embedding. Science **290**(5500), 2323–2326 (2000)
15. Tang, J., Qu, M., Wang, M., Zhang, M., Yan, J., Mei, Q.: Line: Large-scale information network embedding. In: Proceedings of WWW, pp. 1067–1077 (2015)
16. Tang, L., Liu, H.: Relational learning via latent social dimensions. In: Proceedings of ACM SIGKDD, pp. 817–826 (2009)
17. Tang, L., Liu, H.: Scalable learning of collective behavior based on sparse social dimensions. In: Proceedings of ACM CIKM, pp. 1107–1116 (2009)
18. Tang, L., Liu, H.: Leveraging social media networks for classification. Data Min. Knowl. Discov. **23**(3), 447–478 (2011)
19. Wu, X.M., Li, Z., So, A.M., Wright, J., Chang, S.F.: Learning with partially absorbing random walks. In: Proceedings of NIPS, pp. 3077–3085 (2012)
20. Yamaguchi, Y., Faloutsos, C., Kitagawa, H.: Omni-prop: seamless node classification on arbitrary label correlation. In: Proceedings of AAAI, pp. 3122–3128 (2015)
21. Zhou, D., Bousquet, O., Lal, T.N., Weston, J., Schölkopf, B.: Learning with local and global consistency. In: Proceedings of NIPS, pp. 321–328 (2004)
22. Zhu, X., Ghahramani, Z., Lafferty, J.D.: Semi-supervised learning using gaussian fields and harmonic functions. In: Proceedings of ICML, pp. 912–919 (2003)

An Ultrasonic Image Recognition Method for Papillary Thyroid Carcinoma Based on Depth Convolution Neural Network

Wei Ke[1], Yonghua Wang[1,2(✉)], Pin Wan[1], Weiwei Liu[3], and Hailiang Li[4]

[1] School of Automation, Guangdong University of Technology,
Guangzhou 510006, China
1938311796@qq.com, sjzwyh@163.com, wanpin2@163.com
[2] Key Laboratory of Machine Intelligence and Advanced Computing,
Ministry of Education, Sun Yat-Sen University, Guangzhou 510006, China
[3] Sun Yat-Sen University Cancer Center, Guangzhou 510060, China
liuww@sysucc.org.cn
[4] School of Electronics and Information Technology, Sun Yat-Sen University,
Guangzhou 510006, China
lihail@mail2.sysu.edu.cn

Abstract. The ultrasonic image of thyroid papillary carcinoma is characterized by two dimensional gray scale, low resolution, and complicated internal tissue structure. The characteristics of thyroid papillary carcinoma are not obvious and it is difficult to be distinguished. In this paper, the convolution neural network (CNN) theory is introduced for the automatic identification of the ultrasonic image of thyroid papillary carcinoma. Based on the improvement of the Faster RCNN, a detection method for the identification of ultrasonic image features of papillary thyroid carcinoma is proposed, that is, by connecting the fourth and fifth layers of the shared convolution layer in the Faster RCNN, and then normalizing. Secondly, multi-scale ultrasonic images are used in the input. Finally, thyroid papillary carcinoma is classified according to several major characteristics of its ultrasound image.so that the detailed ultrasound image diagnostic report can be received. The experimental results show that the recognition accuracy of the Faster RCNN is higher, the training time is shorter and the efficiency is higher compared with that of the original Faster RCNN.

Keywords: Convolution neural network · Thyroid papillary carcinoma · Ultrasound images

1 Introduction

Thyroid cancer is the most common malignancy in endocrine system, and it takes the first place in the incidence of head and neck cancer. Thyroid papillary carcinoma is the most common, accounting for about 85% of all thyroid cancers [1]. Therefore, the diagnosis of thyroid papillary carcinoma is very important.

© Springer International Publishing AG 2017
D. Liu et al. (Eds.): ICONIP 2017, Part II, LNCS 10635, pp. 82–91, 2017.
https://doi.org/10.1007/978-3-319-70096-0_9

CNN [2] is the fastest growing area in the last five years. It is one kind of artificial neural network, which has become a hotspot in the field of speech analysis and image recognition. The convolution neural network is a machine learning model of deep learning. Its weight sharing network structure reduces the complexity of the network model, reduces the number of weights, and avoids the complex feature extraction and data reconstruction in the traditional recognition algorithm process. CNN has many advantages, but it is rare in the application of ultrasonic image recognition, mainly due to the small samples of ultrasound images, low resolution, and most of them are monochrome images and complex organizational structure, etc., which are the key factors resulting in the rare application of CNN in this area.

In this paper, an improved Faster RCNN was designed by means of CNN-based Faster RCNN network object detection method. By using the layer connection, multi-scale input, multi-classification and fine tuning. A large number of existing cases of ultrasound images was used to extract the characteristics of thyroid papillary carcinoma, a stable, effective, accurate and specific and reliable thyroid papillary carcinoma ultrasound image analysis and diagnosis system was established. This would help to assist clinicians in diagnosing and practicing the training of these types of cancer features. In addition, it can also help non-professionals to understand their condition preliminarily.

2   Related Works

The automatic classification of medical ultrasound images is essentially the similarity problem of the image, or the problem of pattern recognition. In histopathological aspects, Toki and Tanaka [3] used the SIFT method to extract the image to identify prostate cancer. For the incomplete gland features, the accuracy was improved to 6.3%–13.3% comparing to the previous methods. For the color and texture features of biopsy specimens, Niwas and Palanisamy [4] used least squares support vector machine (LS-SVM) for the diagnosis of breast cancer. In many deep learning methods, CNN is the most suitable one for the image feature extraction. Litjens and Sánchez [5] used CNN to idiomatically identify the features of Sentinel and breast cancer metastasis in MR image. This method can reduce the workload of the pathologist and increase the objectivity of the diagnosis. In order to obtain a more accurate model, CNN often needs to train a large number of pictures [5, 6]. In the medicine field, it is impossible to get so many pictures, because the characteristics of histopathological images are more complex than those in nature, and pathological features tend to be very similar or not obvious compared to the surrounding tissue. This leads to the fact that CNN is not widely used in medical imaging. With the CNN's image recognition [7–9] aspects of the development at an alarming rate, Girshick et al. [10] has turned the detection problem into a classification problem, and proposed the RCNN structure. Later, according to the problems of redundant computation and multiple steps requiring in model training in R-CNN, Girshick [11] further proposed the Fast RCNN framework structure, which integrated the whole detection process. It only needs one feature extraction for each image, greatly reducing the redundant computation and improving the detection speed and performance. Fast R-CNN [11] is slow to extract the candidate area and it is the bottleneck of the entire detection network. Ren et al. [12] also proposed the Faster RCNN frame structure, to get the candidate area with CNN. The candidate region extraction network and the target detection network share the feature extraction layer. So the Faster RCNN achieved better detection performance.

In this paper, according to the identification of ultrasound image features of papillary thyroid carcinoma, Faster RCNN made the following improvements:

(1) As the low resolution features of the ultrasonic image, Faster RCNN is not very good for the low-resolution image recognition. By connecting the fourth and fifth layers of the Faster RCNN, the results show that this method increased the number of mAPs (mean Average Precision) of ultrasonic image recognition of thyroid papillary carcinoma by 7.8%, and the accuracy rate increased by 1.7%.

(2) By multi-scale ultrasonic image input, the problem of inaccurate local feature extraction was solved, and the efficiency of ultrasonic image recognition of thyroid papillary carcinoma was further improved. The results show that mAP increased by 3.4% and the accuracy rate increased by 9.2%.

(3) By the multi-classification way, a multi-classification of cancer image was marked, and the system can automatically generate a simple diagnostic report of ultrasonic image.

3   A New Model of the Faster RCNN Network of Ultrasonic Image Features of Thyroid Papillary Carcinoma

Currently, Faster RCNN has achieved the remarkable results in target detection. But our experiments show that it is not very good to directly use for the ultrasound image recognition of thyroid papillary carcinoma. The mAP is only 0.62. The main reason is that the internal structure of ultrasound image is complex, the tissues overlap each other, the boundary is unclear, and the characteristics of malignant cancer ultrasound images and some tissues are very similar. Secondly, the medical ultrasound image is a monochrome image generated from the light spot with different brightness, and it has low resolution.

Because the depth learning model can learn the hidden high-level features from the image, so it can achieve better results in the ultrasound image recognition compared to other shallow learning algorithm with low-level features. In this paper, the Faster RCNN network model was improved, and the features were extracted by combining with deep and shallow learning and multi-scale input, effectively improve the recognition rate of ultrasound images was effectively improved. The improved Faster RCNN network model is shown in Fig. 1.

3.1   Layer Connection

The feature extraction is performed by connecting the deep and shallow layers of the shared convolution layer, then the normalized network model is constructed. Experiments show that the fourth and fifth layers of the shared convolution are better, and this method improves the accuracy of cancer feature recognition.

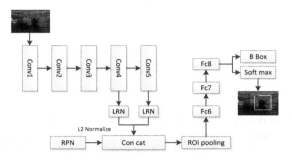

Fig. 1. Faster RCNN frame

3.2 L2 Normalization

As shown in Fig. 1, when connection the fourth and fifth layer of sharing convolution, in order to be able to expand the depth characteristics of definition object in multiple convolution layer, two characteristics tensor for ROI pooling needs to be combined to reduce the dimension. A causal connection between deep and shallow layers can lead to poor performance, because the difference in size has too much effect on the weight below. Therefore, a straightforward solution for this problem is to normalize each ROI pooling tensor before concatenation.

Similar to the original work, L2 normalization to each tensor was applied. The normalization is done within each pixel in the pooled feature map tensor. After the normalization, scaling is applied on each tensor independently as:

$$\hat{x} = \frac{x}{\|x\|_2} \tag{1}$$

$$\|x\|_2 = \left(\sum_{i=1}^{d} |x_i| \right)^{\frac{1}{2}} \tag{2}$$

Where x and $\hat{x}$ stand for the original pixel vector and the normalized pixel vector respectively. d stands for the number of channels in each ROI pooling tensor.

The scaling factor γ_i is then applied to each channel for every ROI pooling tensor:

$$y_i = \gamma_i \hat{x}_i \tag{3}$$

During training, the update for the scaling factor γ and input x is calculated by back-propagation and chain rule:

$$\frac{\partial l}{\partial \hat{x}} = \frac{\partial l}{\partial y} \cdot \gamma \tag{4}$$

$$\frac{\partial l}{\partial x} = \frac{\partial l}{\partial \hat{x}} \left(\frac{I}{\|x\|_2} - \frac{xx^T}{\|x\|_2^3} \right) \tag{5}$$

$$\frac{\partial l}{\partial \gamma_i} = \sum_{y_i} \frac{\partial l}{\partial y_i} \hat{x}_i \qquad (6)$$

Where $y = [y_1, y_2, \cdots, y_d]^T$.

3.3 Multi-scale

Faster R-CNN also uses fixed-size images for training. Through our experiments, we can learn the characteristics of different size ranges, increase the robustness and reduce the influence of the subsampling on the feature representation through the multi-size picture input, improve the extraction efficiency of the original features of the picture, and improve the accuracy of cancer feature recognition.

3.4 Multi-classification

Faster RCNN outputs a rectangle and a category name and a score. For medical diagnosis, the output of more information can provide more diagnostic reference for the doctor. It can be concluded that the main characteristics of ultrasonic image of cancer are: unclear boundary, nonuniform echo, irregular shape, and strong echo intensity (calcification). For the sake of analysis, these characteristics are represented by b, h, x, and q. At the same time, in order to output these cancer characteristics, each cancer area will be marked several times. Each region marks at least one "c", representing a region with cancer characteristics. If any characteristics in the above b h x q is met, the corresponding label would be labeled. In this way, according to the label name and score, a simple diagnostic report will be automatically generated when it is tested. As shown in Fig. 2.

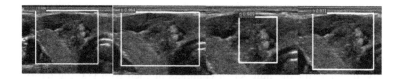

Fig. 2. Thyroid papillary carcinoma report

4 Experiments

4.1 The Build of the Image Data Set

Ultrasound images of 307 people from the Sun Yat-sen University Cancer Center from 2010 to 2014 were collected, including 54 men and 253 women. Each person had 5 to 30 ultrasound images. There were 4,738 ultrasound images totally. In these patients, 256 were diagnosed with thyroid papillary carcinoma and had surgery; 51 were diagnosed with normal thyroid gland. There were 1153 images among 51 people with the normal thyroid gland. Ultrasound images of 200 people who were diagnosed were taken as training sample, and there were 1,367 samples for training sample. The ultrasound images of remaining 107 people were used for testing. In addition, it can be obtained from the diagnostic report that each ultrasound image of the identified person includes 1 to 3 cancer features.

4.2   The Labeling and Classification of Images

We used the annotated software to mark all the diagnostic training images. The ultrasound images used for training meet the XML format files required by the Faster RCNN training, and the annotation of the ultrasonic images for testing was marked as Ground True. Rectangular boxes were used for image tagging. Each cancer area was marked as "c" for each cancer category. If boundary was not clear, the region continued to be marked as "b". If the shape was irregular, the region continued to be marked as "x". If echo is nonuniform, the region continued to be marked as "h". If there was a calcified area or flare, the region continued to be marked as "q". Finally, when the images were tested, the regional characteristics for cancer were determined as long as a regional output is one or more tags from {c b h x q}. In the end, our training cancer images were marked with 3,347 cancer features, and the cancer images used for the test were labeled with 805 cancer features. An XML file for the location coordinates and classification of a region was generated.

4.3   Sample Training

The Faster RCNN network framework for the deep learning python was used; it can be accelerated using GPU. We use the VOC2007 database for pre-training. First, draw the target box and use the opencv dynamic library that others have wrapped up. Then do the XML file, and overwrite the folder corresponding to the VOC2007 database. By modifying the source code of the Faster RCNN, the fourth and fifth layers of the ZF (Shared convolution layer) were connected and normalized.

4.4   Training and Results

Stochastic gradient descent was used to train our network parameters, the learning rate was set to 0.001, and the number of iterations are 40000, 20000, 40000, and 20000.

    Model 1: using the original Faster RCNN network;
    Model 2: using layer connection (layer 4 and layer 5);
    Model 3: using multi-scale input;
    Model 4: using multi-scale input and layer connections;
    The mAP for each model training is shown in Table 1:

Table 1. Performance of models

	Model 1	Model 2	Model 3	Model 4
mAP	0.618	0.696	0.652	0.738

5 Analysis of Experimental Results

To study the effects of our improved data of Faster RCNN on the use of medical imaging, let's examine the methods we use through the cross-testing. The models 1, 2, 3 and 4 correspond to: ID1, ID2, ID3, ID4.

After each method, the results of the test and the relevant data were obtained as shown in Table 2.

Table 2. Performance of strategies

	TP	TPR	FP	FPR	TN	TNR	FN	FNR
Ground truth	805				196			
ID1	604	0.750	57	0.291	139	0.709	201	0.250
ID2	618	0.767	48	0.245	148	0.755	187	0.233
ID3	678	0.842	40	0.204	156	0.796	127	0.158
ID4	715	0.888	31	0.158	165	0.842	90	0.112

In this paper, the automatic identification of ultrasonic image of thyroid papillary carcinoma is studied, and it is closely related to medical science. We use the subject line, that is, the ROC curve. The curve is a comprehensive indicator of the sensitivity and specificity of a continuous variable; it shows a way of revealing the relationship between sensitivity and specificity. A number of different thresholds were set through continuous variables, and a series of sensitivity and specificity was calculated. A curve was draw by using sensitivity as y-coordinate and (1 - specificity) as x-coordinate. The larger area under the curve is, the higher accuracy of the diagnosis is. The ROC curves for all methods are shown in Fig. 3:

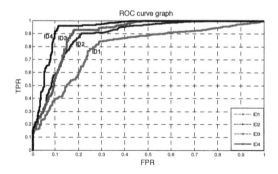

Fig. 3. ROC curve graph

As it can be seen from Fig. 3, the ROC is getting better and better as the methods have been improved. ID4 uses all our methods, and it works best. When TPR <0.5 or FPR >0.5, it doesn't make sense medically. Table 2 was compared with ID1-ID4.

(1) The ID1 VS ID2 (layer connection) is shown in Fig. 3, Because of the connection layer, ID2 is significantly better than ID1 and its ROC curve is closer to the upper left. It can be seen from Table 3 that connecting the fourth and fifth layers increases TP, TN, and reduces FP, FN. In addition, the layer connection makes the model have better recognition effect on the cancer features of irregular shape, the lower resolution, and have less recognition effect on the cancer feature of unclear boundary, as shown in Fig. 4.

Table 3. Improved faster RCNN compared to handcraft performance

	TP	TPR	FP	FPR	TN	TNR	FN	FNR
Ground truth	805				196			
Handcrafted	638	0.793	39	0.199	157	0.801	167	0.207
Faster RCNN	715	0.888	31	0.158	165	0.842	90	0.112

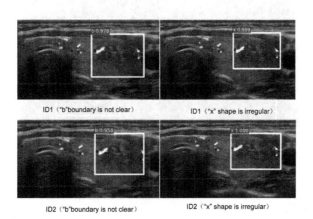

Fig. 4. ID1 vs. ID2

(2) ID3 VS ID1 (multi-scale input) is illustrated in Fig. 3, ID3 uses multi-scale input (This article keeps the original width ratio and uses 800px, 600px and 400px input), its effect is significantly better than ID1 and its ROC curve is closer to the upper left, its AUX value is greater. It can be seen from Table 3 that multidimensional input increases TP, TN, and reduces FP, FN. As shown in Fig. 5, multi-scale inputs are significantly better at identifying cancer features of unclear boundary than the models that do not use this strategy. In addition, for the cancer characterized by calcification or strong light spot, ID3 has strong recognition ability, and is better for the nonuniform echo of ID1.

The experiment result shows that ID4 (improved Faster RCNN) works best for using all the methods, and it is compared with the artificial recognition performance, as shown in Table 3:

As it can be seen from Table 3, for false positives, Faster RCNN and artificial one were very similar; they can reach 19.9% and 15.8%, respectively. The reason is that the characteristics of the pathological image are quite complex. It is hard to distinguish for both Faster RCNN and artificial one. However, the true number and ratio of Faster RCNN are higher than artificial, similar to the true negative. The false negative ratio is one of the most important concerns in the medical field. False negative numbers and ratios are too high to cause very serious miscarriage of justice. Regarding to this, the effect of Faster RCNN is significantly better than the artificial. FNR of Faster RCNN is 11.2% and the artificial one reach 20.7%. Obviously, the effect of Faster RCNN is better than that of artificial one.

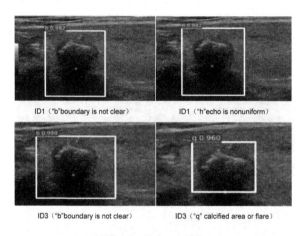

ID1 ("b"boundary is not clear)   ID1 ("h"echo is nonuniform)

ID3 ("b"boundary is not clear)   ID3 ("q" calcified area or flare)

Fig. 5. ID1 vs. ID3

6   Conclusion

By improving the Faster RCNN, after a large number of experiments, the detection model which can identify complex structural cancer characteristics was identified and the recognition effect was better. The results of our experiments show that the proposed network model has a true positive recognition rate of 88.8%, and it is possible to accurately determine whether the ultrasound image of thyroid papillary carcinoma is characterized by cancer. In the future, how to increase the number of samples by combining every medical image training features to improve the true positive rate of cancer needs to be strengthened.

Acknowledgment. This work was supported in part by the Degree and Graduate Education Reform Project of Guangdong Province under Grant No. 2016JGXM_MS_26, Foundation of Key Laboratory of Machine Intelligence and Advanced Computing of the Ministry of Education under Grant No. MSC-201706A and Higher Education Quality Project of Guangdong Province.

References

1. Davies, L., Welch, H.G.: Increasing incidence of thyroid cancer in the United States. JAMA J. Am. Med. Assoc. **295**(18), 2164–2167 (2006)
2. Hinton, G., Deng, L., Yu, D., et al.: Deep neural networks for acoustic modeling in speech recognition. IEEE Signal Process. Mag. **29**(6), 82–97 (2012)
3. Toki, Y., Tanaka, T.: Image feature extraction method with SIFT to diagnose prostate cancer. In: Sice Conference, pp. 2185–2188. IEEE (2012)
4. Niwas, S.I., Palanisamy, P., Zhang, W.J., et al.: Log-gabor wavelets based breast carcinoma classification using least square support vector machine. In: IEEE International Conference on Imaging Systems and Techniques, pp. 219–223. IEEE (2011)
5. Litjens, G., Sánchez, C.I., Timofeeva, N., et al.: Deep learning as a tool for increased accuracy and efficiency of histopathological diagnosis. Sci. Rep. **6**, 26286 (2016)
6. Russakovsky, O., Deng, J., Su, H., et al.: ImageNet large scale visual recognition challenge. Int. J. Comput. Vis. **115**(3), 211–252 (2015)
7. He, K., Zhang, X., Ren, S., et al.: Deep residual learning for image recognition. In: Computer Vision and Pattern Recognition, Las Vegas, Nevada, USA, pp. 770–778 (2016)
8. Zeiler, M.D., Fergus, R.: Visualizing and understanding convolutional networks. In: Fleet, D., Pajdla, T., Schiele, B., Tuytelaars, T. (eds.) ECCV 2014, Part I. LNCS, vol. 8689, pp. 818–833. Springer, Cham (2014). doi:10.1007/978-3-319-10590-1_53
9. He, K., Zhang, X., Ren, S., et al.: Delving deep into rectifiers: surpassing human-level performance on imagenet classification. In: International Conference on Computer Vision, Santiago, Chile, pp. 1026–1034 (2015)
10. Girshick, R., Donahue, J., Darrell, T., et al.: Rich feature hierarchies for accurate object detection and semantic segmentation. In: Proceedings of the IEEE Conference on Computer Vision and Pattern Recognition, Columbus, Ohio, USA, pp. 580–587 (2014)
11. Girshick, R.: Fast R-CNN. In: Proceedings of the IEEE International Conference on Computer Vision, Santiago, Chile, pp. 1440–1448 (2015)
12. Ren, S., He, K., Girshick, R., et al.: Faster R-CNN: towards real-time object detection with region proposal networks. In: Advances in Neural Information Processing Systems, Montréal, Canada, pp. 91–99 (2015)

An STDP-Based Supervised Learning Algorithm for Spiking Neural Networks

Zhanhao Hu[1], Tao Wang[2], and Xiaolin Hu[3(✉)]

[1] Department of Physics, Tsinghua University, Beijing, China
[2] Huawei Technology, Beijing, China
[3] Tsinghua National Laboratory for Information Science and Technology (TNList),
Department of Computer Science and Technology,
Center for Brain-Inspired Computing Research (CBICR),
Tsinghua University, Beijing, China
xlhu@tsinghua.edu.cn

Abstract. Compared with rate-based artificial neural networks, Spiking Neural Networks (SNN) provide a more biological plausible model for the brain. But how they perform supervised learning remains elusive. Inspired by recent works of Bengio et al., we propose a supervised learning algorithm based on Spike-Timing Dependent Plasticity (STDP) for a hierarchical SNN consisting of Leaky Integrate-and-fire (LIF) neurons. A time window is designed for the presynaptic neuron and only the spikes in this window take part in the STDP updating process. The model is trained on the MNIST dataset. The classification accuracy approach that of a Multilayer Perceptron (MLP) with similar architecture trained by the standard back-propagation algorithm.

Keywords: STDP · SNN · Supervised learning

1 Introduction

Rate-based deep neural networks (RDNN) with back-propagation (BP) algorithm have got great developments in recent years [10]. Neurons in these networks deliver information by floating numbers. But in the brain, signals are carried on by spikes, a kind of binary signals. This property can be captured by a spiking neural networks (SNN). But how the SNNs are trained remains largely unknown.

Several works studying supervised algorithm on SNN have made some progress recently. Some works [2,3,7,8,12,17] make use of time coding by spikes. In a very first work [2], each neuron is only allowed to fire a single spike. The model is then expanded to allowing multiple spikes by later studies [3,7]. Networks in these papers usually need to keep multiple channels with independent weights between two neurons. These channels account for different time delays [2] or order numbers of spikes in the spike train [17]. These algorithms are designed to learn spike trains, but classification on large datasets is hard for these models.

© Springer International Publishing AG 2017
D. Liu et al. (Eds.): ICONIP 2017, Part II, LNCS 10635, pp. 92–100, 2017.
https://doi.org/10.1007/978-3-319-70096-0_10

In fact, the algorithms need to convey real numbers to spike trains. Due to the difficulty of this conversion and recognizing ability of the network, these models can only work on very simple datasets.

Recently, Bengio et al. proposes an idea to build a two-phased learning algorithm for energy-based models called e-prop [14]. They implement the algorithm on an energy-based model with input neurons clamped to input data and output neuron variable under target signals. Neurons are free from target signals in the first phase, and the state of which is denoted by s^0. Dynamics of output neurons are changed slightly by target signals in the second phase, and the state of neurons is s^ξ. Let $\rho()$ represent the active function. The weight W_{ij} of synapse between neuron j and neuron i is updated by

$$W_{ij} \leftarrow W_{ij} + \eta \Delta W_{ij}, \tag{1}$$

where

$$\Delta W_{ij} \propto \lim_{\xi \to 0} \frac{1}{\xi}(\rho(s_i^\xi)\rho(s_j^\xi) - \rho(s_i^0)\rho(s_j^0)). \tag{2}$$

And this rule is a symmetric version of another rule

$$\Delta W \propto \dot{s}_i \rho(s_j), \tag{3}$$

which is studied in previous work [1]. In the work a link has been made between (3) and Spike-Timing Dependent Plasticity (STDP) rule.

STDP rule is thought to be an ideal basis of algorithms on SNN. It is first found in physiological experiment [11], defines that the plasticity of a synapse is only dependent on the time difference of spikes from the two neurons attached by this synapse. But computational significance of STDP is not clear. Several works implement STDP on learning algorithms [6,9,13]. They all take an idea that utilizing the simple property that the synaptic weight is strengthened when the postsynaptic spike is after the presynaptic spike, thus a strict order of presynaptic and postsynaptic spike is needed.

In this work we propose a new STDP-based algorithm on SNN. Also, we find that simply computing all of the spikes using the STDP rule results in poor results. We modify the spike pairs that perform STDP rule, and achieve good results on same benchmark image classification dataset. We stress that we do not change the original STDP rule on single pair of spikes, but provide a way that how to use the STDP rule.

2   Method

2.1   The Network

The network is a bidirectionally connected network with asymmetric weights based on the leaky integrate-and-fire (LIF) neuron model [5]. The state of neuron i is described by membrane potential V_i. The dynamics of V_i is:

$$\tau_V \frac{\mathrm{d}V_i}{\mathrm{d}t} = -V_i + E_L - r_m \sum_{j \in \Gamma_i} \bar{g}_{s,ij} P_{s,j}(V_i - E_{s,j}) + R_m I_e, \tag{4}$$

where I_e is input current, E_L is equilibrium potential, $E_{s,j}$ is determined by types of neurotransmitter, τ_V is a time constant, and R_m is a resistance constant. Γ_i is the set of neurons that have synapses to neuron i. The membrane potential V_i triggers the neuron to release a spike when it reaches a threshold V_{th}, and then is reseted to V_{reset} after the spike. $\bar{g}_{s,ij}P_{s,j}$ represents synaptic conductance from neuron j to neuron i, where $\bar{g}_{s,ij}$ represents the maximum strength of the synapse, and $P_{s,j}$ represents the probability of opened neurotransmitter gates. The dynamics of $P_{s,j}$ is

$$\tau_P \frac{dP_{s,j}}{dt} = -P_{s,j} + \sum_k \delta(t - T_j^{(k)}). \tag{5}$$

The variable $P_{s,j}$ increases by a unit amount every time neuron j spikes, and decreases to zero spontaneously. $\delta()$ is a Dirac function, which means $\delta(x) = 0$, $(x \neq 0)$ and $\int_{-\infty}^{\infty} \delta(x)x = 1$. $[T_j^{(1)}, T_j^{(2)}, ...]$ represents for spike train of neuron j.

We set all $E_{s,j}$ to $0\ V$, and the input current I_e to $0\ \mu A$. Also, for the sake of convenience, we write $\bar{g}_{s,ij}$ to W_{ij}, and introduce an input summation for postsynaptic neuron i

$$P_i = \sum_{j \in \Gamma_i} \bar{g}_{s,ij} P_{s,j}, \tag{6}$$

and rewrite the basic dynamics (4) and (5) as

$$\tau_V \frac{dV_i}{dt} = -V_i + E_L - r_m P_i(V_i - E_s), \tag{7}$$

$$\tau_P \frac{dP_i}{dt} = -P_i + \sum_{j,k} W_{ij}\delta(t - T_j^{(k)}). \tag{8}$$

The network consists of an input layer, a hidden layer, and an output layer. We denote the data for supervised learning by normalized input signal v_x and target signal v_y.

For neuron i in the input layer, we simply let it be controlled by input signal $v_{x,i}$:

$$P_i = P_0 v_{x,i}, \tag{9}$$

and P_0 is a constant to convert the scales. Neurons in the input layer fire in a fixed pattern under an input proportional to input signal. The neurons in the hidden layer are not affected by any signals from data directly, and act according to (7) and (8).

Situation for neurons in the output layer is a bit more complicated. Like the e-prop method [14], learning is performed in two phases, named inference phase and learning phase in this paper. The only difference between the two phases is the dynamics of the output layer neurons. In the inference phase, the neurons also act according to (7) and (8). The network gives an inference result by counting the frequency of spikes of output neurons in this phase. And in the learning phase, we add an item represents for effect of target signals:

$$\tau_P \frac{\mathrm{d}P_i}{\mathrm{d}t} = -P_i + \sum_{j,k} W_{ij}\delta(t - T_j^{(k)}) + \beta(P_0 v_{y,i} - P_i), \tag{10}$$

where $v_{y,i}$ is the ith target signal and β controls the effectiveness of target signals.

2.2   The Learning Rule

We adopt the original STDP functions. The STDP function represent the relationship of modification δW_{ij} of the synapse W_{ij} from presynaptic neuron j to postsynaptic neuron i, and the firing time of two spikes fire at t_j and t_i respectively. The commonly used exponential form [15] of STDP function can be

$$\delta W_{ij}(t_i, t_j) = f(t_i - t_j) = \begin{cases} e^{-\frac{t_i - t_j}{\tau_m}}, & \text{when } t_i > t_j \\ 0, & \text{when } t_i = t_j \\ -e^{-\frac{t_j - t_i}{\tau_m}}, & \text{when } t_i < t_j \end{cases} \tag{11}$$

And we can also use a sinusoidal form [16] as

$$\delta W_{ij}(t_i, t_j) = f(t_i - t_j) = \begin{cases} \sin(\frac{t_i - t_j}{\tau_w}\pi), & \text{when } \Delta t \in [-\tau_w, \tau_w] \\ 0, & \text{otherwise} \end{cases}, \tag{12}$$

where τ_w is a time constant. The two functions are plotted in Fig. 1. During the experiment we found that the sinusoidal form resulted in better consequence, so all results presented in the paper are based on (12).

The STDP rule is implemented on a time window in the learning phase after the inference phase. We find that simply summing up all of the spike pairs in a bidirectional network does not work. When the STDP function is approximately anti-symmetric which means $f(\delta t) = -f(-\delta t)$, we have

$$\Delta W_{ij} = \sum_{t_i, t_j} f(t_i - t_j) = -\sum_{t_i, t_j} f(t_j - t_i) = -\Delta W_{ji}. \tag{13}$$

It means that the synapse modifications in two directions of two neurons are always opposite. Consider a situation that two neurons' firing rates are increasing in a same mode, so that average modification of the two synapse are expected to be symmetric, which is $\Delta W_{ij} = \Delta W_{ji}$. Along with (13), we have $\Delta W_{ij} = \Delta W_{ji} = 0$. This makes no sense for learning and implementing this operation can not learn the model well.

For breaking this symmetry we made a slight modification. We redefined the rules of multiple spikes in a time window $[0, T]$. That is, for synapse W_{ij}, spikes

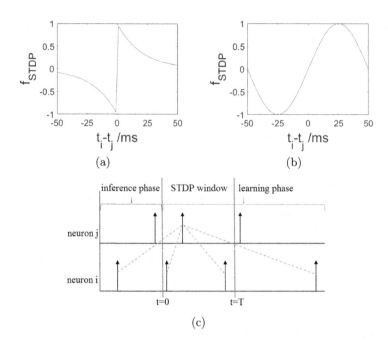

Fig. 1. (a) The exponential form of STDP function. (b) The sinusoidal form of STDP function. (c) Illustration of details of implementing STDP. The learning window is embedded in the learning phase, which is the space between the two vertical lines. Only spike pairs indicated by dotted lines are taken into consider for updating W_{ij}, which is the synaptic weight from presynaptic neuron j to postsynaptic neuron i.

fired by presynaptic neuron j only in time window $[0,T]$, and spikes fired by postsynaptic neuron i in time window $[-\infty,\infty]$ are taken into account:

$$\Delta W_{ij} \propto \int_0^T dt_j \int_{-\infty}^{\infty} dt_i f(t_j - t_i) \sum_{k,l} \delta(t_i - T_i^{(k)})\delta(t_j - T_j^{(j)}). \tag{14}$$

Because of the local property of STDP rule, which means only spikes that the time distance is not larger than τ_w in (12) actually effect, the scope of spikes fired by postsynaptic neuron is $[-\tau_w, T + \tau_w]$ in fact.

In fact, when STDP rule is implemented on time window $[0,T]$, it means the STDP is somehow "turned on" at the time $t = 0$ and "turned off" at the time $t = T$. And more specifically, STDP can be considered as a consequence of some kinds of biochemical signals from both presynaptic neuron and postsynaptic neuron [4]. We propose an idea that STDP is considered to be "turned on" by activating the production or transmission of the biochemical signal triggered by presynaptic neuron spikes, and also it is "turned" off by suppressing these signals, while signals related to postsynaptic spikes are existed all time along.

The learning algorithm is summarized in Algorithm 1.

Algorithm 1. Training the spiking neural network

1: Simulate an inference phase in the time window of $[-t_0, 0]$ and record the spike train $[T_i^{(1)}, T_i^{(2)}, ..., T_i^{(m_i)}]$.
2: Simulate a learning phase in the time window of $[0, T + t_w]$ and record the spike train $[T_i^{(m_i+1)}, T_i^{(m_i+2)}, ..., T_i^{(M_i)}]$.
3: $W_{ij}^{(n+1)} = W_{ij}^{(n)} + \alpha \int_0^T dt_j \int_{-\infty}^{\infty} dt_i f(t_j - t_i) \sum_{k,l} \delta(t_i - T_i^{(k)}) \delta(t_j - T_j^{(j)})$.

3   Results

We implement the model on the MNIST dataset. The dataset contains 60,000 training images and 10,000 test images. And the images are in gray scale and have size 28×28. The size of the network is 784-200-10, which indicates the numbers of neurons in input layer, hidden layer, and output layer, respectively.

We use the Euler method to approximate the differential function (7) and (8). Figure 2 is the simulation illustration of input summation and the membrane potential of 10 output layer neurons with different time step. We set $\tau_V = 20$ ms,

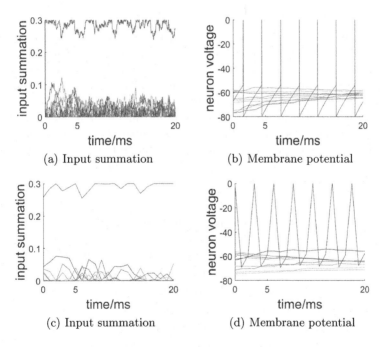

(a) Input summation

(b) Membrane potential

(c) Input summation

(d) Membrane potential

Fig. 2. Simulation illustration of input summation and membrane potential of 10 output layer neurons in an inference phase. The synaptic weights have been trained on MNIST dataset. Only the 8th neuron have a maximal input, and fires in a maximal pattern, while other neurons are not. The simulation for (7) and (8) is processed using Euler method. We have tried different time steps, as 0.01 ms for (a)(b) and 1 ms for (c)(d)

$\tau_P = 10\,\text{ms}$, $E_s = 0$, $E_L = -70\,\text{mV}$, $V_{reset} = -80\,\text{mV}$, $V_{th} = -54\,\text{mV}$, and a hard bound $[0, 0.3]$ for P_i. In fact, we find that a simulation time step of 1 ms is enough to depict the spiking trains, so we use a step of 1 ms in our later experiment.

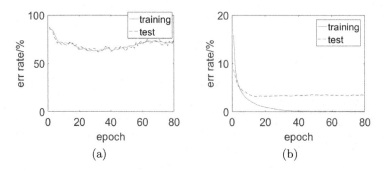

Fig. 3. The error rates against epochs on the MNIST dataset. (a) Simply take all of the spike pairs into account. (b) Use the proposed method.

We test our model on the MNIST dataset (Fig. 3). Using the STDP rule with all of the spikes in the time window taken in to account did not work. By using the proposed method, the error rate on training set is able to decrease to 0.0% in the experiment, which proves the convergence of algorithm experimentally. For comparison, we also implement the e-prop and MLP which have similar architecture to our model (the same number of input, hidden and output neurons). Several other STDP-based algorithms are also compared. The test accuracies on the MNIST dataset are summarized in Table 1. The test accuracy of our method is greater than other STDP-based algorithms, except for the algorithm that use a convolutional architecture [9].

Table 1. Comparison of different algorithms

Model	Neural coding	Test accuracy/%
E-prop	Rate-based	97.5
MLP	Rate-based	98.5
Two layer network [13]	Spike-based	93.5
Two layer network [6]	Spike-based	95.0
Convolutional SDNN [9]	Spike-based	98.4
Proposed model	Spike-based	96.8

4   Discussion

We describe an STDP-based supervised learning algorithm on SNN, and get good results on the MNIST classification task. The accuracy approaches that of an MLP with a similar architecture, which indicates the effectiveness of this algorithm. Compared with existing algorithms for training SNNs, the proposed algorithm have achieved competing results.

The algorithm suggests that biological neurons may not modify their synapses under the STDP rule all the time. STDP takes effect only when the supervisory signals are applied. In addition, the algorithm suggests that not all spikes of the presynaptic neuron participate in the STDP learning process for the synapse. Instead, there may exist a time window and only the spikes during this window should be counted. But biochemical evidence is needed to validate these predictions.

Acknowledgment. This work was supported in part by the National Natural Science Foundation of China under Grant 91420201, Grant 61332007, Grant 61621136008 and Grant 61620106010, in part by the Beijing Municipal Science and Technology Commission under Grant Z161100000216126, and in part by Huawei Technology under Contract YB2015120018.

References

1. Bengio, Y., Mesnard, T., Fischer, A., Zhang, S., Wu, Y.: STDP as presynaptic activity times rate of change of postsynaptic activity. arXiv preprint (2015). arXiv:1509.05936
2. Bohte, S.M., Kok, J.N., La Poutre, H.: Error-backpropagation in temporally encoded networks of spiking neurons. Neurocomputing **48**(1), 17–37 (2002)
3. Booij, O., tat Nguyen, H.: A gradient descent rule for spiking neurons emitting multiple spikes. Inf. Process. Lett. **95**(6), 552–558 (2005)
4. Clopath, C., Büsing, L., Vasilaki, E., Gerstner, W.: Connectivity reflects coding: a model of voltage-based STDP with Homeostasis. Nat. Neurosci. **13**(3), 344–352 (2010)
5. Dayan, P., Abbott, L.F.: Theoretical Neuroscience, vol. 806. MIT Press, Cambridge (2001)
6. Diehl, P.U., Cook, M.: Unsupervised learning of digit recognition using spike-timing-dependent plasticity. Front. Comput. Neurosci. **9**, 99 (2015)
7. Ghosh-Dastidar, S., Adeli, H.: A new supervised learning algorithm for multiple spiking neural networks with application in epilepsy and seizure detection. Neural Netw. **22**(10), 1419–1431 (2009)
8. Gütig, R., Sompolinsky, H.: The tempotron: a neuron that learns spike timing-based decisions. Nat. Neurosci. **9**(3), 420–428 (2006)
9. Kheradpisheh, S.R., Ganjtabesh, M., Thorpe, S.J., Masquelier, T.: STDP-based spiking deep neural networks for object recognition. arXiv preprint (2016). arXiv:1611.01421
10. LeCun, Y., Bengio, Y., Hinton, G.: Deep learning. Nature **521**(7553), 436–444 (2015)

11. Markram, H., Lübke, J., Frotscher, M., Sakmann, B.: Regulation of synaptic efficacy by coincidence of postsynaptic APS and EPSPS. Science **275**(5297), 213–215 (1997)
12. Ponulak, F., Kasiński, A.: Supervised learning in spiking neural networks with resume: sequence learning, classification, and spike shifting. Neural Comput. **22**(2), 467–510 (2010)
13. Querlioz, D., Bichler, O., Dollfus, P., Gamrat, C.: Immunity to device variations in a spiking neural network with memristive nanodevices. IEEE Trans. Nanotechnol. **12**(3), 288–295 (2013)
14. Scellier, B., Bengio, Y.: Equilibrium propagation: bridging the gap between energy-based models and backpropagation. Front. Comput. Neurosci. **11** (2017). Article no. 24
15. Song, S., Miller, K.D., Abbott, L.F.: Competitive Hebbian learning through spike-timing-dependent synaptic plasticity. Nat. Neurosci. **3**(9), 919–926 (2000)
16. Xie, X., Seung, H.S.: Spike-based learning rules and stabilization of persistent neural activity. In: Advances in Neural Information Processing Systems, pp. 199–208 (2000)
17. Xie, X., Qu, H., Yi, Z., Kurths, J.: Efficient training of supervised spiking neural network via accurate synaptic-efficiency adjustment method. IEEE Trans. Neural Netw. Learn. Syst. **28**(6), 1411–1424 (2017)

An End-to-End Approach for Bearing Fault Diagnosis Based on a Deep Convolution Neural Network

Liang Chen[1,2]($\boxtimes$), Yuxuan Zhuang[1], Jinghua Zhang[1],
and Jianming Wang[2]

[1] School of Mechanical and Electric Engineering,
Soochow University, Suzhou, China
chenl@suda.edu.cn
[2] Post-Doctoral Research Center,
Suzhou Asia-Pacific Metals Co. LTD, Suzhou, China

Abstract. Traditional methods for bearing fault diagnosis mostly utilized a shallow model like support vector machine (SVM) that required professional machinery skills and much of knowledge. Deep models like deep belief network (DBN) had shown its advantage in fault feature extraction without prior knowledge. In this paper, an end-to-end approach based on deep convolution neural network (DCNN) is presented. The approach embodying the idea of end to end diagnosis has only one simple and elegant convolution neural network and don't need any exquisite hierarchical structure that was used in the traditional methods. The samples of time-domain signals are inputted into the proposed model without any frequency transformation, and the approach can diagnosis bearing fault types and fault sizes simultaneously as output. Experimental researches had shown that the approach has the advantages such as a simple structure, less iteration and real-time, while its accuracy on the diagnosis of fault types and fault sizes can still be guaranteed.

Keywords: Fault diagnosis · Deep convolution neural network · Bearing · End to end approach

1 Introduction

It's important to research on the fault diagnosis methods for gears which are curial parts in the rotating machinery. Traditional methods for mechanical fault diagnosis mostly used signal processing technologies such as wavelet analysis and support vector machines [1–4]. In the traditional way, a multiscale slope feature extraction approach was usually proposed [5–8]. However, this hierarchy may not necessary if the diagnosis is considered with a deep learning model. Deep neural network (DNN) could be established to extract the useful features from input data and approximate complex non-linear functions [9]. Deep belief network (DBN) is applied to classify the faults of compressor valves by constructing a hierarchical structure [10]. A novel hierarchical diagnosis network (HDN) is proposed by collecting DBNs by layer for the hierarchical identification, which is highly reliable for precise diagnosis [11]. The authors had

© Springer International Publishing AG 2017
D. Liu et al. (Eds.): ICONIP 2017, Part II, LNCS 10635, pp. 101–109, 2017.
https://doi.org/10.1007/978-3-319-70096-0_11

proposed a two-layer model named adaptive deep convolution neural network (ADCNN) in a previous study to diagnosis bearing faults effectively [12]. The ADCNN model like other hierarchical methods [7, 8, 13, 14] were constructed exquisitely but with some inherent weakness such as complex structure, sensitive and fragile for the different samples and most important lack of real-time.

Inspired by the end to end methodology used in the Google Neural Machine Translation System [17], we propose an end-to-end approach based on deep convolution neural network (e2e-DCNN for short) for bearing fault diagnosis. The approach embodying the idea of end to end used a simple and elegant DCNN structure, and don't need any exquisite hierarchical structure that was used in the traditional methods. The samples of time-domain signals are input into the proposed model without any frequency transformation, and the approach can diagnose bearing fault types and fault sizes simultaneously.

2 Convolution Operations and Its Optimization

2.1 A Typical CNN

CNN (convolution neural network) is composed of a convolution layer and a pooling layer. The convolution layer is responsible for converting a former feature map into another identical dimensional feature map to yield more intrinsic structure information. In order to decrease the complexity of feature maps in the neural network, high-dimensional feature maps are inputted into pooling layers for dimension reduction to obtain more sensitive low-dimensional features maps. Figure 1 shows the basic processing of a convolution layer. A refers to a convolution kernel, and B is a pooling kernel.

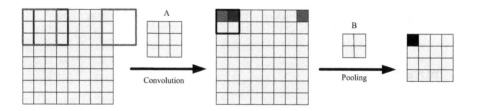

Fig. 1. This is the basic processing of convolution layer.

2.2 The Activation Function and Cost Function

The nonlinear activation function is important to extract effective features from the former map. Non-linear factors are inputted to the adopted model by solving certain complex feature problems, which not only extracts effective characteristics and obtains a better classification results, but also improves the accuracy of fault recognition. The normal form of an activation function is showed below:

$$x_j^n = f(\sum_{i \in M_j} x_i^{n-1} \times w_{ij}^n + b_j^n) \tag{1}$$

Where x_i^{n-1} is the i th feature map of the $n-1$ th layer, and w_{ij}^n denotes the weights of the convolution kernel connecting the i th feature map with j th feature map, b_j^n is given to the bias of each output map and x_j^n refers to the j th feature map of the n th layer. Three activation functions are applied in different operations, i.e. ReLU function, Tanh function and Softmax function. Improper attributes of activation functions may result in updating the weights and biases slowly. The cross-entropy function is calculated by Formula 2. y' is the ideal output of network and y is the actual output. When the ideal output is close to the actual output, the cost value of cross-entropy function approximates to zero ($C = 0^+$). The target of this study is to minimize the cost of cross-entropy function enormously.

$$C = \sum_x [y' \ln y + (1 - y') \ln(1 - y)] \tag{2}$$

3   The Proposed e2e-DCNN Method

3.1   The Construction of e2e-DCNN

In this study, a novel recognition strategy is established for bearing fault diagnosis, which is named as end-to-end DCNN (e2e-DCNN). The e2e-DCNN means that it can recognize the types and sizes of bearing faults simultaneously, and therefore the traditional hierarchical structure is not needed any more.

The e2e-DCNN has performances in extracting superior fault features from a large amount of raw bearing signals and recognizing the type-unknown fault features. The brief framework of e2e-DCNN is presented in Fig. 2. The raw samples are divided into two groups including training datasets and testing datasets. All the datasets are divided into some small sets of samples, and these samples are inputted to the e2e-DCNN repeatedly. The procedure is more concise compared with other hierarchical structures.

3.2   Setting the Parameters

The explicit architecture structure of e2e-DCNN is presented by Fig. 3. There are three convolution layers and two full-connection layers in this architecture. Activation functions are designed for improving the performances of the e2e-DCNN, which include three parts as follows: Firstly, the activation functions of convolution layers are ReLU function. The top two full-connection layers are applied to prepare for recognition, whose activation functions are Tanh functions. The last layer is logistic-regression layer with Softmax activation function, the output of which is a predictive class labels. As shown in Fig. 3, A 1024 vector is reshaped into a 32*32 matrix, which is calculated

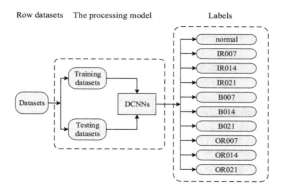

Fig. 2. The framework of e2e-DCNN.

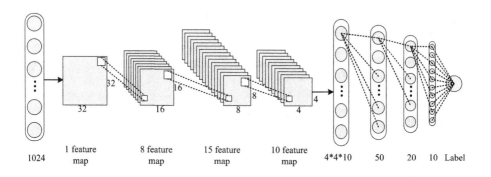

Fig. 3. The structure of e2e-DCNN.

regularly by convolution algorithms. There are three convolution operations including 8, 15 and 10 feature maps (blue planes) separately. Finally, the label of a samples is signed by a series of operations.

There are several parameters playing a crucial role in the training process, such as the size of kernels in max-pooling layers, batch-size and the number of iterations. In this study, the size of kernels in max-pooling layers is a 2*2 matrix. Through these max-pooling kernels, the feature maps are reduced by half. The batch-size is 10, which decides the size of samples in each iteration and affects the training rate. The number of epochs is 1500 in this model, which is smaller than other fault diagnosis methods.

4   The Results and Comparisons

4.1   The Performances of e2e-DCNN

The e2e-DCNN, which is a competitive model for multi-classification to identify fault types and fault sizes. The e2e-DCNN model reduces the total iterations and running time for classification dramatically. The codes of this model are programmed by python on the GPU, so the e2e-DCNN has a strong competitive advantage in iterations and saving times.

Figure 4 shows the accuracy rate of testing datasets during 1500 iterations, and the best result of this model is 97.2%. In addition, it takes only 5 min for training process based on these conditions. The hierarchical ADCNN spends 10 min to finish the same task, which takes more time than the e2e-DCNN. The inputted samples of e2e-DCNN include ten different fault labels, each with the special fault type and fault size. Figure 5 shows the results of classification in the five hundred training samples, the accuracy rate of which reaches 100% approximately. Figure 6 shows that thirteen samples are misjudged in the testing samples apparently, however, the propose method achieves a significant results comparing with other methods.

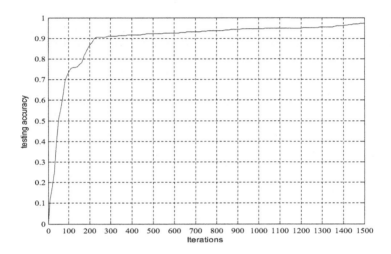

Fig. 4. X-axis represents iterations in training process and Y-axis refers to testing accuracy after each iteration. The accuracy of classification rises quickly during first 300 iterations. After 300 iterations, it grows slowly and the final accuracy rate is 97.2%.

The e2e-DCNN has a great ability in bearing fault diagnosis, according to Table 1 shows more accurate evaluation results of ten different bearing fault types. 50 samples of each bearing fault types are dedicated to train the e2e-DCNN and another 50 samples test the performances of e2e-DCNN for bearing fault diagnosis. From this table, training accuracy mostly reaches 100%. Correspondingly, the mean testing accuracy of ten fault types is 97.2%.

4.2 The Explicit Comparisons

Existing fault diagnosis methods are complex if they were carried out in hierarchical frameworks [7, 8, 13, 14]. For instance, the hierarchical ADCNN as shown in Fig. 7

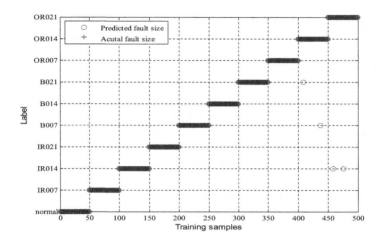

Fig. 5. Predicted ten fault types for training samples are presented in detail. There are four error classification samples in the training samples. The X-axis refers to the number of training samples and the Y-axis refers to ten fault types.

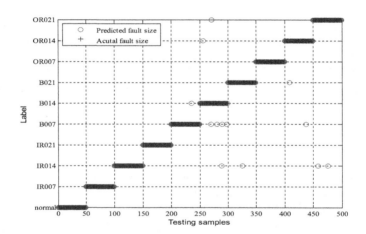

Fig. 6. It shows the testing results of the proposed model. Thirteen samples are misjudged in 500 testing samples, as showed in the figure.

has a huge and complex structure including four ADCNN models. The first ADCNN model divides datasets into three bearing fault types (Inner race fault, Ball fault and Outer race fault). Next, the bearing fault sizes are identified by three ADCNN models separately. These complicated and repeated operations are run by python step by step.

According to Table 2, identical samples are used in the two different operation modes. First, the ADCNN reaches a 96.9% recognition rate on the available equipment in

Table 1. The diagnosis results for e2e-DCNN

Label	Training/testing samples	The number of misclassified samples	Training accuracy/testing accuracy
Normal	50/50	0/0	100/100
IR007	50/50	0/0	100/100
IR014	50/50	0/0	100/100
IR021	50/50	0/0	100/100
B007	50/50	0/1	100/98
B014	50/50	0/7	100/86
B021	50/50	0/1	100/98
OR007	50/50	0/0	100/100
OR014	50/50	2/2	98/98
OR021	50/50	2/2	98/98

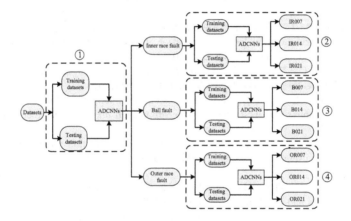

Fig. 7. The hierarchical framework of ADCNN.

Table 2. Comparisons between e2e-DCNN and ADCNN

Methods	Total samples	Recognition rate	Running time	Iterations
The e2e-DCNN	1000	97.2%	4.36 min	1500
The ADCNN	1000	96.9%	6.73 min * 4	8000

the laboratory, which is lower than the e2e-DCNN slightly. Second, as four ADCNN models need to be trained in the hierarchical structure, it is typically very time-consuming to recognize bearing fault both in types and size. Furthermore, the e2e-DCNN model shorten time due to the decrease of iterations, nearly 22.56 min are saved.

5 Conclusions

An end-to-end approach is designed to diagnose bearing fault types and sizes synchronously. The method called e2e-DCNN covers convolution layers, full-connection layers and a logistic-regression layer. This approach is optimized by a number of training samples and tested by test datasets. The proposed method with a high recognition rate has advantages comparing with the ADCNN, which saves considerable times due to less iterations. Therefore, it is suitable and recommended for diagnosing bearing fault due to its excellent advantages.

References

1. Venkatsubramanian, V., Rengaswamy, R., Yin, K., et al.: A review of process fault detection and diagnosis Part I: quantitative model-based methods. Comput. Chem. Eng. **27**, 293–311 (2003)
2. Su, Z., Tang, B., Liu, Z., et al.: Multi-fault diagnosis for rotating machinery based on orthogonal supervised linear local tangent space alignment and least square support vector machine. Neurocomputing **157**, 208–222 (2015)
3. Chen, Z., Li, C., Sanchez, R.: Gearbox fault identification and classification with convolutional neural networks. Shock Vibr. **2015**, 1–10 (2015)
4. Li, C., Sanchez, R., Zurita, G., et al.: Multimodal deep support vector classification with homologous features and its application to gearbox fault diagnosis. Neurocomputing **168**, 119–127 (2015)
5. Li, P., Kong, F., He, Q., et al.: Multiscale slope feature extraction for rotating machinery fault diagnosis using wavelet analysis. Meas. J. Int. Meas. Confederation **46**, 497–505 (2013)
6. Ye, Z., Yang, C.G., Zhang, J., et al.: Fault diagnosis of railway rolling bearing based on wavelet analysis and FCM. Int. J. Digit. Content Technol Appl. **5**, 47–58 (2011)
7. Eslamloueyan, R.: Designing a hierarchical neural network based on fuzzy clustering for fault diagnosis of the Tennessee-Eastman process. Appl. Soft Comput. J. **11**, 1407–1415 (2011)
8. Zhu, K., Song, X., Xue, D.: A roller bearing fault diagnosis method based on hierarchical entropy and support vector machine with particle swarm optimization algorithm. Measurement **47**, 669–675 (2014)
9. Lecun, Y., Bengio, Y., Hinton, G.: Deep learning. Nature **521**, 436–444 (2015)
10. Jia, F., Lei, Y., Lin, J., et al.: Deep neural networks: A promising tool for fault characteristic mining and intelligent diagnosis of rotating machinery with massive data. Mech. Syst. Signal Process. **72–73**, 303–315 (2016)
11. Gan, M., Wang, C., Zhu, C.: Construction of hierarchical diagnosis network based on deep learning and its application in the fault pattern recognition of rolling element bearings. Mech. Syst. Signal Process. **72–73**, 92–104 (2016)
12. Guo, X., Chen, L., Shen, C.: Hierarchical adaptive deep convolution neural network and its application to bearing fault diagnosis. Measurement **93**, 490–502 (2016)
13. Barua, A., Khorasani, K.: Hierarchical fault diagnosis and fuzzy rule-based reasoning for satellites formation flight. IEEE Trans. Aerosp. Electron. Syst. **47**, 2435–2456 (2011)
14. Zhou, S., Lin, L., Xu, J.M.: Conditional fault diagnosis of hierarchical hypercubes. Int. J. Comput. Math. **89**, 2152–2164 (2012)

15. Gu, Z.J., Wang, C.: A hierarchical model of network fault diagnosis. In: International Conference on Convergence Computer Technology, pp. 128–131. IEEE Computer Society, Washington (2012)
16. Hu, B., She, J., Yokoyama, R.: Hierarchical fault diagnosis for power systems based on equivalent-input-disturbance approach. IEEE Trans. Industr. Electron. **60**, 3529–3538 (2013)
17. Wu, Y., Schuster, M., Chen, Z., Le, Q.V., Norouzi, M., et al.: Google's Neural Machine Translation System: Bridging the Gap between Human and Machine Translation (2016)

Morph-CNN: A Morphological Convolutional Neural Network for Image Classification

Dorra Mellouli$^{(\boxtimes)}$, Tarek M. Hamdani, Mounir Ben Ayed, and Adel M. Alimi

REGIM-Lab: REsearch Groups in Intelligent Machines, University of Sfax, National Engineering School of Sfax (ENIS), BP 1173, Sfax 3038, Tunisia
{dorra.mellouli.tn, tarek.hamdani, mounir.benayed, adel.alimi}@ieee.org

Abstract. Deep neural networks, an emergent type of feed forward networks, have gained a lot of interest especially for computer vision problems such as analyzing and understanding digital images. In this paper, a new deep learning architecture is proposed for image analysis and recognition. Two key ingredients are involved in our architecture. First, we used the convolutional neural network, as it is well adapted for image processing since it is the most used form of stored documents. Second, a morphological feature extraction is integrated mainly thanks to its positive impact on enhancing image quality. We have validated our Morph-CNN on multi digits recognition. A study of the impact of morphological operators on the performance measure was conducted.

Keywords: Deep learning · Convolutional neural network · Morphological operators · Morphological convolutional neural network · Image classification

1 Introduction

Several methods have been used for solving pattern recognition problems [22–24]. Deep Learning is a new area of machine learning research that has been introduced in order to move machine learning closer to one of its original goals which is artificial Intelligence [1]. It is based on a set of algorithms that try to model high-level abstractions in data such as images, sound, and text. It helps to solve many big data problems such as computer vision, documents recognition, and natural language processing. One of the goals of deep learning is to replace handcrafted features [16] with efficient algorithms for semi supervised and unsupervised feature learning [2].

Document recognition involves in many fields, therefore several works are proposed reporting new findings and results such in [16–21]. Documents are usually saved as images, convolutional neural networks, a variant of deep neural networks (DNNs) architectures, have shown good results for image analysis and recognition [3]. Convolutional neural network (CNN) is a feed-forward neural network where the neurons connection is inspired by the animal visual cortex organization. The last contains a complex arrangement of cells. A convolution operation is a mathematic approximation of the neuron response to stimuli within its receptive field. The last is a restricted region

© Springer International Publishing AG 2017
D. Liu et al. (Eds.): ICONIP 2017, Part II, LNCS 10635, pp. 110–117, 2017.
https://doi.org/10.1007/978-3-319-70096-0_12

of space where cells respond to stimuli. The receptive fields of different neurons are tiled to cover the entire visual field.

Morphological operations are used to enhance image quality [4]. Therefore, we suggest to use morphological filters for the convolution operation due to the known effect of these filters on images. In Mathematical morphology, basic operators like dilation and erosion consist of computing min/max filters in local neighborhoods defined by structuring elements. By the concatenation of these operators we obtain opening and closing which are operations with scale-space properties and feature selection skills according to the structuring element w.

The main motivation of this paper is that even the filters used in convolutional neural networks are demonstrably powerful, an important information such as the way to choose these filters and the way they work is missed. In addition, to present there is no guarantee a priori that filters will generalize, i.e. they will work on new problems.

To this end, we proposed a new architecture of convolutional neural network based on morphological filters.

2 Background

2.1 Convolutional Neural Network

Convolutional Neural Network is a feed forward deep neural network that is made by three main types of layers which are convolutional layer, pooling layer and fully connected layer [3].

The convolutional Layer is the core building block of a Convolutional Network. Its parameters consist of a set of learnable filters. During the forward pass, each filter is convolved with the image i.e. slide over the image spatially and calculate a dot products between the input and the filter which will produce a feature map with two dimensions. Thus, learnable filters are activated once some type of visual feature is seen.

CNN is a sequence of convolutional layers intercepted with RELU as an activation function. For high-dimensional inputs such as images, it is impractical to connect neurons to all neurons in the previous volume, each neuron is connected to only a small region of the input volume. Rather the connections are local in space, but always full along the entire depth of the input volume. Three parameters control the size of the output volume which are depth, stride and zero-padding.

The pooling Layer is inserted between successive convolutional layers. It down-samples the input and reduces the number of parameters in the network by reducing the spatial size of the representation. Besides it controls the problem of over fitting [5].

In the fully connected layer neurons are fully connected to all activations in the previous layer, it is a standard layer of a multi-layer network.

2.2 Morphological Operators

A wide range of image processing operators are included in the field of mathematical morphology [4] which is based on a simple mathematical concept from set theory. The operators are used for noise removal, edge detection, image segmentation and image enhancement. Morphological techniques explore an image with a structuring element which is a small shape positioned at all possible locations in the image and compared with the corresponding neighborhood of pixels.

The basic morphological operators are dilation, erosion, opening and closing. The dilation is used to enlarge the boundaries of regions of foreground pixels on image. It sets a pixel to the maximum over all pixels in its neighborhood. Dilation increases objects in the image; bright regions are enlarged and dark regions are shrinked.

The erosion is used to erode away the boundaries of regions of foreground pixels on image. It sets a pixel to the minimum over all pixels in its neighborhood. It reduces objects in the image. Thus, small details are eliminated and the holes and gaps between different regions become larger.

Opening is defined by an erosion followed by a dilation. It removes noise from the image, it connects also small dark cracks. Opening is similar to erosion, it removes some of the foreground pixels from the edges of foreground regions pixels. But, it is less destructive than erosion in general.

Closing is defined by a dilation followed by an erosion. It is used to merge or fill structures in an image. It can remove small dark spots and connect small bright cracks. The basic effect of closing is like dilation. It tends to enlarge the boundaries of foreground regions in an image and shrink background color holes of the original boundary shape.

Figure 1 presents an example of these different operations.

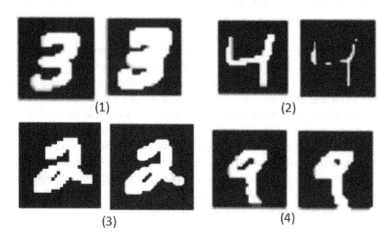

Fig. 1. Example of morphological operation on images: (1) a dilation operation, (2) erosion operation, (3) opening operation, (4) closing operation

3 Morph-CNN: Morphological Convolutional Neural Network

The morphological convolutional layer [6] is based on Counter-Harmonic Mean (CHM) [7] filter formulation for image restoration, which was used to construct robust morphological-like operators [8].

The counter harmonic mean has been considered as an appropriate filter to deal with salt and pepper noise in the state-of-the-art of image processing. More precisely, let f(x) be a 2D real-valued image, i.e., $f : \Omega \subset Z^2 \rightarrow R$, where $x \in \Omega$ denotes the coordinates of the pixel in the image domain.

The CHM filter is obtained as

$$K_w^p f(x) = \frac{(f^{p+1} * w)(x)}{(f^p * w)(x)} = \frac{\int_{y \in w(x)} f^{p+1}(y) w(x-y) dy}{\int_{y \in w(x)} f^p(y) w(x-y) dy} \tag{1}$$

where f^p is an image, where every pixel value in this image is raised to power P, / indicates pixel-wise division, * indicates the convolution operation and w(y) is the filter window, centered at point (y), i.e., the structuring element in the case of morphological operators. Thus, morphological dilation and erosion are the limit cases of the CHM filter, i.e.

$$\lim_{p \to +\infty} K_w^p f(x) = \sup_{y \in w(x)} f(y) = \delta_w(f)(x) \tag{2}$$

$$\lim_{p \to -\infty} K_w^p f(x) = \inf_{y \in w(x)} f(y) = \in_w(f)(x) \tag{3}$$

The morphological convolutional layer based on CHM filter formulation referred to as Morph-Conv layer performs the following operation for a single channel image f(x) and a single filter w(x)

$$MConv(f; w, p)(x) = \frac{(f^{p+1} * w)(x)}{(f^p * w)(x)} = (f *_p w)(x) \tag{4}$$

where p is a scalar which controls the type of operation (P > 0 pseudo-dilation, P < 0 pseudo-erosion and P = 0 standard linear convolution).

Figure 2 illustrates the basic architecture of morphological convolutional neural network. This structure varies in term of the number of performed morphological convolutional layer "Morph-Conv". In the case of a single Morph-Conv layer, erosion or dilation is computed with a negative P and a positive P, respectively. When using

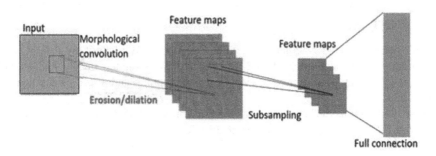

Fig. 2. Basic architecture of Morph-CNN

two Morph-Conv layers, the operators are opening: erosion followed by a dilation (P1 < 0, P2 > 0) and closing: dilation followed by erosion (P1 > 0, P2 < 0).

In this work, we propose to use a morphological convolutional layer instead of a classical random convolutional layer due to the known effect of morphological filters in image processing. The objective is to study the effect of morphological convolutional layer on the classification rate.

4   Experiments

The performances of the different morphological convolutional neural network topologies are elaborated. The approaches are tested on Street View House Numbers (SVHN) and MNIST. In this section, we present our experimental results by giving a description of the datasets and analyzing the performance of our system.

4.1   SVHN

SVHN [9] is obtained from house numbers in Google Street View images. It is a real-world dataset for developing machine learning and object recognition. It is a dataset containing 600 k street numbers with bounding boxes for individual digits.

The images have different dimensions. They are cropped using the bounding boxes location such that all images are of the size 32×32 pixels. They are also converted from 3 channels, color images, to 1 channel, greyscale images. It is important to note that there were originally 73257 digits for training, 26032 digits for testing, and 531131 extra digits.

We used the first format of the dataset which consist of recognizing all the digits presented in the image not the digit in the middle (format 2) which is the widely used format.

Our architecture consists of eight morphological convolutional layers, and two fully connected layer. All morphological convolutional use a filter of size 3*3 the depth of the number of filters in each layer is equal to {16, 32, 64, 64, 128, 128, 512, and 512}. Max-pooling layers are used after each convolution. A dropout of 0.5 is applied to all hidden layers. The zero padding is used to preserve dimensions.

The obtained recognition rate is equal to **97.13%** which is greater than the state of the art [10] 96%.

4.2   MNIST

MNIST dataset (Mixed National Institute of Standards and Technology dataset) is a large data base of handwritten digits. It contains 60,000 training images and 10,000 testing images [11]. This dataset is widely used for training and testing in the field of machine learning.

Our used architecture is composed from four morphological convolutional layers and five MLP-conv [12] layers as illustrated in Table 1. A dropout of 0.5 is used after each pooling.

Table 1. Our used architecture for recognizing MNIST

Layer	Description
Input layer	28*28*1
Morph-conv layer	5*5*192
MLP-conv layer	160
MLP-conv layer	96
Pooling layer	3*3
Morph-conv layer	5*5*192
MLP-conv layer	192
MLP-conv layer	192
Pooling layer	3*3
Morph-conv layer	3*3*192
Morph-conv layer	3*3*192
MLP-conv layer	192
MLP-conv layer	10
Global vote	8*8

The obtained result is compared with previous works that adopted convolutional neural network is presented in Table 2.

We achieve comparable (0.34%) but not better performance results.

Throughout the different results of the different architectures, the effectiveness of using morphological filters in CNN was proved.

The results obtained by Morph-CNN are superior to that obtained by a simple CNN. Also, our results are better than results in [10] using the same number of layers and that prove our contribution by designing a morphological convolutional neural network. The obtained results on MNIST are also comparable to the state of the art.

Table 2. Results on MNIST

Method	Test error
2-Layer CNN + 2-Layer NN [13]	0.53%
Stochastic pooling [13]	0.47%
NIN + Dropout [12]	0.47%
Conv. maxout + Dropout [14]	0.45%
Morph-CNN	**0.34%**

5 Conclusion

In conclusion, we proposed a morphological convolutional neural network architecture which combines convolutional neural network and morphological filters.

The proposed architecture was validated on SVHN and MNIST datasets. Our results show that our architecture achieves good results and higher average recognition rate than a traditional convolutional neural network. And comparing with other architectures, we found good results.

References

1. LeCun, Y., Bengio, Y., Hinton, G.: Deep learning. Nature **521**(7553), 436–444 (2015)
2. Schmidhuber, J.: Deep learning in neural networks: an overview. Neural Netw. **61**, 85–117 (2015)
3. LeCun, Y., Bengio, Y.: Convolutional networks for images, speech, and time series. The Handbook of Brain Theory and Neural Networks, vol. 3361, 10 (1995)
4. Serra, J.: Image Analysis and Mathematical Morphology, vol. 1. Academic Press (1982)
5. Scherer, D., Müller, A., Behnke, S.: Evaluation of pooling operations in convolutional architectures for object recognition. In: Diamantaras, K., Duch, W., Iliadis, L.S. (eds.) ICANN 2010. LNCS, vol. 6354, pp. 92–101. Springer, Heidelberg (2010). doi:10.1007/978-3-642-15825-4_10
6. Masci, J., Angulo, J., Schmidhuber, J.: A learning framework for morphological operators using counter–harmonic mean. In: Hendriks, C.L.L., Borgefors, G., Strand, R. (eds.) ISMM 2013. LNCS, vol. 7883, pp. 329–340. Springer, Heidelberg (2013). doi:10.1007/978-3-642-38294-9_28
7. Bullen, P.S.: Handbook of Means and Their Inequalities, vol. 560. Springer, Netherlands (2013)
8. Angulo, J.: Pseudo-morphological image diffusion using the counter-harmonic paradigm. In: Blanc-Talon, J., Bone, D., Philips, W., Popescu, D., Scheunders, P. (eds.) ACIVS 2010. LNCS, vol. 6474, pp. 426–437. Springer, Heidelberg (2010). doi:10.1007/978-3-642-17688-3_40
9. Netzer, Y., et al.: Reading digits in natural images with unsupervised feature learning. In: NIPS Workshop on Deep Learning and Unsupervised Feature Learning, vol. 2 (2011)
10. Goodfellow, I.J., et al.: Multi-digit number recognition from street view imagery using deep convolutional neural networks. arXiv preprint arXiv:1312.6082 (2013)
11. LeCun, Y., Cortes, C., Burges, C.J.C.: MNIST handwritten digit database. AT&T Labs, 2 (2010), http://yann.lecun.com/exdb/mnist
12. Lin, M., Chen, Q., Yan, S.: Network in network. arXiv preprint arXiv:1312.4400 (2013)
13. Zeiler, M.D., Fergus, R.: Stochastic pooling for regularization of deep convolutional neural networks. arXiv preprint arXiv:1301.3557 (2013)
14. Goodfellow, I.J., et al.: Maxout networks. arXiv preprint arXiv:1302.4389 (2013)
15. Liang, M., Hu, X.: Recurrent convolutional neural network for object recognition. In: Proceedings of the IEEE Conference on Computer Vision and Pattern Recognition (2015)
16. Moussa, S.B., et al.: New features using fractal multi-dimensions for generalized Arabic font recognition. Pattern Recognit. Lett. **31**(5), 361–371 (2010)
17. Bezine, H., Alimi, A.M., Derbel, N.: Handwriting trajectory movements controlled by a beta-elliptic model. TC **1** (2003)
18. Alimi, A.M.: Evolutionary computation for the recognition of on-line cursive handwriting. IETE J. Res. **48**(5), 385–396 (2002)
19. Boubaker, H., Kherallah, M., Alimi, A.M.: New algorithm of straight or curved baseline detection for short arabic handwritten writing. In: 10th International Conference on Document Analysis and Recognition, ICDAR 2009. IEEE (2009)
20. Slimane, F., et al.: A study on font-family and font-size recognition applied to Arabic word images at ultra-low resolution. Pattern Recognit. Lett. **34**(2), 209–218 (2013)
21. Elbaati, A., et al.: Arabic handwriting recognition using restored stroke chronology. In: 10th International Conference on Document Analysis and Recognition, ICDAR 2009. IEEE (2009)

22. Baccour, L., Alimi, A.M., John, R.I.: Similarity measures for intuitionistic fuzzy sets: state of the art. J. Intell. Fuzzy Syst. **24**(1), 37–49 (2013)
23. Dhahri, H., Alimi, A.M.: The modified differential evolution and the RBF (MDE-RBF) neural network for time series prediction. In: International Joint Conference on Neural Networks, IJCNN 2006. IEEE (2006)
24. Bouaziz, S., Dhahri, H., Alimi, A.M., Abraham, A.: A hybrid learning algorithm for evolving flexible beta basis function neural tree model. Neurocomputing **117**, 107–117 (2013)

Combating Adversarial Inputs Using a Predictive-Estimator Network

Jeff Orchard$^{(\boxtimes)}$ and Louis Castricato

Cheriton School of Computer Science, University of Waterloo, Waterloo, Canada
{jorchard,lcastric}@uwaterloo.ca
http://cs.uwaterloo.ca/~jorchard/

Abstract. Deep classification networks have shown great accuracy in classifying inputs. However, they fall prey to adversarial inputs, random inputs chosen to yield a classification with a high confidence. But perception is a two-way process, involving the interplay between feedforward sensory input and feedback expectations. In this paper, we construct a predictive estimator (PE) network, incorporating generative (predictive) feedback, and show that the PE network is less susceptible to adversarial inputs. We also demonstrate some other properties of the PE network.

Keywords: Neural network · Predictive estimator · Autoencoder · Adversarial

1 Introduction

Adversarial input is input chosen specifically to yield a classification with high confidence, and yet not resemble any typical members of that class. For example, a search process found random images (as well as generic patterns) that, when fed into AlexNet [1], were classified with greater than 99.99% confidence [2]. Recent work has looked into overcoming the issue of adversarial input [3,4].

Our hypothesis is that a network with built-in generative capabilities might be able to overcome such adversarial input. Most perceptual networks are feedforward, taking in sensory input and generating a classification as its output [1]. But some networks are also generative; Hinton et al. used RBMs to model the two-way process of recognizing and generating images of hand-written digits, trained on the MNIST dataset [5].

Perception is a two-way process, where sensory inputs interact with expectations, attempting to find a network state that is consistent with both. For example, when you are looking at a raisin, and you are told it looks like a person's face, it shifts your perception; your expectations impinge on the process and your network shifts into a state in which the sensory input of the raisin is meshed with your expectation of a face. You try to see the raisin as a face.

The anatomy of the sensory cortices supports the notion that feedback plays an important role in perception, since most connections between cortical regions are reciprocal (two-way) [6].

© Springer International Publishing AG 2017
D. Liu et al. (Eds.): ICONIP 2017, Part II, LNCS 10635, pp. 118–125, 2017.
https://doi.org/10.1007/978-3-319-70096-0_13

A predictive estimator (PE) is an architecture that has built-in feedback [7]. The higher layers in the perceptual hierarchy send down predictions of what the lower layer should be experiencing, and the lower layers send up the error between that predication and their actual state. However, previous work on PEs have used copied connection weights, where the feedforward connection weights are also used as the feedback connection weights.

In this paper, we aim to generate a predictive estimator network (without weight copying) and see whether the back-and-forth operation of the PE network could be used to combat adversarial inputs. After all, the feedback projections in a PE network contain predictions. These predictions might increase the classification specificity.

2 Methods

Our approach to creating a deep predictive estimator (PE) network is to train a bidirectional network and then use its connections in our PE network.

2.1 Training a Bidirectional Network

Consider the bidirectional network shown in Fig. 1. The network has feedforward connection weights, $\mathbf{W}$ and $\mathbf{P}$, and corresponding biases, a and b, as well as feedback connection weights, $\mathbf{R}$ and $\mathbf{M}$, and biases, c and d.

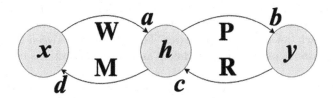

Fig. 1. Simple bidirectional network

If we set the feedback connections to zero (i.e. $\mathbf{M}$, $\mathbf{R}$, c and d are all zeros), then the network simply behaves as a feedforward network. We can train that network using a dataset of (x, y) samples, so that

$$y = \sigma\left(\mathbf{P}h_{\mathrm{ff}} + b\right), \text{ where} \tag{1}$$
$$h_{\mathrm{ff}} = \sigma\left(\mathbf{W}x + a\right), \tag{2}$$

where σ is the logistic activation function. Likewise, if all of the feedforward connections are zero (i.e. $\mathbf{W}$, $\mathbf{P}$, a and b are all zero), then the network behaves in a purely feedback manner. Such a network can be trained so that

$$x = \sigma\left(\mathbf{M}h_{\mathrm{fb}} + d\right), \text{ where} \tag{3}$$
$$h_{\mathrm{fb}} = \sigma\left(\mathbf{R}y + c\right). \tag{4}$$

However, notice that h_{ff} is not necessarily the same as h_{fb}. The intermediate (hidden) representation for the two directions does not have to be the same, especially if the feedforward and feedback connections are learned independently of each other.

Let us suppose that the feedforward and feedback networks were trained using backpropagation so that

$$h = \sigma(\mathbf{W}x + a) \tag{5}$$
$$y = \sigma(\mathbf{P}h + b) \tag{6}$$
$$h = \sigma(\mathbf{R}y + c) \tag{7}$$
$$x = \sigma(\mathbf{M}h + d). \tag{8}$$

It is not sufficient to train $\mathbf{W}$ and $\mathbf{P}$ using simple backpropagation, followed by training $\mathbf{M}$ and $\mathbf{R}$ using backpropagation in the opposite direction. The problem is that the activity in the intermediate layers need to be approximately the same for the feedforward and feedback modes of operation.

Instead of training one direction at a time, we trained one layer at a time as an autoencoder [8]. This is now a fairly common practice. According to the simple network depicted in Fig. 1, we first learn the connection weights $(\mathbf{W}, a)$ and $(\mathbf{M}, d)$ by minimizing the reconstruction error,

$$C\Big(x, \sigma\big(\mathbf{M}\sigma(\mathbf{W}x + a) + d\big)\Big),$$

where C is a cost function such as sum-of-squares, or cross entropy. That is, we project the input x up to the hidden layer, and then project the activity in the hidden layer back down to the input layer. The difference between the input and the reconstruction is used to update the up and down connections between those two layers.

After the first layer is trained as an autoencoder, we train the next layer. If the next layer reaches the output layer of the network, then we train it as an associative memory. This method for learning bidirectional connection weights and biases is similar to the method outlined in [9].

2.2   Predictive Estimator Network

We want to use the learned bidirectional network to generate a continuous-time predictive-estimator network, like the one shown in Fig. 2. The figure shows three PE units. Each PE unit contains a *state* node, denoted x, h and y in the figure, and an *error* node, denoted δ, ε and γ in the figure. Within each PE unit (shown as a shaded box), the state node and the error node are reciprocally connected.

The parameter β can be used to adjust the relative weight of sensory input (coming from the lower levels of the hierarchy on the left) and expectation input (coming from the higher levels on the right). When β is 0, the input to the state nodes comes solely from the feedforward projection. When β is 1, the opposite is true, and the state nodes only receive input from the error node. Hence, when

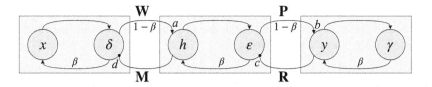

Fig. 2. Diagram of part of a network

$\beta = 1$, the PE network operates in a feedback mode where the state nodes only receive input from higher levels in the hierarchy.

The equations that govern the dynamics of the central PE unit in Fig. 2 are,

$$\tau \frac{dz}{dt} = \mathbf{W}\boldsymbol{\delta} - (\rho + \beta)z \tag{9}$$

$$\tau \frac{dh}{dt} = (1 - \beta)\Big(\sigma(z + a) - h\Big) - \beta\varepsilon \tag{10}$$

$$\tau \frac{d\varepsilon}{dt} = h - \sigma(\mathbf{R}y + c) - \varepsilon \tag{11}$$

where τ represents a time constant. The variable z represents the input current coming from the error node below, and ρ is its default decay coefficient. Roughly speaking, (9) integrates the unit's input current z, (10) converts the input current to an activation h, and (11) tracks the unit's error ε, which is the difference between the unit's state, h, and the predication being sent down from above.

Note that if β is large (close to 1), then the network is operating in a primarily feedback mode, and the last term in (9) causes z to decay quickly and have little influence on h. On the other hand, if β is small (close to 0), then the network is operating in a primarily feedforward mode, and (9) behaves more like an integrator that accumulates the errors being sent from below.

Perhaps the best way to understand the functioning of the PE unit is to study the equilibrium solutions of Eqs. (9)-(11). Consider the equilibrium state of the feedforward system (i.e. set all three derivatives on the left to zero, and let $\beta = 0$). Then Eq. (10) can be written

$$h = \sigma(z + b).$$

This would match (5) if we could show that z must be $\mathbf{W}x$. Suppose, for now, that $\rho = 0$, and consider what happens if we let $z = \mathbf{W}x + \Delta z$. A perturbation analysis (not shown here) seems to suggest that the feedback loop through δ (see Fig. 2) would result in $\frac{dz}{dt} \propto -\Delta z$. Thus, z would be pushed back towards $\mathbf{W}x$.[1]

Equation (11) implies that $\varepsilon \to 0$ since we know that $h = \sigma(\mathbf{R}y + c)$ from (7). Finally, δ would also have to be zero.

If β is equal to 1 instead, we can follow a similar argument to show that $\varepsilon = 0$ (from Eq. (10)), and $h = \sigma(\mathbf{R}y + c)$, and $z = \frac{\mathbf{W}\delta}{\beta + \rho}$. But δ must be zero for the same reason ε is zero. Hence, $z = 0$.

---

[1] The default decay rate of ρ would eventually drive $z \to 0$, but our analysis is relevant as long as ρ is small.

This equilibrium is the goal state of the PE network, in which the error nodes are zero, and the state nodes encode the data to translate between the input and the output (bottom and top) layers.

3   Experiments

3.1   PE Network Behaviour

To get a feel for how the PE network behaves, we ran some experiments using the MNIST dataset. A bidirectional network with five layers (three hidden layers) was trained using the method outlined in Sect. 2.1. The input layer had 784 nodes (the number of pixels in a 28×28 image), and the hidden layers had 100, 80, and 80 nodes. The output layer had 10 nodes. We trained for 30 epochs using stochastic gradient descent with a batch size of 10. Our learning rate was 0.05. We used cross entropy as our cost, and we regularized the connection weights using a decay of 0.001. The parameter τ was set to 0.05 s, and ρ was set to 0.1. After the training, the feedforward part of the network achieved a test accuracy of 76%. We know that other neural networks can do better after more training, but this accuracy was sufficient to serve our purposes.

After training the bidirectional network, we used the connection weights and biases to create our PE network, as outlined in Sect. 2.2. Then we fed a chosen digit as input and simulated the PE network. Note that the PE network receives input at both the bottom layer and the top layer. However, if $\beta = 0$, the network operates in feedforward mode and the top-layer input is ignored. Likewise, if $\beta = 1$, the network operates in feedback mode and the bottom-layer input is ignored.

In these experiments, we ran our network for 1 simulation second, after which we cut off the inputs and simulated some more. The inputs were removed by setting $\beta = 1$ for the bottom layer, and setting $\beta = 0$ for the top layer (each layer can have a different β). The purpose of this sequence is to first allow the input to set the network state, but then remove the inputs and let the PE network "deliberate". After this process, we looked at the top-layer state to see how it compared to the ideal in the test set.

Our PE network yielded a 71% accuracy with $\beta = 0$, using a deliberation time of 0.

Figure 3 shows one example. The true digit (on the left) is a "4". The bidirectional network incorrectly classified this input as a "6" with 41.6% confidence. However, the PE network correctly classified it as a "4" with 23.9% confidence.

Figure 4 shows another example. The bidirectional network classified it as a "3" with 43.8% confidence. In feedforward mode ($\beta = 0$), the PE network classified it as either a "2" or "3" with confidence around 25%. However, we can allow expectation to influence the perception. If β is set to 0.2, then it weights the feedforward/feedback with 80/20. Then the PE network favours the classification of "2" with confidence 28.8%. The corresponding generative images are shown in Fig. 4.

Fig. 3. MNIST example. The image on the left is the original MNIST sample. The middle image was generated using the bidirectional network, (setting the top layer to class 4). The image on the right is the one generated by the PE network.

Fig. 4. MNIST example. The image on the left is the original MNIST sample. The middle image was generated using the bidirectional network (setting the top layer to class 2). The image on the right is the one generated by the PE network with $\beta = 0.2$.

3.2 Susceptibility to Adversarial Input

One of our hypotheses is that the generative, feedback nature of the PE networks will prevent it from being fooled by many adversarial inputs. To test this hypothesis, we ran an experiment on a small dataset, in which binary strings of length 8 are classified into 5 categories.

$$[1, 0, 1, 0, 0, 1, 1, 0] \leftrightarrow [1, 0, 0, 0, 0]$$
$$[0, 1, 0, 1, 0, 1, 0, 1] \leftrightarrow [0, 1, 0, 0, 0]$$
$$[0, 1, 1, 0, 1, 0, 0, 1] \leftrightarrow [0, 0, 1, 0, 0]$$
$$[1, 0, 0, 0, 1, 0, 1, 1] \leftrightarrow [0, 0, 0, 1, 0]$$
$$[1, 0, 0, 1, 0, 1, 0, 1] \leftrightarrow [0, 0, 0, 0, 1]$$

We trained a bidirectional network on that data, and then built the corresponding PE network. The bidirectional network was trained on 300,000 samples, using stochastic gradient descent with a batch size of 10. We used cross entropy as our cost function, and the learning rate was 0.01.

Adversarial input was generated by simply choosing random inputs of 8 values, where each value was chosen randomly from a uniform distribution between 0 and 1. Each sample was fed into the bidirectional network and the PE network. The output of each network was assessed to see if either one yielded a "confident" classification (ie. if the soft-max output gave a value greater than 0.95).

For this experiment, the PE network was run for 1 simulation second with $\beta = 0$ (feedforward mode).

In the adversarial input experiment, the feedforward network yielded a 95% confidence on the random inputs 5% of the time (50 times out of 1000 trials). The PE network did not show a confidence level of 95% on any of the 1000 random strings. However, both the feedforward network and the PE network exhibited 100% accuracy in classifying the true binary strings.

4 Conclusions

The predictive encoder network we created from the connection weights of the bidirectional network exhibited some interesting properties. The feedback inherent in the PE network allowed, in some cases, the network to deliberate and change its mind on an incorrect classification. Moreover, in some cases, allowing an expectation (by setting β to a non-zero value) helped the network to converge to the correct class.

As hypothesized, the predictive estimator network was far less susceptible to adversarial (random) inputs. While the feedforward part of the bidirectional network confidently (mis)classified random inputs 5% of the time, we never observed the PE network confidently misclassify any random inputs. This is despite the fact that both networks exhibited 100% accuracy on the binary dataset.

More study is needed to try to get the accuracy of the bidirectional and PE networks up to contemporary levels on the MNIST dataset (i.e. greater than 98% accuracy). However, we note that the MNIST dataset is not invertible; knowing a digit class is not enough to generate the input image. We plan to investigate stochastic extensions to our method to allow us to generate a variety of inputs, similar to RBMs.

References

1. Krizhevsky, A., Sutskever, I., Hinton, G.E.: ImageNet classification with deep convolutional neural networks. In: Pereira, F., Burges, C.J.C., Bottou, L., Weinberger, K.Q. (eds.) Advances in Neural Information Processing Systems, vol. 25, pp. 1097–1105 (2012)
2. Nguyen, A., Yosinski, J., Clune, J.: Deep neural networks are easily fooled: high confidence predictions for unrecognizable images. In: Computer Vision and Pattern Recognition, pp. 427–436 (2015)
3. Goodfellow, I., Pouget-Abadie, J., Mirza, M.: Generative adversarial networks. In: Ghahramani, Z., Welling, M., Cortes, C., Lawrence, N.D., Weinberger, K.Q. (eds.) Advances in Neural Information Processing Systems, pp. 2672–2680 (2014)
4. Goodfellow, I., Shlens, J., Szegedy, C.: Explaining and harnessing adversarial examples. In: Proceedings of ICLR. arXiv:1412.6572v3 (2015)
5. Hinton, G.E.: A Practical guide to training restricted boltzmann machines. In: Montavon, G., Orr, G.B., Müller, K.-R. (eds.) Neural Networks: Tricks of the Trade. LNCS, vol. 7700, pp. 599–619. Springer, Heidelberg (2012). doi:10.1007/978-3-642-35289-8_32
6. Bastos, A.M., Usrey, W.M., Adams, R., Mangun, G.R., Fries, P., Friston, K.J.: Canonical Microcircuits for Predictive Coding. Neuron **76**(4), 695–711 (2012)

7. Rao, R.P.N., Ballard, D.H.: Predictive coding in the visual cortex: a functional interpretation of some extra-classical receptive-field effects. Nat. Neurosci. **2**(1), 79–87 (1999)
8. Le Cun, Y., Boser, B., Denker, J.S., Henderson, D., Howard, R.E., Hubbard, W., Jackel, L.D.: Handwritten digit recognition with a back-propagation network. In: Advances in Neural Information Processing Systems, pp. 396–404 (1990)
9. Luo, H., Fu, J., Glass, J.: Bidirectional Backpropagation: Towards Biologically Plausible Error Signal Transmission in Neural Networks. arXiv:1702.07097v3 (2017)

A Parallel Forward-Backward Propagation Learning Scheme for Auto-Encoders

Yoshihiro Ohama$^{(\boxtimes)}$ and Takayoshi Yoshimura

Toyota Central Research and Development Laboratories, Inc.,
Aichi 480-1192, Japan
{ohama,yoshimura}@mosk.tytlabs.co.jp

Abstract. Auto-encoders constitute one popular deep learning architecture for feature extraction. Since an auto-encoder has at least one bottle neck layer for feature representation and at least five layers for fitting nonlinear transformations, back-propagation learning (BPL) algorithms with saturated activation functions sometimes face the vanishing gradient problem, which slows convergence. Thus, several modified methods have been proposed to mitigate this problem. In this work, we propose the calculation of forward-propagated errors in parallel with back-propagated errors in the network, without modification of the activation functions or the network structure. Although this scheme for auto-encoder learning has a larger computational cost than that of BPL, processing time until convergence could be reduced by implementing parallel computing. In order to confirm the feasibility of this scheme, two simple problems were examined by training auto-encoders to acquire (1) identity mappings of two-dimensional points along the arc of a half-circle to extract the central angle and (2) hand-writing images to extract labeled digits. Both results indicate that the proposed scheme requires only about half of the iterations to reduce the cost value enough, compared to BPL.

Keywords: Auto-encoder · Vanishing gradient · Credit assignment · Biological plausibility · Feature extraction · Parallel error propagation

1 Introduction

Deep learning is now widely used to develop various applications, such as object detection and classification from image data, automatic translation between different natural languages, speech recognition, and automatic generation of captions from photographs [1]. The back-propagation learning (BPL) algorithm has been widely used for training multi-layered neural models, but a huge number of iterations for updating synaptic weights are required to achieve good performance. The vanishing gradient problem is the primary reason for slow convergence [2], in that back-propagated errors are gradually eliminated because the activation functions in each layer become saturated, which leads to a gradient value too small to propagate errors. To avoid this problem, significant successes were obtained by modified network architectures [3–5], activation functions with mitigated saturation [6, 7], and automatic adjustment of learning rate and momentum [8, 9].

© Springer International Publishing AG 2017
D. Liu et al. (Eds.): ICONIP 2017, Part II, LNCS 10635, pp. 126–136, 2017.
https://doi.org/10.1007/978-3-319-70096-0_14

On the other hand, although neural networks mimic biological information processing, poor biological plausibility of BPL has long been discussed as a drawback [10, 11]. Alternative approaches without back-propagated errors have also been proposed. Perturbation of neural synaptic weights or neural output could behave like reinforcement learning without back-propagated errors [12], but a huge number of iterations are also required. Credit assignment for minimizing the target cost in each layer could be approximated by forward-propagated errors, called forward-propagated learning (FPL) or target-propagation learning (TPL), if multi-layered neural models acquire identity mappings in a neural inverse model [13] or auto-encoder [14]. Recently, it was reported that random synaptic weights for an exclusive error propagation path-way, called feedback-alignment (FA), provide faster convergence than BPL [15, 16]. Some studies have concluded that the rapid convergence of FPL could be regarded as a Newton-like method [13] and that FA could be regarded as a Gauss-Newton method [15]. Since both methods are based on a class of Newton methods, synaptic weights of the neural model should be initialized near the desired weights to realize suitable computation convergence. Thus, biologically plausible approaches might reduce iterations for updating weights but would need to initialize the weights more carefully than for BPL.

Fundamentally, biological plausibility is an important issue but it might be useful to try to use BPL to accelerate learning in artificial intelligence technology. The main purpose of this work is to explore the feasibility of applying such useful features in terms of biological plausibility. Notably, both the forward-propagated errors and the random synaptic feedback errors, named the biologically plausible errors, could individually calculate against the back-propagated errors to implement parallel processing computation. If the biologically plausible errors have significantly good effects for learning in a multi-layered neural model, updating the synaptic weights with the back-propagated errors in parallel to the biologically plausible errors might accelerate learning. Although this idea increases the computational cost, this could be offset using parallel computing.

In this work, we focus on feature extraction using an auto-encoder with a conventional deep learning architecture to discuss the feasibility of the learning procedure using parallel propagated errors. The auto-encoder has at least one bottle neck layer that works as a dimension reduction from activation in the input layer, but the propagated errors for learning are extremely reduced in the bottle neck layer, which causes the vanishing gradient problem. Here, the forward-propagated errors would only be applied as the biologically plausible errors, since it was reported that the random synaptic feedback errors are not effective for training the auto-encoder [15]. In contrast to the back-propagated errors, the forward-propagated errors are gradually eliminated from input layer to output layer. Thus, the vanishing gradient problem might be mitigated by propagating both errors in parallel.

First, two schemes are proposed for introducing parallel error propagation for training the auto-encoder. Next, we will train the auto-encoder to extract a one-dimensional central angle from two-dimensional points along the arc of a half-circle and compare the learning curves and extracted features of each scheme and conventional BPL. After that, the same schemes will be used to extract labeled digits from hand-writing images from the MNIST dataset [17]. Suitability of the labeled features is evaluated by applying conventional classifiers. Finally, the results are discussed and conclusions are given.

2 The Credit Assignment Problem for Auto-Encoders

In order to train a multi-layered model, such as a feed-forward neural network (FNN), a pre-defined cost function that represents the quantified quality of the model must be assigned as errors propagate in each layer during the training period. This problem is known as the credit assignment problem. Let $x_n \in \mathbb{R}^m$ be a column vector as a sample dataset for an auto-encoder, let $X = \{x_1, x_2, \cdots, x_N\}$ represents the dataset, and let $\mathcal{H}(X; \theta, L) = h_L(\theta_{L-1}) \circ h_{L-1}(\theta_{L-2}) \circ \cdots \circ h_2(\theta_1) \circ h_1$ be an auto-encoder where "$\circ$" describes a linear operator and θ_l denotes synaptic weights between the l-th and $l+1$-th layers. Since the auto-encoder will acquire an identity mapping, X is not only the input data but also the desired output data. Conventional mean squared error between the desired output and actual output is used as the cost function to measure the quality of the learning model. In general, the identity mapping learning in the multi-layered model could be described as a minimization problem;

$$\widehat{\theta} = \underset{\theta}{\operatorname{argmin}} J, \tag{1}$$

$$J = \frac{1}{2N} \sum_n \|x_n - \mathcal{H}(X = x_n; \theta, L)\|_2^2, \tag{2}$$

where $\|\cdot\|_2$ denotes the Euclidian norm. Applying the gradient descent method to optimize Eq. (2) iteratively, the iterative equation in the l-th layer could be described using the chain rule for the gradient from the appropriate initial parameter $\widehat{\theta}_{l,0}$ to the i-th iteration;

$$\widehat{\theta}_{l,i+1} = \widehat{\theta}_{l,i} + \varepsilon \nabla_{\widehat{\theta}_{l,i}} J, \tag{3}$$

$$\nabla_{\widehat{\theta}_{l,i}} J = \sum_n \nabla_{\theta_{l,i}} h_{l+1,i,n} \Delta h_{l+1,i,n}^{BPL}, \tag{4}$$

$$\Delta h_{l,i,n}^{BPL} = \begin{cases} x_n - \mathcal{H}\left(X = x_n; \theta = \widehat{\theta}_{l,i}, L\right) & (l = L) \\ \nabla_{h_{l,i,n}} h_{l+1,i,n} \Delta h_{l+1,i,n}^{BPL} & otherwise \end{cases}, \tag{5}$$

where ∇ denotes the partial gradient and ε denotes small positive learning rate. In particular, Eq. (4) is often called the back-propagation learning rule, since the output error would back-propagate through the model from the L-th to l-th layers. In terms of the credit assignment problem, BPL indirectly provides minimization problems in each layer as follows;

$$\widehat{\theta}_{l,i} = \underset{\theta_{l,i}}{\operatorname{argmin}} \frac{1}{2N} \sum_n \left\| \Delta h_{l+1,i,n}^{BPL} \right\|_2^2. \tag{6}$$

If the cost function based on the mean squared error is small enough, the multi-layered model could be approximately regarded as an identity mapping;

$$\mathcal{H}(X; \theta, L) \sim I. \tag{7}$$

The FPL method tries to find the zero point in each layer using a Newton method;

$$\widehat{h}_{l,i+1,n} = \widehat{h}_{l,i,n} - \left[\nabla_{h_{l,i,n}} \nabla_{x_n} h_{l,i,n} \Delta h_{l,i,n}^{FPL} \right]^{-1} \nabla_x h_{l,i,n} \Delta h_{l,i,n}^{FPL}, \tag{8}$$

$$\Delta h_{l,i,n}^{FPL} = \begin{cases} x_n - \mathcal{H}\left(X = x_n; \theta = \widehat{\theta}_{l,i}, L\right) & (l = 1) \\ \nabla_{h_{l-1,i,n}} h_{l,i,n} \Delta h_{l,i,n}^{FPL} & otherwise \end{cases}. \tag{9}$$

By differentiating Eqs. (7) and (8) could be approximately described as follows;

$$\widehat{h}_{l,i+1,n} \sim \widehat{h}_{l,i,n} + \eta \nabla_{x_n} h_{l,i,n} \Delta h_{l,i,n}^{FPL}, \tag{10}$$

where η denotes a small positive learning rate due to the approximation in Eq. (7). Such an approximated Newton method is known as a Newton-like method or the damped Newton method. Thus, FPL directly provides minimization problems in each layer as follows;

$$\widehat{\theta}_{l,i} = \underset{\theta_{l,i}}{\operatorname{argmin}} \frac{1}{2N} \sum_n \left\| \Delta h_{l+1,i,n}^{FPL} \right\|_2^2. \tag{11}$$

3 Parallel Propagated Errors for Training Auto-Encoder Using a Feedforward Neural Network

Using FNN as the learning model, the hypothesis in each layer could be described as;

$$h_{l,n} = \sigma_l\left(s_{l-1,n}\right), \tag{12}$$

$$s_{l,n} = W_{l,i}(\theta_l)h_{l,n} + b_{l,i}(\theta_l), \tag{13}$$

where σ_l is the activation function, $s_{l,n}$ is the net input in the l-th layer, and $W_{l,i}$ is a matrix of synaptic weights from the l-th to the $l+1$-th layers at the i-th iteration. Then, Eqs. (5) and (9) could be respectively re-described as follows;

$$\Delta h_{l,i,n}^{BPL} = \begin{cases} x_n - \mathcal{H}\left(X = x_n; \theta = \widehat{\theta}_{l,i}, L\right) & (l = L) \\ W_{l,i}^T \nabla_{s_{l+1,n}} \sigma_{l+1} \Delta h_{l+1,i,n}^{BPL} & otherwise \end{cases}, \qquad (14)$$

$$\Delta h_{l,i,n}^{FPL} = \begin{cases} x_n - \mathcal{H}\left(X = x_n; \theta = \widehat{\theta}_{l,i}, L\right) & (l = 1) \\ W_{l,i} \nabla_{s_{l,n}} \sigma_l \Delta h_{l,i,n}^{FPL} & otherwise \end{cases}. \qquad (15)$$

The difference between BPL and FPL in terms of error transportation configurations for the credit assignments are illustrated in Fig. 1. Figure 1(a) shows that the back-propagated error in Eq. (14) provides the credit assignment in Eq. (6), while Fig. 1(b) shows that the forward-propagated error in Eq. (15) provides the credit assignment in Eq. (11). Since $\Delta h_{l,i,n}^{FPL}$ and $h_{l,n}$ can be calculated in parallel, and $\Delta h_{l,i,n}^{BPL}$ and $\Delta h_{l,i,n}^{FPL}$ can be calculated independently, providing $\Delta h_{L,i,n}^{BPL}$ as $\Delta h_{1,i,n}^{FPL}$, FPL method might not need to wait for the end of execution $\mathcal{H}$ to update $\widehat{\theta}$. Two examples of the parallel process in case of two 5-layer FNNs, parallel BPL-FPL (PBFPL) and divided BPL-FPL (DBFPL) are illustrated in Fig. 2.

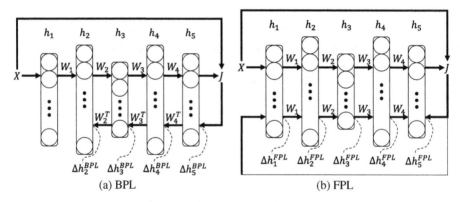

(a) BPL   (b) FPL

Fig. 1. Overview of the difference between BPL and FPL in terms of error transportation configurations for credit assignment.

Figure 2(a) (PBFPL) shows that all synaptic weights are updated by both FPL and BPL, but three computational processes must be completed in time for learning by BPL only, as shown in Fig. 3(a). This scheme, which requires three parallel processes at most, would reduce the required time for the parallel computing implementation in exchange for increasing the computational cost to compute both $\Delta h_{l,i,n}^{BPL}$ and $\Delta h_{l,i,n}^{FPL}$. If the cost function in Eq. (2) could be calculated faster in parallel than BPL and FPL, this scheme would be useful. On the other hand, as shown in Fig. 2(b) (DBFPL), we expected that the vanishing gradient in the first half of synaptic weights might be eased using FPL against BPL, the first half of the synaptic weights are updated by FPL and the other half are updated by BPL. Although this scheme could be implemented using two processes, as shown in Fig. 3(b), implementation using one process might be also

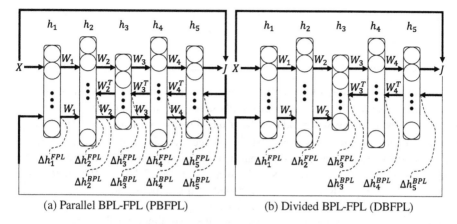

(a) Parallel BPL-FPL (PBFPL)   (b) Divided BPL-FPL (DBFPL)

Fig. 2. Overview of two examples of BPL and FPL execute in parallel in terms of error transportation configurations for credit assignment.

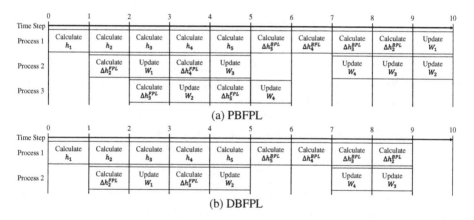

(a) PBFPL

(b) DBFPL

Fig. 3. Timing charts for parallel processing for PBFPL and DBFPL examples in Fig. 2.

useful, if the required iterations for updating the synaptic weights could be reduced by this scheme compared to using only BPL.

4   Numerical Experiments

4.1   Computational Conditions

In this work, numerical experiments were implemented with Python 3.6 code in Linux Ubuntu 14.04 using the Tensor Flow 1.0 library and were computed by an Intel Xeon CPU (2.6 GHz, Broadwell) with 8 GB of memory and NVIDIA Quadro GPU (Maxwell). Although the library might implicitly execute in parallel, parallel computing code was not explicitly described, because the purpose of this work is confirming the feasibility of the learning procedure using parallel propagated errors.

4.2   Extracting Features of a Two-Dimensional Non-Linear Function

To investigate whether PBFPL and DBFPL extract useful features in the hidden bottle - neck layer, several different conditioned FNNs were trained on a two-dimensional non-linear function that was produced by a one-dimensional parameter. The conventional sigmoid function $\{1 + \exp(-s)\}^{-1}$ and rectified linear unit (ReLU) function $\max(0, s)$ [6] were used as the non-linear activation functions. The number of layers was set at 5 or 9. Thus, four FNNs—5 layer - sigmoid, 5 layer - ReLU, 9 layer - sigmoid, and 9 layer - ReLU—were examined in this experiment. The hidden layers (except the bottle-neck layer) had 32 neurons activated by non-linear functions. The two-dimensional input and output layers and the one-dimensional bottle-neck layer used linear activation functions. All synaptic weights were randomly initialized by the uniform distribution within $[-1, 1]$. The two-dimensional non-linear function was described as

$$\begin{cases} x = \cos \varphi \\ y = \sin \varphi \end{cases} \quad (0 \le \varphi \le \pi), \tag{16}$$

where x and y represent the arc of a half-circle and φ is the central angle of the arc. A training dataset sampled 100 points at equal intervals from the range of φ. The ADAM algorithm [9] updated the synaptic weights to minimize the cost function in each layer such as Eq. (6) or Eq. (11).

Learning curves that were defined in Eq. (2) as a cost function are illustrated in Fig. 4. When the cost values fell below 10^{-3}, we visually confirmed by scatter plots that the dataset and the output layer's signals overlapped completely. Figure 4 indicates that PBFPL required about only half of the iterations for updating synaptic weights to reduce the cost value below 10^{-3}, compared to other schemes. On the other hand, the 5-layer FNNs could not minimize the cost values enough using DBFPL. Elapsed times of BPL, PBFPL, and DBFPL were 2.5 ± 0.6 msec/iteration, 5.0 ± 0.9 msec/iteration, and 2.7 ± 0.7 msec/iteration, respectively. The total times required by BPL and DBFPL were similar, but the elapsed time by PBFPL was twice as large as that by BPL; explicit coding in parallel for PBFPL could reduce the total time.

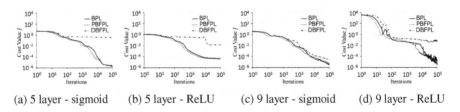

(a) 5 layer - sigmoid   (b) 5 layer - ReLU   (c) 9 layer - sigmoid   (d) 9 layer - ReLU

Fig. 4. Learning curves for acquiring the central angle of a half-circle using different FNNs.

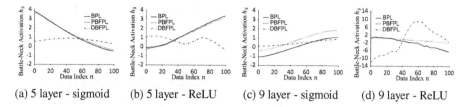

(a) 5 layer - sigmoid   (b) 5 layer - ReLU   (c) 9 layer - sigmoid   (d) 9 layer - ReLU

Fig. 5. Acquired features as central angle using different FNNs after 100,000 iterations.

To confirm the suitability of the extraction feature, the activation signals in the bottle-neck layer after 100,000 iterations are illustrated in Fig. 5 for each FNN. This result indicated that BPL and PBFPL could acquire monotone decrease or increase functions as the central angle of the arc in Eq. (16) for each FNN. The results of the learning curve were evidenced by the fact that the activation signals in the bottle-neck layer using DBFPL could not be regarded as the central angle. Furthermore, the acquired feature of the 9-layer FNNs using DBFPL was outshone by BPL and PBFPL.

4.3   Extracting Two-Dimensional Features of Hand-Written Digit Images

The PBFPL and DBFPL schemes were evaluated using a widely used dataset, MNIST hand written digit images [17]. The dataset consists of 60,000 training binary images and 10,000 test binary images. Since the resolution of the images is 28×28 pixels, 784-dimensional binary sequences were prepared. To conduct the mini-batch learning, the training sequences were divided into 100 batches. A 9-layer FNN with a bottle-neck layer, a 784-900-500-250-2-250-500-900-784 network, was prepared using Hinton's pre-training [3]. The input, output, and bottle-neck layers were activated by linear functions, while the other layers were activated by the conventional sigmoid function.

The learning curves for the test sequences using BPL, PBFPL, and DBFPL are shown in Fig. 6(a). When cost values were lower than 5×10^{-4}, quality of reconstructed images and features were visually good enough. Figure 6(a) shows that PBFPL required only about half of the epochs required by BPL or DBFPL, since the PBFPL cost value was lower than 5×10^{-4} at 8 epochs, but the others were lower at 16 epochs. Elapsed times of BPL, PBFPL, and DBFPL were 11.83 ± 0.09 sec/epoch, 16.47 ± 0.17 sec/epoch, and 12.24 ± 0.07 sec/epoch, respectively. This was a little different from the first experiment (Sect. 4.2), since the elapsed time by PBFPL was less than twice that by BPL. This might be due to library optimization. Figure 6(b) shows averaged images of test data, and Fig. 6(c) shows averaged reconstructed images after pre-training which indicates that pre-training could not learn enough identity mapping. Figures 6(d–f) show averaged reconstructed images after 30 epochs by BPL, PBFPL, and DBFPL, respectively. Since these are similar to each other and the test images, we conclude that all of the schemes could acquire suitable identity mapping.

Scatter plots in Fig. 7 show the activations in the bottle-neck layer using the three schemes after 30 epochs. Clusters in all three scatter plots have similar distributions. To compare how useful features were extracted, three conventional classifiers, the Naïve-Bayes, the linear support vector machine (SVM), and the SVM with Gaussian

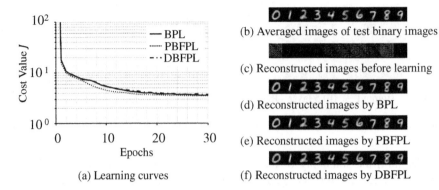

(a) Learning curves

(b) Averaged images of test binary images

(c) Reconstructed images before learning

(d) Reconstructed images by BPL

(e) Reconstructed images by PBFPL

(f) Reconstructed images by DBFPL

Fig. 6. Results of learning for MNIST hand written digit images dataset.

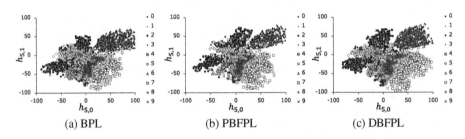

(a) BPL   (b) PBFPL   (c) DBFPL

Fig. 7. Acquired features as clusters for dividing digits after 30 epochs.

kernel, were fitted by the training sequence and used to predict digit labels from the two-dimensional extracted features of the test sequence. Classifier performance is summarized in Table 1. Comparing the accuracies between the raw data column and other columns in Table 1, the two-dimensional extracted features were useful for the Naïve-Bayes classifier but not for the others. Since the gap of accuracies using the SVM, a strong learner, was smaller than that of the linear SVM, essential information might be implicitly preserved in spite of the dimension reduction. Moreover, the accuracy using the extracted features by PBFPL was less than that by BPL and DBFPL. Thus, PBFPL outperformed other methods for all classifiers. The DBFPL performance was similar to that of BPL. In other words, a part of the auto-encoder for dimension reduction could be trained without any back-propagated errors.

Table 1. Accuracies for classifying test binary images by conventional classifier using the two-dimensional extracted features of the test sequence.

Classifier	Raw data	BPL	PBFPL	DBFPL
Naïve Bayes	0.547	0.683	0.733	0.684
Linear SVM	0.917	0.474	0.548	0.494
SVM	0.944	0.858	0.879	0.855

5 Discussion

The experimental results indicate that the PBFPL method reduces the number of iterations required for updating synaptic weights to train the auto-encoders, as compared to BPL. Although the computational cost of PBFPL is larger than that of BPL, implementing PBFPL using parallel computing might reduce computational time for acquiring reasonable representations, such as dimension reduction. Parallel computing has been usually used to update synaptic weights in each layer for BPL in general, but the credit assignment problem must be sequentially solved by the back-propagated error from output layer to input layer. In contrast, PBFPL and DBFPL methods directly solve the credit assignment problem in parallel. Indeed, the proposed schemes indicate that parallel computing could not only apply to updating the weights but also to estimating supervised signals in each layer.

The DBFPL method sometimes demonstrated the same performance as other schemes in the numerical experiments, but it could not perform better than the other methods. This result would not be useful in engineering, but might contribute in a biological context. Biologically plausible deep learning algorithms have been investigated recently. The TPL method [14], which is quite similar to FPL for training auto-encoder, tries to explain Spike-Timing-Dependent Plasticity in the brain. On the other hand, FA [15] and direct feedback-alignment (DFA) methods [16] transport the output error into hidden layers through random synaptic weights, which are path-way exclusive from feedforward synaptic weights. But it is also reported that FA leads to poor performance for the auto-encoder, and the DFA study discussed only a local update rule, which assumed the feedback errors will not propagate over synapses. Since the forward-propagated errors are effective for learning identity mapping even if the derivative of activation function is not known [13], the experimental results indicate that the deeper layers might be able to be trained by the forward-propagated errors. Although combined BPL and FPL reduced computational time using parallel computing in this work, combining FA and FPL might also be an effective approach. If replacing BPL with FA, the learning phase and execution phase would not be separate, which might lead to effective computational implementation in engineering and biological suitability aspects.

6 Conclusion

In this work, we apply the useful features of biological plausibility to train an auto-encoder, using two schemes that combine BPL with FPL in parallel. The PBFPL method outperformed BPL for the two basic numerical experiments, while DBFPL could train a part of the auto-encoder for dimension reduction without any back-propagated errors. Implementing parallel computing and measuring parallel computational time is planned for a future study.

References

1. LeCun, Y., Bengio, Y., Hinton, G.E.: Deep learning. Nature **521**, 436–444 (2015)
2. Hochreiter, S., Bengio, Y., Frasconi, P., Schmidhuber, J.: Gradient flow in reccurent nets: the difficulty of learning long-term dependencies. In: Kremer, C., Kolen, J.F. (eds.) Field Guide to Dynamical Recurrent Neural Networks, pp. 237–244. Wily-IEEE Press, Hoboken (2001)
3. Hinton, G.E., Salakhutdinov, R.R.: Reducing the dimensionality of data with neural networks. Science **313**, 504–507 (2006)
4. Srivastava, R.K., Greff, K., Schmidhuber, J.: Highway Networks. arXiv:1505.00387 (2015)
5. He, K., Zhang, X., Ren, S., Sun, J.: Deep Residual Learning for Image Recognition. arXiv: 1512.03385 (2015)
6. Nair, V., Hinton, G.E.: Rectified linear units improve restricted boltzmann machines. In: 27th International Conference on Machine Learning, pp. 807–814. Omnipress, Madison (2010)
7. Dugas, C., Bengio, Y., Bélisle, F., Nadeau, C., Garcia, R.: Incorporating second-order functional knowledge for better option pricing. In: 13th International Conference on Neural Information Processing Systems, pp. 451–457. MIT Press, Denver (2001)
8. Duchi, J.C., Hazan, E., Singer, Y.: Adaptive subgradient methods for online learning and stochastic optimization. J. Mach. Learn. Res. **12**, 257–269 (2010)
9. Kingma, D.P., Ba, J.: Adam: A Method for Stochastic Optimization. arXiv:1412.6980 (2014)
10. Crick, F.: The recent excitement about neural networks. Nature **337**, 129–132 (1987)
11. Harris, K.D.: Stability of the fittest: organizing learning through retroaxonal signals. Trends Neurosci. **31**, 130–136 (2008)
12. Werfel, J., Xie, X., Seung, H.S.: Learning curves for stochastic gradient decent in linear feedforward networks. Neural Comput. **17**, 2699–2718 (2005)
13. Ohama, Y., Fukumura, N., Uno, Y.: A Simplified Forward-Propagation Learning Rule Applied to Adaptive Closed-Loop Control. In: Duch, W., Kacprzyk, J., Oja, E., Zadrożny, S. (eds.) ICANN 2005. LNCS, vol. 3697, pp. 437–443. Springer, Heidelberg (2005). doi:10.1007/11550907_69
14. Bengio, Y.: How Auto-encoders could Provide Credit Assignment in Deep Networks via Target Propagation. arXiv:1407.7906. (2014)
15. Lillicrap, T.P., Cownden, D., Tweed, D.B., Akerman, C.J.: Random synaptic feedback weights support error backpropagation for deep learning. Nat. Comm. **7**, 13276 (2016)
16. Nøkland, A.: Direct feedback alignment provides learning in deep neural networks. In: 30th International Conference on Neural Information Processing Systems, pp. 1037–1045. MIT Press, Denver (2016)
17. The MNIST database of handwritten digits. http://yann.lecun.com/exdb/mnist

Relation Classification via Target-Concentrated Attention CNNs

Jizhao Zhu[1], Jianzhong Qiao[1(✉)], Xinxiao Dai[2], and Xueqi Cheng[3]

[1] College of Computer Science and Engineering, Northeastern University,
Shenyang 110169, China
zhujz.neu@gmail.com, qiaojianzhong@mail.neu.edu.cn
[2] Shenyang Open University, Shenyang 110003, China
daixx.syou@foxmail.com
[3] CAS Key Laboratory of Network Data Science and Technology,
Institute of Computing Technology, Chinese Academy of Sciences,
Beijing 110190, China
cxq@ict.ac.cn

Abstract. Relation classification is a key natural language processing task that receives much attentions these years. The goal is to assign predefined relation labels to the nominal pairs marked in given sentences. It is obvious that different words in a sentence are differentially informative. Moreover, the importance of words is highly relation-dependent, i.e., the same word may be differentially important for different relations. To include sensitivity to this fact, we present a novel model, referred to as TCA-CNN, which takes the attention mechanism at the word level to pay different attention to individual words according to the semantic relation concentrated when constructing the representation of a sentence. Experimental results show that TCA-CNN achieves a comparable performance compared with the state-of-the-art models on the SemEval 2010 relation classification task.

Keywords: Relation classification · Convolutional Neural Networks · Attention mechanism

1 Introduction

Relation classification is one of the fundamental tasks in natural language processing (NLP). It plays an important role in various scenarios, e.g., information extraction [1], question answering [2], knowledge base construction [3,4], etc. The goal of relation classification is to assign pre-defined relation labels to the nominal pairs marked in given sentences. For instance, given the sentence "Givers gain moral strength and [happiness]$_{e_1}$ from [giving]$_{e_2}$." with the annotated nominal pair, namely e_1 and e_2, the goal would be to automatically

J. Zhu–The work was conducted when Jizhao Zhu visited CAS Key Lab of Network Data Science and Technology.

recognize that this sentence expresses *Cause-Effect* relation between e_1 and e_2, denoted as *Cause-Effect*(e_1, e_2).

Traditional relation classification methods mainly fall into feature- and kernel-based categories. Feature-based methods use a large number of lexical, syntactic or semantic features and feed them into a chosen classifier such as support vector machines (SVM) to classify relations. Conversely, kernel-based do not need much effort on feature engineering, but well-designed kernel functions, which are usually based on syntactic or dependency structures. All these methods have been shown to be effective and yield relatively high performance. However, they strongly depend on extracted features or designed kernels derived from the output of pre-existing NLP tools, which unavoidably lead to the propagation of the errors and hurt the performances of these models. Recently, the methods based on deep neural networks with highly automatic feature learning have made remarkable progress. A large number of works on relation classification use convolutional neural networks (CNN) [5], recursive neural networks (RecursiveNN) [6] and recurrent neural networks (RNN) [7] to reduce the extensive manual feature engineering or other external resources, and have already achieved impressive results.

Although these existing deep neural networks based models have been quite effective, they treat all words equally when composing the representation of the sentence meaning. Obviously, different words in a sentence are differentially informative. For this reason, the attention mechanism was adopted by [8] and the state-of-the-art performance was achieved on the benchmark SemEval 2010 Task 8. However, a word may express kinds of semantic relations with different probabilities. To illustrate, we take the aforementioned sentence as an example. It is intuitive that the importance of word "from" is higher when the semantic relation *Cause-Effect* is concentrated than *Message-Topic* to construct the sentence representation. Therefore, the importance of a word is related to the concentrated semantic relation when constructing the sentence representation, but the existing models have not noticed this yet.

In this paper, we present a novel model, Target-Concentrated Attention Convolutional Neural Networks (TCA-CNN), which takes the attention mechanism at the word level to pay more or less attention to individual words when different semantic relations are concentrated to compose the representation of a sentence. We evaluate our model for relation classification on standard benchmark dataset of SemEval 2010 Task 8. Experimental results show that our proposed method achieves an excellent result compared with existing baselines. The main contributions of our work can be summarized as follows:

- We propose an end-to-end learning model, named TCA-CNN, without extensive feature engineering and external knowledge, and it could capture the key parts of a sentence when different relations are concentrated to compose the sentence representation.
- We present a new pairwise margin-based loss function which is superior to the typical cross-entropy loss functions.

– Experiments conducted on the benchmark dataset of SemEval 2010 Task 8 demonstrate that TCA-CNN achieves a comparable performance with the state-of-the-art models.

2   Related Work

We briefly review the existing studies on relation classification. Traditional methods strongly depend on the extracted features which are often derived from the output of pre-existing NLP tools. So it is unavoidable to the propagation of the errors in the existing tools and the performance of these methods are limited. Recently, deep neural networks have shown promising results and they learn underlying features automatically. Socher et al. [6] proposed MVRNN by using a recursive neural network to tackle relation classification. They managed to capture the compositional aspects of the sentence semantics by exploiting syntactic trees. Zeng et al. [11] exploited DNN to classify relations with lexical, sentence level features and word position features, and they took all of the words as input without complicated pre-precessing. Nevertheless, these methods still depend on additional features from lexical resources and NLP tools. Based on CNNs, Santos et al. [15] proposed the CR-CNN model with special treatment for the *Other* label. Xu et al. [7] leveraged CNNs to learn representation from shortest dependency paths, and address the relation directionality by special treatment on sampling. Additionally, some other deep learning models have been proposed such as [7,16,18]. Since different words in a sentence are differentially informative, Wang et al. [8] introduced the attention mechanism into relation classification task and proposed a novel convolutional neural network architecture relying on two levels of attention in order to better discern patterns in heterogeneous contexts. In this paper, we also adopt attention mechanism to attend to the key parts of a sentence when constructing the representation of then sentence and experimental results show that our model achieves a comparable performance with the state-of-the-art models.

3   Our Proposed Model

In this section, we describe the proposed model for relation classification with target-concentrated attention mechanism. An overview of our architecture is illustrated in Fig. 1. The reason for choosing a CNN rather than other deep neural networks like RNN with long short-term memory unit (LSTM) [9] or gated recurrent unit (GRU) [10], etc., is we argue that CNN is more suitable to detect the key part of sentence relevant to the concentrated relation. The only input for the network is the tokenized text string of the sentence and a semantic relation. First, the input sentence is encoded with the concatenation of word vector and position vectors, where word order is captured by exploiting the positional encoding. Next, the attention mechanism is used to capture the relevance of words with respect to the concentrated relation. After that, a convolutional layer followed by max-pooling is applied to construct a representation of the

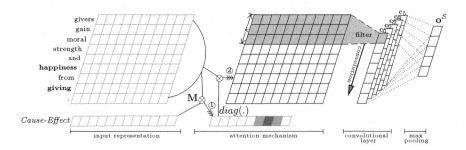

Fig. 1. The architecture of TCA-CNN.

sentence. Finally, by using a scoring function to measure the proximity between the sentence representation and the given relation. In this paper, we use capitalized letter with boldface to denote matrix, and the corresponding lowercase letter with boldface to represent column vector.

3.1   Input Representation

Given a sentence S with words w_i for $i = 1, 2, \ldots, n$, where n is the sentence length, and two marked nominals e_1 and e_2, we first convert each word into a real-valued vector. Let $\mathbf{E}^w \in \mathbb{R}^{d_w \times |V|}$ denote the word embeddings matrix, where V is the input vocabulary and d_w is the word vector dimension. The i-th word in S is transformed into the vector $\mathbf{e}_i^w$ by looking up the word embeddings matrix.

It is obvious that contexts surrounding the nominal pair are critical to determine the semantic relation between marked nominals. Therefore, we also incorporate the word position embedding (position features) proposed by [11] to reflect the relative distances of the current word to the marked nominals e_1 and e_2. Take the sentence shown in Fig. 1 as an example, the relative distances of "from" to "happiness" and "giving" are -1 and 1, respectively. Then, the relative distance is mapped to a vector with size d_p, and d_p is a hyper-parameter to be chosen by the user. Let $\mathbf{e}_{i,1}^p, \mathbf{e}_{i,2}^p \in \mathbb{R}^{d_p}$ denote the position vectors corresponding to the i-th word in a sentence. The overall word embedding $\mathbf{w}_i$ for the i-th word can be obtained by concatenating the word embedding with these two position vectors, namely $\mathbf{w}_i = [\mathbf{e}_i^w; \mathbf{e}_{i,1}^p; \mathbf{e}_{i,2}^p]$ ($[\mathbf{x}_1; \mathbf{x}_2]$ denotes the vertical concatenation of $\mathbf{x}_1$ and $\mathbf{x}_2$). Based on these $\mathbf{w}_i$, the input representation for the sentence S can be represented as a matrix $\mathbf{S} = [\mathbf{w}_1, \mathbf{w}_2, \ldots, \mathbf{w}_n]$.

3.2   Input Attention

Since not all words contribute equally to the representation of the sentence meaning. Moreover, the importance of words are highly relation-dependent, i.e., the same word may be differentially important for different relations. In this paper, we introduce attention mechanism to automatically capture the relevance of words with respect to the concentrated relation when constructing the sentence representation.

On the basis of input representation, we can measure the importance of words in a sentence concentrated on the given semantic relation $r \in R$, where R is the relation set. In this paper, we choose a bilinear function to characterize the importance ξ_i of the i-th word in a sentence with the semantic relation r, given by:

$$\xi_i = \mathbf{w}_i^\top \mathbf{M} \mathbf{r} + b, \tag{1}$$

thereof, $\mathbf{M}$ is a weighting matrix to be learned during the training process, $\mathbf{r} \in \mathbb{R}^{d_r}$ is the embedding of relation r, and $b \in \mathbb{R}$ is the bias term. Then, the normalized importance weight α_i can be obtained through a softmax function, namely:

$$\alpha_i = \frac{\exp(\xi_i)}{\sum_{k=1}^n \exp(\xi_k)}. \tag{2}$$

After that, the diagonal attention matrix $\mathbf{A}$ can be obtained, as follows:

$$\mathbf{A} = diag(\alpha_1, \alpha_2, \ldots, \alpha_n). \tag{3}$$

Finally, the input for the convolutional layer can be get by multiplying $\mathbf{S}$ with $\mathbf{A}$, in the form:

$$\mathbf{Q} = \mathbf{S}\mathbf{A}. \tag{4}$$

3.3 Sentence Representation

The next phrase of our proposed model is to construct the distributed representation $\mathbf{o}^S$ for the input sentence $\mathcal{S}$. The convolutional layer first captures local contextual information with a sliding window of size k over the sentence and the k will be chosen by the user. Afterwards, it combines all local contextual information via a map-pooling operation to obtain a fixed-sized vector for the input sentence. Let $\mathbf{z}_i \in \mathbb{R}^d$ refer to the concatenation of the k successive words embeddings centered around the i-th word:

$$\mathbf{z}_i = [\mathbf{q}_{i-(k-1)/2}; \ldots; \mathbf{q}_{i+(k-1)/2}], \tag{5}$$

where $d = k \times (d_w + 2 \times d_p)$. Since the window may be outside of the sentence boundaries when it slides near the boundary, an extra padding token is repeated multiple times at the beginning and the end of the input. The convolution operation is defined as the dot product of a weight matrix $\mathbf{W}^c \in \mathbb{R}^{d \times l}$ with the matrix $\mathbf{Z} \in \mathbb{R}^{d \times (n-k+1)}$ and then adding a bias vector $\mathbf{b}^c \in \mathbb{R}^l$, where l is the number of filters. We apply a non-linear activation function at the output of the convolutional operation, such as the hyperbolic tangent. For the i-th filter, the convolutional operation can be expressed by:

$$\mathbf{c}_{ij} = \tanh(< \mathbf{w}_i^c, \mathbf{z}_j > + \mathbf{b}_i^c), \tag{6}$$

where $\mathbf{b}_i^c$ is the bias term. Afterwards, the representation vector $\mathbf{o}^S$ for the input sentence can be obtained through the max-pooling operation on each $\mathbf{c}_i = \{\mathbf{c}_{ij}\}$ for $j = 1, 2, \ldots, (n - k + 1)$, so that:

$$\mathbf{o}^S = [\max(\mathbf{c}_1), \max(\mathbf{c}_2), \ldots, \max(\mathbf{c}_l)]^\top. \tag{7}$$

3.4 Scoring

In this work, we propose a new scoring function $\zeta_\theta(\mathcal{S}, r)$ to measure the proximity between the sentence representation $\mathbf{o}^S$ and the given relation r, as follows:

$$\zeta(\mathcal{S}, r) = (\mathbf{o}^S)^\top \mathbf{U} r, \tag{8}$$

where $\mathbf{U}$ is a weighting matrix to be learned during training.

3.5 Model Training

The model could be trained in and end-to-end way with standard back propagation. We define a margin-based pairwise loss function $\mathcal{L}$ based on Eq. (8), in the form:

$$\mathcal{L} = \phi(\zeta(\mathcal{S}, r^-) + \gamma - \zeta(\mathcal{S}, r^+)) + \beta\|\theta\|^2, \tag{9}$$

where $\phi = \log(\exp(x) + 1)$, γ is the margin separating the positive pair from the negative one, $\zeta(\mathcal{S}, r^+)$ is the matching score between the sentence representation $\mathbf{o}^S$ and the ground-truth relation r^+, $\zeta(\mathcal{S}, r^-)$ denote the matching score between $\mathbf{o}^S$ and the incorrect relation r^-, β is the L_2-regularization term and θ is the parameter set consisting of $\mathbf{M}, \mathbf{U}, \mathbf{W}^c, \mathbf{b}^c$.

Table 1. Hyper-parameters used in our experiments.

Parameter	Parameter Name	Value
d_w	word embedding size	100
d_p	word position embedding size	80
d_r	relation embedding size	80
k	filter size	4
l	filter number	1000
γ	margin	1.0
λ	initial learning rate	0.002

In our experiments, we use the publicly available word2vec[1] skip-gram architecture [12] to learn the initial word embeddings on Wikipedia[2]. The embeddings of out-of-vocabulary words and all relations are randomly initialized with

[1] https://code.google.com/p/word2vec/.
[2] https://dumps.wikimedia.org/enwiki/.

uniform samples from $U(-1.0,1.0)$. All hyper-parameters are jointly learned via minimizing the loss function of Eq. (9). Additionally, AdaGrad [13] is used as our optimization method during the training process. Table 1 reports all the hyper-parameters used in the following experiments.

4   Experiments

4.1   Dataset and Evaluation Metrics

To evaluate the performance of TCA-CNN, we conduct experiments on SemEval-2010 Task 8 dataset [14] which is a widely used benchmark for relation classification and freely available[3] on the internet. The dataset contains 10,717 examples, including 8,000 training instances and 2,717 test instances, annotated with 9 directed relation labels and 1 undirected *Other* label. Taking the directionality of the relation labels into account, e.g., *Cause-Effect*(e_1, e_2) and *Cause-Effect*(e_2, e_1) are different relation labels, we treat each directed relation labels as two in our model. We evaluate the model performance by using the SemEval-2010 Task 8 official scorer in terms of the macro-average F1-scores for the 9 directed relations (excluding *Other*).

Table 2. Comparison with other published results of Neural Network models.

Classifier	F1
MVRNN [6]	82.4
CNN+Softmax [11]	82.7
CR-CNN [15]	84.1
DepNN [16]	83.6
depLCNN [17]	83.7
depLCNN+NS [17]	85.6
SDP-LSTM [7]	83.7
DRNNs [18]	85.8
Att-Input-CNN [8]	87.5
TCA-CNN	87.3

4.2   Results and Analysis

The experimental results on the test set are reported in Table 2. MVRNN and DepNN are based on RecursiveNN, whereas DepNN achieves an F1-score of 83.6% exceeding MVRNN with a relative improvement of 1.7% by capturing the features of shortest dependency paths via CNN. Both CNN-based model depLCNN and RNN-based SDP-LSTM leverage the shortest dependency paths

---

[3] http://docs.google.com/View?id=dfvxd49s_36c28v9pmw.

between the marked nominal pair and obtain the identical results. By considering the relation directionality with a negative sampling strategy, depLCNN further improves the result to 85.6%. From the results, we can see that our novel target-concentrated attention based architecture achieves the F1-score of 87.3%, outperforming the well known CR-CNN model by 3.2% and DRNNs by 1.5%, but the accuracy is a slightly lower than the state-of-the-art model Att-Input-CNN. The results indicate that TCA-CNN effectively captures the key part of sentence for constructing the representation of a sentence.

4.3 Visualization of Attention

In order to validate that our model is able to select informative words in a sentence with the semantic relation concentrated, we can obtain the attention weight α in Eq. (2) and visualize the word level attention weights in Fig. 2 for the sentence mentioned in Introduction.

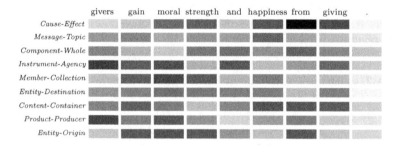

Fig. 2. Visualization of Attention.

Each line in Fig. 2 shows the representation of how attention focuses on words with the interaction of the concentrated semantic relation. The color depth indicates the degree of importance, namely the darker the more important. From the Fig. 2, we can observe that when concentrating on: (1) the ground-truth relation of *Cause-Effect*, the word "from" was assigned the highest attention weight, and the words such as "happiness" and "giving" also are important. However, it is surprised to find that the non-entity tokens "moral" and "strength" are assigned the same level importance as "happiness". After detailed analyzing the sentence, we can know that the "moral strength" also is a result caused by giving; (2) other relations, we first take the relation *Message-Topic* as an example, the key word "from" is assigned a lower attention value, which means "from" is irrelevant with respect to the semantic relation *Message-Topic*. As a result, the output sentence representation would have low matching score with *Message-Topic*. Besides, the similar phenomena can be found when the rest of the other relations are concentrated to compose the sentence representations.

5 Conclusion

In this work we propose an end-to-end learning model, referred to as TCA-CNN, with target-concentrated attention mechanism for relation classification. Our motivation is that different words in a sentence are differentially informative and the importance of words are highly relation-dependent. The experimental results based on the SemEval-2010 Task 8 dataset show that TCA-CNN achieves a comparable performance compared with the state-of-the-art models. In the future, it might be interesting to jointly model the entity pair and relation with attention mechanism, since it is intuitive that the relation interact closely with the entity pair in a sentence.

Acknowledgments. This work is supported by the 973 Program of China under Grant Nos. 2013CB329606 and 2014CB340405, the National Key Research and Development Program of China under Grant No. 2016YFB1000902, the National Natural Science Foundation of China (NSFC) under Grant Nos. 61272177, 61402442, 61572469, 91646120 and 61572473.

References

1. Wu, F., Weld, D.S.: Open information extraction using Wikipedia. In: 48th Annual Meeting of the Association for Computational Linguistics, pp. 118–127. ACL Press, Stroudsburg (2010)
2. Golub, D., He, X.: Character-level question answering with attention. arXiv preprint arXiv:1604.00727 (2016)
3. Shin, J., Wu, S., Wang, F., De Sa, C., Zhang, C., Ré, C.: Incremental knowledge base construction using deepdive. Proc. VLDB Endowment **8**, 1310–1321 (2015)
4. Jia, Y., Wang, Y., Lin, H., Jin, X., Cheng, X.: Locally adaptive translation for knowledge graph embedding. In: 30th AAAI Conference on Artificial Intelligence, pp. 992–998. AAAI Press, Menlo Park (2016)
5. LeCun, Y., Bottou, L., Bengio, Y., Haffner, P.: Gradient-based learning applied to document recognition. Proc. IEEE **86**, 2278–2324 (1998)
6. Socher, R., Huval, B., Manning, C.D., Ng, A.Y.: Semantic compositionality through recursive matrix-vector spaces. In: 2012 Joint Conference on Empirical Methods in Natural Language Processing and Computational Natural Language Learning, pp. 1201–1211. ACL Press, Stroudsburg (2012)
7. Xu, Y., Mou, L., Li, G., Chen, Y., Peng, H., Jin, Z.: Classifying relations via long short term memory networks along shortest dependency paths. In: 2015 Conference on Empirical Methods in Natural Language Processing, pp. 1785–1794. ACL Press, Stroudsburg (2015)
8. Wang, L., Cao, Z., de Melo, G., Liu, Z.: Relation classification via multi-level attention cnns. In: 54th Annual Meeting of the Association for Computational Linguistics, pp. 1398–1307. ACL Press, Stroudsburg (2016)
9. Hochreiter, S., Schmidhuber, J.: Long short-term memory. Neural Comput. **9**, 1735–1780 (1997)
10. Cho, K., Van Merriënboer, B., Bahdanau, D., Bengio, Y.: On the properties of neural machine translation: Encoder-decoder approaches. arXiv preprint arXiv:1409.1259 (2014)

11. Zeng, D., Liu, K., Lai, S., Zhou, G., Zhao, J.: Relation classification via convolutional deep neural network. In: 25th International Conference on Computatinal Linguistics: Technical Papers, pp. 2335–2344. ACM, New York (2014)
12. Mikolov, T., Chen, K., Corrado, G., Dean, J.: Efficient estimation of word representations in vector space. arXiv preprint arXiv:1301.3781 (2013)
13. Duchi, J., Hazan, E., Singer, Y.: Adaptive subgradient methods for online learning and stochastic optimization. J. Mach. Learn. Res. **12**, 2121–2159 (2011)
14. Hendrickx, I., Kim, S. N., Kozareva, Z., Nakov, P., Ó Séaghdha, D., Padó, S., Pennacchiotti, M., Romano, L., Szpakowicz, S.: Semeval-2010 task 8: multi-way classification of semantic relations between pairs of nominals. In: Proceedings of the Workshop on Semantic Evaluations: Recent Achievements and Future Directions, pp. 94–99. ACL Press, Stroudsburg (2009)
15. Santos, C.N.D., Xiang, B., Zhou, B.: Classifying relations by ranking with convolutional neural networks. arXiv preprint arXiv:1504.06580 (2015)
16. Liu, Y., Wei, F., Li, S., Ji, H., Zhou, M., Wang, H.: A dependency-based neural network for relation classification. In: 53rd Annual Meeting of the Association for Computational Linguistics and the 7th International Joint Conference on Natural Language Processing(Short Papers), pp. 285–290. ACL Press, Stroudsburg (2015)
17. Xu, K., Feng, Y., Huang, S., Zhao, D.: Semantic relation classification via convolutional neural networks with simple negative sampling. In: 2015 Conference on Empirical Methods in Natural Language Processing, pp. 536–540. ACL Press, Stroudsburg (2015)
18. Xu, Y., Jia, R., Mou, L., Li, G., Chen, Y., Lu, Y., Jin, Z.: Improved relation classification by deep recurrent neural networks with data augmentation. arXiv preprint arXiv:1601.03651 (2016)

Comparing Hybrid NN-HMM and RNN for Temporal Modeling in Gesture Recognition

Nicolas Granger[✉] and Mounîm A. el Yacoubi

SAMOVAR, Télécom SudParis, CNRS, University of Paris-Saclay,
9 rue Charles Fourier, 91000 Évry, France
{nicolas.granger,mounim.el_yacoubi}@telecom-sudparis.eu

Abstract. This paper provides an extended comparison of two temporal models for gesture recognition, namely Hybrid Neural Network-Hidden Markov Models (NN-HMM) and Recurrent Neural Networks (RNN) which have lately claimed the state-the-art performances. Experiments were conducted on both models in the same body of work, with similar representation learning capacity and comparable computational costs. For both solutions, we have integrated recent contributions to the model architectures and training techniques. We show that, for this task, Hybrid NN-HMM models remain competitive with Recurrent Neural Networks in a standard setting. For both models, we analyze the influence of the training objective function on the final evaluation metric. We further tested the influence of temporal convolution to improve context modeling, a technique which was recently reported to improve the accuracy of gesture recognition.

Keywords: Hybrid NN-HMM · RNN · Gesture recognition · End-to-End learning · Representation learning

1 Introduction

Gestures are composed of movements or poses of the body by which the subject is actively trying to convey a message. The objective of continuous gesture recognition is to detect and recognize the sequence of gestures within a stream of sensory inputs. The latter are generally recorded from cameras, wearable sensors or more recently depth map cameras which further allow reliable body pose detection.

Over the last decade, Deep Neural Networks have been used with spectacular results in many fields ranging from natural image classification to handwriting and speech recognition. Gesture recognition naturally relates to these last two fields and, as expected, has benefited from these models as well. It notably takes advantage from convolutional architectures of neuron connections, which drastically improves learning of local image patterns. As a result, recent contributions now tend to use trainable representation extractors as the first stage in a recognition pipeline.

© Springer International Publishing AG 2017
D. Liu et al. (Eds.): ICONIP 2017, Part II, LNCS 10635, pp. 147–156, 2017.
https://doi.org/10.1007/978-3-319-70096-0_16

For two of the state-of-the-art models for gesture recognition, this representation extractor is followed by an explicit temporal model: the Hybrid Neural Network/Hidden Markov Model, first introduced for speech recognition [1], has been transposed to gesture and sign language recognition [9,16]; Recurrent Neural Networks also provide a flexible model for sequential data. While plagued by weak training signal propagation and short-lived memory in vanilla form, [7] has shown that carefully crafted connections between neurons can eliminate those issues with excellent results obtained on speech [5], handwriting [6] and also gesture recognition [12].

To validate the respective advantages of these two temporal models, we propose a comparative study of the two under similar settings. The validation has been carried out on the Montalbano v2 [3] dataset which contains a series of Italian gestures from 20 different classes captured with a Kinect device. For this paper, we restrict our data to the body pose modality which encodes the position of articulations and other important skeleton points in space.

Our contributions lie in the following aspects: we propose modifications to the training loss functions to alleviate data imbalance issues; we demonstrate that Hybrid-HMM and RNN perform similarly under similar settings; finally, we report an experiment showing that RNNs are less reliant on contextual information than Hybrid NN-HMM models are.

2   Related Work

Traditionaly, gesture recognition has involved two steps, feature extraction and then temporal classification. The former usually relies on engineered features such as handcrafted body pose features or HoG features extracted around the body or the hands from the video frames. For the latter, a lot of effort has been invested into optimizing models to characterize the temporal structure on the gestures, with Probabilistic Graphical Models offering a large range of possibilities: HMM, CRF... [17,18].

Our methodology builds on recent contributions which have focused on learning representations as part of the overall training process. [9] reuses a pre-trained representation extraction stage from a natural image classifier [14]. [16] pre-trains a Deep belief network on body pose features. Both integrate the representation extractor into a Hybrid Neural Network/Hidden Markov Model (NN-HMM).

Instead of considering a temporal model of gestures, [11] concatenates successive input observations at multiple scales, and feed them directly into a deep neural network.

More recently, [12] obtained state-of-the-art performances by using a Convolutional Neural Network (CNN) combined with a Recurrent Neural Network (RNN) to process the video inputs. This model also introduces temporal convolution layers to capture contextual information in the representation extraction stage.

3   Temporal Models for Gesture Recognition

3.1   Representation Learning

To produce task-specific (i.e. gesture) representations, we opted for a multi-layer neural network trained from scratch in a supervised way. In comparison, [16] uses a deep belief network trained in an unsupervised fashion and later fine-tuned for the classification task. To prevent the overfitting and slowness of supervised learning, we have equipped all layers with Batch Normalization [8] and Dropout [13]. Furthermore, activation non-linearities have been set to leaky Rectified Linear Units (ReLU) [10] in order to propagate the training signal more efficiently through the layers.

The information contained in previous and future observations is commonly exploited in speech recognition. For gestures, [11] actually build a model without an explicit temporal model but instead concatenate local observations to provide the local context as input to a classifier. Following the work of [12], we opt for temporal convolution to produce a learned representation which also embeds the local context. Let h_i^t be the activation of the i-th neuron of the previous layer at time-step t. The temporal convolution at t by a filter $\mathbf{w}$ of width $2k+1$ is given by:

$$a^t = \sum_i \sum_{u=-k}^{k} h_i^{t+u} w_{i,k-u} \tag{1}$$

where the result of the temporal convolution a_t becomes the activation of the neuron associated with this filter.

3.2   Hybrid NN-HMM

A Hybrid NN-HMM uses pseudo observations likelihoods instead of true likelihood distributions in its original formulation as given by Eq. 2:

$$P(x_{1:T}, s_{1:T}) = P(s_1)P(x_1|s_1) \prod_{t=2}^{T} P(s_t|s_{t-1})P(x_t|s_t) \tag{2}$$

$$P(x_t|s_t) = \frac{P(s_t|x_t)P(x_t)}{P(s_t)} \propto \frac{P(s_t|x_t)}{P(s_t)} \tag{3}$$

where $P(s_1)$ is a prior on the initial states, $P(s_t|s_{t-1})$ models the transition dynamics between states and $P(x_t|s_t)$ the state conditioned observation likelihood. Using (3) instead of an actual likelihood allows to choose predictive models of the input such as a neural network classifier, the output of which is interpreted as the state posterior probability $p(s_t|x_t)$. For our experiments, the multi-layer representation network from the previous section is plugged into a dense layer with a softmax non-linearity so as to form the trainable predictor $P(s_t|x_t)$.

This posterior model needs to be trained in a supervised fashion, using the alignment of HMM states over the observations for labeling. The overall training process therefore contains two alternating steps: fitting the posterior model on the optimal state alignment given previous HMM iteration, and then fitting the transition probabilities alone.

In our model, gestures are represented by 5 states interconnected by left-to-right transitions, one state skips, and a reverse transition from the fourth to the second as shown on Fig. 1. The first and last states usually absorb transitional movements from non-gesture class segments to an actual gesture segment. Skips let the model ignore unobserved states whereas reverse connections are expected to capture periodicity. A garbage state captures all the non-gesture observations and provides a transition between gestures, leading to a total of $20*5+1 = 101$ states to be predicted by the posterior model $P(s_t|x_t)$.

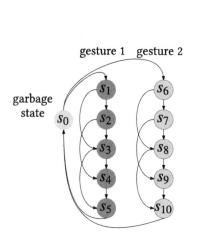

Fig. 1. state transition dynamics for the Hybrid NN-HMM gesture recognition model (self-transitions omitted)

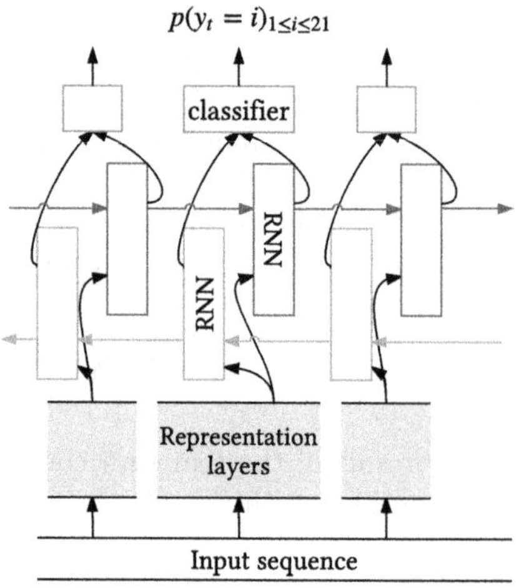

Fig. 2. RNN model for gesture recognition

3.3   Recurrent Neural Network

The purely neuronal solution is chosen to resemble the hybrid model with a recurrent neural network as a drop-in replacement for the HMM. More precisely, the previous multilayer neural network (for image representation learning) is truncated before the softmax layer and connected into two RNNs reading their input sequences in forward and reverse time order respectively. This configuration known as bidirectional RNN [4] helps to generate predictions without delay as one of the RNNs has access to 'future' observations. The outputs of both networks at each time step are then concatenated and fed into a fully connected layer. A final softmax function issues the predictions over the 21 labels (20 gestures + 1 non-gesture class). Figure 2 sums up the whole architecture.

Due to memory limitations, the sequences are split into chunks of 128 time steps. Temporal convolution and RNN are both subject to edge effects due to the use of zero padding and the absence of sufficient context at the edges of the sequences. We therefore drop some warm-up frames at the beginning and the end of the chunks. Experiments have shown that using the size of the padding (half of the temporal kernel size) leaves no noticeable edge effect in terms of frame-wise error rate within the chunks.

4   Experimental Setup

4.1   Dataset and Data Augmentation

The dataset is composed of 340 training, 230 validation and 240 testing recordings. The training set contains approximately 340 instances for each of the 20 gestures. The validation set is solely used for cross-validation because the temporal and class annotations were originally not disclosed during the Chalearn 2014 competition.

In this work, we only use the upper body pose joint locations (hands, elbows, shoulder, heads, hips). Sequences with more than 25 missing observations have been eliminated, while other missing positions have been linearly interpolated. Then, the sequences have been filtered by a Gaussian kernel of unit variance to reduce noise. The dataset was augmented two times with random horizontal flipping and affine space distortions.

4.2   Pre-processing

As in [11] or [16], the positions are transformed, using basic transformations, into the following features:

- raw positions centered around the center point between shoulders, and normalized by the distance between shoulders to eliminate subject size
- first and second order derivatives of the positions
- pairwise position differences (spatial vector connecting any two points)
- pairwise Euclidean distances (spatial distance between any two points)
- cosinus, sinus and orthonormal vector of the angles between successive limbs

which produces a feature vector of 248 components which have been normalized to 0 mean and unit variance.

4.3   Architectural Details

The exact architecture for our experiments begins with a shared multilayer neural network for representation learning:

- Dense layer: 1024 neurons, batch normalization, ReLU, dropout (0.3)
- Dense layer: 1024 neurons, batch normalization, ReLU, dropout (0.3)
- Temporal convolution: 256 filters of width 17, batch normalization, ReLU, dropout (0.3)

For the Hybrid NN-HMM model, an additional dense layer with 101 neurons and a softmax non-linearity complete the state posterior predictor $P(s_t|x_t)$. In the RNN model, the recurrent layers take their inputs directly from the features computed by the temporal convolution layer.

Each of the two RNNs uses 172 Gated Recurrent Units (GRU) [2], a simplified version of the LSTM cells [7]. LSTM cells (and GRU as a consequence) turn vanilla neurons into a structure of gates and bridges, which greatly enhances the propagation of the feed-forward signals and of the back-propagated gradient descent updates.

5   Experiments and Results

5.1   Evaluation Metric and Training Loss Functions

We assess our two models using the Jaccard Index (JI) metric which evaluates both the correctness of the detected labels and the precision of the temporal alignment:

$$J_{r,i} = \frac{G_{r,i} \cap P_{r,i}}{G_{r,i} \cup P_{r,i}} \text{ or } 0 \text{ if } G_{r,i} \cup P_{r,i} = 0 \tag{4}$$

$$J_r = \frac{1}{l_r} \sum_{i=1}^{L} J_{r,i} \qquad JI = \frac{1}{N} \sum_{r=1}^{N} J_r \tag{5}$$

where $G_{r,i}$ (resp. $P_{r,i}$) is the binary vector of the ground-truth (resp. prediction) for class i in recording r, l_r is the number of classes observed in r, L the number of classes and N the number of sequences.

Since this objective is not easily differentiable, the models are usually trained against the categorical cross entropy between the targets classes t and the predictions $\mathbf{p}$ seen as class posterior probabilities:

$$L_{crossentropy}(t, \mathbf{p}) = -\sum_{j} \delta_{j=t} log(p_j) \tag{6}$$

However, the final classification which assigns labels for each time step simply takes the most probable class regardless of how confident the model is. For that reason, we have tried to use the categorical hinge loss function instead, which only seeks to ensure a safety margin Δ between the activity of the neuron for the correct label class and the other neurons:

$$L_{hinge}(t, \mathbf{p}) = \max_{j \neq t}(0, \Delta + p_j - p_t) \tag{7}$$

This function focuses training on the most difficult pairwise decisions. It remains questionable whether a specific but more difficult task is more suitable for training a neural network, especially for the early stage of training. In practice, the hinge loss takes more iterations to trigger early stopping indeed, but leads to better classification scores and smoother (less confident) predictions for the RNN model. On the Hybrid NN-HMM the difference is not significant and cross entropy performs slightly better when it come to training HMM state posteriors.

Because the Jaccard index penalizes spurious predictions of gestures, eliminating very short sequences was found to consistently improve the final score, and more particularly so on the RNN which tends to have more noisy outputs.

The loss functions have been further modified to alleviate the large imbalance of example labels. Indeed, the non-gesture class is 30 times more frequent than the other classes. In the posterior model of the NN-HMM model, observations are further distributed among the 5 states of each gesture, thus amplifying the imbalance problem. This situation is commonly handled by resampling the training observations to eliminate these priors [15], but this approach is not practical with temporal data containing different gesture classes within a single sequence. As an alternative, we have corrected the loss function by the inverse frequency of the classes to predict:

$$L'(t,p) = L(t,p) \times f_t^{-\alpha} \qquad \alpha \in [0,1] \tag{8}$$

where $L(t,p)$ is the original loss function and f denotes the label frequency. Setting the smoothing factor $\alpha = 0$ returns the vanilla cost whereas $\alpha = 1$ should completely counterbalance the effect of priors. In practice, we have found that the non-gesture class was more difficult to learn and that $\alpha = 0.7$ actually leads to more balanced predictions. For the hybrid HMM model, we assume that the modified cost function leads to learn $\frac{P(s|x)}{P(s)}$ instead of $P(s|x)$ and we have therefore removed the division by the priors to compute the pseudo-likelihoods in (3).

Using this configuration, the Hybrid NN-HMM and the RNN obtain very similar performances as shown in Table 1.

Table 1. Performance of our models and other reported experiments on the body pose data (Jaccard Index). *hinge* and *CE* indicate whether the hinge or the cross entropy loss functions were used to train the neural network.

	Val	Test
[16]	0.783	0.779
RNN (*CE*)	0.802	0.796
Hybrid HMM (*hinge*)	0.803	0.797
Hybrid HMM (*CE*)	0.804	0.803
[11]		0.808
RNN (*hinge*)	0.813	0.809

5.2   Influence of Temporal Context

In our models, local context information is brought in by the temporal convolution layer. To assess the influence of context on temporal models, we have tested varying context window sizes. Because the number of parameters varies with the size of the filters, experiments have also been conducted with dilated kernels [19]: the input is subsampled before filtering so that a given kernel can cover multiples of the original temporal window. Results are summarized in Table 2. We observe that increasing the size of the window improves the recognition metric. The Hybrid NN-HMM model is more dependent on contextual information than the RNN model, probably because the latter is able to capture the context through the recurrent layers. Nevertheless, both models perform very similarly when sufficient contextual information is provided.

Table 2. Validation scores of our models under varying context sizes (Jaccard Index)

kernel * dilation	RNN	Hybrid HMM
9 * 1	0.804	0.785
13 * 1	0.809	0.785
9 * 2	0.816	0.796
17 * 1	0.813	0.803
13 * 2	0.811	0.811
25 * 1	0.813	0.811

6   Discussions and Conclusion

We have presented two competing solutions for gesture recognition based on body pose descriptors. Recurrent Neural Networks have recently reached state-of-the-art performances for sequence recognition thanks to several contributions to the architecture and the training methods. However, we demonstrate that the Hybrid NN-HMM also benefits from the improvement of neural network techniques, and compares favorably to its pure neuronal counterpart for gesture recognition. Training the Hybrid model remains more cumbersome than training an end-to-end neural network because of the alternating training steps, but the state-based representation provides more insight about the internals of the model when it comes to interpreting the error or adjusting the meta-parameters. We have also shown that, for our dataset, the hinge loss is more suitable for training a Neural Networks classifier. Future extensions of this work will compare the ability of both models to handle multi-modal inputs by adding the video recordings.

References

1. Bourlard, H., Morgan, N.: A continuous speech recognition system embedding MLP into HMM. In: Advances in Neural Information Processing Systems, pp. 186–193 (1990)
2. Cho, K., Van Merriënboer, B., Gulcehre, C., Bahdanau, D., Bougares, F., Schwenk, H., Bengio, Y.: Learning phrase representations using RNN encoder-decoder for statistical machine translation. arXiv preprint arXiv:1406.1078 (2014)
3. Escalera, S., Baró, X., Gonzàlez, J., Bautista, M.A., Madadi, M., Reyes, M., Ponce-López, V., Escalante, H.J., Shotton, J., Guyon, I.: ChaLearn looking at people challenge 2014: dataset and results. In: Agapito, L., Bronstein, M.M., Rother, C. (eds.) ECCV 2014. LNCS, vol. 8925, pp. 459–473. Springer, Cham (2015). doi:10. 1007/978-3-319-16178-5_32
4. Graves, A., Fernández, S., Schmidhuber, J.: Bidirectional LSTM networks for improved phoneme classification and recognition. In: Duch, W., Kacprzyk, J., Oja, E., Zadrożny, S. (eds.) ICANN 2005. LNCS, vol. 3697, pp. 799–804. Springer, Heidelberg (2005). doi:10.1007/11550907_126
5. Graves, A., Mohamed, A.R., Hinton, G.: Speech recognition with deep recurrent neural networks. In: 2013 IEEE International Conference on Acoustics, Speech and Signal Processing (ICASSP), pp. 6645–6649. IEEE (2013)
6. Graves, A., Schmidhuber, J.: Offline handwriting recognition with multidimensional recurrent neural networks. In: Advances in Neural Information Processing Systems, pp. 545–552 (2009)
7. Hochreiter, S., Schmidhuber, J.: Long short-term memory. Neural Comput. $9(8)$, 1735–1780 (1997)
8. Ioffe, S., Szegedy, C.: Batch normalization: accelerating deep network training by reducing internal covariate shift. In: Bach, F., Blei, D. (eds.) Proceedings of the 32nd International Conference on Machine Learning, Proceedings of Machine Learning Research, vol. 37, pp. 448–456, 07–09 July 2015. PMLR, Lille (2015)
9. Koller, O., Zargaran, S., Ney, H., Bowden, R.: Deep sign: hybrid CNN-HMM for continuous sign language recognition. In: Proceedings of the British Machine Vision Conference 2016, BMVC 2016, York, UK, 19–22 September 2016 (2016)
10. Maas, A.L., Hannun, A.Y., Ng, A.Y.: Rectifier nonlinearities improve neural network acoustic models. In: ICML Workshop on Deep Learning for Audio, Speech and Language Processing (2013)
11. Neverova, N., Wolf, C., Taylor, G.W., Nebout, F.: Multi-scale deep learning for gesture detection and localization. In: Agapito, L., Bronstein, M.M., Rother, C. (eds.) ECCV 2014. LNCS, vol. 8925, pp. 474–490. Springer, Cham (2015). doi:10. 1007/978-3-319-16178-5_33
12. Pigou, L., van den Oord, A., Dieleman, S., Van Herreweghe, M., Dambre, J.: Beyond temporal pooling: recurrence and temporal convolutions for gesture recognition in Video. Int. J. Comput. Vis. 1–10 (2016)
13. Srivastava, N., Hinton, G.E., Krizhevsky, A., Sutskever, I., Salakhutdinov, R.: Dropout: a simple way to prevent neural networks from overfitting. J. Mach. Learn. Res. $15(1)$, 1929–1958 (2014)
14. Szegedy, C., Liu, W., Jia, Y., Sermanet, P., Reed, S., Anguelov, D., Erhan, D., Vanhoucke, V., Rabinovich, A.: Going deeper with convolutions. In: Proceedings of the IEEE Conference on Computer Vision and Pattern Recognition, pp. 1–9 (2015)

15. Tóth, L., Kocsor, A.: Training HMM/ANN hybrid speech recognizers by probabilistic sampling. In: Duch, W., Kacprzyk, J., Oja, E., Zadrożny, S. (eds.) ICANN 2005. LNCS, vol. 3696, pp. 597–603. Springer, Heidelberg (2005). doi:10.1007/11550822_93

16. Wu, D., Pigou, L., Kindermans, P.J., Nam, L.E., Shao, L., Dambre, J., Odobez, J.M.: Deep Dynamic Neural Networks for Multimodal Gesture Segmentation and Recognition. IEEE Trans. Pattern Anal. Mach. Intell. **38**(8), 1583–1597 (2016). doi:10.1109/TPAMI.2016.2537340

17. Yang, H.D., Sclaroff, S., Lee, S.W.: Sign language spotting with a threshold model based on conditional random fields. IEEE Trans. Patt. Anal. Mach. Intell. **31**(7), 1264–1277 (2009)

18. Yin, Y., Davis, R.: Real-time continuous gesture recognition for natural human-computer interaction. In: 2014 IEEE Symposium on Visual Languages and Human-Centric Computing (VL/HCC), pp. 113–120. IEEE (2014)

19. Yu, F., Koltun, V.: Multi-scale context aggregation by dilated convolutions. CoRR abs/1511.07122 (2015)

Patterns Versus Characters in Subword-Aware Neural Language Modeling

Rustem Takhanov$^{(\boxtimes)}$ and Zhenisbek Assylbekov

Nazarbayev University, Astana, Kazakhstan
{rustem.takhanov,zhassylbekov}@nu.edu.kz

Abstract. Words in some natural languages can have a composite structure. Elements of this structure include the root (that could also be composite), prefixes and suffixes with which various nuances and relations to other words can be expressed. Thus, in order to build a proper word representation one must take into account its internal structure. From a corpus of texts we extract a set of frequent subwords and from the latter set we select patterns, i.e. subwords which encapsulate information on character n-gram regularities. The selection is made using the pattern-based Conditional Random Field model [19,23] with l_1 regularization. Further, for every word we construct a new sequence over an alphabet of patterns. The new alphabet's symbols confine a local statistical context stronger than the characters, therefore they allow better representations in $\mathbb{R}^n$ and are better building blocks for word representation. In the task of subword-aware language modeling, pattern-based models outperform character-based analogues by 2–20 perplexity points. Also, a recurrent neural network in which a word is represented as a sum of embeddings of its patterns is on par with a competitive and significantly more sophisticated character-based convolutional architecture.

Keywords: Subword-aware language modeling · Pattern-based conditional random field · Word representation · Deep learning

1 Introduction

The goal of natural language modeling is, given a corpus of texts from a certain language, to build a probabilistic distribution over all possible sequences of words/sentences. Historically, first approaches to the problem [4,16] were highly interpretable, involving syntax and morphology, i.e. the internal structure of such models was of interest even to linguists. Nowadays the best performance is achieved by the so called recurrent neural network language models (RNNLM), which unfortunately lack the desired properties of interpretability.

For rich-resource languages the amount of training data, i.e. a corpus of texts, is bounded only by the computational power of the language modeling method. Due to this, most of RNNLM methods treat text as a sequence of token identifiers, where a token corresponds to either a word, or punctuation mark. Indeed, if any word appears in a text in various different contexts, a

© Springer International Publishing AG 2017
D. Liu et al. (Eds.): ICONIP 2017, Part II, LNCS 10635, pp. 157–166, 2017.
https://doi.org/10.1007/978-3-319-70096-0_17

method can learn high quality word representation without taking into account its morphology. This logics fails when a corpus of texts is not large enough, and the problem is aggravated for morphology-rich languages, such as, e.g., turkic or finno-ugric languages. Thus, the problem of word representation that would take into account an internal structure of a word becomes very actual — recent advances in language modeling are connected with treating words as sequences of characters or other subword units.

Much research has been done on character-level neural language modeling [6,9–11,15,20]. However, not much work exploits character n-grams that occur in a word. In [17] a word is represented using a character n-gram count vector, followed by a single nonlinear transformation to yield a low-dimensional embedding; the word embeddings are then fed into neural machine translation models. In [22] a very similar technique is used and an evaluation on three other tasks (word similarity, sentence similarity, and part-of-speech tagging) is performed; they demonstrate that their method outperforms more complex architectures based on character-level recurrent and convolutional neural networks. Probably closest to ours is an approach from [2] where a word representation is a sum of terms, each term corresponding to a certain n-gram that occurs in that word. One weekness of the mentioned approaches is that all possible n-grams that occur in a corpus of texts are present there in an *a priori* equal way, and a difference in their value for word representation is calculated in the process of learning. Whereas we in advance select a subset of n-grams that could potentially enrich word vectors by subword information. For this purpose we use the pattern-based Conditional Random Field with l_1 regularization.

Our approach also differs in the following aspects: we (i) replace each character by a new symbol which in some way concentrates an information on previous characters, (ii) experiment with several ways of combining subword embeddings to produce word embeddings, and (iii) evaluate our methods on a ubiquitous language modeling task.

2   A New Alphabet for Words

Throughout the paper, we will use the following notation: if $\mathcal{X}$ is an alphabet, then $\mathcal{X}^*$ denotes a set of words over $\mathcal{X}$; for $\alpha, \beta \in \mathcal{X}^*$, $\alpha\beta$ denotes the concatenation of α and β; by $*$ we denote an arbitrary word.

The key trick that we use in this paper is replacing a word $a_1 a_2 \cdots a_k$ (that occurs in some context) over the initial alphabet $\mathcal{A}$ with a word $s_1 s_2 \cdots s_k$ over a new alphabet of states $\mathcal{S}$. Let us describe this substitution. We first define a finite state machine $(\mathcal{A}, \mathcal{S}, \delta, s_0)$, where s_0 is an initial state and $\delta : \mathcal{S} \times \mathcal{A} \to \mathcal{S}$ is a state-transition function. If we are given a sentence $\alpha = b_1 b_2 \cdots b_K$ such that every b_i is a character symbol from $\mathcal{A}$ (it could be a punctuation mark, i.e. a symbol that marks a boundary between words) our state machine reads this sentence and produces a sequence of states: $s_0 s_1 \cdots s_K$. In the latter sequence, every s_i corresponds to a state of our machine after reading a symbol b_i. Thus, every subsequence $b_i b_{i+1} \cdots b_j$ of the initial sentence α corresponds

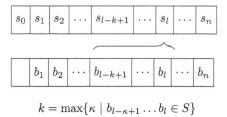

$$k = \max\{\kappa \mid b_{l-\kappa+1} \ldots b_l \in S\}$$

Fig. 1. Finite-state machine.

to a subsequence $s_i s_{i+1} \cdots s_j$ where $1 \leq i \leq j \leq K$. Therefore, if $b_i b_{i+1} \cdots b_j$ corresponds to a word in a sentence α, then we will substitute it with $s_i s_{i+1} \cdots s_j$.

Thus, given such a finite state machine, every word of a sentence can be rewritten over another alphabet S. Let us describe now our finite state machine.

Suppose that after an analysis of a training set, i.e. of a corpus of texts from our language $\mathcal{L}$, we extract a certain finite set of sequences $\Pi_0 \subseteq \mathcal{A}^*$ that we assume not only to be frequent, but in some way statistically characterising our language. A specific way of choosing Π_0 will be given in the following subsection. Any element $\pi \in \Pi_0$ we call *a pattern*. Any such set defines a set of states $S = \{\beta \mid \underset{\pi \in \Pi_0}{\exists} \pi = \beta *\}$, which is, in fact, a set of all prefixes of patterns. We assume that an empty word ε is also in S and define $s_0 = \varepsilon$.

Now we have to define a state-transition function δ. Our idea is to construct it in such a way that after reading the first l symbols of the sentence $b_1 b_2 \cdots b_l$ the machine should be in a state $s_l \in S$ where s_l is the longest word from S for which $b_1 b_2 \cdots b_l = *s_l$ (Fig. 1). The latter decription induces the following definition: for any $\alpha \in S$ and $a \in \mathcal{A}$, $\delta(\alpha, a)$ is the longest word $\beta \in S$ for which $\alpha a = *\beta$.

Patterns

In this subsection we will describe how we extract a set of patterns Π_0 from a corpus of texts (Fig. 2). By a corpus of texts we understand a training set $T = \{\alpha_1, \cdots, \alpha_L\} \subseteq \mathcal{A}^*$ where α_i is a sentence from our language $\mathcal{L}$.

First we extract from our training set T a set of patterns Π' based on the following simple procedure: we fix in advance a threshold f and put to T only those

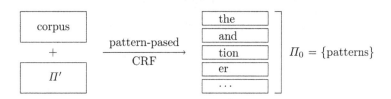

Fig. 2. Pattern mining.

words $\alpha \in \mathcal{A}^*$ that occur in T in more than f places. Then we apply a reduction procedure, i.e. if (a) α is a subword of β, (b) α and β always occur together in T, then we delete α from Π'. A pattern-based conditional random field model for our language is the following probability distribution over $\mathcal{A}^*$ [19,23]:

$$\Pr(b_1 \cdots b_K) = A \cdot e^{-E(b_1 \cdots b_K)},$$

where $E(b_1 \cdots b_K) = \sum_{\alpha \in \Pi'} \sum_{i<j:b_i \cdots b_j = \alpha} c^\alpha$, and c^α, $\alpha \in \Pi'$, are parameters to be learned from T.

The learning is done by the minimization of the negative log-likelihood with L_1-regularization:

$$- \sum_{i=1}^{L} \log \Pr(\alpha_i) + C \sum_{\alpha \in \Pi'} |c^\alpha|. \tag{1}$$

The latter function is convex, an efficient computation of its value and gradient is described in [19]. For the optimization we used the Limited-memory Broyden-Fletcher-Goldfarb-Shanno (L-BFGS) method written by Jorge Nocedal. Via the parameter C one can manage the number of patterns $\alpha \in \Pi'$ for which $c^\alpha \neq 0$. Finally, we define $\Pi_0 = \{\alpha \in \Pi' | c^\alpha \neq 0\}$.

3   Subword-Aware Neural Language Model

In what follows, both regular characters and patterns are referred to as *subwords*. The overall architecture of the subword-aware neural language model is displayed in Fig. 3.

It consists of three main parts: (i) subword-based word embedding model, (ii) word-level recurrent neural network language model (RNNLM), and (iii) softmax layer. Below we describe each part in more detail.

Subword-based word embeddings: A word $w \in \mathcal{W}$ (in a sentence) is defined by the sequence of its subwords $s_1 \ldots s_{n_w} \in \mathcal{X}^*$ ($\mathcal{X} = \mathcal{A}$ in the case of character-based representation, and $\mathcal{X} = \mathcal{S}$ in our pattern-based approach), and each state is embedded into $d_\mathcal{X}$-dimensional space via an embedding matrix $\mathbf{E}_\mathcal{X}^{in} \in \mathbb{R}^{|X| \times d_\mathcal{X}}$ to obtain a sequence of state vectors:

$$\mathbf{s_1}, \ldots, \mathbf{s_{n_w}}. \tag{2}$$

Then we try three different methods to get an embedding of the word w:

– **Concat:** A simple concatenation of state vectors (2) into a single word vector:

$$\mathbf{w} = [\mathbf{s_1}; \mathbf{s_2}; \ldots; \mathbf{s_{n_w}}; \underbrace{\mathbf{0}; \mathbf{0}; \ldots; \mathbf{0}}_{n-n_w}].$$

We either truncate (if w consists of more than n symbols) or zero-pad $\mathbf{w}$ so that all word vectors have the same length $n \cdot d_\mathcal{X}$ to allow batch processing. This approach is motivated by a desire to keep all the information regarding subwords, including the order in which they appear in the word.

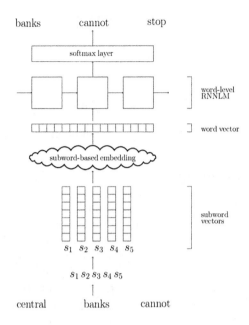

Fig. 3. Subword-aware language model.

– **Sum:** A summation of subword vectors:

$$\mathbf{w} = \sum_{t=1}^{n_w} \mathbf{s_t}. \tag{3}$$

This approach was used by [3] to combine a word and its morpheme embeddings into a single word vector.

– **CNN:** A convolutional model of [9]:

$$\mathbf{w} = \mathrm{CNN}(\mathbf{s_1}, \ldots, \mathbf{s_{n_w}}).$$

This method has already demonstrated excellent performance for character-level inputs, therefore we decided to apply it to patterns as well.

To model interactions between subwords, we feed the resulting word embedding $\mathbf{w}$ into a stack of two highway layers [18] with dimensionality d_{HW} per layer. In cases when dimensionality of $\mathbf{w}$ does not match d_{HW}, we project it into $\mathbb{R}^{d_{\mathrm{HW}}}$.

Word-level RNNLM: Once we have embeddings $\mathbf{w_{1:k}}$ for a sequence of words $w_{1:k}$, we can use a word-level RNN language model to produce a sequence of states $\mathbf{h_{1:k}} \in \mathbb{R}^{d_{\mathrm{LM}}}$ according to

$$\mathbf{h_t} = \mathrm{RNNCell}(\mathbf{w_t}, \mathbf{h_{t-1}}), \qquad \mathbf{h_0} = \mathbf{0}.$$

There is a big variety of RNN cells to choose from. The most advanced recurrent neural architectures, at the time of this writing, are RHN [25] and NAS [26]. However, to make our results directly comparable to the previous work of [9] on character-level language modeling we select a more conventional architecture – a stack of two LSTM cells [8].

Softmax: The last state $\mathbf{h_k}$ from (4) is further used to predict the next word w_{k+1} according to the probability distribution

$$\Pr(w_{k+1}|w_{1:k}) = \text{softmax}(\mathbf{h_k W + b}), \tag{4}$$

where $\mathbf{W} \in \mathbb{R}^{d_{\text{LM}} \times |\mathcal{W}|}$, $\mathbf{b} \in \mathbb{R}^{|\mathcal{W}|}$, and d_{LM} is a hidden layer size of the RNN.

4 Experimental Setup

Data sets: All models are trained and evaluated on the English PTB data set [12] utilizing the standard training (0–20), validation (21–22), and test (23–24) splits along with pre-processing by [14]. Since the PTB is criticized for being small nowadays, we also provide an evaluation on the WikiText-2 data set [13], which is approximately two times larger than PTB in size and three times larger in vocabulary. We do not append any additional symbols at the end of each line in WikiText-2, but remove spaces between equality signs in the sequences "= =" and "= = =", which occur in section titles.

Hyperparameters: The regularization parameter C from (1) is set to 1600, which results in 883 unique patterns ($|\Pi_0| = 883, |\mathcal{S}| = 890$) for the PTB data set (cf. 48 plain characters) and 1440 unique patterns ($|\Pi_0| = 1440, |\mathcal{S}| = 1471$) for the WikiText-2 data set (cf. 281 plain characters). We set the threshold value f to 300 on the PTB and to 700 on the WikiText-2. We experiment with two configurations for the state size d_{LM} of the word-level RNNLM: 300 (small models) and 650 (medium-sized models). Specification of other hyperparameters is given below.

Concat: $d_{\mathcal{A}} = 15$ (for characters), and $d_{\mathcal{S}} = 30$ (for patterns). We give higher dimensionality to patterns as their amount significantly exceeds the amount of characters. n is set to the 95th percentile of word lengths, i.e. 95% of all words have not more than n characters[1]. We do not set $n = \max_{w \in \mathcal{W}} n_w$, as this would result in excessive zero-padding. $d_{\text{HW}} = d_{\text{LM}}$.

Sum: $d_{\mathcal{X}} = d_{\text{HW}} = d_{\text{LM}} \in \{300, 650\}$ for both characters and patterns. We give higher dimensionality to subword vectors here (compared to other models) since the resulting word vector will have the same size as subword vectors (see (3)).

CNN: In character-based models we choose the same values for hyperparameters as in the work of [9]. For pattern-based models we choose: $d_{\mathcal{S}} = 50$ and $d_{\mathcal{S}} = 100$ for small and medium-sized models; filter widths are $[1, 2, 3, 4, 5, 6]$ and $[1, 2, 3, 4, 5, 6, 7]$ for small and medium-sized models; the corresponding depths (number of features per width) are $[100, 50, 75, 100, 100, 100]$ and $[100, 100, 150, 200, 200, 200, 200]$. $d_{\text{HW}} = \sum \text{depths} \in \{525, 1150\}$.

---

[1] Word length in characters and in patterns is the same.

Optimization is done similarly to [5, 9, 24]. Training the models involves minimizing the negative log-likelihood over the corpus $w_{1:K}$:

$$-\sum_{k=1}^{K} \log \Pr(w_k | w_{1:k-1}) \longrightarrow \min,$$

which is typically done by truncated BPTT [6, 21]. We backpropagate for 35 time steps using stochastic gradient descent where the learning rate is initially set to 0.7 and halved if the perplexity does not decrease on the validation set after an epoch. We use a batch size of 20. We train for 65 epochs, picking the best performing model on the validation set. Parameters of the models are randomly initialized uniformly in $[-0.05, 0.05]$, except the forget bias of the word-level LSTM, which is initialized to 1, and the transform bias of the highway, which is initialized to values near -2. For regularization we use variational dropout [5] with dropout rates for small/medium Concat, Sum/medium CNN models as follows: 0.1/0.15/0.2 for the embedding layer, 0.2/0.3/0.35 for the input to the gates, 0.1/0.15/0.2 for the hidden units, and 0.2/0.3/0.35 for the output activations. We clip the norm of the gradients (normalized by minibatch size) at 5.

5   Results

The results of evaluation on PTB and WikiText-2 are reported in Tables 1 and 2 correspondingly. As one can see, models which process patterns consistently outperform those which use characters under small parameter budgets. However, the difference in performance is less pronounced when we allow more parameters.

Also, it is clearly seen that patterns are more beneficial for simple models, such as Concat and Sum, but have less effect on the CNN model, which shrinks the gap between characters and patterns. This is quite natural as patterns carry

Table 1. Results on the PTB for small (left) and medium-sized models.

Model	Characters		Patterns	
	Size	PPL	Size	PPL
Concat	5M	119.2	5M	**99.6**
Sum	5M	108.2	5M	**87.4**
CNN	6M	87.3	6M	**84.8**

Model	Characters		Patterns	
	Size	PPL	Size	PPL
Concat	15M	91.5	15.8M	**83.6**
Sum	15M	91.5	15.5M	**82.1**
CNN	20M	79.6	20.5M	**77.2**

Table 2. Results on WikiText-2 for small (left) and medium-sized models.

Model	Characters		Patterns	
	Size	PPL	Size	PPL
Concat	11.9M	138.2	12.1M	**114.2**
Sum	11.9M	124.0	12.3M	**101.9**
CNN	12.9M	105.2	13.0M	**102.8**

Model	Characters		Patterns	
	Size	PPL	Size	PPL
Concat	30.2M	115.9	30.8M	**99.0**
Sum	30.3M	106.7	31.1M	**94.9**
CNN	34.5M	97.38	35.7M	**94.2**

some information on character n-grams and, hence, can be considered as "discrete convolutions", which makes CNN over patterns not as efficient as CNN over regular characters. However, we notice that in all cases a simple sum of pattern embeddings (Pat-Sum) is on par with a more sophisticated convolution over character embeddings (Char-CNN). Faster[2] training of the Pat-Sum compared to the Char-CNN makes the patterns even more advantageous.

Why does Pat-Sum perform equally well as Char-CNN? As was described in Sect. 3 word embeddings are processed by the two highway layers before they are fed into the RNNLM. Highway is a weighted average between nonlinear and identity transformations of the incoming word embedding:

$$\mathbf{w} \mapsto \mathbf{t} \odot \sigma(\mathbf{wA} + \mathbf{b}) + (\mathbf{1} - \mathbf{t}) \odot \mathbf{w},$$

where $\mathbf{t}$, $\mathbf{A}$ and $\mathbf{b}$ are trainable parameters, $\sigma(\cdot)$ is a non-linear activation, $\mathbf{1}$ is a vector whose all components are 1 and $\odot$ is an operation of component-wise multiplication. The ideal input for the highway is the one that does not need to undergo a nonlinear transformation, i.e. the highway will then be close to an identity operator, and hence in the ideal case we shall have $\mathbf{t} = \mathbf{0}$. But if $\mathbf{w}$ is rather "raw", then the highway should prepare it for the RNN (resulting in $\mathbf{t} \neq \mathbf{0}$). Such extra nonlinearity can measured by the closeness of $\mathbf{t}$ to $\mathbf{1}$. We hypothesize that the reason why Pat-Sum performs well is that the sum of pattern embeddings is *already* a good word representation. Hence the highway in Pat-Sum does less nonlinear work than in Char-CNN: In Pat-Sum it is almost an identical transformation, and such a simple highway is well-trained according to [7]. To validate our hypothesis we compare the distributions of the transform gate $\mathbf{t}$ values from both highway layers of Pat-Sum and Char-CNN. The density plots in Fig. 4 support our hypothesis: Pat-Sum does not utilize much of nonlinearity in the highway layers, while Char-CNN heavily relies on it.

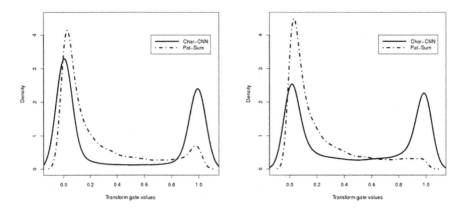

Fig. 4. Kernel density estimations of the transform gate values of the first (left) and second highway layers in Char-CNN and Pat-Sum.

---

[2] Around 1.2x speedup on NVIDIA Titan X (Pascal).

Source code: All models were implemented in TensorFlow [1] and the source code for Pat-Sum is available at https://github.com/zh3nis/pat-sum.

6   Conclusion

Regular characters are rather uninformative when their embeddings are concatenated or summed to produce word vectors, but patterns, on the contrary, carry enough information to make these methods work significantly better. Convolutions over subword embeddings do capture n-gram regularities and, therefore, make the difference between characters and patterns less noticeable. It is noteworthy, that a simple and fast sum of pattern embeddings is on par with more sophisticated and slower convolutions over characters embeddings.

Acknowledgments. We gratefully acknowledge the support of NVIDIA Corporation with the donation of the Titan X Pascal GPU used for this research.

References

1. Abadi, M., Agarwal, A., Barham, P., Brevdo, E., Chen, Z., Citro, C., Corrado, G.S., Davis, A., Dean, J., Devin, M., et al.: Tensorflow: Large-scale machine learning on heterogeneous distributed systems (2016). arXiv preprint: arXiv:1603.04467
2. Bojanowski, P., Grave, E., Joulin, A., Mikolov, T.: Enriching word vectors with subword information (2016). arXiv preprint: arXiv:1607.04606
3. Botha, J., Blunsom, P.: Compositional morphology for word representations and language modelling. In: Proceedings of the 31st International Conference on Machine Learning (ICML 2014), pp. 1899–1907 (2014)
4. Chomsky, N.: Three models for the description of language. IRE Trans. Inf. Theor. **2**(3), 113–124 (1956)
5. Gal, Y., Ghahramani, Z.: A theoretically grounded application of dropout in recurrent neural networks. In: Advances in Neural Information Processing Systems, pp. 1019–1027 (2016)
6. Graves, A.: Generating sequences with recurrent neural networks (2013). arXiv preprint: arXiv:1308.0850
7. Hardt, M., Ma, T.: Identity matters in deep learning (2016). arXiv preprint: arXiv:1611.04231
8. Hochreiter, S., Schmidhuber, J.: Long short-term memory. Neural Comput. **9**(8), 1735–1780 (1997)
9. Kim, Y., Jernite, Y., Sontag, D., Rush, A.M.: Character-aware neural language models. In: Proceedings of the Thirtieth AAAI Conference on Artificial Intelligence, pp. 2741–2749. AAAI Press (2016)
10. Lankinen, M., Heikinheimo, H., Takala, P., Raiko, T., Karhunen, J.: A character-word compositional neural language model for finnish (2016). arXiv preprint: arXiv:1612.03266
11. Ling, W., Dyer, C., Black, A.W., Trancoso, I., Fermandez, R., Amir, S., Marujo, L., Luis, T.: Finding function in form: compositional character models for open vocabulary word representation. In: Proceedings of the 2015 Conference on Empirical Methods in Natural Language Processing, Lisbon, Portugal, pp. 1520–1530. Association for Computational Linguistics, September 2015

12. Marcus, M.P., Marcinkiewicz, M.A., Santorini, B.: Building a large annotated corpus of English: the penn treebank. Comput. Linguist. **19**(2), 313–330 (1993)
13. Merity, S., Xiong, C., Bradbury, J., Socher, R.: Pointer sentinel mixture models. In: Proceedings of ICLR 2017 (2017)
14. Mikolov, T., Karafiát, M., Burget, L., Cernocky̌, J., Khudanpur, S.: Recurrent neural network based language model. In: Interspeech, vol. 2, p. 3 (2010)
15. Mikolov, T., Sutskever, I., Deoras, A., Le, H.S., Kombrink, S., Cernocky, J.: Subword language modeling with neural networks (2012). Preprint (http://www.fit.vutbr.cz/imikolov/rnnlm/char.pdf)
16. Shannon, C.E., Weaver, W.: A mathematical theory of communication (1963)
17. Sperr, H., Niehues, J., Waibel, A.: Letter n-gram-based input encoding for continuous space language models. In: Proceedings of the Workshop on Continuous Vector Space Models and their Compositionality, pp. 30–39 (2013)
18. Srivastava, R.K., Greff, K., Schmidhuber, J.: Training very deep networks. In: Advances in Neural Information Processing Systems, pp. 2377–2385 (2015)
19. Takhanov, R., Kolmogorov, V.: Inference algorithms for pattern-based CRFs on sequence data. In: ICML, vol. 3, pp. 145–153 (2013)
20. Verwimp, L., Pelemans, J., Wambacq, P., et al.: Character-word LSTM language models. In: Proceedings of EACL 2017 (2017)
21. Werbos, P.J.: Backpropagation through time: what it does and how to do it. Proc. IEEE **78**(10), 1550–1560 (1990)
22. Wieting, J., Bansal, M., Gimpel, K., Livescu, K.: Charagram: embedding words and sentences via character n-grams. In: Proceedings of the 2016 Conference on Empirical Methods in Natural Language Processing, EMNLP 2016, Austin, Texas, USA, pp. 1504–1515, 1–4 November 2016
23. Ye, N., Lee, W.S., Chieu, H.L., Wu, D.: Conditional random fields with high-order features for sequence labeling. In: Advances in Neural Information Processing Systems, pp. 2196–2204 (2009)
24. Zaremba, W., Sutskever, I., Vinyals, O.: Recurrent neural network regularization (2014). arXiv preprint: arXiv:1409.2329
25. Zilly, J.G., Srivastava, R.K., Koutník, J., Schmidhuber, J.: Recurrent highway networks (2016). arXiv preprint: arXiv:1607.03474
26. Zoph, B., Le, Q.V.: Neural architecture search with reinforcement learning. In: Proceedings of ICLR 2017 (2017)

Hierarchical Attention BLSTM for Modeling Sentences and Documents

Xiaolei Niu and Yuexian Hou[(⊠)]

School of Computer Science and Technology, Tianjin University, Tianjin, China
{xlniu,yxhou}@tju.edu.cn

Abstract. Recently, neural network based methods have made remarkable progresses on various Natural Language Processing (NLP) tasks. However, it is still a challenge to model both short and long texts, e.g. sentences and documents. In this paper, we propose a Hierarchical Attention Bidirectional LSTM (HA-BLSTM) to model both sentences and documents. HA-BLSTM effectively obtains a hierarchy of representations from words to phrases through the hierarchical structure. We design two attention mechanisms: local and global attention mechanisms. The local attention mechanism learns which components of a text are more important for modeling the whole text, while the global attention mechanism learns which representations of the same text are crucial. Thus, HA-BLSTM can model long documents along with short sentences. Experiments on four benchmark datasets show that our model yields a superior classification performance over a number of strong baselines.

Keywords: BLSTM · Attention · Text modeling

1 Introduction

The goal of text modeling is to represent the meaning of a text. With the distributed representations of the continuous words, such as phrases, sentences, documents achieved great success, it is common practice to present the variable-length sentence or document as a fixed-length vector. The simplest method in this direction probably is continuous Bag-of-words (cBoW), where the representation of a text is achieved by averaging the embeddings of words in the text. However, cBoW does not consider the order of words in the text, causing the difficulty in capturing the structure of sentences or documents. Recently, neural network based text modeling approaches, in which the order of words is taken into consideration, have shown excellent abilities in modeling sequences, such as Recursive Neural Network (RecNN) [1–3], Recurrent Neural Network (RNN) [4–6], and Convolutional Neural Network (CNN) [7,8]. These models apply nonlinear transformations to model the interactions between words, furthermore, the structure of sentences can also be learned by RecNN. However, during the nonlinear transfer process, they can obtain a fixed-length vector that does not retain intermediate representations (multi-level abstractions of the text), which

© Springer International Publishing AG 2017
D. Liu et al. (Eds.): ICONIP 2017, Part II, LNCS 10635, pp. 167–177, 2017.
https://doi.org/10.1007/978-3-319-70096-0_18

may be extremely important to the task in processing. Besides, all components of a text are considered equally important to describe the meaning of the text in the above networks. Intuitively, the importance of each intermediate representation and each component of the text is varying with the task at hand.

In this paper, we propose a Hierarchical Attention BLSTM (HA-BLSTM). It is observed that different words and phrases in a text are differentially informative, thus HA-BLSTM adopts local-level attention mechanism to study which words or phrases are informative in a certain text. Unlike cBoW, CNN, RNN and RecNN, which output a fixed-length vector, the hierarchical structure of HA-BLSTM forms intermediate representations as multi-level abstractions for the text. Obviously, the importance of intermediate representation of each layer in HA-BLSTM is not equal and depends on the text and the task. Therefore, HA-BLSTM uses global-level attention mechanism to study which intermediate representations of the text should be paid more attention.

Our contributions can be summarized into three parts: First, for both sentence and document modeling, we propose a hierarchical architecture with two attention mechanisms, which obtains a hierarchical multi-scale representation of the text rather than a fixed-length vector. Furthermore, the number of the layers in the hierarchical architecture can be changed according to the task, which makes the model more general. Second, we verify that our local and global attention mechanisms are effective for the improvement of the performance. Third, we conduct experiments on four benchmark datasets to show the superiority of our model over previous methods.

2   Hierarchical Attention BLSTM Model

The overall architecture of HA-BLSTM is shown in Fig. 1. The number of the layers in the model can be variable. We take three-layer structure as an example to discuss. It consists of three parts: BLSTM-based sequence encoder, a local-level attention layer and a global-level attention layer.

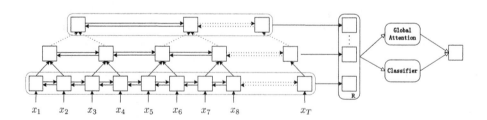

x_1 x_2 x_3 x_4 x_5 x_6 x_7 x_8 x_T

Fig. 1. The overall diagram of HA-BLSTM.

2.1   BLSTM-Based Sequence Encoder

LSTM was presented [9] to specially address the problem about learning long-term dependencies. At each time step t, we define the LSTM units to be a collection of vectors in R^m: an input gate i_t, a forget gate f_t, an output gate o_t, a memory cell c_t and a hidden state h_t. m is the number of the LSTM units. The entries of the gating vectors i_t, f_t and o_t are in $[0, 1]$. The transition equations of LSTM are the following:

$$i_t = \sigma \left(W_i x_t + U_i h_{t-1} + b_i \right), \tag{1}$$
$$f_t = \sigma \left(W_f x_t + U_f h_{t-1} + b_f \right), \tag{2}$$
$$o_t = \sigma \left(W_o x_t + U_o h_{t-1} + b_o \right), \tag{3}$$
$$z_t = \tanh \left(W_z x_t + U_z h_{t-1} + b_z \right), \tag{4}$$
$$c_t = i_t \odot z_t + f_t \odot c_{t-1}, \tag{5}$$
$$h_t = o_t \odot \tanh \left(c_t \right), \tag{6}$$

where x_t is the input at the current time step, σ denotes the logistic sigmoid function and $\odot$ denotes elementwise multiplication. In this paper, we adopt BLSTM to take advantage of additional backward information and thus enhance the memory capability. We encode the hidden state of a unit as following:

$$\tilde{h}_j^l = \left[\overrightarrow{h_j^l} \oplus \overleftarrow{h_j^l} \right], \tag{7}$$

where $\overrightarrow{h_j^l}$ and $\overleftarrow{h_j^l}$ are the same as h_t in formula (6), the $\oplus$ indicates concatenation operation, and $\tilde{}$ stands for the output of BLSTM.

2.2   Attention Mechanism

Local Attention. Not all words and phrases contribute equally to the representation of the text meaning. Therefore, we introduce local attention mechanism (see Fig. 2(a)) to learn which words or phrases are important to the meaning of the sentence or document and aggregate the representations of those informative words or phrases to form a fixed-length continuous vector, which is a summarization of the sentence or document with the appropriate scale.

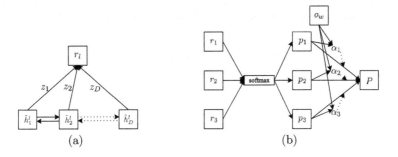

(a)   (b)

Fig. 2. (a) and (b) are the local and global attention mechanisms in HA-BLSTM.

At each layer l, r_l is a representation of the sequence, which is computed as:

$$r_l = \sum_{j=1}^{D} z_j \odot \tilde{h}_j^l, \tag{8}$$

where $l \in [1,3]$, $z_j \in R^d$ ($j \in [1,D]$, $D = T/2^{l-1}$, T is the length of the given sequence),

$$z = \begin{bmatrix} z_1 \\ z_2 \\ \vdots \\ z_D \end{bmatrix} = \begin{bmatrix} 1/Z \\ 1/Z \\ \vdots \\ 1/Z \end{bmatrix} \odot \exp(\begin{bmatrix} u_1^l \\ u_2^l \\ \vdots \\ u_D^l \end{bmatrix}), \tag{9}$$

where $Z \in R^d$ is the vector of the normalization coefficients,

$$Z_k = \sum_{j=1}^{D} [\exp(\begin{bmatrix} u_1^l \\ u_2^l \\ \vdots \\ u_D^l \end{bmatrix})]_{D \times (j-1)+k}, \tag{10}$$

where $1 \leq k \leq d$,

$$u_j^l = \tanh(W_u \tilde{h}_j^l + b_u), \tag{11}$$

where $W_u \in R^{d \times d}$, $b_u \in R^d$ are the parameters.

We first feed a word or phrase annotation $\tilde{h}_j^l$ through a one-layer MLP to get u_j^l as a hidden representation of $\tilde{h}_j^l$, then through a softmax function we obtain the weight vector z_j for the word or phrase annotation $\tilde{h}_j^l$. After that, we compute the representation of the sentence or document r_l as a weighted sum of the word or phrase annotations based on the weight vectors. From another point of view, z_j can be viewed as the update gates in the gate mechanism, the representation of each layer r_l can be regarded as a choice among the word or phrase annotations $\tilde{h}_j^l$.

Global Attention. After the local-level attention layer, we obtain a multi-scale hierarchical representation (R in Fig. 1.) for the given text. Depending on the text and the task, the weights of different levels are not identical. Inspired by [10], we introduce the global attention mechanism (see Fig. 2(b)) to reward representations that are informative to classify the category correctly. Specifically,

$$p_l = P(\cdot \mid x_j; \theta) = \text{softmax}(W_p r_l + b_p), \tag{12}$$

$$o_l = \tanh(W_g p_l + b_g), \tag{13}$$

$$\alpha_l = \frac{\exp(o_l^\top o_g)}{\sum_l \exp(o_l^\top o_g)}, \tag{14}$$

$$P = \sum_l \alpha_l p_l, \tag{15}$$

where $W_p \in R^{c \times d}$, $W_g \in R^{c \times c}$, $b_p \in R^c$, $b_g \in R^c$, $o_g \in R^c$ are the parameters, c is the number of categories. We first compute the class distribution $p_l = \mathrm{P}(\cdot \mid x_j; \theta)$ of each representation. Then we compute a hidden representation of p_l like local attention mechanism, and we measure the reliability of the representations at each level as the similarity of o_l with a vector o_g and get a normalized reliability weight α_l through a softmax function. Finally, we compute the coincident class distribution P.

2.3   Architecture

HA-BLSTM is a hierarchical structure, which is effective to model the combinations of features by mixing the information continuously in a bottom-up manner. When the children nodes are combined into their parent node, the fused information of two children nodes is also merged and preserved by their parent node. The number of the layer in HA-BLSTM is $l \in [1,3]$, at each layer l, the activation of the j-th ($j \in \left[1, T/2^{l-1}\right]$) hidden node $h_j^l \in R^d$ is computed as:

$$h_j^l = \left[\tilde{h}_{2j}^{l-1} \oplus \tilde{h}_{2j+1}^{l-1}\right], \tag{16}$$

$$\tilde{h}_{2j}^{l-1} = \mathrm{BLSTM}(h_{2j}^{l-1}), \tag{17}$$

$$\tilde{h}_{2j+1}^{l-1} = \mathrm{BLSTM}(h_{2j+1}^{l-1}), \tag{18}$$

where $\tilde{h}_{2j}^{l-1}$, $\tilde{h}_{2j+1}^{l-1} \in R^{2m}$ are the outputs of BLSTM units. In the case of text classification, for an input sequence of length T and the corresponding class $y^{(i)}$, we first represent each word x_j ($j \in [1,T]$) into its corresponding vector $h_j^1 \in R^d$, where d is the dimensionality of word embeddings. That is, the embeddings are the input of the first layer, whose outputs are recursively applied to upper layers until it arrives at the third layer. Vividly, $\tilde{h}_j^l$ can be viewed as the annotation for the word or phrase. Through the BLSTM-based sequence encoder, the information in the hidden nodes of the first layer can represent single words, the combined information in the hidden nodes of the second and third layer can represent bi-grams and four-grams.

Table 1. Statistics of the four datasets used in this paper.

Dataset	Type	Train size	Dev. size	Test size	Class	Average length	Vocabulary size
SST-1	Sentence	8544	1101	2210	5	19	18 K
SST-2	Sentence	6920	872	1821	2	18	15 K
TREC	Sentence	5452	-	500	6	10	9.4 K
IMDB	Document	25000	-	25000	2	294	392 K

3   Experiments

3.1   Datasets

We test our model on four benchmarks. Summary statistics of the datasets are in Table 1.

- **SST-1.** Stanford Sentiment Treebank is a movie reviews dataset with one sentence per review [3]. The objective is to classify a review as fine-grained labels (very negative, negative, neutral, positive, very positive).[1]
- **SST-2.** Same as SST-1 but with neutral reviews removed and binary labels.
- **TREC.** Question classification dataset [12]. The task involves classifying a question into 6 question types (abbreviation, description, entity, human, location, and numeric value).[2]
- **IMDB.** The IMDB dataset consists of 100,000 movie reviews with binary classes [13]. Each movie review has several sentences.[3]

3.2   Hyperparameters and Training

In all of the experiments, we adopt the publicly available word2vec vectors, which are pre-trained on 100 billion words from Google News. The vectors have dimensionality of 300 and were trained using the continuous bag-of-words architecture [14]. Words that do not present in the set of pre-trained words are initialized randomly. And the word embeddings are fine-tuned during training to improve the performance. In order to ensure the input vector of each layer has the same dimension, we use 75 as the dimensionality of hidden units. And dropout rate is 0.5, mini-batch size is 64. We choose these hyper-parameters which achieve the best performance on the development set for the final evaluation.

We apply dropout in fully connected layers, which are before softmax layers. The objective of our model is to minimize the cross-entropy error of the predicted and true distributions. The object is to minimize the objective function:

$$J(\theta) = -\frac{1}{n} \sum_{i=1}^{n} \log P_{y^{(i)}}^{(i)}, \tag{19}$$

where $y^{(i)}$ is the corresponding category, n is the number of train sequence and θ denotes all the trainable parameters of our model.

---

[1] http://nlp.stanford.edu/sentiment/ Data is actually provided at the phrase-level and both phrases and sentences are used to train the model, but only sentences are scored at test time [3,7,11]. Thus the training set is an order of magnitude larger than listed in Table 1.

[2] http://cogcomp.cs.illinois.edu/Data/QA/QC/.

[3] http://ai.stanford.edu/~amaas/data/sentiment/.

3.3   Results

Overall Performance. As showed in Table 2, the HA-BLSTM model achieves excellent performance on three out of four tasks compared with other models. In the task of both topic classification (e.g. TREC) and sentiment classification (e.g. SST-1, SST-2 and IMDB), the end-to-end HA-BLSTM shows a promising performance to model sentences and documents without any extra knowledge which is adopted in some tree-based neural network, e.g. Tree-LSTM [4], or multi-task optimization, e.g. Multi-Task [5].

Our model does not get the best accuracy in IMDB dataset, which has longer texts than the other three. The main reason may be the sensitivity of length in

Table 2. Experiment results of HA-BLSTM compared with other models. Performance is measured in accuracy(%). Models are categorized into five classes. The first block is Neural Bag-of-Words (NBOW) model. The second is Paragraph Vector (PV). The third category is RecNN models. CNN models are the fourth block, and the last category is RNN models and their variations. **NBOW:** The NBOW sums the word vectors and applies a non-linearity followed by a softmax classification layer. **PV:** Distributed representations of sentences and documents [11]. **RAE:** Recursive Autoencoders with pre-trained word vectors from Wikipedia [1]. **MV-RNN:** Matrix-Vector RecNN with parse trees [2]. **RNTN:** Recursive Neural Tensor Network with tensor-based feature function and parse trees [3]. **DCNN:** Dynamic CNN with k-max pooling [7]. **CNN-non-static:** CNN with fine-tuned pretrained word-embeddings [8]. **CNN-MC:** CNN with static pretrained and fine-tuned pretrained word-embeddings [8]. **LSTM:** Standard Long Short-Term Memory Network [4]. **BLSTM:** Bidirectional LSTM [4]. **Tree-LSTM:** Tree-Structured LSTM [4]. **Multi-Task:** RNN for Text Classification with Multi-Task Learning [5]. **LSTMN:** Long Short-Term Memory Network for machine reading [6].

Model	SST-1	SST-2	TREC	IMDB
NBOW	42.4	80.5	88.2	-
PV [11]	48.7	87.8	-	**92.6**
RAE [1]	43.2	82.4	-	-
MV-RNN [2]	44.4	82.9	-	-
RNTN [3]	45.7	85.4	-	-
DCNN [7]	48.5	86.8	93.0	-
CNN-non-static [8]	48.0	87.2	93.6	-
CNN-MC [8]	47.4	88.1	92.2	-
LSTM [4]	45.8	86.7	-	-
BLSTM [4]	49.1	86.8	-	-
Tree-LSTM [4]	51.0	88.0	-	-
Multi-Task [5]	49.6	87.9	-	91.3
LSTMN [6]	49.3	87.3	-	-
HA-BLSTM	**51.5**	**88.9**	**93.8**	91.5

RNN (LSTM), which is not effective to model a long text due to the excessively long chain of information transmission even with several gating mechanisms. Furthermore, the long text will lead to a low-variance attention distribution by the softmax operation over all the words. In an extreme condition, the attention distribution over a large number of words will tend to be uniform, which will lose its discriminatory effectiveness.

Visualization of Attention. We visualize the local and global attention mechanisms to validate their ability to select informative words or phrases and to distinguish the suitable levels of representations for higher classification accuracy.

Dateset: TREC Prediction: Location
What is the location of the Sea of Tranquility ?
Dateset: TREC Prediction: Human
What person 's head is on a dime ?

Dateset: SST-1 Prediction: Very Positive
I loved it !
Dateset: SST-1 Prediction: Very Negative
Proves that a movie about goodness is not the same thing as a good movie .

Fig. 3. The darker the color, the greater the weight.

Figure 3 shows that our model can capture discriminatory words for topic classification in the TREC dataset. For example, our model accurately finds out the key words *location* and *Sea* in the first sentence with label 'Location'. For the second sentence with label 'Human', our model localizes the word *person*. Meanwhile, the local attention mechanism also works well for sentiment classification in the SST-1 dataset. Note that our model can find out the sentiment words like *love* and *!* in the third sentence. However the words *goodness* and *good*, which also carrying strong sentiment, are paid little attention. That is, our model can handle complex context to pay more attention to the word *not* in the fourth sentence, which has a label of 'Very Negative'.

To demonstrate the effectiveness of the global attention mechanism, we propose a Hierarchical Local-Attention BLSTM (HLA-BLSTM) without global-attention to compare with HA-BLSTM. Figure 4(a) shows the classification accuracy of HA-BLSTM and HLA-BLSTM. Obviously, HA-BLSTM works better than HLA-BLSTM, especially on SST-1 and TREC datasets. It indicates that our global attention mechanism can accurately find out the representation in which level is informative.

Generally, representations in different hierarchical levels have different degrees of abstraction. The lower-level representations only contain semantics of a single word or phrase, while the higher-level representations would be about the compositional semantics or topic-level information. As showed in Fig. 4(b), we get the average weight of different levels over the four datasets. In different datasets, there is a little difference in the attention distributions over different

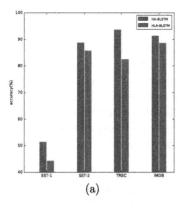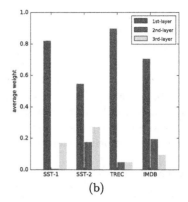

(a)   (b)

Fig. 4. (a) Classification accuracy of HA-BLSTM and HLA-BLSTM. (b) The average weight of different levels over the four datasets.

layers. The first layer undertakes the highest average weight over all datasets, which contributes the most information to the classification task. The higher the layer is, the higher the level of abstraction is, and the less its contributions to the final classification. The reason for the less effectiveness in the higher-level layer may be caused by the low nonlinearity of the textual data and the richness of semantics of a single word. In Computer Vision (CV) which usually adopts a large number of layers for higher abstraction [15], the value of a single pixel can mean nothing, and a block of pixels with compositional semantics may give us a little information and the whole image does mean entire semantics [16]. However, a single word can contain rich semantic information, and a large number of layers in neural network seem to be unnecessary in NLP.

Effect of the Number of Layers. Figure 5 shows the effect of the number of layers among the four datasets. We can see that three-layer BLSTM architecture achieves the best performance compared with deeper or shallower hierarchical structures. Specially, one-layer BLSTM does not get a promising accuracy due to the missing of global attention. In our opinion, the increasing layers of networks indeed learn the semantic representation with high-level abstraction, thus leading to a better performance. However, it tends to be worse when a much deeper hierarchical structure (with more than three layers) is adopted, which is unnecessary for text modeling and introduces redundant noises.

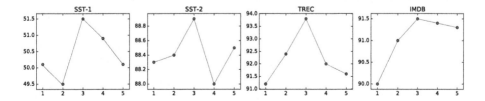

Fig. 5. The classification accuracy of models with different layers from one to five.

4   Conclusion

In this paper, we propose HA-BLSTM, Hierarchical Attention BLSTM for modeling sentences and documents. HA-BLSTM adopts a hierarchical structure to represent a text by a multi-scale summarization instead of a fixed-length vector. The application of BLSTM promotes features mixed better. The local and global attention mechanisms can select the highly informative components and representations of a sequence respectively. The experimental results demonstrate that our model performs better than previous methods.

Acknowledgments. This work is funded in part by the Chinese 863 Program (grant No. 2015AA015403), the Key Project of Tianjin Natural Science Foundation (grant No. 15JCZDJC31100), the Tianjin Younger Natural Science Foundation (Grant no: 14JCQNJC00400), the Major Project of Chinese National Social Science Fund (grant No. 14ZDB153) and MSCA-ITN-ETN - European Training Networks Project (grant No. 721321, QUARTZ).

References

1. Socher, R., Pennington, J., Huang, E.H., Ng, A.Y., Manning, C.D.: Semi-supervised recursive autoencoders for predicting sentiment distributions. In: Proceedings of the Conference on Empirical Methods in Natural Language Processing, pp. 151–161. Association for Computational Linguistics (2011)
2. Socher, R., Huval, B., Manning, C.D., Ng, A.Y.: Semantic compositionality through recursive matrix-vector spaces. In: Proceedings of the 2012 Joint Conference on Empirical Methods in Natural Language Processing and Computational Natural Language Learning, pp. 1201–1211. Association for Computational Linguistics (2012)
3. Socher, R., Perelygin, A., Wu, J.Y., Chuang, J., Manning, C.D., Ng, A.Y., Potts, C., et al.: Recursive deep models for semantic compositionality over a sentiment treebank. In: Proceedings of the Conference on Empirical Methods in Natural Language Processing (EMNLP), vol. 1631, p. 1642. Citeseer (2013)
4. Tai, K.S., Socher, R., Manning, C.D.: Improved semantic representations from tree-structured long short-term memory networks. arXiv preprint (2015). arXiv:1503.00075
5. Liu, P., Qiu, X., Huang, X.: Recurrent neural network for text classification with multi-task learning. arXiv preprint (2016). arXiv:1605.05101
6. Cheng, J., Dong, L., Lapata, M.: Long short-term memory-networks for machine reading. arXiv preprint (2016). arXiv:1601.06733
7. Kalchbrenner, N., Grefenstette, E., Blunsom, P.: A convolutional neural network for modelling sentences. arXiv preprint (2014). arXiv:1404.2188
8. Kim, Y.: Convolutional neural networks for sentence classification. arXiv preprint (2014). arXiv:1408.5882
9. Hochreiter, S., Schmidhuber, J.: Long short-term memory. Neural Comput. **9**(8), 1735–1780 (1997)
10. Yang, Z., Yang, D., Dyer, C., He, X., Smola, A.J., Hovy, E.H.: Hierarchical attention networks for document classification. In: HLT-NAACL, pp. 1480–1489 (2016)
11. Le, Q.V., Mikolov, T.: Distributed representations of sentences and documents. ICML **14**, 1188–1196 (2014)

12. Li, X., Roth, D.: Learning question classifiers. In: Proceedings of the 19th International Conference on Computational Linguistics, vol. 1, pp. 1–7. Association for Computational Linguistics (2002)
13. Maas, A.L., Daly, R.E., Pham, P.T., Huang, D., Ng, A.Y., Potts, C.: Learning word vectors for sentiment analysis. In: Proceedings of the 49th Annual Meeting of the Association for Computational Linguistics: Human Language Technologies, vol. 1, pp. 142–150. Association for Computational Linguistics (2011)
14. Mikolov, T., Sutskever, I., Chen, K., Corrado, G.S., Dean, J.: Distributed representations of words and phrases and their compositionality. In: Advances in Neural Information Processing Systems, pp. 3111–3119 (2013)
15. He, K., Zhang, X., Ren, S., Sun, J.: Deep residual learning for image recognition. In: Proceedings of the IEEE Conference on Computer Vision and Pattern Recognition, pp. 770–778 (2016)
16. Zeng, D., Liu, K., Lai, S., Zhou, G., Zhao, J., et al.: Relation classification via convolutional deep neural network. In: COLING. pp. 2335–2344 (2014)

Bi-Directional LSTM with Quantum Attention Mechanism for Sentence Modeling

Xiaolei Niu, Yuexian Hou$^{(\boxtimes)}$, and Panpan Wang

School of Computer Science and Technology, Tianjin University, Tianjin, China
{xlniu,yxhou,panpan_tju}@tju.edu.cn

Abstract. Bi-directional LSTM (BLSTM) often utilizes Attention Mechanism (AM) to improve the ability of modeling sentences. But additional parameters within AM may lead to difficulties of model selection and BLSTM training. To solve the problem, this paper redefines AM from a novel perspective of the quantum cognition and proposes a parameter-free Quantum AM (QAM). Furthermore, we make a quantum interpretation for BLSTM with Two-State Vector Formalism (TSVF) and find the similarity between sentence understanding and quantum Weak Measurement (WM) under TSVF. Weak value derived from WM is employed to represent the attention for words in a sentence. Experiments show that QAM based BLSTM outperforms common AM (CAM) [1] based BLSTM on most classification tasks discussed in this paper.

Keywords: Attention mechanism · Two-state vector formalism · Weak measurement · Quantum theory

1 Introduction

Recently, neural network based sentence modeling approaches have shown excellent abilities in modeling sentences, such as Recursive Neural Networks (RecNN) [2], Recurrent Neural Networks (RNN) [3] and Convolutional Neural Networks (CNN) [4]. Among these models, LSTM (a kind of RNN) has shown its excellent ability to model the word order and long-term dependencies in sentences. Bi-directional LSTM (BLSTM) was proposed to model the context dependency from past and future. To achieve sentence vectors, BLSTM averages the hidden states of all nodes.[1] However, not all of those hidden nodes have equal importance for sentence representation. Attention Mechanism (AM) was thus introduced to weight the importance of hidden nodes in BLSTM [1]. Although AM can improve the ability of BLSTM for modeling sentences, the additional parameters are also introduced and may cause difficulties of model selection and BLSTM training.

Therefore, this paper attempts to design an economical and effective AM from the perspective of quantum cognition. The new AM will reduce the parameters and the complexity of model selection on the premise of ensuring the

---

[1] http://deeplearning.net/tutorial/lstm.html.

© Springer International Publishing AG 2017
D. Liu et al. (Eds.): ICONIP 2017, Part II, LNCS 10635, pp. 178–188, 2017.
https://doi.org/10.1007/978-3-319-70096-0_19

competitiveness of the model. We regard sentence modeling as the process of human understanding of sentences, which is a cognitive activity. Quantum Theory (QT) is widely used to explain cognitive activities in psychology and cognition science. Wang et al. clarified the potential of using QT to build models of cognition from three aspects: *Why apply quantum concepts to human cognition? How is quantum cognitive modeling different from traditional cognitive modeling? What cognitive processes have been modeled using a quantum account?* The applications of using QT to explain or model cognitive activities have been proposed [5]. Bruza et al. used quantum probability theories to address cognitive phenomena that have been proven recalcitrant to model by means of classical probability theory [6]. Therefore, it is feasible and necessary to model AM from the perspective of quantum cognition.

Before modeling a Quantum Attention Mechanism (QAM), we find the similarity between BLSTM and Two-State Vector Formalism (TSVF). TSVF is a recently concerned formalism for QT. It considers a more complete description for a quantum state [7–9]. The standard QT assumes that a system at a given time t is described completely by a quantum state $|\Psi\rangle$ [10]. Aharonov, Bergmann, Lebowitz (ABL) proposed the TSVF of quantum mechanics, which describes a system at a given time t by a two-state vector $\langle\Phi||\Psi\rangle$ [11]. In TSVF, the quantum state $|\Psi\rangle$ and $\langle\Phi|$ describe the information from history and future respectively. That is, TSVF models the effect on current system state from both the history information and the future information. It is a natural analogy with the exist of forward propagation information and backward propagation information in BLSTM. Therefore, we try to use TSVF to model the effect on current attention from both history and future information.

Human's comprehension of the sentence will gradually change with reading the words one by one. The above change of human's cognition is called cognitive shift [12]. To understand the sentence, people would subconsciously judge the importance of the key words when reading the sentence. The judgement can be seen as a Quantum Measurement (QM). There are two kinds of QM: Standard Quantum Measurement (SQM) and Weak Measurement (WM), and the latter is the generalization of the former [13]. After the measurement, SQM will make the measured system collapse, while WM only makes the system state biased slightly. Therefore, WM can be used to model the measurement process which exerts little effect on the quantum system to be measured. Because the process of human understanding of sentences is gentle, and human's comprehension of the sentence would not be changed a lot after reading a word in most cases. Hence, we assume that the process of the above cognitive shift is often gradual, with a small amount of mutation. It turns out that the general WM framework is more appropriate to model this cognitive shift. In WM, weak value is the statistical average value of the measurement results. Consequently, we propose a Quantum Attention Mechanism (QAM) which employs WM rather than SQM to model the process of human understanding of sentences, and weak value under TSVF to represent the degree of importance of words for human understanding of the sentence.

Our contributions can be summarized as follows: First, we propose a Quantum Attention Mechanism (QAM) which models the different importance of words from a cognitive perspective and does not introduce additional parameters. Second, we qualitatively and quantitatively analyse that QAM is more effective and efficient than CAM for the improvement of the performance. Third, we conduct a large number of experimental studies on five benchmark datasets to show that our mechanism is quite competitive compared with the previous mechanism.

2   Bi-Directional LSTM

LSTM was presented [14] to specially address the problem about learning long-term dependencies. As shown in Fig. 1, the LSTM unit retains a separate memory cell inside that updates and exposes its content only when considered necessary. At each time step t, we define the LSTM units to be a collection of vectors in R^l: an input gate i_t, a forget gate f_t, an output gate o_t, a memory cell c_t and a hidden state h_t. The entries of the gating vectors i_t, f_t and o_t are in $[0, 1]$. The transition equations of LSTM are the following:

$$i_t = \sigma\left(W_i x_t + U_i h_{t-1} + b_i\right), \tag{1}$$

$$f_t = \sigma\left(W_f x_t + U_f h_{t-1} + b_f\right), \tag{2}$$

$$o_t = \sigma\left(W_o x_t + U_o h_{t-1} + b_o\right), \tag{3}$$

$$z_t = \tanh\left(W_z x_t + U_z h_{t-1} + b_z\right), \tag{4}$$

$$c_t = i_t \odot z_t + f_t \odot c_{t-1}, \tag{5}$$

$$h_t = o_t \odot \tanh\left(c_t\right), \tag{6}$$

where x_t is the input at the current time step, σ denotes the logistic sigmoid function and $\odot$ denotes elementwise multiplication. W_i, W_f, W_o, $W_z \in R^{l \times d}$,

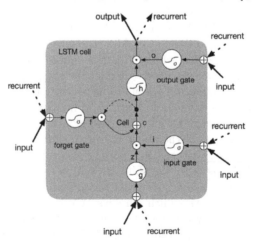

Fig. 1. Schematic of LSTM unit.

U_i, U_f, U_o, $U_z \in R^{l \times l}$ and b_i, b_f, b_o, $b_z \in R^l$ are trainable parameters. Here, l and d are the dimensionality of hidden states and input respectively. As we can see, the forget gate controls the amount of which each unit of the memory cell is erased, the input gate determines how much each unit is updated, and the exposure of the internal memory state is determined by the output gate.

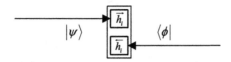

Fig. 2. TSVF in BLSTM.

In this paper, we adopt BLSTM to take advantage of additional backward information and thus enhance the memory capability. We encode the hidden state of a BLSTM unit as following:

$$h_i = \left[\overrightarrow{h_i} \oplus \overleftarrow{h_i} \right], \tag{7}$$

where $\overrightarrow{h_i}$ and $\overleftarrow{h_i}$ are the same as h_t in formula (6), the $\oplus$ indicates concatenation operation. For a node in BLSTM, it acquires the information from both history and future. The above feature of BLSTM is similar to the TSVF (see Fig. 2), which has the **pre-state** $|\Psi\rangle$ and the **post state** $\langle\Phi|$.[2] Thus, we attempt to model the effect on the current attention from both history information and future information through the TSVF.

3   Model

3.1   The Architecture of Our Model

The overall architecture of our model is shown in Fig. 3. In the case of text classification, for an input sequence of length T and the corresponding class $y^{(j)}$ ($j \in [1, m]$, m is the number of training sentences), we first represent each word $x_i \in R^{K_v}$ into its corresponding vector $E_x x_i \in R^d$, where $E_x \in R^{d \times K_v}$, K_y is the vocabulary size of the dataset, and d is the dimensionality of word embeddings. That is, the embeddings are the inputs of BLSTM, whose outputs are the hidden states $h_i \in R^{2l}$. Then, through the common Attention Mechanism (CAM) or the Quantum Attention Mechanism (QAM), the hidden states h_i are integrated into a sentence vector $h \in R^{2l}$. Finally, we calculate the probability of obtaining the corresponding class $y^{(j)}$ through logistic regression.

---

[2] In QT, the quantum probability space is encapsulated in an Hilbert space $\mathbb{H}^n$, which is an abstract vector space processing the structure of the inner product. A finite dimensional space is sufficient for the work reported in this paper. Thus, we limit our researches to a finite real space $\mathbb{R}^n$. With the Dirac's notation, a quantum state can be written as a column vector $|\Psi\rangle$, whose conjugate transpose is a row vector $\langle\Psi|$.

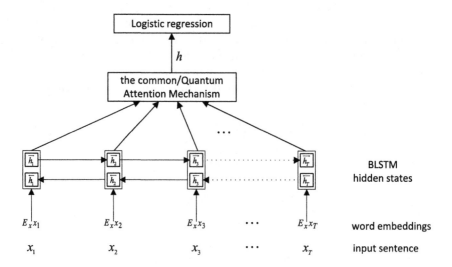

Fig. 3. The overall diagram of the model.

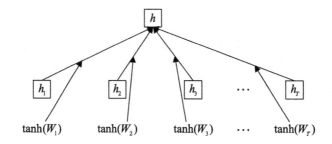

Fig. 4. Quantum Attention Mechanism.

3.2 Quantum Attention Mechanism

Analogy to the Weak Measurement (WM) [13] in physics, in QAM (See Fig. 4), we regard human's understanding to the meaning of the sentence as the **system**, the word embeddings as the **observable variables**, and the importance of the words to the sentence comprehension as the **measurement result**. The **pre-state** is the forward memory cell $c_i^{in} = \vec{c_i} \in R^l$ which contains the information of all words in the past, the **post-state** is the backward memory cell $c_i^{fin} = \overleftarrow{c_i} \in R^l$ which contains the information of all words in the future. Thus, the weak value under the Two-State Vector Formalism (TSVF) is

$$W_i = \frac{\langle c_i^{fin} | E_x x_i | c_i^{in} \rangle}{\langle c_i^{fin} | c_i^{in} \rangle} \tag{8}$$

which can be regarded as the degree of importance of the words to understand the meaning of the sentence at the statistical level.

As a result of several huge weak values produced by the above formula, we apply a non-linear transformation to the weak value:

$$w_i = \tanh(W_i) \tag{9}$$

Finally, QAM computes the sentence vector h as follows:

$$h = \sum_i w_i h_i \tag{10}$$

4   Experiments

4.1   Datasets

We test our model on five benchmarks. Summary statistics of the datasets are in Table 1.

Table 1. Statistics of the five datasets used in this paper. CV means there was no standard train/test split and thus 10-fold CV is used.

Dataset	Train size	Dev. size	Test size	Class	Average length	Vocabulary size
MR	10662	-	CV	2	21	20 K
SST-1	8544	1101	2210	5	19	18 K
SST-2	6920	872	1821	2	18	15 K
Subj	10000	-	CV	2	21	21 K
TREC	5452	-	500	6	10	9.4 K

MR Movie reviews dataset with one sentence per review. The task is to detect positive/negative reviews [15].[3]

SST-1 Stanford Sentiment Treebank is an extension of MR, re-labeled by [2]. The objective is to classify a review as fine-grained labels (very negative, negative, neutral, positive, very positive).[4]

SST-2 Same as SST-1 but with neutral reviews removed and binary labels.

Subj Subjectivity dataset where the task is to classify a sentence as being subjective or objective [17].

TREC Question classification dataset [18]. The task involves classifying a question into 6 question types (abbreviation, description, entity, human, location, and numeric value).[5]

---

[3] https://www.cs.cornell.edu/people/pabo/movie-review-data/.

[4] http://nlp.stanford.edu/sentiment/ Data is actually provided at the phrase level. Hence both phrases and sentences are used to train the model, but only sentences are scored at test time [2,4,16]. Thus the training set is an order of magnitude larger than listed in Table 1.

[5] http://cogcomp.cs.illinois.edu/Data/QA/QC/.

4.2   Hyperparameters and Training

In all of the experiments, we adopt the publicly available word2vec vectors, which are pre-trained on 100 billion words from Google News. The vectors have dimensionality of 300 and are trained using the continuous bag-of-words architecture [19]. Words that do not present in the set of pre-trained words are initialized randomly. And the word embeddings are fine-tuned during training to improve the performance. We use 300 as the dimensionality of hidden units. And dropout rate is 0.5, mini-batch size is 64. We choose these hyper-parameters which achieve the best performance on the development set for the final evaluation.

Early stopping strategy on dev sets is employed to prevent overfitting. We apply dropout in the fully connected layer of logistic regression, which is before the softmax layer of logistic regression. The objective of our model is to minimize the cross-entropy error of the predicted and true distributions. The object is to minimize the objective function:

$$J(\theta) = -\frac{1}{m} \sum_{j=1}^{m} \log P_{y^{(j)}}^{(j)} \tag{11}$$

where $y^{(j)}$ is the corresponding category, θ denotes all the trainable parameters of our model. Examples are padded to the longest sequence in each batch and masks are generated to help identify the padded region. For datasets without a standard dev set, we randomly select 10% of the training data as the dev set. Training is done through stochastic gradient descent over shuffled mini-batches with the Adadelta update rule.

4.3   Results

Overall Performance. As showed in Table 2, Quantum Attention Mechanism based BLSTM (QAM-BLSTM) achieves excellent performance on four out of five tasks compared with the common Attention Mechanism based BLSTM (CAM-BLSTM) and other methods. In the tasks of both topic classification (e.g. TREC) and sentiment classification (e.g. SST-1, STT-2, and Subj), QAM-BLSTM shows a better performance than CAM-BLSTM. There are two reasons to obtain the above experimental results: First, QAM has no extra parameters introduced by CAM and reduces the complexity of model selection. Second, QAM can capture the forward and backward information in the forward and backward memory cell $\overrightarrow{c_i}$ and $\overleftarrow{c_i}$, while CAM does not utilize any contextual information.

QAM-BLSTM gets a lower accuracy than CAM-BLSTM in the task of MR, whose training set is bigger than the other four, as showed in Table 2. The main reason maybe is that the bigger training set makes the additional parameters of CAM learn more information. While the other four datasets do not have so much data to train the additional parameters of CAM.

Table 2. Experiment results of QAM-BLSTM compared with CAM-BLSTM and other methods. The AM in CAM-BLSTM is the same as the AM in [1]. Performance is measured in accuracy(%). **RAE**: Recursive Autoencoders with pre-trained word vectors from Wikipedia [20]. **MV-RNN**: Matrix-Vector RecNN with parse trees [21]. **RNTN**: Recursive Neural Tensor Network with tensor-based feature function and parse trees [2]. **DCNN**: Dynamic CNN with k-max pooling [4]. **NBOW**: The NBOW sums the word vectors and applies a non-linearity followed by a softmax classiffcation layer. **Sent-Parser**: Sentiment analysis-specific parser [22]. **Tree-CRF**: Dependency tree with Conditional Random Fields [23].

Model	MR	SST-1	SST-2	Subj	TREC
CAM-BLSTM [1]	**80.0**	48.7	86.2	92.0	92.0
QAM-BLSTM	79.8	**49.8**	**87.0**	**92.3**	**93.6**
RAE [20]	77.7	43.2	82.4	-	-
MV-RNN [21]	79.0	44.4	82.9	-	-
RNTN [2]	-	45.7	85.4	-	-
DCNN [4]	-	48.5	86.8	-	93.0
NBOW	-	42.4	80.5	-	88.2
Sent-Parser [22]	79.5	-	84.7	-	-
Tree-CRF [23]	77.3	-	-	-	-

Dataset : SST-2   **Actual category** : negative
CAM : Arguably the year 's silliest and most incoherent movie .
(Prediction category : negative, Prediction probability : 0.90)
QAM : Arguably the year 's silliest and most incoherent movie .
(Prediction category : negative, Prediction probability : 0.95)

Dataset : SST-2   **Actual category** : negative
CAM : Frenetic but not really funny .
(Prediction category : positive, Prediction probability : 0.73)
QAM : Frenetic but not really funny .
(Prediction category : negative, Prediction probability : 0.61)

Dataset : SST-2   **Actual category** : positive
CAM : While this film is not in the least surprising , it is still ultimately very satisfying .
(Prediction category : positive, Prediction probability : 0.88)
QAM : While this film is not in the least surprising , it is still ultimately very satisfying .
(Prediction category : positive, Prediction probability : 0.65)

Fig. 5. Visualization of Attention. The darker the color, the greater the weight. The actual category is given by the dataset, the prediction category is predicted by the model and the prediction probability is the probability of achieving the prediction category.

Visualization of Attention. We visualize CAM and QAM to compare their ability to select informative words for higher classification accuracy, as shown in Fig. 5. We select three typical sentences from SST-2 dataset to clarify that QAM does better on capturing informative words than CAM.

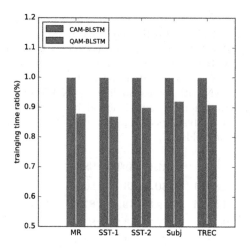

Fig. 6. Training time ratio of CAM-BLSTM and QAM-BLSTM. We assume the training time ratio of CAM-BLSTM is 100%, and the training time ratio of QAM-BLSTM is the proportion of the training time of QAM-BLSTM in the training time of CAM-BLSTM.

For the first sentence, CAM and QAM could accurately find out the sentiment words "silliest" and "incoherent", and the two models both give the right predictions. For the second sentence, QAM-BLSTM gives the right prediction while CAM-BLSTM gives the wrong prediction. CAM and QAM can both find the sentiment words "Frenetic" and "funny", and QAM gives lower weight to the above words than CAM. The reason is that QAM finds and gives more weight to the transitional word "but" and the negative word "not", which are not detected by CAM. That is, QAM can handle more complex contexts than CAM. The above conjecture could also be verified by the third sentence. The two models give the right predictions while the prediction probability given by QAM-BLSTM is lower than CAM-BLSTM, which seems to indicate that CAM-BLSTM does better than QAM-BLSTM on the classification task. However, the sentiment of the first part of the sentence is negative, which is detected by QAM through the high weight given to the word "not". Finally, QAM-BLSTM still gives the right prediction, despite with the lower prediction probability than CAM-BLSTM.

Training Time. Figure 6 shows the training time ratio of the two models. Taken as a whole, the training time of QAM-BLSTM is shorter than CAM-BLSTM as a result of the former without the additional parameters which are introduced by the latter. On average, the training time of QAM-BLSTM is 90% of the training time of CAM-BLSTM, which indicates that the former is more efficient than the latter.

5   Conclusion

In this paper, we propose a parameter-free Attention Mechanism (AM): QAM, Quantum Attention Mechanism for modeling sentences more effectively and efficiently. We first employ Weak Measurement (WM) to model the process of human understanding of sentences from a quantum cognitive perspective. The weak value under the Two-State Vector Formalism (TSVF) represents the importance of words in the sentence. Experimental results demonstrate that QAM based BLSTM (QAM-BLSTM) performs better than common AM based BLSTM (CAM-BLSTM) for modeling sentences in most classification tasks. Qualitative and quantitative results show that QAM is more effective and efficient than CAM in handling complex contexts and training time.

Acknowledgments. This work is funded in part by the Chinese 863 Program (grant No. 2015AA015403), the Key Project of Tianjin Natural Science Foundation (grant No. 15JCZDJC31100), the Tianjin Younger Natural Science Foundation (Grant no: 14JCQNJC00400), the Major Project of Chinese National Social Science Fund (grant No. 14ZDB153) and MSCA-ITN-ETN - European Training Networks Project (grant No. 721321, QUARTZ).

References

1. Yang, Z., Yang, D., Dyer, C., He, X., Smola, A.J., Hovy, E.H.: Hierarchical attention networks for document classification. In: HLT-NAACL, pp. 1480–1489 (2016)
2. Socher, R., Perelygin, A., Wu, J.Y., Chuang, J., Manning, C.D., Ng, A.Y., Potts, C., et al.: Recursive deep models for semantic compositionality over a sentiment treebank. In: Proceedings of the Conference on Empirical Methods in Natural Language Processing (EMNLP), vol. 1631, p. 1642. Citeseer (2013)
3. Liu, P., Qiu, X., Huang, X.: Recurrent neural network for text classification with multi-task learning. arXiv preprint arXiv:1605.05101 (2016)
4. Kalchbrenner, N., Grefenstette, E., Blunsom, P.: A convolutional neural network for modelling sentences. arXiv preprint arXiv:1404.2188 (2014)
5. Wang, Z., Busemeyer, J.R., Atmanspacher, H., Pothos, E.M.: The potential of using quantum theory to build models of cognition. Top. Cogn. Sci. **5**(4), 672–688 (2013)
6. Bruza, P.D., Wang, Z., Busemeyer, J.R.: Quantum cognition: a new theoretical approach to psychology. Trends Cogn. Sci. **19**(7), 383–393 (2015)
7. Aharonov, Y., Vaidman, L.: Complete description of a quantum system at a given time. J. Phys. A: Math. Gen. **24**(10), 2315 (1991)
8. Ravon, T., Vaidman, L.: The three-box paradox revisited. J. Phys. A: Math. Theor. **40**(11), 2873 (2007)
9. Gibran, B.: Causal realism in the philosophy of mind. Essays Philos. **15**(2), 5 (2014)
10. Aharonov, Y., Vaidman, L.: The two-state vector formalism: an updated review. In: Muga, J., Mayato, R.S., Egusquiza, Í. (eds.) Time in Quantum Mechanics. Lecture Notes in Physics, vol. 734. pp. 399–447. Springer, Heidelberg (2008). doi:10.1007/978-3-540-73473-4_13
11. Aharonov, Y., Bergmann, P.G., Lebowitz, J.L.: Time symmetry in the quantum process of measurement. Phys. Rev. **134**(6B), B1410 (1964)
12. Latta, R.L.: The Basic Humor Process: A Cognitive-shift Theory and the Case Against Incongruity, vol. 5. Walter de Gruyter (1999)
13. Tamir, B., Cohen, E.: Introduction to weak measurements and weak values. Quanta **2**(1), 7–17 (2013)

14. Hochreiter, S., Schmidhuber, J.: Long short-term memory. Neural Comput. **9**(8), 1735–1780 (1997)
15. Pang, B., Lee, L.: Seeing stars: exploiting class relationships for sentiment categorization with respect to rating scales. In: Proceedings of the 43rd Annual Meeting on Association for Computational Linguistics, pp. 115–124. Association for Computational Linguistics (2005)
16. Le, Q.V., Mikolov, T.: Distributed representations of sentences and documents. In: ICML 2014, pp. 1188–1196 (2014)
17. Pang, B., Lee, L.: A sentimental education: sentiment analysis using subjectivity summarization based on minimum cuts. In: Proceedings of the 42nd Annual Meeting on Association for Computational Linguistics, p. 271. Association for Computational Linguistics (2004)
18. Li, X., Roth, D.: Learning question classifiers. In: Proceedings of the 19th International Conference on Computational Linguistics, vol. 1, pp. 1–7. Association for Computational Linguistics (2002)
19. Mikolov, T., Sutskever, I., Chen, K., Corrado, G.S., Dean, J.: Distributed representations of words and phrases and their compositionality. In: Advances in Neural Information Processing Systems, pp. 3111–3119 (2013)
20. Socher, R., Pennington, J., Huang, E.H., Ng, A.Y., Manning, C.D.: Semi-supervised recursive autoencoders for predicting sentiment distributions. In: Proceedings of the Conference on Empirical Methods in Natural Language Processing, pp. 151–161. Association for Computational Linguistics (2011)
21. Socher, R., Huval, B., Manning, C.D., Ng, A.Y.: Semantic compositionality through recursive matrix-vector spaces. In: Proceedings of the 2012 Joint Conference on Empirical Methods in Natural Language Processing and Computational Natural Language Learning, pp. 1201–1211. Association for Computational Linguistics (2012)
22. Dong, L., Wei, F., Liu, S., Zhou, M., Xu, K.: A statistical parsing framework for sentiment classification. Comput. Linguist. (2015)
23. Nakagawa, T., Inui, K., Kurohashi, S.: Dependency tree-based sentiment classification using CRFS with hidden variables. In: Human Language Technologies: The 2010 Annual Conference of the North American Chapter of the Association for Computational Linguistics, pp. 786–794. Association for Computational Linguistics (2010)

An Efficient Binary Search Based Neuron Pruning Method for ConvNet Condensation

Boyu Zhang[1(✉)], A.K. Qin[2], and Jeffrey Chan[1]

[1] RMIT University, Melbourne, VIC, Australia
{zhang.boyu,jeffrey.chan}@rmit.edu.au
[2] Swinburne University of Technology, Melbourne, VIC, Australia
kqin@swin.edu.au

Abstract. Convolutional neural networks (CNNs) have been widely applied in the field of computer vision. Nowadays, the architecture of CNNs is becoming more and more complex, involving more layers and more neurons per layer. The augmented depth and width of CNNs will lead to greatly increased computational and memory costs, which may limit CNNs practical utility. However, as demonstrated in previous research, CNNs of complex architecture may contain considerable redundancy in terms of hidden neurons. In this work, we propose a magnitude based binary neuron pruning method which can selectively prune neurons to shrink the network size while keeping the performance of the original model without pruning. Compared to some existing neuron pruning methods, the proposed method can achieve higher compression rate while automatically determining the number of neurons to be pruned per hidden layer in an efficient way.

Keywords: Deep learning · Convolutional neural network · Condensation · Pruning

1 Introduction

Nowadays, convolutional neural networks (CNNs) have achieved great success on image recognition [1], object detection [2] problems. However, the state-of-the-art CNNs always have large quantities of parameters which need hundreds of megabytes for storage. In addition, such large number of parameters can make the testing process very time-consuming, energy-consuming and may demand large amount of RAM. All these problems make the CNNs hard to be deployed on mobile devices or chips whose ROM, RAM and computing ability are limited.

It has been shown there exists much redundancy [3] in CNNs, which is mainly caused by the large amount of parameters in the networks. Many prior researches [4–16] have tried to compress the CNNs while keeping comparative performance as the original model. These studies can be categorized as three directions,

- Network mimicking. The methods in this direction normally train a *"student"* network with much smaller size (e.g., *shallower* [4] or *FitNets* [15]) to mimic a pre-trained large-scale *"teacher"* model's behavior.

© Springer International Publishing AG 2017
D. Liu et al. (Eds.): ICONIP 2017, Part II, LNCS 10635, pp. 189–197, 2017.
https://doi.org/10.1007/978-3-319-70096-0_20

- Weight decomposition. These techniques use low-rank approximation [11,12] to factorize an *n-by-n* weight matrix to one *n-by-1* and one 1-by-n matrix so that both the number of parameters and FLOP decrease. This idea is also borrowed to build the Inception-V3 network [17].
- Neuron pruning. These methods [8,10,13,14,16,18] directly remove the insignificant parameters or neurons in a network to shrink the size. They often apply a retraining process after pruning in order to compensate the performance loss.

Methods in these three categories can cooperate with each other so that better compressing performance can be achieved.

Compared to other two categories, neuron pruning also helps for designing network architecture. When building a CNN, it's easy to set excessive neurons than it actually needs. These redundant neurons can make the network more vulnerable to over-fitting. With neuron pruning, we expect to prune those less important neurons and make the network more robust.

There are two important steps in neuron pruning methods, determining which neurons to prune and deciding the number of neurons to be pruned per layer. In this work, we apply an input and output weight magnitude based method to decide which neurons should be pruned. Compared to other neuron pruning methods, ours can achieve highest compression rate when keeping same or better model performance. Also, we propose an efficient binary search based pruning method to automatically decide the number of neurons per layer to be pruned while others need to manually set the number or prune neurons in an inefficient iterative way.

The structure of this paper is as follows, Sect. 2 introduces the related works. In Sect. 3, we present the details of proposed neuron pruning method. Section 4 shows our experimental results on Lenet-5 and VGG-16 model. Section 5 gives our conclusions.

2   Related Works

Neuron pruning is a straight-forward way to compress the network's size. Given a large-scale neural network, it tries to remove some unimportant neurons which cause least harm to the performance.

The first step of neuron pruning is to decide which neurons should be pruned [10,13,14,16]. The idea in [16] is to wire neuron pairs that have similar input weights in the same layer. [14] preserves those neurons whose weights are the most diverse from others and recover the performance by a re-weighting process. However, both [14] and [16] can only be applied on fully connected layer. [13] prunes the filters of CNN based on the absolute sum of their weights. [10] removes the neurons who generate the least activation on the training data. Nevertheless, [10] just takes the activation of neurons into account while neglecting their output connection weights. If the output connection weights of a neuron are significant, it's important even its activation is insignificant than others.

The second step of neuron pruning is to decide how many neurons should be pruned in one layer. [16] manually sets the number of pruning neurons. [13,14] prune several fixed percentages of neurons to observe the loss brought by pruning. [10] iteratively prunes a small portion of neurons before the loss exceed tolerance. The first three are hard to find the optimal number of neurons to be pruned and the last one can take too long to reach the optimal.

3   Neuron Pruning Method

The term *neuron* in the following part refers to either filter in convolutional layers or unit in fully connected layers. As shown in Fig. 1, when pruning a neuron, we will both prune its input and output connections. In a convolutional layer, it corresponds to prune the filter of a feature map and the kernels connected to it in the next layer's filters.

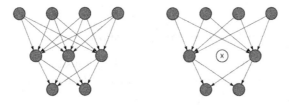

Fig. 1. Before and after pruning

3.1   Determining Which Neurons to Prune

In [13], it defines the importance of a neuron j in layer i by the absolute input weight sum $\sum |W_{i,j}|$. A lower value of $\sum |W_{i,j}|$ means the neuron is less important since it gives an expectation of the magnitude of the output. Neurons with smaller of that value tend to produce weaker activations compared to other neurons. However, even if a neuron's activation is weak, a large enough output connection weight can make it feed a significant input to next layer than other neurons with small output connection. Thus, when considering a neuron's influence on the network, we should take both its input and output connection into account. In this work, we define the importance of neuron j as Eq. 1 where IOM represents input and output magnitude. A neuron with small IOM tends to have less influence on the network than other neurons within the same layer and in a higher priority of being pruned.

$$IOM_j = \sum |W_{j,input}| + \sum |W_{j,output}| \tag{1}$$

Algorithm 1. Binary search based pruning

Input: network model M, original accuracy a, number of neurons n in current layer, minimal percentage of neuron counts $t\%$.

1: Set $p = 0$, $l = n$
2: calculate the IOM of each neuron
3: **while** $l > \max(t\%*n, 1)$ **do**
4:     prune $(p + \frac{1}{2}l)$ neurons of current layer with smallest IOM value in M to form new model M'
5:     retrain M'
6:     Evaluate the accuracy a' of M'
7:     **if** $a' < a$ **then**
8:         break
9:     **else**
10:         Set $p = p + \frac{1}{2}l$, $l = \frac{1}{2}l$
11:     **end if**
12: **end while**
Output: p

3.2 Binary Search Based Pruning Method

Previous works normally decide the number of neurons to be pruned empirically [16,18] or iteratively [10] before the performance decrease too much. [13] measures the sensitivity of layers by sequentially removing 10% neurons of one layer and record the trend of accuracy drop. Then it needs to manually decide what percentage of neurons should be pruned according to how drastically the accuracy drops. This process is a trial and error work, which can be time-consuming when pruning a large-scale network. For the iterative way in [10], it needs to set a parameter for deciding pruning intensity. This parameter needs to be fine-tuned since a lower intensity will lead to slow pruning process while higher intensity will decrease the performance dramatically. In this section, we propose a binary search based pruning (BSBP) method which can automatically decide how many neurons per layer should be pruned in a more efficient way.

The process is illustrated in Algorithm 1 where p and l represents pruned and remaining number of neurons. This idea is inspired by Binary Search which is an efficient searching method on an ordered array. At first, we sort neurons of the current layer by IOM value. Then in each pruning iteration, we try to prune p plus half of the left neurons, which is $\frac{1}{2}l$, and retrain. At the end of each iteration, the p and l will be updated. The algorithm will terminate when l is not higher than 1.

To find an optimal pruning numbers, the time complexity of our method is $O(log(n))$ while the empirical and iterative ways are $O(n)$. However, in practice, it can still take a lot of retraining times if every neuron counts when pruning a layer with excessive neurons. To balance the efficiency and accuracy, we can set a minimal percentage of neuron counted as $t\%$ of the number of neurons n in the layer. We can also set different $t\%$ for layers if the numbers of neurons diverse a lot in different layers. In this case, the stopping criteria turns to be $l \leq \max(t\% * n, 1)$.

4 Experiment

4.1 Experimental Setting

We will evaluate our method *BSBP-IOM* on two networks: LeNet-like net [19] on MNIST dataset and an Imagenet pretrained VGG-16 [20] model fine-tuned by Caltech256 dataset [21]. The baseline methods we compare with are *Network Trimming (NT)* [10] and *Pruning Filters for Efficient ConvNets (PFEC)* [13], which are also neuron pruning based methods and can prune the convolutional layers. Furthermore, we apply *BSBP* to decide the pruning number for *PFEC (BSBP-PFEC)* and compare it with *PFEC* and *BSBP-IOM* to show the efficiency of *BSBP* and the effectiveness of *IOM*.

When evaluating the performance of different pruning methods, there are two conflicting criteria which are accuracy after pruning A_p and compression rate R_c. Often, A_p decreases as R_c increases. In order to make the results comparable, we require the least accuracy after pruning should be no less than the original accuracy A_o, and the one who achieves higher R_c is better. Note this restriction is set to make different methods comparable and the R_c is possible not as high as previous works showed while they allow A_p to be lower than A_o.

To compare the efficiency of different methods, it's not straightforward since some algorithms may terminate quite early with a small number of neurons pruned so they will surely cost less retraining times. Here, we investigate the pruned number at the time step where there is one algorithm first stops. A larger pruned number at this step represents higher efficiency.

Our experiment is run on MXNet [22] and a desktop equipped with a GTX1080 GPU and an i7-7700k CPU.

4.2 Experiment on LeNet

The LeNet-like network we adopt has a structure of (20-50-500-10) where the first two are convolutional layers, the third is a fully-connected layer and the last is an output layer. This network is trained on the full training set of MNIST and achieves an accuracy of 99.169% on the testing set.

In terms of pruning parameter settings, we set the balance parameter $t\%$ as 2% for all layers in our method. For [13], when pruning single layer, it implements the prune-retrain process for nine times to prune 10% to 90% neurons to determine a layer's *sensitivity*. In this experiment, we follow the same process but stops when A_p is lower than A_o. For [10], we follow their prune-retrain process until A_p is lower than A_o. For retraining, we set epoch as 10 and learning rate as $1 * 10^{-3}$.

The layer-wise pruning result is shown in Fig. 2 and Table 1. In Fig. 2, we may find *BSBP-PFEC* is faster than *PFEC*, which proves the *BSBP* method

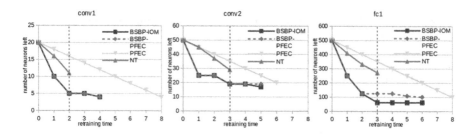

Fig. 2. Layer-wise pruning result

Table 1. Neurons Left (NL) and Compression Rate (CR) for LeNet condensation

Method	conv1		conv2		fc1	
	NL	CR	NL	CR	NL	CR
BSBP-IOM	4	**80.00%**	17	**66.00%**	62	**87.60%**
BSBP-PFEC	4	**80.00%**	19	62.00%	101	79.80%
PFEC	4	**80.00%**	20	60.00%	100	80.00%
NT	11	55.00%	29	42.00%	272	45.60%

is more efficient than the sequential way of *PFEC*. Also, Table 1 illustrates that our method *BSBP-IOM* can achieve higher or at least the same compression rate than any other baselines which shows the effectiveness of *IOM*. Although *NT* takes less retraining times, it decreases the model's performance drastically and terminates the iteration with a low compression rate.

4.3 Experiment on VGG-16

The VGG-16 model is fine-tuned on Caltech256 dataset[1] and achieves 77.47% top-1 accuracy on testing set. For retraining, we set a constant learning rate as $1 * 10^{-4}$ and train 5 epochs in each retraining process. Since layer conv5_3 and fc_6 account for 72.5% parameters, we first implement the pruning methods on these two layers. Furthermore, we take two intermediate layers, say conv2_2 and conv3_3, into account. The other settings are the same as Sect. 4.2.

The result is shown in Fig. 3 and Table 2. From this result, we can observe that *BSBP-IOM* can always obtain higher compression rate than other baselines which further proves the effectiveness of *IOM* pruning criteria. It's also noticeable that *BSBP-PFEC* is not as efficient as *PFEC* on layer conv2_2 and conv5_3. This is reasonable since there is only a few percentage of neurons can be pruned on these two layers and the sequential way will find the point faster than binary way. Once the layers are more robust to pruning like layer conv3_3 and fc_6, the binary way can always be more efficient than the sequential way.

---

[1] The fine-tuning process is the same as https://github.com/dmlc/mxnet-notebooks/blob/master/python/how_to/finetune.ipynb.

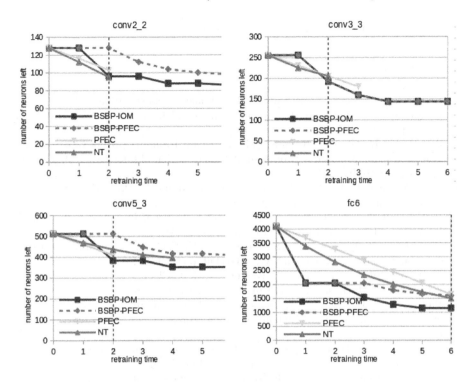

Fig. 3. Layer-wise pruning result

Table 2. Neurons Left (NL) and Compression Rate (CR) for VGG-16 condensation

Method	conv2_2		conv3_3		conv5_3		fc_6	
	NL	CR	NL	CR	NL	CR	NL	CR
BSBP-IOM	**86**	**32.81%**	**144**	**43.75%**	**352**	**31.25%**	**1152**	**71.88%**
BSBP-PFEC	98	23.44%	**144**	**43.75%**	408	20.31%	1600	60.94%
PFEC	103	19.53%	180	29.69%	410	19.92%	1639	59.99%
NT	95	25.78%	205	19.92%	397	22.46%	1504	63.28%

5   Conclusion and Discussion

In this work, we propose an input and output weight magnitude based pruning criteria. The experiments show that the output connection weights are also important when deciding whether a neuron should be pruned. Also, we develop a binary search based neuron pruning method which can automatically determine how many neurons per hidden layer should be pruned. The experimental results on LeNet-5 and VGG-16 show our method can achieve higher compression rate and is more efficient than baseline methods while keeping same or better performance than the original model.

Acknowledgements. This research is supported by Chinese Scholarship Council.

References

1. Krizhevsky, A., Sutskever, I., Hinton, G.E.: Imagenet classification with deep convolutional neural networks. In: Advances in Neural Information Processing Systems, pp. 1097–1105 (2012)
2. Ren, S., He, K., Girshick, R., Sun, J.: Faster r-cnn: Towards real-time object detection with region proposal networks. In: Advances in Neural Information Processing Systems, pp. 91–99 (2015)
3. Denil, M., Shakibi, B., Dinh, L., Ranzato, M., de Freitas, N.: Predicting parameters in deep learning. In: Nips, pp. 2148–2156 (2013)
4. Ba, L., Caurana, R.: Do deep nets really need to be deep? In: Advances in Neural Information Processing Systems 2014, pp. 1–6 (2014)
5. Chen, W., Wilson, J.T., Tyree, S., Weinberger, K.Q., Chen, Y.: Compressing Convolutional Neural Networks. arXiv:1506.04449, pp. 1–9 (2015)
6. Chen, W., Wilson, J.T., Tyree, S., Weinberger, K.Q., Chen, Y.: Compressing neural networks with the hashing trick. CoRR, abs/1504.04788 (2015)
7. Han, S., Mao, H., Dally, W.J.: Deep compression - compressing deep neural networks with pruning, trained quantization and Huffman coding. In: Iclr, pp. 1–13 (2016)
8. Han, S., Pool, J., Tran, J., Dally, W.J.: Learning both weights and connections for efficient neural networks. In: Nips, pp. 1135–1143 (2015)
9. Hinton, G., Vinyals, O., Dean, J.: Distilling the knowledge in a neural network. In: NIPS 2014 Deep Learning Workshop, pp. 1–9 (2015)
10. Hu, H., Peng, R., Tai, Y.W., Tang, C.K.: Network Trimming: A Data-Driven Neuron Pruning Approach towards Efficient Deep Architectures (2016)
11. Jaderberg, M., Vedaldi, A., Zisserman, A.: Speeding up Convolutional Neural Networks with Low Rank Expansions. arXiv preprint arXiv:1405.3866, p. 7 (2014)
12. Lebedev, V., Ganin, Y., Rakhuba1, M., Oseledets, I., Lempitsky, V.: Speeding-up convolutional neural networks using fine-tuned CP-Decomposition. In: Iclr, pp. 1–10 (2015)
13. Li, H., Kadav, A., Durdanovic, I., Samet, H., Graf, H.P.: Pruning Filters for Efficient ConvNets (2016)
14. Mariet, Z., Sra, S.: Diversity networks. In: Iclr, pp. 1–11 (2015)
15. Romero, A., Ballas, N., Kahou, S.E., Chassang, A., Gatta, C., Bengio, Y.: FitNets: Hints for Thin Deep Nets, pp. 1–13 (2014)
16. Srinivas, S., Babu, R.V., Education, S.: Data-free Parameter Pruning for Deep Neural Networks, pp. 1–12 (2015)
17. Szegedy, C., Vanhoucke, V., Ioffe, S., Shlens, J., Wojna, Z.: Rethinking the inception architecture for computer vision. In: Proceedings of the IEEE Conference on Computer Vision and Pattern Recognition, pp. 2818–2826 (2016)
18. He, T., Fan, Y., Qian, Y., Tan, T., Yu, K.: Reshaping deep neural network for fast decoding by node-pruning. In: 2014 IEEE International Conference on Acoustics, Speech and Signal Processing (ICASSP), pp. 245–249. IEEE (2014)
19. LeCun, Y., Bottou, L., Bengio, Y., Haffner, P.: Gradient-based learning applied to document recognition. Proc. IEEE **86**(11), 2278–2324 (1998)

20. Simonyan, K., Zisserman, A.: Very deep convolutional networks for large-scale image recognition. arXiv preprint arXiv:1409.1556 (2014)
21. Griffin, G., Holub, A., Perona, P.: Caltech-256 Object Category Dataset (2007)
22. Chen, T., Li, M., Li, Y., Lin, M., Wang, N., Wang, M., Xiao, T., Xu, B., Zhang, C., Zhang, Z.: Mxnet: a flexible and efficient machine learning library for heterogeneous distributed systems. arXiv preprint arXiv:1512.01274 (2015)

CNN-LSTM Neural Network Model for Quantitative Strategy Analysis in Stock Markets

Shuanglong Liu[1], Chao Zhang[2], and Jinwen Ma[1(✉)]

[1] Department of Information Science, School of Mathematical Sciences and LMAM,
Peking University, Beijing 100871, China
jwma@math.pku.edu.cn
[2] Academy for Advanced Interdisciplinary Studies, Peking University,
Beijing 100871, China

Abstract. In this paper, the convolutional neural network and long short-term memory (CNN-LSTM) neural network model is proposed to analyse the quantitative strategy in stock markets. Methodically, the CNN-LSTM neural network is used to make the quantitative stock selection strategy for judging stock trends by using the CNN, and then make the quantitative timing strategy for improving the profits by using the LSTM. It is demonstrated by the experiments that the CNN-LSTM neural network model can be successfully applied to making quantitative strategy, and achieving better returns than the basic Momentum strategy and the Benchmark index.

Keywords: Neural network · CNN · LSTM · Quantitative strategy · Stock markets

1 Introduction

The complexity of the internal structure in stock price system and the diversity of the external factors (the national policy, the bank rate, price index, the performance of quoted companies and the psychological factors of the investors) determine the complexity of the stock market, uncertainty and difficulty of stock price forecasting task [1]. The stock market has the characteristics of high return and high risk, which has always been concerned on the analysis and forecast in the stock prices [2,3]. One of the main ideas of the quantitative strategy is to predict and judge the future price of the stock by using the trend of the stock market, and draw up the corresponding investment strategy [4].

A convolutional neural network (CNN) is a mapping from input to output in essence, which can study the mapping relationship without precise mathematical expression between any input and output. As long as convolutional network training using the known pattern with a pooling layer to extract the most representative global features, network has the mapping ability between the input and

---

S. Liu and C. Zhang—The two authors contributed equally to this paper.

D. Liu et al. (Eds.): ICONIP 2017, Part II, LNCS 10635, pp. 198–206, 2017.
https://doi.org/10.1007/978-3-319-70096-0_21

output [5]. Thus we can use CNN for stock ranker to achieve the quantitative stock selection strategy.

To achieve better returns, we adopt the recurrent neural networks (RNN) which have proved one of the most powerful models for processing sequential data. Long Short-Term Memory (LSTM) is one of the most successful RNNs architectures to fix the vanishing gradient problem in neural network [6]. LSTM introduces the memory cell, a unit of computation that replaces traditional artificial neurons in the hidden layer of the network. With these memory cells, networks are able to effectively associate memories and input remote in time, hence suit to grasp the structure of stock data dynamically over time with high prediction capacity [7]. Hence we can use LSTM to achieve the quantitative timing strategy.

The experimental results show that this CNN-LSTM neural network model can find potential rules from historical datasets, and the corresponding quantitative selection and timing strategy is valid and profitable. The rest of this paper is organized as follows. In Sect. 2, we give a brief review of the CNN and LSTM, then describe the CNN-LSTM framework. Section 3 presents the CNN-LSTM flow chart, and the experimental results of as well as the comparisons of the basic Momentum strategy and Benchmark index. Finally, we conclude the paper and present future work in Sect. 4.

2 CNN-LSTM Neural Network

2.1 CNN

For supervised classification, CNN is among the most successful models and gets the state-of-the-art result in many benchmarks [8]. Actually, it involves many more connected weights. A form of regularization is realized in the architecture, and some degree of translation invariance is provided automatically. This particular kind of neural network assumes that we wish to learn filters, in a data-driven fashion, as a means to extract features describing the inputs. The full CNN framework and formula derivation can be seen in the literatures [9].

CNNs are hierarchical models whose convolutional layers alternate with subsampling layers, reminiscent of simple and complex cells in the primary visual cortex [10]. At a convolution layer, the previous layer's feature maps are convolved with learnable kernels, which form the output feature map through the activation function. Multiple input maps can be combined as the output with convolutions. For convenience we just introduce the convolution layer:

$$x_j^l = f\left(\sum_{i \in M_j} x_i^{l-1} * k_{ij}^l + b_j^l \right), \tag{1}$$

where M_j represents a selection of input maps.

2.2   LSTM

Recurrent neural networks have the capability to dynamically incorporate past experience due to internal recurrence [11]. RNNs can project the dynamic properties of the system automatically, so they are computationally more powerful than feed-forward networks, and the valuable approximation results are obtained for chaotic time series prediction [12,13]. One of RNN models is long-short-term memory which works when there is a long delay, and the signals with a mixture of low and high frequency components can be able to handled. The learning process of RNN models however requires a relatively long time because there is a recurrent network architecture [14].

A schematic of the vanilla LSTM block [15] can be seen in Fig. 1. It features three gates (input, forget and output), block input, a single cell (the Constant Error Carousel), an output activation function, and peephole connections. The output of the block is recurrently connected back to the block input and all of the gates. The vector formulas for LSTM layer forward pass are given in [15]. In order to facilitate your understanding, just listed below:

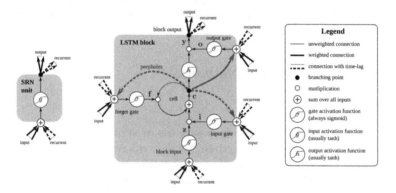

Fig. 1. Detailed Long Short-Term Memory block as used in the hidden layers of a recurrent neural network.

$$z^t = g(W_z x^t + R_z y^{t-1} + b_z) \qquad\qquad block\ input \qquad (2)$$

$$i^t = \sigma(W_i x^t + R_i y^{t-1} + p_i \odot c^{t-1} + b_i) \qquad\qquad input\ gate \qquad (3)$$

$$f^t = \sigma(W_f x^t + R_f y^{t-1} + p_f \odot c^{t-1} + b_f) \qquad\qquad forget\ gate \qquad (4)$$

$$c^t = i^t \odot z^t + f^t \odot c^{t-1} \qquad\qquad cell\ state \qquad (5)$$

$$o^t = \sigma(W_o x^t + R_o y^{t-1} + p_o \odot c^t + b_o) \qquad\qquad output\ gate \qquad (6)$$

$$y^t = o^t \odot h(c^t) \qquad\qquad block\ output \qquad (7)$$

where x^t is the input vector at time t, the W are input weight matrices, the R are square recurrent weight matrices, the p are peephole weight vectors and

b are bias vectors. Functions σ, g and h are point-wise non-linear activation functions: *logistic sigmoid* $\left(\frac{1}{1+e^{-x}}\right)$ is used for as activation function of the gates and hyperbolic tangent is used as the block input and output activation function. The point-wise multiplication of two vectors is denoted as $\odot$. The corresponding Back-Propagation Through Time(BPTT) formulas can be found in [15]'s supplementary material.

2.3 CNN-LSTM Framework

The details of the CNN-LSTM framework are as follows:

Algorithm 1. The CNN-LSTM framework

1: Initialization of parameters and data.
2: **repeat**
3:    **repeat**
4:       CNN-quantitative selection step:
        input: 32*1 dimensional matrix, i.e. the monthly rates of return from the first 13 month to the first 2 month and the daily rates of return from the first 20 day to the first 1 day.
5:    **until** Either the component remains the same in the previous iteration, or the iterations reach certain threshold.
6:    Output the predicted current monthly rate of return.
7: **until** All shares are traversed in the A stock market.
8: Select the top one percent stock in the CNN step output.
9: **repeat**
10:    **repeat**
11:       LSTM-quantitative timing step:
        input: 30*6 dimensional matrix, i.e. before 30 days' features: ['open', 'close', 'high', 'low', 'amount', 'volume'].
12:    **until** Either the component remains the same in the previous iteration, or the iterations reach certain threshold.
13:    Output the predicted next 5 days' rate of return: 1 if positive rate, otherwise -1.
14: **until** All selected shares are traversed.
15: Output the current monthly total return.

---

3 Experiment Results

We implement CNN-LSTM neural network model for quantitative selection and quantitative timing strategy on the training dataset, and verify its performance on the test dataset. We are exploring a parallel implementation of the learning algorithm that could be run on GPUs. Our experiments are implemented in the Linux system (Ubuntu 16.04.2 LTS) with GPU (device 0: GeForce), and 16.00GB RAM with running Python 2.7 source codes.

This approach should lead to a substantial decrease in training time as the algorithm can take advantage of parallelization at the data-level (since it uses mini-batches) as well as at the network layer level. Alternatively, a more straight-forward approach would be to retrain the classifier each month, but update the LSTM more frequently in order to improve profits which are infinitely close to local optimization.

The details of CNN-LSTM flow chart and parameters are described in the Fig. 2 and in the Table 1 as follows:

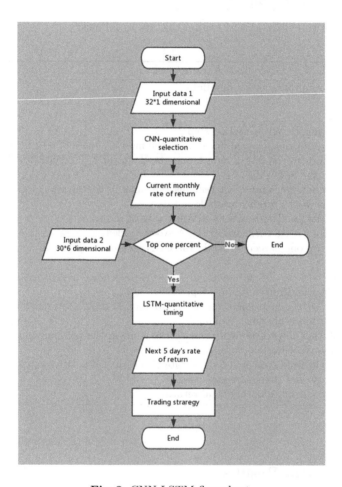

Fig. 2. CNN-LSTM flow chart.

We obtain data on individual Chinesse stocks from the SINA FINANCE web. The training set covers the period from 2007-1-1 to 2013-12-31, and the test set covers the period from 2014-1-1 to 2017-3-31. Data setting and preprocessing of CNN-LSTM neural network are described in the framework.

Table 1. The parameters for CNN-LSTM.

Parameters	CNN	LSTM
Input layer	1	1
Conv/LSTM hidden layer	2	1
FCN hidden Layer	2	1
Output layer	1	1
Epoch	500	100
Activation	ReLU, Tanh	Tanh
Weight	Normal(0,1)	Normal(0,1)
Optimizer	Adam	Adam
Learning rate	0.001	0.001
Objective function	Cross-entropy	Cross-entropy

We did z-score standardization of data when necessary [16]. For every month t, we use the 12 monthly rates of return for month $t-13$ through $t-2$ and the 20 daily rates of return as the input of CNN quantitative selection step, and before 30 days features: ['open', 'close', 'high', 'low', 'amount', 'volume'] as input of LSTM quantitative timing step. Only the features which are to be fed to the neural network are chosen and trained for prediction assigning random biases and weights. In our CNN-LSTM model, the LSTM part is composed of a sequential layers followed by 1 LSTM layer and dense layer with Tanh activation.

Over fitting of neural networks is one of the most difficult things to avoid in training neural networks. Over fitting means that the model performs well in training data, but for the other data the predictor effect is poor. The reason is that "rote" data and noises usually lead to complicated model. To avoid over-fitting of the model, the dropout mechanism is added to the CNN-LSTM model and the regularization term is applied to the weights. Dropout refers to drop some features randomly to improve the robustness of the model. Regularization refers to add an L2 norm in the calculation of the loss function, so that some of the weight values close to 0 avoid forced adaptation for each feature. Then it improves the robustness, also gets the effect of feature choice.

When the LSTM predictive value is equal to 1, we buy and hold 5 days, and if previous positions, update the number of held days as 5 and continue held. When the LSTM predictive value is equal -1, it continues if short positions, and if already held shares, the number of held days will be decreased by one, and if the number of held days is equal to 0, we will sell the share. Figure 3 shows the position ratios of CNN-LSTM model in the test dataset. The gap between two consecutive months means that we make the quantitative stock selection strategy for each month by using the CNN, thus sells all of shares if possible. Meanwhile, the phenomenon that position ratio is less than 1 before the end of the month demonstrates that the LSTM mechanism makes the quantitative timing strategy effectively.

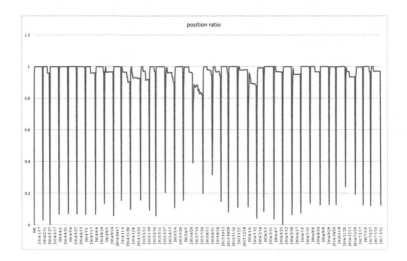

Fig. 3. The position ratios of CNN-LSTM model in the test dataset.

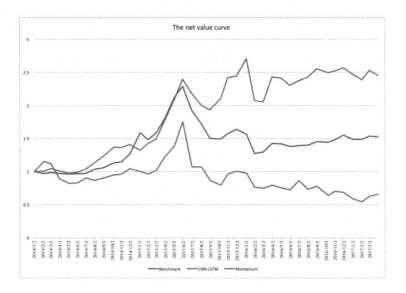

Fig. 4. The net value curves of Benchmark, CNN-LSTM and Momentum.

Table 2. The comparison of the results

	Benchmark	CNN-LSTM	Momentum
Annualized rate of return	0.136	0.309	−0.118
Maximum retracement	0.443	0.241	0.689

We compare the annualized rate of return, the maximum retracement and the net value of our CNN-LSTM model with the basic Momentum strategy and Benchmark index respectively in the Table 2 and Fig. 4. Basic momentum strategy is the empirical finding that stocks with high past returns over 3-to-12 months (winners) continue to perform well over the next few months relative to stocks with low past returns (losers). The net value curves demonstrate a significant increase in the performances qualitatively. During the stock market crash, the maximum retracement of CNN-LSTM is tolerable. The annualized rate of return using our CNN-LSTM neural network model is more than 2 times as large as the annualized rate of return using Benchmark index. Meanwhile, the maximum retracement of CNN-LSTM neural network model is respectively 34%, 54% of the maximum retracement of the basic Momentum strategy and Benchmark index. The experiments fully illustrate our model is efficient and the investment return is impressive, and verify the robustness and practicability of the algorithm as well.

4   Conclusion and Future Work

We have applied the deep learning to stock trading and made two main contributions to the applied machine learning literature. First, we show that CNN can extract useful features even from low signal-to-noise time series data such as financial asset prices if the inputs are appropriately preprocessed. And we make the quantitative stock selection strategy for judging stock trends by using the CNN. Second, we use LSTM neural network to predict a high accuracy in future stock prices and the predicting outcomes are used as timing signals, which significantly improves the retracement of the CNN stock selection model in the backtesting stage. Our model easily accommodates returns of different frequencies as well as nonreturn data and produces investment results that exceed the basic Momentum strategy and Benchmark index in the vast finance literature. We have successfully applied the CNN-LSTM neural network to modeling and making the quantitative stock selection and timing strategy which is feasible, robust and highly profitable.

The issue for future work is reducing computational complexity and increasing computation speed, so that this method can be applied to hours or minutes data instead of the days data. Furthermore, if we apply the model to actual investment decisions, we need to improve on these aspects, such as feature selection, model construction and parameter optimization.

Acknowledgement. This work was supported by the Natural Science Foundation of China for Grant 61171138.

References

1. Fu, C., Fu, M., Que, J.: Prediction of stock price base on radial basic function neural networks. Technol. Dev. Enterp. **4**, 005 (2004)
2. Sun, W., Guo, J., Xia, B.: Discussion about stock prediction theory based on RBF neural network. Heilongjiang Sci. Technol. Inf. **22**, 130 (2010)
3. Liu, S., Ma, J.: Stock price prediction through the mixture of gaussian processes via the precise Hard-cut EM algorithm. In: Huang, D.-S., Han, K., Hussain, A. (eds.) ICIC 2016. LNCS, vol. 9773, pp. 282–293. Springer, Cham (2016). doi:10.1007/978-3-319-42297-8_27
4. Chavarnakul, T., Enke, D.: Intelligent technical analysis based equivolume charting for stock trading using neural networks. Expert Syst. Appl. **34**(2), 1004–1017 (2008)
5. Ding, X., Zhang, Y., Liu, T., Duan, J.: Deep learning for event-driven stock prediction. In: International Conference on Artificial Intelligence, pp. 2327–2333. AAAI Press (2015)
6. Hochreiter, S., Schmidhuber, J.: Long short-term memory. Neural Comput. **9**(8), 1735–1780 (1997)
7. Murtaza, R., Harshal, P., Shraddha, V.: Predicting stock prices using LSTM. Int. J. Sci. Res. (IJSR) **6**(4), 1754–1756 (2017)
8. LeCun, Y., Bottou, L., Bengio, Y., Haffner, P.: Gradient-based learning applied to document recognition. Proc. IEEE **86**(11), 2278–2324 (1998)
9. Bouvrie, J.: Notes on Convolutional Neural Networks. Neural Nets (2006)
10. Hubel, D.H., Wiesel, T.N.: Receptive fields and functional architecture of monkey striate cortex. J. Physiol. **195**(1), 215–243 (1968)
11. Murtagh, F., Starck, J., Renaud, O.: On neuro-wavelet modeling. Decis. Support Syst. **37**(4), 475–484 (2004)
12. Terzija, N.: Robust digital image watermarking algorithms for copyright protection (2006)
13. Sak, H., Senior, A., Beaufays, F.: Long short-term memory recurrent neural network architectures for large scale acoustic modeling. In: Fifteenth Annual Conference of the International Speech Communication Association (2014)
14. Fryzlewicz, P., Bellegem, S., Sachs, R.: Forecasting non-stationary time series by wavelet process modelling. Ann. Inst. Stat. Math. **55**(4), 737–764 (2003)
15. Greff, K., Srivastava, R.K., Koutnik, J., Steunebrink, B.R., Schmidhuber, J.: LSTM: a search space odyssey. IEEE Trans. Neural Netw. Learn. Syst. **pp**(99), 1–11 (2016)
16. Takeuchi, L., Lee, Y.: Applying deep learning to enhance momentum trading strategies in stocks. Working paper, Stanford University (2013)

Learning Inverse Mapping by AutoEncoder Based Generative Adversarial Nets

Junyu Luo, Yong Xu, Chenwei Tang, and Jiancheng Lv[⊠]

Machine Intelligence Laboratory, College of Computer Science, Sichuan University,
Chengdu 610065, People's Republic of China
lvjiancheng@scu.edu.cn

Abstract. The inverse mapping of GANs' (Generative Adversarial Nets) generator has a great potential value. Hence, some works have been developed to construct the inverse function of generator by directly learning or adversarial learning. While the results are encouraging, the problem is highly challenging and the existing ways of training inverse models of GANs have many disadvantages, such as hard to train or poor performance. Due to these reasons, we propose a new approach based on using inverse generator (IG) model as encoder and pre-trained generator (G) as decoder of an AutoEncoder network to train the IG model. In the proposed model, the difference between the input and output, which are both the generated image of pre-trained GAN's generator, of AutoEncoder is directly minimized. The optimizing method can overcome the difficulty in training and inverse model of an non one-to-one function. We also applied the inverse model of GANs' generators to image searching and translation. The experimental results prove that the proposed approach works better than the traditional approaches in image searching.

Keywords: Inverse model · GAN · AutoEncoder network

1 Introduction

Generative adversarial nets (GANs) [1], based on the minimax two-player game theory, show a great power in generating high quality artificial data. And the method of Deep convolutional generative adversarial nets [2] shows the great potential on the mapping between image space X and latent space Z. Lots of papers [2–4] have shown the huge power of inverse model of a generator on semi-supervised learning and adjusting the outputs images of the generators. In addition, finding the inverse mapping of generator can also provide us useful insights to the generator and we may use this to improve the performance of generator. Building on ideas from these many previous works, many works [4–7] have been developed to learn the the inverse mapping of the generator. But, the mapping from latent space Z to image space X is an unidirection mapping and non-linear inverse problem. This brings a great challenge for finding the inverse mapping of generator.

© Springer International Publishing AG 2017
D. Liu et al. (Eds.): ICONIP 2017, Part II, LNCS 10635, pp. 207–216, 2017.
https://doi.org/10.1007/978-3-319-70096-0_22

Dumoulin and Donahue [6,7] proposed a way of learning encoder network E alongside the generator G and discriminator D. The approach successfully avoids the problem of uniderection mapping brought by directly training the inverse model. However, the reconstruction results are not satisfying enough. Creswell's idea [5] can get a good correlation between samples and reconstructions. The approach takes the desired output z as optimization goal. It' very simple but slow, because we have to calculate the z by using multiple gradient descents every step. In other words, the approach is trying to search the z instead of calculating the z. Perarnau proposed a invertible conditional GANs(ICGAN) [4]. In the approach, the inverse model is trained through directly minimizing the difference between (E_z, E_y) and (z, y), where y is the label information of x and z is a noise vector. While the strategy mitigates the effect of the problem that the function of generator is not a one-to-one function, the freedom of latent space Z is restricted by the label information. Due to the approach requires abundant label information, the requirement for data sets is very strict.

In this paper, we propose a new approach to learn the inverse mapping by AutoEncoder based on GANs (AEGAN) as a complement of former works. We use the AutoEncoder to train a inverse model. The pre-trained generator is regarded as the decoder part of an AutoEncoder and the inverse generator is regarded as the corresponding encoder part. This model does not directly minimize the difference between the original noise vector and the reconstructed noise vector, but try to minimize the difference between the generated samples of noise vectors. This strategy not only avoids problems of directly training the inverse model, but also avoids the poor correlation of adversarial training. In addition, we also explore the application value of inverse model in image processing. The corresponding vectors of images contain rich semantic information. Our experiments prove that such semantic information is very helpful in image searching. And by combing the generator model, the inverse model can also be used in image-to-image translation.

2   Primary and Motivation

The existing ways of learning the inverse model of the GANs have made great success, however there still remains many problems waiting for solving. The idea of Dumoulin and Donahue [6,7] is to train encoder network E alongside the generator G and discriminator D. The training objective is defined as a minimax objective:

$$\min_{G,E} \max_{D} V(D,E,G) = \mathbb{E}_{x \sim p_{data}(x)}[\log D(x, E(x))] + \mathbb{E}_{z \sim p(z)}[\log(1 - D(G(z), z))]$$

(1)

Where D,E,G are Discriminator, Encoder, Generator respectively. x is an input sample and z is a noise vector. During the training, the G,E try to minimize the value function and D tries to maximize the value function. This approach successfully avoids the problem of directly training the inverse model. However, this approach also results the poor correlation between samples and reconstructions, because the discriminator only focus on the difference between data sets instead of the difference between two images. So the encoder part can't catch the unique features of one signal image. In addition, the approach needs to train a third network with the generative net, which means that inversion cannot be learned from a pre-trained generative network.

Creswell [5] proposes a different idea that can get a good correlation between samples and reconstructions. The main idea is to directly minimize the difference between generated image $G(z)$ and sample image x through optimizing the value of z, where G is a pre-trained generator. The z is updated by:

$$z = z - \alpha \nabla_z[-x * \log(G(z)) - (1 - x) * \log(1 - G(z))] \tag{2}$$

Where α stands for the learning rate. This approach takes the desired output z as optimization goal. It's easy to implement but poor in effectiveness because it doesn't provide a real inverse function and we have to use gradient descents every time.

The invertible conditional GAN(ICGAN) [4], proposed by Perarnau, tries to solve the problem through conditional GAN. In this model, ICGAN tries to minimize the difference between (E_z, E_y) and (z, y), y is the label information including the gender, age and so on. E_z is the noise vector Encoder and E_y is the label information Encoder. The two training objectives are:

$$L_{ez} = \mathbb{E}_{z \sim p_z, y' \sim p_y} \left\| z - E_z(G(z, y')) \right\|_2^2$$
$$L_{ey} = \mathbb{E}_{x, y \sim p_{data}} \left\| y - E_y(x) \right\|_2^2 \tag{3}$$

The label information limits the freedom of latent space Z. This strategy mitigates the effect of the uniderection mapping problem. But this approach requires abundant label information, which results that it can not be used in unsupervised approach.

3   AutoEncoder Based Generative Adversarial Nets

The details of training and network structure can be found int he Appendix.

3.1   Basic Structure

Our idea of AEGAN is inspired from AutoEncoder. Here we take the generator $G(z; \theta_g)$ as the decoder part of the AutoEncoder and the desired inverse generator $IG(x; \theta_{ig})$ as the encoder part. Figure 1 shows the training process of AEGAN, we try to minimize the difference between generated image x and reconstructed image x'. IG compresses a generated image x into a latent space vector z' and G reconstructs the z' into a new image x'. z' is used as the extracted feature of input sample x and our experiments prove that z' is a very good image feature in image translation and searching. Many previous methods regard the generator as an encoder part instead of a decoder part in training and it's against the nature of AutoEncoder. And the mapping from z to x also brings difficulty to the learning of the encoder part. So in AEGAN, we change our goal into minimizing $|x - x'|$.

The innovation of AEGAN is that we focus on the reconstructed images instead of the reconstructed noise vectors. This model does not directly minimize the difference between z and z', but try to minimize the difference between the x and x'. This strategy not only avoids problems in directly training the inverse model, but also avoids the poor correlation of adversarial training.

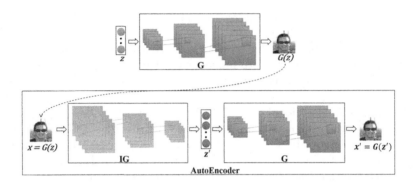

Fig. 1. The training process of AEGAN

3.2   Training Steps

Training the Generator. First we train the GAN's generator G using the approach and the network structure of DCGAN [2]. G is a deconvolutional network with one fully connected layer and four deconvolutional layers with strides $(1, 2, 2, 1)$. The activation function is relu for first four layers and sigmoid for the last layer. The sigmoid layer is aimed at normalizing the generated images. And prior $z \in \mathbb{R} \sim \mathrm{U}(-1, 1)$.

The optimization goal of generator is:

$$\min_{G} \max_{D} V(\theta_d, \theta_g) = \mathbb{E}_{x \sim p_{data}(x)}[\log D(x)] + \mathbb{E}_{z \sim p(z)}[\log(1 - D(G(z)))] \quad (4)$$

Training the Inverse Generator. Then we start to train the inverse generator IG by using the information from a pre-trained generator G. In details, the structures of G and IG are symmetric. The deconvolutional layers of G are replaced with the corresponding convolutional layers. The activation function of output layer is tanh for limiting the range of reconstructed z'. The convolution type in IG is strided convolution [2]. To avoid the difficulty of directly training the encoder we require the value function of IG to minimize the difference between the fake image x generated by G and the reconstructed output x'. We choose the cross-entropy function to define the difference between x and x'. The optimization objective can be defined as:

$$\min_{IG} \mathbb{E}_{x \sim p_{generated}(x)} \{V(x; \theta_{ig})\}$$

$$V(x; \theta_{ig}) = -x * \log x' - (1 - x) * \log(1 - x') \tag{5}$$

$$= -x * \log G(IG(x; \theta_{ig})) - (1 - x) * \log(1 - G(IG(x; \theta_{ig})))$$

Where θ_g, θ_d are the parameters of the generator G and discriminator D. Algorithm 1 shows the detail of training IG.

Algorithm 1. Training the Inverse Generator

---

for number of training iterations **do**

1. Sample minibatch of m noise samples $(z^{(1)}, ..., z^{(m)})$ from noise prior $z \sim p_g(z)$ and use them to generate the training images $(x^{(1)}, ..., x^{(m;\cdot;\cdot)}) \sim p_{generated}(x)$ through the pre-trained generator G.

2. Put the generated image $x(x = G(z))$ into the AutoEncoder part to get the reconstructed image x'.

$$z' = IG(x) = IG(G(x))$$
$$x' = G(z') \tag{6}$$

3. Compute the reconstruction loss $V(x)$ according to Eq. (4).

$$V(x) = -x * \log G(IG(x)) - (1 - x) * \log(1 - G(IG(x))) \tag{7}$$

4. Perform a backpropagation to compute the gradients and only upgrade the parameters of IG.

$$\theta_{ig} = \theta_{ig} - \frac{\alpha}{m} \sum_{i=1}^{m} \frac{\partial V(x^i; \theta_{ig})}{\theta_{ig}} \tag{8}$$

Where α is the learning rate.

end for

---

4   Experiment Results

We evaluate the ability of this inverse model on CelebFaces Attributes Dataset (CelebA) [8]. CelebA is a large-scale face attributes dataset.

4.1   Reconstructing Samples

We take the outputs of generator as the samples and use the inverse mapping from these samples to Z space to generate the reconstructed samples. Here, we compare AEGAN with a directly trained inverse model based on ICGAN [4] and the adversarial inverse model based on BiGAN [6]. The original BiGAN and ICGAN both contain an additional image label information vector. In here we remove the label vectors because of the unsupervised condition. Figure 2 shows the reconstructed results of AEGAN, inverse model and BiGAN. For BiGAN we uses the different original samples because BiGAN can't use a pre-trained generator as base. This is because that in BiGAN the generator and inverse generator are trained in the same time as Eq. (1) shows. So we compare BiGAN with the generated samples from its own generator for fairness. In addition, we use the dHash [9] as standard to evaluate the similarity of generated images. dHash will give every image a special hash code and the difference between hash codes can be used to describe the similarity between images. We take the average similarity as final result. As we can see in Table 1, the result of AEGAN is also the best in this experiment.

original   AEGAN   directly   original-BiGAN   BiGAN

Fig. 2. The reconstructed results

Table 1. Similarity compared with original samples

AEGAN	Directly training	BiGAN
0.8266	0.7944	0.6594

4.2   Searching the Similar Images Using AEGAN

To illustrate the power of AEGAN, we will show its ability in searching the similar images. We only compare with the general image searching algorithm, because our approach is based on unsupervised learning. We compare AEGAN with three general image searching algorithms: dHash, pHash [9] and color histogram [10]. In details, the similarity between two images are based on the Euclidean Distance between the reconstructed z' vectors of them, the smaller the distance, the higher the similarity. We take an image from the original data set celebA and add some other factors such as color transform, adding a sunglasses to the person, to form the 3 test images. Then we implement 4 different algorithms to find the closest images in the first 20,000 images of celebA. The Fig. 3 proves that AEGAN is very suitable for this task. To evaluate the comprehensive performance, the second experiment is aiming at finding the similar images. We compare our algorithm with dHash. We take the first 20,000 images of celebA as the test set and take other 64 images from the celebA as base images. As we can

The test images   color historgram   pHash   dHash   AEGAN

Fig. 3. The searching results.

Fig. 4. The searched results for dHash and AEGAN. The first block contains the base images. And the second one is the searching result of AEGAN. The last one is the result of dHash.

Table 2. Label similarity compared with base samples

AEGAN	dHash
0.7918	0.7483

see from Fig. 4, AEGAN approach is much better than dHash. AEGAN catches the important features of face images such as the face angle, face similarity, hair style and facial expression. In addition, we use the label similarity to evaluate the searching results. There are 40 labels for each image including gender, hair color and so on. The result can be seen from Table 2. Although AEGAN is not a patch on specialized face recognition algorithms in this task, we have to emphasize that this approach is unsupervised and universal. In other words, this idea can easily be implemented in other fields.

4.3 Super-Resolution Using the AEGAN

To prove our approach does learn the major features of face images, we propose the third experiment. In this experiment we take the Gaussian Blur images as inputs of inverse generator IG and then use the output of inverse generator to reconstruct the original images. We choose the generated data as the original examples. As Fig. 5 shows, we can see AEGAN also performs well in super-resolution and we didn't train the AEGAN specially for this task. AEGAN can automatically ignore the abnormal parts of input sample and add the missing features to the reconstructed output. It is worth mentioning that the approach is unsupervised. As we known, the labeled data are extremely rare in most of application. Given the data limitations, the proposed method work surprisingly well for Super-Resolution without label information.

Fig. 5. The results of super-resolution by AEGAN. The first block contains the base image. And the second block contains the images after adding the Gaussian Blur. The last one is the reconstructed result.

5   Conclusion and Further Works

AEGAN uses the idea of Auotoencoder to overcome the difficulty in training a inverse model of generator. And the experiments show that the inverse mapping of generator has a very similar function compared with Word Embedding [11]. Because the inverse out put of an image can be regarded as a vector presentation of the image and this vector presentation can catches the important features of images as Experiment 2 shows. This ability can be very helpful in fields of image and video processing. It's possible to get a universal vector representation of image if we train the AEGAN at large image data sets. In addition, we can use AEGAN to reform the Image-to-Image Translation approach based on GAN [12]. With AEGAN, the training of generator part can be done in unsupervised condition and we only need to train the encoder part in conditional situation. In other words, it's possible to train a Image-to-Image GAN net in semi-supervised condition if we use the structure of AEGAN.

Acknowledgments. This work was supported by the National Science Foundation of China (Grant No. 61375065 and 61625204), partially supported by the State Key Program of National Science Foundation of China (Grant No. 61432012 and 61432014).

Appendix: Network Structures and Training Details

The Adam optimizer is used for all the experiments and the parameters are the same. The learning rate is 0.0002 and beta1 is 0.5. The experiment is trained on complete CelebA dataset. Batch size is 64 (Tables 3, 4, 5 and 6).

Table 3. Generator

Input shape operation	100				
	Kernel	Stride	Filter	BN	Activation
Dense			4*4*64*8	N	
Reshape			4,4,64*8	Y	Relu
Deconv	5*5	2*2	64*4	Y	Relu
Deconv	5*5	2*2	64*2	Y	Relu
Deconv	5*5	2*2	64*1	Y	Relu
Deconv	5*5	2*2	3	N	Sigmoid

Table 4. Discriminator

Input shape operation	64*64*3				
	Kernel	Stride	Filter	BN	Activation
Conv	5*5	2*2	64*1	Y	Lrelu
Conv	5*5	2*2	64*2	Y	Lrelu
Conv	5*5	2*2	64*4	Y	Lrelu
Conv	5*5	2*2	64*8	Y	Lrelu
Reshape			4*4*64*8	N	
Dense			1	N	Sigmoid

Table 5. Inverse generator

Input shape operation	64*64*3				
	Kernel	Stride	Filter	BN	Activation
Conv	5*5	2*2	64*1	Y	Relu
Conv	5*5	2*2	64*2	Y	Relu
Conv	5*5	2*2	64*4	Y	Relu
Conv	5*5	2*2	64*8	Y	Relu
Reshape			4*4*64*8	N	
Dense			100	N	Tanh

Table 6. Discriminator (BiGAN)

Input shape operation	64*64*3, 100				
	Kernel	Stride	Filter	BN	Activation
Conv	5*5	2*2	64*1	Y	Lrelu
Conv	5*5	2*2	64*2	Y	Lrelu
Conv	5*5	2*2	64*4	Y	Lrelu
Conv cond concat			64*4+100	N	
Conv	5*5	2*2	64*8	Y	Lrelu
Conv	5*5	2*2	64*8	Y	Lrelu
Conv	5*5	2*2	64*8	Y	Lrelu
Reshape			1*1*64*8	N	
Dense			1	N	Sigmoid

References

1. Goodfellow, I.J., Pougetabadie, J., Mirza, M., Xu, B., Wardefarley, D., Ozair, S., Courville, A., Bengio, Y., Ghahramani, Z., Welling, M.: Generative adversarial nets. In: Advances in Neural Information Processing Systems, vol. 3, pp. 2672–2680 (2014)
2. Radford, A., Metz, L., Chintala, S.: Unsupervised representation learning with deep convolutional generative adversarial networks (2015). arXiv preprint: arXiv:1511.06434
3. Dong, H., Neekhara, P., Wu, C., Guo, Y.: Unsupervised image-to-image translation with generative adversarial networks (2017). arXiv preprint: arXiv:1701.02676
4. Perarnau, G., van de Weijer, J., Raducanu, B., Alvarez, J.M.: Invertible conditional gans for image editing (2016). arXiv preprint: arXiv:1611.06355
5. Creswell, A., Bharath, A.A.: Inverting the generator of a generative adversarial network (2016). arXiv preprint: arXiv:1611.05644
6. Donahue, J., Krahenbuhl, P., Darrell, T.: Adversarial feature learning (2016). arXiv preprint: arXiv:1605.09782
7. Dumoulin, V., Belghazi, I., Poole, B., Lamb, A., Arjovsky, M., Mastropietro, O., Courville, A.: Adversarially learned inference (2016). arXiv preprint: arXiv:1606.00704
8. Liu, Z., Luo, P., Wang, X., Tang, X.: Deep learning face attributes in the wild. In: Proceedings of the IEEE International Conference on Computer Vision, pp. 3730–3738 (2015)
9. Niu, X.M., Jiao, Y.H.: An overview of perceptual hashing. Acta Electronica Sin. **36**(7), 1405–1411 (2008)
10. Swain, M.J., Ballard, D.H.: Color indexing. Int. J. Comput. Vis. **7**(1), 11–32 (1991)
11. Hinton, G.E.: Learning distributed representations of concepts. In: Proceedings of the Eighth Annual Conference of the Cognitive Science Society, Amherst, MA, vol. 1, p. 12 (1986)
12. Isola, P., Zhu, J.Y., Zhou, T., Efros, A.A.: Image-to-image translation with conditional adversarial networks (2016). arXiv preprint: arXiv:1611.07004

Fast and Accurate Image Super Resolution by Deep CNN with Skip Connection and Network in Network

Jin Yamanaka[1(✉)], Shigesumi Kuwashima[1], and Takio Kurita[2]

[1] ViewPLUS Inc., Chiyoda-ku, Tokyo 102-0084, Japan
{jin,kuwashima}@viewplus.co.jp
[2] Hiroshima University, Hiroshima 739-8527, Japan
tkurita@hiroshima-u.ac.jp

Abstract. We propose a highly efficient and faster Single Image Super-Resolution (SISR) model with Deep Convolutional neural networks (Deep CNN). Deep CNN have recently shown that they have a significant reconstruction performance on single-image super-resolution. The current trend is using deeper CNN layers to improve performance. However, deep models demand larger computation resources and are not suitable for network edge devices like mobile, tablet and IoT devices. Our model achieves state-of-the-art reconstruction performance with at least 10 times lower calculation cost by Deep CNN with Residual Net, Skip Connection and Network in Network (DCSCN). A combination of Deep CNNs and Skip connection layers are used as a feature extractor for image features on both local and global areas. Parallelized 1×1 CNNs, like the one called Network in Network, are also used for image reconstruction. That structure reduces the dimensions of the previous layer's output for faster computation with less information loss, and make it possible to process original images directly. Also we optimize the number of layers and filters of each CNN to significantly reduce the calculation cost. Thus, the proposed algorithm not only achieves state-of-the-art performance but also achieves faster and more efficient computation. Code is available at https://github.com/jiny2001/dcscn-super-resolution.

Keywords: Deep learning · Image super resolution · Deep CNN · Residual net · Skip connection · Network in network

1 Introduction

Single Image Super-Resolution (SISR) was mainly used for specific fields like security video surveillance and medical imaging. But now SISR is widely needed in TV, video playing, and websites as display resolutions are getting higher and higher while source contents remain between twice and eight times lower resolution when compared to recent displays. In other cases, network bandwidth is generally limited while the display's resolution is rather high. Recent Deep-Learning based methods (especially with deeply and fully convolutional networks) have achieved high performance in the problem of SISR from low resolution (LR) images to high resolution (HR) images.

© Springer International Publishing AG 2017
D. Liu et al. (Eds.): ICONIP 2017, Part II, LNCS 10635, pp. 217–225, 2017.
https://doi.org/10.1007/978-3-319-70096-0_23

We believe this is because deep learning can progressively grasp both local and global structures on the image at same time by cascading CNNs and nonlinear layers. However, with regards to power consumption and real-time processing, deeply and fully convolutional networks require large computation and a lengthy processing time. In this paper, we propose a lighter network by optimizing the network structure with recent deep-learning techniques, as shown in Fig. 1. For example, recent state-of-the-art deep-learning based SISR models which we will introduce at Sect. 2 have 20 to 30 CNN layers, while our proposed model (DCSCN) needs only 11 layers and the total computations of CNN filters are 10 to 100 times smaller than the others.

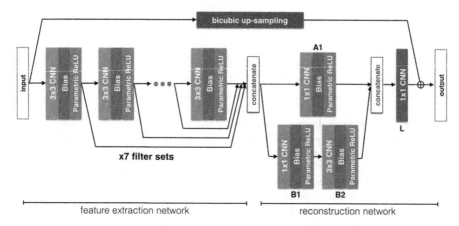

Fig. 1. Our model (DCSCN) structure. The last CNN (dark blue) outputs the channels of the square of scale factor. Then it will be reshaped to a HR image. (Color figure online)

Feature Extraction. In the previous Deep Learning-based methods, an up-sampled image was often used as their input. In these models, the SISR networks can be pixel-wise and its implementation becomes easier. However, they have 20–30 CNN layers in total and heavy computation is required for each up-sampled pixel. Furthermore, extracting features of up-sampled pixel is redundant, especially in the case of a scale factor of 3 or more. We use an original image as an input of our model so that the network can grasp the features efficiently. We also optimize the number of filters of each CNN layer and send those features directly to the image reconstruction network via skip connections.

Image Detail Reconstruction. In the case of data up-sampling, the transposed convolutional layer (also known as a deconvolution layer) proposed by Matthew D. Zeiler [1] is typically used. The transposed convolutional layer can learn up-sampling kernels, however, the process is similar to the usual convolutional layer and the reconstruction ability is limited. To obtain a better reconstruction performance, the transposed convolutional layers need to be stacked deeply, which means the process needs heavy computation. So we propose a parallelized CNN structure like the Network in Network [2], which usually consists of one (or more) 1×1 CNN(s). Remarkably, the 1×1 CNN layer not only reduces the dimensions of the previous layer for faster computation with less information loss, but also adds more nonlinearity to enhance the potential representation of the network. With this structure, we can significantly reduce the number of CNN or transposed CNN filters. 1×1 CNN has 9 times less computation than 3×3 CNN, so our reconstruction network is much lighter than other deep-learning based methods.

2   Related Work

Deep Learning-based methods are currently active and showing significant performances on SISR tasks. Super-Resolution Convolutional Neural Network (SRCNN) [3] is the method proposed at this very early stage. C. Dong et al. use 2 to 4 CNN layers to prove that the learned CNN layers model performs well on SISR tasks. The authors concluded that using a larger CNN filter size is better than using deeper CNN layers. SRCNN is followed by Deeply-Recursive Convolutional Network for Image Super-Resolution (DRCN) [4]. DRCN uses deep (a total of 20) CNN layers, which means the model has huge parameters. However, they share each CNN's weight to reduce the number of parameters to train, meaning they succeed in training the deep CNN network and achieving significant performances.

The other Deep Learning-based method, VDSR [5], is proposed by the same authors of DRCN. VDSR uses Deep Residual Learning [6], which was developed by researchers from Microsoft Research and is famous for receiving first place in ILSVRC 2015 (a large image classification competition). By using residual-learning and gradient clipping, VDSR proposed a way of significantly speeding up the training step. Very deep Residual Encoder-Decoder Networks (RED) [7] are also based on residual-learning. RED contains symmetric convolutional (encoder) and deconvolutional (decoder) layers. It also has skip connections and connects instead to every two or three layers. Using this symmetric structure, they can train very deep (30 of) layers and achieve state-of-the-art performance. These studies therefore reflect the trend of "the Deeper the Better".

On the other hand, Yaniv Romano et al. proposed Rapid and Accurate Image Super Resolution (RAISR) [8], which is a shallow and faster learning-based method. It classifies input image patches according to the patch's angle, strength and coherence and then learn maps from LR image to HR image among the clustered patches. C. Dong et al. also proposed FSRCNN [9] as a faster version of their SRCNN [3]. FSRCNN uses transposed CNN to process the input image directly. RAISR and FRSCNN's processing speeds are 10 to 100 times faster than other state-of-the-art Deep Learning-based methods. However, their performance is not as high as other deeply convolutional methods, like DRCN, VDSR or RED.

3 Proposed Method

We started building our model from scratch. Started from only 1 CNN layer with small dataset and then grow the number of layers, filters and the data. When it stopped improving performance, we tried to change the model structure and tried lots of deep learning technics like mini-batch, dropout, batch normalization, regularizations, initializations, optimizers and activators to learn the meanings of using each structures and technics. Finally, we carefully chose structures and hyper parameters which will suit for SISR task and build our final model.

3.1 Model Overview

Our model (DCSCN) is a fully convolutional neural network. As shown in Fig. 1, DCSCN consists of a feature extraction network and a reconstruction network. We cascade a set of CNN weights, biases and non-linear layers to the input. Then, to extract both the local and the global image features, all outputs of the hidden layers are connected to the reconstruction network as Skip Connection. After concatenating all of the features, parallelized CNNs (Network in Network [2]) are used to reconstruct the image details. The last CNN layer outputs the 4ch (or the channels of square of scale factor) image and finally the up-sampled original image is estimated by adding these outputs to the up-sampled image constructed by bicubic interpolation. Thus the proposed CNN model focusses on learning the residuals between the bicubic interpolation of the LR image and the HR original image.

In the previous studies, an up-sampled image was often used as their input for the Deep Learning-based architecture. In these models, the SISR networks will be pixel-wise. However, 20–30 CNN layers are necessary for each up-sampled pixel and heavy computation (up to 4x, 9x and 16x) is required, as shown in Fig. 2. It also seems inefficient to extract a feature from an up-sampled image rather than from the original image, even from the perspective of the reconstruction process.

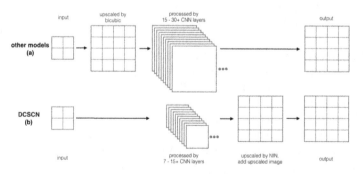

Fig. 2. Simplified process structures of (a) other models and (b) our model (DCSCN).

3.2   Feature Extraction Network

In the first feature extraction network, we cascade 7 sets of 3×3 CNN, bias and Parametric ReLU units. Each output of the units is passed to the next unit and simultaneously skipped to the reconstruction network. Unlike with other major deep-learning based large-scale image recognition models, the number of units of CNN layers are decreased from 96 to 32, as shown in Table 1. As discussed in Yang et al. [10], for model pruning, it is important to use an appropriate number of training parameters to optimize the network. Since the local feature is more important than the global feature in SISR problems, we reduce the features by the following layer and it results in better performance with faster computation. We also use the Parametric ReLU units as activation units to handle the "dying ReLU" problem [11]. This prevents weights from learning a large negative bias term and can lead to a slightly better performance.

Table 1. The numbers of filters of each CNN layer of our proposed model

	Feature extraction network						Reconstruction network				
	1	2	3	4	5	6	7	A1	B1	B2	L
DCSCN	96	76	65	55	47	39	32	64	32	32	4
c-DCSCN	32	26	22	18	14	11	8	24	8	8	4

3.3   Image Reconstruction Network

As stated in the Model Overview, DCSCN directly processes original images so that it can extract features efficiently. The final HR image is reconstructed in the last half of the model and the network structure is like in the Network in Network [2]. Because of all of the features are concatenated at the input layer of the reconstruction network, the dimension of input data is rather large. So we use 1×1 CNNs to reduce the input dimension before generating the HR pixels.

The last CNN, represented by the dark blue color in Fig. 1, outputs 4 channels (when the scale factor s = 2) and each channel represents each corner-pixel of the up-sampled pixel. DCSCN reshapes the 4ch LR image to an HR(4x) image and then finally it is added to the bi-cubic up-sampled original input image. As with typical Residual learning networks, the model is made to focus on learning residual output and this greatly helps learning performances, even in cases of shallow (less than 7 layers) models.

4   Experiments

4.1   Datasets for Training and Testing

For training, 91 images from Yang et al. [12] and 200 images from the Berkeley Segmentation Dataset were used [13]. We then performed data augmentation on those training images. The images are flipped horizontally, vertically and both horizontally and vertically to make 3 more images for each image. While in the training phase, SET 5 [14] dataset is used to evaluate performance and check if the model is likely to overfit or not. The total number of training images is 1,164 and the total size is 435 MB. Color (RGB) images are converted to YCbCr image and only Y-channel is processed. Each training image is split into 32 by 32 patches with stride 16 and 64 patches are used as a mini-batch. For testing, we use SET 5 [14], SET 14 [15], and BSDS100 [13] datasets.

4.2   Training Setup

Each CNN is initialized with the method proposed by He et al. [11] and also initialized to 0 for all biases and PReLUs. During training, dropout [16] with p = 0.8 is applied to each output of PReLU layers. Mean Squared Error (MSE) between the estimated output and ground truth is used as a basic loss value and we also add the sum of L2 norms of each CNN's weight (scaled by the factor of 0.0001) to the loss for regularization. We use Adam [17] with an initial learning rate = 0.002 for the optimization algorithm to minimize loss. When the loss does not decrease after 5 epochs of training steps, the learning rate is decreased by a factor of 2 and training is finished if the learning rates goes lower than 0.00002. We also present a compact version of our proposed network (c-DCSCN) as the parameters are shown in Table 1. An example of the results are shown in Fig. 3.

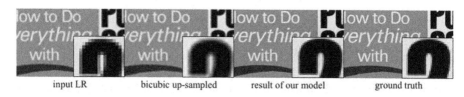

| input LR | bicubic up-sampled | result of our model | ground truth |

Fig. 3. An example of our result of img_013 in set14 [15]

4.3   Comparisons with State-of-the-Art Methods

Comparisons with accuracy. Peak Signal-to-Noise Ratio (PSNR) are used to compare the accuracy of the proposed DCSCN with other Deep Learning-based SR algorithms. Table 2 shows quantitative comparisons for 2x SISR. Red text indicates the

Table 2. Comparisons of accuracy with other SR algorithms. (scale = x2)

Dataset	SRCNN	DRCN	VDSR	RED30	DCSCN (ours)
Set5	36.66	**37.63**	37.53	**37.66**	37.62
Set14	32.45	**33.04**	33.03	32.94	**33.05**
BSDS100	31.36	31.85	31.90	**31.99**	**31.91**

best performance and the blue text indicates the second-best. The result shows our proposed algorithm (DCSCN) has either a best or second-best performance for those datasets.

Comparisons with computation complexity. Since each implementation occurs under different platform and libraries, it's not fair to test execution time to compare these methods. Here we calculate the computation complexity of each method instead. Since deep learning computation is usually difficult to parallelize, computation complexity of 1 pixel is used as a good indicator of computation speed. CNN layers are calculated as $size^2$ times input filters times output filters. Bias, ReLU, adding or multiplying layers are calculated as number of filters. When bicubic up-sampling is needed, we calculate it as 16 multiplications and additions. Thus the approximate computation complexity for each method is shown in Table 3. The complexity calculated may slightly differ from true complexity. For example, FSRCNN [9] and RED [7] contain transposed CNN and it needs to pad 0 before processing. However, those

Table 3. Comparisons of approximate computation complexity. (scale = x2) For comparison, we chose f1, f2, f3, n1, n2 = (9, 5, 5, 64, 32) for SRCNN and d, s, m = (56, 12, 4) for FSRCNN

	SRCNN (9, 5, 5)	FSRCNN (56, 12, 4)	DRCN	VDSR	RED30	DCSCN (ours)	c-DCSCN (ours)
CNN layers	3	8	20	20	30	11	11
CNN filters	32, 64	56, 12	256	64	64	32 to 96	8 to 32
Bias and activation layers	3, 2	7, 7	20, 19	20, 19	0, 36	10, 10	10, 10
Input image size	x4	x1	x4	x4	x4	x1	x1
Complexity [k]	**229.5**	**26.2**	**78,083.2**	**2,668.5**	**4,152.8**	**244.1**	**26.1**

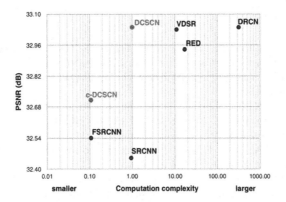

Fig. 4. Comparison between reconstruction performance for set14 vs. computation complexity. DCSCN's complexity is taken as 1.00.

differences are much smaller than CNN calculations and therefore are negligible. So they are ignored to create a brief comparison between performance vs. complexity, as shown in Fig. 4. We can see our DCSCN has a state-of-the-art reconstruction performance, while the computation complexity is at least 10 times smaller than VDSR [5], RED [7] and DRCN [4].

5   Conclusion and Future Works

This paper proposed a fast and accurate Image Super Resolution method based on CNN with skip connection and network in network. In the feature extraction network of our method, the structure is optimized and both local and global features are sent to the reconstruction network by skip connection. In the reconstruction network, network in network architecture is used to obtain a better reconstruction performance with less computation. In addition, the model is designed to be capable of processing original size images. Using these devices, our model can achieve state-of-the-art performance with less computation resources.

Since SISR tasks are now beginning to be used on the network edge (the entry point devices of services like mobile, tablet and IoT devices), building a small but still effective model is rather important. While this model has been proposed through numerous trial and error processes, there should be a better way of tuning the model structure and hyper parameters. Establishment of a method to design suitable model complexity for each problem is needed.

Another noteworthy aspect of this study is the use of the ensemble learning model. Deep Learning itself has a good capacity for complex problems, however, classic ensemble learning tends to lead to good results with less computation, even when there is great diversity within the problem. Also, the ensemble model makes it easier to parallelize for faster computation. Therefore, small sets of Deep-Learning models could be made and combined to work as an ensemble model to fix real and complex problems.

References

1. Zeiler, M.D., Krishnan, D., Taylor, G.W., Fergus, R.: Deconvolutional networks. In: Computer Vision and Pattern Recognition, pp. 2528–2535 (2010)
2. Lin, M., Chen, Q., Yan, S.: Network in network. In: International Conference on Learning Representations (2014)
3. Dong, C., Loy, C.C., He, K., Tang, X.: Learning a deep convolutional network for image super-resolution. In: Fleet, D., Pajdla, T., Schiele, B., Tuytelaars, T. (eds.) ECCV 2014. LNCS, vol. 8692, pp. 184–199. Springer, Cham (2014). doi:10.1007/978-3-319-10593-2_13
4. Kim, J., Lee, J.K., Lee, K.M.: Deeply-recursive convolutional network for image super-resolution. In: Computer Vision and Pattern Recognition, pp. 1637–1645 (2016)
5. Kim, J., Lee, J.K., Lee, K.M.: Accurate image super-resolution using very deep convolutional networks. In: Computer Vision and Pattern Recognition, pp. 1646–1654 (2016)

6. He, K., Zhang, X., Ren, S., Sun, J.: Deep residual learning for image recognition. In: Computer Vision and Pattern Recognition, pp. 770–778 (2016)
7. Mao, X.J., Shen, C., Yang, Y.B.: Image restoration using very deep convolutional encoder-decoder networks with symmetric skip connections. In: Neural Information Processing Systems (2016)
8. Romano, Y., Isidoro, J., Milanfar, P.: RAISR: rapid and accurate image super resolution. IEEE Trans. Comput. Imaging 3(1), 110–125 (2017)
9. Dong, C., Loy, C.C., Tang, X.: Accelerating the super-resolution convolutional neural network. In: Leibe, B., Matas, J., Sebe, N., Welling, M. (eds.) ECCV 2016. LNCS, vol. 9906, pp. 391–407. Springer, Cham (2016). doi:10.1007/978-3-319-46475-6_25
10. Han, S., Mao, H., Dally, W.J.: Deep compression: compressing deep neural networks with pruning, trained quantization and Huffman coding. In: International Conference on Learning Representations (2016)
11. He, K., Zhang, X., Ren, S., Sun, J.: Delving deep into rectifiers: surpassing human-level performance on ImageNet classification. In: IEEE International Conference on Computer Vision, pp. 1026–1034 (2015)
12. Yang, J., Wright, J., Huang, T.S., Ma, Y.: Image super resolution via sparse representation. IEEE Trans. Image Process. 19(11), 2861–2873 (2010)
13. Arbelaez, P., Maire, M., Fowlkes, C., Malik, J.: Contour detection and hierarchical image segmentation. IEEE Trans. Pattern Anal. Mach. Intell. 33(5), 898–916 (2011)
14. Bevilacqua, M., Roumy, A., Guillemot, C., Alberi-Morel, M.L.: Low-complexity single-image super-resolution based on nonnegative neighbor embedding. In: British Machine Vision Conference (2012)
15. Zeyde, R., Elad, M., Protter, M.: On single image scale-up using sparse-representations. In: Boissonnat, J.-D., Chenin, P., Cohen, A., Gout, C., Lyche, T., Mazure, M.-L., Schumaker, L. (eds.) Curves and Surfaces 2010. LNCS, vol. 6920, pp. 711–730. Springer, Heidelberg (2012). doi:10.1007/978-3-642-27413-8_47
16. Hinton, G.E., Srivastava, N., Krizhevsky, A., Sutskever, I., Salakhutdinov, R.R.: Improving neural networks by preventing coadaptation of feature detectors. arXiv preprint arXiv:1207. 0580 (2012)
17. Kingma, D.P., Ba, J.L.: Adam: a method for stochastic optimization. In: International Conference on Learning Representations (2015)

Generative Moment Matching Autoencoder with Perceptual Loss

Mohammad Ahangar Kiasari, Dennis Singh Moirangthem, and Minho Lee$^{(\boxtimes)}$

School of Electronics Engineering, Kyungpook National University,
Daegu, South Korea
ahangar100@gmail.com, mdennissingh@gmail.com, mholee@gmail.com

Abstract. In deep generative networks, one of the major challenges is to generate non-blurry, clearer images. Unlike the generative adversarial networks, generative models such as variational autoencoders, generative moment matching networks etc. use pixel-wise loss which leads to the generation of blurry images. In this paper, we propose an improved generative model called Generative Moment Matching Autoencoder (GMMA) with a feature-wise loss mechanism. We use a pre-trained VGGNet convolutional neural network to compute the loss at the various feature extraction layers. We evaluate the performance of our model on the MNIST and the Large-scale CelebFaces Attributes (CelebA) dataset. Our generative model outperforms the existing models on the log-likelihood estimation test. We also illustrate the effectiveness of our mechanism and the improved generation and reconstruction capabilities. The proposed GMMA with perceptual loss successfully alleviates the problem of blurry image generation.

Keywords: Generative Networks · Moment Matching · Autoencoder · Convolutional Neural Networks · Feature extraction

1 Introduction

Generative models have the capability of producing new samples with properties similar to the training data. Recently, adversarial models like the Generative Adversarial Networks (GAN) [4] have been proved to be very powerful in data generation tasks. Generative models such as Variational Autoencoder (VAE) [12, 20] and Generative Moment Matching Networks (GMMN) [15] have also become popular. These models, unlike the adversarial models, formalize the generation problem in the framework of a probabilistic model with latent variables.

In the current deep learning models, a pixel wise loss like L_2 is commonly used. This is because it is easy to implement and has been proved to be very effective for training the deep networks. The generative models like VAE or GMMN also use this loss for training the network. However, the generated images are smoothened and blurry compared to natural images. This is because the pixel wise loss fails to understand the perceptual difference between the original and the generated images.

© Springer International Publishing AG 2017
D. Liu et al. (Eds.): ICONIP 2017, Part II, LNCS 10635, pp. 226–234, 2017.
https://doi.org/10.1007/978-3-319-70096-0_24

Several recent papers successfully generate images by optimizing the perceptual loss, which is based on the high-level features extracted from pre-trained deep Convolutional Neural Networks (CNNs). Hou et al. [9] constructed a VAE by enforcing deep feature consistency using CNN. Neural style transfer [3] and texture synthesis [2] also jointly minimize high-level feature reconstruction loss and style reconstruction loss by optimization. These models show that the deep representation of the CNN can capture a variety of spatial correlation properties of the input image. This ability to enhance the reconstruction loss of the autoencoder by substituting the pixel-wise loss with feature-wise loss can be applied to other generative models. The feature-wise loss can be presented as the mean square error between two features of input images in each selected layer of a deep pre-trained CNN such as VGGNet [21].

In this work, we address the problem of blurry image generation in the current generative models by introducing a new model with feature-wise loss. We propose the Generative Moment Matching Autoencoder (GMMA) with perceptual loss to alleviate the issues faced by generative models with pixel-wise loss. The GMMA uses a pre-trained VGGNet to extract the features of the generated images and compare it to the original features. We compute the loss at multiple feature levels to improve the generation capability of our model. We use the MNIST [14] and the Large-scale CelebFaces Attributes (CelebA) [16] dataset to evaluate our model. The GMMA can outperform the existing models on the log likelihood estimation tests on the MNIST data. Moreover, the generated results show that our model with perceptual loss can produce clearer images compared to GMMA with pixel-wise loss.

2   Proposed Model

Generative models like VAE, Adversarial Autoencoders [17] suffer from the blurry images generation problem because of the pixel-wise mean square error reconstruction cost function. In order to address this problem, we propose a generative moment matching autoencoder based on a feature level loss using pre-trained networks like AlexNet [13] and VGGNet. In this work, we utilize the VGGNet with 16 layers to compute the perceptual loss. The architecture of our proposed model is shown in Fig. 1. We describe the details of our approach as follows.

2.1   Generative Moment Matching Autoencoder (GMMA)

The proposed Generative Moment Matching Autoencoder (GMMA), in spirit, is similar to the adversarial autoencoder (AAE) [17] and variational autoencoder (VAE) [12] with a difference in the loss function. VAE and AAE use KL divergence and adversarial loss functions respectively while the moment-matching autoencoder uses the Maximum Mean Discrepancy (MMD) loss function in order to keep the distribution of the hidden space under control. MMD is a well-known fitness function to measure the distance between two datasets. The goal is to

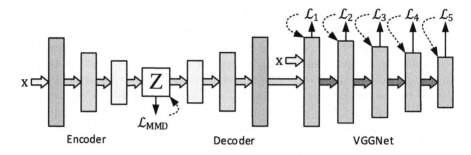

Fig. 1. The proposed GMMA with perceptual loss.

measure how much two datasets belong to the same distribution. In order to answer this question, [5,6] proposed the MMD fitness function shown in Eq. (1).

Let $X = \{x_1, x_2, ..., x_N\}$ be the input of the autoencoder and $\widehat{X} = \{\widehat{x}_1, \widehat{x}_2, ..., \widehat{x}_N\}$ be the reconstructed data and $\widehat{Z} = \{\widehat{z}_1, \widehat{z}_2, ..., \widehat{z}_N\}$ be the latent variables of the input X. In the GMMA, we minimize the mean square error (MSE) of the reconstructed $\widehat{X}$ while minimizing the cost function that is defined as follows:

$$\widehat{\mathcal{L}}^2_{MMD}(Z, \widehat{Z}) = \frac{1}{N^2} \sum_{i=1}^{N} \sum_{j=1}^{N} k\left(\widehat{z}_i, \widehat{z}_j\right) - \frac{2}{NM} \sum_{i=1}^{N} \sum_{j=1}^{M} k\left(\widehat{z}_i, z_j\right)$$
$$+ \frac{1}{M^2} \sum_{i=1}^{M} \sum_{j=1}^{M} k\left(z_i, z_j\right) \tag{1}$$

where $Z = \{z_1, z_2, ..., z_N\}$ with N samples of a known distribution $q(Z)$ (like Gaussian or uniform distributions) which is the target distribution of the latent space $\widehat{Z}$ of the autoencoder. The GMMA attempts to minimize $\widehat{\mathcal{L}}^2_{MMD}(Z, \widehat{Z})$. By minimizing the $\widehat{\mathcal{L}}^2_{MMD}(Z, \widehat{Z})$, the latent variables in the code space will be forced to maintain the same distribution as $q(Z)$. In the proposed model, the encoder is trained using the MSE and MMD loss functions, while the decoder part is trained only by using the MSE loss function. All parameters of the encoder and decoder are optimized with stochastic gradient descent (SGD).

2.2   GMMA with Perceptual Loss

Since, pixel-wise reconstruction loss functions are not proper for generating high quality images, we replace the MSE reconstruction loss function with a feature level loss. Generally each layer in a deep structure defines a specific representation of the input images. Let T and X be the original and generated images using GMMA, and t^l and x^l be the corresponding feature representation in layer l. We can vectorize the original and generated feature map in each convolutional layer of the deep structure in the form of x^l_{ij} and t^l_{ij} respectively, where ij indicates the feature map of the ith channel at position j. The squared-error loss between these two feature maps are presented by:

$$\mathcal{L}_i = \frac{1}{2} \sum_{i=1}^{I} \sum_{j=1}^{J} (t_{ij}^l - x_{ij}^l)^2 \tag{2}$$

where t_{ij}^l and x_{ij}^l are the activation of the ith filter at position j in l^{th} layer.

We then apply the new reconstruction loss function as follows:

$$\mathcal{L}_{rec} = \sum_{i=1}^{N} \mathcal{L}_i \tag{3}$$

where $\mathcal{L}_i$ indicates the feature-level loss of the ith layer in a pretrained VGGNet16. N is the number of layers in VGGNet16.

3   Experiments and Results

We evaluated our proposed model based on two well known datasets, MNIST [14] and Large-scale CelebFaces Attributes (CelebA) dataset [16]. We describe the details of all the experiments and report the results of each experiment as follows.

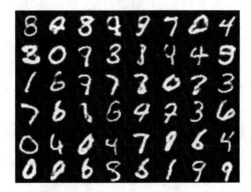

Fig. 2. The generated hand written digits with the proposed model.

MNIST. The MNIST dataset contains 60,000 and 10,000 training and test images, respectively. Each image has a size of 28×28 pixels. We implemented three convolutional layers in the encoder and three deconvolutional [19,23] layers in the decoder part of the autoencoder. The dimension of the code space is set to 10. We used the ADAM [11] optimizer with momentum $\beta_1 = 0.5$, $\beta_1 = 0.999$ and a mini-batch size of 64. All weights were initialized with a normal distribution with standard deviation of 0.002. We used Batch Normalization [10] after each

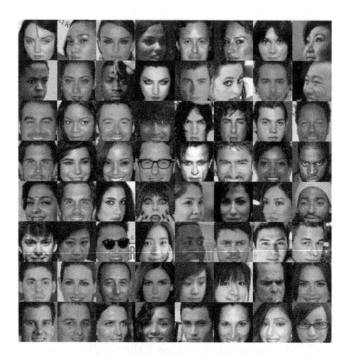

Fig. 3. The original face images.

Fig. 4. The reconstructed faces using GMMA with pixel-wise loss.

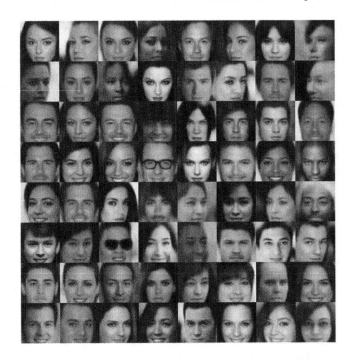

Fig. 5. The reconstructed faces using GMMA with perceptual loss.

layer except for the last layer of the autoencoders. We used the parametric rectified linear (pReLU) [7] activation in each layer except the output layer. We set the learning rate to 0.0005 for both the perceptual loss and the MMD optimizers.

We need to evaluate the generative performance of the proposed GMMA. However, there are no straightforward methods to evaluate the generative models because we cannot compute the probability of a sample directly. We compare our model with the current state-of-the-art generative models using the log-likelihood estimation based method described in some recent works [1,4,22]. We fit a Gaussian Parzen window to the generated samples from the model and then, compute the likelihood of the test samples using that distribution. We selected the scale parameter of the Gaussian probability distribution function via cross-validation. We made the comparison by drawing 10,000 samples and 16,384 samples from our trained model. The log-likelihood estimation results are shown Table 1. The results show that our model outperforms the existing models.

Additionally, in order to generate random images, we feed the decoder part of the autoencoder with random samples from the normal distribution with zero mean and unit variance. The generated images are shown in Fig. 2. The results show that the proposed model can generate new hand written digit samples which are not included in the training data.

CelebA. The CelebA dataset has a total of 202,599 images with 40 attribute annotations per image. The original size of the images is 178×218 but we align and crop the center 64×64 pixels of the images in order to emphasize on the faces. We kept the settings of this experiment same as the MNIST experiment except that the dimension of the code space is set to 100. In order to visually compare the performance of our proposed model, we conducted two experiments. First, we train the GMMA with a pixel-wise MSE loss and we reconstruct a set of images given a batch of input images. The input images and the reconstructed images are shown in Figs. 3 and 4, respectively. In the second experiment, we train our model with the feature-wise MSE loss function using the pre-trained VGGNet features. The reconstructed images given the same input images are shown in Fig. 5. The results show that the proposed model can produce non-blurry face images compared to the images generated using the pixel-wise loss.

Table 1. Log-likelihood estimations for MNIST with 10 K and 16 K drawn samples from the GMMA

Model	MNIST (10 K)	MNIST (16 K)
DBN [8]	138 ± 2	-
Stacked CAE [8]	121 ± 1.6	-
Deep GSN [22]	214 ± 1.1	-
GAN [4]	225 ± 2	305 ± 8.97
GMMN+AE [15]	282 ± 2	-
AAE [17]	340 ± 2	-
VAE [12, 18]	-	445 ± 5.36
GMMA	449 ± 3.26	476 ± 6.15

4   Conclusion

In this paper, we proposed the Generative Moment Matching Autoencoder with perceptual loss that can address blurriness in generated images. The proposed model was constructed using feature-wise loss and was evaluated using the MNIST and CelebA datasets. The proposed model outperforms the existing generative models in the log-likelihood estimation test. The results illustrated that the proposed model improves the quality of the output images.

Acknowledgments. This work was supported by the Industrial Strategic Technology Development Program (10044009) funded by the Ministry of Trade, Industry and Energy (MOTIE, Korea) (50%).

References

1. Bengio, Y., Mesnil, G., Dauphin, Y., Rifai, S.: Better mixing via deep representations. In: ICML (1), pp. 552–560 (2013)
2. Gatys, L., Ecker, A.S., Bethge, M.: Texture synthesis using convolutional neural networks. In: Advances in Neural Information Processing Systems, pp. 262–270 (2015)
3. Gatys, L.A., Ecker, A.S., Bethge, M.: A neural algorithm of artistic style. arXiv preprint (2015). arXiv:1508.06576
4. Goodfellow, I., Pouget-Abadie, J., Mirza, M., Xu, B., Warde-Farley, D., Ozair, S., Courville, A., Bengio, Y.: Generative adversarial nets. In: Advances in Neural Information Processing Systems, pp. 2672–2680 (2014)
5. Gretton, A., Borgwardt, K.M., Rasch, M., Schölkopf, B., Smola, A.J., et al.: A Kernel method for the two-sample-problem. Adv. Neural Inf. Process. Syst. **19**, 513 (2007)
6. Gretton, A., Borgwardt, K.M., Rasch, M.J., Schölkopf, B., Smola, A.: A Kernel two-sample test. J. Mach. Learn. Res. **13**, 723–773 (2012)
7. He, K., Zhang, X., Ren, S., Sun, J.: Delving deep into rectifiers: Surpassing human-level performance on imagenet classification. In: Proceedings of the IEEE International Conference on Computer Vision, pp. 1026–1034 (2015)
8. Hinton, G.E., Osindero, S., Teh, Y.W.: A fast learning algorithm for deep belief nets. Neural Comput. **18**(7), 1527–1554 (2006)
9. Hou, X., Shen, L., Sun, K., Qiu, G.: Deep feature consistent variational autoencoder. In: 2017 IEEE Winter Conference on Applications of Computer Vision (WACV), pp. 1133–1141. IEEE (2017)
10. Ioffe, S., Szegedy, C.: Batch normalization: accelerating deep network training by reducing internal covariate shift. arXiv preprint, arXiv:1502.03167 (2015)
11. Kingma, D., Ba, J.: Adam: a method for stochastic optimization. arXiv preprint, arXiv:1412.6980 (2014)
12. Kingma, D.P., Welling, M.: Auto-encoding variational bayes. arXiv preprint, arXiv:1312.6114 (2013)
13. Krizhevsky, A., Sutskever, I., Hinton, G.E.: Imagenet classification with deep convolutional neural networks. In: Advances in Neural Information Processing Systems, pp. 1097–1105 (2012)
14. LeCun, Y., Bottou, L., Bengio, Y., Haffner, P.: Gradient-based learning applied to document recognition. Proc. IEEE **86**(11), 2278–2324 (1998)
15. Li, Y., Swersky, K., Zemel, R.S.: Generative moment matching networks. In: ICML, pp. 1718–1727 (2015)
16. Liu, Z., Luo, P., Wang, X., Tang, X.: Deep learning face attributes in the wild. In: Proceedings of International Conference on Computer Vision (ICCV) (2015)
17. Makhzani, A., Shlens, J., Jaitly, N., Goodfellow, I.: Adversarial autoencoders. arXiv preprint, arXiv:1511.05644 (2015)
18. Nowozin, S., Cseke, B., Tomioka, R.: f-gan: training generative neural samplers using variational divergence minimization. In: Advances in Neural Information Processing Systems, pp. 271–279 (2016)
19. Radford, A., Metz, L., Chintala, S.: Unsupervised representation learning with deep convolutional generative adversarial networks. arXiv preprint, arXiv:1511.06434 (2015)
20. Rezende, D.J., Mohamed, S., Wierstra, D.: Stochastic backpropagation and approximate inference in deep generative models. In: International Conference on Machine Learning, pp. 1278–1286 (2014)

21. Simonyan, K., Zisserman, A.: Very deep convolutional networks for large-scale image recognition. arXiv preprint, arXiv:1409.1556 (2014)
22. Thibodeau-Laufer, E., Alain, G., Yosinski, J.: Deep generative stochastic networks trainable by backprop (2014)
23. Zeiler, M.D., Krishnan, D., Taylor, G.W., Fergus, R.: Deconvolutional networks. In: 2010 IEEE Conference on Computer Vision and Pattern Recognition (CVPR), pp. 2528–2535. IEEE (2010)

Three-Means Ternary Quantization

Jie Ding[2]([✉]), JunMin Wu[1,2], and Huan Wu[2]

[1] Suzhou Institute for Advanced Study,
University of Science and Technology of China, Suzhou, China
jmwu@ustc.edu.cn
[2] Department of Computer Science and Technology,
University of Science and Technology of China, Suzhou, China
{djl993,wuhuan00}@mail.ustc.edu.cn

Abstract. Deep Convolution Neural Networks (DCNNs) have achieved state-of-the-art results in a wide range of tasks, especially in image recognition and object detection. However, millions of parameters make it difficult to be deployed on embedded devices with limited storage and computational capabilities. In this paper, we propose a new method called Three-Means Ternary Quantization (TMTQ), which can quantize the weights to ternary values $\{-\alpha_1, 0, +\alpha_2\}$ during the forward and backward propagations. Scaling factors $\{\alpha_1, \alpha_2\}$ are used to reduce the loss of quantization. We evaluate this method on MNIST, CIFAR-10 and ImageNet datasets with different network architectures. The results show that the performance of our ternary models obtained from TMTQ is only slightly worse than full precision models but better than recently proposed binary and ternary models. Meanwhile, our TMTQ method achieves up to about $16\times$ model compression rate compared with the 32-bits full precision counterparts, for we just use ternary weights (2-bits) and fixed scaling factors during the inference.

Keywords: Deep learning · Model compression · Neural network quantization · Ternary neural network

1 Introduction

Deep Convolution Neural Networks (DCNNs) have demonstrated breaking results on a variety of computer vision tasks, including but not limited to image classification [1, 2] and object detection [3, 4]. However, deploying Deep Convolution Neural Networks (DCNNs) on embedded devices has been found highly difficult due to the massive amount of storage and multi-accumulate operations. As a result, it remains a great challenge to deploy deep CNNs on embedded devices.

Substantial efforts have been made to solve this problem. The most common method is to compress a full-trained networks directly. [5] proposed vector quantization techniques to compress deep CNNs, by replacing the weights in full connected layers with respective floating-point centers obtained from k-means clustering. HashedNets [6] reduced model sizes by using a hash function to put pre-trained weights into corresponding buckets and force them to share the same value. However, they both concentrated on the full connected layers only.

© Springer International Publishing AG 2017
D. Liu et al. (Eds.): ICONIP 2017, Part II, LNCS 10635, pp. 235–245, 2017.
https://doi.org/10.1007/978-3-319-70096-0_25

Another common method is using lower precision weights, which can not only reduce the size of networks, but also speed up the execution. [7] proposed that using SIMD instructions with 8-bits fixed-point implementation can improve the performance of computing during inference, yielding $3\times$ speed-up over floating-point baseline. [8] trained deep neural networks with low precision multipliers and high precision accumulators. [9] introduced an approach to eliminate the need of float-point multiplication by converting multiplication into binary shift. Moreover, [10] eliminated the need for multiplications by forcing the weights used in forward and backward propagations to be binary (not necessarily 0 and 1), and achieved near state-of-the-art results on MNIST, CIFAR-10 datasets, but performed worse than full precision counterparts by a wide margin on ImageNet [11] dataset. Furthermore, [12] introduced a high performance fixed-point optimization method that allow networks with ternary $\{-1, 0, +1\}$ weights and 2 or 3 bits of fixed-point signals, which can greatly reduce the word-length of weights and signals for implementing networks on embedded devices. However, the performance of networks shows obvious degradation on large datasets. Later, [13] proposed ternary weight networks (TWNs) with weights quantized to $\{-\alpha, 0, +\alpha\}$ to find a balance between high model compression rate and high accuracy, which achieved better performance on large dataset compared with previous quantized networks due to the increased weight precision and scaling factors. However, the same scaling factors for positive and negative weights have limited the expression ability of the ternary weight networks. Recently, lots of new methods have been proposed to train CNNs with low-precision weights, including but not limited to BinaryNet [14], XNOR-Net [15], DoReFa-Net [16], Bitwise Neural Network [17] and TTQ [18].

This paper makes the following contributions:

1: We introduce Three-Means Ternary Quantization (TMTQ), a new method to quantize the weights to ternary values $\{-\alpha_1, 0, +\alpha_2\}$ for each layer during forward and backward propagations (Sect. 3).
2: We show that TMTQ performs better than the existing quantization methods and obtains near state-of-the-art results on MNIST, CIFAR-10 and ImageNet datasets (Sect. 4).

2   Related Quantization Methods

Recently, more and more researchers concentrate on deploying deep neural networks on embedded devices. In order to solve the limitations of storage and computing power, they proposed low-precision alternatives to perform deep learning tasks, following are some latest studies on low-precision network quantization methods.

2.1   BinaryConnect

BinaryConnect [10] proposed a method to quantize full precision weights to binary values, shown in Eq. (1), which constrains the weights to $\{+1, -1\}$ during forward and backward propagations.

$$W_l^b = \begin{cases} +1 & if \; w_l \geq 0, \\ -1 & otherwise \end{cases} \tag{1}$$

The key point of BinaryConnect is that it only binarizes the weights during forward and backward propagations but not during the parameters update when reserved full precision weights are used. And the real-valued are restricted to $[-1, 1]$ to reduce the impact of the large weights. During inference, only binary weights are needed, a $32\times$ smaller model can be deployed on embedded devices.

2.2 Fixed-Point Feedforward Deep Neural Networks

Hwang [12] proposed a direct 3-point quantization method to constrain the weights to $\{-1, 0, +1\}$, which is shown in Eq. (2).

$$W_l^t = \begin{cases} +1 & w_l > +\Delta \\ 0 & |w_l| < \Delta \\ -1 & w_l < -\Delta \end{cases} \tag{2}$$

Here Δ is the threshold used to quantize continuous weights. However, determining threshold Δ is a difficult problem, because there is no clear relation between the parameters and final output errors resulted in by the quantization. Therefore, the threshold Δ is initially determined by using an L2-error minimizing approach, and then fine-tuned by using exhaustive search to find a best value that minimized the output error.

After training, by using 2-bits to store the ternary values, they obtained almost $16\times$ compression rate compared with the full precision weights. The fixed-point networks show only negligible performance loss when compared to full precision counterparts on small datasets according to their paper. Also the "0" value ensure the sparseness of networks, which can prevent the network over-fitting.

2.3 Ternary Weights Networks

Ternary weight networks (TWNs) [13] – neural networks with weights constrained to $\{+\alpha, 0, -\alpha\}$. A scaling factor α is used to reduce the loss between ternary and full-precision weights, shown in Eq. (3).

$$W_l^t = \begin{cases} +\alpha & w_l > +\Delta \\ 0 & |w_l| < \Delta \\ -\alpha & w_l < -\Delta \end{cases} \tag{3}$$

Also, Δ is a threshold used to quantize continuous weights. During training, α and Δ are optimized by minimizing L2-error between full precision and ternary weights. However, because α and Δ are independent factors, this problem has no straightforward solution as [12] (described in Sect. 2.2). To overcome this, approximated values are used, shown in Eqs. (4) and (5).

$$\Delta = 0.7 * E(|w_l|) \tag{4}$$

$$\alpha = \frac{1}{|I_\Delta|} \sum_{i \in I_\Delta} |w_i|, \ I_\Delta = \{i| \, |w_i| > \Delta\} \tag{5}$$

The training process of ternary weight networks is the same as binary weights described before. Also, with this quantization method, the authors obtained $16\times$ smaller models compared with full precision counterparts and achieved near state-of-the-art results on different datasets according to their paper.

3   Three-Means Ternary Quantization

In this section, we give a detailed view of TMTQ, considering how to obtain ternary values from full precision weights and train deep neural networks with ternary weights. We first consider the ternary quantization method and then introduce how to train networks with this method.

3.1   Quantization Method

Our method is shown in (6). First, we set two different thresholds Δ_l^p and Δ_l^n for positive weights and negative weights, and then quantize the full-precision weights to ternary values $\{W_l^p, 0, -W_l^n\}$ by thresholds.

$$W_l^t = \begin{cases} W_l^p & W_l > \Delta_l^p \\ 0 & -\Delta_l^n < W_l < \Delta_l^p \\ -W_l^n & W_l < -\Delta_l^n \end{cases} \tag{6}$$

Here we introduce four independent factors $\{\Delta_l^n, \Delta_l^p, W_l^n, W_l^p\}$ to quantize the continuous full-precision weights. The different thresholds and scaling factors between positive and negative weights enable networks to have stronger learning ability. Unlike previous works which have the thresholds Δ_l^* and scaling factors W_l^* set by experience, we propose a novel algorithm to optimizing these four factors simultaneously from the full precision weights, which is shown in Algorithm 1.

As shown in Algorithm 1, our quantization method is similar to k-means with k = 3, but still have some differences. First, we do not choose centers randomly. If the weights W_l is the first time to be quantized, we just initialize three centers with $Min(W_l)$, 0, $Max(W_l)$ to accelerate clustering convergence [19]. Otherwise, because parameters update is small during each training iteration, using previous training iteration centers is also a good way to reduce the number of clustering iterations. Second, centers are updated during each clustering iteration process except for center[1], we fixed its value equals 0 to make sure the sparseness of the networks which can prevent over-fitting of the networks like dropout. Furthermore, though we quantize the full-precision weights with four independent factors, we do not need to know how to calculate these specific values with our method TMTQ. We get the ternary weights automatically by invisible thresholds after some clustering iterations without setting any approximate value.

The benefits of using TMTQ: (i) TMTQ method obtained all parameters automatically from the weights without any artificial factors, which is easy to be implemented for arbitrary networks and datasets. (ii) The asymmetric of ternary values $\{+W_l^p, 0, -W_l^n\}$ enables networks to have more model capacity.

Algorithm 1: Three-Means Ternary Quantization (TMTQ)

Input: Learned full-precision weights W_l, **MaxIter** is the maximum number of
      clustering iterations.
Output: W_l^t
Begin
  First calculate: $\text{Max}(W_l)$, $\text{Min}(W_l)$
  Set three cluster centers
    if (first quantized) **then**
      center[0] ← $\text{Min}(W_l)$, **[1]** ← 0, **center**[2] ← $\text{Max}(W_l)$ // initialize centers
    else
      center[0] ← center[0], **center**[1] ← 0, **center**[2] ← center[2]
    end
  Assume cluster G_i includes elements nearest to **center**[i] , i $\in \{0,1,2\}$
    for iter ← 0 to **MaxIter do**
      for j ← 0 to N {N is the number of W_l's elements} **do**
        if $\text{Min} \left(W_l^j - \textbf{center}[\text{i}]\right)^2$ $W_l^j \in G_i$
      end
      Update centers
        $\Delta_0 \leftarrow |G_0|$, $\textbf{center}[0] \leftarrow \frac{1}{|\Delta_0|} * \sum_{W_l^j \in G_0} W_l^j$
        $\textbf{center}[1] \leftarrow 0$
        $\Delta_2 \leftarrow |G_2|$, $\textbf{center}[2] \leftarrow \frac{1}{|\Delta_2|} * \sum_{W_l^j \in G_2} W_l^j$
    end
  Update weights
    for j ← 0 to N **do**
      if $W_l^j \in G_i$ $W_l^j \leftarrow \textbf{center}[\text{i}]$, $i \in \{0, 1, 2\}$
    end
End

3.2   Train Ternary Networks with TMTQ

We use ternary weights during forward and backward propagations and update the parameters with reserved full precision weights as described before. Stochastic gradient descent (SGD) is used to train the networks. The training steps are shown in Algorithm 2.

Noting that our training steps are similar to normal training methods except for the ternary weights are used in forward and backward propagations. In addition, some useful tricks are utilized to speed up training process and improve the inference accuracy. Batch Normalization (BN) [20] not only accelerates training by reducing internal covariate shift, but also reduces the impact of weights scales. And also, learning rate scaling and momentum are both effective methods to optimize network training.

Furthermore, our TMTQ method does not increase training time much for we update clustering centers with centers' value obtained from previous training iterations (Algorithm 1). Through this way, 2 clustering iterations are enough to obtain good results during each training iteration.

Algorithm 2: SGD train networks with TMTQ

Input: Learned full-precision weights W_l and b_l for layer l. **L** is the number of layers
       layer l output: a_l, **C** is the loss function of networks
       TMTQ (W_l) means quantize weights with TMTQ.

Begin
  1. **Forward propagation:**
    for l ← 1 to **L-1** do
      $W_l^t \leftarrow$ TMTQ(W_l)
      $a_{l+1} \leftarrow f(W_l^t * a_l + b_l)$ //* means inner product or convolutional operation
    end
  2. **Backward propagation:**
    for l ← **L-1** to 1 do
      $\frac{\partial C}{\partial a_l} \leftarrow \left((W_l^t)^T * \frac{\partial C}{\partial a_{l+1}} \right) \circ f'$ // $\circ$ means element-wise product
      $\frac{\partial C}{\partial W_l} \leftarrow \frac{\partial C}{\partial a_{l+1}} * (a_l)^T$
      $\frac{\partial C}{\partial b_l} \leftarrow \frac{\partial C}{\partial a_{l+1}}$
    end
  3. **Parameter update:**
    for l ← 1 to **L-1** do
      $W_l \leftarrow W_l - \eta * \frac{\partial C}{\partial W_l}$
      $b_l \leftarrow b_l - \eta * \frac{\partial C}{\partial b_l}$
    end
End

3.3   Inference

In previous sections, we have introduced the way to train deep neural networks with TMTQ method. During inference, only the ternary weights and scaling factors are needed. By storing the weights with 2-bits values, we can reduce the mode size by about 16×. Furthermore, due to the W_l^p and W_l^n are fixed during inference, calculating the scaling factors on activate function in advance is an effective way to speed up forward propagation on specialized hardware, for lots of multiplications are replaced with addition or subtract operations.

4   Experiments

In this section, we compare our TMTQ method with different existing quantization methods on three benchmark datasets: MNIST, CIFAR-10 and ImageNet. For fair comparison, the same hyper parameters are used during training, such as network structure, learning rate, regularization method and optimization method (SGD). In addition, MNIST and CIFAR-10 experiments are repeated 4 times to obtain the average results, reducing the effect of random initialization and data augmentation. We implement our experiments on Caffe [21] framework.

4.1   MNIST

The MNIST is an image classification benchmark dataset containing 60 thousand training images and 10 thousand test images. We train LeNet-5 network on MNIST without any data augmentation or preprocessing methods. The LeNet-5 consists of: "32-C5 + MP2 + 64-C5 + MP2 + 512-FC + 10SoftMax". Where 32-C5 means the convolution layer contains 32 kernels with size 5×5, MP2 means 2×2 max-pooling layer, FC is fully connected layer and SoftMax is an output layer. We use SGD to update parameters with momentum equals 0.9. Minibatch size is set to 100. Learning rate is initialized to 0.0001 and reduced by steps. Moreover, we add Batch Normalization layer after every convolution layer to reduce internal covariate shift.

In order to make the quantized network converge as soon as possible, we first train a full precision model on MNIST as a baseline, and then fine-tune the full precision baseline with binary and ternary quantization methods. The training curves are shown in Fig. 1. The result (Table 1) shows that our ternary model obtained from TMTQ outperforms BinaryConnect model and TWNs model by 0.31%, 0.05% respectively and has 0.02% accuracy degradation over full precision model.

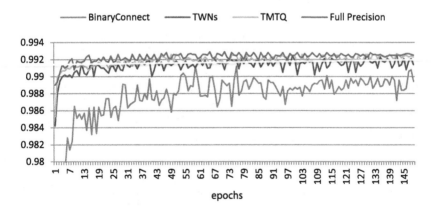

Fig. 1. Test accuracy of Lenet-5 on MNIST with different quantization methods

Table 1. Accuracy rate on MNIST,CIFAR-10 and ImageNet.

Method	MNIST	CIFAR-10	ImageNet(top-1)
TMTQ	99.21	91.33	55.83
TWNs	99.16	90.89	53.41
BinaryConnect	98.90	89.97	–
Full precision	99.23	91.50	56.80
BinaryNet	98.60	89.85	–
XNOR-net	–	–	51.20

4.2 CIFAR-10

The CIFAR-10 is an image classification benchmark dataset containing 50 thousand 32 × 32 RGB training images and 10 thousand test images. We train VGG13 network which is inspired from VGG16 [22] on CIFAR-10 with some data-augmentation operations. We pad 2 pixels in each side of images and randomly crop 32 × 32 size from padded images during training. During inference, original 32 × 32 images are used to test the networks. Our VGG13 networks denoted as: "(2 × 128-C3) + MP2 + (2 × 256-C3) + MP2 + (2 × 512-C3) + MP2 + (2 × 512-C3) + MP2 + (2 × 512-C3) + MP2 + (2 × 1024-FC) + 10-SoftMax". These layers have the same meaning as described in Sect. 4.1. Parameters update by SGD method with momentum equals 0.9 and learning rate is initialized to 0.0001. Minibatch size is set to 100. Furthermore, Batch Normalization (BN) is used after convolution layers to speed up the training process.

Also, we first use a full-trained VGG13 model as a baseline, and then fine-tune the baseline with binary and ternary quantization methods. Training curves are shown in Fig. 2. The result (Table 1) shows that our ternary model obtained from TMTQ out-performs BinaryConnect model and TWNs model by 1.36%, 0.44% respectively, and has 0.17% accuracy degradation over full precision model.

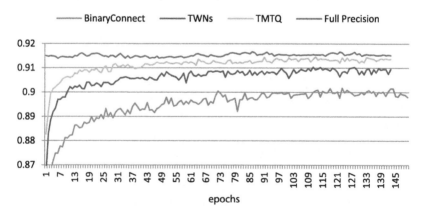

Fig. 2. Test accuracy of VGG13 on CIFAR-10 with different quantization methods.

4.3   ImageNet

ImageNet is an image classification dataset with over 1.28 million training images and 50 thousand validation images. We use AlexNet structure in our experiment with the full precision weights for the first convolution layer and the last full connect layer. During training, images are resized to 256 × 256 and randomly cropped to 227 × 227 before input. SGD method is used to update the parameters with momentum equals 0.9. Minibatch size is set to 256. Learning rate is initialized to 0.0001 and reduced by 0.1 at iteration 200000.

We download a full-trained AlexNet model from caffe model zoo as a baseline and then fine-tune this baseline model with TMTQ and TWNs quantization methods, training curves of top-1 accuracy in validation dataset are shown in Fig. 3. The result (Table 1) shows that our TMTQ model outperforms TWNs model by 2.42% and has only 0.97% accuracy degradation over full precision counterpart.

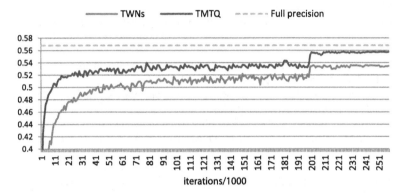

Fig. 3. Validation accuracy of AlexNet on ImageNet with different quantization methods

5   Conclusion

We propose a novel method TMTQ which quantizes continuous weights to ternary values during forward and backward propagations. With TMTQ method, we do not need to set any thresholds Δ_l^* in advance or calculate the scaling factors W_l^* by approximately, all factors are obtained automatically by learning the centers of the full-precision weights. Furthermore, our quantization method reduces the model size by about 16× for we just need ternary weights (2-bits) and scaling factors during inference. The above experiments proved that our method TMTQ performs better than BinaryConnect and TWNs quantization methods on CIFAR-10 and ImageNet datasets, and has only slightly accuracy degradation over full precision counterparts. Future works will extend those results to other models and datasets, and explore the deep relationship between ternary values and network outputs.

References

1. Krizhevsky, A., Sutskever, I., Hinton, G.E.: ImageNet classification with deep convolutional neural networks. In: Proceedings of the Annual Conference on Neural Information Processing Systems, pp. 1097–1105 (2012)
2. Szegedy, C., Liu, W., Jia, Y., et al.: Going deeper with convolutions. In: Proceedings of the IEEE Conference on Computer Vision and Pattern Recognition, pp. 1–9 (2015)
3. Girshick, R., Donahue, J., Darrell, T., et al.: Rich feature hierarchies for accurate object detection and semantic segmentation. In: Proceedings of the IEEE Conference on Computer Vision and Pattern Recognition, pp. 580–587 (2014)
4. Girshick, R.: Fast R-CNN. In: Proceedings of the IEEE Conference on Computer Vision and Pattern Recognition, pp. 1440–1448 (2015)
5. Gong, Y., Liu, L., Yang, M., et al.: Compressing deep convolutional networks using vector quantization (2014). arXiv preprint: arXiv:1412.6115
6. Chen, W., Wilson, J., Tyree, S., et al.: Compressing neural networks with the hashing trick. In: Proceedings of the International Conference on Machine Learning, pp. 2285–2294 (2015)
7. Vanhoucke, V., Senior, A., Mao, M.Z.: Improving the speed of neural networks on CPUs. In: Proceedings of the Annual Conference on Neural Information Processing Systems, pp. 4–8 (2011)
8. Courbariaux, M., Bengio, Y., David, J.P.: Training deep neural networks with low precision multiplications (2015). arXiv preprint: arXiv:1412.7024
9. Lin, Z., Courbariaux, M., Memisevic, R., et al.: Neural Networks with Few Multiplications (2016). arXiv preprint: arXiv:1510.03009
10. Courbariaux, M., Bengio, Y., David, J.P.: Binaryconnect: training deep neural networks with binary weights during propagations. In: Proceedings of the Annual Conference on Neural Information Processing Systems, pp. 3123–3131 (2015)
11. Deng, J., Dong, W., Socher, R., et al.: Imagenet: a large-scale hierarchical image database. In: Proceedings of the IEEE Conference on Computer Vision and Pattern Recognition, pp. 248–255 (2009)
12. Hwang, K., Sung, W.: Fixed-point feedforward deep neural network design using weights +1, 0, and −1 (2014). arXiv preprint: arXiv:1405.3866
13. Li, F., Zhang, B., Liu, B.: Ternary weight networks (2016). arXiv preprint: arXiv:1605.04711
14. Hubara, I., Courbariaux, M., Soudry, D., et al.: Binarized neural networks. In: Proceedings of the Annual Conference on Neural Information Processing Systems, pp. 4107–4115 (2016)
15. Rastegari, M., Ordonez, V., Redmon, J., Farhadi, A.: XNOR-Net: ImageNet classification using binary convolutional neural networks. In: Leibe, B., Matas, J., Sebe, N., Welling, M. (eds.) ECCV 2016, Part IV. LNCS, vol. 9908, pp. 525–542. Springer, Cham (2016). doi:10.1007/978-3-319-46493-0_32
16. Zhou, S., Wu, Y., Ni, Z., et al.: DoReFa-Net: training low bitwidth convolutional neural networks with low bitwidth gradients (2016). arXiv preprint: arXiv:1606.06160
17. Kim, M., Smaragdis, P.: Bitwise Neural Networks (2016). arXiv preprint: arXiv:1601.06071
18. Zhu, C., Han, S., Mao, H.: Trained ternary quantization (2016). arXiv preprint: arXiv:1612.01064
19. Pavan, K., Rao, A., Rao, V., et al.: Robust seed selection algorithm for k-means type algorithms (2012). arXiv preprint: arXiv:1202.1585

20. Ioffe, S., Szegedy, C.: Batch normalization: accelerating deep network training by reducing internal covariate shift. In: Proceedings of the International Conference on Machine Learning, pp. 448–456 (2015)
21. Jia, Y., Shelhamer, E., Donahue, J., et al.: Caffe: convolutional architecture for fast feature embedding. In: Proceedings of the International Conference on Multimedia Retrieval, pp. 675–678 (2014)
22. Simonyan, K., Zisserman, A.: Very deep convolutional networks for large-scale image recognition (2014). arXiv preprint: arXiv:1409.1556

Will Outlier Tasks Deteriorate Multitask Deep Learning?

Sirui Cai, Yuchun Fang[✉], and Zhengyan Ma

School of Computer Engineering and Science, Shanghai University,
Shanghai, China
ycfang@shu.edu.cn

Abstract. Most of the multitask deep learning today use different but correlated tasks to improve their performances by sharing the common features of the tasks. What will happen if we use outlier tasks instead of related tasks? Will they deteriorate the performance? In this paper, we explore the influence of outlier tasks to the multitask deep learning through carefully designed experiments. We compare the accuracies and the convergence rates between the single task convolutional neural network (STCNN) and outlier multitask convolutional neural network (OMTCNN) on facial attribute recognition and hand-written digit recognition. By doing that, we prove that outlier tasks will constrain each other in a multitask network without parameter redundancy and cause a worse performance. We also discover that outlier tasks related to image recognition, like facial attribute recognition and hand-written digit recognition, may not be outlier tasks and have some common features in the bottom layers for the fact that they can use the other one's first convolutional layer to replace theirs without any accuracy losses.

Keywords: Outlier tasks · Multitask learning · Deep learning

1 Introduction

Deep learning [1, 2] is a technique with a long history but hasn't drawn much attention until recent years. With AlexNet [3] winning the ILSVRC in the year of 2012, convolutional neural network [4], a kind of deep learning methods, started to show remarkable performance in computer vision.

Multitask Learning [5] has been widely used in deep learning area. In [6], Biswaranjan, Devries and Taylor demonstrates that learning representations to predict the position and shape of facial landmarks can improve expression recognition from images. In [7], Zhang et al. optimize the detection robustness of facial landmark detection together with heterogeneous but subtly correlated tasks. In [8], Yu and Lane show that by introducing a secondary task we are able to significantly improve the performance of the main task for which the model is trained. Zhang et al. in [9] build a deep convolutional neural network that can simultaneously learn the face/non-face decision, the face pose estimation problem, and the facial landmark localization problem as a post filter to their multi-view face detector.

© Springer International Publishing AG 2017
D. Liu et al. (Eds.): ICONIP 2017, Part II, LNCS 10635, pp. 246–255, 2017.
https://doi.org/10.1007/978-3-319-70096-0_26

All the examples mentioned above use correlated tasks to improve performances of their networks, paying no attention to outlier tasks. What would happen if we apply outlier tasks to the multitask network? Will they deteriorate the performance? In this paper, we try to figure this question out by comparing the performances of single task convolutional neural network (STCNN) and outlier multitask convolutional neural network (OMTCNN).

We choose facial attribute recognition and hand-written digit recognition as our outlier tasks. We suppose outlier tasks would constrain each other and make the performance worse for the reason that they don't have any related information to share.

In the beginning, the OMTCNN perform nearly the same as the STCNN does, which is not what we expect. We think this may be because there are too many parameters in the network for it to perform outlier tasks independently. We prove this by running the experiment with reducing the parameters in the network.

We also find out that outlier tasks related to image recognition, like facial attribute recognition task and hand-written-digit recognition task, may have some common features in the bottom layers, which means they could be related in the bottom level while be isolated in the upper level.

2 Experiments Design

2.1 Experiment Framework

We first directly compare the accuracies during the training between the STCNN and OMTCNN in Sect. 3. These two kinds of network has the same hidden layers and we train them in the exact same way. So the only factor that makes the performance different is whether it perform single task or outlier tasks. In our experiment, the difference between the performances of STCNN and OMTCNN is pretty tiny, which goes against our expectation.

We guess the parameter redundancy in our network structure gives the OMTCNN the ability to perform outlier tasks independently, which makes the loss of performance little. In Sect. 4, we redo the experiment repeatedly while we keep reducing the parameters in the network structure. With the redundancy removed, the difference of the performances between STCNN and OMTCNN become obvious.

However, when the complexity of the structure has been reduced to an extremely small level, the OMTCNN outperform STCNN instead, which implies the two outlier tasks we use might have common features in low level that help the OMTCNN to train. We run another experiment in Sect. 5 to verify this assumption.

2.2 Outlier Tasks and Dataset

Outlier tasks should be tasks that are little correlated. Facial attribute recognition and hand-written digit recognition are our choice. Facial image and hand-written digit image are totally different except for they are both pictures.

We use CelebA dataset, which contains more than 200,000 facial images labeled with 40 attributes, as our dataset for facial attribute recognition and MNIST dataset as our dataset for hand-written digit recognition. We choose 10000 images from each dataset as training set and another 10000 images as testing set.

2.3   Structures of STCNN and OMTCNN

Three kinds of convolutional network are used in our experiments. A STCNN that performs facial attribute recognition, a STCNN that performs hand-written digit recognition and an OMTCNN that does both tasks. These three networks only differ in their output layers, which means they have exactly the same input layers and hidden layers.

As is shown in Fig. 1, the input layers of the three networks have a shape of 100*100*1 and take grey images as inputs. The output layer of the STCNN that recognizes facial attributes is a softmax layer with 2 nodes which represents is or isn't. The output layer of the STCNN that recognizes hand-written digits is a softmax layer with 10 nodes which represents 0 to 9. The OMTCNN has both output layers above.

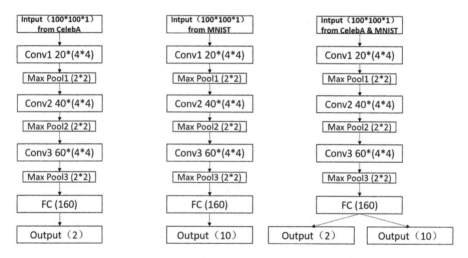

Fig. 1. The basic structure of networks.

In Sect. 4, we keep adjusting the structure of the hidden layers for comparison, so the amount of layers and filters in the hidden layers of these three networks are not fixed. Figure 1 shows the common structure of the hidden layers we use at the beginning in Sect. 3. It has four common hidden layers, which are three convolutional layers and one fully connected layer. The first convolutional layer has 20 4*4 filters, the second convolutional layer has 40 4*4 filters and the third convolutional layer has 60 4*4 filters. Each convolutional layer is followed by a 2*2 max pooling layer.

The fully connected layer at the end has 160 nodes. The activation function used in every layer is ReLU and the cost function we set for all three networks is cross entropy function, both of which are widely used in image recognition task.

3   Influence of Outlier Tasks in OMTCNN

At the beginning, we directly compare the performances of the STCNN and the OMTCNN to see if the outlier tasks worsen the performance.

First, we choose a facial attribute which is labeled in CelebA dataset, for instance, Heavy Makeup, as our target for facial attribute recognition. Then we train the two STCNN with their individual training sets and the OMTCNN with both training sets for 40 epochs. When we train the OMTCNN, we use images from the two training sets in turn, which means if the data of current batch is from CelebA, the data of next batch will be from MNIST. During the entire training, we test the training network with the testing set after each epoch and make record of the accuracies. The accuracies of all three networks on both tasks in 20 epochs are shown in Fig. 2.

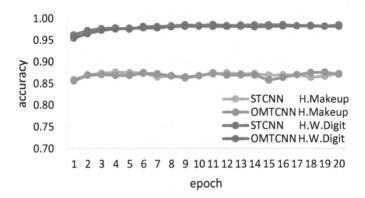

Fig. 2. The accuracies of STCNNs and OMTCNN on heavy makeup recognition and hand-written digit recognition in 20 epochs.

From Fig. 2, we can see that the curves of the accuracies of the STCNN and the accuracies of the OMTCNN nearly overlap no matter in Heavy Makeup recognition or in hand-written digits recognition, which means the OMTCNN of these two outlier tasks has almost the same performance as the STCNN has.

This result is not what we expect. In our hypothesis, outlier tasks will be constrained by each other in multitask network, which makes the performance of OMTCNN worse than the performance of STCNN.

We change the facial attribute from Heavy Makeup to Smiling (Fig. 3) and run the experiment again. The result remains the same.

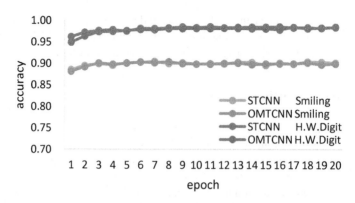

Fig. 3. The accuracies of STCNNs and OMTCNN on Smiling recognition and hand-written digit recognition in 20 epochs.

4   Reducing the Parameter Redundancy

We think the reason that the OMTCNN and STCNN have same performances is the parameters in our network structure are in redundancy. That means the network has enough parameters to perform two outlier tasks independently. So we decide to keep adjusting the structure of the common hidden layers by reducing parameters until we get the result we are looking for or the amount of the parameters are minimized.

4.1   Reducing the Filters in Each Layer

We reduce the parameters of the structure in two ways. One is reducing the number of filters in each convolutional layer and the nodes in the fully connected layer. We reduce half of the filters or nodes of every layer each time. The structures with parameters reduced we use are shown in Table 1.

Table 1. Network structures with different parameter reduction.

Structure	Filters in 1st layer	Filters in 2nd layer	Filters in 3rd layer	Nodes in fc layer
W1	10	20	30	80
W2	5	10	15	40
W3	2	5	7	20
W4	1	2	3	10

We do the same experiment with Heavy Makeup as our facial attribute in this four structures.

From Figs. 4, 5, 6 and 7, we can see that when the number of filters is reduced to a half of the basic structure (W1), the OMTCNN and STCNN still perform pretty closely. When the number of filters is reduced to a quarter of the basic structure (W2), the

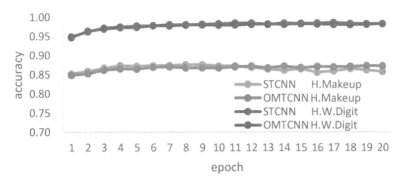

Fig. 4. The accuracies of STCNNs and OMTCNN of W1 structure on heavy makeup recognition and hand-written digit recognition in 20 epochs.

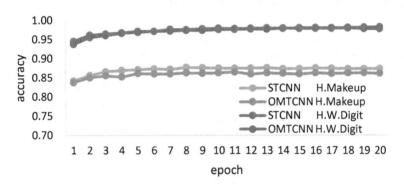

Fig. 5. The accuracies of STCNNs and OMTCNN of W2 structure on heavy makeup recognition and hand-written digit recognition in 20 epochs.

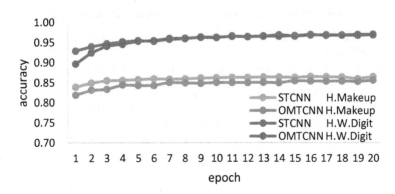

Fig. 6. The accuracies of STCNNs and OMTCNN of W3 structure on heavy makeup recognition and hand-written digit recognition in 20 epochs.

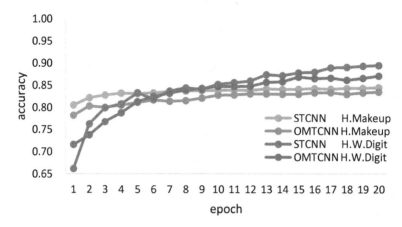

Fig. 7. The accuracies of STCNNs and OMTCNN of W4 structure on heavy makeup recognition and hand-written digit recognition in 20 epochs.

performance of the STCNN on Heavy Makeup recognition is slightly better than that of the OMTCNN. When the number of filters is reduced to one eighth of the basic structure (W3), although both STCNN and OMTCNN reach the same accuracy on hand-written digit recognition, the STCNN converges faster than the OMTCNN. When the number of filters is reduced to one sixteenth of the basic structure (W4), the STCNN performs better than OMTCNN either on Heavy Makeup recognition or on hand-written digit recognition.

In conclusion, with the number of the parameters becoming less, the fact that STCNN outperforms OMTCNN becomes more obvious.

4.2   Reducing the Number of the Layers

The other way we reduce the parameters is reducing the amount of layers of the network. From [10], we know that reducing layers would cost more loss of complexity than reducing filters in each layer. The two structures (D1 and D2) we use are shown below and the result of the experiment we run on them are shown in Figs. 8 and 9.

D1: 40 filters in the 1st layer, 60 filters in the 2nd layer, 160 nodes in fully connected layer.
D2: 60 filters in the 1st layer, 160 nodes in fully connected layer.

From Fig. 8, we can see that, with one layer removed, OMTCNN converges faster than STCNN on Heavy Makeup recognition. And in Fig. 9, with two layers removed, the STCNN can't converge on Heavy Makeup recognition during the whole training while the OMTCNN starts to converge, though very unstable, in the 19th epoch. This is very interesting for we all expect STCNN outperforms OMTCNN but the result goes to the contrary.

There is a mechanism called eavesdropping in multitask learning [5], which says a task can eavesdrop some features it needs but can't extract for some reasons (e.g., lack

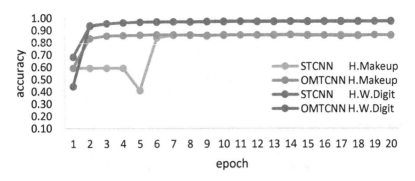

Fig. 8. The accuracies of STCNNs and OMTCNN of D1 structure on heavy makeup recognition and hand-written digit recognition in 20 epochs.

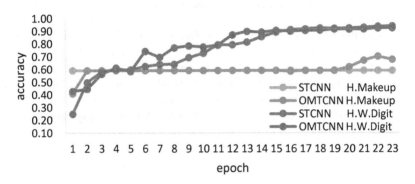

Fig. 9. The accuracies of STCNNs and OMTCNN of D2 structure on heavy makeup recognition and hand-written digit recognition in 23 epochs.

of parameters) from another task that also extracts these features in a multitask network. In our case, we assume the reason that the OMTCNN can converge is that the Heavy Makeup recognition task eavesdrops some features from the hand-written recognition task in our multitask network, which means this two tasks may not be outlier tasks in bottom level layers. They may have some common features in the bottom layers (e.g., outline detection).

5   Common Features in Outlier Tasks

From Figs. 8 and 9, we see that the OMTCNN outperforms the STCNN on Heavy Makeup recognition when the complexity of their network structure is extremely small. According to this situation, we propose a hypothesis that facial attribute recognition task and hand-written digit recognition task may have some common features in the bottom layers that help the OMTCNN.

To verify this hypothesis, we do the following experiment. As is shown in Fig. 10, we use the first convolutional layer of the STCNN for hand-written digit recognition to

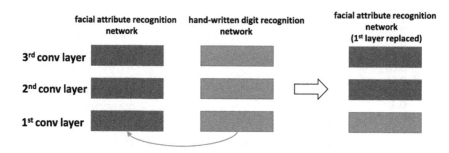

Fig. 10. Replace the facial attribute recognition network's 1st layer with the hand-written digit recognition network's 1st layer.

replace the first convolutional layer of the STCNN for Heavy Makeup recognition and see the difference of performances between this STCNN with 1st layer replaced and the original STCNN.

To obtain the STCNN with 1st layer replaced, we first train the network (in W3 structure) with MNIST dataset for hand-written recognition for 10 epochs (at this moment, it has already converged), then we freeze the first layer of the hidden layers, which means the weights and the biases of it are fixed, and finally, we train the network with CelebA dataset for Heavy Makeup recognition.

The comparison of accuracies between this network and the original one is shown in Fig. 11.

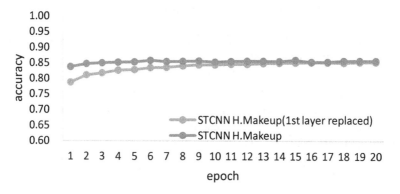

Fig. 11. The accuracies of STCNN and STCNN (1st layer replaced) on heavy makeup recognition in 20 epochs.

From Fig. 11, we can see the STCNN with 1st layer replaced converge to the same accuracy as the original network does, just with a smaller convergence rate. This can prove that the first layer of the network that perform CelebA Heavy Makeup recognition can be replaced by the first layer of the network that perform MNIST hand-written digits recognition, which means this two tasks have some common features in the first layer. We also run the experiment on STCNN for hand-written recognition with 1st layer replaced by STCNN for Heavy Makeup recognition and get the similar result.

6 Conclusions

We first compare the performances between the STCNN and OMTCNN. Then we reduce the parameters in our network structure and do the comparison again to see the difference. By doing this, we find out that in a multitask network, outlier tasks would constrain each other and make the performance of the multitask network worse than that of the single task network, if the parameters of the network are not in redundancy. We also use the first layer of a hand-written digit recognition network (trained with MNIST) to replace the first layer of a Heavy Makeup recognition network (trained with CelebA). Then we compare the performance of this replaced network and the original network. By doing this, we can draw a conclusion that outlier tasks may not always be isolated, they could be correlated or isolated in different level. For outlier tasks related to image recognition, like facial attribute recognition and hand-written digit recognition, they could be correlated in the bottom layers for some basic image processing.

Acknowledgement. The work is funded by the National Natural Science Foundation of China (No. 61170155), Shanghai Innovation Action Plan Project (No. 16511101200) and the Open Project Program of the National Laboratory of Pattern Recognition (No. 201600017).

References

1. Goodfellow, I., Bengio, Y., Courville, A.: Deep Learning. MIT Press, Cambridge (2016)
2. Nielsen, M.: Neural Networks and Deep Learning. Determination Press (2015)
3. Krizhevsky, A., Sutskever, I., Hinton, E.: ImageNet classification with deep convolutional neural networks. In: International Conference on Neural Information Processing Systems (2012)
4. Lecun, Y., Haffner, P.: Gradient-based Learning applied to document recognition. Proc. IEEE **86**, 2278–2324 (1998)
5. Caruana, R.: Multitask learning. Mach. Learn. **28**, 41–75 (1997)
6. Biswaranjan, K., Devries, T., Taylor, G.W.: Multitask learning of facial landmarks and expression. In: 2014 Canadian Conference on Computer and Robot Vision, pp. 98–103 (2014)
7. Zhang, Z., Luo, P., Chen, C.L., Tang, X.: Facial landmark detection by deep multitask learning. In: European Conference on Computer Vision, pp. 94–108 (2014)
8. Yu, B., Lane, I.: Multitask deep learning for image understanding. In: Soft Computing and Pattern Recognition, pp. 37–42. IEEE (2014)
9. Zhang, C., Zhang, Z.: Improving multiview face detection with multitask deep convolutional neural networks. In: IEEE Winter Conference on Applications of Computer Vision, pp. 1036–1041 (2014)
10. Bengio, Y.: Learning Deep Architectures for AI. Now Publishers, Hanover (2009)

The Effect of Task Similarity on Deep Transfer Learning

Wei Zhang, Yuchun Fang$^{(\boxtimes)}$, and Zhengyan Ma

School of Computer Engineering and Science,
Shanghai University, Shanghai, China
ycfang@shu.edu.cn

Abstract. In recent years, with deep learning achieving a great success, deep transfer learning gradually becomes a new issue. Fine-tuning as a simple transfer learning method can be used to help train deep network and improve the performance of network. In our paper, we use two fine-tuning strategies on deep convolutional neural network and compare their results. There are many influencing factors, such as the depth and width of the network, the amount of data, the similarity of the source and target domain, and so on. Then we keep the network structure and other related factors consistent and use the fine fine-tuning strategy to find the effect of cross-domain factor and similarity of task. Specifically, we use source network and target test data to calculate the similarity. The results of experiments show that when we use fine-tune strategy, using different dataset in source and target domain would affect the target task a lot. Besides the similarity of tasks has direction, and to some extent the similarity would reflect the increment of performance of target task when the source and target task use the same dataset.

Keywords: Deep learning · Transfer learning · CNN

1 Introduction

The convolutional neural network(CNN) has achieved a great success in image recognition. With the rapid development of GPU compute capability, large-scale images can be used to train CNN in a relatively acceptable time. CNN model like Krizhevsky et al. [1] has a good performance in recognizing CIFAR-10 dataset. GoogLeNet [2] is a 22 layers deep network which achieves state-of-art performance in the ILSVRC14.

Transfer learning aims to extract the knowledge from source task and apply the knowledge to target task. Pan et al. [3] has a detailed introduction to transfer learning.

It is meaningful to apply transfer learning to CNN so that the performance of CNN could be improved. Many methods of deep transfer learning have been proposed. Ge and Yu [4] use the similar images of source task to improve the performance of target network when training data of target task is insufficient, and they got a good result. Xu et al. [5] use a semi-supervised method to train a network with existing labeled data and no-labeled web data. Long et al. [6] proposed the joint adaptation networks and Ding et al. [7] proposed the task-driven deep transfer network.

© Springer International Publishing AG 2017
D. Liu et al. (Eds.): ICONIP 2017, Part II, LNCS 10635, pp. 256–265, 2017.
https://doi.org/10.1007/978-3-319-70096-0_27

In fact, there are many factors which influence the performance of CNN a lot. Azizpour et al. [8] found those factors such as network width, network depth, early stopping, source task, fine-tuning. In our experiment, we get rid of those factors which are related to structure of network and concentrate on factors of dataset and the label of samples. we want to get some guide conclusions that will help us to choose a better plan to improve the performance of the target network.

In deep learning field, the trained network can be considered as a prediction function [9] which is called 'task' in transfer learning field. Tasks can be divided into source task and target task. Source task is used to help improve the performance of target task. The similarity between source task and target task can influence the performance of target task. We can get the similarity by logic thinking, but how can we choose source task when there are some similar tasks? Logic thinking won't work without a hitch in this case. We try to define similarity mathematically and find a good conclusion.

Transfer learning always uses two domains which is called source domain and target domain individually to name datasets which are used in source task and target task.

There is no doubt that when transferring to the same target task, cross-domain transfer learning and transfer learning whose source domain and target domain are the same would have difference performances. Cross-domain means the dataset of source domain and target domain are drawn from the different feature space and different distribution, which increases the difference of source and target domain. In real world applications, we have to use different datasets for transfer learning when there are few samples for training in target task. Because of those reasons, the need of finding out the influence of cross-domain and same domain on transfer learning arises.

Transfer learning uses the knowledge from source domain and source task to improve the performance of target task. Knowledge learnt from source domain and source task consist in weights and biases of deep network. Fine-tuning, which uses weights and bias of network as the initializing parameter of target network, is a method of deep transfer learning. We use this method to perform some experiments, and it gets good results.

2 Strategies of Deep Transfer Learning

Fine-tuning [10] is a method of transferring knowledge from an existed model to a novel model. Fine-tuning uses the weights and biases of a trained network as the initial weights and biases of novel network before the novel network starts to train. In our experiments, the trained network is called source network and the novel network is called target network. And we use the same CNN architecture in source network and target network.

The other method is called simple deep feature extraction method. This method uses the same network architecture in source network and target network, but the convolution layers are fixed in target network so that low layer of source network could be used as deep feature extractor. Those deep features from different task might be similar, which could be used to transfer as the joint knowledge. In fact, simple deep extraction method uses a simple network architecture in task network because only several layers in network can be trained.

In fact, since the difference between simple feature extraction method and fine-tuning is that the former will fix convolutional layers' weights and biases and the latter set all weights and biases trainable, simple deep feature extraction method is a simplified version of fine-tuning. Before starting to introduce experiments, we would like to name Fine-tuning as strategy I and name simple deep feature extraction method strategy II. The architectures of strategies are depicted in Fig. 1.

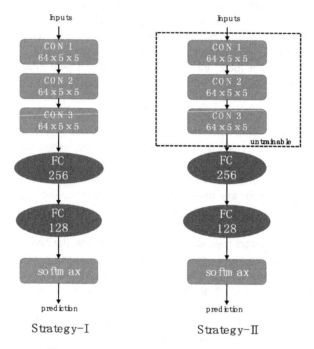

Fig. 1. The CNN architectures in experiments

In the experiments, we consider that the performance which gets from using test dataset of target task to measure the accuracy of source network is associated with the similarity between source task and target task, because the performance of target network could be better when tasks are similar. Validation function $h(D_{test})$ denotes the accuracy of network, which is got with the test dataset D_{test}. We denote the source task validation function and target source task validation function as $h_S(\cdot)$ and $h_T(\cdot)$. $D_{training}^S, D_{test}^S$ stand for training dataset and test dataset of source domain. $D_{training}^T, D_{test}^T$ stand for training dataset and test dataset of target domain. We denote S as the similarity between source task and target task with shown as Eq. (1).

$$S = h_S\left(D_{test}^S\right) \times \ln \frac{h_S\left(D_{test}^S\right)}{h_S\left(D_{test}^T\right)} \tag{1}$$

According to the Eq. (1), the smaller the S, the more similar the source task and target task. There are two similarities S_1, S_2. Note that if source task and target task of S_1 are both different from these of S_2, comparison between S_1 and S_2 is meaningless.

Besides, we assume that the effects of similarity between source task and target task will be exhibited obviously when using a simple network architecture. In other words, as the similarity of task is not the main factors of transfer learning and its effects would be invisible when network is enough complex. In experiments, if performances of target networks which get with strategy I are almost no difference, we could use the strategy II to perform the same experiment so that it could show different experimental results.

3 Experiments

3.1 Data Processing

In experiments, we use gender label, heavy makeup label and lipstick label from CelebA[1] dataset and gender label from CAS-PEAL[2] dataset. CelebA dataset is a large-scale face attributes dataset where images cover large pose variations and background clutter. There are 99594 images in CAS-PEAL dataset that is smaller than CelebA dataset.

Because positive and negative samples have different quantities in CelebA and CAS-PEAL dataset, we tried to remove this effect from experiments. We extract 25000 male label images and 25000 female label images from CelebA dataset so that we get 40000 images as gender training dataset and 10000 images as gender test dataset. Like getting gender training and test dataset, we get the training dataset and test dataset of heavy makeup and lipstick. In CAS-PEAL dataset, we try to flip and rotate the images for getting more samples, and finally we get a gender dataset with 15000 training samples and 5000 test samples.

Furthermore, samples from CelebA dataset and CAS-PEAL have different size, but our network requires a constant input dimension. We fix the samples' size as 80×64.

Finally, we get CelebA gender dataset, CelebA heavy makeup dataset, CelebA lipstick dataset and CAS-PEAL gender dataset for our experiments.

3.2 Training Source Task Network

In order to prove our assumption, we use strategy I and strategy II to do a series of experiments. According to whether cross-domain and cross task, we divide experiments into four parts, that is normal network training, same domain and different tasks training, cross-domain and same task training, cross-domain and different tasks training.

The same domain and different tasks training only uses strategy I when the other transfer learning experiments use both strategy I and strategy II.

---

[1] http://mmlab.ie.cuhk.edu.hk/projects/CelebA.html.

[2] http://www.jdl.ac.cn/peal/.

We trained four networks, which are CelebA gender network, CelebA heavy makeup network, CelebA lipstick and CAS-PEAL Gender network, as the source network from the normal network training experiments. We uses this four source networks to do transfer learning experiments. The performances of source networks are showed in Table 1.

Table 1. Performances of source networks

Lebel	Accuracy
CelebA gender	96.54%
CelebA heavy makeup	90.14%
CelebA lipstick	92.40%
CAS-PEAL gender	98.46%

3.3   Different Performances of Different Transfer Strategies

We use two strategies in our experiments with the result that experiments which use strategy I 2%-6% higher than using strategy II. The Table 2 shows differences of performances when using different strategies. As the strategy II use a simpler network architecture, the result gets a bit lower. In fact, strategy II can't improve performance of target network.

Table 2. Using different strategy, getting different result. The notations Acc-I, Acc-II represent accuracy from the target network which use strategy I and II respectively. The notation Difference represents Acc-I minus Acc-II

Source task label	Target task label	Acc-I	Acc-II	Difference
CAS-PEAL gender	CelebA gender	96.66%	90.74%	+5.92%
CAS-PEAL gender	CelebA heavy makeup	89.90%	84.88%	+5.02%
CAS-PEAL gender	CelebA lipstick	91.88%	87.48%	+4.40%
CelebA gender	CAS-PEAL gender	99.05%	96.56%	+2.49%
CelebA heavy makeup	CAS-PEAL gender	99.05%	95.97%	+3.08%
CelebA lipstick	CAS-PEAL gender	99.13%	95.86%	+3.27%

When training networks, we find that the target networks' cross-entropy loss starts from a low value when the target task and source task are similar as show in Fig. 2. On the contrary, the cross-entropy loss starts from a high value and is sometimes even higher than those using random initializing weights. And have a look at those experiments, they always are cross-domain and have different source task label and target task label. Besides, we get a good performance when epoch of training is low with fine-tuning method, for example experiments of transferring to CelebA Gender label as shown in the Fig. 3.

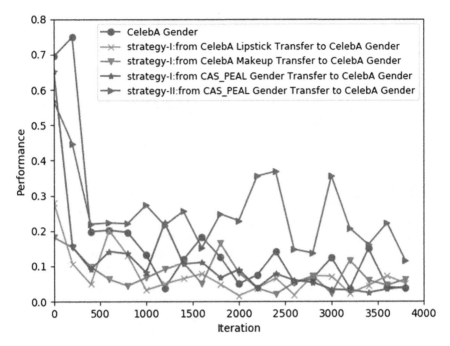

Fig. 2. Comparison of Training loss of transferring to CelebA gender task experiments. Losses of Cross-domain experiments always have higher initial values than those using the same domain.

3.4   Cross-Domain Factor

Different datasets have different feature spaces. It has an impact on transfer learning. We put the experimental results in the Table 3. We find that the results of transfer from the CAS-PEAL network to CelebA lipstick and heavy makeup network experiments didn't achieve the goal of improving performances of target networks. We think that CAS-PEAL samples are grey scale images and there are few helpful features from CAS-PEAL gender network to help improve the performance of CelebA lipstick and makeup network which need more mostly color features. However, it's effective to transfer from the CelebA lipstick or CelebA makeup network to CAS-PEAL gender network, because CelebA samples have ample gender non-Chinese gender characteristics, which is still helpful for transfer to CAS-PEAL gender network (Chinese gender network).

From the Tables 3 and 4, We try to transfer gender task to heavy makeup task and lipstick task. when the source domain and target domain use the same dataset, the task similarity S is close to 0 which means target task is close to source task, and accuracies are higher than those gotten from normal network. When source domain and target domain are different, it always needs an adaption process so that there are more samples with available and helpful features from source task to be used in target task.

The cross-domain factor is easy to consider that different domains mean different space feature and different distribution. And it will reduce the similarity between source

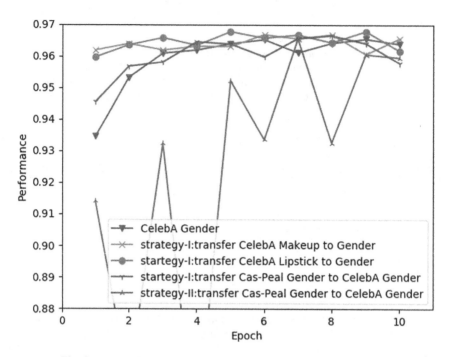

Fig. 3. Accuracies of transferring to CelebA gender task experiments

Table 3. Performance comparison of experiments. Acc represents the accuracy of networks

Source Task	Target Task / Acc	CAS-PEAL	CelebA		
		Gender	Gender	Lipstick	Heavy Makeup
CAS-PEAL	Gender	98.46%	96.66%	91.88%	89.90%
CelebA	Gender	99.08%	96.54%	92.41%	90.64%
	Lipstick	99.13%	96.78%	92.40%	90.73%
	Heavy Makeup	99.05%	96.69%	92.77%	90.14%

task and target task. However, some joint knowledge can still be learned by target task and the quantity of knowledge might be few when the difference between source domain and target domain is high. If target domain has little samples for training, try to find a similar dataset and make S small might be helpful to train and improve the target network's performance.

Table 4. Similarity Comparison. The notation S computed with Eq. (1) represents the similarity of tasks. And the smaller the S, the higher the similarity

S Source Task \ Target Task		CAS-PEAL	CelebA		
		Gender	Gender	Lipstick	Heavy Makeup
CAS-PEAL	Gender	0	0.2674	0.3154	0.3377
CelebA	Gender	0.3263	0	0.08286	0.1333
	Lipstick	0.5241	-0.0069	0	0.0394
	Heavy Makeup	0.5182	0.0197	-0.0076	0

3.5   Transferring in the Same Dataset

When source task and target task use the same dataset, we can ignore dataset adaptation process and pay attention to different tasks. We find that S is smaller when Acc is higher. As shown in Table 4, in transferring to CelebA Gender experiments, the similarity between CelebA lipstick and CelebA Gender is closer than the similarity between CelebA heavy makeup and CelebA Gender, and CelebA lipstick transfer to CelebA gender experiment gets the best performance in the transferring to CelebA Gender experiments.

In our opinion, similarity of tasks has directionality. As shown in Fig. 4, the end of the arrow represents the source task and the head of the arrow represents the target task. Besides we marked similarity and improvement of target task in the middle of the arrow. Note that S can be compared between transfer experiments only when source or

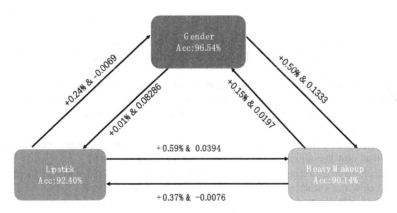

Fig. 4. The similarity and increment of performance of transfer experiments with CelebA dataset

target tasks are the same. Otherwise, it would be meaningless. When we consider to ensure that the source tasks are the same and comparing different target task, there is no clear regularity can be found from S and increment of performance. However, when we keep target task the same and make source task different, we find that the smaller the S, the greater the increment. Different target tasks would have different training difficulties. We make target tasks consistent so that we could get the same criteria. However, it no longer follows the laws when source task and target task use different datasets. We think that the factor of different datasets will affect transfer experiments with different tasks simultaneously.

4 Conclusion

In this paper, we try to use two different strategies as transfer methods. Experimental results show that strategy I is useful and strategy II can't improve the performance of target task. Then we use strategy I to find the regular of cross-domain factors and similarity of tasks. When using different datasets, source task should have sufficient training data and the training samples have similar feature space to those in target domain. Finally, we find the heuristic relevance of the similarity and increment of performance of target network. Nevertheless, our mathematical approach to compute task similarity still needs to be further improved to apply to more different situations. our experimental analysis should go deeper in neural networks and find more transfer strategies in feature investigation.

Acknowledgments. The work is funded by the National Natural Science Foundation of China (No. 61170155), Shanghai Innovation Action Plan Project (No. 16511101200) and the Open Project Program of the National Laboratory of Pattern Recognition (No. 201600017).

References

1. Krizhevsky, A., Sutskever, I., Hinton, G.E.: Imagenet classification with deep convolutional neural networks. In: Pereira, F., Burges, C., Bottou, L., Weinberger, K. (eds.) NIPS 2012, pp. 1097–1105 (2012)
2. Szegedy, C., Liu, W., Jia, Y., Sermanet, P., Reed, S., Anguelov, D., Erhan, D., Vanhoucke, V., Rabinovich, A.: Going deeper with convolutions. In: IEEE CVPR 2015 (2015)
3. Pan, S.J., Yang, Q.: A survey on transfer learning. IEEE Trans. Knowl. Data Eng., 1345–1359 (2010)
4. Ge, W., Yu, Y.: Borrowing treasures from the wealthy: deep transfer learning through selective joint fine-tuning. arXiv preprint arXiv:1702.08690 (2017)
5. Xu, Z., Huang, S., Zhang, Y., Tao, D.: Webly-supervised fine-grained visual categorization via deep domain adaptation. IEEE Trans. Pattern Anal. Mach. Intell. (2016)
6. Long, M., Wang, J., Jordan, M.I.: Deep transfer learning with joint adaptation networks. arXiv preprint arXiv:1605.06636 (2016)
7. Ding, Z., Nasrabadi, N.M., Fu, Y.: Task-driven deep transfer learning for image classification. In: 2016 IEEE International Conference on Acoustics, Speech and Signal Processing, pp. 2414–2418. IEEE (2016)

8. Azizpour, H., Razavian, A. S., Sullivan, J., Maki, A., Carlsson, S.: Factors of transferability for a generic convNet representation. IEEE Trans. Pattern Anal. Mach. Intell., 1790–1802 (2016)
9. A visual proof that neural nets can compute any function, neuralnetworksanddeeplearning. com/chap4.html. Accessed 20 May 2017
10. CS231n Convolutional Neural Networks for Visual Recognition, cs231.github.io/transfer-learning/. Accessed 15 June 2017

Exploiting the Tibetan Radicals in Recurrent Neural Network for Low-Resource Language Models

Tongtong Shen[1], Longbiao Wang[1], Xie Chen[2],
Kuntharrgyal Khysru[1], and Jianwu Dang[1,3(✉)]

[1] Tianjin Key Laboratory of Cognitive Computing and Application,
Tianjin University, Tianjin, China
{ttshen, longbiao_wang, gtjl86}@tju.edu.cn
[2] University of Cambridge, Cambridge, UK
xc257@cam.ac.uk
[3] Japan Advanced Institute of Science and Technology, Ishikawa, Japan
jdang@jaist.ac.jp

Abstract. In virtue of the superiority of handling the sequence data and the effectiveness of preserving long-distance information, recurrent neural network language model (RNNLM) has prevailed in a range of tasks in recent years. However, a large quantities of data are required for language modelling with good performance, which poses the difficulties of modeling for low-resource languages. To address this issue, Tibetan as one of minority languages is instantiated, and its radicals (components of Tibetan characters) are explored for constructing language model. Motivated by the inherent structure of Tibetan, a novel construction of Tibetan character embedding is exploited to RNNLM. The fusion of individual radical embedding is enhanced by three ways, including using uniform weight (TRU), different weights (TRD) and radical combination (TRC). This structure, especially combining with the radicals, can extend the capability to capture long-term context dependencies and solve the low-resource problem to some extent. The experimental results suggest that this proposed structure obtained a better performance than standard RNNLM, yielding 7.4%, 12.7% and 13.5% relative perplexity reduction by using TRU, TRD and TRC respectively.

Keywords: Language model · Low resource · Recurrent neural network · Character embedding · Radical

1 Introduction

Statistical language model (LM) is a crucial component of many applications, such as machine translation, information retrieval and speech recognition [1–3], which provides a high-level understanding of text or speech in statistical point of view.

T. Shen and L. Wang—These authors contributed equally to this work.

© Springer International Publishing AG 2017
D. Liu et al. (Eds.): ICONIP 2017, Part II, LNCS 10635, pp. 266–275, 2017.
https://doi.org/10.1007/978-3-319-70096-0_28

LM aims to calculate the probability of any given word sequence, which allows LM to be incorporated into the statistical models. Meanwhile, the syntactic and semantic attributes of sentences can be encoded implicitly in LM to improve prediction.

The conventional n-gram LM [4–6] has been the dominant LM for several decades due to its easy implementation, fast training and good generalization. For n-gram LM, however, there are two well-known issues. The first is that it cannot capture long-term information due to its n-gram assumption. The second is the data sparsity issue. Recurrent neural network provides a feasible solution for both of these two issues, by projecting each word into a low and continuous space, and using recurrent connection to keep the complete history information. Recently, RNNLM [7–9] has been proved to outperform the traditional n-gram LM to be the state-of-the-art. However, a large quantity of data are required for robust parameter estimation. So data sparsity is still an issue for low-resource languages, which is the research topic in this paper. Tibetan is one of minority languages used in China. And data sparsity issue is also the top priority to be dealt with.

Many different approaches have been explored to address the data sparsity issue. One direction is to reduce the amount of model parameters, including LM based class and LM with compression layer [6, 10]. However, it is still poor to make prediction of rare words even with a smaller amount of model parameters. RNNLM is able to mitigate the sparsity issue by using word embedding as inputs. So another natural approach draws support from richer features [12, 13], which can be exploited to enhance the word embedding and help RNN learn more context information effectively. Subwords [14–16] that contain some smaller units such as characters and morphs are exploited widely. In [17], the morphological structure is leveraged by exploiting the different uses of morphological features both in input layer and output layer. An apparent drawback is that the morph decomposition needs extra tools. Besides, it is inappropriate to Tibetan, in which the concept of morph is not existed. [18] utilized the subword information by a character-level convolutional neural network (CNN). Although the experimental results demonstrated that the model consistently outperforms the standard LSTM baseline, it didn't work well for Tibetan.

But for Tibetan LM, it still remains preliminary stage having not utilizing RNNLM due to the scarcity of the training data. Character is a natural and minimal meaningful unit for Tibetan, which is similar as word in English. By analyzing and exploiting the features of Tibetan character, a new structure exploiting the Tibetan radical (component of Tibetan character) encoding is proposed, which shows high potential to solve the data sparsity issue.

In this paper, our proposed model aims to exploit the particular Tibetan radical unit, and interpolates the radical embeddings into character embedding. To explore different properties of different radicals, factors for different radical embeddings are introduced, which allows the model more flexibility. And every radical embedding can be interpolated according to its contribution to the integral meaning of corresponding character. Besides, there is a radical combination phenomenon in Tibetan. Encoding for radical combination can fully utilize the properties of Tibetan radicals. By the introduction of radical embeddings, the character embedding is enhanced with more useful semantic information, which can help to address the data sparsity issue.

The rest of the paper is organized as follows. Section 2 gives a brief overview of the standard RNNLM. Section 3 describes the proposed RNNLM with structured character embedding enhanced with Tibetan radical encoding. The experimental setup and evaluation results are given in Sect. 4. Section 5 gives a discussion about the experimental results. Finally, we conclude the research and the future work in Sect. 6.

2   Review of Standard RNNLM

Statistical language model is given a sequence of words, then to measure how likely a sentence is by predicting its probability. RNNLM can make use of sequential information well. It preserves long-span context by the introduction of hidden layer which captures information of what has been calculated so far. The standard structure of RNN is depicted in Fig. 1.

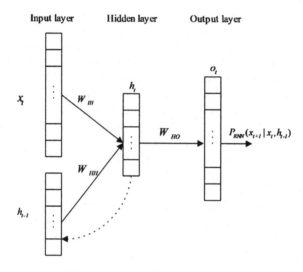

Fig. 1. Structure of standard RNNLM

x_t denotes the input layer of time t, which encodes the present word w_t using one-hot vector whose size is V_{word}. The hidden layer, denoted as h_t, preserves the remaining context information by using the activation function. The output layer of RNNLM is o_t, which is the language model probability of each word at time $t+1$ in vocabulary given the history word sequence $<w_t, \ldots, w_1>$. Input layer, hidden layer and output layer in the propagation process of RNNLM can be computed as follows:

$$h_t = f(W_{IH}x_t + W_{HH}h_{t-1}) \tag{1}$$

$$o_t = g(W_{HO}h_t) \tag{2}$$

$$P_{RNN}(x_{t+1} = k|x_t, h_{t-1}) = o_{t,k} \tag{3}$$

where $f(z)$ and $g(z_m)$ are sigmoid and softmax activation functions:

$$f(z) = \frac{1}{1 + e^{-z}} \tag{4}$$

$$g(z_m) = \frac{e^{z_m}}{\sum_k e^{z_k}} \tag{5}$$

Behind the structure of RNNLM, the idea is to make full use of sequence information in virtue of the hidden layer which is executed repeatedly for each word, so that it can model arbitrarily long span information. But in practice it is limited to looking back only a few steps. Still, RNNLM needs to be modified and interpolated more extra features to model longer context.

3   RNNLM with Tibetan Radical

3.1   Introduction of Tibetan Radical

Tibetan is a low-resource language known as one of minority languages in China. In a sentence, every two characters are separated by a *tsek* (a Tibetan separator). But there is not any symbol to divide the Tibetan word, which makes word segmentation a difficulty. For Tibetan, character is the minimal semantic unit, which is similar as word in English. So character unit is chosen as the input unit.

A Tibetan character has a complex shape, which is actually a group of radicals with size of 1 to 7 as shown is Fig. 2. Each radical has its contribution to produce the meaning of character, therefore, it carries some information to predict the character. Next, different model structures are explored to exploit the properties of Tibetan radicals.

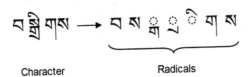

Character   Radicals

Fig. 2. An example of Tibetan character and its radical decomposition

3.2   RNNLM with Structured Character Embedding

In order to enrich the input character embedding with Tibetan radical features, the structured character embedding is proposed, which is interpolated with the weighted sum of Tibetan radical embeddings. Equation (6) shows the structured character embedding with radicals,

$$\vec{c}_r = \vec{c} + \lambda\left(\sum\nolimits_{i \in N} \vec{r}_i\right) \tag{6}$$

where $\vec{c}$ denotes the character embedding, $\vec{r}_i$ represents embedding of the radical that is in position i of the radical sequence and N is the number of radicals of a specific character, which varies between 1 and 7. And a uniform weight λ is introduced to realize the structured character embedding $\vec{c}_r$ with radical embeddings.

$$\vec{c}_r = \vec{c} + \sum\nolimits_{i \in N} \lambda_i \vec{r}_i \tag{7}$$

In order to further explore the property of each radical, different weights λ_i for different radicals are proposed to optimize the structured character embedding as Eq. (7).

The structured RNNLM with Tibetan radicals is illustrated in Fig. 3, and there is also a compression layer which collects both the character embedding and the corresponding radical embeddings. Two main benefits can be obtained by introducing compression layer. First, it compresses the input information and extracts its more meaningful parts. What's more, it reduces the size of the model that becomes larger due to the introduction of radicals. The proposed model can be trained using standard back propagation through time (BPTT) [7] algorithm with slight parameter shift.

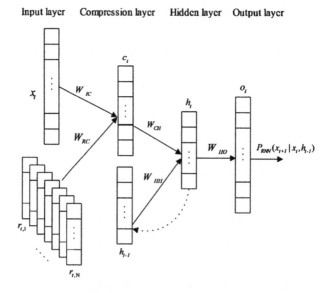

Fig. 3. RNNLM with structured Tibetan character embedding

As illustrated in Fig. 3, the formulas in the propagation process of RNNLM can be rewritten as follows:

$$c_t = f(W_{IC}x_t + \sum_{i \in N} \Lambda_i W_{RC}r_{t,i}) \qquad (8)$$

$$h_t = f(W_{CH}c_t + W_{HH}h_{t-1}) \qquad (9)$$

$$o_t = g(W_{HO}h_t) \qquad (10)$$

where Λ_i is the ith weight matrix for the ith radical, and every Λ_i is equal for TRU, but unequal for TRD. The parameters to be trained involve $\{W_{IC}, W_{RC}, W_{CH}, W_{HH}, W_{HO}, \Lambda_i\}$.

Besides, many different units can be the inputs of RNNLM, such as phrase, word, character, or smaller unit radical in this paper. In small unit based LM, since the number of radicals is small in Tibetan, the radical vocabulary can cover all radicals in data set. It not only simplifies the model structure, but more significantly, avoids out-of-vocabulary (OOV) issue and relieves data sparsity. But large unit is usually necessary because small unit based LM is disadvantaged in capturing long context information under the limit of modeling distance of RNN. So it is vital to achieve a balance between these two cases. By analyzing the property of Tibetan character, it is unnatural to straight decompose the Tibetan character into several radicals. But some combinations of Tibetan radicals carry more semantic information. Added Tibetan structure information of Tibetan can further optimize the representation of Tibetan character. Figure 4 shows an example of Tibetan radical combination. If the structure put in the square is regarded as an integral whole, it is able to preserve more useful information. In this paper, the fixed radical combination is also adopted.

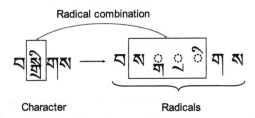

Fig. 4. An example of Tibetan radical combination

4   Experiments and Results

Experiments were conducted to examine the performance of proposed model structures on a small benchmark data set. Perplexity (PPL) is chosen as the evaluation criterion, and a language model with better performance usually has lower PPL. In this section, the experimental corpora are described in detail. Then, results of the baseline LMs are exhibited, which are used as the contrast experiments. Finally, we present the results of RNNLMs with Tibetan radicals.

4.1   Experimental Setup

In this paper, the raw data about news were crawled from the internet, and then checked and cleaned by two Tibetan experts. The clean data were divided into 25 sections, with the standard segmentation method in [7, 18]. Section 0–20 were used as the training set while Section 21–22 and 23–24 were picked out for validation and testing respectively.

The character vocabulary was limited to the top 2472 ranking according to frequency. In addition, an OOV notation was used to present any character not in the chosen vocabulary. The size of the corpora and the percentage of OOV character are illustrated in Table 1. It also shows the information of Tibetan radical covered all characters in the vocabulary, including the single radical and radical combination.

Table 1. Statistics of Tibetan data

Data	# Token	% OOV
Char vocabulary	2472	–
Single radical	57	–
Radical combination	420	–
Training set	1.5 m	1.08
Valid set	125 k	1.12
Test set	126 k	1.11

4.2   Results of RNNLM with Structured Character Embedding

The proposed RNNLMs with Tibetan radical (RNN_TR) were implemented using CUED-RNNLM toolkit [10, 19] and we denoted the baseline RNNLM using Tibetan character only as RNN_TC. For fair comparison, all networks were unfolded 5 times (bptt = 5). The comparison between standard RNN_TC and two kinds of RNN_TR is made in Table 2. It shows that RNN_TR gets a significant PPL improvement over the standard RNN_TC. With the increase of hidden units, the PPL of standard RNN_TC can't be reduced due to its dependency on large amount of data. But for RNN_TR, the performance can get stable improvement, which demonstrates that the introduction of radical can solve the data sparsity issue to some extent.

It is also interesting to explore the properties of different radicals from the same character. As described in Sect. 3, there are two kinds of RNN_TRs, RNNLM with uniform weight (RNN_TRU) and RNNLM with different weights (RNN_TRD) respectively. From Table 2, improvement of RNN_TRD is significantly higher than

Table 2. Evaluation results comparison between RNN_TRU and RNN_TRD

LM	#Hidden Units	PPL			
		_TC	_TRU	_TRD	_TRC
RNN	400	59.9	59.6	56.5	55.9
	500	58.4	58.3	55.8	54.9
	600	61.8	58.0	54.9	54.4
	700	62.2	57.6	54.3	53.8

RNN_TRU. And when hidden units were 700, RNN_TRU and RNN_TRD yield 7.4% PPL reduction and 12.7% PPL reduction. It shows that each component of a Tibetan character has varying contributions to the integrated meaning.

To verify the effectiveness of radical combination, RNN_TRC which denotes RNN_TR with Tibetan radical combination, was trained and evaluated in Table 2. It shows that RNN_TRC achieved sustained performance improvement in 1% relative PPL reduction and radical combination is a more natural semantic unit compared with single radical.

4.3   Results of Interpolation Between RNNLM and N-Gram LM

RNNLMs and n-gram LM, as two inherently different LMs, have their respective modeling power. RNNLMs are usually combined with n-gram LM using a fixed weight by linear interpolation. This part mainly explores the interpolation results and verifies their varying complementary attributes.

With the experimental verification, the best results were obtained when interpolation weight is 0.6 for RNNs. We denoted Kneser-Ney smoothed 3-gram as KN3, and selected the best result for each RNN structure (Hidden units are 500 for RNN_TC, and 700 for three RNN_TRs). In Table 3, we can see that our proposed RNN structures all obtained better results compared with conventional KN3. What's more, when RNNs are combined with KN3, definite improvements are achieved. It demonstrates that RNNs and n-gram both have their complementary contributes and further testify the effectiveness of our modified RNNs in solving the data sparsity issue especially for Tibetan.

Table 3.   Interpolation results between RNNs and KN3 with fixed weight 0.6 for RNNs.

	PPL	
LM	RNN	RNN + KN3
KN3	–	58.5
RNN_TC	58.4	48.0
RNN_TRU	57.6	47.9
RNN_TRD	54.3	47.0
RNN_TRC	53.8	46.9

In this section, the structure of RNNLM with Tibetan radical is explored, and the exploiting of radical embedding in character-based RNNLM achieves coincident improvement in PPL reduction.

5   Discussion

This paper has investigated strategies to solve the problems with low-resource language by exploiting Tibetan radical features in recurrent neural network language models for limited resource scenarios. The experimental results suggest our proposed models are more suitable for Tibetan by using the structured information of Tibetan character.

For this reason, this study proposes a new structure to explore Tibetan radical features by incorporating the radical embeddings in character embedding with three different measures. By exploiting the property of character, RNNLM acquires more information to model longer span context. The experimental results prove that the proposed model yields a better performance ascribed to the introduction of radical embedding. Next, results of different weights for different radicals from one character display a further improvement, which also reveals that radicals have different properties. Roughly speaking, varying positions of radical will change its property lightly, which leaves many issues to explore. More interestingly, some radical combination produces more abundant connotations. In this paper, the fixed combination is used. More dynamic radical combinations should be exploited. Finally, the effectiveness of our models are further testified when interpolated to n-gram.

Because of the limitation of Tibetan corpus, we firstly verify the superiority of the Tibetan radical in our proposed structured character embedding by exploiting it in RNN. And it is easy to migrate this structure to LSTM (long short-term memory). Compared with RNN, LSTM can solve the gradient vanishing problem and then model longer history context. So the performance can be further improved by exploiting the Tibetan radical in LSTM.

6 Conclusion and Future Work

In this study, a new structure of Tibetan character embedding is proposed by analyzing and exploiting the features of Tibetan. By exploiting the features of Tibetan radical, Tibetan character embedding is fused with radical embeddings by three ways, including using uniform weight, using different weights and using radical combination. The proposed model enhances the character embedding and shows a high potential to address the data sparsity issue for low-resource language.

For the future work, this structure will be applied to LSTM to further improve the performance of Tibetan LM. And the relationship between the statistical characteristics of radicals and their weights in RNNLM will be explored. It can be used to guide the parameter initialization to jump out of local optimum to achieve a better result. Besides, the measures of radical combination are also worth investigating to help Tibetan LM model more useful information.

Acknowledgements. The research is partially supported by the National Basic Research Program of China (No. 2013CB329301), and the National Natural Science Foundation of China (No. 61233009). Besides, we are especially grateful to the partial support by JSPS KAKENHI Grant (16K00297).

References

1. Brown, P.F., Cocke, J., Pietra, S.A.D., Pietra, V.J.D., Jelinek, F., Lafferty, J.D., Mercer, R. L., Roossin, P.S.: A statistical approach to machine translation. Comput. Linguist. **16**(2), 79–85 (1990)

2. Zhai, C.X., Lafferty, J.: A study of smoothing methods for language models applied to information retrieval. ACM Trans. Inf. Syst. **22**(2), 179–214 (2004)
3. Kuhn, R., Mori, R.D.: A Cache-Based Natural Language Model for Speech Recognition. IEEE Trans. Pattern Anal. Mach. Intell. **12**(6), 570–583 (1990)
4. Chen, S.F., Goodman, J.: An empirical study of smoothing techniques for language modeling. Comput. Speech Lang. **13**(4), 359–394 (1994)
5. Roark, B., Saraclar, M., Collins, M.: Discriminative N-Gram language modeling. Comput. Speech Lang. **21**(2), 373–392 (2007)
6. Brown, P.F., Desouza, P.V., Mercer, R.L., Pietra, V.J., Vincent, J.D., Lai, J.C.: Class-based N-Gram models of natural language. Comput. Linguist. **18**(4), 467–479 (1992)
7. Mikolov, T., Karafiát, M., Burget, L., Cernocký, J., Khudanpur, S.: Recurrent neural network based language model. In: INTERSPEECH 2010 – 11th Annual Conference of the International Speech Communication Association, Japan, pp. 1045–1048 (2010)
8. Mikolov, T., Kombrink, S., Burget L., Cernocky J.H.: Extensions of recurrent neural network language model. In: ICASSP 2011 - 2011 IEEE International Conference on Acoustics, Speech and Signal Processing, Czech, pp. 5528–5531 (2011)
9. Mikolov, T., Zweig, G.: Context dependent recurrent neural network language model. In SLT 2012 - 2012 IEEE Spoken Language Technology Workshop, USA, pp. 234–239 (2012)
10. Chen, X., Liu, X., Qian, Y., Gales, M.J.F., Woodland, P.C.: CUED-RNNLM — an open-source toolkit for efficient training and evaluation of recurrent neural network language models. In: ICASSP 2016 – 2016 IEEE International Conference on Acoustics, Speech and Signal Processing, China, pp. 6000–6004 (2016)
11. Shi, Y.Z., Zhang, W.Q., Liu, J., Johnson, M.T.: RNN language model with word clustering and class-based output layer. J. Audio Speech Music Process. **2013**(1), 22 (2013)
12. Mousa, E.D., Kuo, H.K.J., Mangu, L., Soltau, H.M.: Morpheme-based feature-rich language models using deep neural networks for LVCSR of Egyptian Arabic. In: ICASSP 2013 - 2013 IEEE International Conference on Acoustics, Speech and Signal Processing, Canada, pp. 8435–8439 (2013)
13. Shi, Y.Y., Wiggers, P., Catholijn, M., Jonker: Towards recurrent neural networks language models with linguistic and contextual features. In: INTERSPEECH 2012 - 13th Annual Conference of the International Speech Communication Association, pp. 1662–1665. (2012)
14. Mousa, E.D., Schluter, R., Ney, H.: Investigations on the use of morpheme level features in language models for Arabic LVCSR. In: ICASSP 2012 - IEEE International Conference on Acoustics, Speech and Signal Processing, USA, pp. 5021–5024 (2012)
15. He, Y.Z., Hutchinson, B., Baumann, P., Ostendorf, M.: Subword-based modeling for handling OOV words inkeyword spotting. In: ICASSP 2014 - 2014 IEEE International Conference on Acoustics, Speech and Signal Processing, Italy, pp. 7864–7868 (2014)
16. He, T.X., Xiang, X., Qian, Y., Yu, K.: Recurrent neural network language model with structured word embeddings for speech recognition. In: ICASSP 2015 - IEEE International Conference on Acoustics, Speech and Signal Processing, Australia, pp. 5396–5400 (2015)
17. Fang, H., Ostendorf, M., Baumann, P., Pierrehumbert, J.: Exponential language modeling using morphological features and multi-task learning. IEEE/ACM Trans. Audio Speech Lang. Process. **23**(12), 2410–2421 (2015)
18. Kim, Y., Jernite, Y., Sontag, D., Rush, A.M.: Character-aware neural language models. In: AAAI 2016 - 30th AAAI Conference on Artificial Intelligence, USA, pp. 2741–2749 (2015)
19. Chen, X., Wang, X., Liu, X., Gales, M.J.F., Woodland, P.C.: Efficient GPU-based training of recurrent neural network language models using spliced sentence bunch. In: INTER-SPEECH 2014 - 15th Annual Conference of the International Speech Communication Association, Singapore, pp. 641–645 (2014)

Learning Joint Multimodal Representation Based on Multi-fusion Deep Neural Networks

Zepeng Gu[✉], Bo Lang, Tongyu Yue, and Lei Huang

State Key Lab of Software Development Environment,
School of Computer Science and Engineering, Beihang University,
Beijing 100191, China
{guzepeng, langbo, yuetongyu,
huanglei}@nlsde.buaa.edu.cn

Abstract. Recently, learning joint representation of multimodal data has received more and more attentions. Multimodal features are concept-level compositive features which are more effective than those single-modality features. Most existing methods only mine interactions between modalities on the top of their networks for one time to learn multi-modal representation. In this paper, we propose a multi-fusion deep learning framework which learns multimodal features richer in semantic. The framework sets multiple fusing points in different level of feature spaces, and then integrates and passes the fusing information step by step from the low level to higher levels. Moreover, we propose a multi-channel decoding network with alternate fine-tuning strategy to fully mine the modality–specific information and cross-modality correlations. We are also the first to introduce deep learning features into multimodal deep learning, alleviating the semantic and statistical property differences between modalities to learn better features. Extensive experiments on real-world datasets demonstrate that, our proposed method achieves superior performance compared with the state-of-the-art methods.

Keywords: Multimodal · Deep learning · Multi-fusion · Semantic integration

1 Introduction

Nowadays, we often encounter data consisting of different modalities in real-world applications. Although every modality has its specific information and statistical properties, different modalities usually share high level concepts and semantic information; hence there exists correlations between different modalities. Multimodal data usually contain more information than any single-modal data. By fusing different modalities together, we can integrate intra-modal information with cross-modal complementary information to get a concept-level compositive feature, with which the performance in retrieval and classification can be improved.

In early stage, many statistical approaches were proposed for multimodal learning. D. M. Blei et al. [1] proposed multimodal-oriented Correspondence LDA model to mine the hierarchy correlation between images and texts. E.P. Xing et al. [2] proposed a dual-wing harmoniums model to learn a joint representation of the image and text modalities.

© Springer International Publishing AG 2017
D. Liu et al. (Eds.): ICONIP 2017, Part II, LNCS 10635, pp. 276–285, 2017.
https://doi.org/10.1007/978-3-319-70096-0_29

Nikhil Rasiwasia et al. [3] proposed a semantic correlation matching (SCM) approach to produce an isomorphic semantic space for cross-modal retrieval. However, due to the poor learning ability of shallow structures, these studies failed to capture high-level concepts from multimodal data to get accurate multimodal features.

Recently, there has been a growing interests in using deep networks for multi-modal learning. Ngiam et al. [4] built a deep autoencoder based on restrict boltzman machine and aggregated speech and video signals to find a shared representation. Srivastava et al. [5, 6] successively introduced the multimodal deep belief net and the multimodal deep boltzmann machine to learn deep generative models over joint space of image and text inputs. Feng et al. [7] proposed a CCA based auto-encoder for multimodal learning, which used CCA to train the network.

The quality of the learned multimodal features heavily depend on the procedure of interaction mining between modalities. However, all of these existing methods adopt single-fusion framework: they only mine interactions between modalities on the top of their networks for one time.

In this paper, we enhance the interaction mining procedure by setting multiple fusing points in different level of feature spaces, each fusing point can integrate the interactions between modalities in current feature space with the interactions from lower level spaces and then pass the information step by step from the low level to higher levels. However, a direct link between different modalities will introduce more noise due to the huge differences in semantic content and statistical properties between modalities. To solve this problem, we introduce deep learning features and utilize a series of normalization methods in multimodal deep learning, for making sure that the input features of the two modalities locate in similar feature space. What's more, in order to train the network to fully mine the modality–specific information and cross-modality correlations, we propose a multi-channel decoding network with alternate training strategy to fine-tune the network. The experimental results show that the performance of our method outperforms the state-of-the-art methods on MIR Flickr [8], NUS-WIDE [9] and PASCAL-sentence [10] databases.

The overall contributions of our paper are as follows.

(1) We propose a novel multimodal deep learning framework to mine the correlations between modalities in different levels, and learn the vertical correlations gradually from low level to higher level feature spaces, so as to reinforce the interactions between modalities.

(2) We propose a general decoding network and corresponding training strategy to fully exploit modality–specific information and cross-modality correlations to fine-tune the feature learning net and learn better multimodal representations.

(3) We introduce CNN visual features and Word2vec textual features into multi-modal learning. As far as we know, this is the first time that deep learning based features have been introduced into multimodal learning. These features have similar statistical properties and abundant semantic information, which improves the accuracy of cross-modality correlation mining and the quality of the learned multi-modal features.

The rest of this paper is organized as follows: Sect. 2 details the multi-fusion multimodal deep learning network; Sect. 3 reports the experimental results on three databases, followed by the conclusion in the last section.

2   Multi-fusion Multimodal Deep Learning Framework

In this section, we first elaborate the motivation and basic component of our multi-fusion multimodal learning framework (MFMDL), and then respectively describe the multi-fusion feature learning model, the multi-channel decoding network and alternate fine-tuning algorithm.

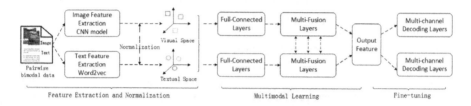

Fig. 1. Concept diagram of our proposed multimodal learning model.

2.1   Motivation and Framework

The key of multimodal learning lies in mining the correlation of different modalities. The existing multimodal learning methods adopt single-fusion framework, i.e., they build separate channel for each modality and only mine interactions between modalities for one time on the top level of their networks to learn a joint multi-modal representation. However, the interactions between modalities have different manifestation in every level of the net and high level feature space may not contain all the useful information. Hence the previous methods have the problem that they can't fully mine the interactions between modalities, which restricts the quality of the output multimodal features.

To solve this problem, we propose the multi-fusion multimodal learning framework. We set multiple fusing points in different levels of the feature learning network to integrate the interactions between modalities in current feature space with the interactions from lower level spaces and then pass the information step by step from the low level to higher levels. As a result, the final joint layer on the topmost hidden layer contains modal-specific information and cross-modal correlations from all different layers of the whole net.

This however brought another problem: when we employ the multi-fusion model straightforward, the quality of output feature from multi-fusion model is even worse than those single-fusion ones. After analysis, we find the problem lies in the significant differences between two modalities. The image and text modality vary a lot in semantic level and statistical properties, making it difficult to project them into a common feature space to mine the correlation between them. So the multi-fusion structure introduces more noise than single-fusion ones and will repeatedly accumulate the noise from low to high, degrading the performance of final learned features. To solve this problem, we import deep learning features into multimodal learning tasks. Compared with traditional features, deep learning features contain richer semantic information and are similar in statistical form. With deep learning features, our multi-fusion model can easily project two modality into common space and mine more accurate correlations from different levels of feature spaces, which makes the best use of our multi-fusion model.

The framework is demonstrated in Fig. 1, which can be split into 3 stages. The first stage is feature extracting and normalization. We use CNN [13] and Word2vec [14] models fine-tuned by corresponding big datasets to extract visual and textual features as the input of our model, then a series of normalization methods like Mean Cancellation, KL Expansion and Covariance Equalization are adopted to balance the statistical difference between modalities. The second stage is multimodal learning. We propose a novel multi-fusion net to learn multimodal features, which consists of full-connected layers and multi-fusion layers. After that, in the third stage, a multi-channel decoding net and corresponding training strategy is proposed to fine-tune the feature learning model in stage 2.

2.2 Multi-fusion Feature Learning Net

As we have mentioned above, to learn better multimodal features, we should mine the interactions between modalities in multiple levels of feature spaces. Inspired by the way of how shortcut connections [11] and residual network [12] use priori knowledge from low levels, we set multiple fusing points in different level of feature space to integrate the interactions between modalities in current feature space and the interactions from lower level spaces.

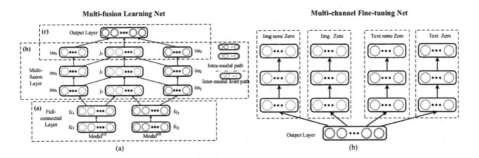

Fig. 2. The structure of MFMDL. (a) The multi-fusion learning net for learning multimodal feature. (b) The multi-channel fine-tuning net to optimize the parameter of (a)

The multimodal learning net is shown in Fig. 2(a), which has 3 parts:

(a) The bottom layers are separate full-connected layers; they map the features from different modalities into similar high level feature space. We build full-connected layers at the bottom of the net by the observation that low level feature spaces usually contain more modal-specific information, and conduct correlation mining between modalities directly from bottom spaces will bring in more noise and degrade the accuracy of the output multimodal features.

(b) The middle part is multi-fusion layers; we add multiple fusing points in this part to mine the vertical correlation between modalities. In this part, there are two kinds of channels: the modality-specific channel and the inter-modal joint channel. The modality-specific channel maps two separate modalities into higher levels of modality-specific feature spaces while the layer in inter-modal joint channel integrate the correlations between modalities in current feature space with the interactions from lower level spaces and then pass the information step by step from the low level to higher levels.

(c) The top layer is the output layer; it is connected to all the hidden nodes of the previous layer to learn a joint multimodal representation.

2.3   Multi-channel Decoding Net with Alternate Fine-Tuning Algorithm

To learn better multimodal feature, we should fully mine the inherent semantic information of every specific modality and the interactions between modalities, named 'intra-modal correlation' and 'cross-modal correlation' respectively.

The intra-modality correlation evaluates multimodal feature's ability of preserving inherent semantic information of every modality. Given multiple modalities (x_{inz}, x_{tnz}), where both modalities are none zero, the output multimodal feature of the model should reconstruct the input features. The loss function of intra-modality correlation is defined as follow:

$$L_{intra} = arg\,min \sum_{i=1}^{K} [\left(\|x_i' - x_{inz}\|_2^2\right) + \left(\|x_t' - x_{tnz}\|_2^2\right)] \tag{1}$$

where $\|\ \|_2$ is the L2 norm and (x_i', x_t') is the reconstruction of the inputs.

On the other hand, the cross-modality correlation mining requires that: when only one modality is present and the rest are absent, the learned feature should have the ability to infer the missing modality. For example, when only image feature is present and text is absent, the loss function of the cross-modality correlation is defined as follow:

$$L_{cross} = arg\,min \sum_{i=1}^{K} (\|x_t'' - x_{tmz}\|_2^2) \tag{2}$$

where x_t'' is the reconstruction of the text feature and x_{tmz} is the original text feature (During training procedure, we have bi-modal data, the text is manually set to zero). The corresponding function when text is present vice versa.

For the aforementioned two loss functions, the 'intra-modality correlation' aims to reconstruct the original input while the 'cross-modality correlation' aims to diverge the original input to infer cross-modal interaction. As a result, these two loss functions are contradictory, and when we want to integrate them into one single model, it will cause fluctuation and make the model deviate far from the true one. In order to meet the requirement of both correlations, we propose a multi-channel decoding net with alternate training strategy.

The framework of the decoding net is shown in Fig. 2(b), which contains two channels for each modality named image-none-zero (**inz**) channel, image-zero (**iz**) channel, text-none-zero (**tnz**) channel and text-zero (**tz**) channel. Considering different possibilities for the bi-modal input data consisting of text and image, i.e., missing text, missing image, and bi-modal input. When both modalities are present, we choose bimodal path *inz*, *tnz* as shown in Fig. 3(a) and use L_{intra} as the loss function to measure the intra-modality correlation. When one modality is absent (the e.g. text feature is zero), we choose unimodal path *inz* and *tz* as shown in Fig. 3(b) and use L_{cross} as the loss function to measure the cross-modality correlation. So the decoding net will alternately choose channel corresponding to different possible condition of the input data.

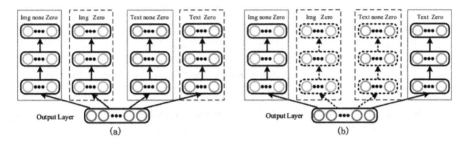

Img none Zero Img Zero Text none Zero Text Zero Img none Zero Img Zero Text none Zero Text Zero

Output Layer (a) Output Layer (b)

Fig. 3. Multi-channel decoding net. (a) Bimodal decoding path. (b) Unimodal decoding path

The fine-tuning algorithm of multi-fusion learning model is presented as follows.

Algorithm1: Fine-tuning of the multi-fusion learning model

Input: Bimodal dataset $X = \{(x_{inz}^{(k)}, x_{tnz}^{(k)})\}_{k=1}^{N}$, net parameters: θ

Output: fine-tuned parameters: θ'

1:**for** i from 1 to N **do**
2: split bimodal data $(x_{inz}^{(k)}, x_{tnz}^{(k)})$ into two unimodal data:
   $(x_{izero}^{(k)}, x_{tnz}^{(k)})$, $(x_{inz}^{(k)}, x_{tzero}^{(k)})$ and the expanded dataset is X'
3:**end for**
4:**repeat**
5: **for**$(x_i^{(k)}, x_t^{(k)})$ in X'**do**
6:**if** x is bimodal data:
7:    Select the output of bimodal decoding path: (x_i', x_t') apply (3.1) to compute L_{intra}
8:    Use back-propagation to tune the parameter θ of the bimodal path
9: **else**:
10:    Select the output of unimodal decoding path: (x_i'', x_t'') apply (3.2) to compute L_{cross}
11:    Use back-propagation to tune the parameter θ of the unimodal path
12: **end for**
13: Shuffling the dataset
14:**until** converge

---

3 Experiments

3.1 Datasets

Flickr. [8] consists of 1 million images crawled from the social photography website Flickr along with their user assigned tags. There are 25000 labelled images with 38 classes and every image may belong to several classes. Among the labelled data, only 22,175 images have corresponding textual tags. We only use the unlabeled data to train the model and randomly select 5000 pairs of the labelled multimodal data as the test set.

NUS-WIDE. [9] is a web image dataset consists of 269,648 image-text multimodal data. A ground-truth for 81 classes in total is provided and each image is labelled by at least one class. In the experiment, we randomly select samples belonging to top 20 largest classes and each sample contains more than 5 tags. The size of the test set is 5849 and the rest serve as training set.

Pascal Sentence. [10] contains 1000 pairs of multimodal data which are randomly selected from 2008 Pa development kit. Each sample consists of one image and five corresponded sentence that describing the content of image. These image-text pairs are labeled by 20 classes, each of which has 50 image-text pairs. We randomly select 40 pairs of data from every class and there is all together 800 samples in training set and the rest 200 samples serve as test set.

3.2 Experiment Settings

For FLICKR and NUS-WIDE, we adopt an 8-layer model: 2 full-connected layers, 3 multi-fusion layers and 3 multi-channel decoding layers. Considering the limited samples in Pascal-Sentence, we adopt a 5-layer model, which consists of 1 full-connected layer, 2 multi-fusion layers and 2 multi-channel decoding layers. The number of units in each layer for a single modality is summarized in Table 1.

Table 1. Number of units in each single-modality layer

Dataset	Full-connected layer	Multi-fusion layer	Multi-channel decoding layer
FLICKR	4096-4096	2048-2048-1024	1024-2048-4096
NUSWIDE	4096-4096	2048-2048-1024	1024-2048-4096
PASCAL	1024	512-256	512-1024

3.3 Results

Effectiveness of the structure of MFMDL
We adopt the controlling variable method to verify the effectiveness of our proposed model. We remove one part of our work every time and generate three models: MFMDL with no bottom full-connected layers, MFMDL without multi-fusion layers,

and MFMDL without multi-channel fine-tuning nets. Then we compare the quality of features learned from these models.

From Fig. 4(a) we can see that:

1. Removing any part of MFMDL will degrade the performance of the learned multimodal features, which proves that all the proposed strategies in this paper do contribute to learning better multimodal features.
2. The performance of features from MFMDL with no full-connected layers degrades more compared with the other models. This proves the correctness of our analysis in Sect. 2.2 that low level feature spaces usually contain more modal-specific information, and conduct correlation mining between modalities directly from bottom space will bring in more noise. Therefore, we can draw the conclusion that in order to learn better feature, we should abort low level cross-modal interactions and mine the correlation between modalities in relatively high level feature spaces.

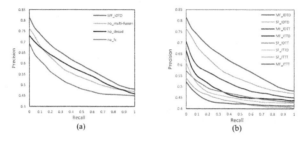

Fig. 4. (a) Different components of our model (b) Different features on different models

Impact of different features on single-fusion model and multi-fusion model

We compare the impact of traditional features and deep learning features on single-fusion model and multi-fusion model respectively. Traditional image features are represented by concatenating Phow, Gist and MPEG-7 descriptors and text feature is Bow. For deep learning features, we use off-the-shelf CNN [13] model and Word2vec [14] model, fine tune them with our multimodal datasets and then use them to extract visual and textual features. We also combine one traditional feature and one deep learning feature as input to learn joint represents. In Fig. 4(b), the 'MF' denotes multi-fusion structure and 'SF' denotes single-fusion structure, 'T' means traditional features while 'D' means deep learning features. For example, 'MF_IDTT' means we use deep image features with traditional text features as input and test on the multi-fusion model.

From Fig. 4(b), we can see that when use deep learning bimodal features, the performances on both single-fusion model and multi-fusion model have significant advantage than other cases. The multi-fusion model remarkably outperforms the single-fusion one.

In most cases, the performances of multi-fusion model are better than single-fusion model except using both traditional features, which demonstrates that our multi-fusion model can better mine correlations between modalities to learn more accurate features than single-fusion model. What's more, multi-fusion model with both traditional features achieves worst performance, we conclude that multi-fusion model is suitable for the case when both modalities are similar in statistical properties and semantic content. When two modalities vary a lot, the multi-fusion structure will bring in more noise and degrades the performance of output features.

Comparison with other baselines
We compare our method with other baselines, including DBN [5], DBM [6], Correspondence-AutoEncoder [15] (Cor-AE) and bimodal-AutoEncoder [4] (Bi-AE). We train every method under same condition. We run each method ten times and report the following average results. The precision-recall curves are shown in Fig. 5.

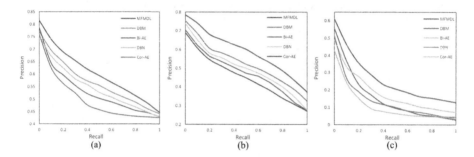

Fig. 5. Precision-recall on three datasets. (a) FLICKR. (b) NUSWIDE. (c) PASCAL.

The comparison results in Fig. 5 show that, our proposed method MFMDL achieves superior performance compared with the state-of-the-art methods in all three datasets. This improvement mainly comes from two folds. Firstly, the multi-fusion structure during feature learning stage enhance the interaction mining procedure and can well mine the correlations between modalities. Secondly, the multi-channel decoding net and alternate fine-tuning algorithm fully exploit both modality–specific information and cross-modality correlations so as to optimize the parameters of the feature learning net and contribute to better multimodal features.

4 Conclusion

In this paper, we propose a novel multi-fusion based multimodal deep learning model. The multi-fusion structure can learn the vertical correlations in different feature spaces; therefore it can reinforce the interactions mining between modalities and learn better multimodal features. Compared with existing single-fusion multimodal learning methods, our method can better mine the interactions between modalities. Moreover, we propose a general multi-channel decoding network and corresponding training strategy that can well integrate modality–specific information and cross-modality correlations to make the multimodal representations more accurate. We are also the first to introduce deep learning features into multimodal learning. These features improve the quality of the multimodal features and our multi-fusion structure can make best use of them than single-fusion methods. Experimental results demonstrate a substantial gain of our method on the three widely used public datasets.

Acknowledgment. This work was supported in part by the grants from the National Natural Science Foundation of China (Grant No: 61370125, the foundation of the State Key Lab of Software Development Environment (Grant No: SKLSDE-2017ZX-03).

References

1. Blei, D.M., Jordan, M.I: Modeling annotated data. In: International ACM SIGIR Conference on Research and Development in Information Retrieval, pp. 127–134. ACM (2003)
2. Xing, E.P., Yan, R., Hauptmann, A.G.: Mining associated text and images with dual-wing harmoniums. In: Computer Science (2005)
3. Rasiwasia, N., Pereira, J.C., Coviello, E., Doyle, G., Lanckriet, G.R.G., Levy, R.: A new approach to cross-modal multimedia retrieval. In: International Conference on Multimedia, pp. 251–260. ACM (2010)
4. Ngiam, J., Khosla, A., Kim, M., Nam, J., Lee, H., Ng, A.Y.: Multimodal deep learning. In: ICML 2011, pp. 689–696. DBLP, Washington (2011)
5. Srivastava, N., Salakhutdinov, R.: Learning representations for multimodal data with deep belief nets. In: International Conference on Machine Learning Workshop (2012)
6. Srivastava, N., Salakhutdinov, R., Hinton, G.: Modeling documents with deep boltzmann machines. In: Uncertainty in Artificial Intelligence, Seattle (2013)
7. Fangxiang, F., Xiaojie, W., Ruifan, L.: Cross-modal retrieval with correspondence Auto-encoder. In: Multimedia 2014, Orlando (2014)
8. Bosch, A., Zisserman, A., Munoz, X.: Image classification using random forests and ferns. In: International Conference on Computer Vision, pp. 1–8. IEEE (2007)
9. Chua, T.S., Tang, J., Hong, R., Li, H., Luo, Z., Zheng, Y.: NUS-WIDE: a real-world web image database from National University of Singapore. In: ACM International Conference on Image and Video Retrieval, p. 48. ACM (2009)
10. Rashtchian, C., Young, P., Hodosh, M., Hockenmaier, J.: Collecting image annotations using Amazon's Mechanical Turk. NAACL Hlt **2010**, 139–147 (2010)
11. Raiko, T., Valpola, H., Lecun, Y.: Deep learning made easier by linear transformations. In: Conference on AI and Statistics, Vol. 22, pp. 924–932 (2011)
12. Kaiming, H.: Deep Residual Learning for Image Recognition (2015)
13. Krizhevsky, A., Sutskever, I., Hinton, G.E.: ImageNet classification with deep convolutional neural networks. ICONIP **25**, 1097–1105 (2012)
14. Mikolov, T., Sutskever, I., Chen, K., Corrado, G., Dean, J.: Distributed representations of words and phrases and their compositionality. Adv. Neural. Inf. Process. Syst. **26**, 3111–3119 (2013)
15. Feng, F., Wang, X., Li, R.: Cross-modal retrieval with correspondence Autoencoder. In: ACM (2014)

DeepBIBX: Deep Learning for Image Based Bibliographic Data Extraction

Akansha Bhardwaj[1,2]($\boxtimes$), Dominik Mercier[1], Andreas Dengel[1],
and Sheraz Ahmed[1]

[1] Smart Data and Services, DFKI Kaiserslautern, Kaiserslautern, Germany
{akansha.bhardwaj,dominik.mercier,andreas.dengel,sheraz.ahmed}@dfki.de
[2] eXascale Infolab, University of Fribourg, Fribourg, Switzerland
akbwaj@exascale.info

Abstract. Extraction of structured bibliographic data from document images of non-native-digital academic content is a challenging problem that finds its application in the automation of cataloging systems in libraries and reference linking domain. The existing approaches discard the visual cues and focus on converting the document image to text and further identifying citation strings using trained segmentation models. Apart from the large training data, which these existing methods require, they are also language dependent. This paper presents a novel approach (DeepBIBX) which targets this problem from a computer vision perspective and uses deep learning to semantically segment the individual citation strings in a document image. DeepBIBX is based on deep Fully Convolutional Networks and uses transfer learning to extract bibliographic references from document images. Unlike existing approaches which use textual content to semantically segment bibliographic references, DeepBIBX utilizes image based contextual information, which makes it applicable to documents of any language. To gauge the performance of the presented approach, a dataset consisting of 286 document images containing 5090 bibliographic references is collected. Evaluation results reveals that the DeepBIBX outperforms state-of-the-art method (ParsCit, 71.7%) for bibliographic references extraction and achieved an accuracy of 84.9% in comparison to 71.7%. Furthermore, in terms of pixel classification task, DeepBIBX achieved a precision and a recall rate of 96.2%, 94.4% respectively.

Keywords: Deep learning · Machine learning · Bibliographic data · Reference linking

1 Introduction

The delivery of knowledge through the digital format has enabled readers to access and share knowledge around the world. This phenomenon has resulted in digital becoming the regular format, owing to the ease of accessing, preserving and sharing content. Though digital content is ubiquitous, the content

D. Liu et al. (Eds.): ICONIP 2017, Part II, LNCS 10635, pp. 286–293, 2017.
https://doi.org/10.1007/978-3-319-70096-0_30

which is not natively-digital continues to lack suitable metadata which makes it difficult for such content to be easily discoverable. The most obvious example of such content is the digitization of old articles, where the scanning process renders a digital image. For the successful implementation of digital libraries, it is important to automate the generation of bibliographic databases for non natively-digital books.

Most of the works done so far on the task of generating bibliographic databases focus on converting the image into text and then further using the text segmentation techniques to structure citation data [1, 2]. This results in the loss of contextual information present in bibliographic document images which has the discriminative ability to identify references from one another. In this work, we introduce an image based reference extraction model where the above problem has been approached from a deep learning perspective.

Deep learning has recently proven to be extremely successful on various tasks of visual recognition [3–5] including semantic segmentation [6]. In this work, we introduce a semantic segmentation model for image based reference extraction. The issue of unavailability of large amount of training data for this model has been bypassed using the transfer learning approach introduced by Carauana [7]. Also, transfer learning benefits by saving the additional cost of time and computational resources needed to perform training on a large scale.

In this work, we have transferred the knowledge gained from the FCN-8s network [6] trained for PASCAL VOC challenge [8] with 21 classes to identifying individual citation strings based on the contextual indentation information present in bibliographic document images.

1.1 Paper Contribution

This paper introduces a novel deep learning based semantic segmentation model fine-tuned for reference extraction in bibliographic document images. The trained model detects individual citation strings in a document image with a precision of 83.9% and a recall of 84.6%. The work also presents a framework in which references are identified in a document image, converted to text and further resolved to structured segmented information for reference linking applications. Further evaluations with the state-of-the-art ParsCit segmentation model [1] show that while ParsCit extracted 71.7% citation strings, our approach extracts 84.9% citation strings on a test set of 286 bibliographic document images. This approach of identifying individual citation strings works for bibliographic document images of any language as it utilizes the contextual indentation information present in document images.

2   Related Works

Procedures for digitization of books have improved considerably in past few years and several ambitious projects with libraries aim to digitize thousands of books.

Google book-scanning project [9] works with libraries to offer digitized books and aims to digitize every book ever printed.

In this phase of transition, digital libraries require automated cataloging process for the purpose of generating bibliographic databases. Several projects have focused on the creation of an electronic card catalog and the success of these endeavors resulted in Online Public Access Catalog (OPAC) replacing the traditional card catalog in many academic, public and special libraries. Bibliographic data has more power now with new technologies assisting it's reuse in research with citation management softwares, linking of data from multiple sources and also in aiding data mining of large datatsets to identify publication trends.

Several projects have focused on automatic identification of references in scholarly PDF documents but, they either rely only on the text [1,2], or employ heuristics based on visual cues [10].

To the best of our knowledge, none of the approaches so far have used deep learning to identify bounding boxes of citation strings in document images.

3   Dataset

The data for this task has been collected from print media (books, journals, articles, etc.) present in libraries arranged in different indentation formats. The bibliographic information belonging to these print media have been scanned at a DPI resolution of 300 or more. For creation of the dataset, an equal number of files are selected from each category of publication to generate a well-balanced dataset of 440 files. These files are manually annotated with bounding boxes around each reference. Figure 1 shows some of the sample data.

This data is further augmented by removing the whitespace around the text area and the final transformed dataset consisted of 574 train images, 50 images for validation and 298 images for test set. All images are further cropped to a $width \times height$ of 500×1500 pixels. The labels of the dataset consist of a rectangular bounding box surrounding each reference, the rest is labeled as background.

(a)   (b)   (c)   (d)

Fig. 1. Examples of various kinds of bibliographic document images in raw dataset

4 DeepBIBX: The Proposed Approach

Extraction of structured data from bibliographic document images starts with pre-processing bibliographic document images, followed by deep learning based reference extraction from document images, and further segmentation of each extracted citation string into structured information like title, author, publisher, volume, pages, etc.

4.1 Preprocessing

Before starting the actual pipeline of reference extraction, it is important to normalize scanned document images for different qualitative distortions. To do so, document binarization is performed to convert color and gray scale documents into binary format. The method described by Breuel [11] is used to perform document binarization and to correct document skew. The binarized and skew corrected document image is then passed to the heart of DeepBIBX, i.e., Image based reference extraction module.

4.2 Image Based Reference Extraction

Architecture. Figure 2 shows the architecture of a deep Fully Convolutional Network (FCN) [6] which is used for semantic segmentation. FCNs take input of arbitrary size and produce correspondingly-sized output with efficient inference and learning. Each layer of data is a three-dimensional array of size $h \times w \times d$, where h and w are $height, width$ respectively, and d is the color channel dimension. Receptive fields are the locations in higher layers which are connected to the locations in the image.

The basic components of an FCN consists of convolution, pooling, and activation functions. They operate on local input regions, and depend only on relative spatial coordinates. If x_{ij} is the data vector at location (i, j) for a particular

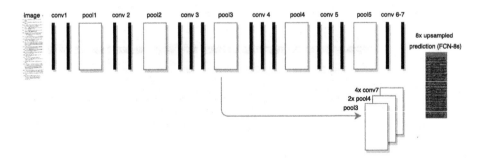

Fig. 2. FCN-8s architecture: Pooling and prediction layers are shown as boxes while intermediate layers are shown as vertical lines. Additional predictions from pool3, at stride 8, provide further precision

layer, and y_{ij} is the data vector for the following layer, these functions compute outputs y_{ij} by

$$y_{ij} = f_{ks}\left(\left\{x_{si+\delta i, sj+\delta j}\right\}_{0 <= \delta i, \delta j <= k}\right)$$

where k is called the kernel size, s is the stride or subsampling factor, and f_{ks} determines the layer type: a matrix multiplication for convolution or average pooling, a spatial max for max pooling, or an element nonlinearity for an activation function. An FCN operates on an input of any size, and produces an output of corresponding spatial dimensions.

A real-valued loss function composed with an FCN defines a task. If the loss function is a sum over the spatial dimensions of the final layer, its gradient will be a sum over the gradients of each of its spatial components, considering all of the final layer receptive fields as a minibatch.

Approach. Deep learning based approaches usually require a lot of training data. However, a large amount of data for our task was unavailable. To resolve this problem, the concept of transfer learning was adopted. In DeepBIBX, FCN-8 network, which was pre-trained on PASCAL VOC 21 class challenge [8] problem, was used to allow for better segmentation for reference extraction. The last layer of original FCN-8 network which in its default settings outputs 21 classes is removed and the activations of the last hidden layer are used as the feature descriptors of the input dataset. A final layer is added which outputs 2 classes, reference area and background.

The network is trained on the dataset for 80 epochs with stochastic gradient descent. The semantic segmentation output generated after training separates the foreground from background roughly (refer Fig. 3d). This output is further post-processed to obtain crisper boundaries using blob identification heuristics and the output is transformed as shown in Fig. 4e. It is important to mention here that these heuristics have been developed only on the validation set. Each

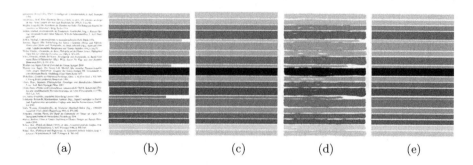

(a)   (b)   (c)   (d)   (e)

Fig. 3. An example from test set where each detected box has an IoU $>= 0.5$ resulting in 100% precision and 100% recall (a) Bibliographic document image (b) Corresponding human annotated bounding boxes, (c) processed human annotated data for evaluation (d) prediction generated by semantic segmentation model (3) identification of bounding boxes after post-processing, each labeled with a different color (Color figure online)

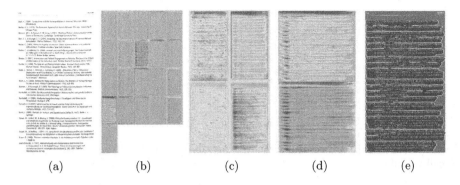

Fig. 4. Visualization of the activation intensities of FCN-8s network at multiple layers during the forward pass of a test image. (a) Source image (b) fuse_pool3 (c) upscore8 (d) score_2 classes (e) inference image

bounding box in the post-processed result is compared to each bounding box present in the ground truth. A box is identified if the Intersection over Union (IoU) ratio for resulting bounding box and processed ground truth bounding box is greater than 0.5. For each document image, these identified bounding boxes are used to calculate precision and recall. Figure 3 shows an example of an image from test set where inferred precision and recall rate is 100%.

In the next experiment, all text lines of the ground truth document image have been replaced with rectangular boxes, the same length and width as that of each text line. Keeping other parameters same as in previous experiment, pre-trained FCN-8s was trained on this transformed dataset as well. Figure 4 shows visualization of the activation intensities at multiple layers during the forward pass of a test image.

4.3   Segmentation of Citation Strings

Once the region of each individual bibliographic entry is identified, OCR is performed for each individual entry [11]. The resulting textual information can be given as an input to any citation string segmentation model like AnyStyle [12], ParsCit [1] to segment it into author, title, DOI, page, publisher, volume and other relevant information which can be used for reference linking applications.

5   Evaluation

Due to varying parameters of the model, a complete match between predicted and ground-truth bounding boxes is unrealistic. Therefore, approaches based on semantic segmentation are evaluated using the IoU metric. This metric rewards predicted bounding boxes for heavily overlapping with the ground-truth bounding boxes.

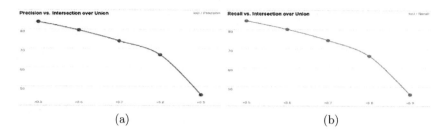

Fig. 5. Precision, Recall results compared to varying IoU (a) Precision vs. IoU (b) Recall vs. IoU

The pixel-wise evaluation for bounding box on document image gives a precision of 96.2% and a recall of 94.4%. It is important to mention here that though the pixel wise evaluation results in good precision and recall, it is not a good evaluation measure as the trained model might simply be a text line recognizer. To make sure that this is not the case, results have been further evaluated for detection of each bounding box.

For further evaluation, a reference box is identified when the IoU of predicted bounding box and labeled bounding box is greater than 0.5 after post-processing. This results in a precision of 82.6% and a recall of 80.0%. In the experiment, where the lines were blurred, a precision of 83.9% and a recall of 84.6% was observed. Figure 5 shows a precision and recall curve with respect to IoU for the case when text lines are blurred (Table 1).

ParsCit is the current state of the art in the area of reference segmentation. Table 2 compares the results from our approach to ParsCit. The results show that on a test set of 286 bibliographic document images, which were converted to text, ParsCit extracted 3645 references and our image based reference extraction model extracted 4323 references out of a total of 5090 references. These results suggest that visual cues are very important during identification of references and should not be discarded.

Table 1. Evaluation of image based extraction results

Category	Precision	Recall
Pixel-wise evaluation	96.2%	94.4%
Bounding box detection on plain document image	82.6%	80.0%
Bounding box detection on document image with blurred lines	83.9%	84.6%

Table 2. Evaluation of results when compared to ParsCit

Category	Number of extracted references	Extracted percentage
ParsCit	3645	71.7%
Proposed approach	4323	84.9%

6   Conclusion and Future Work

This work presents a novel deep learning based semantic segmentation model for identifying references in bibliographical document images. This model is language independent and identifies individual references with a precision of 83.9% and a recall rate of 84.6%. The results have been compared with state-of-the-art text based semantic segmentation model ParsCit where the proposed model outperforms the reference detection task by a margin of more than 13%. These results suggest that utilizing the contextual information present in bibliographic document images is a key factor in extraction of bibliographic data. This work is useful for the automation of library cataloging systems and for reference linking applications. The future work will focus on a comprehensive model for the above tasks and provide a solution for digital libraries.

Acknowledgements. This work was partially supported by the DFG under contract DE 420/18-1 and by the Swiss National Science Foundation under grant number 407540_167320.

References

1. Councill, I.G., Giles, C.L., Kan, M.Y.: Parscit: an open-source CRF reference string parsing package. In: LREC 2008 (2008)
2. Tkaczyk, D., Szostek, P., Fedoryszak, M., Dendek, P.J., Bolikowski, L.: Cermine: automatic extraction of structured metadata from scientific literature. Int. J. Doc. Anal. Recognit. (IJDAR) **18**(4), 317–335 (2015)
3. He, K., Zhang, X., Ren, S., Sun, J.: Deep residual learning for image recognition. In: Proceedings of the IEEE Conference on Computer Vision and Pattern Recognition, pp. 770–778 (2016)
4. Zhang, X., Li, Z., Loy, C.C., Lin, D.: Polynet: a pursuit of structural diversity in very deep networks. arXiv preprint arXiv:1611.05725 (2016)
5. Szegedy, C., Ioffe, S., Vanhoucke, V., Alemi, A.A.: Inception-v4, inception-resnet and the impact of residual connections on learning. In: AAAI, pp. 4278–4284 (2017)
6. Long, J., Shelhamer, E., Darrell, T.: Fully convolutional networks for semantic segmentation. In: Proceedings of the IEEE Conference on Computer Vision and Pattern Recognition, pp. 3431–3440 (2015)
7. Caruana, R.: Multitask Learning. In: Thrun, S., Pratt, L. (eds.) Learning to Learn. Springer, Boston (1998)
8. Everingham, M., Van Gool, L., Williams, C., Winn, J., Zisserman, A.: Pascal visual object classes challenge results **1**(6), 7 (2005), www.pascal-network.org
9. Johnson, R.K.: Special issue: In google's broad wake: taking responsibility for shaping the global digital library. ARL: A bimonthly report on research library issues and actions from ARL, CNI, and SPARC, vol. 250. Association of Research Libraries (2007)
10. Crossref labs pdfextract, https://www.crossref.org/labs/pdfextract/
11. Breuel, T.M.: The ocropus open source OCR system. DRR 6815, 68150 (2008)
12. Anystyle.io, https://anystyle.io

Bio-Inspired Deep Spiking Neural Network for Image Classification

Jingling Li[1,2], Weitai Hu[1,2], Ye Yuan[1,2], Hong Huo[1,2], and Tao Fang[1,2(✉)]

[1] Department of Automation, Shanghai Jiao Tong University, Shanghai, China
tfang@sjtu.edu.cn
[2] Key Laboratory of System Control and Information Processing,
Ministry of Education, Shanghai, China
jinglingli@sjtu.edu.cn

Abstract. Spiking neural networks (SNNs) are a kind of data-driven and event-driven hierarchical networks, and they are closer to the biological mechanism than other traditional neural networks. In SNNs, signals are transmitted as spikes between neurons, and spike transmission is easily implemented on hardware platform for large-scale real-time deep network computing. However, the unsupervised learning methods for spike neurons, such as the STDP learning methods, generally are ineffective in training deep spiking neural networks for image classification application. In this paper, the network parameters (weights and bias) obtained from training a convolution neural network (CNN), are converted and utilized in a deep spiking neural network with the similar structure as the CNN, which make the deep SNN be capable of classifying images. Since the CNN is composed of analog neurons, there will be some transfer losses in the process of conversion. After the main sources of transfer losses are analyzed, some reasonable optimization strategies are proposed to reduce the losses while retain a higher accuracy, such as max-pooling, softmax and weight normalization. The deep spiking neural network proposed in this paper is closer to the biological mechanism in the design of neurons and our work is helpful for understanding the spike activity of the brain. The proposed deep SNN is evaluated on CIFAR and MNIST benchmarks and the experimental results have shown that the proposed deep SNN outperforms the state-of-the-art spiking network models.

Keywords: Spiking neural networks · Convolution neural networks · IF neuron · Image classification

1 Introduction

Spiking neural networks (SNNs) transmit spike signals between neurons. In this kind of event-driven computing systems, power consumptions mainly occur in the current active parts of the networks, so the power can be effectively saved in their inactive parts. This enables SNNs do distributed and asynchronous computing with reduced network time delays. The characteristics of SNNs make them

D. Liu et al. (Eds.): ICONIP 2017, Part II, LNCS 10635, pp. 294–304, 2017.
https://doi.org/10.1007/978-3-319-70096-0_31

more powerful in real time computing [1,2]. In recent years, Convolution Neural Networks [3] (CNNs) have become the most successful network architectures for natural image classification problems. However, a lot of computing resources are required for training and running, which is the shortcomings of CNNs. Obviously, SNNs have the advantages in high speed operation performances, while CNNs have the advantages in classification performances.

Although SNNs have great computing performances, they are still lack of effective learning methods conforming to biological mechanism [4]. The most preferred learning principle used in SNNs is STDP (Spike-timing-dependent plasticity) learning method [4]. However, STDP learning method is still ineffective in training multilayer neural networks. Therefore, instead of training SNNs directly by spike-based learning rules, a converted training way has attracted attention. It starts from a common artificial neural network, and the network is trained through the back propagation algorithm. After training, the network parameters (weights and bias) would be converted in appropriate methods and then utilized in SNNs. Cao et al. tailored a normal CNN to fit the requirements of a SNN, but this approach resulted in performance losses to some degree [5]. Diehl et al. converted a CNN to a SNN by weight normalization, and the network performance was improved as the conversion errors reduce [6]. Hunsberger et al. used LIF neurons in the SNN to improve the conversion performance [7]. In theory, the performance of SNNs is no less than CNNs [8], however, SNNs are difficult to achieve the same performance as CNNs in practice.

In this paper, the work is focused on utilizing the network parameters of CNNs to make deep SNNs be capable of image classification tasks. Since the CNNs are composed of analog neurons, there must be a certain transfer loss in the process of conversion. Therefore, based on the analysis of the main sources of losses, some reasonable optimization strategies are proposed to reduce the conversion errors between these two networks. The experiments on CIFAR and MNIST benchmarks have shown that the proposed deep SNN outperforms the state-of-the-art spiking network models.

This paper is organized as follows: the proposed deep SNN is elucidated in Sect. 2, including the analyses of the problem of CNN-to-SNN conversion and several optimization strategies. The evaluations on CIFAR and MNIST benchmarks are given in Sect. 3. The conclusion is in Sect. 4.

2   Deep Spiking Neural Network

The main difference between SNNs and CNNs are the different forms of input and transfer data. All the data are input to the traditional CNNs at once, and then propagated between the network layers, until some numerical values are output. However, for SNNs, the input is usually a signal sequence that represents an event flow. SNNs can achieve the pseudo-simultaneity of the input and output [9], and handle the time-varying input more effectively [10], and utilize specific hardware for more efficient computing [11].

In this paper, a deep SNN is proposed by combining the advantages of both SNNs and CNNs. Both neural networks have the same architecture, and the

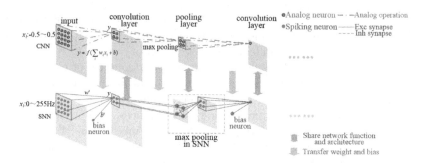

Fig. 1. Architecture sharing and parameter conversion of CNN and SNN.

network parameters (weight and bias) are obtained by training the CNN, and then converted into the SNN. The conversion process is shown in Fig. 1. The upper part of the figure is the CNN (composed of analog neurons), while the bottom part is the SNN (composed of spike neurons). The parameters trained in the CNN will be converted and utilized in the corresponding layer of the SNN. However, there will be significant transfer losses during the conversion [10]. Therefore, both CNN and SNN need to be adjusted to reduce these conversion losses. The conversion method mentioned in paper [5] is used.

2.1 Adjustments on the CNN

Convolution neural networks [12] usually are multi-layer supervised learning neural networks. Convolution layers and pooling layers are their core modules for feature extraction in CNNs. The dimension of the data is reduced by alternative convolutional and pooling layers, and abstract features of the data are extracted at the same time. In order to make use of the advantages of CNNs in classification, following adjustments on the traditional CNNs for converting it into the spiking neural network are made: (1) the bio-inspired neuron activation function is introduced in the CNNs; and (2) the noise is introduced in the training.

Introduce in the Bio-Inspired Activation Function. The activation function in traditional CNNs aims to introduce non-linear factors in the network to enhance the expression of image features. The common activation functions are sigmoid, tanh, etc. These activation functions usually produce negative outputs, which are improper to SNNs. Therefore, the output values of the traditional CNNs must be limited, and a bio-inspired activation function – ReLU (Rectified Linear Units) function is introduced in the CNNs:

$$ReLU(x) = max(0, x). \tag{1}$$

where x denotes the output of a certain layer in the CNNs. The ReLU function ensures that the neurons outputs are always positive. On the other hand, the results obtained by ReLU activation function are proportional to the number of spikes emitted by neurons in the SNN at a given time. In addition, the paper [12] has shown that using ReLU instead of the traditional sigmoid activation function can accelerate the training process, and strengthen the sparseness of neuronal activities, and enhance the generalization ability of neural networks.

Therefore, in this paper, ReLU is used as the activation function in all the layers of the original CNN except the output layer.

Train with Noise. In order to adapt to the spike data transmission in the SNN, additional noise is introduced in the training process of the CNN for better robustness, such as denoising autoencoder [13]. Unlike CNNs using analog values, SNNs accumulate errors when spike signals are transmitted through each layer. For example, the truncation errors will be generated when the spike neurons are saturated. Whats more, quantitative errors occur when discrete fire rates in SNNs are used to represent the analog values in CNNs. These errors are gradually accumulated through the transmission in a multi-layer network, which degrades the performance of the multi-layer spike neural network. Training the CNN with noise can simulate these situations, and improve the performance of conversion.

2.2 Adjustments on the Spiking Neuron Network

Spiking neural networks usually are composed of Integrate-and-fire (IF) neurons. Convolution operations are implemented on spike neurons. Feature selectivity and invariance are realized by using bio-inspired max pooling, normalized weights, biases in each layer, and the transformation of the input data range, and so on.

Integrate-and-Fire Neuron Model. The neuron model used in the SNN is a simple integrate-and-fire (IF) model. The IF neuron dynamics are given by the equation as follows:

$$\frac{dv_{mem}(t)}{dt} = \sum_i \sum_{s \in S_i} w_i \delta \left(t - s \right). \tag{2}$$

where w_i is the synapse weight of i-th input neuron, $\delta\{.\}$ is the Dirac function,and $S_i = \{t_i^0, t_i^0, ...\}$ denotes spike time series of i-th pre-synapse neuron. When the membrane voltage reaches the threshold $v_{thr} = 1.0V$, and the voltage resets to $v_{res} = 0.0V$.

Convolution Operation in Spiking Neuron Network. The convolution operation in the CNN is $y = \sum_i w_i x_i$, where w_i is the weight of the convolution kernel, x_i is the input, and y is the output. The convolution operation in the SNN is similar to that in the CNN. x_i denotes the fire rate of i-th neuron, $|w_i|$ is the synapse weight between i-th neuron and neuron y. If w_i is large than zero, the connection between x_i and y is excitatory synapse, otherwise inhibitory. The fire rate of neuron y corresponds to ReLU output of neuron y' (ReLU(y')) in the CNN. Therefore, the convolution operation can be implemented in the SNN.

Max Pooling in the SNN. Nonlinear pooling operations (such as max pooling) usually exist in CNNs, which are the basis of feature selectivity and invariance. However, since SNNs transmit discrete spike signals, the max pooling cannot be realized by the simple maximum value operation. Although average pooling can be used to substitute max pooling [7], this will lead to undesirable performance errors. Therefore, it is necessary to establish a nonlinear pooling mechanism suitable for spiking neural networks.

The architecture for max pooling used in this paper is a bio-inspired model based on Yu et al. [14]. As shown in Fig. 2, it is a three-layer neural network with an input layer X, an intermediate layer (performing a nonlinear transformation) Y and an output neuron Z. Solid lines with triangular synapses and dashed lines with circular synapses represent excitatory and inhibitory connections, respectively. Each intermediate neuron Y is connected to all other Y neurons, and the neuron Z can output a spike signal which is proportional to the maximum input.

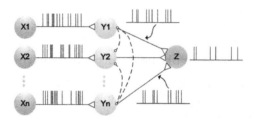

Fig. 2. MAX pooling in the SNN. Solid lines with triangular synapses and dashed lines with circular synapses represent excitatory and inhibitory connections, respectively.

Weight Normalization. The neuron outputs with the activation function (ReLU) of CNNs usually have a range from zero to positive infinity. However, a spike neurons fire rate has a limited range. If the input is too large, the spike neuron will tend to be saturated. Therefore, it is necessary to calculate an appropriate normalization coefficient when converting the network parameters obtained by the CNN.

In [7], the maximum activation value of a CNN in a training set is used to calculate a weight normalization coefficient. In the SNN, the weights of the spike neurons of the corresponding layer are multiplied by this weight normalization coefficient, which ensures that the fire rate of the spike neurons not exceed a certain saturation value. However, this method may make most neurons at a lower fire rate and lead to large quantization errors, which increases the delay of information transmission. In this paper, a robust normalization method is used to select the weight normalization coefficient. The coefficient with which p-percentage of the neurons are activated is chosen.

Taking the CNN with CIFAR10 dataset as an example, the distribution of activation values of the first convolution layer is shown in Fig. 3. The maximum activation value is 11.8, and 99.9% of the data is less than 6.0. The normalization

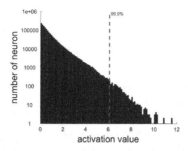

Fig. 3. Distribution of all activation values in the first convolution layer of the CNN.

coefficient is $1/11.8 \approx 0.08$ when calculated with the maximum value (11.8). The coefficient values tend to be $1/6.0 \approx 0.17$ at the position where 99.9% of the neurons fire. This method can guarantee 99.9% of the spike neurons with higher fire rates, which can be enough to compensate for saturation errors caused by the remaining 0.1% of the spike neurons. In this paper, the normalized coefficients are calculated at the activation value where 99.9% of the neurons fire.

Function and Realization of Biases. In addition to the network weights, biases are usually added to change the data range. Most previous spiking neural networks choose to remove the biases, which often causes a certain network transfer loss. In this paper, neurons that continuously release spike signals are used as biases. The values of biases are changed according to the weights of the connections between neurons. Through this way, the spiking neural network could stimulate biases.

Changing the Range of Input Data, Weights and Biases. In some CNNs, the input data will be normalized. For example, the range of input data is changed from 0.0~1.0 to -0.5~0.5 by subtracting the mean value. Whats more, in recent years, BN (Batch Normalization) layer are widely used in CNNs. This method can accelerate the training process by normalizing the data of every layer [15].

In SNNs, fire rates are always positive, so the range of input data need be changed to 0.0~1.0. However, this change will influence the output of this layer. In this paper, the weights and biases of the first convolution layer are changed accordingly from:

$$y_{conv1} = w_{conv1}x_{conv1} + b_{conv1}, x_{conv1} \in [x_{min}, x_{max}] . \tag{3}$$

$$
\begin{aligned}
to : y_{conv1} &= w_{conv1} \frac{x_{conv1} - x_{min}}{x_{max} - x_{min}} + b_{conv1} \\
&= \frac{w_{conv1}}{x_{max} - x_{min}} x_{conv1} + \left(b_{conv1} - \frac{w_{conv1}x_{min}}{x_{max} - x_{min}} \right), x_{conv1} \in [0, 1] .
\end{aligned}
$$

The weights and biases of the first convolution layer are changed accordingly: $w_{conv1} \rightarrow \frac{w_{conv1}}{x_{max}-x_{min}}$, $b_{conv1} \rightarrow b_{conv1} - \frac{w_{conv1}x_{min}}{x_{max}-x_{min}}$. Other layers parameters do not need change because they have no difference to y_{conv1}.

Conversion to a Spiking Neuron Network. The conversion is completed as the following steps: (1) ReLUs is used for all neurons in the CNN; (2) Noise is introduced in the process of training the CNN; (3) The weights in the CNN are mapped directly into the SNN composed of IF neurons; (4) The range of the input data of the spiking neuron network is changed to 0.0∼1.0, while the weights and the biases of the first convolution layer of the SNN are adjusted accordingly; (5) The fire rates of the input neurons in the SNN are proportional to the amplitude of the input image. In this paper, the input range of 0.0∼1.0 is converted into 0∼255 Hz.

There exist local response normalization (LRN) layers in some convolution neural networks, such as Krizhevsky [12] network for CIFAR10 dataset. We remove the LRN layer because it may make the network very complex. After removing the LRN layer, the network accuracy decreased by less than 0.1%, namely, the effects of removing the LRN layer on the results were negligible. In addition, the additional noise is only introduced in the training process, and it will be removed in test.

3   Experiment and Analysis

The network architecture of the proposed deep SNN is shown in Fig. 4. The network is composed of two convolution layers, two maximum pooling layers and three fully connected layers. ReLUs are used as the activation functions in the other convolution layers and the full connection layers, while softmax loss function is used in the last layer to output the classification result.

CIFAR-10 [16] dataset that widely used in image classification tasks is used to test the classification performance of the proposed deep SNN. This dataset contains 60,000 images with 10 classes. The first 50000 images are used for training and the rest 10000 images are for test. The original size of each image is 32×32, and each image is cropped to 24×24. The weight parameters of the CNN are preserved and converted into the SNN with the same architecture.

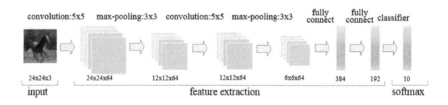

Fig. 4. The architecture of the proposed network.

Factors Affecting the Accuracy of the Proposed SNN. The proposed SNN is evaluated under different optimization strategies.

Figure 5(a) shows the accuracies of different strategies about pooling, changing the range of input data and the introduction of biases. The network accuracy is 82.43% when the SNN uses average pooling, without biases and changes of input. When the range of input data is changed, the accuracy becomes 83.62%. The accuracy rises to 84.88% when biases are introduced. When max pooling is used instead of average pooling, with or without biases, the accuracies are 86.02% and 86.21%, respectively. Introduction of noise in training set can rise the accuracy to 86.29%.

Figure 5(b) shows the accuracies under different normalization strategies. It can be seen that the accuracy is the highest when the normalized coefficients are calculated at the activation value where 99.9% of the neurons fire. The accuracy reaches to 86.43%, which is very closed to the accuracy of 86.48% of the CNN.

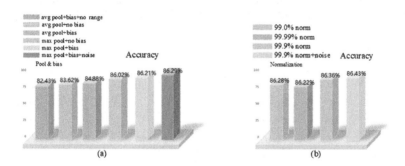

Fig. 5. (a). Test accuracy of the proposed SNN with different pooling, biases and ranges of input. (b). Accuracies under different normalization strategies.

Through the optimization strategies mentioned above, the accuracy of the proposed SNN is effectively improved, which further proves that the network optimization methods are feasible and effective.

Comparison with Other Networks. In this paper, other spiking networks of the same scale are chosen to compare using CIFAR-10 dataset, as shown in the Table 1. Cao's spiking neural network [5] with IF neurons is converted based on Krizhevsky's convolution neural network [12]. Hunsberger's spiking neural network with improved LIF neurons [7] is similar. Although their network conversion errors are less than 2%, there is no weight normalization method in their networks, which may lead to neurons saturation and cause more performance problems. By using the optimization strategies mentioned above, the conversion errors between these two networks are reduced, and the state-of-art result is achieved compared with other networks.

Table 1. Accuracy of different networks.

Network	CIFAR-10 accuracy
CNN of this paper	**86.48%**
SNN of this paper	**86.43%**
CNN of Krizhevsky [12]	85.37%
SNN of Hunsberger [7]	82.59%
SNN of Cao [5]	77.43%

Accuracy-Delay-Tradeoff. The proposed SNN needs to balance the relationship between accuracy and delay, and the network needs a longer time for obtaining a higher accuracy. In this paper, the tradeoff of different normalization methods are compared, as shown in Fig. 6. The curves represent the results of different normalization strategies, and the robust weight normalization factor mentioned in this paper can achieve ideal tradeoff between delay and final accuracy.

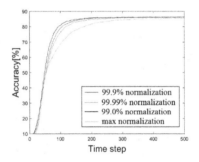

Fig. 6. Accuracy-delay-tradeoff with different normalizations.

Classification Accuracy on MNIST Dataset. The test also conducts on MNIST [3] dataset (a digital handwritten dataset). The accuracy of the CNN is 99.16%, and the accuracy of the proposed deep SNN is 99.09%.

The results on two datasets have shown that the CNN is converted into the SNN with lower losses, and the proposed deep SNN have comparative performances on both classification and computing compared to CNNs.

4   Conclusion

In this paper, a deep SNN is proposed for image classification. The network parameters (weights and bias) are firstly obtained by training a convolution neural networks (CNN), and then are converted and utilized in the SNN. Compared with other spiking neural networks, the proposed deep SNN achieves comparative performances on both classification and computing. Furthermore, it is closer to the biological mechanism in the design of neurons. Our work is helpful for understanding the spike activity of the brain. Future work includes solving the problem of reducing the firing rate of neurons and introducing in more biologically specific neuron models.

Acknowledgments. This study was partly supported by the National Natural Science Foundation of China (No. 41571402), the Science Fund for Creative Research Groups of the National Natural Science Foundation of China (No. 61221003), and Shanghai Jiao Tong University Agri-X Fund (No. Agri-X2015004).

References

1. Neftci, E.O., Pedroni, B.U., Joshi, S., et al.: Stochastic synapses enable efficient brain-inspired learning machines. Front. Neurosci. **10**, 241 (2016)
2. MFolowosele, F., Vogelstein, R.J., Etienne-Cummings, R.: Real-time silicon implementation of V1 in hierarchical visual information processing. In: Biomedical Circuits and Systems Conference, pp. 181–184. IEEE Press (2008)
3. LeCun, Y., Bottou, L., Bengio, Y., Haffner, P.: Gradient-based learning applied to document recognition. Proc. IEEE Press **86**, 2278–2324 (1999). Morgan Kaufmann
4. Brader, J.M., Senn, W., Fusi, S.: Grid Learning real-world stimuli in a neural network with spike-driven synaptic dynamics. Neural Comput. **19**, 2881–2912 (2007)
5. Cao, Y., Chen, Y., Khosla, D.: Spiking deep convolutional neural networks for energy-efficient object recognition. Int. J. Comput. Vis. **113**, 54–66 (2015)
6. Diehl, P.U., Neil, D., Binas, J., et al.: Fast-classifying, high-accuracy spiking deep networks through weight and threshold balancing. In: International Joint Conference on Neural Networks (IJCNN) 2015, IEEE, pp. 1–8. IEEE Press (2015)
7. Hunsberger, E., Eliasmith, C.: Spiking deep networks with LIF neurons. arXiv:1510.08829 (2015)
8. Maass, W., Markram, H.: On the computational power of circuits of spiking neurons. J. Comput. Syst. Sci. **69**, 593–616 (2004)
9. Camunas-Mesa, L., Zamarreno-Ramos, C., Linares-Barranco, A., et al.: An event-driven multi-kernel convolution processor module for event-driven vision sensors. IEEE J. Solid-State Circ. **47**, 504–517 (2012)
10. O'Connor, P., Neil, D., Liu, S.C., et al.: Real-time classification and sensor fusion with a spiking deep belief network. Front. Neurosci. **7** (2013)
11. Foster, I., Kesselman, C., Nick, J., Tuecke, S.: The Physiology of the Grid: an Open Grid Services Architecture for Distributed Systems Integration. Technical report, Global Grid Forum (2002)
12. Krizhevsky, A., Sutskever, I., Hinton, G.E.: Imagenet classification with deep convolutional neural networks. Adv. Neural Inf. Process. Syst. **25**, 1097–1105 (2012)
13. Vincent, P., Larochelle, H., Bengio, Y., et al.: Extracting and composing robust features with denoising autoencoders. In: Proceedings of the 25th international conference on Machine learning. ACM, pp. 1096–1103 (2008)
14. Angela, J.Y., Giese, M.A., Poggio, T.A.: Biophysiologically plausible implementations of the maximum operation. Neural Comput. **14**, 2857–2881 (2002)

15. Ioffe, S., Szegedy, C.: Batch normalization: Accelerating deep network training by reducing internal covariate shift. In: International Conference on Machine Learning, pp. 448–456 (2015)
16. Krizhevsky, A., Hinton, G.: Learning Multiple Layers of Features from Tiny Images (2009)

Asynchronous, Data-Parallel Deep Convolutional Neural Network Training with Linear Prediction Model for Parameter Transition

Ikuro Sato[1(✉)], Ryo Fujisaki[1], Yosuke Oyama[2], Akihiro Nomura[2], and Satoshi Matsuoka[2]

[1] Denso IT Laboratory, Inc., Tokyo, Japan
{isato,rfujisaki}@d-itlab.co.jp
[2] Tokyo Institute of Technology, Tokyo, Japan
{oyama.y.aa,nomura.a.ac}@m.titech.ac.jp,matsu@is.titech.ac.jp

Abstract. Recent studies have revealed that Convolutional Neural Networks requiring vastly many sum-of-product operations with relatively small numbers of parameters tend to exhibit great model performances. Asynchronous Stochastic Gradient Descent provides a possibility of large-scale distributed computation for training such networks. However, asynchrony introduces stale gradients, which are considered to have negative effects on training speed. In this work, we propose a method to predict future parameters during the training to mitigate the drawback of staleness. We show that the proposed method gives good parameter prediction accuracies that can improve speed of asynchronous training. The experimental results on ImageNet demonstrates that the proposed asynchronous training method, compared to a synchronous training method, reduces the training time to reach a certain model accuracy by a factor of 1.9 with 256 GPUs used in parallel.

1 Introduction

One of the findings in the last few years about Convolutional Neural Network (CNN) is that models requiring a relatively large number of sum-of-product Operations Per Parameter (OPP) in the forward step tend to exhibit high accuracies in recognition tasks [1–3]. One such example can be seen in the ILSVRC classification task [4], where GoogLeNet [2], an example of the computationally intensive deep models with about 221 OPP, scored 6.67% top-5 error rate, whereas AlexNet [5], a parameter-rich model with about 11 OPP, scored 16.4%.

Data-parallel computation in a computing cluster provides possibilities of significant speed-up in training of computationally intensive models [2,6–9], by which we mean models requiring a large amount of computation to produce gradients with a relatively small number of parameters, like GoogLeNet. In data-parallelism each processor basically repeats two kinds of processes: (1) the gradient-computing process reads a small set of training data, which we refer to as "sub-batch" in this paper, and computes the gradients of the sub-batch

© Springer International Publishing AG 2017
D. Liu et al. (Eds.): ICONIP 2017, Part II, LNCS 10635, pp. 305–314, 2017.
https://doi.org/10.1007/978-3-319-70096-0_32

cost; and (2) the parameter-update process updates parameters by adding the gradients from all or a part of the processors utilizing high-speed interconnect communication. Data-parallel training of a computationally intensive model is efficient, compared to that of parameter-rich models, because communication burden of the former is relatively low.

Two strategies mainly exist in data-parallel neural network training: Synchronous Stochastic Gradient Descent (SSGD) [7,9] and Asynchronous Stochastic Gradient Descent (ASGD) [6,8,10,11]. In SSGD gradient-computing process and parameter-update process run one after the other, whereas in ASGD these two processes run concurrently without waiting the other to be completed. When compared two strategies under the same computational resources, ASGD generally enjoys higher parameter-update frequency for computationally intensive models. This is because ASGD does not suffer from waiting a relatively long period of gradient computation to complete a parameter update. On the other hand, an expected cost or error rate drop per parameter update of ASGD is smaller than that of SSGD in general [8,10,11]. In ASGD, gradients are computed based on *stale* parameters, whose timestamp is older than the current timestamp. Due to the staleness, the gradient vector computed in ASGD is no longer parallel to the steepest descent direction at current parameters. One technical challenge is to develop a mechanism that can *predict* future parameters, with which gradients are computed. If this parameter-prediction accuracy can be made high enough so that the computed gradient vector restores the steepest descent direction at current parameters to be updated, ASGD acquires nearly equal expected cost or error rate drop per update as SSGD, and as a consequence, ASGD having a relatively high update frequency outperforms SSGD in speed of training a computationally intensive CNN.

We propose an algorithm for stale parameter updates in ASGD, named PP-ASGD (PP stands for "Parameter Predicted"), aiming to improve the cost or error rate drop per parameter update, compared to a naive ASGD. The contributions of this work are as stated below:

- We propose an ASGD algorithm based on a linear prediction model for parameter transition, depending on parameter staleness and stale momentum.
- We show an experimental evidence that the proposed method provides good prediction accuracies of parameter transitions.
- We show experimental evidences that PP-ASGD reduces training time to reach a certain model accuracy, compared to a naive ASGD with no parameter prediction.
- We show an experimental evidence that PP-ASGD reduces training time to reach a certain model accuracy, compared to SSGD, by a factor of 1.9 for a computationally intensive CNN trained on ImageNet with 256 GPUs.

2   Proposed Method

In this section we discuss the proposed method that works efficiently in a type of computing clusters as stated below. Suppose we have a computing cluster, in which each compute node contains the same number of GPUs, and any two nodes can communicate through high-speed interconnect. With such computational environment use of collective communication known as MPI-Allreduce [12] is a reasonable choice for parameter update [7,9]. This routine executes element-wise sum of vectors (gradients, in our case) from every node and places the resultant vector (sum of gradients) to every node. The communication period necessary to run one MPI-Allreduce is typically $O(\log(\#\text{nodes}))$, and this sublinear behavior helps to avoid a communication bottleneck because the communication duration needed for an update grows moderately with respect to the number of nodes. Previous work mostly uses MPI-Allreduce for SSGD [7,9]; however, it brings drawback of low update frequency for computationally intensive models. To overcome this drawback, we introduce an ASGD algorithm with MPI-Allreduce in Sect. 2.1. ASGD generally creates a relatively large staleness value in training a computationally intensive model. In Sect. 2.2, we discuss a parameter prediction model to mitigate this problem.

2.1 ASGD with Collective Communication

In Algorithm 1 we give a data-parallel ASGD algorithm that can yield update frequencies independent of the amount of computation needed to produce gradients [13].[1] The parameter-update thread repeats the update process incessantly. This decouples the parameter-update process from gradient-computing process, thus makes the update frequency F_U independent of the period of gradient computation. The gradient-computation thread uses a GPU to process gradient computation repeatedly and incessantly without any synchronization. Gradient-computation frequency F_G depends on the amount of computation for gradients. For comparison, we give SSGD algorithm with MPI-Allreduce in Algorithm 4, in which update frequency does depend on the load of gradient computation.

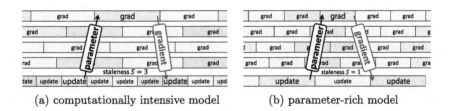

(a) computationally intensive model   (b) parameter-rich model

Fig. 1. Illustration of the time behavior of 4 **grad** threads and 1 **update** thread in ASGD.

A computationally intensive model experiences high staleness compared to a parameter-rich model in ASGD for a given number of nodes. We define time-average staleness, $\overline{S} \in \mathbb{R}$, as

---

[1] Mutexes need to be implemented in appropriate places to avoid read/write collisions.

Algorithm 1. ASGD with MPI-Allreduce

```
input   : w_0,                              /* w_0: initial param. */
        : μ, λ,                  /* μ: momentum rate, λ: learning rate */
        : t_f, G,              /* t_f: max #updates, G: #GPUs in a node */
        : b, X                /* b: sub-batch size, X: training dataset */
output : w
1 begin
2 │   global w, ŵ ← w_0; D_1, D_2, ···, D_G, M ← 0 · w_0; F ← true /* in bold face */
3 │   thread update(w_0, μ, λ, t_f, G)      /* See Algorithm 2 for update(). */
4 │   thread grad(1, b, X)                  /* See Algorithm 3 for grad(). */
5 │   thread grad(2, b, X)                  /* thread lines are        */
6 │   ···                                   /* executed in parallel. */
7 │   thread grad(G, b, X)
8 │   wait thread              /* waits until all the thread complete */
9 │   w ← w
```

Algorithm 2. Function update	**Algorithm 3.** Function grad
1 **Function** update(w_0, μ, λ, t_f, G)	1 **Function** grad(g, b, X)
2 │ **for** t ← 0 **to** t_f − 1 **do**	2 │ **do**
3 │ │ D_L ← D_1 + D_2 + ··· + D_G	3 │ │ **for** k ← 1 **to** b **do**
4 │ │ D_1, D_2, ···, D_G ← 0 · w_0	4 │ │ │ x_k ← randpick(X)
5 │ │ D_A ← MPI-Allreduce(D_L)	│ │ │ /* random sampling */
6 │ │ M ← μM − λD_A	5 │ │ w_ℓ ← ŵ /* local copy */
7 │ │ w ← w + M	6 │ │ D_g ← D_g + Σ_k ∇_w J(x_k; w_ℓ)
8 │ │ ŵ ← f_{⌊S̄⌋}(w, M) /* Eq.(2) */	│ │ /* grad. of cost J() */
9 │ F ← false /* training done */	7 │ **while** F

$$\overline{S} = 1 + F_U / F_G. \tag{1}$$

It is an addition of the count of updates in one gradient computation period and offset one, which comes from the fact that the consecutive updates run incessantly. As illustrated in Fig. 1, ASGD training of a computationally intensive model acquires a relatively large staleness value because it has a relatively large F_U / F_G.

There are mainly two approaches to mitigate problems caused by high staleness: $\overline{S}$-reduction and gradient "quality" improvement. The former approach includes use of small sub-batch size [10], and model-parallelism [5,6,14]. The latter approach includes our momentum-based prediction mechanism as presented next, and a delay compensation technique based on approximated Hessian [8].

2.2   Linear Prediction Model for Parameter Transition

We discuss the proposed method for predicting future parameters to improve an expected cost or error rate drop per update in ASGD. The basic idea is

---

Algorithm 4. SSGD with MPI-Allreduce

```
    input  : w_0, μ, λ, t_f, G, b, X            /* same input as in Algorithm 1 */
    output : w
1 begin
2       global ŵ ← w_0; D_1, D_2, ··· , D_G ← 0 · w_0; F ← false    /* in bold face */
3       w ← w_0, M ← 0 · w_0
4       for t ← 0 to t_f − 1 do
5           thread grad(1, b, X)                    /* thread lines are      */
6           thread grad(2, b, X)                    /* executed in parallel. */
7           ···                                      /* See Algorithm 3 for grad(). */
8           thread grad(G, b, X)        /* do-while part executed only once */
9           wait thread               /* waits until all the thread complete */
10          D_L ← D_1 + D_2 + ··· + D_G
11          D_1, D_2, ··· , D_G ← 0 · w_0
12          D_A ← MPI-Allreduce(D_L)
13          M ← μM − λD_A
14          w ← w + M
15          ŵ ← w + μM                                        /* NAG */
```

---

that right after parameters get updated, the method predicts future parameters, with which gradients are computed, so that the computed gradient vector becomes approximately parallel to the steepest-descent direction at the time of update. Suppose we have a parameter vector $w_t \in \mathbb{R}^D$ (D is the dimension of the parameter space) at timestamp t, compute the forward and backward steps, and then use the computed gradients to update w_{t+S} to w_{t+S+1}. Here, S is an integer-valued staleness, with $S = 0$ being SSGD and $S > 0$ being ASGD. The aim of the proposed method is to design a function that can *predict* parameter vector that is $(S + 1)$-timestamp ahead; *i.e.*, to design $f_S : \mathbb{R}^D \to \mathbb{R}^D$ so that $f_S(w_t, \cdot) \simeq w_{t+S+1}$.

The explicit form of the parameter prediction function that we use is

$$f_S(w_t, M_t) = w_t + M_t \sum_{S'=1}^{S+1} \mu^{S'}, \tag{2}$$

The function depends on M_t, (stale) momentum vector at timestamp t, and S, an integer-valued staleness given by $S = \lfloor \bar{S} \rfloor$, where the time-average staleness $\bar{S}$ is assumed to be measured during training. The prediction model is a natural extension of Nesterov's Accelerated Gradients (NAG) [15] to stale gradients; *i.e.*, when a staleness value is zero (SSGD), the proposed method becomes equivalent to NAG: $f_0(w, M) = w + \mu M$, as in Algorithm 4.

The proposed method is expected to work well in those cases, which the popular momentum method [16] or its variants, such as NAG, can accelerate convergence, or in other words, the gradients are quite correlated between arbitrary two consecutive iterations. If the parameter prediction accuracy can be made very high, PP-ASGD has a huge advantage to speed-up training of a computationally intensive model as PP-ASGD has a higher update frequency than SSGD.

3   Evaluation

We conducted image classification experiments to compare training times between PP-ASGD and ASGD, and between PP-ASGD and SSGD.

We used three datasets for evaluation: (1) **ImageNet-1000** [4][2] –the 1000-class ILSVRC classification dataset; (2) **ImageNet-32** –a subset of ImageNet-1000, consisting of 32 randomly chosen classes by the authors; and (3) **CIFAR-10** [17][3]. For ImageNet training, on-line data augmentation technique including random scaling, cropping and weak elastic distortion [18] was adopted. For CIFAR-10 training, no data augmentation is used. We used the minimum sub-batch size, $i.e.$, $b = 1$, for all ImageNet training.

We used following computational environments. All ImageNet experiments were conducted in TSUBAME-KFC/DL supercomputer[4]. The program of distributed training is written in C++, CUDA and OpenMPI from scratch. All CIFAR-10 experiments were conducted in a single node with one GPU with a program written in MATLAB. To test (PP-)ASGD on CIFAR-10, nonzero staleness was artificially generated.

We used simple CNN architectures as follows. Convolutional kernels always have 3×3 spatial sizes. Non-overlapping maximum-pooling is adapted. Activation function is given by $\max(a, 0.01a)$, similar to ReLU [19]. Cross entropy loss is used with softmax output. CIFAR-10 CNN has a form of CCPCPCPFFF, where 'C' means convolutional, 'P' means pooling, and 'F' means fully-connected layers. Description of the numbers of maps and neurons are omitted. In all experiments the same momentum rate 0.99 is used.

3.1   Training Speed: PP-ASGD Vs ASGD

CIFAR-10. Figure 2 shows classification error rate curves of PP-ASGD and ASGD with staleness values $S = 3, 9, 27$. For $S = 3$ the error rate of PP-ASGD at a given point in epoch is lower than or similar to that of ASGD. For $S = 9$ the error rates of PP-ASGD in the interval of first 7 epochs is clearly lower than that of ASGD. The most notable speed-up is observed for $S = 27$ by roughly 5× to reach the same error rate 0.3. As for generalization ability, PP-ASGD produces a much lower error rate than ASGD for $S = 27$. For the case of $S = 3$ or $S = 9$, though the error rate curve fluctuates time-to-time, the model accuracy produced by PP-ASGD is by and large equal to that produced by ASGD.

---

[2] See http://image-net.org for details.

[3] See https://www.cs.toronto.edu/~kriz/cifar.html for details.

[4] Each compute node of TSUBAME-KFC/DL contains 2 Intel Xeon E5-2620 v2 CPUs and 4 NVIDIA Tesla K80. Since K80 contains 2 GPUs internally, each node has 8 GPUs for total. FDR InfiniBand is equipped for interconnect.

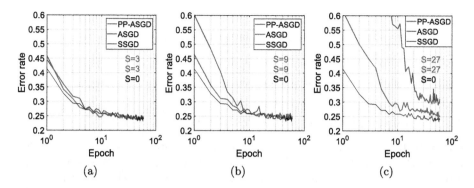

Fig. 2. Classification error rate curves of PP-ASGD, ASGD, and SSGD on the CIFAR-10 validation dataset. Staleness values of PP-ASGD and ASGD are varied: (a) $S = 3$, (b) $S = 9$, and (c) $S = 27$. Horizontal axes are in logarithmic scale.

ImageNet-32. The left side of Fig. 3 shows classification error rate curves of PP-ASGD and ASGD. We used 32 GPUs (4 nodes $\times$ 8 GPUs) in each training. The time-average staleness is about 8.5 for both cases. Note that the computational time for the parameter prediction part is negligible. It is evident from the left side of Fig. 3 that PP-ASGD outperforms ASGD in training speed approximately by a factor of two to reach the same top-5 error rate, say 0.2.

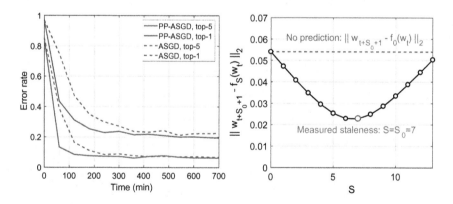

Fig. 3. Left: classification error rate curves of PP-ASGD and ASGD on the ImageNet-32 validation dataset. Right: plot of $\|w_{t+S_0+1} - f_S(w_t)\|_2$ for $S = 0, 1, \cdots, 13$ with measured staleness $S_0 = 7$. Each point is an average of 100 measurements right after 1 epoch. CNN architecture: CPCPCCPCCPCCPCCF. We used 32 GPUs to train each model.

The right side of Fig. 3 shows the parameter prediction error, expressed by $\|w_{t+S_0+1} - f_S(w_t)\|_2$, where S_0 is the measured staleness and S is swept from 0 to 13. From this experiment $\|w_{t+S_0+1} - f_S(w_t)\|_2$ has a minimum at $S = S_0$, indicating that the coefficient in the stale momentum term of the proposed prediction model is indeed appropriate. The horizontal dashed line indicates discrepancy between the stale parameter vector and the future $((S_0 + 1)$-ahead) parameter vector; whereas the red circle indicates discrepancy between the predicted parameter vector by our method and the future $((S_0 + 1)$-ahead) parameter vector. The latter discrepancy (by PP-ASGD) is 42% of the former discrepancy (by ASGD). It is considered that this improvement results in the training speed-up.

3.2 Training Speed: PP-ASGD Vs SSGD

CIFAR-10. Figure 2 also shows classification error rate curves of SSGD, besides PP-ASGD with staleness values $S = 3, 9, 27$. SSGD has the largest error rate drop in the interval of the first few epochs, but PP-ASGD with $S = 3(9)$ reaches very similar error rates as SSGD after $4(9)$-th epoch. As for $S = 27$ case, PP-ASGD clearly produces a degraded generalization performance compared with SSGD.

ImageNet-1000. We conducted large-scale training experiments on ImageNet-1000 by PP-ASGD and SSGD. In Fig. 4 the leftmost figure shows error rate curves, and the middle figure shows the relative training speeds to reach 0.6 top-1 error rate. We ran each training a couple of times with different learning rates, and show the best performing results. The learning rates used for the results shown in Fig. 4 are ranged from 1e–4 to 8e–4.[5] We did not drop learning rate during training. From the figure it is observed that PP-ASGD consistently

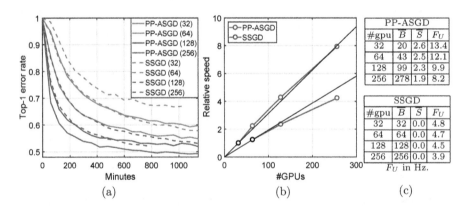

(a)   (b)   (c)

Fig. 4. (a) Classification error rate curves of PP-ASGD and SSGD on the ImageNet-1000 validation dataset. Numbers in parentheses indicate #GPUs. (b) Relative speeds to reach 0.6 top-1 validation error rate. Black lines indicate ideal linear speed-up lines. (c) Time-average batch size $\overline{B}$ (here, "batch" means a set of sub-batches used for an update), time-average staleness $\overline{S}$, and update frequency F_U. All the experiments use the CNN of the same form, CCPCCPCPCCPCF.

---

[5] In every case the learning rate is varied from 0 to the target value linearly from the beginning of the training until the end of the first epoch for stability. After this period, the learning rate is held fixed at the target value.

outperforms SSGD in training speed by a factor of 1.8–1.9 when the same number of GPUs are used. It is also observed that PP-ASGD exhibits a near-linear speed-up behavior with respect to the number of GPUs up to 256-GPU, while SSGD exhibits a sublinear behavior.

4   Discussion and Conclusion

In this work, we proposed PP-ASGD algorithm that uses a parameter prediction model for asynchronous, data-parallel CNN training. The prediction model is based on a linear function of a stale momentum vector with a coefficient depending on measured staleness value. Experiments showed that our model has good parameter prediction accuracies, that result in reduction of training time to reach a certain model accuracy, compared with a naive ASGD. PP-ASGD also outperforms SSGD in training speed to reach the same model accuracy by a factor of 1.9, when a computationally intensive model is trained on ImageNet using 256 GPUs in parallel.

Lastly, we discuss a possibility of further improvement of gradient quality in asynchronous settings. Zheng, *et al.* [8] proposed a delay compensation technique for asynchronous, distributed deep learning. In their method a compute thread computes gradients and an approximated Hessian matrix using stale parameters, and an update thread corrects the stale gradients by the product of the approximated Hessian and the difference vector between the stale and current parameter vectors. Our method differs in that gradients are computed by *predicted* parameters by stale momentum and that Hessian computation is not necessary. Indeed, it is expected that by *combining* the method of Zheng, *et al.* and ours gradient quality can be further improved. In the combined method, a compute thread computes gradients and approximated Hessian matrix using *predicted* parameters, and an update thread corrects the gradients by the product of the approximated Hessian and the difference vector between the *predicted* and current parameter vectors (that is, the parameter-prediction error). Our method can yield small parameter-prediction error, with which the Hessian correction term would further improve the gradient quality.

References

1. He, K., Zhang, X., Ren, S., Sun, J.: Deep residual learning for image recognition. In: IEEE Conference on Computer Vision and Pattern Recognition, pp. 770–778 (2016)
2. Szegedy, C., Liu, W., Jia, Y., Sermanet, P., Reed, S., Anguelov, D., Erhan, D., Vanhoucke, V., Rabinovich, A.: Going deeper with convolutions. In: IEEE Conference on Computer Vision and Pattern Recognition, pp. 1–9 (2015)
3. Lin, M., Chen, Q., Yan, S.: Network in network. In: International Conference on Learning Representations (2014)
4. Russakovsky, O., Deng, J., Su, H., Krause, J., Satheesh, S., Ma, S., Huang, Z., Karpathy, A., Khosla, A., Bernstein, M., Berg, A.C., Fei-Fei, L.: ImageNet large scale visual recognition challenge. Int. J. Comput. Vis. **115**(3), 211–252 (2015)

5. Krizhevsky, A., Ilya, S., Hinton, G.E.: Imagenet classification with deep convolutional neural networks. In: Neural Information Processing Systems, pp. 1097–1105 (2012)
6. Dean, J., Corrado, G.S., Monga, R., Chen, K., Devin, M., Le, Q.V., Mao, M.Z., Ranzato, M., Senior, A., Tucker, P., Yang, K., Ng, A.Y.: Large scale distributed deep Networks. In: Neural Information Processing Systems, pp. 1223–1231 (2012)
7. Iandola, F.N., Ashraf, K., Moskewicz, M.W., Keutzer, K.: Firecaffe: near-linear acceleration of deep neural network training on compute clusters arXiv:1511.00175 (2015)
8. Zheng, S., Meng, Q., Wang, T., Chen, W., Yu, N., Ma, Z., Liu, T.: Asynchronous stochastic gradient descent with delay compensation for distributed deep learning arXiv:1609.08326 (2016)
9. Wu, R., Yan, S., Shan, Y., Dang, Q., Sun, G.: Deep Image: Scaling up image recognition arXiv:1501.02876 (2015)
10. Gupta, S., Zhang, W., Wang, F.: Model accuracy and runtime tradeoff in distributed deep learning: a systematic study. In: IEEE International Conference on Data Mining, pp. 171–180 (2016)
11. Zhang, W., Gupta, S., Lian, X., Liu, J.: Staleness-aware async-SGD for distributed deep learning. In: International Joint Conferences on Artificial Intelligence, pp. 2350–2356 (2016)
12. MPI: A message-passing interface standard. http://mpi-forum.org/docs/mpi-3.1/mpi31-report.pdf
13. Oyama, Y., Nomura, A., Sato, I., Nishimura, H., Tamatsu, Y., Matsuoka, S.: Predicting statistics of asynchronous SGD parameters for a large-scale distributed deep learning system on GPU supercomputers. In: IEEE Big Data, pp. 66–75 (2016)
14. Jaderberg, M., Czarnecki, W.M., Osindero, S., Vinyals, O., Graves, A., Kavukcuoglu, K.: Decoupled neural interfaces using synthetic gradients arXiv:1608.05343 (2016)
15. Nesterov, Y.: A method of solving a convex programming problem with convergence rate $O(1/k^2)$. Sov. Math. Dokl. **27**, 372–376 (1983)
16. Qian, N.: On the momentum term in gradient descent learning algorithms. Neural Netw. **12**(1), 145–151 (1999)
17. Krizhevsky, A.: Learning multiple layers of features from tiny images. Master's thesis, Computer Science Department, University of Toronto (2009)
18. Simard, P.Y., Steinkraus, D., Platt, J.C.: Best practices for convolutional neural networks applied to visual document analysis. In: IAPR International Conference on Document Analysis and Recognition, pp. 958–963 (2003)
19. Nair, V., Hinton, G.E.: Rectified linear units improve restricted Boltzmann machines. In: International Conference on Machine Learning, pp. 807–814 (2010)

Efficient Learning Algorithm Using Compact Data Representation in Neural Networks

Masaya Kibune[(✉)] and Michael G. Lee

Fujitsu Laboratories of America, Inc.,
1240 E. Arques Avenue, Sunnyvale, CA 94085, USA
mkibune@us.fujitsu.com

Abstract. Convolutional neural networks have dramatically improved the prediction accuracy in a wide range of applications, such as vision recognition and natural language processing. However the recent neural networks often require several hundred megabytes of memory for the network parameters, which in turn consume a large amount of energy during computation. In order to achieve better energy efficiency, this work investigates the effects of compact data representation on memory saving for network parameters in artificial neural networks while maintaining comparable accuracy in both training and inference phases. We have studied the dependence of prediction accuracy on the total number of bits for fixed point data representation, using a proper range for synaptic weights. We have also proposed a dictionary based architecture that utilizes a limited number of floating-point entries for all the synaptic weights, with proper initialization and scaling factors to minimize the approximation error. Our experiments using a 5-layer convolutional neural network on Cifar-10 dataset have shown that 8 bits are enough for bit width reduction and dictionary based architecture to achieve 96.0% and 96.5% relative accuracy respectively, compared to the conventional 32-bit floating point.

Keywords: Data representation · Bit width reduction · Dictionary-based method · Uniform/non-uniform initialization · Scaling factor

1 Introduction

In recent years, due to rapid advances in learning algorithms and the exceptional growth of computing power, artificial neural network (ANN) has emerged as a dominant computation model for many real-world problems, including vision recognition, speech recognition, natural language processing, recommendation systems, robotics and autonomous driving vehicles. Although the current computational requirements have been provided by the commercial success of graphic processing units (GPUs), explosive increase in data and network size continues to drive the research in novel computing methods and architectures to provide better speed, accuracy and energy efficiency.

In modern computers, the time and the energy spent on computation are only small fractions of those needed for data communication between data memory and the computation unit (e.g., 0.1pJ/operation for 32-bit addition, 3.0pJ/operation for 32-bit

© Springer International Publishing AG 2017
D. Liu et al. (Eds.): ICONIP 2017, Part II, LNCS 10635, pp. 315–324, 2017.
https://doi.org/10.1007/978-3-319-70096-0_33

multiply, 10-100pJ/transfer for cache, 1.3-2.6nJ/transfer for main memory [1]). Although the data flow and SIMD (Single Instruction Multiple Data) architectures can in principle exploit the program flow predictability to hide the memory transfer latency, the overall energy for computation and communication is the most limiting factor for performance scaling in today's large scale computing systems. Consequently, reduction of the data transfer energy is the most promising approach to facilitate the performance scaling in building the large scale ANN computing systems.

Recently, there has been good interest in reducing the storage, communication and computation complexity of ANN models. [2] reduces data precision down to 16-bit fixed point using stochastic rounding for the weights. [3] reduces it further down to 4-10 bits by applying precision scaling techniques on the weights and activations. Some recent works have shown that more computationally efficient DNN (Deep Neural Network) could be constructed by quantizing most of the parameters during training. Binarized Neural Network [4] constrains the weights and activations to −1 and 1. This approach reduces not only the memory for these parameters but also the complexity of convolution to bitwise XNOR, which in turn makes MAC (Multiply–ACcumulate) operation faster. In a succeeding paper, Quantized Neural Network [5] extends its work to quantize ANNs with 1 bit weights and multi-bit activations and gradients, most operations are done by bitwise operation and the large-size network works well for image recognition. In approaches other than reducing data precision, [6] reduces the storage and communication penalty of weight-dominated ANNs by using a hashing trick to effectively map the weights to a concise table so that each table entry represents multiple weights. In [7], several techniques are used, including network pruning, clustering, and Huffman encoding, to optimize the inference computation of ANNs for mobile applications. Both approaches use parameter sharing with a fixed mapping between the parameters and the shared representatives.

In this paper, we investigate algorithmic and architectural advances that exploit inherent redundancy of the ANNs to optimize the computation speed and efficiency with little or no accuracy loss, thus offering further performance scaling. We introduce two compact data representations: (1) bit width reduction and (2) dictionary-based method with a new training scheme that updates the mapping of weights throughout training to improve the prediction accuracy. These methods explore reduction in memory for the network parameters such as weights and biases in a feedforward ANN, in order to reduce the requirement in communication and storage and to minimize the energy consumption and alleviate the performance scaling limitations. We note that both representations are also applicable to other network parameters such as activations and gradients. Our ultimate goal is to build a specialized ANN computing architecture for both learning and inference, with hardware support for the proposed algorithmic techniques. Thus we propose a new algorithm for selecting the compact data representation values and individually mapping of network parameters. We further propose a new learning algorithm for dictionary-based method which dynamically determines the mapping of the individual parameters to their compact data representations.

We discuss the algorithmic and architecture implications for bit width reduction in Sect. 2 and for dictionary-based method in Sect. 3. Section 4 provides the experimental results and discussion, and Sect. 5 concludes the paper.

2 Bit Width Reduction

There have been several efforts related to reducing the number of bits for data representation in neural networks using fixed-point [2], power-of-two quantization [8] and binary representation [4, 5] to achieve high energy efficiency. The merit of fixed-point approach is less requirement on hardware resources due to simpler arithmetic operating units and smaller memory size compared to floating points, as well as design flexibility for energy-accuracy tradeoff. [9] evaluates the accuracy dependence on the number of bits for network parameters in several neural networks and shows hardware metrics such as design area, energy consumption and delay. However, there are no detailed studies on the number of bits vs accuracy [2] and/or the best combination of integer and decimal bits to achieve comparable training accuracy compared to the conventional floating point [3]. In this paper, we investigate these characteristics and the design flexibility in detail. The conventional round-to-nearest rounding is used for quantization in this study, other rounding schemes, such as truncation and stochastic rounding, are also applicable. The compaction ratio of memory size for the bit width reduction is as follows:

$$N \times 32/(N \times M) \tag{1}$$

Here N is the total number of parameters and M is the number of bits per parameter.

3 Dictionary-Based Method

Throughout the development in the field of ANN, there have been more or less direct indications that large and complex networks usually have significant parameter redundancy [10]. In the past, this redundancy was often deemed as detrimental, and various techniques, such as regularization, dropout and unsupervised pre-training, have been developed to overcome it. We exploit the parameter redundancy to minimize the resources needed for both learning and inference.

3.1 Weights Mapping Scheme

In general terms, this is achieved by defining a many-to-one mapping function fWs: $Ws \rightarrow DWs$, where Ws is the set or subset of network parameters – weights and biases (e.g. all the weights in a layer) and DWs is the set of dictionary entries, and $\|DWs\| < \|Ws\|$, where $\| \ \|$ is the dimension. By storing and transporting only the address of DWs, which are encoded/decoded at the source/destination, we can save $(1-\|DWs\|/\|Ws\|)$ of the required communication and storage for weight at the expense of storing the dictionaries at both source and destination locally, which is relatively inexpensive considering the size of the dictionary. Figure 1 shows a generic computing core.

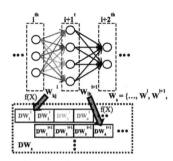

Fig. 1. Mapping from the network parameters to the dictionary entries.

There are several distinct items to fully define the mapping:

(1) Set of network parameters partitioned into disjoint set of domains of fWs: Some of the possible choices are random, one function (i.e. one dictionary) per layer, many functions per layer, many layers per function, one function for all layers.

(2) Definition of the DWs (how are the network parameter dictionary entries generated): Intuitively, they should represent the parameters in Ws as closely as possible to minimize the conversion error. Choices include uniform arrangement, in which only one of the directory entries and the stride need to be specified, and non-uniform arrangement, in which each entry needs to be determined individually using batch or online clustering.

(3) Actual mapping of the function fW: The function can be defined by the nearest neighbors of the dictionary entries.

The dictionary entries could be 32-bit floating point, and the compaction ratio compared to the conventional method is as follows (2):

$$N \times 32/(N \times log_2(L) + L \times 32) \qquad (2)$$

Here N is the total number of parameters and L is the number of the dictionary entries. Compared to (1), this compaction ratio is smaller if L equals to 2^M. The experimental results of comparable accuracy using suitable L and M for the bit width reduction and the dictionary-based method respectively are given in Sect. 4.

3.2 Training with Dictionary-Based Data Representation

In order to use the dictionary-based method for compact parameter representation during the learning phase, we need to be able to train with the dictionary-based data representation. Different from the transition to the bit width reduction after training, described in [3, 7], the network parameters are dynamically mapped to the adequate dictionary entries during training, this task is considerably more difficult than both the conventional training and the static assignment of dictionary entries. When a dictionary entry is shared among many network weights, consequently the error gradient of that shared dictionary entry is the sum of all the gradients of the weights mapped to that entry.

To implement the update of dictionary entries in the backpropagation-based algorithm, we design a simple scheme to re-scale the initial dictionary entries dynamically during the learning phase to generate new dictionary entries, thus this excludes minimum and maximum parameters for every minibatch to realize proper precision and range for better performance, using the following formula.

$$Re\text{-}scale\left(D_p^i\right) = D_{p\_ini}^i \times Range(W_{kj}^i|Lab\left(W_{kj}^i\right) = D_p^i)/Range(D_{p\_ini}^i) \times alpha$$
$$+ Mean(W_{kj}^i|Lab\left(W_{kj}^i\right) = D_p^i) \tag{3}$$

$$Range(X) = Max(X) - Min(X) \tag{4}$$

$$Mean(X) = (Max(X) + Min(X))/2 \tag{5}$$

Here D_p^i is the p-th dictionary entry in the i-th layer, $D_{p\_ini}^i$ is the initial value for the p-th dictionary entry in the i-th layer, and $Range(X)$ and $Mean(X)$ return the range and the mean of variable of X respectively. Both the maximum and the minimum are used because the parameter distribution, i.e. probability density function, is not necessarily symmetric. With a value less than one, the scaling factor $alpha$ would limit the parameter range and ignore large-value parameters, which would otherwise lead to lower precision.

The update of the parameter labels is realized by grouping the updated parameters using the updated dictionary entries and assigning the labels of the dictionary entries to each parameter. Note that relabeling can be used to point a parameter to a dictionary entry with the closet value either directly or after stochastic rounding. The algorithm for simultaneous dictionary and label update is shown in Fig. 2.

The performance of this algorithm and its convergence may depend on the initial distribution of dictionary entries $D_{p\_ini}^i$, which can be random, uniform, or non-uniform such as Gaussian distribution.

```
1. Initialize all dictionary entries Dⁱ with uniform or
non-uniform distribution and pointers Labⁱ
2. Forward propagation
   For i = 1 to L, compute activations Aᵢ using Dᵢ and Labⁱ
3. Backward propagation
   Compute output layer's activations gradient dC/dAᴸ
   For i = 1 to L-1, compute dC/dAⁱ using Dⁱ and Labⁱ
4. Parameter updates
   For i = 1 to L,
      Compute weights gradient dC/dWⁱ using Aᵢ and dC/dAⁱ
      Update weights Wⁱ using dC/dWⁱ and learning rate
      Update Dⁱ based on eq. (3)
      Update Labⁱ to point Dⁱ close to Wⁱ
```

Fig. 2. Algorithm for the update of the dictionary entries and the parameter labels.

4 Experiments and Discussion

We test the two methods for image recognition using Cifar-10 dataset, which consists of 60,000 32 × 32 pixel images in RBG format for training and testing. For the experiments, we implement a CNN (Convolutional Neural Network) with 5-layers (three convolutional layers, one fully-connected layer and one classifier layer) known as CifarQuick [11]. The convolutional layer has either 32 or 64 5 × 5 filters and max pooling over 2 × 2 window size. We also use batch normalization [12] after the max pooling to have better performance. We design codes using Theano Deep Leaning framework for our experiments, the relative prediction accuracy compared to 74.87% by conventional 32-bit floating point used to shown the experimental results of our methods.

Figure 3 (left) shows the relative accuracy of the network with bit width reduction in our experiments, as a function of the number of decimal bits with several curves for several different numbers of integer bits. At 3-bit integer and 5-bit decimal (8 bit in total), it reaches accuracy of 96.0%. Figure 3 (right) depicts the accuracy dependence on the decimal bits, and each curve has the same total number of bits, including integer bits and decimal bits. It is interesting to note that given a fixed number of total bits, the higher numbers of decimal bits do not necessarily lead to better accuracy, which implies the importance of good balance between integer and decimal bits to cover reasonable range and precision for the parameters. We also test the performance of the dictionary-based method with uniform initialization for several scaling factors as shown in Fig. 4 and with non-uniform initialization as shown in Fig. 5. For both initializations, 8-bit dictionary reaches comparable accuracy, 96.2% with a scaling factor of 0.995 and 96.5% with a scaling factor of 0.993 respectively. The results demonstrate that the non-uniform initialization is more suitable to reflect the parameter distribution. The best scaling factors in Fig. 6 are slightly smaller than 1.0 and they substantially excludes the large-value parameters, but they should not be too much smaller than 0.99 because that would exclude too vigorously and increase the approximation error. For example, a scaling factor of 0.985 only achieves 90.9%

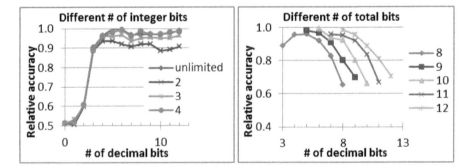

Fig. 3. Relative accuracy for bit width reduction using fixed point data representation. Left: The curves correspond to the different numbers of integer bits. Right: The curves correspond to the different numbers of total bits.

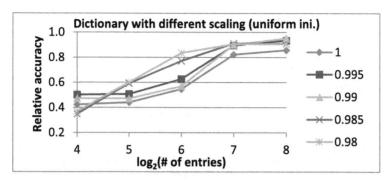

Fig. 4. Relative accuracy for the dictionary-based method using 32-bit floating point data representation with uniform initialization for entries. The curves correspond to the different scaling factors.

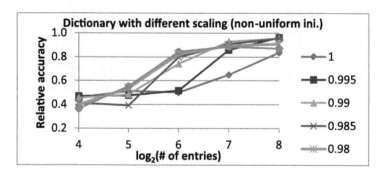

Fig. 5. Relative accuracy for weights sharing using 32-bit floating point data representation with non-uniform initialization for entries. The curves correspond to the different scaling factors.

accuracy, which is 5% smaller than that achieved by a scaling factor of 0.993. Figure 7 shows the histograms of the parameter distribution when different scaling factors are applied. With a scaling factor less than 1.0, the long tails are removed and replaced with higher frequencies at the two edges (in the right figure). The settings in the number of integer bits, the number of decimal bits and scaling factors are important, and they could be optimized during training to achieve even better energy efficiency. Note that the dictionary-based method achieves slightly better accuracy than the bit width reduction, and we believe this is due to the better precision of data representation using 32-bit floating point dictionary entries. More details are illustrated in Table 1.

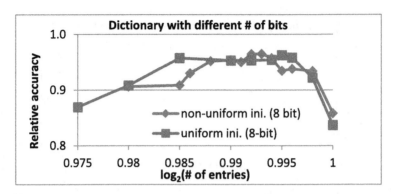

Fig. 6. Relative accuracy for the dictionary-based method using 32-bit floating point data representation with uniform and non-uniform initialization for entries respectively.

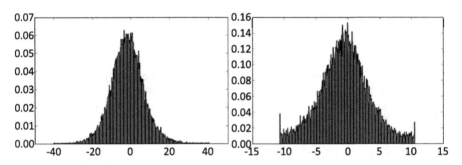

Fig. 7. Parameter distribution in a convolutional layer after learning for dictionary-based method with uniform initialization (Left: scaling factor of 1.0, Right: scaling factor of 0.995).

Table 1. Performance summary

Method	Data representation	Relative accuracy (%)
Conventional	32-bit floating point	100
Bit width reduction	8-bit fixed point (3-bit integer and 5-bit decimal)	96.0
Dictionary-based	32-bit floating for entries	96.5 (non-uniform initialization)

5 Conclusion

In this paper, we have investigated the prediction accuracy by compact data representation via bit width reduction and dictionary-based method respectively, in order to save memory and energy consumption for communication between computation units, and experiments have been done using 5-layer convolutional neural networks on Cifar-10 dataset. We have also proposed a new training scheme to update the parameter labels as well as the dictionary entries with non-uniform initialization and scaling factor to minimize the quantization error and improve the accuracy of the dictionary-based method. Our experimental results have shown that both methods with 8-bit implementations can achieve comparable accuracy of 96.0% and 96.5% respectively. Further work that is planned includes dynamic update of the dictionary entries based on clustering of the parameter values, instead of rescale from the initial dictionary entries. Adjustable setting for network optimization during training, e.g., a good balance between the numbers of integer bits and decimal bits, will also be investigated.

References

1. Horowitz, M.: 1.1 computing's energy problem (and what we can do about it). In: Solid-State Circuits Conference Digest of Technical Papers (ISSCC), pp. 10–14 (2014)
2. Gupta, S., Agrawal, A., Gopalakrishnan, K., Narayanan, P.: Deep learning with limited numerical precision. In: Proceedings of the 32nd International Conference on Machine Learning, pp. 1737–1746 (2015)
3. Moons, B., De Brabandere, B., Van Gool, L., Verhelst, M.: Energy-efficient convnets through approximate computing. In: Applications of Computer Vision (WACV), pp. 1–8 (2016)
4. Courbariaux, M., Hubara, I., Soudry, D., El-Yaniv, R., Bengio, Y.: Binarized neural networks: training deep neural networks with weights and activations constrained to +1 or −1. In: Lee, D.D., Sugiyama, M., Luxburg, U.V., Guyon, I., Garnett, R. (eds.) Advances in Neural Information Processing Systems, vol. 29, pp. 4107–4115. MIT Press, Cambridge (2016)
5. Hubara, I., Courbariaux, M., Soudry, D., El-Yaniv, R., Bengio, Y.: Quantized neural networks: training neural networks with bit width reduction weights and activations (2016). arXiv preprint: arXiv:1609.07061
6. Chen, W., Wilson, J., Tyree, S., Weinberger, K., Chen, Y.: Compressing neural networks with the hashing trick. In: Proceedings of the 32nd International Conference on Machine Learning, pp. 2285–2294 (2015)
7. Han, S., Mao, H., Dally, W.J.: Deep compression: compressing deep neural networks with pruning, trained quantization and huffman coding. In: International Conference on Learning Representations (2016)
8. Lin, Z., Courbariaux, M., Memisevic, R., Bengio, Y.: Neural networks with few multiplications (2015). arXiv preprint: arXiv:1510.03009
9. Hashemi, S., Anthony, N., Tann, H., Bahar, R.I., Reda, S.: Understanding the impact of precision quantization on the accuracy and energy of neural networks. In: 2017 Design, Automation & Test in Europe Conference & Exhibition (DATE), pp. 1474–1479 (2017)

10. Cheng, Y., Yu, F.X., Feris, R.S., Kumar, S., Choudhary, A., Chang, S.F.: An exploration of parameter redundancy in deep networks with circulant projections. In: Proceedings of the IEEE International Conference on Computer Vision, pp. 2857–2865 (2015)
11. Krizhevsky, A., Sutskever, I., Hinton, G.E.: Imagenet classification with deep convolutional neural networks. In: Pereira, F., Burges, C.J.C., Bottou, L., Weinberger, K.Q. (eds.) Advances in Neural Information Processing Systems, vol. 25, pp. 1097–1105. MIT Press, Cambridge (2012)
12. Ioffe, S., Szegedy, C.: Batch normalization: accelerating deep network training by reducing internal covariate shift. In: Proceedings of the 32nd International Conference on Machine Learning, pp. 448–456 (2015)

Regularizing CNN via Feature Augmentation

Liechuan Ou[1], Zheng Chen[3], Jianwei Lu[1,2(✉)], and Ye Luo[1(✉)]

[1] School of Software Engineering, Tongji University, Shanghai, China
{liechuan.ou,jwlu33,yeluo}@tongji.edu.cn
[2] Institute of Translational Medicine, Tongji University, Shanghai, China
[3] College of Architecture and Urban Planning, Tongji University,
Shanghai, China
zhengchen@tongji.edu.cn

Abstract. Very deep convolutional neural network has a strong representation power and becomes the dominant model to tackle very complex image classification problems. Due to the huge number of parameters, overfitting is always a primary problem in training a network without enough data. Data augmentation at input layer is a commonly used regularization method to make the trained model generalize better. In this paper, we propose that feature augmentation at intermediate layers can be also used to regularize the network. We implement a modified residual network by adding augmentation layers and train the model on CIFAR10. Experimental results demonstrate our method can successfully regularize the model. It significantly decreases the cross-entropy loss on test set although the training loss is higher than the original network. The final recognition accuracy on test set is also improved. In comparison with Dropout, our method can cooperate better with batch normalization to produce performance gain.

Keywords: Deep learning · CNN · Overfitting · Model regularization

1 Introduction

Deep Convolutional Neural Network [1] (CNN) has shown significant performance gain two decades ago [1]. The large dataset, ImageNet [2], and powerful computational resources are the main catalysts for the revival of CNN. Following work on weights initialization methods [3, 4] and network architectures [5–7] allow us to train network models with hundreds of layers. The introduction of more layers, enhances the expressive power of the model, but also increases the risk of over-fitting.

Researchers have proposed lots of methods to tackle over-fitting, which can be divided into two main categories. The one is adding an additional constrain on the model, which enforces the model to encode some prior knowledge [8]. It can be also a general preference for simpler models, like ℓ_2 weight decay used in [9]. The other is to increase the number of labeled data. By increasing the size of datasets, most of the machine learning algorithms can achieve better performance. That's because, if the learning process can be viewed as fitting a function, more data can describe the target manifold more accurately which helps the learning get away from outliers and results in a function with better generalization ability. The number of training samples required is

© Springer International Publishing AG 2017
D. Liu et al. (Eds.): ICONIP 2017, Part II, LNCS 10635, pp. 325–332, 2017.
https://doi.org/10.1007/978-3-319-70096-0_34

related to the capacity of the feature space which is exponential to the feature dimensions [10]. The convolutional neural network is very hungry for data due to the high-dimension nature of images. Although ImageNet provides one million labeled images, the winning model in the competitions all utilized data augmentation [5–7, 11].

The problem of insufficient data cannot be simply solved by the data augmentation. Most of the widely used augmentation methods are carried out on the input layer, that is, the original image. We state that such operations can also be applied to the feature maps produced by hidden layers. CNN is a hierarchical feature extractor, in which the output features of the current layer is the input features of its successive layer. From such a perspective, the input image and the feature maps at the intermediate levels have nothing different but data representation at different abstract levels. Therefore, a feature map can be viewed as an image with multiple channels, and data augmentation operations applied to ordinary RGB images can naturally be used to feature maps. We term the augmentation on feature maps as feature augmentation.

In this work, we introduce augmentation layers (AugLayer) into a regular CNN to regularize the network. Within a AugLayer, a certain kind of augmentation operation is performed on the inbound feature map and a modified one with information preserved is generated as output. In order to validate our idea, two operations, contrast adjustment and brightness adjustment are adopted in our experiments. The experimental result of deduced cross-entropy loss and increased classification accuracy on CIFAR10 dataset demonstrates the effectiveness of our proposed feature augmentation method on regularizing CNN model.

2   Related Work

For a long time, data set augmentation is a simple and effective method used in supervised learning to prevent over-fitting. It is particularly popular in computer vision community because it's very easy to generate many variants of an image with the information preserved. Common augmentation methods include random crop, scale jitter, brightness adjustment, contrast adjustment, and other affine transformations. LeCun et al. [12] applied a series of operations on the MNIST dataset while training LeNet, which is the first successful CNN model. Krizhevsky et al. [5] use horizontal flip, random crop and PCA analysis to improve the model robustness, resulting in an increase by over 1% on top-1 accuracy of AlexNet [5]. VGGNet [6], the winning model of 2014 ILSVRC, additionally utilized the scale jitter. Recently Chiyuan Zhang et al. [13] reported that using only random cropping without any other regularization method would allow the recognition rate of Inception Network [11] to increase from 59.80% to 67.18% on ImageNet dataset.

All these augmentation methods are applied to the image at the input layer. To the best of our knowledge, the augmentation in the feature space of CNN received little attention. Terrance et al. [14] proposed a method to augment the feature set. It works by first learning a data representation and then applying interpolation and extrapolation to features mapped to that representation. Our method differentiates from it in two points. One is that the augmentation operations occur simultaneously with the entire training process, and second, our method is specially designed for image data. We employee image enhancement methods and therefore encode domain knowledge. In addition, there are some regularization methods performing implicit augmentation. Dropout [15] mainly used in fully connected layers randomly discards some activations and it can be explained as creating many variants with missing value at dropped dimensions. Our method explicitly augments feature maps. Batch Normalization [16] (BN) is proposed to accelerate training but also plays a role of the regularizer. In conjunction with BN, Dropout has little effect in our experiments. By contrast, our method can still obtain performance gain at the Residual Network [7] (ResNet) which heavily uses BN layers.

3 Model

Our model is based on ResNet. The original ResNet consists of multiple building blocks, each of which includes two convolutions. In our proposed network architecture, the AugLayer is inserted after some convolutions illustrated by Fig. 1. It transforms the input feature map but preserves the spatial appearance of the feature and only functions during training. Without loss of generality, two kinds of augmentation techniques, contrast adjustment and brightness adjustment are used in AugLayer. In the following section, we will provide the details of these two augmentation techniques.

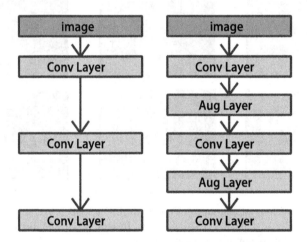

Fig. 1. Common architecture and our proposed architecture.

3.1   Contrast Adjustment

Contrast adjustment is a common method for image enhancement. Contrast is created by the difference of the luminance reflected by the adjacent surfaces. In the physical world, images of the same scene with different contrast are often observed. It's easy to obtain many variants of one image by adjusting its contrast. Contrast adjustment is conducted according to the following equations,

$$I' = (I - m) * f + m \tag{1}$$

$$f \sim U(1 - \alpha, 1 + \alpha) \tag{2}$$

where I is either an image or a feature map, m is the mean of each channel and f is the contrast ratio. α is empirically set to 0.25 in experiments. It's possible to find a better value using grid search. The image contrast will be enhanced if $f > 1$, otherwise weakened.

In our model, the contrast adjustment is applied to the feature maps. f is drawn from a uniform distribution illustrated by Eq. (2). It means that the contrast of some channels is enhanced and other channels weakened. The reason is that for a certain spatial location, the sum of feature values across all channels remains roughly unchanged. We also tried enhancing the contrast of all channels by sampling f on an interval greater than 1, and the results showed a performance drop on test set. That's probably because the augmentation operation introduces a numerical bias between training set and test set. Figure 2 demonstrates an example of contrast adjustment on an image and a feature map, respectively.

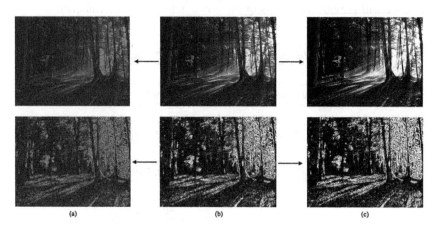

(a)   (b)   (c)

Fig. 2. The effect of contrast adjustment. Column (b) lists a RGB image and one of its feature maps extracted using a trained VGG16 network. Images in column (a) are variants with decreased contrast and column (c) enhanced contrast.

3.2 Brightness Adjustment

The brightness of an image reflects the light intensity of the environment at the time of image generation, and different intensities result in different images. Using a group of determined adjustment operations but performing on different channels also leads to images with different visual appearances. We propose to add similar operations after convolutional layers to augment the feature maps. Therefore, the same image can produce different feature maps when passing through the network with unchanged weights. This makes the network lose the opportunity to remember the sample exactly, thereby improving the generalization of the model. The brightness adjustment in our proposed method is carried out according to the Eq. (3) where $stdv$ is the standard deviation of features on each channel within a mini-batch, and f is the adjustment ratio, which is obtained from a uniform distribution defined by Eq. (4). β is set to 0.05. Larger values like 0.25 and 0.5, are also tried but they lead to poor performance.

$$I^{'} = I + stdv * f \tag{3}$$

$$f \sim U(-\beta, \beta) \tag{4}$$

4   Experiments

4.1   Dataset and Evaluation Metric

To evaluate our method, we use the popular CIFAR10 [9] dataset. It consists of ten categories and 60,000 color images with 32×32 pixels, of which 50,000 are for training and the rest for testing. Like other classification models, our model output the normalized probabilities of one input image belongs to each category and naturally cross-entropy loss is used for training and test. Accuracy is computed to measure the quality of predictions at test. In addition, the gap between training loss and test loss is also be used for evaluation.

4.2   Implementation

We apply the proposed method in the most popular ResNet to test its effectiveness. Basically, we follow the hyper parameters in [7]. The first layer is a 3×3 convolution, and then a stack of 6n layers are used. We call every 2n layers as a stage. After each stage, the feature map size will be halved and the number of filters will be doubled except for the first stage. Following those convolutions, a global average pooling and a fully connected layer are used. The number of trainable layers is 6n+2. We tried $n = \{1, 2, 3, 5, 7\}$, leading to 8, 14, 20, 32 and 44-layer network. There are two strategies of introducing our proposed AugLayer to the model. One option is adding one AugLayer for each stage, and the other is inserting one AugLayer after each convolution. Both are experimented. We compare our method with Dropout and image augmentation respectively. Dropout sets 50% activations of the flattened feature vector to zeros. Image augmentation adjusts the contrast or brightness of input images.

4.3   Training

The training employees SGD optimizer with a momentum of 0.9, an initial learning rate of 0.1, and learning rate decay of 0.0001. At 120th and 160th epoch, the learning rate is dropped by 90%. Batch size is 128 and the training lasts for 200 epochs. We use simple mean/std normalization. The basic data set augmentation method is same as that in [7], where each side of the image is padded by 4 pixels and 32×32 patches are randomly sampled and then flipped horizontally with probability 0.5. Training is conducted on a

NVIDIA GTX1080. One run takes 1–4 h with respect to different network depth. The introduction of AugLayer increase training time by about 5%–10%.

4.4   Results

Feature Contrast Adjustment
Figure 3 demonstrates that contrast adjustment on feature maps can effectively regularize the network. The "normal" means basic configuration consisting of mean-std preprocessing, random crop and random flip. The "image-contrast" additionally adjusts the image contrast randomly. The "feature contrast" introduces three AugLayers while "feature-contrast-more" aggressively inserts more AugLayers after each convolution. All networks can achieve convergence and the loss reaches a plateau at the 120th epoch of the first learning rate drop. The network with AugLayer has lower validation loss in the end although it has higher training loss during the whole training. It means our method can significantly narrow the gap between training and testing. Such phenomenon is more obvious given more AugLayer are introduced. Randomly adjusting the contrast of input images causes a slight performance degradation if measured by loss.

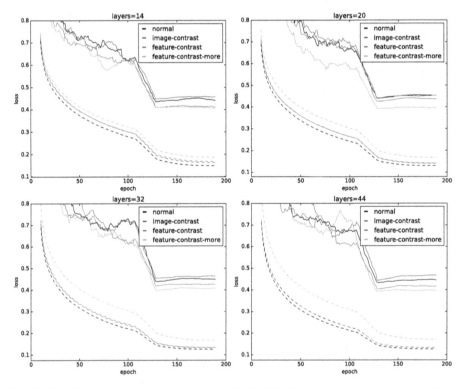

Fig. 3. The figure depicts training curves of 14, 20, 32 and 44-layer network with 4 configurations respectively. Dashed lines denote training loss and solid lines denote test loss.

Table 1. Test loss and classification error on CIFAR10

Config	Normal	Dropout	Image-contrast	Feature-contrast	Feature-contrast-more
8-layer	0.46 (11.6%)	0.48 (13.2%)	0.51 (11.9%)	0.43 (11.2%)	**0.42 (11.7%)**
14-layer	0.45 (9.00%)	0.45 (9.16%)	0.46 (9.52%)	0.41 (8.48%)	**0.41 (8.62%)**
20-layer	0.47 (8.45%)	0.49 (7.92%)	0.48 (8.78%)	0.44 (7.93%)	**0.40 (7.54%)**
32-layer	0.45 (7.70%)	0.59 (7.99%)	0.43 (7.38%)	0.43 (7.07%)	**0.41 (7.10%)**
44-layer	0.45 (7.03%)	0.58 (7.44%)	0.47 (7.24%)	0.42 (6.37%)	**0.39 (6.54%)**

Table 1 illustrates more detailed results. It shows that the AugLayer can consistently help the network generalize better. More AugLayers result in lower test loss. As for the metric of accuracy, similar trend can be observed but more augmentations don't always lead higher accuracy. The third column of Table 1 shows a performance decline if Dropout is inserted after the fully connected layer. We also tried replacing all AugLayers with Dropout and got worse results which are not listed here.

Feature Brightness Adjustment
Adjusting the brightness of each channel of the feature map can also slightly increase the generalization ability of the model. However, the test loss declines less significantly and more AugLayer don't consistently yield better results, either in terms of loss or recognition rate. The effectiveness of feature augmentation by brightness is weaker than by contrast. We don't show results of Dropout here (Table 2).

Table 2. Test loss and classification error on CIFAR10

Config	Normal	Image-bright	Feature-bright	Feature-bright-more
8-layer	0.451 (11.7%)	0.449 (11.6%)	0.442 (11.6%)	**0.438 (11.2%)**
14-layer	0.450 (9.90%)	0.475 (9.79%)	**0.437 (9.04%)**	0.447 (9.09%)
20-layer	0.473 (8.33%)	0.464 (9.36%)	0.457 (8.35%)	**0.446 (7.83%)**
32-layer	0.457 (7.69%)	0.476 (7.82%)	0.447 (7.22%)	**0.445 (7.16%)**
44-layer	0.432 (6.91%)	0.442 (7.20%)	0.445 (6.82%)	**0.438 (6.77%)**

5 Conclusion

In this study, we introduce a concept of the augmentation layer. By employing feature contrast and feature brightness adjustment techniques, we show that augmenting feature maps can regularize a convolutional neural network. Experiments on CIFAR10 verified the effectiveness of our method. Although our model is unable to fit the training samples as well as the original ResNet, it achieved a lower loss on the test set. Our future work will includes introducing other types of augmentation operations, testing compound augmentation operations, experimenting on larger networks, and larger datasets.

Acknowledgements. This work was supported by the General Program of National Natural Science Foundation of China under Grant No. 61572362 and No. 81571347.

References

1. LeCun, Y., Boser, B.E., Denker, J.S., Henderson, D., Howard, R.E., Hubbard, W.E., Jackel, L.D.: Handwritten digit recognition with a back-propagation network. In: Advances in Neural Information Processing Systems, pp. 396–404. Citeseer (1990)
2. Deng, J., Dong, W., Socher, R., Li, L.J., Li, K., Fei-Fei, L.: Imagenet: a large-scale hierarchical image database. In: Proceedings of the IEEE Conference on Computer Vision and Pattern Recognition, pp. 248–255. IEEE (2009)
3. Glorot, X., Bengio, Y.: Understanding the difficulty of training deep feed forward neural networks. In: Proceedings of AISTATS, pp. 249–256 (2010)
4. He, K., Zhang, X., Ren, S., Sun, J.: Delving deep into rectifiers: surpassing human-level performance on imagenet classification. In: Proceedings of the IEEE International Conference on Computer Vision, pp. 1026–1034. IEEE (2015)
5. Krizhevsky, A., Sutskever, I., Hinton, G.E.: Imagenet classification with deep convolutional neural networks. In: Advances in Neural Information Processing Systems, pp. 1097–1105 (2012)
6. Simonyan, K., Zisserman, A.: Very deep convolutional networks for large-scale image recognition. In: ICLR (2015)
7. He, K., Zhang, X., Ren, S., Sun, J.: Deep residual learning for image recognition. In: Proceedings of the IEEE Conference on Computer Vision and Pattern Recognition, pp. 770–778. IEEE (2016)
8. Yang, W., Ouyang W., Li, H., Wang, X.: End-to-end learning of deformable mixture of parts and deep convolutional neural networks for human pose estimation. In: Proceedings of the IEEE Conference on Computer Vision and Pattern Recognition, pp. 3073–3082. IEEE (2016)
9. Krizhevsky, A., Hinton, G.: Learning multiple layers of features from tiny images. Technical report, University of Toronto (2009)
10. Bishop, C.M.: Pattern Recognition and Machine Learning. Information Science and Statistics. Springer, New York (2006)
11. Szegedy, C., Vanhoucke, V., Ioffe, S., Shlens, J., Wojna, Z.: Rethinking the inception architecture for computer vision. In: Proceedings of the IEEE Conference on Computer Vision and Pattern Recognition, pp. 2818–2826. IEEE (2016)
12. LeCun, Y., Bottou, L., Bengio, Y., Haffner, P.: Gradient-based learning applied to document recognition. Proc. IEEE **86**(11), 2278–2324 (1998). IEEE
13. Zhang, C., Bengio, S., Hardt, M., Recht, B., Vinyals, O.: Understanding deep learning requires rethinking generalization. arXiv preprint (2016). arXiv:1611.03530
14. DeVries, T., Taylor, G.W.: Dataset augmentation in feature space. arXiv preprint (2017). arXiv:1702.05538
15. Srivastava, N., Hinton, G.E., Krizhevsky, A., Sutskever, I., Salakhutdinov, R.: Dropout: a simple way to prevent neural networks from overfitting. J. Mach. Learn. Res. **15**(1), 1929–1958 (2014)
16. Ioffe, S., Szegedy, C.: Batch normalization: accelerating deep network training by reducing internal covariate shift. In: International Conference on Machine Learning, pp. 448–456. (2015)

Effectiveness of Adversarial Attacks on Class-Imbalanced Convolutional Neural Networks

Rafael Possas[(⊠)] and Ying Zhou

School of Information Technologies, University of Sydney,
Camperdown, NSW, Australia
{rafael.possas,ying.zhou}@sydney.edu.au
https://sydney.edu.au

Abstract. Convolutional neural networks (CNNs) performance has increased considerably in the last couple of years. However, as with most machine learning methods, these networks suffer from the data imbalance problem - when the underlying training dataset is comprised of an unequal number of samples for each label/class. Such imbalance enforces a phenomena known as domain shift that causes the model to have poor generalisation when presented with previously unseen data. Recent research has focused on a technique called *gradient sign* that intensifies domain shift in CNNs by modifying inputs to deliberately yield erroneous model outputs, while appearing unmodified to human observers. Several commercial systems rely on image recognition techniques to perform well. Therefore, adversarial attacks poses serious threats to their integrity. In this work we present an experimental study that sheds light on the link between adversarial attacks, imbalanced learning and transfer learning. Through a series of experiments we evaluate the *fast gradient sign method* on class imbalanced CNNs, linking model vulnerabilities to the characteristics of its underlying training set and internal model knowledge.

Keywords: Convolutional neural networks · Adversarial examples · Gradient sign · Imbalanced training · Transfer learning

1 Introduction

Convolutional neural networks (CNNs) are a class of non-linear machine learning algorithms known for its state of the art performance on datasets with spatial structure. To date, not much research has been done on adversarial attacks against CNNs - a process on which inputs are changed to manipulate the algorithm outputs. The motivation for adversarial robustness comes largely from being able to shield image recognition systems from behaving unexpectedly. Experimental demonstrations of the effectiveness of adversarial attacks were carried out mainly by [2,5,15] and have heightened the need for improvement on

© Springer International Publishing AG 2017
D. Liu et al. (Eds.): ICONIP 2017, Part II, LNCS 10635, pp. 333–342, 2017.
https://doi.org/10.1007/978-3-319-70096-0_35

the current state of CNNs techniques. Developing robustness to such attacks has become of the utmost importance as many commercial applications are based on the same small group of models.

Domain shift or dataset shift [16] is also a well known cause for low performance of several machine learning algorithms [7,8]. This happens when the joint distribution of inputs and outputs differs between training and testing stages, causing models to perform badly on unseen data. The adverse effect of domain shift is even worse on real world, as data distributions are often skewed and rarely contains enough information to learn all the required features of the data domain. Adversaries have been proven to more readily exploit domain shift [10,12], and the question as to whether imbalanced training sets affects adversarial inputs performance on CNNs is still unanswered.

The effectiveness of an adversarial attack also depends on the internal gradient information of the targeted model. As shown on Papernot et al. (2016), attacks could be classified as both black-box and white-box. The former uses gradient information from a separate model, while the latter uses the target model gradient to generate adversarial inputs. While black-box attack is an approximation of the internal knowledge of the target model, the white-box uses the true representation of the feature space.

Currently, there is no empirical evidence on the effectiveness of adversarial attacks on class-imbalanced CNNs. We designed a set of experiments to investigate how both imbalanced training sets and the model's internal knowledge affects the robustness to such attacks. The main contributions of this work are as follows:

1. To shed new light on how CNNs trained on imbalanced datasets are affected by adversarial attacks
2. Evaluate the impact of transfer learning on imbalanced CNNs and how classes with similar set of features react to the perturbation caused by the gradient sign method

Section 2 of this paper discusses the related work in both CNNs, gradient sign methods, adversarial attacks and imbalanced/transfer learning. Section 3 provides details of the training models, imbalanced datasets and gradient sign methods used in our experiments. Section 4 presents the results on the under-sampled, over-sampled and balanced cases using both black/white-box attacks. Sections 5 is dedicated to drawing conclusions and providing directions to related future work.

2   Related Work

Previous work has shown that the high-dimensional non-linearities of convolutional neural networks [11] creates adversarial pockets of space - places where data points can be placed in order to provide a wrong model output. By exploiting such characteristics, recent methods were able to deliberately create an adversary that produces an incorrect, high confidence prediction for an image without visible distortion [13]. This is achieved by adding intentional noise to each pixel of an image so as to fool the algorithm into predicting an incorrect label [5,14,18].

The gradient sign method was introduced by Goodfellow et al. (2014) and has been used as the foundation of many of the experiments in adversarial attacks on CNNs. The results have shown that convolutional neural networks have linear behavior in very high dimensional spaces [5]. Most inputs were miss-classified not only by Goodfellow et al. (2014) experiments but by others as well [2,15].

The work of Papernot et al. (2016) has shown that one can use transfer learning to perform black-box attacks against CNNs [14,19] and, thus, to intentionally force the model to predict specific labels. The combination of adversaries and transfer learning creates a threat vector for many state of the art methods. Attacks, however, depend on some specific internal information of the target model [12,14]. For instance, the same model trained by two different configurations of the same dataset would have different gradients and thus, would provide different degrees of adversarial perturbations.

Techniques to overcome imbalanced learning have been developed for more general machine learning models. The work of Heibo et al. [6], for instance, provides a technique for doing weighted sampling of minority classes to minimize the effect of imbalanced learning. Another approach could be to incorporate unsupervised clustering on synthetic data generation mechanism in order to avoid wrong generation of synthetic samples [1]. More recent work has used a Bayesian framework to increase l_2 robustness to adversarial examples [2].

3   Experiment Design

Our experiments aims to investigate the relationships of the underlying learning structure of CNNs and the perturbation caused by gradient sign methods. In particular we focus on the investigation of how the gradient step from the sign method moves the points away from their distributions, and how this could be affected by both balanced and imbalanced training sets. This requires class labels of the data set to be non-hierarchical so we can make better assumptions of their distributions.

We use the CIFAR-10 data set [9] in our experiment. CIFAR-10 data is visually rich and empowers the analysis between different class labels. The data set contains 32×32 images in 10 classes, each has 5,000 samples for training and 1,000 for testing. There is not much overlap nor hierarchical relationship between classes. Most CNNs experiments nowadays use the 2014 ImageNet dataset [4]. However, its hierarchically organized categories adds unnecessary complexity to the experiment design and hinders the analysis of the results (e.g. causality relationships).

3.1   Network Architecture and Synthetic Dataset Imbalance

Network Architecture. All the experiments were performed using a modified VGGNet [17] architecture as shown on Fig. 1. The two fully connected 4096 layers at the end were replaced by one single layer with 512 neurons and RELU activations. In addition, the total number of convolutions blocks and pooling layers were reduced to 3, with the first layer having 2 stacked convolution layers followed by a max pooling of stride 2×2 and the last two layers with 3 stacked convolutions also followed by a max pooling of stride 2×2. We have used RMSProp [3] as the optimisation technique with a learning rate of 10^{-4} and a decay 10^{-5}. Figure 2 shows that our model has an overall accuracy of approximately 83%, which is comparable to many state of the art models nowadays.

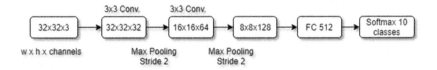

Fig. 1. Adapted VGG architecture

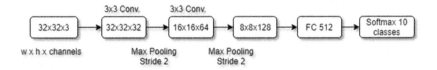

Fig. 2. Results of our adapted VGG architecture on the CIFAR-10 dataset shows comparable overall performance

Dataset Imbalancing. As the CIFAR-10 dataset is not naturally imbalanced, we have artificially created two variations on which we trained the imbalanced models. One dataset consists of a direct under-sample of the target class to 1,000 samples, and the other was changed using an over-sampling of the target class (or an under-sampling of all other classes). We kept the number of samples for the target class at 5,000 while all other classes were reduced to 1,000 samples.

For each class of the two different datasets configurations, a network was then trained until convergence using the same hyper-parameters as the balanced case. Each model was evaluated against a test set of 1,000 samples of the target class which was perturbed by its own under/over-sampled model and the balanced model. The two sources of gradient information are referred as white-box and black-box attacks since the former has complete information of the model weights and biases while the latter uses an approximation of the same parameters.

Both imbalanced models were separately tested for each class on white-box and black-box adversarial attacks. The white-box test was designed to investigate the vulnerability of class imbalance on adversarial examples while the black-box test is designed to verify the robustness on transfer learning environments. In total we evaluated 50 different combinations: 20 for each different imbalanced dataset (same model gradient and balanced model gradient) and 10 for the balanced model using its own gradients on each class. Figure 3 shows the accuracy for the models without any perturbation. It can be seen that the individual class accuracy for the under-sampled case is generally reduced while the same metric is increased on the over-sampling model.

3.2   Gradient Sign Methods

The gradient sign is a method that uses internal gradient information to create directed perturbation to input data. The resulting label will be different whether one adds or subtracts noise according to Eqs. 1 and 2.

$$C(x + \delta) \approx C(x) + \epsilon * sign(\nabla C) \tag{1}$$

$$C(x + \delta) \approx C(x) - \epsilon * sign(\nabla C) \tag{2}$$

The gradient sign equation has a simple interpretation. The main goal is to add a change δ into each pixel of the image so as to make that image closer to the chosen label on which we extracted the gradient from the source model. The sign on our ∇C indicates that we are only interested on the direction of the gradient while the ϵ controls the magnitude of the step.

Suppose the current true label of the class is selected as a gradient candidate, adding noise would mean that we increase the cost function of our input while subtracting noise is the same as minimizing our loss function even further. The equations above are usually referred as ascent and descent methods.

Perturbations could also be applied by two variations of the gradient sign method. While the fast gradient sign method applies a single perturbation to the input, the iterative gradient sign method performs the same perturbation a chosen number of times iteratively [5]. Figure 4 shows an example of adversarial created using the fast method.

In order to enforce consistency throughout our experiments, we have chosen the true sample label as the backpropagated gradient along with the fast gradient sign ascent method. The intuition behind this choice is that we look to increase the cost function of the target class by moving away from the current true label. The ϵ value chosen was 0.01 as it provided the best trade-off between

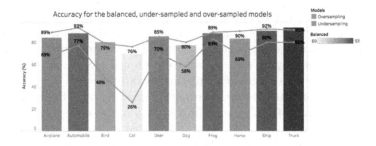

Fig. 3. Individual class accuracy for under-sampled, over-sampled case on the CIFAR-10 modified dataset shows a decrease in accuracy for classes with lower number of samples

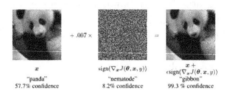

Fig. 4. Adversarial example crafting with fast gradient sign [5].

misclassification rate and the amount of visible change applied to the input image.

4   Results

We use the results of the balanced model on adversarial attacks as the baseline to evaluate whether imbalanced CNNs are more or less vulnerable to adversarial learning. Table 1 shows that the accuracy for all classes is drastically reduced when the balanced model is presented with adversarial examples. Models with under-sampled datasets were even more vulnerable than balanced models. Figure 5 shows the relative difference for all the three different models (balanced, under-sampled and over-sampled). Values were calculated by finding the difference between the perturbed accuracy and the non-perturbed accuracy of each class model. They represent the percentage on which the initial accuracy was reduced. The under-sampled model had the higher relative difference on average, which shows that the imbalanced nature of the dataset ended-up increasing the vulnerability of the model.

Perturbation on the over-sampling case had a weaker effect, as the small push caused by our ε was not enough to move points to outside of their distributions. Objects of the over-sampled classes would need bigger steps in order to successfully create an adversary that leads to a wrong classification label. Accuracy for most of the over-sampling cases was around 45% and the relative difference was the lowest of all three models, which shows robustness of the target over-sampled class.

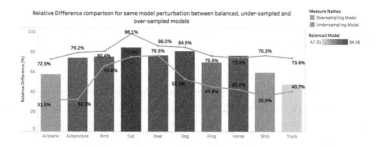

Fig. 5. Relative difference for each model. Higher numbers means more vulnerability

Class imbalanced models are naturally affected by the false positive and false negative trade off shown on Fig. 6. The decision boundaries on such models favor the class with more samples and, hence, increases the accuracy for this class while decreasing for the other classes. The area under the curve for misclassified examples on the under-sampled distribution is bigger, and it is caused by the suboptimal exploration of feature space of that class. This effect is exploited by adversaries as there is an increase on the misclassification rate of distributions with lower amplitude. The increased number of samples of the over-sampled label causes the model to perform a trade-off when optimizing its loss function. For instance, the decision boundary would be chosen in order to minimize the total error of the model. The cost function is lower when the decision boundary minimizes the misclassification of the majority class as there is a higher number of samples. The choice of a biased decision boundary could be one of the factors explaining the higher resilience of over-sampled models.

Table 1. Results for the two different sources of perturbations along with the two different imbalanced datasets. Under-sampling intensifies adversarial attack while over-sampling increases model robustness

Class label	Black-box		White-box		
	Undersample	Oversample	Balanced	Undersample	Oversample
0 - Airplane	60%	87%	36%	19%	61%
1 - Automobile	64%	91%	23%	16%	63%
2 - Bird	38%	73%	20%	9.4%	27%
3 - Cat	21%	72%	11%	0.5%	19%
4 - Deer	58%	80%	20%	9.8%	20%
5 - Dog	47%	76%	15%	9%	38%
6 - Frog	76%	88%	27%	20%	49%
7 - Horse	59%	88%	20%	18%	52%
8 - Ship	69%	89%	37%	19%	59%
9 - Truck	46%	87%	49%	21%	54%

4.1 Transfer Learning and Overlapping Distributions

Transfer Learning. The use of a different model gradient (black-box) for creating adversaries has shown less effective when compared to the same model (white-box) attack. As the overall gradient have not only different direction but also magnitudes, the system has proven to be more robust to the attack. The experiment reveals that although the gradient sign method is quite effective for fooling CNN models it does require a good amount of knowledge from the underlying training parameters so as to unleash its full potential. Attacking an under-sampled/over-sampled model with the gradient of the balanced model did not show to be as effective as using the same model's gradient. The average accuracy of an under-sampled model attack with adversaries generated from a different model was 53.8% while the same metric was 25.8% for the same model attack. Even that our training samples are within the same data domain, there are still huge differences on the gradients learned from the model.

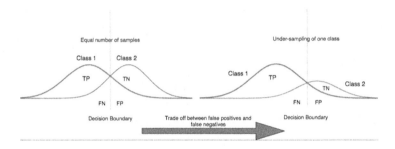

Fig. 6. Dataset imbalance causes models to perform adjustments of decision boundaries leading to an increase on accuracy of the majority class and decrease on the minority class.

Overlapping Distributions. The results for the balanced model on Fig. 2 shows that for the pairs cat/dog and automobile/truck there is already a natural misclassification between one another. For instance 13% of dog samples were misclassified as cat in the original balanced model. Our experiment demonstrates that the adversarial attacks intensify this phenomena in only one of the classes of the pair. While for both under-sampled cat and truck the number of samples misclassified with the similar class has increased, the same did not happen with dog and automobile. Figure 7 shows that cats are increasingly misclassified as dogs when under-sampling on the cat class is used. While on the cat under-sampling case the percentage of samples misclassified as dogs increased from 31% to 39%, the same number decreased from 38% to 32% on the dog under-sampling test.

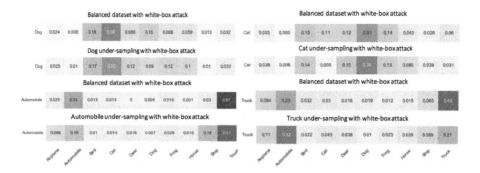

Fig. 7. Under-sample on cat and truck increases misclassification to similar classes, while dog and automobile does not.

5 Conclusion and Future Work

We have shown that adversarial attacks are even more severe on datasets with under-sampled class labels and that the decision boundary trade-off on the over-sampled classes increases their robustness to such attacks. Labels with similar features have only shown higher vulnerability to the fast gradient sign methods in one of the classes of the pair. This specific result shows that similar classes might have degrees of similarities on which could be more or less exploited by the gradient method.

As several commercial applications rely on almost the same group of models, understanding of such properties is of extreme importance. Future work in this field could look further in datasets with a higher number of classes and more complex relationships between labels so as to not only confirm our insights but also discover new interesting properties of class imbalanced CNNs and adversarial attacks. Current applications looking to increase their robustness to the adversarial methods presented in this work can use over-sampling techniques on critical labels so as to shield that label from gradient sign adversarial attacks.

References

1. Barua, S., Islam, M.M., Murase, K.: A novel synthetic minority oversampling technique for imbalanced data set learning. In: Lu, B.-L., Zhang, L., Kwok, J. (eds.) ICONIP 2011, Part II. LNCS, vol. 7063, pp. 735–744. Springer, Heidelberg (2011). doi:10.1007/978-3-642-24958-7_85
2. Billovits, C., Eric, M., Agarwala, N.: Hitting depth: investigating robustness to adversarial examples in deep convolutional neural networks (2016)
3. Dauphin, Y., de Vries, H., Bengio, Y.: Equilibrated adaptive learning rates for non-convex optimization. In: Advances in Neural Information Processing Systems, pp. 1504–1512 (2015)
4. Deng, J., Dong, W., Socher, R., Li, L.J., Li, K., Fei-Fei, L.: Imagenet: a large-scale hierarchical image database. In: IEEE Conference on Computer Vision and Pattern Recognition, CVPR 2009, pp. 248–255. IEEE (2009)

5. Goodfellow, I.J., Shlens, J., Szegedy, C.: Explaining and harnessing adversarial examples (2014). arXiv preprint: arXiv:1412.6572
6. He, H., Bai, Y., Garcia, E.A., Li, S.: Adasyn: adaptive synthetic sampling approach for imbalanced learning. In: IEEE International Joint Conference on Neural Networks, IJCNN 2008 (IEEE World Congress on Computational Intelligence), pp. 1322–1328. IEEE (2008)
7. Japkowicz, N., Stephen, S.: The class imbalance problem: a systematic study. Intell. Data Anal. **6**(5), 429–449 (2002)
8. Krawczyk, B.: Learning from imbalanced data: open challenges and future directions. Prog. Artif. Intell. **5**(4), 221–232 (2016)
9. Krizhevsky, A.: Cifar-10 and cifar-100 datasets (2009). https://www.cs.toronto.edu/~kriz/cifar.html
10. Laskov, P., Lippmann, R.: Machine learning in adversarial environments. Mach. Learn. **81**(2), 115–119 (2010). doi:10.1007/s10994-010-5207-6
11. Lawrence, S., Giles, C.L., Tsoi, A.C., Back, A.D.: Face recognition: a convolutional neural-network approach. IEEE Trans. Neural Netw. **8**(1), 98–113 (1997)
12. Lowd, D., Meek, C.: Adversarial learning. In: Proceedings of the Eleventh ACM SIGKDD International Conference on Knowledge Discovery in Data Mining, KDD 2005, pp. 641–647. ACM, New York (2005). http://doi.acm.org/10.1145/1081870.1081950
13. Papernot, N.: On the integrity of deep learning systems in adversarial settings (2016)
14. Papernot, N., McDaniel, P., Goodfellow, I.: Transferability in machine learning: from phenomena to black-box attacks using adversarial samples (2016). arXiv preprint: arXiv:1605.07277
15. Papernot, N., McDaniel, P., Goodfellow, I., Jha, S., Berkay Celik, Z., Swami, A.: Practical black-box attacks against deep learning systems using adversarial examples (2016). arXiv preprint: arXiv:1602.02697
16. Quionero-Candela, J., Sugiyama, M., Schwaighofer, A., Lawrence, N.D.: Dataset Shift in Machine Learning. The MIT Press, Cambridge (2009)
17. Simonyan, K., Zisserman, A.: Very deep convolutional networks for large-scale image recognition (2014). arXiv preprint: arXiv:1409.1556
18. Szegedy, C., Zaremba, W., Sutskever, I., Bruna, J., Erhan, D., Goodfellow, I., Fergus, R.: Intriguing properties of neural networks (2013). arXiv preprint: arXiv:1312.6199
19. Yosinski, J., Clune, J., Bengio, Y., Lipson, H.: How transferable are features in deep neural networks? In: Advances in Neural Information Processing Systems, pp. 3320–3328 (2014)

Sharing ConvNet Across Heterogeneous Tasks

Takumi Kobayashi[(✉)]

National Institute of Advanced Industrial Science and Technology,
Umezono 1-1-1, Tsukuba, Ibaraki, Japan
takumi.kobayashi@aist.go.jp

Abstract. Deep convolutional neural network (ConvNet) is one of the most promising approaches to produce state-of-the-art performance on image recognition. The ConvNet exhibits excellent performance on the task of the training target as well as favorable transferability to the other datasets/tasks. It, however, is still dependent on the characteristics of the training dataset and thus deteriorates performance on the other types of task, such as by transferring the ConvNet pre-trained on ImageNet from object classification to scene classification. In this paper, we propose a method to improve generalization performance of ConvNets. In the proposed method, the ConvNet layers are partially shared across heterogeneous tasks (datasets) in end-to-end learning, while the remaining layers are tailored to respective datasets. The method provides models of various generality and specialty by controlling the degree of shared layers, which are effectively trained by introducing the diversity into mini-batches. It is also applicable to fine-tuning the ConvNet especially on a smaller-scale dataset. The experimental results on image classification using ImageNet and Places-365 datasets show that our method improves performance on those datasets as well as provides the pre-trained ConvNet of higher generalization power with favorable transferability.

1 Introduction

Image recognition performance has been significantly improved by deep convolutional neural network (ConvNet) [1,2] in the framework of deep learning; it is applied with great success to such as object detection [3] and tracking [4]. The deep ConvNet stacks many convolution layers in order to extract image features of diverse levels and a huge number of parameters contained in those layers are trained in an end-to-end manner through back-propagation. The problem of over-fitting is remedied by leveraging large-scale annotated data [5,6] and some techniques such as rectified linear unit (ReLU) [7], DropOut [8] and BatchNormalization [9].

The so-trained Deep ConvNets exhibit excellent classification performance on the dataset/task of the training target, while being effectively transferable to the other datasets and tasks [10–12]. For example, the ConvNet pre-trained on ImageNet [5] can be applied as an image feature extractor to various image recognition tasks on which hand-crafted features [13,14] have effectively worked; the pre-trained (off-the-shelf) ConvNets produce state-of-the art performance

© Springer International Publishing AG 2017
D. Liu et al. (Eds.): ICONIP 2017, Part II, LNCS 10635, pp. 343–353, 2017.
https://doi.org/10.1007/978-3-319-70096-0_36

on various datasets of even middle scale [10–12]. In the pre-trained ConvNets, however, we can find some dependency on the characteristics of the training dataset. As discussed in [10], the ConvNet pre-trained on ImageNet [5] works well for tasks related to object classification (ImageNet task), but it degrades performance on scene classification tasks which are far from the targets of ImageNet, and vice versa [6]. Thus, for effectively applying those ConvNets as feature extractors, it is required to carefully consider the type of target tasks in advance.

In this paper, we propose a method to improve generalization performance of ConvNets. The proposed method allows the ConvNet to be trained on heterogeneous datasets (tasks) in an end-to-end manner, while it has been usually learned on a single (homogeneous) dataset such as either of ImageNet [5] or Places-365 [6]. Our approach is close to the hybrid method in [6] which trains a single ConvNet on the union of those two datasets through simply concatenating their label sets. In contrast to [6], the proposed method deals with the label sets separately while sharing the network *partially* across heterogeneous datasets. Thus, it can provide various models of different generality and specialty by controlling the degree of the shared network components. Thereby, the method produces the ConvNet improving performance on the task of the training target as well as the one exhibiting better generalization performance with high transferability to (other) various tasks. The multitask learning (MTL) [15,16] is also related to our work in that the network components are shared across several datasets in training. The MTL, however, considers only the *related* (homogeneous) tasks, thereby deteriorating performance on heterogeneous ones. In this work, we effectively treat the heterogeneous tasks by taking into account their diversity in mini-batch construction. And, while it has not been clearly discussed how many network components should be shared, we thoroughly investigate the degree of the shared components in terms of classification performance. Furthermore, we also present an effective approach toward fine-tuning in our framework.

2   Sharing ConvNet

In [6,10], the generality or transferability of the ConvNets is improved by concatenating the ConvNets or the datasets. Let $\mathcal{F}$ indicate the ConvNet architecture, *e.g.*, AlexNet [1], with the parameters denoted by $\boldsymbol{\theta}$. Suppose we have D datasets $\{\mathcal{D}_d\}_{d=1}^{D}$, *e.g.*, $\{\mathcal{D}_d\}_{d=1}^{2} = \{\text{ImageNet, Places-365}\}$, each of which contains pairs of image I and its class label y. The ConvNet is usually trained on respective datasets by

$$\left\{ \min_{\boldsymbol{\theta}_d} \sum_{(I,y)\in\mathcal{D}_d} 1[y, \mathcal{F}(I;\boldsymbol{\theta}_d)] \right\}_{d=1}^{D} \Leftrightarrow \min_{\{\boldsymbol{\theta}_d\}_{d=1}^{D}} \sum_{d=1}^{D} \sum_{(I,y)\in\mathcal{D}_d} 1[y, \mathcal{F}(I;\boldsymbol{\theta}_d)], \quad (1)$$

where 1 indicates the cost function, usually cross-entropy classification loss, and $\boldsymbol{\theta}_d$ is the parameter set for the d-th dataset $\mathcal{D}_d$. In (1), the ConvNet of the parameter $\boldsymbol{\theta}_d$ is individually trained on the dataset $\mathcal{D}_d$. Then, the neuron activations

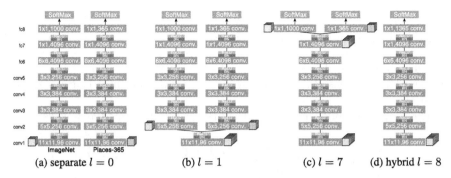

Fig. 1. ConvNet architectures of the proposed model using the AlexNet [1]. We show the models of $l = 0, 1, 7, 8$ in (a,b,c,d), respectively. Note that the separate model of $l = 0$ does not share any layers and are trained individually on the respective datasets, while the hybrid one of $l = 8$ shares all the layers by using the concatenated label sets. At convolution layers, the filter sizes are shown together with the number of output channels. The colored frames shown next to the layers indicate samples in a mini-batch; two colors indicate samples for ImageNet and Places-365, respectively. This figure is best viewed in color.

at the intermediate layer, such as fc7, are employed as transferable features and concatenated across the ConvNets $\{\mathcal{F}(\cdot; \boldsymbol{\theta}_d)\}_{d=1}^{D}$ toward general image features [10].

On the other hand, a single ConvNet equipped with the parameter $\boldsymbol{\theta}_0$ can be trained on the union of the datasets by concatenating $\{\mathcal{D}_d\}_{d=1}^{D}$ [6];

$$\min_{\boldsymbol{\theta}_0} \sum_{(I,y)\in\mathcal{D}_1\cup\cdots\cup\mathcal{D}_D} \mathbb{1}[y, \mathcal{F}(I; \boldsymbol{\theta}_0)], \tag{2}$$

where the label set is also enlarged in accordance with the dataset concatenation. To merge label sets, it is necessary to consider the overlap or correlation among the class categories, though in [6] the label sets of ImageNet and Places-365 are simply concatenated into 1,365 class labels. The so-trained ConvNet $\mathcal{F}(\cdot; \boldsymbol{\theta}_0)$ can be applied as a general feature extractor to both object and scene classifications, which is referred to as the hybrid-ConvNet [6].

In this study, we present an intermediate model between the above-mentioned extreme cases for partially sharing ConvNet (parameters) across datasets. The parameter set $\boldsymbol{\theta}$ of the L-layered ConvNet is decomposed into L subsets $\boldsymbol{\theta}^l$, $l = 1, \cdots, L$, each of which parameterizes each layer, and $\boldsymbol{\theta}^{1:l}$ denotes the set aggregating the parameters from the first layer to the l-th layer. The hybrid-ConvNet (2) shares all the parameters $\boldsymbol{\theta}$ across the datasets (Fig. 1d), while in (1) any ConvNet parameters are not shared but trained individually (Fig. 1a). The proposed model shares a part of the parameter $\boldsymbol{\theta}$ up to the l-the layer, $\boldsymbol{\theta}^{1:l}$, across the datasets, and the others are tailored for respective datasets as shown in Fig. 1b, c. The common part in the ConvNet extracts general characteristics shared across the datasets (tasks) and the remaining part is task-oriented. In contrast to the hybrid model, our model easily accepts multiple datasets due to the task-oriented part without carefully considering the overlaps among the label sets; this is practically useful to free us from manually checking label contents. Through learning on various datasets of heterogeneous tasks, we can enhance the generality of the shared ConvNet, which facilitates classifying both objects (ImageNet) and scenes (Places-365), by extracting fundamental features shared across them.

The proposed model that shares the first l layers is trained as follows.

$$\min_{\boldsymbol{\theta}_0^{1:l}, \{\hat{\boldsymbol{\theta}}_d^{l+1:L}\}_{d=1}^D} \sum_{d=1}^D \sum_{(I,y)\in\mathcal{D}_d} \mathbb{1}[y, \mathcal{F}(I; \boldsymbol{\theta}_d = \{\boldsymbol{\theta}_0^{1:l}, \hat{\boldsymbol{\theta}}_d^{l+1:L}\})], \tag{3}$$

where $\boldsymbol{\theta}_0^{1:l}$ indicates the shared parameters of up to the l-th layer and $\hat{\boldsymbol{\theta}}_d^{l+1:L}$ is the remaining parameter set which is specific to the d-th dataset. In other words, the ConvNet of $\mathcal{F}(I; \boldsymbol{\theta}_d = \{\boldsymbol{\theta}_0^{1:l}, \hat{\boldsymbol{\theta}}_d^{l+1:L}\})$ is trained on the d-th dataset. Note that the shared parameter $\boldsymbol{\theta}_0^{1:l}$ sees all the data while $\hat{\boldsymbol{\theta}}_d^{l+1:L}$ only looks at the data appearing in the d-th dataset $\mathcal{D}_d$. The degree of sharing ConvNet is controlled by the depth l at which the ConvNet branches (Fig. 1). This unified method (3) produces the separate model (1) by $l = 0$ and the hybrid model (2) by $l = L$. We conduct thorough experiments in Sect. 3 by gradually changing the depth l.

To properly learn the ConvNet (3) on heterogeneous datasets, we introduce the diversity into a mini-batch in training as follows. The same number of samples are drawn from respective datasets and packed into a mini-batch in order to fairly take into account the heterogeneous characteristics derived from the datasets at each updating step; for example, we sample 256 images from ImageNet and Places-365, respectively, and concatenate them to construct the mini-batch of 512 samples. Then, as shown in Fig. 1, each sample in the mini-batch is passed through the network differently according to which dataset it belongs to, and at the shared layers the derivatives for those (heterogeneous) samples are merged to update the network parameters $\{\boldsymbol{\theta}_d\}_{d=1}^D$ via mini-batched SGD. Thereby, the updating (derivative) is consistent throughout the end-to-end learning even on the heterogeneous datasets. In contrast, the MTL method [15] fills a mini-batch with *homogeneous* samples all of which are drawn from the randomly selected dataset. This produces consistent updates only when all the tasks are related, *i.e.*, the training datasets are homogeneous. In the case of heterogeneous datasets, however, the derivatives are inconsistent over the training steps since the characteristics of the mini-batches differ at every step according to what type of dataset is selected. This would hamper the learning, as empirically shown in Sect. 3. Note that our mini-batches merging derivatives across heterogeneous samples contribute to proper learning of ConvNet by effectively extracting the common updating information across the heterogeneous datasets.

3   Experimental Results

We apply the proposed method (Sect. 2) to the AlexNet model [1] which is composed of the five convolution and three fully-connected layers ($L = 8$) as shown in Fig. 1; hereafter, we follow the conventional naming of the layers, such as conv1 for the first convolution layer. Note that since the batch normalization [9] is embedded in the ConvNet (Fig. 1), we do not apply DropOut [8]. All the networks are implemented by using MatConvNet toolbox [17].

3.1 Datasets

In this study, we train the ConvNets (3) on two large-scale datasets of ImageNet [5] for object classification and Places-365 [6] for scene classification. The ImageNet contains 1,329,405 training images of 1,000 object classes (ILSVRC2014) and the Places-365 is composed of 1,839,960 images sampled from 365 scene categories. For the hybrid model (2), we simply concatenate those two label sets into 1,365 class labels as in [6].

3.2 Mini-batch

For separately training ConvNets (1) (or (3) of $l = 0$), we apply the mini-batch of 256 samples on the respective datasets. On the other hand, as described in Sect. 2, we draw 256 samples from ImageNet and Places-365, respectively, to construct the (heterogeneous) mini-batch of 512 samples, in a fair manner with the training of the separate model (1). Note that the mini-batch of 512 samples is split into two mini-batches of 256 samples at the branch in our ConvNets (3), as shown in Fig. 1. Since the two datasets contain different numbers of images, *i.e.* ImageNet is smaller than Places-365, we pad ImageNet dataset with images randomly picked up from that dataset so that it has the same number of images as Places-365. Thereby, we can draw the same number of samples from those datasets in constructing the heterogeneous mini-batch.

The mini-batch is filled with images of 224×224 pixels cropped from the original ones with random flipping and jittering in terms of position and pixel values as in [1].

3.3 Learning

The ConvNets are trained by SGD in 20 epochs through decreasing learning rate constantly on log-scale from 10^{-1} to 10^{-4}; the learning rate is determined as $10^{-\frac{16+3t}{19}}$, $t \in \{1, \cdots, 20\}$ where t indicates the epoch. We use the learning parameter of 0.9 for momentum and 0.0005 for weight decay. This training scheme is applied to any ConvNets.

3.4 Performance on ImageNet and Places Datasets

We evaluate performance on the datasets used for training. According to the standard evaluation protocols in ImageNet [5] and Places-365 [6], we measured the top-5 classification error rates on a validation set by applying 10-crop testing procedure to test images [1]. In the hybrid model of (2) (or (3) with $l = 8$), the last fully-connected layer is split so as to produce 1,000 class outputs on ImageNet and 365 on Places-365 after learning, which results in the same architecture as the model of $l = 7$. Note that the separate model (1) corresponds to the original AlexNet model.

Figure 2 shows the performance results. Though the performances are slightly fluctuated due to only 1-shot evaluation, we can see that (1) the proposed model sharing a part of ConvNet improves performance being superior even to the hybrid model [6], and (2) the models sharing smaller part exhibit better performance; the best result is achieved by the model of $l = 1$. The hybrid model of $l = 8$ merges (concatenates) the label sets of ImageNet and Places-365 by force, and thus might take into account the label correlation wrongly, degrading performance, compared especially to our model of $l = 7$. Our method enjoys larger performance improvement on ImageNet than on Places-365 since the samples from Places-365 compensate the smaller-scale ImageNet by favorably exploiting the common characteristics across them. In contrast, the MTL method[1] [15] does not contribute to improvement but degrade the performance. The comparison between ours and the MTL highlights the effectiveness of our heterogeneous mini-batch construction for leveraging the heterogeneous datasets to improve performance. The MTL switches a dataset to produce mini-batches at each SGD step, leading to poor results especially as the shared components increases due to inconsistently updating the network at training steps. On the other hand, our approach makes the update consistent throughout the learning by merging the derivatives at each step to exploit the effective update information which is common across the heterogeneous samples. The heavily shared model of larger l imposes the same feature extractor on these heterogeneous tasks, which slightly deteriorates the performance compared to those of smaller l. Such shared model, however, would contribute to a general feature extractor as described in the next section.

3.5   Transferability

Next, we evaluate the transferability of the above pre-trained ConvNets by applying them to the other datasets than ImageNet and Places-365. The pre-trained ConvNets are tested on various datasets which are categorized into four types in terms of classification targets (Table 1); VOC2007 [18] and Caltech256 [19] for *object* classification, Indoor67 [20], Scene15 [21] and SUN397 [22] for *scene* classification, and Bird200 [23], Flower102 [24] and Pet37 [25] for *fine-grained* classification, and Event8 [26], Action40 [27] and FMD [28] for the *others*.

The image features are extracted by applying the pre-trained Convnet in a convolution manner to a rescaled image of which the minimum side has 256 pixels, and then are max-pooled over the image region. The neuron activations at the intermediate layer are employed to produce holistic image feature vector of fixed

---

[1] In training by the MTL method, for fair comparison, we use the same number of samples as in ours by padding ImageNet dataset.

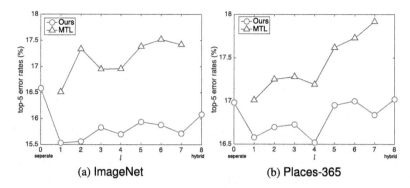

(a) ImageNet   (b) Places-365

Fig. 2. Classification error rate (%) on a validation set of ImageNet/Places-365. The top-5 error rates are measured by applying 10-crop testing procedure [1]. The ConvNets (3) are trained by the MTL approach [15] and ours.

Table 1. Details of the datasets used for evaluating transferability. This table shows the number of training samples, test samples and class categories from the top row to the bottom.

	Object		Scene			
	VOC2007	Caltech256	Indoor67	Scene15	SUN397	
Training samples	5011	15360	5360	1500	19850	
Test samples	4952	9984	1340	2985	19850	
Categories	20 objects	256 objects	67 scenes	15 scenes	397 scenes	
	Fine-grained			Others		
	Bird200	Flower102	Pet37	Event8	Action40	FMD
Training samples	5994	2040	3680	560	4000	500
Test samples	5794	6149	3669	480	5532	500
Categories	200 species	102 species	37 species	8 sports	40 actions	10 materials

dimensionality. As shown in Fig. 3, the ConvNet pre-trained on ImageNet/Places-365 exhibits dependency on the types of the training datasets. For achieving general features, as in [10], we exploit the layers of $fc7^2$ both on ImageNet and Places-365 (see Fig. 1b) and concatenate them into the 8,192-dimensional feature vector for the models of $l = 0, \cdots, 6$. On the other hand, we concatenate $fc6$ and $fc7$ to produce 8,192-dimensional features for $l = 7, 8$ since the layers of $fc6$ and $fc7$ are both shared in those models (see Fig. 1c, d). The features are finally classified by linear SVM [29] and the classification accuracy is measured according to the standard protocol provided in the respective datasets; on Caltech256, we draw 60 training samples on each class, and for the details, refer to the respective papers.

The performance results are shown in Table 2. By combining two type of pre-trained ConvNets for objects (ImageNet) and scenes (Places-365), the

---

[2] $fc7$ outperforms $fc6$ as shown in Fig. 3.

ConvNet features exhibit favorable transferability on various kinds of tasks including both object and scene classifications. The heavily shared models of larger l are superior to those of smaller l, which contrasts to Table 2. By sharing larger part of ConvNet across the heterogeneous datasets, the pre-trained ConvNet achieves better generalization power by exploiting common (general) features. Especially, the model of $l = 7$ produces favorable performance on the tasks of *fine-grained* and *others*. Comparing $l = 7$ with $l = 8$ (hybrid), one can see that splitting fc8 layer is more effective than concatenating label sets for enhancing generalization performance.

We can conclude that (1) the less shared ConvNet of $l = 1$ is effective for improving performance on the task of training target (Fig. 2), and (2) the heavily shared ConvNet of $l = 7$ provides a general feature extractor with better transferability (Table 2).

Table 2. Classification accuracies (%) by the pre-trained ConvNets on various datasets.

Dataset	Separate $l = 0$	$l = 1$	$l = 2$	$l = 3$	$l = 4$	$l = 5$	$l = 6$	$l = 7$	Hybrid $l = 8$
VOC2007	79.97	80.50	80.20	80.52	80.59	80.38	80.15	79.96	80.05
Caltech256	74.27	74.85	75.07	74.39	74.88	74.19	74.78	74.59	74.91
avg. (*object*)	77.12	77.67	77.64	77.46	**77.73**	77.29	77.46	77.28	77.48
Indoor67	74.82	75.56	76.53	76.19	75.40	75.84	75.77	75.38	75.56
Scene15	93.11	93.39	93.47	93.35	93.65	93.31	93.05	93.03	93.06
SUN397	60.63	61.13	61.32	61.05	61.19	60.48	60.13	59.22	59.01
avg. (*scene*)	76.19	76.69	**77.11**	76.86	76.75	76.54	76.32	75.88	75.88
Bird200	63.35	62.82	62.87	62.68	62.34	63.05	63.45	65.29	64.72
Flower102	90.07	90.18	90.79	90.36	90.22	90.32	91.01	90.20	90.60
Pet37	81.92	82.33	82.41	82.10	81.62	81.55	81.66	82.37	81.68
avg. (*fine-grained*)	78.44	78.44	78.69	78.38	78.06	78.31	78.71	**79.29**	79.00
Event8	96.04	95.90	96.04	95.97	96.32	96.11	96.60	96.32	96.11
Action40	62.60	64.21	64.05	64.37	64.70	63.69	63.34	64.67	63.61
FMD	72.85	73.27	73.62	72.19	73.73	73.65	75.13	74.37	72.40
avg. (*others*)	77.16	77.80	77.90	77.51	78.25	77.81	78.35	**78.45**	77.37

3.6 Fine-Tuning

Fine-tuning is employed to further adapt the pre-trained ConvNet to the target dataset, though requiring tedious learning parameter tuning. We fine-tune the pre-trained ConvNet by decreasing the learning rate from 10^{-3} to 10^{-6} over 40 epochs ($10^{-\frac{114+3t}{39}}$, $t \in \{1, \cdots, 40\}$), with the mini-batch of 128 samples. Note that the ConvNet is initialized as the optimized parameter values in Sect. 3.4 except for the last fc8 layer which is randomly initialized.

Based on the results in Table 2, we apply the model of $l = 7$ to the tasks other than *object* and *scene* classifications which are the targets in the pre-training. The performance results are shown in Table 3. By fine-tuning the model,

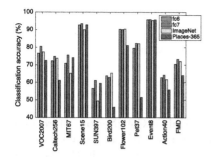

Fig. 3. Performance comparison for `fc6`, `fc7` in the model of $l = 1$ and `fc7` in ConvNets pre-trained on ImageNet/Places-365. The `fc7` features exhibit superior performance to `fc6`, and ImageNet-ConvNet works only on the ImageNet-related tasks, excluding scene classification.

Table 3. Classification accuracies (%) of fine-tuned ConvNet of $l = 7$ pre-trained on both ImageNet and Places-365 in Sect. 3.4.

		Original	Fine-tuned
Fine-grained	Bird200	65.29	65.59
	Flower102	90.20	91.53
	Pet37	82.37	80.24
Others	Event8	96.32	96.60
	Action40	64.67	65.00
	FMD	74.37	76.56

Table 4. Classification accuracies (%) of the pre-trained ConvNets of $l = 7$ which is fine-tuned by our method. All the three datasets are used in our fine-tuning.

	Others		
	Event8	Action40	FMD
Original	96.32	64.67	74.37
Standard fine-tuning	96.60	65.00	76.56
Our fine-tuning	96.81	65.13	78.03

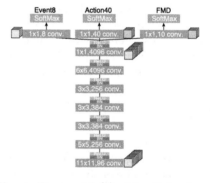

Fig. 4. Our model (3) of $l = 7$ fine-tuned on *others* datasets. Three datasets, Event8, Action40 and FMD, are treated at once.

the performance is favorably improved except for Pet37; the dataset contains images of cats and dogs which are the classification targets in ImageNet, and thus the fine-tuning might deteriorate the generalization power due to over-fitting. In this case, the numbers of training samples in the datasets of *others* task, especially Event8 and FMD, are small, which might make the training less effective.

To cope with such small-scale problem, we again apply the proposed framework (Fig. 1) to the fine-tuning. Namely, all three datasets of *others* task are utilized at once for fine-tuning the ConvNet of $l = 7$ with a mini-batch of $384 = 128 \times 3$ samples as shown in Fig. 4. Table 4 shows the performance results, demonstrating that our fine-tuning further improves performance even compared to the ordinary fine-tuning. Especially, FMD benefits from our fine-tuning since the dataset is quite small-scale containing only 500 training samples

(Table 1). Through our fine-tuning, the ConvNet can see larger number of training samples and effectively exploit common characteristics across the multiple datasets to improve performance on the small-scale dataset.

4 Conclusion

In this paper, we have proposed a method to train a ConvNet on heterogeneous tasks (datasets) for improving performance. In the proposed method, the ConvNet layers are partially shared across the different datasets in the end-to-end learning to enhance generalization power, while the remaining layers are tailored to respective tasks (datasets). By controlling the degree of shared network layers, the method provides various types of ConvNet of different generality. To properly learn the ConvNet on the heterogeneous datasets, we construct a mini-batch so as to fairly contain heterogeneous samples, producing consistent updates (derivatives) throughout the training. The experimental results on ImageNet and Places-365 datasets show that the ConvNet sharing less layers favorably improves performance on those dataset, and that of heavily shared layers exhibits better generalization performance with favorable transferability. We have also demonstrated that the proposed method is applicable to fine-tuning the ConvNet especially on small-scale datasets. Our future works include to apply the method to various ConvNets.

References

1. Krizhevsky, A., Sutskever, I., Hinton, G.E.: Imagenet classification with deep convolutional neural networks. In: NIPS, pp. 1097–1105 (2012)
2. LeCun, Y., Boser, B., Denker, J.S., Henderson, D., Howard, R.E., Hubbard, W., Jackel, L.D.: Backpropagation applied to handwritten zip code recognition. Neural Comput. **1**(4), 541–551 (1989)
3. Ouyang, W., Wang, X., Zeng, X., Qiu, S., Luo, P., Tian, Y., Li, H., Yang, S., Wang, Z., Loy, C., Tang, X.: Deepid-net: deformable deep convolutional neural networks for object detection. In: CVPR, pp. 2403–2412 (2015)
4. Bertinetto, L., Valmadre, J., Henriques, J., Vedaldi, A., Torr, P.: Fully-convolutional siamese networks for object tracking arXiv:1606.09549 (2016)
5. Deng, J., Dong, W., Socher, R., Li, L.J., Li, K., Fei-Fei, L.: Imagenet: a large-scale hierarchical image database. In: CVPR, pp. 248–255 (2009)
6. Zhou, B., Khosla, A., Lapedriza, A., Torralba, A., Oliva, A.: Places: an image database for deep scene understanding. arXiv:1610.02055 (2016)
7. Nair, V., Hinton, G.E.: Rectified linear units improve restricted Boltzmann machines. In: ICML, pp. 807–814 (2010)
8. Srivastava, N., Hinton, G., Krizhevsky, A., Sutskever, I., Salakhutdinov, R.: Dropout: a simple way to prevent neural networks from overfitting. J. Mach. Learn. Res. **15**, 1929–1958 (2014)
9. Ioffe, S., Szegedy, C.: Batch normalization: accelerating deep network training by reducing internal covariate shift. J. Mach. Learn. Res. **37**, 448–456 (2015)

10. Azizpour, H., Razavian, A.S., Sullivan, J., Maki, A., Carlsson, S.: Factors of trans-ferability for a generic convnet representation. IEEE Trans. Pattern Anal. Mach. Intell. **38**(9), 1790–1802 (2016)
11. Oquab, M., Bottou, L., Laptev, I., Sivic, J.: Learning and transferring mid-level image representations using convolutional neural networks. In: CVPR, pp. 1717–1724 (2014)
12. Razavian, A.S., Azizpour, H., Sullivan, J., Carlsson, S.: CNN features off-the-shelf: an astounding baseline for recognition. In: CVPR Workshop, pp. 512–519 (2014)
13. Csurka, G., Bray, C., Dance, C., Fan, L.: Visual categorization with bags of key-points. In: ECCV Workshop, pp. 1–22 (2004)
14. Dalal, N., Triggs, B.: Histograms of oriented gradients for human detection. In: CVPR, pp. 886–893 (2005)
15. Collobert, R., Weston, J.: A unified architecture for natural language processing. In: ICML, pp. 160–167 (2008)
16. Simonyan, K., Zisserman, A.: Two-stream convolutional networks for action recog-nition in videos. In: NIPS, pp. 568–576 (2014)
17. Vedaldi, A., Lenc, K.: MatConvNet - convolutional neural networks for matlab. In: ACM MM (2015)
18. The PASCAL Visual Object Classes Challenge 2007 (VOC 2007). http://www.pascal-network.org/challenges/VOC/voc2007/index.html
19. Griffin, G., Holub, A., Perona, P.: Caltech-256 object category dataset. Technical report 7694, Caltech (2007)
20. Quattoni, A., Torralba, A.: Recognizing indoor scenes. In: CVPR, pp. 413–420 (2009)
21. Lazebnik, S., Schmid, C., Ponce, J.: Beyond bags of features: spatial pyramid matching for recognizing natural scene categories. In: CVPR, pp. 2169–2178 (2006)
22. Xiao, J., Hays, J., Ehinger, K.A., Oliva, A., Torralba, A.: Sun database: large-scale scene recognition from Abbey to zoo. In: CVPR (2010)
23. Wah, C., Branson, S., Welinder, P., Perona, P., Belongie, S.: The Caltech-UCSD birds-200-2011 dataset. Technical report CNS-TR-2011-001, California Institute of Technology (2011)
24. Nilsback, M.E., Zisserman, A.: Automated flower classification over a large num-ber of classes. In: Indian Conference on Computer Vision, Graphics and Image Processing (2008)
25. Parkhi, O.M., Vedaldi, A., Zisserman, A., Jawahar, C.V.: Cats and dogs. In: CVPR, pp. 3498–3505 (2012)
26. Li, L.J., Fei-Fei, L.: What, where and who? classifying events by scene and object recognition. In: ICCV (2007)
27. Yao, B., Jiang, X., Khosla, A., Lin, A., Guibas, L., Fei-Fei, L.: Human action recognition by learning bases of action attributes and parts. In: ICCV (2011)
28. Sharan, L., Rosenholtz, R., Adelson, E.: Material perception: What can you see in a brief glance? J. Vis. **9**(8), 784 (2009)
29. Vapnik, V.: Statistical Learning Theory. Wiley, New York (1998)

Training Deep Neural Networks for Detecting Drinking Glasses Using Synthetic Images

Abdul Jabbar[(⊠)], Luke Farrawell, Jake Fountain, and Stephan K. Chalup

School of Electrical Engineering and Computing, The University of Newcastle,
Callaghan, NSW 2308, Australia
{Abdul.Jabbar,Luke.Farrawell,Jake.Fountain}@uon.edu.au,
Stephan.Chalup@newcastle.edu.au

Abstract. This study presents an approach of using synthetically rendered images for training deep neural networks on object detection. A new plug-in for the computer graphics modelling software Blender was developed that can generate large numbers of photo-realistic ray-traced images and include meta information as training labels. The performance of the deep neural network DetectNet is evaluated using training data comprising synthetically rendered images and digital photos of drinking glasses. The detection accuracy is determined by comparing bounding boxes using intersection over union technique. The detection experiments using real-world and synthetic image data resulted in comparable results and the performance increased when using a pre-trained GoogLeNet model. The experiments demonstrated that training deep neural networks for object detection on synthetic data is effective and the proposed approach can be useful for generating large labelled image data sets to enhance the performance of deep neural networks on specific object detection tasks.

Keywords: Deep learning · Data augmentation · Big data · Image processing · Ray tracing · Object detection · Synthetic data generation

1 Introduction

Deep Learning has achieved excellent results in image classification, object detection and other computer vision and machine learning applications [1–4]. One of the typical issues with deep learning is the requirement of large data sets for training. Although there are various online databases containing millions of images [5], it can be necessary for researchers to create new data sets to better utilize the power of deep neural networks on specific tasks. However, generating a new image data set and labelling it manually can be very time consuming.

Computer graphics techniques such as ray tracing [6] allow the generation of photo-realistic images and in this process the computer can be employed for labelling of those images. As deep neural networks are typically trained on Graphical Processing Units (GPUs), these can also be used to render large quantities of images efficiently.

© Springer International Publishing AG 2017
D. Liu et al. (Eds.): ICONIP 2017, Part II, LNCS 10635, pp. 354–363, 2017.
https://doi.org/10.1007/978-3-319-70096-0_37

The present project utilised the Blender computer graphics modelling software with customisable settings that allows users to design detailed 3-dimensional scenes and objects [7]. A plug-in was developed to automate the generation of variations in the scene during rendering and to combine these with various environmental backgrounds. Due to the software having full access to the scene data, automated labelling of the generated images can produce a metadata file containing information such as the bounding box of the object, the position of the object in the scene and the position of where the image was taken. Although this approach allows the user to be removed from the processes of collecting and manually labelling the data, it still requires the user to initially create the scene.

In a related study Jaderberg et al. [8] presented a framework for the recognition of natural scene text using deep neural network models trained on synthetic text data generated by their text generation engine. Peng et al. [9] used crowd sourced 3D models to generate synthetic non-photorealistic images of objects for bootstrapping deep convolutional neural networks. Rajpura et al. [10] demonstrated that synthetic images generated with Blender can be used to create highly competitive deep convolutional nets for identifying products in refrigerator scenes. They also noted that photorealism may not be necessary to achieve results that compete with networks trained with real images.

The present project, however, uses real drinking glasses and photo-realistic models as the objects to detect. Due to the translucent nature of a drinking glass and its reflective properties, this is a challenging task for detection and also tests the performance of the 3D rendering tool. Traditional image processing techniques were reported to fail in case of translucent or transparent objects and research on their detection is typically restricted to controlled environments, or uses special equipment such as Light Field Cameras [11], Time of Flight Cameras [12], or X-Ray Tomography [13].

The following sections describe the use of the plug-in, demonstrate the viability of the proposed approach of using computer-generated images of drinking glasses for training neural networks. The performance on a new data set of similar real-world images is evaluated for comparison.

2   Methodology and Experimental Setup

Two data sets were created, one containing images of real drinking glasses in real-world environments captured using a digital camera, and the other data set contained similar but synthetically rendered images. Both data sets were divided into training, validation, and test images for training of DetectNet [14]. Detection performance of our data was also evaluated using GoogLeNet [4] trained on ImageNet [5] as a pre-trained network.

Training of the deep neural networks was performed on NVIDIA's Deep Learning GPU Training System (DIGITS) [15] using a workstation equipped with a NVIDIA Quadro K2200 GPU. Each network model was trained for 30 epochs with base learning rate of 0.0001 and solver type Adam. Training and testing was divided into three broader categories corresponding to the training and test data sets which are: (1.) training and testing on real-world images, (2.) training and testing on synthetic images, and (3.) training on synthetic and testing on real-world images.

2.1   Bounding Boxes and Detection Rate

The network output is a list of bounding box coordinates around the detected object. For the comparison of the output with the target bounding box, we are using Intersection over Union (IoU) [16]. This technique is commonly used in object detection challenges such as the PASCAL VOC challenge [17]. The number of successful detections in a test set is counted using IoU, where:

$$IoU = \frac{\text{area of overlap}}{\text{area of union}}$$

The IoU value for each detected bounding box and its corresponding target box is compared with a pre-set IoU value. If it is greater than that pre-set IoU bound then it means that enough area of both bounding boxes overlap to count the network-generated bounding box around the object as a valid object detection.

Fig. 1. Example IoU values of a detection where solid line box is the target bounding box and dashed line box is the network output.

2.2   Real-World Image Data Collection

Images for the real-world data set were collected through three sources. The main source for the real-world data set was a Canon EOS 60D digital camera. Images of six different types of glasses in six surroundings were taken as follows: on a white table, on a white table with black cloth on it, on a stool in living room, on a kitchen shelf, on a brown table in living room, and on a red sofa. The camera resolution was set to 5184 × 3456 pixels, sensitivity to ISO 1000, zoom set to 20 mm and autofocus was turned on. The camera was placed on a tripod and images were taken from different angles and under several different lighting conditions. Using the described approach, 1,728 images were captured and manually labelled.

ImageNet is a very large online database of images involving hundreds of objects [5]. The object list also contains drinking glasses under the containers category. There are over a thousand images of drinking glasses available. Many of these were not useful for our study due to glasses being not clearly visible, occlusions, fluid in the glasses not being in the static state, and non-transparency of the glass or cup. A manual selection was carried out to extract the images suitable to be included in our data set. As a result, 387 images were selected containing glasses in numerous different environments and under different lighting conditions.

Google makes millions of images available from throughout the web [18]. A careful selection was made of useful glass images and 289 of the examined images were determined to be suitable to be included in our data set.

By collecting images from the three described sources, the total number of labelled images in our real-world data set reached 2,404.

2.3 Synthetic Image Data Creation

To assist in the automated creation of large computer-generated data sets of photo-realistic images, a plug-in for the 3D modelling software Blender was developed. This plug-in required minimal user interaction and has powerful features that helped reducing the time it takes to produce the data set. Figure 2 shows the workflow of using the plug-in with Blender. The workflow requires the user to spend the most time in three sections: creating the scene, setting up the cameras and configuring the render properties.

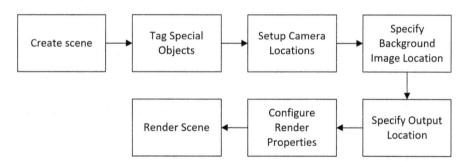

Fig. 2. Flow chart of the process of creating a scene and rendering it with the Deep Learning Renderer plug-in for Blender.

Creating a scene for use with the deep learning renderer requires a similar process to the normal Blender scene creation. This allows for any Blender knowledge to easily be transferable and used with the plug-in. The plug-in aims to simplify tasks within Blender by removing complex tasks from the user by abstracting them into a more simpler task, such as using a file selector to navigate to a directory in which all background images reside. By doing this, the plug-in is able to then find all images in the directory and switch between the backgrounds during the rendering to add variation to the scene background.

Objects in the scene can be tagged in two ways, a controllable object and a surface object. These two tags allow the deep learning renderer to analyse the scene and build up a required function list that will be used during each render iteration. A controllable object tag is used to distinguish which object is the main focus of the scene and the primary target of the computer vision system. Multiple objects can be tagged as a controllable object to allow for different positions or modifications to the object whilst only allowing one object to be rendered at a time. The surface object tag allows for the user to distinguish between different objects that contain the same position, but only one should be rendered at a time. This allows for a variety in what the object is sitting upon to produce different varieties in the environment.

To allow for a large collection of images to be rendered, the user is required to insert Blender camera objects into the scene to act as key points in which a camera can interpolate its position and rotation between the key points whilst rendering the scene (Fig. 3a). This allows for the user to force the camera along a particular path whilst also allowing additional unspecified images to be generated during the camera interpolations.

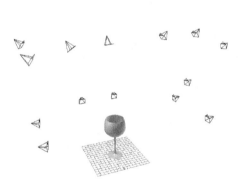

(a) Blender scene with several cameras

(b) A synthetic image rendering of a scene using only a glass and a HDRI background

Fig. 3. Rendering an image from a Blender scene with the use of the plug-in.

For added realism and to reduce the scene creation time, high-dynamic-range imaging (HDRI) [19] images were used to provide realistic backgrounds as well as to leverage the use of rendering techniques such as Image Based Lighting (IBL) [20]. The use of IBL allowed for the reduction in scene creation by removing the requirement of lighting to be set up for the scene as well as allowing for realistic lighting conditions to be used from the background HDRI. This allows for the user to point the plug-in into a folder of HDRI images to allow for automated switching of background images without the user being required to set up multiple scenes with correct lighting conditions.

During the rendering of the images, additional metadata is saved alongside the images. The metadata is a collection of the data that is available from the scene that may provide useful information for computer vision tasks such as the bounding box of the object, what object is currently visible in the scene, the object's x, y and z position and the camera's x, y and z position. By creating the metadata alongside the rendering, a significant reduction in time required for gathering the required data for the deep learning task can be seen compared to a user manually creating the metadata during image capture or after all images are gathered.

Two data sets were produced using this plug-in. The first data set included six different 3D glass renders placed in 13 different HDR 360 degree background images. Each of the six glasses was placed on a 3D rendered flat surface somewhere in the image so that it could be perceived that the glass is standing on an object such as table, bench, floor, or shelf (Fig. 3b). The background and table-like objects in this data set were substantially different from those in the real-world images. The second synthetic data set was created based on a simple description of the backgrounds and glasses in the real-world images with the intention that the new synthetic images of the second synthetic data set would look in principle similar to the images of the real-world data set (Fig. 4).

Fig. 4. A real-world image on the left and a similar-looking synthetically rendered image on the right.

The first data set comprised a total 2,678 images rendered from various angles in 13 different surroundings containing six glasses in several different positions relative to the cameras. Additional two glass models were employed in second data set to generate a total of 5,026 images with surfaces and backgrounds similar to the real-world images.

3   Results

3.1   Training and Testing on Real-World Data

2,404 real-world images were divided into 1600 training, 404 validation, and 400 test images. After training DetectNet [14] on this data, the number of detections was counted on the test images for varying IoU bounds. The detections ranged from 285 to 388 for IoU bounds between 0.9 and 0.5 with a best rate of 97% for IoU $\geq$ 0.5. Repeating training on the same data but using GoogLeNet pre-trained on the ImageNet increased the detection rate for IoU $\geq$ 0.5 to 99.5% (Fig. 5).

3.2   Training and Testing on Synthetically Rendered Data

2,678 synthetically rendered images were divided into 1800 training, 428 validation, and 450 test images. Training was conducted similarly to the real-world case. Detections on the test set without any pre-trained network ranged from 31 for IoU $\geq$ 0.9 to 368 for IoU $\geq$ 0.5 with best detection rate 81.77%. Using the pre-trained GoogLeNet increased the best detection rate to 94.88% for IoU $\geq$ 0.5. The detection rate in this case was relatively low compared to Sect. 3.1 because of having more surroundings and fewer images per surrounding compared to the real-world data (Fig. 5).

3.3   Training on Synthetic and Testing on Real-World Data

In this category, networks were trained on the two synthetic data sets described at the end of Sect. 2.3.

Case 1: Training was conducted on the first data set that comprised 2,678 synthetically rendered images that were very different from the real-world data. These 2,678 images were divided into 1,900 training and 778 validation images. The same 400 real-world images that were used in Sect. 3.1 were employed for testing. The glass detection rate for the network of this case was only 8% for IoU $\geq$ 0.5. It increased to 52.5% for IoU $\geq$ 0.5 when GoogLeNet pre-trained on ImageNet was used.

Case 2: The second set of training experiments employed the same 2,678 images used by the network of Case 1, but in addition the training set included 2,500 randomly selected images from the second synthetically rendered data set which comprised images more closely related to the real-world images (Sect. 2.3). In total the training set of Case 2 consisted of 5,178 images that were divided into 4,000 training and 1,178 validation images. Using the same test set as for the first network, the glass detection rate of the second network was 52.8% for IoU $\geq$ 0.5 and it further increased to 71.14% for IoU $\geq$ 0.5 with the use of weights from GoogLeNet pre-trained on ImageNet. Training of these networks was repeated 10 times for different samples of the 2,500 synthetic images. The detection rates in dependency of increasing IoU bounds are shown in Fig. 5 under the labels S-R and PTS-R only for the best networks of Case 2.

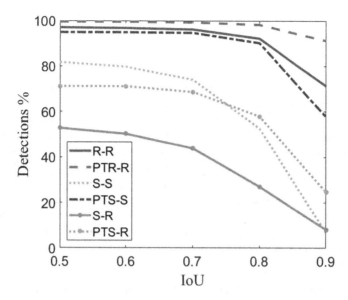

Fig. 5. R-R means the network was trained and tested on real-world data. S-S refers to training and testing on synthetic data. In the case of S-R the network was trained on synthetic data but it was tested on the real world data test set. PT means weights were initialised using a pre-trained GoogLeNet. IoU bounds close to 0.5 can still mean good detection (see Fig. 1).

4   Discussion

Transparent drinking glasses are challenging objects to detect and to render. Due to their transparency, the background in which they are placed highly influences their appearance. Changing backgrounds would have significantly less effect on training using images containing only opaque objects.

The training experiments conducted within the scope of this pilot study triggered a number of interesting observations about how real-world data and synthetic data can be combined and what impact this may have for deep learning. At least three concepts can be distinguished that could be further investigated in this context:

1. Data complementation: The existing data is complemented by other or missing data. For example, real-world data can be complemented by simulated data. Both types of data are equally suitable for training as indicated by our experiments. It would be interesting to investigate what impact different proportions of complementary synthetic data components have on deep learning and how to compose the validation set in combination with the training set when only limited knowledge about the test data is available.
2. Data supplementation: Specific data is added to the training set in order to improve performance. In our study the networks of Sect. 3.3 showed poor performance only when they were trained on very different-looking synthetic data

compared to the real-world data they were tested on (different backgrounds and different glass models). However, the results improved from 8% detection rate (Case 1) to 52% (Case 2) when the training set was supplemented by additional synthetic data that was designed to artificially resemble some basic features of the test data. This improvement in results highlights the fact that synthetic images can be used to improve training of deep neural networks if the supplemented images show general similarities to the test images.

3. Object augmentation: Artificial objects are rendered into an existing scene and the resulting synthetic images can be used for training deep nets on specific object detection. Computer graphics rendering and ray-tracing can take lighting and reflections into account and allow even challenging objects such as drinking glasses to be realistically augmented into a scene. The results of the reported pilot experiments could probably be further improved if 360 degree background images would be used by the plug-in that were captured at the same or similar-looking locations where the real-world test data was collected.

The new Blender plug-in can be used to augment objects into scenes and supplement smaller training sets by complementing them with large amounts of synthetic data. The improvement in detection accuracy on real-world test data by addition of similar-looking synthetic images to the training data reported in Sect. 3.3 demonstrates that the plug-in is capable of producing synthetic data that is sufficiently similar to the real-world data.

5   Conclusion

This collaboration of deep learning and computer graphics research proposed and demonstrated an approach for the generation of synthetic data and training deep neural networks on that data. This can help researchers to use larger more diverse pre-labelled data sets for training their networks on specific tasks, without having to spend too much time on manually collecting and labelling of images. Our trained networks showed comparable results on both real-world and synthetic data sets. The detection rate increased in every case when GoogLeNet trained on ImageNet was employed as a pre-trained network. The presented pilot experiments also indicate that a suitable selection of synthetically rendered training data can help to improve the detection rate on real-world image data.

Acknowledgements. AJ was supported by a UNRSC50:50 scholarship. JF was supported by an Australian Government Research Training Program scholarship. LF was supported by a summer scholarship and sponsorship through 4Tel Pty. In this paper AJ focused on data generation and deep learning, JF and LF focused on development of the Blender plugin for the generation of synthetic data and SKC supervised the project.

References

1. Goodfellow, I., Bengio, Y., Courville, A.: Deep Learning. MIT Press (2016)
2. Krizhevsky, A., Sutskever, I., Hinton, G.E.: Imagenet classification with deep convolutional neural networks. In: Pereira, F., Burges, C.J.C., Bottou, L., Weinberger, K.Q. (eds.) Advances in Neural Information Processing Systems (NIPS 2012), vol. 25, pp. 1097–1105. Curran Associates, Inc. (2012)
3. Simonyan, K., Zisserman, A.: Very deep convolutional networks for large-scale image recognition. CoRR abs/1409.1556 (2014), http://arxiv.org/abs/1409.1556
4. Szegedy, C., Liu, W., Jia, Y., Sermanet, P., Reed, S., Anguelov, D., Erhan, D., Vanhoucke, V., Rabinovich, A.: Going deeper with convolutions. In: 2015 IEEE Conference on Computer Vision and Pattern Recognition (CVPR), pp. 1–9 (2015)
5. Imagenet, http://www.image-net.org/. Accessed 03 June 2017
6. Shirley, P., Morley, R.K.: Realistic Ray Tracing, 2nd edn. A. K. Peters Ltd., Natick (2003)
7. Blender Foundation: Blender, https://www.blender.org/. Accessed 27 May 2017
8. Jaderberg, M., Simonyan, K., Vedaldi, A., Zisserman, A.: Synthetic data and artificial neural networks for natural scene text recognition. CoRR abs/1406.2227 (2014), http://arxiv.org/abs/1406.2227
9. Peng, X., Sun, B., Ali, K., Saenko, K.: Learning deep object detectors from 3D models. In: Proceedings of the IEEE International Conference on Computer Vision, pp. 1278–1286 (2015)
10. Rajpura, P.S., Hegde, R.S., Bojinov, H.: Object detection using deep CNNs trained on synthetic images arXiv:1706.06782 [cs] (2017)
11. Xu, Y., Nagahara, H., Shimada, A., Taniguchi, R.: Transcut: Transparent object segmentation from a light-field image. CoRR abs/1511.06853 (2015), http://arxiv.org/abs/1511.06853
12. Klank, U., Carton, D., Beetz, M.: Transparent object detection and reconstruction on a mobile platform. In: IEEE International Conference on Robotics and Automation (ICRA), Shanghai, China, 9–13 May (2011)
13. Ihrke, I., Kutulakos, K., Lensch, H., Magnor, M., Heidrich, W.: State of the art in transparent and specular object reconstruction. In: EUROGRAPHICS Star Proceedings, pp. 87–108, EG, Crete, Greece (2008)
14. Tao, A., Barker, J., Sarathy, S.: Detectnet: Deep neural network for object detection in digits (2016), https://devblogs.nvidia.com/parallelforall/detectnet-deep-neural-network-object-detection-digits/. Accessed 20 June 2017
15. Barker, J., Prasanna, S.: Deep learning for object detection with digits (2016), https://devblogs.nvidia.com/parallelforall/deep-learning-object-detection-digits/. Accessed 12 June 2017
16. Michael, L., David, W.: Distance between sets. Nature **234**, 34–35 (1971)
17. Everingham, M., Van Gool, L., Williams, C.K.I., Winn, J., Zisserman, A.: The pascal visual object classes (voc) challenge. Int. J. Comput. Vision **88**(2), 303–338 (2010)
18. Google images, https://images.google.com/
19. Chaurasiya, R.K., Ramakrishnan, K.R.: High dynamic range imaging. In: 2013 International Conference on Communication Systems and Network Technologies. pp. 83–89, April 2013
20. Debevec, P.: A tutorial on image-based lighting. IEEE Comput. Graph. Appl. (2002), http://ict.usc.edu/pubs/Image-Based%20Lighting.pdf

Image Segmentation with Pyramid Dilated Convolution Based on ResNet and U-Net

Qiao Zhang[1,2], Zhipeng Cui[1], Xiaoguang Niu[1], Shijie Geng[1], and Yu Qiao[1(✉)]

[1] Intelligence Learning Laboratory, Institute of Image Processing
and Pattern Recognition, Department of Automation,
Shanghai Jiao Tong University, Shanghai, China
qiaoyu@sjtu.edu.cn
[2] The Fu Foundation School of Engineering and Applied Science,
Columbia University, New York, USA

Abstract. Various deep convolutional neural networks (CNNs) have been applied in the task of medical image segmentation. A lot of CNNs have been proved to get better performance than the traditional algorithms. Deep residual network (ResNet) has drastically improved the performance by a trainable deep structure. In this paper, we proposed a new end-to-end network based on ResNet and U-Net. Our CNN effectively combine the features from shallow and deep layers through multi-path information confusion. In order to exploit global context features and enlarge receptive field in deep layer without losing resolution, We designed a new structure called pyramid dilated convolution. Different from traditional networks of CNNs, our network replaces the pooling layer with convolutional layer which can reduce information loss to some extent. We also introduce the LeakyReLU instead of ReLU along the downsampling path to increase the expressiveness of our model. Experiment shows that our proposed method can successfully extract features for medical image segmentation.

Keywords: Deep learning · Semantic image segmentation · Convolutional neural network · Medical image · Ultrasound Nerve Segmentation

1 Introduction

It has been widely accepted that CNNs have an impressive performance in computer vision tasks in recent years. CNNs have also been widely applied to the field of medical image segmentation and gain great popularity.

Brebisson et al. [1] apply the CNNs for anatomical brain segmentation and get good result. Zhang et al. [2] has designed deep convolutional neural networks for segmenting isointense stage brain tissues using multi-modality MR images. Li et al. [3] use the CNNs to learn the intrinsic image features of lung image patches. However, a lot of methods were based on the sliding-window technique which was proposed by Ciresan et al. [4]. This method could lead to storage overhead and ineffectiveness if we process a high resolution image. This method would

© Springer International Publishing AG 2017
D. Liu et al. (Eds.): ICONIP 2017, Part II, LNCS 10635, pp. 364–372, 2017.
https://doi.org/10.1007/978-3-319-70096-0_38

also lead to hierarchical global information loss. Long et al. [5] proposed Fully Convolutional Networks (FCN), which is based on VGG-16 [6]. FCN is an end-to-end network which can effectively solve the overstorage problem. It is widely acknowledged that the deeper architecture would achieve better performance. However, the training error rate in a deeper plain network would even be higher because the gradient would disappear more easily in a deeper architecture. He et al. [7] proposed deep residual network which makes the deep network training possible and achieves compelling accuracy. Furthermore, the repeated pooling layers and convolution strides in traditional CNNs would largely reduce receptive filed which is quite important for dense prediction tasks. The deconvolution process would not successfully recover the detail information which are lost in the downsampling process. Fisher et al. [8] proposed dilated convolution, which can effectively enlarge receptive field without losing resolution. It has been proved to improve the performance in VGG-16 network and accelerate convergence.

In this paper, we propose a new network based on ResNet and U-Net [9]. It can effectively combine the features from shallow and deep layers through multi-path confusion. We design a new structure called pyramid dilated convolution, which aims to exploit global context features with multi-scale. Furthermore, we apply the LeakyReLU [10] instead of ReLU [11] at downsampling path to increase the expressiveness of our model. Our network was applied to the Ultrasound Nerve Segmentation task and achieved good result.

2 Methodology

2.1 Pyramid Dilated Res-U-Net

In this paper, we propose a new segmentation architecture named Pyramid Dilated Res-U-Net. It is based on ResNet and U-Net with pyramid dilated convolution unit. This network structure is illustrated in Fig. 1. We use the deformed residual unit as shown in Fig. 2(b) to extract the feature map. We apply U-Net structure to combine multi-path feature maps from intermediate and deep layers. We refine the deep feature map from the 4th block of ResNet with multi-scale

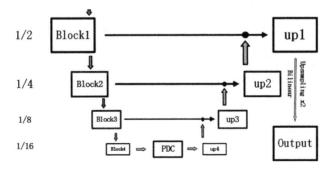

Fig. 1. Pyramid Dilated Res-U-Net

dilated convolution to fuse global context information. As for the first block of ResNet, we apply filter size of 5 instead of 3. Output from fusion is upsampled by bilinear interpolation with a factor of 2 to achieve an end-to-end training.

2.2   BN-LeakyReLU Residual Unit

The basic residual unit in ResNet is shown in Fig. 2(a). The following form denotes the basic unit:

$$y_k = F(x_k; W_l) + h(x_k) \tag{1}$$

$$x_{k+1} = f(y_k) \tag{2}$$

where x_k and x_{k+1} represent the input and output of the k-th unit, and h is an identity mapping function, F is a residual function and f represents activation function. He et al. [12] proposed that pre-activation of the weight layers (Fig. 2(b)) would be much easier to train and generalize better than post-activation structure (Fig. 2(a)). According to [12], we can use the chain rule of backpropagation [13] to get the following form:

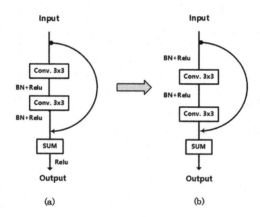

Fig. 2. Basic residual unit (a) and deformed residual unit (b).

$$\frac{\partial \varepsilon}{\partial x_k} = \frac{\partial \varepsilon}{\partial x_K} \frac{\partial x_K}{\partial x_k} = \frac{\partial \varepsilon}{\partial x_K} (1 + \frac{\partial}{\partial x_k} \sum_{i=k}^{K-1} F(x_i, W_i))) \tag{3}$$

where ε denotes the loss function, x_k denotes the feature of k-th layer and x_K denotes the feature of K-th layer. This structure could propagate information directly and through weight layers. Therefore, we implement this technique into our Network (Fig. 2(b)). As for the first block, we use a filter size of 5 instead of 3 in order to get a better basic feature map. The activation function is LeakyReLU instead of ReLU. LeakyReLU is denoted as the following form.

$$f(x) = \begin{cases} \alpha x & \text{if}(x < 0) \\ x & \text{if}(x > 0) \end{cases} \tag{4}$$

It allows a small, non-zero gradient when the unit is not active. So it would enlarge the expressiveness of our network to some extent.

2.3 Pyramid Dilated Convolution Unit

Fisher et al. [8] proposed dilated convolution which can exponentially enlarge receptive field without losing resolution. It is widely known that the receptive field affects the extent to which we exploit the context information. The context information is of great importance for accurate segmentation. However, Zhou et al. [14] presents that the actual receptive field of CNNs in deep layer is much smaller than the theoretical calculation.

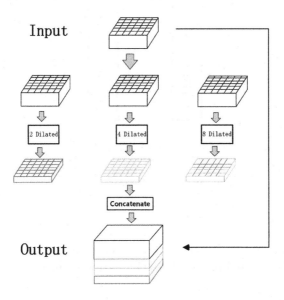

Fig. 3. Given an input feature map, we separately use dilated convolution with different factors to extract information. The corresponding three extracted feature maps are then concatenated with the input feature map to get the output.

We address this issue by designing a new structure, called Pyramid Dilated Convolution Unit shown in Fig. 3. We apply dilated convolution with 2, 4, 8 factors at the 4th block of ResNet to refine the feature map. It can effectively extract global context information through multi-scale dilated convolution. This unit could also enlarge receptive field without losing resolution.

The refined feature maps of different factors generated by dilated convolution are finally concatenated together with input image. Through concatenation operation, we can combine the raw feature information and the information in hierarchical structure. Then the fused feature map is fed to upsampling process. Experiment results show that the Pyramid Dilated Convolution Unit can successfully refine feature map with global context information.

2.4   Multi-path Fusion

As we know the feature map in the deep layer is usually of small size and it would lead to drastically information loss if we upsample directly. The low-level features embedded in intermediate layers are very necessary for accurate high resolution segmentation. In our network, we implement the U-Net-like structure to deal with multi-path fusion. Therefore, the shallow layer information and deep layer information together make the final segmentation more reliable. Specifically, feature map from the 5th block of ResNet is fed to the ReLU-Conv Unit (Fig. 4). This unit could be used to fine tune the weights effectively. The output of it is upsampled by bilinear interpolation and then concatenates the feature map from 4th block. In this way, we get fused output of half the input image size.

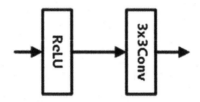

Fig. 4. ReLU_Conv Unit

3   Experiments

Our proposed method is applied on the segmentation problem of medical image. The method is evaluated in the Ultrasound Nerve Segmentaiton datasets and it achieves good result.

3.1   Implementation Details

Our network is based on top of keras with the backend of tensorflow. We implement data augmentation method to generate more training data. Specifically, we adopt small rotation, translation, random resize and random mirror. Inspired by [9], we use the "Adam" gradient descent optimizer with 0.00002 learning rate. For the training process, we assume that "batchsize" is of great importance because it affects the stability of the gradient and batch normalization [15]. However, we set the "batchsize" to 12 during training because of limitation of physical memory on GPU.

3.2   Ultrasound Nerve Segmentation

Ultrasound Nerve Segmentation task is required to identify nerve structures called the Brachial plexus in ultrasound images. This help inserting a patient's

Table 1. As for the network, baseline is ResNet54 (with ReLU and Pyramid Dilated Convolution). In our test, $\alpha = 0.2$ yields the best corresponding this network structure.

Parameter α	Dice coefficient(%)
ResNet54 (without LeakyRelU)	64.21
ResNet54 (with $\alpha = 0.1$)	67.12
ResNet54 (with $\alpha = 0.2$)	69.15
ResNet54 (with $\alpha = 0.3$)	65.26
ResNet54 (with $\alpha = 0.4$)	63.17

pain management catheter. The dataset are consisted of grayscale images with the corresponding binary masks. However, the dataset contains quite a lot contradictory images, therefore we pre-process the images and keep 4102 training images out of the 5500 in the end. The original images have a size of 580×420, we resize the images into 160×128 since the images are quite noisy and limitation of our memory resources. For the evaluation part, we use dice coefficient as a loss and also try binary cross-entropy. The two methods get roughly the same result.

To evaluate our network, we conduct experiments with several different settings. As for downsampling, we do experiment with pooling downsampling and convolution downsampling. We try different alpha of LeakyReLU in the downsampling process (Table 1).

Table 2. Deeper structure could yield better performance. However, deep network would be harder to train and occupy more resources. So in our experiment, we choose to use the ResNet54. PDC means Pyramid Dilated Convolution Unit.

Depth of ResNet	Dice coefficient(%)
ResNet34+PDC	68.52
ResNet54+PDC	69.15
ResNet72+PDC	69.31
ResNet101+PDC	69.39

It is widely known that deeper neutral networks could yield better segmentation accuracy, however the deep architecture could result in astounding cost of training time and GPU resources. We conduct experiments for various depths of deformed ResNet of 34,54,72,101 as shown in Table 2. We try different filter size to extract features of first block. We find that filter size of 5 could yield a better result than 3 and 7 in our problem.

We also compare Dilated Res-U-Net with other architectures (Table 3). Figure 5 presents the segmentation results of ultrasound nerve images with

Table 3. In this table, fs means filter size of the first block of ResNet. All experiments are on the preprocessed dataset and the U-Net experiment is based on the original dataset.

Method	Dice coefficient(%)
ResNet54+PDC+fs3	69.01
ResNet54+PDC+fs5(Ours)	**69.15**
ResNet54+PDC+fs7	69.11
ResNet54+PDC+pooling	68.73
ResNet54(fs3)	64.52
U-Net(without prepocess)	56.00

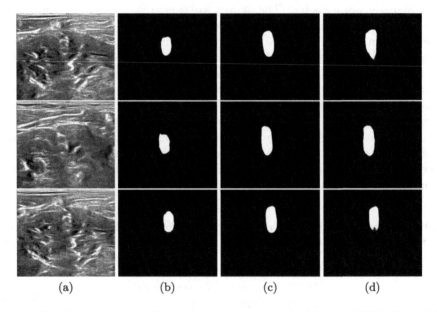

(a)	(b)	(c)	(d)

Fig. 5. Samples of ultrasound nerve segmentation with different CNNs. From left to right: (a) Input image, (b) U-Net, (c) Dilated-Res-U-Net, (d) Dilated-Res-U-Net(without PDC). PDC means Pyramid Dilated Convolution Unit

different CNNs. U-Net is restored following the link https://github.com/jocicmarko/ultrasound -nerve-segmentation. Figure 5 shows that Dilated-Res-U-Net could get a more complete structure than the network without Pyramid Dilated Convolution Unit. Table 3 demonstrates that this structure could effectively improve the accuracy by 4.6%. Therefore, the Pyramid Dilated Convolution Unit can successfully refine feature map with global context information.

4   Conclusions

In this paper, we have proposed an effective semantic segmentation network based on ResNet and U-net. We have developed a new structure Pyramid

Dilated Convolution Unit for exploitation of global context information. This unit also enlarges the receptive field without losing resolution. We also introduce LeakyReLU in the downsampling process instead of ReLU. We designed a structure without pooling operation and conduct experiment of different filter size in the extraction of basic features. Experiment results on Ultrasound Nerve Segmentation dataset show that our proposed method could effectively extract features in medical image for segmentation.

Acknowledgments. This research is partly supported by NSFC (No: 61375048).

References

1. Brebisson, A.D., Mountana, G.: Deep neural networks for anatomical brain segmentation. In: Proceedings of the IEEE Conference on Computer Vision and Pattern Recognition Workshops (2015)
2. Zhang, W., Li, R., Deng, H., Wang, L.: Deep convolutional neural networks for multi-modality isointense infant brain image segmentation. NeuroImage **108**, 214–224 (2015)
3. Li, Q., Cai, T., Wang, X., Zhou, Y., Feng, D.: Medical image classification with convolutional neural network. In: the 13th International Conference on Control Automation Robotics & Vision (ICARCV). IEEE (2014)
4. Ciresan, D.C., Meier, U., Masci, J., Gambardella, L.M., Schmidhuber, J.: Flexible, high performance convolutional neural networks for image classification. In: Twenty-Second International Joint Conference on Artificial Intelligence (2011)
5. Long, J., Shelhamer, E., Darrell, T.: Fully convolutional networks for semantic segmentation. In: Proceedings of the IEEE Conference on Computer Vision and Pattern Recognition (2015)
6. Simonyan, K., Zisserman, A.: Very deep convolutional networks for large-scale image recognition. ArXiv preprint arXiv:1409.1556 (2014)
7. He, K., Zhang, X., Ren, S., Sun, J.: Deep residual learning for image recognition. In: Proceedings of the Institute of Electrical and Electronics Engineers Conference on Computer Vision and Pattern Recognition (2016)
8. Yu, F., Koltun, V.: Multi-scale context aggregation by dilated convolutions, arXiv preprint arXiv:1511.07122 (2015)
9. Ronneberger, O., Fischer, P., Brox, T.: U-Net: convolutional networks for biomedical image segmentation. In: Navab, N., Hornegger, J., Wells, W.M., Frangi, A.F. (eds.) MICCAI 2015. LNCS, vol. 9351, pp. 234–241. Springer, Cham (2015). doi:10.1007/978-3-319-24574-4_28
10. Xu, B., Wang, N., Chen, T., Li, M.: Empirical evaluation of rectified activations in convolutional network. arXiv preprint arXiv:1505.00853 (2015)
11. Nair, V., Hinton, G.E.: Rectified linear units improve restricted boltzmann machines. In: Proceedings of the 27th International Conference on Machine Learning (ICML 2010) (2010)
12. He, K., Zhang, X., Ren, S., Sun, J.: Identity mappings in deep residual networks. In: Leibe, B., Matas, J., Sebe, N., Welling, M. (eds.) ECCV 2016. LNCS, vol. 9908, pp. 630–645. Springer, Cham (2016). doi:10.1007/978-3-319-46493-0_38
13. LeCun, Y., Boser, B.E., Denker, J.S., Henderson, D., Howard, R.E., Hubbard, W.E., Jackel, L.D.: Backpropagation applied to handwritten zip code recognition. Neural Comput. **1**(4), 541–551 (1989)

14. Zhou, B., Khosla, A., Lapedriza, A., Oliva, A., Torralba, A.: Object detectors emerge in deep scene cnns. arXiv preprint arXiv:1412.6856 (2014)
15. Ioffe, S., Szegedy, C.: Batch normalization: Accelerating deep network training by reducing internal covariate shift. arXiv preprint arXiv:1502.03167 (2015)

Deep Clustering with Convolutional Autoencoders

Xifeng Guo[1(✉)], Xinwang Liu[1], En Zhu[1], and Jianping Yin[2]

[1] College of Computer, National University of Defense Technology,
Changsha 410073, China
guoxifeng13@nudt.edu.cn
[2] State Key Laboratory of High Performance Computing,
National University of Defense Technology, Changsha 410073, China

Abstract. Deep clustering utilizes deep neural networks to learn feature representation that is suitable for clustering tasks. Though demonstrating promising performance in various applications, we observe that existing deep clustering algorithms either do not well take advantage of convolutional neural networks or do not considerably preserve the local structure of data generating distribution in the learned feature space. To address this issue, we propose a deep convolutional embedded clustering algorithm in this paper. Specifically, we develop a convolutional autoencoders structure to learn embedded features in an end-to-end way. Then, a clustering oriented loss is directly built on embedded features to jointly perform feature refinement and cluster assignment. To avoid feature space being distorted by the clustering loss, we keep the decoder remained which can preserve local structure of data in feature space. In sum, we simultaneously minimize the reconstruction loss of convolutional autoencoders and the clustering loss. The resultant optimization problem can be effectively solved by mini-batch stochastic gradient descent and back-propagation. Experiments on benchmark datasets empirically validate the power of convolutional autoencoders for feature learning and the effectiveness of local structure preservation.

Keywords: Deep clustering · Convolutional autoencoders · Convolutional neural networks · Unsupervised learning

1 Introduction

Given a large collection of unlabeled images represented by raw pixels, how to divide them into K groups in terms of inherent latent semantics? The traditional way is first extracting feature vectors according to domain-specific knowledges and then employing clustering algorithm on the extracted features. Thanks to deep learning approaches, some work successfully combines feature learning and clustering into a unified framework which can directly cluster original images with even higher performance. We refer to this new category of clustering algorithms as *Deep Clustering*.

© Springer International Publishing AG 2017
D. Liu et al. (Eds.): ICONIP 2017, Part II, LNCS 10635, pp. 373–382, 2017.
https://doi.org/10.1007/978-3-319-70096-0_39

Some researches have been conducted, but what are the critical ingredients for deep clustering still remains unclear. For example, what types of neural networks are proper for feature extraction? How to provide guidance information i.e. to define clustering oriented loss function? Which properties of data should be preserved in feature space? In this paper, we focus on the first and third questions and conclude that Convolutional AutoEncoders (CAE) and locality property are two of key ingredients for deep clustering algorithms.

The most widely used neural networks in deep clustering algorithms are Stacked AutoEncoders (SAE) [12,13,16,18]. The SAE requires layer-wise pre-training before being finetuned in an end-to-end manner. When the layers go deeper, the pretraining procedure can be tedious and time-consuming. Furthermore, SAE is built with fully connected layers, which are ineffective for dealing with images. The work in [8] is the first trial to train CAE directly in an end-to-end manner without pretraining.

In terms of properties of data to preserve in feature space, the primitive work considers sparsity or graph constraints by adding prior knowledges to the objective [13,15]. They are two-stage algorithms: feature learning and then clustering. Latter, algorithms that jointly accomplish feature learning and clustering come into being [16,19]. The Deep Embedded Clustering (DEC) [16] algorithm defines an effective objective in a self-learning manner. The defined clustering loss is used to update parameters of transforming network and cluster centers simultaneously. However, they ignore the preservation of data properties, which may lead to the corruption of feature space. We improve DEC algorithm by preserving local structure of data generating distribution and by incorporating convolutional layers.

Our key idea is that CAE is beneficial to learning features for images and preserving local structure of data avoids distortion of feature space. The contributions are:

- A Convolutional AutoEncoders (CAE) that can be trained in end-to-end manner is designed for learning features from unlabeled images. The designed CAE is superior to stacked autoencoders by incorporating spacial relationships between pixels in images. We show that convolutional layer, convolutional transpose layer and fully connected layer are sufficient for constructing an effective CAE.
- The local structure preservation is considered during tuning network parameters according to clustering oriented loss function. We demonstrate that preserving local structure helps stabilize the training procedure and avoid the corruption of feature space.
- We propose the Deep Convolutional Embedded Clustering (DCEC) algorithm to automatically cluster images. The DCEC takes advantages of CAE and local structure preservation. And the resulting optimization problem can be efficiently solved by mini-batch stochastic gradient descent and backpropagation.
- Extensive experiments are conducted on benchmark image datasets. The results validate the effectiveness of CAE and local structure preservation.

2   Convolutional AutoEncoders

A conventional autoencoder is generally composed of two layers, corresponding to encoder $f_W(\cdot)$ and decoder $g_U(\cdot)$ respectively. It aims to find a code for each input sample by minimizing the mean squared errors (MSE) between its input and output over all samples, i.e.

$$\min_{W,U} \frac{1}{n} \sum_{i=1}^{n} \|g_U(f_W(x_i)) - x_i\|_2^2 \tag{1}$$

For fully connected autoencoder,

$$\begin{aligned} f_W(x) &= \sigma(Wx) \equiv h \\ g_U(h) &= \sigma(Uh) \end{aligned} \tag{2}$$

where x and h are vectors, and σ is activation function like ReLU, sigmoid. Note that the bias is omitted for convenient description. After training, the embedded code h serves as the new representation of input sample. Then h can be fed into another autoencoder to form Stacked AutoEncoders (SAE). To exploit the spacial structure of images, convolutional autoencoder is defined as

$$\begin{aligned} f_W(x) &= \sigma(x * W) \equiv h \\ g_U(h) &= \sigma(h * U) \end{aligned} \tag{3}$$

where x and h are matrices or tensors, and "$*$" is convolution operator. The Stacked Convolutional AutoEncoders (SCAE) [10] can be constructed in a similar way as SAE.

We propose a new Convolutional AutoEncoders (CAE) that does not need tedious layer-wise pretraining, as shown in Fig. 1. First, some convolutional layers are stacked on the input images to extract hierarchical features. Then flatten all units in the last convolutional layer to form a vector, followed by a fully connected layer with only 10 units which is called embedded layer. The input 2D image is thus transformed into 10 dimensional feature space. To train it in the unsupervised manner, we use a fully connected layer and some convolutional transpose layers to transform embedded feature back to original image. The parameters of encoder $h = F_\omega(x)$ and decoder $x' = G_{\omega'}(h)$ are updated by minimizing the reconstruction error:

$$L_r = \frac{1}{n} \sum_{i=1}^{n} \|G_{\omega'}(F_\omega(x_i)) - x_i\|_2^2 \tag{4}$$

where n is the number of images in dataset, $x_i \in \mathbb{R}^2$ is the ith image.

The key factor of the proposed CAE is the aggressive constraint on the dimension of embedded layer. If the embedded layer is large enough, the network may be able to copy its input to output, leading to learning useless features. The intuitive way of avoiding identity mapping is to control the dimension of latent

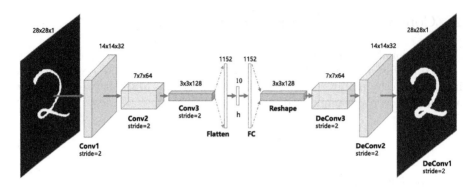

Fig. 1. The structure of proposed Convolutional AutoEncoders (CAE) for MNIST. In the middle there is a fully connected autoencoder whose embedded layer is composed of only 10 neurons. The rest are convolutional layers and convolutional transpose layers (some work refers to as Deconvolutional layer). The network can be trained directly in an end-to-end manner.

code h lower than input data x. Learning such under-complete representations forces the autoencoder to capture the most salient features of the data. Thus we force the dimension of embedded space to equal to the number of clusters of dataset. In this way, the network can be trained directly in an end-to-end manner even without any regularizations like Dropout [14] or Batch Normalization [5]. The learned compact representations are proved effective for clustering task.

Another factor is that we utilize convolutional layer with stride instead of convolutional layer followed by pooling layer in the encoder, and convolutional transpose layer with stride in the decoder. Because the convolutional (transpose) layers with stride allow the network to learn spacial subsampling (upsampling) from data, leading to higher capability of transformation.

Note that we do not aim at the state-of-the-art clustering performance, so we do not adopt fancy layers or techniques like BatchNormalization layer, LeakyReLu activation or layer-wise pretraining. We only show the CAE is superior to fully connected SAE in image clustering task.

3   Deep Convolutional Embedded Clustering

As introduced in Sect. 2, the CAE is a more powerful network for dealing with images compared with fully connected SAE. So we extend Deep Embedded Clustering (DEC) [16] by replacing SAE with CAE. Then we argue that the embedded feature space in DEC may be distorted by only using clustering oriented loss. To this end, the reconstruction loss of autoencoders is added to the objective and optimized along with clustering loss simultaneously. The autoencoders will preserve the local structure of data generating distribution, avoiding the corruption of feature space. The resulting algorithm is termed as Deep Convolutional Embedded Clustering (DCEC). In the following sections, we first give the structure of DCEC, then introduce the clustering loss and local structure preservation mechanism in detail. At last, the optimization procedure is provided.

3.1 Structure of Deep Convolutional Embedded Clustering

The DCEC structure is composed of CAE (see Fig. 1) and a clustering layer which is connected to the embedded layer of CAE, as depicted in Fig. 2. The clustering layer maps each embedded point z_i of input image x_i into a soft label. Then the clustering loss L_c is defined as Kullback-Leibler divergence (KL divergence) between the distribution of soft labels and the predefined target distribution. CAE is used to learn embedded features and the clustering loss guides the embedded features to be prone to forming clusters.

The objective of DCEC is

$$L = L_r + \gamma L_c \tag{5}$$

where L_r and L_c are reconstruction loss and clustering loss respectively, and $\gamma > 0$ is a coefficient that controls the degree of distorting embedded space. When $\gamma = 1$ and $L_r \equiv 0$, (5) reduces to the objective of DEC [16].

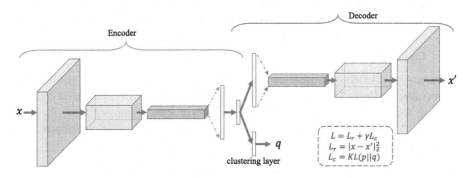

Fig. 2. The structure of deep convolutional embedded clustering (DCEC). It is composed of a convolutional autoencoders and a clustering layer connected to embedded layer of autoencoders.

3.2 Clustering Layer and Clustering Loss

The clustering layer and loss are directly borrowed from DEC [16]. We briefly review their definitions for completeness of DCEC structure.

The clustering layer maintains cluster centers $\{\mu_j\}_1^K$ as trainable weights and maps each embedded point z_i into soft label q_i by Student's t-distribution [9]:

$$q_{ij} = \frac{(1 + \|z_i - \mu_j\|^2)^{-1}}{\sum_j (1 + \|z_i - \mu_j\|^2)^{-1}} \tag{6}$$

where q_{ij} is the jth entry of q_i, representing the probability of z_i belonging to cluster j.

The clustering loss is defined as

$$L_c = KL(P\|Q) = \sum_i \sum_j p_{ij} \log \frac{p_{ij}}{q_{ij}} \tag{7}$$

where P is the target distribution, defined as

$$p_{ij} = \frac{q_{ij}^2 / \sum_i q_{ij}}{\sum_j \left(q_{ij}^2 / \sum_i q_{ij} \right)} \tag{8}$$

3.3   Reconstruction Loss for Local Structure Preservation

DEC [16] abandons the decoder and finetunes the encoder using clustering loss L_c. However, we suppose that this kind of finetuning could distort the embedded space, weaken the representativeness of embedded features and thereby hurt clustering performance. Therefore, we propose to keep the decoder untouched and directly attach the clustering loss to embedded layer.

As shown in [13] and [4], autoencoders can preserve local structure of data generating distribution. Under this condition, manipulating embedded space slightly using clustering loss L_c will not cause corruption. So the coefficient γ is better to be less than 1, which will be empirically fixed to 0.1 for all experiments.

3.4   Optimization

We first pretrain the parameters of CAE by setting $\gamma = 0$ to get meaningful target distribution. After pretraining, the cluster centers are initialized by performing k-means on embedded features of all images. Then set $\gamma = 0.1$ and update CAE's weights, cluster centers and target distribution P as follows.

Update autoencoders' weights and cluster centers. As $\frac{\partial L_c}{\partial z_i}$ and $\frac{\partial L_c}{\partial \mu_j}$ are easily derived according to [16], then the weights and centers can be updated by using backpropagation and mini-batch SGD straightforwardly.

Update target distribution. The target distribution P serves as ground truth soft label but also depends on predicted soft label. Therefore, to avoid instability, P should not be updated at each iteration using only a batch of data. In practice, we update target distribution using all embedded points every T iterations. See (6) and (8) for the update rules.

The training process terminates if the change of label assignments between two consecutive updates for target distribution is less than a threshold δ.

4   Experiment

4.1   DataSets

The proposed DCEC method is evaluated on three image datasets: **MNIST-full**: The MNIST dataset [7] consists of total 70000 handwritten digits of

28×28 pixels. **MNIST-test**: The test set of MNIST, containing 10000 images. **USPS**: The USPS dataset contains 9298 gray-scale handwritten digit images with size of 16×16 pixels.

4.2 Experiment Setup

Comparing methods. We demonstrate the effectiveness of our DCEC algorithm mainly by comparing with **DEC** [16]. The two-stage deep clustering algorithm is denoted as **SAE+k-means** (or **CAE+k-means**), i.e. performing k-means on embedded features of pretrained SAE (or CAE). **IDEC** [17] denotes the algorithm that adds reconstruction loss L_r to DEC's objective. **DEC-conv** is the structure that directly replaces SAE in DEC with CAE but without L_r. **DCEC** is the proposed structure, which adds both L_r and convolutional layers to DEC. For the sake of completeness, two traditional and classic clustering algorithms, k-**means** and Spectral Embedded Clustering (**SEC**) [11], are also included in comparison.

Parameters setting. For SAE+k-means, DEC [16] and IDEC [17], the encoder network is set as a fully connected multilayer perceptron (MLP) with dimensions d-500-500-2000-10 for all datasets, where d is the dimension of input data (features). And the decoder network is a mirror of encoder, i.e. a MLP with dimensions 10-2000-500-500-d. Except for input, output and embedding layers, all internal layers are activated by ReLU nonlinearity function [3]. The SAE is pretrained end-to-end for 400 epochs using SGD with learning rate 0.01 and momentum 0.9.

For CAE+k-means, DEC-conv and DECE, the encoder network structure is $\text{conv}_{32}^5 \rightarrow \text{conv}_{64}^5 \rightarrow \text{conv}_{128}^3 \rightarrow \text{FC}_{10}$ where conv_n^k denotes a convolutional layer with n filters, kernel size of $k \times k$ and stride length 2 as default. The decoder is a mirror of encoder. The CAE is pretrained end-to-end for 200 epochs using Adam [6] with default parameters. The convergence threshold is set to $\delta = 0.1\%$. And the update intervals $T = 140$. Our implementation is based on Python and Keras [2] and the code is available at https://github.com/XifengGuo/DCEC.

Evaluation Metric. All clustering methods are evaluated by clustering accuracy (ACC).

4.3 Results

The clustering results are shown in Table 1. Our DCEC algorithm outperforms all opponents in terms of clustering accuracy on all datasets.

Advantage of CAE. SAE+k-means, DEC and DEC-reco share the same pretrained SAE network structure and weights. As a counterpart, CAE+k-means, DEC-conv and DCEC use the same CAE structure and weights. By comparing each pair of equivalents (like DEC-reco and DCEC), we see that methods using CAE outperform their counterparts that use SAE by a large margin. Notice that, At pretraining stage, CAE is trained for 200 epochs while SAE for 400 epochs.

Table 1. Comparison of clustering performance in terms of accuracy (%). The results of DEC† is obtained by using the code published by authors.

Methods	MNIST-full	MNIST-test	USPS
k-means	53.24	54.72	66.82
SEC [11]	80.37	N/A	N/A
DEC† [16]	86.55	82.36	73.68
SAE+k-means	78.17	66.81	61.65
DEC	84.08	69.94	69.28
DEC-reco	84.21	71.45	72.10
CAE+k-means	84.90	79.00	74.15
DEC-conv	88.63	84.83	77.90
DCEC	**88.97**	**85.29**	**79.00**

And at clustering stage, methods with CAE converge much faster than SAE counterparts. This demonstrates that CAE is superior to SAE in image clustering task.

Local structure preservation. We can see the effect of adding reconstruction loss by comparing DEC and DEC-reco (or DEC-conv and DCEC). The clustering accuracies of DEC-reco are higher than that of DEC. And the same is true for DEC-conv and DCEC. We assume that this superiority is due to the fact that autoencoders can preserve local structure of data by minimizing the reconstruction loss. We validate this property by visualizing the embedded features. The t-SNE [9] visualization on a random subset of MNIST-full with 1000 samples is shown in Fig. 3. For DCEC, the "shape" of each cluster is almost maintained compared with pretrained CAE. Furthermore, when you focus on clusters colored by red and blue (digits 4 and 9), in DCEC they are still somehow separable but totally distinguishable in DEC-conv. It can be concluded that the autoencoder can preserve the intrinsic structure of data generating distribution and hence help clustering loss to manipulate the embedded feature space *appropriately*.

5   Related Work

Existing deep clustering algorithms broadly fall into two categories: (i) two-stage work that applies clustering after having learned a representation, and (ii) approaches that jointly optimize the feature learning and clustering.

The former category of algorithms directly take advantage of existing unsupervised deep learning frameworks and techniques. For example, [1,13,15] use autoencoder to learn low dimensional features of original graph or data samples, and then runs conventional clustering algorithm like k-means and non-parametric maximum-margin clustering on learned representations.

The other category of algorithms try to explicitly define a clustering loss, simulating classification error in supervised deep learning. [19] proposes a recurrent

Pretrained CAE

DEC-conv

DCEC

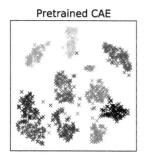
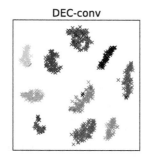
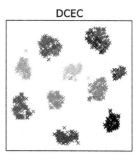

Fig. 3. Visualization of clustering results on subset of MNIST-full. Different colors mark different clusters. The data structure in DCEC is preserved better than DEC-conv. Note points with red and blue colors, they are totally mixed together in DEC-conv while still somehow separable in our DCEC.

framework, which integrates feature learning and clustering into a single model with a unified weighted triplet loss and optimizes it end-to-end. DEC [16] learns a mapping from the observed space to a low-dimensional latent space with SAE, which can obtain feature representations and cluster assignments simultaneously. DBC [8] improves DEC by replacing SAE with CAE.

The proposed DCEC falls into the second category. It excels [19] by simplicity without recurrent and outperforms DEC in terms of clustering accuracy and feature's representativeness. DBC [8] studied the CAE but still neglected the local structure preservation problem. Our DCEC takes care of both convolutional networks and local structure preservation.

6 Conclusion

This paper proposes a Deep Convolutional Embedded Clustering (DCEC) algorithm to take advantage of both convolutional neural networks and local structure preservation mechanism. DCEC is a framework that jointly learns deep representations of images and performs clustering. It learns good features with local structure preserved by using Convolutional AutoEncoders (CAE) and manipulates feature space by incorporating a clustering oriented loss. The experiment empirically demonstrates the effectiveness of DCEC on image clustering task and validates that both convolutional networks and local structure preservation mechanism are vital to deep clustering for images.

Acknowledgments. This work was financially supported by the National Natural Science Foundation of China (Project no. 60970034, 61170287, 61232016 and 61672528).

References

1. Chen, G.: Deep learning with nonparametric clustering. arXiv preprint arXiv:1501.03084 (2015)

2. Chollet, F., et al.: Keras (2015). https://github.com/fchollet/keras
3. Glorot, X., Bordes, A., Bengio, Y.: Deep sparse rectifier neural networks. J. Mach. Learn. Res. **15**, 315–323 (2011)
4. Goodfellow, I., Bengio, Y., Courville, A.: Deep Learning. MIT Press (2016)
5. Ioffe, S., Szegedy, C.: Batch normalization: accelerating deep network training by reducing internal covariate shift. In: International Conference on Machine Learning (ICML), pp. 448–456 (2015)
6. Kingma, D., Ba, J.: Adam: A method for stochastic optimization. arXiv preprint arXiv:1412.6980 (2014)
7. LeCun, Y., Bottou, L., Bengio, Y., Haffner, P.: Gradient-based learning applied to document recognition. Proc. IEEE **86**(11), 2278–2324 (1998)
8. Li, F., Qiao, H., Zhang, B., Xi, X.: Discriminatively boosted image clustering with fully convolutional auto-encoders. arXiv preprint arXiv:1703.07980 (2017)
9. Maaten, L.V.D., Hinton, G.: Visualizing data using t-SNE. J. Mach. Learn. Res. **9**, 2579–2605 (2008)
10. Masci, J., Meier, U., Cireşan, D., Schmidhuber, J.: Stacked convolutional auto-encoders for hierarchical feature extraction. In: Honkela, T., Duch, W., Girolami, M., Kaski, S. (eds.) ICANN 2011. LNCS, vol. 6791, pp. 52–59. Springer, Heidelberg (2011). doi:10.1007/978-3-642-21735-7_7
11. Nie, F., Zeng, Z., Tsang, I.W., Xu, D., Zhang, C.: Spectral embedded clustering: a framework for in-sample and out-of-sample spectral clustering. IEEE Trans. Neural Netw. **22**(11), 1796–1808 (2011)
12. Peng, X., Feng, J., Lu, J., Yau, W.Y., Yi, Z.: Cascade subspace clustering. In: AAAI Conference on Artificial Intelligence (AAAI), pp. 2478–2484 (2017)
13. Peng, X., Xiao, S., Feng, J., Yau, W.Y., Yi, Z.: Deep subspace clustering with sparsity prior. In: International Joint Conference on Artificial Intelligence (IJCAI) (2016)
14. Srivastava, N., Hinton, G.E., Krizhevsky, A., Sutskever, I., Salakhutdinov, R.: Dropout: a simple way to prevent neural networks from overfitting. J. Mach. Learn. Res. **15**(1), 1929–1958 (2014)
15. Tian, F., Gao, B., Cui, Q., Chen, E., Liu, T.Y.: Learning deep representations for graph clustering. In: AAAI Conference on Artificial Intelligence (AAAI), pp. 1293–1299 (2014)
16. Xie, J., Girshick, R., Farhadi, A.: Unsupervised deep embedding for clustering analysis. In: International Conference on Machine Learning (ICML) (2016)
17. Guo, X., Gao, L., Liu, X., Yin, J.: Improved deep embedded clustering with local structure preservation. In: International Joint Conference on Artificial Intelligence (IJCAI-17), pp. 1753–1759 (2017). doi:10.24963/ijcai.2017/243
18. Yang, B., Fu, X., Sidiropoulos, N.D., Hong, M.: Towards k-means-friendly spaces: simultaneous deep learning and clustering. arXiv preprint arXiv:1610.04794 (2016)
19. Yang, J., Parikh, D., Batra, D.: Joint unsupervised learning of deep representations and image clusters. In: Conference on Computer Vision and Pattern Recognition (CVPR), pp. 5147–5156 (2016)

An Incremental Deep Learning Network for On-line Unsupervised Feature Extraction

Yu Liang, Yi Yang, Furao Shen$^{(\boxtimes)}$, Jinxi Zhao, and Tao Zhu

National Key Laboratory for Novel Software Technology,
Department of Computer Science and Technology,
Collaborative Innovation Center of Novel Software Technology and Industrialization,
Nanjing University, Nanjing, China
frshen@nju.edu.cn

Abstract. In this paper, we propose an incremental deep learning network for on-line unsupervised feature extraction. This deep learning network is based on 3 data processing components: (1) cascaded incremental orthogonal component analysis network (IOCANet); (2) binary hashing; and (3) blockwise histograms. In this architecture, IOCANet can process online data and get filters to do convolutions. Binary hashing is used to enhance the nonlinearity of IOCANet and reduce the quantity of the data. Eventually, the data is encoded by blockwise histograms. Experiments demonstrate that the proposed architecture has potential results for on-line unsupervised feature extraction.

Keywords: Deep learning · On-line unsupervised feature extraction

1 Introduction

Computer vision is an interdisciplinary field that deals with how computers can be made to gain high-level understanding from digital images or videos. Many significant fields such as artificial intelligence, neurobiology are closely related to computer vision. However, similar images may have different lighting conditions, misalignment, non-rigid deformations, occlusion and corruptions, which brings great difficulties to computer vision. Hence, scientists want to extract features from images to overcome the intra-class variability. Representative examples are Gabor features and local binary patterns (LBP) for texture and face classification and SIFT and HOG features for object recognition [3]. These artificial features have achieved great success in corresponding tasks. However, these features can not be adapted to the new conditions.

Deep neural networks (DNNs) are proposed to overcome the weakness of hand-crafted features. The main idea of DNNs is that higher level features can represent more abstract semantics of the data, which means that the intra-class variability will only have little affect upon the features. Therefore these features can achieve great results on image classification. One key ingredient to the success of deep learning in image classification is the use of convolutional

© Springer International Publishing AG 2017
D. Liu et al. (Eds.): ICONIP 2017, Part II, LNCS 10635, pp. 383–392, 2017.
https://doi.org/10.1007/978-3-319-70096-0_40

architectures [1], which is called ConvNet. A convolution operation on small regions of input is introduced to reduce the number of free parameters and improve generalization. One major advantage of convolutional networks is the use of shared weight in convolutional layers, which means that the same filters (weights bank) are used for each pixel in the layer; this both reduce memory footprint and improve performance [4].

Although ConvNet has achieved great success in different vision tasks, it still can not process the online and incremental data. Besides, although ConvNet adopts convolution operation to reduce the number of parameters, it still needs to train a mass of parameters, which takes a lot of time and computing resources.

The initial motivation of our study is to resolve the problem that current deep learning has no way to process online incremental data, which means that if new data comes, our only way is to train all the data again. This would waste a lot of computing resources. What's more, we want to design a simple deep learning network. This network does not need to train a large amount of parameters.

Hence, we propose an Online Incremental Orthogonal Component Analysis Network (IOCANet). The core of our method is to use online incremental orthogonal component analysis method to generate the convolution kernels. After that, like ConvNet, we will do convolution operation to extract features. However, different from ConvNet, IOCANet is simple, but efficient and effective. Compared with ConvNet, it has lower time complexity and both mass data and small amount of data are suitable for IOCANet.

2 Related Work

In recent years, incremental learning has attracted great attention due to the increasing demand for systems have the ability of learning and evolving. When new data is input, incremental learning methods updated the learned model without recalculating the whole model repeatedly. Obviously, these methods enjoy a great advantage: their computational and storage cost is greatly reduced while the performance is improved [2].

Hence, we propose online incremental orthogonal component analysis (IOCA) to deal with incremental learning problem. And in IOCANet, IOCA algorithm is used to generate the convolution kernels (filters), which are the basis in the feature subspace of IOCA. The main principle of IOCA is "entities should not be multiplied unnecessarily". As is shown in Fig. 1 and we give the detailed incremental orthogonal component analysis algorithm in Algorithm 1. In the beginning, feature subspace S is initialized as a zero-dimensional space. Suppose when the t-th data x_t is input, $b_1, b_2, ..., b_k$ are the k basis vectors have been learned, IOCA tries to update S by extracting candidate basis vectors b_{k+1} from x_t and outputs $x_t{}'s$ low-dimensional representation y_t. Then, IOCA continues to process the t+1th data until there is no new data.

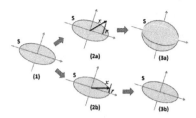

Fig. 1. S is the feature subspace. Input vector x is projected onto S and its complemented subspace $S^\perp$. $\|r\|_2$ measures the linear dependence between x and S. The adaptive threshold T is represented by the red line. (2a) If $\|r\|_2$ is larger than T, (3a) IOCA will extract a new base vector and enlarge S. (2b) Otherwise, (3b) no new base vector will be extracted and S remains unchanged.

Algorithm 1. Incremental Orthogonal Component Analysis

Initialize basis $B = \varnothing$ and its dimension k = 0.
Initialize $L_{MAX} = 0$
for each input x_i **do**
  if $\|x_i\|_2 > L_{max}$ **then**
    $L_{max}^t = \|x_i\|_2$
  end if
  Let $r_t = x_t$
  for i=1:k **do**
    Compute $y_t^i = r_t^T b_i$, let $y_{t,i}$ be the i-th entry of y_t.
    Compute $r_t^i = r_t - y_{t,i} b_i$
  end for
  Compute $b_{k+1} = \frac{r_t}{\|r_t\|_2}$
  if $\frac{\|r_t\|_2}{L_{max}^{(t)}} \geq f(\frac{f}{d})$ **then**
    Accepted b_{k+1} as a component and let $B^{(k+1)} = [B^{(k)}, b_{k+1}]$.
    Let $y_{t,k+1} = \|r_t\|_2$ be the $(k+1)^{th}$ entry of y_t
    Update basis dimension $k = k + 1$
  end if
end for

The time complexity of IOCA is $O(Ndk)$, N is the training set size, d is the dimension of original data, and k is the number of basis eventually learned by the algorithm. Note that the algorithm of IOCA is concise and its time complexity is low. Therefore, the proposed method enjoys a low computational load and high numerical stability. Because of its simplicity, IOCA has few limits in applications and has the potential to be a universal approach in feature extraction.

PCANet [3] is a simple deep learning network that shares various similarities with IOCANet. PCANet uses PCA algorithm to generate the convolution kernels. PCANet needs all the data input at once and process them together, besides, the number of convolution kernels should be given before the training, which may require a priori information about the data. However, presumably, it is exactly in the absence of such information. And we always need to attempt some values to decide which value is suitable. For IOCANet, we don't have to worry about this situation. IOCANet will tell you the appropriate number of convolution kernels. Experiment in the fourth section demonstrates this.

3   Proposed Method

As shown in Fig. 2, we use two stages IOCANet as an example to describe the proposed incremental deep learning architecture. In the first stage, we mainly introduce the structural characteristic of each layer in IOCANet. In the second stage, for the reason that layers are similar to each other, we mainly put the focus on the structure between layers. In the output stage, we introduce binary hashing and blockwise histograms to realize non-linear feature extraction.

3.1   Structures of the IOCA Network (IOCANet)

Suppose that we are given N input training images $\{I_i\}_{i=1}^N$ of size $m \times n$, and we assume that the patch size (or 2D filter size) is $k_1 \times k_2$ at all stages. Because our algorithm is online and incremental, only one image will be input at a time. Here we assume that I_i is input.

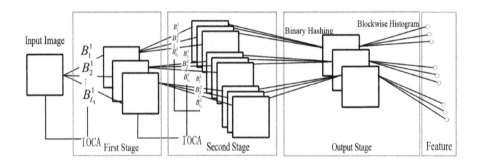

Fig. 2. The overall view of two-stage IOCANet

The First Stage. For input image I_i, around each pixel, we take a $k_1 \times k_2$ patch and we collect all (overlapping) patches, i.e., $x_{i,1}, x_{i,2}, ...x_{i,\widetilde{m}\widetilde{n}}$, where each $x_{i,j}$ denotes the j-th vectorized patch in I_i, $\widetilde{m} = m - k_1 + 1, \widetilde{n} = n - k_2 + 1$. After that we can obtain matrix X

$$X = [x_{i,1}, x_{i,2}, ...x_{i,\widetilde{m}\widetilde{n}}] \in R^{k_1 k_2 \times \widetilde{m}\widetilde{n}} \tag{1}$$

With matrix X, we use incremental orthogonal component analysis to generate the convolution kernel. After that, the basis B captures the main variation of all of the training patches and that is the convolution kernels (or filters) we want to get. Of course, similar to ConvNet, we can stack multiple stages of IOCANet filters to extract higher level features.

The Second Stage. The operation in the second stage is the same as the first stage. Let the l-th filter output of the first stage be:

$$I_i^l = I_i * B_l^1, i = 1, 2, ..., N \tag{2}$$

where $*$ denotes 2D convolution, and the boundary of I_i is zero-padded before convolving with B_l^1, so as to make I_i^l have the same size as I_i. As in the first stage, we collect all of the overlapping patches of I_i^l, and form $Y_i^l = [y_{i,l,1}, y_{i,l,2}, ...y_{i,l,\tilde{m}\tilde{n}}] \in R^{k_1 k_2 \times \tilde{m}\tilde{n}}$, where each $y_{i,l,j}$ denotes the j-th vectorized patch in I_i^l. Furthery, we collect all the l-th filters output and define

$$Y = [Y_i^1, Y_i^2, ..., Y_i^{L1}] \tag{3}$$

where L_1 is the num of filters in the first stage. After that, with the IOCA algorithm, the filters of the second stage B_l^2 are then obtained. We set the number of the filters in the second stage to L_2. For each input I_i^l of the second stage, one will output L_2 images of size $m \times n$, and each convolves I_i^l with B_l^2 for $l = 1, 2, 3, ..., L_2$

$$O_i^l = \{I_i^l * B_l^2\}_{l=1}^2 \tag{4}$$

The number of output images at the second stage is $L_1 \times L_2$. If more stages are helpful for us to extract suitable feature, we can repeat the above process to build more stages.

Output Stage (Hashing and Histograms). For the input image I_i, we get L_1 images with the process of the first stage, then repeat the process, we get $L_1 \times L_2$ images with the process of the second stage. In this section, we will reduce the number of images and extract features in an unsupervised manner.

For the images in O_i^l, we binarise these images and obtain $H(O_i^l)$, where $H()$ is a Heaviside step (like) function, whose value is one for positive entries and zero otherwise.

Around each pixel, we view the vector of L_2 binary bits as a decimal number. This converts the L_2 outputs in O_l^l back into a single integer-valued image:

$$T_i^l = \sum_{i=1}^{L2} 2^{l-1} H(I_i^l * B_l^2) \tag{5}$$

Hence, every pixel is an integer in the range $[0, 2^{L_2-1}]$. Besides, the value of the pixel is different from the common number. We treat the L_2 outputs equally and the order and weights are irrelevant, which means that the distance between 0 and 2^{L_2-1} equals to the distance between 0 and 1.

Each of the L_1 images $T_i^l, l = 1, 2, ..., L_1$, is partitioned into N blocks, for each blocks, we compute the histogram (with 2^{L_2} bins) of the decimal values and then concatenate all N blocks into one vector and denote as $hist(T_i^l)$. After that, we will concatenate all L_1 images into one vector:

$$f_i = [hist(T_i^1), hist(T_i^2), ..., hist(T_i^{L^1})] \tag{6}$$

The local blocks can be either overlapping or non-overlapping, it depends on the input data, we will walk through this in detail in an upcoming section.

The parameters of the IOCANet include the filter size k_1, k_2, the number of stages, and the block size for local histograms in the output layer. The number of filters in each stage L_1, L_2 can be decided by IOCA automatically.

3.2 Computational Complexity

In this section, we give you the computational complexity of IOCANet. We take two-stage IOCANet-2 as an example. For an input image, it has $\widetilde{m} \times \widetilde{n}$ patches and the patches size is $k_1 \times k_2$. Hence, in the first stage, the complexity of IOCA is $O(k_1 k_2 \widetilde{m} \widetilde{n} L_1)$. After that, the complexity of convolution operation is $O(L_1 k_1 k_2 \widetilde{m} \widetilde{n})$, therefore, the overall computational complexity of first stage is $O(L_1 k_1 k_2 \widetilde{m} \widetilde{n})$. In the second stage, the number of input images is L_1 and the computational complexity of second stage is $O(L_1 L_2 k_1 k_2 \widetilde{m} \widetilde{n})$. In the output stage, the complexity of binary hashing is $O(L_2 mn)$, and the naive histogram operation is of complexity $mnL_2 \frac{1}{1-BOR} log2$, where BOR is block overlap ratio and the range of BOR is 0 to 1. The overall computational complexity of IOCANet is

$$O(mnk_1 k_2 L_1 L_2 N)$$

where $m \times n$ is the size of input images, $k_1 \times k_2$ is the size of patches, L_1 is the number of filters in the first stages and L_2 is the number of filters in the second stages. N is the number of images in input to the network in an on-line way.

Beyond that, the space complexity of IOCANet is low. After we extract features from an input image, we throw the input image away to make room for the next image, which means that the space complexity of IOCANet is independent of the number of images in the data set. That is particulary suited for big data.

4   Experiment

In this section, we first explore how the proposed IOCANet performs in handwritten digit recognition tasks. Then we do the experiment on face recognition, which would explain the performance of IOCANet on different tasks. Here we introduce RandNet to illustrate the effectiveness of IOCANet. Compared with IOCANet, RandNet replaces the IOCA filters with completely random filters.

4.1   Digit Recognition on MNIST Datasets

The MNIST database (Mixed National Institute of Standards and Technology database) is a large database of handwritten digits that is commonly used for training various image processing systems. We use this database to measure the effectiveness of IOCANet on mass data.

Databases. The MNIST database of handwritten digits has a training set of 60,000 examples, and a test set of 10,000 examples. These examples are 28×28 grayscale images of handwritten digits 0–9.

Classifiers. A linear SVM classifier is used in this section.

Number of Filters. In this section, experiments will tell whether the number of filters decided by IOCANet is suitable. The block size in this experiment is 7×7, the block overlap ratio is 0.5, and the filter size is 7×7.

Firstly, for the one-stage network, we get the result that $L_1 = 8$ automatically. Regarding the two-stage networks, we can get the result that $L_1 = 8, L_2 = 16$.

After that, we remove the threshold $f(\frac{f}{d})$, with this threshold, we can determine whether a new filter is needed and get the number of filters automatically. Then we vary the number of filters in the one-stage networks IOCANet-1 from 2 to 12. Regarding the two-stage networks IOCANet-2, we set $L_1 = 8$ and change L_2 from 4 to 24. The result is shown in Fig. 3.

We can see that in IOCANet-1, $L_1 = 8$ is suitable for the reason that more filters will only bring little benefit, which is in tune with the number of filters determined automatically by our algorithm. Regarding the two-stage networks, $L_1 = 8, L_2 = 16$ is appropriate too. What's more, Fig. 3 illustrates that the number of filters decided by IOCANet also is reasonable for RandNet and PCANet, which validates the effectiveness of our algorithm.

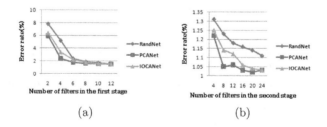

(a)   (b)

Fig. 3. Error rate of RandNet, PCANet and IOCANet on MNIST test set. For (a), we vary the number of filters in the first stage from 2 to 12. For (b), we set $L_1 = 8$ and vary the number of filters in the second stage from 2 to 12

Comparison with State of the Art. We compare IOCANet with RandNet, PCANet, ConvNet and other state of the art methods. Regarding the parameters of RandNet, we set the block size to 7×7. In PCANet, we set the filter size 7×7 and the number of PCA filters $L_1 = L_2 = 8$. The block overlap ratio is set to 0.5.

Table 1. Comparison of error rates(%) of the methods on MNIST test set

Methods	MNIST	Methods	MNIST
HSC [5]	0.77	RandNet-1	1.32
K-NN-SCM [6]	0.63	RandNet-2	0.63
K-NN-IDM [7]	0.54	PCANet-1	0.94
CDBN [8]	0.82	PCANet-2	0.66
Stochastic pooling ConvNet [9]	0.47	IOCANet-1	2.98
Conv. Maxout+Dropout [10]	0.45	IOCANet-2	0.92

The testing error rates of the various methods on MNIST are shown in Table 1. We know that the best result is 0.23% [4]. We see from the table that IOCANet is comparable with the state-of-the-art methods on this standard MNIST task. However, IOCANet does not need to set the number of filters on every stage, and if new training images input, PCANet needs to combine original training set and the new training set, then redo the experiment. For IOCANet, we only need to input the images one by one, then we can get the feature and do the classification.

4.2 Face Recognition on ORL Dataset

In this section, we do experiment on ORL dataset to explore how IOCANet performs in face verification task. And for the reason that ORL dataset has 400 images, we use this dataset to check the performance of IOCANet on small amount of data.

Databases. ORL dataset contains 40 people and per person has 10 images. The image size is 112×92. All the images are frontal and slight tilt of the head. For every person, we randomly choose 8 images as training images and the remaining images as testing images.

Classifiers. A nearest neighbor (NN) classifier is employed in this section. Linear SVM are not selected because every person only has few images, which may not be suitable for Linear SVM classifier.

Number of Filters. The effectiveness of the number of filters decided by IOCANet is studied here. The filter size of the network is 17×17. The block size is 19×19 and the block overlap ratio is 0.

For one stage network IOCANet-1, with out algorithm, we can get the number of filters in the first stage $L_1 = 8$. Regarding the two-stage networks, we can get that $L_1 = 8, L_2 = 18$.

After that, we vary number of filters in the first stage L_1 from 2 to 12. Regarding two stage network IOCANet-2, we set $L_1 = 8$, change L_2 from 4 to

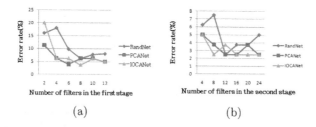

Fig. 4. Error rates of RandNet, PCANet and IOCANet on ORL test set. For (a), we vary the number of filters in the first stage from 2 to 12. For (b), we set $L_1 = 8$ and vary the number of filters in the second stage from 4 to 24

24. The result is shown in Fig. 4. We can see that $L_1 = 8$ is suitable for IOCANet-1, which equals the number of filters decided by our method. For IOCANet-2, $L_1 = 8, L_2 = 18$ be slightly more than the best result, but it still is appropriate for the reason that it has almost no effect on the performance of IOCANet.

Comparison with State of the Art. We compare IOCANet with RandNet and PCANet. We set the parameters of PCANet to the filter size 17×17, the number of filters $L_1 = 8, L_2 = 12$ and 19×19 block size. The filters size of IOCANet is 17×17. Besides, the block size of IOCANet is 19×19.

The performances of all methods are given in Table 2. One can observe that PCANet and IOCANet achieve similar result, but both PCANet and IOCANet perform better than RandNet. What's more, two-stages network also performs better than one-stage network.

Table 2. Comparison of error rates(%) of the methods on ORL test set

Methods	Orl	Methods	Orl
RandNet-1	6.25	PCANet-2	2.5
RandNet-2	2.5	IOCANet-1	3.75
PCANet-1	5	IOCANet-2	2.5

5   Conclusion

In this paper, we proposed an incremental deep learning network for online unsupervised feature extraction – IOCANet. IOCANet is a simple deep learning network, it only has few parameters must be given to and some of parameters can be decided by itself. When the parameters are set, this algorithm is simple and effective. IOCANet has low time complexity, which means that IOCA has few limits in applications and has the potential to be a universal approach. What's more, IOCANet is able to keep learning from on-line and incremental data, which means that if new training data input, IOCANet can extract features directly. For classical feature extraction algorithms such as ConvNet, they need to combine original training set and the new training set, then redo the training process, which wastes large amount of computing resources. Besides, both mass data and small amount of data are suitable for IOCANet.

The experiments demonstrate that IOCANet can achieve reasonable result for digit recognition and face recognition. Although the performance of the other methods sometimes is slightly better in certain aspect, IOCANet fulfills simple architecture, reasonable classification result and low time complexity. When the learning is online and incremental, the performance of IOCA is outstanding.

Acknowledgments. This work is supported in part by the National Science Foundation of China under Grant Nos. (61373130, 61375064, 61373001), and Jiangsu NSF grant (BK20141319).

References

1. Kavukcuoglu, K., Sermanet, P., Boureau, Y.L., et al.: Learning convolutional feature hierarchies for visual recognition. In: International Conference on Neural Information Processing Systems, Vancouver, British Columbia, Canada, pp. 1090–1098. Curran Associates Inc. (2010)
2. Tao, Z., Ye, X., Furao, S., et al.: An online incremental orthogonal component analysis method for dimensionality reduction. Neural Netw. **85**, 33–50 (2016)
3. Chan, T.H., Jia, K., Gao, S., et al.: PCANet: a simple deep learning baseline for image classification? IEEE Trans. Image Process. **24**(12), 5017–5032 (2015). A Publication of the IEEE Signal Processing Society
4. Dan, C., Meier, U., Schmidhuber, J.: Multi-column deep neural networks for image classification. In: IEEE Conference on Computer Vision and Pattern Recognition, pp. 3642–3649. IEEE Computer Society (2012)
5. Yu, K., Lin, Y., Lafferty, J.: Learning image representations from the pixel level via hierarchical sparse coding. In: IEEE Conference on Computer Vision and Pattern Recognition, pp. 1713–1720. IEEE Computer Society (2011)
6. Salve, S.G., Jondhale, K.C.: Shape matching and object recognition using shape contexts. In: IEEE International Conference on Computer Science and Information Technology, pp. 471–474. IEEE (2010)
7. Keysers, D., Deselaers, T., Gollan, C., et al.: Deformation models for image recognition. IEEE Trans. Pattern Anal. Mach. Intell. **29**, 1422–1435 (2007)
8. Lee, H., Grosse, R., Ranganath, R., et al.: Convolutional deep belief networks for scalable unsupervised learning of hierarchical representations. In: International Conference on Machine Learning, pp. 609–616. ACM (2009)
9. Zeiler, M.D., Fergus, R.: Stochastic Pooling for Regularization of Deep Convolutional Neural Networks. Eprint Arxiv (2013)
10. Goodfellow, I.J., Wardefarley, D., Mirza, M., et al.: Maxout networks. Comput. Sci. **28**, 1319–1327 (2013)

Compressing Low Precision Deep Neural Networks Using Sparsity-Induced Regularization in Ternary Networks

Julian Faraone[1,2]($\boxtimes$), Nicholas Fraser[1,2], Giulio Gambardella[2], Michaela Blott[2], and Philip H.W.Leong[1]

[1] School of Electrical and Information Engineering,
The University of Sydney, Sydney, Australia
julian.faraone@sydney.edu.au
[2] Xilinx Research Labs, Dublin, Ireland

Abstract. A low precision deep neural network training technique for producing sparse, ternary neural networks is presented. The technique incorporates hardware implementation costs during training to achieve significant model compression for inference. Training involves three stages: network training using L2 regularization and a quantization threshold regularizer, quantization pruning, and finally retraining. Resulting networks achieve improved accuracy, reduced memory footprint and reduced computational complexity compared with conventional methods, on MNIST and CIFAR10 datasets. Our networks are up to 98% sparse and 5 & 11 times smaller than equivalent binary and ternary models, translating to significant resource and speed benefits for hardware implementations.

Keywords: Deep Neural Networks · Ternary Neural Network · Low-precision · Pruning · Sparsity · Compression

1 Introduction

Deep Neural Networks (DNNs) have revolutionized a wide range of research fields including computer vision [1] and natural language processing [2]. However, along with excellent prediction capabilities, the state-of-the-art architectures are both computationally and memory intensive due to their vast number of model parameters. Ultra-low precision DNNs replace most floating point arithmetic with bitwise or addition operations which greatly reduces computational complexity and power consumption. These representations also significantly reduce hardware complexity and memory bandwidth, allowing implementations of state-of-the-art architectures on constrained hardware environments. As a result, there's been a growing interest in specialized hardware solutions for ultra-low precision DNNs and specifically, Binarized Neural Networks (BNNs) [3,4], and Ternary Neural Networks (TNNs) [5]. These networks constrain either weights alone or

© Springer International Publishing AG 2017
D. Liu et al. (Eds.): ICONIP 2017, Part II, LNCS 10635, pp. 393–404, 2017.
https://doi.org/10.1007/978-3-319-70096-0_41

weights and activations, leading to extremely efficient hardware implementations. In the present work, we enhance the inherent sparsity of TNNs whilst maintaining the advantages of multiplierless computations. We use similar Convolutional Neural Networks (CNNs) to [6] for CIFAR10 classification and achieve similar accuracies, although their network has a full precision 1st layer compared to our ternary weights. Regularization techniques and reduced precision weight representations have been extensively studied for compression, acceleration and power minimization. Many efforts have concentrated on building efficient computational structures from floating point networks through sparse weight representations and quantization [7,8]. Such networks still require fixed-point multiply-accumulate operations which limits power savings and speed. Instead of considering sparsity and reduced precision separately, we explore sparse TNNs which don't require multiplies in any layers. Pruning the fully connected layers of BNNs and TNNs was proposed in [9] to reduce the number of model parameters for efficient hardware implementations. We prune all layers and focus on inference acceleration. With recent breakthroughs in low precision deep learning, specialized hardware solutions have been increasingly investigated. FINN implements scalable BNN accelerators on FPGAs [10] and we use this framework to explore performance advantages of sparse TNNs.

In this paper we propose a three-stage training approach for TNNs which is able to reduce hardware costs for inference. Firstly, the network is trained using L2 regularization and a quantization threshold regularizer, secondly we use quantization pruning whereby the sparsity pruning threshold is the same as the quantization threshold and thirdly we retrain the network. During training, the network learns in a sparse environment. This has significant benefits as we can determine the sensitivity of the weights to sparsity regularizers, i.e. measure the sensitivity of weights in different layers and advantageously utilize a quantization pruning method. The contributions of this paper are thus as follows:

- The first reported low-precision training method which minimizes hardware costs as part of the objective function. This uses a quantization threshold regularizer and L2 regularization to encourage sparsity during training.
- A layer-based quantization pruning technique which utilizes sparsity information obtained during training.
- A quantitative comparison of our proposed sparse TNN with state-of-the-art multiplierless networks in terms of accuracy, memory footprint, computational requirements and hardware implementation costs.
- We achieve between 2 and 11x compression. For memory bound hardware architectures, this would directly translate into speed-up.

2   Sparse TNN Training

The key idea in this work is to introduce sparsity in TNN weight representations through regularization. TNN training consists of real-valued weight parameters, w_r, which are quantized deterministically to w_q using a quantization threshold, η.

$$w_q = \begin{cases} 1 & \text{if} & w_r > \eta \\ 0 & \text{if} & -\eta \leq w_r \leq \eta \\ -1 & \text{if} & w_r < -\eta \end{cases} \tag{1}$$

For the forward path, w_q is computed and used for inference. For the backward path, the gradients are computed with w_q and parameter updates are then applied to w_r. In training DNNs, generally many values for w_r can achieve the same training loss and regularization techniques incorporate a preference for certain weight representations. We use several regularization techniques to minimize the number of nonzero parameters and induce sparsity. Our regularization scheme considers the hardware costs not only during the fine-tuning stage, but also during training.

Quantization Threshold Regularization. Deterministic rounding requires partitioning the w_r weight space by setting a threshold hyperparameter η. Typically different values for η are set for different assumptions made on w_r. To uniformly partition the weight space $\eta = 0.33$ [9] or to minimize quantization error $\eta = 0.5$. In our case we increase η to make 0's consume a large portion of the weight space (upto 95%) which induces a similar sparsity effect to L1 regularization. However, L1 regularization has a continous shrinkage effect which induces sparsity amongst all w_r but not necessarily w_q. Increasing the threshold on the other hand, induces sparsity directly amongst w_q and parameter updates for w_r are either penalized or rewarded based purely on the gradients. An example of the regularization effect is shown in Fig. 1(a). By partitioning the weight space by 90%, the network is initialized with high sparsity and takes longer to converge than training with a uniformly distributed weight space.

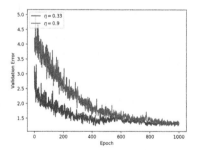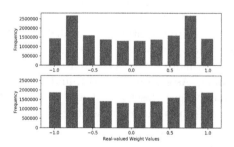

Fig. 1. (a)Validation error convergence on MNIST. (b) Weight distribution for w_r for MLP Layer in MNIST training. With L2 regularization (top) and without (bottom), for $\eta = 0.9$.

L2 Regularization. In traditional TNN training the cost function C can be represented as the average loss L_i over all training examples n:

$$C(w_q) = \frac{1}{n} \sum_{i=1}^{n} L_i(w_q) \tag{2}$$

L2 regularization has the property of penalizing peaky weights to generate a more diffused set of weights. We add L2 regularization, as a function of the quantized weights, directly into the cost function to penalize nonzeros and induce sparsity:

$$C(w_q) = \underbrace{\frac{1}{n} \sum_{i=1}^{n} L_i(w_q)}_{\text{data loss}} + \underbrace{\lambda R(w_q)}_{\text{regularization loss}} \tag{3}$$

where the regularization term is the quadtratic penalty over all parameters,

$$R(w_q) = \frac{1}{2} w_q^2 \tag{4}$$

and the gradient contribution from the regularization term becomes:

$$\frac{dC(w_q)}{dR(w_q)} = \lambda w_q \tag{5}$$

where λ is the regularization strength hyperparameter. With L2 regularization, each epoch becomes a greedy search to reduce hardware costs as only the corresponding w_r for each nonzero in w_q is penalized by λ. From (5) and (1) it is evident the regularization term will only effect the corresponding parameter updates on w_r for nonzero w_q. This is desirable when used in conjunction with a large η as peaky weights (close -1 and 1 in this case) are more likely to be pulled below the threshold for a given regularization strength. Also, it avoids L2 regularization from continually penalizing weights, making them stuck at low values. This allows for weight values which are penalized in earlier training epochs, to then be more easily recovered through parameter updates if required later in training. As seen in Fig. 1(b), under L2 regularization the frequency shrinks for weight values closer to -1 and 1. It is also evident that many weights clump around values closer to the threshold of 0.9.

Quantization Pruning. L2 and threshold regularization achieve a certain sparsity before accuracy starts to degrade. This is addressed via quantization pruning by utilizing weight sensitivity information after the initial training phase and eliminating a subset of weights in w_r which all quantize to zero. We then retrain the network, using a masking vector w_m which sets the pruned weights to zero:

$$w_m = \begin{cases} 1 & \text{if} \quad w_r < -\sigma \\ 0 & \text{if} \quad -\sigma \leq w_r \leq \sigma \\ 1 & \text{if} \quad w_r > \sigma \end{cases} \tag{6}$$

In sensitivity pruning, the sparsity hyperparameter σ is optimized by setting different sparsities for different layers. Depending on the type and order of layer, they have a different sensitivity to pruning. In our method, by forcing sparsity through regularization during training, the gradient descent minimization process converges on the inherent sparsity sensitivity of each layer. We then utilize the ratio of zeros in each layer from the first training phase by pruning only w_r below or equal to the quantization threshold.

$$\sigma \leq \eta \tag{7}$$

Weight initialization for retraining then becomes the elementwise multiplication w_{r_2}.

$$w_{r_2} = w_{r_1} \odot w_m \tag{8}$$

For retraining, w_{r_2} is updated but the pruned weights are fixed at zero. Also, the threshold is set to the same value as in the initial training phase.

Weight Representations. When implementing TNNs for inference on computer hardware, the real valued weights in w_r are discarded and only w_q is stored. In order to demonstrate the benefits of the sparse nature of these networks, we use two different compression techniques which can be utilized for different embedded device and specialized hardware applications depending on memory and resource requirements. Due to the high data regularity of the weight representations, storing all the ternary weights as 2-bits is not necessary. To conveniently store the unstructured sparse weight values, we use two compression methods. The first is Run Length Encoding (RLE), which stores only the index differences between each nonzero and also a sign bit which defines the type of operation. In our second method we use Huffman Coding (HC) on the index differences to assign variable length codewords whereby the most frequently occurring indexes are represented with shorter length codes and vice versa. HC has higher complexity for its decoder implementation and a higher compression rate than RLE.

Algorithm. Algorithm 1 is the compression process and consists of four parts. Part (1) represents typical TNN training and additionally requires hyperparameters λ and η to be set as in Algorithm 2. In Part (2) the masking vector is computed and used for retraining in Part (3). After the network is trained, the real-valued weights are discarded and the quantized weights are encoded for Part (4). Outputs and inputs for each layer are represented by y and x respectively; b is the bias term (if applicable); L is the learning rate; and CGU is compute gradient updates.

Algorithm 1	Algorithm 2
1. Train	**-Forward Pass:**
Set λ and η for sparsity requirements and implement Algorithm 2	**for** each weight layer p **do** $w_{q_p} = Q(w_{r_{1_p}})$ **with threshold** η
2. Prune	**end for**
Compute w_m **with** $\sigma = \eta$	**for** each layer i in range(1,N) **do**
3. Retrain	Compute y_i **with** w_q, x_i
Keep λ and η the same	**end for**
Repeat Step 1. **with** $w_{r_2} = w_{r_1} \odot w_m$ and λ, η	**-Backward Pass:**
4. Encode	Compute cost: $C(w_q)$ **with** y_N, λ
Apply HC or RLE on resulting w_q	**for** each weight layer j **do**
	CGU: $g_1 = \dfrac{dC(w_{q_j})}{dw_{q_j}} + \lambda w_{q_j}$
	CGU: $g_2 = \dfrac{dC(w_{q_j})}{db_j}$
	Updates: $w_{r_{1_j}} = w_{r_{1_j}} - Lg_1$ $b_j = b_j - Lg_2$
	end for

3 Sparsity and Networks

We evaluate our training methods on two image classification benchmarks, MNIST and CIFAR10. We apply our training technique and compare directly against results from BinaryConnect [3] and BinaryNet [4]. BinaryConnect uses floating point ReLu activation functions and BinaryNet uses binary activation functions. Their results are represented in Figs. 3 and 5 as 'model-a-b' where a is the weight bitwidth and b is the activation bitwidth (bitwidth = 32 is for floating point, bitwidth = 1 is for binary and bitwidth = 2 is for ternary equivalents of these architectures with a uniformly distributed weight space). Our results are reported as TNN with resulting sizes represented as x/y which represents the sizes after encoding in RLE/HC respectively. For all results, we report the number of weight parameters (Params) in millions, percentage of zero-valued parameters, the error-rate and size of the network in megabytes (MB). In all our models we used only one pruning iteration except for the MLP with floating point activations for which we used two iterations.

MNIST. The MNIST dataset consist of 70k 28×28 images of grey-scale handwritten digits. The networks used for classification consist of 3 hidden layers of 4096 neurons for the network with binary activations and 1024 neurons for the network with floating point activations. We train the network for 1000 epochs and choose the network which produces the best validation error rate. We first analyse the effect of quantization pruning on the MNIST dataset for different threshold settings. No L2 regularization is used in these numbers in order to focus on the effect of different pruning thresholds. Setting a higher threshold allows for more aggressive pruning at the threshold. The results are displayed in

Fig. 2 and although other threshold settings achieve similar accuracies, setting both $\eta = \sigma = 0.9$ achieves significantly more sparsity. At this setting we can prune 80% of weights without pruning away any nonzeros. It is evident that pruning nonzeros impinges on the network performance and hence the quantization threshold is an effective indicator for which weights can be pruned. Pruning at a lower sparsity threshold maintains accuracy benefits, although results in more nonzeros and to highly sparsify the network, it would have to be repeatedly pruned. This could require several iterations and take days/weeks as each training iteration takes days itself. The results are displayed in Fig. 3. Using the network with binary activations produces up to 97.6% sparsity and over 5× compression over its binarized network (BNet) with better accuracy and approximately 11× its ternary network with the same accuracy. The network with a floating point activation function, achieves 92.8% sparsity and 3.5× compression over its binarized equivalent network. For these networks we used $\eta = 0.9$.

η	σ	Pruned	Error-rate	Nonzeros
0.9	0.95	91%	1.08	1,220,468
0.9	**0.9**	**80%**	**0.92**	**1,863,521**
0.9	0.65	50%	0.96	3,826,912
0.7	0.8	76%	0.98	3,595,898
0.7	0.7	64%	0.91	5,243,764
0.7	0.58	50%	0.92	6,863,798
0.5	0.9	89%	1.14	2,448,073
0.5	0.75	74%	1.04	5,416,539
0.5	0.5	74%	0.98	10,396,476

Fig. 2. Quantization pruning for TNN (Binary Activations) on MNIST, without L2 regularization

Model	Params	Zeros	Error-rate	Size (MB)
MLP-2-1	36.4	54%	0.92	9.12
MLP-1-1	36.4	0%	0.96	4.56
TNN	36.4	97.6%	0.93	0.83/1.59
MLP-2-32	2.91	34%	1.23	0.72
MLP-1-32	2.91	0%	1.29	0.36
TNN	2.91	92.8%	1.22	0.07/0.11

Fig. 3. Classification accuracies for Sparse TNNs for MLPs on MNIST with L2 regularization and pruning

CIFAR10. The CIFAR10 dataset is benchmark dataset consisting of 32×32 colour images with 10 categories. We use a VGG-derivative architecture inspired by BinaryConnect [3]. From Fig. 5, we see that there is an improvement in accuracy and/or compression for both networks in contrast to their binarized and ternary equivalents. The convolutional layers are less robust to the threshold regularizer and hence we set a lower value for the convolutional layers $\eta_1 = 0.8$ and a higher value for the fully connected layer $\eta_2 = 0.9$. We show the accuracy and sparsity relationship in Fig. 4(a) for varying thresholds and show that threshold regularization improves accuracy. The leftmost point is the fully dense binarized network where $\eta = 0$ and as we introduce the threshold regularization, the error-rate drops by up to 1.4% as the sparsity is increased. In Fig. 4(b), we plot the percentage of nonzeros for each layer in the CNN for varying values of the threshold regularizer. By increasing the threshold, the robustness of each layer under sparsity becomes more prominent. For most of the networks,

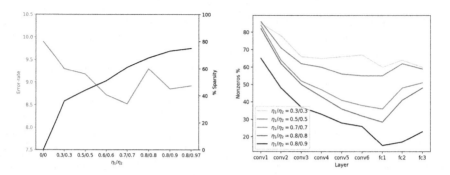

Fig. 4. (a) Accuracy vs Sparsity for CIFAR10 with varying η, without pruning. (b) Per Layer Sparsity for different threshold values on CIFAR10, no regularization or pruning

Model	Params	Zeros	Error-rate	Size (MB)
VGG-2-1	14.02	65%	11.2	3.52
VGG-1-1	14.02	0%	11.4	1.76
TNN	14.02	92.3%	10.8	0.88/1.05
VGG-2-32	14.02	35%	9.2	3.52
VGG-1-32	14.02	0%	9.9	1.76
TNN	14.02	90.1%	9.6	0.96/1.22

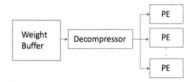

Fig. 5. Classification accuracies for Sparse TNNs for CNNs on CIFAR10 with L2 regularization and pruning

Fig. 6. Diagram of decompressor feeding multiple processing elements with data reuse

the first two convolutional layers are the most sensitive to sparsity and consist of around 80% nonzeros and the last convolutional and first fully connected layers are the least sensitive. These are similar conclusions to [8] who pruned each layer independantly to determine their sparsity sensitivity. In our case, the network learns these sensitivities by training in sparse environments. This is advantageous as efficient sparsity parameters are determined for any layer type or order and don't require a hyperparameter search. Varying the threshold provides sensitivity information for the sparsity of each layer and quantization pruning takes advantage of this by pruning each layer according to the threshold and hence these ratios.

4   Hardware Implications of Sparse TNNs

In this section, we explore the hardware implications of implementing TNNs with unstructured sparse data representations. Storing the weights in a compressed format, requires a decompressor which incurs some overheads on hardware designs. A fully parallel architecture would require a decompressor for every weight in the convolution or fully connected layer and decompressors in this case would consume significant amounts of resources. For sparse TNNs, we can take advantage of data reuse patterns which are present within convolution layers and fully connected layers (when batching is applied) to increase the ratio of processing elements (PEs) to decoders. When the sparsity of these networks is taken into consideration, the number of *effective operations* (discussed later in this Section) increases the potential performance of TNNs to values well beyond those of BNNs. For conventional computing platforms (e.g., CPUs and GPUs), the main benefit of sparsity and compression is the increase in operational intensity that is achieved for a particular layer. Sequential processors, (such as CPUs) will also be able to benefit from the reduction in required operations per layer, as a result of the high sparsity of TNNs. For parallel processors, (such as GPUs, FPGAs and ASICs) it is a lot more difficult to take advantage of this benefit due to the irregular data access patterns. We describe a hardware decompressor, a corresponding parallel architecture suitable for FPGAs and the potential performance of that architecture in terms of effective operations per second.

Hardware Decompressor. Our proposed hardware decompressor iterates through a list of weights, stored in a sign–magnitude form in on-chip memory. In each cycle, the hardware decompressor outputs the complement of the sign bit to represent the weight value and adds the magnitude value to an internal counter, which is used to generate the address of the value to be accessed from the input vector. The RLE decoder consists of a counter which controls the address of the input to feed into the PE for computation. The resource and performance estimates given by Vivado HLS of the resultant hardware description are that the design can produce an address and a weight every cycle at 250 MHz while using 112 LUT resources on the FPGA.

A Sparse TNN Accelerator. Three types of low precision networks are described in this paper: (1) networks with binary activations (VGG/MLP-1/2-1); and (2) networks with floating point activations (VGG/MLP-1/2-32). For all networks, the predominant calculations for inference are multiply accumulate operations (MACs). For type (1) networks, this corresponds to XNOR-popcount operations [4], where a popcount is the number of set bits in a word. For type (2) networks, this corresponds to an XNOR operation on the sign bit of a floating point value, followed by a floating point accumulate.

Accelerator Architecture. Our proposed accelerator architecture is based on that generated by FINN [10]. In particular, we propose a design which has processing engines with a similar datapath to FINN. To compute the input-weight matrix in specialized hardware implementations, typically a series or array of PEs are used to receive input data and a weight value to perform the multiply accumulate operations, as required for the datatype. For the compressive format described in Sect. 2, these implementations require a decompressor between the weight matrix and the PE as represented in Fig. 6. For type (1), we estimate resource usage on the roofline given by [10], which is reported to have an average cost of 5 LUTs for both an XNOR and popcount operation.[1] For type (2), we estimate the resource usage by instantiating a Xilinx Floating Point 7.1 IP core addition module. The peak throughput numbers are what can be achieved if 70% of the LUTs or 100% of the DSPs are used on the target device, a Xilinx KU115 running at 250 MHz. These are 46.4 TOPs for type (1) and 1.3 TOPs for type (2). The total KU115 resources are 663k LUTs and 5,520 DSPs.

Exploiting Sparsity Through Data Reuse. Convolutional layers require many operations on different input pixels to the same weight value. Hence, we can utilize data re-use optimizations [11] to instantiate a decompressor for a specific weight and calculate several MAC operations on different input pixels. This greatly reduces the average resource usage of the decompressor per operation. Similar optimizations can be utilized for the fully connected layers, whereby batching can be applied to allow a single weight to calculate several MAC operations across multiple input vectors.

Let us introduce a data re-use factor, R, which denotes the total amount of data re-use available in a particular layer. For fully connected layers, $R = B$, where B is the batch size. For convolutional layers, $R = B \times P$, where P is the number of output pixels in the output image. Furthermore, our RLE decoder allows us to easily avoid calculating any zero valued weights. In comparison to the benchmark BNNs, which have strictly dense weights, only the non-zero weight computations need to be calculated. Our sparsity factor, then becomes a multiplier which significantly reduces our cost per operations and hence the regularization techniques discussed in the paper directly minimize hardware costs during training. To this end, we introduce an *effective operation* cost, given by: $C_e = \gamma * (C_{op} + C_d/R)$, where γ is ratio of non-zero weight values to total weights in the layer, C_{op} is the proportion of the KU115 which is utilised by a single operation and C_d is the proportion of the KU115 which is utilised by the decoder. [2] An *effective throughput* can then be calculated as: $T_e = 1/C_e * 250$MHz. Figures 7(a) and (b) show the effective throughput of type (1) & (2) networks respectively, while varying γ and R. The horizontal lines represent the benchmark BNN networks, MLP and VGG (VGG is labelled as CNN in figures) from the results in Figs. 3 and 5 and the other percentages represent networks of the same type with varying sparsities. Note that these are theoretical peak values and further overheads are likely for all datapoints when they are implemented in a real system. For type (2), a lower sparsity factor is required to improve on the benchmark throughput as these operations are more expensive and hence every zero weight has a greater hardware benefit than for the type (1).

---

[1] FINN quotes 2.5 LUTs per operation, which is multiplied by 2 to get LUTs/per MAC.

[2] Assuming 70% of the LUTs and 100% of the DSPs can be utilised for compute.

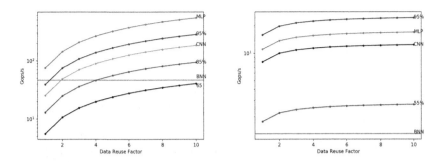

Fig. 7. (a) Effective throughput: BNNs vs TNNs (type 3) while varying γ and R. (b) Effective throughput: BNNs vs TNNs (type 1) while varying γ and R. Note: VGG is labelled as CNN.

5   Conclusion and Future Work

This paper contributes to the applicability of Deep Neural Networks on embedded devices and specialized hardware. We introduce a TNN training method which uses a quantization threshold hyperparameter, complemented by L2 regularization and quantization pruning to substantially reduce the memory requirements and computational complexity. This was shown using different network topologies on the MNIST and CIFAR10 benchmarks. Future work in the area will look into extending this quantization technique to other low precision networks for more difficult datasets, improving accuracy whilst maintaining sparsity and also sparse TNN hardware accelerator designs.

Acknowledgements. This research was partly supported under the Australian Research Councils Linkage Projects funding scheme (project number LP130101034) and Zomojo Pty Ltd.

References

1. Simonyan, K., Zisserman, A.: Very deep convolutional networks for large-scale image recognition (2014)
2. Luong, M.-T., Pham, H., Manning, C.D.: Effective approaches to attention-based neural machine translation (2015)
3. Courbariaux, M., Bengio, Y., David, J.-P.: Binaryconnect: training deep neural networks with binary weights during propagations (2015)
4. Courbariaux, M., Bengio, Y.: Binarynet: training deep neural networks with weights and activations constrained to +1 or −1 (2016)
5. Li, F., Liu, B.: Ternary weight networks (2016)
6. Venkatesh, G., Nurvitadhi, E., Marr, D.: Accelerating deep convolutional networks using low-precision and sparsity (2016)
7. Han, S., Mao, H., Dally, W.J.: Deep compression: compressing deep neural networks with pruning, trained quantization and Huffman coding. In: International Conference on Learning Representations (2015)

8. Han, S., Pool, J., Tran, J., Dally, W.: Learning both weights and connections for efficient neural network. In: Advances in Neural Information Processing Systems (NIPS), pp. 1135–1143 (2015)
9. Ardakani, A., Condo, C., Gross, W.J.: Sparsely-connected neural networks: towards efficient VLSI implementation of deep neural networks (2016)
10. Umuroglu, Y., Fraser, N.J., Gambardella, G., Blott, M., Leong, P.H.W, Jahre, M., Vissers, K.A.: FINN: a framework for fast, scalable binarized neural network inference (2016)
11. Fraser, N.J., Umuroglu, Y., Gambardella, G., Blott, M., Leong, P.H.W., Jahre, M., Vissers, K.A.: Scaling binarized neural networks on reconfigurable logic (2017)

A Feature Learning Approach for Image Retrieval

Junfeng Yao[1], Yao Yu[1], Yukai Deng[1], and Changyin Sun[2(✉)]

[1] School of Automation and Electrical Engineering,
University of Science and Technology Beijing, Beijing 100083, China
[2] School of Automation, Southeast University, Naijing 210096, China
cysun@seu.edu.cn

Abstract. Extraction of effective image features is the key to the content-based image retrieval task. Recently, deep convolutional neural networks have been widely used in learning image features and have achieved top results. Based on CNNs, metric learning methods like contrastive loss and triplet loss have been proved effective in learning discriminative image features. In this paper, we propose a new supervised signal to train convolutional neural networks. This step could ensure that the features obtained are well differentiated in space, which is very suitable for image retrieval task. We give an example on MNIST to illustrate the intent of this loss function. Also, we evaluate our method on two datasets including CUB-200-2011, CARS196. The experimental results show that the retrieval effect is fairly good on this two datasets. Besides, our loss function is much easier to implement and train.

Keywords: Image retrieval · Convolutional neural networks · Metric learning

1 Introduction

How to judge the similarity between images is a key to many visual problems. For content-based image retrieval task, we usually first extract image features, then calculate distances of those features to determine how similar they are, finally according to the similarity of images return search results. Therefore, extracting features with high robustness is the key to improve the retrieval performance. Previously, handcrafted features such as [1, 2] were often used. These handcrafted features are usually very complex and not robust enough. Recently, with the development of deep learning, some state of the art deep convolution neural networks, such as [3–5], have been proved to have excellent feature extraction capabilities. In general, the traditional classification of convolutional neural networks could already be used to extract image features, but it is not good enough. For specific tasks, many researchers design different supervised signals to make the features learned from networks fit the task better. In 2015 Bell et al. used contrastive loss [6] to train convolutional neural networks for visual search in interior design. In the same year, FaceNet [7] used triplet loss method to train the network for face classification. After that, Song et al. [8] used a Lifted Structured loss to train the network for image retrieval. These supervised signals, or loss functions, have achieved very good results and some commonly used supervised

D. Liu et al. (Eds.): ICONIP 2017, Part II, LNCS 10635, pp. 405–412, 2017.
https://doi.org/10.1007/978-3-319-70096-0_42

signals have been widely used in different fields, including face recognition, image retrieval etc.

However, for some reasons, the methods mentioned above are more difficult to train than traditional classification networks. The above loss functions, in general, require that in a mini batch, the features of the samples of the same class are brought together, and the features of samples of different classes are far apart. Although the definitions of those loss functions are simple, but for large data sets, the conflict among each batch would increase during the process of stochastic gradient descent. Therefore, the network would be easy to diverge in training. An important measure to solve the problem is to pick appropriate sample pairs or triples for each batch, which increases the complexity of training. Besides, there are no specific rules on how to choose sample pairs and triples, which also puzzles other researchers who want to use these methods. Nowadays, researchers [9–11] often add some supervised signal based on the classification network. On the one hand, a classification network could guarantee the stability of training. On the other hand, additional supervised signal could also optimize the classification loss for specific tasks. This is also the design direction of this paper. In 2016, [12] designed center loss when training classification network in the face recognition task, and the supervised signal was simple and effective which also inspired the design of the loss function in this paper. Based on the above research, the main works of our paper are as follows:

We design a new supervised signal suitable for image retrieval tasks. With the joint supervision of softmax loss and our supervised signal, the highly discriminative features could be obtained.

We show this loss is very easy to implement and train.

We evaluate our method on two datasets. The experimental results show that the retrieval effect is fairly good.

1.1 Our Loss Function

For a given network, the softmax loss could be presented as follows:

$$L_s = -\sum_{i=1}^m log \frac{e^{W_{y_i}^T x_i + b_{y_i}}}{\sum_{j=1}^n e^{W_j^T x_i + b_j}} \tag{1}$$

In Eq. 1, $x_i \in \mathbb{R}^d$ denotes the ith deep feature, belonging to the y_i th class. d is the feature dimension. $W_j \in \mathbb{R}^d$ denotes the jth column of the weights $W \in \mathbb{R}^d$ in the last fully connected layer and $b \in \mathbb{R}^n$ is the bias term. The size of the mini-batch and the number of the class is m and n, respectively.

From experiments in [12], we know that under the supervision of softmax, the deeply learned features are separable but not discriminative enough. In order to develop an effective loss function to improve the discriminative power of the deeply learned features, we add two different supervised signals to the softmax loss. As shown in Fig. 1, our loss function consists of three parts, including L_s part, L_c part, and L_m part.

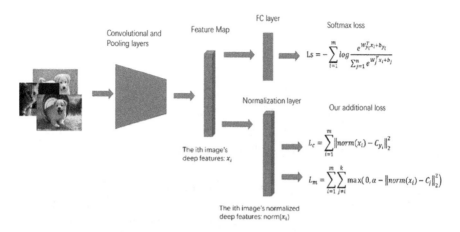

Fig. 1. Composition of our loss function

For L_c part, the part of loss is calculated as Eq. 2:

$$L_c = \frac{1}{2} \sum_{i=1}^{m} \left\| norm(x_i) - C_{y_i} \right\|_2^2 \tag{2}$$

The $x_i \in \mathbb{R}^d$ denotes the ith deep feature, and $norm(x_i)$ means that the feature x_i is normalized before we calculate the L_c part. The $C_{y_i} \in \mathbb{R}^d$ denotes the y_i th class center of deep features. Ideally, in each iteration we need to calculate the whole training set to get the centers of every class, which is inefficient and even impractical. [12] has given a solution that centers are updated based on mini-batch rather than the whole training set. The L_c part here is designed to bring the normalized features of samples of same class in a mini batch together which is directly shown in Eq. 2

For L_m part, the part of loss is calculated as Eq. 3:

$$L_m = \frac{1}{2} \sum_{i=1}^{m} \sum_{j \neq y_i}^{n} \max\left(0, \alpha - \left\| norm(x_i) - C_j \right\|_2^2\right) \tag{3}$$

The n denotes the number of the classes and the C_j denotes the jth center. The α is a parameter set by us to control the distance boundary. As we can see from Eq. 2, if a sample in a mini batch is close to the center it does not belong to and the distance between them is smaller than α, this sample would contribute loss for L_m. Therefore, L_m part here is designed to separate the features of samples of different classes in a mini batch away from each other.

Here we should notice two points. The first one is that the L_c part and L_m part themselves are unstable just like the contrastive loss and triplet loss, but combined with softmax loss, they would play a much better role. The second one is we do not need to select the training samples for every mini batch which is quiet common when the loss is contrastive loss or triplet loss. In other words, the training process is as easy as classification networks and very stable due to the control of softmax loss.

The whole loss is formulated as Eq. 4:

$$L = L_s + \lambda_1 L_c + \lambda_2 L_m$$
$$= -\frac{1}{m}\sum_{i=1}^{m} log \frac{e^{W_{y_i}^T x_i + b_{y_i}}}{\sum_{j=1}^{n} e^{W_j^T x_i + b_j}}$$
$$+ \lambda_1 \frac{1}{2m}\sum_{i=1}^{m} \left\| norm(x_i) - C_{y_i} \right\|_2^2$$
$$+ \lambda_2 \frac{1}{2m}\sum_{i=1}^{m}\sum_{j \neq y_i}^{n} \max\left(0, \alpha - \left\| norm(x_i) - C_j \right\|_2^2\right)$$

(4)

The λ_1 and λ_2 is used to balance the three loss functions. The conventional softmax loss can be considered as special case of this joint supervision. The loss that L defines can be optimized by standard SGD. The learning algorithm is very similar to the Algorithm 1 in [12]. A little difference is that after updating the centers, all centers would be normalized before we use to calculate loss next iteration. This is designed to keep the length of the vector of every center is equal to 1.

1.2   An Example of MNIST

Here like the toy example in [12], we also use an example of MNIST to show the intention of our loss function. We use CaffeNet provided by Caffe [13], which is a popular deep learning framework, and apply our loss function. All the dropout layers in CaffeNet are removed and the output number of last hidden layer is set to 3. The λ_1, λ_2 and distance bound α is set to 0.1,0.01 and 1,respectively. After training, we plot the features of test images on 3-D space to see what loss function have done. The features in the 3-D space are shown as Fig. 2.

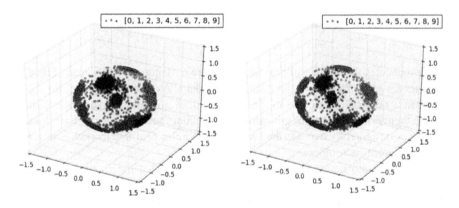

Fig. 2. Features of test images are extracted when the iteration is 1000 (left) and 9000(left). Notice: In fact, the blue points are located at other side of the global surface, they are not facing us like the red and brown points. (Color figure online)

As we can see from the Fig. 2, our loss is designed to force the points of same color on the global surface to come together as possible as they can and also make the distance of points of different colors larger than the margin we set. It is obvious that the features extracted at 9000 iterations are more discriminative, for the points of same colors are closer and the points of different colors are further away from each other. The reason we choose the normalized features is that it is more convenient for us to measure the similarity of two picture based on the Euclidean distance or Cosine distance of high dimensional features.

2   Experiments

2.1   Implementation Details

For all evaluated data sets, data sets are divided into training sets and test sets. We guarantee that there is no intersection between the set of classes used for training versus testing, so we can test the network's ability to extract the features of images from previously unseen classes.

We use GoogleNet [4] as a classification network for extracting features, for which the number of output of the final hidden layer is set to 64. In other words, the dimension of the extracted features is 64. Contrastive, loss, triplet loss and our loss function are applied respectively to train the GoogleNet. Experiments have proved that dropout [3] trick has a great influence on the updating of centers when using our loss. In order to ensure the training convergence, dropout layers in GoogleNet are removed when optimizing our loss function. To speed up training, we use a pretrained model on the ILSVR ImageNet [14] and the fully connected layer (the last layer) is initialized with random weights. In the following experiments, we will detail the network parameters on each data set.

2.2   Evaluation

For the features extracted by different networks, we evaluate them from two aspects including the clustering quality and retrieval quality. For clustering quality, we use the F_1 and NMI [15] metrics. As shown in Eq. 5, F_1 metric computes the harmonic mean of precision and recall.

$$F_1 = \frac{2PR}{P+R} \tag{5}$$

Given a set of cluster $\Omega = \{w_1, \cdots, w_K\}$ and a set of ground truth classes $\mathbb{C} = \{c_1, \cdots, c_K\}$, the normalized mutual information(NMI) metric can be computed. w_i denotes the set of example with cluster assignment i. c_j denotes the set of examples with the ground truth class label j. As shown in Eq. 6, NMI is defined by the ratio of mutual information and the average entropy of clusters and the entropy of labels.

$$\text{NMI}(\Omega, \mathbb{C}) = \frac{I(\Omega, \mathbb{C})}{2(H(\Omega) + H(\mathbb{C}))} \tag{6}$$

Recall@K [16] metric is used to evaluate the retrieval quality. Each test image (query) first retrieves K nearest neighbors from the test set and receives score 1 if an image of the same class is retrieved among the K nearest neighbors and 0 otherwise.

2.3   Cars196

The CARS196 data set [17] has 198 classes of cars with 16,185 images. We split the first 98 classes for training (8054 images) and the other 98 classes for testing (8131 images). On this dataset, maximum training iteration is set to 15000 for all experiments. The base learning rate is 0.01. The margin parameter α is set to 1. The batch size is set to 64 for contrastive, triplet and our method. The parameter λ_1 and λ_2 in our loss is set to 0.1 and 0.01 respectively. From Fig. 3, we can observe that features learned from our loss function have much higher NMI, F_1 and Recall@K {K = 1, 2, 4, 8, 16, 32} score than other two methods on this dataset. The retrieval examples are shown in Fig. 4.

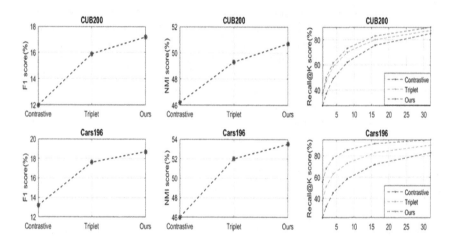

Fig. 3. The NMI, F_1 and Recall@K score on dataset CUB-200-2011 (upper) and Cars196 (lower) for three supervised signals.

2.4   CUB-200-2011

The CUB-200-2011 dataset [18] has 200 classes of birds with 11,788 images. We split the first 100 classes for training (5,864 images) and the rest of the classes for testing (5,924 images). On this dataset, maximum training iteration is set to 10000 for all experiments. The base learning rate is 0.01. The margin parameter α is set to 1. The batch size is set to 64 for contrastive, triplet and our method. The parameter λ_1 and λ_2 in our loss is set to 0.1 and 0.01 respectively. From Fig. 3. We can observe features learned from our loss function also have higher NMI, F_1 and Recall@K {K = 1, 2, 4, 8, 16, 32}

Fig. 4. The retrieval examples on dataset Cars196 using our method

Fig. 5. The retrieval examples on dataset CUB-200-2011 using our method

score than other two methods on this dataset but not as much on Cars196 dataset. Maybe further data preprocessing is needed but the effectiveness our method is proved. The retrieval examples are shown in Fig. 5.

3   Conclusion

In this paper, we design a new supervised signal which is very easy to implement on the basis of softmax loss. With the joint supervision of softmax loss and our supervised signal, the highly discriminative features could be obtained. The experimental results on CUB-200-2011, CARS196 datasets show quiet good performance of our methods for image retrieval task. Further researches like the influence of data processing and experiments on more complicated datasets are waited to be done. In this paper, the design of the loss is accomplished and the effectiveness has been proved on two datasets.

References

1. Lowe, D.G.: Distinctive image features from scale-invariant key points. Int. J. Comput. Vision **60**(2), 91–110 (2004)
2. Mikolajczyk, K., Schmid, C.: A performance evaluation of local descriptors. IEEE Trans. Pattern Anal. Mach. Intell. **27**(10), 1615–1630 (2005)
3. Krizhevsky, A., Sutskever, I., Hinton, G.: ImageNet classification with deep convolutional neural networks. In: 26th International Conference on Neural Information Processing Systems, pp. 1097–1105. Curran Associates Inc., Harrahs and Harveys, Lake Tahoe (2012)
4. Szegedy, C., Liu, W., Jia, Y.: Going deeper with convolutions. In: 2015 IEEE Conference on Computer Vision and Pattern Recognition, pp. 1–9. IEEE Computer Society, Boston (2015)
5. He, K., Zhang, X., Ren, S.: Deep residual learning for image recognition. In: 2016 IEEE Conference on Computer Vision and Pattern Recognition, pp. 770–778. IEEE Computer Society, Las Vegas (2016)
6. Bell, S., Bala, K.: Learning visual similarity for product design with convolutional neural networks. ACM Trans. Graph. **34**(4), 98 (2015)
7. Schroff, F., Kalenichenko, D., Philbin, J.: Facenet: a unified embedding for face recognition and clustering. In: 2015 IEEE Conference on Computer Vision and Pattern Recognition, pp. 815–823. IEEE Computer Society, Boston (2015)
8. Song, H.O., Xiang, Y., Jegelka, S., Savarese, S.: Deep metric learning via lifted structured feature embedding. In: 2016 IEEE Conference on Computer Vision and Pattern Recognition, pp. 4004–4012. IEEE Computer Society, Las Vegas (2016)
9. Sun, Y., Wang, X., Tang, X.: Deep learning face representation from predicting 10,000 classes. In: 2014 IEEE Conference on Computer Vision and Pattern Recognition, pp. 1891–1898. IEEE Computer Society, Columbus (2014)
10. Sun, Y., Chen, Y., Wang, X., Tang, X.: Deep learning face representation by joint identification-verification. In: 24th International Conference on Neural Information Processing Systems, pp. 107–114. Curran Associates Inc., Montréal (2014)
11. Parkhi, O.M., Vedaldi, A., Zisserman, A.: Deep face recognition. In: British Machine Vision Conference, pp. 41.1–41.12. BMVC, Swansea (2015)
12. Wen, Y., Zhang, K., Li, Z., Qiao, Yu.: A discriminative feature learning approach for deep face recognition. In: Leibe, B., Matas, J., Sebe, N., Welling, M. (eds.) ECCV 2016. LNCS, vol. 9911, pp. 499–515. Springer, Cham (2016). doi:10.1007/978-3-319-46478-7_31
13. Caffe homepage, http://caffe.berkeleyvision.org/
14. Russakovsky, O., Deng, J., Su, H.: ImageNet large scale visual recognition challenge. Int. J. Comput. Vision **115**(3), 211–252 (2015)
15. Sanderson, M., Christopher, D.: Introduction to Information Retrieval. Cambridge University Press, Cambridge (2010)
16. Jegou, H., Douze, M., Schmid, C.: Product quantization for nearest neighbor search. IEEE Trans. Pattern Anal. Mach. Intell. **33**(1), 117 (2011)
17. Cars196 homepage, http://ai.stanford.edu/~jkrause/cars/car_dataset.html
18. CUB-200-2011 homepage, http://www.vision.caltech.edu/visipedia/CUB-200-2011.html

Soft-Margin Softmax for Deep Classification

Xuezhi Liang[1,2,3], Xiaobo Wang[1,3(✉)], Zhen Lei[1,3], Shengcai Liao[1,3],
and Stan Z. Li[1,2,3]

[1] Center for Biometrics and Security Research and National Laboratory of Pattern
Recognition Institute of Automation, Chinese Academy of Sciences, Beijing, China
[2] Center for Internet of Things, Chinese Academy of Sciences, Wuxi, China
[3] University of Chinese Academy of Sciences, Beijing, China
xzliang@cbsr.ia.ac.cn, {xiaobo.wang,zlei,scliao,szli}@nlpr.ia.ac.cn

Abstract. In deep classification, the softmax loss (Softmax) is arguably
one of the most commonly used components to train deep convolutional
neural networks (CNNs). However, such a widely used loss is limited
due to its lack of encouraging the discriminability of features. Recently,
the large-margin softmax loss (L-Softmax [1]) is proposed to explicitly
enhance the feature discrimination, with hard margin and complex forward and backward computation. In this paper, we propose a novel soft-
margin softmax (SM-Softmax) loss to improve the discriminative power
of features. Specifically, SM-Softamx only modifies the forward of Softmax by introducing a non-negative real number m, without changing the
backward. Thus it can not only adjust the desired continuous soft margin
but also be easily optimized by the typical stochastic gradient descent
(SGD). Experimental results on three benchmark datasets have demonstrated the superiority of our SM-Softmax over the baseline Softmax, the
alternative L-Softmax and several state-of-the-art competitors.

Keywords: CNN · Softmax · L-Softmax · SM-Softmax · Classification

1 Introduction

Classification is a fundamental yet still challenging problem in machine learning
and computer vision community. Over the past years, convolutional neural networks (CNNs) have shown significant improvements in many classification tasks,
such as hand-written digit recognition [2], object recognition [3,4] and face recognition [5,6]. To train a deep CNN model, large scale training set and the end to
end learning framework are indispensable. Facing the increasingly more complex
data, CNNs can continuously be improved with dropout [3], deeper structure [7],
new non-linear activations [8], regularization [9], stochastic pooling [10] and so
on. Besides the above efforts, a renewed trend towards boosting the classification
performance is to learn discriminative features with well-designed loss functions.
However, this is non-trivial since a new loss function usually should be easily
optimized by the typical stochastic gradient descent.

Intuitively, the learned features are good if their intra-class compactness and
inter-class separability are well maximized. Based on such idea, the contrastive

© Springer International Publishing AG 2017
D. Liu et al. (Eds.): ICONIP 2017, Part II, LNCS 10635, pp. 413–421, 2017.
https://doi.org/10.1007/978-3-319-70096-0_43

loss [5] and triplet loss [11] were proposed to enlarge the inter-class distinction as well as alleviate the intra-class variance. However, the number of training pairs and triplets are needed to be elaborately selected. The complexity can go up to $O(N^2)$ where N is the total number of training samples. Considering that CNNs often handle large scale training sets, the training processing may be inefficient. The hinge loss was adopted in [12] for classification. However, it is usually unstable to learn discriminative features. The softmax loss is widely used in many CNNs due to its simplicity and probabilistic interpretation. Despite its popularity, current softmax loss does not explicitly encourage the intra-class compactness and inter-class separability. The center loss was introduced in [13] and was combined with the softmax loss to enhance the intra-class compactness. It has achieved a promising performance on face recognition task. However, as pointed out in [14], combing a Euclidean based loss with softmax loss to construct a joint supervision may not be optimal. The Sparsemax [15] designed a new activation function similar to the softmax, but able to output sparse probabilities. The L-softmax loss [1] was developed to explicitly enforce the angle margin between different classes. However, the angle margin is a hard one since the corresponding parameter should be an integer. Moreover, the forward and backward computation of L-Softmax are complex.

In this paper, inspired by the recent work [1], we propose a novel soft-margin softmax (SM-Softmax) loss to effectively learn the discriminative features. Specifically, rather than introducing a hard angle margin as the work [1] does, we design a soft distant margin to enlarge the intra-class compactness and inter-class separability. In this way, we only need to change the forward computation of Softmax, without modifying the backward computation. Thus our SM-Softmax loss can be easily optimized by the standard stochastic gradient descent. Moreover, the designed soft distant margin theoretically contains all the hard angle margin in L-Softmax [1] and the degenerative margin (0) in Softmax. Thus the proposed SM-Softmax not only inherits all merits from Softmax and L-Softmax but also learns features with large soft margin between different classes. For clarity, the contribution of this paper can be summarized as follows:

- We design a new simple and powerful loss function namely SM-Softmax to strengthen the intra-class compactness and inter-class separability between learned features.
- We show that the proposed SM-Softmax loss is trainable and can be directly optimized by the typical stochastic gradient descent (SGD).
- Extensive experiments on MNIST, CIFAR10/CIFAR10+ and CIFAR100 datasets demonstrate the superiority of our SM-Softmax over the baseline Softmax, the alternative L-Softmax and several state-of-the-art methods.

2   Related Work

To learn discriminative CNNs features, existing works can be mainly classified into two categories: (1) Improving the deep CNN structures; (2) Designing better loss functions.

CNN Structures: The NiN [17] was instantiated the misro neural network with a multi-layer perceptron to enhance model discriminability for local patches within the receptive field. The Maxout [18] was designed for leveraging the dropout technique by enforcing the output to be the max of a set of inputs. The FitNet [19] was to address the network compression by introducing intermediate-level hints. The DSN [20] aimed to simultaneously minimizes classification error while making the learning process of hidden layers direct and transparent. The All-CNN [21] consisted solely of convolution layers by simply replacing the max-pooling into convolutional layer with increased layer. The R-CNN [22] resorted to a recurrent CNN for visual classification by incorporating recurrent connections into each convolutional layer. The GenPool [23] generalized the pooling operations in current CNNs to play a central role. Although existing CNN structures have achieved promising results for classification, they still suffer from the limited discrimination problem because of softmax loss.

Loss Functions: Currently many loss functions including contrastive loss [5], triplet loss [11], center loss [13], L-Softmax loss [1], softmax loss *etc.* have been used to train the CNNs. To make inter-class dispension and intra-class compactness as much as possible. The work [5] combined the softmax loss and the contrastive loss to jointly supervise the CNNs, with pairs of training samples as inputs. The work [11] adopted the triplet loss to encourage a distance constraint, requiring three (or a multiple of three) training samples as input at a time. The work [13] developed the center loss and fused it with softmax loss to learn discriminative features. The softmax loss is widely used in many CNNs and it can be written as follows:

$$L_{Softmax} = -\log\left(\frac{e^{W_{y_i}^T x_i}}{\sum_j^K e^{W_j^T x_i}}\right) = -\log\left(\frac{e^{\|W_{y_i}\|\|x_i\|\cos(\theta_{y_i})}}{\sum_j^K e^{\|W_j\|\|x_i\|\cos(\theta_j)}}\right), \quad (1)$$

where $\mathbf{x}_i$ denotes the deep feature of the i-th training sample. y_i is its corresponding label. $\mathbf{W} = [\mathbf{W}_1, \mathbf{W}_2, \ldots, \mathbf{W}_K]^T$ is the parameters of the last fully connected layer, which can be also seen as the classifiers. K is the total number of classes. θ_j is the angle between the vector $\mathbf{W}_j$ and $\mathbf{x}_i$. The L-Softmax [1] loss employed a hard angle margin constraint in the original softmax loss, encouraging angular decision margin between classes to learn more discriminative features. Specifically, it can be formulated as:

$$L_{L-Softmax} = -\log\left(\frac{e^{\|W_{y_i}\|\|x_i\|\cos(a\theta_{y_i})}}{e^{\|W_{y_i}\|\|x_i\|\cos(a\theta_{y_i})} + \sum_{j\neq y_i}^K e^{\|W_j\|\|x_i\|\cos(\theta_j)}}\right), \quad (2)$$

where a is an integer that is closely related to the classification margin.

3   Soft-Margin Softmax Loss

To formulate our soft-margin softmax (SM-Softmax) loss, we first give a simple example to describe our intuition. Consider the binary classification and we have

---

Algorithm 1: Training a L-layers CNN supervised by SM-softmax loss.

Input: Training data $\{\mathbf{x}_i\}$. Initialized parameters $\mathbf{\Theta}$ in convolution layers.
Parameters $\mathbf{W}$ in SM-Softmax loss layer. Hyperparameter m.

while *not converged* **do**

    Compute the forward propagation by the modified soft-margin Softmax (5);

    Compute the standard backward propagation;

    Update the parameters $\mathbf{W}$;

    Update the parameters $\mathbf{\Theta}$.

end

Output: The parameters $\mathbf{\Theta}$ and the weight $\mathbf{W}$.

---

a sample $\boldsymbol{x}$ from class 1. The original softmax classifier is to enforce $\boldsymbol{W}_1^T \boldsymbol{x} > \boldsymbol{W}_2^T \boldsymbol{x}$ (*i.e.*, $\|\boldsymbol{W}_1\|\|\boldsymbol{x}\| \cos(\theta_1) > \|\boldsymbol{W}_2\|\|\boldsymbol{x}\| \cos(\theta_2)$) to classify $\boldsymbol{x}$ correctly. To make the classification more rigorous, the work L-Softmax [1] introduces an angle margin as

$$\|\boldsymbol{W}_1\|\|\boldsymbol{x}\| \cos(\theta_1) \geq \|\boldsymbol{W}_1\|\|\boldsymbol{x}\| \cos(a\theta_1) > \|\boldsymbol{W}_1\|\|\boldsymbol{x}\| \cos(\theta_2), \qquad (3)$$

and uses the intermediate value $\|\boldsymbol{W}_1\|\|\boldsymbol{x}\| \cos(a\theta_1)$ to replace $\|\boldsymbol{W}_1\|\|\boldsymbol{x}\| \cos(\theta_1)$ in the training. In that way, the class 1 and class 2 are explicitly separated. However, to make $\cos(a\theta_1)$ expand into Taylor series, a should be a positive integer. In other words, this margin cannot go through all possible angles and is a *hard* one. Moreover, the forward and backward computation are complex due to the angle margin involved. To address these issues, we here introduce a *soft* margin and simply let

$$\boldsymbol{W}_1^T \boldsymbol{x} \geq \boldsymbol{W}_1^T \boldsymbol{x} - m > \boldsymbol{W}_2^T \boldsymbol{x}, \qquad (4)$$

where m is a non-negative real number and is a distant margin. In the training phase, we employ $\boldsymbol{W}_1^T \boldsymbol{x} - m$ to replace $\boldsymbol{W}_1^T \boldsymbol{x}$, thus our multi-class soft-margin softmax (SM-Softmax) classifier can be defined as:

$$s_i = \frac{e^{\boldsymbol{W}_{y_i}^T \boldsymbol{x}_i - m}}{e^{\boldsymbol{W}_{y_i}^T \boldsymbol{x}_i - m} + \sum_{j \neq y_i}^{K} e^{\boldsymbol{W}_j^T \boldsymbol{x}_i}}. \qquad (5)$$

Finally, the soft-margin softmax (SM-Softmax) loss is formulated as

$$L_i = -\log\left(\frac{e^{\boldsymbol{W}_{y_i}^T \boldsymbol{x}_i - m}}{e^{\boldsymbol{W}_{y_i}^T \boldsymbol{x}_i - m} + \sum_{j \neq y_i} e^{\boldsymbol{W}_j^T \boldsymbol{x}_i}} \right). \qquad (6)$$

Obviously, when m is set to zero, the SM-Softmax loss becomes identical to the original softmax loss. The advantages of the soft margin (4) can be summarized into two aspects. One is that the soft margin m can go through all the possible desired margins, and includes the hard margin a. The other one is that the SM-Softmax loss is easy to implement since it only changes the forward computation of Softmax. For clarity and completeness, we summarize the major optimization scheme in Algorithm 1.

4   Experiments

Following the protocol in [1], we demonstrate the effectiveness of the proposed
SM-Softmax loss on three benchmark datasets and compare it with the baseline
Softmax, the alternative L-Softmax [1] and several state-of-the-art competitors.

4.1   Dataset Description

Three benchmark datasets adopted in the experiments are those widely used for
evaluating the performance of deep classification, including:

MNIST [24] is a dataset of handwritten digits (from 0 to 9) composed of 28×28
pixel gray scale images. It consists 60k training images and 10k test images. We
scaled the pixel values to the [0,1] range before inputting to the CNN architecture.

CIFAR10 [25] is a set of natural color images of 32×32 pixels. It contains 50k
training samples and 10k test samples. We adopt two commonly used comparison
protocols on this dataset. We first compare our SM-Softmax with others under no
data augmentation. For the data augmentation, we follow the standard technique
in [1] for training, that is, 4 pixels are padded on each side, and a 32×32 crop is
randomly sampled from the padded image or its horizontal flip. In test, we only
evaluate the single view of the original 32×32 image. In addition, we subtract the
per-pixel mean computed over the training set from each image before putting
the images into the network.

CIFAR100 [25] is with the same size and format as the CIFAR10 dataset,
except it has 100 classes containing 600 images each. There are 500 training
images and 100 testing images per class. The 100 classes in the CIFAR100 are
grouped into 20 superclasses.

Table 1. The detailed CNN architecture used in our work. Conv1.X, Conv2.X,
Conv3.X denote convolution units that may contain multiple convolution layers. *E.g.*,
$[3 \times 3,64] \times 4$ denotes 4 cascaded convolution layers with 64 filter of size 3×3.

Layer	Mnist	Cifar10/Cifar10+	Cifar100
conv0.X	$[3 \times 3,64] \times 1$	$[3 \times 3,64] \times 1$	$[3 \times 3,96] \times 1$
conv1.X	$[3 \times 3,64] \times 3$	$[3 \times 3,64] \times 4$	$[3 \times 3,96] \times 4$
Pool1	2×2 Max, Stride 2		
conv2.X	$[3 \times 3,64] \times 3$	$[3 \times 3,96] \times 4$	$[3 \times 3,192] \times 4$
Pool2	2×2 Max, Stride 2		
conv3.X	$[3 \times 3,64] \times 3$	$[3 \times 3,64] \times 4$	$[3 \times 3,384] \times 4$
Pool3	2×2 Max,Stride 2		
Fully connected	256	256	512

4.2 Compared Methods

We compare our SM-Softmax loss with the hinge loss, the commonly used Softmax loss, the recently proposed L-Softmax [1] and several state-of-the-art methods including the CNN [16], the DropConnect [2], the FitNet [19], the NiN [17], the Maxout [18], the DSN [20], the ALL-CNN [21], the R-CNN [22], the ResNet [4], the GenPool [23]. The results of all the compared methods are cropped from the original paper [1].

4.3 Implementation Details

We use Caffe [26] libary with our modifications to implement the proposed SM-Softmax loss. For the adopted CNN architecture, we follow the design philosophy of VGG-net [27], as the work [1] does. Specifically, for convolution layers, the kernel size is 3×3 and 1 padding (if not specified) to keep the feature map unchanged. For pooling layers, if the feature map size is halved, the number of filter is doubled to keep preserve the time complexity per layer. The detailed CNN architecture for each dataset are described in Table 1. For all experiments, We adopt the Relu [28] as the activation function and batch size is 128. We train all our models on a Nvidia Titan-X GPU and use the Caffe deep learning framework. CNN training is done with SGD with momentum 0.9 and weight decay of 0.0005. For the training, two stepwise strategy is adopted. We first train our CNN network supervised by softmax loss to obtain a good initialization. Then, we fine tune the CNN network supervised by our SM-Softmax loss based on the pre-trained model, with a small learning rate 0.01.

4.4 Performance Comparison

Table 2 provides the quantitative comparison among all the competitors on three benchmark datasets. The bold numbers in each column is the best performance. On MNIST, it is well-known that this dataset is typical and easy in deep classification. Almost all thee competitors can achieve under 1% error rate. The improvement of our SM-Softmax is not visibly big. On CIFAR10 and CIFAr10+, we can see that our SM-Softmax achieves about 2% improvement over the baseline Softmax and slightly better than the hard margin L-Softmax. On CIFAR100, a similar trend as that shown in MNIST and CIFAR10 is provided. In summary, the experiments have validated that the proposed SM-Softmax is significant better than Softmax due to its explicit discrimination on features, and is slightly better than the hard-margin L-Softmax because of its soft continuous margin.

4.5 Experiments on the Parameter m

The parameter m represent the soft margin between different classes. We investigate the sensitiveness of m on CIFAR10 and CIFAR100 as an example. Specifically, we vary the soft margin m from 0 to 0.9, with the stepsize of 0.1. From the

Table 2. Recognition error rate(%) on MNIST, CIFAR10 and CIFAR100 datasets. CIFAR10 denotes the performance without data augmentation, while CIFAR10+ is with data augmentation.

Method	MNIST	CIFAR10	CIFAR10+	CIFAR100
CNN [16]	0.53	N/A	N/A	N/A
DropConnect [2]	0.57	0.41	9.32	N/A
FitNet [19]	0.5	N/A	8.39	35.04
NiN [17]	0.47	10.47	8.81	35.68
Maxout [18]	0.45	11.68	9.38	38.57
DSN [20]	0.39	9.69	7.97	34.57
ALL-CNN [21]	N/A	9.08	7.25	N/A
R-CNN [22]	0.31	8.69	7.09	31.75
ResNet [4]	N/A	N/A	6.43	N/A
GenPool [23]	0.3	7.62	6.05	32.37
Hingeloss	0.47	9.91	6.96	32.90
Softmax	0.40	9.05	6.50	32.74
L-softmax [1]	0.31	7.58	5.92	29.53
SM-softmax	**0.30**	**7.50**	**5.73**	**29.28**

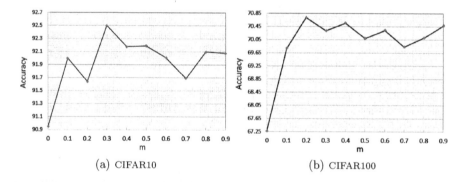

(a) CIFAR10   (b) CIFAR100

Fig. 1. Classification accuracy on CIFAR10 and CIFAR100 with different m.

curves in Fig. 1, we can observe that, as m grows, the accuracy rate grows gradually at the beginning and changes very slightly in a relatively large range of m. Moreover, we can clearly see that it reveals the effectiveness of our SM-Softmax ($m \neq 0$) in comparison with the baseline Softmax ($m = 0$).

5   Conclusions

This paper has proposed a novel soft-margin softmax (SM-Softmax) loss for deep classification tasks. The SM-Softmax achieves the discrimination of features by introducing a soft margin m between different classes. SM-Softmax only changes the forward of Softmax. Thus it can be easily optimized by the SGD. Extensive experiments have shown the advantages of our SM-Softmax over the baseline Softmax, the alternative L-Softmax and several state-of-the-art competitors.

Acknowledgments. This work was supported by the National Key Research and Development Plan (Grant No. 2016YFC0801002), the Chinese National Natural Science Foundation Projects #61473291, #61572501, #61502491, #61572536, #61672521 and AuthenMetric R&D Funds.

References

1. Liu, W., Wen, Y., Yu, Z.: Large-margin softmax loss for convolutional neural networks. In: ICML (2016)
2. Wan, L., Zeiler, M., Zhang, S.: Regularization of neural networks using dropconnect. In: ICML (2013)
3. Krizhevsky, A., Sutskever, I., Hinton, G.E.: Imagenet classification with deep convolutional neural networks. In: NIPS (2012)
4. He, K., Zhang, X.: Deep residual learning for image recognition. In: CVPR (2016)
5. Sun, Y., Chen, Y., Wang, X.: Deep learning face representation by joint identification-verification. In: NIPS (2014)
6. Taigman, Y., Yang, M., Ranzato, M.A.: Deepface: closing the gap to human-level performance in face verification. In: CVPR (2014)
7. Szegedy, C., Liu, W., Jia, Y.: Going deeper with convolutions. In: CVPR (2015)
8. He, K., Zhang, X., Ren, S.: Delving deep into rectifiers: surpassing human-level performance on imagenet classification. In: CVPR (2015)
9. Srivastava, N., Hinton, G.E., Krizhevsky, A.: Dropout: a simple way to prevent neural networks from overfitting. JMLR (2014)
10. Zeiler, M.D., Fergus, R.: Stochastic pooling for regularization of deep convolutional neural networks. arXiv preprint arXiv:1301.3557 (2013)
11. Schroff, F., Kalenichenko, D., Philbin, J.: Facenet: A unified embedding for face recognition and clustering. In: CVPR (2015)
12. Tang, Y.: Deep learning using linear support vector machines. arXiv preprint arXiv:1306.0239 (2013)
13. Wen, Y., Zhang, K., Li, Z., Qiao, Y.: A discriminative feature learning approach for deep face recognition. In: Leibe, B., Matas, J., Sebe, N., Welling, M. (eds.) ECCV 2016. LNCS, vol. 9911, pp. 499–515. Springer, Cham (2016). doi:10.1007/978-3-319-46478-7_31
14. Liu, W., Wen, Y., Yu, Z.: SphereFace: deep hypersphere embedding for face recognition. In: CVPR (2017)
15. Martins, A., Astudillo, R.: From softmax to sparsemax: a sparse model of attention and multi-label classification. In: ICML (2016)
16. Jarrett, K., Kavukcuoglu, K., LeCun, Y.: What is the best multi-stage architecture for object recognition? In: ICCV (2009)
17. Lin, M., Chen, Q., Yan, S.: Network in network. In: ICLR (2014)
18. Goodfellow, I.J., Warde-Farley, D., Mirza, M.: Maxout Networks. In: ICML (2013)
19. Romero, A., Ballas, N.: Fitnets: Hints for thin deep nets. In: ICLR (2013)
20. Lee, C.Y., Xie, S., Gallagher, P.W.: Deeply-supervised nets. AISTATS (2015)

21. Springenberg, J.T., Dosovitskiy, A., Brox, T.: Striving for simplicity: The all convolutional net. In: ICLR (2015)
22. Liang, M., Hu, X.: Recurrent convolutional neural network for object recognition. In: CVPR (2015)
23. Lee, C.Y., Gallagher, P.W., Tu, Z.: Generalizing pooling functions in convolutional neural networks: mixed, gated, and tree. AISTATS (2016)
24. LeCun, Y. The MNIST database of handwritten digits (1998), http://yann.lecun.com/exdb/mnist/
25. Krizhevsky, A., Geoffrey, H.: Learning multiple layers of features from tiny images (2009)
26. Jia, Y., Shelhamer, E., Donahue, J.: Caffe: Convolutional architecture for fast feature embedding. In: ACM (2014)
27. Simonyan, K., Zisserman, A.: Very deep convolutional networks for large-scale image recognition. arXiv preprint arXiv:1409.1556 (2014)
28. Glorot, X., Bordes, A., Bengio, Y.: Deep sparse rectifier neural networks. AISTATS (2011)

Temporal Attention Neural Network
for Video Understanding

Jegyung Son, Gil-Jin Jang, and Minho Lee[✉]

School of Electronics Engineering, Kyungpook National University,
1370 Sankyuk-Dong, Puk-Gu, Taegu 702-701, South Korea
wprud4@gmail.com, mholee@gmail.com, gjang@knu.ac.kr

Abstract. Deep learning based vision understanding algorithms have recently approached human-level performance in object recognition and image captioning. These performance evaluations are, however, limited to static data and these algorithms are also limited. Few limitations of these methods include their inability to selectively encode human behavior, movement of multiple objects and time-varying variations in the background. To address these limitations and to extend these algorithms for analyzing dynamic videos, we propose a temporal attention CNN-RNN network with motion saliency map. Our proposed model overcome scarcity of usable information in encoded data and efficiently integrate motion features by incorporating dynamic nature of information present in successive frames. We evaluate our proposed model over UCF101 public dataset and our experiments demonstrate that our proposed model successfully extract motion information for video understanding without any computationally intensive preprocessing.

Keywords: Video understanding · Action recognition · Saliency map · Convolutional neural network · Long short term memory · Deep learning

1 Introduction

Understanding of sensory information is essential in various real life tasks like speech recognition, natural language processes, and computer vision. Visual information, in particular that correspond to around 70% of sensory information is the most valuable for understanding our environment. Various studies have demonstrated human-level performance on static data understanding such as object recognition [1] and image captioning [2]. These successes in vision for static data have motivated works in a direction towards understanding dynamic applications like videos. As an example of such studies, Karpathy *et al.* proposed a basic Convolutional Neural Network (CNN) with Recurrent Neural Network (RNN) model for action recognition [3]. Likewise, Donahue et al. improved Long Short Term Memory (LSTM) for video understanding [4]. Venugopalan et al. developed video caption system based on prior art researches [5]. These studies, however, failed to enjoy equitable success compared to what has been achieved in case of static datasets. Difficulties in selectively encoding important information out of numerous information in videos is the primary reason behind the failure of these methods over dynamic application scenarios. Another challenge in capturing the

© Springer International Publishing AG 2017
D. Liu et al. (Eds.): ICONIP 2017, Part II, LNCS 10635, pp. 422–430, 2017.
https://doi.org/10.1007/978-3-319-70096-0_44

necessary information in dynamic scenarios arise from the fact that the scale of necessary information to understand videos is too small and the scene keeps changing with time. Some studies are undertaken to address this problem. Srivastava et al. proposed unsupervised learning with RNN Autoencoder [6]. Tran et al. proposed a 3D CNN structure [7]. These methods, however, did not yield satisfactory performance despite having used large datasets for training. After having known the shortcomings of these models in dynamic scenarios, image processing techniques such as optical flow [8], Dynamic Saliency Map (DSM) [9] or Improved Dense Trajectory (IDT) [10] offer better approach to video understanding problems and also exhibit better performance. It is to remark that these image processing methods are heuristics and require large computational resources. To this end, we propose a temporal attention network with motion saliency map for efficient video understanding. The proposed model captures additional motion information in a computationally efficient manner and exhibits satisfactory performance compared to the state-of-the-art methods.

2 Related Works

2.1 Long Short-Term Memory

RNN and its variants incorporate feedback loops to store memory which is important in sequential data. LSTM [11], a variant of RNN can efficiently train recurrent neural network on even very long sequence without suffering from long-term dependency problem (Fig. 1).

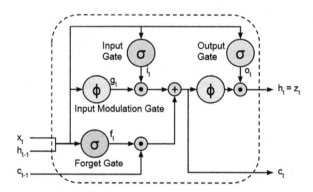

Fig. 1. LSTM unit

LSTM improve upon RNN by so-called gating mechanism. We briefly introduce operations of gates in LSTM as follows:

$$i_t = \sigma(W_{xi}x_t + W_{hi}h_{t-1} + b_i) \tag{1}$$

$$f_t = \sigma(W_{xf}x_t + W_{hf}h_{t-1} + b_f) \tag{2}$$

$$o_t = \sigma(W_{xo}x_t + W_{ho}h_{t-1} + b_o) \tag{3}$$

$$g_t = tanh(W_{xc}x_t + W_{hc}h_{t-1} + b_c) \tag{4}$$

$$c_t = f_t \odot c_{t-1} + i_t \odot g_t \tag{5}$$

$$h_t = o_t \odot tanh(c_t) \tag{6}$$

σ denotes sigmoid function $(1 + e^{-x})^{-1}$ which squashes real-value within a range [0, 1], $\odot$ means element-wise multiplication.

When input x_t is given at a time t, input gate i_t, forget gate f_t, output gate o_t, cell candidate (input modulation gate) g_t are calculated. If the current input has more important information compared to the previous input then i_t would be close to 1 and f_t would be close to 0 that makes LSTM forget previous data and update based on the current input. By incorporating this mechanism, LSTM selectively stores information from long sequential data and prevents long term dependency problem.

2.2   CNN-RNN Architecture

A combined model comprising CNN and RNN, which we refer as CNN-RNN is one of the most successful network in terms of performance and applicability in various areas. At each time step, a frame is input to the CNN and a corresponding feature vector is obtained. An LSTM RNN processes this feature vector as its input in each step and encodes it with previous information into hidden states that represents the given frames till the current time step. The hidden state of the LSTM is used to predict the labels and it is compared with the target. Basic CNN-RNN network generates prediction label at every time step. This LSTM classifier was proposed in [6]. It is natural since basic CNN-RNN network primarily focus on spatial information such as objects and background. Therefore it can predict action labels at every time step and improve test (generalization) performance by predicting based on a single frame as well as multiple frames.

3   Proposed Model

The proposed method consists of a two flow network as shown in Fig. 2. One is a basic CNN-RNN network that mainly deals with static information such as objects and backgrounds with little motion information. The other one is a temporal attention network that handles additional motion information. The proposed model, temporal attention network, can successfully extract motion information by using three consecutive frames as input. If we compare different actions in videos with similar background having similar objects then the basic CNN-RNN model that captures spatial information cannot classify the actions correctly. In this case, the proposed temporal attention network will be able to complement the spatial information with additional motion information, thereby, improving the video understanding capability of the combined network.

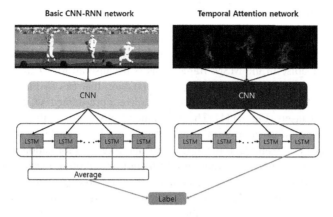

Fig. 2. Architecture of the proposed model

3.1 Motion Saliency Map

Motion information is important for better performance in action recognition and has to be incorporated despite being computationally intensive to obtain it. We proposed motion saliency map, an innovative framework that allows to extract motion information without time-consuming preprocessing. Motion Saliency Map (MSM) is a modified version of DSM to obtain motion information in a simple and efficient manner. DSM is used to analyze the dynamics of the successive static saliency maps, and can localize an attention region in dynamic scenes to focus on specific moving objects. In processing for creating the static saliency map, center-surround difference is used to remove non-dominant and remain dominant region. For MSM, dynamics of the successive input images are considered in the center-surround difference as shown in Fig. 3. The center image is obtained by concatenation of three gray scale images from t to $t + 2$. The color region of center image include motion information. To highlight motion information, MSM is obtained by subtracting the surround image, which is average image of three gray scale images from t to $t + 2$.

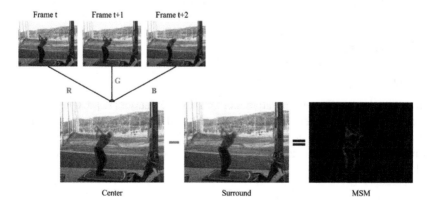

Fig. 3. Flow graph of MSM

3.2 Temporal Attention Network

As described in the previous section, we build the MSM that carries motion information. However, encoding motion information is challenging as it is too sensitive to the presence of noise in the MSM frame. This is because an MSM frame consists of only important information such as shape and position that can be highly affected by the noise. In order to overcome this issue, we utilize a pre-trained VGGNet trained on ILSVRC2012 datasets (Fig. 4) [1]. The pre-trained CNN is not easily distracted by the noise such as non-informative lines or patterns since it has a tendency to focus on the shape of objects. For example, if the input frame has motion information with noise, the CNN can selectively choose the motion information by ignoring meaningless patterns which are generated by unstable camera or changing backgrounds. Therefore, by combining the pre-trained CNN with the proposed MSM, we are able to develop an efficient network for motion information extraction. However, we need to carefully control the weights of the network in such a way that we retain the benefits of the pre-trained CNN and also optimize the network for the current task. On the other hand, if we train the network with random initialization, it would lose the aforementioned advantages of a pre-trained CNN.

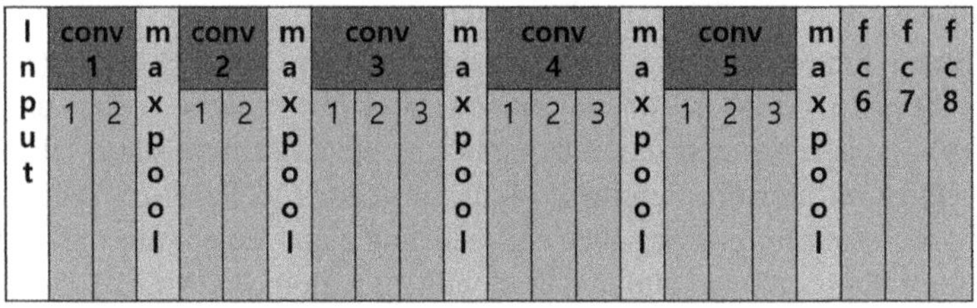

Fig. 4. Structure of VGGNet

We train our proposed model by initializing the weights of the convolution layers with the pre-trained model but randomly initializing the fully connected layers. In addition, we fixed the weights of the first three convolution layers and optimize the remaining layers on the action recognition dataset.

4 Experiments

4.1 Dataset

In this paper, we evaluate proposed model on UCF101 dataset [12]. UCF101 consist of 101 action classes in over 13 k clips with 27 h of video data. Videos are realistic user-uploaded which are containing camera motion and cluttered background. This database is the most challenging dataset in action recognition because of large number of classes and unconstrained nature of such clip.

4.2   Implementation Details

Our proposed network can be trained together with simple backpropagation in an end-to-end manner. However the database we are using for evaluation has less number of videos. Hence we train each network separately in order to impart enough gradient information to motion attention network. We assign 1024 units for LSTM and use orthogonal initializer. For CNN, initialize convolution layers with pre-trained weights and fix the weights of layer 1, 2, 3. We extracted 40 frames for every video thus LSTM step is set as 40. However, for the temporal attention network has 38 MSMs since the raw frames are to be concatenated. The code is implemented in Tensorflow [13]. For optimization, we use the Adam Optimizer [14] with learning rate 0.00001.

4.3   Results and Discussion

Table 1 presents the action recognition accuracy of the proposed method compared to two baselines and current the state-of-the-art methods. The upper section of the table shows the results of the two baselines. The middle section present the results of the methods that use only RGB frames as inputs. And the lower section reports the performance of models using optical flows. Our proposed method shows the best performance among models that use only RGB frames except C3D + linear SVM [7]. However, the higher accuracy in C3D + linear SVM model mainly comes from the linear SVM classifier where the features are the same as in C3D + fc6 [15]. Based on these results, we claim that our method is better in terms of feature extraction for video understanding.

Table 1. Action recognition results on UCF101

Method	Accuracy
Imagenet + linear SVM	68.8
iDT w/BoW + linear SVM [10]	76.2
Deep networks [3]	65.4
LRCN-fc6 [4]	68.2
Spatial Convolutional Net [8]	73.0
LSTM composite model [6]	75.8
C3D + fc6 [15]	76.4
Proposed model	**79.1**
C3D + linear SVM [7]	82.3
LRCN with Flow [4]	80.90
LSTM composite model [6]	84.3

LRCN with Flow [4] uses optical flow with basic CNN-RNN network and shows similar result with ours. This illustrates that our method successfully extract motion information from videos without the computationally expensive optical flow preprocessing mechanism.

In order to understand the contribution of the basic CNN-RNN and the temporal attention network in the proposed model, we estimate the accuracy of the basic CNN-RNN and the temporal attention network separately on every task in the dataset. For example, in the action recognition task shown in Fig. 5(a), the basic CNN-RNN and temporal attention network shows 41.67% and 83.33% accuracy respectively. We analyzed the result to understand the performance difference between the two networks and we found that the basic CNN-RNN network misclassify Fig. 5(a) as Fig. 5(b), since Figs. 5(a) and (b) exhibits similar spatial information. But the dynamic information in both videos are different. In Fig. 5(a) the bowler 'runs' to throw the ball however in Fig. 5(b) the batsman 'swings' to hit the ball and runs. Therefore, because of the big difference in the dynamic information, the temporal attention network shows higher accuracy. In another example, for Fig. 5(c), the basic CNN-RNN network and the temporal attention network show 47.06% and 94.12% accuracy respectively. Figures 5(c) and (d) includes a similar object that are types of rope. The dynamic information in Fig. 5(c) is jumping but Fig. 5(d) mainly consists of hand movements. Therefore, temporal attention network shows much better performance in classifying those videos.

(a) CricketBowling   (b) CricketShot   (c) Jumprope   (d) Nunchuck

Fig. 5. Examples of datasets

According to our analysis, we conclude that the basic CNN-RNN cannot fully understand video without the help of temporal information. On the contrary, a standalone temporal attention network without the help of spatial information may have difficulties in understanding the videos entirely. Thus both network should be combined in order to harmonize spatial and temporal information for understanding the total information present in videos.

5   Conclusion

In this paper, we proposed a video understanding model that consists of a temporal attention network and a basic CNN-RNN network. The temporal attention network focusses on temporal information whereas the CNN-RNN network captures spatial information. We argue that the basic CNN-RNN by itself is not sufficient to fully understand videos without the help of temporal information. Hence, we integrated these two networks in order to enhance the performance of our model. This combined model offers an efficient feature extraction method for video understanding without complex preprocessing and is comparable to the current state-of-the-art action recognition models.

In the future, we plan to improve the proposed model by introducing hierarchical structure in the temporal attention network and enhance the motion information extraction ability by training it on larger kinetics dataset.

Acknowledgement. This work was partly supported by Institute for Information & communications Technology Promotion (IITP) grant funded by the Korea government (MSIT) (R7124-16-0004, Development of Intelligent Interaction Technology Based on Context Awareness and Human Intention Understanding) (50%) and the National Research Foundation of Korea (NRF) grant funded by the Korea government (MSIP) (No. NRF-2016R1E1A2020559) (50%).

References

1. Simonyan, K., Zisserman, A.: Very deep convolutional networks for large-scale image recognition. arXiv preprint arXiv:1409.1556 (2014)
2. Vinyals, O., Toshev, A., Bengio, S., Erhan, D.: Show and tell: a neural image caption generator. In: Proceedings of the IEEE Conference on Computer Vision and Pattern Recognition, pp. 3156–3164 (2015)
3. Karpathy, A., Toderici, G., Shetty, S., Leung, T., Sukthankar, R., Fei-Fei, L.: Large-scale video classification with convolutional neural networks. In: Proceedings of the IEEE conference on Computer Vision and Pattern Recognition, pp. 1725–1732 (2014)
4. Donahue, J., Anne Hendricks, L., Guadarrama, S., Rohrbach, M., Venugopalan, S., Saenko, K., Darrell, T.: Long-term recurrent convolutional networks for visual recognition and description. In: Proceedings of the IEEE Conference on Computer Vision and Pattern Recognition, pp. 2625–2634 (2015)
5. Venugopalan, S., Rohrbach, M., Donahue, J., Mooney, R., Darrell, T., Saenko, K.: Sequence to sequence-video to text. In: Proceedings of the IEEE International Conference on Computer Vision, pp. 4534–4542 (2015)
6. Srivastava, N., Mansimov, E., Salakhudinov, R.: Unsupervised learning of video representations using lstms. In: International Conference on Machine Learning, pp. 843–852 (2015)
7. Tran, D., Bourdev, L., Fergus, R., Torresani, L., Paluri, M.: Learning spatiotemporal features with 3d convolutional networks. In: Proceedings of the IEEE International Conference on Computer Vision, pp. 4489–4497 (2015)
8. Simonyan, K., Zisserman, A.: Two-stream convolutional networks for action recognition in videos. In: Advances in Neural Information Processing Systems, pp. 568–576 (2014)
9. Ban, S.W., Lee, I., Lee, M.: Dynamic visual selective attention model. Neurocomputing **71**(4), 853–856 (2008)
10. Wang, H., Schmid, C.: Action recognition with improved trajectories. In: Proceedings of the IEEE International Conference on Computer Vision, pp. 3551–3558 (2013)
11. Hochreiter, S., Schmidhuber, J.: Long short-term memory. Neural Comput. **9**(8), 1735–1780 (1997)
12. Soomro, K., Zamir, A.R., Shah, M.: UCF101: a dataset of 101 human actions classes from videos in the wild. arXiv preprint arXiv:1212.0402 (2012)

13. Abadi, M., Agarwal, A., Barham, P., Brevdo, E., Chen, Z., Citro, C., Ghemawat, S.: Tensorflow: large-scale machine learning on heterogeneous distributed systems. arXiv preprint arXiv:1603.04467 (2016)
14. Kingma, D., Ba, J.: Adam: a method for stochastic optimization. arXiv preprint arXiv:1412.6980 (2014)
15. Tran, D., Bourdev, L.D., Fergus, R., Torresani, L., Paluri, M.: C3D: generic features for video analysis. CoRR, abs/1412.0767, **2**(7), 8 (2014)

Regularized Deep Convolutional Neural Networks for Feature Extraction and Classification

Khaoula Jayech[✉]

LATIS Research Lab, National Engineering School of Sousse,
University of Sousse, Sousse, Tunisia
ljayech_k@yahoo.fr

Abstract. Deep Convolutional Neural Networks (DCNNs) are the state-of-the-art in fields such as visual object recognition, handwriting and speech recognition. The DCNNs include a large number of layers, a huge number of units, and connections. Therefore, with the huge number of parameters, overfitting can occur. In order to prevent the network against this problem, regularization techniques have been applied in different positions. In this paper, we show that with the right combination of applied regularization techniques such as fully connected dropout, max pooling dropout, L2 regularization and He initialization, it is possible to achieve good results in object recognition with small networks and without data augmentation.

Keywords: Deep learning · Deep convolutional neural networks · Object recognition · Fully connected dropout · Max pooling dropout · L2 regularization

1 Introduction

Visual object recognition is an extremely hard computational problem in computer vision research. It has a lot of potential applications that touch a lot of areas of artificial intelligence including video data mining, object identification for mobile robots, and image retrieval. It searches to identify and localize categories, places and objects in order to recognize and classify images.

Visual object recognition has gained the interest of the research community and has been further applied successfully to a lot of other application areas [1–5]. However, it is still an open problem and a challenging task. The core problem is due to the high variability of the objects constituting an image. In fact, the object may have variation in the view point, the illumination, the scale and the imaging conditions [6, 7].

Recently, deep learning, especially the Convolutional Neural Networks (CNNs), has attracted huge attention among computer vision research communities thanks to its high performance in classification tasks [8, 9]. It has produced extremely promising results for various tasks of pattern recognition issues like handwritten digits, face recognition, sentiment analysis, object detection and image classification [9–11]. Those models have some advantages and disadvantages. Indeed, the main advantage of Deep

© Springer International Publishing AG 2017
D. Liu et al. (Eds.): ICONIP 2017, Part II, LNCS 10635, pp. 431–439, 2017.
https://doi.org/10.1007/978-3-319-70096-0_45

CNNs (DCNNs) is their accuracy in image recognition problems. Also, they are very good at discovering high-dimensional data having intricate structures [8]. On the other hand, they have some disadvantages such as the high computational cost, so if you do not have a good GPU, they will quite slow to train the model (for complex tasks) and they will need a lot of training data.

This paper introduces a DCNN model to obtain a high multi-classification accuracy on object recognition. The architecture of the CNN model is neatly elaborated to extract deep hidden features and model small training datasets, which fits well for the used datasets. The CIFAR-10 and STL-10 datasets are labeled subsets of an 80-million-tiny-image dataset. These datasets are used to evaluate the performance of the CNN model. The experiment results prove that the CNN model with the right combination of regularization techniques has an adaptive accuracy rate on classification.

The main contributions of this study are the following:

– The method uses the CNN to classify images into 10 categories and produce an accuracy of 97% utilizing the CIFAR-10 and 75.4% using the STL-10.
– The CNN model utilizes three convolution layers, a regularization layer, and a high efficiency optimizer to be adaptive to the CIFAR and STL datasets.

The remaining of this paper is set as follows: In the second section, we present some related work. In the third section, we describe the details of applying the CNN model to object recognition. Our experimental study and results using this system are provided in the fourth section. In the final section, we present some concluding remarks and future directions.

2 Related Work

Although the problem of object recognition is still a very active and challenging task, good results have been recorded thanks to the new learning capabilities offered by deep neural networks.

In this context, Tobias et al. in [10] presented the implementation of light-weight CNN schemes on mobile devices for domain-specific objection recognition tasks. In the same optic, the DCNNs were investigated by Lorandet et al. in [12] for RGB-D based object recognition. The DCNNs outperformed other classifiers and proved a significant classification accuracy.

Krizhevsky in [13] suggested a large DCNN to classify 1.2 million high-resolution images in the ImageNet LSVRC-2010 contest into 1000 different classes. The model achieved top-1 and top-5 error rates. The neural network was composed of five convolutional layers, some of which were followed by max-pooling layers and three fully-connected layers with a final 1000-way softmax. In order to accelerate the training process, non-saturating neurons and a very efficient GPU implementation of the convolution operation were used. Nevertheless, to minimize overfitting, some regularization techniques like the dropout proved to be very effective.

In handwritten digit recognition, Calderon et al. in [14] and Alwzwazy in [15] proposed a robust DCNN for classification, which achieved superior results. A combination of the CNNs and the RNNs was presented by Peris in [16] and applied for the generation of video and image descriptions. These models demonstrated that they outperformed the previous state of the art.

Indeed, Haiteng in [11] put forward advanced DCNNs for body constitution to simulate the function of pulse diagnosis, which is able to classify an individual's constitution, based on their pulse. The CNN model employed the latest activation unit and rectified the linear unit and the stochastic optimization. This model attained a recognition accuracy of 95% on classifying nine constitutional types.

Peyrard et al. in [17] proposed a blind approach to super-resolution based on the CNN architecture. The network could deal with different blur levels without any a priori knowledge of the actual kernel utilized to give LR images. The obtained results showed the success of the suggested approach for the blind set-up and were comparable with non-blind approaches.

A deep-neural-network-based estimation metric was investigated by Sholomon et al. in [18] to solve the jigsaw puzzle problem. The proposed metric indicated an extremely high precision even without extracting any manual feature.

Two CNN architectures were presented by Garcia et al. in [19] for emotion recognition in order to classify images into seven emotions. The first architecture checked the effects of minimizing the number of deep learning layers. However, the second architecture horizontally divided the given image into two streams based on eye and mouth positions. This method performed good results compared it other approaches proposed in the literature.

3   Object Recognition Based on DCNN Model

The success of any DCNN comes from the efficient use of GPUs, Rectified Linear Units (ReLUs), a new regularization technique such as a max pooling dropout, a fully connected dropout, and techniques for data augmentation to generate more training examples by deforming the existing ones. In the following section, we describe the major improvements and overall architecture of the DCNN model.

3.1   Initialization and Stochastic Optimization

Before starting to learn the parameters of the network, we must initialize its parameters. An initialization establishes the probability distribution function for the initial weights. The model uses a uniform initialization such as the He weight initialization. This initialization method effectively resolves the bottleneck of the extremely deep neuronal network training [11]. Yet, in order to optimize and update various CNN parameters, the Adam algorithm is used. It is a simple and efficient computational algorithm for optimization based on the gradients of stochastic objective functions. This algorithm is well suited for a CNN with a complex structure and large parameter spaces and it combines the strength of two newly popular optimization methods: the ability of AdaGrad to cope with sparse gradients and the ability of RMSProp to handle non-stationary objectives.

3.2 Leaky Rectified Linear Unit

In general, to learn a neural network, the saturated counterpart, such as a hyperbolic tangent or a logistic sigmoid, is used. However, in recent years, the most popular activation function for the deep network is the ReLU. It calculates the following function:

$$f(x) = \max(0, x). \tag{1}$$

There are some advantages in using the ReLU. First, the ReLU is faster to calculate because it does not require any normalization or exponential calculation (like those required in sigmoid activations or tanh). Second, the use of the ReLU accelerates the convergence of the stochastic gradient descent. This is argued to be caused by its linear and non-saturating form. Third, it does not face the problem of gradient degradation as for the sigmoid and tanh functions. It has been demonstrated that deep networks can be trained effectively utilizing the ReLU even without pre-training.

3.3 Over-Fitting Prevention and Regularization

Learning the CNNs uses a large number of layers, a huge number of units, and connections related to its complex structure and numerous filters in each convolutional layer. These are prone to overfitting, which is a serious problem. To deal with this problem, dropout learning and regularization methods have been developed to improve the CNN performance and reduce overfitting.

L2 and ridge regularization
In order to reduce the regression coefficient overfitting, regularization penalties are appended to CNN parameters. In fact, the L2 regularization and ridge are used in a fully connected layer. L2 weight regularization penalizes weight values by adding the sum of their squared values to the error term to drive all weights to smaller values. Nevertheless, ridge regularization decreases the approximated regression coefficients towards surmount overfitting, which is caused by high dimensionality [7]. The penalty parameter is set to 0.01.

Max pooling dropout
In recent years, Wu and Gu in [20] proposed to use a special dropout variant with the CNN, known as the max pooling dropout. Actually, the traditional CNN is composed of alternating convolutional and pooling layers, with fully-connected layers on top. However, the max pooling dropout can be seen as a special variant of stochastic pooling. It is used within the pooling layers to introduce stochasticity into the learning process with the difference that activations are utilized with a probability proportional to their rank, instead of the strength of their activation.

Fully connected dropout
Dropout learning is used in deep learning to avoid overfitting. A small number of data compared with the size of a network may cause overfitting [21]. Dropout learning follows two processes. At the training stage, some hidden units are neglected with a probability p, and this process reduces the network size. If a dropout probability p of

0.5 is used, roughly half of the activations in each layer will be deleted for every training sample, thus preventing hidden units from relying on other hidden units being present. At the testing stage, the neglected inputs and hidden units are combined with the learned hidden units and multiplied by p to express the final output. As a result, the weights are rescaled proportional to the dropout probability. For example, for a dropout probability of 0.5, all weights are divided by two [21]. This regularization can improve the network performance and significantly reduce the error rate.

3.4   Architecture of Proposed DCNN

The suggested system is presented in Fig. 1. The CNN architecture is composed of six layers: three convolutional layers with 15, 20 and 25 filters, where each filter has a size of 5*5 and each convolutional layer is followed by a max pooling layer of a size of 2*2; two fully connected layers with 600 and 300 units performed after the convolutional layers, and the softmax layer, which is the final layer of the CNN model classifying the output into 10 class labels.

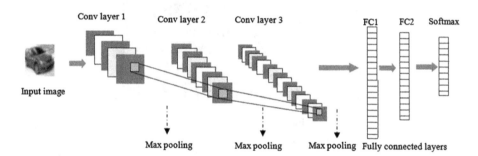

Fig. 1. Overall CNN architecture

A dropout layer is applied to the output with a probability of 0.5 on the 1st, 2nd and 3rd convolutional layers and to two fully connected layers. With this fixed architecture we then proceed to test the effects of the different regularization techniques on the set classification task.

4   Experimentation

We conduct our experimental studies using the proposed DCNN for object recognition. This architecture and the previously described regularization methods are trained and tested to classify images from two datasets: CIFAR-10 and STL-10. The next section introduces the dataset and the overall performance of the DCNN model.

4.1 Database Description

To evaluate the performance of the proposed system, the experiments are conducted on the benchmark object recognition datasets: CIFAR-10 and STL-10.

The CIFAR-10 dataset [13] consists of 60,000 color images of 32×32 pixels in 10 classes: airplanes, automobiles, birds, cats, deers, dogs, frogs, horses, ships, and trucks. The total dataset is split into 50,000 training images and 10,000 testing ones. The last 10,000 training images are used for validation. Here are the classes in the dataset, as well as 10 random images from each class (Fig. 2):

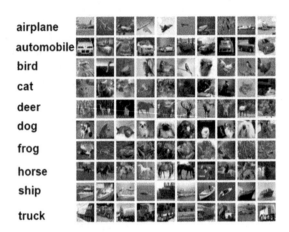

Fig. 2. CIFAR-10 dataset

We use also the STL-10 dataset that contains 96×96 RGB images in 10 categories. This dataset has 5,000 labeled training images and 8,000 test images. Additionally, it includes 100,000 unlabeled images for unsupervised learning algorithms, which are extracted from a similar but broader distribution of images [22].

4.2 Results and Discussion

We perform classification experiments on CIFAR-10 and STL-10. Then, we proceed to compare the effects of various regularization methods on seven different classifiers. The following seven settings are tested:

1. No regularization
2. CNN withLReL
3. CNN with LReL, max pooling dropout
4. CNN with LReL, max pooling dropout, fully connected dropout
5. CNN with LReL, max pooling dropout, fully connected dropout, L2
6. CNN with LReL, max pooling dropout, fully connected dropout, L2, ADASYS
7. CNN with LReL, max pooling dropout, fully connected dropout, L2, He

The results of each method are illustrated in Fig. 3a and b. Rate recognition is defined as to the number of correctly recognized samples divided by the total number of test samples. The objective is to classify the input image into 10 class labels. Using CIFAR-10, the initial CNN model achieves a higher recognition rate of 75.5% with the LReL as shown by Fig. 3a. With the LReL and the max pooling dropout, the recognition rate significantly increases by 25.5%. With the addition of the fully connected dropout, the recognition rate goes up by 3.08%. Applying the L2 regularization slightly raises the rate to 94.3%. With the ADASYS method, the rate decreases to 90.07%. The final CNN model with the He initialization gives the highest performance of 97.15%.

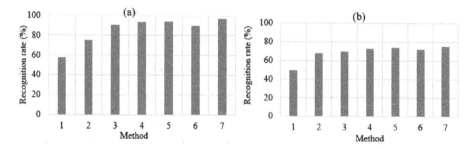

Fig. 3. (a) Comparison of results on CIFAR-10 dataset and (b) Comparison of results on STL dataset

The experimental results show the outperformance of the DCNN based on the max pooling dropout and the fully connected dropout compared to the standard CNN. In fact, the DCNN model demonstrates its superiority based on a very complex and high dimensional dataset with limited samples and without any data augmentation. However, the training and test DCNNs are time-consuming tasks due to the implementation of the fully connected dropout and the max pooling dropout.

5 Conclusion

In this paper, we have presented a DCNN model for object recognition and examined the effects of regularization techniques on the training of DCNNs. This regularized model is able to surmount the shortcomings of traditional recognition methods and improves the multi-classification recognition rate. The experiments have proven that the combination of the DCNN with the max pooling dropout and fully connected dropout can avoid the problem of overfitting. In addition, we have shown that the right combination of regularization techniques can have a big impact on the performance of DCNNs and their trained features by giving an adaptive recognition rate on an extremely complex dataset. As a perspective, these regularization techniques can be used together with data augmentation and more complex CNNs with more filters or more layers, to potentially achieve good results and minimize the execution time on challenging datasets.

References

1. Bai, S.: Growing random forest on deep convolutional neural networks for scene categorization. Expert Syst. Appl. **71**, 279–287 (2017)
2. Zhao, W., Xiong, L., Ding, H.: Automatic recognition of loess landforms using Random Forest method. J. Mt. Sci. **14**(5), 885–897 (2017)
3. Krizhevsky, A., Hinton, G.: Learning multiple layers of features from tiny images (2009)
4. Gecer, B., Azzopardi, G., Petkov, N.: Color-blob-based COSFIRE filters for object recognition. Image Vis. Comput. **57**, 165–174 (2017)
5. Liang, M., Hu, X.: Recurrent convolutional neural network for object recognition. In: IEEE Conference on Computer Vision and Pattern Recognition, pp. 3367–3375 (2015)
6. Dicarlo, J., Cox, D.: Untangling invariant object recognition. Trends Cogn. Sci. **11**(8), 333–341 (2007)
7. Zhang, L., He, Z., Liu, Y.: Deep object recognition across domains based on adaptive extreme learning machine. Neurocomputing **239**, 194–203 (2017)
8. Lecun, Y., Bengio, Y., Hinton, G.: Deep learning. Nature **521**(7553), 436–444 (2015)
9. Chen, W., Wilson, J.T., Tyree, S., Weinberger, K.Q., Chen, Y.: Compressing convolutional neural networks. arXiv preprint arXiv:1506.04449 (2015)
10. Tobias, L., Ducournau, A., Rousseau, F.: Convolutional neural networks for object recognition on mobile devices: a case study. In: IEEE 23rd International Conference on Pattern Recognition (ICPR), pp. 3530–3535 (2016)
11. Li, H., Xu, B., Wang, N., Liu, J.: Deep convolutional neural networks for classifying body constitution. In: Villa, A.E.P., Masulli, P., Pons Rivero, A.J. (eds.) ICANN 2016. LNCS, vol. 9887, pp. 128–135. Springer, Cham (2016). doi:10.1007/978-3-319-44781-0_16
12. Madai-Tahy, L., Otte, S., Hanten, R., Zell, A.: Revisiting deep convolutional neural networks for RGB-D based object recognition. In: Villa, A.E.P., Masulli, P., Pons Rivero, A. J. (eds.) ICANN 2016. LNCS, vol. 9887, pp. 29–37. Springer, Cham (2016). doi:10.1007/978-3-319-44781-0_4
13. Krizhevsky, I., Sutskever, A., Hinton, G.E.: ImageNet classification with deep convolutional neural networks. In: Advances in Neural Information Processing Systems (NIPS), pp. 1097–1105 (2012)
14. Calderon, A., Roa, S., Victorino, J.: Handwritten digit recognition using convolutional neural networks and gabor filters. In: Proceedings of the International Congress on Computational Intelligence (2003)
15. Alwzwazy, H.A., Albehadili, H.M., Alwan, Y.S.: Handwritten digit recognition using convolutional neural networks (2016)
16. Peris, Á., Bolanos, M., Radeva, P.: Video description using bidirectional recurrent neural networks. arXiv preprint arXiv:1604.03390 (2016)
17. Peyrard, C., Baccouche, M., Garcia, C.: Blind super-resolution with deep convolutional neural networks. In: Villa, A.E.P., Masulli, P., Pons Rivero, A.J. (eds.) ICANN 2016. LNCS, vol. 9887, pp. 161–169. Springer, Cham (2016). doi:10.1007/978-3-319-44781-0_20
18. Sholomon, D., David, Omid E., Netanyahu, Nathan S.: DNN-Buddies: a deep neural network-based estimation metric for the jigsaw puzzle problem. In: Villa, A.E.P., Masulli, P., Pons Rivero, A.J. (eds.) ICANN 2016. LNCS, vol. 9887, pp. 170–178. Springer, Cham (2016). doi:10.1007/978-3-319-44781-0_21
19. Ruiz-Garcia, A., Elshaw, M., Altahhan, A., Palade, V.: Deep learning for emotion recognition in faces. In: Villa, A.E.P., Masulli, P., Pons Rivero, A.J. (eds.) ICANN 2016. LNCS, vol. 9887, pp. 38–46. Springer, Cham (2016). doi:10.1007/978-3-319-44781-0_5

20. Wu, H., Gu, X.: Towards dropout training for convolutional neural networks. Neural Netw. **71**, 1–10 (2015)
21. Hara, K., Saitoh, D., Shouno, H.: Analysis of dropout learning regarded as ensemble learning. arXiv preprint arXiv:1706.06859 (2017)
22. Miclut, B.: Committees of deep feedforward networks trained with few data. In: Jiang, X., Hornegger, J., Koch, R. (eds.) GCPR 2014. LNCS, vol. 8753, pp. 736–742. Springer, Cham (2014). doi:10.1007/978-3-319-11752-2_62

Soccer Video Event Detection Using 3D Convolutional Networks and Shot Boundary Detection via Deep Feature Distance

Tingxi Liu[1], Yao Lu[1(✉)], Xiaoyu Lei[1], Lijing Zhang[1], Haoyu Wang[1], Wei Huang[1], and Zijian Wang[1,2]

[1] Beijing Laboratory of Intelligent Information Technology,
School of Computer Science, Beijing Institute of Technology, Beijing 100081, China
{liutx,vis_yl,leixiaoyu,focus_zlj,2120161052,whuang}@bit.edu.cn,
wangzijian@cctv.com
[2] China Central Television, Beijing, China

Abstract. In this work, we propose a novel framework combining temporal action localization and play-break (PB) rules for soccer video event detection. Firstly we treat event detection task in action-level, and adopt 3D convolutional networks to perform action localization. Then we employ PB rules to organize actions into events using long view and replay logo detected in the first step. Finally, we determine the semantic classes of events according to principal actions which contain key semantic information of highlights. For long untrimmed videos, we propose a shot boundary detection method using deep feature distance (DFD) to reduce the number of proposals and improve the performance of localization. Experiment results verify the effectiveness of our framework on a new dataset which contains 152 classes of semantic actions and scenes in soccer video.

Keywords: Soccer event detection · Temporal action localization · 3D convolutional networks · Deep feature distance

1 Introduction

Soccer video analysis is widely applied in many fields like TV program production, match summarization, tactical analysis, etc. The semantic information learned from soccer video could be utilized to produce high-quality programs and provide valuable advices to coaches.

Audience always prefer the highlights such as goal, shot, penalty, free kick and so on, but these highlights are commonly extracted from match video manually, which is rather time-consuming. Meanwhile, the development of hardware leads to improvement on video resolution and sharp growth of storage cost.

Automatic soccer event detection is a brilliant solution to solve the problems mentioned above. Recent years, a large number of approaches are proposed for

© Springer International Publishing AG 2017
D. Liu et al. (Eds.): ICONIP 2017, Part II, LNCS 10635, pp. 440–449, 2017.
https://doi.org/10.1007/978-3-319-70096-0_46

this task [1,2]. Prior methods define an event as a multi-shot video segment, and train different classifiers like SVM [1], CNN+LSTM [2] in event-level directly. In fact, semantic information captured from events is coarse and ambiguous due to the presence of those shots with poor semantic support, e.g. passing, ordinary close-up view, spectator activities and so on.

In this work, we consider soccer event detection in action-level, and adopt action localization methods [3,4] based on 3D convolutional networks for soccer videos. After localization, we utilize the Play-Break (PB) rules as a mapping from actions to events. As the key elements of PB rules, long view and replay logo are recognized by extra classifiers in [1,2], while we eliminate the classification procedure by regarding them as two classes of actions and applying PB rules in action sequences directly. Finally, the semantic class of each event is determined by the principal action (e.g. goal, shooting, penalty, yellow/red card) which has the highest confidence inside the event.

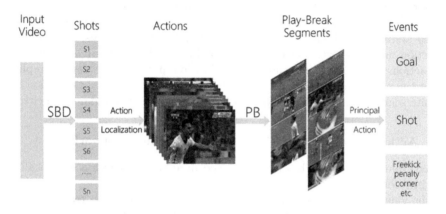

Fig. 1. Our detection framework firstly pre-trim entire video into shots using DFD-based SBD, and perform action localization in every shot. Following PB rules, we organize actions into event sequences, and finally determine the semantic class according to principal action which achieves the highest confidence.

Popular action localization methods [4–7] usually start with a proposal generation process to obtain candidate segments from untrimmed videos. In this paper, we present a novel shot boundary detection (SBD) method based on Deep Feature Distance (DFD) to pre-trim the entire long soccer videos into shots, which can significantly reduce the number of proposals. Unlike prior SBD methods using pixel difference [8], histogram [9], perceptual hash and so on, our method extracts the deep feature of each frame by Convolutional Neural Networks (CNNs) and then calculates Euclidean distance of feature vectors as the measurement of the difference between two adjacent frames. The experimental results show that our SBD method is more effective and efficient with the support of GPU accelerating.

The main contributions of our work are summarized as follows:

1. Different with methods in [1,2], we consider soccer event detection task in action-level, and combine the strength of temporal action localization and Play-Break rules.
2. Instead of extra classification procedure of long/non-long view and logo shots in [1,2], we regard long view and replay logo as two separate action classes, so that PB rules could be applied in action localization results directly.
3. For better performance in action localization, we propose a shot boundary detection method using Deep Feature Distance to pre-trim videos into shots accurately and efficiently.

2   Action-Level Soccer Event Detection

As mentioned in Sect. 1, event-level semantic information captured by [1,2] is coarse and ambiguous due to the presence of those shots with poor semantic support. Our experiments show that with the increase of semantic event classes (from 5 to 8), the performance of classifiers in [1,2] will decline in varying degrees.

To address this issue, we treat an event as a set of actions, and perform detection in action-level. For example, a goal event should be divided into several actions: (1) passing, (2) shot, (3) celebration and (4) multi-camera replays (start and end with a logo respectively). Comparing with event, every action has definite semantic information, which could describe the video more explicitly.

2.1   Action Localization Using 3D Convolutional Networks

Remarkable development has been achieved in action recognition and localization in recent years.

For video action clips trimmed manually, [10,11] use dense trajectories to encode video sequences and classify them using SVM, [12] fuses two streams of features: temporal (still images) and spatial (dense optical flow) to predict video classes, and [3,13] employ 3D convolutional networks to learn spatiotemporal feature from video volumes directly.

For untrimmed long videos, the basic framework of many action localization methods is the combination of a proposal generator and an action classifier. The common used proposal generation methods include sliding window [4,6] and RNN sequence encoder [5,7].

In our framework, we adopt 3D convolutional networks like C3D [3] and SCNN [4] in action-level soccer video event detection because of their excellent efficiency comparing with state-of-the-art two-stream methods [12,14].

C3D [3] is an architecture of 3D ConvNets using $3 \times 3 \times 3$ convolution kernels in all layers. It learns both appearance and motion features from video volumes (typically 16 frames) directly, and produces classification results after a standard softmax layer.

The training examples of SCNN are the proposals generated by sliding window, and corresponding overlap values with ground truth instances measured by Intersection-over-Union (IoU). As illustrated in Fig. 2, SCNN consists of three

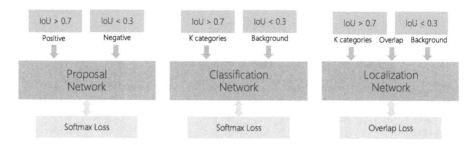

Fig. 2. Flowchart of Segment-CNN (SCNN), which consists of three 3D ConvNets (C3D).

networks similar to C3D: (1) a **proposal network** trained on positive samples $P_{IoU>0.7}$ and negative samples $P_{IoU<0.3}$, which is used to remove background proposals; (2) a **classification network** for action categories trained on $P_{IoU>0.7}$ and $P_{IoU<0.3}$ (as background); (3) a **localization network** trained on the same dataset used in (2) but with a new loss function which takes overlap into account.

For each mini-batch that contains N samples, the standard softmax loss is defined as

$$L_{softmax} = \frac{1}{N} \sum_n \left(-log(P_n^{k_n})\right), \tag{1}$$

where k_n denotes the positive label, and $P_n^{k_n}$ is the prediction score vector after the softmax layer. The overlap loss is defined as

$$L_{overlap} = \frac{1}{N} \sum_n \left(\frac{1}{2} \cdot \left(\frac{(P_n^{k_n})^2}{(v_n)^\alpha} - 1\right) \cdot [k_n > 0]\right), \tag{2}$$

where v_n denotes the overlap measured by IoU. $[k_n > 0]$ equals 0 when $k_n = 0$, which means the sample is a background proposal. If the sample is an action proposal, $[k_n > 0] = 1$. The loss function of localization network $L_{loc} = L_{softmax} + \lambda \cdot L_{overlap}$, λ is a balance parameter and equals 1 in [4].

2.2   Play-Break: Mapping from Actions to Events

Recent works like [1,2] use Play-Break rules to form shots into semantic event sequences. The key idea is that in soccer match video, long and non-long view shots always switch frequently. Specifically, consecutive multiple non-long view shots and replay logos usually appear during the breaks of the match. A typical Play-Break segment is illustrated in Fig. 3.

Similar to methods in [1,2], we summarize the basic rules of Play-Break as follows:

1. Consecutive non-long shots (break) that contain a total of more than T_{break} frames (T_{break} is the break threshold) is defined as a Break.

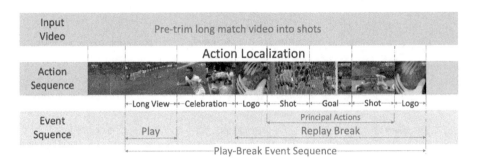

Fig. 3. A typical instance of play-break in action sequences: (1) A long view scene followed by non-long view actions, and (2) several principal actions surrounded by a pair of replay logos. These two segments are regarded as a Play and a Break respectively, and contribute to a Play-Break event sequence. In this example, the principal action 'goal' achieves the highest confidence and determines the semantic class of this event.

2. Shot sequences surrounded by a pair of replay logos form a Break.
3. The last long view shot in front of a Break is defined as a Play. We regard the action sequences from Play to Break as an event.

In our dataset Soccer-152A, long view shot and replay logo are defined as two separate classes. Therefore, temporal actions can be organized into event sequences following PB rules directly. To determine the semantic classes of events, we specify 8 classes of actions as **Principal Action**, including goal, shot, penalty, yellow/red card, free kick, corner, etc. The semantic class of an event depends on the principal action which achieves the highest confidence in the event sequence.

2.3   Shot Boundary Detection Using Deep Feature Distance

An entire soccer match video often has a duration of almost 100 min. Obviously, generating proposals from entire videos is inefficient because of massive overlapping proposals and time-consuming location procedure.

Naturally, an automatic video pre-trimming method is needed to solve the problem. SBD is widely used in video retrieval, indexing, analysis, etc. There are two common types of shot boundary: abrupt and gradual transition, while we focus primarily on abrupt shot boundary in soccer match video.

The key problems of SBD are how to measure the difference between adjacent frames, and select a proper threshold to determine the boundaries. Prior SBD methods calculate frame difference using pixel-level difference [9], histogram [8], block histogram, perceptual hash and so on. One of the common disadvantages of these methods is that the features used to represent the picture are sensitive to illumination, motion and camera movements, which affects the accuracy of detection results.

Inspired by image classification and image retrieval tasks, we propose a SBD method which extracts features from video frames using convolutional neural networks (CNNs), and calculates Euclidean distance of deep feature vectors to evaluate the difference between two adjacent frames. The procedure of DFD-based SBD is described as follows:

1. Feed CNN models (e.g. LeNet, ResNet50) with a sequence of video frames $V\{v_1, v_2, ..., v_n\}$;
2. Obtain the output vector $f_i^{1 \times k}$ from full connected (FC) layer in CNNs (specifically, average pooling layer in ResNet), k denotes the size of output vector after FC layer;
3. Normalize the feature vector using Min-Max Normalization:

$$\hat{f}_i = \frac{f_i - min(f_i)}{max(f_i) - min(f_i)} \tag{3}$$

4. Calculate Euclidean distance between every two adjacent frames.

$$d = \sqrt{\sum_{j=1}^{k} (\hat{f}_i^j - \hat{f}_{i-1}^j)^2} \tag{4}$$

5. Select a boundary-labeled video as ground truth and search the optimum threshold that achieves the highest F1 value, then set the threshold as abrupt threshold T_{abrupt} which determines shot boundaries.

We test the performance of different CNNs pre-trained on ImageNet 2014 and SSID dataset [2] respectively. SSID is a soccer semantic image dataset in which soccer video shots are divided into nine types of camera views. Experimental results show that models pre-trained with ImageNet achieve best performance.

3 Experiments

3.1 Soccer-152A: Semantic Soccer Actions and Scenes

To verify the effectiveness of our detection framework, we collect 14 matches (10 matches for training and 4 for testing) in FIFA World Cup 2014, and segment them into 152 classes of actions. These actions include not only the behaviors of players, coaches, referees and spectators, but also some specific semantic scenes like long view, replay logo, starting line-up, etc. In particular, the presence of long view and replay logo is the prerequisite of Play-Break rules.

Another vital property of soccer actions is that one single shot in soccer video always contains one or more actions (including background), and this property ensures the effectiveness of our DFD-based SBD method.

We organize the dataset named Soccer-152A in the format similar to THUMOS 2014 [15] and UCF-101 [16].

3.2   Shot Boundary Detection Using DFD

As mentioned in Sect. 2.3, we calculate DFD using CNNs pre-trained on ImageNet and SSID respectively. For experiments, we select four matches in FIFA
World Cup 2014 and label 1248 abrupt boundaries manually. The performance
comparison of prior SBD methods and DFDs based on ResNet-50 is given in
Table 1

Table 1. Performance of DFDs comparing with prior SBD methods

Method	Precision	Recall	F1	fps
Pixel level	60.8%	63.6%	62.1%	2.6
Histogram	70.6%	78.4%	74.2%	21.7
Perceptual Hash	71.4%	80.9%	75.8%	11.3
DFD-SSID	75.5%	86.7%	80.7%	**51.6**
DFD-ImageNet	**81.3%**	**89.1%**	**85.0%**	51.5

The results show that the DFD using Resnet-50 trained on ImageNet achieves
the best performance in shot boundary detection. Meanwhile, with the support
of GeForce Titan X GPU, our DFD method reaches a processing speed of 51
frames per second and outperforms prior methods significantly.

3.3   Action Localization in Soccer-152A

According to the distribution of action durations shown in Fig. 4, we set the
lengths of sliding window to 32, 64, 128, 256, 512, 1024 frames, and generate
proposals in 10 training videos using sliding window. Then we calculate overlap values of each proposal evaluated by IoU. If a proposal straddles two or
more ground truth instances, we assign the maximum of IoU and corresponding
category of the instance to the proposal.

Follow the steps described in Sect. 2.1, we select two kinds of proposals
$P_{IoU>0.7}$ and $P_{IoU<0.3}$ as the train samples. Firstly we train the proposal network
using $P_{IoU>0.7}$ and $P_{IoU<0.3}$ as positive and negative samples respectively. Then
we train the classification network with 152 categories of actions in $P_{IoU>0.7}$, and
background samples in $P_{IoU<0.3}$. Finally, the localization network fine-tunes on
the classification network with overlap loss function defined in Eq. 2.

The networks we use in localization are based on Caffe [17] and trained with
a Nvidia GeForce Titan X GPU. All the networks are trained with an initial
learning rate of 10^{-4} and a momentum of 0.9, and optimize the parameters
using stochastic gradient decent (SGD) for 15000 iterations. The results of action
localization are shown in Table 2. SW and Prop stand for initial sliding window
and background filtering by the proposal network respectively.

After action localization, we use Play-Break and 8 classes of principal actions
to perform event detection. For comparison, we implement the method in [2]

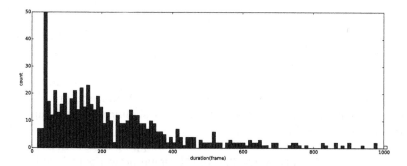

Fig. 4. The distribution of action durations in our dataset.

Table 2. Performance of action localization

Method	Number of Proposals		mAP		
	SW	Prop	tIoU=0.4	tIoU= 0.6	tIoU= 0.8
SCNN	15691	12074	0.44	0.35	0.23
DFD+SCNN	**12337**	**10035**	0.41	**0.36**	**0.26**

using Keras 1.2.2 and train the models on a dataset which contains 8 categories of event. The performance of event detection is given in Table 3

Table 3. Performance of action Event Detection

Event	Total	Precision(%)		Recall(%)	
		[2]	Ours	[2]	Ours
Goal	13	53.8	70	71.4	76.9
Shot	41	58.8	65.2	81.6	78.4
Free kick	15	33.3	66.7	69.2	60
Penalty	2	50	100	100	100
Fault	63	79.3	71.4	83.8	90.4
Corner	19	73.6	60.8	80	84.2
Yellow/Red Card	14	42.8	60	81.8	64.2
Offside	9	44.4	66.7	58.3	77.8

4   Conclusion

We propose a novel soccer video event detection framework combining the strength of temporal action localization and Play-Break rules. We abstract soccer video highlights into 152 classes of actions, and perform action localization based on them using 3D convolutional networks. Then we employ PB rules to organize the action sequences into events by means of long view and replay logo localized by 3D ConvNets. Finally, we determine the class of events according to the principal action which achieves the highest confidence.

To reduce the number of proposals in entire match video, we propose a shot boundary detection method based on Deep Feature Distance to pre-trim videos into shots, which outperforms prior SBD methods significantly and improve the performance of proposal generation.

In this work, we use Play-Break rules as the mapping from actions to events. In the future, we would like to use 3D convolutional networks trained in action-level as visual encoders, and add a Recurrent Neural Network layer as a sequence encoder to generate proposals and perform End-to-End localization in event-level directly.

Acknowledgments. This work was supported by the National Natural Science Foundation of China (No. 61273273).

References

1. Zhao, W., Lu, Y., Jiang, H., Huang, W.: Event detection in soccer videos using shot focus identification. In: 3rd IAPR Asian Conference on Pattern Recognition (ACPR) 2015, pp. 341–345. IEEE (2015)
2. Jiang, H., Lu, Y., Xue, J.: Automatic soccer video event detection based on a deep neural network combined cnn and rnn. In: IEEE 28th International Conference on Tools with Artificial Intelligence (ICTAI) 2016, pp. 490–494. IEEE (2016)
3. Tran, D., Bourdev, L., Fergus, R., Torresani, L., Paluri, M.: Learning spatiotemporal features with 3d convolutional networks. In: Proceedings of the IEEE International Conference on Computer Vision, pp. 4489–4497 (2015)
4. Shou, Z., Wang, D., Chang, S.F.: Temporal action localization in untrimmed videos via multi-stage cnns. In: CVPR (2016)
5. Escorcia, V., Caba Heilbron, F., Niebles, J.C., Ghanem, B.: DAPs: deep action proposals for action understanding. In: Leibe, B., Matas, J., Sebe, N., Welling, M. (eds.) ECCV 2016. LNCS, vol. 9907, pp. 768–784. Springer, Cham (2016). doi:10.1007/978-3-319-46487-9_47
6. Shou, Z., Chan, J., Zareian, A., Miyazawa, K., Chang, S.F.: Cdc: Convolutional-de-convolutional networks for precise temporal action localization in untrimmed videos. arXiv preprint arXiv:1703.01515 (2017)
7. Buch, S., Escorcia, V., Shen, C., Ghanem, B., Niebles, J.C.: Sst: Single-stream temporal action proposals. In: CVPR (2017)
8. By, H.A.: Shot-boundary detection: unraveled and resolved. IEEE Trans. Circ. Syst. Video Technol. **12**(2), 90–105 (2010)
9. Tsamoura, E., Mezaris, V., Kompatsiaris, I.: Gradual transition detection using color coherence and other criteria in a video shot meta-segmentation framework. In: IEEE International Conference on Image Processing, pp. 45–48 (2008)
10. Wang, H., Klaser, A., Schmid, C., Liu, C.L.: Action recognition by dense trajectories. In: Computer Vision and Pattern Recognition, pp. 3169–3176 (2011)
11. Wang, H., Schmid, C.: Action recognition with improved trajectories. In: Proceedings of the IEEE International Conference on Computer Vision, pp. 3551–3558 (2013)

12. Simonyan, K., Zisserman, A.: Two-stream convolutional networks for action recognition in videos. In: Advances in Neural Information Processing Systems, pp. 568–576 (2014)
13. Ji, S., Xu, W., Yang, M., Yu, K.: 3d convolutional neural networks for human action recognition. IEEE Trans. Pattern Anal. Mach. Intell. **35**(1), 221–231 (2013)
14. Wang, L., Xiong, Y., Wang, Z., Qiao, Y., Lin, D., Tang, X., Gool, L.V.: Temporal segment networks: towards good practices for deep action recognition. In: European Conference on Computer Vision, pp. 20–36 (2016)
15. Jiang, Y.G., Liu, J., Roshan Zamir, A., Toderici, G., Laptev, I., Shah, M., Sukthankar, R.: THUMOS challenge: Action recognition with a large number of classes (2014). http://crcv.ucf.edu/THUMOS14/
16. Soomro, K., Zamir, A.R., Shah, M.: Ucf101: A dataset of 101 human actions classes from videos in the wild. Computer Science (2012)
17. Jia, Y., Shelhamer, E., Donahue, J., Karayev, S., Long, J., Girshick, R., Guadarrama, S., Darrell, T.: Caffe: Convolutional architecture for fast feature embedding, pp. 675–678 (2014)

Very Deep Neural Networks for Hindi/Arabic Offline Handwritten Digit Recognition

Rolla Almodfer[1], Shengwu Xiong[1,2], Mohammed Mudhsh[1], and Pengfei Duan[1,2(✉)]

[1] School of Computer Science and Technology,
Wuhan University of Technology, Wuhan 430070, China
duanpf@whut.edu.cn
[2] Hubei Key Laboratory of Transportation Internet of Things,
Wuhan University of Technology, Wuhan 430070, China

Abstract. Handwritten Digit Recognition (HDR) has become one of the challenging areas of research in the field of document image processing during the last few decades. In this paper, inspired by the success of the very deep state-of-the-art VGGNet, we proposed VGG_No for HDR. VGG_No is fast and reliable, which improved the classification performance effectively. Besides, this model has also reduced the overall complexity of VGGNet. VGG_No constructed by thirteen convolutional layers, two max-pooling layers, and three fully connected layers. A Cross-Validation analysis has been performed using the 10-Fold Cross-Validation strategy, and 10-Fold classification accuracies of 99.57% and 99.69% have been obtained for ADBase database and MNIST database, respectively. The classification performance of VGG_No is superior to existing techniques using multi-classifiers since it has achieved better results using very simple and homogeneous architecture.

Keywords: VGGNet · Digit recognition · ADBase · MNIST

1 Introduction

Handwritten digit recognition (HDR) is a difficult task that has been intensely studied for many years in the field of handwritten recognition. Recognition of digits, whether handwritten or machine typed, belongs to the field of optical character recognition (OCR) which is one of the preliminary applications of the Pattern Recognition (PR) and Computer Vision (CV) techniques [1]. However, HDR is a challenging problem due to unlimited variation in shapes and sizes of handwritten digits. It has a wide variety of applications including reading the amounts in cheque, mail sorting, reading aid for the blind and so on. Therefore, HDR methods should be investigated with due importance.

The existing approaches of HDR can generally be divided into two groups: Handcrafted approach and unsupervised/supervised learning approach. For the first group, the most commonly used methods are Hidden Markov Model (HMM) [2, 3], Support Vector Machine (SVM) [4] and Histogram of Oriented Gradient (HOG) [5]. The second group is known as the group of deep learning approaches. This approach has acquired a reputation for solving many computer vision problems, and its

© Springer International Publishing AG 2017
D. Liu et al. (Eds.): ICONIP 2017, Part II, LNCS 10635, pp. 450–459, 2017.
https://doi.org/10.1007/978-3-319-70096-0_47

application to the field of handwritten recognition has been shown to provide significantly better results than traditional methods.

Arabic is one of the most spoken languages; it is the fifth most popular language in the world [6]. About 267 million people use Arabic as their speaking and writing purpose in their daily life. Despite this fact, past and recent works in the field of HDR have extensively investigated on various languages, Arabic is still a mostly unexplored field of study. The important distinction between Arabic and other languages is that Arabic words are written from right to left. Nonetheless, digits of an Arabic number is written from left to right [7]. A major obstacle to research on Hindi/Arabic handwritten digit recognition is the nonexistence of benchmark databases. Unlike Latin, Previous research was reported by databases collected in laboratory environments. While several standard databases, such as NIST, MNIST [8] and CEDAR [9] are available for Latin digits. Various methods have been proposed for the recognition of Arabic handwritten digits. Al-Omari and Al-Jarrah [10] presented a recognition system for online handwritten Arabic digit one to nine. The system skeletonizes the digits, and then geometrical features of the digits are extracted. Probabilistic neural networks (PNNs) are used for recognition. The developed system is translation, rotation, and scaling invariant. Abdelazeem [11] studied the performance of a different set of classifiers for Arabic digit recognition. Some different features were used, and various combinations of features and classifiers were investigated. Gradient features with SVM (RBF kernel) gave the best results of 99.48% for the ADBase database. Parvez and Mahmoud [12] used a polygonal approximation of character contour and a classifier based on turning functions for isolated Arabic alphanumeric character recognition. The authors obtained over 97% accuracy for the ADBase database for Arabic digits.

Recently, Deep Neural Networks (DNN) has achieved great success for object recognition, and several successful architectures were proposed for image classification such as Alex net [13] and GoogLeNet [14]. In 2014, Simonyan and Zissermaanother presented VGGNet [15]. VGGNet is a very deep architecture has achieved a high classification accuracy of the massive Imagenet database [16]. However, this network has a high number of parameters compared to other Deep Convolutional Neural Networks (DCNN), which makes it computationally more expensive to evaluate and requires a significant amount of memory for optimizing the learning parameters.

In this paper, inspired by the success of VGGNet, we proposed VGG_NO for Hindi/Arabic HDR. VGG_NO is straightforward to implement and shows effectiveness in improving classification performance. Moreover, it reduces the overall complexity of VGGNet while keeping the same excellent performance of the net. To improve the generalization capability of the VGG_No, the dropout regularization method is adopted. A Cross-Validation analysis has also been performed, and a 10-Fold classification accuracy of 99.57% has been obtained from the ADBase database [17]. We also VGG_No on the MNIST handwritten digit database, and a 10-Fold classification accuracy of 99.69% has been obtained.

The remainder of the paper consists of the following. Section 2 gives an overview of standard VGGNet and our proposed VGG_NO. Section 3 describes the databases used and our training scheme, and in Sect. 4 we report on results. Finally, conclusion and future work are drawn in Sect. 5.

2   Offline Handwritten Digit Recognition

In this section, we briefly summarize standard VGGnet. We then describe our proposed VGG_No for offline handwritten digit recognition.

2.1   VGGNet Architecture

The VGGnet [15] created by Simonyan and Zisserman presents a very deep, very simple and homogeneous architecture. In VGGNet, a given image is passed through a stack of convolutional layers; the filters are generally with size: 3 × 3. The stride and the spatial padding are both fixed to 1 pixel. The width of convolutional layers starts from 64 to 512. Max pooling layers are followed some of the convolutional layers.

Max pooling is performed over a 2 × 2 pixel window, with stride 2. Finally, three Fully-Connected (FC) layers follow the stack of convolutional layers: the first two have 4096 channels each, the third contains 1000 channels. The final layer is the softmax layer. All convolutional layers are equipped with the rectified function (Relu), which is formulated by:

$$f(x) = max\{0, x\} \tag{1}$$

where x denotes a feature value produced over the former layer. The architectures of VGG_16 is shown in Fig. 1.

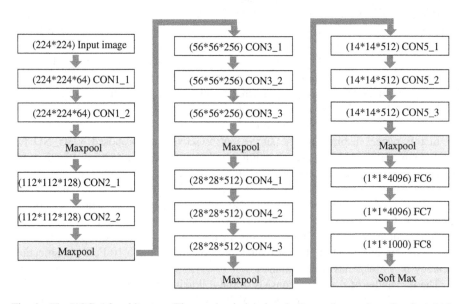

Fig. 1. The VGG_16 architecture. The number in brackets indicates the number of nodes within a layer of the neural network. CON = convolutional layer, FC = fully connected layer

2.2   VGG_NO

In this section, we introduce our proposed architecture that improves the recognition performance of the given databases. The architecture of the VGG_No is shown in Fig. 2. VGG_No follows the standard model of VGGNet, which contains 16 layers with some differences. The filters numbers divided by factor of 8 throughout the network. The filters numbers in a convolutional layer set to 8, 16, 32, and 64 and the first two fully connected layers set to 512. Since the original VGGNet was trained on 1000 classes, its last fully connected layer produces 1000 outputs. We replace this layer with a new fully connected layer that has as many outputs as the number of classes (10 for the ADBase database). The final layer is the soft-max layer.

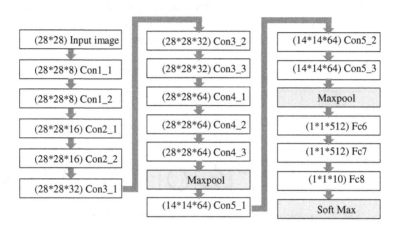

Fig. 2. The architecture of VGG_NO. The number in brackets indicates the number of nodes within a layer of the neural network. CON = convolutional layer, FC = fully connected layer

The important issue in VGG_No design is the selection of input image size. When the image size is set to 28 × 28, the complexity of the network is very low. However, there are several drawbacks, which cannot be ignored using this setting. In one hand, the max-pooling layers have significance to the performance of a deep network. Max pooling partitions the input image into a set of non-overlapping rectangles and, for each such sub-region, outputs the maximum value. It leads to faster convergence rate by selecting superior invariant features, which improve generalization performance. When the image size is 28 × 28, the number of max-pooling layers is hard to determine. However, after several experiments, we kept the fourth and the fifth max-pooling layer and discarded the first three. On the other hand, if we want to remove all the max-pooling layers, the deep model size will be very large since the number of weights in fully connected layers increases significantly. The number of parameters of the VGG_No is very low compared to the number of parameters of standard VGG_16 when applied to binary images. In Table 1 we report the number of parameters for each network configuration. In spite of a large depth, the number of parameters in our networks is around 2 million while VGG_16 is higher than 138 million.

Table 1. Number of parameters

Network	VGG_16	VGG_No
Number of parameters	138,357,544	2,104,354

3   Experiments Setup

3.1   Databases

ADBase database. The ADBase is composed of 70,000 digits written by 700 participants. Each participant wrote each digit (from '0' to '9') ten times. The database is partitioned into two sets: a training set (60,000 digits to 6,000 images per class) and a test set (10,000 digits to 1,000 images per class). This database is available on the website [17]. Sample images of digits from the ADBase database is shown in Fig. 3.

Arabic digit	1	2	3	4	5	6	7	8	9	0
English digit	1	2	3	4	5	6	7	8	9	0
Image										

Fig. 3. Sample images of digits (0–9) from the ADBase database.

MNIST database. The MNIST digit database is composed of 60,000 images of 10 digit classes in the training set and 10,000 digit images in the test set for 70,000 images in the database. The spatial resolution of the images is 28×28 pixels, and all images are grayscale images. This database is available at the website maintained by Lecun et al. at [18]. Sample images of digits from the MNIST database is shown in Fig. 4.

3.2   Training

The architecture of VGG_NO is composed of 13 convolution layers and two max-pooling layers. The layer 10 and layer 13 are followed by a max-pooling layer, with a pooling size of 2×2 and a stride of 2 pixels. The receptive field of each convolutional layer is 3×3. The convolution stride is fixed to 1 pixel; the spatial padding of convolution layer input is such that the spatial resolution is preserved after convolution. Three Fully-Connected (FC) layers follow the stack of convolutional layers: the first two have 512 channels each. Since the original VGG net was trained on 1000 classes, its last fully connected layer produces 1000 outputs. We replace this layer with a new fully connected layer that has as many outputs as the number of classes (10 for the ADBase and MNIST databases). The final layer is the soft-max layer.

Fig. 4. Sample images of digits (0–9) from the MNIST database.

The training is carried out by using Adam optimization algorithm. Adam is a first-order gradient-based algorithm, developed for the optimization of stochastic objective functions with adaptive weight updates based on lower-order moments. Adam optimizer has four parameters: one is the learning rate, exponential decay rates (beta_1) for the moving averages of the gradient, the squared gradient (beta_2) and the smoothing term (epsilon). After related experiments, we left the parameters to their default values, learning rate equal to 0.001, decay rates equal to 0.9, the squared gradient was equal to 0.999 and the smoothing term was equal to 1e-08.. The batch size was set to 256 and the momentum to 0.9. The training was regularized with the weight of $5 \cdot 10^{-4}$ and dropout regularization for the first two fully-connected layers (dropout ratio set to 0.5).The type of nonlinearity used is Rectified Linear Unit *(ReLU)*. VGG_NO was trained for 30 epochs. The whole training procedure for a single network took at most 3 h on a desktop PC with an Intel i7 3770 processor, a NVidia GTX780 graphics card and 16 GB of onboard RAM.

4 Results

To determine the performance of VGG_NO, we have conducted a large number of experiments. The *k*-Fold cross-validation methodology has been used to determine the classification performance of VGG_NO. The classifier performance has been measured regarding Classification Accuracy.

4.1 Performance of the VGG_NO on the k-Fold Cross Validation (CV)

Cross validation is a technique by which we split our training data into complementary subset to then conduct analysis and validation on different sets, aiming to reduce over-fitting and increase out-of-sample performance. To obtain the *k*-Fold cross-validation performance, the available training Set and test Set are first concatenated to get an overall dataset of 70,000 digit images. We then performed a 3-fold, 5-fold, and 10-fold cross-validation and got classification performance averaged over each fold. In the 10-fold cross-validation strategy, the available database is divided into 10-folds with nine folds used for training and the remaining 10th fold used for testing. The process is repeated for all ten folds in turn, and the performance is averaged over the ten folds.

To improve the generalization capability of the VGG_No, the fully connected layers is regularized by 0.5 dropout ratio. Dropout consists of setting to zero the output of each hidden neuron with probability 0.5. If the neurons in CNN are dropped out, they do not contribute to the forward pass and do not participate in back propagation. During testing, we use all the neurons but multiply their outputs by 0.5. However, VGG_No suffered slightly from overfitting even it dropped out values for the fully connected layers. During training, the dropout with probability 0.5 is added to the fully connected layers and the two Max pool layers. The final training and k-fold cross-validation accuracies are reported in Table 2. We evaluate the performance without dropout and with dropout: Overall, without dropout, 3-fold, 5-fold and 10-fold classification accuracies of 98.33%, 98.47%, and 98.80% have been achieved for the ADBase database, and 99.47%, 99.49%, and 99.53% have been achieved for the MNIST database. Figure 5 displays the classification accuracy attained by a VGG_NO on the training and cross-validation data without dropout at different training epochs. With dropout, the accuracy of the network increases, a 3-fold, 5-fold and 10-fold classification accuracies of 99.13%, 99.34%, and 99.57% have been obtained for the ADBase database, and 99.55%, 99.61%, and 99.69% have been obtained for the MNIST database. Figure 6 displays the classification accuracies attained by a VGG_NO on the training and cross validation data with dropout at different training epochs.

Table 2. Top-k accuracy on ADBase and MNIST database.

Database	Top-3 (%)		Top-5 (%)		Top-10 (%)	
	NO dropout	Dropout	NO dropout	Dropout	NO dropout	Dropout
ADBase	98.33	99.13	98.47	99.34	98.80	99.57
MNIST	99.47	99.55	99.49	99.61	99.53	99.69

4.2   Performance Comparison with State-of-the-Art

Unlike Latin, the task of Arabic handwritten digits recognition suffers from the lack of benchmarking database. To the best of our knowledge, this is the first work incorporate deep learning approach for recognizing ADBase database digits. In this subsection, to evaluate the effect of our proposed deep model, we compared the performance of the model with those used ADBase database. Our classification accuracy achieved 99.57% (0.43% of error rate). Table 3 compares the classification accuracy of different methods on ADBase database. Particularly, our best performance is noticeably higher than the result achieved by other methods. From Table 3 the work of Abdelazeem et al. [11] have reached recognition accuracy near to ours (i.e., greater than 99% recognition accuracy). However, this result is obtained by using ensemble methods of RBF kernal and SVM. In contrast, our model is quite simple and generic to apply so it may also work well with handwritten characters such as Latin or Arabic characters. We achieved

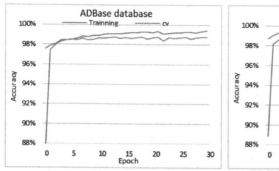
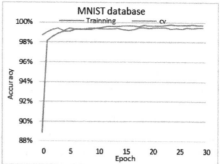

Fig. 5. Training vs. cross validation accuracies for ADBase database and MNIST database without dropout

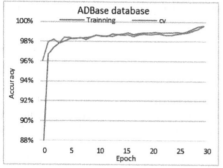
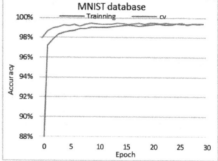

Fig. 6. Training vs. cross validation accuracies for ADBase database and MNIST database with dropout

Table 3. Comparison regarding classification accuracy between our model (highlighted) and the state-of-the-art methods on ADBase

Author(s)	Method	Accuracy (%)
Parvez et al. [12]	Fuzzy turning function	97.17%
Abdelazeem et al. [11]	SVM with RBF kernal	99.48%
Proposed	**VGG_NO**	**99.57%**

of 99.69% recognition rate (0.31% of error rate) on the MNIST benchmark database. The homepage of the MNIST database lists the best performances on their database achieved by various methods [18]. The lowest error rate on the list is 0.23% obtained by [19]. The best result was obtained by committees of many DCNNs, not by single classifiers.

5 Conclusion

In this paper, we proposed VGG_No net for Hindi/Arabic handwritten digit recognition task. VGG_No is an optimized version of the very popular VGGNet. We show incremental improvements of the digits recognition comparable to approaches used Support Vector Machine (SVM) or Fuzzy Logic (FL). VGG_No improved the classification accuracy and reduced the overall complexity of VGGNet by factor 8. We evaluated our network on two databases. We achieved very promising results with validation accuracy of 99.57% (error rate of 0.43%) using dropout regularization technique. As a future work, we plan to experiment the various VGGNet architectures (VGG_11, VGG_13, and VGG_19) on Arabic handwritten digits, characters and words recognition.

Acknowledgments. This research was supported in part by Science & Technology Pillar Program of Hubei Province under Grant (#2014BAA146), Nature Science Foundation of Hubei Province under Grant (#2015CFA059), Science and Technology Open Cooperation Program of Henan Province under Grant (#152106000048).

References

1. Schantz, H.F.: The history of OCR. Recognition Technology Users Association, VT (1982)
2. Cosi, P.: Hybrid HMM-NN architectures for connected digit recognition. In: Proceedings of the IEEE-INNS-ENNS International Joint Conference on Neural Networks, IJCNN 2000, vol. 5 (2000)
3. Al-Haddad, S.A.R., Samad, S.A., Hussain, A., Ishak, K.A., Mirvaziri, H.: Decision fusion for isolated Malay digit recognition using dynamic time warping (DTW) and hidden Markov model (HMM). In: 5th Student Conference on Research and Development, SCOReD 2007, pp. 1–6. IEEE (2007)
4. Drewnik, M., Pasternak-Winiarski, Z.: SVM kernel configuration and optimization for the handwritten digit recognition. In: Saeed, K., Homenda, W., Chaki, R. (eds.) CISIM 2017. LNCS, vol. 10244, pp. 87–98. Springer, Cham (2017). doi:10.1007/978-3-319-59105-6_8
5. Kim, E.H., Kim, B.Y., Oh, S.K.: Design of digits recognition system based on RBFNNs: a comparative study of pre-processing algorithms. Trans. Korean Inst. Electr. Eng. **66**(2), 416–424 (2017)
6. Summary by language size — ethnologue. https://www.ethnologue.com/statistics/size. Last accessed 25 Dec 2016
7. Mahmoud, S.: Recognition of writer-independent off-line handwritten Arabic (Indian) numerals using hidden Markov models. Signal Process. **88**(4), 844–857 (2008)
8. Lécun, Y., Bottou, L., Bengio, Y.: Gradient-based learning applied to document recognition. Proc. IEEE **86**(11), 2278–2324 (1998)
9. Hull, J.J.: A database for handwritten text recognition research. IEEE Trans. Pattern Anal. Mach. Intell. **16**(5), 550–554 (1994)
10. Al-Omari, F.A., Al-Jarrah, O.: Handwritten Indian numerals recognition system using probabilistic neural networks. Adv. Eng. Inf. **18**(1), 9–16 (2004)
11. Abdleazeem, S., El-Sherif, E.: Arabic handwritten digit recognition. Int. J. Doc. Anal. Recogn. (IJDAR) **11**(3), 127–141 (2008)

12. Parvez, M.T., Mahmoud, S.A.: Arabic handwritten alphanumeric character recognition using fuzzy attributed turning functions. In: Proceedings of the Workshop in Frontiers in Arabic Handwriting Recognition, 20th International Conference in Pattern Recognition (ICPR) (2012)
13. Krizhevsky, A., Sutskever, I., Hinton, G.E.: Imagenet classification with deep convolutional neural networks. In: Advances in Neural Information Processing Systems, pp. 1097–1105 (2012)
14. Szegedy, C., Liu, W., Jia, Y., Sermanet, P., Reed, S., Anguelov, D., Rabinovich, A.: Going deeper with convolutions. In: Proceedings of the IEEE Conference on Computer Vision and Pattern Recognition 2015, pp. 1–9 (2015)
15. Simonyan, K., Zisserman, A.: Very deep convolutional networks for large-scale image recognition (2014). arXiv preprint: arXiv:1409.1556
16. Deng, J., Dong, W., Socher, R., Li, L. J., Li, K., Fei-Fei, L.: Imagenet: a large-scale hierarchical image database. In: IEEE Conference on Computer Vision and Pattern Recognition (CVPR 2009), pp. 248–255 (2009)
17. Arabic Handwritten Digits Databases ADBase & MADBase. http://datacenter.aucegypt.edu/shazeem/. Last accessed 10 Aug 2017
18. The MNIST Database of Handwritten Digits. http://yann.lecun.com/exdb/mnist/. Last accessed 10 Aug 2017
19. Ciregan, D., Meier, U., Schmidhuber, J.: Multi-column deep neural networks for image classification. In: IEEE Conference on Computer Vision and Pattern Recognition (CVPR 2012), pp. 3642–3649 (2012)

Layer Removal for Transfer Learning with Deep Convolutional Neural Networks

Weiming Zhi[1($\boxtimes$)], Zhenghao Chen[2], Henry Wing Fung Yueng[2], Zhicheng Lu[2], Seid Miad Zandavi[2], and Yuk Ying Chung[2]

[1] Department of Engineering Science, University of Auckland, Auckland 1010, New Zealand
wzhi262@aucklanduni.ac.nz
[2] School of Information Technologies, University of Sydney, Sydney, NSW 2006, Australia
{zhenghao.chen,hyeu8081,zhlu2106,miad.zandavi,vera.chung}@sydney.edu.au

Abstract. It is usually difficult to find datasets of sufficient size to train Deep Convolutional Neural Networks (DCNNs) from scratch. In practice, a neural network is often pre-trained on a very large source dataset. Then, a target dataset is transferred onto the neural network. This approach is a form of transfer learning, and allows very deep networks to achieve outstanding performance even when a small target dataset is available. It is thought that the bottom layers of the pre-trained network contain general information, which are applicable to different datasets and tasks, while the upper layers of the pre-trained network contain abstract information relevant to a specific dataset and task. While studies have been conducted on the fine-tuning of these layers, the removal of these layers have not yet been considered. This paper explores the effect of removing the upper convolutional layers of a pre-trained network. We empirically investigated whether removing upper layers of a deep pre-trained network can improve performance for transfer learning. We found that removing upper pre-trained layers gives a significant boost in performance, but the ideal number of layers to remove depends on the dataset. We suggest removing pre-trained convolutional layers when applying transfer learning on off-the-shelf pre-trained DCNNs. The ideal number of layers to remove will depend on the dataset, and remain as a parameter to be tuned.

Keywords: Convolutional neural networks · Transfer learning · Deep learning

1   Introduction

Deep Convolutional Neural Networks (DCNNs) have achieved great success in large-scale image recognition. This success is partially due to the availability of large public image databases, such as ImageNet [5]. The ImageNet dataset contains over 1.2 million labeled images, belonging to a thousand distinct object

© Springer International Publishing AG 2017
D. Liu et al. (Eds.): ICONIP 2017, Part II, LNCS 10635, pp. 460–469, 2017.
https://doi.org/10.1007/978-3-319-70096-0_48

classes. However, data acquisition can often be difficult, and obtaining high-quality annotation may be costly. For many specific areas, no large scale database similar to ImageNet exists. For example, the unavailability of labeled medical data is a hindrance for greater use of DCNNs in medical imaging tasks [14].

Transfer learning [2–4] is an increasingly popular approach to alleviate the problem of insufficient training data. This approach generally involves pre-training [7,13,19] a DCNN with a very large *source* dataset. Then, a smaller *target* dataset is "transferred" onto the pre-trained DCNN. This approach has allowed deep networks, such as GoogLeNet [17], and VGGNet [15] to achieve impressive results [6,11] for image detection and classification tasks, even when very little data is provided.

Research has been conducted on the transferability of features during transfer learning [18]. The lower layers of the DCNN contain more general features, while upper layers contain more specific information about the source dataset. In particular, the first layer contains features resembling Gabor filters and colour blobs [18]. The transferability of features decreases significantly in higher layers, as there are discrepancies between the domains of the source and target datasets. In other words, the features contained in the higher layers of a pre-trained DCNN depend relatively heavily on the source dataset and task it has been trained on, and may be less useful when transferred to a new task. An approach often employed is to only retain pre-trained features up to a certain layer, and re-train layers above the chosen layer from randomised weights. Empirical results [18] show that having pre-trained upper layers performs better than having randomised upper layers, if a fine-tuning process is undertaken after the initial transfer. However, the effect of completely removing the upper convolutional layers from pre-trained DCNNs before applying the transfer, has not been considered nor investigated. To the best of our knowledge, there currently exists no framework or approach that utilises layer removal on off-the-shelf pre-trained architectures to improve performance.

As pre-training a DCNN on a large source dataset may be very time-consuming and hardware-demanding, off-the-shelf pre-trained DCNNs [12] are often used in transfer learning. These off-the-shelf DCNNs are publicly available, and have weights pre-trained on ImageNet. The availability of pre-trained off-the-shelf DCNNs have allowed transfer learning to be applied widely. Many previous studies done on specific tasks [9,10,14] involve transferring small target datasets onto pre-trained off-the-shelf DCNNs. However, these attempts focused on selecting the best off-the-shelf pre-trained model for a specific problem, with no modifications to the pre-trained convolutional layers of the off-the-shelf model. The results in this paper show that modifying, in particular removing, a certain number of convolutional layers will improve the performance of transfer learning. Removing convolutional layers will retain the pre-trained weights in the remaining layers, and not require any extra training on a source dataset. Hence, this option provides an efficient way to increase performance for transfer learning on off-the-shelf pre-trained models.

In this paper, we make the following contributions:

1. We suggest an efficient procedure that enhances performance, when applying transfer learning: to remove a suitable number of upper convolutional layers, before applying transfer learning to an off-the-shelf pre-trained model. The ideal number of layers to remove will depend on the dataset, and remain as a parameter to be tuned.
2. We demonstrate that removing upper pre-trained convolutional layers can improve the performance of transfer learning on off-the-shelf pre-trained architectures. This result is unintuitive, as results from Yosinski et al. [18] suggest that networks with fine-tuned pre-trained upper convolutional layers outperform those containing upper convolutional layers re-trained from randomised weights.
3. We perform transfer learning on over ten different convolutional neural networks, each with a different number of layers removed or with no layers removed, derived from an off-the-shelf pre-trained architecture. The trends of how the performance of the networks change, as the number of layers removed changes, are investigated.

2   Approach

2.1   Creating Different Networks by Removing Layers

Yosinski et al. [18] showed that for an eight layer CNN, having any number of upper convolutional layers with randomised weights in a pre-trained network results in worse performance than a network with pre-trained weights in all convolutional layers. However, although the approach of re-training these upper layers have been considered, there has yet to be any study that has looked into completely removing these upper layers. There have also not been any attempts to enhance performance by removing pre-trained convolutional layers. In this paper, we focus on investigating the effect of the removal of upper convolutional layers. In particular, we are interested in seeing whether we can significantly surpass naively applying transfer learning to a pre-trained model, by simply removing these upper convolutional layers.

We base our experiments on an off-the-shelf VGGNet-16 architecture. VGGNet-16 uses very small (3 × 3) convolutional filters, and contains 16 weighted layers, of which the lower 13 are convolutional layers. Convolutional layers in the model are assembled into blocks, with a maxpooling layer after each block. We replace the upper fully connected dense layers, with a global average pooling layer followed by two fully connected dense layers and a dropout layer [16] sandwiched between fully connected layers. The maxpooling layers associated with specific convolutional layers remain untouched. Other networks will be derived from this architecture by removing convolutional layers.

Using the popular off-the-shelf VGGNet architecture with weights pre-trained on ImageNet, we remove the upper-most convolutional layers, layer by layer. A different CNN is created every time a convolutional layer is removed from the top. In total, twelve networks are created. The deepest network contains 13 convolutional layers and the most shallow contains 2. Each network has 2 fully-connected layers on top of the convolutional layers. The uppermost fully-connected layer contains as many neurons as the number of classes in the target dataset. The fully-connected layers have randomised initial weights. A softmax activation function is used to output the predictions. A dropout layer with dropout probability 0.5 is also added between the two fully-connected layers. All of the convolutional layers in each network contain weights pre-trained on ImageNet.

2.2   Details on Transferring

Transfer learning is applied to the different networks we have derived. Transferring includes training on fixed features and fine-tuning. They are done in the following manner:

1. **Training fully connected layers with features extracted from fixed convolutional layers:** The fully connected layers in each network have randomly initialised weights. We freeze the convolutional layers of the networks, and only train the fully connected layers using our training data. The top fully-connected layers are used for classification, these layers are trained on the features extracted from the fixed convolutional layers.
2. **Fine-tuning all the layers:** The convolutional layers of each network are then un-frozen, and the entire network is fine-tuned on the training data. This involves re-training the CNN, starting from the retained weights, and using a very small step size. In our experiments, the step size used for fine-tuning was 1000 times smaller than that used to exclusively train the fully connected layers.

2.3   Datasets

We apply transfer learning on each different pre-trained network. Two different benchmark datasets were used.

The datasets used in our experiments are the CIFAR-10 [1] dataset and the Flowers dataset. The CIFAR-10 dataset includes coloured images belonging to 10 classes (Airplane, Automobile, Bird, Cat, Deer, Dog, Frog, Horse, Ship, Truck), each of which contains 5000 images for training, and 1000 images for testing. All of the images in the CIFAR-10 dataset are of size 32×32 pixels. The Flowers dataset was released with the Tensorflow deep learning library. The Flowers dataset includes images from 5 classes (Daisy, Dandelion, Rose, Sunflower, Tulip), with each containing over 600 images. The images in the Flowers dataset are not of uniform size, and have different aspect ratios. We randomly split the dataset into a training set and testing set, adhering to an 8:2 ratio. Data augmentation is performed by zooming into the images by a factor 0.2, and horizontally flipping them. Data augmentation is done randomly on-line.

2.4 Training Details

During the training fully connected layers with features from fixed convolutional layers, a Stochastic Gradient Descent (SGD) optimiser with a step size 0.01 is used to train the data in batches of 128. The loss function is cross entropy. During fine-tuning, a SGD optimiser with a step size of 0.00001 is used to train the data in batches of 128. All of the images used for training and testing are resized to 224 × 224 pixels, in accordance to the size of the input layer of VGGNet. The classification accuracy of each network is tested using the testing data, and recorded at each training epoch.

We train the Flowers dataset for 40 epochs in total. The convolutional layers are frozen in the first 20 epochs, and the fine-tuning of the entire network occurs in epochs 21–40. We train the CIFAR-10 dataset for 80 epochs in total. The convolutional layers are frozen in the first 40 epochs, and the fine-tuning of the entire network occurs in epochs 41–80.

3 Results

3.1 Performance of Each Network

We apply transfer learning, starting from the network with the most convolutional layers to that with the fewest. We stop when a sufficiently large drop in performance is observed in the network with the fewest pre-trained convolutional layer relative to that of the previous.

The top-1 testing classification accuracies of the different models, at each epoch of training, are shown in Figs. 2 and 3. The final top-1 classification accuracies for the networks, each with a different number of convolutional layers, are presented in Figs. 1 and 4.

4 Discussion

4.1 The Effect of Removing Upper Convolutional Layers

The experiments conducted on pre-trained networks of different layers show that the performance of the network after transfer learning generally increases when pre-trained convolutional layers are removed. Accuracy on CIFAR-10 dataset may be affected by the up-sizing of CIFAR-10 images of size 32 × 32 to the VGGNet input size of 224 × 224. Our experiments on the CIFAR-10 dataset show that the classification accuracy of the network with one convolutional layer removed is 87.43%. This represents a roughly 2% increase of the performance of transferring to a vanilla off-the-shelf pre-trained VGGNet (85.57% accuracy). Further improvements in performance, of up to nearly 10%, occurs when more convolutional layers are taken away. Similar effects can be observed in the experiments on the Flowers dataset. The off-the-shelf pre-trained VGGNet, with no upper convolutional layers removed, can achieve a classification accuracy of around 84.76% on the Flowers dataset. After two upper convolutional layers have been removed, the accuracy rises up to over 90.61%.

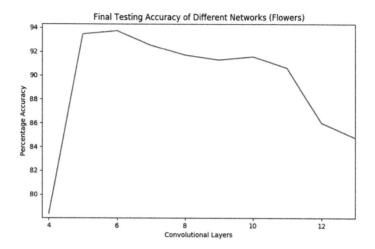

Fig. 1. Final testing accuracies of different models on the Flowers dataset

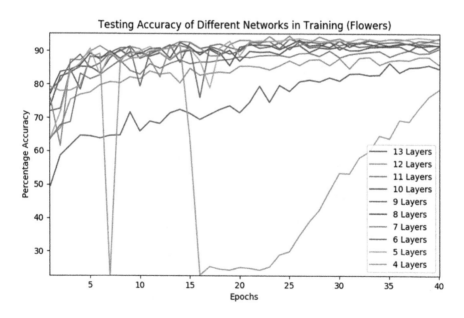

Fig. 2. Testing accuracies of different models during training on the Flowers dataset

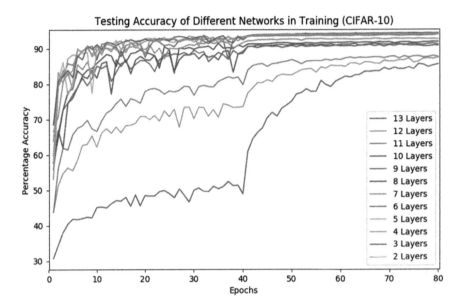

Fig. 3. Testing accuracies of different models during training on the CIFAR-10 dataset

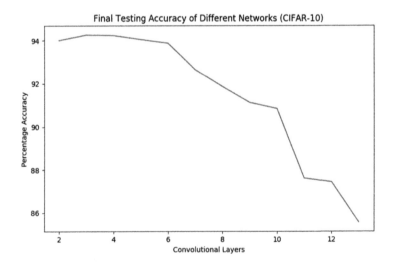

Fig. 4. Final testing accuracies of different models on the CIFAR-10 dataset

4.2   Trends in the Removal of Upper Convolutional Layers

The final accuracies of the networks that have been transferred, using the Flowers dataset, as shown in Fig. 1, gradually increase up to the network with 6 convolutional layers. The performance of the network with 5 convolutional layers is comparable to the one with 6. However, upon taking away another convolutional layer, the performance worsens rapidly. As shown in Fig. 2, the testing accuracy of the 4 convolutional layer network, during training, exhibited massive fluctuates, indicating instability. This points to the existence of a limit to how many layers can be removed. If we remove pre-trained convolutional layers beyond this limit, important information that is useful for the classification task becomes lost, and performance decreases.

As shown in Fig. 4, the final accuracies of the networks with CIFAR-10 as the target dataset gradually increase up to the network with 4 convolutional layers. The network with 3 convolutional layers performs similarly to that with 4 convolutional layers. However, the performance drops when another convolutional layer is removed. Looking at the testing accuracies of the networks while training, shown in Fig. 3, none of the models exhibit the unsteadiness found in the experiment on the Flowers dataset. Nevertheless, the existence of a limit, at which performance cannot be further improved by layer removal is evident.

We can also see that the marginal improvement in performance is more significant when the upper convolutional layers are removed. For the Flowers dataset, the boost in accuracy from removing convolutional layers 11–13 (the top 3 convolutional layers) is much more marked than that resulting from further removing convolutional layers 6–10. Similarly, for the CIFAR-10 dataset, removal of convolutional layers 11–13 (the top 3 convolutional layers) causes the greatest performance enhancement. This observation corroborates with the results of Yosinski et al., suggesting that the upper convolutional layers are less transferable.

4.3   Recommendations for Applying Transfer Learning to Off-the-shelf Pre-trained DCNNs

The networks with the best performance on the benchmark datasets are relatively shallow. This suggests that the suitable depth of the architecture used for transfer learning on small datasets may not be very deep. Very significant improvements have been observed upon removing convolutional layers for transfer learning, using both benchmark datasets tested. By simply using the bottom 3 convolutional layers of VGGNet, we achieved a classification accuracy of 94.26%, comparable to the state-of-the-art performance of 96.53% [8]. It is likely performance improvements in transfer learning, achieved by removing convolutional layers, also apply to many other datasets of similar size and nature. Potential performance benefits can be gained with little trade-off, as removing upper convolutional layers before applying transfer learning is not a time-consuming nor cumbersome task.

Comparisons between the experiments on the two datasets show that the most suitable number of layers to remove before applying transfer on each dataset is different, and depends on the nature of the dataset. The best performance on the Flowers dataset occurred when 6 convolutional layers remain, while the best performance for CIFAR-10 occurred when 3 convolutional layers remain. Hence, it may be useful to set the number of layers to remove from an off-the-shelf pre-trained architecture as a tunable parameter.

It should also be noted that networks with more convolutional layers removed from off-the-shelf architectures tend to reach steady-state in less epochs, as shown in Fig. 2. Therefore, in practice, we can apply transfer learning to the networks with fewer layers for a few number of epochs.

5   Conclusion

We have investigated the effect of removing convolutional layers of pre-trained DCNNs, when using transfer learning. In particular, we have conducted experiments on two benchmark datasets, the CIFAR-10 dataset and the Flowers dataset. Performance was found to improve when upper convolutional layers were removed from an off-the-shelf pre-trained model. An improvement of up to nearly 10% in classification accuracy could be achieved by reducing the number of convolutional layers in the pre-trained model.

We also observed that the number of layers was negatively correlated to performance, up to a given limit. Removal of the uppermost layers had a greater marginal improvement to accuracy than removing the middle convolutional layers.

Many studies have achieved outstanding results by applying transfer learning to off-the-shelf pre-trained DCNNs [9,10,14], without any alteration. Our results suggest that performance improvements are likely to occur if layer removals are performed on off-the-shelf pre-trained DCNNs. Furthermore, the ideal number of convolutional layers to remove varies with the dataset. Therefore, we propose the procedure of removing a suitable number of pre-trained convolutional layers before performing transfer learning on off-the-shelf DCNNs. As the most suitable number of layers to remove varies, the number of pre-trained layers to remove before transferring should be left as a parameter to tune.

References

1. Krizhevsky, A., Hinton, G.: Learning multiple layers of features from tiny images. Technical report (2009)
2. Bengio, Y.: Deep learning of representations for unsupervised and transfer learning. In: JMLR W&CP: Proceedings of Unsupervised and Transfer Learning (2011)
3. Bengio, Y., Bastien, F., Bergeron, A., Boulanger-Lew, N., Breuel, T., Chherawala, Y., Cisse, M., Côté, M., Erhan, D., Eustache, J., Glorot, X., Muller, X., Lebeuf, S.P., Pascanu, R., Rifai, S., Savard, F., Sicard, G.: Deep learners benefit more from out-of-distribution examples. In: JMLR W&CP: Proceedings of AISTATS 2011 (2011)

4. Caruana, R.: Learning many related tasks at the same time with backpropagation. In: Advances in Neural Information Processing Systems, pp. 657–664. Morgan Kaufmann (1995)
5. Deng, J., Dong, W., Socher, R., Li, L., Li, K., Fei-Fei, L.: ImageNet: a large-scale hierarchical image database. In: Computer Vision and Pattern Recognition. IEEE (2009)
6. Donahue, J., Jia, Y., Vinyals, O., Hoffman, J., Zhang, N., Tzeng, E., Darrell, T.: DeCAF: A deep convolutional activation feature for generic visual recognition. CoRR abs/1310.1531 (2013)
7. Girshick, R., Donahue, J., Darrell, T., Malik, J.: Rich feature hierarchies for accurate object detection and semantic segmentation. In: Computer Vision and Pattern Recognition. IEEE (2014)
8. Graham, B.: Fractional max-pooling. CoRR abs/1412.6071 (2015)
9. Hu, F., Xia, G.S., Hu, J., Zhang, L.: Transferring deep convolutional neural networks for the scene classification of high-resolution remote sensing imagery. Remote Sens. 7(11), 14680–14707 (2015)
10. Mehdipour Ghazi, M., Yanikoglu, B., Aptoula, E.: Plant identification using deep neural networks via optimization of transfer learning parameters. Neurocomputing 235, 228–235 (2017)
11. Oquab, M., Bottou, L., Laptev, I., Sivic, J.: Learning and transferring mid-level image representations using convolutional neural networks. In: IEEE Conference on Computer Vision and Pattern Recognition, CVPR 2014. IEEE (2014)
12. Razavian, A.S., Azizpour, H., Sullivan, J., Carlsson, S.: CNN features off-the-shelf: an astounding baseline for recognition. In: Computer Vision and Pattern Recognition Workshops, CVPRW 2014. IEEE (2014)
13. Sermanet, P., Eigen, D., Zhang, X., Mathieu, M., Fergus, R., Lecun, Y.: OverFeat: integrated recognition, localization and detection using convolutional networks. In: International Conference on Learning Representations (2014)
14. Shin, H., et al.: Deep convolutional neural networks for computer-aided detection: CNN architectures, dataset characteristics and transfer learning. IEEE Trans. Med. Imaging 35, 1285–1298 (2016)
15. Simonyan, K., Zisserman, A.: Very deep convolutional networks for large-scale image recognition. CoRR abs/1409.1556 (2014)
16. Srivastava, N., Hinton, G., Krizhevsky, A., Sutskever, I., Salakhutdinov, R.: Dropout: a simple way to prevent neural networks from overfitting. J. Mach. Learn. Res. 15(1), 1929–1958 (2014)
17. Szegedy, C., et al.: Going deeper with convolutions. In: Computer Vision and Pattern Recognition. IEEE (2015)
18. Yosinski, J., Clune, J., Bengio, Y., Lipson, H.: How transferable are features in deep neural networks?. In: Advances in Neural Information Processing Systems (2014)
19. Zeiler, M.D., Fergus, R.: Visualizing and understanding convolutional networks. In: Fleet, D., Pajdla, T., Schiele, B., Tuytelaars, T. (eds.) ECCV 2014. LNCS, vol. 8689, pp. 818–833. Springer, Cham (2014). doi:10.1007/978-3-319-10590-1_53

Music Genre Classification Using Masked Conditional Neural Networks

Fady Medhat$^{(\boxtimes)}$, David Chesmore, and John Robinson

Department of Electronic Engineering, University of York, York, UK
{fady.medhat,david.chesmore,john.robinson}@york.ac.uk

Abstract. The ConditionaL Neural Networks (CLNN) and the Masked ConditionaL Neural Networks (MCLNN) exploit the nature of multi-dimensional temporal signals. The CLNN captures the conditional temporal influence between the frames in a window and the mask in the MCLNN enforces a systematic sparseness that follows a filterbank-like pattern over the network links. The mask induces the network to learn about time-frequency representations in bands, allowing the network to sustain frequency shifts. Additionally, the mask in the MCLNN automates the exploration of a range of feature combinations, usually done through an exhaustive manual search. We have evaluated the MCLNN performance using the Ballroom and Homburg datasets of music genres. MCLNN have achieved accuracies that are competitive to state-of-the-art handcrafted attempts in addition to models based on Convolutional Neural Networks.

Keywords: ConditionaL Neural Networks (CLNN) · Masked ConditionaL Neural Networks (MCLNN) · Conditional Restricted Boltzmann Machine (CRBM) · Deep Belief Nets (DBN) · Music Information Retrieval (MIR)

1 Introduction

Automating the feature extraction is currently an active research field aiming to learn enhanced representations directly from the raw data rather than hand-crafting them. Neural Network based architectures have been used in this regard for image recognition [13] and sound [1]. The adoption of these architectures to sound recognition usually occurs after they gain wide acceptance in other application domains such as image recognition. For example, stacked Restricted Boltzmann Machines (RBM) [5] forming a Deep Belief Net (DBN) [9] to extract features were initially introduced to showcase the capability of these stacked generative layers to be used as a dimensionality reduction technique when applied on images of handwritten digits. Later, Hamel et al. [8] trained a DBN of three RBM layers over frames of a spectrogram to extract abstract representations from music files that were classified using a Support Vector Machine (SVM) [37] for a music genre classification task. Convolutional Neural Networks (CNN) as

© Springer International Publishing AG 2017
D. Liu et al. (Eds.): ICONIP 2017, Part II, LNCS 10635, pp. 470–481, 2017.
https://doi.org/10.1007/978-3-319-70096-0_49

well were initially introduced in the work of LeCun et al. [14] for images, and later attempts followed to use it for sound [11,28,30].

Despite the success of these architectures for images, they are not designed to exploit the time-frequency representation of sound efficiently. For example, DBNs ignore the inter-frames relation by treating a spectrogram's frame in isolation from neighboring frames, and CNNs depend on weight sharing, which does not preserve the spatial locality of the learned features.

The ConditionaL Neural Networks (CLNN) [20] and the Masked ConditionaL Neural Networks (MCLNN) [20] are designed to preserve the spatial locality of the learned features, where there is a dedicated link for every feature in a feature vector compared to the weight sharing using the CNN. The CLNN preserve the temporal relation between the frames by considering a window rather than the isolated frame used in the RBM, and the mask in the MCLNN enforces a systematic sparseness over the network's links. The mask design follows a band-like pattern, which allows the network to be frequency shift-invariant mimicking a filterbank. Additionally, the mask explores several feature combinations concurrently analogous to handcrafting the optimum combination of features through a mix-and-match operation, while preserving the spatial locality of the features.

2   Related Models

The Conditional Restricted Boltzmann Machine (CRBM) [35] by Taylor et al. extended the RBM to the temporal dimension to allow an RBM to learn about a temporal window of frames rather than being trained on static bag-of-frames. To fulfill this aim, the CRBM adapted conditional links to capture the influence of the previous frames on the current one. Figure 1 shows a CRBM layer, where the normal RBM is represented with the bidirectional connections $\hat{W}$ going across the visible vector $\hat{v}_0$ and the hidden nodes $\hat{h}$. The $\hat{B}$ links in the figure represent the conditional links from the previous visible vectors $(\hat{v}_{-1}, \hat{v}_{-2}, ..., \hat{v}_{-n})$ to the hidden layer $\hat{h}$. Similarly, the $\hat{A}$ links capture the autoregressive relation from the previous visible vectors to the current one $\hat{v}_0$. Layers of a CRBM can be stacked over each other similar to a DBN, where Taylor et al. trained a CRBM to model the human motion over a multichannel signal of human joints activity. Mohamed et al. [22] extended the CRBM with the Interpolating Conditional Restricted Boltzmann Machine (ICRBM), which showed an enhanced performance by including the influence of the future frames in addition to the past ones for phoneme recognition. The work of Battenberg et al. [3] was another attempt to use the CRBM for sound, where they used the CRBM to analyze drum patterns.

Similar modifications were introduced to the CNN to fit the time-frequency representation. The CNN architecture, shown in Fig. 2, is based on the two primary operations: convolution and pooling. The convolution operation scans the 2-dimensional representation with a small weight matrix (or filter), e.g. 5×5, where a form of a weighted sum is generated from the element-wise multiplication between the filter and the region of the image being scanned. The output of each

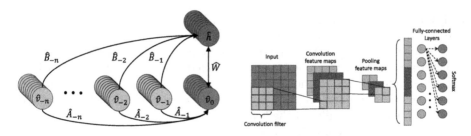

Fig. 1. Conditional RBM   **Fig. 2.** Convolutional neural network

step of the filter is a scalar value positioned in a new representation of the image known as the feature map. The convolutional layer generates several feature maps. The number of feature maps matches the number of filters used. Mean or max pooling follows the convolution to reduce the resolution of the feature maps. These two operations are consecutively repeated to form a deep architecture of a CNN, where the output of the final layer is flattened to a single feature vector to be fed to a fully connected neural network for the final classification. CNN depends on weight sharing, which performs well in favor of large images without the need to have a dedicated weight going across each pixel and the network's hidden layer. Weight sharing does not preserve the spatial locality of the learned features, which is practical for images, but not for time-frequency representation. This is related to the influence of the location of the detected feature at a specific frequency as a property to distinguish between sounds. The work of Abdel-Hamid et al. [1] approached this problem by redesigning the convolutional filters to operate over bands. Another attempt was in [28], where they proposed using separate filters to convolve each of the time and frequency dimensions separately combined in the same model.

The Masked ConditionaL Neural Network (MCLNN) was introduced in [20] with an analysis of the influence of the data split on model accuracy. In this work, we further evaluate the MCLNN performance on the music genre classification task.

3   Conditional Neural Networks

The ConditionaL Neural Network (CLNN) [20] is a discriminative model that extends from the generative Conditional Restricted Boltzmann Machine (CRBM) [35] discussed earlier. The CLNN adapts the conditional previous visible to hidden links proposed in the CRBM, and it further extends the connections to the future frames as presented in the ICRBM [22].

The CLNN is formed of a vector shaped hidden layer, similar to a conventional multi-layer perceptron, having e dimensions. The input layer accepts a number of frames in a window of size d, where the window's middle frame is conditioned on the past and future frames. The width of the window follows (1)

$$d = 2n + 1, \; n \geq 1 \tag{1}$$

where the 1 refers to the window's central frame and the n frames refer to the neighboring frames to the middle one (2 is to account for the past and future directions). There are dense connections between each vector in the input window and the hidden layer. Accordingly, there are $2n + 1$ weight matrices forming a tensor. The weight tensor dimensions are [feature vector length l, hidden layer width e, window's depth d]. Each vector of length l in the input window of size d has a corresponding dedicated weight matrix in the weight tensor. The new vectors generated from the vector-matrix multiplication between each feature vector and its corresponding weight matrix are summed together feature-wise before applying a nonlinear transformation. The activation of a hidden node is given in (2)

$$y_{j,\,t} = f \left(b_j + \sum_{u=-n}^{n} \sum_{i=1}^{l} x_{i,\,u+t}\ W_{i,\,j,\,u} \right) \tag{2}$$

where $y_{j,\,t}$ is the activation at node j of the hidden layer for the window's middle frame at index t of the segment. The segment, discussed later in detail, is a chunk of frames of a minimum size equal to the window. f is the transfer function and b_j is the bias at the jth node. $x_{i,\,u+t}$ is the ith feature of the feature vector x. u refers to the index within the window and t refers to the window's middle frame (having $u = 0$ in the window), which is at the same time the index of the middle frame in the input segment. $W_{i,\,j,\,u}$ is the weight between the ith feature of the vector at position u in the window and the jth neuron in the hidden layer. u is the index of a frame in the window and also the index of its corresponding weight matrix in the weight tensor. The hidden layer activation can be reformulated in a vector form in (3).

$$\hat{y}_t = f \left(\hat{b} + \sum_{u=-n}^{n} \hat{x}_{u+t} \cdot \hat{W}_u \right) \tag{3}$$

where the hidden layer activation vector $\hat{y}$ for the window's middle frame x_t conditioned on the n neighboring frames in either direction is given by the transfer function f, the bias vector $\hat{b}$ and the $vector - matrix$ multiplication between the feature vector $\hat{x}_u$ at index u and its corresponding weight matrix $\hat{W}_u$ at the same index. The number of matrices in the weight tensor is equal to $2n + 1$ matching the number of frames in the window, where each frame is processed by its dedicated matrix. The conditional distribution is formulated in $p(\hat{y}_t | \hat{x}_{-n+t}, ..., \hat{x}_{-1+t}, \hat{x}_t, \hat{x}_{1+t}, ..., \hat{x}_{n+t}) = \sigma(...)$, where σ is a logistic function such as a Sigmoid or the output layer Softmax.

Figure 3 shows two CLNN layers of order $n = 1$ followed by a global pooling layer [17] that aggregates the features over k extra frames before feeding them to a fully connected network for classification. Each CLNN layer consumes 2n frames generating a fewer number of frames. Accordingly, a CLNN is trained over segments of size following (4)

$$q = (2n)m + k, \quad n,\, m \text{ and } k \geq 1 \tag{4}$$

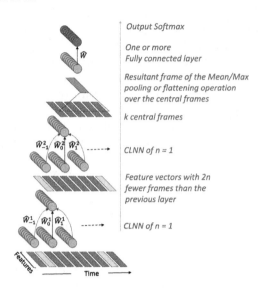

Output Softmax

One or more
Fully connected layer

Resultant frame of the Mean/Max
pooling or flattening operation
over the central frames

k central frames

CLNN of n = 1

Feature vectors with 2n
fewer frames than the
previous layer

CLNN of n = 1

Fig. 3. Two CLNN layers with $n = 1$.

where q is the segment size, the order n is for the number of frames in a single direction (the 2 is for the past and future frames), m is the number of layers, and k is for the extra frames to be pooled across beyond the CLNN layers. For example, at $n = 4$, $m = 3$ and $k = 5$, a segment of size $(2 \times 4) \times 3 + 5 = 29$ frames is presented at the input of the first CLNN layer. The second CLNN layer will receive $29 - (2 \times 4) = 21$ vectors at its input and consequently will generate $21 - (2 \times 4) = 13$ vectors as an output. Similarly, the third layer will generate $13 - (2 \times 4) = 5$ vectors, which undergo flattening or pooling to a single vector before the fully-connected layers.

4   Masked Conditional Neural Networks

Spectrograms represent the energy at different frequency bins as the signal progresses through time. Despite the usefulness of such representations for signal analysis, they are susceptible to the frequency shifts, which could provide different spectral representations for very similar sounds. Frequency shift involves a smearing in the energy of a frequency bin across nearby bins due to uncontrolled factors affecting the signal propagation. Filterbanks tackle the frequency shifts in raw spectrograms. A filterbank is a group of filters used to subdivide the spectrograms into frequency bands allowing the new representation to be frequency shift-invariant. They are the principal operating component of Mel-scaled transformations such as the MFCC. The Masked ConditionaL Neural Networks (MCLNN) [20] embed a filterbank-like behaviour within the network by enforcing a systematic sparseness over the network's links that follows a band-like pattern.

The mask design is controlled by two tunable hyper-parameters: the Bandwidth and the Overlap. Figure 4a shows a masking pattern with a Bandwidth

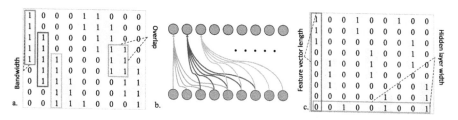

Fig. 4. Masking patterns. (a) *Bandwidth* = 5 and *Overlap* = 3, (b) the active links following the masking pattern in a. (c) *Bandwidth* = 3 and *Overlap* = −1

of 5 and an Overlap of 3. The Bandwidth values refer to the successive 1's in a column, and the Overlap refers to the superposition of the patterns between one column and another. Figure 4b depicts the active connections following the mask in Fig. 4a. Each neuron in the hidden layer of Fig. 4b has a focused spatial region of the feature vector to observe. Figure 4c shows a mask with a negative overlap depicting the non-overlapping distance between two columns. The linear indexing of the binary values of a mask is formulated in (5)

$$lx = a + (g - 1)(l + (bw - ov)) \qquad (5)$$

where the linear index lx is given by the bandwidth bw, the overlap ov and the feature vector length l. a takes the values in $[\,0,\ bw - 1\,]$ and g is in the interval $[\,1, \lceil (l \times e)/(l + (bw - ov)) \rceil\,]$. The mask plays another role of exploring a range of feature combinations analogous handcrafting the optimum feature combinations. This operation is applied in the MCLNN for several feature combinations concurrently as shown in Fig. 4c, where the 2nd set of three columns holds a shifted version of the 1st three columns and similarly for the 3rd set. In a closer analysis, each hidden node (mapped to a column in the mask) will have a different input to observe. For example, the input at the 1st node is the first three features of the feature vector, the 4th node's input is the first two features, and the 7th node is the first feature. The masking is applied through an element-wise multiplication following (6).

$$\hat{Z}_u = \hat{W}_u \circ \hat{M} \qquad (6)$$

where $\hat{W}_u$ is the original weight matrix at index u, $\hat{M}$ is the masking pattern and $\hat{Z}_u$ is the masked weight matrix to replace the original one in (3).

Figure 5 shows a single MCLNN step, where a window of frames of size $2n+1$ is processed with a matching count of matrices. Each frame in the window has a corresponding matrix to process. The vector-matrix multiplication generates d new vectors, which are summed feature-wise before applying the nonlinearity by a transfer function. The output of a single step over the window is a resultant single frame. The highlighted cells in each matrix depict the active links enforced through the mask.

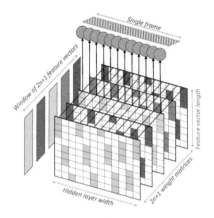

Fig. 5. Single MCLNN step.

5   Experiments

We evaluated the performance of the MCLNN using the Ballroom [6] and the Homburg [10] datasets widely adapted for Music Information Retrieval tasks including genre classification.

The *Ballroom* dataset is composed of 698 music clips of 30 s each, unevenly partitioned across 8 music genres: Cha Cha (CC), Jive (Ji), Quickstep (Qs), Rumba (Ru), Samba (Sa), Tango (Ta), Viennese Waltz (VW) and Slow Waltz (SW).

The *Homburg* dataset contains 1886 music clips of 10 s each, distributed across 9 classes: Alternative (Al), Blues (Bl), Electronic (El), FolkCountry (FC), FunkSoulRnb (FS), Jazz (Ja), Pop (Po), RapHiphop (RH) and Rock (Ro).

All files for both datasets were transformed to a logarithmic mel-scaled spectrogram of 256 bin using an FFT of 2048 and 1024 hop size. Segments were extracted following (4) and the z-score parameters of the training data were used to standardize the testing and validation sets. Experiments were carried out using a 10-folds cross-validation with the mean accuracy across the folds reported. The hyper-parameters used for the MCLNN are listed in Table 1.

Table 1. MCLNN hyper-parameters for the Ballroom and the Homburg

Layer	Hidden nodes	Mask bandwidth	Mask overlap	Order n (Ballroom)	Order n (Homburg)
1	220	40	−10	15	5
2	200	10	3	15	5

The two MCLNN layers are followed by a global single dimension pooling layer to pool feature-wise over the k extra frames. The global pooling emulates

Table 2. Reported accuracies on Ballroom

Classifier and features	Ac.%
SVM + 28 feature, Tempo [26]	96.13
KNN + Modulation Scale Spec. [19]	93.12
Manhattan Dist. + Block-Level feat. [32]	92.44
MCLNN + Mel−Spec. (this work)	**90.40**
SVM + Rhyth., Hist., Stat., Onset, etc. [16]	90.40
KNN + 15 MFCC-like desc., Tempo [7]	90.10
KNN + Rhythm and Timbre [27]	89.20
SVM + 28 features without Tempo [26]	88.00
CNN + Mel-Scaled Spectrogram [28]	87.68
SVM + Rhyth., Hist., Statist. [15]	84.20
KNN + Tempo [7]	82.30

Table 3. Reported accuracies on Homburg

Classifier and features	Ac.%
JSLRR + Cortrical Representations [25]	63.46
LRSM + Cort., MFCC, Chro. [24]	62.40
MCLNN + Mel−Spec. (this work)	**61.45**
KNN + LFP, VDSP, CP, SCP [33]	61.20
SVM + ESA-MFCC [2]	57.81
KNN + Rhythm and Timbre [27]	57.00
KNN + mcRBM, PCA, MVG-MFCC [23]	55.30
SVM + Marsyas features [21,36]	55.00
KNN + Multiple features [10]	53.23
SVN + Novelty Functions [18]	51.10
KNN+ mcRBM, PCA, Mel-Spec. [31]	45.50

the aggregation over a musical texture window, which was studied by Bergstra et al. [4]. We used $k = 11$ and $k = 2$ for the Ballroom and the Homburg, respectively. Two densely connected layers of 50 and 10 nodes followed the global pooling layer, before the final Softmax. The model was trained using ADAM [12] to minimize the categorical cross-entropy between the predicted vector and the target label. Dropout [34] was used as a regularizer. The final decision of the clip's category is decided using probability voting across the frames of the clip.

As listed in Tables 2 and 3, MCLNN achieved an accuracy of 90.4% and 61.45% on the Ballroom and the Homburg, respectively, which surpasses several neural network based architectures in addition to hand-crafted attempts on both datasets. MCLNN achieved the mentioned accuracies without a special design to exploit musical perceptual properties compared to other attempts. In the work of Peeters [26], he achieved 96.13% on the Ballroom using the Tempo annotations released with the dataset. Peeters reapplied his proposed handcrafted features without Tempo data, and the accuracy was 88%, which shows the influence of the tempo annotations. In a similar type of analysis, Gouyon et al. [7] used the Tempo annotations as a baseline to benchmark their proposed handcrafted features, where the Tempo annotations alone achieved 82.3% and their proposed features with the Tempo achieved 90.1%. The work of Marchand et al. [19] achieved 93.12% using multiple processing stages including on-set energy calculation, autocorrelation, modulation scale spectra and dimensionality reduction to exploit rhythmic pattern in a music clip. Seyerlehner et al. [32] achieved 92.44% using several features extracted from blocks of the spectrogram. A neural network based attempt in the work of Pons et al. [28] achieved 87.68% using a shallow CNN architecture with pre-trained filters convolving the time and spectral dimensions separately in the same model. Handcrafted features for the Homburg dataset has been explored as well. The work of Panagakis et al. [25] achieved 63.46% using the auditory cortical representations in combination with their introduced classifier. Their work reports the accuracy achieved on the Ballroom dataset using the same features (cortical representations) and the classifier used for the Homburg, where they achieved 81.93% on the Ballroom dataset. The work in [24] achieved 62.4% on the Homburg dataset using auditory cortical representations, MFCC and Chroma as features. A neural network based attempt on the Homburg dataset in the work of Schluter et al. [31] achieved 45.5% using mcRBM [29], a variant of the RBM, applied on a mel-spectrogram.

Figures 6 and 7 show the confusion matrix for Ballroom and the Homburg datasets, respectively. High confusion is noticed for the Rumba and the Waltz genres with the Slow Waltz, which overlap with the findings in [18]. For the Homburg dataset, less confusion is noticed with the availability of more samples in the genre category.

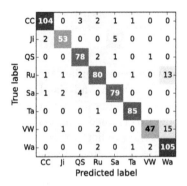

Fig. 6. Ballroom confusion using the MCLNN.

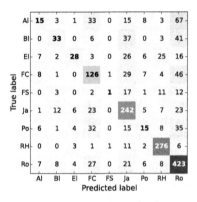

Fig. 7. Homburg confusion using the MCLNN.

6   Conclusions and Future Work

In this work, we have explored the applicability of the ConditionaL Neural Network (CLNN) and the Masked ConditionaL Neural Network (MCLNN) on the music genre classification task. The CLNN preserves the inter-frames relation of a temporal signal and the spatial locality of the features. The MCLNN extends the CLNN by enforcing a systematic sparseness over the network's links following a band-like pattern, which mimics a filterbank. The filterbank-like pattern induces the network to learn in frequency bands. The mask also automates the exploration of several feature combinations concurrently, which is usually a manual process of handcrafting the optimum feature combinations. The MCLNN has achieved competitive accuracies on the Ballroom and the Homburg music datasets compared to several handcrafted attempts, in addition to state-of-the-art Convolutional Neural Networks. The MCLNN has achieved these accuracies without depending on any musical perceptual properties used in several hand-crafted attempts, which allow the MCLNN to generalize to other types of multi-dimensional temporal signals. Future work, we will consider using deeper MCLNN architectures with more optimization to the masking patterns used, in addition to using different orders across the layers. We will also explore applying the MCLNN to multi-dimensional temporal representations other than spectrograms.

Acknowledgments. This work is funded by the European Union's Seventh Framework Programme for research, technological development and demonstration under grant agreement no. 608014 (CAPACITIE).

References

1. Abdel-Hamid, O., Mohamed, A.R., Jiang, H., Deng, L., Penn, G., Yu, D.: Convolutional neural networks for speech recognition. IEEE/ACM Trans. Audio Speech Lang. Process. **22**(10), 1533–1545 (2014)
2. Aryafar, K., Shokoufandeh, A.: Music genre classification using explicit semantic analysis. In: International ACM Workshop on Music Information Retrieval with User-Centered and Multimodal Strategies (MIRUM) (2011)
3. Battenberg, E., Wessel, D.: Analyzing drum patterns using conditional deep belief networks. In: International Society for Music Information Retrieval, ISMIR (2012)
4. Bergstra, J., Casagrande, N., Erhan, D., Eck, D., Kgl, B.: Aggregate features and adaboost for music classification. Mach. Learn. **65**(2–3), 473–484 (2006)
5. Fahlman, S.E., Hinton, G.E., Sejnowski, T.J.: Massively parallel architectures for AI: NETL, Thistle, and Boltzmann machines. In: National Conference on Artificial Intelligence. AAAI (1983)
6. Gouyon, F., Klapuri, A., Dixon, S., Alonso, M., Tzanetakis, G., Uhle, C., Cano, P.: An experimental comparison of audio tempo induction algorithms. IEEE Trans. Audio Speech Lang. Process. **14**(5), 1832–1844 (2006)
7. Gouyon, F., Dixon, S., Pampalk, E., Widmer, G.: Evaluating rhythmic descriptors for musical genre classification. In: International AES Conference (2004)
8. Hamel, P., Eck, D.: Learning features from music audio with deep belief networks. In: International Society for Music Information Retrieval Conference, ISMIR (2010)
9. Hinton, G.E., Salakhutdinov, R.R.: Reducing the dimensionality of data with neural networks. Science **313**(5786), 504–507 (2006)
10. Homburg, H., Mierswa, I., Moller, B., Morik, K., Wurst, M.: A benchmark dataset for audio classification and clustering. In: International Symposium on Music Information Retrieval (2005)
11. Kereliuk, C., Sturm, B.L., Larsen, J.: Deep learning and music adversaries. IEEE Trans. Multimedia **17**(11), 2059–2071 (2015)
12. Kingma, D., Ba, J.: Adam: a method for stochastic optimization. In: International Conference for Learning Representations, ICLR (2015)
13. Krizhevsky, A., Sutskever, I., Hinton, G.E.: Imagenet classification with deep convolutional neural networks. In: Neural Information Processing Systems, NIPS (2012)
14. LeCun, Y., Bottou, L., Bengio, Y., Haffner, P.: Gradient-based learning applied to document recognition. Proc. IEEE **86**(11), 2278–2324 (1998)
15. Lidy, T., Rauber, A.: Evaluation of feature extractors and psycho-acoustic transformations for music genre classification. In: International Conference on Music Information Retrieval, ISMIR (2005)
16. Lidy, T., Rauber, A., Pertusa, A., Inesta, J.M.: Improving genre classification by combination of audio and symbolic descriptors using a transcription system. In: International Conference on Music Information Retrieval (2007)
17. Lin, M., Chen, Q., Yan, S.: Network in network. In: International Conference on Learning Representations, ICLR (2014)

18. Lykartsis, A., Lerch, A.: Beat histogram features for rhythm-based musical genre classification using multiple novelty functions. In: Conference on Digital Audio Effects (DAFx 2015) (2015)
19. Marchand, U., Peeters, G.: The modulation scale spectrum and its application to rhythm-content description. In: International Conference on Digital Audio Effects (DAFx) (2014)
20. Medhat, F., Chesmore, D., Robinson, J.: Masked conditional neural networks for audio classification. In: International Conference on Artificial Neural Networks (ICANN) (2017)
21. Moerchen, F., Mierswa, I., Ultsch, A.: Understandable models of music collections based on exhaustive feature generation with temporal statistics. In: ACM SIGKDD International Conference on Knowledge Discovery and Data Mining (KDD) (2006)
22. Mohamed, A.R., Hinton, G.: Phone recognition using restricted Boltzmann machines. In: IEEE International Conference on Acoustics Speech and Signal Processing, ICASSP (2010)
23. Osendorfer, C., Schluter, J., Schmidhuber, J., van der Smagt, P.: Unsupervised learning of low-level audio features for music similarity estimation. In: Workshop on Speech and Visual Information Processing in Conjunction with the International Conference on Machine Learning (ICML) (2011)
24. Panagakis, Y., Kotropoulos, C.: Music classification by low-rank semantic mappings. EURASIP J. Audio Speech Music Process. **2013**(1), 1–13 (2013)
25. Panagakis, Y., Kotropoulos, C.L., Arce, G.R.: Music genre classification via joint sparse low-rank representation of audio features. IEEE/ACM Trans. Audio Speech Lang. Process. **22**(12), 1905–1917 (2014)
26. Peeters, G.: Spectral and temporal periodicity representations of rhythm for the automatic classification of music audio signal. IEEE Trans. Audio Speech Lang. Process. **19**(5), 1242–1252 (2011)
27. Pohle, T., Schnitzer, D., Schedl, M., Knees, P., Widmer, G.: On rhythm and general music similarity. In: International Society for Music Information Retrieval, ISMIR (2009)
28. Pons, J., Lidy, T., Serra, X.: Experimenting with musically motivated convolutional neural networks. In: International Workshop on Content-Based Multimedia Indexing, CBMI (2016)
29. Ranzato, M., Hinton, G.E.: Modeling pixel means and covariances using factorized third-order Boltzmann machines. In: IEEE Conference on Computer Vision and Pattern Recognition (CVPR), pp. 2551–2558 (2010)
30. Salamon, J., Bello, J.P.: Deep convolutional neural networks and data augmentation for environmental sound classification. IEEE Signal Process. Lett. 24(3), March 2017
31. Schluter, J., Osendorfer, C.: Music similarity estimation with the mean-covariance restricted Boltzmann machine. In: International Conference on Machine Learning and Applications, ICMLA, pp. 118–123 (2011)
32. Seyerlehner, K., Schedl, M., Pohle, T., Knees, P.: Using block-level features for genre classification, tag classification and music similarity estimation. In: Music Information Retrieval eXchange, MIREX (2010)
33. Seyerlehner, K., Widmer, G.: Fusing block-level features for music similarity estimation. In: International Conference on Digital Audio Effects (DAFx 2010) (2010)
34. Srivastava, N., Hinton, G., Krizhevsky, A., Sutskever, I., Salakhutdinov, R.: Dropout: a simple way to prevent neural networks from overfitting. J. Mach. Learn. Res. JMLR **15**, 1929–1958 (2014)

35. Taylor, G.W., Hinton, G.E., Roweis, S.: Modeling human motion using binary latent variables. In: Advances in Neural Information Processing Systems, NIPS, pp. 1345–1352 (2006)
36. Tzanetakis, G., Cook, P.: Musical genre classification of audio signals. IEEE Trans. Speech Audio Process. **10**(5), 293–302 (2002)
37. Vapnik, V., Lerner, A.: Pattern recognition using generalized portrait method. Autom. Remote Control **24**, 774–780 (1963)

Reinforced Memory Network
for Question Answering

Anupiya Nugaliyadde[(✉)], Kok Wai Wong, Ferdous Sohel,
and Hong Xie

Murdoch University, Perth, WA, Australia
{a.nugaliyadde, k.wong, f.sohel, h.xie}@murdoch.edu.au

Abstract. Deep learning techniques have shown to perform well in Question
Answering (QA) tasks. We present a framework that combines Memory Net-
work (MN) and Reinforcement Learning (Q-learning) to perform QA, termed
Reinforced MN (R-MN). We investigate the proposed framework by the use of
Long Short Term Memory Network (LSTM) and Dynamic Memory Network
(DMN). We call them Reinforced LSTM (R-LSTM) and Reinforced DMN
(R-DMN), respectively. The input text sequence and question are passed to both
MN and Q-Learning. The output of the MN is then fed to Q-Learning as a
second input for refinement. The R-MN is trained end-to-end. We evaluated
R-MNs on the bAbI 1 K QA dataset for all of the 20 tasks. We achieve superior
performance when compared to conventional method of RL, LSTM and the
state of the art technique, DMN. Using only half of the training data, both
R-LSTM and R-DMN achieved all of the bAbI tasks with high accuracies. The
experimental results demonstrated that the proposed framework of combining
MN and Q-learning enhances the QA tasks while using less training data.

Keywords: Question Answering · Long Short Term Memory Network ·
Reinforcement Learning · Dynamic Memory Network

1 Introduction

Question Answering (QA) is one of the most complex tasks in Natural Language
Understanding (NLU) [1]. QA requires recalling, reasoning and understanding the
question and context in which the answer is embedded [2]. Deep learning techniques
have shown to enhance the performance of the QA tasks [3]. QA can benefit significantly by using past information. Memory Networks (MNs) [2] such as Long Short
Term Memory Network (LSTM) and Dynamic Memory Network [4] (DMN) have the
ability to recall information from the memory, which makes them suitable for QA tasks
[5–7]. LSTM [8] can hold information over a long time period and LSTM based
techniques can achieve most QA tasks due this characteristic [4, 6, 9]. Another MN
approach, DMN has been used in recent years for QA tasks [4]. It looks at the question
and uses gates to identify the related answer. However, MN is not capable of achieving
QA on its own because MN is not capable of modeling dynamics of question-fact
interaction and complex reasoning in achieving some category of the QA tasks [10].

© Springer International Publishing AG 2017
D. Liu et al. (Eds.): ICONIP 2017, Part II, LNCS 10635, pp. 482–490, 2017.
https://doi.org/10.1007/978-3-319-70096-0_50

Reinforcement Learning (RL) has been shown to perform at human level and can surpass human performance in games, which require reasoning [11]. RL is capable of performing complex reasoning in order to achieve a given goal. Deep neural networks, e.g., deep Q-learning can outperform humans on a number of games [12] due to the ability to use past information. Apart from this, Branavan et al. [13] show that RL is capable of learning from action based on read instructions. To the best of our knowledge, Q-learning has not been used with MN for QA tasks.

In this paper, we propose a framework that combines MN with Q-learning for QA tasks, termed as Reinforced MN (R-MN). As LSTM [5, 6] and DMN [4] are the two MN techniques used for QA in recent publications, we illustrated the proposed R-MN framework by using LSTM and DMN, named as R-LSTM and R-DMN in this paper. MN is used to hold prior information to generate the answer. Q-learning is added to the memory network in order to compare and refine results created by the MN using the reasoning capabilities it holds. Our experiments show that R-LSTM and R-DMN generate accuracies of 99.02% and 98.72% respectively. We compare our results with the state-of-the-art DMN, LSTM and basic RL. R-LSTM has the capability of recalling more information compared to R-DMN and produces better results. We also show that using only half of the training data we can achieve the state-of-the-art performance.

2 Background

Deep learning uses multilevel data processing, which enables machines to understand complex patterns [3]. This has prominently been used in NLP tasks. Yu et al. [14] use to match the answer sentence to a given question using deep learning. Furthermore, this avoids feature selection and linguistic data. The use of deep learning has improved how the QA task can be processed more efficiently.

There have been a number of QA datasets released in the recent years. Weston et al. [2] introduced the challenging bAbI dataset, which holds 20 different types of QA tasks. They show a baseline method using strongly supervised memory networks. They use Adaptive Memory Network combined with N-gram and non-linear matching function, which achieved 16 of the bAbI tasks.

DMN [4], introduced by Kumar et al. has achieved the current state-of-the-art results on bAbI. DMN identifies the question and tracks the answer through the content. The gates used in the DMN is trained to identify the answer and remove the irrelevant information. Despite using all of the training datasets, DMN can achieve 18 out of 20 bAbI tasks. DMN failed on two tasks (i.e., path finding and position reasoning) which require a high level of reasoning capability. LSTM performs similar to a DMN [4]. However, LSTM holds more information in the memory through the gates and removes fewer information compared to DMN. LSTM is more data intensive compared to DMN. The bAbI tasks cover a variety of topic and are not specified into a particular area. Therefore, the tasks are complex to achieve using only a memory network.

Neural network based reasoning [10] is explored for the two specific bAbI tasks in which the DMN fails. Although neural network reasoning achieved better results compared to DMN for those two tasks, it still could not technically achieve those tasks (because the accuracy was less than 95%).

Guo et al. [15] use an RL based memory network to achieve the QA tasks. In the experiments, two methods are followed: baseRL [15] and impRL. In impRL, the memory network is integrated to baseRL. ImpRL was only tested on two tasks: supporting fact and bAbI dialog.

Bakker [16] shows that Reinforcement Learning (RL) and LSTM complement each other in T-maze tasks and pole balancing tasks. LSTM provides the memory in order to support RL and supports the long path to the reward. This shows the capability to improve RL tasks using the memory of memory networks. Memory for the pole balancing and T-maze tasks supports the predictions by holding past information.

To summarise, to the best of our knowledge memory networks with reinforcement learning have not been proposed for QA tasks. None of the existing techniques has reported to achieve all the tasks in the bAbI dataset.

3   The Proposed R-MN Framework

The main architecture of the proposed framework is shown in Fig. 1. It consists of three modules: input module, MN module and Q-learning module. In order to explain the proposed framework, LSTM is used as the MN method for the MN module, which is the R-LSTM in this paper. The proposed R-DMN is using the same architecture as described here, with DMN as the MN method for the MN module. The input sequence is first fed into both Q-Learning and MN. The output of the MN, which we call a coarse result, is passed to Q-learning as the second input. Q-learning first checks (comparison module) if the coarse result is already a correct answer. If it is a correct answer, Q-learning simply passes that coarse result as the final results. Otherwise, Q-learning refines the coarse results to a final result.

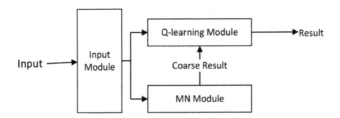

Fig. 1. The architecture of the proposed technique. The input sequence is passed to both LSTM and Q-learning. MN generates an output (coarse result) and passes to Q-learning for checking and refinement. The Q-learning module generates the final result.

3.1   Input Module

We followed the same protocol as [4] for this module. The Gated Recurrent Network (GRU) [17] is used to embed both the input sequence and the answer. Time step t, input x_t and hidden state h_t can be used to define the GRU:

$$h_t = GRU(x_t, h_{(t-1)}) \tag{1}$$

Details can be found in [4]. The input module encodes the sentence sequence, the questions and the answers. The encoded sentence sequence will be the input to the MN with the question. Encoded answers are then used to train the MN in this stage (Fig. 2).

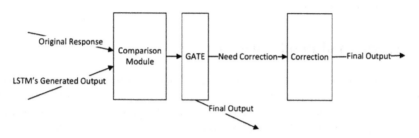

Fig. 2. The Comparison Module: in the training phase, it takes the *original response* (the labelled answer in the training data, i.e., the expected output from the LSTM) and the output of the LSTM. The original response is treated as an award state. If the LSTM output is in the award state, the gate passes the final output. Otherwise, it becomes a correction state and it is corrected through the actions (DQ learning) to the award state.

LSTM and DMN as shown in [4] exhibit the state-of-the-art-performance by achieving 18 bAbI tasks. LSTM's capability of recalling and passing information from one sequence to the next is vital for performing QA tasks.

3.2   Q-Learning

The output of the LSTM is then passed to the Q-Learning module. In the training phase, this module compares the LSTM generated result with the original response. If the result and the original response are not the same, we say that there is an error. The Q-learning module will then refine the result to correct the error. The Q-Learning is trained to achieve its goal of generating the best answer. Q-Learning is trained to identify and generate the best result it requires. The module acts as a correction module to refine the LSTM result to match the correct answer. The module will be trained by using the output of the LSTM and the training result.

The initial comparison module would compare the output of the LSTM's result with the original response. The expected result and the LSTM generated result are compare. If the expected result and the LSTM generated result is the same, the gate will pass the LSTM generated output forward. If the results are different, using the concept of RL, the results are corrected and passed as the output. Q-Learning can be denoted by:

$$Q(s, a) = r + \gamma(max(Q(s', a'))) \tag{2}$$

where s, a, r represent the state, action, and the current reward, respectively. $\gamma(max(Q(s', a')))$ represent the maximum discounted reward for predicted s' state for a predicted action a'. The Q-Learning predicts the best action or set of actions to leads to the maximum reward state.

In training Q-learning observes LSTM output and the expected result. The Q-learning learns to generate 1 for the correct answer (goal state) and 0 for any other answer. When the LSTM generates an answer which is not the goal state (correct answer) the Q-learning learns to change from the current state to the goal state to generate the current answer.

4   Experimental Results and Analysis

We evaluated the proposed framework on the bAbI dataset for QA. The two proposed methods of R-LSTM and R-DMN were compared to the conventional method of RL, and the state of art methods of LSTM and DMN. The objective of the comparative experiment is to find which method can complete all the bAbI tasks with less training data. Our experiments were developed using Python. We used Keras (Theano as the back end), Tensorflow and NumPy to develop the deep neural networks. Q-learning was developed using Gym library.

4.1   The bAbI Tasks Dataset

The bAbI dataset [2] contains 20 different types of QA tasks. It has been benchmarked that the task needs to obtain more than 95% of accuracy to be considered as *achieved*. Otherwise, the task is considered a *fail*. The tasks are different from one another. The training for each task consists of 1 K sets of data, where each set contains context, question and an answer. It has been mentioned that in order to show adaptability, a technique should be trained using a subset of the training set, and then tested on the full test set. For example, the training dataset size can be reduced to 500 for each task and test to see if they can achieve more than 95% accuracy. Accuracy is defined by:

$$Accuracy = \frac{Number\ of\ Correctly\ Answered\ Questions}{Number\ of\ All\ the\ questions\ in\ testing\ dataset} \tag{3}$$

4.2   Results from DMN and LSTM

For the first set of experiments, we implemented DMN and LSTM based methods. The results are summarized in Table 1. Our results are very similar to those reported in [4]. As shown in Table 1, DMN and LSTM produce comparable results. Eighteen out of 20 tasks were achieved. Two tasks i.e., 'position reasoning' and 'path finding' scored low accuracy for both LSTM and DMN methods. They failed these two tasks because the memory networks are not capable of modeling dynamics of question-fact interaction and complex reasoning. Additionally, the capability of recalling information can be prone to recalling information, which may not be relevant. This irrelevant information can create a burden on the memory network by lowering the accuracy.

Table 1. DMN, LSTM, RL results for 1000 training datasets and R-DMN and R-LSTM for 500 training datasets

	Tasks	Accuracy (%)				
		1000 Training dataset			500 Training dataset	
		DMN	LSTM	RL	R-DMN	R-LSTM
1	Single supporting fact	100	100	76.3	100	100
2	Two supporting facts	98.2	97.5	83.6	98.8	99.1
3	Three supporting facts	95.2	96	96.2	96.5	97.2
4	Two argument relations	100	99.1	95.7	99.6	99.5
5	Three argument relations	99.3	98.7	90.89	99	99.6
6	Yes/No questions	100	100	96.1	100	100
7	Counting	96.9	97.2	55.4	97.3	97.6
8	Lists/Sets	96.5	96.1	66.1	96.7	97.2
9	Simple negation	100	99.3	53.2	100	100
10	Indefinite knowledge	97.5	98.1	73.6	99	98.9
11	Basic co-reference	99.9	100	79.3	100	100
12	Conjunction	100	100	95.3	99.5	100
13	Compound co-reference	99.8	99.2	91.5	99	100
14	Time reasoning	100	99.6	89.2	99.6	100
15	Basic deduction	100	100	93.5	100	100
16	Basic induction	99.4	99.1	88.52	100	99.7
17	Positional reasoning	59.6	57.2	96.4	96.2	97.5
18	Size reasoning	95.3	96.5	95.5	96.2	96.5
19	Path finding	34.5	38.2	96.9	97.1	97.6
20	Agent's motivations	100	100	89.2	99.8	100
	Mean	93.6	93.59	85.12	**98.72**	**99.02**

4.3 Results of RL

As shown in Table 1, RL can achieve 'path finding' and 'position reasoning' tasks. However, RL failed to achieve, single supporting factor, two supporting factors, three argument relation, counting, Lists/set, Simple negation, indefinite knowledge basic co-reference, compound co-reference, time reasoning, basic deduction, basic induction, agents motivations tasks. This shows that most of the tasks RL fails is in which memory should play a key role. From the results in Table 1, it can also be concluded that neither RL nor LSTM/DMN can independently achieve all tasks but they complement each other. However, the overall performance in achieving the bAbI tasks are higher in LSTM and DMN than RL as shown in the Table 1.

4.4 Results of R-DMN

From Table 1, it can be observed that R-DMN can achieve all the bAbI tasks. R-DMN outperforms the RL, the LSTM and DMN methods. R-DMN structure uses gates to retain only the specific information that is required to generate the results, and thus can perform better for all the tasks. R-DMN combined the capability of recalling information as well as the enhancement of performing complex reasoning.

4.5   Results of R-LSTM

The experiment shows that the R-LSTM outperforms the R-DMN using the same proposed R-MN framework. As shown in Table 1, both R-LSTM and R-DMN can achieve all the bAbI tasks. However, the R-DMN underperforms slightly when compared to R-LSTM. For instance, R-LSTM and R-DMN achieved overall accuracies of 99.02% and 98.72%, respectively. This is because DMN forgets more important information when compared to LSTM. Consequently, DQ-learning has less influence in correcting the result that is generated by the DMN. This is due to the functionality of the gates in which LSTM retains more information compared to DMN. Further, removes the irrelevant information to produce a better result as it is capable of retaining more information which support the Q-learning compared with DMN.

4.6   Training Data Analysis

Another area of comparison beside accuracies of achieving the tasks is the number of training data used to establish the model. Table 1 shows the accuracies achieved for the testing dataset. The testing set is the set of available data left after the training data set

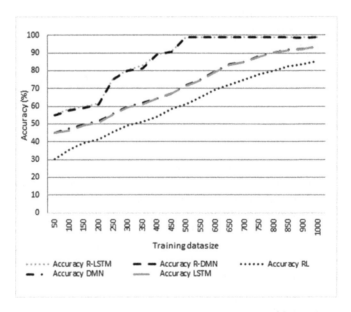

Fig. 3. Accuracy versus training data size. The plot shows the over-all mean accuracy for R-LSTM, R-DMN, RL, DMN and LSTM. The training size was increased starting from 50 to 1000 and tested on the full testing dataset. This shows that the results for R-LSTM and R-DMN peaked at 500 training size (only at half of the training data).

has been randomly selected. In this experiment, in order to see the impact of the number of training data required to achieve the tasks, the training data-size have been randomly selected from 50 to 1000. Figure 3 shows the increment of the overall accuracy for the whole testing dataset. It shows that at 500 training data-size for R-LSTM and R-DMN, the accuracies have plateaued. As for the RL, DMN and LSTM, the accuracies are still lower than R-LSTM and R-DMN at 1000 training data-size. This implies R-LSTM and R-DMN can achieve all the tasks with less training data, while RL, DMN and LSTM cannot achieve all of the tasks even with the full 1000 training data-size.

5   Conclusion

We proposed a framework to combine the memory networks with reinforcement learning to achieve QA tasks. R-MNs' memory networks hold information and RL supports complex reasoning in achieving tasks. DMN and LSTM is used in our experiments for the memory networks. We have achieved all 20 of the 1 K bAbI tasks using R-DMN and R-LSTM with a mean accuracy of 98.72% and 99.02% respectively. This sets new state-of-the-art on the 1 K bAbI dataset. The proposed R-MN can achieve such high accuracy only using half of the training dataset.

Acknowledgment. This work was partially supported by a Murdoch University internal grant.

References

1. Cambria, E., White, B.: Jumping NLP curves: a review of natural language processing research. IEEE Comput. Intell. Mag. **9**(2), 48–57 (2014)
2. Weston, J., Bordes, A., Chopra, S., Rush, A.M., van Merriënboer, B., Joulin, A., Mikolov, T.: Towards ai-complete question answering: a set of prerequisite toy tasks. arXiv preprint arXiv:1502.05698 (2015)
3. LeCun, Y., Bengio, Y., Hinton, G.: Deep learning. Nature **521**(7553), 436–444 (2015)
4. Kumar, A., Irsoy, O., Ondruska, P., Iyyer, M., Bradbury, J., Gulrajani, I., Zhong, V., Paulus, R., Socher, R.: Ask me anything: dynamic memory networks for natural language processing. In: International Conference on Machine Learning (2016)
5. Sukhbaatar, S., Weston, J., Fergus, R.: End-to-end memory networks. In: Advances in Neural Information Processing Systems, pp. 2440–2448 (2015)
6. Bordes, A., Usunier, N., Chopra, S., Weston, J.: Large-scale simple question answering with memory networks. arXiv preprint arXiv:1506.02075 (2015)
7. Weston, J., Chopra, S., Bordes, A.: Memory networks. arXiv preprint arXiv:1410.3916 (2014)
8. Hochreiter, S., Schmidhuber, J.: Long short-term memory. Neural Comput. **9**(8), 1735–1780 (1997)
9. Tan, M., Santos, C.d., Xiang, B., Zhou, B.: LSTM-based deep learning models for non-factoid answer selection. arXiv preprint arXiv:1511.04108 (2015)
10. Peng, B., Lu, Z., Li, H., Wong, K.F.: Towards neural network-based reasoning. arXiv preprint arXiv:1508.05508 (2015)

11. Mnih, V., Kavukcuoglu, K., Silver, D., Rusu, A.A., Veness, J., Bellemare, M.G., Graves, A., Riedmiller, M., Fidjeland, A.K., Ostrovski, G.: Human-level control through deep reinforcement learning. Nature **518**(7540), 529–533 (2015)
12. Mnih, V., Badia, A.P., Mirza, M., Graves, A., Lillicrap, T., Harley, T., Silver, D., Kavukcuoglu, K.: Asynchronous methods for deep reinforcement learning. In: International Conference on Machine Learning, pp. 1928–1937 (2016)
13. Branavan, S.R., Chen, H., Zettlemoyer, L.S., Barzilay, R.: Reinforcement learning for mapping instructions to actions. In: Proceedings of the Joint Conference of the 47th Annual Meeting of the ACL and the 4th International Joint Conference on Natural Language Processing of the AFNLP (2009)
14. Yu, L., Hermann, K.M., Blunsom, P., Pulman, S.: Deep learning for answer sentence selection. arXiv preprint arXiv:1412.1632 (2014)
15. Guo, X., Klinger, T., Rosenbaum, C., Bigus, J.P., Campbell, M., Kawas, B., Talamadupula, K., Tesauro, G., Singh, S.: Learning to query, reason, and answer questions on ambiguous texts. In: 5th International Conference on Learning Representations (2017)
16. Bakker, B.: Reinforcement learning with long short-term memory. In: Neural Information Processing Systems (2002)
17. Cho, K., Van Merriënboer, B., Bahdanau, D., Bengio, Y.: On the properties of neural machine translation: encoder-decoder approaches. arXiv preprint arXiv:1409.1259 (2014)

Hybrid Deep Learning for Sentiment Polarity Determination of Arabic Microblogs

Sadam Al-Azani and El-Sayed M. El-Alfy$^{(\boxtimes)}$

Information and Computer Science Department,
College of Computer Sciences and Engineering,
King Fahd University of Petroleum and Minerals, Dhahran 31261, Saudi Arabia
{g201002580,alfy}@kfupm.edu.sa

Abstract. In this study, we investigate various deep learning models based on convolutional neural networks (CNNs) and Long Short Term Memory (LSTM) recurrent neural networks for sentiment analysis of Arabic microblogs. Unlike English, the Arabic language has several specifics which complicate the process of feature extraction by traditional methods. We adopted a neural language model created at Google, known as word2vec, for vectorizing text. We then designed and evaluated several deep learning architectures using CNN and LSTM. The experiments were run on two publicly available Arabic tweets datasets. Promising results have been attained when combining LSTMs and compared favorably with most related work.

Keywords: Word embedding · Long short-term memory · Convolutional neural network · Arabic sentiment analysis · Deep learning

1 Introduction

Sentiment analysis or opinion mining is one of the very active research areas in natural language processing (NLP). It is widely studied for mining and summarizing opinions of social media on the Web. This field of study is important to the extent that it has spread to other sciences such as management, politics, economics, and sociology. According to Liu [1], sentiment analysis is defined as "the field of study that analyzes people's opinions, sentiments, evaluations, appraisals, attitudes, and emotions towards entities such as products, services, organizations, individuals, issues, events, topics, and their attributes". The task of sentiment analysis has several variants including: opinion extraction, sentiment mining, subjectivity analysis, affect analysis, emotion analysis, review mining, etc.

Similar to other applications of supervised machine learning, the systematic approach for sentiment analysis is composed of three main phases, namely: feature extraction, feature selection and classification. In the first phase, several feature extraction methods can be applied to vectorize text including bag-of-words, part-of-speech tags, etc. However, this might generate a large number of features which

© Springer International Publishing AG 2017
D. Liu et al. (Eds.): ICONIP 2017, Part II, LNCS 10635, pp. 491–500, 2017.
https://doi.org/10.1007/978-3-319-70096-0_51

lead to more complex models and poor performance due to the curse of dimensionality phenomenon to analyze data in a high-dimensional space. Here, feature selection techniques can be employed, in the second phase, to reduce these features by eliminating redundant and/or irrelevant features. This class of methods depends on a feature scoring criterion such as mutual information or correlation. Alternatively, a reduced set of new features can be generated using techniques such as PCA (Principle Component Analysis) or LSA (Latent Semantic Analysis). The last phase utilizes some machine learning mechanisms for classification, such as support vector machines (SVM), k-NN, Naïve Bayes (NB), etc.

Recently, due to the remarkable success of deep learning in computer vision, it has been attempted for other domains including natural language processing. Deep neural language models have been successfully applied for feature extraction. The main advantage of these models is that they don't require any feature engineering for learning continuous text representation from data. Instead, deep contextual features about words are extracted in a lower dimensional space. Many techniques have been proposed for learning word vectors such as word2vec [2,3]. Other deep learning models that have been applied to NLP include Convolutional Neural Networks (CNNs) [4–6] and Long Short-Term Memory (LSTM) [7]. For instance, Kalchbrenner et al. [5] introduced a dynamic CNN for modeling sentences and evaluated it for sentiment prediction and question classification demonstrating good performance. Kim [4] presented an improved scheme based on CNN which employs dynamic and static word embeddings simultaneously for sentence classification and evaluated it on English sentiment analysis.

Unlike the English language, the research on Arabic sentiment analysis is still in its infancy. Arabic is spoken by 500+ million people worldwide (as the first or second language) in 58 countries with complex word structures and numerous morphological forms. A number of approaches have been proposed to address the Arabic sentiment analysis and opinion mining tasks including supervised and unsupervised machine-learning-based, lexicon-based and hybrid approaches. Various machine learning techniques have been applied including SVMs [8–13], Naïve Bayes [8–10,12,13], k-NN [8–10], decision trees [8,12,13], logistic regression [12,13] and SGD [12,13]. Ensemble classification methods have also been investigated [8,14,15].

Most of the work on Arabic sentiment analysis is based on hand-crafted features for either sentiment classification [8–10,12,13,16–19] or sentiment intensity prediction [20] and such approaches can be referred to as traditional models. An alternative approach has been proposed to address sentiment analysis based on joining feature extraction and classification in a single integrated scheme [21–23]. Such method is referred to as end-to-end learning, feature learning or deep learning model. Al-Sallab et al. [21] presented a deep learning framework for Arabic text sentiment classification based on Deep Belief Networks, Deep Auto Encoder and Recursive Auto Encoder. However, the input data model is based on the traditional Bag-of-Words (BoW). Altowayan and Tao [22] trained word embeddings based on CBOW (continuous bag-of-words) method and used them for training several binary classifiers (SVMs, Decision trees, Naïve Bayes, and Random forests) to detect subjectivity and sentiment in both Standard Arabic and Dialectal Arabic. Dahou et al. [23] investigated different neural word embedding architectures using a corpus of 3.4 billion words chosen from a collected web-crawled corpus of 10 billion words. Then, a CNN architecture similar to [4] was trained on top of the pretrained word embeddings to classify sentiments. However, that work only explored the non-static model.

The intension of our work is to investigate various CNN and LSTM models for sentiment analysis of Arabic microblogs. Arabic word vectors from an unsupervised neural language model (word2vec) are used as input to the investigated models. In addition, we proposed five novel combinations of deep learning models and evaluated them for Arabic sentiment analysis on two benchmark Arabic tweet datasets.

The remaining of this paper is organized as follows. Section 2 describes the framework and adopted methods. Section 3 describes the datasets used to train and evaluate the models and discusses the results from several experiments. Section 4 concludes the paper.

2   Framework and Methods

Figure 1 shows the layout of the investigated deep learning framework for polarity determination of Arabic text. The Arabic text is first preprocessed, e.g. removing non-Arabic symbols, removing diacritics (harakat), removing punctuation marks, removing stretching character (tatweel or kashida), and removing duplicate characters. Then, various deep learning models are developed and applied. Each of the main operations in this block diagram is described in details in the following subsections.

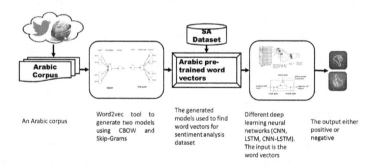

Fig. 1. Investigated framework for Arabic sentiment polarity determination using various deep learning methods

2.1   Word Embedding

In order to convert text into vectors, we adopted word2vec, which is an unsupervised word embedding neural model developed by Tomas Mikolov et al. at Google in 2013 [2,3]. It computes real-valued word vector representations in a relatively lower-dimensional vector space. It is proved to be an efficient and a successful technique in the applications of NLP. Word vectors are located in the vector space such that words that have similar semantic and share common contexts are mapped nearby each other in the space. Word2vec has two neural network architectures: continuous bag-of-words (CBOW) and skip-gram (SG). Both CBOW and SG employ a probabilistic prediction method capable of obtaining syntactic and semantic information to reflect word similarities and relationships. With word embedding, word relations are measured by simply using the distance between two embedding vectors, e.g. (King + Woman − Man) = Queen. CBOW and SG architectures are algorithmically similar. However, CBOW is trained to predict the current word with the help of its given context (surrounding words) whereas SG is trained to predict the context (surrounding words) of a given word.

2.2   Arabic Sentiment Analysis Using CNN

A CNN architecture similar to Kim [4] with minor changes is investigated. Assume a sentence S of n words, $S = \{m_1, m_2, ..., m_n\}$, where m_i is the ith word in S and the task is to predict the sentiment polarity as *positive* or *negative*. The sentence S is represented by an $n \times k$ matrix, where the element in the ith row corresponds to a k-dimensional vector $x_i \in \mathbb{R}^k$ of the ith word. To conduct convolution operation, a filter $w \in \mathbb{R}^{h \times k}$ is applied to a window of h words to generate a new feature. For each possible window in the sentence $\{x_{1:h}, x_{2:h+1}, ..., x_{n-h+1:n}\}$, the filter is applied to each possible window of words in the sentence to produce a feature map $c = [c_1, c_2, ..., c_{n-h+1}]$, where $c \in \mathbb{R}^{n-h+1}$. The next layer is a polling operation such as max, average or L_2-norm is applied to the feature map. Max-polling is the most common one and takes the maximum of feature map, i.e. $\hat{c} = max\{c\}$. Average-pooling was often used historically but has recently fallen out of favor compared to max-pooling in computer vision, especially object recognition [24]. We validated this claim by conducting some experiments using Arabic Sentiment Tweets Dataset (ASTD) where max-pooling performed better than the average-pooling operation.

In order to generate multiple features, multiple filters are used with different window sizes. This forms a vector $z = [\hat{c}_1, \hat{c}_2, ..., \hat{c}_m]$, where m is the number of filters, in the penultimate layer, which is then passed to a fully connected softmax layer. The final output is the probability distribution over classes. Although deep neural networks are very powerful machine-learning systems, a main problem related to them due to a large number of parameters is overfitting. Additionally, these networks are slow to use when they are large; making it difficult to deal with overfitting by combining the predictions of many different large neural nets at test time. This problem is addressed by randomly dropping out a proportion p of the hidden units in the penultimate layer during training [25]. In forward propagation the output unit y without dropout is $y = w.z + b$, while with dropout it becomes $y = w.(z \circ r) + b$, such that $r \in \mathbb{R}^m$ is a vector of Bernoulli random variables with probability p of being 1, and $\circ$ is element-wise multiplication operator. During testing, the learnt weight vectors are scaled by p such that $\hat{w} = pw$ then $\hat{w}$ is used to score the testing sentences.

The main steps of the adopted CNN method are shown in Fig. 2. We used three convolutional filters (3, 5, 7) and used max-over-sampling pooling filter since it reflects the most significant feature [4]. The dropout rate is set to 0.5, and a sigmoid function is applied to generate the final classification.

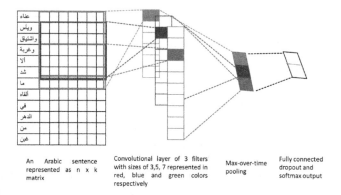

An Arabic sentence represented as n x k matrix   Convolutional layer of 3 filters with sizes of 3,5, 7 represented in red, blue and green colors respectively   Max-over-time pooling   Fully connected dropout and softmax output

Fig. 2. Adopted CNN architecture for Arabic sentiment analysis

2.3 Arabic Sentiment Analysis Using LSTM Models

We investigated four paradigms of LSTM recurrent neural network models to predict the sentiment polarity of Arabic text. Considering the opinion as a word sequence, LSTM has the advantage of recalling long-term spatial and temporal dependencies by linking past contexts to present one. For implementation of LSTM models, we used the Keras deep learning package with Theano backend [26].

The models considered here are as follows:

– Simple LSTM: Here, each word m_i is represented using one-hot encoding. LSTM model then takes this vector and converts it into a *word embedding* dependent vector.
– CNN-LSTM: We added an LSTM layer to a CNN model and the resulting model is referred to as CNN-LSTM.
– Stacked LSTM: Three LSTM layers are stacked on top of each other allowing the model to learn higher-level temporal representations. The first two LSTMs return their full output sequences, but the last one only returns the last step in its output sequence, thus dropping the temporal dimension (i.e. converting the input sequence into a single vector).
– Combined LSTM: We proposed an architecture based on LSTM by combining two LSTMs with dropout probabilities of 0.2 and 0.5, respectively. We investigated different combination methods including: summation, multiplication and concatenation. The layout of this model is shown in Fig. 3.

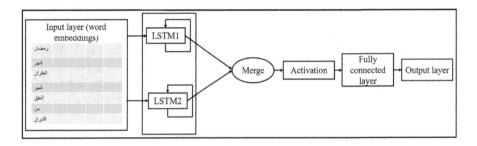

Fig. 3. Combined LSTMs for Arabic sentiment analysis

3   Experiments

3.1   Datasets and Preprocessing

Our focus is on predicting the positive and negative polarity sentiment of Arabic microblogs. Hence, we evaluated various models using two datasets of Arabic tweets: Arabic Sentiment Tweets Dataset (ASTD) [12], which is composed of over 10,000 tweets, and Arabic sentiment analysis (ArTwitter) [27], which consists of 2000 Arabic tweets. For ASTD, we used the balanced dataset preprocessed by Dahou et al. [23] and for ArTwitter we used the dataset preprocessed by Altowayan and Tao [22]. We conducted other preprocessing operations, including removing non-Arabic symbols, removing dialectical marks, removing punctuation marks, removing Tatweel, and removing duplicate character.

3.2   Pre-trained Arabic Word Vectors

We used an Arabic corpus of around 190 million words compiled from various sources (Quran-text, Watan-2004, CNN-Arabic, BBC-Arabic and consumer review) [22] to train CBOW and SG. These models were implemented in Python using gensim package with the parameters described in Table 1. After comparing different vector sizes in our experiments, the reported results are for a vector size of 300.

Table 1. Training parameters of Arabic word vectors

Model	Dimensionality	Window	Sampling	Negative	Min_count	Iterations
CBOW	300	10	0.0001	10	5	15
Skip-Gram	300	10	0.0001	10	5	15

3.3   Results

We conducted several experiments and compared the various models using four evaluation measures: precision (Prc), recall (Rec), accuracy (Acc), and F_1 score.

We first conducted experiments to compare CBOW and skip-grams using different deep learning models on both datasets (ASTD and ArTwitter). Following Kim [4], two model variations are experimented in our work including static and non-static (dynamic) word initialization. Table 2 shows the results of the tested models. The highest results are presented in bold. In general, non-static models with the combined LSTMs give better results.

Table 2. Performance comparison of various models on ASTD and ArTwitter datasets with static and non-static initializations for CBOW and skip-gram word embeddings

Word2vec	Dataset	Method	Static				Non-Static			
			Prec	Rec	Acc	F1	Prec	Rec	Acc	F1
CBOW	ASTD	CNN	74.86	74.40	74.40	74.43	74.12	74.10	74.10	74.11
		LSTM	75.04	74.70	74.70	74.74	80.12	80.12	80.12	80.07
		CNN-LSTM	71.18	68.07	68.07	67.58	76.92	73.49	73.49	72.00
		Stacked-LSTM	72.98	65.66	65.66	63.90	73.60	70.18	70.18	69.70
		Combined-LSTM-SUM	79.04	78.31	78.31	78.33	81.02	81.02	81.02	80.98
		Combined-LSTM-MUL	78.43	77.41	77.41	77.40	**82.32**	**81.63**	**81.63**	**81.64**
		Combined-LSTM-CONC	78.64	77.11	77.11	77.05	80.45	80.42	80.42	80.35
	ArTwitter	CNN	77.47	77.21	77.21	77.06	78.13	77.82	77.82	77.67
		LSTM	83.22	83.16	83.16	83.17	84.59	84.39	84.39	84.40
		CNN-LSTM	79.78	78.23	78.23	78.10	81.79	80.70	80.70	80.63
		Stacked-LSTM	82.54	82.34	82.34	82.35	82.12	81.93	81.93	81.85
		Combined-LSTM-SUM	82.58	82.55	82.55	82.55	84.80	84.80	84.80	84.80
		Combined-LSTM-MUL	83.01	82.96	82.96	82.96	85.42	85.42	85.42	85.42
		Combined-LSTM-CONC	83.22	82.96	82.96	82.96	**86.46**	**86.45**	**86.45**	**86.45**
Skip-grams	ASTD	CNN	73.96	61.45	61.45	57.5	73.96	66.57	66.57	64.90
		LSTM	76.85	76.51	76.51	76.54	77.88	77.41	77.41	77.44
		CNN-LSTM	76.35	75.90	75.90	75.56	75.34	71.99	71.99	71.58
		Stacked-LSTM	70.79	68.98	68.98	68.80	77.02	76.51	76.51	76.54
		Combined-LSTM-SUM	78.31	78.31	78.31	78.31	79.01	78.92	78.92	78.94
		Combined-LSTM-MUL	77.82	77.11	77.11	77.13	78.73	76.20	76.20	76.02
		Combined-LSTM-CONC	79.09	78.61	78.61	78.64	**80.90**	**80.42**	**80.42**	**80.45**
	ArTwitter	CNN	81.2	75.56	75.56	74.73	84.2	83.16	83.16	83.11
		LSTM	82.49	80.90	80.9	80.79	83.62	83.57	83.57	83.54
		CNN-LSTM	78.51	73.92	73.92	72.45	84.24	84.19	84.19	84.20
		Stacked-LSTM	82.21	81.72	81.72	81.72	82.95	82.96	82.96	82.95
		Combined-LSTM-SUM	83.04	82.55	82.55	82.54	85.64	85.63	85.63	85.61
		Combined-LSTM-MUL	82.28	81.72	81.72	81.71	85.83	85.83	85.83	85.82
		Combined-LSTM-CONC	81.45	81.31	81.31	81.32	**87.36**	**87.27**	**87.27**	**87.28**

Different optimizers can be used to compile models on Keras[1] including: Adagrad, Adam, Rmsprop and SGD. The previous experiments were carried out using Adam optimizer [28]. We investigated their impact on various models with their default parameters on ArTwitter dataset and non-static CBOW model. As shown in Table 3, the average performance of Rmsprop is the best followed by Adam. Moreover, the highest results obtained for ArTwitter dataset is obtained using Rmsprop in case of the combined LSTMs with non-static word initialization model.

---

[1] https://keras.io/optimizers/.

Table 3. Compilation optimizers with ArTwitter and non-static CBOW model

Method	Adagrad		Adam		Rmsprop		SGD	
	Acc	F_1	Acc	F_1	Acc	F_1	Acc	F_1
CNN	52.36	35.99	77.82	77.67	78.85	78.84	79.67	79.64
LSTM	85.83	85.84	84.39	84.40	84.19	84.19	68.79	68.77
CNN-LSTM	80.29	80.24	80.70	80.63	82.75	82.72	82.34	82.30
Stacked-LSTM	84.19	84.19	81.93	81.85	84.19	84.19	57.49	53.89
Combined-LSTM-SUM	84.80	84.81	84.80	84.80	83.37	83.38	66.74	66.30
Combined-LSTM-MUL	85.01	85.02	85.42	85.42	86.65	86.65	64.07	64.08
Combined-LSTM-CONC	86.04	86.04	86.45	86.45	**87.06**	**87.07**	65.71	65.72
Average	79.79	77.45	83.07	83.03	83.87	83.86	69.26	68.67

Finally, we compared the highest attained performance with that in the literature as shown in Table 4. It is clear that our proposed method of combining LSTMs compares favorably with other work.

Table 4. Comparisons with other related approaches

Dataset	Approach	Technique	Accuracy
ASTD	Dahou et al. [23]	CNN non-static	75.90
	Our work	Combined-LSTM-Mul, non-static, CBOW, Adam optimizer	**81.63**
ArTwitter	Dahou et al. [23]	CNN non-static	85.01
	Abdulla et al. [27]	Root-stemmer + SVM	85.00
	Our work	Combined-LSTM-CONC, non-static, Skip-gram, Adam optimizer	**87.27**

4   Conclusion

In this work, we evaluated several deep learning methods based on convolutional neural network and long short-term memory models for sentiment analysis of Arabic microblogs. We trained neural language models using two different word2vec based technique: CBOW and skip-gram. The top layer of those architectures are designed to include different approaches: static and non-static word initialization. The experiments showed using word2vec vectors updated during learning achieves the highest results in nearly all cases. In addition, the experiments showed that LSTM performs better than CNN. Moreover, the proposed combined LSTM architectures perform better than other models. Our plan for future work is to investigate different language models generated using large corpora and optimization of parameters for the proposed architectures for further enhancements of the results.

Acknowledgments. The authors would like to acknowledge the support provided by the Deanship of Scientific Research at King Fahd University of Petroleum and Minerals (KFUPM), Saudi Arabia, during this work.

References

1. Liu, B.: Sentiment analysis and opinion mining. Synth. Lect. Hum. Lang. Technol. **5**(1), 1–167 (2012)
2. Mikolov, T., Chen, K., Corrado, G., Dean, J.: Efficient estimation of word representations in vector space. In: Proceedings of Workshop at International Conference on Learning Representations (2013)
3. Mikolov, T., Sutskever, I., Chen, K., Corrado, G.S., Dean, J.: Distributed representations of words and phrases and their compositionality. In: Advances in Neural Information Processing Systems, pp. 3111–3119 (2013)
4. Kim, Y.: Convolutional neural networks for sentence classification. arXiv preprint arXiv:1408.5882 (2014)
5. Kalchbrenner, N., Grefenstette, E., Blunsom, P.: A convolutional neural network for modelling sentences. In: Proceedings of the 52nd Annual Meeting of the Association for Computational Linguistics (2014)
6. Shen, Y., He, X., Gao, J., Deng, L., Mesnil, G.: Learning semantic representations using convolutional neural networks for web search. In: Proceedings of the 23rd International Conference on World Wide Web, pp. 373–374. ACM (2014)
7. Hochreiter, S., Schmidhuber, J.: Long short-term memory. Neural Comput. **9**(8), 1735–1780 (1997)
8. Al Shboul, B., Al-Ayyoub, M., Jararweh, Y.: Multi-way sentiment classification of arabic reviews. In: Proceedings of the 6th IEEE International Conference on Information and Communication Systems (ICICS), pp. 206–211 (2015)
9. Brahimi, B., Touahria, M., Tari, A.: Data and text mining techniques for classifying arabic tweet polarity. J. Digital Inf. Manage. **14**(1), 15 (2016)
10. Omar, N., Albared, M., Al-Moslmi, T., Al-Shabi, A.: A comparative study of feature selection and machine learning algorithms for arabic sentiment classification. In: Jaafar, A., Mohamad Ali, N., Mohd Noah, S.A., Smeaton, A.F., Bruza, P., Bakar, Z.A., Jamil, N., Sembok, T.M.T. (eds.) AIRS 2014. LNCS, vol. 8870, pp. 429–443. Springer, Cham (2014). doi:10.1007/978-3-319-12844-3_37
11. Mohammad, S., Salameh, M., Kiritchenko, S.: How translation alters sentiment. J. Artif. Intell. Res. **55**, 95–130 (2016)
12. Nabil, M., Aly, M., Atiya, A.F.: Astd: Arabic sentiment tweets dataset. In: Proceedings of the International Conference on Empirical Methods in Natural Language Processing, pp. 2515–2519 (2015)
13. ElSahar, H., El-Beltagy, S.R.: Building large arabic multi-domain resources for sentiment analysis. In: Gelbukh, A. (ed.) CICLing 2015. LNCS, vol. 9042, pp. 23–34. Springer, Cham (2015). doi:10.1007/978-3-319-18117-2_2
14. Khasawneh, R.T., Wahsheh, H.A., Alsmadi, I.M., AI-Kabi, M.N.: Arabic sentiment polarity identification using a hybrid approach. In: Proceedings of the 6th IEEE International Conference on Information and Communication Systems (ICICS), pp. 148–153 (2015)
15. Al-Azani, S., El-Alfy, E.S.M.: Using word embedding and ensemble learning for highly imbalanced data sentiment analysis in short arabic text. Procedia Comput. Sci. **109**, 359–366 (2017)

16. Duwairi, R., Ahmed, N.A., Al-Rifai, S.Y.: Detecting sentiment embedded in arabic social media-a lexicon-based approach. J. Intell. Fuzzy Syst. **29**(1), 107–117 (2015)
17. Al-Kabi, M.N., Al-Ayyoub, M.A., Alsmadi, I.M., Wahsheh, H.A.: A prototype for a standard arabic sentiment analysis corpus. Int. Arab J. Inf. Technol. (IAJIT) **13** (2016)
18. Rabab'ah, A.M., Al-Ayyoub, M., Jararweh, Y., Al-Kabi, M.N.: Evaluating sentistrength for arabic sentiment analysis. In: Proceedings of the 7th IEEE International Conference on Computer Science and Information Technology (CSIT), pp. 1–6 (2016)
19. Refaee, E., Rieser, V.: An Arabic twitter corpus for subjectivity and sentiment analysis. In: Proceedings of the 4th International Conference on Language Resources and Evaluation (LREC), pp. 2268–2273 (2014)
20. Refaee, E., Rieser, V.: iLab-Edinburgh at SemEval-2016 Task 7: a hybrid approach for determining sentiment intensity of Arabic twitter phrases. In: Proceedings 10th International Workshop on Semantic Evaluation SemEval-2016, SemEval 2016, San Diego, California, June 2016
21. Al-Sallab, A.A., Baly, R., Badaro, G., Hajj, H., El-Hajj, W., Shaban, K.B.: Deep learning models for sentiment analysis in Arabic. In: ANLP Workshop, vol. 9 (2015)
22. Aziz, A., Tao, L.: Word embeddings for arabic sentiment analysis. In: IEEE International Conference on Big Data, vol. 7, pp. 3820–3825 (2016)
23. Dahou, A., Xiong, S., Zhou, J., Haddoud, M.H., Duan, P.: Word embeddings and convolutional neural network for arabic sentiment classification. In: Proceedings of the 26th International Conference on Computational Linguistics (COLING 2016), pp. 2418–2427 (2016)
24. Scherer, D., Müller, A., Behnke, S.: Evaluation of pooling operations in convolutional architectures for object recognition. In: Diamantaras, K., Duch, W., Iliadis, L.S. (eds.) ICANN 2010. LNCS, vol. 6354, pp. 92–101. Springer, Heidelberg (2010). doi:10.1007/978-3-642-15825-4_10
25. Srivastava, N., Hinton, G., Krizhevsky, A., Sutskever, I., Salakhutdinov, R.: Dropout: a simple way to prevent neural networks from overfitting. J. Mach. Learn. Res. **15**(1), 1929–1958 (2014)
26. Chollet, F., et al.: Keras (2015), https://github.com/fchollet/keras
27. Abdulla, N.A., Ahmed, N.A., Shehab, M.A., Al-Ayyoub, M.: Arabic sentiment analysis: lexicon-based and corpus-based. In: IEEE Jordan Conference on Applied Electrical Engineering and Computing Technologies (AEECT), pp. 1–6 (2013)
28. Kingma, D., Ba, J.: Adam: a method for stochastic optimization. arXiv preprint arXiv:1412.6980 (2014)

Low Frequency Words Compression in Neural Conversation System

Sixing Wu[1], Ying Li[2(✉)], and Zhonghai Wu[2]

[1] School of Software and Microelectronics, Peking University, Beijing, China
[2] National Research Center of Software Engineering, Peking University,
Beijing, China
li.ying@pku.edu.cn

Abstract. Recently, Encoder-Decoder, a framework for sequence-to-sequence (seq2seq) tasks has been widely used in the open domain generation-based conversation system. One of the most difficult challenges in Encoder-Decoder based open domain conversation systems is the Unknown Words Issue, that is, numerous words become out-of-vocabulary words (OOVs) due to the restriction of vocabulary's volume, while a conversation system always tries to avoid their appearances. This paper proposes a novel approach named Low Frequency Words Compression (LFWC) to address this problem by selectively using K-Components shared symbol for word representations of low frequency words. Compared to the standard Encoder-Decoder works at word-level, our LFWC Encoder-Decoder works at symbol-level, and we propose Sequence Transform to transform a word-level sequence into a symbol-level sequence and LFWC-Predictor to decode from a symbol-level sequence into a word-level sequence. To measure the interference of OOVs in neural conversation system, besides log-perplexity (LP), we apply two more suitable metrics UP-LP and UP-Delta to evaluate the interference of OOVs. The experiment shows that the performance of decoding from compressed symbol-level sequences to word-level sequences achieves a recall@1 score of 60.9%, which is much above 16.7% of baseline, with the strongest compression ratio. It also shows our approach outperforms the standard Encoder-Decoder model in reducing interference of OOVs, which achieves almost the half score of UP-Delta in the most of configurations.

Keywords: seq2seq · Conversation system · Vocabulary · Encoder-Decoder · OOVs

1 Introduction

Neural conversation system is a challenging natural language processing task, which involves natural language understanding, inference and generation. In the early stage, researchers focus on the rule-based methods [1] which are skilled in performing conversations with specific processes since they are guided by the hand-crafted rules but hard to extend to the open domain. Thanks to the explosive growth of the Internet, now we can obtain massive data from the Internet. Hence, data-driven approach is recently playing a leading role in the open domain conversation. Data-driven conversation

© Springer International Publishing AG 2017
D. Liu et al. (Eds.): ICONIP 2017, Part II, LNCS 10635, pp. 501–511, 2017.
https://doi.org/10.1007/978-3-319-70096-0_52

methods can be divided into two categories: retrieval-based and generation-based. The idea of retrieval-based method is to retrieve the best-matched response from the already existing database based on the post, whereas the generation-based method is considered as a seq2seq task that tries to understand the meaning of the post sequence and then learn to generate natural language sequence as a response.

A framework for data-driven seq2seq tasks is proposed by [2], which mapping a sequence into another sequence and then it has evolved to Encoder-Decoder framework [3–5]. The Encoder-Decoder framework first summarizes the source sequence as a context, then feeds this context into Decoder to generate target sequence. In a standard conversation system, Encoder and Decoder share a same modest-sized vocabulary. For the out of vocabulary words (OOVs), a universal special symbol *unk* is applied to replace all of them. Unsurprisingly, if there are many OOVs, it is hard for a conversation system to understand the post and generate the response. Due to the computational complexity and memory capacity, the size of vocabulary in a practical system is often restricted, and we called this issue as Unknown Words Issue.

In this paper, we present a novel method called Low Frequency Words Compression (LFWC) to address this Issue. By reviewing many corpus of natural language, we verified an empirical fact called Zipf's Law that the frequency of one word is inversely proportional to its rank in the frequency table, so the low-frequency words have fewer chances to appear in an utterance. Considering this, we take a novel way to represent low-frequency words. In a regular word-level Encoder-Decoder, each word in vocabulary occupies one record, which is too expensive for low-frequency words because they are seldom used. So, in our approach we let k different low-frequency words share a single symbol, thus compresses the vocabulary size and then reduce the appearances of OOVs. We also implement the LFWC Encoder-Decoder framework, which compromises the Sequence Transform, symbol-level Encoder-Decoder, and LFWC-Predictor. We first construct the mapping dictionary based on the mentioned idea that k low-frequency words share a symbol so we can use the Sequence Transform to encode a word-level sequence into a symbol-level sequence as the input of Encoder. Then the symbol-level Encoder-Decoder reads it and generates a symbol-level sequence as output. Finally, we use LFWC-Predictor to decoding from the output of Decoder to a word-level sequence as the natural language response. We perform experiments on the mixture of two public datasets, the results show that the performance of decoding from a compressed symbol-level sequence to a word-level sequence achieves a recall@1 score of 60.9% in average when we use 6-Component shared symbol, which is a great improvement over the baseline Random Choice (16.7%). LFWC Encoder-Decoder outperforms the standard Encoder-Decoder model in both UP-LP (reduced by 0.07 to 0.24) and UP-Delta (reduced by 50% in almost configurations), which indicates that our approach can improve the performance of the dialogue system under the same volume of vocabulary, thus address the Unknown Words Issue.

2   Related Work

Recently, there have been several works that try to solve the problem caused by the OOVs, and these works can be divided into two categories. The first category tries to bypass the issue of limited volume of vocabulary directly. Working at character-level [6] or the hybrid [7] of character-level and word-level is the typical way, which decomposes all OOVs into characters. However, it prolongs the lengths of both input and output sequences, which raises computational complexity significantly. And it just works well within the language composed by a small alphabet. The second category works try to reduce the computational complexity, for instance, adopting the sampled-softmax [8] to reduce the complexity on softmax operation, or using a binary tree to represent a hierarchical clustering of words [9]. These methods speed up the training process by more efficient operations, but still be restricted by memory capacity because they cannot reduce the size of model.

3   Method and Implementation

3.1   Low Frequency Words Compression

Low Frequency Words. Ordinarily, Encoder-Decoder based neural conversation models are trained and operated at word-level. Due to the computational complexity and memory grows linearly with the vocabulary size $|V|$, these models only use the Top-K most frequent words, and the OOVs are replaced by a universal symbol *unk*. Evidently, OOVs reduce the ability to understand dialogue contexts and the quality of generated response texts in Encoder-Decoder models. Zipf's law, an empirical law formulated using mathematical statistics, says a fact that in a common natural language corpus, a word's frequency is inversely proportional to its rank in the frequency table, thus only a small part of words is used frequently. Given a corpus, we illustrate this law by defining a metric $DataCoverage = \frac{\#allwords - \#OOVs}{\#allwords}$, where $\#(x)$ means the counts of x.

As shown in Fig. 1(a), we compute the *DataCoverage* rates on the full Chinese Wikipedia corpus, which has 167 M terms and 312 K unique words. The top-5 K most frequent words already hold approximately 60% share. With the incensement of the vocabulary size, the earnings growth rate of *DataCoverage* is falling, which reflects the low-frequency words are massive but rarely used in most utterances.

LFWC Method. Assuming one vocabulary maintains at most $|V|$ records, then a regular Encoder-Decoder only recognizes and generates $|V|$ words because one record simply represents a word, which is inefficient. Here, we propose a novel method called Low Frequency Words Compression (LFWC) to alleviate it by selectively using k-Components shared symbol to represent low frequency words. As shown in Fig. 1(b), LFWC let m symbols keep the way that one symbol denotes a word, and use $n(n + m = |V|)$ symbols to represent $k * n$ words, where k is a parameter. Thus, LFWC represents $(k - 1) * n$ more words compared to original one. LFWC comprises the following key steps:

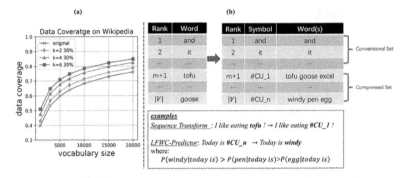

Fig. 1. Results of data coverage and an example of LFWC. (a) The data coverage rates on original way and compressed by LFWC. (b) An example of LFWC.

Preparation. Extracts the top $m + k * n$ most frequent words from the corpus and divides them into two sets: the first is Conventional set that contains top m words and another is Compressed set that contains the rest $k * n$ words. In the Conventional set, the representation is still using one symbol to represent one word. But in the Compressed set, the way is changed to one symbol represents k different words. For convenience, the symbol in the first set is called Raw-Unit, the symbol in the second set is called Compressed-Unit, and the rules that map words to symbols are stored in a dictionary.

Sequence Transform. In our approach, Encoder-Decoder works at symbol-level, so we develop this process to transform from word-level to symbol-level. Given a word-level sequence $\mathbf{w} = \{w_1, \ldots, w_L\}$, we map $\mathbf{w}$ to a symbol-level sequence $\mathbf{s} = \{s_1, \ldots, s_L\}$ as:

$$s_i = cmp\_seq(w_i) = \begin{cases} sid_j, & if \ w_i \ in \ cmp\_lookup(sid_j) \\ unk, & otherwise \end{cases} \tag{1}$$

Where the function *cmp_lookup* is used to look up a word w_i or a group of words $\{w_1, \ldots, w_k\}$ correspond to symbol s_i.

LFWC-Predictor. Now, we discuss how to decode from a symbol-level sequence $\mathbf{s}$ to a word-level sequencec $\mathbf{w}$. Because one Compressed-Unit symbol represents k words, LFWC-Predictor predicts the target word from k candidate words by its context. Given $\mathbf{s} = \{s_1, \ldots, s_L\}$, if s_i is a Raw-Unit, the result w_i can be obtained directly because there are just one candidate, but if s_i is a Compressed-Unit, we let all previously known Raw-Units symbols $\{s_r | r < i, s_r \ is \ a \ RawUnit\}$ as *context_seq*, and compute the context encoding vector $\mathbf{c}_{raw}$ by applying a RNN on the top of the word embeddings of *context_seq* and then select the last hidden state $\mathbf{h}_{rl}^{sr}$ as $\mathbf{c}_{raw}$:

$$\{\mathbf{h}_1^{sr}, \ldots, \mathbf{h}_{rl}^{sr}\} = RNN(context\_seq) \tag{2}$$

Then we use $\mathbf{c}_{raw} = \mathbf{h}_{rl}^{sr}$ to predict a word that is most likely the answer from k words in this Compressed-Unit. We take *raws_context* and all candidates' word-embeddings $\{e_1^{word}, \ldots, e_k^{word}\}$ as inputs, and train a classifier. We use a bilinear term $\mathbf{W}_p$ to compute the possibility between c_{raw} and e_i^{word}:

$$P(w_i|c_{raw}) = softmax(c_{raw}\mathbf{W}_p e_i^{word}) \tag{3}$$

3.2 Encoder-Decoder Framework

In a standard Encoder-Decoder framework, Encoder summarizes the input into a context and Decoder utilizes this context to generate a sequence as output. Encoder applies a RNN to read a source sequence of $\mathbf{x} = \{x_1, \ldots, x_L\}$, into a context vector c, which is considered to have summarized all information of source sequence:

$$c = q(\{\boldsymbol{h}_1, \ldots, \boldsymbol{h}_L\}) \tag{4}$$

Where hidden states $\{\boldsymbol{h}_1, \ldots, \boldsymbol{h}_L\}$ are computed by RNNs, and q is a nonlinear function. Generally, we use $q(\{\boldsymbol{h}_1, \ldots, \boldsymbol{h}_L\}) = \boldsymbol{h}_L$.

Decoder uses another RNN to generate the target sequence $\mathbf{y} = \{y_1, y_2, \ldots, y_M\}$, which maximizes the conditional probability of $\mathbf{y}$ given the context vector c:

$$P(\mathbf{y}|c) = \prod_{t'=1}^{M} P(y_{t'}|\{y_1, \ldots, y_{t'-1}\}, \mathbf{x}) \tag{5}$$

$$P(y_{t'}|\{y_1, \ldots, y_{t'-1}\}, \mathbf{x}) = g(y_{t'-1}, z_{t'}, c) \tag{6}$$

Where $z_{t'}$ is the hidden state of Decoder's RNNs at time t'. g is a nonlinear function that outputs the probability of $y_{t'}$.

To boost the performance, it's common to implement with Attention [4]. Instead of using a fixed context vector c, with Attention, at each time t' the Decoder dynamically computes a context vector $c_{t'}$ to replace the vector c in Eqs. (5, 6).

3.3 LFWC Encoder-Decoder Framework

As it shown in Fig. 2, in our framework, all the word-level sequence will be processed by Sequence Transform before they are fed into Encoder and the symbol-level sequence generated by Decoder would be decoded into word-level sequence by the LFWC-Predictor. The dictionary that saved the mapping rules between words and symbols is developed in advance, and then keep unchanged. One important thing should be noted, the essence of our work is that LFWC-Predictor should be trained beforehand, instead of being jointly trained with Encoder Decoder. The prediction process of LFWC-Predictor doesn't ask for the hidden states of Decoder's RNN because it only relies on the word embeddings of previously known Raw-Units symbols. This design makes the computational complexity and memory capacity of our model rely on the size of unique symbols rather than the size of words. Another advantage is that this design allows us to utilize most natural text corpus besides

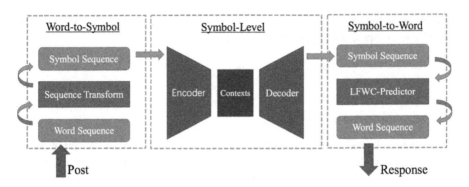

Fig. 2. LFWC encoder-decoder framework

conversation texts to train LFWC-Predictor, which is numerous and much easier to obtain from Web.

Encoder. Existing Encoders often take word-embeddings as input, but we add an additional feature, i.e., part-of-speech embeddings. We map all part-of-speech tags into p_e-dimensional vectors of real numbers. Given a raw word input sequence $\mathbf{w}^x$ and its part-of-speech tag sequence $\mathbf{p}^x$, we transform $\mathbf{w}^x$ into a symbol sequence $\mathbf{s}^x$ by Sequence Transform, then we calculate its word embeddings and part-of-speech embeddings and their concatenation is the input for Encoder. For word-embedding matrix $\mathbf{E}^{word}$, duo to the Raw-Unit symbols are raw words themselves, their word-embedding values are obtained from pre-trained resources. The Compressed-Unit symbols are some special symbols that only appears in our work, therefore, the word-embeddings of Compressed-Unit symbols are initialized as the average of k candidate's embedding values and then jointly training them with Encoder-Decoder. The part-of-speech embedding matrix $\mathbf{E}^{pos}$ is fully jointly learned with Encoder-Decoder.

Decoder. The Decoder is essentially a standard RNN language model. Decoder outputs a sequence of symbols $\mathbf{s}^y$ (not raw words directly) based on the hidden states generated by Encoder, and the generation probability of the i-th symbol is calculated by:

$$P\left(s_i^y | s_{i-1}^y, \ldots, s_1^y, \mathbf{s}^x\right) = g\left(s_{i-1}^y, z_t, c_t\right) \tag{7}$$

Where $g(\cdot)$ is a nonlinear function as Eq. 6, z_t is the hidden state of Decoder at time t, which is calculated by $z_t = RNN\left(s_{i-1}^y, z_{t-1}, c_t\right)$. c_t is a dynamically calculated context vector based on Attention Mechanism.

Training, Evaluation and Inference. The training and inference in our approach are similar to the way standard Encoder-Decoder works. In the training stage, LFWC-Predictor is not required because all the datasets should be firstly transformed to symbol-level by Sequence Transform, then minimize the cross-entropy between the generated symbol sequence and the target symbol sequence. In the inference or evaluation stage, we search for the most likely symbol-level sequence using the left-to-right beam search method. After that, we apply the pre-trained LFWC-Predictor to decode and finally output the most likely word-level sequence $\mathbf{w}^y$, which calculates the probability of a raw word as:

$$P(w_i^y) = \begin{cases} P(s_i^y), & \text{if } s_i^y \in Conventional\ Set \\ P(s_i^y) * P(w_i^y | c_{raw}), & \text{if } s_i^y \in Compressed\ Set \end{cases} \tag{8}$$

4 Experiment

4.1 Settings

Datasets. We evaluate our approach on the mixture of a dataset released by Shang [3] and a dataset from a GitHub project[1]. Shang's dataset is crawled from Weibo, which contains various topics and plentiful rare words. The dataset from GitHub contains many semi-structured dialogues organized by human. We extract 900 K post-response dialogue pairs from each dataset, then randomly divide these 1.8 M pairs into to train set (70%) and test set (30%). We pre-trained a Word2Vec model with the corpus of Wikipedia[2] with dimension = 200. For all datasets, we apply the toolkit jieba[3] to segment and figure out part-of-speech tags.

Implement Details. For LFWC-Predictor, we use a 3-layer bi-directional LSTM with 128 hidden units for context encoding. The baseline for LFWC-Predictor is Random Choice. For LFWC Encoder-Decoder, we use a 3-layer bi-directional LSTM with 256 hidden units for Encoder, and a 3-layer LSTM with 256 hidden units for Decoder. Here the baseline is standard Encoder-Decoder with Attention. All the training examples are divided into mini-batches of 256 examples each. For both, dropout with $p = 0.5$ is applied to all hidden units of LSTMs, and Adam algorithm is used to optimize.

4.2 Results and Analysis

Analysis on Efficiency of LFWC. As mentioned, decoding from a compressed symbol-level sequence into a word-level sequence is a key phrase. Hence, we analysis the efficiency of LFWC on different parameter configurations. We use *LFWC-Predictor* to decode symbol sequences generated by *Sequence Transform* on the corpus. For a Compressed-Unit symbol in a sequence, *LFWC-Predictor* is used to predict the right one from k candidate words given its all previously known Raw-Unit symbols. For evaluation, we use the average of Recall@1 results of all Compressed-Units samples. The parameters include size of symbol vocabulary v of 3 k, 5 k, 7 k, compression ratio $r = \frac{n}{n+m}$ of 0.3, 0.5, 0.7, and bin size k of 2, 4, 6. A higher score of Recall@1 means *LFWC-Predictor* has more chance to restore a fully correct raw word sequence.

---

[1] https://github.com/rustch3n/dgk_lost_conv/tree/master/results.

[2] http://download.wikipedia.com/zhwiki/latest/.

[3] https://github.com/fxsjy/jieba.

As it shown in Fig. 3, our approach performs much better than the baseline method that randomly choose a candidate, which demonstrates LFWC-Predictor is a feasible model to select the right word from a lot of candidates. With the increase of parameter k, one Compressed-Unit represents more words, and our approach can keep an acceptable Recall@1 ($\sim 60\%$) while the random choice method is decreased sharply, which shows that LFWC-Predictor can utilize all previous known Raw-Units as context to predict the correct raw word even when a Compressed Unit symbol represents many words simultaneously. For the parameter compression ratio r, it doesn't affect the performance much if the volume of vocabulary is not too small (see Fig. 3b and c). It's also found in the experiment that if the volume of vocabulary is very small, then, a lower compression ratio r is a better choice because a lower r can protect high frequency words from being compressed.

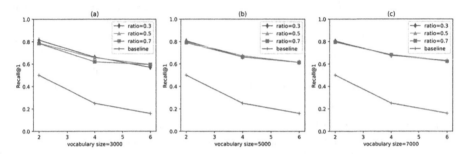

Fig. 3. Performance comparison between LFWC and the baseline method.

Analysis on LFWC Encoder-Decoder. $perplexity = \exp(-\frac{1}{M}\sum_{i=1}^{M}\log p(y_i))$ or it's log version *log-perplexity* (LP) is the most popular automatic metric for language modeling and conversation system, the lower LP is, the better performance is. However, perplexity has several flaws, the biggest one is that *perplexity* is not appropriate in evaluating a model with many OOVs because a model can get a good LP by simply predicting any *unk* word as *unk* class [10]. For instance, when all words in a sentence are OOVs, a model predicting every word as *unk* will obtain an extremely good perplexity. Obviously, *unk* symbols can't provide useful information in a conversation system, and influences the accuracy of the evaluation. To this end, we use the *unknown penalized log-perplexity* (UP-LP) proposed by Ahn [10]. UP-LP penalizes the likelihood of unknown words as follows:

$$p_{up}(y_{unk}) = \frac{p(y_{unk})}{|V_{all}\backslash V_{vocab}|} \qquad (9)$$

Where V_{all} is the full set of words, V_{vocab} is the global vocabulary used for Encoder-Decoder. The set of OOVs is $V_{all}\backslash V_{vocab}$. UP-LP theoretically has a higher value than LP because of the penalization of OOVs, hence the difference between LP and UP-LP can figure out the bad impacts of OOVs in a model. Considering this, we propose a metric named UP-Delta to evaluate the bad impacts of OOVs, which equals to UP-LP minus LP. Here, the less UP-Delta is, the fewer OOVs appear in our model.

Table 1 shows that our LFWC framework outperforms than the standard Encoder-Decoder framework. For LFWC Encoder-Decoder, the configuration with the best comprehensive performance is selected here. Compared to the standard framework, our approach significantly reduces the UP-Delta, where LFWC with $v = 3000$ has a lower UP-Delta compare to baseline with $v = 7000$. Meanwhile, our experiment

Table 1. LFWC vs baseline

Model	Configurations	LP	UP-LP	UP-Delta
Std. Encoder-Decoder	$v = 3000$	4.75	5.21	0.46
Std. Encoder-Decoder	$v = 5000$	5.08	5.38	0.30
Std. Encoder-Decoder	$v = 7000$	5.32	5.54	0.23
LFWC Encoder-Decoder	$v = 3000, k = 4, r = 0.5$	4.75	4.97	0.22
LFWC Encoder-Decoder	$v = 5000, k = 4, r = 0.5$	5.09	5.22	0.13
LFWC Encoder-Decoder	$v = 7000, k = 4, r = 0.5$	5.38	5.47	0.09

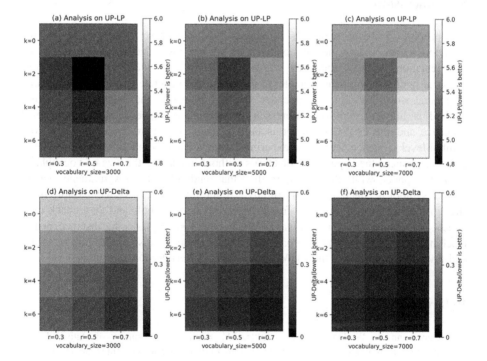

Fig. 4. The results of UP-LP and UP-Delta on different combinations of k and r. The y-axis and x-axis of each plot correspond to the k and r. Each pixel shows the value of UP-LP or UP-Delta corresponds the combination of its coordinate. Specially, values of the row that $k = 0$ are same, which is the result of the baseline model. (a–c) show the result of UP-LP on different vocabulary size, and (d–f) show the result of UP-Delta on different vocabulary size.

results also show that LFWC could reduce the UP-LP, especially in the low configuration situations. The decreases of UP-Delta and UP-LP indicate that our approach LFWC has the ability to address the problem of OOVs.

Sensitivity Analysis. Two parameters are important to our approach: bin size k and compression ratio r. Thus, to figure out the sensitivity of these two parameters, we experiment on several different parameter combinations between k and r.

As shown the Fig. 4, we see that our model doesn't outperform the baseline model in all configurations if only focus on UP-LP. The reason behinds this is that our model actually handles $(k - 1) * n$ more words compared to baseline (see Sect. 3). Although a larger vocabulary is helpful, the more words a vocabulary handles, the higher LP/UP-LP is, which can be verified in Table 1. If we compare our model with baseline according to the volume of known words instead of vocabulary size, it can be found our model still perform better. We find that our model completely outperforms than baseline model if focus on UP-Delta, which indicates our model reduced the problem of OOVs significantly. Meanwhile, we find that $r = 0.5$ is a right choice in most situations which has the balance of the performance of UP-LP and UP-Delta.

5 Conclusion

We propose a novel approach to address the Unknown Words Issue in the Encoder-Decoder based neural conversation system by selective compressing the representations of low frequency words. Our LFWC Encoder-Decoder framework works at symbol-level, which enables to recognize and generate more words compared to general word-level Encoder-decoder. In the framework, the Sequence Transform method is implemented to compress a word-level sequence into a symbol-level sequence and the LFWC-Predictor is built to recover a word-level sequence from symbol-level sequence. Results of experiment indicate that our model has achieved the goal that reduces the appearance of OOVs without increasing the size of vocabulary.

In this paper, while the LFWC method that randomly let k low frequency words share a symbol is effective, it still primitive. In the future work, we will explore more strategies about how to map low frequency words into symbols and then check their effects. Meanwhile, we aim to extend LFWC to other seq2seq tasks, for instance, neural machine translation and text summarization. Meanwhile, we also aim to design a fully end-to-end training across the LFWC-Predictor and Encoder-Decode.

References

1. Schatzmann, J., Weilhammer, K., Stuttle, M., Young, S.: A survey of statistical user simulation techniques for reinforcement-learning of dialogue management strategies. Knowl. Eng. Rev. **21**, 97–126 (2006)
2. Sutskever, I., Vinyals, O., Le, Q.V: Sequence to sequence learning with neural networks. In: Ghahramani, Z., Welling, M., Cortes, C., Lawrence, N.D., Weinberger, K.Q. (eds.) Advances in Neural Information Processing Systems, pp. 3104–3112. Curran Associates, Inc. (2014)

3. Shang, L., Lu, Z., Li, H.: Neural responding machine for short-text conversation. In: Annual Meeting of the Association for Computational Linguistics, pp. 1577–1586 (2015)

4. Bahdanau, D., Cho, K., Bengio, Y.: Neural machine translation by jointly learning to align and translate. In: International Conference on Learning Representations, pp. 1–15 (2014)

5. Vinyals, O., Le, Q.: A neural conversational model (2015)

6. Lee, J., Cho, K., Hofmann, T.: Fully character-level neural machine translation without explicit segmentation. In: Annual Meeting of the Association for Computational Linguistics, pp. 1693–1703 (2016)

7. Luong, M.-T., Manning, C.D.: Achieving open vocabulary neural machine translation with hybrid word-character models. In: Annual Meeting of the Association for Computational Linguistics, pp. 1054–1063 (2016)

8. Jean, S., Cho, K., Memisevic, R., Bengio, Y.: On using very large target vocabulary for neural machine translation. In: Annual Meeting of the Association for Computational Linguistics, pp. 1–10 (2015)

9. Mnih, A., Hinton, G.E.: A scalable hierarchical distributed language model. In: Advances in Neural Information Processing Systems, pp. 1–8 (2008)

10. Ahn, S., Choi, H., Pärnamaa, T., Bengio, Y.: A neural knowledge language model. arXiv. 1–12 (2016)

A Width-Variable Window Attention Model for Environmental Sensors

Cuiqin Hou[1], Yingju Xia[1(✉)], Jun Sun[1], Jing Shang[2], Ryozo Takasu[3], and Masao Kondo[1]

[1] Fujitsu Research and Development Center Co., LTD.,
355 Unit 3F, Gate 6, Space 8, Pacific Century Place,
No. 2A Gong Ti Bei Lu, Chaoyang District, Beijing, China
yjxia@cn.fujitsu.com
[2] College of Environmental Sciences and Engineering, Peking University,
Beijing, China
[3] Fujitsu Laboratories LTD., Kawasaki, Japan

Abstract. Air pollution is a major problem in modern cities and developing countries. Fine particulate matter (PM2.5) is a growing public health concern and become the most serious air pollution. In this study, we formulate the PM2.5 inference problem in conventional environmental sensors as a sequence-to-sequence problem. We adopt the encoder-decoder LSTM (Long short term memory) framework to solve the PM2.5 inference problem. A novel width-variable window attention mechanism is proposed for the encoder-decoder LSTM system. The proposed method learn the position and width of the attention window simultaneously. The proposed method is evaluated on large scale data and the experimental results show that it achieves better performance on two datasets with different concentration of PM2.5.

Keywords: LSTM · Attention model · RNN

1 Introduction

Real-time information about the air quality, especially the concentration of Particulate Matter 2.5 (PM2.5), is of vital importance to protect human health and monitor environment in urban city and developing countries. PM2.5 denotes fine particles with a diameter of 2.5 μm or less. Many countries have established standards for concentration of PM2.5. The unit $\mu g/m^3$ is specified for calculating the particulate contribution to the air quality index. High concentration PM2.5 considerably leads to respiratory illnesses and even increases daily death rates [1–3]. For every increase of 10 $\mu g/m^3$ in PM2.5, the lung cancer rate rose 9% [4].

Nowadays, air quality is monitored by networks of air quality measurement stations operated by official authorities. These stations are highly reliable and can accurately measure a broad range of air pollutants. However, the expensive cost of acquiring and maintaining measurement stations results in insufficient installations. For instance, Beijing of area 16410 km^2 only has 35 air quality measurement stations as illustrated in Fig. 1. Unfortunately, the concentration of PM 2.5 is affected by traffic, industrial

© Springer International Publishing AG 2017
D. Liu et al. (Eds.): ICONIP 2017, Part II, LNCS 10635, pp. 512–520, 2017.
https://doi.org/10.1007/978-3-319-70096-0_53

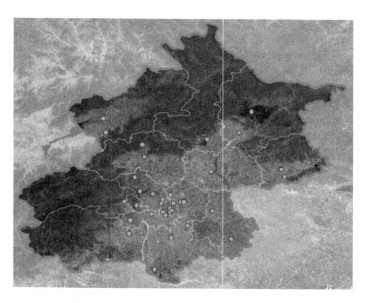

Fig. 1. Air quality measurement stations in Beijing.

installations, meteorology, urban structure and so on and it varies by locations non-linearly [4]. Additionally, indoor PM2.5 concentration and outdoor concentration differs from each other. Furthermore, the air measurement stations report the average value of the concentration of PM2.5 every hour. However, sometimes, especially encountering severe air pollution, the concentration of PM2.5 dramatically increases within half an hour as shown in Fig. 2. To use the accurate and real-time measurement of a concentration of PM2.5 in local and small area, a calibration method for conventional environment sensors has been reported in [5].

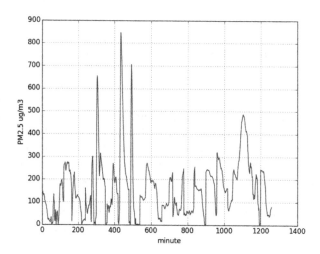

Fig. 2. The PM2.5 concentration segments.

In this paper, we infer the real-time and accurate PM2.5 concentration with deep learning using a conventional PM sensor device. As the Fig. 3 shows, the current PM2.5 concentration is not only related to the current measurements of particulate matters, temperature, humidity and air pressure, it also related to their history measurements as well. Here, the x-axis shows the timeline in minutes and y-axis shows the correlation coefficient. Additionally, it is useful to provide the entire varying tendency of PM2.5. Therefore, we formulate a sequence to sequence problem to infer the PM2.5 concentration. There are many literatures on this topic [6], from traditional machine learning method [7–9] to the popular deep learning method [10, 11]. In this study we propose a variable-width window attention model to solve the problem. We evaluate the proposed model on large scale data and the experimental results show that the proposed model achieve better performance.

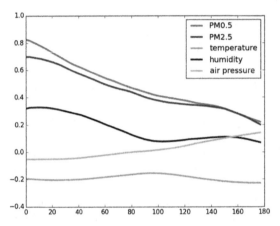

Fig. 3. The Pearson product-moment correlation coefficient between the current true value of the PM2.5 and current measure values of PM0.5, PM2.5, temperature, humidity and air pressure and their history values.

2   Width-Variable Window Attention Model

In our experiment, we find that the current PM2.5 concentration obtained by a conventional sensor device is not only related to the current measurements of particulate matters, temperature, humidity and air pressure, it also related to their history measurements as well as shown in Fig. 3. In addition, it is useful to provide the entire varying tendency of PM2.5. Therefore, we formulate the calibration problem to a sequence to sequence problem. More specifically, we obtain the sequence data of small particles and large particles by air quality monitor and the sequence data of temperature, humidity and air pressure by other sensors. We calibrate the current PM2.5 value and its history values simultaneously. Formally, we observe the input vector sequence $X = (X_1, X_2, \ldots, X_T)$ and we predict the true output vector sequence $Y = (Y_1, Y_2, \ldots, Y_T)$, where X_i denotes the values of small particles, large particles, temperature, humidity and air pressure at time i, and Y_i denotes the value of PM2.5 in $\mu g/m^3$ at time i.

The deep RNN (Recurrent Neural Network) model can be adopted to this problem. In the Encoder-Decoder framework, an encoder reads a sequence of vectors $X = (X_1, X_2, \ldots, X_T)$ into a vector c. The decoder is trained to predict the value of Y_i given the input representation vector c and all the previous predicted values $\{Y_1', Y_2', \ldots, Y_{t-1}'\}$. However, the RNN model suffers the vanishing gradient problem. It cannot long-term dependencies. The LSTM (Long-Short Term Memory), a special kind of RNN, is explicitly designed to avoid the long-term dependency problem. Remembering information for long periods of time is practically their default behavior.

The LSTMs have the form of a chain of repeating modules of neural network. The repeated models have the following structure:

$$f_t = \sigma\left(W_f[h_{t-1}, x_t] + b_f\right) \tag{1}$$

$$i_t = \sigma(W_i[h_{t-1}, x_t] + b_i) \tag{2}$$

$$O_t = \sigma(W_O[h_{t-1}, x_t] + b_O) \tag{3}$$

$$C_t' = tanh(W_C[h_{t-1}, x_t] + b_C) \tag{4}$$

$$C_t = f_t * C_{t-1} + i_t * C_t' \tag{5}$$

$$h_t = O_t * \tanh(C_t) \tag{6}$$

where f_t, i_t, and O_t are "forget gate layer", "input gate layer" and "output gate layer"; C_t' is the new candidate values for the cell state, C_t is the new cell state, h_t is the output of the LSTM model at step t; σ denotes a sigmoid function. We use $C = (h_1, h_2, \ldots, h_T)$ to encode the input vector sequence.

In order to predict more accurate values, attention-based encoder selects different parts of the vector c for each step. Bahdanau et al. [13] propose to compute different context vector by $C_i = \sum_{j=1}^{T} \alpha_{ij} h_j$, where the scores α_{ij} are computed on an attention module. As shown in the Fig. 4, the attention module takes both the decoder's previous state S and the encoder's state h into account. It scores the element of h regardless of their position in the sequence, so it belongs to content-based attention mechanism [14]. This model actually make different weights for elements of the encoder's state h at different step inspired by human vision attention mechanism [15].

However, the previous attention model only handle fixed window size and the position of the window is also predetermined. In many cases, only a small size of window need to be watched and the position of the window is also variable. Therefore, we propose a width-variable window attention model to generate context from the encoder's state for the decoder at different steps. The Fig. 5 shows the proposed model. At each step, the proposed attention model only focus on a window of the encoder's state h and the size of the window is variable. The location and size of the window is learned from the decoder's previous state and the encoder's state. More specifically, we design the width-variable window attention model as follows:

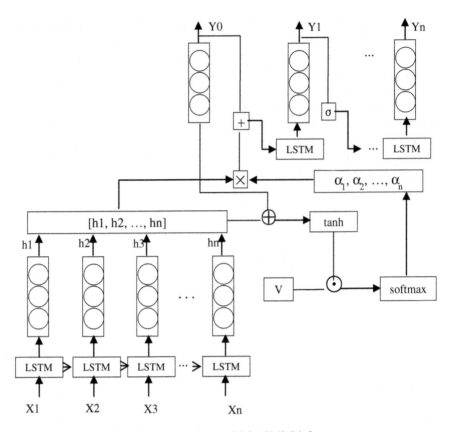

Fig. 4. The attention model for PM2.5 inference

$$contex = V \odot \tanh([s_{t-1}, h_1, h_2, \ldots, h_T]) \tag{7}$$

$$P_t = T * sigmod(W_p * contex + b_p) \tag{8}$$

$$L_t = \frac{1}{2}T * sigmod(W_L * contex + b_L) \tag{9}$$

$$\alpha_i = Relu(L_t - abs(i - P_t)) \qquad i \in \{1, 2, \ldots, T\} \tag{10}$$

Where P_t is the center of the window, L_t is the half size of the window and α_i takes values decreasing from the window center and takes 0 outside the window. The scores α_i take non-zero values on window, so the proposed attention module only attends the window part of the input representation.

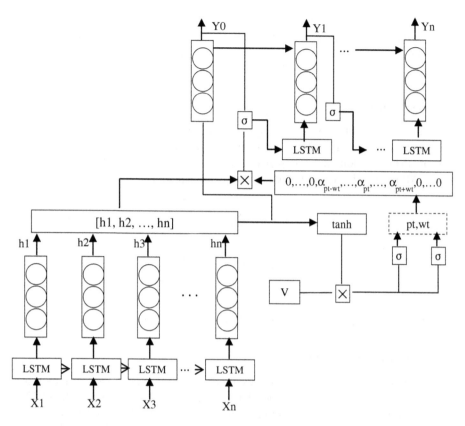

Fig. 5. The width-variable window attention model for PM2.5 inference

3 Experiments

3.1 Data Collection

In our experiments, we use a device Dylos dc1100 to measure the concentration of PM2.5. The device Dylos dc1100 uses light scattered from laser to count particles passing through a chamber. The device report two values, the first value shows the number of particles which diameter is larger than 0.5um, and the second value shows the number of particles which diameter is larger than 2.5um. Since the unit of PM2.5 is unit $\mu g/m^3$, it is necessary to infer the PM2.5 index from the particles numbers. However, most devices cannot give high accuracy particle number due to different size, shape of fine dust and refractive index [12]. Therefore, we added sensors to our device to measure the humidity, temperature and air pressure to calibrate the measurement value about PM2.5.

The ground truth of the PM2.5 is also prepared, as follows. Since the air quality measurement stations report the concentration of PM2.5 per hour, it's difficult to get enough data for training and testing. In this study, the PM2.5 concentration per minute data, obtained by a high performance particulate monitoring analyzer. The two devices measure data every minute. Since the PM2.5 concentration is quite difference in different seasons, especially in winter and summer, we split our data into two datasets according to the concentration of PM2.5 to evaluate the models.

3.2   Evaluation

We evaluate the calibration system by two criterions, one is the MSE (mean square error) and the other is TIC (Theil Inequality Coefficient). TIC is a common criterion to evaluate the regression model. In general, the smaller the value of TIC, the better of the model. MSE and TIC are computed by following equations.

$$\text{MSE} = \frac{1}{n} \sum_i (P_i - M_i)^2 \tag{11}$$

$$\text{TIC} = \frac{\sqrt{\frac{1}{n} \sum_i (P_i - M_i)^2}}{\sqrt{\frac{1}{n} \sum_i P_i^2} + \sqrt{\frac{1}{n} \sum_i M_i^2}} \tag{12}$$

Where P is the prediction value and M is the true values.

3.3   Experimental Results

The proposed model is compared with two other models. The first model is a traditional LSTM model, which directly calibrates PM2.5 values by adding a layer to the LSTM's state. The second model is an attention mechanism based encoder-decoder model and it adopt the attention mechanism proposed in [13]. We evaluate these three models on our two datasets and the experiments are shown in Tables 1 and 2. There are 48,559 data in dataset1 and 124,960 data in dataset2. The evaluation is conducted by 10-fold Cross-validation. From Tables 1 and 2, we can find that the attention-based encoder-decoder systems achieve better performance than the simple LSTM model. It is because the encoder-decoder system considers both the previous input representation and the later information at one step. Hence the encoder-decoder framework systems obtain better performance. From the experimental results, we can also find that our

Table 1. TIC of the system

	LSTM	Attention	Variable Window
DataSet1	0.2553	0.2514	**0.2149**
DataSet2	0.1243	0.1077	**0.096**

Table 2. MSE of the System

	LSTM	Attention	Variable Window
DataSet1	18.18	17.74	**16.92**
DataSet2	41.42	36.69	**33.79**

proposed width-variable window attention module is better than the common attention module. Here, the constrained attention mechanism and the variable width all contribute to the better performance.

4 Conclusion

In this paper, we formulate the PM2.5 inference problem by environmental sensors to a sequence-to-sequence problem. We propose a width-variable window attention mechanism for the adopted encoder-decoder structure system. The proposed attention mechanism learn the position and width of the attention window from the context of encoder and decoder model. We compare our proposed model with the other two models. Experimental results on large scalar dataset show that the proposed width-variable window attention model achieve better performance.

References

1. Dockery, D.W., Xu, X., Spengler, J.D.: An association between air pollution and mortality in six U.S. cities. N. Engl. J. Med. **329**, 1753–1759 (1993)
2. Pope, C.A., Bates, D.V., Raizenne, M.E.: Health effects of particulate air pollution: time for reassessment. Environ. Health Perspect. **103**, 472–480 (1995)
3. Mage, D., Ozolins, G., Peterson, P.: Urban air pollution in megacities of the world. Atmos. Environ. **30**, 681–686 (1996)
4. Hamra, G.B., Guha, N., Cohen, A.: Outdoor particulate matter exposure and lung cancer: a systematic review and meta-analysis. Environ. Health Perspect. **122**, 906–912 (2014)
5. Takasu, R.: Development of compact and low-cost PM2.5 mass concentration measurement equipment and its application to high-frequency mobile monitoring in a local area. In: 2016 International Conference on Agriculture, Energy and Environment Engineering, Bangkok (2016)
6. Oprea, M., Mihalache, S.F., Popescu, M.: A comparative study of computational intelligence techniques applied to PM2. 5 air pollution forecasting. In 6th International Conference on Computers Communications and Control, Oradea, Romania, pp. 103–108 (2016)
7. Park, D., Kwon, S.B., Cho, Y.: Development and calibration of a particulate matter measurement device with wireless sensor network function. Int. J. Environ. Monit. Anal. **1**, 15–20 (2013)
8. Gao, M., Cao, J., Seto, E.: A distributed network of low-cost continuous reading sensors to measure spatiotemporal variations of PM2. 5 in Xi'an, China. Environ. Pollut. **199**, 56–65 (2015)
9. Dong, Y., Wang, H., Zhang, L.: An improved model for PM2. 5 inference based on support vector machine. In: 17th International Conference on Software Engineering, Artificial Intelligence, Shanghai, China, pp. 27–31 (2016)
10. Srimuruganandam, B., Nagendra, S.M.S.: ANN-based PM prediction model for assessing the temporal variability of PM10, PM2. 5 and PM1 concentrations at an urban roadway. Int. J. Environ. Eng. **7**, 60–89 (2015)
11. Zheng, Y., Liu, F., Hsieh, H.P.: U-Air: When urban air quality inference meets big data. In: 19th ACM SIGKDD International Conference on Knowledge discovery and Data Mining, New York, pp. 1436–1444 (2013)

12. Coffey, C.C., Pearce, T.A.: Direct-reading methods for workplace air monitoring. J. Chem. Health Saf. **17**, 10–21 (2010)
13. Bahdanau, D., Cho, K.H., Bengio, Y.: Neural Machine Translation by Jointly Learning to Align and Translate. arXiv preprint arXiv:1409.0473 (2014)
14. Chorowski, J.K., Bahdanau, D., Serdyuk, D.: Attention-based models for speech recognition. In: 29th Annual Conference on Neural Information Processing Systems, Quebec, Canada, pp. 577–585 (2015)
15. Gregor, K., Danihelka, I., Graves, A.: DRAW: A recurrent neural network for image generation. arXiv preprint arXiv:1502.04623 (2015)

Memorizing Transactional Databases Compressively in Deep Neural Networks for Efficient Itemset Support Queries

Yi Ji$^{(\boxtimes)}$ and Yukio Ohsawa

The University of Tokyo, Hongo, Bunkyo, Tokyo 113-8654, Japan
jiyi@g.ecc.u-tokyo.ac.jp, ohsawa@sys.t.u-tokyo.ac.jp

Abstract. Can a deep neural network memorize a database? Though deep artificial neural networks are remarkable for large memory capacity that makes fitting any dataset possible, memorizing a database is a novel learning task unlike other popular tasks which intrinsically model mappings rather than "memorize" information internally. We give a positive answer to the question by showing that through training with maximal/minimal and frequent/infrequent patterns of a transactional database, a dynamically constructed deep net can support random itemset support queries with relatively high precision in regard to data compression ratio. Due to the compressive memorization, the amount of transactions in the database becomes irrelevant to the query time cost in our efficient method. We further discuss the potential interpretation of learnt database representation by analyzing corresponding statistical features of the database and activation patterns of the neural network.

Keywords: Transactional database · Artificial neural network · Approximation query · Pattern mining · Data compression

1 Introduction

In the past few years, deep learning has achieved significant improvement of performance on many machine learning applications such as image recognition, speech recognition, natural language processing, even knowledge representation and reasoning [1]. Despite their massive size, deep artificial neural networks of different kinds can almost infinitely fit any large scale dataset and exhibit remarkably small generalization error. A recent research [2] even shows deep neural networks easily fit random labels, thus raising the question whether deep neural networks learn via memorization. Researchers with different opinion argue that deep neural networks first learn and then refine simple patterns from training data and only incorporate more case-by-case memorization as a later resort [3].

© Springer International Publishing AG 2017
D. Liu et al. (Eds.): ICONIP 2017, Part II, LNCS 10635, pp. 521–531, 2017.
https://doi.org/10.1007/978-3-319-70096-0_54

1.1   Our Contributions

So far, the term "memorization" in deep learning refers to driving down training loss by fitting training dataset without capitalizing on any patterns in the data. In this paper, we propose to memorize transactional databases as the learning task itself but not the means. As shown in Fig. 1, we generate training data from a transactional database by pattern mining algorithms and train a deep neural network for a regression task which takes any itemset as input, and outputs itemset support, i.e., frequency of the itemset being contained by transactions, thus equivalently memorizing the transactional database in the deep net compressively. The compression is lossy due to training loss but highly effective especially when the transaction-item ratio is extremely large, because the width of our deep net mainly depends on the item number and the depth increases with the transaction number logarithmically. The compact size of our deep net significantly accelerates itemset support query by reducing computational complexity, compared to any other query method that requires transaction-level traversal.

Our database memorization task has three major differences compared to brute-force dataset memorization: (i) the target transactional database is not used as training data directly, (ii) the learning task is semi-supervised because only partial itemset support information in the complete power set of items is used to learn the structural representation of a transactional database, (iii) our deep net does not memorize by simply cramming transactional data, whereas stored information of the database is learned and constructed internally in the parameter space.

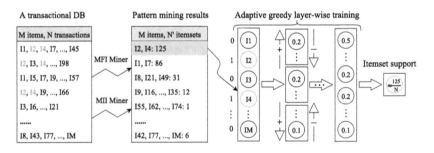

Fig. 1. System architecture of the training process

1.2   Related Work

Related researches have been focusing on information retrieval in databases via deep autoencoders. This task derives the common benefits from dimensionality reduction by deep autoencoders, but also derives the additional benefit that retrieval can become extremely efficient in certain kinds of low dimensional spaces. Semantic hashing [4] is proposed to learn a deep graphical model of the word-count vectors obtained from a large set of documents, in order to extend the efficiency of hash-coding to approximate matching query by mapping documents to memory addresses in such a way that semantically similar documents are located at nearby addresses. The idea of training a hashing representation has been further explored in several directions, including learning similarity preserving hash functions that map high dimensional data onto binary codes [5]. Although deep learning techniques have been applied to various kinds of information retrieval tasks, the main focus in related research is still generalizing from data rather than memorizing information precisely by representation construction.

Ideas for approximation of itemset frequency queries have also been proposed before. A special data structure called Free-Sets [6] is presented for compressing frequent itemsets defined by a certain threshold, whereas not entire information of the database is represented and condensed.

2   Training Data Generation

For being used as a training dataset for a deep neural network, a transactional database typically has far less transactions than the exponential size of the power set of its items, for example, the commonly used dense dataset *Mushroom* has 119 items and only 8124 ($\ll 2^{119}$) transactions. Even if the transaction number is large enough to serve as training data, every transaction's constant support of 1 still causes a deep net to yield prediction values that are narrowed in an extremely small range. Therefore, pattern mining algorithms are applied to original database to generate valid training data. Moreover, the itemset empirical distribution can be derived from the deterministic data generation scheme and database statistics to fine-tune the training optimization.

2.1   Pattern Mining in Transactional Databases

Pattern mining is a traditional research area in the field of data mining. In general, pattern mining tasks in transactional databases focus on finding out most representative itemsets, including but not limited to frequent itemsets, infrequent itemsets, maximal frequent itemsets (MFI) and minimal infrequent itemsets (MII). Given a transactional dataset $\mathcal{T} = \{t_1, t_2, ..., t_n\}$ where each transaction t_q ($q \in [1, n]$) consists of items in $\mathcal{I} = \{i_1, i_2, ..., i_m\}$, the terms *itemset* and *support* refer to a set of items $I \subseteq \mathcal{I}$ and the frequency of an itemset defined as $Supp^{\mathcal{T}}(I) = |\{t_q \in \mathcal{T} : I \subseteq t_q\}|$, respectively. In addition, we say an itemset I with a threshold τ is:

- *τ-frequent* if $Supp^{\mathcal{T}}(I) \geq \tau$ holds;
- *τ-infrequent* if $Supp^{\mathcal{T}}(I) < \tau$ holds;
- *maximal τ-frequent* if it is τ-frequent and all of its proper supersets are τ-infrequent; and
- *minimal τ-infrequent* if it is τ-infrequent and all of its proper subsets are τ-frequent.

For generating training data, the fact that it is impractical to exhaustively enumerate all itemsets in the item power set naturally leads to the idea that we selectively mine most representative itemsets to construct a training dataset of a reasonable size. Based on the instinctive thought that MFIs and MIIs contain more information and less redundancy about the original database than randomly sampled itemsets, we apply two mining algorithms, MAFIA [7] and MIWI-Miner [8], to generate pattern itemsets[1] for training dataset construction. For constantly growing databases and streaming data, which are common in practice, incremental itemset mining algorithms [9,10] can be used instead, so that after slightly fine-tuning with newly generated training data, our model is updated for following support queries.

Specifically, we run two algorithms for a transactional database under a range of support thresholds $[\tau_{\min}, \tau_{\max}]$ and aggregate all MFIs and MIIs together. In the combination procedure, we first uniquify the mining results because of duplicate itemsets, i.e., an itemset I can be maximal/minimal τ_k-frequent/infrequent for different k at the same time, and then we normalize the itemset support distribution by filling the dataset with non-maximal frequent and non-minimal infrequent itemsets of minority supports to approximate a uniform output in training data. The amounts of pattern itemsets under different thresholds and unnormalized itemset support distribution are shown in Fig. 2.

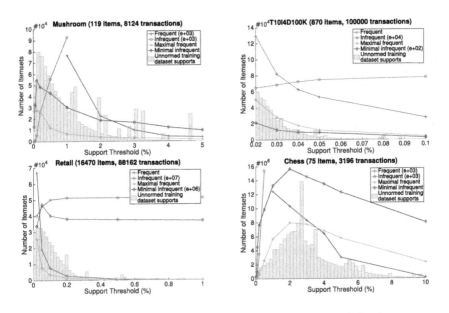

Fig. 2. Training data generation on 4 example transactional databases

---

[1] Zero-support (1-infrequent) itemsets are truncated due to excessive cardinality.

2.2   Itemset Empirical Distribution

In our database memorization task scenario, the performance measure P is intractable for its combinatorial property. We therefore optimize P indirectly by reducing a query cost function $J(\boldsymbol{\theta})$ in the hope that doing so is sufficient to guide the learning process of a deep net to construct an approximate representation inside. Typically, the cost function can be written as

$$J(\boldsymbol{\theta}) = \mathbb{E}_{(\boldsymbol{x},y)\sim p_{\text{data}}} L(f(\boldsymbol{x};\boldsymbol{\theta}), y), \tag{1}$$

where L is the mean square error function, $f(\boldsymbol{x},\boldsymbol{\theta})$ is the predicted itemset support when the input is $\boldsymbol{x}$, and p_{data} is the itemset distribution. In most machine learning problems, we do not know much about $p_{\text{data}}(\boldsymbol{x}, y)$ but only have a training set of samples. In order to minimize the empirical risk, we generally replace the true distribution p_{data} with the empirical distribution $\hat{p}_{\text{data}}$ by averaging on the training set

$$J(\boldsymbol{\theta}) = \mathbb{E}_{\boldsymbol{x},y\sim \hat{p}_{\text{data}}}[L(f(\boldsymbol{x};\boldsymbol{\theta}), y)] = \frac{1}{m}\sum_{i=1}^{m} L(f(\boldsymbol{x}^{(i)};\boldsymbol{\theta}), y^{(i)}). \tag{2}$$

Nevertheless, in practice we can achieve a more authentic itemset empirical distribution by postulating a data generation model and deducing from statistical features of the original database. Synthetic transactional datasets have been widely used for evaluating the performance of pattern mining algorithms over a wide range of data characteristics. The Quest dataset generation scheme [14] successfully mimics the transactions in the retailing environment by picking transaction size from a Poisson distribution and then assigning a series of potentially large itemsets to the transaction. According to a theoretical analysis toward Quest scheme [15], for each item $i \in \mathcal{I}$, the random variable for the number of transactions in $\mathcal{T}$ containing i complies with binomial distribution, so the itemset possibility in training data is

$$p(\boldsymbol{x}) = 1 - \prod_{\tau_{\min}\leq\tau\leq\tau_{\max}} [(1 - p(\hat{f}(\boldsymbol{x}) \geq \tau \mid \boldsymbol{\theta}))(1 - p(\hat{f}(\boldsymbol{x}) < \tau \mid \boldsymbol{\theta}))], \tag{3}$$

and by Bayes' rule, the itemset-support probability function can be derived as

$$p(\boldsymbol{x}, y) = p(y \mid \boldsymbol{x})p(\boldsymbol{x}) = \sum_{d=0}^{y}(\frac{1}{n})^d(1 - \frac{1}{n})^{y-d} \sum_{i_1,\dots,i_d} \prod_{j=0}^{d} \frac{1}{2^{x_j+1} - 1}. \tag{4}$$

Under such a data generation model, we can determine the itemset empirical distribution for adjusting the weight of training samples. In order to estimate the parameters of the generation model, we adopt maximum likelihood estimation method fitting the given transactional dataset

$$\boldsymbol{\theta}_{\text{ML}} = \arg\max_{\boldsymbol{\theta}} \mathbb{E}_{\boldsymbol{x}\sim \hat{p}_{\text{data}}} \log p_{\text{model}}(\boldsymbol{x}; \boldsymbol{\theta}). \tag{5}$$

3   Network Architecture and Training Algorithm

As shown in Fig. 1, our deep neural network for memorizing transactions must have an input layer of an identical width, i.e., the number of activation units, with the number of items in the database. Any itemsets can be represented by a binary vector in such a way for our training process. The output unit of our deep net is a single real value, representing the itemset support normalized into $[0, 1]$ by dividing by the number of transactions. Therefore, the input and output of our deep net have a similar form of an ordinary regression task.

Although different network architectures may have similar memory capacity, past research has shown that dynamic structuring neural network can provide stable and adaptive control of nonlinear systems [11]. In our case, the architecture directly affects the learnt representation and the limitation of compression ratio as well. To this end, a deep learning technique called adaptive greedy layer-wise training is proposed to help us determine the optimal depth and width for each hidden layer. This method is adaptive because the optimal depth and width are not decided before training but dynamically updated during training by a greedy layer-wise approach, which is fully presented in Algorithm 1.

Algorithm 1. Adaptive greedy layer-wise training

Input: α = adjustment factor, M = maximum iterations, TOL = loss tolerance

1 Initialize the deep net with only input layer and output unit
2 **while** *validation error decrease* $-\Delta J(\theta) > TOL$ **do**
3   Initialize hidden layer L of same width as input layer
4   Insert L into the network as the last layer
5   Train 1 epoch
6   **while** *iteration* $< M$ **do**
7   Initialize hidden layer L_+ with $(1 + \alpha)$ width of L by copy-and-fill
8   Initialize hidden layer L_- with $(1 - \alpha)$ width of L by random dropout
9   Replace L with L_+ and L_- respectively
10   Train $1/M$ epochs separately
11   **if** $-\Delta J_+(\theta) < TOL$ and $-\Delta J_-(\theta) < TOL$ **then**
12   **break**
13   **end**
14   **if** $-\Delta J_+(\theta) > -\Delta J_-(\theta)$ **then**
15             $L \leftarrow L_+$
16   **else**
17             $L \leftarrow L_-$
18   **end**
19   **end**
20 **end**

As for the network depth, our adaptive method continuously adds single hidden layer between the current last hidden layer and the output unit, until evaluation result on validation set stops improving significantly. This process resembles greedy layer-wise training except that we do not have prior knowledge about the optimal depth at all. For each hidden layer, the width is determined by a greedy search. The linear adjustment factor α in Algorithm 1 allows for expanding or shrinking the searching space, obtaining a trade-off balance between computational cost and searching granularity. Note that when hidden layer L_+ is initialized, the related weights are first copied from layer L and then residual connections are created; when hidden layer L_- is initialized, all weights without random dropout are simply kept, so that the computational cost for subsequent training is minimized.

Figure 3 reveals how the network architecture is dynamically constructed and affected by the statistical features of a series of synthetic transactional database. It is implied that our adaptive method enables the deep neural network to structure an optimal architecture by adjusting depth and width dynamically, and the generally believed logarithmic relation between network depth and number of training samples is testified, as well as the influence of number of items on the memorization task.

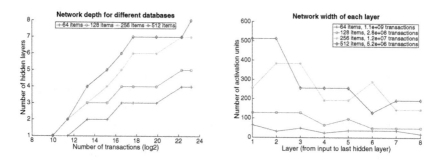

Fig. 3. Dynamically constructed network architecture

The internal relevance between the network architecture and learnt database representation is further analyzed. Inspired by other efforts for improving deep neural network interpretability by contingent means [12, 13], we reasonably speculate that the internal structure of representation is organized in such a manner that activation units are gradually polarized along with depth increase in regard to different clusters of itemsets.

In order to quantify the neuron differentiation, we select the first, middle and last hidden layers of a series of trained deep nets and run k-means clustering for pattern itemsets with cluster numbers equal to the width of selected layers k_1, k_2, k_3. The Euclidean distance of binary itemset vectors is adopted for clustering process. Next, we calculate the average output unit response for each pair of itemset cluster and activation unit, with result shown in Fig. 4. The pattern clearness is enhanced as depth increases and activation unit specialization corresponding to pattern itemset clusters grows prominently as width decreases. In the last layer, it can be clearly observed that for each row that stands for an activation unit, there usually exists one and only one highlighted response column that stands for a itemset cluster, which implies that a structural database representation is learnt through our adaptive training.

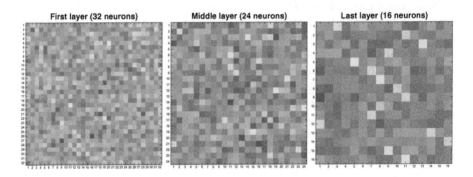

Fig. 4. Neuron activation patterns at different depth and width

4   Experiments

We conduct our training process and itemset support query tests on both synthetic datasets and real-world datasets. Synthetic datasets T10I4D100K.dat and T40I10D100K.dat are sparse, generated by IBM Quest Generator [17] and constructed according to the properties of typical weakly correlated data. Real-world datasets we used in our experiments include mushroom.dat, a dense and highly correlated dataset which describes mushrooms characteristics and kasumi.dat, a recently collected supermarket basket data from Data Jackets [16].

Training data is generated from these datasets as described in Sect. 2. As for validation and test dataset, we sample random itemsets by picking itemset size from Binomial distribution, filling in items with uniform probability and pre-calculate the true support in the database. The evaluation criterion in our experiments is the mean value of support absolute error on test set. For each dataset, we test all combinations of pattern itemsets or randomly sampled itemsets as training data and dynamically constructed or stationary network architecture. For fair comparisons, we impose approximately equal number of parameters on different network architectures. The stationary network architecture has same width with item number for each hidden layer, and the depth is decided under the parameter number restriction.

The experimental results on different datasets are shown in Fig. 5. The advantages of our pattern mining based training data generation and adaptive training algorithm for dynamic architecture construction are illustrated with faster convergence and lower support error on all datasets. Specifically, the data generation scheme seems to have more significant influence on the query precision than network architecture. In the best case, our method reaches a mean itemset support query error less than 0.001, which can be quite satisfying for approximation queries. As for database compression, when the transaction number is large enough, the compression ratio approaches 100:1 (assuming the database is stored using binary vectors), because the compression is essentially a special kind of transformation where only itemset support query is allowed, whereas reconstructing original database can be extremely rough and time consuming.

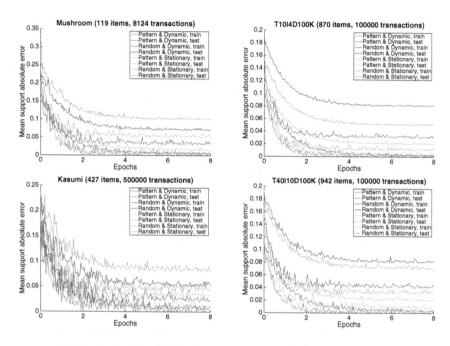

Fig. 5. Training loss and query test precision on 4 datasets

5   Conclusion and Future Work

In this work we presented a novel learning, memorizing transactional databases by constructing structural representation in deep neural networks, and an effective method, utilizing pattern mining and an adaptive greedy layer-wise training algorithm for dynamically building network architecture. With solid experimental results and analysis, we conclude that deep neural networks are capable of precisely memorizing and compressing information other than generalizing knowledge from information. Our method can be applied for approximate itemset support queries, with relatively high precision but low cost in both aspects of time and space complexity, and the compressive memorization is especially efficient in practice for offline processing and reducing concurrency control in database access.

Our activation pattern analysis for deep nets is helpful for interpreting the constructed representation yet insufficient for fully understanding the principles.

While similar techniques have been employed for other deep nets, more general methods for universal interpretation of deep learning models for various tasks should be considered in future study.

Acknowledgments. This work was supported by JST CREST Grant Number JPMJCR1304, JSPS KAKENHI Grant Numbers JP16H01836, and JP16K12428.

References

1. Goodfellow, I., Bengio, Y., Courville, A.: Deep Learning. MIT Press, Cambridge (2016)
2. Zhang, C., Bengio, S., Hardt, M., Recht, B., Vinyals, O.: Understanding deep learning requires rethinking generalization. In: 5th International Conference on Learning Representations, ICLR, Toulon, France (2017)
3. Krueger, D., Ballas, N., Jastrzebski, S., Arpit1, D., Kanwal, M.S., Maharaj, T., Bengio, E., Fischer, A., Courville, A.: Deep nets don't learn via memorization. In: Workshop track of the 5th International Conference on Learning Representations, ICLR, Toulon, France (2017)
4. Salakhutdinov, R., Hinton, G.: Semantic hashing. Int. J. Approximate Reasoning **50**(7), 969–978 (2009)
5. Norouzi, M., Fleet, D.: Minimal loss hashing for compact binary codes. In: 28th International Conference in Machine Learning, ICML, Washington (2011)
6. Boulicaut, J.F., Bykowski, A., Rigotti, C.: Approximation of frequency queris by means of free-sets. In: Proceedings of the 4th European Conference on Principles of Data Mining and Knowledge Discovery, Freiburg, Germany, pp. 75–85 (2000)
7. Burdick, D., Calimlim, M., Gehrke, J.: MAFIA: A maximal frequent itemset algorithm for transactional databases. In: Proceedings of the 17th International Conference on Data Engineering, pp. 443–452. IEEE Press, Washington (2001)
8. Cagliero, L., Garza, P.: Infrequent weighted itemset mining using frequent pattern growth. IEEE Trans. Knowl. Data Eng. **26**(4), 903–915 (2014)
9. Mundra, A., Singh, A., Tomar, P.: Incremental frequent pattern mining: a recent review. Int. J. Eng. Res. Technol. **1**(8) (2012)
10. Dong, W., Jiang, H., Chen, L., Liu, G.: Incremental updating algorithm for infrequent itemsets on weighted condition. In: International Conference on Computer Design and Applications, ICCDA, Qinhuangdao, China (2010)
11. Lei, J.: Dynamic structure neural network for stable adaptive control of non-linear systems. IEEE Trans. Neural Networks **7**(5), 1151–1167 (1996)
12. Dong, Y., Su, H., Zhu, J., Zhang, B.: Improving Interpretability of Deep Neural Networks with Semantic Information. CoRR, http://arxiv.org/abs/1703.04096 (2017)
13. Tan, S., Sim, K., Gales, M.: Improving the interpretability of deep neural networks with stimulated learning. In: IEEE Workshop on Automatic Speech Recognition and Understanding, Scottsdale, USA (2015)
14. Agrawal, R., Srikant, R.: Fast algorithms for mining association rules in large databases. In: Proceedings of the 20th International Conference on Very Large Data Bases, VLDB, pp. 487–499. Morgan Kaufmann, San Francisco (1994)

15. Cooper, C., Zito, M.: Realistic synthetic data for testing association rule mining algorithms for market basket databases. In: Kok, J.N., Koronacki, J., Lopez de Mantaras, R., Matwin, S., Mladenič, D., Skowron, A. (eds.) PKDD 2007. LNCS, vol. 4702, pp. 398–405. Springer, Heidelberg (2007). doi:10.1007/978-3-540-74976-9_39

16. Ohsawa, Y., Kido, H., Hayashi, T., Liu, C.: Data jackets for synthesizing values in the market of data. Procedia Comput. Sci. 22(1), 709–716 (2013)

17. IBM: Quest Synthetic Data Generator (2009). http://www.almaden.ibm.com

Offensive Sentence Classification Using Character-Level CNN and Transfer Learning with Fake Sentences

Suin Seo and Sung-Bea Cho[✉]

Department of Computer Science, Yonsei University,
50 Yonsei-ro, Seodaemun-gu, Seoul, Republic of Korea
{tndls9304,sbcho}@yonsei.ac.kr
http://sclab.yonsei.ac.kr

Abstract. There are two difficulties in classifying offensive sentences: One is the modifiability of offensive terms, and the other is the class imbalance which appears in general offensive corpus. Solving these problems, we propose a method of pre-training fake sentences generated as character-level to convolution layers preventing under-fitting from data shortage, and dealing with the data imbalance. We insert the offensive words to half of the randomly generated sentences, and train the convolution neural networks (CNN) with theses sentences and the labels of whether offensive word is included. We use the trained filter of CNN for training new CNN given original data, resulting in the increase of the amount of training data. We get higher F1-score with the proposed method than that without pre-training in three dataset of insult from kaggle, Bullying trace, and formspring.

Keywords: Text classification · Convolution neural networks · Character-level model · Transfer learning

1 Introduction

Offensive sentence classification is the problem like spam filtering which can resolve with traditional text processing algorithm. In few recent years, Social Network Service (SNS) has extended a lot, and the number of replies, tweets, and comments on the internet also increased at the same time; and these contain many profanities, insulting words, and hate speeches. Besides, many people on the web have been modifying their words to non-general forms when they want to write offensive words on the internet to avoid simple filter of profanities. These obfuscated offensive words use special characters, digits, and non-English characters are called *"profanitype"* or *"symbol swearing."* As the form of offensive words become diverse for this way, traditional text processing algorithms are inappropriate to catch the features of these words in nowadays.

Because there is no way for the classifier to automatically detect whether the input text is offensive or not in training process; many researchers have chosen

© Springer International Publishing AG 2017
D. Liu et al. (Eds.): ICONIP 2017, Part II, LNCS 10635, pp. 532–539, 2017.
https://doi.org/10.1007/978-3-319-70096-0_55

supervised learning approach giving the sentence with the label which indicates offensiveness of the expression together. There are many different offensive sentences on the web, though, to apply supervised learning of each sentence are required, and the more sentences, the more expensive the cost is, so the resources for learning is limited in quantity. Besides, the rate of offensive sentences in the whole corpus is relatively lower than that of non-offensive ones. This characteristic causes data imbalance and results in the inappropriate update of the classifier.

We use the character-level model to deal with modified words and use transfer learning to reduce the effects of data imbalance. The method is similar to the oversampling method in the view of making over-sampled data but is different to oversampling, using trained layer, not data themselves (Table 1).

Table 1. Previous studies on detecting offensive words

Authors	Feature extraction	Classification	Dataset
Chen, et al.	n-gram of BoW	SVM, NB	Youtube
Sood, et al.	n-gram of BoW	SVM	News comments
Xiang, et al.	lexicon features	DT, SVM, LR, RF	Twitter
Djuric, et al.	paragraph2vec	Unsupervised	Yahoo finance
Zhao, et al.	embedding w/BoW	SVM	Bullying traces
Nabata, et al.	embedding w/features	Regression	Yahoo finance

2   Related Works

Previous studies about the classification of offensive sentences used conventional machine learning methods. The simplest way is extracting features from sentences with Bag-of-Word (BoW) (n-gram of BoW), and classifying with Support Vector Machine (SVM) [1,2]. However, as described previously, the difficulty of the task becomes higher; the conventional approach does not work like as before.

Recently, many text processing approaches are being tried to overcome the weaknesses of standard machine learning algorithms, especially in the large and noisy dataset like SNS [3]. Djuric, et al. used word embedding to extract offensive features from the many text data; though the processing speed got faster due to the reduction of the feature vector size, the difference of AUC score with BoW was just 1.18% [4]. After this result, the approaches of recent research have changed to applying additional information. Semantic, linguistic, and other bullying features are used for classifying offensive sentences including hate speeches [5,6].

As described in above, the data-driven approach does not work well in offensive sentence classification. We thought that the reason is for data imbalance. Therefore we tried to decrease the effect of data imbalance, and one approach is transfer learning whose training data is free for imbalance.

3   Offensive Sentence Classification

3.1   Character-Level Convolution Neural Networks

We propose Convolution Neural Networks (CNN) with character-level [7] as a classifier for classifying offensive sentences. Though character-level CNN is already known as a useful method for text classification, this model is helpful to get the robustness in the noisy environment such as SNS including modified offensive sentences. Since the CNN model makes the noise of given texts during convolution and pooling process; CNN adapts to words having changed characters.

The details concerning the equations of character-level CNN are found in [7], but as an important part of our approach, transfer learning of CNN, we introduce a few equations about the processes updating the weight of each CNN filter.

When feature vector x_i and output of the l-1 th convolution layer y^{l-1} are given, the weight of $m \times m$ sized filter w from the lth layer is applied as follows.

$$c_{xy}^l = \sum_{a=0}^{m-1} \sum_{b=0}^{m-1} w_{ab} \, y_{(x+a)(y+b)}^{l-1} \tag{1}$$

The output of convolution layer c^{l-1} passes max-pooling operation, in $k \times k$ sized field, given pooling stride T, $N \times N$ sized output vector p_{xy}^l is calculated as follows.

$$p_{xy}^l = \max c_{xy \times T}^{l-1} \tag{2}$$

During this process, the noise of feature vector is generated and applied in weight of CNN filters. Passing several convolution and max-pooling layers, and finally at the fully-connected layer, CNN model predicts the attributes of the feature vector.

3.2   Generating Fake Sentences

First, we make fake sentences with randomly selected characters. As the input to classifier is character-level, the fake sentences used for transfer learning also generate in character-level. These random sequences of characters reflect the characteristics of typical sentences.

Using a random generator $R_{sentence}$, fake sentence S is chosen to be

$$R_{sentence}(x) = S \in C^n \quad \text{where} \quad S = (c_1, c_2, ..., c_n), \quad c_i \in C \tag{3}$$

Where the Eq. (3), x denotes the seed of random generator, n the length of sentence, and C set of overall characters (Fig. 1).

Then, we make the sentences which have characteristics of offensive words. These sentences are the sequences of characters with inserted offensive words. The offensive words come from the offensive wordlist which the web service

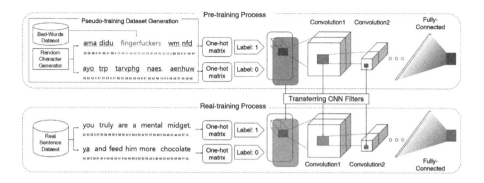

Fig. 1. Training process of proposed method using transfer learning

providers such as google, twitter, and facebook want to block. We extract the offensive words W_{bad}, whose length is k from the list.

$$R_{bad-word}(x) = W_{bad} = (w_1, w_2, ..., w_k) \quad and \quad w_i \in W \tag{4}$$

We insert an extracted word from Eq. (4) to sentence S generated by Eq. (3) at the index chosen by random generator R_{index} in Eq. (5), and then this process makes the sentence offensive.

$$c_{i+k} = w_k \ for \ k = 1, 2, ..., |W_{bad}|, \quad i = R_{index}(x) \in \{1, ..., n\}$$
$$S' = (c_1, c_2, ..., w_1, w_2, ..., w_k, c_{i+k+1}, ..., c_n) \tag{5}$$

We label the sentence S' as the offensive sentence and the sentence S as the non-offensive sentence. The number of each marked sentence is controllable, solving data imbalance. These fake sentences are used for transfer learning.

3.3 Transfer Learning Process

Transfer learning is the method using the weights from the pre-training. In pre-training process, the classifier learns the features of offensive words from the pseudo-training dataset which is generated by above section. Normal sentences are generated from Eq. (3), and offensive sentences from Eq. (5). If the sentence contains a word from the bad-words dataset, we label the sentence as 1, if not, we label 0. Then, we train the pair of sentence and label to character-level CNN model by supervised approach. By doing so, the filters of CNN learn to the way of classifying normal one and offensive one.

After pre-training, filters of the trained CNN have the characteristics of classifying the offensive sentences with normal sentences. Therefore CNN model which using the transferred filters starts the training with some pre-knowledge with the task, whereas CNN with no transfer learning starts the training at the initial state. This difference makes the different point of convergence, and the model with transfer learning gets the higher score.

Table 2. Imbalance of each dataset used in experiment

Dataset	# of total sentences	# of offensive sentences	Ratio of offensive words
insults [8]		2818	31.92%
	8815		
bullyingV3 [9]		1226	25.86%
	4742		
formspring [10]	25825	2360	
			9.14%

4   Experiments

4.1   Dataset

We have used three datasets, Kaggle's "Detecting insults in Data Commentary" (insults) [8], "Bullying trace data set" (bullyingV3) [9], and formspring dataset [10]. Table 2 shows the statistics of each dataset. All datasets have data imbalance, and consist of the relatively small amount of sentences compared to the number of texts used in general text processing tasks.

Table 3. Sample sentences expressing the nature of each dataset.

Dataset	Label	Sample sentence
insults	1	Eat shit and die Andrew
		um holy fuck i need a cigarette
	0	That guy is a real fuckstick.
		needs to give me a fucking like hows everyone doin?
bullyingV3	1	D: I'm not a bully.
		your just bullying me, you love me so..
	0	Fuck me Flights are expensive these days
		lol. I'll bully u!
formspring	1	ilOVEU fAtASS ! <3
		w@n+ y0 b!q d!(k $uRf@(!n m@ l!pSz
	0	iguess yew dnt fucks wit mhe anymo
		w@N+ yUh +0 $M@(K m3 m@k3 dH@ SEx w!Ld n h0+

Table 3 shows the example sentences of each dataset. The insults dataset tends to label as semantic insulting, and has several mislabeled sentences, the noise of data. The bullyingV3 dataset includes the smallest number of sentences among three datasets. Since the number of data is small, it is hard to learn the features of offensive texts, which we want to classify. The formspring dataset has

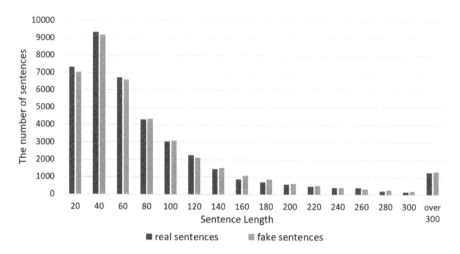

Fig. 2. Length distribution of real sentences and generated fake sentences.

very high data imbalance. Also, there are many words modified by omitting the character, capitalizing the character, and replacing to symbols.

4.2 Deciding the Parameters

Using the method in described in Sect. 3.2, we generate the fake sentences for transfer learning. We configure one sentence as 300 characters; about 95% of sentences in all datasets are matched in this condition.

We have found that the distribution of sentence length follows F distribution approximately. Figure 2 shows that the distribution of the length of original sentences in the corpus and of the lengths of fake sentences chosen by the probability of F distribution is similar.

We use *google-bad-words* for the word-list used in Eq. (4). The word-list includes 550 words banned in the web from google.

The character set has 69 characters including 26 English alphabet, ten digits, and 33 special characters. Below is the set of characters used for creating fake sentences in ascending order of ASCII.

$$\text{.!"}\#\$\%\&\text{'()}*+,\text{-.}/0123456789\text{:;}<=>?$$
$$@[]\char`\^\_\text{`abcdefghijklmnopqrstuvwxyz}\{|\}\sim$$

If the fake sentence is generated with the same probability for all characters, the sentence is far different from the original sentence. In most sentences, however, the frequency of occurrence of each character is similar. Therefore, we generate the sentence depending on the probability of the occurrence of each character. The generated sentence is similar to the actual sentence at the signal level.

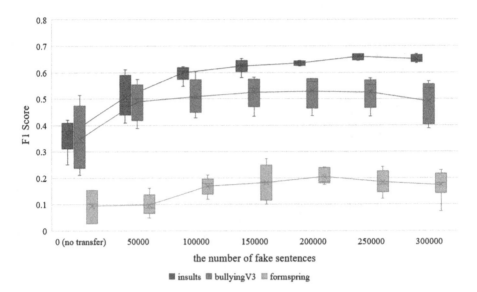

Fig. 3. Variation of the F1 score on the number of sentences for each dataset.

We generate the fake sentences with the methods and the parameters described above, divide into training and validation sets with the ratio of 7:3. Then, we train CNN filters with these sentences.

4.3   Results

We have applied the original training sentences and the test sentences divided into 6:4 respectively, and compared one CNN whose filter is learning the fake data in the previous section with another CNN whose filter is a default.

Since the imbalance of dataset is high, the accuracy is not appropriate to evaluate the model. Therefore, we calculate the F1 score used as test measures of binary classification. The score indicates how well the model works.

As shown in Fig. 3, the F1 score is higher than when transfer learning applied than the case which transfer learning does not apply to all datasets. This result means transfer learning with fake sentences helps the classifier to get higher performance. However, the number of the fake sentences is not a significant variable which affects the performance of the classifier. The filter of CNN changes similarly regardless of the number of fake sentences.

Though we evaluate our method with F1 score, there is no comparative research. For bullyingV3 dataset, [5] got 0.78 of F1 score. For the other datasets, unfortunately, there is no comparable result.

5   Conclusion

Original character-level CNN does not show good performance in offensive classification because the dataset is not enough to train the features. For solving the problem, we propose a method of pre-training with generated fake sentences. In this paper, we apply the method to only offensive classification with the bad words list, but, the method is applicable regardless of the words in the dictionary, and it means the method is also used for any kinds of syntactic searching.

We know the transfer learning helps the model to learn the features though, exact mechanism and principle of the method are veiled. Future work will be the investigation of how the method works and how it differs from without transfer learning.

Acknowledgments. This work was supported by Institute for Information & Communications Technology Promotion (IITP) grant funded by the Korea government (MSIP) (R0124-16-0002), Emotional Intelligence Technology to Infer Human Emotion and Carry on Dialogue Accordingly.

References

1. Chen, Y., Zhou, Y., Zhu, S., Xu, H.: Detecting offensive language in social media to protect adolescent online safety. In: International Conference on Social Computing Privacy, Security, Risk and Trust (PASSAT), pp. 71–80. IEEE (2012)
2. Sood, S.O., Churchill, E.F., Antin, J.: Automatic identification of personal insults on social news sites. J. Assoc. Inf. Sci. Tech. **63**, 270–285 (2012)
3. Xiang, G., Fan, B., Wang, L., Hong, J., Rose, C.: Detecting offensive tweets via topical feature discovery over a large scale twitter corpus. In: 21st International Conference on Information and Knowledge Management, pp. 1980–1984. ACM (2012)
4. Djuric, N., Zhou, J., Morris, R., Grbovic, M.: Hate speech detection with comment embeddings. In: 24th International Conference on WWW, pp. 29–30. ACM (2015)
5. Zhao, R., Zhou, A., Mao, K.: Automatic detection of cyberbullying on social networks based on bullying features. In: 17th International Conference on Distributed Computing and Networking, p. 43. ACM (2016)
6. Nabata, C., Tetreault, J., Thomas, A., Mehdad, Y., Chang, Y.: Abusive language detection in online user content. In: 25th International Conference on WWW, pp. 145–153 (2016)
7. Zhang, X., Zhao, J., LeCun, Y.: Character-level convolutional networks for text classification. In: Advances in Neural Information Processing Systems, pp. 649–657 (2015)
8. Detecting Insults in Data Commentary, Kaggle. https://www.kaggle.com/c/detecting-insults-in-social-commentary
9. Xu, J.-M., Jun, K.-S., Zhu, X., Bellmore, A.: Learning from bullying traces in social media. In: Proceedings of Conference of NAACL-HLT, pp. 656–666. ACL (2012)
10. Formspring Labeled for Cyberbullying. http://www.chatcoder.com/Data Download

Hierarchical Hybrid Attention Networks for Chinese Conversation Topic Classification

Yujun Zhou[1,2,3], Changliang Li[1(✉)], Bo Xu[1], Jiaming Xu[1], Jie Cao[1,2,3],
and Bo Xu[1]

[1] Institute of Automation, Chinese Academy of Sciences,
Beijing, People's Republic of China
{zhouyujun2014,changliang.li,boxu,jiaming.xu,caojie2014,xubo}@ia.ac.cn
[2] University of Chinese Academy of Sciences, Beijing, People's Republic of China
[3] Jiangsu Jinling Science and Technology Group Co., Ltd., Nanjing, People's
Republic of China

Abstract. Topic classification is useful for applications such as forensics analysis and cyber-crime investigation. To improve the overall performance on the task of Chinese conversation topic classification, we propose a hierarchical neural network with automatic semantic features selection, which is a hierarchical architecture that depicts the structure of conversations. The model firstly incorporates speaker information into the character- and word-level attentions and generates sentence representation, then uses attention-based BLSTM to construct the conversation representation. Experimental results on three datasets demonstrate that our model achieves better performance than multiple baselines. It indicates that the proposed architecture can capture the informative and salient features related to the meaning of a conversation for topic classification. And we release the dataset of this paper that can be obtained from https://github.com/njoe9/H-HANs.

Keywords: Hierarchical attention networks · Chinese conversation · Topic classification · Recurrent neural networks

1 Introduction

Conversational texts have a variety of sources, such as Instant Message (IM, e.g. WhatsApp and WeChat), Social Networking Site (SNS, e.g. Facebook and Weibo) and speech to text, which play an important role in many applications. For example, instant messaging communications were utilized in forensics analysis [1], and chat conversations from SNS can be used for cyber-crime investigation [2]. In a typical application, the user firstly need to get a set of utterances about some particular topics that he/she has interests in, e.g. sports and entertainment. Keyword retrieval is usually employed as the first method. However, it cannot achieve satisfactory results due to low precision and recall. The topic of a conversation containing the keyword "sports" may not belong to the sports, e.g. the sports park means a place. Hence, topic classification is introduced to make

© Springer International Publishing AG 2017
D. Liu et al. (Eds.): ICONIP 2017, Part II, LNCS 10635, pp. 540–550, 2017.
https://doi.org/10.1007/978-3-319-70096-0_56

more sophisticated decisions to improve performance, which is a multi-class text classification problem. Given a set of predefined topics, each conversation must be categorized into one of them. In some occasions, a conversation may be classified into more than one class, these are multiple topic classification systems. In this work, we assume that each conversation only can be categorized into one class.

A conversation is usually a sequence of many utterances, which is composed of two utterances at least. Without considering the speakers, a conversation is similar to a document that is a sequence of many sentences. There are many document classification methods, including traditional methods (e.g. SVM classifier with Bag-Of-Words [3]) and deep learning methods (e.g. Recurrent Convolutional Neural Networks [4]). Meanwhile, short text classification is also being well studied [5]. These above classification approaches can be immediately applied to categorize conversations into topics. Nevertheless, they may not achieve the desired performance. Furthermore, according to our review, there are few researches in the literatures to classify the topics of Chinese conversation. These motivate our work to explore an appropriate method for Chinese conversation topic classification.

Table 1. A typical example of the Chinese conversation corpus. $\{A_{s_1}, A_{s_2}\}$ and $\{B_{s_1}, B_{s_2}\}$ are the utterances of speakers A and B respectively.

Utterance	Conversation Content
A_{s_1}	下午好，先生。要一杯茶吗？ Good afternoon, sir. Would you like a tea?
B_{s_1}	我想喝一杯咖啡。 I'd rather have a cup of coffee.
A_{s_2}	没问题，先生。你要在咖啡里加糖和牛奶吗？ Of course, sir. Would you like milk and sugar with that?
B_{s_2}	好的，来点牛奶和两块糖。 Yes, please. Milk and two sugars.

In this paper, we propose a neural model, named Hierarchical Hybrid Attention Networks (H-HANs), which combines attention-based Recurrent Neural Networks (RNN) with word and character embeddings to classify Chinese conversation. Firstly, we build a hierarchical attention-based neural model to generate sentence-level and conversation-level representations jointly. The model makes the classification decision through two levels, i.e. sentence and conversation levels. Sentence-level representation captures the salient words and characters in each utterance, which can determine the meaning of the utterance. Conversation-level representation selects the informative sentences of the conversation by the salient words and characters. Secondly, we explore the value of the speaker based attention. The model incorporates each speaker into the sentence representation. Furthermore, to address the problem of lack of Chinese conversation corpus, we introduce a dataset of Chinese conversation based on the real-world topic instances, which will be released to public. Table 1 shows an example of the Chinese conversation corpus. Experimental results show that our model outperforms baseline methods for Chinese conversation topic classification.

The main contributions of this work are as follows: (1) we propose an effective neural topic classification model for Chinese conversation by taking the combination of word- and character-level attentive features into consideration. (2) we explore the influence of speakers information for Chinese conversation representation. (3) we construct and release a dataset for Chinese conversation with specific topics.

The remainder of this paper is organized as follows: Sect. 2 briefly introduces the works related to this study. Section 3 describes the H-HANs model in detail. Experimental results and discussion are reported in Sect. 4. Section 5 concludes this paper.

2   Related Work

Our work aims to classify Chinese conversation within the given classes (topics). This work is related to topic identification techniques, such as Latent Dirichlet Analysis (LDA), Latent Semantic Analysis (LSA) and Latent Semantic Indexing (LSI), which apply unsupervised learning (clustering) approaches to infer possible topic classes. In contrast, our work uses supervised learning (classification) method to assign a predefined class to a conversation. The followings are more closely related to ours.

There are some works about social media topic classification. Kinsella et al. [6] used the Multinomial Naive Bayesian with the metadata retrieved from external hyperlinks in user-generated posts to improve topic classification of social media. Fei and Liu [7] put forward a center-based similarity space (CBS-L) method to get relevant posts accurately about a topic from social media, which transformed document representation from the traditional n-gram feature space to a center-based similarity (CBS) space where the covariate shift problem was significantly mitigated. For twitter trending topic classification, Lee et al. [8] proposed twitter social network-based approach to predict the class of a topic knowing the classes of its similar topics, which made use of topic-specific influential users that were identified using twitter friend-follower network. Husby and Barbosa [9] employed distant supervision with Freebase[1] to categorize topics of blog posts. For Chinese topic classification, Chen et al. [10] introduced a semi-supervised Bayesian network model for microblog topic classification and deeply exploited the hidden information from unlabeled data and related text resources.

Some neural networks have been proposed for text classification, such as Convolutional Neural Networks (CNN) [11], character-level convolutional networks [12]. Traditional approaches to text classification depend on hand-crafted

---

[1] http://www.freebase.com/.

feature extraction, which are not enough to capture the complete semantics of text. For instance, the word order in the Bag-Of-Words (BOW) model is missing while it is very important for understanding the semantics. Yet these proposed neural network based methods can learn low-dimensional text features (i.e. word embedding [13]) without feature engineering, and achieved state-of-the-art performance. For Chinese text classification, Zhou et al. [5] indicated that the combination of word and character embeddings can achieve better performance. Recently, attention-based neural networks have been introduced to improve further performance for text classification [14–16]. Experimental results showed that the attention-based neural models can select informative words or sentences in a document. Since a conversation consists of a sequence of sentences (i.e. utterances), we assume that some words or sentences hint the topic.

Motivated by the successful utilization of attention mechanism in machine translation [17], there are also some works that incorporate attention signals into CNN and RNN. Zhang et al. [18] introduced attention pooling-based convolutional neural network for classification, which used bidirectional LSTM (BLSTM) to generate the intermediate sentence representation and then compared it with local representations generated by the convolutional layer to calculate the attention weights. Yang et al. [15] proposed the Hierarchical Attention Network (HAN) for document classification, which applied word- and sentence-level attentions to capture qualitatively informative words and sentences in a document. Furthermore, Chen et al. [19] proposed a hierarchical neural LSTM model which incorporated user and product information via word- and sentence-level attentions to improve document sentiment classification. Zhou et al. [16] introduced a hybrid neural networks (HANs) with character- and word-level attentions for Chinese short text classification. Of these our model is most closely relative to the HAN model [15] and the HANs model [16]. We use the HANs model to represent each utterance of a conversation. However, we explore the structure of Chinese conversation and represent the whole text with character-, word- and sentence-level attentions. Moreover, we incorporate the speakers information that those documents do not have into the hierarchical neural networks.

3   Methods

Before formulating our approach, we first define some notations. A Chinese conversation is composed of two or more sentences. Postulated that there are two speakers (i.e. A and B) who talk to each other about some topics, the conversation is denoted by the following set $S^L = \{A_{s_1}, B_{s_1}, ..., A_{s_m}, B_{s_n}\}$, where m and n are the number of sentences that the speaker A and B said respectively and L is the total of sentences. The conversation is associated with a predefined class c_i with belonging to $C = \{c_1, c_2, ..., c_k\}$. We aim to predicate the category label with H-HANs for each Chinese conversation. The model comprises four parts: embedding layer, sentence representation layer, attention and conversation layer, and classification layer. The overall architecture of H-HANs is shown in Fig. 1.

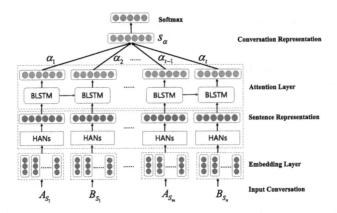

Fig. 1. The architecture of the hierarchical hybrid attention networks, where $\{A_{s_1}, ..., A_{s_m}\}$ and $\{B_{s_1}, ..., B_{s_n}\}$ are the sequences of different speaker utterances and α is the weight given by sentence-level attention.

3.1   Embedding Layer

Each sentence in a Chinese conversation is considered as two sequences, i.e. word sequence $\{w_1, w_2, ..., w_i\}$ and character sequence $\{ch_1, ch_2, ..., ch_j\}$, where $i \in \{1, L_w\}$ and $j \in \{1, L_c\}$, L_w and L_c are the lengths of the word and character sequences respectively. We map each word into its embedding representation $E_{w_i} \in R_d$ and each character into its embedding representation $E_{ch_j} \in R_d$, where d is the dimension of a word or character vector. As a result, the input conversations are mapped into a series of word embedding vectors $\{E_{w_1}, E_{w_2}, ..., E_{w_i}\}$ and character embedding vectors $\{E_{ch_1}, E_{ch_2}, ..., E_{ch_j}\}$ respectively.

3.2   Sentence Representation

Zhou et al. [16] introduced the hybrid attention networks that represents a Chinese short text and captures its semantics effectively. For a Chinese conversation, each utterance is a Chinese short text. Therefore we apply the idea to represent each utterance in a Chinese conversation. It is a noteworthy fact that each utterance is owned to a particular speaker. Hence we contact the speaker information with his/her utterance and feed the sequence into the HANs model. The model firstly builds text representation from word and character levels respectively, then concatenates two intermediate vectors into the final vector representation which is the utterance representation. Finally, the model outputs the sequential sentence representations, i.e. $\{S_1, S_2, ..., S_L\}$.

3.3   Attention and Conversation Layer

It is observed that not all utterances in a conversation contribute equally to the representation of the conversation meaning. When reading a Chinese conversation, people usually can roughly judge which sentences in the conversation are more important. We implement this idea using BLSTM-based attention mechanism in our model from sentence-level attention.

LSTM is an effective way to represent sequential text. However, one directional forward LSTM cannot capture long-range semantic dependency from future context when predicting the semantics in the beginning or middle of an input sequence. Bidirectional LSTM (BLSTM) provides an improved way to capture the semantics from both directions at the same time. In our model, the output of sentence representation layer is fed into the forward LSTM layer and the reverse of the output is fed into the backward LSTM layer. Assume that the LSTM layer outputs the vectors $[h_1, h_2, ..., h_L]$. Correspondingly the new representation S_α of a Chinese conversation is computed by an attention-weighted sum of these output vectors, which is defined as Eq. (1). The attention weight is computed by the Eqs. (2) and (3), where $\alpha_t \in R$.

$$S_\alpha = \sum_{t=1}^{L} \alpha_t h_t \tag{1}$$

$$u_t = \tanh(W_h h_t + b_h) \tag{2}$$

$$\alpha_t = softmax(W_\alpha u_t) \tag{3}$$

According to above equations, we employ attention mechanism to compute the new representation $\overrightarrow{S_\alpha}$ and $\overleftarrow{S_\alpha}$ for the output of forward and backward LSTM respectively, and concatenate $\overrightarrow{S_\alpha}$ and $\overleftarrow{S_\alpha}$ to obtain the attentive representation S_α of the BLSTM layer.

Figure 2 describes the architecture of the BLSTM-based attention layer. The output of this layer is the conversation representation that can capture as many salient utterances in a conversation from both directions as possible. The output represents the semantics of a Chinese conversation and is used to determine which topic of the conversation.

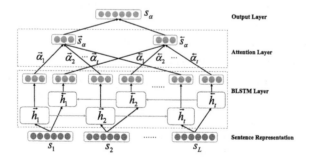

Fig. 2. The architecture of the BLSTM-based attention layer in our model.

3.4   Topic Classification

The final vector S_α is a high level representation of the Chinese conversation and is fed into the top supervised classifier. We apply a linear transformation layer and a softmax layer to produce conditional probabilities. The linear layer converts conversation representation S_α to a real-valued vector whose dimension is the number of topics, and the softmax layer maps each real value to a conditional probability that is computed by Eq. (4).

$$P_c = softmax(W_c S_\alpha + b_c) \tag{4}$$

4   Experiments

In this section, we introduce the experimental datasets, settings and results on the task of Chinese conversation topic classification.

4.1   Datasets

We collect Chinese conversation corpus from some English learning websites and tag them with 9 topic classes, including banking, dating, diet, health, job, sentiment, shopping, sports and travel. From this corpus, we build three experimental datasets with 5-class, 7-class and 9-class respectively. The 5-class dataset (#DataSet1) consists of the conversations with banking, diet, sentiment, shopping and travel. The 7-class dataset (#DataSet2) consists of the conversations with banking, dating, diet, job, sentiment, shopping and travel. The 9-class dataset is the whole corpus, i.e. #DataSet3. We show the corpus statistics in Table 2.

Table 2. The statistics of the experimental datasets.

Dataset statistics	#DataSet1	#DataSet2	#DataSet3
The number of conversations	1,994	2,799	3,415
The number of total sentences	13,590	20,225	25,602
Max/Avg. sentences per conversation	34/7	34/7	34/7
Max/Avg. length per sentence	277/18	415/18	415/18

For each dataset, we choose 80% of the samples for training and 20% for test. We release the corpus on the GitHub[2].

---

[2] https://github.com/njoe9/H-HANs.

4.2 Baselines

We compare our models with several neural network based approaches as follows. Most neural methods applied to text classification are variants of convolutional or recurrent networks. We select four neural network baselines including RCNN, C-LSTMs/BLSTMs, HAN and HANs.

RCNN: Lai et al. [4] introduced a two-layer model, the first layer represented the documents using a bi-directional recurrent structure, and the second layer selected the informative features in the documents by a max-pooling mechanism. We implement the RCNN baseline with word embedding and LSTM-RNNs instead of vanilla RNNs.

C-LSTMs/BLSTMs: Zhou et al. [5] put forward a compositional recurrent neural networks with LSTM or BLSTM, which concatenated the word- and character-level representations into a sentence vector for Chinese short text classification.

HAN: Yang et al. [15] proposed the HAN model for document classification. Inspired by this idea, we firstly concatenate word- and character-level attentive representations for each utterance to get a sentence representation, then use sentence-level attention mechanism to generate conversation representation for classification. We apply LSTM and BLSTM to model sentence and conversation attentive representations respectively, i.e. HAN-LSTM and HAN-BLSTM.

HANs: Zhou et al. [16] developed the model for Chinese short text classification. We explore the effectiveness of the model on the task of topic classification for longer text.

4.3 Experimental Setup

Different from western languages (e.g. English), there have no delimiter between the words or characters in a Chinese text. Therefore, for each utterance text, we apply Jieba[3] to conduct Chinese word segmentation, and initialize the lookup tables of input texts with the 100-dimensional pre-trained word and character embeddings [5] respectively. The hyperparameters of our model are tuned on the validation set and early stopping is utilized within 20 epoches. Dropout rate of 0.4 is set to obtain better performance. We use Stochastic Gradient Descent (SGD) to train all models with learning rate of 0.01 and momentum of 0.9. Table 3 shows the hyper parameter settings in detail.

4.4 Results and Analysis

For the baselines except HAN model, we concatenate all utterances in each conversation to form a long text which is the input (we assume that the max length of each text is 600). For the HAN and H-HANs models, utterances in each conversation are fed into the models in temporal sequence, and their hyperparameters are the same. Table 4 shows the experimental results.

---

[3] https://github.com/fxsjy/jieba.

Table 3. The experimental parameter settings in our model.

Parameter	Choice	Experiment range
Max sentences per conversation	10	10, 15, 20
Max length per sentence	140	100, 140, 200, 600
Word/Character embedding dimension	100	50, 100, 300
LSTM/CNN hidden layer size	100	64, 100, 128, 256
Dropout rate	0.4	0.4, 0.5
Epoch size	20	10, 15, 20
Mini-batch size	8	8, 16, 32, 64

Table 4. Results in percent of weighted-average. **H-HANs+BL** and **H-HANs+BB** denote the model with sentence representation using HANs-BLSTM, and conversation representation using LSTM and BLSTM respectively. **H-HANs+BB+Speaker** denotes the model H-HANs+BB combined with the speakers.

Methods	F_1 (Precision, Recall)		
	#DataSet1	#DataSet2	#DataSet3
RCNN [4]	86.3 (87.4, 86.5)	80.8 (81.4, 80.9)	83.2 (83.2, 83.7)
C-LSTMs [5]	44.5 (60.3, 47.4)	34.7 (55.0, 39.8)	33.6 (43.1, 38.9)
C-BLSTMs [5]	43.2 (50.1, 45.9)	31.7 (36.0, 36.2)	27.8 (42.5, 31.2)
HAN-LSTM [15]	78.3 (79.2, 78.7)	73.1 (74.2, 73.4)	84.9 (85.0, 85.1)
HAN-BLSTM [15]	81.9 (83.8, 82.5)	77.2 (79.7, 77.7)	80.0 (80.6, 79.8)
HANs-BLSTM [16]	86.1 (86.3, 86.0)	82.1 (83.1, 82.1)	85.2 (85.9, 85.5)
H-HANs+BL	88.7 (89.2, 88.7)	83.8 (83.9, 83.9)	83.4 (84.2, 84.0)
H-HANs+BB	**89.9** (89.9, 90.0)	**84.5** (84.7, 84.6)	**85.5** (85.6, 85.5)
H-HANs+BB+Speaker	**91.8** (92.2, 91.7)	**85.8** (86.2, 85.7)	**87.5** (87.9, 87.4)

The experimental results from Rows 4 to 5 show that LSTM or BLSTM have different effectiveness on different datasets. The results reveal that HAN-BLSTM is better than HAN-LSTM on #DataSet1 and #DataSet2 while it is opposite on #DataSet3. The results in Rows 1 to 6 imply that HANs-BLSTM almost achieves better performance than other baselines, which is the basis of our model. In our model, we firstly apply HANs to represent each utterance in a conversation, then feed each sentence representation into the attention-based LSTM/BLSTM layer. Rows 7 and 8 show the results with attention-based LSTM and BLSTM respectively.

Among all baselines, C-LSTMs/BLSTMs obtain lowest performance although they can achieve better performance for Chinese short text classification [5]. It may be concluded that C-LSTMs/BLSTMs are not applied to our corpus. However, Row 6 shows that on the basis of C-LSTMs/BLSTMs, HANs model builds word- and character-level attentions with BLSTM, and improves performance further. Compared Row 5 with Row 6, it indicates that sentence representation plays a leading role in hierarchical attention networks. HAN-BLSTM only uses attention-based BLSTM to represent each utterance, while HANs-BLSTM combines the C-LSTMs/BLSTMs and attention-based BLSTM.

Compared Row 7 with Row 8, it shows that our attention-based BLSTM for conversation representation achieves better performance than attention-based LSTM. In Fig. 2, our model firstly computes the attentive representation for the forward and backward LSTM layer respectively, then concatenates the two outputs to generate the representation of the input text. Therefore the attentive representation from both directions picks out the informative sentences in a conversation.

Row 9 shows that our model can significantly improve the performance with the consideration of speaker information. It proves that not all utterances in a conversation contribute equally to the conversation meaning for different speaker. Comparison with H-HANs+BB model, H-HANs+BB+Speaker further improves the F_1-score by 1.9%, 1.3% and 2.0% on three datasets respectively. Experimental results indicate that our model effectively captures the informative and salient utterances in a conversation.

5   Conclusion

In this paper, we propose a hierarchical hybrid neural networks (H-HANs) for topic classification of the whole Chinese conversation, which incorporates speakers information into character- and word-level attentions for sentence representation and use attention-based BLSTM to generate conversation representation. Experimental results indicate that our approach can effectively select the salient utterances in a conversation with attentive mechanism, which are important to judge the topic of a conversation. Meanwhile, we release the corpus, a new dataset for Chinese conversation topic classification.

Acknowledgments. This work is supported by the National Natural Science Foundation (No. 61602479), National High Technology Research and Development Program of China (No. 2015AA015402) and National Key Technology R&D Program of China under No. 2015BAH53F02.

References

1. Orebaugh, A., Allnutt, J.: Classification of instant messaging communications for forensics analysis. Int. J. Forensic Comput. Sci. **1**, 22–28 (2009)
2. Husin, N., Abdullah, M.T., Mahmod, R.: A systematic literature review for topic detection in chat conversation for cyber-crime investigation. Int. J. Digital Content Technol. Appl. **8**(3), 22 (2014)
3. Tang, D., Qin, B., Liu, T.: Document modeling with gated recurrent neural network for sentiment classification. In: Proceedings of the 2015 Conference on EMNLP 2015, pp. 1422–1432 (2015)

4. Lai, S., Xu, L., Liu, K., Zhao, J.: Recurrent convolutional neural networks for text classification. In: AAAI 2015, pp. 2267–2273 (2015)
5. Zhou, Y., Xu, B., Xu, J., Yang, L., Li, C., Xu, B.: Compositional recurrent neural networks for Chinese short text classification. In: 2016 IEEE/WIC/ACM International Conference on Web Intelligence, pp. 137–144 (2016)
6. Kinsella, S., Passant, A., Breslin, J.G.: Topic classification in social media using metadata from hyperlinked objects. In: Clough, P., Foley, C., Gurrin, C., Jones, G.J.F., Kraaij, W., Lee, H., Mudoch, V. (eds.) ECIR 2011. LNCS, vol. 6611, pp. 201–206. Springer, Heidelberg (2011). doi:10.1007/978-3-642-20161-5_20
7. Fei, G., Liu, B.: Social media text classification under negative covariate shift. In: EMNLP 2015, pp. 2347–2356 (2015)
8. Lee, K., Palsetia, D., Narayanan, R., Patwary, M.M.A., Agrawal, A., Choudhary, A.N.: Twitter trending topic classification. In: 2011 IEEE 11th International Conference on Data Mining Workshops (ICDMW), pp. 251–258 (2011)
9. Husby, S.D., Barbosa, D.: Topic classification of blog posts using distant supervision. In: Proceedings of the Workshop on Semantic Analysis in Social Media, pp. 28–36. Association for Computational Linguistics (2012)
10. Chen, Y., Li, Z., Nie, L., Hu, X., Wang, X., Chua, T., Zhang, X.: A semi-supervised Bayesian network model for microblog topic classification. In: COLING 2012, pp. 561–576 (2012)
11. Kim, Y.: Convolutional neural networks for sentence classification. In: Proceedings of the 2014 Conference on EMNLP, pp. 1746–1751 (2014)
12. Zhang, X., Zhao, J., LeCun, Y.: Character-level convolutional networks for text classification. In: NIPS 2015, pp. 649–657 (2015)
13. Mikolov, T., Sutskever, I., Chen, K., Corrado, G.S., Dean, J.: Distributed representations of words and phrases and their compositionality. In: NIPS 2013, pp. 3111–3119 (2013)
14. Martins, A.F.T., Astudillo, R.F.: From softmax to sparsemax: a sparse model of attention and multi-label classification. In: ICML 2016, pp. 1614–1623 (2016)
15. Yang, Z., Yang, D., Dyer, C., He, X., Smola, A., Hovy, E.: Hierarchical attention networks for document classification. In: NAACL HLT 2016 (2016)
16. Zhou, Y., Xu, J., Cao, J., Xu, B., Li, C., Xu, B.: Hybrid attention networks for Chinese short text classification. In: CICLing 2017 (2017)
17. Bahdanau, D., Cho, K., Bengio, Y.: Neural Machine Translation by Jointly Learning to Align and Translate. CoRR (2014)
18. Zhang, Y., Er, M.J., Wang, N., Pratama, M.: Attention pooling-based convolutional neural network for sentence modelling. Inf. Sci. **373**, 388–403 (2016)
19. Chen, H., Sun, M., Tu, C., Lin, Y., Liu, Z.: Neural sentiment classification with user and product attention. In: EMNLP 2016, pp. 1650–1659 (2016)

Aggregating Class Interactions for Hierarchical Attention Relation Extraction

Kaiyu Huang[(✉)], Si Li, and Guang Chen

Beijing University of Posts and Telecommunications, Beijing, China
{huangky,lisi,chenguang}@bupt.edu.cn

Abstract. Distantly supervised relation extraction is a powerful learning method to recognize relations of entity pairs. However, wrong label problem is inevitable among large-scale training data. In this work we propose a hierarchical attention neural network to effectively alleviate the impact of noise instances. Moreover under distantly supervised scenario, connections and dependencies widely appear among relation classes, which we call class interactions. Previous end-to-end methods that considered the relations as independent failed to make use of these interactions. To better utilize these important interactions, we propose a soft target as training objective to learn class relationships jointly. Experiments show that our model outperforms state-of-the-art methods.

Keywords: Distant supervision · Hierarchicial attention · Soft target

1 Introduction

Traditional relation extraction, which aims to recognize the relationship between two named entities, is inevitably limited by the lack of labeled data. In recent years, the utilization of large-scale knowledge bases (KBs) like Freebase [2] has arisen in many NLP tasks. The KBs are built up with relation triples that contain a pair of entity and their relationship, e.g., (*Steve Jobs*, **founder**, *Apple*). Since data labeling is time consuming and labor intensive, [9] proposed distantly supervised (DS) relation extraction which can automatically generate labeled data. The DS method assumes that if an entity pair has a specific relation in the KBs, then all sentences containing the entity pair, which are called relation mentions, also express this relation. Training data is generated by aligning relation triples in KBs to free texts. However, under this assumption, data could be very noisy since not all the sentences containing the entity pair exactly express such relations. Thus, DS relation extraction suffers from wrong labeling problem.

To relax the wrong label problem, [6,11,14] adopted multi-instance relation extraction. However, these methods with manual feature engineering deeply depends on NLP tools so that noises will also be generated during sentence annotation and parsing. Recently, the utilization of deep neural networks [12,16,18] has relaxed relation extraction from handcraft features. [7,19] utilized convolutional neural networks (CNN) in DS relation extraction. Since recurrent neural

© Springer International Publishing AG 2017
D. Liu et al. (Eds.): ICONIP 2017, Part II, LNCS 10635, pp. 551–561, 2017.
https://doi.org/10.1007/978-3-319-70096-0_57

networks (RNN) have the strength at modeling sequences, in this work we employ a bidirectional RNN with gated recurrent units (GRU) as our sentence encoder.

The effectiveness of attention mechanism [1] has been proved in several NLP works. [17] applied hierarchical attention networks to boost document classification. [7,21] also respectively used word and sentence level attention in relation extraction. In this work, we follow the previous multi-instance learning framework, and employ both word and sentence level attentions to alleviate noises from all aspects. In the hierarchical attention structure, word level attentions recognize the segments strongly suggesting these relations and the following sentence level attentions dynamically select the convincing instances and relax the impact from noisy instances.

Previous DS approaches assign exactly one certain relation label to individual sentences and entity pairs. However, they failed to consider the internal interactions among relations. As [6] argued, the fact that more than one relation classes are expressed in a relation mention is common in DS scenario. We further find that relations that appear simultaneously usually have inherent interactions. Taking the sentence *that is one reason that Hunan's fast-growing provincial capital, Changsha, is beginning to siphon some workers back from Guangdong* for example, the relation *contains* and *capital of* are both expressed in the sentence for the entity pair **Hunan** and **Changsha**. If a relation mention expresses the relation *capital of*, the relation *contains* must be expressed at the same time. Here is another example that the appearance of relation *place of birth* sometimes suggest the relation *place of live*. Interactions among relations are common and important in relation extraction. The dependencies and connections between relations can be expressed by their co-occurrence. In this work, we design a novel scheme to model the interactions. Inspired by [5], we heuristically propose a soft target (ST) by modifying the labels of relation mentions. In the modified labels, the value of each class is set as the probability of the relation mention being classified to this class, instead of a binary value. By the soft target, we jointly aggregate the class interactions during training that leads to a better model performance.

Figure 1 shows the overall structure of our proposed model. Words in input sentences are initialized with pre-trained word embeddings [8] and position embeddings [18]. We first embed the sentences into semantic vector space by a bi-GRU with word attentions, then all the sentence embeddings are weighted by sentence attentions as the embedding of the entity pair. Finally the embeddings are learned to fit the soft target.

The contributions of this work are summarized as follows: (1) We argue that class interactions are important for distantly supervised relation extraction and propose a soft target to enhance relation extraction by jointly learning the class interactions. (2) We propose a hierarchical attention network that is powerful to alleviate wrong label problem and restrain noises from all aspects.

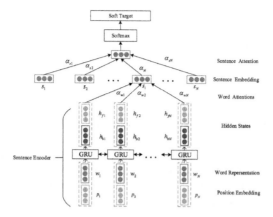

Fig. 1. Hierarchical attention network with soft target

2   Related Work

Relation extraction is a fundamental task in natural language processing. Traditional relation extraction is limited by the expensive annotated training data. Thus, [9] addressed the DS method to generate training data. To address the wrong label problem, [11] introduced multi-instance method and [6,14] adopted multi-instance multi-label learning. Multi-instance learning considers the label of a bag of instances instead of individual instances. However, these methods deeply rely on traditional handcraft features that suffer from error propagation. [19] incorporated multi-instance learning with neural networks. [7] utilized sentence level attentions to selectively combine information from multiple instances and achieved the state-of-the-art performance. These end-to-end methods simply used naive neural network structures and failed to consider the internal interactions between relations. [4] proposed a global learning method that jointly model relation mentions and relation facts in a Markov random field. [20] modeled relation likelihood via learning to rank algorithm. Our work is closely related to these two works that considered relation interactions during learning.

Deep learning is reported to gain considerable promotions in many NLP tasks. As for relation extraction, [13] used recursive neural networks to extract relations. [12,18] used end-to-end CNNs in relation extraction. Meanwhile in [3,10], several variants of RNN is also designed for relation extraction. The attention mechanism has shown its effectiveness in several previous relation extraction works. [15,21] reported their attention based neural relation extraction and showed promising results. Base on these previous works, we utilize a bidirectional RNN to effectively encode the relation mentions and design a hierarchical attention structure to furthest alleviate the harm from noises.

3   Model

3.1   Embedding Layer

The raw input for the network is a sentence x. We first embed every words in the sequence to distributed vectors. The embedding for every token includes following two parts.

Word Embedding. We use a word embedding matrix to transfer words into distributed representations. Given a sentence $x_i = \{w_1, w_2, \cdots, w_m\}$ with m words, every word w_i is encoded to a real-value vector. The embedding matrix $V \in \mathbb{R}^{d \times |V|}$ where d denotes the dimension of word vectors and $|V|$ denotes the size of vocabulary. The column vectors of V are initialized by pre-trained word vectors that contain syntactic and semantic information of the words.

Position Embedding. Following [18], we use position embeddings that specified by the relative distance between current word and entity pair. The distance between the ith word and the entity word at jth place is defined as $i - j$. Two distances towards the entity pair are calculated for every words and then mapped into fixed size vectors. We concatenate two parts of embeddings and the input matrix is denoted as $\mathbf{w} = \{\mathbf{w_1}, \mathbf{w_2}, \cdots, \mathbf{w_m}\}$ where $\mathbf{w_i} \in \mathbb{R}^{d_w + 2 \times d_p}$. d_w denotes the dimension of word vectors and d_p denotes the dimension of position vectors.

3.2   Sentence Encoder

We embed sentences by a bidirectional RNN with gated recurrent units (GRU). The GRU [1] traces the historical hidden states by gating mechanism. GRU keeps two types of gates called reset gate r_t and update gate z_t to decide the way to process previous information. At time t, the GRU updates a new state

$$h_t = (1 - z_t) \odot h_{t-1} + z_t \odot \tilde{h}_t \qquad (1)$$

where $\odot$ denotes element wise product. In this equation, hidden state from previous time step h_{t-1} and current state $\tilde{h}_t$ are reorganized by the update gate z_t which controls the proportion of information from two parts. z_t is calculated as

$$z_t = \sigma(W_z x_t + U_z h_{t-1} + b_z) \qquad (2)$$

x_t is the input vector at time t. Then the candidate state $\tilde{h}_t$ is calculated as

$$\tilde{h}_t = \tanh(W_h x_t + r_t \odot U_h h_{t-1} + b_h) \qquad (3)$$

r_t is the reset gate that determine how much previous information is kept for candidate state. The reset gate is computed as

$$r_t = \sigma(W_r x_t + U_r h_{t-1} + b_r) \qquad (4)$$

For a input sentence s_j, the network updates a forward hidden state $\overrightarrow{h_{it}}$ and a backward hidden state $\overleftarrow{h_{it}}$ separately, we add the two hidden states

$$h_{it} = \overrightarrow{h_{it}} + \overleftarrow{h_{it}} \qquad (5)$$

as the hidden state at time t.

We employ word level attentions to determine important segments in sentences. For each output state h_{it}, we compute its attention weight α_{wt} as

$$u_{it} = tanh(h_{it}) \tag{6}$$

$$\alpha_{wt} = \frac{\exp(u_{it}^T u_w)}{\sum_t \exp(u_{it}^T u_w)} \tag{7}$$

u_w is a query vector and we acquire the sentence represent s_i as

$$s_i = \sum_t \alpha_{wt} h_{it} \tag{8}$$

and s_i is the attention weighted sentence representation.

3.3   Scoring Instances with Sentence Attention

To alleviate the wrong labeling problem, we apply sentence attentions to dynamically evaluate the reliability of instances. During training, sentence attention weights are learned for every instance. The final representation of the entity pair is a linear combination of all the sentence embeddings weighted by attentions.

Specifically, for each sentence s_i we compute an attention α_{si} and the representation of entity pair s is weighted as

$$s = \sum_i \alpha_{si} s_i \tag{9}$$

$$\alpha_{si} = \frac{\exp(e_i)}{\sum_k \exp(e_k)} \tag{10}$$

e_i is a sentence score computed from a bilinear query function as

$$e_i = s_i A r \tag{11}$$

where A is a diagonal matrix represent and r is a query vector.

In order to measure the similarity between relations and entity pairs, the model also learns relation embeddings locating in the same feature space with sentence embeddings. Then we use a score function to determine confidence of entity pairs being classified to each relation. Scores for a entity pair with a representation s is computed as

$$c = sR + b \tag{12}$$

where $R \in \mathbb{R}^{d_h \times |r|}$ is a relation embedding matrix. Column vector in R are representations of relations. d_h is the dimension of sentence embeddings and $|r|$ is the number of relations. Each element in c is a relation score.

3.4   Learning Class Interactions with Soft Target

As introduced above, in this work we employ soft target instead of one-hot labels as our learning objective. Since entity pairs often contain multiple relations that have inherent interactions, soft target model that interactions into the network. Here we define soft target as

$$\pi = \{p_1, p_2, \cdots p_r\} \tag{13}$$

where $\sum_i p_i = 1$. p_i is the probability that the entity pair is assigned to the ith class. And class scores in Eq. (12) are normalized by a softmax layer as the probabilities to classify the entity pair to each relation

$$p(r|S, \theta) = \frac{\exp(c_r)}{\sum_{i=1}^{|r|} \exp(c_i)} \tag{14}$$

Where S represents the input instances, θ is the set of parameters and $|r|$ is the number of relations. We use cross-entropy objective to measure empirical risk

$$L(\theta) = \sum_{i=1}^{N} \pi_i \log p(r_i|S_i, \theta) \tag{15}$$

where N is the total number of entity pairs. In this work the class interactions are mainly considered on the co-occurrence of relation classes. We simply consider positive classes have the same probability.

4   Experiments

4.1   Dataset and Evaluation Metrics

Our experiments are implemented on a widely used dataset that developed by [11] and has been used by [6,7,14,19]. The dataset was generated by aligning the relation facts discovered in Freebase with free texts from New York Times corpus (NYT). There are 53 kinds of relations including a Not Related relation in the corpus. There are 522,611 sentences, 281,270 entity pairs and 18,252 relation facts contained in the training data, and 172,448 sentences, 96,678 entity pairs and 1850 relational facts in the testing set.

We evaluate our model with metrics similar to [9]. We adopt held-out evaluation in all of our experiments. Both precision/recall curves and precision@N (P@N) is reported as evaluation criterion of the model.

4.2   Experiment Settings

Word Embedding: In this work, we use the word2vec tool [8] to pre-train word embeddings with NYT corpus. Words that appear less than 100 times in the corpus are aborted and a UNK symbol is assigned for the rare words whose embedding is randomly initialized. The word embedding matrix is updated during training.

Parameter Settings: Following previous works, we use three-fold validation on the training data to tune the parameters and mini-batches are fed into the network randomly. We use grid search to determine the optimal hyper-parameters. Batch size is set as {60, **120**, 240, 480}. Word embedding size is tuned as {**50**, 100, 150, 200}. We select learning rate among {0.1, 0.05, **0.01**, 0.005, 0.001}. We keep other hyper-parameters same as [7,19]: the size of sentence embedding is 230, position embedding size is set to 5 and dropout rate is set as 0.5.

4.3   Comparison with Baseline

We select following models for comparison through held-out evaluation:

Mintz [9] the first work on distant supervised relation extraction.
MultiR [6] a graphical model based multi-instance learning method.
MIML [14] a multi-label method to address relation overlapping.
PCNN+ATT   [7]   neural   method   that   achieved   the   state-of-the-art
     performance.

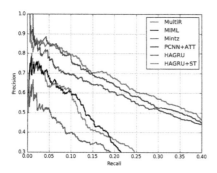

Fig. 2. PR curves of our model and the baselines.

Figure 2 shows the precision/recall curves of our model and baselines. Both HAGRU and HAGRU+ST significantly outperforms previous conventional and neural methods. The precision of PCNN+ATT drops fast after the recall rate reaching 0.025 while ours keeps a considerable precision. The superiority of our method derives from its model structure and the ability of organizing potential interactions of relation facts. The attentive GRU encoder alleviates noises at word and instance aspect and adequately captures the latent features since the inter-class information is propagated through the network via the soft target. These mechanisms guarantee the model to be effective from different aspects. We notice that when recall is tiny, the PCNN model works better than our RNN based models. This may because for some straightforward sentences, local features extracted by CNN work better for the classification.

4.4   Effect of GRU with Hierarchical Attentions

To evaluate the impact of attentions at different level, we train several models with different attention mechanism. The results are presented in Fig. 3 and Table 1. In the experiments, We train a GRU encoder with only word attentions (GRU+WATT) that combines the sentence embeddings by averaging. GRU+WATT shows comparable performance with PCNN+ATT even without sentence level attentions, which proves that word level attention precisely concentrates on important segments in sentences for relation extraction. Meanwhile the fact that GRU encoder with only sentence attentions (GRU+SATT) works not so good also suggests that word attentions is quite important. And when sentence level is further applied, HAGRU is shown much more powerful than PCNN+ATT and GRU+WATT. From these facts, it is concluded that hierarchical attention mechanism which denoises at multiple levels well boosts the model's ability of extracting relation facts.

Table 1. P@N for relation extraction with different number of sentences.

P@N(%)	100	200	300	400	500	Mean
GRU+SATT	80.0	69.5	64.3	58.8	58.2	66.2
GRU+WATT	83.0	80.0	74.0	68.8	66.0	74.4
HAGRU	**87.0**	79.0	74.3	69.8	67.4	75.5
HAGRU+ST	85.0	**81.0**	**77.3**	**71.0**	**70.4**	**76.0**

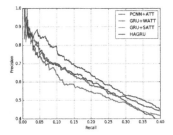

Fig. 3. mpact of different attentions.

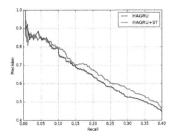

Fig. 4. Impact of soft target.

4.5   Effect of Soft Target

The effectiveness of soft target is shown in Fig. 4 and Table 1. We observe from the PR curves that when more positive classes are recalled, HAGRU+ST keeps a higher precision rate than HAGRU. HAGRU suffers a steep reduction of precision when recall rate reaches 0.05 while HAGRU+ST keeps a long range higher precision. The soft target implies the co-occurrence and dependency among the

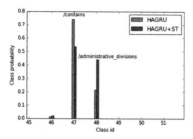

Fig. 5. Class probabilities of the entity pair in different model

classes. Under this objective, embeddings of related classes are restricted closer while the margins between irrelevant classes are maximized. Hence, our model gains the ability to precisely assign relations for entity pairs and recall the fine-grained relations that usually related to coarse-grained ones.

4.6   Case Study

To demonstrate the effectiveness of soft target, we randomly select a entity pair **China** and **Inner Mongolia** which simultaneously express the relation of */location/contains* and */country/administrative_divisions* as our study case. Then we inspect the label distribution to discover how the model works.

As shown in Fig. 5, the output probability of *administrative divisions* significantly increases after the class relationship is jointly learned by soft target which indicates the two classes are learned to be closer. Another benefit brought by joint learning is that fine-grained relations like *administrative divisions* are more likely to be recalled. If learned with single label, these relations are easy to be masked by vast coarse-grained labels.

5   Conclusion

In this paper, we introduce a hierarchical attention network to model relations between entities and eliminate noise. A soft target is further proposed to jointly learn the interactions among relations. This novel scheme is shown to be powerful for relation extraction under distant supervision.

Acknowledgments. This work is supported by the Fundamental Research Funds for the Central Universities (2017RC02) and Beijing Natural Science Foundation (4174098).

References

1. Bahdanau, D., Cho, K., Bengio, Y.: Neural machine translation by jointly learning to align and translate. Computer Science (2014)
2. Bollacker, K., Evans, C., Paritosh, P., Sturge, T., Taylor, J.: Freebase: a collaboratively created graph database for structuring human knowledge. In: Proceedings of the 2008 ACM SIGMOD International Conference on Management of Data, pp. 1247–1250. ACM (2008)
3. Cai, R., Zhang, X., Wang, H.: Bidirectional Recurrent Convolutional Neural Network for Relation Classification. In: Meeting of the Association for Computational Linguistics, pp. 756–765 (2016)
4. Han, X., Sun, L.: Global distant supervision for relation extraction. In: Proceedings of the Thirtieth AAAI Conference on Artificial Intelligence, pp. 2950–2956. AAAI Press (2016)
5. Hinton, G., Vinyals, O., Dean, J.: Distilling the knowledge in a neural network. Comput. Sci. **14**(7), 38–39 (2015)
6. Hoffmann, R., Zhang, C., Ling, X., Zettlemoyer, L., Weld, D.S.: Knowledge-based weak supervision for information extraction of overlapping relations. In: Meeting of the Association for Computational Linguistics: Human Language Technologies, pp. 541–550. Association for Computational Linguistics (2011)
7. Lin, Y., Shen, S., Liu, Z., Luan, H., Sun, M.: Neural relation extraction with selective attention over instances. In: Meeting of the Association for Computational Linguistics, pp. 2124–2133 (2016)
8. Mikolov, T., Chen, K., Corrado, G., Dean, J.: Efficient estimation of word representations in vector space. Computer Science (2013)
9. Mintz, M., Bills, S., Snow, R., Jurafsky, D.: Distant supervision for relation extraction without labeled data. In: Joint Conference of the, Meeting of the ACL and the, International Joint Conference on Natural Language Processing of the AFNLP, pp. 1003–1011. Association for Computational Linguistics (2009)
10. Miwa, M., Bansal, M.: End-to-end relation extraction using LSTMs on sequences and tree structures. arXiv preprint arXiv:1601.00770 (2016)
11. Riedel, S., Yao, L., McCallum, A.: Modeling relations and their mentions without labeled text. In: Balcázar, J.L., Bonchi, F., Gionis, A., Sebag, M. (eds.) ECML PKDD 2010. LNCS, vol. 6323, pp. 148–163. Springer, Heidelberg (2010). doi:10.1007/978-3-642-15939-8_10
12. Santos, C.N.D., Xiang, B., Zhou, B.: Classifying relations by ranking with convolutional neural networks. Computer Science (2015)
13. Socher, R., Huval, B., Manning, C.D., Ng, A.Y.: Semantic compositionality through recursive matrix-vector spaces. In: Joint Conference on Empirical Methods in Natural Language Processing and Computational Natural Language Learning, pp. 1201–1211 (2012)
14. Surdeanu, M., Tibshirani, J., Nallapati, R., Manning, C.D.: Multi-instance multi-label learning for relation extraction. In: Joint Conference on Empirical Methods in Natural Language Processing and Computational Natural Language Learning, pp. 455–465 (2012)
15. Wang, L., Cao, Z., Melo, G.D., Liu, Z.: Relation classification via multi-level attention CNNs. In: Meeting of the Association for Computational Linguistics, pp. 1298–1307 (2016)
16. Yan, X., Mou, L., Li, G., Chen, Y., Peng, H., Jin, Z.: Classifying relations via long short term memory networks along shortest dependency path. Computer Science (2015)

17. Yang, Z., Yang, D., Dyer, C., He, X., Smola, A., Hovy, E.: Hierarchical attention networks for document classification. In: Conference of the North American Chapter of the Association for Computational Linguistics: Human Language Technologies, pp. 1480–1489 (2016)
18. Zeng, D., Liu, K., Lai, S., Zhou, G., Zhao, J.: Relation classification via convolutional deep neural network. In: COLING, pp. 2335–2344 (2014)
19. Zeng, D., Liu, K., Chen, Y., Zhao, J.: Distant supervision for relation extraction via piecewise convolutional neural networks. In: Conference on Empirical Methods in Natural Language Processing, pp. 1753–1762 (2015)
20. Zheng, H., Li, Z., Wang, S., Yan, Z., Zhou, J.: Aggregating inter-sentence information to enhance relation extraction. In: Proceedings of the Thirtieth AAAI Conference on Artificial Intelligence, pp. 3108–3114. AAAI Press (2016)
21. Zhou, P., Shi, W., Tian, J., Qi, Z., Li, B., Hao, H., et al.: Attention-based bidirectional long short-term memory networks for relation classification. In: Meeting of the Association for Computational Linguistics (2016)

Tensorial Neural Networks and Its Application in Longitudinal Network Data Analysis

Mingyuan Bai[1(✉)], Boyan Zhang[2], and Junbin Gao[1]

[1] The University of Sydney Business School, The University of Sydney,
Sydney, NSW 2006, Australia
mbai8854@uni.sydney.edu.au, junbin.gao@sydney.edu.au
[2] The School of Information Technologies, The University of Sydney,
Sydney, NSW 2006, Australia
bzha8220@uni.sydney.edu.au

Abstract. The traditional neural networks are only able to process vectorial data, resulting in the loss of spatial information in high-dimensional structural data when vectorising data. The matrix neural networks (MatNet), a new approach, is only capable of capturing structural information on the first and the second dimension/mode of matrix data. Although the state-of-the-art method multilinear tensor regression (MLTR) manages to capture the linear relational information in high dimensions, the possible nonlinear relationships within multidimensional data may be ignored. To analyse both linear and nonlinear relationships among each mode of the multidimensional relational data, a new model, named tensorial neural networks, is proposed. Within the tensorial neural networks, the hidden layers are in high-dimensions rather than one dimension or two dimensions. The backpropagation algorithm for tensorial neural networks is derived and provided. The performance of the new approach is assessed in analysing longitudinal network data which contains weekly international relationships among 25 countries from 2004 to mid-2014 from World-Wide Integrated Crisis Early Warning System. In other words, the application of this newly proposed method, tensorial neural networks, is on international relationship study in this paper. The dependencies among the international relationship data are generally reciprocity and transitivity which are also the interests of the research.

Keywords: Tensorial neural networks · Longitudinal networks · International relationships · Machine learning

1 Introduction

In recent years, machine learning has drawn incredibly increasing attention in many research areas and the request of processing large volume of data with a higher speed has been highly demanded. Data acquired from science and technology is remarkable not merely for the often-mentioned volume, but also multi- and high-dimensional with the rapid proliferation in new data types. The rise of

© Springer International Publishing AG 2017
D. Liu et al. (Eds.): ICONIP 2017, Part II, LNCS 10635, pp. 562–571, 2017.
https://doi.org/10.1007/978-3-319-70096-0_58

massive multi-dimensional data has led to new demands for Machine Learning (ML) systems to learn complex models with millions to billions of parameters for new types of data structures, that promise adequate capacity to digest massive datasets and offer powerful predictive analytics thereupon. The data types are, not limited to, e.g., the 2D data like digital images[1], 3D data like videos[2] and multispectral images in remote sensing[3] and longitudinal network data from social and political networks[4].

Most traditional learning algorithms only deal with vectorial data. Vectorising multi-dimensional data results in even higher dimensions, demanding powerful computing equipment and more efficient algorithms. In some cases such as in political network analysis, it has been proved that vectorising network data is not a good choice for representing data, see [1]. Hence exploring new machine learning algorithms to directly deal with the data in specially organised data structures has been a challenge in the last decade. We have seen a number of state-of-the-art development in new algorithm design taking care of special data structures like multi-dimensional data and even manifold-valued data, see [2]. In literature, multidimensional data is usually called tensorial data, as the extension of the ordinary vectorial data, see [3]. A number of linear analysis tools or techniques for tensorial data, in the case of multilinear analysis mentioned, have been well studied in the last two decades. The new techniques are making their ways to other disciplines.

To analyse longitudinal relational data, Hoff [4] applied the multilinear tensor regression. With this approach, this linear model is able to process the multidimensional data which are autocorrelated (for example, as a time series). Thus this method can capture the spatial information, such as the long-term longitudinal dependence between the data and the transitivity and the reciprocity of the data. Minhas *et al.* [1] also proposed a method which can capture the interdependence among the data points with the tensor regression based network approach to estimate parameters. These parameters are able to describe the effect of one pair of nodes on the other pair(s) of nodes (one element of the tensor, $x_{i_1,i_2,t}$ where i_1 and i_2 are one pair of nodes, describes the relationship between this pair of nodes at time t). These approaches are parsimonious and also reduce the number of parameters to estimate significantly.

Given the fact that the multidimensional data such as longitudinal relational data (as a time series) are highly complicated, all the aforementioned multilinear analysis may not be able to reveal any hidden complex nonlinear relationship between the independent variables and the dependent variables, to detect possible interactions between the predictors, or to enable the flexibility of the model to capture the information in the data sufficiently.

There was a new approach proposed to enable neural networks to handle the input data in matrix structure, which increases the speed of the process,

---

[1] http://sipi.usc.edu/database/database.php?volume=misc.
[2] https://www.youtube.com/watch?v=OeyZyrXGgtM.
[3] http://dx.doi.org/10.5067/ASTER/AST_L1T.003.
[4] http://snap.stanford.edu/data.

reduces the size of the parameters significantly and captures the spatial information which is in 2 dimensions, see [5]. However, this approach can be applied to the longitudinal relational data which is actually in tensor form. In addition, during the vectorization or matricisation, the solution space is significantly large. Thus the probability to obtain a meaningful local minimum is decreased, since the domain of the sub-optimum is large. What is more, as the model complexity increases, the learning capacity of the model tends to be deteriorated. The computational cost is also significantly high.

The objective of this paper is, under the deep learning neural network framework, to propose a new nonlinear machine learning algorithm which is able to explore nonlinear relations among multidimensional data, specially for the longitudinal relational data, and to preserve and capture spatial features of the data, for example, tensor structured time series with interdependent elements. This method will take tensors directly as the input. In other words, the input layer neurons form a tensor and each neuron represents an element of the tensor. Each neuron receives the information which is summarized through the multilinear mapping of the outputs from the neurons of the immediate previous layer, plus an offset term which is the bias. Then the neurons are activated with a specific activation function. In terms of obtaining the most optimal parameters, the backpropagation will be proposed to train tensorial neural networks (TNN). In addition, the tensorial neural network (TNN) will not only further reduce the solution space, but also in consequence reduce the model complexity, increasing the chance to reach a meaningful local minimum compared with the classic neural networks or the matrix neural networks (MatNet) [5]. After we completed this work based on MatNet, we note the recent work on the same topic in [6].

The paper is organized as follows. In Sect. 2, we propose the new tensorial neural networks and investigate the BP algorithms and relevant regularisations. Section 3 focuses on assessing the performance of the proposed TNNs, evaluated on a real-world dataset. Finally, conclusions and suggestions for future work are provided in Sect. 4.

2   Tensorial Neural Networks

2.1   Preliminaries

Our purpose in this study is to propose a deep learning for tensorial data based on the new neural network structure. We will follow the tensor notation used in [3]. A tensor is a multidimensional array. It is higher-order generalization of scalar (zeroth-order tensor), vector (first-order tensor), and matrix (second-order tensor). In this paper, lowercase italic letters (x, y, $\cdots$) denote scalars, boldface lowercase letters ($\mathbf{x}$, $\mathbf{y}$, $\cdots$) denote vectors, boldface uppercase letters ($\mathbf{X}$, $\mathbf{Y}$, $\cdots$) denote matrices, and boldface Euler script letters ($\mathcal{X}$, $\mathcal{Y}$, $\cdots$) denote tensors. Specifically a K-order tensor $\mathcal{X}$ is an element of the tensor product of K vector spaces with K coordinates index by $(i_1, i_2, ..., i_k)$, denoted by

$$\mathcal{X} = (x_{i_1,i_2,...,i_K})_{1 \le i_1 \le I_1, 1 \le i_2 \le I_2, ..., 1 \le i_K \le I_K}$$

where K is called the order/dimensionality and $I_1, I_2, ..., I_K$ are the relevant dimension along each of K modes of the tensor. Thus all the $I_1 \times I_2 \times \cdots \times I_K$ elements of the tensor $\mathcal{X}$ are arranged in the high-dimensional rectangular structure.

The k-mode product of an K-order tensor $\mathcal{X}$ with a matrix $\mathbf{U}_k = (u_{j_k, i_k}) \in \mathbb{R}^{J_k \times I_k}$ is denoted by $\mathcal{X} \times_k \mathbf{U}_k$. The result is a K-order tensor of dimension $I_1 \times \cdots \times I_{k-1} \times J_k \times I_{k+1} \times \cdots \times I_K$. Elementwise, the k-mode product can be expressed as $(\mathcal{X} \times_k \mathbf{U}_k)_{i_1, \cdots, i_{k-1}, j_k, i_{k+1}, \cdots, i_K} = \sum_{i_k=1}^{I_k} x_{i_1, \cdots, i_{k-1}, i_k, i_{k+1}, \cdots, i_K} u_{j_k, i_k}$.

In this paper, we are particularly interested in the following multiple linear transformation defined by the so-called Tucker multiplication, see [3],

$$\mathcal{X} \rightarrow \mathcal{Y} = \mathcal{X} \times_1 \mathbf{U}_1 \times_2 \mathbf{U}_2 \times_3 \cdots \times_K \mathbf{U}_K \triangleq [\mathcal{X}; \mathbf{U}_1, \mathbf{U}_2, ..., \mathbf{U}_K]. \tag{1}$$

2.2   Tensorial Network Settings

The tensorial neural networks that we propose consists of L layers of K-order tensorial structure, the neighbouring layers of which are connected by the multiple linear mappings defined by (1) with appropriate bias tensors. Specifically, let $\mathcal{X}^{(l)} \in \mathbb{R}^{I_{l1} \times \cdots \times I_{lK}}$ be the tensorial variable at layer l where $l = 0, 1, ..., L$. The layer 0 is called the input layer and the layer L is called the output layer. Layer $l-1$ and layer l ($l = 1, ..., L$) is connected as

$$\mathcal{X}^{(l)} = \sigma^{(l)}(\mathcal{X}^{(l-1)}, \mathcal{W}^{(l)}) = \sigma(\mathcal{X}^{(l-1)} \times_1 \mathbf{U}_1^{(l)} \times_2 \cdots \times_K \mathbf{U}_K^{(l)} + \mathcal{B}^{(l)}). \tag{2}$$

where $\mathcal{B}^{(l)} \in \mathbb{R}^{I_{l1} \times \cdots \times I_{lK}}$, $\mathbf{U}_k^{(l)} \in \mathbb{R}^{I_{lk} \times I_{(l-1)k}}$ ($k = 1, 2, ..., K$), and $\mathcal{W}^{(l)} = \{\mathbf{U}_1^{(l)}, ..., \mathbf{U}_K^{(l)}, \mathcal{B}^{(l)}\}$ denotes the parameters/weights between layers $l-1$ and l with an appropriate activation function σ such as the sigmoid function.

The overall function defined by these L layers networks is given by, based on the notation in (2),

$$f = \sigma^{(L)} \circ \sigma^{(L-1)} \circ \cdots \circ \sigma^{(1)} : \mathbb{R}^{I_{01} \times \cdots \times I_{0K}} \rightarrow \mathbb{R}^{I_{L1} \times \cdots \times I_{LK}}, \tag{3}$$

which is parameterised on the parameter set $\mathcal{W} = \{\mathcal{W}^{(l)}\}_{l=1}^L$.

2.3   Loss Function and Regularisation

The basic principal of any neural network learning for a given set of training $\mathcal{D} = \{(\mathcal{X}_t, \mathcal{Y}_t)\}_{t=1}^N$ and a loss function ℓ is to use the empirical risk minimization. It suffices to minimize the following empirical risk to learn a function that will do well in general, i.e.,

$$\min_{\mathcal{W}} \frac{1}{N} \sum_{t=1}^N \ell(f(\mathcal{X}_t, \mathcal{W}), \mathcal{Y}_t). \tag{4}$$

The loss function ℓ can be chosen as the squared error for regression problems and typical softmax loss for classification problems, see [7].

To maintain a stable training process, as usual, we also add the following regularisation term to the loss function (4), $\|\boldsymbol{W}\|^2 := \sum_{l=1}^{L} \sum_{k=1}^{K} \|\mathbf{U}_{lk}\|_F^2$. In fact, this regularisation term can be replaced with more strong constraints $\|\mathbf{U}_{lk}\|_F^2 = 1$ where $1 \le k \le K - 1$ on each layer to maintain scale uncertain in multiple products. However our experiments have shown that the previous ridge regularisation is sufficient in most cases.

As a common practice, we prefer sparse response inside hidden layers. In particular, we impose a sparsity constraint on the hidden neurons. For this purpose, define $\overline{p}^{(l)} = \frac{1}{N} \sum_{t=1}^{N} \mathcal{X}_t^{(l)}$, the average activations of hidden layer l (averaged over the training set). We wish the average tensor to be a given constant tensor with all the elements to be a given constant ρ. We utilise the following entropy measure to enforce the sparsity:

$$R_l = \mathrm{sum}\left(\rho \log \frac{\rho}{\overline{p}^{(l)}} + (1 - \rho) \log \frac{1 - \rho}{1 - \overline{p}^{(l)}} \right), \tag{5}$$

where $\mathrm{sum}(\mathcal{M})$ means the sum of all the elements of tensor $\mathcal{M}$, and log and / are applied to tensor elementwise.

2.4   Optimisation and Implementation

Finally the overall objective function for training tensorial neural networks has become

$$\ell = \frac{1}{2N} \sum_{t=1}^{N} \|\mathcal{Y}_t - f(\mathcal{X}_t, \boldsymbol{W})\|_F^2 + \lambda \|\boldsymbol{W}\|^2 + \beta \sum_{l=1}^{L} R_l. \tag{6}$$

The classic deep learning neural network training relies on one of gradient descent optimisation algorithm. Given the forward-feed structure of the proposed tensorial neural networks, we can present an effective Backpropagation (BP) algorithm to back-pass the computation of the gradient of the loss function with respect to each of tensorial neural network parameters/weights $\boldsymbol{W}$ for efficient training or learning. We refer readers to [5] for the computation of gradients of two regularisation terms in (6).

In the BP algorithm, the core is to derive the derivatives of the overall loss function with respect to both the parameters and activation variables $\mathcal{X}^{(l)}$ on each hidden layer, as suggested in [8].

The BP algorithm recursively computes gradients with respect to both the inputs to the layers and their parameters by making use of the chain rule. To be concrete, denote by $\ell^{(l)} = \ell \circ \sigma^{(L)} \circ \sigma^{(L-1)} \circ \cdots \circ \sigma^{(l)}$ the loss as a function of the layer $\mathcal{X}^{l-1}$. This notation is convenient because it conceptually separates the network architecture from the layer design.

For a data tuple $(\mathbfcal{X}_t, \mathbfcal{Y}_t)$ and a layer l this is computing

$$\frac{\partial \ell^{(l)}(\mathbfcal{X}_t^{(l-1)}, \mathbfcal{Y}_t)}{\partial \mathbfcal{W}^{(l)}} = \frac{\partial \ell^{(l+1)}(\mathbfcal{X}_t^{(l)}, \mathbfcal{Y}_t)}{\partial \mathbfcal{X}_t^l} \frac{\partial \sigma^{(l)}(\mathbfcal{X}_t^{(l-1)})}{\partial \mathbfcal{W}^{(l)}}, \tag{7}$$

$$\frac{\partial \ell^{(l)}(\mathbfcal{X}_t^{(l-1)}, \mathbfcal{Y}_t)}{\partial \mathbfcal{X}_t^{l-1}} = \frac{\partial \ell^{(l+1)}(\mathbfcal{X}_t^{(l)}, \mathbfcal{Y}_t)}{\partial \mathbfcal{X}_t^l} \frac{\partial \sigma^{(l)}(\mathbfcal{X}_t^{(l-1)})}{\partial \mathbfcal{X}_t^{(l-1)}}, \tag{8}$$

where $\mathbfcal{X}_t^{(l)} = \ell^{(l)}(\mathbfcal{X}_t^{(l-1)}, \mathbfcal{W}^{(l)})$ is the function from the input layer to layer l. Here (7) and (8) define the backpropagation algorithm. All variables $\mathbfcal{X}$s are tensors, so the products in the chain rules are actually the contraction products of relevant tensors, see [3]. For our convenience, we define

$$\mathbfcal{N}^{(l)} = \mathbfcal{X}^{(l)} \times_1 \mathbf{U}_1^{(l)} \times_2 \cdots \times_K \mathbf{U}_K^{(l)} + \mathbfcal{B}^{(l)}. \tag{9}$$

Then it is not hard to prove the following lemma according to the derivative formula in [9]

Lemma 1. *Denote by* $K(l) = I_{l1} \cdot I_{l2} \cdots I_{lK}$ *(*$l = 0, 1, ..., L$*), then*

$$\left(\frac{\partial \mathbfcal{N}^{(l)}}{\partial \mathbfcal{X}^{(l-1)}} \right)_{(K^{(l)} \times K^{(l-1)})} = \mathbf{U}_K^{(l)} \otimes \cdots \otimes \mathbf{U}_1^{(l)}, \tag{10}$$

where the matriced form has been applied and $\otimes$ *means the Kronecker product of matrices.*

To save the space, we present the following derivative formulas in the following theorem without proof.

Theorem 1 (Backpropagation Derivatives). *Suppose the sigmoid activation function is applied on all the hidden layers of the tensorial neural networks, then the derivatives* $\frac{\partial \sigma^{(l)}(\mathbfcal{X}_t^{(l-1)})}{\partial \mathbfcal{W}^{(l)}}$ *and* $\frac{\partial \sigma^{(l)}(\mathbfcal{X}_t^{(l-1)})}{\partial \mathbfcal{X}_t^{(l-1)}}$ *used in the BP algorithm (7) and (8) can be calculated as follows,*

$$\frac{\partial \sigma^{(l)}(\mathbfcal{X}_t^{(l-1)})}{\partial \mathbfcal{X}_t^{(l-1)}} = \sigma'(\mathbfcal{N}^{(l)}) \frac{\partial \mathbfcal{N}_t^{(l)}}{\partial \mathbfcal{X}_t^{(l-1)}} = \sigma(\mathbfcal{N}_t^{(l)}) \odot (1 - \sigma(\mathbfcal{N}_t^{(l)})) \frac{\partial \mathbfcal{N}_t^{(l)}}{\partial \mathbfcal{X}_t^{(l-1)}}; \tag{11}$$

$$\frac{\partial \sigma^{(l)}(\mathbf{X}_t^{(l-1)})_{(k)}}{\partial \mathbf{U}_d^{(l)}} = [(\mathbf{U}_K^{(l)} \otimes \cdots \otimes \mathbf{U}_{k+1}^{(l)} \otimes \mathbf{U}_{k-1}^{(l)} \otimes \cdots \otimes \mathbf{U}_1^{(l)}) \mathbf{X}_{t(k)}^{(l-1)\top}] \otimes \mathbf{I}_{I_k}; \tag{12}$$

$$\frac{\partial \ell^{(l)}(\mathbfcal{X}_t^{(l-1)}, \mathbfcal{Y}_t)}{\partial \mathbfcal{B}^{(l)}} = \sigma(\mathbfcal{N}_t^{(l)}) \odot (1 - \sigma(\mathbfcal{N}_t^{(l)})) \odot \frac{\partial \ell^{(l+1)}(\mathbfcal{X}_t^{(l)}, \mathbfcal{Y}_t)}{\partial \mathbfcal{X}_t^l}. \tag{13}$$

where $\mathbf{M}_{(k)}$ *is the* k*-unfolded matrix of tensor* $\mathbfcal{M}$ *([3]),* $\mathbf{I}$ *is the identity matrix of relevant size, and* $\odot$ *means Hadamard product of tensors, i.e., the elementwise product.*

Remark: The backpropagation derivatives in the above theorem are presented for the case of sigmoid activation function. For any other activation function we can replace $\sigma'(\mathbf{N}^{(l)}) = \sigma(\mathbf{N}_t^{(l)}) \odot (1 - \sigma(\mathbf{N}_t^{(l)}))$. This is simply the derivative of activation function applied on a tensor elementwise.

It is easy to take (10) and (11)-(13) into (7) and (8) to implement the entire BP algorithm over the proposed tensorial neural networks. Our implementation in Mathwork® Matlab based on the tensor toolbox [10,11]. All the experiments were conducted on a laptop with a CPU Intel i7-4980HQ and an memory size of 16 GB.

3   Applications and Experiments

3.1   Longitudinal Network Data

To utilise the new method TNN in the real data, an empirical study should be conducted. In this study, the real data is collected from Integrated Crisis Warning System (ICEWS)[5] which is the same weekly dataset applied in the study of MLTR [4] for the relationship between 25 countries in four types of actions: material cooperation, material conflict, verbal cooperation and verbal conflict, from 2004 to mid-2014. Thus at any particular time point, the data is a 3D tensor of dimensions $25 \times 25 \times 4$. That is, each input $\mathbf{X}_t \in \mathbb{R}^{25 \times 25 \times 4}$. To explore different types of patterns often seen in relational data and social networks, we organise explanatory tensors $\mathbf{X}$ in the following different ways.

Case I: As done in [4] we construct the target tensor $\mathbf{y}_t$ at time t as the lagged $\mathbf{X}_{t-1}$. In total, we construct an overall dataset $\{(\mathbf{X}_t, \mathbf{y}_t)\}_{t=1}^{543}$ of size 543 in which all $\mathbf{X}_t$ and $\mathbf{y}_t$ are 3D tensors.

Case II: In order to explore the pattern of tendency for actions from one country to another country, we organise the explanatory tensor $\mathbf{X}_t \in \mathbb{R}^{25 \times 25 \times 8}$ such that $\mathbf{X}_t(i, j, k) = \mathbf{X}_t(j, i, k-4)$ for $k = 5, 6, 7, 8$ while keeping $\mathbf{y}_t$ unchanged from Case I. That is, slices $k = 5, 6, 7, 8$ are actually the transposed version of slices $k = 1, 2, 3, 4$ respectively.

Case III: To reveal third-order dependence known as transitivity among action data, we further extend the explanatory tensor as $\mathbf{X}_t \in \mathbb{R}^{25 \times 25 \times 12}$ such that, for $k = 9, 10, 11, 12$, $\mathbf{X}_t(i, j, k) = \sum_{l=1}^{25}(\mathbf{X}_t(i, l, k-8) + \mathbf{X}_t(l, i, k-8))$ $(\mathbf{X}_t(j, l, k-8) + \mathbf{X}_t(l, j, k-8))$.

To eliminate the missing values, the NaN elements in the tensors are transformed into 0. After standardising the dataset, the two tensors are split into the training set of the first 400 weeks with the size of $25 \times 25 \times 4$(or 8 or 12) $\times 400$ and the test set of the last 134 weeks with the size of $25 \times 25 \times 4$(or 8 or 12) $\times 134$.

3.2   Experiment Setting

For each of three cases described above, we train TNNs with two hidden layers also in tensor shape. We set the size of hidden layers $8 \times 8 \times 4$(or 8 or 12) and

---

[5] http://www.lockheedmartin.com/us/products/W-ICEWS/iData.html.

$12 \times 12 \times 4$(or 8 or 12) for one of three cases. For TNN training, we randomly initialize all the matrix parameters $\mathbf{U}$'s. To determine the appropriate value of the parameters λ and the sparsity ρ in the training loss function, we use the alternative grid search method to find the best λ and ρ which generate the smaller test errors over testing dataset. We obtained the proper λ's for *Case I*, *Case II* and *Case III* as 0.0012, 0.0017 and 0.15 respectively, and ρ's with 0.010, 0.012 and 0.019, respectively.

3.3 Experiment Results and Analysis

In all three cases, the output layer of TNN is a $25 \times 25 \times 4$ tensor, i.e., $\mathbf{\mathcal{Y}}_t$. The performance of TNN is evaluated based on the relationships revealed among 25 countries and the test error, which can demonstrate the sufficiency of the spatial information captured by TNN in the high-dimensional data. After training the TNN (with two hidden tensor layers), we collect weights matrices $\mathbf{U}_i^l$ with $i = 1, 2, 3$ and $l = 1, 2, 3$ where $i = 3$ refers to the action/reciprocity/transitivity mode. We suggest to define the following overall matrices

$$\mathbf{B}_1 = \mathbf{U}_1^{(3)} \times \mathbf{U}_1^{(2)} \times \mathbf{U}_1^{(1)}; \text{ and } \mathbf{B}_2 = \mathbf{U}_2^{(3)} \times \mathbf{U}_2^{(2)} \times \mathbf{U}_2^{(1)} \qquad (14)$$

and use them to infer the relationship among the 25 countries. The relation can be revealed in a network graph where each node represents each country and each arc with a number (the element in $\mathbf{B}_1$ or $\mathbf{B}_2$) represents the strength of the likelihood of the relationship between each pair of countries. Note both $\mathbf{B}_1$ and $\mathbf{B}_2$ contain the information from four actions (Case I), or four actions with reciprocity (Case II) or four actions with transitivity and reciprocity (Case III), respectively. For $\mathbf{B}_1$, each ij element reveals how likely there will be a relationship between Country i and Country k for each type of action, considering the reciprocity and transitivity information, given that there has been a relationship between Country j and Country k. Similarly, for $\mathbf{B}_2$, each lk element measures how likely there will be a relationship between Country j and Country l for each type of action, considering the reciprocity and transitivity information, given that there has been a relationship between Country j and Country k. Thus for $\mathbf{B}_1$ and $\mathbf{B}_2$ together, what they measure is that when there has been a relationship between Country j and k for each type of action considering reciprocity and transitivity, how likely there will be a relationship between Country i and Country l.

As a demonstration, Fig. 1 shows the relations revealed by TNN for Case I, where the color map shows the countries in the data. Similar results are shown in Fig. 2(a) and (d) for Case II. However more interesting findings are presented in Fig. 2(b), (c), (e) and (f). Both of them demonstrate the relations that are more likely to happen than not, i.e. with highest half chance to happen. It is clear to see that our method has revealed more informative results. The relational graphs of the results from MLTR demonstrates that MLTR does not provide necessary information on the relationships between countries, since the network is overcomplicated. It is hard to find any significant relationships between the

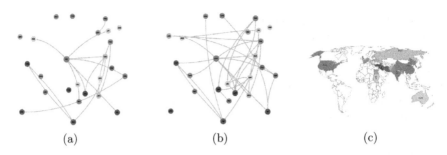

Fig. 1. Learned Coefficients of Networks for Case I: (a) $\mathbf{B}_1$; (b) $\mathbf{B}_2$ and (c) map with colour for referencing countries.

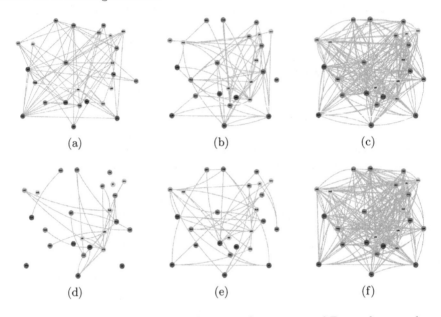

Fig. 2. Learned Coefficients of Networks $\mathbf{B}_1$ on the top row and $\mathbf{B}_2$ on the second row: Case II (a) and (d); Case III (b) and (e) (Our method), (c) and (f) (Hoff's model).

countries. On the contrary, TNN generates comparatively clearer relationships between the countries. From Fig. 2(b) and (e), we can see that Afghanistan, Iran, North Korea, Pakistan, USA, France, Lebanon, Russia, Ukraine and Syria are the centres of the international actions in the world. This result aligns with the common impression of the international relationship events during these decades. Thus TNN captures more structural international relationship information than the previous method MLTR in the longitudinal case.

4   Conclusion

This paper proposes the tensorial neural networks for learning from multidimensional data. We have derived the BP algorithm for the new neural networks and demonstrated the algorithm performance by applying the proposed method for the longitudinal network data. The experiment results show the new method can actually reveal the nonlinear relations which might be missed out the multiple linear regression models. We would also like to point out that the current method should be improved to have a more stable algorithm. All the mode transform matrices $\mathbf{U}$'s are regularised by the so-called ridge regulariser. However the ideal regularisation should be normalisation thus removing the identifiability of all the matrices in multiple production in the basic multiple linear transformation.

In general, TNN outperforms the previous method MLTR which is applied in longitudinal international relationship network analysis. TNN captures more structural information and reveals a more informative picture of the international relationships. This method has the significances in business, social science and science and technology fields. The application of TNN on the social network and international relationship networks is also novel in the machine learning field and the research on international relationship.

References

1. Minhas, S., Hoff, P.D., Ward, M.D.: A new approach to analyzing coevolving longitudinal networks in international relations. J. Peace Res. **53**(3), 491–505 (2016)
2. Wang, B., Hu, Y., Gao, J., Sun, Y., Yin, B.: Laplacian LRR on product grassmann manifolds for human activity clustering in multi-camera video surveillance. IEEE Trans. Circ. Syst. Video Technol. **27**(3), 554–566 (2017)
3. Kolda, T.G., Bader, B.W.: Tensor decompositions and applications. SIAM Rev. **51**(3), 455–500 (2009)
4. Hoff, P.D.: Multilinear tensor regression for longitudinal relational data. Ann. Appl. Stat. **9**(3), 1169–1193 (2015)
5. Gao, J., Guo, Y., Wang, Z.: Matrix neural networks. In: Cong, F., Leung, A., Wei, Q. (eds.) ISNN 2017. LNCS, vol. 10261, pp. 313–320. Springer, Cham (2017). doi:10.1007/978-3-319-59072-1_37
6. Chien, J.T., Bao, Y.T.: Tensor-factorized neural networks. IEEE Trans. Neural Netw. Learn. Syst. (2017), http://ieeexplore.ieee.org/document/7902201/
7. Bishop, C.M.: Pattern Recognition and Machine Learning. Information Science and Statistics. Springer, New York (2006)
8. Vedaldi, A., Lenc, K.: MatConvNet: convolutional neural networks for MATLAB. In: Proceedings of the 23rd ACM International Conference on Multimedia, MM 2015, NY, USA, pp. 689–692. ACM, New York (2015)
9. Kolda, T.G.: Multilinear Operators for Higher-Order Decompositions. Technical report, Sandia National Laboratories (2006)
10. Bader, B.W., Kolda, T.G., et al.: MATLAB Tensor Toolbox Version 2.6 (2015), http://www.sandia.gov/tgkolda/TensorToolbox/
11. Bader, B.W., Kolda, T.G.: Algorithm 862: MATLAB tensor classes for fast algorithm prototyping. ACM TOMS **32**(4), 635–653 (2006)

3HAN: A Deep Neural Network for Fake News Detection

Sneha Singhania$^{(\boxtimes)}$, Nigel Fernandez, and Shrisha Rao

International Institute of Information Technology - Bangalore, Bangalore, India
{sneha.a,nigelsteven.fernandez}@iiitb.org, shrao@ieee.org

Abstract. The rapid spread of fake news is a serious problem calling
for AI solutions. We employ a deep learning based automated detector
through a three level hierarchical attention network (3HAN) for fast,
accurate detection of fake news. 3HAN has three levels, one each for
words, sentences, and the headline, and constructs a news vector: an
effective representation of an input news article, by processing an article
in an hierarchical bottom-up manner. The headline is known to be a distinguishing feature of fake news, and furthermore, relatively few words
and sentences in an article are more important than the rest. 3HAN gives
a differential importance to parts of an article, on account of its three
layers of attention. By experiments on a large real-world data set, we
observe the effectiveness of 3HAN with an accuracy of 96.77%. Unlike
some other deep learning models, 3HAN provides an understandable output through the attention weights given to different parts of an article,
which can be visualized through a heatmap to enable further manual
fact checking.

Keywords: Fake news · Deep learning · Text representation · Attention
mechanism · Text classification

1 Introduction

The spread of fake news is a matter of concern due to its possible role in manipulating public opinion. We define fake news in line with The New York Times
as a "made up story with the intention to deceive, often with monetary gain as
a motive" [1]. The fake news problem is complex given its varied interpretations
across demographics.

We present a three level hierarchical attention network (3HAN) which creates
an effective representation of a news article called *news vector*. A news vector
can be used to classify an article by assigning a probability of being fake. Unlike
other neural models which are opaque in their internal reasoning and give results
that are difficult to analyze, 3HAN provides an importance score for each word
and sentence of an input article based on its relevance in arriving at the output
probability of that article being fake. These importance scores can be visualized

---

S. Singhania and N. Fernandez—These authors contributed equally to this work.

D. Liu et al. (Eds.): ICONIP 2017, Part II, LNCS 10635, pp. 572–581, 2017.
https://doi.org/10.1007/978-3-319-70096-0_59

through a heatmap, providing key words and sentences to be investigated by human fact-checkers.

Current work in detecting misinformation is divided between automated fact checking [2], reaction based analysis [3] and style based analysis [4]. We explore the nascent domain of using neural models to detect fake news. Current state-of-the-art general purpose text classifiers like Bag-of-words [5], Bag-of-ngrams with SVM [6], CNNs, LSTMs and GRUs [7] can be used to classify articles by simply concatenating the headline with the body. This concatenation though, fails to exploit the article structure.

In 3HAN, we interpret the structure of an article as a three level hierarchy modelling article semantics on the principle of compositionality [8]. Words form sentences, sentences form the body and the headline with the body forms the article. We hypothesize forming an effective representation of an article using the hierarchy and the interactions between its parts. These interactions take the form of context of a word in its neighbouring words, coherence of a sentence with its neighbouring sentences and stance of a headline with respect to the body. Words, sentences and headline are differentially informative dependent on their interactions in the formation of a news vector. We incorporate three layers of attention mechanisms [9] to exploit this differential relevance.

The design of 3HAN is inspired by the hierarchical attention network (HAN) [10]. HAN is used to form a general document representation. We design 3HAN unique to the detection of fake news. When manually fact-checking an article the first thing that catches the eye is the headline. We observe a headline to be (i) a distinctive feature of an article [11], (ii) a concise summary of the article body and (iii) inherently containing useful information in the form of its stance with respect to the body. We refer to these observations as our *headline premise*. The third level in 3HAN is especially designed to use our headline premise.

From our headline premise, we hypothesize that a neural model should accurately classify articles based on headlines alone. Using this hypothesis, we use headlines to perform a supervised pre-training of the initial layers of 3HAN for a better initialization of 3HAN. The visualization of attention layers in 3HAN indicates important parts of an article instrumental in detecting an article as fake news. These important parts can be further investigated by human fact-checkers.

We compare the performance of 3HAN with multiple state-of-the-art traditional and neural baselines. Experiments on a large real world news data set demonstrate the superior performance of 3HAN over all baselines with 3HAN performing with an accuracy of 96.24%. Our pre-trained 3HAN model is our best performing model with an accuracy of 96.77%.[1]

2   Model Design

The architecture of 3HAN is shown in Fig. 1. We define a news vector as a projection of a news article into a vector representation suitable for effective

---

[1] Our code is available at: https://github.com/ni9elf/3HAN.

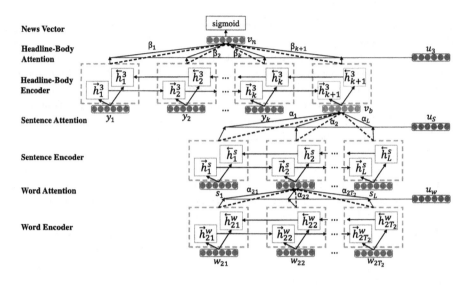

Fig. 1. Model Architecture of 3HAN

classification of articles. A news vector is constructed using 3HAN. To capture the body hierarchy and interactions between parts when forming the news vector, 3HAN uses the following parts from HAN [10]: word sequence encoder, word level attention (Layer 1), sentence encoder, sentence level attention (Layer 2). In addition to the preceding parts, we exploit our headline premise by adding: headline-body encoder and headline-body level attention (Layer 3).

Sequence Encoder using GRU. A Gated Recurrent Unit (GRU) [12] adaptively captures dependencies between sequential input sequences over time. Gating signals control how the previous hidden state h_{t-1} and current input x_t generate an intermediate hidden state $\tilde{h}_t$ to update the current hidden state h_t. GRU consists of a reset gate r_t and an update gate z_t. r_t determines how to combine x_t with h_{t-1} while z_t determines how much of h_{t-1} and $\tilde{h}_t$ to use. $\odot$ denotes the Hadamard product. The GRU model is presented at time t as:

$$\tilde{h}_t = \tanh\left(W_h x_t + U_h\left(r_t \odot h_{t-1}\right) + b_h\right) \tag{1}$$

$$h_t = (1 - z_t) \odot h_{t-1} + z_t \odot \tilde{h}_t \tag{2}$$

with the gates presented as:

$$z_t = \sigma\left(W_z x_t + U_z h_{t-1} + b_z\right), \; r_t = \sigma\left(W_r x_t + U_r h_{t-1} + b_r\right) \tag{3}$$

Word Encoder. We denote word j of sentence i by w_{ij} with sentence i containing T_i words. Each word w_{ij} is converted to a word embedding x_{ij} using GloVe [13] embedding W_e ($x_{ij} = W_e\left(w_{ij}\right)$). We use a bidirectional GRU [9] to form an annotation of each word which summarizes the *context* of the word with preceding and following words in the sentence. A bidirectional GRU consists of a forward $\overrightarrow{\text{GRU}}$ and backward $\overleftarrow{\text{GRU}}$. The overhead arrow in our notation does not denote a vector, it instead denotes the direction of the GRU run. $\overrightarrow{\text{GRU}}$ reads the word embedding sequence ordered $(x_{i1}, x_{i2}, \ldots, x_{iT_i})$ to form forward annotations using hidden states $\left(\overrightarrow{h}{}_{i1}^{w}, \overrightarrow{h}{}_{i2}^{w}, \ldots, \overrightarrow{h}{}_{iT_i}^{w} \right)$. Similarly $\overleftarrow{\text{GRU}}$ reads the word embedding sequence ordered $(x_{iT_i}, x_{iT_i-1}, \ldots, x_{i1})$ to form backward annotations $\left(\overleftarrow{h}{}_{iT_i}^{w}, \overleftarrow{h}{}_{iT_i-1}^{w}, \ldots, \overleftarrow{h}{}_{i1}^{w} \right)$. h_{ij}^{w} is formed as $\left[\overrightarrow{h}{}_{ij}^{w}, \overleftarrow{h}{}_{ij}^{w} \right]$ (concatenation).

$$\overrightarrow{h}{}_{ij}^{w} = \overrightarrow{\text{GRU}}\left(x_{ik}\right), k \in [1, j] \tag{4}$$

$$\overleftarrow{h}{}_{ij}^{w} = \overleftarrow{\text{GRU}}\left(x_{ik}\right), k \in [T_i, j] \tag{5}$$

$$h_{ij}^{w} = \left[\overrightarrow{h}{}_{ij}^{w}, \overleftarrow{h}{}_{ij}^{w} \right] \tag{6}$$

Word Attention. A sentence representation is formed using an attention layer to extract relevant words of a sentence. The word annotation h_{ij}^{w} is fed through a one-layer MLP to get a hidden representation u_{ij} [10]. The similarity of each word u_{ij} with a *word level relevance vector* u_w decides the attention weights α_{ij} normalized using a softmax function [10]. The sentence encoding s_i is a weighted attentive sum of the word annotations. The relevance vector can be interpreted as representing the contextually most relevant word over all words in the sentence. u_w is fixed over all inputs as a global parameter of our model and jointly learned in the training process.

$$u_{ij} = \tanh\left(W_w h_{ij}^{w} + b_w \right) \tag{7}$$

$$\alpha_{ij} = \frac{\exp\left(u_{ij}^T u_w \right)}{\sum_j \exp\left(u_{ij}^T u_w \right)}, \; s_i = \sum_j \alpha_{ij} h_{ij}^{w} \tag{8}$$

Sentence Encoder. Similar to the word encoder, a bidirectional GRU is applied to $(s_1, s_2, \ldots, s_L)$ to compute the forward annotations $\overrightarrow{h}{}_{i}^{s}$ and backward annotations $\overleftarrow{h}{}_{i}^{s}$ for each sentence. These annotations capture the *coherence* of a sentence with respect to its neighbouring sentences in both directions of the body. h_i^s is formed as $\left[\overrightarrow{h}{}_{i}^{s}, \overleftarrow{h}{}_{i}^{s} \right]$.

Sentence Attention. Similar to word attention, we identify relevant sentences in the formation of the body vector v_b by using an attention layer. A *sentence level relevance vector* u_s decides attention weights α_i for sentence annotation h_i^s. u_s can be interpreted as representing the coherently most relevant sentence over all sentences in the body. v_b is composed using $\sum_i \alpha_i h_i^s$.

Headline Encoder. To exploit our headline premise we design a third layer of encoding and attention with the headline being inputted word by word. We denote the k words of the headline by w_{01} to w_{0k}. The word embedding y_i for word w_{0i} is obtained using GloVe embeddings (W_e) by $y_i = W_e(w_{0i})$. We denote v_b as y_{k+1}. A bidirectional GRU is run on $(y_1, y_2, \ldots, y_{k+1})$ to compute the forward and backward annotations of each word. These annotations capture the *stance of the headline* words with respect to the body word. The digit 3 in our notation denotes the third level. h_i^3 is formed as $\left[\overrightarrow{h}_i^3, \overleftarrow{h}_i^3\right]$.

$$\overrightarrow{h}_i^3 = \overrightarrow{\mathrm{GRU}}\left(y_j\right), j \in [1, i], \ \overleftarrow{h}_i^3 = \overleftarrow{\mathrm{GRU}}\left(y_j\right), j \in [k+1, i] \qquad (9)$$

Headline Attention. A *relevance vector* u_3 is used to compute the attention weights β_i for annotation h_i^3. The news vector v_n is formed as the weighted sum of the annotations h_i^3 with β_i as the weights.

$$u_i = \tanh\left(W_3 h_i^3 + b_3\right) \qquad (10)$$

$$\beta_i = \frac{\exp\left(u_i^T u_3\right)}{\sum_i \exp\left(u_i^T u_3\right)}, \ v_n = \sum_i \beta_i h_i^3 \qquad (11)$$

News Vector for Classification. We use the news vector v_n as a feature vector for classification. We use the sigmoid layer $z = \mathrm{sigmoid}\left(W_c v_n + b_c\right)$ as our classifier with binary cross-entropy loss $L = -\sum_d p_d \log q_d$ to train 3HAN. In the loss function q_d is the predicted probability and p_d is the ground truth label (either fake or genuine) of article d.

Supervised Pre-training using Headlines We propose a supervised pre-training of Layer 1 consisting of the word encoder and an attention layer of 3HAN for a better initialization of the model. The pre-training is performed using the headlines only. The output label for a headline input is the corresponding article label.

3   Experiments

3.1   News Data Set

Due to the high turnaround time of manual fact-checking, the number of available manually fact-checked articles is too few to train deep neural models. We shift our fact-checked requirement from an article level to a website level. Keeping with our definition of fake news, we assume that every article from a website shares the same label (fake or genuine) as its containing website. PolitiFact [14] a respected fact-checking website released a list of sites manually investigated and labelled. We use those sites from this list labelled fake. Forbes [15] compiled a list of popular genuine sites across US demographics. Statistics of our data set is provided in Table 1. To maintain a similar distribution as fake articles, we use genuine articles from January 1, 2016 to June 1, 2017, with 65% coming from the 2016 US elections and politics, 15% from world news, 15% from regional news and 5% from entertainment.

3.2   Baselines

To validate the effectiveness of our model, we compare 3HAN with current state-of-the-art traditional and deep learning models. The input is the article text formed by concatenating the headline with the body.

Table 1. Dataset Statistics: (average words per sentence, average sentences per article)

Type	Sites	Articles	Average Words	Average Sentences
Fake	19	20,372	34.20	16.44
Genuine	9	20,932	32.78	27.55

Word Count Based Models. These methods use a hand crafted feature vector derived from variations of frequency of words of an article. A binomial logistic regression is used as the classifier.

1. *Majority* uses the heuristic of taking the majority label in the training set as the assigning label to every point in the test set.
2. *Bag-of-words and its TF-IDF* constructs a vocabulary of the most frequent 50,000 words [5]. The count of these words is used as features. The TF-IDF count is used as features in the other model variant.
3. *Bag-of-ngrams and its TF-IDF* uses the count of the 50,000 most frequent ngrams ($n <= 5$). The features are formed as in the previous model.
4. *SVM+Bigrams* uses the count of the 50,000 most frequent bigrams as features with an SVM classifier [6].

Neural Models. The classifier used is a dense sigmoid layer.

1. *GloVe-Ave* flattens the article text to a word level granularity as a sequence of words. The GloVe embeddings of all words are averaged to form the feature vector.
2. *GRU* treats the article text as a sequence of words. A GRU with an annotation dimension of 300 is run on the sequence of GloVe word embeddings. The hidden annotation after the last time step is used as the feature vector.
3. *GRU-Ave* runs a GRU on the sequence of word embeddings and returns all hidden annotations at each time step. The average of these hidden annotations is used as the feature vector.
4. *HAN and Variants* include HAN-Ave, Han-Max and HAN [10]. HAN uses a two level hierarchical attention network. HAN-Ave and Han-Max replaces the attention mechanism with average and max pooling for composition respectively. Since the code is not officially released we use our own implementation.

3.3 Experimental Settings

We split sentences of bodies and tokenized sentences and headlines into words using Stanford CoreNLP [16]. We lower cased and cleaned tokens by retaining alphabets, numerals and significant punctuation marks. When building the vocabulary we retained words with frequency more than 5. We treat words appearing exactly 5 times as a special single unknown token (UNK). We used 100 dimensional GloVe embeddings to initialize our word embedding matrix and allowed it to be fine tuned. For missing words in GloVe, we initialized their word embedding from a uniform distribution on $(-0.25, 0.25)$ [17].

We padded (or truncated) each sentence and headline to an average word count of 32 and each article to an average sentence count of 21. Hyper parameters are tuned on the validation set. We used 100 dimensional GloVe embeddings and 50 dimensional GRU annotations giving a combined annotation of 100 dimensions. The relevance vector at word, sentence and headline-body level are of 100 dimensions trained as a parameter of our model. We used SGD with a learning rate of 0.01, momentum of 0.9 and mini batch size of 32 to train all neural models. Accuracy was our evaluation metric since our data set is balanced.

3.4   Results and Analysis

We used a train, validation and test split of 20% | 10% | 70% for neural models and a train and test split of 30% | 70% for word count based models. In 3HAN-Ave vectors are composed using average, in 3HAN-Max vectors are composed using max pooling, 3HAN is our proposed model with an attention mechanism for composition and 3HAN+PT denotes our pre-trained 3HAN model. Results are reported in Table 2 and demonstrate the effectiveness of 3HAN and 3HAN+PT due to their best performance over all models.

Neural models using the hierarchical structure (HAN and variants, 3HAN and variants) give a higher accuracy than other baselines. The attention mechanism is a more effective composition operator than average or max pooling.

Table 2. Accuracy in Article Classification as Fake or Genuine

Word Count Based Models

Model	Accuracy
Majority	49.42%
Bag-of-words	90.21%
Bag-of-words +TFIDF	91.92%
Bag-of-ngrams	91.41%
Bag-of-ngrams +TFIDF	92.47%
SVM+Bigrams	83.12%

Neural Network Models

Model	Accuracy
GloVe-Ave	93.63%
GRU	91.11%
GRU-Ave	95.65%
HAN-Ave	94.91%
HAN-Max	94.66%
HAN	95.4%
3HAN-Ave	94.81%
3HAN-Max	95.25%
3HAN	**96.24%**
3HAN+PT	**96.77%**

This is demonstrated by the higher accuracy of 3HAN against 3HAN-Ave and 3HAN-Max. Our headline premise is valid since 3HAN which devotes a separate third level in the hierarchy for the headline performs better than HAN. HAN is indifferent to the headline and focuses its two hierarchical levels only on words and sentences. Pre-training helps in better initialization of 3HAN with 3HAN+PT outperforming 3HAN.

4   Discussion and Insights

The visualization of attention layers provides evidence. An advantage of attention based neural models is the visualization of attention layers which provides insight into the internal classification process. On the other hand, non-attention based models work like a black box. 3HAN provides attention weights to words, sentences and headline of an article. These attention weights are useful for further human fact-checking. A human fact-checker can focus on verifying sentences with high attention weights. Similarly, words with high attention weights can be investigated for inaccuracies.

We visualize the attention weights given to words, sentences and the headline for a sample article through a heatmap in Fig. 2. The sentences with the top five attention weights and the first eight words in each sentence are shown for clarity. Word attention weights α_w are normalized using sentence attention weights α_s by $\alpha_w = \sqrt{\alpha_s}\alpha_w$. Sentence attention weights are shown on the extreme left edge. We observe that sentence 5 and has been assigned the highest weight (0.287). Interestingly, sentence 5 which states "Even refugee welcoming Canada levies a 12 percent penalty on immigrant money" is a factually incorrect sentence.

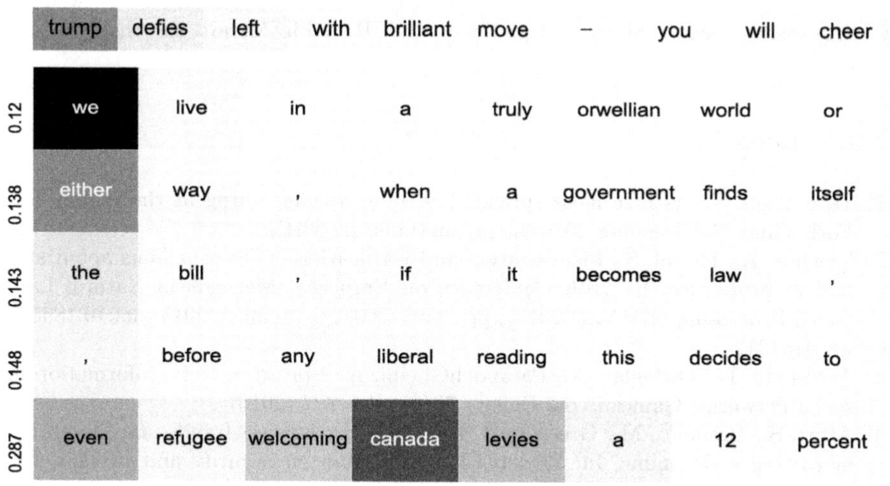

Fig. 2. Visualization of Attention Layers in a Fake News Article with Headline "Trump Defies Left with Brilliant Move - You Will Cheer"

Word count based models perform well. The high accuracy of simple word count based models which do not take into account word ordering or semantics is an indication of vocabulary and patterns of word usage from the vocabulary being a distinguishing feature between fake news and true news.

The attention mechanism is effective. This is observed through the superior performance of HAN compared to non-attention based 3HAN-Max and 3HAN-Ave.

Our headline premise is valid. This is observed from the superior performance of 3HAN to HAN with the third hierarchical level of 3HAN especially designed for our headline premise playing a role.

The inverted pyramid style of writing is used. Inverted pyramid refers to distributing information in decreasing importance in an article. We inferred the usage of the inverted pyramid through our experiments from the small improvement in accuracy even with higher padding sentence counts. Fake news articles tend to be repetitive in information content [11].

5   Conclusion and Future Work

In this paper, we presented 3HAN which creates news vector, an effective representation of an article for detection as fake news. We demonstrated the superior accuracy of 3HAN over other state-of-the-art models. We highlighted the use of visualization of the attention layers. We plan to deploy a web application based on 3HAN which provides detection of fake news as a service and learns in a real time online manner from new manually fact-checked articles.

Acknowledgements. We thank the anonymous ICONIP reviewers as well as G. Srinivasaraghavan, Shreyak Upadhyay and Rishabh Manoj for their helpful comments.

References

1. Tavernisen, S.: As fake news spreads lies, more readers shrug at the truth. New York Times, 6 December 2016. http://nyti.ms/2lw56HN
2. Vlachos, A., Riedel, S.: Identification and verification of simple claims about statistical properties. In: 20th Conference on Empirical Methods in Natural Language Processing (EMNLP 2015), pp. 2596–2601, September 2015. doi:10.18653/v1/d151312
3. Acemoglu, D., Ozdaglar, A., ParandehGheibi, A.: Spread of (mis) information in social networks. Games Econ. Behav. **70**(2), 194–227 (2010)
4. Afroz, S., Brennan, M., Greenstadt, R.: Detecting hoaxes, frauds, and deception in writing style online. In: 33rd IEEE Symposium on Security and Privacy (SP 2012), pp. 461–475. IEEE, May 2012
5. Joachims, T.: Text categorization with Support Vector Machines: Learning with many relevant features. In: Nédellec, C., Rouveirol, C. (eds.) ECML 1998. LNCS, vol. 1398, pp. 137–142. Springer, Heidelberg (1998). doi:10.1007/BFb0026683

6. Wang, S., Manning, C.D.: Baselines and bigrams: Simple, good sentiment and topic classification. In: 50th Annual Meeting of the Association for Computational Linguistics (ACL 2012), pp. 90–94, July 2012

7. Tang, D., Qin, B., Liu, T.: Document modeling with gated recurrent neural network for sentiment classification. In: 20th Conference on Empirical Methods in Natural Language Processing (EMNLP 2015), pp. 1422–1432, September 2015

8. Frege, G.: Sense and reference. Philos. Rev. **57**(3), 209–230 (1948)

9. Bahdanau, D., Cho, K., Bengio, Y.: Neural machine translation by jointly learning to align and translate. In: 3rd International Conference on Learning Representations (ICLR 2015), May 2015

10. Yang, Z., Yang, D., Dyer, C., He, X., Smola, A., Hovy, E.: Hierarchical attention networks for document classification. In: 15th Annual Conference of the North American Chapter of the Association for Computational Linguistics: Human Language Technologies (NAACL HLT 2016), pp. 1480–1489, June 2016

11. Horne, B., Adali, S.: This just in: fake news packs a lot in title, uses simpler, repetitive content in text body, more similar to satire than real news. In: Workshop of the 11th International AAAI Conference on Web and Social Media (ICWSM 2017), May 2017

12. Cho, K., Van Merriënboer, B., Gulcehre, C., Bahdanau, D., Bougares, F., Schwenk, H., Bengio, Y.: Learning phrase representations using rnn encoder-decoder for statistical machine translation. In: 19th Conference on Empirical Methods in Natural Language Processing (EMNLP 2014), pp. 1724–1734, October 2014

13. Pennington, J., Socher, R., Manning, C.D.: Glove: Global vectors for word representation. In: 19th Conference on Empirical Methods in Natural Language Processing (EMNLP 2014), pp. 1532–1543, October 2014

14. Gillin, J.: Politifact's guide to fake news websites and what they peddle. Pundit-Fact, 20 April 2017. http://bit.ly/2pHYKDV

15. Glader, P.: 10 journalism brands where you find real facts rather than alternative facts. Forbes, 1 February 2017. http://bit.ly/2sXPpvf

16. Manning, C.D., Surdeanu, M., Bauer, J., Finkel, J., Bethard, S.J., McClosky, D.: The Stanford CoreNLP natural language processing toolkit. In: 52nd Annual Meeting of the Association for Computational Linguistics (ACL 2014), pp. 55–60, June 2014

17. Kim, Y.: Convolutional neural networks for sentence classification. In: 19th Conference on Empirical Methods in Natural Language Processing (EMNLP 2014), pp. 1746–1751, October 2014

Hierarchical Parameter Sharing in Recursive Neural Networks with Long Short-Term Memory

Fengyu Li[1(✉)], Mingmin Chi[2], Dong Wu[2], and Junyu Niu[2]

[1] Software School, Fudan University, Shanghai, China
lifengyu@fudan.edu.cn
[2] School of Computer Science, Fudan University, Shanghai, China
mmchi@fudan.edu.cn

Abstract. Parameter Sharing (or weight sharing) is widely used in Neural Networks, such as Recursive Neural Networks (RvNNs) and its variants, to control model complexities and extract prior knowledge. The parameter sharing in RvNNs for language model assumes that non-leaf nodes in treebanks are generated by similar semantic compositionality, where hidden units of all the non-leaf nodes in RvNNs share model parameters. However, treebanks have several semantic levels with significantly different semantic compositionality. Accordingly, this leads to a poor classification performance if nodes in high semantic levels share the same parameters with those in low levels. In the paper, a novel parameter sharing strategy in a hierarchical manner is proposed over Long Short-Term Memory (LSTM) cells in Recursive Neural Networks, denoted as shLSTM-RvNN, in which weight connections in hidden units are clustered according to hierarchical semantic levels defined in Penn Treebank tagsets. Accordingly, the parameters in the same semantic level can be shared but those in different semantic levels should have different sets of connections weights. The proposed shLSTM-RvNN model is evaluated in benchmark data sets containing semantic compositionality. Empirical results show that the shLSTM-RvNN model increases classification accuracies but significantly reduces time complexities.

Keywords: Recursive neural networks · Long short-term memory networks · Sentiment analysis · Parameter sharing

1 Introduction

Parameter sharing (or weight sharing) has been widely used in neural networks to control model complexities [1–3]. Here, parameter sharing refers to clusters of weights shared among many connections in network connections so that it reduces model complexities yet with a better generalization of neural networks. To make parameter sharing effective, it is important to specify in advance which parameters should be identical in problems being addressed such that the parameters can be shared in network connections with similar properties or structures [4].

© Springer International Publishing AG 2017
D. Liu et al. (Eds.): ICONIP 2017, Part II, LNCS 10635, pp. 582–592, 2017.
https://doi.org/10.1007/978-3-319-70096-0_60

This idea of parameter sharing has been successfully applied to Convolutional Neural Networks (CNNs) [3] and Recurrent Neural Networks (RNNs) [5–7].

Language models are usually modeled by a RNN network with a recursive structure, i.e., Recursive Neural Networks (RvNNs) [8]. The RvNN networks inherits the idea of parameter sharing but nodes are connected in a recursive structure defined by Penn Treebank [9]. In RvNN networks, all semantic structures are projected into a low dimensional vector space represented by units in hidden layers, where the connections from hidden layers to output ones share the same parameters in all the nodes. In this way, it assumes that all semantic relationships from children nodes to parent nodes follow the same pattern of compositionality. According to Penn Treebank tagsets, non-leaf nodes can be grouped to at least three semantic levels, such as words, phrases and clauses. Therefore, it violates the idea of parameter sharing in which nodes with the same structure share the connection weights. Usually, Long Short-Term Memory (LSTM) is designed to capture long-term temporal dependencies in RNN networks by introducing a memory cell and input/output gates to solve the gradient exploding or vanishing problem in recurrent neural networks [10,11].

In the paper, a hierarchical strategy of parameter sharing is proposed over simplified Long Short-Term Memory cells in Recursive Neural Networks to extract different semantic composition patterns in treebank, which is denoted as shLSTM-RvNN. In particular, parameters of hidden LSTM cells are clustered hierarchically into word, phrase and clause levels based on types of node tags defined in Penn Treebank tagsets. Here, nodes of the same hierarchy share the same connection weights, while those in different hierarchies use different sets of parameters. The proposed shLSTM-RvNN model is evaluated in the benchmark data sets containing semantic compositionality, i.e., sentiment analysis on Stanford Sentiment Treebank and semantic relatedness on SICK (Sentences Involving Compositional Knowledge) data set.

According to the statistics of different sentiment compositions, three different strategies of clustering Penn Treebank tagsets are adopted to cluster tagsets into semantic levels. Empirical results show that it outperforms state-of-art RNN, RvNN and LSTM networks by increasing classification accuracies of nodes not only in sentence level, but all the nodes of treebank. By clustering Penn Treebank tagsets, our model achieves better classification accuracies over all nodes compared to the state-of-the-art. Simultaneously, it can significantly decrease computational complexities.

The rest of the paper is organized as follows. The next section describes the preliminary work on Recursive Neural Networks (RvNNs) and Long Short-Term Memory (LSTM) model. In the following, a novel strategy for parameter sharing in a hierarchy is proposed for weight connections over the LSTM-RvNN model, denoted as shLSTM-RvNN in Sect. 3. Section 4 illustrates the data sets used in the experiments, and reports and discusses the results provided by the proposed shLSTM-RvNN model and state-of-the-art neural networks. Finally, Sect. 5 draws the conclusions of this paper.

2   Preliminary Works

A treebank is a parsed text corpus that annotates a syntactic or semantic sentence structure in linguistics [12] and the popular structure is in a tree schema for the ease of reading. To model the semantic compositionality of treebank in natural language, Recursive Neural Networks are often introduced to model recursive semantic structures, where words, phrases, and clauses can be projected into the same vector space [8], and thus all the semantic structures can be classified with unique text classifier.

To attack the problem of gradient vanishing, the hierarchical strategy is carried out over LSTM cells in Recursive Neural Networks (RvNNs). In the following, Recursive Neural Networks is firstly introduced in recursive grammar structures with parameter sharing. Next, LSTM cells in RvNN networks are briefly described based on recently proposed work in [13,14], where [13] also includes peephole connections to the model, denoted as LSTMp-RvNN in the paper.

2.1   Recursive Neural Networks

As shown in Fig. 1(a), every node is a fully connected three-layer neural network connected recursively with its parent node. There are two types of nodes in RvNNs: leaf nodes and non-leaf nodes. Leaf nodes get external word vectors as inputs, predict with fully connected networks with activation function of σ, and share parameters with other leaf nodes, as denoted by green hidden units in Fig. 1(a).

The three-layer neural networks with yellow hidden units are non-leaf nodes, which get hidden layers of children as inputs, propogate through fully connected networks and activation function of σ, and share parameters with other non-leaf nodes, as denoted in Eq. 1.

$$
\begin{aligned}
h_t &= \sigma(W_L^{(n)} h_L + W_R^{(n)} h_R + b^{(w)}), \\
o_t &= f(W_s h_t + b_s),
\end{aligned}
\tag{1}
$$

where W_s is the fully connected parameters from hidden layer to output layer, $W_{L^{(n)}}$ and $W_{R^{(n)}}$ are full connected parameters from left hidden layer h_L and right hidden layer h_R of parent nodes, respectively.

2.2   LSTM Cells in Recursive Neural Networks

The key idea in Long Short-Term Memory (LSTM) neural network [11] and its variants [13–17] is to introduce memory cells to maintain states over time and to solve the gradient exploding or vanishing problem in recurrent neural networks [10]. Long Short-Term Memory is extended to a hierarchical structure in Recursive Neural Networks, where a memory cell can reflect the history memories of multiple child cells [13,14].

LSTM cells in Recursive Neural Networks inherit LSTM structures in Recurrent Neural Networks by introducing two forget gates controlling the information

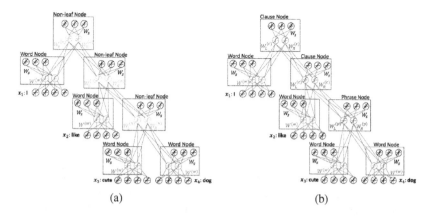

(a)   (b)

Fig. 1. Language Models with LSTM cell in Recursive Structures with parameter sharing in the traditional way shown in (a) and in a hierarchical way shown in (b), where, green units denote shared parameters in leaf nodes (word level), yellow units in non-leaf nodes, blue units in phrase level, and red units in clause level.

flow from two children to their parent. At each time t for non-leaf nodes, the LSTM cell is composed of a collection of vectors in $\mathcal{R}_d$: an input gate i_t, a left forget gate f_t^L, a right forget gate f_t^R, an output gate o_t, an update gate u_t, a memory cell c_t, and a hidden state h_t, where d is the memory dimension of the LSTM cells. And leaf nodes get inputs from word vectors.

3   LSTM Networks with Hierarchical Parameter Sharing

The LSTM-RvNN model described above shares parameters within leaf nodes and non-leaf nodes, respectively, as the structures in leaf and non-leaf nodes are significantly different. Furthermore, non-leaf nodes can be clustered to phrases and clauses levels based on the definition of Penn Treebank, which is shown in Table 1. According to the idea of parameter sharing, weight sharing of non-leaf nodes in the proposed model is carried out in a hierarchical way in terms of different semantic levels, i.e., phrase and clause levels.

In the recently proposed LSTM-RvNN models [13,14], all leaf and non-leaf nodes have input gates shown in Fig. 2(a). However, non-leaf nodes receive information from the hidden layers of their left and right children and they can ignore input gates. Accordingly, LSTM models can be simplified to be introduced in the following.

3.1   Simplified Version of LSTM Cells

After removing input gates in non-leaf nodes, the LSTM cells can be simplified to two structures: leaf structure with input gates (word vectors as input) shown in Fig. 2(c) and non-leaf structure without input gates shown in Fig. 2(b).

Accordingly, output, left and right forget, hidden gates in non-leaf nodes can be summarized as follows:

$$o_t = \sigma(W_{L(o)}h_L + W_{R(o)}h_R + b_{(o)}),$$
$$f_t^L = \sigma(W_{L(fl)}h_L + W_{R(fl)}h_R + b_{(fl)}),$$
$$f_t^R = \sigma(W_{L(fr)}h_L + W_{R(fr)}h_R + b_{(fr)}), \qquad (2)$$
$$c_t = f_t^L \times c_{t-1}^L + f_t^R \times c_{t-1}^R,$$
$$h_t = o_t \times tanh(c_t),$$

As shown in Sect. 4.5, the simplified version of LSTM-RvNN model, denoted as sLSTM-RvNN, slightly improves classification accuracies, while it can significantly reduces temporal and spatial complexities. The modified LSTM model can help to reduce spatial complexity of the proposed hierarchical parameter sharing strategy. Note that the two models have the same structure in leaf nodes shown in Fig. 2(c).

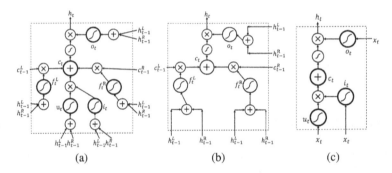

Fig. 2. Structures of LSTM cells: recently proposed LSTM models in [14] and in [13] without peephole connections shown in (a), non-leaf structure of simplified LSTM cells shown in (b), and leaf structure of simplified LSTM cells shown in (c).

3.2 Hierarchical Parameter Sharing

In LSTM cells of RvNN networks, leaf nodes are grouped to the cluster in word level with shared parameters $W^{(w)}$. Furthermore, non-leaf nodes are clustered in phrase and clause levels and thus connection weights are shared in the corresponding level of non-leaf nodes in a hierarchical way, denoted as hLSTM-RvNN. The structure is shown in Fig. 1(b), where green units denote shared parameters in leaf nodes (word level), blue and red units show parameter sharing in phrase and clause levels respectively, in non-leaf nodes. Similar to (2), output, left and right forget, and hidden gates in non-leaf nodes can be summarized as follows:

$$o_t = \sigma(W_{L(o)}^{(s)} h_L + W_{R(o)}^{(s)} h_R + b_{(o)}^{(s)}),$$
$$f_t^L = \sigma(W_{L(fl)}^{(s)} h_L + W_{R(fl)}^{(s)} h_R + b_{(fl)}^{(s)}),$$
$$f_t^R = \sigma(W_{L(fr)}^{(s)} h_L + W_{R(fr)}^{(s)} h_R + b_{(fr)}^{(s)}),$$
$$c_t = f_t^L \times c_{t-1}^L + f_t^R \times c_{t-1}^R,$$
$$h_t = o_t \times tanh(c_t),$$

$$(3)$$

where $W_{L(g)}^{(s)}$, $W_{R(g)}^{(s)}$ and $b_{(g)}^{(s)}$ (g representing o, fl, and fr) are parameters shared in cluster p, and are assigned by the following strategy:

$$W_{L(g)}^{(s)} = \begin{cases} W_{L(g)}^{(c)} & \text{node t in clause level,} \\ \\ W_{L(g)}^{(p)} & \text{node t in phrase level.} \end{cases} \qquad (4)$$

In the following, a hybrid LSTM model is proposed to integrate LSTM cells in a simplified version and LSTM cells in hierarchical parameter sharing, denoted as shLSTM-RvNN. Experimental results show that the shLSTM-RvNN model can achieve the best classification performance with less temporal complexity compared to the state-of-the-art.

3.3 Prediction

In recursive structure, each node will be given a class label $\hat{y}$ from a discrete set of classes Φ, and the class label of each node is assigned to the subtree whose root is that node. Two NLP tasks, i.e., sentiment analysis and sentiment relatedness, are adopted to validate the effectiveness of representing semantic features of texts classified by the proposed LSTM model and the variants of LSTM, RNN and RvNN networks in the following.

Sentiment Analysis. In this task, at each node a softmax classifier is applied to predict the label $\hat{y}_t$. The hidden state h_t at the node is input to the classifier.

$$\hat{p}_\theta(y|x_t) = softmax(W^{(s)} h_t + b^{(s)}),$$
$$\hat{y}_t = argmax_y \hat{p}_\theta(y|x_t),$$

$$(5)$$

where θ is a set of model parameters, $W^{(s)}$ is a $d \times m$ matrix, and $b^{(s)}$ is a m-dimension vector, in which m is the number of classes.

Semantic Relatedness. The task of semantic relatedness is to predict sentence relatedness in pair. For example, 'car' is related to 'road' and 'driving'. Score of relatedness is in $[1, K]$ where $K > 1$ is an integer, and a higher score indicates a greater degree of relatedness. In the tree-structured network, two sentences can be represented by two hidden vectors, h^L and h^R, respectively. According to [14], the relatedness score $\hat{y}$ between two generated representations can be calculated by a two-layer neural network, in which both distance and angle of the representations are as inputs.

4   Experimental Results

To validate the effectiveness of generated semantic representation of the proposed Long-Short Memory in Recursive Neural Networks with hierarchical parameter sharing, in this section, the following experiments are conducted on two NLP tasks: (1) sentiment analysis on Stanford Sentiment Treebank (SST) [18], and (2) semantic relatedness prediction on the SICK data set [18].

The corpus can be represented in Contituency treebank (denoted as "Con-" in the following experiments) and Dependency treebank (denoted as "Dep-" in the following experiments). Accordingly, the methods are denoted by combining the form of structures and different variants of LSTM-RvNN with hierarchical weight sharing, a simplified strategy and/or peephole connections, e.g., Con-hLSTM-RvNN denotes to use the proposed LSTM-RvNN with hierarchical parameter sharing.

4.1   Clusters of Node Types in Constituency Treebank

In order to obtain semantic information in a hierarchical structure, three strategies are adopted based on Penn Treebank. The details are shown in Table 1. Here, strategy-I is generated by the definition of Penn Treebank II [19]. To obtain finer semantic levels, strategy-II and strategy-III are developed in terms of the strategy-I by counting composition types in train dataset of Stanford Sentiment Treebank. As the strategies in Constituency treebank tagsets, Dependency tagsets [20] are grouped by counting sentiment composition types in training dataset of Stanford Sentiment Treebank.

Table 1. Clusters of parameter sharing in Constituency treebank tagsets in non-leaf nodes

Strategies	Clusters	Tagsets
Strategy-I	Clauses	ROOT, S, SBAR, SBARQ, SINV, SQ
	Phrases	ADJP, ADVP, CONJP, FRAG, INTJ, LST, NAC, NP, NX, WHPP, PP, PRN, PRT, QP, RRC, UCP, VP, WHADJP, WHAVP, WHNP
Strategy-II	Clauses	ROOT, S, SBARQ, SINV, SQ
	Phrases	other non-leaf tags
Strategy-III	Clauses	ROOT, S
	Phrases	other non-leaf tags

4.2   Sentiment Analysis on Sentence Level

In Stanford Sentiment Treebank (SST), there are two subtasks: binary classification and fine-grained classification [18]. In binary classification, sentences are classified to negative and positive classes while in fine-grained classification, there are five classes of sentences: very negative, negative, neutral, positive and very positive.

The SST dataset is divided into train, dev and test sets. In binary classification, we use train/dev/test splits of 6920/872/1821 sentences and in fine-grained classification, the splits of 8544/1101/2210 sentences are used. The data of Constituency treebank is from the Stanford Sentiment Treebank, and the data of Dependency treebank is generated by the dependency parser of Stanford [21].

From Table 2, one can see that the proposed model achieves best classification accuracies in both binary and fin-granted sentiment classification tasks. Due to hierarchical parameter sharing, the number of parameters could be at least increased to two folds compared to state-of-the-art networks. In the experiments, for fair comparison the internal memory of all the parameters are kept the same so that the dimensionality d of hidden layers is decreased. However, integrated with simplified version of LSTM, the hybrid models can obtain the best accuracies as well as significantly decrease temporal and spatial complexities of LSTM structures.

Table 2. Accuracies of average sentiment analysis with standard deviation and average results of Semantic Relatedness with standard deviation, over 10 runs

Method	Fine-grained (%)	Binary (%)	Pearson γ
MV-RvNNs [14]	44.4	82.4	-
RNTN [14]	45.7	85.4	-
LSTM [14]	46.4(1.1)	84.9(0.6)	0.8528 ± 0.0031
Bidirectional LSTM [14]	49.1(1.0)	87.5(0.6)	0.8567 ± 0.0028
Con-LSTM-RvNN [14]	51.0(0.5)	88.0(0.3)	0.8582 ± 0.0038
Dep-LSTM-RvNN [14]	48.4(0.4)	85.7(0.4)	0.8676 ± 0.0030
Con-LSTMp-RvNN	49.2(0.3)	87.7(0.2)	0.8454 ± 0.0049
Dep-LSTMp-RvNN	48.2(0.2)	85.7(0.2)	0.8583 ± 0.003
Con-sLSTM-RvNN	51.1(0.3)	88.2(0.4)	0.8602 ± 0.0025
Dep-sLSTM-RvNN	48.5(0.4)	86.0(0.2)	0.8679 ± 0.0019
Con-hLSTM-RvNN	51.3(0.2)	88.3(0.4)	0.8611 ± 0.0020
Dep-hLSTM-RvNN	48.7(0.4)	86.0(0.3)	0.8698 ± 0.0016
Con-shLSTM-RvNN	**51.7(0.2)**	**88.9(0.3)**	0.8651 ± 0.0014
Dep-shLSTM-RvNN	49.0(0.2)	86.1(0.2)	**0.8713 ± 0.0018**

4.3 Semantic Relatedness

Semantic Relatedness is validated on the Sentence Involving Composition Knowledge (SICK) data set [18] with a split of 4500/500/4927 for train/dev/test data sets. The sentences are derived from existing image and video description.

Each pair of sentences is annotated with a score $y \in [1, 5]$. $y = 1$ means that the two sentences are obviously unrelated, and $y = 5$ means that the two sentences are tightly related.

In Table 2, the proposed model with Dependency treebank achieves the best performance on semantic relatedness, while both mLSTM-RvNN and hLSTM-RvNN contribute to the performance.

4.4   Sentiment Analysis on All Nodes

From Table 3, one can see that, in constituency treebank, the performance of sentiment analysis becomes worse with higher semantic levels. The proposed model significantly improves the performance of sentiment analysis on all nodes, and achieves best accuracies with Strategy-II. Meanwhile, the results show that the performance of the three strategies differs in clause level, which contains root nodes and determines the performance on sentence level.

Table 3. Accuracies of sentiment analysis on all nodes of Constituency treebank, with three strategies of parameter sharing.

Clusters (%)	LSTM -RvNN	shLSTM -RvNN	LSTM -RvNN	shLSTM -RvNN	LSTM -RvNN	shLSTM -RvNN
Strategy	Strategy-I		Strategy-II		Strategy-III	
Roots	88.23	88.76	88.23	**88.90**	88.23	88.63
All-Nodes	91.78	92.13	91.78	**92.24**	91.78	92.01
Cluster-1	87.87	88.30	87.79	88.43	87.83	88.18
Cluster-2	90.46	90.76	90.61	90.91	90.60	90.83
Words	97.76	**98.15**	97.76	98.14	97.76	98.12

Table 4. Average results of sentiment analysis and semantic relatedness over 10 runs

Method	Sentiment analysis		Semantic relatedness	
	Time (s)	Memory (KB)	Time (s)	Memory (KB)
Con-LSTM-RvNN	116.0	309.4	38.2	221.0
Dep-LSTM-RvNN	91.1	264.8	41.5	198.6
Con-sLSTM-RvNN	75.8	220.9	23.7	128.1
Dep-sLSTM-RvNN	71.6	172.5	23.7	128.1
Con-hLSTM-RvNN	162.3	442.1	54.1	333.5
Dep-hLSTM-RvNN	139.6	393.7	63.2	284.5
Con-shLSTM-RvNN	104.2	352.6	31.7	245.7
Dep-shLSTM-RvNN	98.9	290.2	37.9	211

4.5 Spatial and Temporal Complexities

The running time is an average one over the first ten epochs by running the same neural network model. Spatial complexity is measured by the number of composition function parameters in neural networks in memory. From Table 4, one can see that sLSTM-RvNN can achieve better performance with less spatial and temporal complexity in both two tasks.

5 Conclusion

Both the simplified LSTM cells and hierarchical parameter sharing help improve the performance, while the hybrid of them achieves better performance. The proposed model improves the accuracies of classification of all the semantic structures, especially for those in high semantic levels, and significantly reduces the temporal complexity. With a finely tuned strategy of clusters on semantic levels, the proposed model achieves best performance, which proves that parameters should be shared among network connections with similar properties or values.

Acknowledgments. This work was supported in part by the Natural Science Foundation of China under Contract 71331005 and in part by the State Key Research and Development Program of China under Contract 2016YFE0100300.

References

1. Rumelhart, D.E., Mcclelland, J.L.: Parallel Distributed Processing: Explorations in the Microstructure of Cognition: Foundations. Parallel Distributed Processing (1986)
2. Lang, K.J., Waibel, A.H., Hinton, G.E.: A time-delay neural network architecture for isolated word recognition. Neural Netw. **3**(1), 23–43 (1990)
3. Lecun, Y.: Generalization and network design strategies. Connectionism in Perspective, pp. 143–155 (1989)
4. Nowlan, S.J., Hinton, G.E.: Simplifying neural networks by soft weight-sharing. Neural Comput. **4**(4), 473–493 (1992)
5. Bengio, Y., Ducharme, R., Vincent, P., Jauvin, C.: A neural probabilistic language model. J. Mach. Learn. Res. **3**, 1137–1155 (2003)
6. Robinson, A.J.: An application of recurrent nets to phone probability estimation. IEEE Trans. Neural Netw. **5**(2), 298–305 (1994)
7. Duda, R.O., Hart, P.E., Stork, D.G.: Pattern Classification. Wiley (2012)
8. Socher, R., Manning, C.D., Ng, A.Y.: Learning continuous phrase representations and syntactic parsing with recursive neural networks. In: Proceedings of the NIPS-2010 Deep Learning and Unsupervised Feature Learning Workshop, pp. 1–9 (2010)
9. Marcus, M.P., Marcinkiewicz, M.A., Santorini, B.: Building a large annotated corpus of English: the penn Treebank. Comput. Linguist. **19**(2), 313–330 (1993)
10. Bengio, Y., Simard, P., Frasconi, P.: Learning long-term dependencies with gradient descent is difficult. IEEE Trans. Neural Netw. **5**(2), 157–166 (1994)
11. Hochreiter, S., Schmidhuber, J.: Long short-term memory. Neural Comput. **9**(8), 1735–1780 (1997)

12. Clark, A., Fox, C., Lappin, S. (eds.).: The Handbook of Computational Linguistics and Natural Language Processing. Wiley, Malden (2013)
13. Zhu, X., Sobihani, P., Guo, H.: Long short-term memory over recursive structures. In: International Conference on Machine Learning, pp. 1604–1612 (2015)
14. Tai, K.S., Socher, R., Manning, C.D.: Improved semantic representations from tree-structured long short-term memory networks. In: Proceedings of Association for Computational Linguistics (2015)
15. Gers, F.A., Schmidhuber, J., Cummins, F.: Learning to forget: continual prediction with LSTM (1999)
16. Gers, F.A., Schmidhuber, J.: Recurrent nets that time and count. In: Proceedings of the IEEE-INNS-ENNS International Joint Conference, vol. 3, pp. 189–194 (2000)
17. Graves, A., Schmidhuber, J.: Framewise phoneme classification with bidirectional LSTM and other neural network architectures. Neural Netw. $18(5)$, 602–610 (2005)
18. Socher, R., Perelygin, A., Wu, J.Y., Chuang, J., Manning, C.D., Ng, A.Y., Potts, C.: Recursive deep models for semantic compositionality over a sentiment Treebank. In: Proceedings of the Conference on Empirical Methods in Natural Language Processing, pp. 1631–1642 (2013)
19. Bies, A., Ferguson, M., Katz, K., Macintyre, R., Tredinnick, V., Kim, G., Schasberger, B.: Bracketing guidelines for Treebank II style penn Treebank project. University of Pennsylvania, pp. 97–100 (1995)
20. De Marneffe, M.C., Manning, C.D.: Stanford typed dependencies manual. Technical report, Stanford University, pp. 338–345 (2008)
21. Chen, D., Manning, C.D.: A fast and accurate dependency parser using neural networks. In: Conference on Empirical Methods in Natural Language Processing, pp. 740–750 (2014)

Robust Deep Face Recognition with Label Noise

Jirui Yuan[1(✉)], Wenya Ma[2], Pengfei Zhu[2], and Karen Egiazarian[1]

[1] Tampere University of Technology, Tampere, Finland
jirui.yuan@student.tut.fi, karen.egiazarian@tut.fi
[2] School of Computer Science and Technology, Tianjin University, Tianjin, China
{wyma,zhupengfei}@tju.edu.cn

Abstract. In the last few years, rapid development of deep learning method has boosted the performance of face recognition systems. However, face recognition still suffers from a diverse variation of face images, especially for the problem of face identification. The high expense of labelling data makes it hard to get massive face data with accurate identification information. In real-world applications, the collected data are mixed with severe label noise, which significantly degrades the generalization ability of deep learning models. In this paper, to alleviate the impact of the label noise, we propose a robust deep face recognition (RDFR) method by automatic outlier removal. The noisy faces are automatically recognized and removed, which can boost the performance of the learned deep models. Experiments on large-scale face datasets LFW, CCFD, and COX show that RDFR can effectively remove the label noise and improve the face recognition performance.

Keywords: Deep learning · Noise removal · Face recognition

1 Introduction

Deep learning has achieved consistent breakthroughs in different tasks, including face recognition [1], scene understanding [2], and image caption [3]. The superior performance of deep learning owns to the representations of data with multiple levels of abstraction and massive labelled training data [4]. However, the lack of accurate label information makes it hard to learn a well-trained deep model with only a few labelled samples. For face recognition, despite the success of deep learning in face verification [5,6], it is hard to achieve satisfactory recognition accuracy without sufficient training data, especially when there are a large number of subjects in face identification. DeepFace uses a large-scale face dataset that consists of 4 millions face images of 4000 subjects [1]. FaceNet is learned on a much larger dataset with 200 millions of 8 millions subjects [5]. The large-scale face databases with accurate labels dramatically improve the performance of face recognition in that the deep learning models can be well trained.

How to acquire correctly labeled face dataset is one of the key challenges in constructing a successful face recognition system. One intuitive way is to manually collect and label the face images. The other way is a semiautomatic

© Springer International Publishing AG 2017
D. Liu et al. (Eds.): ICONIP 2017, Part II, LNCS 10635, pp. 593–602, 2017.
https://doi.org/10.1007/978-3-319-70096-0_61

annotation by online image searching. The searching results contain massive label noise, which should be manually corrected. However, manual annotation suffers from high time consumption, labelling expense and inevitable labelling error [7]. Hence, there is a need to construct an effective face tagging method that can automatically remove noise, and allow collection of a large-scale face dataset with accurate identification information.

To deal with label noise, there are mainly three types of methods: noise-robust, noise-removal, and noise-tolerant. The first category of methods learn models that are robust to label noise. Manwani et al. proposed that when the loss functions are given, the learned model is claimed to be robust to noise if the misclassification probability is irrelevant to label noise [8]. Patrini et al. proposed to improve label noise robustness by loss factorization in weakly supervised learning [9]. Gao et al. divided the loss function into two parts: one irrelevant to noise and the other related with noise, by risk minimization [10]. The second type of methods consider that the noisy face images can be relabelled or directly discarded by a filter. These methods need to manually set a threshold for noise removal [11]. Wilson et al. reviewed the noise removal methods based on locality smoothness. Brodley et al. proposed to detect noisy samples by classification confidence scores [12]. The third type of methods model the noise distribution. Thus, the classification model and the noise model are directly separated. The most common noise modeling method is to estimate the noise distribution by the Bayesian methods.

For face recognition, noise removal aims to clean the noisy samples of each subject and then get a clean face dataset. Beside visual information, the side information can help to correct the label noise. Schroff et al. proposed to fuse visual and textual information to reorder the face images [13]. Li proposed to reorder the samples by incremental model learning using the searching results as the initialized rank [14]. Collins et al. used active learning to label a subset of face images helping noise removal. In real-world applications, the small-scale manually labelled face dataset and the side information maybe can be not reliable [15]. Hence, it is one of the most challenging issues to automatically detect noise samples in unsupervised setting and develop robust deep face recognition model.

In this paper, we propose a robust deep face recognition method by automatic label noise removal. A deep CNN model is firstly trained on a clean dataset with a small sample size. Deep features are extracted for a large-scale noisy face dataset by the pre-trained deep model. Then label noise is automatically removed by unsupervised one class learning (UOCL). Finally, a deep model is trained on the clean large-scale face dataset and tested on a validation set. This process is repeated until the recognition accuracy on the validation set does not increase. We use MS-Celeb-1M as the large-scale noisy dataset. Experiments on LFW, CCFD, and COX datasets shows that the proposed method can effectively alleviate the impact of label noise and improve the recognition performance of the learned deep models.

2   Robust Deep Learning

This section presents the proposed robust deep face recognition method.

2.1   Framework

The lack of data with accurate identification information blocks the improvement of the face recognition performance. Although it is easy to collect massive face images, the label noise may greatly degrade the performance of the recognition system. To make the best use of the large-scale noisy data, we propose a robust deep face recognition (RDFR) method by an automatic noisy removal. The framework is given in Fig. 1. Firstly, a deep model is trained on a clean dataset with a small sample size. The deep features are extracted for a large-scale noisy face dataset by the pre-trained deep model. Then, the noisy samples are removed by unsupervised one class learning (UOCL). This process is repeated to remove the noisy samples until the recognition rate on the validation set does not increase. RDFS aims to extract a clean subset from the large-scale noisy data to train a better deep model.

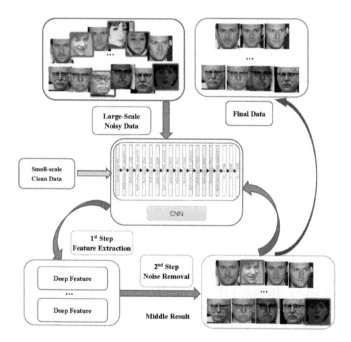

Fig. 1. The flowchart of robust deep face recognition via automatical label removal.

2.2   Unsupervised One Class Learning

In real-world applications, face images are more easily available and reliable compared to other information. Severe outliers should be removed from the large-scale dataset to make the visual information of face images well utilized. The common strategy to deal with a label noise is to transform outlier removal to an unsupervised one-class learning task. The representative methods are robust kernel density estimation (RKDE) [16] and sparse modeling for finding representative objects (SMRS) [17]. In this work, we introduce an efficient automatic noise removal method, namely, unsupervised one class learning (UOCL) [18]. UOCL is built upon two intuitive assumptions: (1) outliers originate from low-density samples, and (2) neighboring samples tend to have consistent classifications.

Given an unlabeled dataset $\mathcal{X} = \{x_i \in \mathbb{R}^d\}_{i=1}^n$ we aim to get a classification function $f : \mathbb{R}^d \mapsto \mathbb{R}$, which is similar to one class SVM. By leveraging a kernel function $\kappa : \mathbb{R}^d \times \mathbb{R}^d \mapsto \mathbb{R}$ that induces the Reproducing Kernel Hilbert Space (RKHS) the target classification function is in the following expression:

$$f(x) = \sum_{i=1}^n \kappa(x, x_i)\alpha_i, \tag{1}$$

where α_i is the expansion coefficient contributed by the functional base $\kappa(\cdot, x_i)$. Let us introduce a soft label assignment $\mathcal{Y} = \{y_i \in \{c^+, c^-\}\}_{i=1}^n$, where c^+ is a positive value for positive samples and c^- is a negative value for outliers. Let $y = [y_1, \cdots, y_n]^T$ be the vector representation of $\mathcal{Y}$.

Now we establish the UOCL model as minimizing the following objective:

$$\min_{f \in \mathcal{H}, \{y_i\}} \sum_{i=1}^n (f(x_i) - y_i)^2 + \gamma_1 \|f\|_{\mathcal{M}}^2 - \frac{2\gamma_2}{n^+} \sum_{i,y_i>0} f(x_i)$$

$$\text{s.t.} \quad y_i \in \{c^+, c^-\}, \forall i \in [1:n],$$

$$0 < n^+ = |\{i|y_i > 0\}| < n, \tag{2}$$

where $\gamma_1, \gamma_2 > 0$ are two trade-off parameters controlling the model, $\|f\|_{\mathcal{M}}^2$ is the manifold regularization item.

2.3   Deep Model

For label noise removal, we use VIPLFaceNet and in the stage of face recognition, we use Resnet-VIPL. VIPLFaceNet contains 7 convolution layers and 3 full connected layers. Resnet-VIPL is modified from the classic Resnet [19], and consists of 82 convolution layers and 2 full connected layers. Compared with Resnet-101, Resnet-VIPL greatly reduces the computation burden while keeps the performance.

3   Experiments

Experiments are conducted on large-scale face databases to evaluate the performance of the proposed method (Fig. 2).

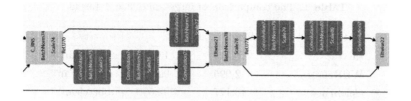

Fig. 2. A part of Resnet-VIPL.

3.1 Datasets

We use a large-scale noisy face dataset MS-Celeb-1M for training. The performance is evaluated on three datasets, including LFW, CCFD and COX.

MS-Celeb-1M is a large-scale noisy dataset from Microsoft [20]. MS dataset has 8,456,240 real-world facial images of 99,891 identities. It is a large-scale dataset that contains large variations in age, pose and so on. There are severe label noises, which may degrade the performance of deep models.

CCFD (Chinese Celebrity Face Dataset) is a large-scale real-world face dataset collected by VIPL. This dataset consists of 263,696 images of 1,001 subjects, with two subsets for training and testing. The training set contains 171,792 images of 701 subjects and the testing set contains 91,904 images of 301 subjects. Facial images in CCFD are collected from the internet and have large variations in age, expression, light, occlusion and pose.

LFW (Labeled Faces in the Wild) is a classic face dataset that consists of 13,233 images of 5,749 identities [21].

CASIA-WebFace is a public face dataset that consists of 494,414 images of 10,575 subjects [22].

COX consists of the gallery set and probe set. The gallery set contains 20,312 face images of 20,312 subjects. The images in the gallery set are the face images of the Chinese identity card. The probe set contains 1,102 test images, which are collected in the wild.

The comparison of different large-scale face datasets are illustrated in Table 1. The test protocols of the three datasets are different.

CCFD: The test set of CCFD contains 91,904 face images of 301 subjects. The test set is divided into the target set and the query set. The verification rate under different false acceptance rate is used to evaluate the recognition performance. Here, the verification rate when FAR is 0.1 is reported.

COX: The ROC curse is used to evaluate the performance.

LFW: The average face verification rate of ten folds are used. There are 300 positive pairs and 300 negative samples per fold.

3.2 Experimental Settings

Face preprocessing. The face images of differen datasets are all resized to 256×256. Deep features are extracted for label noise removal and

Table 1. The comparison of large-scale face datasets

Datasets	Subject	Image	Property
LFW	5,749	13,233	public(clean)
WDRef	2,995	99,773	private(clean)
CelebFace	10,177	202,599	public(clean)
MSRA-CFW	1,583	202,792	public(clean)
CCFD	1,001	270,706	private(clean)
CASIA-WebFace	10,575	494,414	public(clean)
SFC	4,030	4,400,000	private(clean)
MS-Celeb-1M	99,891	8,456,240	public(noise)
Google	8,000,000	200,000,000	private(clean)

face recognition. The deep feature dimension for noise removal is 2,048 and the dimension for face recognition is 1,024.

Parameter setting. The platform of our experiments is Caffe. SGD is utilized to train the VIPLFaceNet and Resnet-VIPL. For VIPLFaceNet, we set the base_lr as 0.06, mini-batch size as 128, iter_size as 1, total iteration in pre-train process as 120,000, momentum as 0.9, and weight-decay as 0.0002. The learning rate is decreased according to the polynomial policy with *gamma* value equals to 0.5. For Resnet-VIPL, we set the base_lr as 0.04, mini-batch size as 32, iter_size as 4, total iteration in pre-train process as 300,000, momentum as 0.9, and weight-decay as 0.0002. For UOCL, we use Gaussian kernel $k(x, y) = exp(-\|x - y\|^2) / 2\sigma^2)$, where $\sigma = \sum_{i,j=1}^{n} \|x_i - y_i\|^2 / n^2$ (Fig. 3).

Fig. 3. The process of label removal on MS-Celeb-1M database. Red bounding box represents the correctly labelled samples while green bounding box represents noisy samples. The face images of one person is taken as example. (Color figure online)

3.3 Experimental Analysis

We use CASIA-WebFace as the clean dataset with small sample size to train a CNN model. Noisy samples are iteratively removed from MS-Celeb-1M. We compare the recognition rate of the raw noisy dataset and the clean dataset after noise removal. Figure 4 shows that by automatical noise removal, the noisy

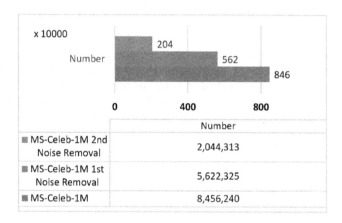

Fig. 4. The number of face samples in MS-Celeb-1M before and after noise removal.

Table 2. The face verification rate on LFW dataset

Method	Training dataset	Accuracy
Resnet-VIPL	MS-Celeb-1M	99.25%
Resnet-VIPL	MN_01	99.40%
Resnet-VIPL	MN_02	99.25%
DeepFace	SFC	97.35%
WSTFusion	WSTFusion	98.73%
VGGFace	VGGFace	98.95%
DeepID2+	DeepID2+	99.47%
FaceNet	Google	99.63%

Table 3. The face recognition rate on CCFD dataset

Method	Training dataset	Finetune	Accuracy
Resnet-VIPL	MS-Celeb-1M	No	58.10%
Resnet-VIPL	MN_01	No	64.72%
Resnet-VIPL	MN_02	No	61.19%
Resnet-VIPL	MS-Celeb-1M	Yes	65.04%
Resnet-VIPL	MN_01	Yes	70.66%
Resnet-VIPL	MN_02	Yes	68.41%

samples are partially removed after then first iteration. Then in the second iteration, all noisy samples are removed together with some clean samples. Hence, noise removal may discard also many clean face samples.

Figure 4 shows the number of samples left in MS-Celeb-1M. After the first iteration, about three million face images are removed while during the second iteration, the other three million samples are removed. The number of removed samples shows that during the iterations, we should carefully use the noise removal algorithm.

Table 2 shows the face verification rate on LFW dataset. MN_01 and MN_02 represent the results of the 1st and the 2nd noise removal. The results show that compared with the raw noisy data, the verification rate is improved by 0.25% after the 1st noise removal. Compared with DeepFace, VGGFace and DeepID2+, the performance of the proposed method is superior or comparable.

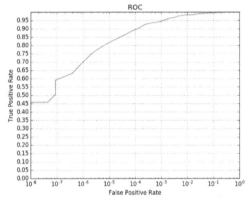

(a) The ROC curve when MS-Celeb-1M is used for training

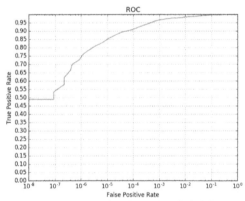

(b) The ROC curve when the cleaned MS-Celeb-1M is used for training

Fig. 5. The comparison of ROC curve on COX dataset

FaceNet achieves 99.63% in that it uses 200 million face images to train the deep model. After the second iteration, the recognition rate is the same as the raw noisy data. However, the number of training samples is only a quarter of the raw data. Hence, the time consumption and storage burden is greatly reduced.

Table 3 shows the recognition rate on CCFD dataset. Note, that the face images in MS-Celeb-1M are all collected from European and American while CCFD contains only the face images of Chinese Celebrities. To reduce the gap across different ethnic groups, we finetune the parameters on the training set of CCFD to improve the recognition performance. From the result, we can see that similar to LFW, the model trained on MN_01 is much better than on MS-Celeb-1M. Compared with the result without finetuning, the recognition rate is much improved. Note that after the second noise removal, the rate slightly decreases, since too many clean data have been removed together with the noisy face images.

Figure 5 shows results on COX dataset. The ROC curves before and after label noise removal clearly reflect the effectiveness of the proposed method.

4   Conclusions and Future Work

In this paper, we proposed a robust deep face recognition method by automatical noise removal. Because of the parameter explosion in deep learning techniques, a large-scale face dataset with correct label information is badly needed to train an accurate deep learning model. Unsupervised one-class learning is used to remove the massive noisy face images. Experiments on large-scale face datasets in the wild validate the effectiveness of the proposed method. In the future, we will focus on end-to-end robust deep face recognition model.

Acknowledgements. This work was supported by the National Program on Key Basic Research Project under Grant 2013CB329304, the National Natural Science Foundation of China under Grants 61502332, 61432011, 61222210.

References

1. Taigman, Y., Yang, M., Ranzato, M., Wolf, L.: Deepface: closing the gap to human-level performance in face verification. In: Computer Vision and Pattern Recognition (CVPR), pp. 1701–1708. IEEE (2014)
2. Cordts, M., Omran, M., Ramos, S., Rehfeld, T., Enzweiler, M., Benenson, R., Franke, U., Roth, S., Schiele, B.: The cityscapes dataset for semantic urban scene understanding. In: Proceedings of the IEEE Conference on Computer Vision and Pattern Recognition, pp. 3213–3223 (2016)
3. You, Q., Jin, H., Wang, Z., Fang, C., Luo, J.: Image captioning with semantic attention. In: Proceedings of the IEEE Conference on Computer Vision and Pattern Recognition, pp. 4651–4659 (2016)
4. LeCun, Y., Bengio, Y., Hinton, G.: Deep learning. Nature **521**(7553), 436–444 (2015)
5. Schroff, F., Kalenichenko, D., Philbin, J.: Facenet: a unified embedding for face recognition and clustering. In: Computer Vision and Pattern Recognition (CVPR), pp. 815–823 (2015)

6. Sun, Y., Liang, D., Wang, X., Tang, X.: Deepid3: Face recognition with very deep neural networks (2015). arXiv preprint: arXiv:1502.00873

7. Ariz, M., Bengoechea, J.J., Villanueva, A., Cabeza, R.: A novel 2d/3d database with automatic face annotation for head tracking and pose estimation. In: Computer Vision and Image Understanding, vol. 148, pp. 201–210 (2016)

8. Manwani, N., Sastry, P.S.: Noise tolerance under risk minimization. IEEE Trans. Cybern. **43**(3), 1146 (2011)

9. Patrini, G., Nielsen, F., Nock, R., Carioni, M.: Loss factorization, weakly supervised learning and label noise robustness. In: International Conference on International Conference on Machine Learning, pp. 708–717 (2016)

10. Gao, W., Wang, L., Li, Y.F., Zhou, Z.H.: Risk minimization in the presence of label noise. In: AAAI, pp. 1575–1581 (2016)

11. Zhang, J., Sheng, V.S., Li, T., Wu, X.: Improving crowdsourced label quality using noise correction. IEEE Trans. Neural Netw. Learn. Syst. (2017)

12. Brodley, C.E., Friedl, M.A.: Identifying and eliminating mislabeled training instances. In: Thirteenth National Conference on Artificial Intelligence, pp. 799–805 (1996)

13. Schroff, F., Criminisi, A., Zisserman, A.: Harvesting image databases from the web. IEEE Trans. Pattern Anal. Mach. Intell. **33**(4), 754–766 (2011)

14. Li, L.J., Fei-Fei, L.: Optimol: automatic online picture collection via incremental model learning. Int. J. Comput. Vis. **88**(2), 147–168 (2010)

15. Collins, B., Deng, J., Li, K., Fei-Fei, L.: Towards scalable dataset construction: an active learning approach. In: Forsyth, D., Torr, P., Zisserman, A. (eds.) ECCV 2008, Part I. LNCS, vol. 5302, pp. 86–98. Springer, Heidelberg (2008). doi:10.1007/978-3-540-88682-2_8

16. Kim, J., Scott, C.D.: Robust kernel density estimation. J. Mach. Learn. Res. **13**, 2529–2565 (2012)

17. Elhamifar, E., Sapiro, G., Vidal, R.: See all by looking at a few: sparse modeling for finding representative objects. In: 2012 IEEE Conference on Computer Vision and Pattern Recognition (CVPR), pp. 1600–1607. IEEE (2012)

18. Liu, W., Hua, G., Smith, J.R.: Unsupervised one-class learning for automatic outlier removal. In: Proceedings of the IEEE Conference on Computer Vision and Pattern Recognition, pp. 3826–3833 (2014)

19. He, K., Zhang, X., Ren, S., Sun, J.: Deep residual learning for image recognition (2015). arXiv preprint: arXiv:1512.03385

20. Guo, Y., Zhang, L., Hu, Y., He, X., Gao, J.: MS-Celeb-1M: a dataset and benchmark for large-scale face recognition. In: Leibe, B., Matas, J., Sebe, N., Welling, M. (eds.) ECCV 2016, Part III. LNCS, vol. 9907, pp. 87–102. Springer, Cham (2016). doi:10.1007/978-3-319-46487-9_6

21. Huang, G.B., Ramesh, M., Berg, T., Learned-Miller, E.: Labeled faces in the wild: a database for studying face recognition in unconstrained environments. Technical report 07-49, University of Massachusetts, Amherst, October 2007

22. Yi, D., Lei, Z., Liao, S., Li, S.Z.: Learning face representation from scratch (2014). arXiv preprint: arXiv:1411.7923

Weakly-Supervised Dual Generative Adversarial Networks for Makeup-Removal

Xuedong Hou[1,2(✉)], Yun Li[1,2], and Tao Li[1,2]

[1] School of Computer Sciences, Nanjing University
of Posts and Telecommunications, Nanjing, China
1070111933@qq.com, {liyun,towerlee}@njupt.edu.cn
[2] Jiangsu Key Laboratory of Big Data Security and Intelligent Processing,
Nanjing University of Posts and Telecommunications, Nanjing, China

Abstract. With the improvement of face recognition precision, face recognition system is used in many fields. However, the face recognition system sometimes cannot recognize the makeup face. In this paper, a new image-to-image translation algorithm based on GAN and dual learning is proposed to remove the makeup. Especially, the proposed algorithm is weakly supervised and it combines the paired and unpaired image-to-image translation model. The dual model is firstly trained using a small number of paired data, then the performance of the model is improved by large number of unpaired data. The proposed weakly-supervised image-to-image translation algorithm is applied into makeup-removal task, and the experimental results demonstrate its higher performance than other algorithms.

Keywords: Image-to-image translation · Dual learning · GAN · Makeup-removal

1 Introduction

With the improvement of face recognition precision, face recognition system has been used in many scenes such as station, airport, bank and so on. Nowadays, makeup is becoming more and more popular. However, makeup faces are usually different from corresponding makeup-free faces, which will reduce the accuracy of the face recognition system. Our goal is to propose a makeup-removal model to recover the makeup-free face from the corresponding makeup ones.

Image-to-image translation task has made great progress recently. Similar to language translation, the image-to-image translation task is to convert an image from one domain to another domain. Many problems can be described as image-to-image translation, for example the makeup removal task. Conditional GAN [1] has been used to implement image-to-image translation, such as image super-resolution, image inpainting, image manipulation and video prediction [2–5]. The "pix2pix" framework [6] uses conditional GAN to learn a mapping from the input image to the target image. All of these tasks are based on supervised framework with paired input and output images $\{x, y\}$ (Fig. 1.left) can be obtained. These models are trained by combining content loss and adversarial loss.

© Springer International Publishing AG 2017
D. Liu et al. (Eds.): ICONIP 2017, Part II, LNCS 10635, pp. 603–611, 2017.
https://doi.org/10.1007/978-3-319-70096-0_62

Paired   Unpaired

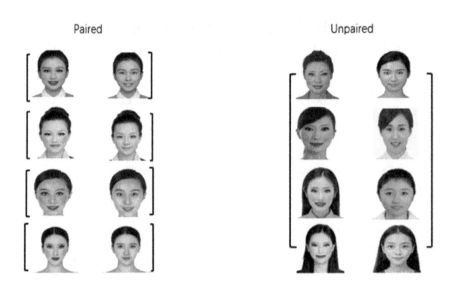

Fig. 1. Paired image data(left) consists of paired training examples $\{x_i, y_i\}$, unpaired image data (right) consisting of source set $\{x_j\} \in X$ and a target set $\{y_j\} \in Y$.

Furthermore, some models have been proposed to consider the unpaired setting. CoupledGAN [7] learns the relationship between two fields or the joint distribution by sharing the parameters of the partial layer of the generator and the discriminator in GAN. DualGAN [8], CycleGAN [9], DiscoGAN [10] train dual generation models $G : x \to y$ and $F : y \to x$ simultaneously which could form an image translation cycle. For each image x, the image translation cycle should be able to bring x back to the original image, i.e. $x \to G(x) \to F(G(x)) \approx x$. For each image y, the cycle should also satisfy the constrain:$y \to G(y) \to G(F(y)) \approx y$. This is called feedback consistency and is used to train the model. However, paired images can be obtained in some situations so we could use these data to train the model. Our goal is to train image-to-image translation model using paired and unpaired images.

In this paper, we propose a new image-to-image translation model using paired and unpaired images and use it in the makeup-removal task. We are given two data sets, one is a paired image dataset (Fig. 1.left) which consists of paired training examples $\{x_i, y_i\}$, where the y_i corresponds to each x_i. The other is unpaired datasets dataset (Fig. 1.right) consisting of a source set $\{x,\} \in X$ and a target set $\{y_j\} \in Y$, without any information to indicate that which x_j matches which y_j. Firstly we train $G : x \to y$ and $F : y \to x$ dual model with a small number of paired input-output images, and then use a large number of unpaired images to improve the performance of the model. We use a GAN discriminator [1] D_Y to classify $G(x)$ apart from y to train the G translates the domain X to a domain distributed identically to Y and add a feedback consistency loss that encourages $F(G(x)) \approx x$. Similarly, we use a GAN discriminator [11] D_X to classify $F(y)$ apart from x to train the F that translates the domain Y to a domain distributed identically to X and add a feedback consistency loss that encourages $G(F(y)) \approx y$. G and F are trained simultaneously. Our primary contribution is to propose a new algorithm which combines paired and unpaired image-to-image translation methods. Our second contribution is to propose a makeup-removal algorithm and obtain good results. As far as we know, this is the first makeup-removal algorithm based on GAN.

The paper is organized as follow. Section 2 introduces the related work. Section 3 presents the proposed method. Section 4 presents the experiments with results and discussion. Section 5 concludes the paper with insights for future work. Our code is available at: https://github.com/houxuedong/makeup-removal .

2   Related Work

Generative adversarial networks (GANs). GAN [11] can learn a generator to capture the distribution of real data by introducing an adversarial discriminator that evolves to discriminate between the real data and the fake. Generative adversarial networks are paired networks: one of which is a generator network, learns to create new samples from a probability distribution defined by a series of training examples; the other is a discriminator network that tries to discriminate between the real data and the fake. Every time the discriminator notices a difference between the two distributions, the generator adjusts its parameters slightly to make it go away. Until at the end the generator exactly reproduces the true data distribution and the discriminator is guessing at random, unable to find a difference. However, the original GAN has many disadvantages, such as training instability, non-convergence, gradient missing, model collapse and so on. Subsequently, many methods and techniques have been proposed to solve these problem [1, 12, 13]. We introduce an adversarial loss to learn the mapping such that the translated image cannot be distinguished from images in the target domain.

Dual learning. Dual learning [14] was first proposed to reduce the requirement on labeled data in training English-to-French and French-to-English translators. The key idea of dual learning is to set up a dual-learning game which involves two agents, each of them only understands one task, but two dual tasks can form a closed-loop feedback system. It can evaluate the consistency between feedback content and original input, which allows us to obtain feedback information from unlabeled data. Then, we can use the feedback information to improve the models in dual tasks. In our case, the GAN is utilized to generate images same as the distribution of target images, and feedback consistency loss is adopted to constrain the feedback content to consist with the original input.

3   Method

Our goal is to learn mapping functions between two domains X and Y. We are given two datasets, one is a paired image dataset which consists of paired training examples $\{x_i, y_i\}$. The other is unpaired dataset consisting of a source set $\{x_j\} \in X$ and a target set $\{y_j\} \in Y$. The paired dataset has a few images, so the model will not work well if we train the model using paired data only. Our algorithm train the model by combining paired and unpaired data. The training procedure is divided into two steps: we use the paired data to train dual model $G : x \rightarrow y$ and $F : y \rightarrow x$ firstly, then improve the model's performance using the unpaired data.

3.1 Paired Image-to-Image Translation

At the first step, paired images are used to train image to image translation model, which is illustrated in Fig. 2(a): we train $G : x \rightarrow y$ and $F : y \rightarrow x$ networks using the paired dataset at the same time. $L1$ norm loss is applied to both mapping functions as $L1$ distance encourages less blurring than $L2$. We also tried adding the $L1$ norm loss with an adversarial loss between $G(x)$ and y, and between $F(y)$ and x, but did not get better result. For the mapping function $G : x \rightarrow y$, we express the objective as:

$$\ell_{paired}(G, x, y) = \|G(x) - y\|_1 \tag{1}$$

For the mapping function $F : y \rightarrow x$, the objective is:

$$\ell_{paired}(F, y, x) = \|F(y) - x\|_1 \tag{2}$$

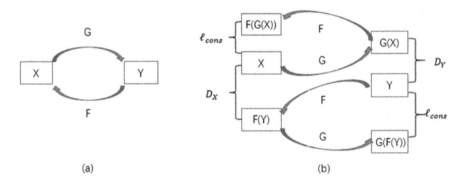

(a)   (b)

Fig. 2. (a) Our model learning two mapping functions $G : x \rightarrow y$ and $F : y \rightarrow x$ using paired data. (b) We train the model using unpaired data. Our objective contains two terms: an adversarial loss and a feedback consistency loss.

3.2 Unpaired Image-to-Image Translation

At second step, image-to-image translation is trained using unpaired data which is illustrated in Fig. 2(b). The objective contains two terms: an adversarial loss to match the distribution of generated images with the data distribution of the target images, and a feedback consistency loss to prevent the learned mappings G and F from contradicting each other [9].

Adversarial Loss. A GAN discriminator is used to classify $G(x)$ apart from y and train the G translates the domain X to a domain distributed identically to Y. The objective is formulated as:

$$\ell_{GAN}(G, D_Y, x, y) = log D_Y(y) + \log(1 - D_Y(G(x))) \tag{3}$$

A similar adversarial loss for the mapping function $F : y \rightarrow x$ is defined as follows:

$$\ell_{GAN}(F, D_X, y, x) = log D_X(x) + \log(1 - D_X(F(y))) \tag{4}$$

Feedback consistency loss. The feedback consistency loss is introduced to push G and F to generate images constrained by input images. For each image x from domain X, the image translation cycle should be able to bring x back to the original image, i.e. $x \rightarrow G(x) \rightarrow F(G(x)) \approx x$. For each image y from domain Y, the image translation cycle should also be able to bring y back to the original image, i.e. $y \rightarrow F(y) \rightarrow G(F(y)) \approx y$ [8–10]. We call this feedback consistency, and it can be expressed as:

$$\ell_{cons}(G, F, x, y) = \|F(G(x)) - x\|_1 + \|G(F(y)) - y\|_1 \tag{5}$$

Full objective. To train the unpaired image-to-image translation model, it is like to minimize the combination of adversarial loss and feedback consistency loss. The full objective of unpaired image-to-image translation is expressed as:

$$\ell_{unpaired}(G, D_Y, x, y) = \ell_{GAN}(G, D_Y, x, y) + \ell_{GAN}(G, D_Y, y, x) \\ + \lambda \ell_{cons}(G, F, x, y) \tag{6}$$

Where λ controls the relative importance of the two terms.

4 Experimental Results

We apply the proposed weakly-supervised image-to-image translation algorithm to makeup-removal task. To demonstrate the effectiveness of our proposed method, we create a new dataset with paired makeup and makeup-free faces.

Datasets. We collect around 100 makeup-free faces images from the Internet, then synthesized makeup face through a makeup website TAAZ [15]. One makeup-free face image can produce different makeup face images using different makeup templates. We synthesize 800 around paired images (Fig. 1.left) and divide the data into training dataset consists of 700 around paired images and test dataset consists of 100 around paired images. The makeup-free face images is different in training and test datasets.

The training data was used in two steps: At first step, we randomly select 100 paired images to train paired image-to-image model. Then we use all makeup images and makeup-free images in training dataset to train unpaired image-to-image model. All images was resized to 128×128 pixels. Figure 1 illustrates some examples of makeup-free and makeup faces.

Baselines. Our method is compared with different baseline image-to-image translation methods on makeup-removal task where ground truth output images are available for evaluation. These methods could be roughly divided into three categories: supervised learning, unsupervised learning, and semi-supervised learning.

cGAN. This method [6] trains a conditional GAN to generate makeup-free face from makeup ones. The discriminator D is trained to identify whether the image is real or generated images. The generator is trained to fool the discriminator. Unlike an unconditional GAN, both the generator and the discriminator observe an input image [2].

L1. This method trains the model using L1 norm loss to minimize the distance between output images and target images.

Pre-training + L1. This method uses unsupervised pre-training to improve image-to-image translation model's performance. An autoencoder is used to pre-train the model using training images, then L1 norm loss is adopted to minimize the distance between output images and target images.

L1 + GAN(pix2pix). This method [6] trains the image-to-image translation model by combining adversarial loss and L1 norm loss. This method is based on supervised learning and paired images are used to train the model.

DualGAN. This method [8] trains two models G and F at the same time, which contains two loss terms: an adversarial loss for matching the distribution of generated images to the distribution in the target domain, and a reconstructed loss to prevent the learned mappings G and F from contradicting each other.

Implementation and training details. We adapt "U-net" [6, 16] as the architecture for our generative networks which add skip connections between each layer i and layer $n - i$, where n is the total number of layers. Such a design enables low-level information to be shared between the input and output, which is beneficial because many image translation problems implicitly demand alignment between input and output structure (e.g., objects, shapes, edges, textures, clutters, etc.) [8]. For the discriminator networks we use 70×70 PatchGANs [6, 8, 17], which tries to classify whether 70×70 overlapping image patches are real or fake. Such a patch-level discriminator architecture has fewer parameters than a full-image discriminator, and can be applied to arbitrarily-sized images in a fully convolutional fashion.

To stabilize our model training procedure, we replace the negative log likelihood objective of GAN by a least square loss [18]. This loss performs more stably during training and generates higher quality results. We alternate between one gradient de-scent step on discriminator, then one step on generator. For all the experiments, we set $\lambda = 100$ in Eq. 6. The RMSProp solver [19] with a batch size of 1 is used. All networks were trained with learning rate of 0.00005 for 100 epochs and a rate of 0.00003 for the next 100 epochs if the model is trained in two steps. At inference time, the generator net is run in exactly the same manner as during the training phase, please see [6, 8, 9] for more details (Table 1).

Comparison against baselines. In Fig. 3, we select three makeup faces corresponding to different people and translate these faces to makeup-free using different methods. The results shows that our method can recover makeup-free images quiet well.

Table 1. Translation performance for different methods

Method	Aver-image *L1* dist.	Method	Aver-image *L1* dist.
cGAN	0.078	*L1*	0.089
Pre-train + L1	0.063	*L1 + GAN*	0.022
DualGAN	0.054	ours	**0.031**

In Fig. 4, we choose three makeup faces of one person with different makeup style and translate these faces to makeup-free using different methods. The experiments results also show that our method can recover the makeup-free faces from different makeup style.

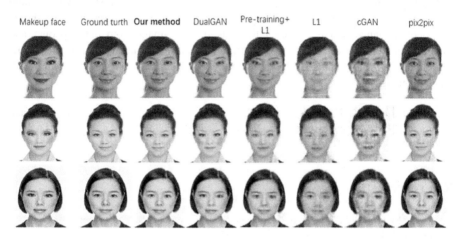

Fig. 3. Different methods for makeup-removal task

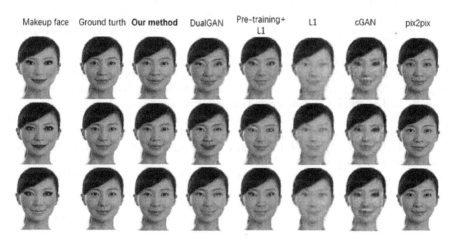

Fig. 4. Makeup-removal task for same women wearing different makeups

Furthermore, we evaluate the quality of makeup-removal results produced by different image-to image translation methods using averaged *L1* distance between output images and target images in test dataset. The smaller distance the better. Our method can achieve better results than *cGAN*, *L1*, *Pre-training + L1* and *DualGAN* models, and obtain similar result to *L1 + GAN (pix2pix)* model. However, *L1 + GAN (pix2pix)* is a supervised model, which need many paired images to train and can not utilize the unpaired images.

5   Conclusion

In this paper, we propose a new weekly-supervised image-to-image translation model and apply it into makeup-removal task. Our method consists of two steps where paired and unpaired images data are used respectively. The experimental results have shown our methods can effectively recover the makeup free image from makeup ones and usually achieve better results in most cases. In the future, we intend to reduce the model complexity by only using GAN in second step and apply our method into other image-to-image tasks.

Acknowledgment. This research was partially supported by National Natural Science Foundation of China (NSFC 61603197), Natural Science Foundation of Jiangsu Province (BK20140885) and NUPTSF (NY2141).

References

1. Mirza, M., Osindero, S.: Conditional generative adversarial nets. arXiv preprint arXiv:1411. 1784 (2014)
2. Ledig, C., Theis, L., Huszár, F., Caballero, J., Cunningham, A., Acosta, A., Aitken, A., Tejani, A.,Totz, J., Wang, Z.: Photo-realistic single image super-resolution using a generative adversarial network. arXiv preprint arXiv:1609.04802 (2016)
3. Pathak, D., Krahenbuhl, P., Donahue, J., Darrell, T., Efros, A.A.: Context encoders: feature learning by inpainting. In: IEEE Conference on Computer Vision and Patten Recognition (2016)
4. Zhu, J.Y., Krahenbuhl, P., Shechtman, E., Efros, A.A.: Generative visual manipulation on the natural image manifold. In: European Conference on Computer Vision (2016)
5. Mathieu, M., Couprie, C., LeCun, Y.: Deep multiscale video prediction beyond mean square error. In: International Conference on Learning Representations (2016)
6. Isola, P., Zhu, J.Y., Zhou, T., Efros, A.A.: Image to-image translation with conditional adversarial networks. arXiv preprint arXiv:1611.07004 (2016)
7. Liu, M.Y., Tuzel, O.: Coupled generative adversarial networks. In: Neural Information Processing Systems, pp. 469–477 (2016)
8. Yi, Z., Zhang, H., Tan, P., Gong, M.: DualGAN: Unsupervised Dual Learning for Image-to-Image Translation. arXiv preprint arXiv:1704.02510 (2017)
9. Zhu, J.Y., Park, T., Isola, P., Efros, A.A.: Unpaired Image-to-Image Translation using Cycle-Consistent Adversarial Networks. arXiv preprint arXiv:1703.10593 (2017)

10. Kim, T., Cha, M., Kim, H., Lee, J.K., Kim, J.: Learning to Discover cross-domain relations with generative adversarial networks. In: International Conference on Machine Learning (2017)
11. Goodfellow, I., Pouget-Abadie, J., Mirza, M., Xu, B., Warde-Farley, D., Ozair, S., Courville, A., Bengio. Y.: Generative adversarial nets. In: Neural Information Processing Systems, pp. 2672–2680 (2014)
12. Radford, A., Metz, L., Chintala, S.: Unsupervised representation learning with deep convolutional generative adversarial networks. arXiv preprint arXiv:1511.06434 (2015)
13. Wu, H., Zheng, S., Zhang, J., Huang, K.: GP-GAN: Towards Realistic High-Resolution Image Blending. arXiv preprint arXiv:1703.07195 (2017)
14. Xia, Y., He, D., Qin, T., Wang, L., Yu, N., Liu, T.Y., Ma, W.Y.: Dual learning for machine translation. arXiv preprint arXiv:1611.00179 (2016)
15. TAAZ Homepage, http://www.springer.com/lncs. Accessed 5 June 2017
16. Ronneberger, O., Fischer, P., Brox, T.: U-Net: Convolutional Networks for Biomedical Image Segmentation. In: Navab, N., Hornegger, J., Wells, William M., Frangi, Alejandro F. (eds.) MICCAI 2015. LNCS, vol. 9351, pp. 234–241. Springer, Cham (2015). doi:10.1007/978-3-319-24574-4_28
17. Li, C., Wand, M.: Precomputed real-time texture synthesis with markovian generative adversarial networks. In: European Conference on Computer Vision (2016)
18. Mao, X., Li, Q., Xie, H., Lau, R.Y., Wang, Z.: Multiclass generative adversarial networks with the l2 loss function. arXiv preprint arXiv:1611.04076 (2016)
19. Tieleman, T., Hinton, G.: Lecture 6.5-rmsprop: divide the gradient by a running average of its recent magnitude. COURSERA: Neural Netw. Mach. Learn. **4**(2) (2014)

Analysis of Gradient Degradation and Feature Map Quality in Deep All-Convolutional Neural Networks Compared to Deep Residual Networks

Wei Gao[✉] and Mark D. McDonnell

Computational Learning Systems Laboratory,
School of Information Technology and Mathematical Sciences,
University of South Australia, Mawson Lakes, SA 5095, Australia
gaowy009@mymail.unisa.edu.au

Abstract. The introduction of skip connections used for summing feature maps in deep residual networks (ResNets) were crucially important for overcoming gradient degradation in very deep convolutional neural networks (CNNs). Due to the strong results of ResNets, it is a natural choice to use features that it produces at various layers in transfer learning or for other feature extraction tasks. In order to analyse how the gradient degradation problem is solved by ResNets, we empirically investigate how discriminability changes as inputs propagate through the intermediate layers of two CNN variants: all-convolutional CNNs and ResNets. We found that the feature maps produced by residual-sum layers exhibit increasing discriminability with layer-distance from the input, but that feature maps produced by convolutional layers do not. We also studied how discriminability varies with training duration and the placement of convolutional layers. Our method suggests a way to determine whether adding extra layers will improve performance and show how gradient degradation impacts on which layers contribute increased discriminability.

Keywords: Convolutional Neural Networks · Deep residual networks · Deep features · Image classification · Phoneme classification · CIFAR · TIMIT

1 Introduction

The recent trend in deep CNNs has been for the number of layers of trained weights to become larger and the convolutional kernels to become smaller [1–3]. The trend has been exemplified by the consecutive winning approaches in ILVSRC computer vision competitions [1–3]; however, the increasing depth exacerbates the problem of gradients degradation in deep CNNs, which was previously investigated by [4]. This induced the advent of deep residual network that effectively solves the problem [5]. ResNets have rapidly become an architecture of choice since firstly showing its strength by winning the ImageNet Challenge in 2015 [5].

© Springer International Publishing AG 2017
D. Liu et al. (Eds.): ICONIP 2017, Part II, LNCS 10635, pp. 612–621, 2017.
https://doi.org/10.1007/978-3-319-70096-0_63

Prior to all-convolutional CNNs, the widely shared architecture of advanced CNNs such as AlexNet [1] and the VGG model [2], were constructed by generally stacking convolutional weights layers, pooling layers and then several fully-connected layers at the end. All-convolutional CNNs were firstly designed by [6] in which the pooling layers and all-to-all layers (as in [1]) were replaced by stride-2 convolutional layers and a global average pooling layer respectively.

Derived from the all-convolutional structure, the deep residual network in [5] introduced the idea of residual learning, which enables processed data and gradients to bypass certain layers during training and deployment. A following paper [7] discussed various mapping mechanisms for skip connections, as well as the sequence of applying activation functions and batch normalisation, the latter of which [8] has largely superseded dropout [9] as the preferred method of regularisation in deep CNNs. In order to further understand residual networks, a lesion study was performed [10], demonstrating that what makes deep residual networks outperform their plain counterparts is not the depth, but the implicit ensembling of many shallower networks with shared weights. The idea of *wide ResNets* was then proposed by Zagouruyko and Komodakis [11] who explored the capability of residual networks in terms of width, specifically by increasing the number of channels in each convolutional layer instead of stacking layers deeper. It turned out that wide residual networks can improve accuracy in less-deep residual networks at the cost of significantly more trainable weights. Crucially, however, they also showed that for the same number of parameters, better performance can be achieved with a wide network than with a very deep network, in a shorter run-time.

In this paper, we investigate empirically the superiority of residual networks in comparison with networks without skip-connections, by quantifying the discriminability of the feature maps following intermediate layers from ResNets and all-convolutional networks. This enables us to cast light on the gradient degradation problem and how it is alleviated by ResNets. Similar to [12], we do not propose a new algorithm for training deep CNNs; rather, our results provide analysis and insight into what is learnt by different layers in deep CNNs, so as to suggest how to optimise the design of models to be trained on a specific dataset, such as CIFAR10/100 and TIMIT datasets.

The paper is structured as follows. In Sect. 2 we describe how this paper relates to prior work. Then in Sect. 3 we outline the datasets we use and our methods for comparing residual networks with plain deep CNNs, before Sect. 4 presents our results. The paper is concluded in Sect. 5 with discussion and suggestions for further research.

2   Prior Work

The term *deep-features* was coined in [13] to describe the result of applying multiple layers of pre-trained convolutional kernels to a new training set, and using the results to train the simple classifier—see e.g. [13,14]. The focus of [13] was on demonstrating the utility of deep-features extracted from distinct new training sets after processing of data through the final layer of a pre-trained deep CNN. It was shown that performance declines when deep-features are instead extracted from layers closer to the input.

Our paper has related objectives to Zeiler and Fergus [12], who used a novel deconvolutional approach to determine what image input features individual units in a deep CNN that become tuned to respond to. They showed that the trend is for hidden units further from the input layer to have learnt to respond invariantly to increasingly complex features in comparison with units close to the input layer. The work in [15] proposed *linear classifier probes* where such probes were added to each layer of pre-trained LeNets and also networks with 128 fully-connected layers, so as to interpret the internal state of those models. However, to our knowledge, there has been no comprehensive comparison of deep-features obtained from residual networks versus plain deep CNNs.

To quantify discriminability in this paper we use a similar approach to that of [14], where a so-called *extreme-learning machine* (ELM) [16] was employed as a simple classifier that received as input deep-features obtained from training a deep CNN on the ImageNet dataset. The ELM approach has several advantages over support vector machines or other simple classifiers, such as being trainable without iterations, being amenable to large input data dimensionality, and yet being very powerful when applied to datasets that have high inherent discriminability [16, 17].

3   Methods

3.1   Datasets and Preprocessing

CIFAR-10 and CIFAR-100. Originally released by [18], the CIFAR-10 dataset consists of 60,000 32 × 32 pixel RGB color images in total. The standard training set of CIFAR-10 is comprised of 50,000 images, distributing uniformly amongst 10 labelled classes, while the test set contains the remaining 10,000 images. The CIFAR-100 dataset shares similar features to the CIFAR-10 dataset except that all 60,000 images are uniformly distributed among 100 pre-labelled classes, which makes its classification task more challenging than that of CIFAR-10.

TIMIT. The TIMIT dataset consists of approximately four hours of speech recorded at 16 KHz from 630 speakers, well labelled into 61 phonemes. Following standard practise, we reduced the number of phoneme labels from 61 to 39 [19]. For the purposes of analyzing deep residual networks, we synthesised static 50 × 50 pixel greyscale images from each labelled phoneme in the TIMIT speech data. To do this, we used a "cochleagram" approach [20]. Each wav file was processed in its entirety by a 50-channel bank of length-64 fourth-order gammatone digital bandpass filters, with centre frequencies between 100 and 8000 Hz. The result for each channel was then half-wave rectified and low-pass filtered by 400-sample boxcar kernels, which recovers the envelope of the narrow-band responses in each channel. Next, the 50×50 representation of each phoneme was obtained by downsampling in each channel to 50 samples uniformly spaced between the phoneme boundaries. The net result is a training set of 142910 greyscale images from 4620 wav files and a test set of 51681 images from 1680 wav files, all categorized into 39 classes.

3.2 Deep CNN Architecture and Training

Implementation Details. The architecture of the deep residual network we used was the version with identity mappings applied to CIFAR-10 in [7]. As in [5], the plain CNN we used was identical to the residual network, but with the skip connections removed. We trained 56-layer non-wide networks, as well as "wide" 20-layer networks with three times the number of channels per layer than the deep networks applied to CIFAR in [5], for comparing the enhanced training process due to residual learning in both cases. A batch-normalization layer was applied directly to the input data, which was different to the set-up [7]. As we used batch-normalisation after each weight layer, all biases were set to zero. This approach was identical for both residual and plain networks.

The mini-batch size was 125, with momentum of 0.9 and weight decay with parameter 0.0005 for stochastic gradient descent (SGD). We used warm restart techniques to manage the learning rate schedule [21], with learning rate constantly dropping between 0.1 and 1×10^{-5} before resetting to 0.1 at Epoch 3, 7, 15 and 31, and terminating training after 62 epochs. For comparison, we also trained 56-layer networks on CIFAR-100 for 126 epochs, with a reduced initial learning rate of 0.05. We performed standard light augmentation of each training images, i.e. random horizontal flips and random crops were applied to each image throughout the training phase.

3.3 Analysis of Deep Features

ELM Classifiers. Thanks to its simplicity, training speed and accuracy, the ELM classifier [16, 17] was utilised for analysing discriminability of deep-features. These classifier have the architecture of a single-hidden-layer neural network, but due to having a linear output layer, can be trained by applying multi-class least squares regression to the hidden-layer responses for all training data in a single batch. The input layer weights are selected randomly and are not learnt, and hence hidden layer sizes need to be increased from typical values to compensate.

We use Identical random weight layers of size $M \times L$ were used whenever the deep CNN layers produced identical feature dimensionality, where M is the number of hidden units and L is the product of the number of channels and the x and y dimensions of each layer's feature map. We also used ridge-regression as in [17].

We trained ELM classifiers on the responses to the entire training set of all layers in the CNNs. This included input layers, weights layers, batch normalization layers (BN) with ReLU activations, global average pooling layers, residual-sum layers and softmax layers. The ELM classifier probes were inserted prior to each warm restart, i.e. at epoch 2, 6, 14, 30, 62, 126.

4   Results

Figures 1 and 2 show our results quantifying the discriminability of different layers in deep CNNs applied to the CIFAR-10 and CIFAR-100 test sets. We noticed that the BN and ReLU activations showed similar behaviours and error rates to the weights layers among the experiments we did, so we do not show any results for them in this paper. However, due to the residual-sum layer placed at the front which processed weights from the early layers, the overall discriminability of BN layers with ReLU activations was suffering larger fluctuation than that of weights layers. We found that reducing learning rate can ameliorate such discriminability fluctuation for activated BN layers.

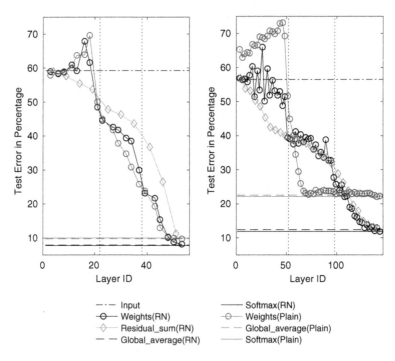

Fig. 1. Comparison for CIFAR-10 of deep-feature discriminability in 20-layer (left) versus 56-layer (right) CNNs after completing 62 epochs of training. The black dot-dashed horizontal lines indicates the classified input data, and dotted vertical lines indicate the layers that perform downsampling. The other lines denote the test errors of the ELM classifier probe inserted at those layers as indicated by the legends. The x-axis shows layer indexes for the residual network; the points for the plain network were shifted to align with the layer indexes in the residual network. Clearly, residual-sum layers show improved discriminability throughout training, and this is not the case for weights layers in either network.

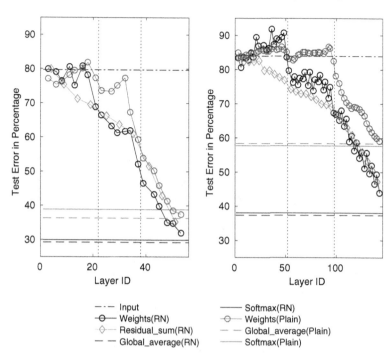

Fig. 2. Comparison for CIFAR-100 of deep-feature discriminability in 20-layer (left) versus 56-layer (right) CNNs after completing 62 epochs of training. The same trends as for CIFAR-10 are evident.

In general, the discriminability of residual-sum layers among layers closer to the input is superior to that of convolutional weights layers. However, for ResNets trained on CIFAR-10, the high variability disappears after the first downsampling, while weight layer discriminability becomes superior to that of residual-sum layers. Such a turning point is detected at the second downsampling when ResNets were trained on CIFAR-100. Although we only show the results of the ELM classifier probe after 62 epochs of training, it was observed that these trends held throughout training. The variability in ELM discriminability almost disappears after the first downsampling of ResNets trained on CIFAR-10; for CIFAR-100, such fluctuation is gradually reduced after the downsampling each time.

We also observe that the residual networks show a consistent decrease in error rate with depth away from the input, whereas the plain networks do not. This trend is consistent with previous discussion of the benefits of using skip connections in residual networks [5,7]. For the plain networks trained on CIFAR-10, we see a sharp decline in the discriminability spanning roughly 9 weights layers in the 56-layer network, which resembles the constant decrease of error rates spanning 12 weights layers in the 20-layer network. For CIFAR-100, learning in the 56-layer network prior to the second downsampling layer is almost entirely absent, with ELM classification saturating at the level of classifying the input layer or even leading to worse error rates as the training proceeds. This could

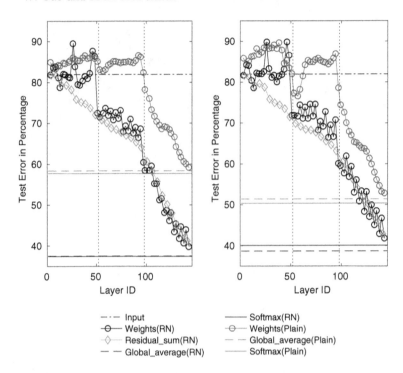

Fig. 3. Comparison for CIFAR-100 of deep-feature discriminability in 56-layer CNNs after 62 epochs of training (left) and after 126 epochs of training (right). The data indicates very deep plain networks that are subject to gradient degradation take more epochs to train to their best performance than their residual network counterparts, possibly due to the reduced number of layers that contribute to discriminability.

reflect the fact that in a plain deep network, CIFAR-100 requires much longer training and a smaller learning rate than CIFAR-10 to achieve good performance.

We further observe that for 20-layer networks trained on both CIFAR-10 and CIFAR-100, the discriminability of feature maps following weights layers in residual networks is comparable to that of weight layers in plain networks. Specifically, after 14 epochs of training, the error rates obtained by the ELM classifier probe continually decreases with distance from the input while the overall discriminability can be slightly improved as trainings continue until Epoch 62. This is not so much the case for 56-layer network where the discriminability of weights layers in plain network show a distinct non-monotonic trend, in stark contrast to weights layers in residual network.

Figure 3 shows the ELM features extracted from 56-layer networks trained on CIFAR-100, after completing 62 epochs of training and 126 epochs of training. Compared to the residual networks shown in Fig. 2, simply reducing the learning rate cannot improve the accuracy of the probe on the softmax layer but it reduces the error rates at intermediate features. Neither can training ResNets longer improve discriminability as measured by the ELM probe. The plain networks are also unable to learn better with a reduced maximum learning rate. Another 62 epochs of training is required to contribute to the reduction of test error.

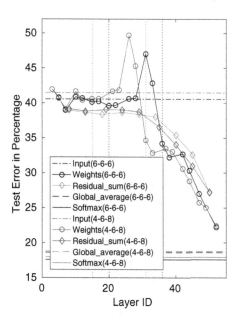

Fig. 4. Comparison for TIMIT of deep-feature discriminability in 20-layer ResNets with difference placement of convolutional layers. The numbers in legends indicate how many weight layers placed at the stages before or after each downsampling

The previous experiments indicate the fact that the discriminability of feature maps following weights layers does not undergo a smooth decline trend as the inputs propagate through the network. We assume that there is redundancy in weights at layers which are closer to the input. In order to verify this, we trained another 20-layer ResNet and its ELM classifiers on TIMIT dataset, but with different structure where a residual block placed before the first downsampling was shifted to somewhere after the second downsampling. This change results in 25% more parameters to be trained but 6% improvement of training speed, since some convolutional calculations for high dimensional feature maps have been replaced with such calculations for lower dimensional data. Figure 4 compares its result with the ELM classifiers trained on standard 20-layer after 30 epochs training. Both ELMs show similar behaviours and also similar quantitative outcomes in terms of the discriminability of intermediate layers.

5 Discussion and Future Work

The poor and highly fluctuating test error rates of ELM classifier probes for layers close to the input (comparable to that from directly classifying the raw input pixels using an ELM) are in part due to the fact that we did not attempt to optimise the ELM classifiers, and in the early layers they were applied to very high-dimensional data. We observed that experiments with increasing M

(hidden layer size of the ELM probe) led to the error rates coming down, but achieving the lowest possible error rate is not the point of this paper. Rather, we are interested in comparative results using vanilla classifiers. Also, tuning the ridge regression parameter λ in the ELM probe did not ameliorate this issue; therefore in this paper, we do not report the exact values of M or λ used for each experiment. A suggesting range for the number of hidden units M is from 500 up to 5,000. For the choice of λ, we tried various values between 1×10^{-6} and 1×10^{6}.

The comparison made between weights layers of the plain networks trained on CIFAR-10 supports the argument that networks with deeper architecture may harm the classification capability, due to gradient degradation [5], which partially reflects the success of wide residual network. The observed monotonic improvement with depth in residual networks is absent in the plain version, consistent with the view that skip-connections overcome gradient degradation in very deep network and adds further support to the demonstrated importance of skip-connections for training very deep CNNs.

We trained networks longer and changed the learning rate schedule for the results shown in Fig. 3, since the analysis of the intermediate features in previous experiments suggests doing so. Then in Fig. 4, we slightly altered the placements of convolutional layers in 20-layer ResNets showing almost no loss in test accuracy compared to the standard ResNet. It is demonstrated that inserting ELM probes into pre-trained networks can provide intuition and evidence on how to optimise the models trained on a specific dataset.

Moreover, our results suggest which feature maps of a residual network are best for discriminability when used in transfer learning or feature extraction tasks; closer to the input layer, residual-sum layers provide better discriminability, whereas closer to the output, the feature maps following convolutional layers may be better.

In future work, we will repeat the experiments of injecting ELM classifiers into pre-trained networks on larger datasets, such as tiny ImageNet dataset and the complete ImageNet, so as to verify the generality of the observations made in this paper. It will also be interesting to examine if our method can be used to determine quickly how many layers will provide benefits in very deep networks.

Acknowledgements. This work is funded by Australian Government Research Training Program (RTP) Scholarship.

References

1. Krizhevsky, A., Sutskever, I., Hinton, G.E.: ImageNet classification with deep convolutional neural networks. In: Advances in Neural Information Processing Systems, vol. 25, pp. 1097–1105, Lake Tahoe (2012)
2. Simonyan, K., Zisserman, A.: Very deep convolutional networks for large-scale image recognition. In: International Conference on Learning Representations, Banff (2014)

3. Szegedy, C., Liu, W., Jia, Y., Sermanet, P., Reed, S., Anguelov, D., Erhan, D., Vanhoucke, V., Rabinovich, A.: Going deeper with convolutions. In: The IEEE Conference on Computer Vision and Pattern Recognition, Las Vegas (2015)
4. Glorot, X., Bengio, Y.: Understanding the difficulty of training deep feedforward neural networks. In: International Conference on Artificial Intelligence and Statistics, Sardinia (2010)
5. He, K., Zhang, X., Ren, S., Sun, J.: Deep residual learning for image recognition. In: Proceedings of IEEE Conference on Computer Vision and Pattern Recognition, Las Vegas (2015)
6. Springenberg, J.T., Dosovitskiy, A., Brox, T., Riedmiller, M.: Striving for simplicity: the all convolutional net. In: Proceedings of International Conference on Learning Representations, San Diego (2015)
7. He, K., Zhang, X., Ren, S., Sun, J.: Identity mappings in deep residual networks. Preprint arXiv.1603.05027, Microsoft Research (2016)
8. Ioffe, S., Szegedy, C.: Batch normalization: accelerating deep network training by reducing internal covariate shift. In: Proceedings of 32nd International Conference on Machine Learning, Lille (2015)
9. Srivastava, N., Hinton, G., Krizhevsky, A., Sutskever, I., Salakhutdinov, R.: Dropout: a simple way to prevent neural networks from overfitting. J. Mach. Learn. Res. **15**, 1929–1958 (2015)
10. Velt, A., Wilber, M., Belongie, S.: Residual networks are exponential ensembles of relatively shallow networks. Preprint arXiv.1605.06431 (2016)
11. Zagoruyko, S., Komodakis, N.: Wide residual networks. Preprint arXiv.1605.07146 (2016)
12. Zeiler, M.D., Fergus, R.: Visualizing and understanding convolutional networks. In: European Conference on Computer Vision, Zurich (2014)
13. Sullivan, J., Razavian, A., Azizpour, H., Carlsson, S.: CNN features off-the-shelf: an astounding baseline for recognition. In: Proceedings of IEEE Conference on Computer Vision and Pattern Recognition, pp. 512–519, Columbus (2014)
14. McDonnell, M.D., Vladusich, T.: Enhanced image classification with a fast-learning shallow convolutional neural network. In: Proceedings of 2015 International Joint Conference on Neural Networks, Ireland (2015)
15. Guillaume, A., Bengio, Y.: Understanding intermediate layers using linear classifier probes. Preprint arXiv.1610.01644 (2016)
16. Huang, G.-B., Zhu, Q.-Y., Siew, C.-K.: Extreme learning machine: theory and applications. Neurocomputing **70**, 489–501 (2006)
17. McDonnell, M.D., Tissera, M.D., Vladusich, T., van Schaik, A., Tapson, J.: Fast, simple and accurate handwritten digit classification by training shallow neural network classifiers with the extreme learning machine algorithm. PLoS One **10**, 1–20 (2015). Article no. e0134254
18. Krizhevsky, A.: Learning multiple layers of features from tiny images. Ph.D. thesis, University of Toronto (2005)
19. Mohamed, A., Dahl, G.E., Hinton, G.E.: Deep belief networks for phone recognition. In: Workshop of Advances in Neural Information Processing Systems, Vancouver (2009)
20. Sainath, T.N., Weiss, R.J., Senior, A., Wilson, K.W., Vinyals, O.: Learning the speech front-end with raw waveform CLDNNs. In: Proceedings of Interspeech, Dresden (2015)
21. Loshchilov, I., Hutter, F.: SGDR: Stochastic gradient descent with restarts. Preprint arXiv.1608.03983 (2016)

Single-Image Super-Resolution for Remote Sensing Data Using Deep Residual-Learning Neural Network

Ningbo Huang[1], Yong Yang[2], Junjie Liu[1], Xinchao Gu[1], and Hua Cai[3(✉)]

[1] School of Computer Science and Technology,
Changchun University of Science and Technology, Changchun, China
[2] Changchun Normal University, Changchun, China
[3] School of Electronic Information Engineering,
Changchun University of Science and Technology,
No. 7089, Weixing Road, Changchun 130022, Jilin Province, China
caihua@cust.edu.cn

Abstract. Single image super-resolution (SISR) plays an important role in remote sensing image processing. In recent years, deep convolutional neural networks have achieved state-of-the-art performance in the SISR field of common camera images. Although the SISR method based on deep learning is effective on general camera images, it is not necessarily effective on remote sensing images because of the significant difference between remote sensing images and common camera images. In this paper, the VDSR network (proposed by Kim et al. in 2016) was found to be invalid for Sentinel-2A remote sensing images; we then proposed our own neural network, which is called the remote sensing deep residual-learning (RS-DRL) network. Our network achieved better performance than VDSR on Sentinel-2A remote sensing images.

Keywords: Single-Image · Super-Resolution · Residual-Learning · Sentinel-2A · Deep convolution neural network

1 Introduction

Single image super-resolution (SISR) has important application value in improving the spatial resolution of remote sensing images. On one hand, although there is a revisit time for the earth observation satellite to allow access to the same location of the scene, the acquired image is likely to be changed when the satellite revisits the same place and shoots again, affected by clouds, shelters, and the motion of objects. On the other hand, the spatial resolution of remote sensing images is determined by the optical hardware and sensor of the remote sensing satellite. However, the satellite's hardware capabilities limits improving the spatial resolution of remote sensing images because the distance between the spaceborne sensor and perceived objects is very large. Therefore, the SISR technology is of great significance to boost the spatial resolution of remote sensing images for facilitating subsequent processing, such as classification [1], segmentation [2], and so on. SISR is designed to generate a high-resolution (HR) image from a

© Springer International Publishing AG 2017
D. Liu et al. (Eds.): ICONIP 2017, Part II, LNCS 10635, pp. 622–630, 2017.
https://doi.org/10.1007/978-3-319-70096-0_64

low-resolution (LR) image. However, the SISR process is an ill-posed, underdetermined inverse problem, that is, there are many corresponding HR images for a single LR image.

In recent years, thanks to big data, GPU, and rectified linear unit (ReLu) [3] activation function, deep neural networks have achieved great success in computer vision. In 2012, Krizhevsky proposed the AlexNet convolutional neural network [4], which showed higher image classification accuracy compared with the runner up by a large margin on the ImageNet Large Scale Visual Recognition Challenge 2012 [5]. In the SISR field of common camera images, deep convolutional neural networks have achieved state-of-the-art performance. The SRCNN network proposed by Dong et al. [6] used three-layer convolutional networks to learn an end-to-end mapping from LR to HR. Although SRCNN has the powerful ability to extract more discriminative features than traditional methods, the authors found that the deeper SRCNN was hard to train and could not achieve better performance. However, the VDSR network [7] (as shown in Fig. 1) successfully includes 20 convolutional layers through learning residuals, and achieves better performance than the SRCNN network. The VDSR network also has faster convergence speed and a larger receptive field than SRCNN.

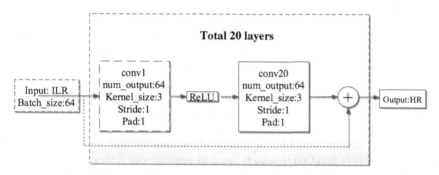

Fig. 1. Architecture of the VDSR network. As paper [7] points out, an interpolated low-resolution (ILR) image directly adds the output of the twentieth convolutional layer.

There are great differences in term of the spatial resolution and radiometric resolution between remote sensing images and common camera images. Here the Sentinel-2A remote sensing images are employed as an example. The size of 492 × 492 px Sentinel-2A remote sensing images may contain a whole town. However, the same size of common camera images may contain only a house and a few trees. The radiometric resolution of the Sentinel-2A is 12 bit [8], which enables the image to be acquired over a range of 0 to 4095 light intensity values, but the radiometric resolution of a common camera is only 8 bit. These differences may make it difficult to train a deep convolutional neural network on Sentinel-2A remote sensing images.

In paper [9], the training dataset was generated from Level-1C of Sentinel-2A on the B02, B03, and B04 band images (10 m resolution) corresponding to RGB and the scale denominator was set to 2. Then, the authors retrained the SRCNN for about 20 days on the Tesla K40c without changing any parameters introduced in [6], but failed eventually. Then they changed the learning rate from 0.0001 to 0.01, and the mini-batch size employed by the Gradient descent algorithm [10] from 64 to 256. The convergence speed of the SRCNN network was still slow (approximately 10 days on the Tesla K40c), and their experimental results showed that the difference of the average peak signal-to-noise ratio (PSNR) between the reconstructed images and the interpolation images was less than 0.4 on their B02, B03, and B04 band test dataset. In this paper, the VDSR network was trained on our training dataset, but failed (as shown in Sect. 3.1). Then, a new neural network called the remote sensing deep residual-learning (RS-DRL) network was designed for remote sensing images, combining VDSR and SRCNN. Our proposed network converged as fast as VDSR. Our experimental results showed that the difference of the PSNR between the reconstructed images and the interpolation images was larger than 0.9 on our B02, B03, and B04 band test dataset, which is significantly superior to VDSR. Since training the SRCNN is very difficult [7], the proposed network was only compared with the VDSR network.

2   Training Dataset and Proposed Neural Network

2.1   Training Dataset

The European Space Agency is developing a new family of missions called Sentinels, and provides free access to observation data [11]. Each Sentinel mission is based on a constellation of 2 satellites. Sentinel-2 is a HR, multi-spectral imaging mission. Sentinel-2 carries an optical instrument payload that samples 13 spectral bands: 4 bands at 10 m, 6 bands at 20 m, and 3 bands at 60 m spatial resolution. The Level-1C orthorectified product of Sentinel-2A, which is encoded in 16 bit/px JPEG2000 format, was used to generate our dataset. Our source dataset contains 5 Sentinel-2A granules acquired in the eastern United States without cloud coverage and no-data values. Only B02, B03, and B04 band images were used to generate our training set and test set. Each image was 10980×10980 px, and was subdivided into 484 tiles of 492×492 px, 22 tiles of 156×492 px, 22 tiles of 492×156 px, and 1 tile of 156×156 px. For each band type, 2420 tiles of 492×492 px were used to generate the training dataset, and 225 tiles of 3 different size images were used to generate the test dataset. LR simulation images were generated by sampling those tiles down and up again using bicubic interpolation at a scale denominator of 2. All tiles were cut into 41×41 patches, and then those patches were stored in HDF5 [12] format.

2.2   Proposed Neural Network

In this section, the RS-DRL network (as shown in Fig. 2), which integrates SRCNN and VDSR, is proposed. Our network consisted of 17 convolutional layers. From the second to the sixteenth layer, each layer had 64 filters of the size $3 \times 3 \times 64$. The first convolutional layer had 64 filters of the size 9×9, and the last layer had a single filter of the size $3 \times 3 \times 64$ to reconstruct the image. After each convolutional operation, the size of the output data was reduced. In order to maintain the same size of the input data for each convolutional layer, 0 was filled around the input data before the

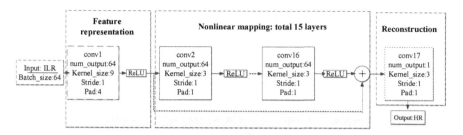

Fig. 2. Architecture of our RS-DRL network. The first layer of this network extracts a set of feature maps. There are 15 convolutional layers in the residual unit, which are used for nonlinear mapping. The last layer produces the final HR image.

convolutional operation. The sum of the output of the first layer and the sixteenth layer was inputted into the seventeenth layer. In order to make the input data and the receptive field of our network have the same size (41×41), the filter size of the first convolutional layer was set to 9×9. Let y_i denote a ground truth image and x_i denote an interpolated LR image. Let $\{(x_i, y_i)\}_{i=1}^{N}$ denote our training data. Our goal was to learn a model f that predicted values $a_i = f(x_i)$, where a_i was a reconstructed image. The equation $loss = \frac{1}{2N} \sum_{i=1}^{N} \|y_i - a_i\|^2$ was expected to be optimized to minimum.

3   Experiments

3.1   Training VDSR Network

The VDSR network used the residual structure proposed by He et al. [13], which makes it possible to train a deeper convolutional neural network. In this section, the *Caffe* framework [14] was used to train the VDSR network on our dataset described in Sect. 2.1. Firstly, the size of the mini-batch was set to 64. The learning rate was set to 0.1, and then decayed 0.1 times every 20 epochs. The technique of adjustable gradient clipping used in [7] is an improvement on the standard gradient clipping technique, which is usually used to suppress exploding gradients [15]. In *Caffe*, the technique of adjustable gradient clipping can be achieved through *clip_gradients* parameter after modifying the *Caffe* framework. In this section, the *clip_gradients* parameter was set to 0.01. The momentum parameter was set to 0.9, and the weight decay parameter was set to 0.0001. The approach depicted in [16] was used for weight initialization. Secondly, the size of the mini-batch was changed to 256 as in [9], and then the VDSR was trained without changing other parameters. The *matcaffe*, which is the MATLAB interface of *Caffe*, was used to test the test dataset on a GPU GTX1080. The VDSR network was trained on the GPU GTX1080 with 80 epochs based on early stopping theory [17]. The average PSNR and average structural similarity (SSIM) [18] of 2 experiments on our test dataset are shown in Tables 1 and 2.

Table 1. Average quantitative index of the VDSR network when mini-batch was set to 64.

Band	Measure	Bicubic	Reconstruction	Difference
B02(Blue)	PSNR	65.2317	65.1921	–0.0396
	SSIM	0.9995	0.9995	0
B03(Green)	PSNR	64.0410	63.7381	–0.3029
	SSIM	0.9994	0.9994	0
B04(Red)	PSNR	61.5956	61.5885	–0.0071
	SSIM	0.9991	0.9991	0

Table 2. Average quantitative index of the VDSR network when mini-batch was set to 256.

Band	Measure	Bicubic	Reconstruction	Difference
B02(Blue)	PSNR	65.2317	65.2271	–0.0046
	SSIM	0.9995	0.9995	0
B03(Green)	PSNR	64.0410	64.0379	–0.0031
	SSIM	0.9994	0.9994	0
B04(Red)	PSNR	61.5956	61.5677	–0.0279
	SSIM	0.9991	0.9991	0

3.2   Training Our RS-DRL Network

In *Caffe*, gradient clipping can be achieved through the *clip_gradients* parameter. In this paper, the RS-DRL network was trained without using adjustable gradient clip-ping, but the *clip_gradients* parameter was set to 1. The learning rate was set to 0.0005, and then decayed 0.97 times every 10 epochs. The momentum parameter was set to 0.9, and the weight decay parameter was set to 0.0001. The mini-batch size was set to 64. The bias was initialized to the constant 0. The method depicted in [16] was used for weight initialization. *Matcaffe* was used to test the test dataset on a GPU GTX1080. All experiments in this section were performed on the GPU GTX1080 with 80 epochs. The average PSNR and average SSIM of our RS-DRL network on our test dataset are shown in Table 3. Train and test loss curves, and qualitative (visual effect) results are shown in Figs. 3, 4 and 5 respectively.

Table 3. Average quantitative index of the RS-DRL network when mini-batch was set to 64.

Band	Measure	Bicubic	Reconstruction	Difference
B02(Blue)	PSNR	65.2317	66.1615	0.9298
	SSIM	0.9995	0.9996	0.0001
B03(Green)	PSNR	64.0410	65.0622	1.0212
	SSIM	0.9994	0.9996	0.0002
B04(Red)	PSNR	61.5956	62.8303	1.2347
	SSIM	0.9991	0.9993	0.0002

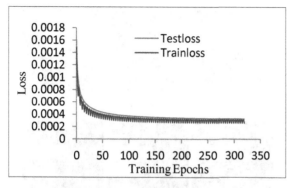

(a) Loss curves of B02 band

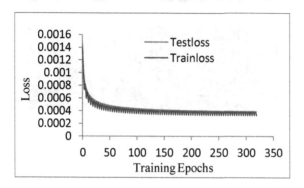

(b) Loss curves 0f B03 band

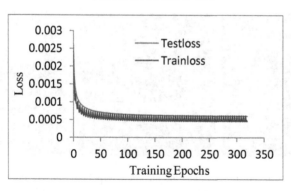

(c) Loss curves of B04 band

Fig. 3. Train and test loss curves of our RS-DRL network. Each experiment was trained for 80 epochs, and each epoch was iterated for 5444 times. The *Caffe* was set to display test loss every 1361 iterations.

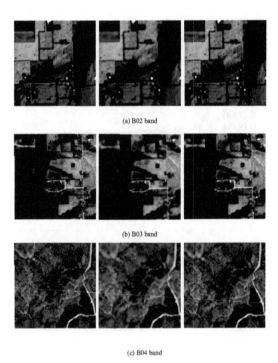

(a) B02 band

(b) B03 band

(c) B04 band

Fig. 4. From left to right, the ground truth image, the bicubic interpolation image, and the reconstructed image respectively.

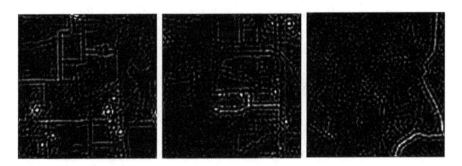

Fig. 5. The reconstructed image minus the bicubic interpolation image. From left to right, the B02 band, B03 band, and B04 band.

4   Discussion

As described in [6], the third convolutional layer of the SRCNN directly outputs re-construction images. In VDSR, the network learns residual images, and reconstruction images are generated by the input of VDSR plus the output of the twentieth layer. This significant change greatly improves the experimental effect and convergence speed on common camera images. However, this change is found to be invalid for remote sensing images. The results in Table 2 show that the difference of the average PSNR between reconstructed images and interpolation images was close to 0 when the mini-batch was set to 256. That is, VDSR had not learned the HF information described in [7] successfully. In order to force the VDSR network to learn the HF information successfully, the VDSR's deep residual unit was replaced with the non-linear mapping convolutional layer of SRCNN in this paper. However, the receptive field size of our proposed network was the same as the VDSR network's because the residual block of the proposed network only had 15 convolutional layers. As shown in Table 3, the difference on our B02, B03, and B04 band test dataset was larger than 0.9, which is better than the results shown in Tables 1 and 2. As shown in Fig. 4, it seems difficult to discern the added details of the reconstructed image compared with the bicubic interpolation image without remote sensing software. In this paper, the added detail information is showed through the reconstructed image minus the bicubic interpolation image (as shown in Fig. 5).

5   Conclusions and Future Work

In this paper, the VDSR network was found to be invalid for remote sensing images, and we proposed the RS-DRL network for SISR on remote sensing images. Our RS-DRL network achieved a better result than VDSR, and converged as fast as VDSR. At present, our network is effective when the scale denominator is 2. In the future, the quantitative indicators and visual effects will continue to be improved, and our net-work will be expanded to any denominator.

Acknowledgment. This work was supported by the development plan project of Jilin province Science and Technology Department under Grant No. 20160101260JC.

References

1. Liu, P., Choo, K.-K.R., Wang, L., Huang, F.: SVM or deep learning? a comparative study on remote sensing image classification. Soft Comput. 1–13 (2016). doi:10.1007/s00500-016-2247-2
2. Mitra, P., Uma Shankar, B., Pal, S.K.: Segmentation of multispectral remote sensing images using active support vector machines. Patt. Recognit. Lett. **25**, 1067–1074 (2004)
3. Glorot, X., Bordes, A., Bengio, Y.: Deep sparse rectifier neural networks. In: AISTATS 2011 Proceedings of 14th International Conference on Artificial Intelligence and Statistics, vol. 15, pp. 315–323 (2011)
4. Krizhevsky, A., Sutskever, I., Hinton, G.E.: ImageNet classification with deep convolutional neural networks. In: Advances in Neural Information Processing Systems, vol. 25, pp. 1–9 (2012)
5. Deng, J., Berg, A., Satheesh, S., Su, H., Khosla, A., Fei-Fei, L.: ImageNet Large Scale Visual Recognition Competition 2012 (ILSVRC 2012). http://www.image-net.org/challenges/LSVRC/2012/

6. Dong, C., Loy, C.C., He, K., Tang, X.: Image super-resolution using deep convolutional networks. IEEE Trans. Pattern Anal. Mach. Intell. **38**, 295–307 (2016)

7. Kim, J., Lee, J.K., Lee, K.M.: Accurate image super-resolution using very deep convolutional networks. CVPR **2016**, 1646–1654 (2016)

8. Sentinel-2 User Handbook. https://earth.esa.int/documents/247904/685211/Sentinel-2_User_Handbook

9. Liebel, L., Körner, M.: Single-image super resolution for multispectral remote sensing data using convolutional neural networks. In: ISPRS - International Archives of the Photogrammetry, Remote Sensing and Spatial Information Sciences, vol. XLI-B3, pp. 883–890 (2016)

10. LeCun, Y., Boser, B., Denker, J.S., Henderson, D., Howard, R.E., Hubbard, W., Jackel, L. D.: Backpropagation Applied to Handwritten Zip Code Recognition (1989)

11. Sentinel-2: Copernicus Sentinel Data. https://scihub.copernicus.eu/dhus

12. The HDF Group: Hierarchical Data Format. https://www.hdfgroup.org/HDF5

13. He, K., Zhang, X., Ren, S., Sun, J.: Deep Residual Learning for Image Recognition Arxiv. Org. **7**, 171–180 (2015)

14. Jia, Y.: Caffe: An Open Source Convolutional Architecture for Fast Feature Embedding. http://caffe.berkeleyvision.org/

15. Pascanu, R., Mikolov, T., Bengio, Y.: On the difficulty of training recurrent neural networks. In: Proceedings of 30th International Conference on Machine Learning, pp. 1310–1318 (2012)

16. He, K., Zhang, X., Ren, S., Sun, J.: Delving deep into rectifiers: surpassing human-level performance on imagenet classification. In: Proceedings of the IEEE International Conference on Computer Vision, pp. 1026–1034 (2016)

17. Bengio, Y.: Practical recommendations for gradient-based training of deep architectures. In: Montavon, G., Orr, G.B., Müller, K.-R. (eds.) Neural Networks: Tricks of the Trade. LNCS, vol. 7700, 2nd edn, pp. 437–478. Springer, Heidelberg (2012). doi:10.1007/978-3-642-35289-8_26

18. Wang, Z., Bovik, A.C., Sheikh, H.R., Simoncelli, E.P.: Image quality assessment: from error visibility to structural similarity. IEEE Trans. Image Process. **13**, 600–612 (2004)

Layer-Wise Training to Create Efficient Convolutional Neural Networks

Linghua Zeng and Xinmei Tian[✉]

CAS Key Laboratory of Technology in Geo-spatial Information Processing
and Application System, University of Science and Technology of China,
Hefei 230027, Anhui, China
zenglh@mail.ustc.edu.cn, xinmei@ustc.edu.cn

Abstract. Recent large CNNs have delivered impressive performance but their
storage requirement and computational cost limit a wide range of their applications in mobile devices and large-scale Internet industry. Works focusing on
storage compression have led a great success. Recently how to reduce computational cost draws more attention. In this paper, we propose an algorithm to
reduce computational cost, which is often solved by sparsification and matrix
decomposition methods. Since the computation is dominated by the convolutional
operations, we focus on the compression of convolutional layers. Unlike sparsification and matrix decomposition methods which usually derive from mathematics, we receive inspiration from transfer learning and biological neural
networks. We transfer the knowledge in state-of-the-art large networks to compressed small ones, via layer-wise training. We replace the complex convolutional
layers in large networks with more efficient modules and keep their outputs in
each-layer consistent. Modules in the compressed small networks are more efficient, and their design draws on biological neural networks. For AlexNet model,
we achieve 3.62× speedup, with 0.11% top-5 error rate increase. For VGG
model, we achieve 5.67× speedup, with 0.43% top-5 error rate increase.

Keywords: Deep learning · Network compression · Layer-wise training

1 Introduction

Large CNNs have recently demonstrated state-of-the-art performance in image classification task, which is treated as an important benchmark for computer vision [10].
A well-known competition, Large Scale Visual Recognition Challenge (ILSVRC) [10],
and its database have given birth to lots of famous CNNs. These networks (e.g. AlexNet
[1] and VGG [2]) are powerful and possess great representation capability. Usually very
similar models are used in the training stage and the deployment stage despite their
enormously different requirements. In the training stage, most state-of-the-art CNNs
focus on decreasing classification error rate. Thus, CNNs are usually designed to have
parameters as many as possible if they could achieve lower error rate. Consequently, a
huge number of redundant parameters will be generated in this stage [4]. In deployment
stage, apart from the error rate, there are strict requirements on storage and computational cost [6]. Improving the efficiency of CNNs is of critical importance.

© Springer International Publishing AG 2017
D. Liu et al. (Eds.): ICONIP 2017, Part II, LNCS 10635, pp. 631–641, 2017.
https://doi.org/10.1007/978-3-319-70096-0_65

To address these issues, there is growing concern about network compression in recent years. It can be roughly divided into storage compression and computation compression. The study of storage compression has been considerably thorough [6]. As a representative work, a three stage pipeline was introduced by Han et al. [6]. Pruning, trained quantization and Huffman coding worked together to reduce the storage requirement by $35\times$ to $49\times$ without increasing the error rate. However, storage compression methods are not remarkably efficient for computation compression. Sparsification and matrix decomposition are fundamental approaches in computation compression. Denton et al. [3] exploited the linear structure of the parameters and found appropriate low-rank approximation of the parameters in different layers. Zhang et al. [5] enabled an asymmetric reconstruction that reduced the rapidly accumulated error when multiple layers were compressed, achieving $5\times$ FLOPs reduction with 1.0% top-5 error rate increase ($5\times$ /+1.0) on VGG model. Figurnov et al. [7] sped up the bottleneck convolutional layers by skipping their evaluation in some of the spatial positions, achieving $2\times$ /+2.0 on AlexNet and $1.9\times$ /+2.5 on VGG. Kim et al. [8] used Tucker Decomposition on each layer with the rank determined by a global analytic solution of VBMF, achieving $2.67\times$ /+1.70 on AlexNet and $4.93\times$ /+0.50 on VGG.

These computation compression methods mainly focus on decomposition algorithms [5, 8] or position choosing algorithm [7] deriving from mathematics. Different from them, we focus on training algorithm inspired by transfer learning. We study how to transfer knowledge in state-of-the-art (big model) networks to compressed networks (small model). Since the computation is dominated by the convolutional operations [3], we focus on the compression of convolutional layers. Firstly we train a big model with redundant parameters to reach the highest possible performance. After that, we propose "layer-wise training", to compress the redundant parameters in the big model and transfer its useful information into the small model. An earlier work proposed by Hinton et al. [4] utilized the last layer output of the big model to train a small model. However, not all of the big model knowledge is included in the last-layer output. Feature maps, generated by convolutional layers, including knowledge about how the network identifies objects, are helpful to teach the small model. For example, when we teach a baby to identify a car, we will not only tell him that this is a car but also tell him that a car has four wheels, the anterior window and others. In our layer-wise training algorithm, we teach the small model not only what the image is but also how to identify the image. Efficient modules in the small model are designed to replace conventional convolutional layers in the big model. We keep the each-layer outputs of the small model and the big model to be consistent. The design of modules draws on biological neural networks, and they also can be explained from the perspective of matrix decomposition.

This paper has the following major contributions:

(1) We propose the layer-wise network training to compress a big model into a small model to reduce computational cost.
(2) We design a set of novel and efficient modules inspired by biological neural networks for layer-wise training and it is the first trying on network compression. Besides they can also be explained from the perspective of matrix decomposition.

(3) We evaluate our methods on large datasets, achieving 3.62× FLOPs reduction with 0.11% top-5 error rate increase on AlexNet model, and 5.67× FLOPs reduction with 0.43% top-5 error rate increase on VGG model.

2 Layer-Wise Training to Create Efficient CNNs

2.1 Overall Framework

In this section, we introduce the scheme of our layer-wise training method. Our scheme consists of three steps: the big model training, layer-wise training for compression, and the small model fine-tuning. Here we use AlexNet [1] as an example, as illustrated in Fig. 1.

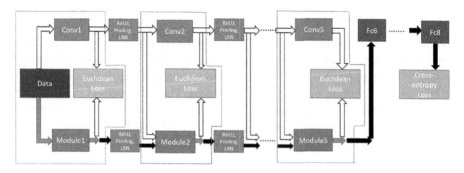

Fig. 1. The scheme of training algorithm. The upper flow in this chart, from conv1 to conv5, represents convolutional layers in the big model. The lower flow, from module1 to module5, represents modules in the small model. The rest part, fc6, fc7, and fc8, represent fully connected layers shared by both big model and small model. Data means input image or we can say training data. Euclidean Loss means the Euclidean Loss layer which computes loss and generate gradients. The red frames are blocks. Since we focus on convolutional layers, ReLU, Pooling and LRN [1] are omitted and represented in a box. (Color figure online)

In the first step, we train a big redundant model (e.g. AlexNet [1], VGG [2]) to achieve the highest possible performance. In the second step, we train modules in the small model to replace convolutional layers in the big model. We keep the each-layer outputs of them to be consistent. We choose Euclidean-Loss function,

$$E = \frac{1}{2} \|x - m\|_2^2. \tag{1}$$

where x and m are the outputs of convolutional layers in the big model and modules in the small model respectively. In this step, as shown in Fig. 1, only white and grey lines work, and the black lines are cut off. The training unit is a block, marked with a red frame. Each block consists of a convolutional layer and a module. In fact, we train modules in each block independently, which means no back propagation between blocks.

In the third step, we fine-tune the small model using cross-entropy loss. Since we use softmax function after the last layer output, we combine it with loss function,

$$E = -log \frac{e^{f_l}}{\sum_{j=1}^{c} e^{f_j}} = log \sum_{j=1}^{c} e^{f_j} - f_l, \tag{2}$$

where f is the output of last fully connected layer in the small model, c is the channel (dimension) of this output, l is the label index of the training image, and f_l is the scalar of f on label index. Image is filled with noise obstructing the classification, and it is learned by parameters. The experiment on AlexNet shows the existence of noise along parameters after layer-wise training. So we fine-tune the whole network after layer-wise training. In this step, only grey and black lines in Fig. 1 work, and the white lines are cut off. The fully connected layers in the small model are copied from the big model, and they share the same parameters.

2.2　Matrix Decomposition

In this section, we introduce matrix decomposition theory in our work. Formally, each convolutional layer takes a stack of feature maps as input, a 3-D tensor denoted as $Z \in \mathbb{R}^{c \times h \times w}$, where h and w are the height and width of feature maps respectively, and c is the number of feature maps also called channel. The parameters of convolutional layers, also called kernels, are denoted as $W \in \mathbb{R}^{n \times c \times d \times d}$, where n is the number of output feature maps, c is the number of input feature maps also called input channels, and $d \times d$ is the spatial kernel size. The output of a convolutional layer, $A \in \mathbb{R}^{n \times h' \times w'}$ is,

$$A_{u,i,j} = \sum_{v=1}^{c} \sum_{m=1}^{d} \sum_{n=1}^{d} Z_{v,(i-1)s+m-p,(j-1)s+n-p} W_{u,v,m,n} \tag{3}$$
$$i.e. \ A = Z \otimes W,$$

where p and s are padding size and convolutional stride respectively, and $\otimes$ represents spatial convolution. If we decompose W into two matrices, denoted as $P \in \mathbb{R}^{c \times k}$ and $Q \in \mathbb{R}^{n \times k \times d \times d}$,

$$W_{u,v,m,n} = \sum_{l=1}^{k} P_{v,l} Q_{u,l,m,n}. \tag{4}$$

$$A_{u,i,j} = \sum_{v=1}^{c} \sum_{m=1}^{d} \sum_{n=1}^{d} Z_{v,(i-1)s+m-p,(j-1)s+n-p} \sum_{l=1}^{k} P_{v,l} Q_{u,l,m,n}$$
$$= \sum_{l=1}^{k} \sum_{m=1}^{d} \sum_{n=1}^{d} \left(\sum_{v=1}^{c} Z_{v,(i-1)s+m-p,(j-1)s+n-p} P_{v,l} \right) Q_{u,l,m,n} \tag{5}$$
$$i.e. \ A = Z \otimes P \otimes Q.$$

This formula means that the origin convolutional layer can be decomposed into two sequentially connected convolutional layers: one layer with 1×1 kernels and the other with $d \times d$ kernels. Besides, if we exchange the orders of P and Q, we have

$$W_{u,v,m,n} = \sum_{l=1}^{k} Q_{v,l,m,n} P_{l,u}. \tag{6}$$

In this way, we can obtain a variant of sequentially-connected convolutional layers, which are one layer with $d \times d$ kernels and the other with 1×1 kernels.

2.3   Modules Inspired by Biological Neural Networks

In this section we introduce the principles behind our module design method. The Ventral Stream, going through V1, V2, V4 and the inferior temporal lobe area, is involved in object identification and recognition [9]. We design three kinds of modules, called MODULE-A, MODULE-B, and MODULE-C, shown in Fig. 2. Following the inspiration from Ventral Stream, MODULE-A corresponds to V1 and V2. MODULE-B and MODULE-C correspond to V4 and the inferior temporal lobe area respectively.

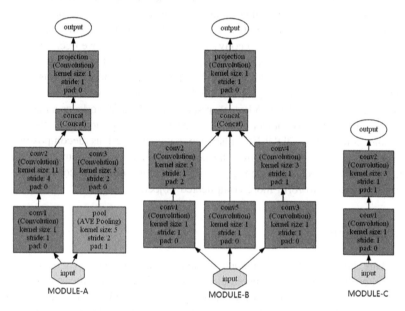

Fig. 2.   Three kinds of modules used in our model. A concatenate layer (Concat) concatenates two or more outputs of convolutional layers along the channel axis.

MODULE-A usually takes the role of the first layer in the small model. Similarly V1 and V2 are in the front of visual cortex. Color and shape are treated in different areas in V1 and V2 [9]. As shown in Fig. 2, MODULE-A has two paths which learn shape and color respectively: one path consists of conv1 and conv2, and the other consists of average pooling and conv3. The number of output feature map of conv1 is 1, which means conv1 translates the input color image into a colorless image. Therefore conv2 can only learn the shape. Average pooling is used to decrease the size of input, because we find the color path requires lower resolution. Conv3 receives all color channels, reflecting the color path. The output of MODULE-A is a linear combination of conv2 and conv3 via projection (convolution with 1×1 kernels). The structure of MODULE-A can also be explained from the perspective of matrix decomposition introduced in Sect. 2.2. Firstly we decompose the original convolutional layer into conv' and projection. Then conv' can be divided into two parts along channel axis, noted as conv2' and conv3'. Then we decompose conv2' into conv1 and conv2. And we decrease kernel size of conv3' to obtain conv3. To keep the receptive fields of two paths consistent, we add an average pooling layer before conv3.

Our MODULE-B, similar with V4, replaces the middle convolutional layers in the big model. V4 has a significant function in visual attention [13]. Inspired by this, MODULE-B focuses on the important part of feature maps and filters the jamming information. MODULE-B has three paths representing different scales of attention. The kernel sizes in conv3, conv4 and conv5 are 5×5, 3×3, and 1×1 respectively. Finally we combine different scales of attentions together via projection. There is also another explanation for MODULE-B from matrix decomposition scheme in Sect. 2.2. Firstly we decompose the original convolutional layer into conv' and projection. Then conv' can be divided into three parts along channel axis, noted as conv1', conv3', and conv5. We decompose conv1' into conv1 and conv2. Similarly we decompose conv3' into conv3 and conv4. Finally we decrease the kernel sizes of conv4 and conv5.

In deeper layers, we adopt MODULE-C. The inferior temporal lobe is capable of remembering particular objects [12]. MODULE-C is very simple, consisting of conv1 and conv2, with 1×1 and 5×5 kernels respectively. Conv2 works as a memory unit, storing the information of object. Conv1 fuses feature maps to match the memory. Conv1 and conv2 in MODULE-C also can be considered as decomposition of a convolutional layer. If we exchange the position of conv1 and conv2, we obtain a variant of MODULE-C. Here conv2 is still a memory unit, but conv1 copes with memory information to form more complicated object.

3   Experiment

To validate our algorithm, we reduce computational complexity of state-of-the-art CNNs without much error rate increase. Following [5, 7, 8], we measure the computational complexity as the number of floating point multiply accumulate operations (FLOPs) in the forward propagation through convolutional layers. In our method, conventional convolutional layers in large CNNs are replaced with our proposed modules that need much fewer FLOPs. All CNNs are implemented using Caffe [11]. The layer-wise training adopts batch gradient descent method.

3.1   MNIST

MNIST is a large database of handwritten digits. We introduce lenet-conv, a model in Caffe [11], consisting of two convolutional layers and two fully connected layers. The validation error rate of lenet-conv is 1.03%. We use a variant of MODULE-C to replace convolutional layers in lenet-conv and the new model is denoted as lenet-conv-dec, as shown in Table 1.

Table 1. The structure of lenet-conv and lenet-conv-dec. Conv1, conv2, fc1, and fc2 are layer names. (K × K, N) denotes a convolutional layer with N kernels of K × K size. Fc1 has 500 neurons and fc2 has 10.

model	conv1		conv2		fc1	fc2
lenet-conv	5×5,20		5×5,50		500	10
lenet-conv-dec	5×5,4	1×1,20	5×5,10	1×1,50	500	10

We compare our layer-wise training algorithm with Distilling [4] and label training, to prove that our algorithm enables faster convergence rate. We didn't compare with other methods [5, 7, 8], because they were designed for large networks and results on this small database were not reported. Label training is the original training algorithm of lenet-conv. Distilling and label training run 15K iterations, and the lowest error rates and corresponding iterations were recorded, shown in Table 2. Our algorithm run 500 iterations on layer-wise training and 5000 iterations on fine-tuning. In the compare of error rates, they are all close to lenet-conv, but ours is a little lower. In the compare of training iterations, our algorithm has an advantage.

Table 2. Error and training iterations of different algorithms. Our algorithm run 500 iterations on layer-wise training and 5000 iterations on fine-tuning.

Algorithm	Error	Training iterations
Label training	1.07	12500
Distilling [4]	1.04	11500
Layer-wise training	**0.99**	**500 + 5000**

3.2 ILSVRC

The ImageNet Large Scale Visual Recognition Challenge (ILSVRC) [10] evaluates algorithms for image classification at large scale. We adopt two famous CNN models, AlexNet [1] (CaffeNet [11] as a variant) and VGG-16 [2], as our baselines. The AlexNet and VGG-16 are directly downloaded from Caffe's [11] model zoo. In the following experiment, we adopt the increase of top-5 error rate and reduction of FLOPs as benchmarks to compare different algorithms. In this section, we prove our algorithm is better than previous algorithms [5, 7, 8] in both the error rate and compression rate. All cited results come from their papers. We didn't compare Distilling method [4] because the results on this large database were not reported and we achieve poor results with this method.

AlexNet Model

Structures of different models are detailed in Table 3. The increase of top-5 error rate and reduction of FLOPs are given in Table 4. The alex-base model is the original AleNet, with 19.78% top-5 error rate and 666M FLOPs.

Table 3. The structures of five variants of AlexNet. The labels, from conv1 to conv5, represent layer names of five convolutional layers. (K × K, N, %G, /S) represents a convolutional layer with N kernels of K × K size, S strides and G groups. If a hyper-parameter is omitted, it is 1. (avepool5×5, /2) means an average pooling layer with 5 × 5 kernel size and 2 strides.

Layer	alexnet-base	alexnet-dec-base	alexnet-dec-back	alexnet-dec-front	alexnet-dec-mod		
conv1	11×11,96,/4	11×11,96,/4	11×11,48,/4	11×11,96,/4	1×1,1		avepool5×5,/2
					11×11,24,/4		5×5,40,/2
			1×1,96		1×1,96		
conv2	5×5,256,%2	5×5,256,%2	5×5,128,%2	1×1,48,%2	1×1,16	1×1,12	1×1,16
						3×3,48	5×5,64
			1×1,256,%2	5×5,256,%2	1×1,256		
conv3	3×3,384	3×3,384	3×3,192	1×1,128	1×1,128		
			1×1,384	3×3,384	3×3,384,%2		
conv4	3×3,384,%2	3×3,384,%2	3×3,192,%2	1×1,192,%2	1×1,96		
			1×1,384,%2	3×3,384,%2	3×3,384,%2		
conv5	3×3,256,%2	3×3,256,%2	3×3,128,%2	1×1,192,%2	1×1,128		
			1×1,256,%2	3×3,256,%2	3×3,256,%4		

Table 4. Comparison of top-5 error rate increase and FLOPs reduction based on AlexNet.

Model	alexnet-dec-base	alexnet-dec-back	alexnet-dec-front	alexnet-dec-mod	Kim's [8]	Figurnov's [7]
error↑	+0.01	+0.04	−0.10	**+0.11**	+1.70	+2.0
FLOPs↓	1×1	2.16×	1.65×	**3.62×**	2.67×	2.0×

alexnet-dec-base

This model is used to show that layer-wise training can reproduce convolutional layers in alexnet-base from scratch. The structure of alexnet-dec-base is the same with alexnet-base and convolutional layers in alexnet-dec-base work as modules. We use the convolutional layer in alexnet-dec-base to learn the one in alexnet-base. We did not fine-tune the network after layer-wise training. The error rate of this model is close to alexnet-base. We visualized the kernels of conv1 in two models, and discovered they were almost the same except that kernels in alexnet-dec-base had more noise. Though noise didn't jeopardize this model, it become complicated when models have less redundancy. So in the following experiments we fine-tune the model after layer-wise training.

alexnet-dec-back and alexnet-dec-front

These two models are used to validate our decomposition scheme in Sect. 2.2. We replace each convolutional layer in alexnet-base with a sequence of two convolutional layers, consisting of d × d kernels and 1 × 1 kernels respectively, and the new model is called alexnet-dec-back. The alexnet-dec-front is similar but its first layer is unchanged. Our alexnet-dec-back model achieved 2.16× FLOPs reduction, with 0.04% increase in the error rate. It proved that decomposition were capable of achieving an acceptable compression rate with little increase in the error rate. Our alexnet-dec-front achieved

1.65× FLOPs reduction, lower than alexnet-dec-back but it achieved 0.10% decrease in the error rate. It proved the existence of redundant parameters.

alexnet-dec-mod

Finally we used the modules in Sect. 2.3. The first convolutional layer is replace with MODULE-A, the second layer is replaced with MODULE-B, and the following layers are replaced with MODULE-C. We try to imitate the structure of Ventral Stream. We achieve 3.62× FLOPs reduction, with 0.11% increase in the error rate (3.62× /+0.11). Comparing to the methods of Kim (2.67× /+1.70) [8] and Figurnov (2× /+2.0) [7], our method has enormous advantages for the error rate and compression rate.

VGG-16

VGG-16 has 15.35G FLOPs, with 10.10% top-5 error rate. Structures of vgg-base (VGG-16) and our vgg-dec-mod model are shown in Table 5. The increase of top-5 error rate and reduction of FLOPs are given in Table 6.

Conv1_1 is unchanged. MODULE-B is used to replace conv1_2, conv2_1, conv2_2, conv3_1, and conv3_2. MODULE-C is used to replace the other convolutional layers. Here MODULE-B is a little different from the prototype. The kernel size of original convolutional layers is 3 × 3. So the convolutional layer with 5 × 5 kernel size in MODULE-B and the layer in front of it are not necessary. Finally we achieve 5.67× FLOPs reduction, with 0.43% increase in top-5 error rate (5.67× /+0.43). Comparing to the methods of Kim (4.93× /+0.50%) [8], Figurnov (1.9× /+2.5%) [7] and Zhang (5× /+1.0%) [5], our method has advantages on both the error rate and compression rate.

Table 5. The structure of vgg-16-base (original VGG-16) and vgg-dec-mod. The meaning of each label is the same with Table 3.

Layer	vgg-16-base	vgg-dec-mod		Layer	vgg-16-base	vgg-dec-mod	
conv1_1	3×3,64	3×3,64		conv1_2	3×3,64	1×1,12	1×1,8
						3×3,24	
						1×1,64	
conv2_1	3×3,128	1×1,24	1×1,8	conv2_2	3×3,128	1×1,36	1×1,16
		3×3,48,%2				3×3,48,%2	
		1×1,128				3×3,512,%2	
conv3_1	3×3,256	1×1,36	1×1,16	conv3_2	3×3,256	1×1,48	1×1,32
		3×3,96,%2				3×3,96,%2	
		1×1,256				1×1,256	
conv3_3	3×3,256	1×1,96		conv4_1	3×3,512	1×1,96	
		3×3,256,%2				3×3,512,%2	
conv4_2	3×3,512	1×1,144		conv4_3	3×3,512	1×1,128	
		3×3,512,%2				3×3,512,%2	
conv5_1	3×3,512	1×1,256		conv5_2	3×3,512	1×1,256	
		3×3,512,%4				3×3,512,%4	
conv5_3	3×3,512	1×1,256					
		3×3,512,%4					

Table 6. Comparison of top-5 error rate increase and FLOPs reduction based on VGG-16.

Model	vgg-16-dec-mod	Kim's [8]	Figurnov's [7]	Zhang's [5]
error↑	**+0.43**	+0.50	+2.5	+1.0
FLOPs↓	**5.67×**	4.93×	1.9×	5×

4 Conclusion

In this work, we propose a layer-wise training algorithm to create efficient convolutional neural networks and achieve better results than previous works, validated by better compression rate, lower error rate and faster convergence rate. Inspiration from visual cortex of brain help us design efficient modules to replace conventional convolutional layers. Besides our method is extremely flexible. It is easy to adopt other module design methods to achieve higher compression rate and lower error rate in the future.

Acknowledgements. This work is supported by the 973 project 2015CB351803, NSFC No. 61572451 and No. 61390514, Youth Innovation Promotion Association CAS CX2100060016, and Fok Ying Tung Education Foundation WF2100060004.

References

1. Krizhevsky, A., Sutskever, I., Hinton, G.: Imagenet classification with deep convolutional neural networks. In: Advances in Neural Information Processing Systems, pp. 1106–1114 (2012)
2. Simonyan, K., Zisserman, A.: Very deep convolutional networks for large-scale image recognition (2014). arXiv preprint: arXiv:1409.1556
3. Denton, E., Zaremba, W., Bruna, J., LeCun, Y., Fergus, R.: Exploiting linear structure within convolutional networks for efficient evaluation. In: Advances in Neural Information Processing Systems, pp. 1269–1277 (2014)
4. Hinton, G., Vinyals, O., Dean, J.: Distilling the knowledge in a neural network (2015). arXiv preprint: arXiv:1503.02531
5. Zhang, X., Zou, J., He, K., Sun, J.: Accelerating very deep convolutional networks for classification and detection. IEEE Trans. Pattern Anal. Mach. Intell. **38**(10), 1943–1955 (2016)
6. Han, S., Mao, H., Dally, W.J.: Deep compression: Compressing deep neural networks with pruning, trained quantization and huffman coding (2015). arXiv preprint: arXiv:1510.00149
7. Figurnov, M., Ibraimova, A., Vetrov, D.P., Kohli, P.: PerforatedCNNs: acceleration through elimination of redundant convolutions. In: Advances in Neural Information Processing Systems, pp. 947–955 (2016)
8. Kim, Y.D., Park, E., Yoo, S., Choi, T., Yang, L., Shin, D.: Compression of deep convolutional neural networks for fast and low power mobile applications (2015). arXiv preprint: arXiv:1511.06530
9. Nicholls, J.G., Martin, A.R., Wallace, B.G., Fuchs, P.A.: From Neuron to Brain. Sinauer Associates, Sunderland (2001)
10. Russakovsky, O., Deng, J., Su, H., Krause, J., Satheesh, S., et al.: Imagenet large scale visual recognition challenge. Int. J. Comput. Vis. **115**(3), 211–252 (2015)

11. Jia, Y., Shelhamer, E., Donahue, J., Karayev, S., Long, J., et al.: Caffe: convolutional architecture for fast feature embedding. In: Proceedings of the 22nd ACM International Conference on Multimedia, pp. 675–678 (2014)
12. Chelazzi, L., Miller, E.K., Duncanf, J.: A neural basis for visual search in inferior temporal lobe. Nature **363**(6427), 345–347 (1993)
13. Roe, A.W., Chelazzi, L., Connor, C.E., Conway, B.R., Fujita, I., et al.: Toward a unified theory of visual area V4. Neuron **74**(1), 12–29 (2012)

Learning Image Representation Based on Convolutional Neural Networks

Zhanbo Yang[1], Fei Hu[1,2], Jingyuan Wang[1], Jinjing Zhang[1], and Li Li[1(✉)]

[1] School of Computer and Information Science, Southwest University,
Chongqing 400715, China
perphyoung@email.swu.edu.cn, lily@swu.edu.cn
[2] Network Centre, Chongqing University of Education, Chongqing, China

Abstract. Image similarity is widely applicable in image understanding and object tracking. It is easy for human to fulfill while difficult for machines. In this paper, we present a simple but efficient end-to-end mechanism to transfer an image into its corresponding representation in vector space based on Convolutional Neural Networks supervised by word2vec, which can then be applied to applications such as image classification and object detection, and a further work of image caption/description. We describe how we train the model to achieve a deep semantic understanding of the image along with its caption. We train our method on Flickr8k and Flickr30k datasets respectively, and evaluate on Corel1k benchmark dataset. Through the visualization of how our model extracts the features of images and produces similar vectors for similar images, we demonstrate the effectiveness of our proposed model.

Keywords: Image similarity · Vector space · Convolutional neural network · Word2vec

1 Introduction

Humans can easily distinguish whether two images are similar or not. However, this remarkable ability is a difficult task for visual recognition systems. To cope with this problem, image representation is proposed. The image representation allows the use of learning techniques for the analysis of images (for computer vision) as well as for the synthesis of images (for computer graphics) [1]. Currently, two main directions of computer vision domain are image classification and image caption. Image representation is more advanced than image classification, as well as the middle-layer for image caption.

In order to generate a discriminative image representation, efforts combining with hand-crafted local features and Bag-of-Feature (BoF) [2] have been made, and its improved approaches, such as Vector of the Locally Aggregated Descriptors (VLAD) [3] and Fisher Vector (FV) [4]. With the rapid development of machine learning, especially the deep learning [5], Convolutional Neural Networks (CNNs) [6] are proposed to tackle with image-oriented problems.

© Springer International Publishing AG 2017
D. Liu et al. (Eds.): ICONIP 2017, Part II, LNCS 10635, pp. 642–652, 2017.
https://doi.org/10.1007/978-3-319-70096-0_66

In this paper, we take advantage of various CNNs to generate the image representation in a vector space, with the output of the word2vec as the exemplar. Concretely, our main contributions are twofold:

- We develop an end-to-end mechanism that produce a characteristic image representation in vector space based on Convolutional Neural Networks.
- We take advantage of the word2vec model to supervise the quality of the image representation.

The remainder of this paper is organized as follows. The related work is provided in Sect. 2. In Sect. 3, we provide a brief overview of our proposed mechanism. Section 4 describe our experiments, and in Sect. 5, we evaluate our model as an application. We conclude the paper in Sect. 6.

2   Related Work

2.1   Image Representation

Our model is mainly inspired by the previous works on image representation while with a more advanced and efficient approach. Sivic et al. [2] studied the BoF representation which groups local descriptors. Schmid et al. [3] proposed an efficient way of aggregating local features into a vector of fixed dimension, namely VLAD. And a formulated probabilistic version of VLAD called Fisher Vector was addressed by Perronnin et al. [4]. Our model takes advantage of Convolutional Neural Networks and produce an end-to-end mechanism for image representation in vector space.

2.2   Image Caption

The most promising application in computer vision domain is image caption, or called image description. Some pioneering methods that address the challenge have been developed [7,8]. However, these approaches often rely on hard-coded visual concepts and sentence templates, which imposes limits on their variety. Kiros et al. [9] firstly take the neural networks to generate sentence for image by proposing an image-text multimodal log-bilinear neural language model. In [10], a multimodal Recurrent Neural Networks model is proposed for image caption, which directly models the probability of generating a word given previous words and image. Furthermore, Vinyals et al. [11] propose an end-to-end neural networks system by utilizing LSTM to generate sentence for image. These models enlighten our direction, and our model can make a step further to learn how to generate a description giving an image.

2.3   Word2vec

In Natural Language Processing (NLP) domain, representation of words has been explored by several pioneers. A very popular model [12] called Neural Network

Language Model (NNLM) was proposed, where a feedforward neural network with a linear layer and a non-linear hidden layer was used to learn jointly the word vector representation and a statistical language model. In 2013, Mikolov et al. [13] produce a powerful tool which provides an efficient implementation of the continuous bag-of-word and skip-gram architectures for computing vector representations of words[1]. Our model uses the word2vec to obtain the ideal vector for the supervised approach.

2.4   CNNs in Visual Domains

Multiple methods have been developed for representing images in higher level representations. Convolutional Neural Networks (CNNs) have recently emerged as a powerful set of models for image classification and object detection [14]. LeNet [6] is the first successful application of CNN, which was proposed by LeCun et, al. to recognize the handwriting digits. AlexNet [15] is a mightier as well as more complex model, which won the Imagenet Large Scale Visual Recognition Challenge 2010 (ILSVRC-2010). In recent years, more powerful architectures of Convolutional Neural Network have been proposed, such as VGG-Net [16], ResNet [17] and Inception [18]. In our proposed mechanism, we choose the LeNet and AlexNet to be the more advanced training models, as well as the classic convolutional one.

3   Our Model

Our model is a supervised approach based on CNNs and word2vec. A high-level overview of our model is presented in Fig. 1.

There are two parts in our model. On the *left* side of Fig. 1 (Train stage), we transfer an image to vector1, and its corresponding caption to vector2 by means of word2vec. Then we train the CNN to learn how to represent an image in its correlative vector by minimizing the difference between vector1 and vector2. On the *right* side (Test stage), we have obtained the trained CNN (CNN*), then we feed test images to it and measure the similarity among their generated vectors. Our approach can further be applied to image classification and object detection.

For an input image and its corresponding caption, the main steps are as follows:

1. CNN is used to transfer an image to a vector (vector1)
2. Word2vec is used to convert a caption to a vector (vector2)
3. Learning a deep semantic understanding of the image along with its caption

---

[1] https://code.google.com/archive/p/word2vec/.

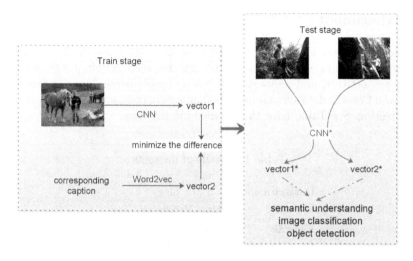

Fig. 1: Overview of our approach

3.1   Weight Updating

Generally, the basic math representation of convolution operation can be described like:

$$f(x,y) \circ w(x,y) = \sum_{s=-a}^{a} \sum_{t=-b}^{b} w(s,t) f(x-s, y-t) \tag{1}$$

For image-oriented task, $f(x,y)$ is the pixel value of image, and $w(x,y)$ is the convolution kernel, while a and b define the kernel size.

Take the classic convolution network as an example, the detailed form of our approach is as follows:

$$x_{ij} = tanh((W_c \times I)_{ij} + b_c) \tag{2}$$
$$h_k = max((x_{ij})_k), \quad for \ x \in kernel_{ij} \tag{3}$$
$$v_k = tanh((W_v \times h_k) + b_v) \tag{4}$$

where I is the image, and x_{ij}, h_k, v_k are the output of convolution, max-pooling and dense (fully connected) layer, respectively. Because the element of the vector that generated by word2vec is between -1 and 1, we choose $tanh()$ to be the activation function, which is a hyperbolic tangent that ensures the output values are between the same interval.

In our proposed approach, I is resize to 224×224, and the max-pooling layer has the kernel of size 3×3. In the end, every image is represented as a set of 128-dimensional vectors.

The other corresponding vector is provided by word2vec, then we apply MSE to compute the loss and adjust the parameters W_c, Wv and the respective biases b_c, b_v through backpropagation algorithm.

4 Experiment

Datasets. We use Flickr8k [19], Flickr30k [20] and Corel1k [21] benchmark datasets in our experiments. The former two datasets contain 8,000 and 31,000 images respectively, and annotated with 5 sentences using Amazon Mechanical Turk. And Corel1k dataset contains 1,000 images of common objects for standard image testing. See Table 1 for the detailed information.

Table 1: Details of datasets

Dataset name	Size		
	Train	Validation	Test
Flickr8k	6,000	1,000	1,000
Flickr30k	28,000	1,000	1,000
Corel1k	-	-	1,000

Data Preprocessing. We alter all sentences to lowercase, discard non-alphanumeric characters. We filter words to those which occur at least 2 times in the whole caption set. Then we apply *gensim*'s Word2Vec() function to train the corresponding model for the Flickr8k and Flickr30k, respectively. This operation results in a less number of vocabulary set for the model. In detail, each word in the vocabulary set is convert to a 128-dimensional vector. For the sentence, we just take the dimension-wise mean of each word vector as the ultimate vector, which is the corresponding one the CNNs endeavor to learn.

CNN Models. In our experiments, we use three type of CNN architectures, namely simple Conv, LeNet and AlexNet. The detailed information can be seen from Table 2.

In Table 2, the conv($a \times a, b, c$) stands for convolution layer with kernel size $a \times a$, strides b, and output size c; max-pooling and dense layer are present as max_pool(pool size, strides, output size) and dense(output size), respectively. The total params denotes the parameters the model need to learn.

4.1 From Image to Vector

Convolutional Neural Networks are widely used and studied in computer vision domain for their excellent performance for image tasks, and are currently state-of-the-art for object recognition, detection and localization [14]. For our method, we begin with a simple CNN with one convolution layer followed by one max-pooling layer. Then a LeNet-like model [6] is used to take the depth of network

Table 2: Details of CNN models

	Conv	LeNet	AlexNet
Layer name	conv(11×11,4,96)	conv(11×11,4,96)	conv(11×11,4,96)
	max_pool(3×3,2,96)	max_pool(3×3,2,96)	max_pool(3×3,2,96)
	dense(128)	conv(5×5,1,256)	conv(5×5,1,256)
	-	max_pool(3×3,2,256)	max_pool(3×3,2,256)
	-	dense(128)	conv(3×3,1,384)
	-	-	conv(3×3,1,384)
	-	-	conv(3×3,1,256)
	-	-	max_pool(3×3,2,256)
	-	-	dense(4096)
	-	-	dense(4096)
	-	-	dense(128)
Layer depth	3	5	11
Total params	8,341,760	3,926,528	22,105,600

into consideration. Lastly, an AlexNet-like architecture [15] is applied to improve the performance.

For the original LeNet is utilized to train on small resolution images for handwriting digit recognition, we modify the convolution filter to a larger size to process the Flickr8k and Flickr30k datasets (the same as the first few layers of AlexNet, for simplicity), and the output is a 128-dimensional vector.

AlexNet is a more powerful model to extract the features of an image. In our framework, we slightly modify the last layer to 128 dimension so as to keep consistent with the output of word2vec.

4.2   From Caption to Vector

For the Flickr8k [19] and Flickr30k [20] datasets, each image is paired with five different captions which provide clear descriptions of the salient entities and events.

We first concatenate the five captions into only one and generate the tokenized words. For simplicity, we convert all the letter to lower case, remove the punctuation and stop words. Then there comes the word2vec, the most important preprocess part of our model. Word2vec is a group of related models that are used to produce word embeddings. In our framework, $nltk^2$ and $gensim^3$ are used to obtain the vector that CNNs endeavor to learn.

---

[2] http://www.nltk.org/.
[3] http://radimrehurek.com/gensim/.

4.3 Learning Deep Semantics by Minimizing the Difference

We train our model on the *keras*[4] platform with *TensorFlow*[5] as the backend. Keras is a high-level neural networks API, written in Python and capable of running on top of either *TensorFlow* or *Theano*[6]. And TensorFlow is an open source deep learning software library for numerical computation using data flow graphs powered by Google Inc.

The CNN is trained to minimize the difference between two vectors, thus two images looks alike will be similar. Our method is able to differentiate utterly-alike and generally-alike, since varying weights apply the MSE (Mean Squared Error) loss function to evaluate the quality of the CNNs.

4.4 Generating Vector for Image

We first investigate the quality of the generated vector. For all of our experiments, we limit the size of the vocabulary to 128, so is the dimension of the generated vector.

Results of our experiment are depicted in Table 3. And the detailed loss during training through 50 epochs can be found in Fig. 2.

Table 3: MSE losses of our approach

Model	Flickr8k			Flickr30k		
	Train	Validation	Test	Train	Validation	Test
Conv(3)	0.3593	0.3780	0.3793	0.3764	0.3930	0.3575
LeNet(5)	0.0527	0.0491	0.0515	0.0872	0.0893	0.0879
AlexNet(11)	**0.0470**	**0.0444**	**0.0475**	**0.0800**	**0.0818**	**0.0804**

In Table 3, the number behind the model name is the total amount of layers (including the output layer, but not the input one). Conv is the model of 1 convolution layer following by 1 max-pooling layer, and a dense (fully connected) layer. LeNet is the modified of the standard one, so is the AlexNet. We take the MSE to measure the performance of the quality of models (lower is better).

Figure 2 shows the MSE losses of the experiments. (We omit the curves of Conv for its scores are too high.) (a) For the Flickr8k, the losses are less than that of Flickr30k, but the validation losses are higher than the train ones. We will talk about this phenomenon again later on. (b) For the Flickr30k, the losses are a little higher, but the performance of the model is better.

---

[4] https://keras.io/.
[5] https://www.tensorflow.org/.
[6] http://deeplearning.net/software/theano/.

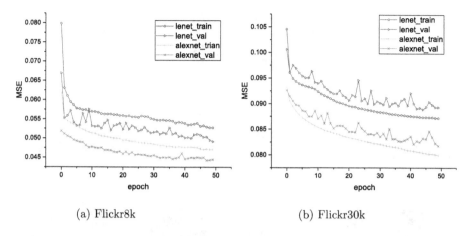

(a) Flickr8k   (b) Flickr30k

Fig. 2: MSE losses of the experiments during training (val: validation)

The Impact of Data Scale on Performance. From Table 3, we can see that with the increment of the amount of layers, all MSE losses are obviously dropped. But there is something abnormal we need to notice: for the Flickr8k dataset, the train losses are lower than the validation ones. For the reason that the performance of the model on Flickr30k, which shows that the validation losses are slightly higher than that of the train ones, we can guess that this is due to the inadequacy of the data scale. We can further infer that with the augmentation of the data scale, our model can perform better.

5   Applications

Our proposed model has potential applications in image classification and object detection, where measuring image similarity is important in both scenarios.

We now evaluate the ability of our model with Cosine Similarity Score (CSC) as the metric to measure the similarity between images. We firstly select a sample image from Corel1k dataset and compute the CSC, then we compute the CSCs of all the images in the whole dataset. Finally, we choose the ones whose CSC to the sample one is greater than 0.990, 0.985 and 0.900 (higher is more similar), respectively. The result of this experiment is shown in Fig. 3.

In Fig. 3, the center image is the sample, and the numbers denote the image order and the correlative CSC. We sort the images in a clockwise direction following the decrease of CSC. The images on the top, right and left of the dashed line is the ones whose CSC to the sample one is greater than 0.990, 0.985 and 0.900, respectively. Although all the images are similar to some extent, our approach can still find the differences between them. For example, the 6th image differs slightly from the sample one in flower's color, and the 7th image has a quite different pose and without green leaves. Whereas the 8th and 9th images are varying obviously in flower's color, thus get the much lower CSC.

Fig. 3: Illustration of similarity between images: flowers (Color figure online)

As we can observe in Fig. 3, the model learns image similarity that agree very strongly with human intuition. The above experiment demonstrates that our model can extract the features and learn the image representation well, and that the effectiveness of our model.

6   Conclusion

In this paper, we propose a simple but efficient end-to-end mechanism to produce a vector representation for image based on Convolutional Neural Networks. We train our model in Flickr8k and Flickr30k datasets respectively, and evaluate it on Corel1k dataset, and showing that our model is capable of extract the features from image and generate similar vectors for similar images with cosine similarity score as the metric. Our work is promising in computer vision domain for image classification and object detection.

Acknowledgments. The authors would also like to thank the anonymous referees for their valuable comments and helpful suggestions. The work was supported by the Fundamental Research Funds For the Central Universities (No. XDJK2017D059). Li Li is the corresponding author for the paper.

References

1. Poggio, T.: Image representations for visual learning. In: Bigün, J., Chollet, G., Borgefors, G. (eds.) AVBPA 1997. LNCS, vol. 1206, pp. 143–143. Springer, Heidelberg (1997). doi:10.1007/BFb0015989
2. Sivic, J., Zisserman, A., others: Video google: a text retrieval approach to object matching in videos. In: International Conference on Computer Vision, pp. 1470–1477 (2003)
3. Schmid, C., Patrick, P.: Aggregating local descriptors into a compact image representation. In: Computer Vision and Pattern Recognition, pp. 3304–3311 (2010)
4. Perronnin, F., Sánchez, J., Mensink, T.: Improving the fisher kernel for large-scale image classification. In: Daniilidis, K., Maragos, P., Paragios, N. (eds.) ECCV 2010. LNCS, vol. 6314, pp. 143–156. Springer, Heidelberg (2010). doi:10.1007/978-3-642-15561-1_11
5. LeCun, Y., Bengio, Y., Hinton, G.: Deep learning. Nature **521**, 436–444 (2015)
6. LeCun, Y., Bottou, L., Bengio, Y., Haffner, P.: Gradient-based learning applied to document recognition. Proc. IEEE **86**, 2278–2323 (1998)
7. Farhadi, A., Hejrati, M., Sadeghi, M.A., Young, P., Rashtchian, C., Hockenmaier, J., Forsyth, D.: Every picture tells a story: generating sentences from images. In: Daniilidis, K., Maragos, P., Paragios, N. (eds.) ECCV 2010. LNCS, vol. 6314, pp. 15–29. Springer, Heidelberg (2010). doi:10.1007/978-3-642-15561-1_2
8. Kulkarni, G., Premraj, V., Ordonez, V., Dhar, S., Li, S., Choi, Y., Berg, A.C., Berg, T.L.: Baby talk: Understanding and generating simple image descriptions. IEEE Trans. Pattern Anal. Mach. Intell. **35**, 2891–2903 (2013)
9. Kiros, R., Salakhutdinov, R., Zemel, R.: Multimodal neural language models. In: Proceedings of the 31st International Conference on Machine Learning (ICML 2014), pp. 595–603 (2014)
10. Mao, J., Xu, W., Yang, Y., Wang, J., Yuille, A.L.: Explain images with multimodal recurrent neural networks. arXiv Preprint arXiv:1410.1090 (2014)
11. Vinyals, O., Toshev, A., Bengio, S., Erhan, D.: Show and tell: lessons learned from the 2015 MSCOCO image captioning challenge. IEEE Trans. Pattern Anal. Mach. Intell. **39**, 652–663 (2017)
12. Bengio, Y., Ducharme, R., Vincent, P., Jauvin, C.: A neural probabilistic language model. J. Mach. Learn. Res. **3**, 1137–1155 (2003)
13. Mikolov, T., Chen, K., Corrado, G., Dean, J.: Efficient Estimation of Word Representations in Vector Space. arXiv Preprint arXiv:1301.3781 (2013)
14. Russakovsky, O., Deng, J., Su, H., Krause, J., Satheesh, S., Ma, S., Huang, Z., Karpathy, A., Khosla, A., Bernstein, M., Berg, A.C., Fei-Fei, L.: ImageNet large scale visual recognition challenge. Int. J. Comput. Vis. **115**, 211–252 (2015)
15. Krizhevsky, A., Sutskever, I., Hinton, G.E.: Imagenet classification with deep convolutional neural networks. In: Advances in Neural Information Processing Systems, pp. 1097–1105 (2012)
16. Simonyan, K., Zisserman, A.: Very Deep Convolutional Networks for Large-Scale Image Recognition. arXiv Preprint arXiv:1409.1556 (2014)
17. Dosovitskiy, A., Springenberg, J.T., Brox, T.: Deep residual learning for image recognition. In: Proceedings of the IEEE Computer Society Conference on Computer Vision and Pattern Recognition, pp. 1538–1546 (2015)
18. Szegedy, C., Vanhoucke, V., Ioffe, S., Shlens, J., Wojna, Z.: Rethinking the inception architecture for computer vision. In: Proceedings of the IEEE Computer Society Conference on Computer Vision and Pattern Recognition (CVPR), pp. 2818–2826 (2016)

19. Hodosh, M., Young, P., Hockenmaier, J.: Framing image description as a ranking task: data, models and evaluation metrics. J. Artif. Intell. Res. **47**, 853–899 (2013)
20. Young, P., Lai, A., Hodosh, M., Hockenmaier, J.: From image descriptions to visual denotations: new similarity metrics for semantic inference over event descriptions. Trans. Assoc. Comput. Linguist. **2**, 67–78 (2014)
21. Wang, J.Z., Li, J., Wiederhold, G.: SIMPLIcity: semantics-sensitive integrated matching for picture libraries. IEEE Trans. Pattern Anal. Mach. Intell. **23**, 947–963 (2001)

Heterogeneous Features Integration in Deep Knowledge Tracing

Lap Pong Cheung[1(✉)] and Haiqin Yang[2]

[1] Computer Science and Engineering, The Chinese University of Hong Kong,
Shatin, Hong Kong
lpcheung@link.cuhk.edu.hk
[2] Department of Computing, Hang Seng Management College, Shatin, Hong Kong
hqyang@ieee.org

Abstract. Knowledge tracing is a significant research topic in educational data mining. The goal is to automatically trace students' knowledge states by analyzing their exercise performance. Recently proposed Deep Knowledge Tracing (DKT) model has shown a significant improvement to solve this task by applying deep recurrent neural networks to learn interaction between knowledge components and exercises. The input of the model is only the one-hot encoding to represent the exercise tags and it excludes all other heterogeneous features, which may degrade the performance. To further improve the model performance, researchers have analyzed the heterogeneous features and provided manual ways to select the features and discretize them appropriately. However, the feature engineering efforts are not feasible for data with a huge number of features. To tackle with them, we propose an automatic and intelligent approach to integrate the heterogeneous features into the DKT model. More specifically, we encode the predicted response and the true response into binary bits and combine them with the original one-hot encoding feature as the input to a Long Short Term Memory (LSTM) model, where the predicted response is learned via Classification And Regression Trees (CART) on the heterogeneous features. The predicted response plays the role of determining whether a student will answer the exercise correctly, which can relieve the effect of exceptional samples. Our empirical evaluation on two educational datasets verifies the effectiveness of our proposal.

Keywords: Recurrent neural networks · Knowledge tracing · Decision tree

1 Introduction

Recently, Massive Online Open Course (MOOC) platforms, such as Coursera, Edx, and Khan Academy, have provided high quality online courses, which attract a large amount of enrolled users worldwide [1]. Data collected from these platforms enables researchers to investigate and monitor the learning process of students, which triggers more attention on educational data mining (EDM) [2,3].

© Springer International Publishing AG 2017
D. Liu et al. (Eds.): ICONIP 2017, Part II, LNCS 10635, pp. 653–662, 2017.
https://doi.org/10.1007/978-3-319-70096-0_67

Knowledge tracing is a significant research topic in EDM, where its goal is to model students' knowledge state over time so that we can estimate their learning progress of mastering the required knowledge components [4]. Inferring student knowledge allows us to adapt to the levels of students and to recommend suitable exercises and learning materials to students according to their needs [5,6].

In the literature, there are two main streams of approaches to solve this task. One is Bayesian Knowledge Tracing (BKT) [4,7,8], which applies a Hidden Markov Model (HMM) to model the knowledge components. The hidden states are updated according to each student's responses to the exercises. The other is Deep Knowledge Tracing (DKT) [9,10], which utilizes deep recurrent neural networks (RNN) to discover the hidden structure of the correlation of exercises by analyzing students' responses to the exercises. It is shown that DKT can achieve 25% gain in AUC when compared to BKT [9], though some researchers later argue that, with suitable extensions, BKT can achieve performance comparable with DKT [2]. More applications of DKT are also investigated in [11–13].

In DKT models, the input is only a one-hot encoding of the exercise tags [9]. It excludes many rich features, such as the exercise title, the number of attempts to answer, and the duration time of answers. These heterogeneous features not only provide additional exercise information, but also capture students' exercise behaviors. They indeed will help to trace students' learning procedures. Researchers then try to incorporate various features [14,15], such as measuring the effect of students' individual characteristics, assessing the effect in tutor system and measuring the effect of subskills. In [15], a manual method is proposed to analyze the features and to select appropriate features for discretization based on the statistics of the features. This method is restricted in two aspects: (1) they require sufficient domain knowledge to understand the data. This may introduce bias when practitioners do not fully explore the data. (2) They are infeasible to discretize the features when they are huge.

To resolve the above problems, we propose an automatic and intelligent approach to integrate the heterogeneous features into the DKT model. More specifically, we conduct a preprocessing step via the Classification And Regression Trees (CART) to predict whether a student can answer an exercise correctly given the heterogeneous features. Here, we consider CART because it is one of the most popular data mining algorithms for classification and also outputs meaningful and interpretable features for decision making [16,17]. We then encode the predicted response and the true response into a 4-bit binary code and combine them with the original one-hot encoding feature as the input to feed into a Long Short Term Memory (LSTM) model. Although the preprocessing step is simple, we believe that the predicted response can provide information of the performance of a student and how the student deviates from others based on the collected features. Our empirical evaluation on two educational datasets verifies our conjecture and demonstrates the effectiveness of our proposal.

The rest of the paper is organized as follows: Sect. 2 details the overall architecture of our proposal. Especially, how the heterogeneous features are learned and incorporated. Section 3 presents the datasets, the experimental setup, and the experimental results with explanation. Finally, Sect. 5 concludes the whole paper with some future work.

2   Our Proposal

Figure 1 illustrates the overall architecture of the proposed model, Deep Knowledge Tracing with Decision Trees (DKT-DT). The bottom part is the preprocessing procedure for the heterogeneous features, which are learned by CART to predict whether a student will answer the exercise correctly. The predicted response and the true response are then encoded into a 4-bit binary code and concatenated with the original one-hot encoding on the exercise tag as a new input. This input is fed into a LSTM [18] to learn the similarity of exercises and trace the knowledge components mastered by the students. Figure 1 shows a vanilla RNN for simplicity, the knowledge tracing model can be implemented by either a vanilla RNN or an LSTM.

2.1   Input and Output

Consider a specific student practicing an exercise at the t-th time stamp, let e_t and a_t be the exercise tag and the heterogeneous features, respectively. c_t

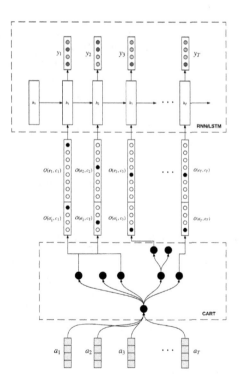

Fig. 1. The architecture of our proposal, see detailed explanation in the text.

denotes whether the student will answer the exercise correctly. c_t is 1 for correctly answering and 0 for others. As shown in Fig. 1, CART will take a_t as the input and try to predict whether the student will correctly answer the exercise. The corresponding predicted response is then denoted as a'_t.

All the features, including the exercise tags, the predicted responses, and the true responses, are represented in the one-hot encoding by $O(\cdot, \cdot)$, where $O(e_t, c_t)$ is the original one-hot encoding for an exercise tag and $O(a'_t, c_t)$ is a newly learned one-hot encoding from CART. Suppose M is the number of all exercises, the size of $O(e_t, c_t)$ is $2M$. Suppose the current exercise is the i-th in the whole quiz set, if the exercise is correctly answered, 1 will be denoted at the i-th index of the feature; otherwise, 1 will be denoted at the $i + M$-th index of the feature. Similarly, $O(a'_t, c_t)$ is represented into a feature of four bits. If CART predicts the student will correctly answer the exercise and the true response is correct, then the representation of $O(a'_t, c_t)$ is 1010. It is similar to define other cases. The concatenation of $O(e_t, c_t)$ and $O(a'_t, c_t)$ generates the input of LSTM x_t to train the corresponding model, which outputs a vector y_t with the size of M to denote the predicted probability of whether a student will answer the question correctly. In Fig. 1, different color grade in the nodes of y_t represents different level of the probability.

2.2   The Model

CART is utilized to automatically partition the feature space and outputs predicted response about whether a student will correctly answer a question. We briefly introduce the splitting criteria of CART in the following.

At each node, CART continuously conducts binary partitioning to group the interaction of the same class by maximizing the gini index or information gain. Given a set S at a node contains training data $a_t \in \mathbb{R}^n$ and the corresponding labels $c_t \in \{0, 1\}$, CART partitions the data into two subsets

$$S_l = (a_t, c_t) | a_{t,j} < t, \quad \text{and} \quad S_r = S \setminus S_l \tag{1}$$

where j is the splitting variable and t is the threshold determined by minimizing the impurity H, which are defined as follows:

$$(j^*, t^*) = \arg \min_{j,t} G(S, j, t) := \frac{|S_l|}{|S|} H(S_l) + \frac{|S_r|}{|S|} H(S_r), \tag{2}$$

where $|\cdot|$ denotes the size of the set. $H(\cdot)$ defines impurity measured by the cross entropy. For region R with N observations, the cross entropy H is defined as

$$H(X) = - \sum_k p_k \log(p_k), \quad \text{where } p_k = \frac{1}{N} \sum_{a_t \in R} I(c_t = k), \tag{3}$$

In binary classification, $k \in \{0, 1\}$.

By minimizating cross entropy, CART learns a set of classification rules. At time t, a_t is fed into the root of CART and follows the path assigned by the classification rules until getting a prediction a'_t. It is noted that the information of heterogeneous features is absorbed by a'_t. The role is to encode the performance of a student and to measure how it deviates from other students. This can be viewed as a key factor of personalized effect, which helps the training of the LSTM.

The input $x_t = [O(e_t, c_t), O(a'_t, c_t)]$, capturing students' previous exercise performance, is fed into a LSTM to learn the hidden structure and to predict the probability that a student will correctly answer the question in the next time stamp. The similarities between previous questions and students' responses are then learned via the LSTM. The LSTM then outputs y_t, a vector denoting the predicted probability that a student will answer the exercise correctly. We need to predict all M exercises because we do not know which exercise a student is going to answer in the next time stamp. The probabilities are then updated in each time stamp.

In the test, the average loss is computed by the binary cross entropy defined as follows:

$$L = \frac{1}{N} \sum_{n=1}^{N} \sum_{t=t_0^n}^{t_0^n + T^n} c_{t+1}^n \log \hat{y}_t^n + (1 - c_{t+1}^n) \log(1 - \hat{y}_t^n), \tag{4}$$

where N is the number of students, t_0^n is the starting index for the n-th student in the test set and T^n is the number of exercises for the student. The predicted value $\hat{y}_t^n$ is the inner product of predicted output and the one-hot encoding of the exercises conducted by the student n, i.e., $\hat{y}_t^n = y_t^{n\top} O(e_{t+1}^n)$ because $\hat{y}_t^n$ can output the corresponding predicted probability that the student n can answer the question correctly in the next time stamp.

3   Experiments

3.1   Datasets

Two educational datasets collected from the computer-based online learning platforms are test in the experiments [15]. They are:

ASSIStments 2009-2010[1] [15]: The dataset consists of 4,151 students exercising on 124 knowledge components with 332 thousands interactions. It is also called the mastery learning data because a student is considered to have mastered a skill when certain criterion is met. This is the dataset selected in [15]

---

[1] https://sites.google.com/site/assistmentsdata/home/assistment-2009-2010-data/skill-builder-data-2009-2010.

Junyi Academy[2]: The dataset is collected from a Chinese e-learning platform established on the basis of the open-source code released by the Khan Academy. The dataset contains students' practicing log in hundreds of mathematics exercises. We select 1,000 most active students for the practicing log, which consists of 657 knowledge components and 971 thousands interactions.

3.2   Experimental Setup

A 5-fold student level cross-validation is conducted in the test. The results are evaluated by the Area Under the ROC Curve (AUC) and R^2, two standard metrics for evaluation the predicted performance [9,15,19–21]. The following models with different ways of feature processing are compared in the experiment:

- **Deep Knowledge Tracing (DKT)** [9]: the input feature is one-hot encoding of the exercise tags.
- **Deep Knowledge Tracing with Feature Engineering (DKT-FE)** [15]: Feature engineering has been conducted by manually selecting a subset of heterogeneous features and discretizing them by a certain pre-determined criterion while reducing the dimensionality of the input via autoencoder. The learned feature is concatenated with one-hot encoding of the exercise tags as the input.
- **Deep Knowledge Tracing without Feature Engineering (DKT-W)**: The selected heterogeneous features are the same as those of DKT-FE, but without any further feature processing. The selected feature is directly concatenated with one-hot encoding of the exercise tags as the input.
- **Deep Knowledge Tracing with Decision Trees (DKT-DT)**: This is our proposed method, where all available features except those cannot easily be represented in the numerical form are applied on CART to extract the predicted response. The number of selected features for the ASSIStments dataset and the Junyi Academy dataset is 12 and 10, respectively. The predicted response and the true response are concatenated with the one-hot encoding as the input.

For the LSTM, we set the hidden dimensionality to 200 and train it via the stochastic gradient descent on the size of a mini-batch as 5. Other parameters are set default in the Tensorflow.

3.3   Results

Table 1 reports the results of all four methods. We have the following observations:

- Our proposed DKT-DT achieves significantly better performance than other methods in terms of both the AUC and R^2 metrics on both datasets. Notably, our proposed DKT-DT attains 13% gain than DKT in the R^2 metric.

---

[2] https://pslcdatashop.web.cmu.edu/DatasetInfo?datasetId=1198.

Table 1. AUC and R^2 results

Model	ASSISTments		Junyi	
	AUC (%)	R^2	AUC (%)	R^2
DKT	73.8 ± 0.7	0.161 ± 0.010	72.5 ± 0.4	0.076 ± 0.014
DKT-FE	73.1 ± 1.0	0.163 ± 0.010	68.8 ± 0.5	0.039 ± 0.004
DKT-W	60.9 ± 0.2	0.010 ± 0.012	70.0 ± 0.6	0.052 ± 0.005
DKT-DT	**74.9 ± 0.6**	**0.182 ± 0.7**	**73.0 ± 1.1**	**0.086 ± 0.011**

- An interesting observation is that including heterogeneous features without appropriate preprocessing degrades the performance of DKT. We conjecture this may be due to the introduction of noise, which intervenes DKT to extract the similarity between exercises.
- The degrading effect of DKT-W is highly dependent on the size of dataset. The size of the Junyi dataset is much larger than that of the ASSISTments dataset and it may help to relieve the effect of training the LSTM.
- The performance of DKT-FE is slightly poor than that of DKT-W in the Junyi dataset. The reason is that we adopt the same criterion to process the feature as the ASSISTment data shown in [15]. The provided criterion is not extensible to the new Juny dataset.
- Overall, the experimental results show that including additional features may improve the prediction accuracy, but it requires proper preprocessing.

4 Detailed Study

In the following, we further investigate the data to understand how the decision tree helps on prediction.

Figure 2 illustrates parts of the decision tree learned from both datasets. It clearly shows how the splitting by the decision tree can help us to determine the

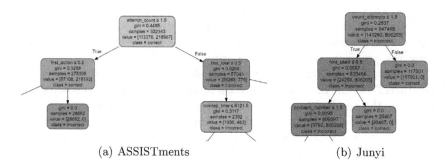

(a) ASSISTments   (b) Junyi

Fig. 2. Trees learned by CART on the **ASSISTments** dataset and the **Junyi** dataset are partially shown.

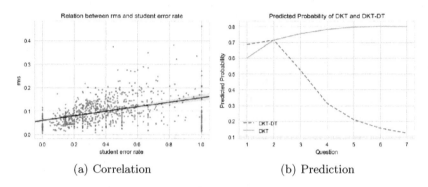

(a) Correlation　　　　　　　　　　　(b) Prediction

Fig. 3. (a) Correlation of the error rate and the root mean square of the difference between the predicted probabilities given by DKT and DKT-DT. (b) Predicted probabilities of DKT and DKT-DT on a student with the largest **rms**.

importance of the features and divide them without manual efforts. For example, sme features, such as "attempt counts" and "the total usage of hints", appear in the root nodes for both datasets. This conforms to our intuition that repeated attempts or using hints can effectively boost students' performance.

Figure 3(a) shows the effect of decision tree by comparing the predicted probabilities given by DKT and DKT-DT on the **ASSISTment** dataset. Due to the space limitation, we only show the results from the **ASSISTment** dataset. For the **Junyi** dataset, the results are similar. In this figure, the error rate of a student is defined by $|Q \setminus Q_c|/|Q|$ and the root mean square (RMS) is defined by $\sqrt{\sum_{t=1}^{T}(p_{DKT}^t - p_{DKT-DT}^t)^2/T}$, where Q is the question set of the student exercises and Q_c is the set of questions correctly answered by the student. p_{DKT}^t and p_{DKT-DT}^t denote the predicted probabilities of the t-th question given by DKT and DKT-DT, respectively. The results show that there is a significant correlation between the error rate and RMS. The difference between DKT and DKT-DT gets larger if a student gives more wrong answers. This implies that the decision tree can adjust the predicted probabilities according to the performance history of students.

We then select the student with the largest RMS from the testing set. The student tried to answer 7 questions of the same skill, but yielded wrong answers. We show the predicted probabilities of correctly answering these questions by DKT and DKT-DT in Fig. 3(b). The result shows the predicted power of our proposed DKT-DT: at the beginning, both models attain similar predicted performance. As the number of practices increases, DKT tends to increase the predicted probability by assuming that the student can gain proficiency by repeating practices, but DKT-DT can reduce the predicted probabilities after learning the additional heterogeneous features. By further scanning the features, such as "attempt count" and "first action", we can observe that this student never attempt to answer the same question again and asked for hint immediately without trying to attempt. The student may be reluctant to repeated training and cannot gain proficiency and hance yield repeated errors. The observation again confirms the power of our proposed DKT-DT in utilizing the heterogeneous features sufficiently.

5   Summary and Future Work

We have proposed an effective method to preprocess the heterogenous features and to integrate them in the original deep knowledge tracing model. The preprocessing step is conducted by CART to output the predicted response of a student whether he/she will answer the current exercise correctly given the heterogenous features. This allows us to capture students' behaviors in the exercises and to provide a good initialization to the DKT model. Our experiments on two educational datasets demonstrate the effectiveness of our proposed feature processing scheme.

Several interesting future work can be considered: First, decision trees have the power of interpreting the data. How to utilize the learned features from CART to guide educational practitioners needs further investigation. Second, there are many types of decision trees and variants of recurrent neural networks. It is worthwhile to investigate how to integrate them seamlessly to further boost the model performance. Third, it is valuable to further extend the current model to provide personalized recommendation for students to select appropriate exercises and to conduct selective practice.

Acknowledgment. The work described in this paper was partially supported by the Research Grants Council of the Hong Kong Special Administrative Region, China (Project No. UGC/IDS14/16).

References

1. Czerniewicz, L., Deacon, A., Glover, M., Walji, S.: MOOC - making and open educational practices. J. Comput. High. Educ. **29**(1), 81–97 (2017)
2. Khajah, M., Lindsey, R.V., Mozer, M.: How deep is knowledge tracing?. In: EDM (2016)
3. Labutov, I., Studer, C.: Calibrated self-assessment. In: EDM (2016)
4. Corbett, A.T., Anderson, J.R.: Knowledge tracing: modelling the acquisition of procedural knowledge. User Model. User Adapt. Interact. **4**(4), 253–278 (1994)
5. Agrawal, R.: Data-driven education: some opportunities and challenges. In: EDM, p. 2 (2016)
6. Sweeney, M., Lester, J., Rangwala, H., Johri, A.: Next-term student performance prediction: a recommender systems approach. In: EDM, p. 7 (2016)
7. Baker, R.S.J., Corbett, A.T., Aleven, V.: More accurate student modeling through contextual estimation of slip and guess probabilities in bayesian knowledge tracing. In: Woolf, B.P., Aïmeur, E., Nkambou, R., Lajoie, S. (eds.) ITS 2008. LNCS, vol. 5091, pp. 406–415. Springer, Heidelberg (2008). doi:10.1007/978-3-540-69132-7_44
8. Pardos, Z.A., Heffernan, N.T.: Modeling individualization in a bayesian networks implementation of knowledge tracing. In: De Bra, P., Kobsa, A., Chin, D. (eds.) UMAP 2010. LNCS, vol. 6075, pp. 255–266. Springer, Heidelberg (2010). doi:10.1007/978-3-642-13470-8_24

9. Piech, C., Bassen, J., Huang, J., Ganguli, S., Sahami, M., Guibas, L.J., Sohl-Dickstein, J.: Deep knowledge tracing. In: NIPS, pp. 505–513 (2015)
10. Xiong, X., Zhao, S., Inwegen, E.V., Beck, J.: Going deeper with deep knowledge tracing. In: EDM, pp. 545–550 (2016)
11. Huang, Y., Guerra, J., Brusilovsky, P.: A data-driven framework of modeling skill combinations for deeper knowledge tracing. In: EDM, pp. 593–594 (2016)
12. Wang, L., Sy, A., Liu, L., Piech, C.: Deep knowledge tracing on programming exercises. In: Proceedings of the Fourth ACM Conference on Learning@ Scale, pp. 201–204. ACM (2017)
13. Zhang, J., Shi, X., King, I., Yeung, D.: Dynamic key-value memory networks for knowledge tracing. In: WWW, pp. 765–774 (2017)
14. Huang, Y., González-Brenes, J.P., Brusilovsky, P.: General features in knowledge tracing to model multiple subskills, temporal item response theory, and expert knowledge. In: EDM, pp. 84–91 (2014)
15. Zhang, L., Xiong, X., Zhao, S., Botelho, A., Heffernan, N.T.: Incorporating rich features into deep knowledge tracing. In: Proceedings of the Fourth ACM Conference on Learning @ Scale, L@S 2017, pp. 169–172. Cambridge, 20–21 April 2017
16. Breiman, L., Friedman, J., Stone, C.J., Olshen, R.A.: Classification and Regression Trees. CRC Press, Boca Raton (1984)
17. Quinlan, J.R.: C4. 5: Programs for Machine Learning. Elsevier, San Francisco (2014)
18. Hochreiter, S., Schmidhuber, J.: Long short-term memory. Neural Comput. 9(8), 1735–1780 (1997)
19. Hu, J., Yang, H., King, I., Lyu, M.R., So, A.M.C.: Kernelized online imbalanced learning with fixed budgets. In: AAAI. Austin Texss, USA (2015)
20. Hu, J., Yang, H., Lyu, M.R., King, I., So, A.M.C.: Online nonlinear AUC maximization for imbalanced data sets. In: IEEE Transactions on Neural Networks and Learning Systems (2017)
21. Yang, H., Lyu, M.R., King, I.: Efficient online learning for multi-task feature selection. ACM Trans. Knowl. Discov. Data 7(2), 1–27 (2013)

Boxless Action Recognition in Still Images via Recurrent Visual Attention

Weijiang Feng, Xiang Zhang$^{(\boxtimes)}$, Xuhui Huang, and Zhigang Luo$^{(\boxtimes)}$

College of Computer, National University of Defense Technology, Changsha, China
zhangxiang_43@aliyun.com, zgluo@nudt.edu.cn

Abstract. Boxless action recognition in still images means recognizing human actions in the absence of ground-truth bounding boxes. Since no ground-truth bounding boxes are provided, boxless action recognition is more challenging than traditional action recognition tasks. Towards this end, AttSPP-net jointly integrates soft attention and spatial pyramid pooling into a convolutional neural network, and achieves comparable recognition accuracies even with some bounding box based approaches. However, the soft attention of AttSPP-net concentrates on only one fixation, rather than combining information from different fixations over time, which is the mechanism of human visual attention. In this paper, we take inspiration from this mechanism and propose a ReAttSPP-net for boxless action recognition. ReAttSPP-net utilizes a recurrent neural network model of visual attention in order to extract information from a sequence of fixations. Experiments on three public action recognition benchmark datasets including PASCAL VOC 2012, Willow and Sports demonstrate that ReAttSPP-net can achieve promising results and obtains higher recognition performance than AttSPP-net.

Keywords: Action recognition · Convolutional neural network · Soft attention · Recurrent neural network · Spatial pyramid pooling

1 Introduction

Boxless action recognition in still images aims at recognizing human actions without the supervision of ground-truth bounding boxes. Compared with traditional ground-truth based action recognition, boxless action recognition is much more challenging, not only due to quick changes in appearance and clutter background confronting to traditional action recognition, but also owing to the requirement for locating the actors just like the bounding boxes do meanwhile reducing the negative effect of action deformation without any supervised knowledge. However, benefiting from the removal of requirement for bounding boxes, boxless action recognition greatly extends still image based action recognition to practical applications.

Several works have tried to tackle challenging boxless action recognition problem. Zhang *et al.* [23] perform boxless action recognition by first utilizing a five-step iterative optimization pipeline for unsupervised discovery of a foreground

© Springer International Publishing AG 2017
D. Liu et al. (Eds.): ICONIP 2017, Part II, LNCS 10635, pp. 663–673, 2017.
https://doi.org/10.1007/978-3-319-70096-0_68

action mask of current image, then designing dedicated feature representation from the action mask for recognition purpose. Compared with their complexity, we have proposed an attention focused spatial pyramid pooling (SPP) network, i.e., AttSPP-net (Attention SPP network) [4] that makes straightforward and lightweight modification to the existing deep convolutional neural network (CNN) architecture. Specifically, AttSPP-net jointly integrates a soft attention layer and a SPP layer into a CNN. By assigning large weights to feature bins of SPP layer which corresponds to salient image regions through a soft attention layer, AttSPP-net can readily locate the action performer of interest, thus conducts action recognition without the supervision of ground-truth bounding boxes. AttSPP-net also exploits SPP to boost robustness to action deformation as well as respects spatial structures among image pixels. The end-to-end AttSPP-net shows effectiveness for boxless action recognition.

However, the soft attention mechanism utilized in AttSPP-net considers only one fixation, rather than combining information from different fixations over time to build up the representation of an image. We humans usually focus attention selectively on parts of the visual space with different locations to be fixated on over a sequence of time and currently acquired information guiding future eye movements, i.e., future fixations [14]. In this paper, we take inspiration from these facts and embed the soft attention mechanism within a recurrent model in order to combine information from different fixations over time.

Similar to AttSPP-net, our proposed Recurrent AttSPP-net, termed ReAttSPP-net, jointly integrates a recurrent visual attention layer and SPP into a CNN. The recurrent model is a recurrent neural network (RNN). With the sequential modeling capability of RNN, ReAttSPP-net can locate salient image regions at different time with the salient information at current time guiding the locating of salient image regions at subsequent time. But the RNN also introduces difficulty for training ReAttSPP-net. To evaluate the effectiveness of ReAttSPP-net, we conduct experiments on three public benchmark datasets including PASCAL VOC 2012 [3], Willow [1], and Sports [8]. Experimental results demonstrate higher mean recognition accuracy than AttSPP-net and promise of ReAttSPP-net for boxless action recognition in still images.

2   Related Work

Still image based action recognition has long been a popular topic in visual applications. For a comprehensive study on this topic, we refer interested readers to the survey paper [16]. According to whether to use ground-truth bounding box or not, we classify action recognition methods into bounding box based approaches and boxless ones.

For bounding box based action recognition in still images, most methods adopt the BoW [11,18] approach. The BoW approach firstly detects key-point regions, describes these regions with local features, and finally quantizes these features against a learned visual vocabulary. Besides, some methods combine part-based information within the BoW framework [12,19].

Compared with traditional methods [7,13,20,21], CNNs have achieved more astonishing results on various computer vision tasks, and researchers have exploited CNNs to automatically extract features for action recognition. Oquab *et al.* [15] utilize a CNN to extract features of the bounding boxes and further obtain a small gain in performance against previous methods. Hoai [9] employ the *fc7* features of a network trained on ImageNet dataset to weight different image regions. Gkioxari *et al.* [5] train body part detectors based on the *pool5* features and then combine them with the bounding box to jointly train a CNN. Later on, they use a CNN to extract features from the bounding box region and the candidate regions generated by the bottom up region proposals method, and then combine the features of the bounding box region and the most informative candidate region to make the final prediction [6].

The aforementioned methods strongly rely on the prior knowledge of the ground-truth bounding boxes. They can be regarded as weak supervised methods and may be fragile in real-world applications. For boxless action recognition free from the ground-truth bounding boxes in a completely unsupervised manner, there are only a few works. Zhang *et al.* [23] perform boxless action recognition by discovering a foreground action mask of current image in an unsupervised manner. Feng *et al.* [4] propose an AttSPP-net that utilizes a soft attention mechanism to automatically focus on salient action region.

3   Recurrent Visual Attention Focused SPP Network

In this section, we are ready to present our network model, i.e., ReAttSPP-net. The overall structure is illustrated in Fig. 1(a). ReAttSPP-net is based on AttSPP-net [4], with a recurrent visual attention layer replacing the soft attention layer of AttSPP-net. The recurrent visual attention layer is modeled with a RNN, as pictured in Fig. 1(c). By assigning large weights to feature bins of SPP layer (shown in Fig. 1(b)) which corresponds to salient image regions through the soft attention mechanism, and incrementally combining information from different fixations at a sequence of time through the recurrent model, the recurrent visual attention layer of ReAttSPP-net can locate the action performer of interest, thus conducts action recognition without the supervision of ground-truth bounding boxes.

Particularly, given an image I, ReAttSPP-net first extracts features with the convolutional layers, and then pools the extracted features using three-level spatial pyramid pooling. Subsequently, the recurrent visual attention layer assigns a weight to each spatial bin at each time step with the weights at current time step guiding the weights at subsequent time steps, and derives the aggregated features by weighted summation at the final time step. Then, ReAttSPP-net feeds the aggregated features as input of the fully-connected layers, and in the final softmax layer outputs probabilities of each action.

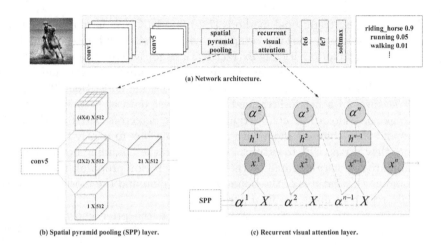

Fig. 1. The schematic structure of our ReAttSPP-net. (a) Overall network structure. (b) The detailed spatial pyramid pooling layer. (c) The detailed recurrent visual attention layer.

3.1 The Recurrent Visual Attention Layer

ReAttSPP-net utilizes the recurrent visual attention mechanism to automatically focus on salient image regions, and model the recurrent visual attention layer with a RNN.

Same to AttSPP-net [4], we represent the spatial bins of the SPP layer as a feature matrix:

$$X = [X_{1,1}, X_{2,1}, \cdots, X_{h,4^{h-1}}] \in \mathbb{R}^{s \times D}, \tag{1}$$

where h denotes number of spatial levels, s denotes the total number of spatial bins, D denotes the feature dimensionality of each spatial bin, and $X_{i,j}$ corresponds to the i−th scale and j−th region of each image.

Assuming the total time steps of the RNN is n. For each spatial feature column $X_{i,j}$, the RNN generates a positive weight $\alpha_{i,j}^t$ at time step t ($t \in [1, n]$) representing the relative importance to give to the spatial bin when aggregating $X_{i,j}$ together. To compute α^1, the recurrent visual attention layer uses a perceptron network taking the SPP feature X as input:

$$
\begin{aligned}
e_{i,j}^1 &= W^T X_{i,j} + b \\
\alpha_{i,j}^1 &= \frac{\exp(e_{i,j}^1)}{\sum_{p=1}^{h} \sum_{q=1}^{4^h-1} \exp(e_{p,q}^1)},
\end{aligned}
\tag{2}
$$

where W and b are parameters of the perceptron network.

For time step $t \in [1, n-1]$, the input x^t of the RNN is the weighted summation of feature matrix X using weights α^t. Once the weights α^t are computed, the recurrent visual attention layer computes $x^t \in \mathbb{R}^D$ as following:

$$x^t = \sum_{i=1}^{h} \sum_{j=1}^{4^h-1} \alpha_{i,j}^t X_{i,j}. \tag{3}$$

The recurrent hidden units h^t of the RNN at time step $t \in [1, n-1]$ aggregate information from the beginning to the current time step by taking hidden units h^{t-1} at previous time step as extra inputs:

$$h^t = \tanh\left(W_i x^t + W_h h^{t-1}\right), \tag{4}$$

where W_i and W_h are the input-to-hidden and hidden-to-hidden weight parameters of the RNN. Note that h^1 do not have previous hidden units as extra inputs. The number of hidden units in our experiments is 256.

The output of the RNN at time step $t \in [1, n-1]$ are the fixation weights α^{t+1} of the spatial bins at time step $t+1$:

$$\begin{aligned}
e_{i,j}^{t+1} &= W_o h^t \\
\alpha_{i,j}^{t+1} &= \frac{\exp\left(e_{i,j}^{t+1}\right)}{\sum_{p=1}^{h} \sum_{q=1}^{4^h-1} \exp\left(e_{p,q}^{t+1}\right)}.
\end{aligned} \tag{5}$$

where W_o is the hidden-to-output weight parameter of the RNN.

The output of the RNN is the input x^n at the final time step n. ReAttSPP-net then feeds x^n to the fully-connected layer $fc6$. ReAttSPP-net is smooth and differentiable under the deterministic soft attention mechanism, and the end-to-end learning can be optimized by standard back-propagation.

3.2   Loss Function

To train ReAttSPP-net, we use cross-entropy loss together with weight decay. The loss over a mini-batch of training examples $B = \{I_i, y_i\}_{i=1}^M$ is given by

$$\text{loss}\,(B) = -\frac{1}{M} \sum_{i=1}^{M} \sum_{c=1}^{C} y_{i,c} \log \hat{y}_{i,c} + \lambda \sum_j \theta_j^2, \tag{6}$$

where y_i and $\hat{y}_i$ are the one hot label vector and class probabilities vector of image I_i respectively, C is the number of action classes, λ is the weight decay coefficient, and θ represents all the model parameters.

4   Experimental Results

In this section, we evaluate the effectiveness of ReAttSPP-net for action recognition in still images on the PASCAL VOC 2012 dataset [3], the Willow dataset [1], and the Sports dataset [8] by comparing with AttSPP-net [4], VGG19_SPP which removes the recurrent visual attention layer from ReAttSPP-net, and the baseline VGG19 model which removes both the recurrent visual attention layer and SPP layer from ReAttSPP-net. During the testing time, we estimate probabilities for all actions for every example, and compute AP for each action and the mean AP.

We train our model with stochastic gradient descent (SGD) using back-propagation. Based on the learned model parameters of 19-layer VGGNet, we first fine-tune ReAttSPP-net on the ImageNet [2] dataset for the image classification task. We set the learning rate to 0.001, the batch size to 32, and the weight decay coefficient to 0.0002. We fine-tune for 230 K iterations on ImageNet dataset under Caffe [10] framework. After the fine-tuning, we train our model on each action recognition dataset for 50 K iterations with a batch size of 32.

4.1 PASCAL VOC 2012 Dataset

The PASCAL VOC 2012 Action dataset consists of 10 different actions, *Jumping, Phoning, Playing Instrument, Reading, Riding Bike, Riding Horse, Running, Taking Photo, Using Computer, Walking*. Since ReAttSPP-net can only recognize one action from one image for this moment, we ignore images occurred more than one action in the same image. The final training dataset consists of 1865 images and the testing dataset contains 1848 images.

For this dataset, we use the validation set for testing and ReAttSPP-net obtains a mean AP of 78.08%. We show the comparison of ReAttSPP-net with other approaches in Table 1. The upper part of Table 1 is the result of bounding box based methods, and the lower part of methods without bounding boxes. Our experiments show that ReAttSPP-net performs effectively, and achieves higher mean AP compared with AttSPP-net, demonstrating effectiveness of the recurrent model for visual attention. In spite of no ground-truth bounding boxes available, ReAttSPP-net obtains higher AP for some action categories like *Phoning and Reading*, though lower AP for *Running, Walking* compared with Hoai *et al.* [9] and Oquab *et al.* [15]. In terms of mean AP, ReAttSPP-net achieves better result than these two bounding box based methods, showing the effectiveness of ReAttSPP-net for boxless action recognition.

4.2 Willow Dataset

The Willow dataset contains 7 classes of actions in 968 images. The actions are *interacting with computer, photographing, playing instrument, riding bike, riding horse, running, walking*. Similar to PASCAL VOC 2012 dataset, we do not consider images with more than one action, and the final training set has 429 images, and the testing set has 484 images. ReAttSPP-net achieves a mean AP of 88.84% on the test set. The performance varies from 72.22% for *walking* to 96% for *riding horse*. The full confusion matrix obtained by ReAttSPP-net is shown in Fig. 2.

In Table 2, we compare our methods with existing approaches on the Willow test set. The upper and lower part of Table 2 correspond to bounding box based and boxless action recognition results, respectively. PBoW [1] uses bag-of-features methods as well as part-based representation and obtains 59.6% mean AP. The Dsal [18] uses the saliency map and semantic pyramid to find semantically meaningful regions and obtain a mean AP of 65.9%. The EPM [19] achieves a mean AP of 67.6%. The CF [11] obtains a mean AP of 70.1%. The SMP [12]

Table 1. Comparison of different approaches on the PASCAL VOC dataset.

AP(%)	Jumping	Phoning	Playing instrument	Reading	Riding bike	Riding horse	Running	Taking photo	Using computer	Walking	Mean AP
Oquab et al. [15]	74.8	46.0	75.6	45.3	93.5	95.0	86.5	49.3	66.7	69.5	70.2
Hoai et al. [9]	82.3	52.9	84.3	53.6	95.6	96.1	89.7	60.4	76.0	72.9	76.3
Gkioxari et al. [5]	84.7	67.8	91.0	66.6	96.6	97.2	90.2	76.0	83.4	71.6	82.6
Gkioxari et al. [6]	**91.5**	**84.4**	93.6	**83.2**	**96.9**	**98.4**	**93.8**	**85.9**	**92.6**	**81.8**	**90.2**
Zhang et al. [23]	86.68	72.22	**93.97**	71.30	95.37	97.63	88.54	72.42	88.81	65.31	83.23
VGG19	74.86	66.34	82.33	66.21	82.35	84.82	67.63	56.38	78.19	48.67	71.27
VGG19_SPP	80.33	68.78	83.26	73.97	82.35	89.53	72.66	64.36	77.13	58.67	75.49
AttSPP-net	75.41	73.17	83.26	74.43	86.47	91.1	71.22	61.7	79.26	62	76.19
ReAttSPP-net	83.61	69.76	85.58	74.89	87.65	92.67	72.66	68.09	84.57	56.67	78.08

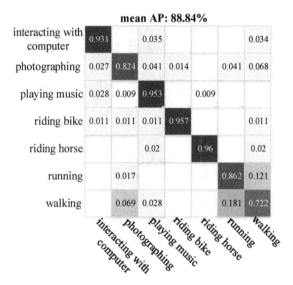

Fig. 2. The confusion matrix obtained by ReAttSPP-net on the Willow dataset.

Table 2. Comparison of different approaches on the Willow dataset.

AP(%)	int. computer	Photographing	Playing music	Riding bike	Riding horse	Running	Walking	Mean AP
PBoW [1]	58.2	35.4	73.2	82.4	69.6	44.5	54.2	59.6
Dsal [18]	59.7	42.6	74.6	87.8	64.2	56.1	56.5	65.9
EPM [19]	64.5	40.9	75.0	91.0	87.6	55.0	59.2	67.6
CF [11]	61.9	48.2	76.5	90.3	84.3	64.7	64.6	70.1
SMP [12]	66.8	48.0	77.5	93.8	87.9	67.2	63.3	72.1
GSPM [24]	67.9	49.1	86.5	93.0	86.2	65.7	**72.6**	74.4
VGG19	89.66	68.92	84.11	93.62	96	72.41	69.44	80.79
VGG19_SPP	**96.55**	**82.43**	92.52	**96.81**	**98.0**	79.31	72.22	85.95
AttSPP-net [4]	93.1	78.4	90.7	93.6	92.0	84.5	70.8	86.2
ReAttSPP-net	93.1	**82.43**	**95.33**	95.74	96.0	**86.21**	72.22	**88.84**

reaches a mean AP of 72.1%. The GSPM [24] introduces a generalized symmetric pair model and achieves a mean AP of 74.4%. Again, ReAttSPP-net achieves higher mean AP than AttSPP-net on the Willow dataset.

4.3   Sports Dataset

The Sports dataset consists of 6 different actions in different sports. These sports are *cricket batting, cricket bowling, tennis serve, tennis forehand, volleyball serve, and croquet shot*. There are 300 images in total with 50 images per action, 180 images for training, and 120 images for testing. ReAttSPP-net achieves a mean AP of 98.33% on the test set, and 100% AP for *cricket batting, cricket bowling, croquet shot, and tennis forehand*. Figure 3 shows the confusion matrix obtained using ReAttSPP-net. We also show all the failure cases in the figure. The failure case in the *tennis serve* is due to the scenes in *tennis forehand* and *tennis serve* are exactly the same. And because the poses during *volleyball serve* and *tennis serve* are quite similar, *volleyball serve* includes one image misclassified into *tennis serve*.

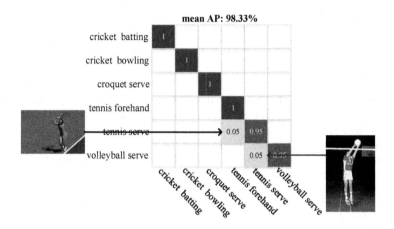

Fig. 3. The confusion matrix obtained by ReAttSPP-net on the Sports dataset.

We compare ReAttSPP-net with others on the Sports dataset in Table 3. The SFC [8] method applies spatial and functional constraints on perceptual elements for coherent semantic interpretation and obtains a mean AP of 79.0%. By modeling interactions between humans and objects, the HMI [17] method obtains a recognition rate of 83.0%. The HOI [22] method jointly models the mutual context of objects and human poses and achieves an action recognition accuracy of 87.0%. The SMP [12] method obtains a mean AP of 92.5% on this dataset. On the Sports dataset, ReAttSPP-net also achieves higher accuracy than AttSPP-net.

Table 3. Comparison of different approaches on the Sports dataset.

Method	SFC	HMI	HOI	SMP	VGG19	VGG19_SPP	AttSPP-net	ReAttSPP-net
Mean AP(%)	79.0	83.0	87.0	92.5	95.0	95.8	97.5	**98.33**

5 Conclusion

This paper develops a simple yet effective model termed ReAttSPP-net for action recognition in still images. It is able to automatically pay attention to different image regions of the action and combine information from these fixations over a sequence of time without the supervision of the ground-truth bounding boxes and provide an alternative way for real-world situations. Experiments show that ReAttSPP-net achieves higher mean recognition accuracy than AttSPP-net, demonstrating the effectiveness of the recurrent neural network model for visual attention. Modifying the recurrent visual attention layer by concatenating information at every time step is our future work.

Acknowledgments. This work is supported by National High Technology Research and Development Program (under grant No. 2015AA020108) and National Natural Science Foundation of China (under grant No. U1435222).

References

1. Delaitre, V., Laptev, I., Sivic, J.: Recognizing human actions in still images: a study of bag-of-features and part-based representations. In: British Machine Vision Conference (2010)
2. Deng, J., Dong, W., Socher, R., Li, L.J., Li, K., Fei-Fei, L.: ImageNet: a large-scale hierarchical image database. In: IEEE Conference on Computer Vision and Pattern Recognition, pp. 248–255 (2009)
3. Everingham, M., Van Gool, L., Williams, C.K., Winn, J., Zisserman, A.: The pascal visual object classes (VOC) challenge. Int. J. Comput. Vis. **88**(2), 303–338 (2010)
4. Feng, W., Zhang, X., Huang, X., Luo, Z.: Attention focused spatial pyramid pooling for boxless action recognition in still images. In: International Conference on Artificial Neural Networks. Springer (2017)
5. Gkioxari, G., Girshick, R., Malik, J.: Actions and attributes from wholes and parts. In: IEEE International Conference on Computer Vision, pp. 2470–2478 (2015)
6. Gkioxari, G., Girshick, R., Malik, J.: Contextual action recognition with R*CNN. In: IEEE International Conference on Computer Vision, pp. 1080–1088 (2015)
7. Guan, N., Tao, D., Luo, Z., Yuan, B.: NeNMF: an optimal gradient method for non-negative matrix factorization. IEEE Trans. Sig. Process. **60**(6), 2882–2898 (2012)
8. Gupta, A., Kembhavi, A., Davis, L.S.: Observing human-object interactions: using spatial and functional compatibility for recognition. IEEE Trans. Patt. Anal. Mach. Intell. **31**(10), 1775–1789 (2009)
9. Hoai, M.: Regularized max pooling for image categorization. J. Brit. Inst. Radio Eng. **14**(3), 94–100 (2014)
10. Jia, Y., Shelhamer, E., Donahue, J., Karayev, S., Long, J., Girshick, R., Guadarrama, S., Darrell, T.: Caffe: Convolutional architecture for fast feature embedding. In: ACM International Conference on Multimedia, pp. 675–678 (2014)
11. Khan, F.S., Anwer, R.M., van de Weijer, J., Bagdanov, A.D., Lopez, A.M., Felsberg, M.: Coloring action recognition in still images. Int. J. Comput. Vis. **105**(3), 205–221 (2013)
12. Khan, F.S., van de Weijer, J., Anwer, R.M., Felsberg, M., Gatta, C.: Semantic pyramids for gender and action recognition. IEEE Trans. Image Process. **23**(8), 3633–3645 (2014)
13. Liu, T., Tao, D.: Classification with noisy labels by importance reweighting. IEEE Trans. Patt. Anal. Mach. Intell. **38**(3), 447–461 (2016)
14. Mnih, V., Heess, N., Graves, A., et al.: Recurrent models of visual attention. In: Advances in Neural Information Processing Systems, pp. 2204–2212 (2014)

15. Oquab, M., Bottou, L., Laptev, I., Sivic, J.: Learning and transferring mid-level image representations using convolutional neural networks. In: IEEE Conference on Computer Vision and Pattern Recognition, pp. 1717–1724 (2014)
16. Poppe, R.: A survey on vision-based human action recognition. Image Vis. Comput. **28**(6), 976–990 (2010)
17. Prest, A., Schmid, C., Ferrari, V.: Weakly supervised learning of interactions between humans and objects. IEEE Trans. Patt. Anal. Mach. Intell. **34**(3), 601–614 (2012)
18. Sharma, G., Jurie, F., Schmid, C.: Discriminative spatial saliency for image classification. In: IEEE Conference on Computer Vision and Pattern Recognition, pp. 3506–3513 (2012)
19. Sharma, G., Jurie, F., Schmid, C.: Expanded parts model for human attribute and action recognition in still images. In: IEEE Conference on Computer Vision and Pattern Recognition, pp. 652–659 (2013)
20. Tao, D., Li, X., Wu, X., Maybank, S.J.: General tensor discriminant analysis and gabor features for gait recognition. IEEE Trans. Patt. Anal. Mach. Intell. **29**(10), 1700–1715 (2007)
21. Tao, D., Tang, X., Li, X., Wu, X.: Asymmetric bagging and random subspace for support vector machines-based relevance feedback in image retrieval. IEEE Trans. Patt. Anal. Mach. Intell. **28**(7), 1088–1099 (2006)
22. Yao, B., Fei-Fei, L.: Recognizing human-object interactions in still images by modeling the mutual context of objects and human poses. IEEE Trans. Patt. Anal. Mach. Intell. **34**(9), 1691–1703 (2012)
23. Yu, Z., Li, C., Wu, J., Cai, J., Do, M.N., Lu, J.: Action recognition in still images with minimum annotation efforts. IEEE Trans. Image Process. **25**(11), 5479–5490 (2016)
24. Zhao, Z., Ma, H., Chen, X.: Generalized symmetric pair model for action classification in still images. Patt. Recogn. **64**, 347–360 (2017)

Compositional Sentence Representation from Character Within Large Context Text

Geonmin Kim[(✉)], Hwaran Lee, Bokyeong Kim, and Soo-young Lee

Korea Advanced Institute of Science and Technology, Deajeon, South Korea
{gmkim90,hwaran.lee,bokyeong1015,sy-lee}@kaist.ac.kr

Abstract. This paper describes a Hierarchical Composition Recurrent Network (HCRN) consisting of a 3-level hierarchy of compositional models: character, word and sentence. This model is designed to overcome two problems of representing a sentence on the basis of a constituent word sequence. The first is a data sparsity problem when estimating the embedding of rare words, and the other is no usage of inter-sentence dependency. In the HCRN, word representations are built from characters, thus resolving the data-sparsity problem, and inter-sentence dependency is embedded into sentence representation at the level of sentence composition. We propose a hierarchy-wise language learning scheme in order to alleviate the optimization difficulties when training deep hierarchical recurrent networks in an end-to-end fashion. The HCRN was quantitatively and qualitatively evaluated on a dialogue act classification task. In the end, the HCRN achieved the *state-of-the-art* performance with a test error rate of 22.7% for dialogue act classification on the SWBD-DAMSL database.

Keywords: Rare word · Inter-sentence dependency · Hierarchical recurrent neural network · Hierarchy-wise learning · Dialogue act

1 Introduction

Sentence representations are usually built from representations of constituent word sequences using a compositional word model. Many compositional word models based on neural networks have been proposed, and have been used for sentence classification [15,21] or generation [11,24] tasks. However, learning to represent a sentence on the basis of constituent word sequences involves two difficulties. First, estimating the embedding of rare words suffers from the data-sparsity problem and poorly estimated embedding can cause sentence representations of inferior quality. Second, conventional sentence representation does not take into account inter-sentence dependency, which is an important linguistic context for understanding the intention of the sentence.

In this paper, we propose a Hierarchical Composition Recurrent Network (HCRN), which consists of a hierarchy of 3 levels of compositional models: character, word and sentence. Sequences at each level are composed by a Recurrent

D. Liu et al. (Eds.): ICONIP 2017, Part II, LNCS 10635, pp. 674–685, 2017.
https://doi.org/10.1007/978-3-319-70096-0_69

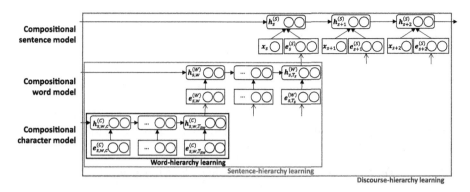

Fig. 1. Illustration of the hierarchical composition recurrent network. The thick arrows indicate affine and non-linear transformation, the thin arrows indicate identity transformation. For simplicity, each level is shown with one layer.

Neural Network (RNN). In the HCRN, the output of the lower levels of the compositional model is fed into the higher levels. Sentence representation by the HCRN enjoys several advantages compared to sentence representation by a single compositional word model. From the compositional character model, the word representation is built from characters by modeling morphological processes shared by different words. In this way, the data-sparsity problem with rare words is resolved. From the compositional sentence model, inter-sentence dependency can be embedded into sentence representation. Sentence representation with inter-sentence dependency is able to capture implicit intention as well as explicit semantics of a given sentence. Training the HCRN in an end-to-end fashion has optimization difficulties because a deep hierarchical recurrent network may suffer from the vanishing gradient problem across different levels in the hierarchy. To alleviate this, a hierarchy-wise language learning algorithm is proposed, and it is empirically shown that it improves the network's optimization. The efficacy of the proposed method is verified on a spoken dialogue act classification task. The task is to classify the communicative intentions of sentences in spoken dialogues. Compared to conventional sentence classification, this task presents two challenging problems. First, it requires that the model estimate representations of spoken words which often include rare and partial words. Second, understanding the dialogue context is often required to clarify meanings of sentences within a given dialogue. The HCRN with the hierarchy-wise learning algorithm achieves *state-of-the-art* performance on the SWBD-DAMSL database. The source code of this work is available at github.com/gmkim90/HCRN_DA.

2   Method

2.1   Hierarchical Composition Recurrent Network

Figure 1 shows our proposed Hierarchical Composition Recurrent Network (HCRN). Consider a dialogue D consisting of sentence sequences $s_{1:T_D}$ and its associated label $t_{1:T_D}$. The HCRN consists of a hierarchy of RNNs with compositional character, compositional word and compositional sentence levels. At each level, each sequence encoding($\mathbf{e}$) is obtained by the hidden neuron($\mathbf{h}$) of RNN at the end of the sequence [3,25]. Compositional Sentence model additionally takes a binary vector which indicates speaker identity change across dialogue. The composition rule is summarized in Table 1. The notation of well-known transformations are represented as follows: gating units such as LSTM or GRU are represented as g, and Multi Layer Perceptron with Softmax non-linearity as r.

Table 1. Composition rules used in each hierarchy of HCRN

Compositional character	Compositional word	Compositional sentence
$\mathbf{h}_{s,w,c}^{(C)} = g(\mathbf{h}_{s,w,c-1}^{(C)}, \mathbf{e}_{s,w,c}^{(C)})$	$\mathbf{h}_{s,w}^{(W)} = g(\mathbf{h}_{s,w-1}^{(W)}, \mathbf{e}_{s,w}^{(W)})$	$\mathbf{h}_s^{(S)} = g(\mathbf{h}_{s-1}^{(S)}, \mathbf{e}_s^{(S)}, \mathbf{x}_s)$
$\mathbf{e}_{s,w}^{(W)} = \mathbf{h}_{s,w,T_{sw}}^{(C)}$	$\mathbf{e}_s^{(S)} = \mathbf{h}_{s,T_s}^{(W)}$	$P(y_s|\mathbf{s}_{1:s}) = r(\mathbf{h}_s^{(S)})$

Loss is defined as the negative log-likelihood of the label of the sentences within dialogue.

$$L(s_{1:T_D}) = -logP(y_{1:T_D}|s_{1:T_D}) = -\sum_{t=1}^{T_D} logP(y_t|s_{1:t})$$

One advantage of the HCRN is its ability to learn long character sequences. For example, in our experiment, the sentence becomes a much longer sequence when represented by characters (37.92) compared to words (8.28), in average. While conventional stacked RNNs have difficulty when dealing with very long sequences [1,8], the hierarchy of the HCRN deals with segmented short sequences at each level so vanishing gradient problems during back-propagation through time are relatively insignificant. Each level of the HCRN uses a different speed of dynamics during sequence processing, so that the model can learn both short-range and long-range dependencies in large text samples. The following abbreviations are used for the rest of this paper: the compositional character model (CC), the compositional word model (CW), the compositional sentence model (CS), and the multi layer perceptron (MLP).

2.2 Hierarchy-Wise Language Learning

To alleviate the optimization difficulties of end-to-end training of HCRN, hierarchy-wise language learning is proposed. In the hierarchy of composition models, the lower level composition network is trained first, higher level composition layers are gradually added after the lower level network is optimized for a given objective function. This approach is inspired by the unsupervised layer-wise pre-training algorithm in [7], which is known to provide better initialization for subsequent supervised learning. Word-hierarchy proceeds in an unsupervised way by reconstructing the character sequence of each word using

RNN Autoencoder, proposed in [22]. This stage is viewed as *learning to spell*. Sentence-hierarchy and Discourse-hierarchy learning proceed in a supervised way to classify the given label of the sentence.

3 Experiments

3.1 Task and Dataset

The HCRN was tested on a spoken dialogue act classification task. The dialogue act (DA) is the communicative intention of a speaker in each sentence. We chose the SWBD-DAMSL database[1], which is a subset of the Switchboard-I (LDC97S62) dialogue corpus annotated with DA for each sentence. The SWBD-DAMSL has 1155 dialogues on 70 pre-defined topics, 0.22M sentences, 1.4M word tokens and a 42-class tagset shown in Table 2. The number of elements in the character dictionary is 31 including 26 letters, - (indicating a partial word), '(indicating possessive case), . (indicating abbreviation), <noise> (indicating non-verbal sound) and <unk> (indicating unknown symbols) for all other characters. We follow the train/test set division in [23]: 1115/19 dialogues, respectively. Validation data includes 19 dialogues chosen from the training data. After pre-processing of the corpus, the number of sentences in the train/test/validation sets are 197370, 4190 and 3315 respectively. All letters are converted into lowercase. Disfluency tags and special punctuation marks such as (? ! ,) which cannot be produced by a speech recognizer are removed.

3.2 Common Settings

We employ the Gated Recurrent Unit (GRU) as a basic unit of the RNN [4,12]. The configuration of the HCRN is represented by the hierarchy of the compositional level and its size, $CC_{size} - CW_{size} - CS_{size}$ as shown in Table 3. In all supervised learning, the classifier consists of 3-layers and 128 hidden units MLP with Rectified Linear Units and Softmax non-linearity. A common hyperparameter setting is used in all experiments. All weights are initialized from a uniform distribution within $[-0.1, 0.1]$ except for the pre-trained weights. We optimized all networks with adadelta [26] with decay rate (ρ) 0.9 and constant (ϵ) 10^{-6}, gradient clipping with threshold 5, and batch size of 64, 64, 8 for word, sentence and discourse hierarchy learning. Early stopping based on validation loss was used to prevent overfitting.

3.3 Unsupervised Word-Hierarchy Learning

During word-hierarchy learning, CC is jointly trained with the RNN Decoder to reconstruct input character sequences. The number of all unique words in the training set is 19353. The *end of word* token is appended to every end of the

---

[1] The dataset is available at https://web.stanford.edu/~jurafsky/swb1_dialogact_annot.tar.gz.

Table 2. 42-class tagset of dialogue act provided from SWBD-DAMSL. Classes are sorted from the most frequent to the least frequent, from top-left to bottom-right with column-major order.

Non-opinion	Declarative question	Other answers
Backchannel	Backchannel(question)	Opening
Opinion	Quotation	Or clause
Abandoned	Summarize	Dispreferred answer
Agreement	Non-yes answer	3rd party talk
Appreciation	Action-directive	Offers
Yes-No-Question	Completion	Self talk
Non-verbal	Repeat phrase	Downplayer
Yes answer	Open question	Accept part
Closing	Rhetorical question	Tag question
Wh-question	Hold before answer	Declartive question
No answer	Reject	Apology
Acknowledgment	Non-no answer	Thanking
Hedge	Non-understand	Others

Table 3. Size of compositional model at each level, represented by (# layers) × (# cell in each layer). Note that the complexity of the model increases as the level of hierarchy increases, following the assumption that the complexity of composition increases as the level of language increases.

	CC	CW	CS
Small	1×64	2×128	2×256
Large	2×128	3×256	3×512

character sequence. Learning is terminated if validation loss fails to decrease by 0.1% for three consecutive epochs.

Pre-training performance itself is evaluated by sequence reconstruction ability. For reconstruction, the RNN Decoder generates character sequences from the encoder vector which is the last time step hidden neuron of CC. Generation is performed based on greedy sampling at each time step. The performance is evaluated on two measures: Character Prediction Error Rate (CPER) and Word Reconstruction Fail Rate (WRFR). CPER measures the ratio of incorrectly predicted characters to the reconstructed sequence. WRFR is the ratio of words where complete reconstruction fails out of the total words in the test set. The reconstruction performance of the RNN Encoder-Decoder on words both in vocabulary and out-of-vocabulary (OOV) is summarized in Table 4. Overall, the model almost perfectly reconstructs the character sequences of the training data, and even generalizes well for the unseen words. The large size model out-

Table 4. Reconstruction performance of the RNN Encoder-Decoder on words in the vocabulary and out-of-vocabulary (OOV). The length column presents the mean and standard deviation (in parentheses) of the character length of words for which complete reconstruction failed.

Model	In vocabulary			Out of vocabulary		
	CPER (%)	WRFR (%)	Length	CPER (%)	WRFR (%)	Length
$CC_{1\times64}$	0.39	2.25	13.1(2.6)	2.06	9.17	12.3(2.2)
$CC_{2\times128}$	0	0	-	1.21	5.28	12.7(2.4)

performs the small size model. Almost all cases in which reconstruction failed involved sequences longer than 12 characters on average.

3.4 Supervised Word-Hierarchy and Sentence-Hierarchy Learning

Initialization of CC: Random VS. Pre-trained. The performance of sentence-hierarchy learning with and without the word-hierarchy learning are compared to evaluate how the pre-trained CC provides useful initialization for sentence-hierarchy learning. With the pre-trained CC, at first, the parameters of the CC are frozen, and the CW and MLP are trained for 1 epoch[2]. After that, the whole architecture consisting of the CC, CW and MLP is jointly trained. Evaluation was performed on architectures with different CC and CW sizes (see Table 3).

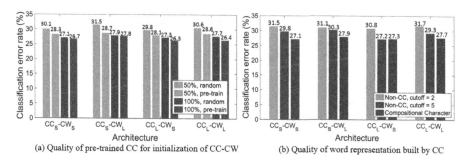

(a) Quality of pre-trained CC for initialization of CC-CW

(b) Quality of word representation built by CC

Fig. 2. Result to show the quality of our pre-trained CC for initialization on sentence-hierarchy learning. (a) Test error rate (%) of comparing learning CC-CW with different initialization: pre-trained CC and random. (b) Test error rate (%) of comparing learning CC-CW and CW. At each level, size is represented as either small (S) or large (L) in Table 3.

In addition, pre-training on two different training dataset sizes (50% and 100%) are compared. The results are shown in Fig. 2(a). Pre-training consistently

---

[2] The number of epochs to freeze the pre-trained model is chosen as the best parameter from preliminary experiments on the validation set.

reduces the test error rate on the various architectures, especially when fewer training data are available.

CC VS. non-compositional word embedding. We compare two different methods to build word representation in this section: CC and conventional non-compositional word embedding (=non-CC). Since CC is used to learn the morphological structures of words, it is not comparable with widely used pre-trained word embedding such as Word2Vec [19], which aims to learn semantic/syntactic similarities between different words. Therefore, for a fair comparison we randomly initialized both models rather than employing pre-trained word embedding. For the non-CC embedding method, we set two different cutoff frequencies: $\tau_c = 5$ (6294 words), $\tau_c = 2$ (11746 words). Word embedding size is 64 and 128 for both CC and non-CC. Figure 2(b) shows the comparison of test error rates on the above settings. Non-compositional word embedding with the high cutoff ($\tau_c = 5$) outperforms the low cutoff ($\tau_c = 2$). This is because the data sparsity problem during the estimation of rare words is more severe for the model with the lower cutoff setting. Compared to the non-CC, CC outperforms or is on a par, with fewer parameters.

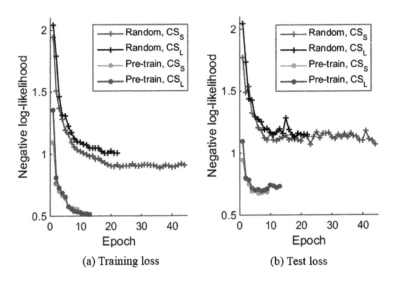

(a) Training loss   (b) Test loss

Fig. 3. Learning curve on (a) training data and (b) test data. The objective function is converged to a much lower value when the model employs initialization from the pre-trained model resulting from sentence-hierarchy learning.

3.5 Discourse-Hierarchy Learning

During discourse-hierarchy learning, the CS on top of the $CC_{2\times 128} - CW_{2\times 128}$ is trained. For the first 5 epochs, the network is trained with the CC and CW frozen. Then, the whole network is jointly optimized.

Optimization difficulty of end-to-end learning. We compared the learning curves of discourse-hierarchy learning using two different model initializations: with the pre-trained model from sentence-hierarchy learning, and with random initialization (end-to-end learning). The learning curve in Fig. 3 clearly shows that initializing with the pre-trained model significantly alleviates optimization difficulties.

Table 5. Test error rate of sentence hierarchy learning and discourse hierarchy learning. Discourse-hierarchy learning outperforms Sentence-hierarchy learning.

Hierarchy	Model	Err (%)
Sentence	$CC_{2\times128} - CW_{2\times128}$	26.27
Discourse	$CC_{2\times128} - CW_{2\times128} - CS_{2\times256}$	**22.73**
	$CC_{2\times128} - CW_{2\times128} - CS_{3\times512}$	22.99

Effects of dialogue context on sentence representation. Table 5 shows the test classification error rate of sentence-hierarchy learning and discourse-hierarchy learning. Compared to sentence-hierarchy learning, discourse-hierarchy learning improves performance significantly.

Table 6. An example of dialogue segment containing 8 sentences. Predictions of label from model of sentence-hierarchy learning (without dialogue-context) and discourse-hierarchy learning (with dialogue-context) are provided along with true labels.

Dialogue segment	True	Without context	With context
A: and uh quite honestly i just got so fed up with it i just could not stand it any more	S	S	S
B: is that right	**BQ**	**YQ**	**BQ**
A: yeah	**A**	**B**	**A**
A: i mean this is the kind of thing you look at	**S**	**O**	**S**
B: yeah	B	B	B
A: you sit there	S	S	S
A: and when you are writing up budgets you wonder okay how much money do we need	**S**	**WQ**	**S**

* S = Statement, A = Agreement, B = Backchannel, WQ = Wh-Question.
YQ = Yes-No-Question, O = Opinion, BQ = Backchannel-Question.

To qualitatively analyze the improvement, we show examples of sentences on the test set for which prediction is improved by dialogue context. Analysis is done with model $CC_{2\times128} - CW_{2\times128} - CS_{2\times256}$, which achieved the best test accuracy during discourse-hierarchy learning. Table 6 shows a dialogue example including 8 sentences, comparing sentence-hierarchy and discourse-hierarchy learning. Highlighted sentences indicate cases where discourse-hierarchy learning predicts correctly while sentence-hierarchy learning fails to predict. For example, "yeah" in the 3rd sentence of the example can be interpreted as both Agreement and Backchannel, and an informed decision between the two is only possible when the dialogue context is available. This example demonstrates that sentence representation with dialogue context helps to distinguish confusing dialogue acts.

Comparison with other methods. Several other methods for dialogue act classification are compared with our approach in Table 7. Our approach outperforms the other benchmarks, achieving 22.7% classification error rate on the test set. Similar approaches employ a neural network based model that hierarchically composes sequences starting from word sequences [10,14,20]. We conjecture that the improvement demonstrated by our model is due to two factors. First, our model build word representations from constituent characters and so suffers less from the data sparsity problem when learning the embedding of rare words. Second, the hierarchy-wise language learning method alleviates the optimization difficulties of the deep hierarchical recurrent network.

Table 7. Performance comparison with other methods for dialogue act classification on SWBD-DAMSL.

Method	Test err. (%)
Class based LM + HMM [23]	29.0
RCNN [14]	26.1
HCRN with word as basic unit + End-to-End learning[a] [20]	24.9
Utterance feature + Tri-gram context + Active learning + SVM [6]	23.5
Discourse model + RNNLM [10]	23.0
HCRN with character as basic unit + Hierarchy-wise learning	**22.7**

[a] We evaluated this performance by ourselves due to task difference.

4   Related Works

The difficulty for RNNs in learning long-range dependencies within character sequences has been addressed in [2]. Hierarchical RNNs have been proposed as one possible solution, which design RNN architecture in which different layers learn at different speeds of dynamics [5,13,17]. Compared with these models, the HCRN deals with segmented shorter sequences at each level, and thereby the vanishing gradient problem is rendered relatively insignificant. There are several recent studies on representing large context text hierarchically for document classification [25] and on the dialogue response model [20]. These approaches benefit from hierarchical representations that represent long sequences as a hierarchy of shorter sequences. However, the basic unit used in these approaches is the word, and models that begin at this level of representation open themselves to the data sparsity problem. This problem is somewhat resolved by building word representations from character sequences. Successful examples can be found in language modeling [16,18] and machine translation [9].

5   Conclusion

In this paper, we introduced the Hierarchical Composition Recurrent Network (HCRN) model consisting of a 3-level hierarchy of compositional models: character, word and sentence. The inclusion of the compositional character model improves the quality of word representation especially for rare and OOV words. Moreover, the embedding of inter-sentence dependency into sentence representation by the compositional sentence model significantly improves the performance of dialogue act classification. The HCRN is trained in a hierarchy-wise language learning fashion, alleviating optimization difficulties with end-to-end training. In the end, the proposed HCRN using the hierarchy-wise learning algorithm achieves *state-of-the-art* performance with a test classification error rate of 22.7% on the dialogue act classification task on the SWBD-DAMSL database.

Acknowledgments. This work was supported by Institute for Information and communications Technology Promotion (IITP) grant funded by the Korea government (MSIT) [2016-0-00562(R0124-16-0002), Emotional Intelligence Technology to Infer Human Emotion and Carry on Dialogue Accordingly].

References

1. Bengio, Y., Simard, P., Frasconi, P.: Learning long-term dependencies with gradient descent is difficult. IEEE Trans. Neural Netw. **5**(2), 157–166 (1994)
2. Bojanowski, P., Joulin, A., Mikolov, T.: Alternative structures for character-level RNNs (2016). arXiv preprint: arXiv:1511.06303
3. Cho, K., van Merrienboer, B., Gulcehre, C., Bahdanau, D., Bougares, F., Schwenk, H., Bengio, Y.: Learning phrase representations using RNN encoder-decoder for statistical machine translation. In: Proceedings of the 2014 Conference on Empirical Methods in Natural Language Processing (EMNLP), pp. 1724–1734 (2014)
4. Chung, J., Gulcehre, C., Cho, K., Bengio, Y.: Empirical Evaluation of Gated Recurrent Neural Networks on Sequence Modeling (2014). arXiv preprint: arXiv:1412.3555v1
5. Chung, J., Gulcehre, C., Cho, K., Bengio, Y.: Gated feedback recurrent neural networks. In: Proceedings of the 32nd International Conference on Machine Learning (ICML), vol. 37, pp. 2067–2075 (2015)
6. Gambäck, B., Olsson, F., Täckström, O.: Active learning for dialogue act classification. In: Proceedings of Interspeech 2011 (2011)

7. Hinton, G.E., Osindero, S., Teh, Y.W.: A fast learning algorithm for deep belief nets. Neural Comput. **18**(7), 1527–1554 (2006)
8. Hochreiter, S.: The vanishing gradient problem during learning recurrent neural nets and problem solutions. Int. J. Uncertainty Fuzziness Knowl. Based Syst. **6**, 107–116 (1998)
9. Jason, L., Kyunghyun, C., Thomas, H.: Fully character-level neural machine translation without explicit segmentation (2017). arXiv preprint: arXiv:1610.03017
10. Ji, Y., Haffari, G., Eisenstein, J.: A Latent Variable Recurrent Neural Network for Discourse Relation Language Models (2016). arXiv preprint: arXiv:1603.01913
11. Jonas, G., Michael, A., David, G., Denis, Y., Yann, N.: Convolutional Sequence to Sequence Learning (2017). arXiv preprint: arXiv:1705.03122
12. Jozefowicz, R., Zaremba, W., Sutskever, I.: An empirical exploration of recurrent network architectures. In: Proceedings of the 32nd International Conference on Machine Learning (ICML), pp. 171–180 (2015)
13. Junyoung, C., Sungjin, A., Yoshua, B.: Hierarchical multiscale recurrent neural network. In: International Conference of Learning Representation (ICLR) (2017)
14. Kalchbrenner, N., Blunsom, P.: Recurrent convolutional neural networks for discourse compositionality. In: ACL WS on Continuous Vector Space Models and Their Compositionality, pp. 119–126 (2013)
15. Kim, Y.: Convolutional neural networks for sentence classification. In: Proceedings of the 2014 Conference on Empirical Methods in Natural Language Processing (EMNLP), pp. 1746–1751 (2014)
16. Kim, Y., Jernite, Y., Sontag, D., Rush, A.M.: Character-aware neural language models. In: Proceedings of Association for the Advancement of Artificial Intelligence (2016)
17. Koutnik, J., Greff, K., Gomez, F., Schmidhuber, J.: A clockwork RNN. In: Proceedings of the 31st International Conference on Machine Learning (ICML), vol. 32, pp. 1863–1871 (2014)
18. Ling, W., Luis, T., Marujo, L., Astudillo, R.F., Amir, S., Dyer, C., Black, A.W., Trancoso, I.: Finding function in form: compositional character models for open vocabulary word representation. In: Proceedings of Empirical Methods on Natural Language Processing (EMNLP), pp. 1520–1530 (2015)
19. Mikolov, T., Chen, K., Corrado, G., Dean, J.: Distributed representations of words and phrases and their compositionality. In: Advances in Neural Information Processing Systems (NIPS) (2013)
20. Serban, I.V., Sordoni, A., Bengio, Y., Courville, A., Pineau, J.: Building end-to-end dialogue systems using generative hierarchical neural network models. In: Special Track on Cognitive Systems at AAAI (2016)
21. Socher, R., Manning, C.D., Ng, A.Y.: Learning continuous phrase representations and syntactic parsing with recursive neural networks. In: NIPS-2010 Deep Learning and Unsupervised Feature Learning Workshop (2010)
22. Srivastava, N.: Unsupervised learning of video representations using LSTMs. In: Proceedings of International Conference of Machine Learning 2015, vol. 37 (2015)
23. Stolcke, A., Ries, K., Coccaro, N., Shriberg, E., Bates, R., Jurafsky, D., Taylor, P., Martin, R., Ess-Dykema, C.V., Meteer, M.: Dialogue act modeling for automatic tagging and recognition of conversational speech. Comput. Linguist. **26**(3), 339–373 (2000)
24. Sutskever, I., Vinyals, O., Le, Q.V.: Sequence to sequence learning with neural networks. In: Advances in Neural Information Processing Systems (NIPS), pp. 3104–3112 (2014)

25. Tang, D., Qin, B., Liu, T.: Document modeling with gated recurrent neural network for sentiment classification. In: Proceedings of the 2015 Conference on Empirical Methods in Natural Language Processing, pp. 1422–1432 (2015)
26. Zeiler, M.D.: ADADELTA: an adaptive learning rate method (2012). arXiv preprint: arXiv:1212.5701

Ultra-deep Neural Network for Face Anti-spoofing

Xiaokang Tu and Yuchun Fang[⊠]

School of Computer Engineering and Science, Shanghai University, Shanghai, China
ycfang@shu.edu.cn

Abstract. Face anti-spoofing is a hot research area in computer vision. With the progress of Deep Neural Networks (DNNs) in computer vision, some work has introduced neural networks into face anti-spoofing. However, the neural networks that most of the approaches use consist of only a few layers due to the limitation of training data. Inspired by the fact that deep efficiently trained neural networks are often possible to learn better representation than shallow networks. In this paper, we propose a fully data-driven ultra-deep model based on transfer learning. The model adopts a pre-trained deep residual network to learn highly discriminative features, and combines it with the Long Short-Term Memory (LSTM) units to discover long-range temporal relationships of from video frames for classification. We conduct extensive experiments on two most common benchmark datasets, namely, REPLAY-ATTACK and CASIA-FASD. Experimental results demonstrate that our ultra-deep network framework archives state-of-the-art performance.

Keywords: Face anti-spoofing · Face liveness detection · Deep learning · Transfer learning

1 Introduction

Face recognition is one of the most commonly used techniques in application of biometrics. One of the main obstacles of applying face recognition systems are especially vulnerable to spoofing attacks made by spoofing faces. Face spoofing attacks can be performed in a variety and relatively cheap ways such as *print attack, photo attack, video attack* or *3DMask attack*. A print attack, one of the most common and simple among the afore-mentioned spoofing attack type, refers to facial spoofing carried out by presenting a printed photo to a vision senser. Different from print attacks, a photo attack is a way to spoof biometric system via target's photo on digital media, such as mobile phone, tablet. A video attack exploits target's face video to intrude biometric systems. With the development of 3D reconstruction and 3D print technologies, 3D masks can easily be made with one or few client's face images to spoof the face recognition system.

In recent years, Deep Learning has achieved impressive results in computer vision and speech recognition relying on efficiently training DNNs from the raw

© Springer International Publishing AG 2017
D. Liu et al. (Eds.): ICONIP 2017, Part II, LNCS 10635, pp. 686–695, 2017.
https://doi.org/10.1007/978-3-319-70096-0_70

inputs directly. It is often possible to learn better representations than hand-crafted features, by feeding with sufficient data. The leading results [1–3] on the challenging ImageNet dataset [4] also show that depth of network is of crucial importance for many computer vision tasks. Driven by the significance of depth [5], In this paper, we propose a method which use a ultra-deep neural network to learn effective and powerful representations for face anti-spoofing.

The rest of this paper is organized as follows: We begin with a review of the related work in Sect. 2. Section 3 describes about the system design. The experiments and results obtained to validate our scheme, including data preparation and evaluation metrics are reported in Sect. 4. Section 5 presents conclusion and future work.

2   Related Works

A number of face anti-spoofing approaches had been developed to enhance the reliability of face recognition systems. The topic of anti-spoofing methods has been reviewed in detail in a number of recent review article [6,7]. The countermeasures of 2D face spoofing attacks detection generally can be divided into two main categories: those based on *static features* and those based on *dynamic features*, depending on the type of features used.

Static features based methods assume that there are inherently different texture properties between genuine faces and fake ones. The analysis of facial features is done by using various feature extraction algorithms such as Histogram of Oriented Gradient (HOG) [8], Local Binary Pattern (LBP) and its variants [9,10]. Li *et al.* [11] argue that the frequency distributions on the image of a live person and the image of an attack are different. In [12], micro texture patterns for printed artifacts are analyzed by using a multi-scale LBP method. A Support Vector Machine (SVM) was utilized to discriminate between the genuine face and fake face. In [10], a liveness detection algorithm based on color texture analysis was proposed. The LBP descriptor is used to characterize the image by combining the color (RGB, HSV and YCbCr) texture information. In [13], the authors derive a new multi-scale space to represent the face images before texture features extraction. The new multi-scale space representation is derived through multiscale filtering. Recently [14] achieved excellent performance on detecting spoofing attempts via extracting block-wise Haralick texture features from redundant discrete wavelet transformed frames obtained from a video. The proposed algorithm yields an equal error rate (EER) of 6.7% with 30 frames experiment and 1.1% with all frames experiment.

Dynamic features based methods tend to exploit motion information of detected faces as cues to recognize the attack using a sequence of input frames. In [15], the authors employed a multi-resolution strategy in a single descriptor from three orthogonal planes of the local binary pattern (LBP-TOP) that combines the space and time information. The authors reported a HTER of 7.6% on the REPLAY-ATTACK database and EER of 10.0% on the CASIA-FASD database. Santhosh *et al.* [16] performed his analysis on image spoofing based on printed pictures and replayed video. The authors used a pipeline of Dynamic mode decomposition, LBP and SVM with a histogram intersection kernel. It was proved that the pipeline is efficient, convenient and effective to use. Yang *et al.* [17] use Convolutional Neural Networks (CNNs) to extract static features from the original image and dynamic features from the dynamic maps. The face liveness detection result is obtained from the output of the SVM classifier. In [18], DOFV (displacement of optical flow vector) was extracted, and then use kNN for classifing. The authors reported a HTER of 22.81% on the REPLAY-ATTACK database.

In the previous work [19], the authors construct a deep neural network classifier by putting a LSTM layer above a convolutional architecture which contains two convolutional layer with max pooling after each. But the structure is too shallow to learn powerful representations of input frames, and yields a ERR of 5.93% on CASIA-FASD. In order to make up for the weakness of the previous work, we propose an improved method in this paper. The key factor of our method is that we extract spacial features of sequenced frames using a very deep pre-trained neural network. Then, the sequenced extracted spacial features are fed into long short-term memory (LSTM) units to extract temporal features which are useful for final classification. Despite its simplicity, we found our method to be surprisingly effective. A detailed explanation will be described in the following sections.

3   Proposed Method

The performance of those CNN-based approaches heavily rely on the availability of annotated images for training. Due to the limitation of training data in face anti-spoofing databases, it is quite hard to train a high performance entire large network classifier. A common way used to avoid overfitting a large network is using transfer learning when there is not enough data to train it from scratch. Ours face anti-spoofing method use a pre-trained network called "ResNet-50" to discover high-level semantic information and meaningful hidden representations. Then, LSTM units are used to learn temporal features of images sequences. Finally, the learned features are used to distinguish genuine faces from fake ones.

3.1   Deep Residual Networks

Deep Residual Networks (ResNets) [3] lead a recent and dramatic increase in both depth and accuracy of CNNs, facilitated by constraining the network to learn residuals. ResNets are built up by stacking residual units, see Fig. 1. For residual unit i, let x and y be the input and output vectors of layers considered. The $\mathcal{F}(\cdot)$ be its trainable non-linear residual mappings. The output of residual unit i can be expressed as:

$$y = \mathcal{F}(x, \mathcal{W}_i) + x \qquad (1)$$

where $\mathcal{W}_i$ denotes the trainable parameters of i-th residual unit. ResNets can be intuitively understood by thinking of residual functions as paths through which information can propagate easily. This means that, in every layer, a ResNet learns more complex feature combinations, which it combines with the shallower representation from the previous layer. This architecture allows for the construction of much deeper networks.

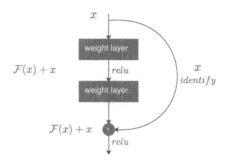

Fig. 1. Residual networks block illustration.

3.2 Long Short-Term Memory

Different from feed-forward CNN which can only discover spacial information, Long short-term memory (LSTM) units [20] are capable of learning long-range temporal dependencies from input sequences. The core idea behind the LSTM architecture is a memory cell which can maintain its state over time, and non-linear gating units which regulate the information flow into and out of the cell. Using LSTM-CNN architecture can combine the advantages of CNN and LSTM to extract spatial-temporal information from videos. Therefore we put a LSTM layer above the ResNet-50 model except for the top layers, which forms our LSTM-ResNet architecture. The framework of introduced scheme is illustrated in Fig. 2.

3.3 Model Details

In this study, we use a fixed weights pre-trained on ImageNet database to initial our ResNet-50 model. To adapt the ResNet-50 model for our face anti-spoofing task, we directly output the spatial average of the feature map via applying a global average pooling [21] to the output of last convolutional layer. The input of each timestep is normalized color image of shape $3 \times 224 \times 224$. After the features are extracted layer by layer, we get a 2048 dimensions feature vector output from the ResNet-50 model. Moreover, the feature vector is fed into LSTM layers which consists of 256 internal units. Here, the output of LSTM layer each timestep will be stacked and passed to a full-connected layer with 512

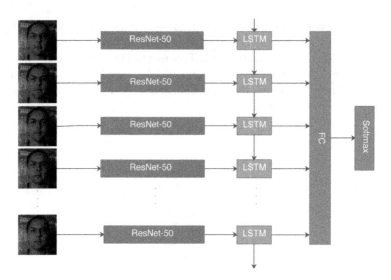

Fig. 2. Brief illustration of the LSTM-ResNet Architecture of the proposed method.

neurons. To avoid over-fitting, the full-connected layer is followed by a dropout layer. Finally, considering face anti-spoofing as binary classification problem. we choose softmax as the decision function for classification and use cross entropy loss function to optimize the classifier. We train with a batch size of 16 using Adam with a learning rate of 1×10^{-4} without weight decay.

4   Experiments

In this section, we implement our algorithm on two challenging face spoofing databases: REPLAY-ATTACK [22] and CASIA-FASD [23]. We provide an in-depth analysis of the results obtained with the proposed method. The following experiments were performed on a INTEL(R) CORE(TM) i7-7700K (4.20 GHz) processor and a Nvidia GTX 1080 GPU with 8 Gbyte RAM.

4.1   Experimental Databases

This section presents an overview of the two selected databases which consist of a number of real access attempts and fake face attacks under different conditions. The details of the all the databases are discussed below.

CASIA-FASD Database consists of 600 videos from 50 subjects in which 20 subjects are used for training and 30 subjects are used for testing as defined in the protocol. Total 12 videos are recorded for each subject with 3 different camera resolutions: low, normal and high. Three different kinds of attacks with two different support conditions were considered. The database is divided into: (1) Training set and (2) Test set with 20 and 30 independent subjects, respectively. Some samples of the database are shown in Fig. 3.

Fig. 3. Example of real accesses and attacks in different scenarios.

Replay-Attack Database consists of 1, 200 short video recordings of real accesses and attack attempts of 50 clients. A set of videos were recorded of each clients in the database under two different illumination conditions: controlled and adverse. The first condition was with uniform background and office lights turned on. The second condition was under following scene: non uniform background and the office lights were out. All subjects in database are partitioned into three non-overlapped sub-sets with 15, 15, and 20 subjects respectively: (1) Training set, to tune parameters of the classifier; (2) Development set, to fix the decision threshold; (3) Test set, to evaluate final classification performance. Figure 4 shows some frames of the captured spoofing attempts.

Fig. 4. Example of real accesses and attacks in different scenarios. In first row, samples from adverse scenario. In the second row, samples from controlled scenario. Columns from left to right show examples of real access, printed photograph, mobile phone and tablet attacks.

4.2 Experiment Setup

We follow the official overall test protocols of two selected face anti-spoofing databases. For each database, we use the training set to train the classifier, and the development set to tune the classifier for good performance. For evaluating the performance of the model, the test set is intended to be used. It should be remarked that CASIA-FASD database is lack of the specific development set, we split the training set into five folds, use one of them as development set and the other for training. As for REPLAY-ATTACK database, the development set is already given, there is no need to divide the original sets.

4.3   Data Augmentation

Our method takes a video as the input. Pan *et al.* [24] exploited the observation that humans blink once every 2–4 s, therefore, we divide each video into two second (50 frames at 25 fps) video clips in our experiments. Then, each video clip is subsampled to 25 frames to reduce the complexity for brevity. A horizontal flip strategy is applied to all video clip to generate more training data. The face coordinates are determined using machine learning toolbox Bob[1] [25]. we calculate the region-of-interest (ROI) which is the minimum bounding box that contains all the face regions of its frames of each sample. Following the method proposed in [17], the background information is useful for classifying, we enlarge the face bounding box by factor of 2.0 to make use of the information of background. The pixels which exceed the border of video frames will simply filled with zero. Finally all input frames are resized into 224×224 before being fed into neural networks.

4.4   Performance Measure

In the performance measurement, to make fair comparison with other related works, the performance evaluations of the studied anti-spoofing algorithm are measured in terms of the equal error rate (EER) and half total error rate (HTER). The EER is a biometric security system algorithm used to predetermining the threshold value which defined as the common value when the false acceptance rate (FAR) and false rejection rate (FRR) are equal. HTER is defined as

$$HTER = \frac{FAR(\tau, D) + FRR(\tau, D)}{2} \tag{2}$$

where FRR is the proportion of fake images misclassified as real, FAR means the proportion of fake images misclassified as real, the threshold τ corresponds to the EER operating point of the used development set, and D is the test sub-set. We use overall results combined all the quality and attack sets to report the final performance of the two benchmark databases.

4.5   Experimental Results

Firstly, to prove the effectiveness of our approach, we compare the performance with the results of other state-of-the-art approaches in Table 1. The overall

---

[1] http://www.idiap.ch/software/bob/.

test of our proposed algorithm obtains a HTER of 1.22% (EER is 1.00%) on CASIA-FASD and a HTER of 1.18% (EER is 1.03%) on REPLAY-ATTACK with 25 frames experiment, respectively. There is a HTER of 5% performance improvement in face spoofing attacks detection comparing with first LSTM-CNN method [19] on CASIA-FASD. It clearly shows that our proposed method is better than most of the previous works on two selected databases. The slightly lower performance than the [14] is most likely due to that DNNs need large amount of data to train. Meanwhile, different with DMD [16], our approach gives robust results on both two databases.

Table 1. Comparative test results for different databases among our method and state-of-the-art methods.

Databases	CASIA-FASD		REPLAY-ATTACK	
	EER (%)	HTER (%)	EER (%)	HTER (%)
LBP-TOP + SVM [15]	10.00	-	7.8	7.60
Context based [8]	-	-	-	5.11
Haralick feature + SVM [14]	-	1.1	-	-
LSTM-CNN [19]	5.17	5.93	-	-
CNN [17]	-	5.08	-	2.43
DPCNN [26]	2.9	6.1	4.5	-
DMD [16]	21.7	-	5.3	3.7
Scale space + LBP [13]	4.2	-	0.7	3.1
Non-linear diffusion [27]	-	-	-	10.00
Proposed[a]	1.63	1.80	1.16	1.28
Proposed[b]	**1.00**	1.22	1.03	**1.18**

[a] trained with single input frame per sample
[b] trained with 25 input frames per sample

Secondly, using 25 frames for face spoofing attacks detection may be time-consuming for certain hardware conditions. Therefore, we perform an additional experiment to explore the performance of our architecture on single frame based classification via feeding only one frame each sample into our network when training. As it shown in Table 1, the HTER has relative increased by 50.0% on CASIA-FASD and 8.7% on REPLAY-ATTACK datasets, respectively. The result indicates the positive effect of temporal features extracted from 25 frames on face anti-spoofing task. Despite the performance has declined, it still has comparable performance with state-of-the-art methods. It means that there is a good compromise between complexity cost and performance.

5   Conclusions

In this paper, we introduced an utlra-deep neural network approach to address the problem of face anti-spoofing using sequenced frames. We use data augmentation strategies to generate more training data and utilize background information and spacial-temporal features for face spoofing attacks detection. Experimental results on two challenging databases demonstrate that our proposed method makes a significant improvement compared with other shallow neural networks [17,19,26] and achieves state-of-the-art results in overall protocol for video based anti-spoofing. It clearly shows that our network framework is more effective and powerful.

For future work, we think it is worth exploring other CNN architectures and different complex benchmarks. We also plan to test our approach on other databases and improve the generalization ability of the countermeasures.

Acknowledgements. The work is funded by the National Natural Science Foundation of China (No. 61371149, No. 61170155), Shanghai Innovation Action Plan Project (No. 16511101200) and the Open Project Program of the National Laboratory of Pattern Recognition (No. 201600017).

References

1. Srivastava, R.K., Greff, K., Schmidhuber, J.: Training very deep networks. CoRR abs/1507.06228 (2015)
2. Szegedy, C., Liu, W., Jia, Y., Sermanet, P., Reed, S.E., Anguelov, D., Erhan, D., Vanhoucke, V., Rabinovich, A.: Going deeper with convolutions. CoRR abs/1409.4842 (2014)
3. He, K., Zhang, X., Ren, S., Sun, J.: Deep residual learning for image recognition. CoRR abs/1512.03385 (2015)
4. Deng, J., Dong, W., Socher, R., Li, L.J., Li, K., Fei-Fei, L.: ImageNet: a large-scale hierarchical image database. In: CVPR 2009 (2009)
5. Larsson, G., Maire, M., Shakhnarovich, G.: Fractalnet: ultra-deep neural networks without residuals. CoRR abs/1605.07648 (2016)
6. Chingovska, I., Yang, J., Lei, Z., Yi, D.: The 2nd competition on counter measures to 2d face spoofing attacks. In: International Conference on Biometrics, pp. 1–6 (2013)
7. Galbally, J., Marcel, S., Fierrez, J.: Biometric antispoofing methods: a survey in face recognition. IEEE Access **2**, 1530–1552 (2015)
8. Komulainen, J., Hadid, A., Pietikainen, M.: Context based face anti-spoofing. In: IEEE Sixth International Conference on Biometrics: Theory, Applications and Systems, pp. 1–8 (2013)
9. Diviya, M., Mishra, S.: A novel approach for detecting facial image spoofing using local ternary pattern. In: 2016 Second International Conference on Science Technology Engineering and Management (ICONSTEM), pp. 61–66. IEEE (2016)
10. Boulkenafet, Z., Komulainen, J., Hadid, A.: Face spoofing detection using colour texture analysis. IEEE Trans. Inf. Forensics Secur. **11**(8), 1818–1830 (2016)
11. Li, J., Wang, Y., Jain, A.K.: Live face detection based on the analysis of Fourier spectra. Proc. SPIE **5404**, 296–303 (2004)
12. Maatta, J., Hadid, A., Pietikainen, M.: Face spoofing detection from single images using micro-texture analysis. In: International Joint Conference on Biometrics, pp. 1–7 (2011)
13. Boulkenafet, Z., Komulainen, J., Feng, X., Hadid, A.: Scale space texture analysis for face anti-spoofing. In: International Conference on Biometrics, pp. 1–6 (2016)

14. Agarwal, A., Singh, R., Vatsa, M.: Face anti-spoofing using Haralick features. In: IEEE International Conference on Biometrics Theory, Applications and Systems (2016)
15. Pereira, T.D.F., Anjos, A., Martino, J.M.D., Marcel, S.: LBP - top based counter-measure against face spoofing attacks. In: International Conference on Computer Vision, pp. 121–132 (2012)
16. Tirunagari, S., Poh, N., Windridge, D., Iorliam, A., Suki, N., Ho, A.T.S.: Detection of face spoofing using visual dynamics. IEEE Trans. Inf. Forensics Secur. **10**(4), 762–777 (2015)
17. Yang, J., Lei, Z., Li, S.Z.: Learn convolutional neural network for face anti-spoofing. Comput. Sci. **9218**, 373–384 (2014)
18. Yin, W., Ming, Y., Tian, L.: A face anti-spoofing method based on optical flow field. In: 2016 IEEE 13th International Conference on Signal Processing (ICSP), pp. 1333–1337. IEEE (2016)
19. Xu, Z., Li, S., Deng, W.: Learning temporal features using LSTM-CNN architecture for face anti-spoofing. In: Pattern Recognition, pp. 141–145 (2016)
20. Hochreiter, S., Schmidhuber, J.: Long short-term memory. Neural Comput. **9**(8), 1735 (1997)
21. Lin, M., Chen, Q., Yan, S.: Network in network. CoRR abs/1312.4400 (2013)
22. Chingovska, I., Anjos, A., Marcel, S.: On the effectiveness of local binary patterns in face anti-spoofing. In: Biometrics Special Interest Group, pp. 1–7 (2012)
23. Zhang, Z., Yan, J., Liu, S., Lei, Z.: A face antispoofing database with diverse attacks. In: IAPR International Conference on Biometrics, pp. 26–31 (2012)
24. Pan, G., Wu, Z., Sun, L.: Liveness Detection for Face Recognition. InTech (2008)
25. Anjos, A., Shafey, L.E., Wallace, R., Günther, M., McCool, C., Marcel, S.: Bob: a free signal processing and machine learning toolbox for researchers. In: 20th ACM Conference on Multimedia Systems (ACMMM), Nara, Japan. ACM Press, October 2012
26. Li, L., Feng, X., Boulkenafet, Z., Xia, Z., Li, M., Hadid, A.: An original face anti-spoofing approach using partial convolutional neural network. In: 2016 Sixth International Conference on Image Processing Theory, Tools and Applications (IPTA), pp. 1–6, December 2016
27. Alotaibi, A., Mahmood, A.: Deep face liveness detection based on nonlinear diffusion using convolution neural network. Signal Image Video Process. **11**(4), 1–8 (2016)

License Plate Detection Using Deep Cascaded Convolutional Neural Networks in Complex Scenes

Qiang Fu, Yuan Shen, and Zhenhua Guo[✉]

Graduate School at Shenzhen, Tsinghua University, Shenzhen 518055, China
fuq15@mails.tsinghua.edu.cn,
zhenhua.guo@sz.tsinghua.edu.cn

Abstract. License plate detection plays an important role in intelligent transportation system. However, it is still a challenging task due to plenty of complex scenes. Recent studies show that deep learning approaches achieve prominent results on general object detection. Therefore, in this paper, we propose a deep cascaded convolutional neural network for improving license plate detection in complex scenes. Firstly, we utilize convolutional features to generate candidate vehicles proposals. Then a network is used to detect a license from each vehicle proposal by analyzing the correlation between vehicles and licenses. Finally, we enhance detection performance by processing license boundary. Experimental results on a large dataset demonstrate that our method works effectively in a variety of complex scenes.

Keywords: License plate detection · Cascaded convolutional neural network · Vehicle proposals

1 Introduction

Due to the development of intelligent transportation system, license plate detection, as an important part of the system, has received considerable attention. It has numerous potential applications, such as traffic monitoring and road accidents remote processing [1]. However, it is still not easy to detect license plates in an open environment. The difficulty does lie in the influence of complex environmental factors, for example, different illumination, weather and patterns similar to plates. Besides, the variation of the plates, for instance, plate location, size, and occlusion also affect final detection results. Previous work on license plate detection mainly use some handcrafted features to estimate the possibility of the plate. Since some features may be sensitive in complex environment, some approaches can only be effective in certain circumstances and generate many false positives in other scenes [2].

Owing to its ability to acquire multi-scale discriminative representations of the objects, deep convolutional neural network (CNN) [3] obtains remarkable achievements in object detection. One of the classical object detection work is R-CNN [4]. It extracts certain amounts of candidate regions, and then uses CNN for feature extraction and classification for the regions. The following state-of-the-art methods such as Fast

© Springer International Publishing AG 2017
D. Liu et al. (Eds.): ICONIP 2017, Part II, LNCS 10635, pp. 696–706, 2017.
https://doi.org/10.1007/978-3-319-70096-0_71

R-CNN [5] and Faster R-CNN [6] adopt similar idea. Faster R-CNN utilizes a region proposal network (RPN) which combines object proposal and detection into an integrated network. Thanks to RPN, Faster R-CNN achieves accuracy improvement and time-consumption reduction. Inspired by the good effect of CNNs in generic categories, some of the CNNs based specific categories such as face and pedestrian detection have been proposed in recent years [7–9].

Similarly, as a specific category detection, CNN can also extract more expressive discriminative features from license plate so as to improve the accuracy of detection. Despite CNN has such a big advantage, these approaches still have some drawbacks which makes them less adaptable. They cannot handle the balance between small objects and high confidence because the bounding boxes may not contain enough features for detection if they are too small. In complex scenes, the proportion of license plate in an image is usually small, which makes it difficult to detect. However, some of the available plate detection methods ignore the correlation between vehicles and licenses. In real world, a license plate may only appear within vehicle. In addition, both the ratio of a license plate in a car and the ratio of a car in an image are in a suitable range. This inherent correlation may make detection more accurate.

In this paper, we propose a framework to utilize unified cascaded CNNs. The proposed CNNs consist of two stages. In the first stage, it produces vehicles proposals through a CNN. Then, we detect license plates from the proposals which have been extracted in former stage through a more powerful CNN. Finally, we refine each bounding box according to the boundary of license plate region. Using this framework, we can detect license plates with different variations such as colors, fonts or sizes in complicated environments. Extensive experiments on a set of real traffic images with day and night illuminations show that the proposed method could get performance than state-of-the-art methods in license plates detection.

The rest of paper is organized as follows. Section 2 discusses related work. Section 3 presents the proposed method. Section 4 reports and analyzes experimental results. Finally, Sect. 5 concludes our work.

2   Related Work

2.1   License Plate Detection

Although plenty of plate detection methods have been proposed in recent years, it is still a challenging problem because of free viewpoint and presence of various illumination situations. In general, a license plate consists of three parts, edges, plate and characters. So the detection based on handcrafted features can be roughly classified into three types: edge based methods [10, 11], plate feature based methods [12, 13] and character based methods [14–16].

Edge based approaches try to find regions with obvious edge density as license plates. In [10, 11], these license plate localization methods used edge detector combining with some geometric transformation to search the rectangles which can be regarded as candidate license plates. This strategy performs well in relatively simple scenarios. However, it is difficult to find license plates if their edges are blurry.

Plate features mainly includes color and texture. Both of them can be used because they are usually different from other parts of the vehicle body. Deb et al. [13] proposed HSI color model to detect candidate license plate regions. Giannoukos et al. [12] advanced Sliding Concentric Window (SCW) to confirm license plate based on the local irregularity texture characteristic of the plate. It performs as well as edge based method in simple scenarios. However, they are too sensitive to unwanted similar features which are very common in natural scene images.

Characters are the most important elements of license plates and the easiest feature to distinguish the plate region. Matas et al. [14] introduced the well-known character feature detector Maximally Stable Extremal Region (MSER) to detect license plates and other traffic signs. As the MSERs are highly robust against environmental changes, many researchers utilize MSER combing with conditional random model [15] or label-moveable clique [16] to remove unwanted character regions. However, the method [16] which was introduced by Gu et al. is hard to recognize the right order of the characters and Li et al.'s [15] approach is unable to detect multi-scale license plates.

2.2   CNN for Object Detection

With the outstanding results on image classification, CNN has been applied to object detection and achieves exceptional performances. In [17], detection problem is treated as a regression problem to object bounding box's location. Sermanet et al. [18] used a pre-trained classification network to predict object bounding box in a tedious and computationally expensive way. Girshick et al. [4] proposed R-CNN which uses object proposals generated by selective search to choose the object region for detection tasks. To reduce the computation of each proposal in R-CNN, Fast R-CNN [5] has been introduced by sharing convolutional features and dealing with object proposals from the last convolutional layer. Recently, Faster R-CNN [6] substituted RPN for the object proposals generated by selective search and obtained higher accuracy with faster speed. SSD [19] segmented the input image into some grids and predicted the object bounding box through the grids in CNN. In addition to detect general categories, CNN has used in the detection of specific categories. Angelova et al. [7] applied CNN in pedestrian detection and achieved high accuracy. Yang et al. [20] trained CNNs for facial attribute recognition to generate candidate facial region, which also obtained remarkable effect. Chen et al. [21] used convolutional features to replace hand-crafted features and detected the location in image pyramid by traditional sliding window scheme.

2.3   Cascaded Network

The cascade face detector proposed by Viola and Jones [22] utilized Haar-like features and AdaBoost to train cascaded classifiers. The idea of reduce candidates by combining a number of simple features is also applied to CNNs. Li et al. [8] used a shallow network to reject easy non-face samples at first, then eliminated more negatives through two deeper networks. Zhang et al. [9] proposed cascaded CNNs by multi-task learning for joint face detection and alignment, each detection network can benefit from the result of previous network. Angelova et al. [7] cascaded a shallow deep network and a fine-tune Alexnet to achieve real-time pedestrian detection. The shallow network removed amounts of candidates and reserved an appropriate number of candidates for the following CNN to detect.

3 Approach

3.1 Cascaded Convolutional Neural Network

The overall structure of our approach is shown in Table 1. The proposed cascaded CNN is composed of two stages. We employ similar structure of Faster R-CNN with different convolutional layers for feature map extraction in each stage of CNN. We use RPNs [6] to predict object region proposals with different scales and ROI pooling layer [5] to classify and localize in both of the stages. As a RPN outputs multi-scale candidate boxes with class confidence, we just use a single-scale image whose shorter side is re-scaled to 600 pixels, instead of resizing it many times to build an image pyramid.

Table 1. The overall structure of our cascaded CNN

Stage 1 CNN		Stage 2 CNN	
Input		Input	
Convolution(kernel: 7 × 7, stride: 2)		Convolution(kernel: 3 × 3, stride: 1)	
		Convolution(kernel: 3 × 3, stride: 1)	
		Max pooling(kernel: 2 × 2, stride: 2)	
Max pooling(kernel: 3 × 3, stride: 2)		Convolution(kernel: 3 × 3, stride: 1)	
		Convolution(kernel: 3 × 3, stride:1)	
Convolution(kernel: 5 × 5, stride: 2)		Max pooling(kernel: 2 × 2, stride: 2)	
		Convolution(kernel: 3 × 3, stride: 1)	
		Convolution(kernel: 3 × 3, stride: 1)	
Max pooling(kernel: 3 × 3, stride: 2)		Convolution(kernel: 3 × 3, stride: 1)	
		Max pooling(kernel: 2 × 2, stride: 2)	
Convolution(kernel: 3 × 3, stride: 1)		Convolution(kernel: 3 × 3, stride: 1)	
		Convolution(kernel: 3 × 3, stride: 1)	
		Convolution(kernel: 3 × 3, stride: 1)	
Convolution(kernel: 3 × 3, stride: 1)		Max pooling(kernel: 2 × 2, stride: 2)	
		Convolution(kernel: 3 × 3, stride: 1)	
		Convolution(kernel: 3 × 3, stride: 1)	
Convolution (kernel: 3 × 3, stride: 1)	RPN	Convolution (kernel: 3 × 3, stride: 1)	RPN
ROI pooling		ROI pooling	
Fully connected (4096)		Fully connected (4096)	
Fully connected (4096)		Fully connected (4096)	
Fully connected	Fully connected	Fully connected	Fully connected
Softmax(4)	Bounding box regression(16)	Softmax(2)	Bounding box regression(8)

Note: ReLU which is not shown in the table is followed by every convolution layer

Stage 1: we train a simple CNN which includes 5 convolutional layers with a RPN to generate three categories of candidate vehicles proposals from the last convolutional layer. The stage 1 CNN can get the vehicle proposal with the highest Intersection-over-Union (IoU) overlap with a ground-truth box. The threshold setting for IoU is not too high to ensure all vehicles can be extracted.

Stage 2: each vehicle proposal with high confidence is fed to another powerful CNN after padding with 50% on each side. In this network, we use the architecture of VGG16 [23] with RPN to get better detection results because of two reasons: the first one is that a car is changed from foreground to background making background more complex; the other one is that license detection, similar as face detection, needs more discrimination features to get better performance [8].

For each proposal, we need to get a ground-truth class u and bounding-box regression target v. v is a vector with 4 values which represents coordinates of left top, height and width respectively. Therefore, the learning target of joint classification and bounding-box regression can be formulated as:

$$L(p, u, t, v) = L_{cls}(p, u) + \lambda * p_t L_{reg}(t, v) \tag{1}$$

where $L_{cls}(p, u)$ is cross-entropy loss for true class u. p is the probability computed by the network that the proposal belongs to the true class. t is the coordinated vector of the ground-truth box associated with the proposal. For the regression loss, we use $L_{reg}(t, v) = L_1(t - v)$ where L_1 is the robust loss function (smooth L_1) defined in [15]. The term $p_t L_{reg}(t, v)$ means it is activated only for the object proposal ($p_t = 1$) and not used otherwise ($p_t = 0$).

3.2 Bounding Box Refinement

After detection by cascaded CNNs, we find that some detected bounding boxes cannot surround the license plate completely. For example, Fig. 1(a) only contains the left part of the license plate. It may not be considered as a license plate and then be rejected by CNN because of the low IoU. Therefore, we perform a simple process for refining bounding box according to edge feature of license plate. For each bounding box of a license plate with the highest IoU, we enlarge its edges with 30% on each side. Then we utilize Canny operator on the enlarged region of license plate to perform edge detection. We can find the top and bottom boundaries by horizontal projection. Similarly, the left and right boundaries can be found by vertical projection. Figure 1(b) shows an example of bounding box refinement.

Fig. 1. (a) and (b) represent the bounding box before and after refinement, respectively.

3.3   Training Details

The convolutional layers for feature extraction in our CNN model is initialized by pre-training on the ImageNet [24], and all rest of new layers are randomly initialized by a zero-mean Gaussian distribution with standard deviation 0.01. We randomly sample 128 positive and negative object proposals to compute the learning target function of a mini-batch to avoid detecting. We sample positive proposals from all proposals if an IoU ratio is higher than 0.7 for any ground-truth box and assign a negative label to the proposal that has an IoU overlap lower than 0.3. At the beginning of training, we flip the input image horizontal for data augmentation. We use a learning rate of 0.001 for 60 K iterations and decrease it to 0.0001 for the last 20 K iterations in each training phase. We use a momentum of 0.9 and a weight decay of 0.0005 [25]. In the first stage of the networks, we set the IoU threshold value of 0.4 to ensure that all of the vehicle proposals can be extracted. Our network is implemented by Caffe [26].

4   Experimental Results

4.1   Dataset

Since there are few public Chinese license plate datasets available, we collected a challenging dataset including 30975 images to test our approach. The dataset is taken from different real traffic monitoring scenes with various illumination conditions, including sunny, cloudy, daytime, nighttime and different kinds of vehicle (bus, truck, car, etc.). Some samples from dataset are shown in Fig. 2. Resolution of the images is 2048 × 1536 pixels. Detailed description of the dataset is listed in Table 2. In the experiment, the proportion of train set, validation set and test set is 4:1:1. Ground-truth of vehicle and license plate location are manually labeled.

Fig. 2. Some samples of our dataset. A number of images in the dataset contain more than one vehicle or license plate.

4.2   Weighting Parameter

The weighting parameter λ manages the balance between the two loss functions. As stated in [2], there is no uniform way to evaluate performance of different license plate detection systems. In this paper, we follow the general evaluation criterion for detection results using precision and recall rate. Precision is defined as the number of correctly detected license plates divided by the total number of detected regions. Recall is defined as the number of correctly detected license plates divided by the total number

Table 2. Detail of the dataset

Category	License Plate	Car	Bus	Truck
Number	32038	28854	1125	2006

of ground-truth boxes. A detection is considered as correct if the IoU between the detection and ground-truth bounding box is greater than 0.5. To evaluate the impact of λ, we conduct experiments comparing the average precision (AP) of our approach at $\lambda = \{0.01, 0.1, 1, 10, 100\}$. Figure 3 shows that our approach performs the best when λ is near to 1. Therefore, for simplify, we set the weighting parameter $\lambda = 1$.

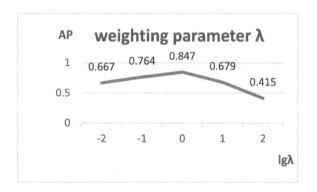

Fig. 3. Evaluation of the weighting parameter λ.

4.3   Detection Results

We give a comparison between our approach and some previous methods in Table 3. We choose Faster R-CNN [6] and SSD [19] for comparison because both of them achieve good effect in detection task. Li et al. [15] 's method used character with conditional random field model and edges to detect license plates and works effectively. Statistical analysis is shown in Table 3 and some of detection results are illustrated in Fig. 4. Based on the evaluation criterion described above, our approach outperforms the other methods in both precision and recall, which is higher 0.26% and 0.90% than the second best method, respectively. Figure 5 shows an example of detection result. As shown in Fig. 5(c), the method proposed by Yuan et al. [11] approach cannot detect license plate correctly because the hand-crafted features are sensitive to noise in natural scene. Because of gaining enough discriminant features, our method can detects both plates as shown in Fig. 5(d) and Fig. 5(e). However, faster R-CNN fails to detect one plate. These results indicate that our approach is more robust to image size, illumination and orientation.

The Fig. 6 shows the candidate proposals which are extracted from a region of a bus. CNN detect the license plate correctly and regard the other proposals as background because only a proposal which contains a plate can achieve high probability.

Table 3. Comparison of plate detection results by different methods. Our cascaded CNN approach in bold

Method	Precision (%)	Recall (%)
Li *et al.* [15]	97.19	89.61
SSD [19]	97.83	84.54
Faster R-CNN [6]	98.16	86.68
Our approach	**98.42**	**90.51**

Fig. 4. Some of successful results. Red bounding boxes labeled in the first picture in each line are the vehicle proposal. The boxes in remaining pictures in each group are the detected locations of license plates in the corresponding vehicle proposals. Better viewed by zooming. (Color figure online)

Fig. 5. An example of detection result by different methods. (a) Original image with red bounding which are vehicle proposals. (b) is result of Faster R-CNN, (c) is result of the method proposed by Yuan et al.'s [25] and (d), (e) are results of our approach. Better viewed by zooming. (Color figure online)

This successful detection demonstrates outstanding discrimination power of CNN. We can also find that the recall rate of Faster R-CNN is lower than Li et al. [15] 's method. This result reveals the Faster R-CNN's shortcoming that it cannot detect small object in

Fig. 6. Some of the proposals extracted from stage 2 of the proposed CNN. Only the first image is recognized as the license plate and the other are regarded as the background.

a large background because of lacking enough features. However, our approach enhances the recall rate by generating proposals from vehicles which turns the area of a license plate into an appropriate size.

Figure 7 shows some of detection failure examples. In Fig. 7(a), the license plate is too small for stage 2. In Fig. 7(b), our approach omits the license plate since it is located in the top of the picture and the car which owning this plate is not detected by our CNN.

Fig. 7. Some of our failures. Our approach only generates the vehicle proposal in stage 1, but fail to detect the license plate.

5   Conclusion

In this paper, we have proposed a license plate detection system using the cascaded convolutional neural networks. A simple CNN is used to generate the candidate vehicle proposals and then a deep CNN detects a license plate carefully in the proposal according to the relationship between vehicles and licenses. We fine-tune the bounding box of a license plate through its edges. Experimental result shows that this approach can produce effective performance in complex scenes. Our future work is to further explore proposal for detecting small object easily, based on the limitations in our current work. Another direction is to transform the cascaded networks into an end-to-end network which can get a variety of vehicle and license information.

Acknowledgement. This work is partially supported by Shenzhen fundamental research fund (Grant No. JCYJ20170412170438636) and the Natural Science Foundation of China (NSFC) (No. 61772296). We gratefully acknowledge the support of NVIDIA Corporation with the donation of the Tesla K40 GPU used for this research.

References

1. Kranthi, S., Pranathi, K., Srisaila, A.: Automatic number plate recognition. Int. J. Adv. Tech. **2**(3), 408–422 (2011)
2. Du, S., Ibrahim, M., Shehata, M., Badawy, W.: Automatic license plate recognition (alpr): a state-of-the-art review. IEEE Trans. Circuits Syst. Video Technol. **23**(2), 311–325 (2013)
3. LeCun, Y., Bengio, Y.: Deep learning. Nature **521**(7553), 436–444 (2015)
4. Girshick, R., Donahue, J., Darrell, T., Malik, J.: Rich feature hierarchies for accurate object detection and semantic segmentation. In: CVPR, pp. 580–587 (2014)
5. Girshick, R: Fast R-CNN. ICCV (2015)
6. Ren, S., He, K., Girshick, R.B., Sun, J.: Faster R-CNN: towards real-time object detection with region proposal networks. In: NIPS (2015)
7. Angelova, A., Krizhevsky, A., Vanhoucke, V., Ogale, A., Ferguson, D.: Real-time pedestrian detection with deep network cascades. In: BMVC (2015)
8. Li, H., Lin, Z., Shen, X., Brandt, J., Hua, G.: A convolutional neural network cascade for face detection. In: CVPR, pp. 5325–5334 (2015)
9. Zhang, Z., Luo, P., Loy, C.C., Tang, X.: Facial landmark detection by deep multi-task learning. In: ECCV, pp. 94-108 (2014)
10. Lalimia, M.A., Ghofrania, S.: A vehicle license plate detection method using region and edge based methods. Comp. Electr. Eng. **39**, 834–845 (2013)
11. Yule, Y., Wenbin, Z., Yong, Z., Xinan, W., Xuefeng, H., Nikos, K.: A robust and efficient approach to license plate detection. IEEE Trans. Image Proces. **26**(3), 1102–1113 (2017)
12. Giannoukos, I., Anagnostopoulos, C.-N., Loumos, V., Kayafas, E.: Operator context scanning to support high segmentation rates for real time license plate recognition. Pattern Recogn. **43**(11), 3866–3878 (2010)
13. Deb, K., Jo, K.: HSI color based vehicle license plate detection. In: Proceedings of International Conference on Control Automation System, pp. 687-691 (2008)
14. Matas, J., Chum, O., Urban, M., Pajdla, T.: Robust wide-baseline stereo from maximally stable extremal regions. Image Vis. Comput. **22**(10), 761–767 (2004)
15. Li, B., Tian, B., Li, Y., Wen, D.: Component-based license plate detection using conditional random field model. IEEE Trans. Intell. Transp. Syst. **14**(4), 1690–1699 (2013)
16. Gu, Q., Yang, J., Kong, L., Cui, G.: Multi-scaled license plate detection based on the label-moveable maximal mser clique. Opt. Rev. **22**(4), 669–678 (2015)
17. Szegedy, C., Toshev, A., Erhan, D.: Deep neural net-works for object detection. In: NIPS, pp. 2553–2561 (2013)
18. Sermanet, P., Eigen, D., Zhang, X., LeCun, Y.: Overfeat: integrated recognition, localization and detection using convolutional networks. CoRR, abs/1312.6229 (2013)
19. Liu, W., Anguelov, D., Erhan, D., Szegedy, C., Reed, S., Fu, C., Berg, A.C.: SSD: single shot multibox detector. arXiv preprint, arXiv:1512.02325 (2015)
20. Yang, S., Luo, P., Loy, C.C., Tang, X.: From facial parts responses to face detection: a deep learning approach. In: ICCV, pp. 3676-3684 (2015)
21. Ying-Nong, C., Chin-Chuan, H., Cheng-Tzu, W., Bor-Shenn, J., Kuo-Chin, F.: The application of a convolution neural network on face and license plate detection. In: ICPR, vol. 4 (2006)
22. Viola, P.A., Jones, M.J.: Rapid object detection using a boosted cascade of simple features. In: CVPR, pp. 511–518 (2001)
23. Simonyan, K., Zisserman, A.: Very deep convolutional networks for large-scale image recognition. In: ICLR (2015)

24. Russakovsky, O., Deng, J., Su, H., Krause, J., Satheesh, S., Ma, S., Huang, Z., Karpathy, A., Khosla, A., Bernstein, M., Berg, A.C., Fei-Fei, L.: Imagenet large scale visual recognition challenge. In: IJCV, pp. 1–42, April (2015)
25. Krizhevsky, A., Sutskever, I., Hinton, G.: Imagenet classification with deep convolutional neural networks. In: NIPS (2012)
26. Jia, Y., Shelhamer, E., Donahue, J., Girshick, R., Guadarrama, S., Darrell, T.: Caffe: convolutional architecture for fast feature embedding. Eprint Arxiv, pp. 675-678 (2014)

Brain-Computer Interface

Task-Free Brainprint Recognition Based on Degree of Brain Networks

Wanzeng Kong$^{(\boxtimes)}$, Qiaonan Fan, Luyun Wang, Bei Jiang, Yong Peng, and Yanbin Zhang

School of Computer Science, Hangzhou Dianzi University, Hangzhou, China
{kongwanzeng,yongpeng,zhyb}@hdu.edu.cn, fanqiaonn@163.com,
18868876785@163.com, jiangbei_1991@163.com,

Abstract. Personal identification plays an important role in the information society. However, the traditional methods of identification cannot fully guarantee security. As a new type of biometrics, brainprint has remarkable advantages of non-stealing and unforgeability. It is a more secure biometrics for personal identification. In this paper, we propose a new method for brainprint recognition based on brain networks of electroencephalogram (EEG) signals. Firstly, we construct the brain functional networks upon the phase synchronization of EEG channels. Then, the degree of brain networks is computed to form a novel feature vector. Lastly, we utilize linear discriminant analysis (LDA) to classify extracted features. Experiments are conducted on four data sets. The average recognition accuracy of each data set is over 0.937 and the best one reaches 0.993.

Keywords: EEG · Brainprint recognition · Brain networks · Phase synchronization

1 Introduction

Nowadays, the security of personal information becomes more important [1]. Most of existing biometric personal identification methods, such as fingerprint, palm vein and face, suffer from the risk of being copied or forged easily. Different from these identification approaches, brainprint [2] has unique advantages. For example, it can not be stolen or forged, and only alive person can produce it.

The concept of brainprint was firstly proposed by Armstrong et al. [2] in 2014. They used the components of event-related potential (ERP) as characteristics to identify 45 subjects, the accuracy rate was in the range of 82%-97%. Further, these features were stable over time. Brainprint refers to a unique and durable biometric, which is produced by the brain. At present, there are many methods and applications for brainprint recognition. Das et al. [3] used visually evoked neural activity for discriminating individuals and analyzed EEG data in a holistic manner. Discriminative spatio-temporal filters were utilized to extract features. Then they used LDA and support vector machines (SVM) to classify

© Springer International Publishing AG 2017
D. Liu et al. (Eds.): ICONIP 2017, Part II, LNCS 10635, pp. 709–717, 2017.
https://doi.org/10.1007/978-3-319-70096-0_72

20 subjects. Recognition rates ranged from 75% to 94%. Yeom et al. [4] found that everyone would produce a different reaction when he confronted self-face and non-self-face, which can be measured by EEG. So they proposed a new biometric system and devised a novel stimulus presentation paradigm for personal authentication. The mean accuracy rate was 86.1%. Gui et al. [5] used wavelet packet decomposition to extract frequency features from 32 subjects, and performed classification based on an artificial neural network. The classification rate can reach around 90%. Maiorana et al. [6] extracted features through eigenbrains or eigentensorbrains for recognition. Principal component analysis (PCA) and multilinear PCA (MPCA) were used to define two bases for EEG signals. They evaluated the method on a database comprising EEG recordings acquired from 30 subjects. The accuracy rate of the experiment was 87.9%.

As described above, researches of brainprint recognition were based on the amplitude of the EEG signals. In fact, EEG signals consist of amplitude and phase information. Both the phase and the amplitude contain important EEG information. However, due to the lack of measurement and calculation models, the phase information has been rarely analyzed and implemented. The phase synchronization of the EEG signals is based on phase information of EEG signals. Using phase synchronization to study EEG signals, we can find new solutions that have not been found in amplitude studies. Phase synchronization calculates the instantaneous phase values between different channel pairs by the Hilbert transform (HT), so as to compare the phase difference of the two oscillatory sequences. Instantaneous phase extracts from observed signals, but neglects the effect of instantaneous amplitude. Relevant studies have shown that the phase synchronization of EEG signals is a reflection of the differences in white matter architecture in individuals [7,8]. Therefore, we use the relationship between phase synchronization and the physiological features of the brain, analyze the phase synchronization features of each channel to obtain the phase synchronization matrix, and then extract features for recognition. Besides, methods of existing brainprint recognition generally were tested on one data set with specific task in their work. Therefore, the methods they used can not be widely applied.

In this paper, a method is proposed for brainprint recognition. First, phase locking value (PLV) is computed to measure phase synchronization. The coherent matrix constructed by PLV will obtain a weighted undirected network. Then, the degree of brain networks is utilized to form a feature vector. Finally, we use LDA to obtain the classification results. Phase synchronization of EEG signals is considered in our experiment rather than amplitude information. It not only describes the interaction of channel pairs, but also reflects the relationship of instantaneous phase between channels. Different from one type of EEG signals from one task, the proposed method evaluates on four different data sets from diverse tasks, namely two public data sets [9,10] and other two data sets collected by our laboratory [11,12].

2 Methods

2.1 Preprocessing

In our experiments, EEG data are filtered 2 Hz to 47 Hz by using bandpass filters. The value of every channel has been dealing with common average reference (CAR) [13]. Then, Butterworth band-pass filters are used to select corresponding band, namely theta (4–8 Hz), alpha (8–13 Hz), beta (13–30 Hz) and gamma (>30 Hz).

2.2 Phase Synchronization

Phase synchronization analyzes the interrelation of EEG signals based on phase and synchronization angles [14]. It can retain phase components of EEG signals and inhibit the impact of amplitude [15].

First, the analytical signal $Z_x(t)$ of EEG signal $x(t)$ is defined as:

$$Z_x(t) = x(t) + j\tilde{x}(t) = A_x(t)e^{j\Phi_x(t)} \tag{1}$$

where $A_x(t)$ and $\Phi_x(t)$ are instantaneous amplitude and instantaneous phase of $x(t)$, respectively.

The Hilbert transform $\tilde{x}(t)$ for the given continuous time series $x(t)$ is:

$$\tilde{x}(t) = \frac{1}{\pi} P \int_{-\infty}^{+\infty} \frac{x(\tau)}{t - \tau} d\tau \tag{2}$$

where P denotes the Cauchy principal value.

$\Phi_x(t)$ can be defined as:

$$\Phi_x(t) = \arctan \frac{\tilde{x}(t)}{x(t)} \tag{3}$$

And $\Phi_y(t)$ has the similar definition.

Phase-locking value (PLV) is used to measure the phase synchronization information [16], which is defined as follows::

$$PLV = |< \exp(j\{\Phi_x(t) - \Phi_y(t)\}) >| \tag{4}$$

where $< . >$ means the averaging operator of a continues time t.

PLV can be calculated with an one-second time window. There are H non-overlapping time segmentations of each sample. The average PLV is the mean of H seconds PLV. One channel EEG signals are as a time series. Different channel pairs can be constructed by pair-wise channels. Then we can get a $n \times n$ symmetric matrix $\mathbf{V}$ as below:

$$\mathbf{V} = \begin{bmatrix} 1 & v_{12} & \cdots & v_{1n} \\ v_{21} & 1 & \cdots & v_{2n} \\ \vdots & \vdots & \vdots & \vdots \\ v_{(n-1)1} & v_{(n-1)2} & \cdots & v_{(n-1)n} \\ v_{n1} & v_{n2} & \cdots & 1 \end{bmatrix} \tag{5}$$

Figure 1 shows the symmetric matrix **V**. We use it as the coherence matrix of brain networks [17].

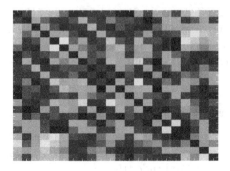

Fig. 1. The symmetric matrices V obtained from a data set with 22 channels

2.3   Degree of Brain Networks

The concept of brain network is derived from graph theory [18]. Generally, a weighted undirected graph G consists of a set of nodes N, a set of undirected edges between nodes E and a set of weights W that describes the strength of the connections, namely $G = \{N, E, W\}$.

In this paper, each channel is considered as a node in brain networks. Phase synchronization between channels is used as the connection strength. We describe the phase synchronization of EEG signals by using PLV. The degree of brain networks is used as features for brainprint recognition.

The degree of brain networks represents the number of edges connected to the node, which is an essential attribute of the graph. For an undirected graph G, the degree of node k_i^w represents the sum of the connection strength of the connected edge, $w_{ij} \in W$. It is defined as below:

$$k_i^w = \sum_{j \in N} w_{ij} \tag{6}$$

Linear discriminant analysis (LDA) is a typical data analysis method for dimension reduction and classification [19]. We utilize it to classify the extracted features for brainprint recognition.

2.4   Summary of the Proposed Method

The detailed steps of the method are shown in Fig. 2. The method includes several stages: signal preprocessing, calculate the mean PLV symmetric matrix as a coherence matrix of the brain function network, use the degree of nodes of the brain network as features for brainprint recognition, utilize LDA for classification.

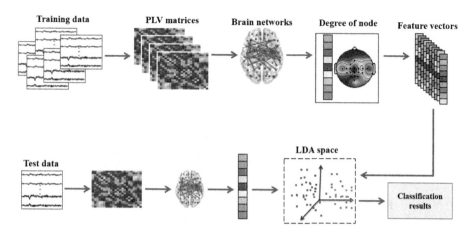

Fig. 2. Framework of the proposed method.

3 Experiments

3.1 Data Acquisition

We focus on studying brainprint recognition in task-free state, so that four data sets are used in this paper. The first data set obtains from BCI Competition 2008 - Graz data set A [9]. It contains 9 subjects. We call it **BCI data**. The second data set obtains from the BNCI Horizon 2020 project [10]. It is a two-class motor imagery task data set. There are 14 participants. We talk about it as **Motor data**. The third data set is collected from an experiment with 20 subjects [11]. We call it **NMk data**. The fourth data set is collected through a fatigue driving experiment [12]. This experiment includes 12 subjects aged between 23 and 25. We talk about it as **DRI data**.

For each dataset, we intercept 480s long raw data of each subject. 30s prolonged non-overlap segments are selected to calculate the mean PLV which is used to construct brain networks. There are 16 samples collected from each subject. For each subject, half of the samples are used as training samples. The other half is used as test samples.

3.2 Feature Analysis

The degree of brain networks is used as the features of brainprint recognition, which has certain particularity for each subject. In a brain functional network based on EEG signals, an electrode channel represents a node. The degree of brain networks is an important feature for brainprint recognition. We obtain the mean value of the degree of brain networks for all samples of each subject. These mean values are used as EEG information carried by each channel. We draw the brain topographic maps to show the features in a visual way. The DRI data are taken as examples shown in Fig. 3.

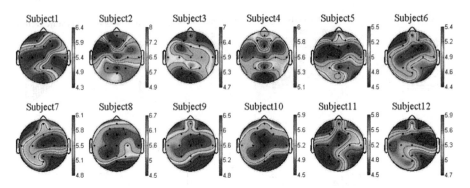

Fig. 3. Brain topographic maps of 12 subjects in DRI data.

Figure 3 shows the brain topographic map of 12 subjects. In DRI dataset, the subjects are asked to perform simulated driving tasks and have to drive under different conditions. It consists of eight conditions or stages. Fatigue driving tasks are complex. Cognitive reactions of subjects are distinct for different tasks. It can be seen from the figure, for each subject, the distribution of the strength shows significant differences. The same statement does not exist between every two subjects. This indicates that the degree of brain networks of each subject is unique.

In order to better prove the conclusion, we calculate the mean value of the average of the degree of brain networks among each subjects. A mean value represents a subject. Then the variance of each subject is calculated. Furthermore, we also calculate the variance of all subjects. The BCI data set is taken as an example and the results are shown in Fig. 4.

It can be seen from the figure, the variances of each subject and the variance of all subjects (i.e., within-class variance and between-class variance) have a significant gap. All subjects' variance is larger than each subject's variance.

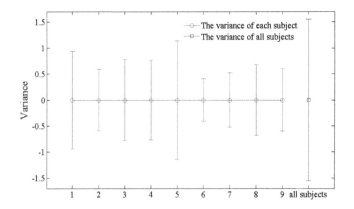

Fig. 4. The variance of each subject and all subjects

3.3   Classification Results

EEG signals are rhythmic and behave differently in different frequency bands. Four bands are used to study the brainprint recognition based on EEG signals. We make a comparison to explore in which band the degree of brain networks would have better performance. For each data set, the samples are randomly divided into test set and training set. Ten times are performed. Then classification accuracies can be obtained. Figure 5 is the result of four frequency bands on four data sets.

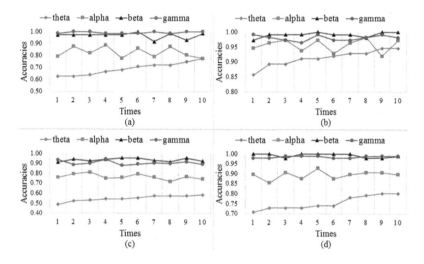

Fig. 5. Four frequency bands classification accuracies for datasets. (a) BCI data; (b) Motor data; (c) NMK data; (d) DRI data.

It can be seen that the accuracies of beta and gamma frequency bands are significantly higher than that of alpha and theta frequency bands in four data sets. According to the experimental results, based on the phase information of EEG signals, we believe that brainprint recognition based on brain networks will achieve better performance in beta and gamma frequency bands.

Average values of ten times recognition accuracies are computed. Table 1 show the recognition accuracies of four data sets in the beta frequency band.

As can be seen from Table 1, the average accuracies of ten times are above 0.99 for Motor data and DRI data. Results show that the degree of brain networks is well done in brainprint recognition for different data sets.

In addition, we compare the experimental results with [20]. Nguyen et al. used the mel-frequency cepstral coefficients (MFCCs) to extract features and evaluated this method in EEG-based datasets, which included BCI data. The recognition accuracy rate was 46.24%. Compared with the MFCCs, our method has significant advantages (50.57% higher). The results are shown in Table 2.

Table 1. Average recognition accuracies of four data sets

	1	2	3	4	5	6	7	8	9	10	Average
BCI data	0.972	0.972	0.972	0.972	0.972	1	0.917	0.986	0.931	0.986	**0.968**
Motor data	0.973	0.991	0.991	0.991	1	0.991	0.991	0.982	1	1	**0.991**
NMk data	0.913	0.944	0.925	0.944	0.956	0.956	0.931	0.919	0.956	0.925	**0.937**
DRI data	1	1	0.979	1	1	1	1	0.979	0.979	0.990	**0.993**

Table 2. Brainprint recognition accuracy of BCI data obtained by degree of brain network and mel-frequency cepstral coefficients

	Recognition accuracy
Degree of brain network	96.81%
Mel-frequency cepstral coefficients	46.24%

4   Conclusion

In this paper, we have carried out the research on brainprint recognition of different data sets. The symmetric matrix is used as the coherence matrix of brain network, which is constructed by PLV. The degree of brain networks is used to form feature vectors. LDA is classifying the test sample to obtain the final result. We evaluate this method on four EEG data sets that subjects execute different tasks. The average recognition accuracies are all above 0.93. The best accuracy of this method is above 0.99. The beta and gamma frequency bands have better recognition result based on the phase information of the EEG signals. During the experiment, we find that degree of brain networks is of considerable difference among different subjects. It is clear evidence that the feature vectors combined with the degree of brain networks are effective for brainprint recognition.

Acknowledgments. This work was supported by National Natural Science Foundation of China (Grant No. 61671193), International Science & Technology Cooperation Program of China (Grant No. 2014DFG12570)

References

1. Huang, X., Altahat, S., Tran, D., Sharma, D.: Human identification with electroencephalogram (EEG) signal processing. In: 12th International Symposium on Communications and Information Technologies, pp. 1021–1026. IEEE Press, Gold Coast (2012)
2. Armstrong, B.C., Ruiz-Blondet, M.V., Khalifian, N., Kurtz, K.J., Jin, Z., Laszlo, S.: Brainprint: assessing the uniqueness, collectability, and permanence of a novel method for ERP biometrics. Neurocomputing **166**, 59–67 (2015)
3. Das, K., Zhang, S., Giesbrecht, B., Eckstein, M.P.: Using rapid visually evoked EEG activity for person identification. In: 31st Annual International Conference of the IEEE Engineering in Medicine and Biology Society, Minneapolis, pp. 2490–2493 (2009)

4. Yeom, S.K., Suk, H.I., Lee, S.W.: Person authentication from neural activity of face-specific visual self-representation. Pattern. Recogn. **46**(4), 1159–1169 (2013)
5. Gui, Q., Jin, Z., Xu, W.: Exploring EEG-based biometrics for user identification and authentication. In: 2014 IEEE Signal Processing in Medicine and Biology Symposium (SPMB), Philadelphia, pp. 1–6 (2014)
6. Maiorana, E., Rocca, D.L., Campisi, P.: Eigenbrains and eigentensorbrains: parsimonious bases for EEG biometrics. Neurocomputing **171**, 638–648 (2016)
7. Valdéshernández, P.A., Ojeda-González, A., Martínez-Montes, E., Lage-Castellanos, A., Virués-Alba, T., Valdés-Urrutia, L., Valdés-Sosa, P.A.: White matter architecture rather than cortical surface area correlates with the EEG alpha rhythm. Neuroimage **49**(3), 2328–2339 (2010)
8. Stam, C.J., Straaten, E.C.W.V.: Go with the flow: use of a directed phase lag index (DPLI) to characterize patterns of phase relations in a large-scale model of brain dynamics. Neuroimage **62**(3), 1415–1428 (2012)
9. Brunner, C., Leeb, R., Mller-Putz, G., Schlögl, A.: Bci competition 2008 graz data set a. Putz (2008)
10. Steyrl, D., Scherer, R., Faller, J.: Random forests in non-invasive sensorimotor rhythm brain-computer interfaces: a practical and convenient non-linear classifier. Biomed. Eng. **61**(1), 77–86 (2016)
11. Kong, W., Zhao, X., Hu, S., Vecchiato, G., Babiloni, F.: Electronic evaluation for video commercials by impression index. Cogn. Neurodyn. **7**(6), 531–535 (2013)
12. Kong, W., Lin, W., Babiloni, F., Hu, S., Borghini, G.: Investigating driver fatigue versus alertness using the granger causality network. Sensors **15**(8), 19181–19198 (2015)
13. Mcfarland, D.J., Mccane, L.M., David, S.V., Wolpaw, J.R.: Spatial filter selection for EEG-based communication. Electroencephalogr. Clin. Neurophysiol. **103**(3), 386–394 (1997)
14. Kong, W., Zhou, Z., Jiang, B., Babiloni, F., Borghini, G.: Assessment of driving fatigue based on intra/inter-region phase synchronization. Neurocomputing **219**, 474–482 (2017)
15. Sun, J., Hong, X., Tong, S.: Phase synchronization analysis of EEG signals: an evaluation based on surrogate tests. IEEE Trans. Biomed. Eng. **59**(8), 2254–2263 (2012)
16. Rosenblum, M.G., Pikovsky, A.S., Kurths, J.: Synchronization approach to analysis of biological systems. Fluct. Noise. Lett. **04**(1), L53–L62 (2012)
17. Chavez, M., Valencia, M., Latora, V., Martinerie, J.: Complex networks: new trends for the analysis of brain connectivity. Int. J. Bifurcat. Chaos. **20**(06), 1677–1686 (2010)
18. Bullmore, E., Sporns, O.: Complex brain networks: graph theoretical analysis of structural and functional systems. Nat. Rev. Neurosci. **10**(3), 186–198 (2009)
19. Kim, T.K., Kim, H., Hwang, W., Kee, S.C.: Face description based on decomposition and combining of a facial space with LDA. In: 2003 International Conference on Image Processing, Barcelona, pp. 877–880 (2003)
20. Nguyen, P., Tran, D., Huang, X., Sharma, D.: A proposed feature extraction method for EEG-based person identification. In: Proceedings of the 2012 International Conference on Artificial Intelligence, Las Vegas, pp. 826–831 (2012)

Optimized Echo State Network with Intrinsic Plasticity for EEG-Based Emotion Recognition

Rahma Fourati[1][✉], Boudour Ammar[1], Chaouki Aouiti[2],
Javier Sanchez-Medina[3], and Adel M. Alimi[1]

[1] REGIM-Lab.: REsearch Groups in Intelligent Machines,
National Engineering School of Sfax (ENIS), University of Sfax,
BP 1173, 3038 Sfax, Tunisia
{rahma.fourati.tn,boudour.ammar,adel.alimi}@ieee.org
[2] Research Units of Mathematics and Applications UR13ES47,
Department of Mathematics, Faculty of Sciences of Bizerta,
University of Carthage, Zarzouna, 7021 Bizerta, Tunisia
chaouki.aouiti@fsb.rnu.tn
[3] CICEI: Innovation Center for the Information Society,
University of Las Palmas de Gran Canaria, Las Palmas de Gran Canaria, Spain
javier.sanchez.medina@ieee.org

Abstract. Reservoir Computing (RC) is a paradigm for efficient training of Recurrent Neural Networks (RNNs). The Echo State Network (ESN), a type of RC paradigm, has been widely used for time series forecasting. Whereas, few works exist on classification with ESN. In this paper, we shed light on the use of ESN for pattern recognition problem, i.e. emotion recognition from Electroencephalogram (EEG). We show that the reservoir with its recurrence is able to perform the feature extraction step directly from the EEG raw. Such kind of recurrence rich of nonlinearities allows the projection of the input data into a high dimensional state space. It is well known that the ESN fails due to the poor choices of its initialization. Nevertheless, we show that pretraining the ESN with the Intrinsic Plasticity (IP) rule remedies the shortcoming of randomly initialization. To validate our approach, we tested our system on the benchmark DEAP containing EEG signals of 32 subjects and the results were promising.

Keywords: Echo state network · Intrinsic plasticity · Feature extraction · Classification · Electroencephalogram · Emotion recognition

1 Introduction

Emotion is defined as a mental state and an affective reaction towards an event based on subjective experience [1]. In psychology, there is a difference between discrete emotions and affective states. Ekman [2] grouped emotions into six different categories such that happiness, sadness, surprise, disgust, anger, and fear. While, Russell [3] defined emotions in the bipolar model, valence and arousal dimensions are explored. The valence is ranged from negative (unpleasant) to positive (pleasant), and the arousal is the activation level of the emotion. Later, a three-dimensional Pleasure-Arousal-Dominance (PAD) model was proposed by Mehrabian and Russell in [4]. In this model, a third

© Springer International Publishing AG 2017
D. Liu et al. (Eds.): ICONIP 2017, Part II, LNCS 10635, pp. 718–727, 2017.
https://doi.org/10.1007/978-3-319-70096-0_73

dimension is added called dominance. It represents the controlling and dominant nature of the emotion. It ranges from submissive (or without control) to dominant (or in control/empowered).

Emotion recognition is a pattern recognition problem. Thus, the recognition process involves all basic steps in that area beginning with preprocessing, dimensionality reduction and classification. Dimensionality reduction basically consists in feature extraction selection. For instance, in a handwritten recognition problem, several works proposed new features [5, 6] while other approaches focus on the learning process to achieve better recognition rate [7–10]. For the case of EEG signals, the main goal is to be able of training the classifier in such a way that when new instances are presented, they are correctly classified. The current work deals with the proposition of a new method for feature extraction, to know, the use of the hidden layer of the Echo State Network (ESN) [11] pretrained with the intrinsic plasticity rule (IP) [12] for the feature extraction from the preprocessed EEG raw data.

In this paper, we proposed an ESN for EEG-based emotion recognition adopting the two-dimensional model of emotions. We have not found any other methodology using ESNs for emotion classification with EEG signals as input. We don't make use of signal processing techniques to do that, but we input a temporal signal to the ESN. Furthermore, we have not found any other work using RNN to test the DEAP benchmark [13]. It contains 1280 EEG trials of 32 subjects using a Biosemi cap with 32 channels. These are our two main contributions to the state of art in this topic.

The remainder of this paper is organized as follows: Sect. 2 gives an overview of the proposed approaches for EEG-based emotion recognition. Section 3 first presents the general architecture of ESN, secondly, introduces the IP rule and details the proposed approach. Section 4 first describes the DEAP dataset and then gives the experimental results and discussion. Section 5 summarizes the paper and outlines our future work.

2 Related Works on Emotion Recognition

During the past few years, EEG-based emotion recognition research has progressed rapidly. In this section, we provide an overview of the current state-of-the art EEG-based emotion recognition with the recognized emotions in Table 1. Most of works, classify emotions into positive and negative (P/N) of valence dimension and LA/HA according to the excitation level of arousal dimension. Four classes can be composed by combining Low/High Arousal and Low/High Dominance, which includes HAHD, HALD, LAHD and LALD. Besides, combination of valence, arousal and dominance can give 8 emotional states that we will explore in Sect. 4.

Most of the existing approaches are based on the power spectral features using Short-Time Fourier Transform [14] and statistical methods like Fractal dimension [14]. Moreover, Recurrence Plot analysis is used for the extraction of non-linear features as in [15]. In contrast, few works as in [18, 19] didn't perform the feature extraction step and classified the raw EEG signals using the Hidden Markov Model (HMM) and Deep Belief Network (DBN). In the current work, ESN has as input the preprocessed EEG raw and the classification is also performed by the readout layer.

Table 1. Existing methods for emotion recognition form DEAP dataset

Refs	EEG Features	Classification	Emotions	Accuracy (%)
[13]	Power spectral features	SVM	2 (LA/HA)	62
			2 (P/N)	57.6
[14]	Statistical features, fractal dimension features and power bands features	SVM	HAHD, HALD, LAHD, LALD	63.04
[15]	Non-linear features	KNN	2 (P/N)	58.05 ± 0.093
			2 (LA/HA)	64.56 ± 0.107
[16]	Ontological concepts	Ontological model	2 (P/N)	75.19
			2 (LA/HA)	81.74
[17]	Two-part generative model representation from Segment level features	SVM	2 (P/N)	70.9 ± 11.4
			2 (LA/HA)	67.1 ± 14.2
[18]	raw EEG signal	HMM	2 (P/N)	58.75 ± 3.8
			2 (LA/HA)	55 ± 4.5
[19]	raw EEG signal	DBN	2 (P/N)	58.4
			2 (LA/HA)	64.3
[20]	Differential entropy features	GELM	HAHD, HALD, LAHD, LALD	69.67

According to Table 1, it is clear that several approaches are based on Support Vector Machines (SVM) [13, 14, 17]. Whereas, other approaches are based on the use of deep neural networks such as DBN [19] and Graph regularized Extreme Learning Machine (GELM) [20]. Note that, [14, 16] have selected only 10 and 8 participants EEG signals, respectively, from DEAP dataset for classification.

Bozkhov et al. [21] fed the ESN with all data from a private EEG dataset. They only used the hidden layer of ESN pretrained with IP to have a new representation of the EEG dataset. Next, a feature selection step is done by using projection of 2D, 3D and 4D of the new representation. They achieved 76.9% with using Linear Discriminant Analysis (LDA). But, the projection step is very complex and hence the computational time is high. The main difference between our work and that of [21] is that we use ESN as an architecture for both representation of input data and its classification. This will be detailed in the next section.

3   The Proposed System for Emotion Recognition

In the current work, we proposed a novel approach for emotion recognition. It consists in using the reservoir computing for feature extraction and classification. Our approach is mainly based on two pioneering works [12, 21]. In this line, we explore the ESN model and the adaptation of its internal dynamic with the IP.

3.1 Echo State Network Model

ESNs are a kind of recurrent neural network originally proposed by Jager [11]. It consists of a three layered network: the input layer which contains the input, the hidden layer called the reservoir and the output layer often called readout layer. It looks like the basic feedforward neural network, but enriched with recurrence in the reservoir W^{res}, possible feedback connection from the output layer to the reservoir W^{fb} and a possible connection from the input to the output layer. Jager *et al.* [11] proposed the ESN accelerating the learning process. The manner to get such situation is through the random initialization of weights of the network and selecting just the weights from the connections between the hidden units and the readout units to be trained. Many models were proposed for time series prediction (e.g. [22, 23]), but ESN as a model outperforms existing works in that field as in [24].

ESNs are powerful tools for data representation yet quite algorithmically simple. Input data is encoded through a non-linear transformation into a high dimensional state space. Note that, the recurrent connections implement a short-term memory by means of transient network states. The non-linearity with the memory allows us to capture the EEG dynamics signals and to represent them as spatio-temporal patterns. We believe that the reservoir is able to perform to the feature extraction, a fundamental and very important step in the emotion recognition process.

Figure 1 illustrates the proposed architecture, the recurrent connections are only in the hidden layer, there is not feedback connections.

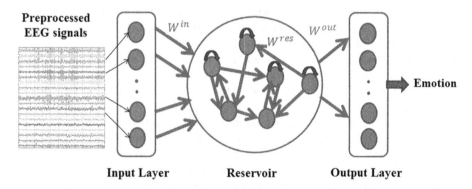

Fig. 1. The proposed architecture for EEG-based emotion recognition

As input, the ESN capture the preprocessed EEG signals. The reservoir generates a new representation of the input data. The activation states of the reservoir are considered as a feature vector. The last layer is the classification step. The latter is performed using the following equation:

$$y(t) = W^{out}(x(t)) \tag{1}$$

where $x(t)$ is the activation state vector at time step t.

Fast training, dynamic non-linear behavior in the reservoir and having the memory thanks to the recurrent connections are all the key ingredients of the success of the ESN. Nevertheless, many works have reported that due to the initial random states the reservoir has not or has a late stable behavior. The question, here, is how to guarantee a stable behavior in the reservoir.

As a first initiative, Jager proposed to use the so called "echo state property". The maximal absolute eigenvalue of the reservoir connections weights should be less than one $\rho(W^{res}) < 1$, this is the so called "spectral radius". The new matrix connections will be the division of the randomly generated W^{res} by the calculated spectral radius $\rho(W^{res})$. This condition ensures that the ESN have validated the echo state property and in this manner the reservoir will be sparse. However, the sparsity still does not guarantee that the ESN will converge in all cases. Besides, several approaches have been proposed for the optimization of the ESNs using Particle Swarm Optimization as in [24, 25].

From a biological point of view, Triesh [12] was the first who proposed the use of IP in the neurobiological model.

Since we have used the IP as a pretraining algorithm, we did not give here the basic mathematical representation of the ESN as proposed by Jager [11]. Instead, we present the adapted equations by the IP rule in the next sub-section.

3.2   The Pretraining with the Intrinsic Plasticity Rule

In order to achieve an optimization of the reservoir, we follow previous works in which they used the IP rule [12, 26–28]. Inspired by biology, Triesch [12] proposed the concept of intrinsic plasticity. It is thought of as changes to neuron's activation function from $f(x)$ to $f(ax + b)$, it is not an update of weights that traditional training algorithms realize. Actually, the biological neuron does not adapt its synapses, it adapts its intrinsic parameters. Triesch derived the IP rule for fermi activation function and for an exponential desired distribution. Thereafter, Schrauwen et al. [28] extended IP considering also hyperbolic tangent as an activation function with Gaussian desired distribution.

The aim of the IP is to maximize information at the output of a single neuron, it contains the maximum information about its input. Entropy maximization ensures the information maximization. So, the neuron will be able to adapt its response in an autonomous way to the desired distribution. Equation (2) measures the distance between the actual probability density $p(x)$ of the neuron's output and the targeted probability density $p_d(x)$ using the Kullback-Leiber divergence metric [12].

$$D_{KL}(p(x), p_d(x)) = \int p(x) log\left(\frac{p(x)}{p_d(x)}\right) dx \qquad (2)$$

With respect to the Gaussian distribution with μ as mean and σ as a standard deviation, the Kullback-Leiber divergence becomes as shown in Eq. (3).

$$D_{KL}(p(x), p_d(x)) = -H(x) + \frac{1}{2\sigma^2} E\left((x - \mu)^2\right) + log\frac{1}{\sigma\sqrt{2\pi}} \qquad (3)$$

Therefore, IP will be a compromise between the maximization of the actual entropy H and the minimization of the expected entropy E. To achieve this balance, at each time step the neuron's gain a and bias b are updated using Eqs. (4) and (5) where η represents the learning rate.

$$\Delta a = \frac{\eta}{a} + \Delta b(W^{in} + W^{res}x) \tag{4}$$

$$\Delta b = -\eta\left(-\frac{\mu}{\sigma^2} + \frac{x}{\sigma^2}\left(2\sigma^2 + 1 - x^2 + \mu x\right)\right) \tag{5}$$

Thus, the activation state of the hidden neural units is defined by Eq. (6).

$$x(t) = f^{res}(diag(a)(W^{in}in(t) + W^{res}x(t-1)) + b) \tag{6}$$

The update of the gain and bias in the IP with both the hyperbolic tangent and Gaussian distribution has the exactly same effect as when using fermi and exponential distribution. For this reason, Schrauwen et al. [28] claimed that the relation is independent of the chosen non-linearity function and the targeted distribution.

4 Experimental Results

In this section, we aim to validate our proposed approach. So, it was tested on the DEAP benchmark in order to be able to compare our results to the current state-of-the-art methods. Thereafter, we have studied the effectiveness of IP on the emotion recognition process, as well as on the size of the reservoir.

4.1 DEAP Dataset Description

The DEAP dataset is a challenging benchmark. It provides up to 1280 EEG trials. The format varies from the EEG raw data with noise (file extension is.bdf) to the preprocessed EEG raw data. The emotions in the DEAP dataset are expressed in the three-dimensional space such that arousal, valence and dominance. Consequently, we have used it for binary classification problem to discriminate positive and negative emotions, low and high arousal. Besides, Table 2 shows 8 emotional states as done in [14].

4.2 Experiment Settings

For the ESN model, the input size depends on the EEG signals and the output size is determined by the classes of emotions to discriminate. Actually, the ESN performance is conditioned by the selection of a number of hypermeters which are:

- Reservoir size N_R: It is the number of neurons in the hidden layer of the ESN. In fact, when the fixed size is superior to the length of the input signal, the role of reservoir is the expansion of the input into a high dimensional space. Otherwise, the reservoir role is the compression of the input signal, which is our case.

Table 2. Mapping emotional states into the VAD model

Valence	Arousal	Dominance	Emotional state
Positive	Low	Low	Protected
Positive	Low	High	Satisfied
Positive	High	Low	Surprised
Positive	High	High	Happy
Negative	Low	Low	Sad
Negative	Low	High	Unconcerned
Negative	High	Low	Frightened
Negative	High	High	Angry

- Spectral radius $\rho(W^{res})$: Jaeger [11] has recommended to satisfy the Echo State Property. And this is by setting the $\rho(W^{res})$ below 1. We remind that the spectral radius is defined as the largest absolute eigenvalue of the internal weight matrix, W^{res}. Scaling the latter will ensure that the length of the activity vector stays about the same after each iteration. This allows the input to echo around the network for a long time.
- Sparsity degree: It consists in setting most of the weights to zero. So, two cases are envisaged, ESN model will be either densely connected with smaller internal weights, or sparsely connected with higher internal weights [11]. Stability can be maintained in either case, however, other characteristics of the network may change, and an excessive sparsity degree will lead to stronger coupling of neural internal states and reduce the diversity of the neuronal states in the reservoir.
- Input scaling $W_{in} \in [W_{in}^{min}, W_{in}^{max}]$: It is very important to set the random connections very carefully so the ESN does not explode or die [11]. The scaled inputs need to drive the loosely coupled oscillators without wiping out the information from the past that they already contain.

Unfortunately, while the setting of ESN model was recommended to be done carefully, there is not an automated method allowing us to determine the optimal hyperparameters values. So, we fixed varied values and we have tested the ESN model on DEAP benchmark. The input weights were scaled between −0.1 and 0.1. The internal weights W^{res} values were scaled between −0.5 and 0.5. We also varied the reservoir size from 500 to 1500. In other words, each EEG preprocessed signal is encoded into a 500-D or 1000-D or 1500-D vector by ESN with IP for final classification.

Schrauwen et al. [28] proved that the reservoir states converged to the targeted distributions. They suggested to use zero value for the mean, 0.1 for the variance and for 0.0005 the learning rate. For the gain vector, it is also initialized to ones et the bias vector is initialized with zeros. It has been showed that the IP training can be stopped after performing 5 to 10 iterations. Koprinkova-Hristova [29] has found the same conclusion. The author added that unlike supervised algorithms which look to fit the output to a target data, the IP procedure aims to fit the internal units' responses to reflect input data structure.

4.3   Results and Discussion

We have evaluated the performance of our system on the DEAP dataset. The influence of the number of iterations of IP is studied as well as the number of neurons in the reservoir. We examine the binary classification problem depending on the level of the valence or the arousal as well as a multi-labels classification problem, i.e. the case of 8 emotional states.

Each EEG channel signal is encoded in 8064 data for a period of 60s. ESN-IP was fed with a single channel data with each correspondent label. ESN output is the predicted label for one channel. To classify an EEG trial, we averaged all predicted labels of 32 channels to get a percentage. Next, the label is the one which has the higher percentage.

According to Table 3, our proposed approach shows higher recognition rate than the existing approaches. Thereby we report the best results found with reservoir size 1500 and 10 IP iterations.

Table 3. ESN-IP results for emotion discrimination in comparison with existing methods

References	Valence accuracy (%)	Arousal accuracy (%)
System based on HMM [18]	58.75 ± 3.8	55 ± 4.5
System using DBN [19]	58.4	64.3
The proposed ESN based on IP	$\mathbf{71.03 \pm 1.2}$	$\mathbf{68.28 \pm 1.7}$

There is only one work using 8 emotional states [30] which found 69.53% as result. When compared with this work, our system has relatively lower accuracy classification up 68.79%. But, we recall that the input type is not the same and this influences on the performance measure.

Throughout the experimental results, we have validated the effectiveness of the ESN model for ensuring the emotion recognition process. When compared with one or two works having the same input as ours, i.e. a raw EEG signal, the ESN model outperforms the proposed systems in [18, 19]. The main contribution of the current work is to prove that the ESN, more specifically the reservoir, is able to generate a feature vector for classification of emotions.

5   Conclusion

The goal of this paper is to understand the ability of the ESNs for feature extraction and classification. Actually, our system captures the EEG raw signal and relays it to the reservoir. The latter plays the role of a kernel such that it projects the input into a high dimensional space. More specifically, the reservoir performs the extraction of spatio-temporal features from EEG signals. It is believed that the random initializations of the ESNs are their big flaw, but in our work, we address this problem by using the IP rule which guarantees to have a Gaussian distribution of reservoir neurons responses, in other words stable behavior of the reservoir. Comparing to the state-of-the-art methods, we have found encouraging results on the DEAP benchmark.

The proposed system is the first to consider the EEG as spatio-temporal input for the ESN, it is neither a feature vector nor a power spectral density. Nevertheless, the current study was mainly conducted to ensure the emotion recognition task. The choice of the ESN hyperparameters was not varied, hence a future sensitivity analysis of the performance on these hyperparameters will be conducted. This is due to lack of existing tools for finding the optimized values of ESN hyperparameters. Until now, these choices are test and trial. Moreover, we will focus on studying the plasticity effect on the reservoir for the emotion recognition problem as well.

Acknowledgment. The research leading to these results has received funding from the Ministry of Higher Education and Scientific Research of Tunisia under the grant agreement number LR11ES48.

References

1. Mauss, I.B., Robinson, M.D.: Measures of emotion: a review. Cogn. Emot. **23**, 209–237 (2009)
2. Ekman, P.: Basic Emotions in Handbook of Cognition and Emotion. Wiley, New York (1999)
3. Russell, J.A.: Affective space is bipolar. J. Pers. Soc. Psychol. **37**, 345–356 (1979)
4. Mehrabian, A.: Pleasure-arousal-dominance: a general framework for describing and measuring individual differences in temperament. Current Psychol. **14**, 261–292 (1996)
5. Bezine, H., Alimi, A.M., Derbel, N.: Handwriting trajectory movements controlled by a bêta-elliptic model. In: Proceedings of the International Conference on Document Analysis and Recognition, ICDAR, p. 1228 (2003)
6. Ben Moussa, S., Zahour, A., Benabdelhafid, A., Alimi, A.M.: New features using fractal multi-dimensions for generalized Arabic font recognition. Pattern Recognition Letters, vol. 31 (5), pp. 361–371 (2010)
7. Alimi, A.M.: Evolutionary computation for the recognition of on-line cursive handwriting. IETE J. Res. **48**(5), 385–396 (2002). SPEC
8. Boubaker, H., Kherallah, M., Alimi, A.M.: New algorithm of straight or curved baseline detection for short arabic handwritten writing. In: Proceedings of the International Conference on Document Analysis and Recognition, ICDAR, p. 778 (2009)
9. Elbaati, A., Boubaker, H., Kherallah, M., Alimi, A.M., Ennaji, A., Abed, H.E.: Arabic handwriting recognition using restored stroke chronology. In: Proceedings of the International Conference on Document Analysis and Recognition, ICDAR, p. 411 (2009)
10. Slimane, F., Kanoun, S., Hennebert, J., Alimi, A.M., Ingold, R.: A study on font-family and font-size recognition applied to Arabic word images at ultra-low resolution. Pattern Recogn. Lett. **34**(2), 209–218 (2013)
11. Jaeger, H.: A tutorial on training recurrent neural networks, covering bppt, rtrl, ekf and the echo state network approach. Technical report, German National Research Center for Information Technology (2013)
12. Triesch, J.: A gradient rule for the plasticity of a neuron's intrinsic excitability. In: Duch, W., Kacprzyk, J., Oja, E., Zadrożny, S. (eds.) ICANN 2005. LNCS, vol. 3696, pp. 65–70. Springer, Heidelberg (2005). doi:10.1007/11550822_11

13. Koelstra, S., et al.: DEAP: a database for emotion analysis using physiological signals. IEEE Trans. Affective Comput. **3**, 18–31 (2012)
14. Liu, Y., Sourina, O.: Real-time fractal-based valence level recognition from EEG. In: Gavrilova, Marina L., Tan, C.J.Kenneth, Kuijper, A. (eds.) Transactions on Computational Science XVIII. LNCS, vol. 7848, pp. 101–120. Springer, Heidelberg (2013). doi:10.1007/978-3-642-38803-3_6
15. Bahari, F., Janghorbani, A.: EEG-based emotion recognition using recurrence plot analysis and k nearest neighbor classifier. In 20th Iranian Conference on Biomedical Engineering (ICBME), pp. 228–233 (2013)
16. Zhang, X., Hu, B., Chen, J., Moore, P.: Ontology-based context modeling for emotion recognition in an intelligent web. World Wide Web **16**(4), 497–513 (2013)
17. Zhuang, X., Rozgic, V., Crystal, M.: Compact unsupervised EEG response representation for emotion recognition. In: International Conference on Biomedical and Health Informatics (BHI), pp. 736–739 (2014)
18. Torres-Valencia, C., Garcia-Arias, H., Alvarez Lopez, M., Orozco-Gutierrez, A.: Comparative analysis of physiological signals and electroencephalogram (EEG) for multimodal emotion recognition using generative models. In: XIX Symposium on Image, Signal Processing and Artificial Vision (STSIVA), pp. 1–5 (2014)
19. Li, X., Zhang, P., Song, D., Yu, G., Hou, Y., Hu, B.: EEG based emotion identification using unsupervised deep feature learning. In: SIGIR2015 Workshop on Neuro-Physiological Methods in IR Research (2015)
20. Zheng, W.-L., Zhu, J.-Y., Lu, B.-L.: Identifying stable patterns over time for emotion recognition from EEG. IEEE Trans. Affective Comput. **8** (2017)
21. Bozhkov, L., Koprinkova-Hristova, P., Georgieva, P.: Reservoir computing for emotion valence discrimination from EEG signals. Neurocomputing **231**, 28–40 (2017)
22. Dhahri, H., Alimi, A.M.: The modified differential evolution and the RBF (MDE-RBF) neural network for time series prediction. In: Proceedings of IEEE International Conference on Neural Networks, p. 2938 (2006)
23. Bouaziz, S., Dhahri, H., Alimi, A.M., Abraham, A.: A hybrid learning algorithm for evolving flexible beta basis function neural tree model. Neurocomputing **117**, 107–117 (2013)
24. Chouikhi, N., Ammar, B., Rokabni, N., Alimi, A.M., Abraham, A.: PSO-based analysis of Echo State Network parameters for time series forecasting. Appl. Soft Comput. **55**, 211–225 (2017)
25. Chouikhi, N., Fdhila, R., Ammar, B., Rokbani, N., Alimi, A.M.: Single- and multi-objective particle swarm optimization of reservoir structure in echo state network. In: IEEE International Joint Conference on Neural Networks, Vancouver, Canada (2016)
26. Steil, J.J.: Online reservoir adaptation by intrinsic plasticity for backpropagation-decorrelation and echo state learning. IEEE Trans. Neural Netw. **20**(3), 353–364 (2007)
27. Wardermann, M., Steil, J.J.: Intrinsic plasticity for reservoir learning algorithms. In: Verleysen, M. (ed.) Advances in Computational Intelligence and Learning (ESANN 2007), pp. 513–518 (2007)
28. Schrauwen, B., Wandermann, M., Verstraeten, M., Steil, J.J., Stroobandt, D.: Improving reservoirs using intrinsic plasticity. Neurocomputing **71**, 1159–1171 (2008)
29. Koprinkova-Hristova, P.: On effects of IP improvement of ESN reservoirs for reflecting of data structure. In: IEEE International Joint Conference on Neural Networks (2015)
30. Liu, Y., Sourina, O.: EEG databases for emotion recognition. In: International Conference on Cyberworlds (2013)

A Computational Investigation of an Active Region in Brain Network Based on Stimulations with Near-Infrared Spectroscopy

Xu Huang[1(✉)], Raul Fernandez Rojas[1], Allan C. Madoc[2],
Keng-Liang Ou[3], and Sheikh Md. Rabiul Islam[4]

[1] Faculty of Education, Science, Technology and Mathematics,
University of Canberra, Canberra, Australia
{Xu.Huang,raul.fermandezrojas}@canberra.edu.au
[2] Technology and E-Commerce, Institutional Banking Markets,
Commonwealth Bank, Sydney NSW 2000, Australia
[3] Taipei Medical University, 250 Wuxing Street, Taipei, Taiwan
[4] Department of Electronics and Communication Engineering,
Khulna University of Engineering and Technology, Khulna, Bangladesh

Abstract. Near-infrared spectroscopy (NIRS) has been widely used in medical imaging to observe oxygenation and hemodynamic responses in the cerebral cortex. In this paper, the major target is reporting our current study about the computational investigation of functional near infrared spectroscopy (fNIRS) in the somatosensory region with noxious stimulations. Based on signal processing technologies within communication network, the related technologies are applied, including cross correlation analysis, optic flow, and wavelet. The visual analysis exposed pain-related activations in the primary somatosensory cortex (S1) after stimulation which is consistent with similar studies, but the cross correlation results strongly evidenced dominant channels on both cerebral hemispheres. Our investigation also demonstrated that the spatial distribution of the cortical activity origin can be described by the hemodynamic responses in the cerebral cortex after evoked stimulation using near infrared spectroscopy. The current outcomes of this computational investigation explore that it is good potential to be employed to deal with pain assessment in human subjects.

Keywords: Brain-computational investigation · Brain-machine interface · Brainwave feedback

1 Introduction

1.1 A Subsection Sample

Brain activity and its related research have been drawing huge attention from various researchers in different areas, such as biomedical science, medical science and engineering. The current research in this paper is a part of the collaborations between the University of Canberra, Australia and Taipei Medical University, Taiwan.

© Springer International Publishing AG 2017
D. Liu et al. (Eds.): ICONIP 2017, Part II, LNCS 10635, pp. 728–738, 2017.
https://doi.org/10.1007/978-3-319-70096-0_74

As pain detections for non-verbal people (or patients) would be a big challenge in clinical processing. We are primarily expecting our research outcomes will explore some relevant information between pain and pain-control for those people who have oral and/or writing difficulties to make a communication to a doctor, such that it could, in the foreseeable future, improve the quality of medical services in real time. As an example, it may be possible for mitigating the pain for a patient who is undergoing an oral operation in real time.

We have gained from the rapid developments of high technologies, including medical science, such as applications of near-infrared spectroscopy (NIRS). An NIRS is a non-invasive optical imaging technique that can be used as a non-invasive neuroimaging method to obtain brain activity by measuring real-time changes of oxygenated (HbO) and deoxygenated haemoglobin (Hb) in real time. The NIRS technology can make a design of lower cost, portable equipment, and wearable imaging caps with real-time processing. This neuroimaging technique can be used to assess cortical activity in diverse experimental and clinical applications. As an outcome, it has been successfully applied in both research and medical settings to assess cerebral functioning. In particularly, functional NIRS (fNIRS) has many applications in brain computer interface (BCI) [1, 2] brain activity studies in active and resting states, pain research [3, 4] face processing [5, 6], and language training and improvements [7, 8].

In order to take the challenge for an effective detection of cortical activity in a brain many researchers have used different methods to improve the cortical activity, such as contrast to noise ratio (CNR) [8], principal component analysis (PCA) [9], and probabilistic analysis for a brain network [10]. However, there is little description about the relation mapping active region in a brain responding to evoked stimulations.

In this paper, we shall demonstrate our novel algorithm for a close look at spatiotemporal characteristics of brain activities in NIRS responding to the evoked stimulations from near infrared spectroscopy. The medical images clearly present the obtained oxygenation and hemodynamic response in the cerebral cortex. The features against the hemodynamic responses after acupuncture stimulations are also presented. In Sect. 2, it is describing experiment design and related theoretical analysis methods. Section 3 is about the experimental results and discussions. Finally in Sect. 4, a conclusion for this paper will be presented. These outcomes of the computational investigation strongly recommended that the obtained spatiotemporal features are helpful for understanding the function of active regions in the brain. Those features explored will be expected for the future real life applications, such as pain mitigation.

2 Experiment Designs and Theoretical Analysis Methods

2.1 Experiment Designs

For our experiments, there is a group randomly picked up from the volunteers, healthy individuals (1/3 females, 2/3 males) with ages between 25 to 35 years old. No participants reported a prior history of neurological or psychiatric disorder. All the stimulations are running at right-handed. The participating people were examined again before our experimental works to make sure all the subjects have no significant medical disorder and any current unstable medical condition or currently under any medication.

The configuration for the current experiment was using two probes of 12 channels each to measure neurologic activity, which is shown in Fig. 1. The area examined was the bilateral motor cortex area, where it is expected to have hemodynamic responses in the somatosensory cortex area (S1) [11, 12]. According to the international EEG 10–20 system [13], the probes were centered on the C3 and C4 position.

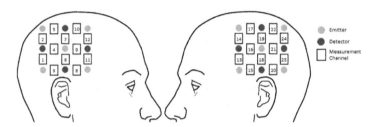

Fig. 1. The probes locations and their channels. The measuring probes were centered on the C3 and C4 of the international 10–20 system; right hemisphere (channels 1–12) and left hemisphere (channels 13–24).

2.2   Implementing Experiments

This investigation is part of research collaboration between the School of Oral Medicine of Taipei Medical University (TMU, Taiwan) and the University of Canberra, Australia (UC, Australia). The study and methods were carried out in accordance with the guidelines of the Declaration of Helsinki (DoH) and approved by full-board review process of the TMU-Joint Institutional Review Board under contract number 201307010.

Hemodynamic data were collected using an optical topography system (ETG-4000, Hitachi Medical Corporation, Tokyo, Japan). All experiments were carried out at the Laboratory at TMU with the conditions of a quiet, room temperature (22–24°) and room humidity (40–50%) via a controller at the laboratory room. The experiments were done in the morning (10:00 am–12:00 pm) and each experiment lasted around 30 min. In order to obtain stimulation-related activation in the cerebral cortex, acupuncture was used to induce pain stimulation in a safe manner. Traditional Chinese acupuncture techniques were performed by a professional acupuncturist of TMU Hospital. The acupuncture point (acupoint) used for the stimulation was at the "hegu point," which is located between the thumb and forefinger in the back of the hand. The acupuncture procedure consisted of three types of acupuncture stimulations (tasks) [14]: the first stimulation is needle insertion (T1), the three following stimulations are needle twirl to increase Qi (T2), and the last stimulation is needle removal (T3). All acupuncture stimulations lasted five seconds. Pre-time and resting time (Rt) between acupuncture stimulations was 30 s, post-time was 10 s. The complete data experiment is described in [14], this data set was used as primary source of our study.

2.3   Channel Cross Correlation Analysis

In order to investigate the relations against the time base, cross correlation is used to calculate the temporal similarity among the channels and identify the dominant channels on both hemispheres. This time-dependent analysis provides evidence for the presence of regions where the cortical activity can be associated with increased localized cerebral blood flow. The time cross correlation function was running among channels 1 to 12 in the right probe and 13 to 24 in the left probe (refer to Fig. 1). The time cross correlation between two waveforms $x(t)$ and $y(t)$ can be defined as Eq. (1) as follows:

$$r_{xy}(\tau) = \sum_{-\infty}^{\infty} x(t)y(t - \tau).$$ (1)

Here, τ is dummy variable for the time-lag between $x(t)$ and $y(t)$, the variable of Y_{xy} represents the difference (lag/lead) between channel signal $y(t)$ and channel signal $x(t)$. The cross correlation values between the two channels in the same probe are done by the stimulation from –40 s to +40 s at a sampling rate of 10.

2.4   Optical Flow Analysis

Optical flow (OF) can be defined as a "flow" of pixel values at the image plane in terms of time varying for the images. It is an algorithm that performs at pixel level and estimate local displacement or checking the change velocity between two temporally-consecutive images. In other words, optical flow is referring to the perceived motion of an object in a field of view by an image sensor or human eye [15, 16]. In our case, we applied an optical flow algorithm to evaluate the time and spatial relationship between channels, in terms of intensity of distributions of stimulations. To the best of our knowledge, this is the first study where OF is used as dynamic analysis method of activation of NIRS signals.

2.5   Wavelet Analysis

It is obviously the fact that the brain's responses to the stimulations signals are the functions of both time and spatial. Hence, we can analysis the responses and obtain the information of brain activity in terms of temporal domain, or in terms of spatial domain, however, we could not obtain the information from both temporal and spatial domains simultaneously due to "Heisenberg uncertainty principle".

Fortunately we can use wavelets to create a way to do so at a reasonable level. Mallat algorithm is one of the most popular wavelet algorithms used in different areas of research. The algorithm is based on a multi-resolution pyramid decomposition and synthesis method. Similarly, Cohen-Daubechies-Feauveau (CDF) 9/7 wavelet transform (WT) is another lifting scheme based wavelets transform that can reduce the computational complexity [17, 18]. Following the notations used in our previous research [17, 18] the mathematical representations of y_L and y_H can be defined as below:

$$\begin{cases} y_L(n) = \sum_{i=0}^{N_L-1} \hat{h}(i)x(2n-i) \\ y_H(n) = \sum_{i=0}^{N_H-1} \hat{g}(i)x(2n-i) \end{cases},$$

where the variables N_L and N_H are the lengths of low pass and high pass filters respectively. The current aim is to find out when the signal response in the brain network is actually completed after the stimulations. We assume that the objective of compressive sensing de-noising process is to estimate the original image x with dimension $N \times N$, pixels by corrupted together with noise (or a disturbance based on the stimulation), n, from the following equation:

$$f = x + n \tag{2}$$

The real sample of signal, f, that could be represented by transform coefficients x, which is

$$f = \Psi x = \sum_{i=1}^{N} x_i + n_i)\psi_i. \tag{3}$$

Here $\psi = [\psi_1, \psi_2, \ldots, \psi_N]$ is the transform basis matrix using by sparsity transform and $s = [(x + n)_1, (x + n)_2, \ldots, (x + n)_N]$ being an N-vector of coefficients and there are only with $S < <N$ significant elements in x. Hence, we sample from mixing matrix or measurement matrix F that is stable and incoherence with matrix transform Y:

$$Y = \Phi f = \Phi \Psi x = \Theta(x + n) \tag{4}$$

Here Θ is the compressive sensing matrix. We need to reconstruct the original signal from the observation. It is well know that sparsity is a fundamental principle in fidelity reconstruction, and noise is not sparse in the standard domain. Therefore, we can reconstruct the exact signal due to sparsity. Our major interest is to find out how does the "n" decay to the value less than the threshold value we designed, which indicates the "stimulation processing" is approximately close to the completed status. The flow chart of computing this situation is shown in Fig. 2. We take the ith n, denoted as n_i, and comparing it with the threshold at $t = i$, denoted as, $thred_i$. If n_i is larger than the threshold, $thred_i$ then we shall take this case as that the active region in the brain is keep going (hence, no reaction will take), or if it is less than the threshold at this time, we shall take the case that at $t = i$, the activity brain is approximately close to the end of process and will be picked it up as targeted image.

We are, from [17], [18], applying them in different way as we are interested in when the stimulation processing is effectively completed after the current stimulation, which is given by

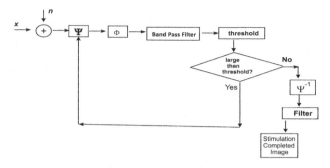

Fig. 2. Proposed image de-noise framework based on compressive sensing can be used for checking whether the "stimulation completed" is done or not.

$$T(j,l) = \beta \frac{\sigma_{j,l}^2}{\sigma_{w,j,l}^2}$$
$$\sigma_{j,l}^2 = \left(\frac{median(|HP_{j,l}|)}{0.6745}\right)^2 \tag{5}$$
$$\hat{\sigma}_{w,j,l}^2 = \max(\hat{\sigma}_y^2 - \hat{\sigma}, 0),$$

where, $\hat{\sigma}_y^2 = \frac{1}{M \times N} \sum_{j,l=1}^{M,N} y_{j,l}^2$, β is the parameter define by threshold. With proposed threshold, a "de-noised" (for this paper, it is for separating the original part and the changed part) OMP/BP (optimum pass/bandpass) coefficient $\hat{x}_{Tj,l}$ is calculated as follows:

$$\hat{x}_{Tj,l} = \begin{cases} \frac{x_{r,j,l}[x_{r,j,l}-T^\alpha]}{|x_{r,j,l}|} \text{ for } |x_{r,j,l}| \geq T(j,l) \\ 0 \text{ for } |x_{r,j,l}| < T(j,l) \end{cases} \tag{6}$$

where, $x_{r,j,l}$ is the coefficients value after image reconstruction by OMP/BP. Here, α and β are smooth signal parameters and we have chosen $\alpha = 20$ and $\beta = 0.3$ due to the experimental base [17, 18].

3   Experimental Results and Discussions

When it is completed for the applications of the noxious stimulation to the subject, we observed the responses of Oxyhemoglobin (HbO) in different channels on both hemispheres. The purpose of this observation is to find out whether the obtained visual results can show any relation between significant active areas and patters in the NIRS data. The analysis showed dominant areas where the HbO concentration was higher and also showed propagation delays from more-active areas to less-active areas. As examples, three images are shown in Fig. 3 for subject 4 and subject 5.

From Fig. 3, it is observed that these two examples showed the regions with higher activation after the stimulation. The NIRS data exhibited these areas in all subjects on

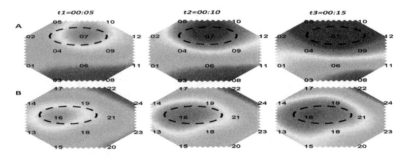

Fig. 3. Activated areas present in the NIRS data. "A" (see the top row) Dominant region around Ch7 on right hemisphere in subject 4. "B" (see the bottom row) Dominant region around Ch16 on left hemisphere in subject 5.

both hemispheres. These patterns present the activation area on the cerebral cortex. We can observe that the brain activity response increased to channel 7 (Ch7 in subject 4) on the right hemisphere and the area around channel 16 (Ch16 in subject 5) on the left hemisphere. These two areas are part of the postcentral gyrus in the parietal lobe.

The postcentral gyrus is the location of the primary somatosensory cortex (S1) area that is involved with the perception and modulation of painful somatosensory sensations. It is important to confirm the fact that the cortical activity presented a bilateral S1 activation after the acupuncture stimulation. Our experimental results and confirmations are consistent with other similar studies. Nevertheless, other experiments have reported that pain activation can also be detected in the secondary somatosensory cortex (S2), the anterior cingulate cortex (ACC), and the insular cortex (IC) [11, 26].

We can obtain the brain activation by using the stimulation reactions from the color patterns or OFs. As the distributions of the intensity and direction represent the activity features, we can also make the prediction of the activity. As shown in Fig. 4, two examples of the optical flows predict the progressions of activated areas in time are presented.

In the top panel of Fig. 4, two image frames (*t1* and *t2*) showed a constant increase (expansion) of cortical activity in the dominant region, it is noted that the weak regions

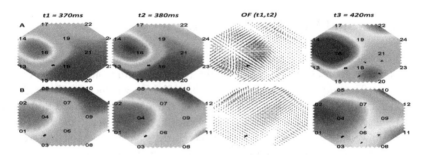

Fig. 4. Optical flow for movement prediction for cortical activity. (A) The top panel is the images taken on the left hemisphere (Ch13 to Ch24) from the subject 3. (B) The bottom panel represents the frames taken on the right hemisphere (Ch1 to Ch12) from subject 6.

shrink (dotted circle). In fact, the colour pattern also showed that the weaker areas become stronger; this indicates that the stimulations are in continuous process. This phenomenon is more evidence using the motion vectors of the optical flow result; in this image we can see the expansion (outer movement) of OF vectors from dominant channel Ch16 and the contraction (inner movement) of OF vectors to Ch18.

Therefore, these results show that by using the optical flow field it could be possible to predict the direction of the cortical activity.

It is interesting that we can further show the relations between the OxyHemoglobin samples and the OF, which are shown in Fig. 5.

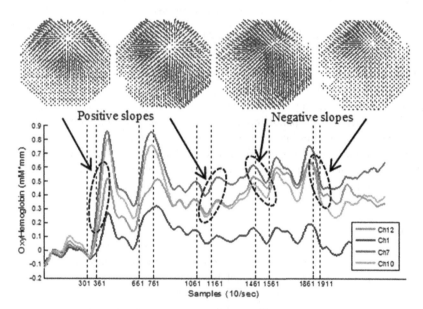

Fig. 5. The slope direction (bottom panel) heavily links the distributions of the OF (top panel) directions and intensities. This observations showed that NIRS data can also be reflected by the OF. The dash lines represent the duration of the acupuncture stimulation processing.

From the above descriptions and observations, we come to the fact that a stimulation is a processing and its behaviors can be expressed partially by either OxyHemoglobin time waves (hence we can calculate its speed information) or OF or colour activity areas (hence we have spatial information). However, if we would like to know both exact time and spatial information simultaneously about the stimulation process, it would be impossible due to "Heisenberg uncertainty principle" which is one of physics principles [22].

If we take the intensity as the two parts showed in Eq. (2), namely x is the original value and n is the changed value after the current invoked stimulation. Now the target is finding the value n and comparing it with the threshold that was described in [17, 18].

The experimental results of the wavelet tracking algorithm are shown in Fig. 6.

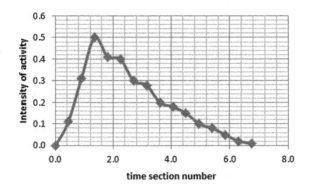

Fig. 6. Wavelet tracking results in terms of time section number.

Figure 6 clearly shows that after the current stimulation about 6.3 normalized sub-sections, the stimulation process is virtually completed. As we expected that the response was not uniformly changed. The wavelet analysis also presented the most of the brain activity of the spatiotemporal distribution for the current stimulation as it would be the point of intensity, n, changing from increasing to decreasing (as shown in Fig. 6, around the time section 1.34). Also as an example, in Fig. 4, at $t = 420$ ms the n value is significantly changed so the brain activity around $t = 420$ ms was the highest (refer to the top "A" row).

4 Conclusions

We have first shown our investigations on spatiotemporal analysis of brain active region in a brain network with optical flow and wavelet using near-infrared spectroscopy (NIRS). The outcomes of this investigation, including there is a dominated channel, the stimulations are not decayed uniformly, and active region that reflected the "pain" can be visualized by our technologies such as OF. All research outcomes have potential applications for the research in the analysis of brain activities such as brain computer interface, pain research, vision impaired, and for people with intellectual disability to enable a choice to understand their pain sensation.

The wavelet technology also allows us to monitor the stimulation processing in both time and spatial regions simultaneously. The wavelet algorithm also offered the information about the process completion information.

This study presented a new method to analyze functional near-infrared spectroscopy (NIRS) data. The NIRS data represented the cortical activation in subjects after noxious stimuli. It is important to investigate the significance of these cortical areas in response to the acupuncture stimulation in the future. Finally, NIRS-based analysis in conjunction with wavelet coherence offered a powerful method to study functional connectivity of somatosensory stimuli in humans.

References

1. Coyle, S.M., Ward, T.E., Markham, C.M.: Brain-computer interface using a simplified function near-infrared spectroscopy system. J. Neural Eng. **4**, 208–219 (2007)
2. Boecker, M., Buecheler, M.M., Schroeter, M.L., Gauggel, S.: Prefrontal brain activation during stop-signal response inhibition: an event-related functional near-Infrared Spectroscopy study. Behav. Brain Res. **176**, 259–266 (2007)
3. Bartocci, M., Bergqvist, L.L., Lagercrantz, H., Anand, K.: Pain activates cortical areas in the preterm newborn brain. Pain **122**, 109–117 (2006)
4. Fernandez-Rojas, R., Huang, X., Ou, K.L.: Spatiotemporal analysis of brain activity response using near infrared spectroscopy. Int. J. Pharm. Med. Biol. Sci. **5**, 1–6 (2016)
5. Kobayashi, M., Otsuka, J.Y., Nakato, E., Kanazawa, S., Yamaguchi, M.K., Kakigi, R.: Do infants represent the face in a viewpoint-invariant manner? Neural adaptation study as measured by near-infrared spectroscopy. Front. Hum. Neurosci. **5**, 23–30 (2011)
6. Honda, Y., Nakato, E., Otsuka, Y., Kanazawa, S., Kojima, S., Yamaguchi, M.K., et al.: How do infants perceive scrambled face? A near-infrared spectroscopic study. Brain Res. **1308**, 137–146 (2010)
7. Gervain, J., Macagno, F., Cogoi, S., Peña, M., Mehler, J.: The neonate brain detects speech structure. Proc. Natl. Acad. Sci. U.S.A. **105**, 14222–14227 (2008)
8. Song, X., Pogue, B.W., Jiang, S., Doyley, M.M., Dehghani, H., Tosteson, T.D., et al.: Automated region detection based on the contrast-to-noise ratio in near-infrared tomography. Appl. Opt. **43**, 1053–1062 (2004)
9. Kovelman, I., Shalinsky, M., Berens, M.S., Petitto, L.A.: Shining new light on the brain's "bilingual signature: a functional Near Infrared Spectroscopy investigation of semantic processing. Neuroimage **39**, 1457–1471 (2008)
10. Verner, M., Herrmann, M.J., Troche, S.J., Roebers, C.M., Rammsayer, T.H.: Cortical oxygen consumption in mental arithmetic as a function of task difficulty: a near-infrared spectroscopy approach. Front. Hum. Neurosci. **7**, 47–51 (2013)
11. Hofbauer, R.K., Rainville, P., Duncan, G.H., Bushnell, M.C.: Cortical representation of the sensory dimension of pain. J. Neurophysiol. **86**, 402–411 (2001)
12. Bushnell, M., Duncan, G., Hofbauer, R., Ha, B., Chen, J.I., Carrier, B.: Pain perception: is there a role for primary somatosensory cortex? Proc. Natl. Acad. Sci. U.S.A. **96**, 7705–7709 (1999)
13. Homan, R.W., Herman, J., Purdy, P.: Cerebral location of international 10–20 system electrode placement. Electroencephalogr. Clin. Neurophysiol. **66**, 376–382 (1987)
14. Fernandez Rojas, R., Huang, X., Ou, K.L., Tran, D., Islam, S.M.R.: Analysis of pain hemodynamic response using near-infrared spectroscopy (NIRS). Int. J. Mult. Appl. **7**, 31–42 (2015)
15. Horn, B.K., Schunck, B.G.: Determining optical flow. Technical Symposium East, pp. 319–331 (1981)
16. Horn, B.: Robot Vision. MIT press, Cambridge (1986)
17. Islam, Sheikh Md.Rabiul, Huang, X., Ou, K.L., Rojas, R.F., Cui, H.: Novel information processing for image de-noising based on sparse basis. In: Arik, S., Huang, T., Lai, W.K., Liu, Q. (eds.) ICONIP 2015. LNCS, vol. 9491, pp. 443–451. Springer, Cham (2015). doi:10. 1007/978-3-319-26555-1_50
18. Islam, Sheikh Md.Rabiul, Huang, X., Le, K.: A novel adaptive shrinkage threshold on shearlet transform for image denoising. In: Loo, C.K., Yap, K.S., Wong, K.W., Beng Jin, A. T., Huang, K. (eds.) ICONIP 2014. LNCS, vol. 8836, pp. 127–134. Springer, Cham (2014). doi:10.1007/978-3-319-12643-2_16

19. Bushnell, M., Duncan, G., Hofbauer, R., Ha, B., Chen, J.I., Carrier, B.: Pain perception: is there a role for primary somatosensory cortex? Proc. Nat. Acad. Sci. **96**, 7705–7709 (1999)
20. Sutherland, M.T., Tang, A.C.: Reliable detection of blateral activation in human primary somatosensory cortex by unilateral median nerve stimulation. Neuroimage **33**, 1042–1054 (2006)
21. Coghill, R.C., Sang, C.N., Maisog, J.M., Iadarola, M.J.: Pain intensity processing within the human brain: a bilateral, distributed mechanism. J. Neurophysiol. **82**, 1934–1943 (1999)
22. Zarate, O., McEvoy, J.P.: Introducing Quantum Theory: A Graphic Guide. Icon Books Ltd, London, 06 September 2007. ISBN: 9781840468502

An Algorithm Combining Spatial Filtering and Temporal Down-Sampling with Applications to ERP Feature Extraction

Feifei Qi, Yuanqing Li, Zhenfu Wen, and Wei Wu$^{(\boxtimes)}$

Center for Brain Computer Interfaces and Brain Information Processing,
South China University of Technology, Guangzhou 510641, China
auweiwu@scut.edu.cn

Abstract. Event-related potentials (ERP) based brain-computer interfaces (BCI) is a promising technology for decoding mental states. Due to the high trail-to-trial variability and low signal-to-noise ratio caused by volume conduction, analyzing brain states corresponding to ERP on a single trial is a challenging task. In this paper, we propose a computationally efficient method for ERP feature extraction, termed spatial filtering and temporal down-sampling (SFTDS). The spatial filters and the temporal down-sampling weight vectors can be optimized under a single objective function by SFTDS. Experiments on real P300 data from 10 subjects show the superiority of SFTDS over other algorithms.

Keywords: ERP · Spatial filter · Weighted down-sampling · Regularization

1 Introduction

Brain-computer interfaces (BCI) aims at designing an effective communication interface between human brain and external control devices. Event-related potentials (ERP), which is usually measured by electroencephalogram (EEG), is a popular noninvasive technology for detecting brain activities. In recent years, ERP based BCI have gained more and more attention [1–3]. However, the characteristics of ERP signal make the utility of ERP based BCI extremely challenging: (1) The ERP signal is often contaminated with strong task-unrelated noises, and the recorded ERP signal of a single channel is a mixed activity from multiple brain sources due to volume conduction [4]. (2) The correlation between the temporal features of ERP signal is relatively strong due to the high dimensionality. Therefore, how to enhance the signal-to-noise ratio (SNR) and apply efficient down-sampling strategy on the ERP signal, plays an important role in feature extraction and classification stage for the ERPs based BCI.

Coherent averaging method averages the ERP signal over a large number of trials to enhance the SNR [6], however, performing single-trial classification is of tremendous importance considering the real-time requirement of BCI. As coherent averaging neglects the spatial information of the multichannel EEG signal.

© Springer International Publishing AG 2017
D. Liu et al. (Eds.): ICONIP 2017, Part II, LNCS 10635, pp. 739–747, 2017.
https://doi.org/10.1007/978-3-319-70096-0_75

Spatial filtering techniques were introduced for ERP analysis, as the ERP sources and other noises usually exhibit distinct spatial patterns. Several blind source separation such as principle component analysis (PCA), independent component analysis (ICA) and its variants, sparse component analysis (SCA), have been widely applied in EEG signal analysis [7–10]. Several tensor decomposition techniques have been introduced into EEG analysis, to decompose the EEG signal as several sources corresponding to distinct modes [11, 12].

Other supervised spatio-temporal filtering algorithms were devised for ERP feature extraction. The signal-to-noise ratio maximizer (SIM) algorithm [13] was designed by maximizing the SNR of the ERPs, which was based on a probabilistic generative model to estimate the ERP components. And then a Bayesian model for ERP analysis from multichannel EEG was proposed [14], and the number of ERP components can be automatically determined by sparse Bayesian learning. The discriminative spatial patterns (DSP) method [15] and spatial-temporal discriminant analysis (STDA) method [16] maximize Fisher criterion. However DSP did not involve the extraction of temporal patterns, and STDA optimized the spatial filters and temporal filters iteratively.

In view of the real-time requirement of BCI, we propose an efficient feature extraction method for ERP analysis, which optimizes the spatial filters and the weighted down-sampling vectors under a single objective function. This method is named spatial filtering and temporal down-sampling (SFTDS). In pursuing the optimal parameters, SFTDS maximizes the ERP power while minimizes the power of the noises. Moreover, to enhance the generalization capacity of SFTDS, a regularization term was introduced to constrain the model complexity. Experimental results show that with SFTDS applied in ERP signal analysis, we get a superior performance than other methods.

The rest of the paper is structured as follows. In Sect. 2, the methodology formulation of SFTDS is presented, and the efficacy of SFTDS on a real ERP data set over other algorithms is demonstrated in Sect. 3. Finally Sect. 4 concludes this paper.

2   SFTDS

In this section, we describe the mathematical formulation of SFTDS in details. SFTDS is motivated by the following hypothesis:

- The ERP signal is approximately identical for each trial, which is time-locked and phase-locked to external stimuli.
- The evoked potentials related to the target stimuli can be enhanced by spatial filtering.
- The source signal at distinct time points is strongly correlated, and it is helpful to reduce the redundancy by linearly superimposing the signals at distinct time points.

2.1   Spatial Fitering

The primary problem of ERP signal analysis is the low SNR. We expect to maximize the energy of the evoked ERP responses while minimize the uncorrelated background noises by spatial filtering. The basic assumption is that the ERP signal is stable under different trials, and the background EEG signal can be modeled by zero-mean Gaussian distribution.

Let C denotes the number of recorded channels, T denotes the number of sample points, R denotes the number of recorded trials of ERP signal. The multichannel signal is presented as $\mathbf{X}_r, r = 1, 2, \cdots, R$, by which the ERP signal is estimated as

$$\mathbf{S} = \frac{1}{R} \sum_{r=1}^{R} \mathbf{X}_r \tag{1}$$

Then the noise signal of the r-th trial is $\mathbf{N}_r = \mathbf{X}_r - \mathbf{S}$. Actually, $\mathbf{S}$ is the least-squares solution that minimizes the total noise energy of the R trials. The objective function of spatial filter $\mathbf{w} \in \mathbb{R}^{C \times 1}$ is as follows:

$$\max_{\mathbf{w}} \frac{\mathbf{w}^\top \mathbf{D} \mathbf{w}}{\mathbf{w}^\top \mathbf{R} \mathbf{w}} \tag{2}$$

where $\mathbf{D}$ is the covariance matrix of the estimated ERP signal $\mathbf{S}$, $\mathbf{R}$ is the covariance matrix of the sum of background noise $\mathbf{N}_r$. The definition of $\mathbf{D}$ and $\mathbf{R}$ are:

$$\mathbf{D} = \mathbf{S} \cdot \mathbf{S}^\top, \quad \mathbf{R} = \frac{1}{R} \sum_{r=1}^{R} \mathbf{N}_r \cdot \mathbf{N}_r^\top \tag{3}$$

The final problem can be solved by generalized eigenvalue decomposition (GED). The generalized eigenvectors corresponding to the generalized eigenvalues, is the resulted spatial filters.

2.2   Temporal Down-Sampling

Most of the existing algorithms ignore the correlation of ERP signals in the temporal domain, even assume that the signal samples at different time points are statistically independent. Superimposing the signals at adjacent time points is a common approach for suppressing high frequency noises [6]. Therefore, we expect to enhance the superability of the ERP features by superimposing the temporal signal, while eliminating the redundant information.

Let M denotes the dimension of the weighted down-sampling vectors $\mathbf{a}$, T denotes the number of sample points of the recorded data, then the number of samples after superimposed by $\mathbf{a}$ is demoted as P. For a one-dimension signal $\mathbf{x} \in R^{1 \times T}$, the i-th feature of the temporal signal after processed by $\mathbf{a}$ can be presented as:

$$v_i = \sum_{k=1}^{M} \mathbf{a}(k) \cdot \mathbf{x}((i-1) \cdot M + k), \quad i = 1, 2, \cdots, P \tag{4}$$

where the down-sampled signal $\mathbf{v} \in \mathbb{R}^{P \times 1}$.

To control the model complexity, we constrain that one single channel shares a single weight vector. Denote the weight vector for the c-th channel as $\mathbf{a}_c \in \mathbb{R}^{M \times 1}$, $c = 1, 2, \cdots, C$. Let $\bar{*}$ represents the weighted down-sampling processing, then for the ERP signal of the c-th channel $\mathbf{S}_c$, the down-sampled signal can be presented as:

$$\mathbf{v}_c = \mathbf{a}_c \bar{*} \mathbf{S}_c \tag{5}$$

Let

$$\tilde{\mathbf{S}} = \begin{pmatrix} \bar{\mathbf{S}}_{(1)} \\ \bar{\mathbf{S}}_{(2)} \\ \vdots \\ \bar{\mathbf{S}}_{(N)} \end{pmatrix} \tag{6}$$

where $\bar{\mathbf{S}}_{(k)} = (S_{(:,k)}, \ S_{(:,M+k)}, \ \cdots, \ S_{(:,(P-1) \times M+k)})$ Then the ERP signal $\mathbf{S}$ after spatial filtered by $\mathbf{w}$ and weighted down-sampled can be presented as:

$$\mathbf{Y} = (w_1, w_2, \cdots, w_C) \begin{pmatrix} \mathbf{a}_1 \bar{*} \mathbf{S}_{(1,:)} \\ \mathbf{a}_2 \bar{*} \mathbf{S}_{(2,:)} \\ \vdots \\ \mathbf{a}_C \bar{*} \mathbf{S}_{(C,:)} \end{pmatrix} = \tilde{\mathbf{w}} \cdot \tilde{\mathbf{S}} \tag{7}$$

here $\tilde{\mathbf{w}} = \text{vec}((\mathbf{w}^\top \odot \mathbf{A})^\top) = [w_1 \mathbf{a}_1(1), w_2 \mathbf{a}_2(1), \cdots, w_C \mathbf{a}_C(1), \cdots, w_1 \mathbf{a}_1(M), w_2 \mathbf{a}_2(M), \cdots, w_C \mathbf{a}_C(M)]$ is a reparametered vector encompassing both spatial filter $\mathbf{w}$ and weighted down-sampling vector matrix $\mathbf{A}$, where $\mathbf{A} = [\mathbf{a}_1^\top, \mathbf{a}_2^\top, \cdots, \mathbf{a}_C^\top] \in R^{C \times M}$.

By this way, we can optimize the spatial filter and channel-specific weighted down-sampling vectors under a single objective function, and the ultimate optimization function is:

$$\max_{\tilde{\mathbf{w}}} \frac{\tilde{\mathbf{w}}^\top \tilde{\mathbf{S}} \tilde{\mathbf{S}}^\top \tilde{\mathbf{w}}}{\tilde{\mathbf{w}}^\top (\frac{1}{R} \sum_{r=1}^{R} \tilde{\mathbf{N}}_r \tilde{\mathbf{N}}_r^\top) \tilde{\mathbf{w}}} \tag{8}$$

where $\tilde{\mathbf{N}}_r$ is the noise signal processed by (6) as the ERP signal. In this paper, we choose the $\tilde{\mathbf{w}}$'s corresponding to the three largest eigenvalues.

2.3 l_2-norm Regularization

As the number of unknown parameters is relatively larger (MC), the model tends to overfit the training data. One feasible way for controlling the model complexity is incorporating regularization term to restrict the parameter space. In this paper, we employ l_2-norm penalty to seek the tradeoff between the generalization capacity and the model complexity. Actually, l_2-norm regularization has been widely used, and the GED problem can be efficiently optimized with l_2-norm penalty incorporated. The optimization problem of SFTDS is:

$$\max_{\tilde{\mathbf{w}}} \mathcal{L}(\tilde{\mathbf{w}}) = \frac{\tilde{\mathbf{w}}^\top \tilde{\mathbf{S}} \tilde{\mathbf{S}}^\top \tilde{\mathbf{w}}}{\tilde{\mathbf{w}}^\top (\frac{1}{R} \sum_{r=1}^{R} \tilde{\mathbf{N}}_r \tilde{\mathbf{N}}_r^\top + \rho \cdot \mathbf{I}) \tilde{\mathbf{w}}} \tag{9}$$

where ρ is the regularization parameter, we set it as $\rho = 0.5$ in this paper.

Furthermore, the features of ERP signal and non-ERP signal extracted by SFTDS, are used to construct a one-way feature vector. Finally, Fisher linear discriminant analysis (FLDA) is applied to classify this two types of features, with the performance is evaluated by mean classification accuracies.

3 Data Analysis and Results

The data set used to evaluate the performance of SFTDS is from ten healthy subjects (S1-S10), who participated a P300-speller experiments. The interface was composed of 36 virtual buttons (letter or digit), with six rows by six columns (the interface was presented in Fig. 1). The ERP data were sampled at 200 Hz, recorded by a Neuroscan SynAmps system with 30 recorded channels. There were 12 epochs for each subject, and each buttons intensified 15 times randomly during one acquisition. Therefore for each epoch, a total of 180 trials were obtained, with 30 targets and 150 non-targets. As the determination of P300 basically components can be viewed a binary classification problem, then for each subject, a total of 240 trials (with 120 targets and 120 non-targets) and 1820 trials (with 240 targets and 1680 non-targets) were derived as the training data set, and the testing data set. The EEG data were digitally filtered at 1-15 Hz, and time segments of 0.1-0.7 s were used for analysis.

Fig. 1. The P300-speller interface.

Two feature extraction methods were considered, named STDA from [16] and Raw-Channels from [17] (the six channels were Fz, Cz, Pz, Oz,PO7, PO8), with the down-sampling rate $M \in \{1, 5, 10, 15, 20\}$. To evaluate the performance of weighted down-sampling and the classic down-sampling method, we also considered the R-SFTDS (with $M = 1$ in SFTDS, and down-sampled the spatially

filtred ERP data manually). The classification performance of the four methods
are presented in table 1. It can also be observed that the performance of SFTDS
are increased over STDA and Raw-Channels substantially. The superiority of
SFTDS over R-SFTDS indicates the advantage of weighted down-sampling.

Table 1. The classification performances (%) of SFTDS, R-SFTDS, STDA, the Raw-
Channels algorithm (select six channels by experience), when the number of training
samples for the target is 120.

SFTDS					R-SFTDS					
M	5	10	15	20	M	1	5	10	15	20
S1	87.40	88.59	89.74	92.08	S1	80.36	82.19	88.07	85.57	84.58
S2	77.66	79.53	82.03	84.48	S2	70.68	71.20	81.15	79.27	81.20
S3	81.93	87.40	87.55	88.49	S3	78.59	83.07	85.52	83.28	83.44
S4	75.68	80.73	84.01	84.43	S4	71.61	75.31	77.55	75.52	70.63
S5	79.95	83.59	85.52	85.36	S5	74.58	78.49	84.58	81.25	78.65
S6	70.99	76.98	78.13	79.95	S6	69.58	71.15	75.68	72.55	72.86
S7	85.63	86.25	85.68	87.86	S7	80.57	84.01	88.59	84.17	79.11
S8	80.47	82.45	84.22	87.03	S8	76.88	77.34	82.08	75.78	79.90
S9	88.13	90.26	90.94	90.83	S9	78.33	86.72	90.42	85.36	80.63
S10	76.56	79.27	77.55	74.84	S10	72.50	77.19	83.70	82.66	76.25
ave	**80.44**	83.51	**84.54**	**85.54**	ave	75.37	78.67	**83.73**	80.54	78.72
std	5.49	4.46	4.42	5.11	std	4.11	5.30	4.76	4.56	4.40
STDA					Raw-Channels					
M	5	10	15	20	M	1	5	10	15	20
S1	70.05	76.09	80.31	79.01	S1	55.78	68.80	80.63	77.24	80.63
S2	72.97	74.90	79.11	73.59	S2	59.74	67.71	75.16	75.94	72.50
S3	64.64	70.42	70.63	76.41	S3	60.36	71.61	79.53	75.94	75.26
S4	65.94	63.85	67.24	62.86	S4	56.04	64.69	68.13	71.25	63.70
S5	72.76	71.93	73.70	70.68	S5	56.15	69.53	73.75	73.07	67.29
S6	57.66	60.52	63.13	62.40	S6	61.56	59.64	63.65	64.38	65.16
S7	64.38	70.36	73.59	70.21	S7	63.91	72.71	80.63	77.03	71.51
S8	69.69	71.77	68.23	73.18	S8	58.39	66.46	69.11	68.85	66.25
S9	76.67	79.53	77.29	78.49	S9	57.92	70.73	81.72	77.76	74.74
S10	63.07	66.98	68.18	66.41	S10	55.10	72.76	79.38	81.93	76.93
ave	67.78	70.64	72.14	71.32	ave	58.49	68.46	75.17	74.34	71.40
std	5.67	5.69	5.63	5.98	std	2.88	4.08	6.33	5.06	5.62

We highlight the results by showing the extracted spatial filters and the
resulted temporal features of subject S1 in Fig. 2, To be specific, the curves

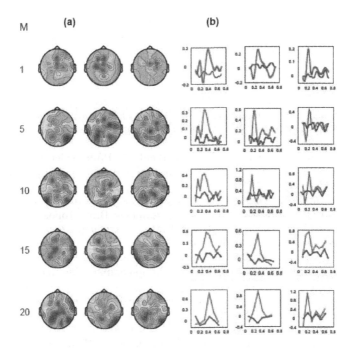

Fig. 2. (a) The topological distribution of the three spatial filter for subject S1 under different down-sampling rate M. (b) The curves connected by the temporal features for subject S1 averaged by 120 trials, which are obtained by the ERP signal after spatial filtering and wieghted down-sampling processing. (Color figure online)

in sub-figure (b) of Fig. 2, are connected by the temporal features for subject S1 averaged by 120 trials (with the red lines denote the target, and the blue lines denote the non-target), which are obtained by the ERP signal after spatial filtering and temporally down-sampling processing.

4   Conclusions

We propose an algorithm SFTDS for ERP feature extraction, which optimizes the spatial filters and weighted sown-sampling vectors under a single objective function. Therefore, the SNR can be enhanced by SFTDS, and the discriminative features in temporal domain can be extracted. SFTDS was applied to the single-trial binary classification of a P300 data set. The classification performance indicated the efficacy of SFTDS over other algorithms.

Acknowledgments. This work was supported by 973 Program of China (No. 2015CB351703), the National Natural Science Foundation of China (No. 61403144, No. 61633010), the tip-top Scientific and Technical Innovative Youth Talents of Guangdong special support program (No. 2015TQ01X361).

References

1. Zhang, Y., Zhao, Q., Jin, J., Wang, X., Cichocki, A.: A novel BCI based on ERP components sensitive to configural processing of human faces. J. Neural Eng. **9**(2), 026018 (2012)
2. Wolpaw, J., Birbaumer, N., McFarland, D., Pfutscheller, G., Vaughan, T.: Brain-computer interfaces for communication and control. Clin. Neurophysiol. **113**(6), 767–791 (2002)
3. Koenig, T., Stein, M., Grieder, M., Kottlow, M.: A tutorial on data-driven methods for statistically assessing ERP topographies. Brain Topogr. **27**(1), 72–83 (2014)
4. Baillet, S., Mosher, J.C., Leahy, R.M.: Electromagnetic brain mapping. IEEE Sig. Process. Mag. **18**, 14–30 (2001)
5. Lotte, F., Congedo, M., Lécuyer, A., Lamarche, F., Arnaldi, B.: A review of classification algorithms for EEG-based brain-computer interfaces. J. Neural Eng. **4**(2), R1 (2007)
6. Luck, S.J.: An Introduction to the Event-Related Potential Technique. The MIT Press, Massachusetts (2005)
7. Chapman, R.M., McCrary, J.W.: EP component identification and measurement by principal components analysis. Brain Cogn. **27**(3), 288–310 (1995)
8. Makeig, S., Bell, A.J., Jung, T.P., Sejnowski, T.J.: Independent component analysis of electroencephalographic data. Adv. Neural Inf. Process. Syst. **8**, 145–151 (1996)
9. Zibulevsky, M., Zeevi, Y.Y.: Extraction of a source from multichannel data using sparse decomposition. Neurocomputing **49**(1), 163–173 (2002)
10. Makeig, S., Westerfield, M., Jung, T.P., Enghoff, S., Townsend, J., Courchesne, E., Sejnowski, T.J.: Dynamic brain sources of visual evoked responses. Science **295**, 690–694 (2002)
11. Morup, M., Hansen, L.K., Herrmann, C.S., Parnas, J., Arnfred, S.M.: Parallel factor analysis as an exploratory tool for wavelet transformed event-related EEG. NeuroImage **29**(3), 938–947 (2006)
12. Lee, H., Kim, Y.D., Cichocki, A.: Nonnegative tensor factorization for continuous EEG classification. Int. J. Neural Syst. **17**, 305–317 (2007)
13. Wu, W., Gao, S.: Learning event-related potentials (ERPs) from multichannel EEG recordings: a spatio-temporal modeling framework with a fast estimation algorithm. In: 2011 Annual International Conference of the IEEE Engineering in Medicine and Biology Society, pp. 6959–6962. IEEE Press, Boston (2011)
14. Wu, W., Wu, C., Gao, S., Liu, B., Li, Y., Gao, X.: Bayesian estimation of ERP components from multicondition and multichannel EEG. NeuroImage **88**(1), 319–339 (2014)
15. Liao, X., Yao, D., Wu, D., Li, C.: Combining spatial filters for the classification of single-trial EEG in a finger movement task. IEEE Trans. Biomed. Eng. **54**(5), 821–831 (2007)

16. Zhang, Y., Zhou, G., Zhao, Q., Jin, J., Wang, X., Cichocki, A.: Spatial-temporal discriminant analysis for ERP-based brain-computer interface. IEEE Trans. Neural Syst. Rehabil. Eng. **21**(2), 233–243 (2013)
17. Krusienski, D.J., Sellers, E.W., McFarland, D.J., Vaughan, T.M., Wolpaw, J.R.: Toward enhanced P300 speller performance. J. Neurosci. Methods **167**(1), 15–21 (2008)

Intent Recognition in Smart Living Through Deep Recurrent Neural Networks

Xiang Zhang[1]($\boxtimes$), Lina Yao[1], Chaoran Huang[1], Quan Z. Sheng[2],
and Xianzhi Wang[3]

[1] University of New South Wales, Sydney, Australia
xiang.zhang3@student.unsw.edu.au
[2] Macquarie University, Sydney, Australia
[3] Singapore Management University, Singapore, Singapore

Abstract. Electroencephalography (EEG) signal based intent recognition has recently attracted much attention in both academia and industries, due to helping the elderly or motor-disabled people controlling smart devices to communicate with outer world. However, the utilization of EEG signals is challenged by low accuracy, arduous and time-consuming feature extraction. This paper proposes a 7-layer deep learning model to classify raw EEG signals with the aim of recognizing subjects' intents, to avoid the time consumed in pre-processing and feature extraction. The hyper-parameters are selected by an Orthogonal Array experiment method for efficiency. Our model is applied to an open EEG dataset provided by PhysioNet and achieves the accuracy of 0.9553 on the intent recognition. The applicability of our proposed model is further demonstrated by two use cases of smart living (assisted living with robotics and home automation).

Keywords: Intent recognition · Deep learning · EEG · Smart home

1 Introduction

Smart living involves a collection of technologies that monitor and control domestic living environments, intended to support residents' routine activities to improve their quality of lives. However, the existing smart living control technologies (e.g., voice control [1] and application-based control [2]), may still be found difficult in situations that people have troubles in motor abilities, such as aged individuals, people having motor neuron disease (e.g., Parkinson disease, cord injury, brain-stem stroke) or disabilities.

Thus, to assist such individuals, new smart home systems based on intent recognition are essential, which likely can alleviate aforementioned issues.

Electroencephalography (EEG) signals reflect activities on certain brain areas not requiring any initiative actions such as gesture, voice, or so on. EEG data is generated when a subject imagines performing a certain action such as close hands. Therefore, EEG signal are widely captured to recognize one's intent, with

© Springer International Publishing AG 2017
D. Liu et al. (Eds.): ICONIP 2017, Part II, LNCS 10635, pp. 748–758, 2017.
https://doi.org/10.1007/978-3-319-70096-0_76

the intent of using it as input to communicate or interact with external smart devices such as wheelchairs or service robots a real-time brain-computer interface (BCI) systems [3].

So far, existing EEG-based intent recognition approaches face several challenges. First, the data pre-processing, parameters selection and feature engineering are time-consuming and highly dependent on human expertise. Second, current accuracies mostly center around $60 \sim 85\%$ [4–6], which are too low for real-world deployment. Finally, existing research mainly focus on binary intents recognition while multi-intent scenario dominates the practical applications.

On the other hand, deep learning based approaches are capable of modelling high level representations as well as capturing complex relationships, which are often hidden in raw data, via stacking multiple layers of information processing modules in hierarchical architectures [7]. Recurrent Neural Networks (RNNs) is one example making use of sequential information. In particular, Long Short-Term Memory (LSTM) is one RNN architecture designed to model temporal sequences and their long-range dependencies, and often results in higher accurate compared to conventional RNNs [8]. In this paper, we propose a deep recurrent neural network model for intent recognition in smart living, to help individuals with motor impairments. Reusable source code and dataset are provided to reproduce the results[1]. Our main contributions of this paper are highlighted as below:

- We propose a LSTM recurrent neural network for smart living intent recognition, which directly processes raw EEG data under multi-class scenario.
- We apply Orthogonal Array experiment method for hyper-parameters tuning, which saves 98.4% of time compared to exhausting tuning.
- We evaluate our approach over an open EEG dataset and achieves 0.9553 of accuracy. We also demonstrate the applicability of proposed intent recognition in two real use cases.

2   Related Work

The current application of EEG signals is mainly in medicine and neurology. [9] proposes a Logistic Regression (LR) approach to analyse EEG signals to detect seizure patient and achieves as high as 91% of accuracy. Wavelet analysis [10] is employed to carry on a diagnosis of Traumatic Brain Injury (TBI) by quantitative EEG (qEEG) data and reaches 87.85% of accuracy. Power spectral density [11] are extracted as EEG data features to input into SVM, extreme learning machine and linear discriminant analysis to predict the outcome of Transcranial direct current stimulation (TDCS) treatment. The work achieves 76% accuracy with the data from FC4 $\sim$ AF8 channels and 92% with the data from CPz $\sim$ CP2 channels.

All the aforementioned literature uses binary classification and extracts features in different areas manually. Recent research focuses more on the performance comparison of different classifiers. [12] builds one deep belief net (DBN)

---

[1] https://github.com/xiangzhang1015/EEG-based-Control.

classifier for each channel and combines them through Ada-boost algorithm and classifies the left and right hand motor imagery. The work achieves average 83% accuracy. [5] adopts SVM as the classifier and achieves an average accuracy of 65% with the input data being denoised by a wavelet denoising algorithm before power spectral density (PSD) feature selection. [13] yields an accuracy of 80% with the foundational universal background models (UBMs) classifier after the data is processed by I-vectors and Joint Factor Analysis (JFA). [14] combined convolutional neural networks (CNN) and stacked autoencoders (SAE) to classify EEG Motor Imagery signals and results 90% accuracy. The application of related methods in smart living in relatively limited. As an example, [15] uses high pass and low pass filter to reduce the noise signal interference and extracts EEG features by fisher distance. The switch control experiment results show that their approach achieves an accuracy of 86%.

3   The Proposed Approach

In this section we introduce the flow chart of the proposed approach at first and then involve to more details. The architecture of our approach is shown in Fig. 1. The system consists of two components: the online component and the offline component.

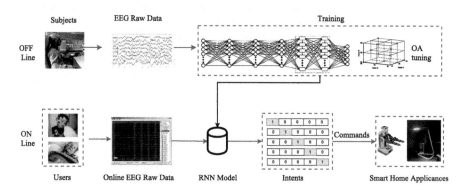

Fig. 1. Workflow of the proposed approach

In the online component, raw EEG data, collected from subjects, are used to train a deep recurrent neural network model (Sect. 3.1). The model directly works on raw EEG data without any pre-processing, smoothing, filtering or feature extraction. The parameters in the deep learning model are optimized by the Orthogonal Array experiment (Sect. 3.2). In the offline component, the user's willing (EEG signal) is sent to above pre-trained RNN model and then recognized as specific intent. The intent is subsequently used to command devices, such as turning lights on/off or driving a robot to serve a cup of water.

3.1 LSTM Recurrent Neural Network

RNN, as a class of deep neural networks, can help to explore the feature dependencies over time through an internal state of the network, which allows us to exhibit dynamic temporal behavior. In order to precisely recognize the user's intent in smart living surrounding, we propose a 7-layer LSTM Recurrent Neural Network model including three components: 1 input layer, 5 hidden layers, and 1 output layer. In hidden layers, two of them are consisted of LSTM cells [16] (shown as the rectangles in Fig. 1).

Assume one collection of EEG signals is $E = \{E_1, E_2, ..., E_j, ..., E_{bs}\}, E_j \in \mathbb{R}^K$ with n_{bs} denotes the batch size, j denotes the j-th EEG sample, and K denotes the number of dimensions in each EEG raw signal ($K = 64$ in this paper). And in the RNN model, we denote the i-th layer ($i = 1, 2, \cdots, I, I = 7$ in this paper) $X_i^r = \{X_{ijk}^r | k = 1, 2, \cdots, K_i\}, X_i^r \in \mathbb{R}^{[n_{bs}, 1, K_i]}$ ($K_1 = K = 64$), where K_i denotes the dimension of the layer. Note that the number of dimension equals to the amount of neurons accordingly in each layer. When the input only contains one EEG sample, the first layer can be $X_1^r = E_j$.

Weights between layer i and layer $i+1$ can be denoted as $W_{i,(i+1)}^r \in \mathbb{R}^{[K_i, K_{i+1}]}$, for instance, $W_{1,2}^r$ describes the weight between layer 1 and layer 2. $b_i^r \in \mathbb{R}^{K_i}$ denotes the biases of i-th layer. The connection between the i-th and $(i + 1)$-th layer will be $X_{i+1}^r = X_i^r * W_{i,i+1}^r + b_i^r$.

Please note the sizes of X_i^r, $W_{i,i+1}^r$ and b_i^r must match. For example, in Fig. 1, the transformation between H1 layer and H2 layer, the sizes of X_3^r, X_2^r, $W_{[2,3]}^r$, and b_2^r are correspondingly $[n_{bs}, 1, K_3]$, $[n_{bs}, 1, K_2]$, $[K_2, K_3]$, and $[n_{bs}, 1]$. The 5-th and 6-th layers here are LSTM layers, and they can be connected by:

$$f_i = sigmoid(T(X_{(i-1)j}^r, X_{(i)(j-1)}^r))$$

$$f_f = sigmoid(T(X_{(i-1)j}^r, X_{(i)(j-1)}^r))$$

$$f_o = sigmoid(T(X_{(i-1)j}^r, X_{(i)(j-1)}^r))$$

$$f_m = tanh(T(X_{(i-1)j}^r, X_{(i)(j-1)}^r))$$

$$c_{ij} = f_f \odot c_{i(j-1)} + f_i \odot f_m$$

$$X_{ij}^r = f_o \odot tanh(c_{ij})$$

where f_i, f_f, f_o and f_m represent the input gate, forget gate, output gate and input modulation gate accordingly, and $\odot$ denotes the element-wise multiplication. The c_{ij} denotes the state (memory) in the j-th LSTM cell in the i-th layer, which is the most significant part to explore the time-series relevance between samples. The $T(X_{(i-1)j}^r, X_{(i)(j-1)}^r)$ denotes the operation as follows:

$$X_{(i-1)j}^r * W + X_{(i)(j-1)}^r * W' + b$$

where W, W' and b denote the corresponding weights and biases. At last, we obtain the RNN predict results X_7^r and employ the cross-entropy as the cost function. The ℓ_2 norm is selected as the regularization function and the cost is optimized by the AdamOptimizer algorithm [17].

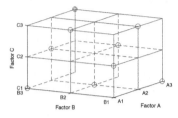

Fig. 2. OA selection

Table 1. Factors and levels

	Level 1	Level 2	Level 3	Level 4
λ	0.002	0.004	0.006	0.008
lr	0.005	0.01	0.015	0.02
K_i	16	32	48	64
I	5	6	7	8
n_b	1	3	6	13

3.2 Orthogonal Array Experiment Method

Although deep learning algorithms can generally achieve good performance in many areas, tuning the hyper-parameters (e.g., the number of layers, the number of nodes in each layer and the learning rate) is time-consuming and dependent on one's experience. This paper employs the Orthogonal Array (OA) experiment method [18] to select the hyper-parameters, which works *much faster* than traditional hyper-parameters tuning methods. OA[2] is widely used in *design of experiments, coding theory, and cryptography*, however, to our best knowledge, this paper is the very first work to apply OA of the parameter tuning in machine learning and data mining areas.

OA is a systematic and statistical method and its principle is to compare the dependent variable which is resulted from a different combination of independent variables. It chooses certain representative combinations instead of all combinations for testing. In this method, independent variable is called "factor" and different values of factor are called "levels". For instance, if the program has three factors and each of them has three levels, which are represented by a cube with 27 nodes (each node represents one combination of hyper-parameters), OA only chooses 9 representative groups of parameters to optimize the selection. As shown in Fig. 2, A_1, A_2, A_3 represent 3 levels of factor A, while factors B, C are by the same token (the factor is supposed to be statistically independent with the others). The 9 circled nodes are the nine groups selected by OA. Each edge (totally 27 edges) in the cube has one circled node and each face (totally 9 faces) has three circled nodes.

For different number of factors and levels, corresponding OA table is provided. Generally, an OA table can be written as $Ln_a(n_b^{n_c})$, where n_a denotes the number of hyper-parameter combination, n_b denotes the number of levels of each factor and n_c denotes the number of factors.

---

[2] https://www.york.ac.uk/depts/maths/tables/taguchi_table.htm.

Table 2. Intents and corresponding label and function in case studies

Intent	Label	Robot (Case 1)	Household Appliance (Case 2)
Eye Closed	1	Walk Ahead	Turn on Blue LEDs
Left Fist	2	Turn Left	Turn on White LED
Right Fist	3	Turn Right	Turn on Yellow LED
Both Fists	4	Grasp	Turn on Red LED
Both Feet	5	Unloose	Turn on All LEDs

Table 3. The confusion matrix of 5-classes classification

	Ground Truth					Evaluation			
	0	1	2	3	4	Precision	Recall	F1	AUC
Predicted 0	2062	19	23	18	22	0.9618	0.9380	0.9497	0.9982
Label 1	17	1120	19	15	20	0.9404	0.9084	0.9241	0.9977
2	2	13	1146	14	11	0.9574	0.9257	0.9413	0.9990
3	10	5	7	1162	10	0.9732	0.9028	0.9367	0.9990
4	18	21	15	23	1197	0.9396	0.9392	0.9394	0.9987
Total	2120	1178	1210	1232	1260	4.7723	4.6140	4.6911	4.9926
Average						0.9545	0.9228	0.9382	0.9985

4 Experiments

4.1 Dataset

We select the widely used EEG data from PhysioNet eegmmidb (*EEG motor movement/imagery database*) database[3] to evaluate the proposed approach. The EEG signals we selected are under 5 categories of intents. The intents are shown in Table 2. In our work, we select 280,000 EEG samples from 10 subjects (28,000 samples each subject) for the experiment. Every sample is a vector of 64 elements corresponding to 64 channels.

4.2 Overall Comparison

This section is aimed to demonstrate the efficiency of the proposed approach, for which we compare our approach with the state-of-the-art methods. Our model is composed of 7 layers RNN with 2 LSTM layers, the learning rate and the λ are set as 0.004 and 0.005, the number of the nodes in each hidden layer is 64 and the number of batches n_b is 3 (detailed in Sect. 4.3).

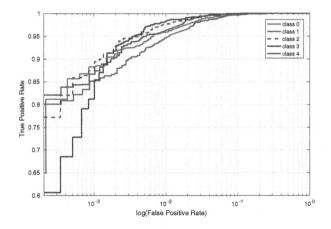

Fig. 3. ROC curves. X-axis is the logarithmic of the False Positive Rate.

---

[3] https://www.physionet.org/pn4/EEGmmidb/.

Our intent recognition result, the confusion matrix and the corresponding evaluation are presented in Table 3. It can be read that our approach produces a mean accuracy of **0.9553**, in tests of five intents recognition on 10 subjects. The ROC (Receiver Operating Characteristic) curves of five intents are displayed in Fig. 3. Additionally, comparison with the state-of-the-art methods is shown in Table 5 (the Binary/Multi column refers binary intents recognition or multi-intents recognition). The KNN sets the number of neighbors as 3; the SVM adopts One-vs-the-rest (OvR) multi-class strategy and the estimator is LinearSVC; the RF sets the number of estimators as 300; the AdaBoost adopts the number of estimators as 50 and the learning rate as 0.3; all the not mentioned parameters are set as default values. We can perceive that the proposed approach significantly outperforms all the state-of-the-art methods, by a large margin of 10%.

4.3   Hyper-parameter Tuning

The intent recognition results rely on hyper-parameters since we adopt deep learning model. To achieve optimal recognition accuracy, we employ OA to optimize the hyper-parameters. In this paper, we select five most common hyper-parameters including λ (the coefficient of ℓ_2 norm), lr (learning rate), K_i (the hidden layer nodes size), I (the number of layers), and n_b (the number of batches[4]), and they are shown in Table 1. Since this OA experiment contains 5 factors and 4 levels, the total number of factor combinations can be found in *the standard orthogonal experiment table*[5]. As shown in the standard orthogonal experiment table, 5 factors with 4 levels OA experiment has 16 different combine ways, which means 16 experiments should be conducted to optimize the hyper-parameters. The combination of hyper-parameters and the range analysis of results of the experiment, are shown in Table 4. The optical λ, lr, K_i, I, and n_b tuned by OA are 0.004, 0.005, 64, 7, and 3, respectively. The parameter selection of 5 factors and 4 levels needs $1024 = 4^5$ combinations in an exhaustive method, while with OA only 16 combinations are needed. This means $(1 - 16/1024) = $ **98.4%** of time are saved. In Table 4, $R_{level i}$ is the sum of accuracy of all the combinations contains $level_i$. We selected the best levels listed in Table 4 for training the model and obtain an accuracy of **0.9553**.

4.4   Feature Evolution

To better understand the essence of the proposed model, we graphically describe the feature evolution procedures. Figure 4 shows the revolution of variations between samples from different classes. In the input layer, the samples are chaotic entangled; and they become clear and observable in the last LSTM layer after

---

[4] The size of training dataset and testing dataset depends on n_b since the total dataset is fixed, e.g., if n_b equals 1, there will be 14,000 training dataset and 14,000 testing dataset. If n_b equals 3, we will have 21,000 training dataset and 7,000 testing dataset.

[5] https://www.york.ac.uk/depts/maths/tables/l16b.htm.

Table 4. OA experiment factor analysis

No.	1	2	3	4	5	6	7	8	9	10	11	12	13	14	15	16	R_{level1}	R_{level2}	R_{level3}	R_{level4}	Best level
λ	0.002	0.002	0.002	0.002	0.004	0.004	0.004	0.004	0.006	0.006	0.006	0.006	0.008	0.008	0.008	0.008	3.159	**3.26**	2.441	2.44	**0.004**
lr	0.005	0.01	0.015	0.02	0.005	0.01	0.015	0.02	0.005	0.01	0.015	0.02	0.005	0.01	0.015	0.02	**3.47**	2.875	2.747	2.208	**0.005**
K_i	16	32	48	64	32	16	64	48	48	64	16	32	64	48	32	16	2.132	2.886	3.011	**3.271**	**64**
I	5	6	7	8	7	8	5	6	8	7	6	5	6	5	8	7	2.326	2.932	**3.048**	2.894	**7**
n_b	1	3	6	13	13	6	3	1	3	1	13	6	6	13	1	3	2.969	**3.088**	2.907	2.336	**3**
acc	0.689	0.91	0.893	0.667	0.925	0.717	0.848	0.77	0.926	0.826	0.322	0.367	0.93	0.422	0.684	0.404					

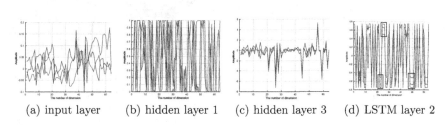

(a) input layer   (b) hidden layer 1   (c) hidden layer 3   (d) LSTM layer 2

Fig. 4. Feature evolution. The black rectangles in (d) indicate the features which can clearly show the difference between the various intents.

the training through several hidden layers. Particularly, in Fig. 4(d), the black rectangles display parts of the dimensions which can clearly show the difference between the intents. Conclusively, the proposed approach is enabled to automatically extract distinguishable features (Fig. 4(d)) from the chaotic raw EEG data (Fig. 4(a)).

4.5 Deployment

In this section, the efficiency of intent recognition is demonstrated by two applications. The structure of RNN and the corresponding parameters used in this section are the same as the counterparts in Sect. 4.2.

Assisted Living with Mind-controlled Mobile Robot. A simulated robot is navigated by our system, which learns user's intent from EEG recordings, to take a can of beverage from a table in the kitchen and put it in a table in living room. This case randomly selects some EEG raw data from Subject 1 dataset as simulation inputs. The path is shown in Fig. 5, which is designed for the EEG data to drive PR2 to implement its service task. Starting from near the Kitchen's table, the PR2 robot walks forward and holds its hand to grasp the beverage can. Then it turns back and walks along the path to the table in living room and unlooses hands to put the beverage on the table. It shows that the robot can precisely grasp and unloose target according to the path planned in the subject's mind. The simulation platform is in Gazebo toolbox[6] and the robot controlling program is powered by Robot Operating System (ROS)[7]. The

---

[6] http://gazebosim.org/.
[7] http://www.ros.org/.

Table 5. Performance comparison with the state of the art methods. RF: Random Forest, LDA: Linear Discriminant Analysis. **All the methods are evaluated using the same database.**

	Index	Methods	Binary/Multi	Accuracy
State of the art	1	Almoari [3]		0.7497
	2	Sun [5]		0.65
	3	Major [4]	Binary	0.68
	4	Shenoy [6]		0.8206
	5	Tolic [19]		0.6821
	6	Ward [13]	Multi (3)	0.8
	7	Pinheiro [20]	Multi (4)	0.8505
Baselines	8	KNN (k=3)		0.8369
	9	SVM		0.5082
	10	RF		0.7739
	11	LDA	Multi (5)	0.5127
	12	AdaBoost		0.3431
	13	CNN		0.8409
	14	Ours		**0.9553**

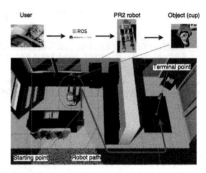

Fig. 5. Use Case 1: mind-controlled PR2 assistive robot performs a daily task: reaching a cup of water in kitchen area and getting it back onto a table in living room.

simulation environment is depicted in Fig. 5 and the demo can be found at here[8]. The robot executes 5 actions according to 5 commands described in Table 2.

Assisted Living with Mind-Controlled Appliances. The most common scenario in a smart home would be controlling household appliances. In this case, we control four LEDs ON/OFF through intents. LED commands corresponding to specific intents are mentioned in Table 2. For every command, the corresponding LED keeps on for 2 s and then turns off. Such test is conducted 10 times with totally 80 commands, and our model accomplishes *100%* of accuracy, which indicates that the EEG-based mind control have potential to be significant in household in the future.

5   Conclusion and Futurework

In this paper, we present an LSTM-RNN approach to recognize the smart living user intents in EEG raw signals. By experimenting on large scale EEG dataset, we can claim that our proposed approach significantly outperforms a series of the state-of-the-art methods by achieving 0.9553 of accuracy. It provides insight into feature revolution by visualizing the data shape, waveform fluctuation flowing through each layer of our proposed model. Moreover, we demonstrate the applicability of the approach by implementing two use cases, wherein an assistive robot performs a physical task, and household appliances are interacted, based on intent recognition. Our prior work atop multi-task learning based framework [21] shows the capability to capture certain underlying local commonalities under

---

[8] https://www.youtube.com/watch?v=VZYX1095Vkc.

the intra-class variabilities shared by all the activities of different subjects. Our future works will focus on improving the accuracy in *person-independent* scenario, wherein the training and testing data can be from different subjects.

References

1. Muhammad, G., Alhamid, M.F., Hossain, M.S., et al.: Enhanced living by assessing voice pathology using a co-occurrence matrix. Sensors **17**(2), 267 (2017)
2. Kumar, S.: Ubiquitous smart home system using android application. arXiv preprint arXiv:1402.2114 (2014)
3. Alomari, M.H., Abubaker, A., Turani, A., Baniyounes, A.M., Manasreh, A.: EEG mouse: a machine learning-based brain computer interface. Int. J. Adv. Res. Comput. Sci. Appl. **5**, 1–6 (2014)
4. Major, T.C., Conrad, J.M.: The effects of pre-filtering and individualizing components for electroencephalography neural network classification. In: SoutheastCon, 2017. IEEE (2017)
5. Sun, L., et al.: Classification of imagery motor EEG data with wavelet denoising and features selection. In: 2016 International Conference on Wavelet Analysis and Pattern Recognition (ICWAPR) (2016)
6. Shenoy, H.V., Vinod, A., Guan, C.: Shrinkage estimator based regularization for EEG motor imagery classification. In: 2015 10th International Conference on Information, Communications and Signal Processing (ICICS). IEEE (2015)
7. LeCun, Y., Bengio, Y., Hinton, G.: Deep learning. Nature **521**(7553), 436–444 (2015)
8. Sak, H., Senior, A.W., Beaufays, F.: Long short-term memory recurrent neural network architectures for large scale acoustic modeling. In: Interspeech (2014)
9. Page, A., Sagedy, C., Smith, E., Attaran, N., Oates, T., Mohsenin, T.: A flexible multichannel EEG feature extractor and classifier for seizure detection. IEEE Trans. Circ. Syst. II Express Briefs **62**, 109–113 (2015)
10. Albert, B., Zhang, J., Noyvirt, A., Setchi, R., Sjaaheim, H., Velikova, S., Strisland, F.: Automatic EEG processing for the early diagnosis of traumatic brain injury. In: World Automation Congress (WAC) (2016)
11. Al-Kaysi, A.M., Al-Ani, A., Loo, C.K., et al.: Predicting tDCS treatment outcomes of patients with major depressive disorder using automated EEG classification. J. Affect. Disord. **208**, 597–603 (2017)
12. An, X., Kuang, D., Guo, X., Zhao, Y., He, L.: A deep learning method for classification of EEG data based on motor imagery. In: Huang, D.-S., Han, K., Gromiha, M. (eds.) ICIC 2014. LNCS, vol. 8590, pp. 203–210. Springer, Cham (2014). doi:10.1007/978-3-319-09330-7_25
13. Ward, C., Picone, J., Obeid, I.: Applications of UBMS and I-vectors in EEG subject verification. In: 2016 IEEE 38th Annual International Conference of the Engineering in Medicine and Biology Society (EMBC) (2016)
14. Tabar, Y.R., Halici, U.: A novel deep learning approach for classification of EEG motor imagery signals. J. Neural Eng. **14**, 016003 (2016)
15. Mu, Z., Yin, J., Hu, J.: Design of smart home system using EEG signal. Metall. Min. Ind. **2015**(6), 436–441 (2015)
16. Zaremba, W., Sutskever, I., Vinyals, O.: Recurrent neural network regularization. arXiv preprint arXiv:1409.2329 (2014)

17. Kingma, D., Ba, J.: Adam: A method for stochastic optimization. arXiv preprint arXiv:1412.6980 (2014)
18. Taguchi, G.: System of Experimental Design: Engineering Methods to Optimize Quality and Minimize Costs. UNIPUB/Kraus International Publications, White Plains (1987)
19. Tolić, M., Jović, F.: Classification of wavelet transformed EEG signals with neural network for imagined mental and motor tasks. Kineziologija **45**(1), 130–138 (2013)
20. Pinheiro, O.R., Alves, L.R., Romero, M., de Souza, J.R.: Wheelchair simulator game for training people with severe disabilities. In: International Conference on Technology and Innovation in Sports, Health and Wellbeing (TISHW). IEEE (2016)
21. Yao, L., Nie, F., Sheng, Q.Z., et al.: Learning from less for better: semi-supervised activity recognition via shared structure discovery. In: Proceedings of the 2016 ACM International Joint Conference on Pervasive and Ubiquitous Computing. ACM (2016)

Recognition of Voluntary Blink and Bite Base on Single Forehead EMG

Jianhai Zhang$^{(\boxtimes)}$, Wenhao Huang, Shaokai Zhao, Yanyang Li, and Sanqing Hu

College of Computer Science, Hangzhou Dianzi University,
Hangzhou 310018, Zhejiang, China
{jhzhang,sqhu}@hdu.edu.cn, hwhzzly@gmail.com, lnkzsk@126.com,
lyyzzly@gmail.com

Abstract. With the development of intelligent wearable technology, the need for a more effective and practical means of human-computer interaction is becoming increasingly urgent. In this paper, we used only one forehead Electromyogram (EMG) channel to accurately recognize at least 6 different voluntary blink and bite patterns as output interactive commands. Differential square moving average (DSMA) and square moving average (SMA) were used to distinguish blink and bite, voluntary blink and natural blink, respectively. Then, random forests classifier was employed to classify the 6 blink and bite patterns with extracted time-domain features. The accuracy of 92.60 $\pm$ 2.55 was obtained for the dataset of 10 subjects. It provides an effective human-computer interaction method with the advantages of rich commands, good real-time performance, low cost and small individual differences. The method proposed can be conveniently embedded in wearable device as an alternative of interaction.

Keywords: Human-computer interaction · Wearable device · EMG · Blink recognition · Bite recognition

1 Introduction

In recent years, intelligent wearable technology has been gaining more and more attention from the academic and the business community around the world, which has been considered as the core and main form of the next generation of smart device [1,2]. However, the lack of an effective human-computer interaction hinders its further development in practical applications.

At present, the interaction methods based on speech and gesture recognition are dominant in wearable device [3,4]. But these methods can't be applied to many practical situation, such as in the meeting. Recently, Brain-computer interface (BCI) technology begins to attract attention, and is considered as the most appropriate, natural way of interaction [5]. Facebook by Mark Zuckerberg and Neuralink by Elon Musk has put forward ideas from "speech-to-text" to "thought-to-text" using BCI technology. Despite the rapid development, BCI based on EEG (such as P300 [6], Motor imagination [7], SSVEP [8]) is still

© Springer International Publishing AG 2017
D. Liu et al. (Eds.): ICONIP 2017, Part II, LNCS 10635, pp. 759–766, 2017.
https://doi.org/10.1007/978-3-319-70096-0_77

mainly used by patients, subject to the richness and accuracy of output commands and individual differences. As well known, however, a variety of Electromyogram (EMG) signals caused by facial muscle movements are captured as artifacts while recording scalp EEG. Can we recognize the voluntary facial muscle movements from these EMG signals to interact with computer? Some work has been done for this. Bo Ning [9] and Mihai Duguleana [10] have tried to control wheelchair and robot by eye blink.

In this paper, we employed less EMG electrodes (single electrode located on forehead) to accurately recognize more voluntary facial muscle movements (at least 6 as in this paper: single eyes blink, double eyes blink, long eyes blink, single bite, double bite, long bite). With this, we can provide an effective human-computer interaction method with the advantages of rich and accurate interactive commands, good real-time performance, low cost, easy to carry and small individual differences. The method we proposed can be conveniently embedded in wearable device as an alternative of interaction.

2   Materials and Methods

2.1   Materials

Mindwave Mobile headset by Neurosky Company was used for forehead EMG signal recording with sampling rate of 512 Hz. Mindwave Mobile headset is an embedded system with a single bio-sensor to acquire forehead EMG and EEG signals. The sensor is placed on forehead at FP1 location and a reference electrode is connected to the ear lobe [11], using Bluetooth to transmit recorded data. This headset has been used in lots of research works. Abo-zahad et al. [12] used it to study blink signals as human identification. Adnan Mehmood Bhatti et al. [11] used it to study emotion recognition based on EEG signals. Alpha-Trainer [16] used it to implement a Brain-computer interface system based on android.

In this paper, we want to recognize six kinds of voluntary facial muscle movements, including single blink, double blink, long blink, single bite, double bite, long bite. These six motions are easy to implement by every person and have obvious characteristics in their EMG waveform, as shown in Fig. 1.

In this paper, the dataset is recorded from ten healthy adult subjects (21–25 years old, 5 males and 5 females). The purpose of the experiment is to acquire subjects' forehead EMG signals while they are biting or voluntary blinking. During the recording, the subjects were seated in front of a screen and implement the facial movements by instruction. Ten 5-minutes trials were done for every subject. In each trial, every motion of six voluntary blink and bite patterns was implemented 10 times. The first 30 s of each trial doesn't include any voluntary motions with rest state and natural blink. Each motion was required to be finished within 1 s. There are 10 s interval between two facial movements. All the trials were finished within 2 weeks. So, we obtained 100 samples of every voluntary facial motion for each subject, and the total of 6000 samples.

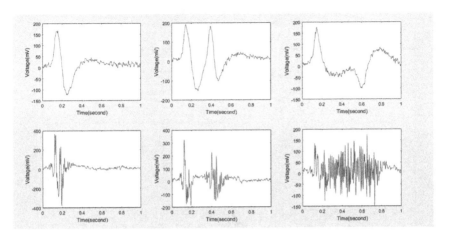

Fig. 1. EMG signals for single blink, double blink, long blink from left to right on top panel, and EMG signals for single bite, double bite, and long bite from left to right on bottom panel.

2.2 Signal Preprocessing

Firstly, the data for each subject was preprocessed as follows:

Step 1. Subtract mean value for each trial to eliminate the baseline drift;
Step 2. Merge all trials of the subject into one new trial X;
Step 3. Normalization of X to [−1,1], denoted as X′;
Step 4. Squared moving average (SMA) method and differential squared moving average (DSMA) method [13] are used to calculate two kinds of short time energy of the data X′. The formulas of SMA and DSMA are as follows. The moving step of two methods is 0.1 s.

Square moving average method (SMA):

$$SMA(i) = \frac{1}{52} \sum_{j=0}^{51} X(i+j)^2 \qquad (1)$$

Differential square moving average method (DSMA):

$$DSMA(i) = \frac{1}{52} \sum_{j=1}^{51} [X(i+j) - X(i+j-1)]^2 \qquad (2)$$

where $i = 1, 2, ..., L - 51$; L is the length of X'. And the performance of this step is shown in Fig. 2.

Step 5. Calculate basic segmenting threshold T. Firstly, calculate the short-time energy of the first 30-seconds rest state data by SMA. The basic segmenting threshold T is set as 0.1 times of the maximum of the short energy.

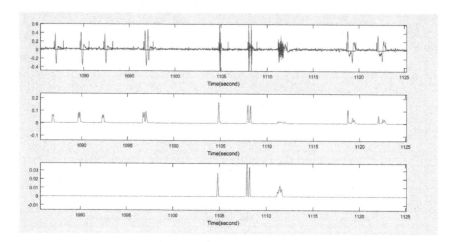

Fig. 2. The upper sub-figure shows the normalized data. The middle sub-figure shows the data after square moving average. And the bottom sub-figure shows the data after differential square moving average. SMA and DSMA method are used as preclassification methods. The red line segment the bite group data and the black line segment the blink group data.

Step 6. Data segmentation. The threshold T is used to automatically segment data X′ into sample data containing interesting motion data. While a data point's SMA value is higher than T, choosing this point as the starting point, and the 1-second length data after the starting point is segmented as a sample data. The result of this step is shown in Fig. 3.

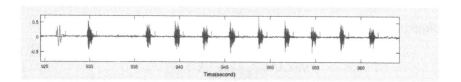

Fig. 3. Data segmentation

2.3 Feature Extraction

21 time domain features are extracted for classification. Every 1-second sample data is divided into ten 100-ms segments, then the positive and negative energy of each segment is calculated as the first twenty features. The last feature is the total energy of this sample.

Positive Energy:

$$E_+(i) = \sum_{j=1}^{51} X(i * 51 + j) \tag{3}$$

Where $X(i * 51 + j) > 0$, $i = 0, 1, 2, ..., 9$

Negative Energy:

$$E_-(i) = \sum_{j=1}^{51} X(i * 51 + j) \tag{4}$$

Where $X(i * 51 + j) < 0$, $i = 0, 1, 2, ..., 9$

Total Energy:

$$E_{all} = \sum_{i=1}^{512} X(i) \tag{5}$$

2.4   Classification

Just as mentioned in step 4 of 2.2, the pre-classification step are as follows.

(1) Distinguish the bite sample and blink sample. For each sample, if any DSMA value is higher than the threshold T, this sample is classified into the bite group or into the blink group.
(2) Distinguish natural blink and voluntary blink. For each blink sample, if the number of the data points with SMA value higher than T is bigger than 77 (about 0.15 s), it will be categorized into voluntary blink group or into natural blink group.

Now, we have two sample groups, one for voluntary blink and another for bite. Each group contains 3 different motion patterns (single blink, double blink, long blink for blink group data, single bite, double bite, long bite for bite group data). Random forests classifier [14] with 200 sub-trees is employed for each group to distinguish the 3 patterns. The random forests classifier is suitable for dealing with the problem of multi-class classification [15]. And the all process of forehead EMG recognition is shown in Fig. 4.

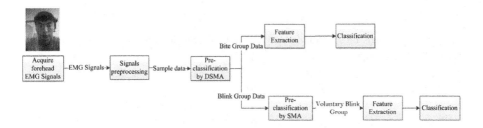

Fig. 4. The process of recognition

3   Result

For comparison, we also directly feed the original 512 sample data into classifier as features. Table 1 shows the average classification accuracy and standard deviation of each subject. 5-fold cross validation were applied to increase the reliability of the classification results. The average classification accuracy and standard deviation of 87.88 ± 3.84 and 92.60 ± 2.55 across subjects were obtained using 512 original data and 21 time-domain features respectively.

Table 2 shows the average confusion matrix across subjects. Table 2 shows the average confusion matrix across subjects with feature data. From Table 2, we can found that the misclassification rates between voluntary blink group and bite group are zero. This verifies the effectiveness of the pre-classification step.

Table 1. The average classification accuracy and standard deviation of each subject with 5-fold cross validation.

Sub no.	Original data (%)	Feature data (%)
01	94.83 ± 5.99	96.33 ± 3.04
02	86.83 ± 3.30	90.67 ± 1.60
03	81.50 ± 5.15	89.17 ± 5.24
04	86.33 ± 5.16	90.17 ± 7.30
05	89.83 ± 2.73	92.33 ± 3.41
06	91.00 ± 6.49	94.00 ± 5.25
07	84.33 ± 4.22	90.50 ± 4.19
08	89.50 ± 9.51	96.00 ± 3.46
09	89.67 ± 4.66	92.00 ± 3.26
10	85.00 ± 6.77	94.83 ± 3.08
Mean	87.88 ± 3.84	92.60 ± 2.55

Table 2. Confusion matrix obtained by random forests and feature data across subjects (%).

	Single blink	Double blink	Long blink	Single bite	Double bite	Long bite
Single blink	94.00	2.3	3.7	0	0	0
Double blink	2.7	95.0	2.3	0	0	0
Long blink	2.5	2.9	94.6	0	0	0
Single bite	0	0	0	90.6	6.1	3.3
Double bite	0	0	0	9.2	89.0	1.8
Long bite	0	0	0	4.3	3.3	92.4

4   Conclusions

The method presented in this paper achieves a good recognition performance (mean: 92.60 ± 2.55) for six kinds of facial muscle movements. Our method is convenient and economical with only one channel located on forehead. Moreover, the calculation speed of this method can meet the requirements of the online system. Our future works include: (1) applying this method to the online recognition system; (2) further improving the classification performance; (3) improving the adaptive ability for different people.

Acknowledgments. This work was supported in part by the National Natural Science Foundation of China under Grant 61100102 and Grant 61473110 and Grant 61633010, in part by the International Science and Technology Cooperation Program of China under Grant 2014DFG12570.

References

1. Kumari, P., Mathew, L., Syal, P.: Increasing trend of wearables and multimodal interface for human activity monitoring: a review. Biosens. Bioelectr. **90**, 298–307 (2017)
2. Chan, M., Esteve, D., Escriba, C., Campo, E.: A review of smart homes - present state and future challenges. Comput. Meth. Prog. Biomed. **91**(1), 55–81 (2008)
3. Wu, W., Hsu, C., Yang, S.: Smart wearable device design for bicycle lights direction control with speech-recognition function. In: International Symposium on Computer, Consumer and Control, Xian, pp. 53–56. IEEE (2016)
4. Lopez-Nava, I., Munoz-Melendez, A.: Wearable inertial sensors for human motion analysis: a review. IEEE Sens. J. **16**(22), 7821–7834 (2016)
5. Ali, B., Mehrdad, F., Rabab, K., Gary, E.: A survey of signal processing algorithms in brain-computer interfaces based on electrical brain signals. J. Neural Eng. **4**(2), R32–R57 (2007)
6. Zhang, R., Yuan, L., Yong, Y., Hao, Z., et al.: Control of a wheelchair in an indoor environment based on a brain-computer interface and automated navigation. IEEE Trans. Neural Syst. Rehabil. Eng. **24**(1), 128–139 (2016)
7. Vourvopoulos, A., Badia, S., Liarokapis, F.: EEG correlates of video game experience and user profile in motor-imagery-based brain-computer interaction. Vis. Comput. **33**(4), 533–546 (2017)
8. Vialatte, F., Maurice, M., Dauwels, J., Cichocki, A.: Steady-state visually evoked potentials: focus on essential paradigms and future perspectives. Prog. Neurobiol. **90**(4), 418–438 (2010)
9. Ning, B., Li, M., Liu, T., Shen, H., Hu, L., Fu, X.: Human brain control of electric wheelchair with eye-blink electrooculogram signal. In: Su, C.-Y., Rakheja, S., Liu, H. (eds.) ICIRA 2012, Part I. LNCS (LNAI), vol. 7506, pp. 579–588. Springer, Heidelberg (2012). doi:10.1007/978-3-642-33509-9_58
10. Duguleana, M., Mogan, G.: Using eye blinking for EOG-based robot control. In: Camarinha-Matos, L.M., Pereira, P., Ribeiro, L. (eds.) DoCEIS 2010. IFIP AICT, vol. 314, pp. 343–350. Springer, Heidelberg (2010). doi:10.1007/978-3-642-11628-5_37

11. Adnan, M., Muhammad, M., Syed, M., Bilal, K.: Human emotion recognition and analysis in response to audio music using brain signals. Comput. Hum. Behav. **65**, 267–275 (2016)
12. Abo-Zahhad, M., Ahmed, S., Abbas, S.: A novel biometric approach for human identification and verification using eye blinking signal. IEEE Signal Process. Lett. **22**(7), 876–880 (2015)
13. Zhao, Z., Chen, X., Zhang, X., Yang, J., Tu, Y., Lantz, V., Wang, K.: Study on online gesture sEMG recognition. In: Huang, D.-S., Heutte, L., Loog, M. (eds.) ICIC 2007. LNCS, vol. 4681, pp. 1257–1265. Springer, Heidelberg (2007). doi:10.1007/978-3-540-74171-8_128
14. Breiman, L.: Random forests. Mach. Learn. **45**, 5–32 (2001)
15. Prinzie, A., Van, D.: Random forests for multiclass classification: random multinomial logit. Expert Syst. Appl. **34**(3), 1721–1732 (2008)
16. AlphaTrainer. http://alphatrainer.github.io/mscthesis/ch-experiment/index.html

Multimodal Classification with Deep Convolutional-Recurrent Neural Networks for Electroencephalography

Chuanqi Tan, Fuchun Sun[✉], Wenchang Zhang, Jianhua Chen, and Chunfang Liu

State Key Laboratory of Intelligent Technology and Systems,
Tsinghua National Laboratory for Information Science
and Technology (TNList), Department of Computer Science and Technology,
Tsinghua University, Beijing, China
chuanqi.tan@gmail.com, fcsun@mail.tsinghua.edu.cn

Abstract. Electroencephalography (EEG) has become the most significant input signal for brain computer interface (BCI) based systems. However, it is very difficult to obtain satisfactory classification accuracy due to traditional methods can not fully exploit multimodal information. Herein, we propose a novel approach to modeling cognitive events from EEG data by reducing it to a video classification problem, which is designed to preserve the multimodal information of EEG. In addition, optical flow is introduced to represent the variant information of EEG. We train a deep neural network (DNN) with convolutional neural network (CNN) and recurrent neural network (RNN) for the EEG classification task by using EEG video and optical flow. The experiments demonstrate that our approach has many advantages, such as more robustness and more accuracy in EEG classification tasks. According to our approach, we designed a mixed BCI-based rehabilitation support system to help stroke patients perform some basic operations.

Keywords: Multimodal · EEG classification · Optical flow · Deep learning · CNN · RNN

1 Introduction

For patients suffering from stroke, it is very meaningful to provide a communication method to deliver brain messages and commands to the external world apart from the normal nerve-muscle output pathway. Due to natural and non-intrusive characteristics, most BCI systems select the EEG signal as input [1]. The biggest challenge in BCI is EEG classification, aiming to translate raw EEG signal into the commands of the human brain. This can be used to control external equipment, such as rehabilitation devices and other devices, when the EEG signal is decoded correctly. However, traditional EEG classification methods can not obtain satisfactory result, one of the reasons is that some useful

D. Liu et al. (Eds.): ICONIP 2017, Part II, LNCS 10635, pp. 767–776, 2017.
https://doi.org/10.1007/978-3-319-70096-0_78

information has been ignored. Deep learning, as a new classification platform, has recently received increased attention from researchers [2,3]. It has been successfully applied to many classification problems, such as image classification [4], video classification [5] and speech recognition [6]. However, deep learning has not been fully explored in EEG classification. Similar to the structure of the human brain, deep learning is particularly suitable for classification problems from which it is hard to extract hand-designed features. Therefore, deep learning has very promising prospects in the EEG classification field.

The contributions of this paper are as follows. Firstly, our approach reduces the EEG classification problem to a video classification problem, which is designed to utilize multimodal information. Secondly, optical flow has been introduced into this field to characterize the variant of EEG signal in the temporal dimension. Thirdly, a deep CNN-RNN network has been constructed, which is designed for EEG videos and optical flow. Finally, a mixed BCI-based rehabilitation support system is built using our approach.

The rest of this paper is organized as follows. Firstly, we will review related works in Sect. 2. Secondly, the method we proposed will be described in Sect. 3. Third, findings of our experiments will be presented in Sect. 4. Finally, conclusions and further steps will be discussed in Sect. 5.

2   Related Work

In order to improve the accuracy of EEG classification, a lot of work has been carried out. The performance of this pattern recognition like system depends on both the features selected and the classification algorithms employed. Traditionally, a great variety of hand-designed features have been proposed such as band powers (BP) [7], power spectral density (PSD) values [8] and so on. In recent years, the common spatial pattern (CSP) [9] has been proved to be an expressive feature of EEG signal. A lot of related work has been proposed such as CSSP, WCSP and SCSSP [10]. Unlike these single modal approaches, there are many researchers focusing on how to extract multimodal information from the EEG signal [11,12] and how to fuse this information [13].

From hand-designed to data-driven features, deep learning has played a significant role in diverse fields where the artificial intelligence (AI) community has struggled for many years. Certainly, bioinformatics can also benefit from deep learning. In recent years, many public reviews [14,15] have been proposed to discuss deep learning applications in bioinformatics research. For example, [16] applying deep belief networks (DBN) to the frequency components of EEG signal to classify left-hand and right-hand motor imagery skills. [17] used CNN to decode P300 patterns, and [18] used CNN to recognize rhythm stimuli. [19] conducted an emotion detection and facial expressions study with both EEG signal and face images by RNN.

3 Method

3.1 Preprocessing

We are only interested in certain brain activities, and these signals need to be separated from background noise, and unnecessary artifacts must be eliminated. In the preprocessing phase, we first apply the Butterworth filter with 0.5-50 Hz as a bandpass filter to remove high-order noise in the signal. Then, a denoise Autoencoder (DAE) [20] as a symmetrical neural network is used to denoise in an unsupervised manner. It is trained to rebuild the input to construct a robust feature representation. Autoencoders, like the principal components analysis (PCA), are usually trained to perform dimension reduction tasks, but the DAE is more useful in learning sparse representations of input. This means that a high-dimensional original signal can be represented by using a few representative atoms on a low-dimensional manifold, which is similar to sparse coding.

3.2 EEG Videos and Optical Flow

Similar to speech signal, the most notable features of EEG signal reside in the frequency dimension, which is usually studied using a spectrogram of the signal. The feature vector formed by aggregating spectral measurements of all electrodes is the traditional method in EEG data analysis. However, these methods clearly ignore the locations of electrodes and the inherent information in spatial dimension. In our approach, for representing multimodal information, we propose to preserve the spatial structure by EEG image, apply frequency filters to represent the spectral dimension, and utilize the EEG videos to account for temporal evolutions in brain activity.

Firstly, filtering is performed by using five frequency filters (α: 8-13 Hz, β: 14-30 Hz, γ: 31-51 Hz, δ: 0.5-3 Hz, θ: 4-7 Hz) to represent different EEG signal rhythms which correspond to different brain activity. According to the frequency characteristics of the EEG signal, we produced five different EEG dataset by these filters. Secondly, EEG images are generated for each EEG frame in time dimension. We project the 3D locations of electrodes (shown in Fig. 1(a), unit of percentage) to 2D points by azimuthal equidistant projection (AEP) which borrows from mapping applications, and interpolate them to a 32*32 gray image. We refer to the collection of these EEG images on the time-line as EEG video. Compare to the EEG topographic maps used for EEG visualization, EEG images generated by AEP can maintain the distance between electrodes more accurately, which reflect more useful information in spatial dimension. Finally, we split each EEG video into 12 segments and perform average operation in each segment. In this way, each EEG video is compressed into a 12-frame short video. The frames of a sample EEG video are shown in Fig. 1(b).

Reducing the EEG classification problem to a video classification problem brings many benefits. The spatial structure of the electrodes has been preserved clearly. Many of the video classification techniques can also be applied to

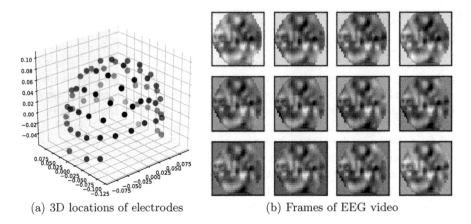

(a) 3D locations of electrodes   (b) Frames of EEG video

Fig. 1. Frames of EEG video generated from EEG signal by project the 3D locations of electrodes to 2D points via AEP algorithm

EEG signal. Due to the inherent structure of CNNs, it is more suited to image and video data classification. Moreover, there are many excellent CNNs such as AlexNet and GoogLeNet that can be used for EEG videos.

Optical flow [21] has been introduced by our approach to represent the variant information of EEG signal. Optical flow is widely used in most video classification method, because it can describe the obvious motion of objects in a visual scene by calculate the motion between two image frames which are taken at times t and $t+\Delta t$ at every pixel position. Consider $f(x, y, t)$ is the pixel of location (x, y) at time t, it moves by distance $(\Delta x, \Delta y)$ in next frame taken at $x + \Delta t$. These pixels has the same value, and the following brightness constancy constraint can be given:

$$f(x, y, t) = f(x + \Delta x, y + \Delta y, t + \Delta t) \qquad (1)$$

Assuming the movement to be small, take Taylor series approximation of right-hand side and ignoring higher-order terms in the Taylor series, we can get the following equation:

$$f(x + \Delta x, y + \Delta y, t + \Delta t) = f(x, y, t) + \frac{\partial f}{\partial x}\Delta x + \frac{\partial f}{\partial y}\Delta y + \frac{\partial f}{\partial t}\Delta t + \ldots \qquad (2)$$

Then remove common terms and divide by Δt to get:

$$\frac{\partial f}{\partial x}\frac{\Delta x}{\Delta t} + \frac{\partial f}{\partial y}\frac{\Delta y}{\Delta t} + \frac{\partial f}{\partial t}\frac{\Delta t}{\Delta t} = \frac{\partial f}{\partial x}u + \frac{\partial f}{\partial y}v + \frac{\partial f}{\partial t} = 0 \qquad (3)$$

where $u = \Delta x/\Delta t$ and $v = \Delta y/\Delta t$. In this equation, (u, v) is the value of optical flow at $f(x, y, t)$ which are responding to magnitude and direction respectively.

To utilize existing implementations and networks used for frame of EEG video, we store optical flow as an image and rescale it to a $[0,255]$ range, and the visualization images are shown in Fig. 2 by mapping direction to Hue value and

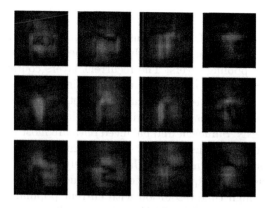

Fig. 2. Visualization of optical flow extracted from EEG video

mapping magnitude to Value plane on HSV image. In this way, optical flow can be processing using the same way as EEG image to learn the global description of EEG videos.

3.3 Network Architecture

We constructed a deep network containing a CNN part and a RNN part for the classification of EEG data. The architecture of our network is shown in Fig. 3. The CNN part and the RNN part were combined through a reshaping operation. Firstly, EEG videos and optical flow were fed into the CNN part. Secondly, a reshaping operation merged and converted the outputs of the CNN part into a 2-dimensional feature vector. Then, the feature vector was fed into the RNN

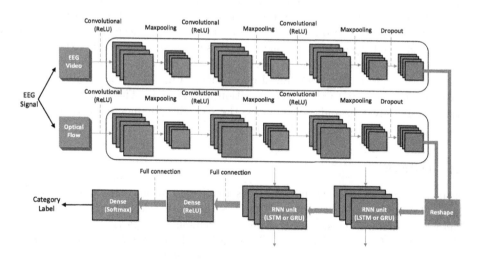

Fig. 3. Architecture of our deep CNN-RNN network

part with two recurrent layers. Finally, the outputs of the RNN part were fed into a dense layer with ReLU and a dense layer with softmax, to obtain a final category label. In our network, we apply 4*4 kernel for convolution layers and 3*3 kernel for max pooling layers. The recurrent layers contain 128 nodes and the full connection layer after the RNN unit contains 64 nodes.

There were two difficulties in training the network, including insufficient dataset and vanishing gradient problem in the time dimension while training the recurrent unit in RNN. Sufficient and balanced data are most important assumes in deep learning to satisfy the necessity of optimizing a tremendous number of weight parameters in neural networks. Unfortunately, this is usually not true for EEG signal because data acquisition is complex and expensive. However, EEG signal have a very high time resolution with current popular signal acquisition equipment. Herein, we train the CNN part with fully sampled video and use 12 frames of short video to train the RNN part. To against vanishing gradient problems while training the RNN part, replacing the simple perceptron hidden units with more complex units, such as Long-Short Term Memory (LSTM) [22] or Gated Recurrent Unit (GRU) [23] which function as memory cells, can help significantly.

4   Experiments

We implemented a mixed BCI-based rehabilitation support system for stroke patients with the EEG classification approach we proposed. Firstly, we obtained the image and depth of the operating platform by Microsoft Kinect2, and then applied a computer vision algorithm to identify targets and show them in the software interface. Then, choices were shown flickering in different frequencies, and the subjects utilized steady state visually evoked potential (SSVEP) to select one of them. Movement destination can be controlled by MI when the system is in move mode. Finally, the operation was performed by a robot arm with fingers.

With our rehabilitation support system, the subjects successfully performed some predefined operations through brain signals. In the grasp experiment (Fig. 4(a)), the subjects select a target, grasp it, move it to another position and put it down. In the pour liquid experiment (Fig. 4(b)), the subjects grasp a water cup, move it to the target position and pour it. These operations are critical for daily life, and can enhance the capacity for independent living of some special patients such as stroke patients.

4.1   Dataset

In the following analysis, we use the dataset collected by our system, from the MI data, while the four health subjects chooses the move direction in our software. The power spectral density after using five frequency filters is shown in Fig. 5. They contain four categories (up, down, left and right imagined movements) signals for control movement direction, which are collected in 2 s time-windows

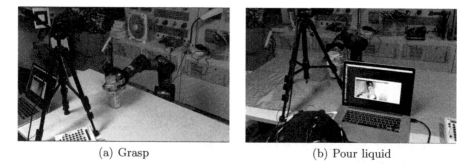

(a) Grasp   (b) Pour liquid

Fig. 4. Mixed BCI-based rehabilitation support system for stroke patients

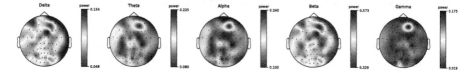

Fig. 5. Visualization of power spectral density on our dataset

by 1000 Hz sampling rate. Totally, we extracted dataset from 10 sessions, and used cross validation to distinguish training sets and test sets.

In addition, we apply our approach on the dataset IIa from BCI competition IV. It contains EEG signal from nine subjects who perform four kinds of motor imagery (right hand, left hand, foot and tongue). These signals are recorded using 22 electrodes by 250 Hz sampling rate and band-pass filtered between 0.5 and 100 Hz. For each subject, two sessions on different days were recorded and thus there are a total of 576 trials.

4.2   Results

We compared our approach against various classifiers commonly used in the field, including support vector machines (SVM), linear discriminant analysis (LDA), CSP+LDA, Autoencoder, Conv1D. SVM, LDA are the classic methods of machine learning. CSP is the most classical hand-designed feature and has been popular in this field for a long time. Autoencoder was introduced to this field recently. Conv1D is an intuitive attempt to apply CNNs to EEG classification. In our experiments, respectively, we tested the performance of these methods and our approach by applying LSTM or GRU as the basic elements of the RNN unit. We repeated many times by using every method we mentioned above, each time taking 9 sessions of data as training sets and 1 session of data as a test set. The performance results are shown in Fig. 6(a) with offline training. The experimental results show that our proposed approach can achieve more accuracy and stability, which is obviously superior to the traditional methods. There is no obvious difference between when we apply LSTM or GRU as the

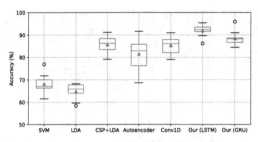
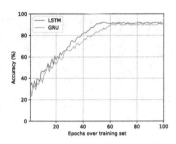

(a) Classification accuracy (%) obtained from 10-flod cross validation

(b) Accuracy of each epoch when training by our approach

Fig. 6. Experiment results between our CNN-RNN network and other approaches based on the dataset collected from our rehabilitation support system.

basic element of RNN, but it can reduce training time when applying GRU as the basic element of RNN. Moreover, it can be demonstrated that our approach can converge quickly and stably (Fig. 6(b)).

Furthermore, Table 1 presents the performance of our approach and traditional approaches on dataset IIa from BCI competition IV. It is clear that the our approach presented in this paper provides a significant improvement in classification accuracy over the traditional approaches. Results also suggested that our approach can achieve better performance when using LSTM. These differences between LSTM and GRU can be due to the fact that LSTM has a more complex structure than GRU.

Table 1. Experiment results (%) on dataset IIa from BCI competition IV, Sn is subject n in the dataset.

	$S1$	$S2$	$S3$	$S4$	$S5$	$S6$	$S7$	$S8$	$S9$	Avg	Std
SVM	78.8	51.7	83.0	61.8	54.2	39.2	83.0	82.6	66.7	66.78	15.25
CSP+LDA	78.1	44.4	81.9	59.0	39.6	50.0	80.9	68.4	77.1	64.38	15.62
Conv1D	78.8	53.1	82.6	60.4	59.0	43.8	82.6	83.3	81.2	69.42	14.45
Our approach (LSTM)	78.8	62.5	83.0	63.5	67.7	45.8	90.3	85.8	72.6	72.22	13.17
Our approach (GRU)	90.6	41.0	95.1	68.1	47.6	54.9	90.3	64.9	80.6	70.34	18.79

Our approach achieves superior accuracy over the traditional methods. However, due to the complexity of the network, careful design and optimization is needed to obtain satisfactory results. Herein, the training time of our network is much longer than other traditional methods because of two-step training strategy, especially when apply LSTM as the RNN unit.

5 Conclusions

In this paper, we propose a novel EEG classification approach, and build a mixed BCI-based rehabilitation support system. This rehabilitation support system can help stroke patients achieve a level of independence. The EEG classification problem is reduced to a video classification problem by converting EEG signal to gray-scale EEG videos. Moreover, optical flow has been introduced into this field, which can characterize the variant of EEG signal in the temporal dimension. To utilize the multimodal information of EEG, we project the position of electrodes to preserve the spatial information, apply multiple frequency filters to represent the spectral information, and utilize the time sequences information of EEG videos and optical flow to represent temporal information. We have constructed a deep neural network designed for these EEG videos and optical flow, and have partially solved the problem of insufficient EEG datasets by training the network in two steps. In future, EEG classification may be improved by state-of-the-art approaches from image classification and video classification. Particularly, we will apply the trained networks from image classification and video classification by transfer learning to solve the problem of insufficient EEG dataset.

Acknowledgments. This work was supported by the National Natural Fund: 91420302 and 91520201. Thanks to the contributors of the open source software used in our system.

References

1. Amiri, S., Fazel-Rezai, R., Asadpour, V.: A review of hybrid brain-computer interface systems. Adv. Hum. Comput. Interact. **2013**, 1 (2013)
2. LeCun, Y., Bengio, Y., Hinton, G.: Deep learning. Nature **521**(7553), 436–444 (2015)
3. Min, S., Lee, B., Yoon, S.: Deep learning in bioinformatics. Briefings in Bioinformatics, p. bbw068 (2016)
4. Schmidhuber, J.: Deep learning in neural networks: an overview. Neural networks **61**, 85–117 (2015)
5. Ng, Y.H., Hausknecht, M., Vijayanarasimhan, S., Vinyals, O., Monga, R., Toderici, G.: Beyond short snippets: deep networks for video classification. In: Computer Vision and Pattern Recognition, pp. 4694–4702 (2015)
6. Yu, D., Deng, L.: Automatic Speech Recognition: A Deep Learning Approach. Springer, London (2014). doi:10.1007/978-1-4471-5779-3
7. Kaiser, V., Kreilinger, A., Müller-Putz, G.R., Neuper, C.: First steps toward a motor imagery based stroke bci: new strategy to set up a classifier. Front Neurosci. **5**, 86 (2011)
8. Waldert, S., Pistohl, T., Braun, C., Ball, T., Aertsen, A., Mehring, C.: A review on directional information in neural signals for brain-machine interfaces. J. Physiol. Paris **103**(3), 244–254 (2009)
9. Ramoser, H., Muller-Gerking, J., Pfurtscheller, G.: Optimal spatial filtering of single trial EEG during imagined hand movement. IEEE Trans. Rehabil. Eng. **8**(4), 441–446 (2000)

10. Aghaei, A.S., Mahanta, M.S., Plataniotis, K.N.: Separable common spatio-spectral patterns for motor imagery bci systems. IEEE Trans. Biomed. Eng. **63**(1), 15–29 (2016)

11. Verma, G.K., Tiwary, U.S.: Multimodal fusion framework: a multiresolution approach for emotion classification and recognition from physiological signals. NeuroImage **102**, 162–172 (2014)

12. Bashivan, P., Rish, I., Yeasin, M., Codella, N.: Learning representations from EEG with deep recurrent-convolutional neural networks. Computer Science (2015)

13. Tan, C., Sun, F., Zhang, W., Liu, S., Liu, C.: Spatial and spectral features fusion for EEG classification during motor imagery in bci. In: 2017 IEEE EMBS International Conference on Biomedical & Health Informatics (BHI), pp. 309–312. IEEE (2017)

14. Mamoshina, P., Vieira, A., Putin, E., Zhavoronkov, A.: Applications of deep learning in biomedicine. Mol. Pharm. **13**(5), 1445 (2016)

15. Greenspan, H., Ginneken, B.V., Summers, R.M.: Guest editorial deep learning in medical imaging: overview and future promise of an exciting new technique. IEEE Trans. Med. Imaging **35**(5), 1153–1159 (2016)

16. An, X., Kuang, D., Guo, X., Zhao, Y., He, L.: A deep learning method for classification of eeg data based on motor imagery. In: International Conference on Intelligent Computing, pp. 203–210 (2014)

17. Cecotti, H., Graser, A.: Convolutional neural networks for p300 detection with application to brain-computer interfaces. IEEE Trans. Pattern Anal. Mach. Intell. **33**(3), 433 (2011)

18. Stober, S., Cameron, D.J., Grahn, J.A.: Using convolutional neural networks to recognize rhythm stimuli from electroencephalography recordings. In: Advances in Neural Information Processing Systems, pp. 1449–1457 (2014)

19. Soleymani, M., Asghariesfeden, S., Pantic, M., Fu, Y.: Continuous emotion detection using EEG signals and facial expressions. In: IEEE International Conference on Multimedia and Expo, pp. 1–6 (2014)

20. Li, J., Struzik, Z., Zhang, L., Cichocki, A.: Feature learning from incomplete EEG with denoising autoencoder. Neurocomputing **165**, 23–31 (2015)

21. Farneback, G.: Two-frame motion estimation based on polynomial expansion. In: Scandinavian Conference on Image Analysis, pp. 363–370 (2003)

22. Gers, F.A., Schmidhuber, J., Cummins, F.: Learning to forget: continual prediction with lstm. neural computation. Neural Comput. **12**(10), 2451–2471 (2000)

23. Cho, K., Merrienboer, B.V., Gulcehre, C., Bahdanau, D., Bougares, F., Schwenk, H., Bengio, Y.: Learning phrase representations using rnn encoder-decoder for statistical machine translation. Computer Science (2014)

An Improved Visual-Tactile P300 Brain Computer Interface

Hongyan Sun, Jing Jin$^{(\boxtimes)}$, Yu Zhang, Bei Wang, and Xingyu Wang

Key Laboratory of Advanced Control and Optimization for Chemical Processes,
Ministry of Education, East China University of Science and Technology,
Shanghai, China
jinjingat@gmail.com

Abstract. Recently, the bimodal BCI has attracted more and more attention. Previous studies have reported that the classification performance of bimodal system was better than that of unimodal system. Based on the fundamental visual-tactile P300 BCI, this paper made a change on the flash pattern of visual stimuli expecting to improve its performance by enhancing the link between visual and tactile modalities. Two patterns were tested in this paper, which respectively were picture-vibrate pattern (producing the visual effect of vibration) and color-change pattern (changing blue to green). The results showed that the picture-vibrate pattern achieved higher classification accuracy and information transfer rate than color-change pattern. The average online bit rate of picture-vibrate pattern including the breaking time between selections, reached 12.49 bits/min, while the color-change pattern's online bit rate reached 8.87 bits/min on average.

Keywords: Brain computer interface · P300 · Visual-tactile · Picture-vibrate pattern · Color-change pattern

1 Introduction

Brain-computer interface (BCI) is a human-computer interaction technique, which uses electroencephalogram (EEG) to control external device directly without the involvement of peripheral nerves or muscle tissues [1, 2]. The P300 based BCI is one of the most popular system because of its high accuracy and information transfer rate [3, 4]. P300 can be evoked by different stimulus modalities, such as visual [4–6], audio [7] or tactile [8]. Some studies have compared these modalities' influences on BCIs [9, 10]. Even though the tactile stimuli achieved lowest accuracy than other modalities for healthy users [9], it outperformed for ALS patients [10]. Therefore, tactile P300 BCI is a viable alternative for patients with visual or audio dysfunction [11].

Several tactile P300 BCIs have been tested successfully. An influential study was conducted by Brouwer and van Erp in 2010 [8]. Six vibrators were placed evenly around subject's waist, and different stimulus onset asynchronies (SOA) were measured by grouping different on- and/or off-time. The result showed that the optimal SOA was close to SOAs of visual P300 BCIs, which provided a baseline for the tactile BCI studies. In recent years, tactile stimuli have been delivered to different parts of the

© Springer International Publishing AG 2017
D. Liu et al. (Eds.): ICONIP 2017, Part II, LNCS 10635, pp. 777–785, 2017.
https://doi.org/10.1007/978-3-319-70096-0_79

human body, such as fingers, chest, head, et al. [12–14], and the tactile BCI system was also used to control a wheelchair successfully [15, 16].

To further improve the performance of tactile P300 BCI, multisensory modalities based BCI systems have also been investigated. Brouwer et al. [17] combined tactile stimuli with visual stimuli, and found that the bimodal stimuli achieved highest classification accuracy compared to unimodal stimuli. Thurlings et al. [18] studied the visual-tactile gaze-independent BCI system, and surveyed the effects of location-congruency and selective attention to modality on the bimodal ERP-BCI. The result showed that location-congruent bimodal stimuli could improve ERP-BCIs, but selective attention to modality had fewer influence on classification performance. In a recent study, an auditory-tactile bimodal P300 BCI was investigated by Yin et al. [19], in which the direction-congruency was also used. And the author found that the proposed bimodal stimulation achieved higher classification accuracy and information transfer rate than unimodal stimulation.

Driver et al. [20] pointed out that the information received from one sensory channel can affect the original feeling obtained from another sensory channel. For example, when the auditory stimuli were delivering, presenting the corresponding visual stimuli would strengthen the understanding of auditory information. In this paper, based on the fundamental visual-tactile P300 BCI system (color-change pattern) [17], we proposed an improved visual-tactile P300 BCI system (picture-vibrate pattern) with the aim of enhancing the link between visual and tactile modalities. The two patterns differed only on the flash pattern of visual stimulation, while the tactile stimulation patterns were all the same.

2   Methods and Materials

2.1   Subjects and Data Acquisition

Six healthy subjects (one female and five males, aged 22–28 years old) participated in this study, which were pad 100 RMB and labeled as S1, S2, S3, S4, S5 and S6. All of them had intact tactile sensation.

EEG data were recorded by a g.USBamp and a g.EEGcap (Guger Technologies, Graz, Austria). The bandpass filter was set between 0.1 Hz–30 Hz, and the sample rate was 256 Hz. According to the international 10-20 system, 14 electrodes were selected, which were Fz, FC1, FC2, C3, Cz, C4, CP3, CP1, CP2, CP4, P3, Pz, P4 and Oz (see Fig. 1). The right mastoid was used as the reference, and front electrode (FPz) was selected as the ground electrode.

2.2   Stimuli and Procedure

In this paper, the visual and tactile stimuli were synchronous and location-congruent [14]. The vibrotactile stimuli were delivered by g.VIBROstims which were powered by a g.STIMbox (g.tec Medical Engineering GmbH, Schiedlberg, Austria). Five parts of body were selected to place vibrators: left wrist, right wrist, abdomen, left ankle and right ankle. The visual stimuli were presented on a 24in. LED monitor (see Fig. 2).

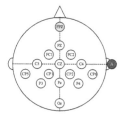

Fig. 1. Electrodes configuration.

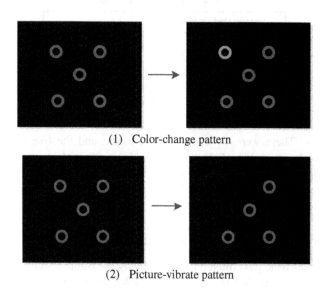

(1) Color-change pattern

(2) Picture-vibrate pattern

Fig. 2. The display during the online runs. The left-upper circle represents the vibrator placed on the left wrist. The right-upper circle represents the vibrator placed on the right wrist. The middle circle represents the vibrator placed on the abdomen. The left-lower circle represents the vibrator placed on the left ankle. The right-lower circle represents the vibrator placed on the right ankle.

The background was black, and the blue circles represented vibrators on corresponding parts of body. Referencing Brouwer's work [8, 17], the stimulus-on time was 200 ms, and the inter-stimulus interval was 400 ms.

In the color-change pattern, the circles changed green during the stimulus-on time, and then reverted to blue during the stimulus-off time. In the picture-vibrate pattern, to produce the visual effect of vibration, the white rectangle moved to the right and left respectively for 50 ms, and backed to the original position respectively for 50 ms (see Fig. 3).

2.3   Offline and Online Protocols

In this study, offline training block and online testing block were all included (see Fig. 4). The offline training block was consisted of three runs, when each run included

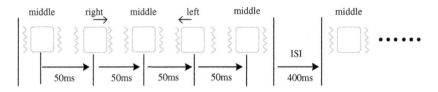

Fig. 3. The presenting sequence of picture-vibrate pattern.

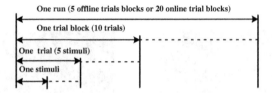

Fig. 4. The flowchart of stimuli.

five trial blocks. There were 10 trials per trial block, and the five stimulators were selected randomly in each trial. In the online block, 20 trial blocks were included, which means that the five targets were tested for four times. Besides, the online block was an adaptive system proposed by Jin et al. [5]. The system would feedback the classification result when the two consecutive outputs were consistent.

2.4   Feature Extraction Procedure and Classification Scheme

The EEG data was band pass filtered (0.1–30 Hz) by the Butterworth filter of 3th order, and down-sampled from 203 Hz to 29 Hz by selecting every seventh sample. Consequently, the size of the feature vector was 14×29 (14 represents the number of the channels and 29 denotes the samples). Bayesian linear discriminant analysis (BLDA) was chosen as the classifier because of its great classification performance by avoiding over-fitting [21].

2.5   Data Analysis

To compare different paradigms' performance, bit rate is an objective measure. Raw bit rate (RBR) was defined by Wolpaw in 2002 [2], which was calculated via

$$B = \{\log_2 N + P \log_2 P + (1 - P) \log_2[(1 - P)/(N - 1)]\} \times T \tag{1}$$

Where P denotes the classification accuracy, N denotes the number of target every trial and T denotes the completion time of the target selection task.

3 Results

3.1 Offline Analysis

Figure 5 shows the averaged ERP amplitude of target across 6 participants over 14 electrodes. The R-squared value is common method to show the time energy of ERP signal, the definition is $r^2 = \left(\frac{\sqrt{N_1 N_2}}{N_1 + N_2} \cdot \frac{\text{mean}(X_1) - \text{mean}(X_2)}{\text{std}(X_1 \cup X_2)}\right)^2$, where X is the features of class, and N is the number of samples. The two patterns' R-square values are shown in Fig. 6.

Figure 7 shows the offline classification accuracies and raw bit rates of each participant overlapped over 1–10 trials. Obviously, the picture-vibrate pattern achieved better offline classification performance than color-change pattern. Figure 8 shows the

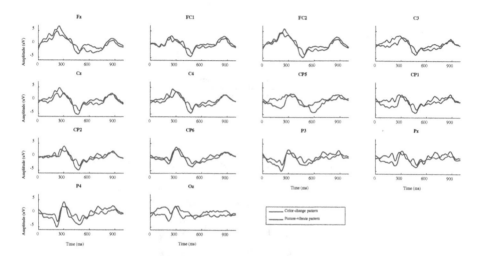

Fig. 5. Grand averaged ERPs of targets across 6 subjects over 14 electrodes.

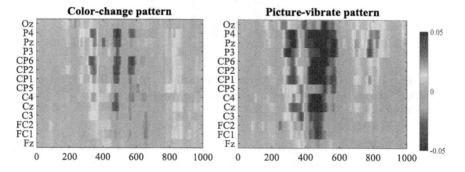

Fig. 6. R-squared values of ERPs from 0 to 1000 ms averaged across 6 subjects.

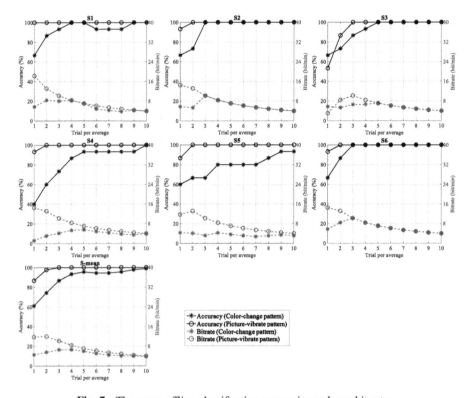

Fig. 7. The mean offline classification accuracies and raw bit rates.

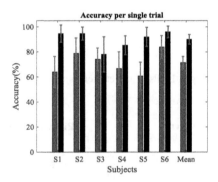

Fig. 8. The mean single-trial classification accuracies across 6 subjects. The red bar represents the average value of color-change pattern, and the black bar represents the average value of picture-change pattern. (Color figure online)

single-trial accuracy of each participant. Paired sample t-test was used to show the difference between the two patterns, and the result shown that picture-vibrate pattern was significantly higher than color-change pattern in single-trial classification accuracy ($t = -4.304$, $p = 0.008$).

3.2 Online Performance

Table 1 shows each participant's online classification performance. The online classification accuracy and required trials were achieved by the classification and identification of BLDA model, and the raw bit rates were calculated by Formula (1). The paired sample t-test showed that the picture-vibrate pattern required significantly fewer trials than color-change pattern ($t = 3.25$, $p = 0.023$). The online classification accuracies and raw bit rates were higher for the picture-vibrate pattern, but the difference between the two patterns were not significant ($t = -1.995$, $p = 0.108$; $t = -2.389$, $p = 0.062$).

Table 1. The online classification accuracies, raw bit rates and average numbers of trials

Subjects	Color-change pattern			Picture-vibrate pattern		
	ACC (%)	RBR (bit/min)	AVT	ACC (%)	RBR (bit/min)	AVT
S1	100	11.81	2.40	100	12.61	2.15
S2	100	11.81	2.40	100	12.78	2.10
S3	90	8.30	2.45	100	11.51	2.50
S4	70	4.39	2.30	100	13.14	2.00
S5	75	4.95	2.55	100	12.61	2.15
S6	100	11.96	2.35	100	12.27	2.25
AVG	89	8.87	2.41	100	12.49	2.19
STD	14	3.54	0.09	0	0.55	0.17

[*] ACC = classification accuracy; RBR = raw bit rate (bit/min); AVT = average number of trials used to classify each target; AVG = average value; STD = standard deviation.

4   Discussion

This paper tested two visual-tactile stimulation patterns: color-change pattern and picture-vibrate pattern. The offline and online results showed that the picture-vibrate pattern achieved higher classification accuracy and information transfer rate than color-change pattern.

In 2014, Thurlings et al. [18] found that bimodal system could evoke larger P300 than unimodal system measured by tAUC. This paper used R-square to represent the energy of ERP signal (see Fig. 6). The red component represented positive potential, and the blue component represented negative potential. It was obvious that the energy of ERP was stronger in the picture-vibrate pattern.

With respect to the offline classification accuracy and raw bit rates (see Fig. 7), all subjects achieved better classification performance in the picture-vibrate pattern. The single trial accuracy of each subject was further calculated in the Fig. 8. The result of paired samples t-test showed that the difference between the two patterns was significant ($p < 0.05$).

During the online block, the subject completed the test of 20 targets. From Table 1 we can see that picture-vibrate pattern obtained higher online classification accuracy and information transfer rate, and required fewer trials to classify each target than color-change pattern. But the result of t-test showed that only the difference of required trials was significant ($p < 0.05$). Because that number of samples were fewer and the data didn't coincided with normal distribution law, which may cause the difference of accuracy and bit rate were not significant ($p > 0.05$).

Some limitations still exist in this paper. The picture-vibrate pattern achieved significantly better classification accuracy than color-change pattern. However, this result may attribute to the difference of visual stimulation. That is, the stronger intensity of visual stimulation may contribute to better classification performance of the bimodal system. The proposal of the picture-vibrate pattern aimed to improve the performance by strengthening the link between different modalities. Therefore, unimodal system in the two patterns should be further conducted and compared with the bimodal system to demonstrate its effectiveness.

5   Conclusion

Based on the previous studies of visual-tactile P300 BCI, this paper made an improvement on the visual stimulation pattern, which used picture-vibrate pattern to substitute traditional color-change pattern for the purpose of enhancing the link between different modalities. The online and offline results showed that the proposed picture-vibrate pattern achieved significantly higher classification accuracy and information transfer rate than color-change pattern, but further studies should been conducted to verify its effectiveness. In general, there are still a lot of rooms for improvement on the bimodal BCI by changing stimulation patterns.

Acknowledgement. This work was supported by the Grant National Natural Science Foundation of China, under Grant Nos. 91420302, 61573142. This work was also supported by the Fundamental Research Funds for the Central Universities (WH1516018, 222201717006) and Shanghai Chenguang Program under Grant 14CG31.

References

1. Mak, J.N., Wolpaw, J.R.: Clinical applications of brain-computer interfaces: current state and future prospects. IEEE Rev. Biomed. Eng. **2**, 187–199 (2009)
2. Wolpaw, J.R., Birbaumer, N., Mcfarland, D.J., Pfurtscheller, G., Vaughan, T.M.: Brain-computer interfaces for communication and control. Clin. Neurophysiol. **113**(6), 767–791 (2002)
3. Farwell, L.A., Donchin, E.: Talking off the top of your head: toward a mental prosthesis utilizing event-related brain potentials. Electroencephalogr. Clin. Neurophysiol. **70**(6), 510–523 (1988)
4. Sellers, E.W., Mcfarland, D.J.: Toward enhanced P300 speller performance. J. Neurosci. Meth. **167**(1), 15–21 (2008)
5. Jin, J., Sellers, E.W., Zhou, S., Zhang, Y., Wang, X., Cichocki, A.: A p300 brain-computer interface based on a modification of the mismatch negativity paradigm. Int. J. Neural Syst. **25**(3), 595–599 (2015)

6. Jin, J., Allison, B.Z., Zhang, Y., Wang, X., Cichocki, A.: An ERP-based BCI using an oddball paradigm with different faces and reduced errors in critical functions. Int. J. Neural Syst. **24**(8), 1450027 (2014)
7. Hill, N.J., Lal, T.N., Bierig, K., Birbaumer, N., Schölkopf, B.: An auditory paradigm for brain–computer interfaces. In: Saul, L.K., Weiss, Y., Botton, L. (eds.) Advances in Neural Information Processing Systems, vol. 17, pp. 569–576. MIT Press, Cambridge (2005)
8. Brouwer, A.M., van Erp, J.B.F.: A tactile P300 brain-computer interface. Front. Neurosci. **4**, 19 (2010)
9. Aloise, F., Lasorsa, I., Schettini, F., Brouwer, A., Mattia, D., Babiloni, F., Salinari, S., Marciani, M.G., Cincotti, F.: Multimodal stimulation for a P300-based BCI. Int. J. Bioelectromagn. **9**(3), 128–130 (2007)
10. Kaufmann, T., Holz, E.M., Kübler, A.: Comparison of tactile, auditory, and visual modality for brain-computer interface use: a case study with a patient in the locked-in state. Front. Neurosci. **7**, 129 (2012)
11. Ortner, R., Lugo, Z., Prückl, R., Hintermüller, C., Noirhomme, Q., Guger, C.: Performance of a tactile P300 speller for healthy people and severely disabled patients. In: Conference Proceedings of IEEE Engineering in Medicine and Biology Society, pp. 2259–2262. IEEE Press, Osaka (2013)
12. van der Waal, M., Severens, M., Geuze, J., Desain, P.: Introducing the tactile speller: an ERP-based brain-computer interface for communication. J. Neural Eng. **9**(4), 045002 (2012)
13. Mori, H., Makino, S., Rutkowski, Tomasz M.: Multi–command chest tactile brain computer interface for small vehicle robot navigation. In: Imamura, K., Usui, S., Shirao, T., Kasamatsu, T., Schwabe, L., Zhong, N. (eds.) BHI 2013. LNCS, vol. 8211, pp. 469–478. Springer, Cham (2013). doi:10.1007/978-3-319-02753-1_47
14. Rutkowski, T.M., Mori, H.: Tactile and bone-conduction auditory brain computer interface for vision and hearing impaired users. J. Neurosci. Methods **244**, 45–51 (2015)
15. Kaufmann, T., Herweg, A., Kübler, A.: Toward brain-computer interface based wheelchair control utilizing tactually-evoked event-related potentials. J. Neuroeng. Rehabil. **11**(1), 7 (2014)
16. Herweg, A., Gutzeit, J., Kleih, S., Kübler, A.: Wheelchair control by elderly participants in a virtual environment with a brain-computer interface (BCI) and tactile stimulation. Biol. Psychol. **121**, 117–124 (2016)
17. Brouwer, A.M., Erp, J.B.F.V., Aloise, F., Cincotti, F.: Tactile, visual, and bimodal P300s: could bimodal P300s boost BCI performance. SRX Neurosci. **2010**, 1–9 (2010)
18. Thurlings, M.E., Brouwer, A.M., Erp, J.B.F.V., Werkhoven, P.: Gaze-independent ERP-BCIs: augmenting performance through location-congruent bimodal stimuli. Front. Neurosci. **8**, 143 (2014)
19. Yin, E., Zeyl, T., Saab, R., Hu, D., Zhou, Z., Chau, T.: An auditory-tactile visual saccade-independent P300 brain–computer interface. Int. J. Neural Syst. **26**(1), 1650001 (2016)
20. Driver, J., Noesselt, T.: Multisensory interplay reveals crossmodal influences on 'Sensory-specific' brain regions, neural responses, and judgments. Neuron **57**(1), 11–23 (2008)
21. Hoffmann, U., Vesin, J.M., Ebrahimi, T., Diserens, K.: An efficient P300-based brain-computer interface for disabled subjects. J. Neurosci. Meth. **167**(1), 115–125 (2008)

A New Hybrid Feature Selection Algorithm Applied to Driver's Status Detection

Peng-fei Ye, Lan-lan Chen[✉], and Ao Zhang

Key Laboratory of Advanced Control and Optimization for Chemical Processes,
Ministry of Education, East China University of Science and Technology, 130
Meilong Road, Shanghai 200237, China
llchen@ecust.edu.cn

Abstract. This research introduces a framework based on multimodal feature analysis and hybrid feature selection algorithm for improving the recognition rate of driver's status. In order to provide rich information about physiological conditions of human operators, a variety of physiological features are widely extracted from time, spectral, wavelet and nonlinear domains. The redundant and noisy parts of the original feature set could negatively influence the identification performance and occupy limited computing resource. Therefore, a new hybrid feature selection approach is proposed to handle the high dimensionality of feature space and improve classification precision simultaneously. Decision Tree and Sparse Bayesian Learning were employed to generate the initial feature subset that could be further optimized by the adaptive tabu search with Fisher classifier. Finally, three-level driver's stress statuses were discriminated by using support vector machine. Our experimental results show that the proposed algorithm has achieved satisfactory identification rate of driver's status with compact feature vector.

Keywords: Driver's status detection · Multiple physiological signals analysis · Hybrid feature selection · Tabu search

1 Introduction

Driving safety requires driver under a relaxed mind and high vigilance level. Various types of unfit driving statuses, such as stress, drowsy, fatigue and distraction, deteriorate the performance of a driver and may lead to dangerous behavior even fatal traffic accidents [1]. Recently, government and automakers pay more attention to the highly integrated and economic solutions for in-vehicle safety assistant systems.

Researchers in the past have validated the analysis of physiological signals as an effective approach to evaluate stress level, fatigue and emotion statuses of human operators [2]. In literature, multiple kinds of physiological signals such as galvanic skin response (GSR), skin temperature (ST), blood volume pulse (BVP), electrocardiogram (ECG), respiration and electroencephalogram (EEG) have been reported for the detection of driver's status [3, 4]. Multi-modal features have been extracted from time, spectral, wavelet even nonlinear analysis. However, diverse bio-signals and multi-modal feature generation inevitably produce a high dimensional feature space.

© Springer International Publishing AG 2017
D. Liu et al. (Eds.): ICONIP 2017, Part II, LNCS 10635, pp. 786–795, 2017.
https://doi.org/10.1007/978-3-319-70096-0_80

The redundant and noisy parts of the original feature set could negatively influence the identification performance and occupy limited computing resource. Recently, many hybrid strategies have been applied efficiently to solve the challenges in high-dimensional dataset and made a good compromise between categorization performance and computational efficiency. This paper attempts to propose a novel feature selection method to eliminate the redundant and noisy part of features, shorten the computational time of model training, and improve the performance of categorization task.

2   Experimental Materials

First, we will introduce the driving dataset containing different driving stress conditions which we want to classify. The signals used in this research were contributed to NIH PhysioBank Database by Healey and Picard [5]. Totally 27 drive runs were recorded from nine drivers while they were driving on a prescribed route. The signals were recorded during three different driving conditions and related to low, medium and high stress statuses. Four channels of physiological signals were analyzed: ECG with the sampling frequency (F_S) of 496 Hz, GSR recorded on the left hand and the left foot with the F_S of 31 Hz, and respiration measured through chest cavity expansion with the F_S of 31 Hz.

For each drive test, three 10-min data were selected from low, medium and high stress driving periods respectively. The selected data is further divided into 100-sec segments with an advance of 10 s. For each drive test, three 10-min data were selected from low, medium and high stress driving periods respectively. The selected data is further divided into 100-sec segments with an advance of 10 s.

3   Methods

The general process of the proposed system is illustrated in Fig. 1. This research is mainly concentrated on feature generation and feature selection procedure to search for the most relevant and useful feature subset from the original high-dimensional feature space.

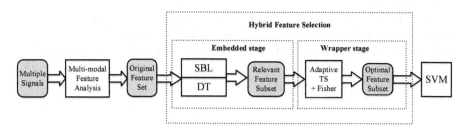

Fig. 1. The general process of the proposed system.

3.1   Feature Extraction

After initial preprocessing, multimodal features are extracted from the time, spectral, wavelet and nonlinear analysis for each segment. Totally, 154 features are obtained and the overview of all the features extracted from multiple physiological signals is listed in Table 1.

Table 1. Multi-modal features extracted from multiple physiological signals

Domain	Features	Signals
Time	Statistics for raw signals: mean, standard deviation (STD), variance, root mean square (RMS), maximum (max), minimum (min)	ALL
	Waveform features: peak number sum, magnitude sum, duration sum and area sum	FGSR
	Statistics for the first order difference sequence (FOD) and the second order difference (SOD) sequence	HGSR
Spectral	Spectral power in 0–0.1 Hz, 0.1–0.2 Hz, 0.2–0.3 Hz, 0.3–0.4 Hz, and total band	Respiration
	Spectral energy in 0–0.04 Hz (VLF), 0.04–0.15 Hz (LF), 0.15–0.5 Hz (HF), total band and the ratio of them	HR
	Statistic features of spectral power in 0–0.5 Hz	GSR
Wavelet	The mean and STD of relevant wavelet coefficients computed from five detail signals and approximation signal, which were generated by wavelet decomposition with db4 wavelet family	ALL
Non-linear	Approximate Entropy, C0 Complexity, Sample Entropy, Hurst Exponent, Permutation Entropy, Fractal Dimension	ALL

3.2   Feature Selection

The design framework for the proposed hybrid feature selection method is also presented in Fig. 1. In the embedded stage, two approaches are employed to generate the initial feature subset that could be further optimized by the wrapper method with corresponding classifier in the next stage.

Embedded stage

The embedded stage is an important part for the proposed hybrid strategy which could initially eliminate the irrelevant, redundant and ineffective feature. Here, Decision Tree (DT) and Sparse Bayesian Learning (SBL) are employed in the embedded stage.

Decision Tree builds classification or regression models in the form of a tree structure, which can handle both nominal and numerical data. It breaks down a dataset into smaller and smaller subsets while at the same time an associated decision tree is incrementally developed. A decision tree can easily be transformed into a set of rules by mapping from the root node to the leaf nodes one by one. Once the decision rules have been determined, it is possible to use the rules to predict new node values based on new or unseen data. In the literature, Decision Tree has been applied in the selection process of features [6].

Sparse Bayesian Learning (SBL) was originally proposed as a machine learning algorithm by Tipping. The solution of SBL has a strong sparseness, since the parametric Gaussian distribution is used as the prior distribution of the solution in SBL. The sparse solution obtained by SBL can greatly reduce the redundancy and complexity of the model. Zhang et al. recommended a sparse Bayesian method for selecting the important P300 features from EEG in the application of brain-computer interfaces [7].

Wrapper stage

Another indispensable part of the hybrid strategy is the wrapper stage, where adaptive Tabu search algorithm combined with Fisher classifier is utilized. TS algorithm was proposed by Glover to solve combinational optimization problem. Recently, Tabu search algorithm has obtained promising results on feature selection tasks especially when the search space is noisy with numerous local optima [8].

The detailed process for the Tabu search algorithm is introduced below. The algorithm starts with an initial solution generated by one of the embedded methods. Then it is during the phase of initialization including initializing tabu list, constructing objective function, deciding the aspiration criterion and setting termination condition. This is followed by treating initial solution as the current best solution and evaluating its cost value. Next is the key step of TS. Setting the current solution as the starting point, the neighborhood and candidate list are generated via replacing one feature from the current solution in each iteration. The neighborhood optimal solution is found according to the principle that the chosen solution has the minimum of cost value from candidate list. The current best solution and the new starting point are replaced with the neighborhood optimal solution if the minimum is smaller than the cost value of the current best solution, otherwise the new starting point is regarded from the candidate list that doesn't belong to tabu list. Start the next iteration cycle from the new starting point if termination condition isn't satisfied after updating tabu list, otherwise finish the search and return the best solution.

Algorithm 1. Hybrid Algorithm for Feature Selection

Step1: Using embedded methods to generate the initial solution S;

Step2: Initialize tabu list, objective function $Cost(S)$ and aspiration criterion

Step3: $S^* \leftarrow S$,evaluate $Cost(S^*)$

Step4: WHILE (termination condition is not satisfied) do

      Begin

        (1) Generate neighborhood of S via replacing one feature for each iteration;

        (2) Set candidate solution set OpenList(S) by selecting a certain number of
solutions from the neighborhood of S;

        (3) while OpenList(S)$\neq \Phi$ do

            Find the best neighborhood solution S' from OpenList(S) which makes
$Cost(S')$ become the minimum value;

            IF $Cost(S')<Cost(S^*)$

                $S^* = S'$;

                $S = S'$;

            Else

                Find the best solution S' that is not in tabu list T;

                $S = S'$;

            End IF

            End while

        (4) Update tabu list;

      End

    End WHILE

Step5: End search and return best solution.

Several crucial factors in Tabu search algorithm should be carefully determined as shown in Fig. 2.

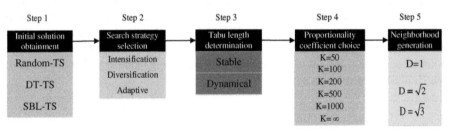

Fig. 2. The crucial factors determination for adaptive Tabu search

(1) Initial solution

Here, initial solution has been obtained by Decision Tree (DT) and Sparse Bayesian Learning (SBL) methods instead of the random manner, since the embedded methods can eliminate the irrelevant and redundant features effectively.

(2) Search strategy

Usually, intensification search strategy (ISS) and diversification search strategy (DSS) could be used to establish candidate list. ISS can intensify and achieve more sufficient search in the neighborhood of current best solution. While DSS has more possibilities to realize global optimization since DSS helps to escape from local optimum by changing the search direction. To combine the merits of both approaches, an adaptive search strategy based on intensification and diversification search strategy (ASS-ID) is adopted to optimize search result.

(3) Tabu length

Tabu length defines the iterations in which the solutions can't be selected unless aspiration criterion is met. Usually, stable tabu length runs more effectively while it tends to fall into cycle dilemma which indicates the algorithm can't escape from local optimal plight based on the current tabu length. In this case, tabu length can be regarded as a dynamical variable, here change rule is set according to search performance and the nature of problem.

(4) Objective function and proportionally coefficient

Two items have been considered into the objective function as shown in Eq. 1, where *rate* and *num* reflect classification performance and the number of selected features respectively. *rate* is the sum-of-squares of $error_1$, $error_2$ and $error_3$, which indicate the wrong identification rate for each stress level. Additionally, proportionally coefficient K is defined as the ratio of k_1/k_2, where k_1 and k_2 are the weight coefficients of classification rate and feature number.

$$Cost = k_1 \cdot rate + k_2 \cdot num \qquad (1)$$

$$rate = error_1^2 + error_2^2 + error_3^2 \qquad (2)$$

$$K = k_1/k_2 \qquad (3)$$

(5) Neighborhood

Neighborhood could be gained by randomly inverting d features from N original features when $d = D^2$, which can include $N!/[(N-d)! \times d!]$ possible solutions. Then candidate list is acquired via abstracting part of solutions from neighborhood.

3.3 Classification

We have two links to the classifier. The first link lies in TS algorithm, which incorporates Fisher classifier to assess the identification capacity of the generated feature set. The second link lies in the last procedure of the identification task, which uses SVM with linear kernel as the final classifier. Totally, fourteen sets of drive data are utilized, one set of data is randomly conscripted as the test set, and the remaining 13 sets of data

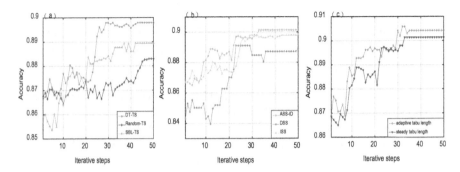

Fig. 3. Determination of crucial factors for hybrid feature selection method. (a) Results for different kinds of initial solution. (b) Results of TS for three kinds of search strategies, i.e., ISS, DSS and ASS-ID. (c) Results of TS based on stable and adaptive tabu length.

are used as the training set. 14-fold cross validation is performed and the mean results of 14 times cross validation is regarded as the final result.

4 Results

4.1 Determination of Several Crucial Factors for Hybrid Algorithm

We show the results using different initial solution, search strategies and tabu length in Fig. 3 and compare the results of TS algorithm based on different Euclidean distance and different proportionality coefficient in Fig. 4.

The search results for different initial solutions generated by SBL, DT and random manner are presented in Fig. 3a. Hybrid algorithms excelled TS with random initial solution in search results. Furthermore, the result of DT-TS was distinctly superior to those of SBL-TS and random manner in both accuracy and convergence rate.

The search results using three kinds of search strategies are illustrated in Fig. 3b. ASS-ID inherited the advantages of ISS and DSS. The speed of accuracy was rising gently, which was similar to ISS. Furthermore, obvious promotion appeared at some iteration steps (such as the 23rd iteration), which indicated the algorithm jumped out of local optimal plight thanks to the characteristic of DSS. In conclusion, an effective improvement on the quality of search result could be achieved by ASS-ID.

Additionally, both the classification accuracy and convergence rate using adaptive tabu length presented some improvements compared to those with stable tabu length (Fig. 3c).

Figure 4 illustrates the results of TS algorithm based on different Euclidean distance and different proportionality coefficient. First, we discuss the choice of proportionality coefficient. Figure 4a, b and c show the trend of identification accuracy in iterations while the feature reduction rate is illustrated in Fig. 4d, e, and f. $K = 50$, 100 and 200 should be discarded according to the change trend of accuracy, and $K = $ infinity was also unsuitable for application with the consideration of feature reduction. The acceptable accuracy was obtained under proportionally coefficient

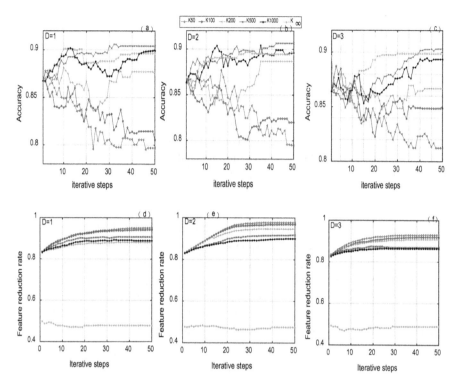

Fig. 4. Results of algorithm based on different Euclidean distance and different proportionality coefficient

$K = 500$ and 1000 and finally $K = 500$ was chosen for adoption because its results were slightly superior to that of $K = 1000$.

Furthermore, we discuss the selection for appropriate neighborhood D (i.e., Euclidean distance $d = D^2$). A moderate scale of candidate list is helpful to reduce the calculation amount and find a better solution faster. Moreover, this finite search in the solution space does not have a bad effect on the quality of the solution from a global perspective. Here, the candidate list contained 80 solutions, which was a subset of the neighborhood space. When $D = \sqrt{2}$ and $D = \sqrt{3}$, the scale of neighborhood was so large that could produce many possibilities of solutions while only a small part of them which belong to candidate list were searched and used. That is to say, large amount of solutions in neighborhood were never searched and used by our proposed algorithm. While choosing which part of the neighborhood space for further searching brought about another problem, i.e., the randomness and instability of solutions. This was the main limitation of bigger Euclidean distance. In conclusion, neighborhood solution space generated by $D = 1$ was more appropriate for Tabu search algorithm especially when original feature dimension was high.

4.2   Comparison of Different Feature Selection Methods

Table 2 makes a comparison for the classification performance tested on the original full feature set and the selected feature set using different feature selection techniques. In single embedded mode, the cost value presented an obvious reduction although the identification precision using single SBL approach was a little lower than that using original feature set. In single wrapper mode, the identification precision on basic TS is improved but no so significant. Additionally, the effect of feature reduction was not as obvious as that of single embedded method. The results of the hybrid mode were the best. As for the proposed DT-TS algorithm, not only the identification precision but also the feature reduction rate were superior to those of the above five situations.

Table 2. Results for different methods in feature selection process

Methods		Sensitivity	Specificity	Precision	Feature number	Cost value
Raw	All features	0.878	0.939	0.892	154	18.14
Embedded	SBL	0.866	0.933	0.883	28	6.12
	DT	0.871	0.935	0.896	27	5.47
Wrapper	TS	0.879	0.940	0.893	51	7.4
Hybrid	SBL-TS	0.897	0.948	0.901	24	4.44
	DT-TS	0.905	0.949	0.914	15	3.07

5   Discussions and Conclusions

An effective driver's status detection system with multi-modal physiological feature generation and hybrid feature selection algorithm has been developed and tested in this research. The main contribution of this paper is to improve the recognition rate of driver's status under different driving stress conditions using optimal physiological sensors and feature sets. Several explanations for the obtained results are listed as follows.

In order to provide rich information about the physiological conditions of human operators, multimodal feature generation is proposed. The larger the number of features adopted, the larger the possibility of searching for an optimal feature subset.

Compared with single feature selection method, the hybrid approach can improve the identification rate of drive stress using more economic feature set and make a good compromise between the operation efficiency and effectiveness. There are possible reasons for its superiority. The first reason is that the approaches in the embedded stage initially eliminate the irrelevant, redundant and ineffective features which could greatly reduce the computational complexity and enhance the feasibility for the successive wrapper method. The second reason is that in the wrapper stage the Tabu search with adaptive search strategy, variable tabu length and optimized objective function makes it more capable to find the better solution and escape from local optimal plight.

Future work can be carried out from the following aspects. First, the combination of other algorithms for feature selection can be employed, such as the incorporation of different filter, embedded and wrapper methods. Second, in the wrapper stage, the combination of global search methods (genetic algorithm, neural network) and local search algorithms (simulated annealing, Hill climbing) could be explored in depth. Third, other physiological signals like EEG, BVP, EMG and EOG can be researched.

Acknowledgement. This work is partly supported by National Natural Science Foundation of China (Nos. 61201124, 51407078) and Fundamental Research Funds for the Central Universities (222201717006, WH1414022).

References

1. Ji, Q., Zhu, Z., Lan, P.: Real-time nonintrusive monitoring and prediction of driver fatigue. IEEE Trans. Veh. Technol. **53**, 1052–1068 (2004)
2. Conati, C.: Probabilistic assessment of user's emotions in educational games. J. Appl. Artif. Intell. **16**(7–8), 555–575 (2002)
3. Fu, R., Wang, H., Zhao, W.: Dynamic driver fatigue detection using hidden Markov model in real driving condition. Expert Syst. Appl. **63**, 397–411 (2016)
4. Sahayadhas, A., Sundaraj, K., Murugappan, M., et al.: Physiological signal based detection of driver hypovigilance using higher order spectra. Expert Syst. Appl. **42**(22), 8669–8677 (2015)
5. Healey, J.A., Picard, R.W.: Detecting stress during real-world driving tasks using physiological sensors. IEEE Trans. Intell. Transp. Syst. **6**(2), 156–166 (2005)
6. Dębska, B., Guzowska-Świder, B.: Decision trees in selection of featured determined food quality. Anal. Chim. Acta **705**(1), 261–271 (2011)
7. Zhang, Y., Zhou, G., Jin, J., et al.: Sparse bayesian classification of EEG for brain–computer interface. IEEE Trans. Neural Netw. Learn. Syst. **27**(11), 2256–2267 (2015)
8. Ghadyani, M., Shahzadi, A.: Adaptive joint sparse recovery algorithm based on Tabu search. Neurocomputing **224**, 9–18 (2017)

Deep Learning Method for Sleep Stage Classification

Ling Cen[1](✉), Zhu Liang Yu[2], Yun Tang[1], Wen Shi[1],
Tilmann Kluge[3], and Wee Ser[1]

[1] School of Electrical and Electronic Engineering, Nanyang Technological University,
Singapore, Singapore
{cenling,shiwen,ewser}@ntu.edu.sg, YTANG014@e.ntu.edu.sg
[2] South China University of Technology, Guangzhou, China
zlyu@scut.edu.cn
[3] Austrian Institute of Technology, GmBH,
Donau City Strasse 1, 1220 Vienna, Austria
tilmann.kluge@ait.ac.at

Abstract. When humans fall asleep, they go through five sleep stages,
i.e. wakefulness, stages of non-rapid eye movement consisting of N1, N2
and N3, and rapid eye movement (REM). Monitoring the proportion and
distribution of sleep stages can help to diagnose sleep disorder and measure sleep quality. Traditional process of sleep scoring by well-trained
experts is quite subjective and time-consuming. Automatic sleep staging analysis has demonstrated a lot of usefulness and attracted increasing attentions. With the massively growing size of accessible data and
the rapid development of computational power, Deep Learning (DL)
has achieved significant improvement in a lot of areas. In this work,
an intelligent system for sleep stage classification is developed by using
polysomnographic (PSG) data including electroencephalogram (EEG),
electrooculogram (EOG) and electromyogram (EMG) based on a DL
architecture. In our method, the Convolutional Neural Network (CNN)
is employed as the feature detector, which is combined with a Hidden
Markov Model (HMM) for its strengths of dealing with temporal data.
Experiment results have shown a performance improvement compared to
those methods with hand-crafted features or unsupervised feature learning by Deep Brief Learning (DBN).

Keywords: Sleep stage · Machine Learning (ML) · Classification · Deep
Learning (DL) · Convolutional Neural Network (CNN) · Hidden Markov
Model (HMM)

1 Introduction

When humans fall asleep at night, they can typically pass through several
sleep transitions or sleep stages that consist of wakefulness (W), stages of
non-rapid eye movement that are divided into 4 stages of N1-N4 based on

© Springer International Publishing AG 2017
D. Liu et al. (Eds.): ICONIP 2017, Part II, LNCS 10635, pp. 796–802, 2017.
https://doi.org/10.1007/978-3-319-70096-0_81

Rechtschaffen & Kales rules [1] or 3 stages by combining N3 and N4 into one stage based on Academy of Sleep Medicine (AASM) [2], and Rapid Eye Movement (REM). Monitoring the proportion and distribution of sleep stages can help to diagnose sleep disorder and measure sleep quality [3]. Sleep stages can be classified by measuring electrophysiological signals such as Electroencephalogram (EEG), Electrocardiogram (ECG), Electrooculogram (EOG) and Electromyogram (EMG), etc. Deeper sleep pattern is in general marked by the appearance of a slow wave (delta) on EEG, which is followed by an increase in the amplitude value. When the deepest stages is reached, however, the amplitude is decreased. The similar phenomena can be observed in EMG signals. As for EOG signals, the fluctuation of amplitude occurs typically when sleep stages getting deeper and the peak of amplitude change takes place when the REM is reached where the activity of eye movement will happen. Traditionally, sleep stages are manually evaluated and monitored by well-trained experts. It is, however, a subjective process and a tedious task requiring much time and effort of physician [4]. With the rapid development of Artificial Intelligence (AI), intelligent systems for automatic stage scoring and sleep quality monitoring have attracted increasing attentions and efforts from scholars.

With the massively growing size of accessible data and the rapid development of computational power, Deep Learning (DL) has achieved significant improvement in many areas, e.g. natural language processing, object recognition, speech recognition, handwriting recognition, biomedical signal processing, etc., in comparison with other state-of-the-art machine learning methods. Recently, researchers start to apply deep learning in sleep studies [4–8]. When evaluating sleep stages based on polysomnographic (PSG) data by using machine learning technologies, due to the complexity of multi-modal sleep data, feature extraction is quite difficult, and moreover, the size of the feature space may grow to quite large, which makes feature selection ultimately necessary. Deep learning is able to automatically learn feature representation from raw data with various deep architectures in either unsupervised or supervised fashions. In [5], deep belief networks (DBNs) were employed for unsupervised feature learning from handcraft features or raw sleep data, which gave a higher classification accuracies compared to fine-tuned hand-crafted features with a Gaussian observation hidden Markov model (GOHMM). It has been demonstrated that deep learning can model data with complex structures and address the variant problem caused by various subjects in sleep data [9, 10].

In this work, an automatic system for sleep stage scoring is developed by taking advantages of powerful DL technologies. The PSG data including EEG, EOG and EMG are used for sleep stage classification. A deep feed-forward Neural Network, Convolutional Neural Network (CNN) is employed to learn the characteristics of the high-order correlation among the visible data and corresponding labels as a feature detector, which eliminates the need of hand-crafted feature extraction and selection. The CNN is then combined with a Hidden Markov Model (HMM) for its strengths of dealing with temporal data bearing sequential nature for sleep stage classification.

The remainder of the paper is organized as follows. In Sect. 2, the proposed system for classifying sleep stages is presented. The experimental results obtained through model evaluation are summarized in Sect. 3, followed with concluding remarks provided in Sect. 4.

2   Prediction Model

Sleep staging is evaluated based on different types of PSG signals that are collected from various subjects, either healthy people or patients with different disorders, which leads to complex data characteristics and variant problem. The success of classification is heavily dependent on effective feature engineering when traditional shallow learning algorithms are employed. To address this in our method, we take advantages of powerful deep learning technologies as feature detectors, which eliminates the need of hand-crafted feature extraction and selection.

Deep learning, developed since 2006 [11], refers to a class of machine learning techniques and architectures, in which many layers of non-linear information processing stages are exploited in hierarchical architectures for feature representation learning and pattern classification or recognition [12]. Compared to shallow models like Support Vector Machines (SVM), deep learning networks represent multi-layer neural networks with deeper structures, in which the data are processed at and in between of the multiple layers. Such networks are theoretically capable of implementing any non-linear functions for modeling the relationship between the inputs and outputs. The strength of DL networks lies in their abilities to identify structures in the lower-level data representations and use them to clean, cluster and provide much more organized features as input for the learning at the higher levels of data abstraction. In recent years with drastically increased chip processing abilities, e.g. GPU units, significantly lowered cost of computing hardware, and recent advances in research of machine learning and signal/information processing, DL techniques have gain increasing attention and popularity [12]. The DL can adjust the structure and its depth to fit and accommodate the complexity of various predictive problems at hand, which have been successfully applied in various areas, e.g. visual object recognition, image processing, speech recognition, phonetic recognition, voice search, speech and image feature coding, semantic utterance classification, hand-writing recognition, natural language processing, information retrieval, etc. [12].

Depending on the applications, DL techniques can be broadly categorized into 3 architectures: generative deep architectures associated with unsupervised feature learning, discriminative deep architectures for discrimination purpose in pattern classification by characterizing the posterior distributions of classes conditioned on the visible data, and hybrid deep architectures with the goal of discrimination assisted with outcomes of generative architectures [12]. Convolutional Neural Network (CNN) is one of the most popular deep learning methods for discriminative deep architectures. A CNN can be seen as a feed-forward neural network, in which each module consists of a convolutional layer and a pooling layer that subsamples the output of the convolutional layer and reduces the data rate from the layer below. The weight sharing in the convolutional layer, together with appropriately chosen pooling schemes, endows the CNN with some invariance properties (e.g., translation invariance), which, commonly used in computer vision and image recognition, have been found highly effective.

In our method, sleep stage classes are automatically evaluated by combining a CNN and a HMM. Figure 1 shows the flowchart of the whole system. The CNN is employed as a feature detector to characterize the high-order correlation properties of the PSG data for sleep staging analysis. Considering the sequential nature of sleep data, the CNN is combined with the Hidden Markov Model (HMM) for its strengths of dealing with temporal data, in which the output from the last fully-connected layer of the CNN are fed into HMM to yield final labels in sleep stage classification.

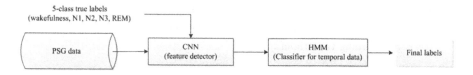

Fig. 1. Flowchart of the learning model in the system.

3   Experiments

To evaluate the effectiveness of the proposed method, the experiment was carried out on the benchmark dataset used in [5]. The dataset, which can be downloaded in PhysioNet [13], was provided by St. Vincent's University Hospital and University College Dublin. The dataset consists of 25 acquisitions from subjects with suspected sleep disordered breathing, which is described in Table 1. Five sleep stages, i.e. wakefulness, N1, N2, N3, and REM, were evaluated by a sleep expert. Their composition is illustrated in Fig. 2.

The data were preprocessed as described in [5], which can be concluded as:

1. processed by notch filtering at 50 Hz for canceling out power line disturbances;
2. filtered with a band-pass filter of 0.3 to 32 Hz for EEG and EOG, and 10 to 32 Hz for EMG;
3. down-sampled to 64 Hz;
4. removing each epoch before and after a sleep stage switch from the training set to avoid possible subsections of mislabeled data within one epoch;
5. normalized with zero mean and unit standard deviation.

One EEG channel of C3-A2, two EOG channels and one EMG channel were used in our experiment. Each sample was stored in a 4×64 matrix that was reshaped with a dimension of 16×16 as input of the CNN. There are two stacks of convolutional and sub-sampling layer in the CNN model. The first convolutional layer has 6 feature maps and a kernel size of 5×5, and the second convolutional

Table 1. Description of the database.

	Proportion (%)
No. acquisitions	25
Gender	21 males
	4 females
Average age	50
Average height (cm)	173
Average weight (kg)	95
PSG data	2 EEG channels (C3-A2 and C4-A1)
	2 EOG channels
	1 EMG channel using $10 - 20$ electrode placements system
Sampling rate (Hz)	128 Hz for EEG
	64 Hz for EOG and EMG
Average recording time (hours)	6.9

Sleep stage composition

■ Awake ■ N1 ■ N2 ■ N3 ■ REM

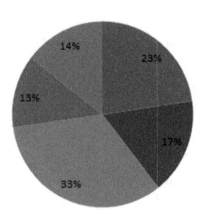

Fig. 2. Data proportion of sleep stages in the dataset.

layer doubles the feature maps to 12 while using the same kernel size. The scale sizes in the 2 sub-sampling layers are both 2.

A leave-one-out cross-validation was conducted, in which each time one acquisition was selected from the 25 acquisition for testing and the other acquisitions were for model training. The average classification accuracy across wakefulness, N1, N2, N3, and REM is 69.78%. Compared to the results having an average accuracy of 67.4% achieved by employing the DBN to learn features from raw

PSG data and the HMM as the classifier in [5], the developed DL based model can achieve more accurate classification outcome. If using 28 handmade features carefully extracted according to the characteristics of stages in both time and frequency domain, the average accuracy with a Gaussian observation hidden Markov model (GOHMM) is only 63.9% [5], which is, as shown in Fig. 3, much lower than those based on feature representation learned by using the DL methods.

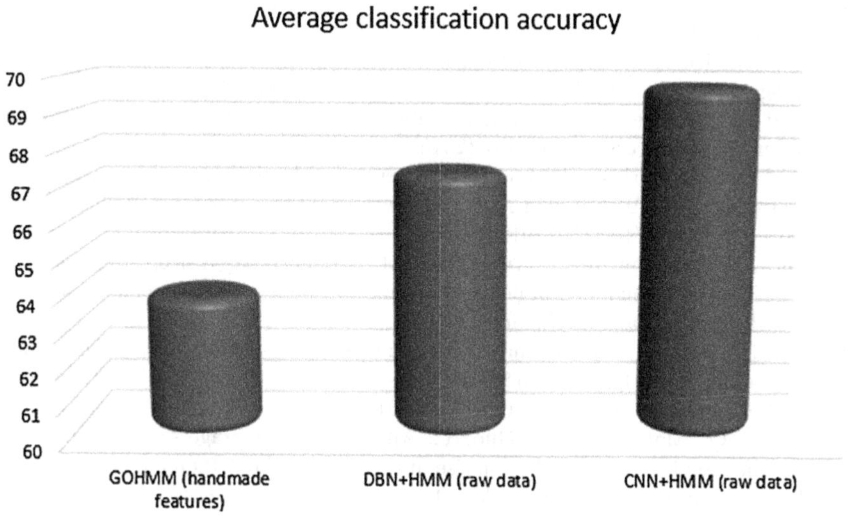

Average classification accuracy

Fig. 3. Comparison among different models.

4   Conclusions

This work intends to explore sleep stage scoring by using the deep learning architecture, in which sleep stages are classified into wakefulness, N1, N2, N3 of non-Rapid Eye Movement (non-REM), and REM by developing a learning model based on Convolutional Neural Network (CNN) and Hidden Markov Model (HMM) with polysomnographic (PSG) data including electroencephalogram (EEG), electrooculogram (EOG) and electromyogram (EMG) signals. The CNN is employed to characterize the high-order correlation properties of the PSG data, which is combined with the Hidden Markov Model (HMM) for its strengths of dealing with temporal data in sleep stage classification. It has been shown from the experimental results that classification performance can be improved compared to those achieved by using hand-crafted features or features learned with Deep Brief Networks (DBN).

Acknowledgements. This work was supported in part by the National Natural Science Foundation of China under Grants 61573150 and 61573152, Guangdong innovative project 2013KJCX0009, Guangzhou project 201604016113 and 201604046018.

References

1. Rechtschaffen, A., Kales, A.: A Manual of standardized terminology, techniques and scoring system for sleep stages of human subjects, pp. 3–7. Government Printing Office, Public Health Service, Washington DC (1968)
2. Iber, C., Ancoli-Israel, S., Chesson, A.L., Quan, S.F.: The AASM Manual for the Scoring of Sleep and Associated Events: Rules, Terminology, and Technical Specifications. American Academy of Sleep Medicine, Westchester (2007)
3. Carskadon, M.A., Rechtschaifen, A.: Monitoring and staging human sleep. In: Kryger, M.H., Rpth, T., Dement, W.C. (eds.) Principles and Practice of Sleep Medicine, 4th edn. Saunders Elsevier (2005)
4. Zhang, J.M., Wu, Y., Bai, J., Chen, F.Q.: Automatic sleep stage classification based on sparse deep belief net and combination of multiple classifiers. Trans. Inst. Measure. Control **38**(4), 435–451 (2016)
5. Langkvist, M., Karlsson, L., Loutfi, A.: Sleep stage classification using unsupervised feature learning. Advances in Artificial Neural Systems, vol. 2012, 9 pages (2012), http://dx.doi.org/10.1155/2012/107046
6. Yulita, I.N., Fanany, M.I., Arymurthy, A.M.: Sequence-based sleep stage classification using conditional neural fields. In: Computational and Mathematical Methods in Medicine. Hindawi Publishing (2016)
7. Giri, E.P., Fanany, M.I., Arymurthy, A.M.: Combining Generative and Discriminative Neural Networks for Sleep Stages Classification. In: Computational Intelligence and Neuroscience. Hindawi Publishing (2016)
8. Tsinalis, O., Mathews, P.M., Guo, Y.: Automatic sleep stage scoring using time-frequency analysis and stacked sparse autoencoders. Ann. Biomed. Eng. (2015)
9. Glorot, X., Bordes, A., Bengio, Y.: Deep sparse rectifier neural networks. Aistats **15**, 315–323 (2011)
10. Supratak, A., Wu, C., Dong, H., Sun, K., Guo, Y.: Survey on feature extraction and applications of biosignals. In: Holzinger, A. (ed.) Machine Learning for Health Informatics. LNCS (LNAI), vol. 9605, pp. 161–182. Springer, Cham (2016). doi:10.1007/978-3-319-50478-0_8
11. Hinton, G.E., Salakhutdinov, R.R.: Reducing the dimensionality of data with neural networks. Science **313**, 504–507 (2006)
12. Deng, L.: Three classes of deep learning architectures and their applications: a tutorial survey. APSIPA Trans. Sig. Inf. Process. (2012)
13. Goldberger, A.L., Amaral, L.A., Glass, L., et al.: PhysioBank, PhysioToolkit, and PhysioNet: components of a new research resource for complex physiologic signals. Circulation **101**(23), 215–220 (2000)

Composite and Multiple Kernel Learning for Brain Computer Interface

Minmin Miao$^{(\boxtimes)}$, Hong Zeng, and Aimin Wang

School of Instrument Science and Engineering, Southeast University, No.2 Sipailou,
Nanjing 210096, China
15006187659@163.com, {hzeng,101004143}@seu.edu.cn

Abstract. High-performance feature engineering and classification
algorithms are significantly important for motor imagery (MI) related
brain-computer interface (BCI) applications. In this research, we offer a
new composite kernel support vector machine (CKSVM) based method
to extract significant common spatial pattern (CSP) feature components
from multiple temporal-frequency segments in a data-driven manner.
Furthermore, we firstly introduce a multiple kernel discriminant analysis
(MKDA) method for MI EEG classification. The experimental results on
BCI competition IV data set 2b clearly showed the effectiveness of our
method outperforming other similar approaches in the literature.

Keywords: Brain computer interface · Motor imagery · Composite kernel support vector machine · Multiple kernel discriminant analysis

1 Introduction

A brain computer interface (BCI) system supplies a new communication path
between the brain and other external devices [1]. It translates human intentions into instructions to control an outer machine by analyzing and classifying
different brain states. One of the most widely analyzed brain state is event-
related desynchronization/synchronization (ERD/ERS) which can be typically
measured by electroencephalogram (EEG) [2]. ERD/ERS phenomenon always
appears when people do motor imagery (MI) tasks. Generally, the study of MI
EEG related BCI can be well treated as a pattern recognition problem and various methods were proposed for MI EEG feature extraction and classification.

Firstly, for the issue of feature engineering, common spatial pattern (CSP)
[3] has proven to be a very useful method and has been frequently adopted in
MI EEG feature extraction. However, the performance of CSP algorithm mainly
depends on the frequency band-pass filtering of the EEG signals, the selection
of the temporal window for analysis and the subset of CSP filters used [4]. It is
widely known that using subject-specific parameters such as discriminative frequency sub-band(s), temporal window of maximum separability can enhance the
performance of a BCI system. In recent years, three kinds of methods have been
mainly proposed to solve the problem of frequency band selection. The first one

© Springer International Publishing AG 2017
D. Liu et al. (Eds.): ICONIP 2017, Part II, LNCS 10635, pp. 803–810, 2017.
https://doi.org/10.1007/978-3-319-70096-0_82

is simultaneous optimization of spectral filters within the CSP [5]. The second one is searching the optimal frequency band based on evolutionary algorithm [6]. The third one is selection of significant features from multiple frequency bands [2,7]. Moreover, several algorithms have been proposed to select the optimal temporal window for feature extraction automatically [4].

Secondly, for the classification problem, because of its fine classification performance and simplicity, linear discriminant analysis (LDA) has been most frequently adopted as a linear classification algorithm in the BCI field. As may be seen from BCI literature, kernel methods such as support vector machine (SVM) can sometimes achieve better results than linear methods [8]. Kernel discriminant analysis (KDA) [8] was proposed to extend LDA to the non-linear case, further equipped with efficient implementation by Cai et al. [9], KDA has been a competitive non-linear classification algorithm. It is well known that in kernel methods, the choice of kernel function is extremely important, since it completely defines the embedding of the data samples in the feature space. In practical applications, the "optimal" embedding is always analyzed as following: given multiple kernels capturing different views of the problem, how to learn an "optimal" combination of them [10].

In this paper, to further improve the effect or performance of feature extraction and classification for MI EEG based BCI. We propose a composite kernel learning method and a multiple kernel learning method for feature selection and feature classification, respectively. The main contributions of our work are twofold as follows: (1) As an extension of optimal filter band selection methods [2,7], We propose a novel composite kernel support vector machine (CKSVM) based method to select significant CSP features from multiple temporal-frequency segments. (2) We firstly introduce a multiple kernel discriminant analysis (MKDA) method for MI EEG classification.

2   Materials and Methods

2.1   EEG Data Set Description

In this study, BCI competition IV data set 2b was used to evaluate the performance of our method. This data set consists of EEG data from 9 subjects and EEG signals were recorded from 3 electrodes (C3, Cz, and C4). Each subject provides 5 sessions of EEG recording. All of these sessions include no less than 120 trials and two classes of motor imageries, namely left hand and right hand. The EEG signals were band-pass filtered between 0.5 Hz and 100 Hz and sampled at 250 Hz. To compare with the first placed winner of the competition under the same condition, we used the same session(s) for training and testing for each subject. Since continuous classification output is required for evaluation, the class labels are evaluated on sliding windows. The EEG signals between 3 s and 7.5 s after the beginning of the trials are extracted for training. Class label is evaluated on each sliding window of length 4.5 s after the beginning of each trial. Moreover, the moving step of the sliding window is 25 samples.

2.2   Proposed Method

Feature Extraction and Selection. At first, we decompose the raw EEG signals into multiple time-frequency segments. For BCI competition IV data set 2b, totally 16 band-pass filters of uniform bandwidth 4 Hz are adopted to cover the frequency components from 6 to 40 Hz, and the overlap between two neighboring sub-bands is 2 Hz. Time segmentation uses rectangular time windows, and length of each time segment is set to 2 s. Moreover, the overlap between each other is 0.5s, therefore totally 6 time segments are obtained.

Within each decomposed component, which is one T-segment of one f-band, traditional CSP algorithm is used on the training data. It is important to remark that in this study we use only one pair of spatial filters since only 3 channels are available. For the spatial filtered EEG signal, band power is then computed as feature. As a result, the feature vector of each temporal-frequency segment is two-dimensional. Two dimensional features of all segments are then concatenated to form a $D(D = 2 \times 16 \times 6 = 192)$ dimensional feature vector. In this research, each temporal-frequency segment is mapped into a Hilbert space individually. Composite kernels are then utilized to determine the relevance of each temporal-frequency segment to discriminate tasks, by using the SVM parameters of each segment. Let feature vector $\mathbf{f}_{i,l}$ represents features from temporal-frequency segment l for trial i where $1 \leq l \leq 96$. Each feature vector is mapped to a Hilbert space through a transformation $\varphi(\cdot)$ provided:

$$\langle \varphi_l(\mathbf{f}_{i,l}), \varphi_l(\mathbf{f}_{j,l}) \rangle = k_l(\mathbf{f}_{i,l}, \mathbf{f}_{j,l}) \tag{1}$$

where $\langle \cdot \rangle$ is an inner product operator and $k_l(\cdot, \cdot)$ denotes a Mercer's kernel function. Note that j denotes trial j. We have used linear kernel in this study which is defined as:

$$k_l(\mathbf{f}_{i,l}, \mathbf{f}_{j,l}) = \mathbf{f}_{i,l}{}^{\mathrm{T}} \cdot \mathbf{f}_{j,l} \tag{2}$$

Stacking all the feature vectors from different segments (totally $16 \times 6 = 96$ segments) in a single feature vector for trial i, we have

$$\varphi(\mathbf{f}_i) = \left[\varphi_1^{\mathrm{T}}(\mathbf{f}_{i,1}) \cdots \varphi_{96}^{\mathrm{T}}(\mathbf{f}_{i,96}) \right]^{\mathrm{T}} \tag{3}$$

The inner product between these feature vectors is then given as:

$$\langle \varphi(\mathbf{f}_i), \varphi(\mathbf{f}_j) \rangle = \sum_{l=1}^{96} k_l(\mathbf{f}_{i,l}, \mathbf{f}_{j,l}) \tag{4}$$

The resulting kernel obtained after summation is known as composite kernel. The composite kernel SVM learning machine [11] for the training samples is given by the following optimization problem:

$$\max_{\alpha} -\frac{1}{2} \sum_{i,j} \alpha_i \alpha_j y_i y_j \sum_{l=1}^{96} k_l(\mathbf{f}_{i,l}, \mathbf{f}_{j,l}) + \sum_i \alpha_i$$
$$s.t. \begin{cases} \sum_i \alpha_i y_i = 0 \\ 0 \leq \alpha_i \leq C \end{cases} \tag{5}$$

where C is a SVM regularization parameter and y denotes the class label, in this work C is set to 1 empirically. After learning parameters of SVM, the quadratic norm of each temporal-frequency segment can be computed as:

$$\|\mathbf{h}_l\|^2 = \alpha^{\mathrm{T}}\mathbf{K}_l\alpha \tag{6}$$

where $\mathbf{K}_l$ is the kernel matrix obtained in terms of the inner product of training vectors of segment l. Temporal-frequency segments are ranked on the basis of their quadratic norm. Higher is the value of quadratic norm, more is the relevancy of that segment to motor imagery tasks. Therefore, the features of segments with high values of quadratic normal form are selected.

Feature Classification. Based on the selected features of training set, we design our classifier for classification. As a non-linear extension of LDA, KDA is a classifier, in a similar way to LDA, seeks directions that improve class separation. However, KDA considers the problem in the feature space $\Im$ induced by some nonlinear mapping $\phi : \Re^{N_F} \to \Im$, where N_F is the dimension of feature vector. The objective function of KDA to find the optimal projective vector $\mathbf{v}_{opt}$ is as follows:

$$\mathbf{v}_{opt} = \arg\max \frac{\mathbf{v}^{\mathrm{T}}\mathbf{S}_B^\phi\mathbf{v}}{\mathbf{v}^{\mathrm{T}}\mathbf{S}_W^\phi\mathbf{v}} \tag{7}$$

where $\mathbf{v} \in \Im$. $\mathbf{S}_B^\phi$ and $\mathbf{S}_W^\phi$ are the between-class and within-class scatter matrices in $\Im$, i.e.

$$\mathbf{S}_B^\phi = \sum_{k=1}^{S} M_k(\mu_\phi^{(k)} - \mu_\phi)(\mu_\phi^{(k)} - \mu_\phi)^{\mathrm{T}} \tag{8}$$

and

$$\mathbf{S}_W^\phi = \sum_{k=1}^{S} \left(\sum_{i=1}^{M_k} \left(\phi(\mathbf{x}_i^{(k)}) - \mu_\phi^{(k)} \right) \left(\phi(\mathbf{x}_i^{(k)}) - \mu_\phi^{(k)} \right)^{\mathrm{T}} \right) \tag{9}$$

S is the number of classes, $\mu_\phi^{(k)}$ and μ_ϕ are the mean of of the k-th class and the golbal mean, respectively, in the feature space, and M_k is the number of feature vectors in the k-th class. It can be proved that the above maximization problem can be solved by *kernel trick*. For a chosen mapping function ϕ, an inner product $\langle\cdot\rangle$ can be defined on $\Im$, which makes for the so-called reproducing kernel Hilbert space (RKHS) $\langle\varphi(\mathbf{x}), \varphi(\mathbf{y})\rangle = k(\mathbf{x}, \mathbf{y})$, where $k(\mathbf{x}, \mathbf{y})$ is a positive semi-define kernel function. Then from the theory of RKHS, we know that any solution $\mathbf{v}_{opt} \in \Im$ must lie in the span of all training samples in $\Im$. There exist coefficients β_i such that

$$\mathbf{v}_{opt} = \sum_{i=1}^{M} \beta_i\phi(\mathbf{x}_i) \tag{10}$$

where M is the number of total training samples. Let $\beta_{opt} = [\beta_1, \beta_2, \cdots, \beta_M]$, then the maximization problem in Eq. (7) corresponds to the following eigenvalue decomposition problem

$$\mathbf{KVK}\beta = \lambda\mathbf{KK}\beta \tag{11}$$

where $\mathbf{K}$ is the kernel matrix $\mathbf{K}_{i,j} = k(\mathbf{x}_i, \mathbf{x}_j)$, and V is defined as

$$\mathbf{V}_{i,j} = \begin{cases} 1/M_k, & \text{if } \mathbf{x}_i \text{ and } \mathbf{x}_j \text{ both belongs to the } k\text{-th class} \\ 0, & \text{otherwise} \end{cases} \tag{12}$$

Each eigenvector β_{opt} gives the projection of a new testing sample $\widetilde{\mathbf{x}}$ onto $\mathbf{v}$ in the feature space. For $\widetilde{\mathbf{x}}$ we have

$$\langle \mathbf{v}, \phi(\widetilde{\mathbf{x}}) \rangle = \sum_{i=1}^{M} \beta_i k(\mathbf{x}_i, \widetilde{\mathbf{x}}) \tag{13}$$

Finally, $\widetilde{\mathbf{x}}$ is classified on the basis of the Euclidean distance to the projected mean for each class

$$\widetilde{l} = \arg \max_k \left\| \langle \mathbf{v}, \phi(\widetilde{\mathbf{x}}) \rangle - \left\langle \mathbf{v}, \mu_\phi^{(k)} \right\rangle \right\| \tag{14}$$

As we can see that KDA uses kernel function for non-linear mapping and the choice of kernel function is critically important, since it completely determines the embedding of the data in the feature space. Ideally, this embedding should be learnt from training data. In this study, we propose a multiple kernel discriminant analysis (MKDA) method. For M samples in the training set, our goal is to learn the optimal kernel weight ε for a linear combination of linear kernel and gaussian kernel as follows:

$$k_{opt}(\mathbf{x}, \mathbf{y}) = \varepsilon(\mathbf{x}^T \mathbf{y}) + (1 - \varepsilon) \exp(-\|\mathbf{x} - \mathbf{y}\|^2 / 2\delta^2) \tag{15}$$

Note that when only linear kernel is selected, MKDA degenerates into LDA. Besides, MKDA with single gaussian kernel becomes KDA. We choose these two kernel functions to capturing different "views" of linear and non-linear and to learn a "optimal combination of them". In this study, δ is set to 10 for gaussian kernel. For the choice of ε, we define optimality in terms of Fisher's linear discriminant analysis (FDA), that is, the learnt kernel weight ε is optimal, if the ratio of the projected between-class distance to inter-class distance is maximised.

3   Results and Discussion

Since the kappa coefficient was used as a performance measure in the BCI competition IV, it is used in this part of the experiment to measure the maximum kappa value evaluated on the testing data. The performance of our proposed method is compared with some other famous methods OSTP, DCSP, FBCSP and results of the 1st, 2nd, 3rd and 4th placed submissions for the competition. Note that the results of OSTP, DCSP and FBCSP are presented in [4]. Table 1 shows the performance comparison of the proposed method with other competitors. From Table 1 we observe that our method outperforms all other algorithms in terms of the average kappa value including the 1st placed winner of the competition though there is no significant difference ($p=0.76$) in the statistical analysis,

Table 1. Performance comparison of the proposed method,OSTP, DCSP, FBCSP and top four methods in the BCI competition in terms of kappa value. SD means standard deviation and the maximum kappa value is marked in boldface.

Subject	Our	OSTP	DCSP	FBCSP	1st	2nd	3rd	4th
1	**0.4875**	0.431	0.419	0.356	0.40	0.42	0.19	0.23
2	0.2429	0.207	0.236	0.171	0.21	0.21	0.12	**0.31**
3	0.1938	**0.238**	0.194	0.169	0.22	0.14	0.12	0.07
4	0.925	0.944	0.938	**0.963**	0.95	0.94	0.77	0.91
5	**0.8687**	0.844	0.850	0.850	0.86	0.71	0.57	0.24
6	**0.625**	0.594	0.613	0.594	0.61	0.62	0.49	0.42
7	0.5062	0.581	0.556	0.556	0.56	**0.61**	0.38	0.41
8	0.8062	**0.863**	0.838	0.856	0.85	0.84	0.85	0.74
9	**0.7875**	0.663	0.681	0.750	0.74	0.78	0.61	0.53
Average	**0.6048**	0.5961	0.5917	0.585	0.6	0.5856	0.4556	0.4289
SD	0.2669	0.2658	0.2673	0.2982	0.2762	0.2767	0.2725	0.2639
p-value	-	0.69	0.44	0.35	0.76	0.45	0.0029	0.031

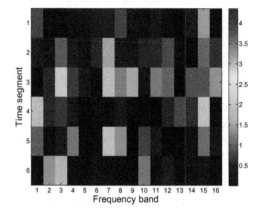

Fig. 1. Distribution of significant temporal-frequency segments for subject 1. Frequency bands indicated as 1,2,$\cdots$,16 correspond to filter subbands 6–10 Hz, 8–12 Hz,$\cdots$, 36–40 Hz, respectively. Time segments indicated as 1,2,$\cdots$,6 correspond to the temporal windows 0–2 s, 0.5–2.5 s,$\cdots$,2.5–4.5 s, respectively. Different colors correspond to different values of quadratic normal.

paired T-test. Moreover, our approach outperforms the 3rd and 4rd placed submissions of the competition significantly ($p<0.05$). Figure 1 depicts the distribution of significant temporal-frequency segments for subject 1. It can be seen that the segments with high values of quadratic normal are mainly located in sensory motor rhythms, (i.e., μ-rhythms 8–13 Hz and β-rhythms 14–30 Hz). In addition, CKSVM allows a measure of the relevance of each segment to a particular task.

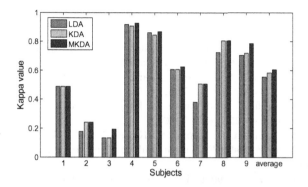

Fig. 2. Classification accuracy comparisons between LDA, KDA and MKDA.

Only the relevant and informative segments are selected for classification. We believe that decomposing a multi-channel EEG into multiple time-frequency segments for more precise analysis helps to improve the classification accuracy. In this study, we sort the values of quadratic normal in descend order and choose the first ϑ corresponding temporal-frequency segments for analysis. Note that the parameter ϑ is determined by the average classification accuracy of 5×5-fold cross validation on the training set, that is, the ϑ with the highest accuracy is selected. As described above, the optimal kernel weight ε is determined by the value of FDA. In this work, we set $\varepsilon \in \{0, 0.002, 0.004, \cdots 0.998, 1\}$ and select the optimal one. In order to evaluate the effectiveness of MKDA, we also used LDA ($\varepsilon = 1$) and KDA ($\varepsilon = 0$) for classification, and the classification accuracies for all subjects are depicted in Fig. 2. From Fig. 2 we can see that MKDA gives an equal or better result than LDA and KDA for each subject and yields higher overall result over LDA and KDA.

4 Conclusions

In this paper, we have proposed to select discriminative temporal-frequency features by CKSVM in a data-driven manner. Furthermore, to improve the classification accuracy, we introduce multiple kernel into KDA for MI EEG classification. The experiment results on BCI competition IV data set 2b show that our proposed method outperforms the state-of-the-art approaches, which are also devoted to optimizing feature selection and classification for MI EEG in BCI.

Acknowledgments. This work was supported by the National Major Scientific Instruments and Equipment Development Program of China under Grant 2013YQ17052502, Nation Nature Science Foundation of China under Grant 61673105, Jiangsu Province Science and Technology Support Program of China under Grant BE2012740.

References

1. Arvaneh, M., Guan, C.T., Ang, K.K., Quek, C.: Optimizing spatial filters by minimizing within-class dissimilarities in electroencephalogram-based brain-computer interface. IEEE Trans. Neural Netw. Learn. Syst. **24**, 610–619 (2013)
2. Zhang, Y., Zhou, G.X., Jin, J., Wang, X.Y., Cichocki, A.: Optimizing spatial patterns with sparse filter bands for motor-imagery based brain-computer interface. J. Neurosci. Methods **255**, 85–91 (2015)
3. Blankertz, B., Tomioka, R., Lemm, S., Kawanabe, M., Muller, K.R.: Optimizing spatial filters for robust EEG single-trial analysis. IEEE Sig. Process. Mag. **25**, 41–56 (2008)
4. Ang, K.K., Chin, Z.Y., Zhang, H.H., Guan, C.T.: Mutual information-based selection of optimal spatial-temporal patterns for single-trial EEG-based BCIs. Pattern Recogn. **45**, 2137–2144 (2012)
5. Lemm, S., Blankertz, B., Curio, G., Muller, K.R.: Spatio-spectral filters for improving the classification of single trial EEG. IEEE Trans. Biomed. Eng. **52**, 1541–1548 (2005)
6. Xu, P., Liu, T.J., Zhang, R., Zhang, Y.S., Yao, D.Z.: Using particle swarm to select frequency band and time interval for feature extraction of EEG based BCI. Biomed. Sig. Process. Control **10**, 289–295 (2014)
7. Thomas, K.P., Guan, C.T., Lau, C.T., Vinod, A.P., Ang, K.K.: A new discriminative common spatial pattern method for motor imagery brain-computer interfaces. IEEE Trans. Biomed. Eng. **56**, 2730–2733 (2009)
8. Nicolas-Alonso, L.F., Corralejo, R., Gomez-Pilar, J., Alvarez, D., Hornero, R.: Adaptive semi-supervised classification to reduce intersession non-stationarity in multiclass motor imagery-based brain-computer interfaces. Neurocomputing **159**, 186–196 (2015)
9. Cai, D., He, X.F., Han, J.W.: Speed up kernel discriminant analysis. Vldb J. **20**, 21–33 (2011)
10. Yan, F., Kittler, J., Mikolajczyk, K., Tahir, A.: Non-sparse multiple kernel fisher discriminant analysis. J. Mach. Lear. Res. **13**, 607–642 (2012)
11. Castro, E., Martinez-Ramon, M., Pearlson, G., Sui, J., Calhoun, V.D.: Characterization of groups using composite kernels and multi-source fMRI analysis data: application to schizophrenia. Neuroimage **58**, 526–536 (2011)

Transfer Learning Enhanced Common Spatial Pattern Filtering for Brain Computer Interfaces (BCIs): Overview and a New Approach

He He and Dongrui Wu[(✉)]

School of Automation, Huazhong University of Science and Technology,
Wuhan, China
{hehe91,drwu}@hust.edu.cn

Abstract. The electroencephalogram (EEG) is the most widely used input for brain computer interfaces (BCIs), and common spatial pattern (CSP) is frequently used to spatially filter it to increase its signal-to-noise ratio. However, CSP is a supervised filter, which needs some subject-specific calibration data to design. This is time-consuming and not user-friendly. A promising approach for shortening or even completely eliminating this calibration session is transfer learning, which leverages relevant data or knowledge from other subjects or tasks. This paper reviews three existing approaches for incorporating transfer learning into CSP, and also proposes a new transfer learning enhanced CSP approach. Experiments on motor imagery classification demonstrate their effectiveness. Particularly, our proposed approach achieves the best performance when the number of target domain calibration samples is small.

Keywords: Brain computer interface · Common spatial pattern · Motor imagery · Transfer learning

1 Introduction

Brain computer interfaces (BCIs) [10,19] provide a direct communication pathway for a user to interact with a computer or external device by using his/her brain signals, which include electroencephalogram (EEG), magnetoencephalogram (MEG), functional magnetic resonance imaging (fMRI), functional near-infrared spectroscopy (fNIRS), electrocorticography (ECoG), and so on. EEG-based BCIs have attracted great attention because they have little risk (no need for surgery), are convenience to use, and offer high temporal resolution. They have been used for robotics, speller, games, and medical applications [6,14].

However, there are still many challenges for wide-spread real-world applications of EEG-based BCIs [10,13]. One of them is related to the EEG signal quality. EEG signals can be easily contaminated by various artifacts and noise, including muscle movements, eye blinks, heartbeats, environmental electromagnetic fields, etc. Common approaches to clean EEG signals including time-domain filtering and spatial filtering. Common spatial pattern (CSP) filtering

© Springer International Publishing AG 2017
D. Liu et al. (Eds.): ICONIP 2017, Part II, LNCS 10635, pp. 811–821, 2017.
https://doi.org/10.1007/978-3-319-70096-0_83

[3,17,21,26] is one of the most popular and effective spatial filters for EEG to increase its signal-to-noise ratio.

CSP performs supervised filtering, which requires some subject-specific calibration data to design. This is time-consuming and not user-friendly. A promising approach for shortening or even completely eliminating this calibration session is transfer learning (TL) [15], which has already been extensively used to handle individual differences and non-stationarity in EEG-based BCI [8,18,20,22–25]. TL leverages relevant data or knowledge from other subjects or tasks to reduce the calibration effort for a new subject or task. Traditionally, EEG signal processing (e.g., CSP filtering) and classification (e.g., TL) are performed sequentially and independently. However, recent research has shown that TL may be used to directly enhance CSP for better filtering performance [4,9,12].

This paper focuses on TL enhanced CSPs. Its main contributions are:

1. We group existing TL enhanced CSPs into two categories and give a comprehensive review of them. To our knowledge, this is the first review in this direction.
2. We propose a novel TL enhanced CSP approach, and demonstrate its performance against existing approaches on EEG-based motor imagery classification.

The rest of this paper is organized as follows: Sect. 2 introduces CSP and TL, and gives an overview of existing approaches for incorporating TL into CSP. Section 3 proposes a new instance-based TL approach to enhance CSP. Section 4 compares the performance of all these approaches. Finally, Sect. 5 draws conclusions and points out several future research directions.

2 Existing TL Enhanced CSP Filters

This section briefly introduces CSP and TL, and reviews three existing approaches for integrating them.

2.1 Common Spatial Pattern (CSP)

Let $X \in \mathbb{R}^{C \times T}$ be an EEG epoch, where C is the number of channels and T the number of time samples. For simplicity, only binary classification is considered in this paper.

CSP [3,17,21] separates a multivariate signal into additive subcomponents which have maximum differences in variance between the two classes. Specifically, CSP finds a filter matrix to maximize the variance for one class while minimizing it for the other:

$$W_0 = \arg\max_{W} \frac{\mathrm{tr}(W^T \bar{\Sigma}_0 W)}{\mathrm{tr}(W^T \bar{\Sigma}_1 W)} \tag{1}$$

where $W_0 \in \mathbb{R}^{C \times F}$ is the filter matrix consisting of F filters, $\mathrm{tr}(\cdot)$ is the trace of a matrix, $\bar{\Sigma}_0$ and $\bar{\Sigma}_1$ are the mean covariance matrices of epochs in Classes 0 and 1, respectively. The solution W_0 is the concatenation of the F eigenvectors associated with the F largest eigenvalues of the matrix $\bar{\Sigma}_1^{-1}\bar{\Sigma}_0$.

In practice, we often construct a CSP filter matrix $W_* = [W_0, W_1] \in \mathbb{R}^{C \times 2F}$, where

$$W_1 = \arg\max_W \frac{\text{tr}(W^T \bar{\Sigma}_1 W)}{\text{tr}(W^T \bar{\Sigma}_0 W)} \tag{2}$$

i.e., W_1 maximizes the variance for Class 1 while minimizing it for Class 0. Similar to W_0, W_1 is the concatenation of the F eigenvectors associated with the F largest eigenvalues of the matrix $\bar{\Sigma}_0^{-1}\bar{\Sigma}_1$. Since $\bar{\Sigma}_1^{-1}\bar{\Sigma}_0$ and $\bar{\Sigma}_0^{-1}\bar{\Sigma}_1$ have the same eigenvectors, and the eigenvalues of $\bar{\Sigma}_1^{-1}\bar{\Sigma}_0$ are the inverses of the eigenvalues of $\bar{\Sigma}_0^{-1}\bar{\Sigma}_1$, W_1 actually consists of the F eigenvectors associated with the F smallest eigenvalues of the matrix $\bar{\Sigma}_1^{-1}\bar{\Sigma}_0$. So, only one eigen-decomposition of the matrix $\bar{\Sigma}_1^{-1}\bar{\Sigma}_0$ (or $\bar{\Sigma}_0^{-1}\bar{\Sigma}_1$) is needed in computing W_*.

Once W_* is obtained, CSP projects an EEG epoch $X \in \mathbb{R}^{C \times T}$ to $X' \in \mathbb{R}^{2F \times T}$ by:

$$X' = W_*^T X \tag{3}$$

Usually $2F < C$, so CSP can increase the signal-to-noise ratio and reduce the dimensionality simultaneously.

After CSP filtering, the logarithmic variance feature vector is then calculated as [4]:

$$\mathbf{x} = \log\left(\frac{\text{diag}(X'X'^T)}{\text{tr}(X'X'^T)}\right) \tag{4}$$

where $\text{diag}(\cdot)$ returns the diagonal elements of a matrix. $\mathbf{x}$ can be used as the input to a classifier, e.g., linear discriminant analysis (LDA).

2.2   Transfer Learning (TL)

TL has been extensively used in BCIs to reduce their calibration effort [8,18,20,23,24]. Some basic concepts of TL are introduced in this subsection.

A *domain* [11,15] $\mathcal{D}$ in TL consists of a feature space $\mathcal{X}$ and a marginal probability distribution $P(\mathbf{x})$, i.e., $\mathcal{D} = \{\mathcal{X}, P(\mathbf{x})\}$, where $\mathbf{x} \in \mathcal{X}$. Two domains $\mathcal{D}_s$ and $\mathcal{D}_t$ are different if $\mathcal{X}_s \neq \mathcal{X}_t$, and/or $P_s(\mathbf{x}) \neq P_t(\mathbf{x})$.

A *task* [11,15] $\mathcal{T}$ in TL consists of a label space $\mathcal{Y}$ and a conditional probability distribution $Q(y|\mathbf{x})$. Two tasks $\mathcal{T}_s$ and $\mathcal{T}_t$ are different if $\mathcal{Y}_s \neq \mathcal{Y}_t$, or $Q_s(y|\mathbf{x}) \neq Q_t(y|\mathbf{x})$.

Given a *source domain* $\mathcal{D}_s$ with n labeled samples, and a *target domain* $\mathcal{D}_t$ with m_l labeled samples and m_u unlabeled samples, TL learns a target prediction function $f : \mathbf{x} \mapsto y$ with low expected error on $\mathcal{D}_t$, under the assumptions $\mathcal{X}_s \neq \mathcal{X}_t$, $\mathcal{Y}_s \neq \mathcal{Y}_t$, $P_s(\mathbf{x}) \neq P_t(\mathbf{x})$, and/or $Q_s(y|\mathbf{x}) \neq Q_t(y|\mathbf{x})$.

For example, in EEG-based motor imagery classification studied in this paper, a source domain consists of EEG epochs from an existing subject, and the target domain consists of EEG epochs from a new subject. When there are Z source domains $\{\mathcal{D}_s^z\}_{z=1,...,Z}$, we can perform TL for each of them separately and then aggregate the Z classifiers, or treat the combination of the Z source domains as a single source domain.

2.3 Incorporating TL into CSP: Covariance Matrix-Based Approaches

Since covariance matrices are used in CSP, whereas the target domain does not have enough labeled samples to reliably estimate them, a direction to incorporate TL into CSP is to utilize the source domain covariance matrices to enhance the estimation of the target domain ones.

Kang et al. [9] proposed a subject-to-subject transfer approach, which emphasizes the covariance matrices of source subjects who are more similar to the target subject. They computed the dissimilarity between the target subject and each source subject by Kullback-Leibler (KL) divergence between their data distributions, and then used the inverses of these dissimilarities as weights to combine the source domain covariance matrices.

Let p_s^z be the EEG data distribution in the zth source domain $\mathcal{D}_s^z$, which is assumed to be C-dimensional Gaussian with zero mean and covariance matrix Σ_s^z, i.e., $p_s^z \sim N(\mathbf{0}, \Sigma_s^z)$. Let p_t be the data distribution in the target domain $\mathcal{D}_t$, which is C-dimensional Gaussian with zero mean and covariance matrix Σ_t, i.e., $p_t \sim N(\mathbf{0}, \Sigma_t)$. The KL divergence between p_s^z and p_t is computed as [9]:

$$KL(p_s^z, p_t) = \frac{1}{2}\left\{\log\left(\frac{|\Sigma_t|}{|\Sigma_s^z|}\right) + \text{tr}[\Sigma_t^{-1}\Sigma_s^z] - C\right\}, \quad z = 1, ..., Z \quad (5)$$

where $|\cdot|$ is the matrix determinant.

Then, the TL-enhanced covariance matrix for the target subject is computed as:

$$\widetilde{\Sigma}_t = (1 - \lambda)\Sigma_t + \lambda \sum_{z=1}^{Z} \alpha_z \Sigma_s^z \quad (6)$$

where λ is an adjustable parameter to balance the information from the target subject and source subjects, and

$$\alpha_z = \frac{1}{\gamma} \cdot \frac{1}{KL(p_s^z, p_t)} \quad (7)$$

in which $\gamma = \sum_{z=1}^{Z} \frac{1}{KL(p_s^z, p_t)}$ is a normalization factor.

Lotte and Guan [12] proposed a similar approach for incorporating TL into CSP, based on the covariance matrices:

$$\widetilde{\Sigma}_t = (1 - \lambda)\Sigma_t + \frac{\lambda}{|S_t(\Omega)|} \sum_{z \in S_t(\Omega)} \Sigma_s^z \quad (8)$$

where Ω is the set of subjects whose data have been recorded previously, $S_t(\Omega)$ is a subset of subjects from Ω, $|S_t(\Omega)|$ is the number of subjects in $S_t(\Omega)$, and $\lambda \in [0,1]$ is defined by

$$\lambda = \begin{cases} 1, & targetAcc \leq randAcc \\ 0, & targetAcc \geq selectedAcc \\ \frac{selectedAcc-targetAcc}{1-randAcc}, & \text{otherwise} \end{cases} \tag{9}$$

in which $targetAcc$ is the leave-one-out validation accuracy on the target domain labeled samples when the classifier is trained by using only the target domain labeled samples, $selectedAcc$ is the accuracy on the target domain labeled samples when the classifier is trained by using only the labeled samples from the selected source subjects in $S_t(\Omega)$, and $randAcc$ is the classification accuracy at the chance level (e.g., 50% for binary classification). The algorithm for determining $S_t(\Omega)$ can be found in [12].

2.4 Incorporating TL into CSP: A Model-Based Approach

Instead of learning a single set of CSP filters by aggregating information from the target subject and all (or a subset of) source subjects, as introduced in the previous subsection, Dalhoumi et al. [4] proposed an approach to design a set of CSP filters for each source subject, train a classifier for each source subject according to the extracted features, and then aggregate all these source classifiers to obtain the target classifier.

Let W^z and f^z be the CSP filter matrix and classifier trained for the zth source subject, respectively, and $\{(X_j, y_j)\}_{j=1,...,m}$ be the labeled target domain data. We first filter each X_j by W^z, extract the corresponding feature vector $\mathbf{x}_j^z$ using (4), and then feed $\mathbf{x}_j^z$ into model f^z to obtain its classification $f^z(\mathbf{x}_j^z)$. The final classifier is:

$$f(\mathbf{x}) = \sum_{z=1}^{Z} w^z f^z(\mathbf{x}) \tag{10}$$

where the weights $\mathbf{w}_* = (w^1, ..., w^Z)$ are determined by solving the following constrained minimization problem:

$$\mathbf{w}_* = \arg\min_{\mathbf{w}} \sum_{j=1}^{m} \ell \left(\sum_{z=1}^{Z} w^z f^z(\mathbf{x}_j^z), y_j \right) \tag{11}$$

$$s.t. \quad \sum_{z=1}^{Z} w^z = 1$$

$$w^z \geq 0, \ z = 1, ..., Z$$

where $\ell \left(\sum_{z=1}^{Z} w^z f^z(\mathbf{x}_j^z), y_j \right)$ is the loss between $\sum_{z=1}^{Z} w^z f^z(\mathbf{x}_j^z)$ and y_j.

Dalhoumi et al. [4] also constructed another CSP filter matrix and the corresponding classifier using the target domain data only, and compared its leave-one-out validation performance with that of $f(\mathbf{x})$ to determine which one should be used as the preferred classifier. Because the goal of this paper is to compare different TL enhanced CSP approaches, we always use $f(\mathbf{x})$.

3   Incorporating TL into CSP: Instance-Based Approaches

This section introduces our proposed approach for incorporating TL into CSP. It's an instance-based approach, meaning that the source domain labeled samples are combined with the target domain labeled samples in a certain way to design the CSP.

The simplest instance-base approach is to directly combine the labeled samples from the target domain and all source domains. However, this is usually not optimal because it completely ignores the individual difference: some source domain samples may be more similar to the target domain samples, so they should be given more consideration.

So, a better approach is to re-weight the source domain samples according to their similarity to the target domain samples, and then use them in the CSP. The main problem is how to optimally re-weight the source samples. We adopt the approach proposed by Huang et al. [7], which is a generic method for correcting sample collection bias and has not been used for CSP and BCIs. It assigns different weights to the source domain samples to minimize the Maximum Mean Discrepancy [2] between the source and target domains after mapping onto a reproducing kernel Hilbert space. More specifically, it solves the following constrained minimization problem:

$$\min_{\boldsymbol{\beta}} \left\| \frac{1}{n} \sum_{j=1}^{n} \beta_j \phi(\mathbf{x}_s^j) - \frac{1}{m} \sum_{j=1}^{m} \phi(\mathbf{x}_t^j) \right\|_H^2 \tag{12}$$

$$s.t. \quad 0 \leq \beta_j \leq b, \quad j = 1, ..., n$$

$$\left| \sum_{j=1}^{n} \beta_j - n \right| \leq n\epsilon$$

where $\mathbf{x}_s^j$ is the jth source domain sample, $\mathbf{x}_t^j$ is the jth target domain sample, $\phi(\mathbf{x})$ is a feature mapping onto a reproducing kernel Hilbert space H, $\boldsymbol{\beta} = (\beta_1, ..., \beta_n)$ is the weight vector for the source domain samples, n is the number of source domain samples, m is the number of target domain samples, and b and ϵ are adjustable parameters.

The source domain samples are then re-weighted by $\boldsymbol{\beta}$ and combined with the target domain samples to design a CSP filter matrix.

4   Experiment and Results

This section presents a comparative study of the above TL-enhanced CSP algorithms.

4.1   Dataset and Preprocessing

We used Dataset 2a from BCI competition IV[1], which consists of EEG data from 9 subjects. Every subject was instructed to perform four different motor imagery tasks, namely the imagination of movement of the left hand, right hand, both feet, and tongue. A training session and a test session were recorded on different days for each subject and each session is comprised of 288 epochs (72 for each of the four classes). The signals were recorded using 22 EEG channels and 3 EOG channels at 250 Hz and bandpass filtered between 0.5 Hz and 100 Hz.

Only the 22 EEG channels were used in our study. We further processed them using the Matlab EEGLAB toolbox [5]. They were first down-sampled to 125 Hz. Next a bandpass filter of 8–30 Hz was applied as movement imagination is known to suppress idle rhythms in this frequency band contra-laterally [16]. As we consider binary classification in this paper, only EEG signals corresponding to the left and right hand motor imageries were used. More specifically, EEG epochs between 1.5 and 3.5 s after the appearance of left or right hand motor imagery cues were used.

4.2   Algorithms

We compared the performance of the following seven CSP algorithms:

1. *Baseline 1 (BL1)*, which uses only the small amount of target domain labeled samples to design the CSP filters and the LDA classifier, and applies them to target domain unlabeled samples. That's, BL1 does not use any source domain samples.
2. *Baseline 2 (BL2)*: which combines all source domain samples to design the CSP filters and the LDA classifier, and applies them to target domain unlabeled samples. That's, BL2 does not use any target domain labeled samples.
3. *Baseline 3 (BL3)*, which directly combines all source domain samples and target domain labeled samples, designs the CSP filters and the LDA classifier, and applies them to target domain unlabeled samples.
4. *Covariance matrix-based approach 1 (CM1)*, which is the approach proposed by Kang et al. [9], as introduced in Sect. 2.3. $\lambda = 0.5$ was used in our study.
5. *Covariance matrix-based approach 2 (CM2)*, which is the approach proposed by Lotte and Guan [12], as introduced in Sect. 2.3.
6. *Model-based approach (MA)*, which is the approach introduced in Sect. 2.4.

---

[1] http://www.bbci.de/competition/iv/.

7. *Instance-based approach (IA)*, which is our proposed algorithm: it first solves the constrained optimization problem in (12) for the weights of the source domain samples, then combines target domain labeled samples and the weighted source domain samples to train CSP filters and the LDA classifier, and next applies them to target domain unlabeled samples.

There were 9 subjects in our dataset. Each time we picked one as our target subject, and the remaining 8 as the source subjects. For the target subject, we randomly reserved 40 epochs (20 epochs per class) as the training data pool, and used the remaining 104 epochs as our test data. We started with zero target domain training data, trained different CSP filters using the above 7 algorithms, and evaluated their performances on the test dataset. We then sequentially added 2 labeled epochs (1 labeled epoch per class) from the reserved training data pool to the target domain training dataset till all 40 epochs were added. Each time we trained different CSP filters using the above 7 algorithms and evaluated their performances on the test dataset. We repeated this process 30 times to obtain statistically meaningful results.

4.3   Results

The performances of the 7 algorithms are shown in Fig. 1, where the first 9 subfigures show the performances on the individual subjects. Observe that some subjects, e.g., Subjects 2 and 5, were more difficult to deal with than others, and there was no approach that always outperformed others; however, when m, the number of target domain labeled epochs, was small, our proposed algorithm (IA) achieved the best performance for 5 out of the 9 subjects.

The last subfigure of Fig. 1 shows the average performance across the 9 subjects. Observe that:

1. When m was small, all other methods outperformed BL1. Particularly, when $m = 0$, BL1 cannot build a model because it used only subject-specific calibration data, but all other algorithms can, because they can use data from the source subjects. This suggests that all TL-enhanced CSP algorithms are advantageous when the target domain has very limited labeled epochs.
2. BL2 outperformed BL1 and BL3 when m was small, but as m increased, all other algorithms outperformed BL2. This suggests that there is large individual difference among the subjects, so incorporating target domain samples is necessary and beneficial.
3. Generally, all TL-enhanced CSP algorithms outperformed the three baselines, suggesting the effectiveness of TL. Particularly, our proposed algorithm (IA) achieved the best performance when m was small. This is favorable, as we always want to achieve the best calibration performance with the smallest number of subject-specific calibration samples.

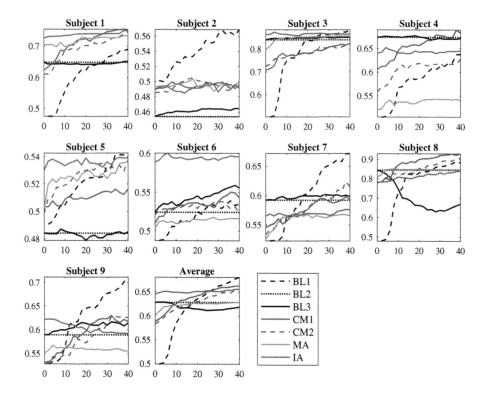

Fig. 1. Classification accuracies of the 7 CSP approaches, when the number of target domain labeled samples increases.

5   Conclusions

CSP is a popular spatial filtering approach to increase the signal-to-noise ratio of EEG signals. However, it is a supervised approach, which needs some subject-specific calibration data to design. This is time-consuming and not user-friendly. A promising approach for shortening or even completely eliminating this calibration session is TL, which leverages relevant data or knowledge from other subjects or tasks. This paper reviewed three existing approaches for incorporating TL into CSP, and also proposed a new TL enhanced CSP approach. Experiments on motor imagery classification demonstrated the effectiveness of these approaches. Particularly, our proposed approach achieved the best performance when the number of target domain calibration epochs is small.

The following directions will be considered in our future research:

1. Use the Riemannian mean instead of the Euclidean mean in estimating the mean class covariance matrices in CSP [1]. As the covariance matrix of each epoch is semi-positive definite, they are located on a Riemannian manifold instead of in an Euclidean space. So, the Riemannian means may be more reasonable than the Euclidean means in CSP.

2. Use also TL enhanced classifiers, e.g., weighted domain adaptation [20,24].
3. Extend the TL enhanced CSPs from classification to regression, using a fuzzy set based approach similar to the one proposed in [21].

References

1. Barachant, A., Bonnet, S., Congedo, M., Jutten, C.: Common spatial pattern revisited by Riemannian geometry. In: IEEE International Workshop on Multimedia Signal Processing, London, UK, pp. 472–476, October 2010
2. Belkin, M., Niyogi, P., Sindhwani, V.: Manifold regularization: a geometric framework for learning from labeled and unlabeled examples. J. Mach. Learn. Res. **7**, 2399–2434 (2006)
3. Blankertz, B., Tomioka, R., Lemm, S., Kawanabe, M., Muller, K.R.: Optimizing spatial filters for robust EEG single-trial analysis. IEEE Sig. Process. Mag. **25**(1), 41–56 (2008)
4. Dalhoumi, S., Dray, G., Montmain, J.: Knowledge transfer for reducing calibration time in brain-computer interfacing. In: Proceedings of IEEE 26th International Conference on Tools with Artificial Intelligence, Limassol, Cyprus, November 2014
5. Delorme, A., Makeig, S.: EEGLAB: an open source toolbox for analysis of single-trial EEG dynamics including independent component analysis. J. Neurosci. Methods **134**, 9–21 (2004)
6. van Erp, J., Lotte, F., Tangermann, M.: Brain-computer interfaces: beyond medical applications. Computer **45**(4), 26–34 (2012)
7. Huang, J., Smola, A.J., Gretton, A., Borgwardt, K.M., Scholkopf, B.: Correcting sample selection bias by unlabeled data. In: Proceedings of International Conference on Neural Information Processing Systems, Vancouver, Canada, pp. 601–608, December 2006
8. Jayaram, V., Alamgir, M., Altun, Y., Scholkopf, B., Grosse-Wentrup, M.: Transfer learning in brain-computer interfaces. IEEE Comput. Intell. Mag. **11**(1), 20–31 (2016)
9. Kang, H., Nam, Y., Choi, S.: Composite common spatial pattern for subject-to-subject transfer. Sig. Process. Lett. **16**(8), 683–686 (2009)
10. Lance, B.J., Kerick, S.E., Ries, A.J., Oie, K.S., McDowell, K.: Brain-computer interface technologies in the coming decades. Proc. IEEE **100**(3), 1585–1599 (2012)
11. Long, M., Wang, J., Ding, G., Pan, S.J., Yu, P.S.: Adaptation regularization: a general framework for transfer learning. IEEE Trans. Knowl. Data Eng. **26**(5), 1076–1089 (2014)
12. Lotte, F., Guan, C.: Learning from other subjects helps reducing brain-computer interface calibration time. In: Proceedings of IEEE International Conference on Acoustics Speech and Signal Processing (ICASSP), Dallas, TX, March 2010
13. Makeig, S., Kothe, C., Mullen, T., Bigdely-Shamlo, N., Zhang, Z., Kreutz-Delgado, K.: Evolving signal processing for brain-computer interfaces. In: Proceedings of the IEEE 100 (Special Centennial Issue), pp. 1567–1584 (2012)
14. Nicolas-Alonso, L.F., Gomez-Gil, J.: Brain computer interfaces, a review. Sensors **12**(2), 1211–1279 (2012)
15. Pan, S.J., Yang, Q.: A survey on transfer learning. IEEE Trans. Knowl. Data Eng. **22**(10), 1345–1359 (2010)
16. Pfurtscheller, G., Brunner, C., Schlogl, A., da Silva, F.L.: Mu rhythm (de)synchronization and EEG single-trial classification of different motor imagery tasks. NeuroImage **31**(1), 153–159 (2006)

17. Ramoser, H., Muller-Gerking, J., Pfurtscheller, G.: Optimal spatial filtering of single trial EEG during imagined hand movement. IEEE Trans. Rehabil. Eng. **8**(4), 441–446 (2000)
18. Waytowich, N.R., Lawhern, V.J., Bohannon, A.W., Ball, K.R., Lance, B.J.: Spectral transfer learning using Information Geometry for a user-independent brain-computer interface. Front. Neurosci. **10**, 430 (2016)
19. Wolpaw, J.R., Birbaumer, N., McFarland, D.J., Pfurtscheller, G., Vaughan, T.M.: Brain-computer interfaces for communication and control. Clin. Neurophysiol. **113**(6), 767–791 (2002)
20. Wu, D.: Online and offline domain adaptation for reducing BCI calibration effort. IEEE Trans. Hum.-Mach. Syst. **47**(4), 550–563 (2017)
21. Wu, D., King, J.T., Chuang, C.H., Lin, C.T., Jung, T.P.: Spatial filtering for EEG-based regression problems in brain-computer interface (BCI). IEEE Trans. Fuzzy Syst. (2017, accepted)
22. Wu, D., Lance, B.J., Lawhern, V.J.: Active transfer learning for reducing calibration data in single-trial classification of visually-evoked potentials. In: Proceedings of IEEE International Conference on Systems, Man, and Cybernetics, San Diego, CA, October 2014
23. Wu, D., Lawhern, V.J., Gordon, S., Lance, B.J., Lin, C.T.: Driver drowsiness estimation from EEG signals using online weighted adaptation regularization for regression (OwARR). IEEE Trans. Fuzzy Syst. (2016, in press)
24. Wu, D., Lawhern, V.J., Hairston, W.D., Lance, B.J.: Switching EEG headsets made easy: reducing offline calibration effort using active weighted adaptation regularization. IEEE Trans. Neural Syst. Rehabil. Eng. **24**(11), 1125–1137 (2016)
25. Wu, D., Lawhern, V.J., Lance, B.J.: Reducing offline BCI calibration effort using weighted adaptation regularization with source domain selection. In: Proceedings of IEEE International Conference Systems, Man and Cybernetics, Hong Kong, October 2015
26. Wu, D., Lawhern, V.J., Lance, B.J., Gordon, S., Jung, T.P., Lin, C.T.: EEG-based user reaction time estimation using Riemannian geometry features. IEEE Trans. Neural Syst. Rehabil. Eng. (2017, in press)

EEG-Based Driver Drowsiness Estimation Using Convolutional Neural Networks

Yuqi Cui and Dongrui Wu$^{(\boxtimes)}$

School of Automation, Huazhong University of Science and Technology,
Wuhan, Hubei, China
{yuqicui,drwu}@hust.edu.cn

Abstract. Deep learning, including convolutional neural networks (CNNs), has started finding applications in brain-computer interfaces (BCIs). However, so far most such approaches focused on BCI classification problems. This paper extends EEGNet, a 3-layer CNN model for BCI classification, to BCI regression, and also utilizes a novel spectral meta-learner for regression (SMLR) approach to aggregate multiple EEGNets for improved performance. Our model uses the power spectral density (PSD) of EEG signals as the input. Compared with raw EEG inputs, the PSD inputs can reduce the computational cost significantly, yet achieve much better regression performance. Experiments on driver drowsiness estimation from EEG signals demonstrate the outstanding performance of our approach.

Keywords: Brain-computer interface · Convolutional neural network · Drowsiness estimation · EEG · Spectral meta-learner for regression

1 Introduction

Drowsy driving is one of the most important causes of traffic accidents, following only to alcohol, speeding, and inattention [28]. As a result, it is very important to monitor the driver's drowsiness level and take actions accordingly. There have been many different approaches [1,6,22,29] for doing so, which can be roughly categorized into two groups:

1. *Contactless detection approaches*, which do not require the driver to physically wear any sensors. Their main advantage is the convenience to use. Contactless detection approaches can be further classified into two categories:

   (a) *Computer vision based detection approaches*, which can be applied to either the driver or the vehicle.

   When applied to the driver, a typical practice is to place some cameras behind the windshield, which capture the driver's head in realtime. From the video we can compute the eye blink frequency [12,21], the percentage of eye closure (PERCLOS) [11,31], the eye movement [15,16], the head pose [12,27], etc., which are indicators of drowsiness. The main drawback

© Springer International Publishing AG 2017
D. Liu et al. (Eds.): ICONIP 2017, Part II, LNCS 10635, pp. 822–832, 2017.
https://doi.org/10.1007/978-3-319-70096-0_84

of these approaches is that they can be easily affected by the lighting condition.

When applied to the vehicle, usually some cameras are used to capture the relative position of the vehicle in the lane. From lane departure events we can estimate the driver drowsiness [6,15,29]. The main drawback of this approach is that it can also be easily affected by lighting and weather, and it may not work when the lane markers are unclear or missing.

(b) *Driver-vehicle interaction based detection approaches*, which use various sensors to measure the driving patterns, e.g., speeding, tailgating, abrupt braking, inappropriate steering wheel adjustments, etc. [23,29], to infer if the driver is drowsy.

2. *Contact sensor based detection approaches*, which require the driver to physically wear some sensors to measure his/her physiological signals, e.g., electroencephalogram (EEG) [26,34–36], electrocardiography [20,26], electromyography [2,19], respiration [30,32], galvanic skin response [5,15], etc. Theoretically, physiological signals are more accurate and reliable drowsiness indicators, as they originate directly from the human body. Their main disadvantages include: (1) the driver's body movements may introduce artifacts and noise to the physiological signals, and hence reduce the detection accuracy; and, (2) the driver may feel uncomfortable to wear such body sensors.

This paper focuses on the contact sensor based detection approaches. More specifically, we consider EEG-based driver drowsiness detection. The main reason is that EEG signals, which directly measure the brain state, have the potential to predict the drowsiness before it reaches a dangerous level. Hence, compared with other approaches, there is ample time to alert the driver to avoid accidents.

There has been research on using deep learning [17,18] for driver drowsiness classification. This paper considers regression instead of classification. It makes the following three contributions:

1. It extends EEGNet [24], a convolutional neural network (CNN) originally designed for classification problems in brain-computer interface (BCI), to regression problems.
2. It uses spectral meta-learner for regression (SMLR) [37], an unsupervised ensemble regression approach, to aggregate multiple EEGNet regression models for improved performance.
3. Instead of using raw EEG signals as the input to EEGNet, it uses their power spectral density (PSD) at certain frequencies as the input, which significantly saves the computational cost, and also improves the regression performance.

The remainder of this paper is organized as follows: Sect. 2 introduces our proposed EEGNet-PSD-SMLR approach. Section 3 presents the details of a drowsy driving experiment in a virtual reality (VR) environment, and the performance comparison of EEGNet-PSD-SMLR with several other approaches. Finally, Sect. 4 draws conclusions and points out a future research direction.

2   The EEGNet-PSD-SMLR Model

This section introduces our proposed EEGNet-PSD-SMLR model for driver drowsiness estimation.

2.1   EEGNet for Regression

The CNN regression model used in this paper is modified from the EEGNet classification model [24], which has demonstrated outstanding performance in four different BCI applications, i.e., P300 visual-evoked potential, error-related negativity, movement-related cortical potential, and the sensory motor rhythm.

Denote an EEG epoch as $\mathbf{x} \in \mathbb{R}^{C \times T}$, where C is the number of channels and T is the number of time samples (or features) per channel. The EEGNet classification and regression architectures are given in Table 1, where N is the number of classes in classification. Observe that the two architectures are identical for the first three layers; the only difference occurs at the fourth layer. The EEGNet classification architecture uses softmax regression for classification, whereas the EEGNet regression architecture uses a dense layer followed by an activation layer for regression. We have tested different activation functions (ReLU, sigmoid, tanh, and linear), and found linear activation gave the best results. So, linear activation was adopted in this paper.

Table 1. EEGNet architectures for classification and regression.

Layer	Input size	Operation	Output size	Number of parameters
1	$C \times T$	$16 \times \text{Conv1D}(C,1)$	$16 \times 1 \times T$	$16C + 16$
	$16 \times 1 \times T$	BatchNorm	$16 \times 1 \times T$	32
	$16 \times 1 \times T$	Reshape	$1 \times 16 \times T$	
	$1 \times 16 \times T$	Dropout(0.25)	$1 \times 16 \times T$	
2	$1 \times 16 \times T$	$4 \times \text{Conv2D}(2,32)$	$4 \times 16 \times T$	$4 \times 2 \times 32 + 4 = 260$
	$4 \times 16 \times T$	BatchNorm	$4 \times 16 \times T$	8
	$4 \times 16 \times T$	Maxpool2d(2,4)	$4 \times 8 \times T/4$	
	$4 \times 8 \times T/4$	Dropout(0.25)	$4 \times 8 \times T/4$	
3	$4 \times 8 \times T/4$	$4 \times \text{Conv2D}(8,4)$	$4 \times 8 \times T/4$	$4 \times 4 \times 8 \times 4 + 4 = 516$
	$4 \times 8 \times T/4$	BatchNorm	$4 \times 8 \times T/4$	8
	$4 \times 8 \times T/4$	Maxpool2d(2,4)	$4 \times 4 \times T/16$	
	$4 \times 4 \times T/16$	Dropout(0.25)	$4 \times 4 \times T/16$	
4 (Class.)	$4 \times 4 \times T/16$	Softmax Regression	N	$TN + N$
4 (Regr.)	$4 \times 4 \times T/16$	Dense	1	T or $T+1$
	1	Activation	1	1
Total		Classification		$16C + N(T+1) + 840$
		Regression		$16C + T + 841$

2.2 SMLR for EEGNet Regression Model Aggregation

It's well-known that neural network models can be easily trapped at local minima. Since the EEGNet regression model is compact and can be trained quickly, we can use ensemble learning to increase its robustness. More specifically, we train 10 different EEGNet regression models by bootstrapping, and then use SMLR [37] to aggregate them.

Consider a regression problem with a continuous value input space $\mathcal{X}$ and a continuous value output space $\mathcal{Y}$. Assume there are n unlabeled samples, $\{\mathbf{x}_j\}_{j=1}^n$, with unknown true outputs $\{y_j\}_{j=1}^n$, and m base regression models, $\{f_i\}_{i=1}^m$. The ith regression model's prediction for $\mathbf{x}_j$ is $f_i(\mathbf{x}_j)$. The goal of SMLR is to accurately estimate y_j by optimally combining $\{f_i(\mathbf{x}_j)\}_{i=1}^m$. As shown in Algorithm 1, SMLR consists of two steps: (1) estimate the accuracy of each base regression model; (2) select and combine the strong base regression models.

Algorithm 1: The SMLR algorithm [37].

Input: n unlabeled samples, $\{\mathbf{x}_j\}_{j=1}^n$;
  m base regression models, $\{f_i\}_{i=1}^m$.
Output: The n estimated outputs, $\{f(\mathbf{x}_j)\}_{j=1}^n$.
Apply each f_i to $\{\mathbf{x}_j\}_{j=1}^n$ to obtain the estimates $\{f_i(\mathbf{x}_j)\}_{j=1}^n$ and assemble them into a vector $\mathbf{f}_i(\mathbf{x})$;
Compute the covariance matrix $Q \in \mathbb{R}^{m \times m}$ of $\{\mathbf{f}_i(\mathbf{x})\}_{i=1}^m$;
Compute the first leading eigenvector, $\boldsymbol{\mu}_0$, of Q;
Perform k-means clustering ($k = 3$) on the absolute values of the elements of $\boldsymbol{\mu}_0$;
Identify S, the subset of the strong regression models, as those belong to the cluster with the maximum centroid;
Return $f(\mathbf{x}_j) = \frac{\sum_{i \in S} \mu_{0,i} f_i(\mathbf{x}_j)}{\sum_{i \in S} \mu_{0,i}}, \quad j = 1, ..., n.$

---

3 Experiment and Results

3.1 Dataset

The experiment setup used in this paper was identical to that in [34,37]. Sixteen healthy subjects with normal or corrected-to-normal vision were recruited to participant in a sustained-attention driving experiment [7,8], which consisted of a real vehicle mounted on a motion platform with six degrees of freedom immersed in a 360-degree VR scene. Each subject performed the experiment for about 60–90 min in the afternoon when the circadian rhythm of sleepiness reached its peak. To induce drowsiness during driving, the VR scene simulated monotonous driving at 100 km/h on a straight and empty highway. During the experiment, random lane-departure events were introduced every 5–10 s, and participants were instructed to steer the vehicle to compensate for them immediately. Their response time was recorded and later converted to a drowsiness index (see the next subsection), as research has shown that it has strong correlation with fatigue [21]. Participants' scalp EEG signals were recorded using a 500 Hz 32-channel Neuroscan system (30-channel EEGs plus 2-channel earlobes).

3.2   Preprocessing

The 16 subjects had different lengths of experiment, because the disturbances were presented randomly every 5–10 s. Data from one subject was not recorded correctly, so we used only 15 subjects. To ensure a fair comparison, we used the first 3,600 s data for each subject.

We defined a function [34,37] to map the response time τ to a drowsiness index $y \in [0,1]$:

$$y = \max \left\{ 0, \ \frac{1 - e^{-(\tau - \tau_0)}}{1 + e^{-(\tau - \tau_0)}} \right\} \tag{1}$$

$\tau_0 = 1$ was used in this paper, as in [34,37]. The drowsiness indices were then smoothed using a 90-second square moving-average window to reduce variations. This does not reduce the sensitivity of the drowsiness index because previous research showed that the cycle lengths of drowsiness fluctuations are longer than four minutes [25].

We used EEGLAB [10] for EEG signal preprocessing. A 1–50 Hz band-pass filter was applied to remove high-frequency muscle artifacts, line-noise contamination and direct current drift. Next the EEG data were downsampled from 500 Hz to 250 Hz and re-referenced to averaged earlobes.

We tried to predict the drowsiness index for each subject every 3 s. All 30 EEG channels were used in feature extraction. We epoched 30-second EEG signals right before each sample point, computed the power spectral density (PSD) in the theta and alpha bands (4–12 Hz) for each channel using Welch's method [33], and converted them into dBs. Each channel had 67 such PSD points at different frequencies. Some channels may have dBs significantly larger than others, which degraded the regression performance. So we removed channels which had at least one dB larger than 20, and normalized the dBs of all remaining channels to mean zero and standard deviation one. Assume the number of remaining channels is C' (usually C' is about 30). Then, the input matrix to our EEGNet regression model has dimensionality $C' \times 67$.

3.3   Algorithms

We used data from 14 subjects to build a regression model for the 15th subject, simulating the scenario that we already collected data from 14 subjects and need to use their data to help estimate the drowsiness level for a new driver. We repeated this process 15 times so that each subject had a chance to be the "new" driver.

We compared the performance of the following five algorithms:

1. *Ridge regression based on principal component features* (RR), which is the baseline. This method was first used in [34]. It combined data from all existing 14 subjects and extracted average PSDs in the theta band as features. Similar to the case in Sect. 3.2, some channels may have extremely large average PSDs, which were removed (using a 20 dB threshold) for better regression performance. We then normalized the dBs of each remaining channel to mean zero and standard deviation one, and extracted a few (usually around 10) leading principal components, which accounted for 95% of the variance. The projections of the dBs onto these principal components were then used as our features. At last we built a ridge regression model for the 15th subject.
2. *RR based on principal component features and SMLR* (RR-SMLR). This is the method proposed in [37]. We built 14 RR models, each one using only one source subject's data as the training dataset. Feature extraction was the same as in RR. After obtaining 14 models trained on different datasets, we used SMLR to aggregate them for the target subject.
3. *EEGNet regression model using band-passed EEG inputs* (EEGNet), which used the EEGNet regression architecture described in Sect. 2.1. EEG signals, after 1–50 Hz band-pass filtering, were used as input. So, the input dimensionality was 30×7500 (the second dimensionality was 7500 because we used 30-second EEG signals for estimation, and the sampling rate was 250 Hz).
4. *EEGNet regression model using the PSD features* (EEGNet-PSD). The EEGNet regression architecture was identical to the one in EEGNet, but the $C' \times 67$ PSD features described in Sect. 3.2 were used as its input.
5. EEGNet-PSD *with SMLR* (EEGNet-PSD-SMLR), which was the above EEGNet-PSD model combined with SMLR ensemble learning, as described in Sect. 2.2.

Each algorithm was repeated 10 times so that statistical meaningful results can be obtained. The performance measures were the root mean square error (RMSE) and the correlation coefficient (CC), as in [34,37].

3.4 Results and Discussions

The experimental results are shown in Fig. 1 and Table 2. Observe that:

1. EEGNet, which used band-passed EEG signals as the input, had the worst RMSE and CC for most subjects and also on average. This is because the input feature had very large dimensionality ($T = 7500$ in Table 1), so there were about 8820 parameters in this model. On the contrary, there were only $1200 \times 14 = 12800$ training samples, which may not be enough to fully optimize these parameters.
2. EEGNet-PSD, which had about 67 PSD points in each channel, achieved better RMSE and CC than both RR and EEGNet for most subjects. This demonstrates that the PSD features are better than the band-passed EEG temporal features. Because of the much smaller dimensionality, training time of EEGNet-PSD was also reduced significantly compared with EEGNet.

3. EEGNet-PSD-SMLR, which is an ensemble of multiple EEGNet-PSD aggregated by the SMLR, achieved comparable performance with RR-SMLR, which was our best approach on this driving dataset. On average its RMSE was 1.99% smaller than EEGNet-PSD, and its CC was 2.65% larger than EEGNet-PSD. This suggests that SMLR can indeed improve the learning performance.

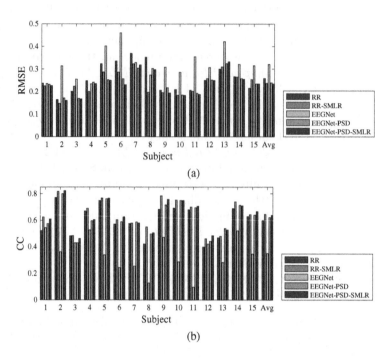

Fig. 1. (a) RMSEs and (b) CCs of the five approaches on the 15 subjects. The last group in each subfigure shows the average performance across the 15 subjects.

Table 2. Average performances of the five algorithms on the 15 subjects.

	RR	RR-SMLR	EEGNet	EEGNet-PSD	EEGNet-PSD-SMLR
RMSE	0.2587	0.2371	0.3208	0.2394	**0.2347**
CC	0.5994	**0.6446**	0.3499	0.6215	0.6379

We also performed a two-way Analysis of Variance (ANOVA) for the five algorithms to check if the RMSE and CC differences among them were statistically significant, by setting the subjects as a random effect. The results are shown in Table 3, which shows that there were statistically significant differences (at 5% level) for both RMSEs and CCs.

Table 3. p-values of two-way ANOVA tests for the five algorithms.

	RMSE	CC
p	$< .0001$	$< .0001$

Then, non-parametric multiple comparison tests based on Dunn's procedure [13,14] were used to determine if the difference between any pair of algorithms was statistically significant, with a p-value correction using the False Discovery Rate method [4]. The p-values are shown in Table 4, where the statistically significant ones are marked in bold. Observe that the RMSE differences and the CC differences between EEGNet-PSD-SMLR and RR/EEGNet were statistically significant, but the differences between EEGNet-PSD-SMLR and EEGNet-PSD/RR-SMLR were not.

Table 4. p-values of non-parametric multiple comparisons for the five algorithms.

		RR	RR-SMLR	EEGNet	EEGNet-PSD
RMSE	RR-SMLR	**.0040**			
	EEGNet	**.0000**	**.0000**		
	EEGNet-PSD	**.0087**	.3757	**.0000**	
	EEGNet-PSD-SMLR	**.0007**	.3239	**.0000**	.2416
CC	RR-SMLR	**.0015**			
	EEGNet	**.0000**	**.0000**		
	EEGNet-PSD	.0731	.0767	**.0000**	
	EEGNet-PSD-SMLR	**.0055**	.3226	**.0000**	.1550

4   Conclusions

This paper focused on the much under-studied regression problems in BCI, particularly, driver drowsiness estimation from EEGs. It has extended EEGNet, a 3-layer CNN model for BCI classification, to BCI regression, and also utilized SMLR to aggregate multiple EEGNets for improved performance. Another novelty of our model is that it uses the PSD of EEG signals as the input, instead of raw EEG signals. In this way it can reduce the computational cost significantly, yet achieve much better regression performance. Experiments showed that EEGNet-PSD-SMLR achieved comparable performance with our best regression model proposed recently.

Recently Riemannian geometry features have demonstrated outstanding performance in several BCI classification applications [3,9]. Our latest research [38] has also showed that Riemannian geometry features can outperform the traditional powerband features in an EEG-based BCI regression problem. Our future research will investigate Riemannian geometry features in the EEGNet and SMLR framework.

References

1. Abbood, H., Al-Nuaimy, W., Al-Ataby, A., Salem, S.A., AlZubi, H.S.: Prediction of driver fatigue: approaches and open challenges. In: Proceedings of the 14th UK Workshop on Computational Intelligence, Bradford, UK, pp. 1–6, September 2014
2. Akin, M., Kurt, M.B., Sezgin, N., Bayram, M.: Estimating vigilance level by using EEG and EMG signals. Neural Comput. Appl. **17**(3), 227–236 (2008)
3. Barachant, A., Bonnet, S., Congedo, M., Jutten, C.: Classification of covariance matrices using a Riemannian-based kernel for BCI applications. Neurocomputing **112**, 172–178 (2013)
4. Benjamini, Y., Hochberg, Y.: Controlling the false discovery rate: a practical and powerful approach to multiple testing. J. R. Stat. Soc. Ser. B (Methodological) **57**, 289–300 (1995)
5. Boon-Leng, L., Dae-Seok, L., Boon-Giin, L.: Mobile-based wearable-type of driver fatigue detection by GSR and EMG. In: Proceedings of the IEEE Region 10 Conference, pp. 1–4, November 2015
6. Chacon-Murguia, M.I., Prieto-Resendiz, C.: Detecting driver drowsiness: a survey of system designs and technology. IEEE Consum. Electron. Mag. **4**(4), 107–119 (2015)
7. Chuang, C.H., Ko, L.W., Jung, T.P., Lin, C.T.: Kinesthesia in a sustained-attention driving task. Neuroimage **91**, 187–202 (2014)
8. Chuang, S.W., Ko, L.W., Lin, Y.P., Huang, R.S., Jung, T.P., Lin, C.T.: Co-modulatory spectral changes in independent brain processes are correlated with task performance. Neuroimage **62**, 1469–1477 (2012)
9. Congedo, M., Barachant, A., Andreev, A.: A new generation of brain-computer interface based on Riemannian geometry (2013). arXiv:1310.8115
10. Delorme, A., Makeig, S.: EEGLAB: an open source toolbox for analysis of single-trial EEG dynamics including independent component analysis. J. Neurosci. Methods **134**, 9–21 (2004)
11. Dinges, D., Grace, R.: PERCLOS: a valid psychophysiological measure of alertness as assessed by psychomotor vigilance. Technical report FHWA-MCRT-98-006, US Department of Transportation, Federal highway Administration (1998)
12. Dinges, D.F., Mallis, M.M.: Evaluation of techniques for ocular measurement as an index of fatigue and as the basis for alertness management. Technical report DOT HS 808 762, National Highway Traffic Safety Administration (1998)
13. Dunn, O.: Multiple comparisons among means. J. Am. Stat. Assoc. **56**, 62–64 (1961)
14. Dunn, O.: Multiple comparisons using rank sums. Technometrics **6**, 214–252 (1964)
15. Edwards, J.D., Sirois, W., Dawson, T., Aguirre, A., Davis, B., Trutschel, U.: Evaluation of fatigue management technologies using weighted feature matrix method. In: Proceedings of the 4th International Driving Symposium on Human Factors in Driver Assessment, Training and Vehicle Design, Stevenson, WA, pp. 146–152, July 2007
16. Eriksson, M., Papanikotopoulos, N.P.: Eye-tracking for detection of driver fatigue. In: Proceedings of the Conference on Intelligent Transportation Systems, pp. 314–319, November 1997

17. Hajinoroozi, M., Mao, Z., Huang, Y.: Prediction of driver's drowsy and alert states from EEG signals with deep learning. In: Proceedings of the 6th IEEE International Workshop on Computational Advances in Multi-Sensor Adaptive Processing, Cancun, Mexico, pp. 493–496, December 2015
18. Hajinoroozi, M., Mao, Z., Jung, T.P., Lin, C.T., Huang, Y.: EEG-based prediction of driver's cognitive performance by deep convolutional neural network. Signal Process. Image Commun. **47**, 549–555 (2016)
19. Hu, S., Zheng, G.: Driver drowsiness detection with eyelid related parameters by support vector machine. Expert Syst. Appl. **36**(4), 7651–7658 (2009)
20. Jahn, G., Oehme, A., Krems, J.F., Gelau, C.: Peripheral detection as a workload measure in driving: effects of traffic complexity and route guidance system use in a driving study. Transp. Res. Part F Traffic Psychol. Behav. **8**(3), 255–275 (2005)
21. Ji, Q., Zhu, Z., Lan, P.: Real-time nonintrusive monitoring and prediction of driver fatigue. IEEE Trans. Veh. Technol. **53**(4), 1052–1068 (2004)
22. Kang, H.B.: Various approaches for driver and driving behavior monitoring: a review. In: Proceedings of the IEEE International Conference on Computer Vision Workshops, pp. 616–623, December 2013
23. Krajewski, J., Sommer, D., Trutschel, U., Edwards, D., Golz, M.: Steering wheel behavior based estimation of fatigue. In: Proceedings of the 5th International Driving Symposium on Human Factors in Driver Assessment, Training and Vehicle Design, Big Sky, Montana, pp. 118–124, June 2009
24. Lawhern, V.J., Solon, A.J., Waytowich, N.R., Gordon, S.M., Hung, C.P., Lance, B.J.: EEGNet: a compact convolutional network for EEG-based brain-computer interfaces. CoRR abs/1611.08024 (2016). http://arxiv.org/abs/1611.08024
25. Makeig, S., Inlow, M.: Lapses in alertness: coherence of fluctuations in performance and EEG spectrum. Electroencephalogr. Clin. Neurophysiol. **86**, 23–35 (1993)
26. Michail, E., Kokonozi, A., Chouvarda, I., Maglaveras, N.: EEG and HRV markers of sleepiness and loss of control during car driving. In: Proceedings of the 30th Annual International Conference of the IEEE Engineering in Medicine and Biology Society, Vancouver, BC, Canada, pp. 2566–2569, August 2008
27. Murphy-Chutorian, E., Trivedi, M.M.: Head pose estimation and augmented reality tracking: an integrated system and evaluation for monitoring driver awareness. IEEE Trans. Intell. Transp. Syst. **11**(2), 300–311 (2010)
28. Sagberg, F., Jackson, P., Kruger, H.P., Muzer, A., Williams, A.: Fatigue, sleepiness and reduced alertness as risk factors in driving. Technical report TOI Report 739/2004, Institute of Transport Economics, Oslo (2004)
29. Sahayadhas, A., Sundaraj, K., Murugappan, M.: Detecting driver drowsiness based on sensors: a review. Sensors **12**(12), 16937–16953 (2012)
30. Sharma, M.K., Bundele, M.M.: Design & analysis of K-means algorithm for cognitive fatigue detection in vehicular driver using respiration signal. In: Proceedings of the IEEE International Conference on Electrical, Computer and Communication Technologies, Tamil Nadu, India, pp. 1–6, March 2015
31. Sommer, D., Golz, M.: Evaluation of PERCLOS based current fatigue monitoring technologies. In: Proceedings of the Annual International Conference of the IEEE Engineering in Medicine and Biology, Buenos Aires, Argentina, pp. 4456–4459, August 2010
32. Tayibnapis, I.R., Koo, D.Y., Choi, M.K., Kwon, S.: A novel driver fatigue monitoring using optical imaging of face on safe driving system. In: Proceedings of the International Conference on Control, Electronics, Renewable Energy and Communications, pp. 115–120, September 2016

33. Welch, P.: The use of fast Fourier transform for the estimation of power spectra: a method based on time averaging over short, modified periodograms. IEEE Trans. Audio Electroacoust. **15**, 70–73 (1967)
34. Wu, D., Chuang, C.H., Lin, C.T.: Online driver's drowsiness estimation using domain adaptation with model fusion. In: Proceedings of the International Conference on Affective Computing and Intelligent Interaction, Xi'an, China, pp. 904–910, September 2015
35. Wu, D., Lawhern, V.J., Gordon, S., Lance, B.J., Lin, C.T.: Driver drowsiness estimation from EEG signals using online weighted adaptation regularization for regression (OwARR). IEEE Trans. Fuzzy Syst. (2016)
36. Wu, D., Lawhern, V.J., Gordon, S., Lance, B.J., Lin, C.T.: Offline EEG-based driver drowsiness estimation using enhanced batch-mode active learning (EBMAL) for regression. In: Proceedings of the IEEE International Conference on Systems, Man and Cybernetics, Budapest, Hungary, pp. 730–736, October 2016
37. Wu, D., Lawhern, V.J., Gordon, S., Lance, B.J., Lin, C.T.: Spectral meta-learner for regression (SMLR) model aggregation: towards calibrationless brain-computer interface (BCI). In: Proceedings of the IEEE International Conference on Systems, Man and Cybernetics, Budapest, Hungary, pp. 743–749, October 2016
38. Wu, D., Lawhern, V.J., Lance, B.J., Gordon, S., Jung, T.P., Lin, C.T.: EEG-based user reaction time estimation using Riemannian geometry features. IEEE Trans. Neural Syst. Rehabil. Eng. (2017)

Real-Time fMRI-Based Brain Computer Interface: A Review

Yang Wang and Dongrui Wu[✉]

School of Automation, Huazhong University of Science and Technology,
Wuhan, Hubei, China
{wangyang_sky,drwu}@hust.edu.cn

Abstract. In recent years, the rapid development of neuroimaging technology has been providing many powerful tools for cognitive neuroscience research. Among them, the functional magnetic resonance imaging (fMRI), which has high spatial resolution, acceptable temporal resolution, simple calibration, and short preparation time, has been widely used in brain research. Compared with the electroencephalogram (EEG), real-time fMRI-based brain computer interface (rtfMRI-BCI) not only can perform decoding analysis across the whole brain to control external devices, but also allows a subject to voluntarily self-regulate specific brain regions. This paper reviews the basic architecture of rtfMRI-BCI, the emerging machine learning based data analysis approaches (also known as multi-voxel pattern analysis), and the applications and recent advances of rtfMRI-BCI.

Keywords: Brain Computer Interface · Functional Magnetic Resonance Imaging · Machine learning · Multi-voxel pattern analysis

1 Introduction

A brain computer interface (BCI) uses neurophysiological signals from the brain, e.g., electrocorticography (ECoG), electroencephalogram (EEG), and functional magnetic resonance imaging (fMRI), to control external devices or computers [3]. Among these signals, fMRI non-invasively measures the task-induced blood-oxygen-level-dependent (BOLD) changes related to brain neuronal activities. Unlike EEG, fMRI has excellent spatial resolution and whole brain coverage, so it can accurately locate activation areas in the brain.

This paper reviews the basic architecture of real-time fMRI-based BCI (rtfMRI-BCI), an emerging machine learning based data analysis approach (also known as multi-voxel pattern analysis), and the applications and recent advances of rtfMRI-BCI.

2 The Architecture of rtfMRI-BCI

Different from conventional fMRI, in which image analysis can only be performed after all scans are finished, rtfMRI-based BCI allows the simultaneous

© Springer International Publishing AG 2017
D. Liu et al. (Eds.): ICONIP 2017, Part II, LNCS 10635, pp. 833–842, 2017.
https://doi.org/10.1007/978-3-319-70096-0_85

acquisition, analysis and visualization of whole brain images. A typical closed-loop rtfMRI-BCI system consists of four components: image acquisition, image preprocessing, image analysis, and feedback.

1. *Image acquisition:* According to some pre-defined scanning parameters, a MRI scanner uses an echo planar imaging sequence to stimulate brain MRI echo signals and then records them. An image reconstruction workstation then assembles these signals into three-dimensional images.

2. *Image preprocessing:* fMRI images need to be preprocessed to improve their quality before further analyses can be performed. This usually involves the following steps:

    (a) *Slice timing correction:* An fMRI image consists of multiple slices that are sampled sequentially at different time instances, so the same region from different slices are shifted in time relative to each other. Slice timing correction interpolates the slices so that they can be viewed as being sampled at exactly the same time [36], as shown in Fig. 1.

    (b) *Realignment:* Any head motion of the subject can contaminate the neighboring voxels. A common practice for motion correction is to treat the brain as a rigid body, and then calculate its translation and rotation relative to a reference image [13].

    (c) *Coregistration:* fMRI images typically have low spatial resolution and do not include enough anatomical details, so they are usually registered to a high resolution structural MRI image of the same subject before presentation [45].

    (d) *Normalization:* Group analysis requires the voxels from the same brain location of different subjects are comparable. Normalization is used to register a subject's anatomical structure to a standardized stereotaxic space defined by a template, such as the Montreal Neurological Institute or Talairach brain [2].

    (e) *Spatial smoothing:* This is usually performed by convolving the functional image with a Gaussian kernel. Smoothing can suppress random noise, and hence increase the signal-to-noise ratio. However, it also reduces the actual spatial resolution and blurs the details, so generally it is not used in machine learning based fMRI analysis.

3. *Image analysis:* This step locates the real-time activation areas within the brain and then performs univariate or multivariate analysis. Typical tasks include statistical analysis of a specific region of interest (ROI) to determine its activation level, and online classification of brain states to find the subject's intention.

    Univariate analysis measures brain activities from thousands of locations repeatedly, and then analyzes each location individually to understand how a particular perceptual or cognitive state is encoded [18]. If the response at a certain location in the brain is different between two states, then the voxel strength at that location can be used to decode the state. Therefore, univariate analysis uses statistical analysis to identify the voxels that are significantly correlated to a specific task, and hence the regions that are significantly activated in the brain, which are called ROIs or functional areas.

While the majority of work in rtfMRI-BCI is done through conventional univariate analysis, there is a growing interest in machine learning based multivariate analysis, particularly, in the emerging field of brain state classification, i.e., decoding the brain state to determine the intention of the subject. This typically includes feature extraction, feature selection/dimensionality reduction, and classification.

(a) *Feature extraction:* The resting-state fMRI is commonly used to diagnose mental diseases. In addition to calculating regional attributes such as the amplitude of low-frequency fluctuations [48] and regional homogeneity [49], functional connections between different regions can also be calculated, and the connection matrix can be used to compute its network properties [50]. For the task-based fMRI, in addition to calculating the functional connections between different regions, the voxel intensities at different times can also be used as features in pattern analysis, and the resulting method is called multi-voxel pattern analysis (MVPA).

(b) *Feature selection/dimensionality reduction:* Feature selection selects the most useful features from a feature set and discards the rest, so it also results in dimensionality reduction. It is an important data preprocessing process that can alleviate the curse of dimensionality and simplify the subsequent learning tasks. Dimensionality reduction maps the original high-dimensional feature space to a low-dimensional subspace using a mathematical transformation. The new features are linear or nonlinear combinations of the original features, and are usually more informative [25].

(c) *Classification:* Simple linear classifiers, such as correlation-based classifier [15, 39], neural networks without hidden layers [28], linear discriminant analysis [7, 16, 17, 27], linear support vector machine (SVM) [9, 20, 24], and Gaussian naive Bayes classifiers [24], are frequently used in MVPA. They compute a weighted sum of the voxel intensities and pass it to a decision function to classify the brain state. Nonlinear classifiers, such as nonlinear SVM [10, 24] and multi-layer neural networks [14], have also been used in MVPA. Compared with linear classifiers, nonlinear ones can capture more complex mappings between features and the brain states. Though theoretically nonlinear classifiers can implement more complex mappings, there is no guarantee that they can significantly outperform linear classifiers in MVPA [9]. This may be because nonlinear classifiers generally need a large amount of training data to achieve their best performance, which may not be easily available in neuroimaging. Additionally, by using a simple linear classifier one can visualize and explain which voxels are more important in decision making, but it is much more difficult to do so for a nonlinear classifier. As a result, the linear SVM classifier is frequently used in fMRI research.

4. *Feedback:* This step feeds the online analysis results back to the subject in real-time, so that the subject can voluntarily self-regulate his/her cognitive function or state. It also presents task-related stimuli to the subject.

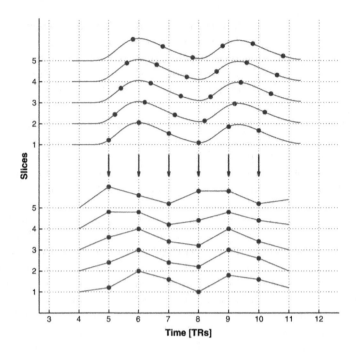

Fig. 1. Illustration of slice timing correction. Adopted from [36].

3   Applications of rtfMRI-BCI

The applications of rtfMRI in BCI can be roughly partitioned into two categories: (1) neurofeedback, in which a subject can voluntarily self-regulate his/her brain activity in a specific region through the feedback of the activation level there; and, (2) brain state decoding, which analyzes the subject's fMRI data to determine his/her intention, which can be then used to control an external device or computer.

3.1   Neurofeedback

Because fMRI has high spatial resolution and can image the entire brain, rtfMRI-BCI can extract the activation levels of specific anatomical locations (ROIs) as feedback. Among the various feedback modalities (auditory, visual, verbal, olfactory, and tactile), visual feedback has been the most popular one. The form of visual feedback also changes with the purpose of the experiment. deCharms et al. [8] introduced a flame-like feedback in a pain-related study, as shown in Fig. 2(a), where the intensity of the flame increases with the intensity of the signal. Sitaram et al. [6] described a thermometer feedback, where red and blue colors are used to indicate whether the signal is above or below a baseline, as shown in Fig. 2(b). Weiskopf et al. [43] used the differential feedback intensity curve as feedback, where an upward arrow indicates an activity enhancement, as shown in Fig. 2(c).

The seminal rtfMRI-BCI work by deCharms et al. [8] on chronic pain is worth special mentioning here. The purpose was to find out whether adjusting the activity on the rostral part of the anterior cingulate cortex (rACC) can affect the perception of pain. Their study showed that the pain introduced by noxious stimulus may be perceived differently if the subject intentionally induces an increase or inhibition in the BOLD level of rACC. Through rtfMRI-based neurofeedback, subsequent experiments have been able to voluntarily adjust the level of activity in many other brain regions, including the anterior cingulate cortex [44], the insula [6], the motor area [47], the amygdala [29], the inferior frontal gyrus [30], and the parahippocampal place area [42]. After enough training, a subject can even voluntarily adjust the corresponding brain region without neurofeedback, and this ability can last for some time after the training.

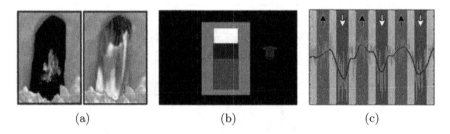

| (a) | (b) | (c) |

Fig. 2. Three different forms of visual feedback. (a) flame, adopted from [8]; (b) thermometer, adopted from [6]; (c) intensity curve, adopted from [43].

These research results suggest that rtfMRI-BCI provides a new approach in neuroscience for studying brain plasticity and functional reorganization through sustained training of specific brain regions [34]. One potential application of neurofeedback is clinical rehabilitation, e.g., reducing the effects of abnormal brain activities, overcoming stroke-induced dyskinesia and Parkinson, relieving chronic pain, and treating depression and other neurological problems such as psychosis, social phobia and addiction [5, 31–33, 40, 41].

3.2   Brian State Decoding

Another main application of rtfMRI-BCI is similar to "brain reading", which classifies a subject's brain state to determine his/her intention. Its implementation can be divided into two categories: (1) pattern matching based on task-specific ROIs, and (2) machine learning based brain state classification.

Pattern matching was used by Yoo et al. [46] in 2004 to perform BCI-based spatial navigation, in which a subject's brain signal was classified into four states so that they can control the computer to navigate through a maze. [4, 23, 26, 35,

37] reported similar work. In all these studies the number of classifiable brain states did not exceed four.

In 2007, Sorger et al. [38] used pattern matching to distinguish among 27 brain states, and implemented the world's first rtfMRI-BCI based spelling system. In this system, a subject can independently alter three aspects of the BOLD signal:

1. The location of the signal source, by performing three different mental tasks (motor imagery, mental calculation, and inner speech).
2. Delay of the mental task start time (0 s, 10 s, and 20 s).
3. The duration of the mental task, which in turn determines the duration of the brain signal (10 s, 20 s, and 30 s).

The combination of these aspects resulted in 27 unique brain responses, which can be assigned to 27 characters, as shown in Fig. 3.

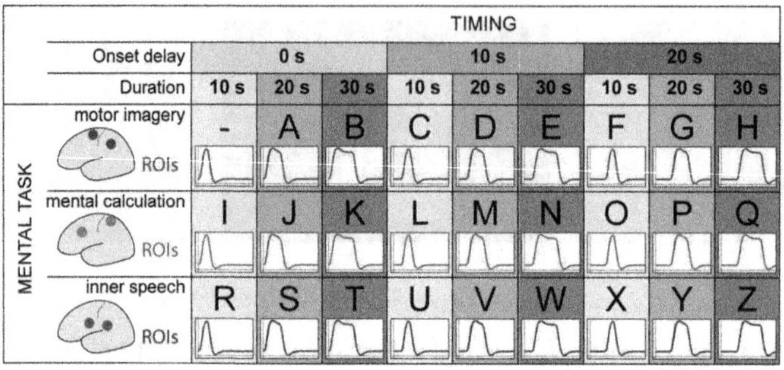

Fig. 3. Letter coding scheme. Adopted from [38].

The spelling system required very little pre-training to help patients in locked-in syndrome to communicate in real time. Its main disadvantage is that the information transfer rate was very low (on average 50 s per letter).

In summary, pattern matching based on task-specific ROIs needs very little pre-training and preparation to implement a BCI system, but generally has low transfer efficiency. Machine learning based brain state classification, also known as MVPA, is expected to improve it. Its main advantages include: (1) it does not require *a priori* assumptions about the functional positioning and individual performance strategies, and (2) it can significantly improve the sensitivity of human neuroimaging analysis by considering the full spatial pattern of brain activities that are measured at many locations.

The application of MVPA to offline fMRI data analysis originated from Haxby et al.'s work [15] in 2001. Since then, cognitive neuroscience research has witnessed a rapidly growing interest on brain state classification using fMRI and experimental designs.

In 2007, LaConte et al. [21] performed online classification of the left and right index finger movement using SVM, which verified the feasibility of using machine learning to implement a BCI system. They first trained a SVM classifier on offline fMRI data, then applied it to online fMRI images to predict the brain state, and next updated the computer-presented stimulus accordingly. This study also showed that machine learning based stimulus feedback can respond to changes in the brain state much earlier than the time-to-peak limitation of the BOLD response, i.e., the former has higher sensitivity. In 2009 Eklund et al. [12] used a neural network to classify three activities (left hand movement, right hand movement, and resting) from rtfMRI, and then controlled the balance of a virtual reality inverted pendulum. In 2011, Hollmann et al. [19] used relevance vector machine to predict a person's decision in the game. In 2013, Andersson et al. [1] used SVM to classify visuospatial attentions based on the fMRI data collected by an ultrahigh field MRI scanner (7 Tesla). Four subjects succeeded in navigating a robot with virtually no training. Compared with methods based on the local activation of ROIs, MVPA has significantly higher information transfer rate.

4   Future Developments and Ethical Considerations

In BCIs, EEG has excellent temporal resolution but poor spatial resolution, whereas fMRI has high spatial resolution and low temporal resolution. Recent advances in sensing hardware have enabled the simultaneous acquisition of EEG and fMRI signals, but sophisticated signal processing and machine learning approaches are still needed to optimally integrate these two modalities to achieve both high temporal resolution and high spatial resolution [11, 22, 51]. Then, brain stimulation techniques like the transcranial magnetic stimulation (TMS) can be better used to treat brain disorders.

The rapid development of BCIs also raises ethical concerns. Both structural and functional brain signals are related to mental states and traits, which could potentially be used to reveal sensitive private information [18]. So, ethics and regulations are also very important to the healthy development of BCIs.

5   Conclusions

This paper has introduced the architecture of rtfMRI based BCI, which includes image acquisition, image preprocessing, image analysis, and feedback. Among them, image preprocessing and analysis are the most important components. Though there have been lots of algorithms for offline fMRI data processing and analysis, how to modify and optimize them for online real-time tasks still calls for more research.

We also reviewed the applications of rtfMRI in BCI, which can be divided into two directions: neuralfeedback and brain state decoding. Both can be of great significance to clinical rehabilitation and cognitive neuroscience research.

References

1. Andersson, P., Pluim, J.P., Viergever, M.A., Ramsey, N.F.: Navigation of a telepresence robot via covert visuospatial attention and real-time fMRI. Brain Topogr. **26**(1), 177–185 (2013)
2. Ashburner, J., Friston, K., et al.: The role of registration and spatial normalisation in detecting activations in functional imaging. Clin. MRI **7**(1), 26–27 (1997)
3. Birbaumer, N., Cohen, L.G.: Brain-computer interfaces: communication and restoration of movement in paralysis. J. Physiol. **579**(3), 621–636 (2007)
4. Bleichner, M., Jansma, J., Salari, E., Freudenburg, Z., Raemaekers, M., Ramsey, N.: Classification of mouth movements using 7 T fMRI. J. Neural Eng. **12**(6), 066026 (2015)
5. Buyukturkoglu, K., Roettgers, H., Sommer, J., Rana, M., Dietzsch, L., Arikan, E.B., Veit, R., Malekshahi, R., Kircher, T., Birbaumer, N., et al.: Self-regulation of anterior insula with real-time fMRI and its behavioral effects in obsessive-compulsive disorder: a feasibility study. PLoS One **10**(8), e0135872 (2015)
6. Caria, A., Veit, R., Sitaram, R., Lotze, M., Weiskopf, N., Grodd, W., Birbaumer, N.: Regulation of anterior insular cortex activity using real-time fMRI. Neuroimage **35**(3), 1238–1246 (2007)
7. Carlson, T.A., Schrater, P., He, S.: Patterns of activity in the categorical representations of objects. J. Cogn. Neurosci. **15**(5), 704–717 (2003)
8. deCharms, R.C., Maeda, F., Glover, G.H., Ludlow, D., Pauly, J.M., Soneji, D., Gabrieli, J.D., Mackey, S.C.: Control over brain activation and pain learned by using real-time functional MRI. Proc. Natl. Acad. Sci. USA **102**(51), 18626–18631 (2005)
9. Cox, D.D., Savoy, R.L.: Functional magnetic resonance imaging (fMRI) brain reading: detecting and classifying distributed patterns of fMRI activity in human visual cortex. Neuroimage **19**(2), 261–270 (2003)
10. Davatzikos, C., Ruparel, K., Fan, Y., Shen, D., Acharyya, M., Loughead, J., Gur, R., Langleben, D.D.: Classifying spatial patterns of brain activity with machine learning methods: application to lie detection. Neuroimage **28**(3), 663–668 (2005)
11. Deshpande, G., Rangaprakash, D., Oeding, L., Cichocki, A., Hu, X.P.: A new generation of brain-computer interfaces driven by discovery of latent EEG-fMRI linkages using tensor decomposition. Front. Neurosci. **11**, 246 (2017)
12. Eklund, A., Ohlsson, H., Andersson, M., Rydell, J., Ynnerman, A., Knutsson, H.: Using real-time fMRI to control a dynamical system by brain activity classification. In: Yang, G.-Z., Hawkes, D., Rueckert, D., Noble, A., Taylor, C. (eds.) MICCAI 2009. LNCS, vol. 5761, pp. 1000–1008. Springer, Heidelberg (2009). doi:10.1007/978-3-642-04268-3_123
13. Friston, K.J., Frith, C.D., Frackowiak, R.S., Turner, R.: Characterizing dynamic brain responses with fMRI: a multivariate approach. Neuroimage **2**(2), 166–172 (1995)
14. Hanson, S.J., Matsuka, T., Haxby, J.V.: Combinatorial codes in ventral temporal lobe for object recognition: Haxby (2001) revisited: is there a face area? Neuroimage **23**(1), 156–166 (2004)
15. Haxby, J.V., Gobbini, M.I., Furey, M.L., Ishai, A., Schouten, J.L., Pietrini, P.: Distributed and overlapping representations of faces and objects in ventral temporal cortex. Science **293**(5539), 2425–2430 (2001)
16. Haynes, J.D., Rees, G.: Predicting the orientation of invisible stimuli from activity in human primary visual cortex. Nat. Neurosci. **8**(5), 686 (2005)

17. Haynes, J.D., Rees, G.: Predicting the stream of consciousness from activity in human visual cortex. Curr. Biol. **15**(14), 1301–1307 (2005)
18. Haynes, J.D., Rees, G.: Decoding mental states from brain activity in humans. Nat. Rev. Neurosci. **7**(7), 523 (2006)
19. Hollmann, M., Rieger, J.W., Baecke, S., Lützkendorf, R., Müller, C., Adolf, D., Bernarding, J.: Predicting decisions in human social interactions using real-time fMRI and pattern classification. PLoS One **6**(10), e25304 (2011)
20. Kamitani, Y., Tong, F.: Decoding the visual and subjective contents of the human brain. Nat. Neurosci. **8**(5), 679–685 (2005)
21. LaConte, S.M., Peltier, S.J., Hu, X.P.: Real-time fMRI using brain-state classification. Hum. Brain Mapp. **28**(10), 1033–1044 (2007)
22. Laufs, H.: A personalized history of EEG-fMRI integration. Neuroimage **62**(2), 1056–1067 (2012)
23. Lee, J.H., Ryu, J., Jolesz, F.A., Cho, Z.H., Yoo, S.S.: Brain-machine interface via real-time fMRI: preliminary study on thought-controlled robotic arm. Neurosci. Lett. **450**(1), 1–6 (2009)
24. Mitchell, T.M., Hutchinson, R., Niculescu, R.S., Pereira, F., Wang, X., Just, M., Newman, S.: Learning to decode cognitive states from brain images. Mach. Learn. **57**(1), 145–175 (2004)
25. Mwangi, B., Tian, T.S., Soares, J.C.: A review of feature reduction techniques in neuroimaging. Neuroinformatics **12**(2), 229–244 (2014)
26. Naito, M., Michioka, Y., Ozawa, K., Ito, Y., Kiguchi, M., Kanazawa, T.: A communication means for totally locked-in ALS patients based on changes in cerebral blood volume measured with near-infrared light. IEICE Trans. Inf. Syst. **90**(7), 1028–1037 (2007)
27. O'toole, A.J., Jiang, F., Abdi, H., Haxby, J.V.: Partially distributed representations of objects and faces in ventral temporal cortex. J. Cogn. Neurosci. **17**(4), 580–590 (2005)
28. Polyn, S.M., Natu, V.S., Cohen, J.D., Norman, K.A.: Category-specific cortical activity precedes retrieval during memory search. Science **310**(5756), 1963–1966 (2005)
29. Posse, S., Fitzgerald, D., Gao, K., Habel, U., Rosenberg, D., Moore, G.J., Schneider, F.: Real-time fMRI of temporolimbic regions detects Amygdala activation during single-trial self-induced sadness. Neuroimage **18**(3), 760–768 (2003)
30. Rota, G., Sitaram, R., Veit, R., Erb, M., Weiskopf, N., Dogil, G., Birbaumer, N.: Self-regulation of regional cortical activity using real-time fMRI: the right inferior frontal gyrus and linguistic processing. Hum. Brain Mapp. **30**(5), 1605–1614 (2009)
31. Ruiz, S., Birbaumer, N., Sitaram, R.: Abnormal neural connectivity in Schizophrenia and fMRI-brain-computer interface as a potential therapeutic approach. Front. Psychiatry **4**, 17 (2013)
32. Ruiz, S., Buyukturkoglu, K., Rana, M., Birbaumer, N., Sitaram, R.: Real-time fMRI brain computer interfaces: self-regulation of single brain regions to networks. Biol. Psychol. **95**, 4–20 (2014)
33. Sitaram, R., Caria, A., Veit, R., Gaber, T., Ruiz, S., Birbaumer, N.: Volitional control of the anterior insula in criminal psychopaths using real-time fMRI neurofeedback: a pilot study. Front. Behav. Neurosci. **8**, 344 (2014)
34. Sitaram, R., Weiskopf, N., Caria, A., Veit, R., Erb, M., Birbaumer, N.: fMRI brain-computer interfaces. IEEE Signal Process. Mag. **25**(1), 95–106 (2008)

35. Sitaram, R., Zhang, H., Guan, C., Thulasidas, M., Hoshi, Y., Ishikawa, A., Shimizu, K., Birbaumer, N.: Temporal classification of multichannel near-infrared spectroscopy signals of motor imagery for developing a brain-computer interface. NeuroImage **34**(4), 1416–1427 (2007)
36. Sladky, R., Friston, K.J., Tröstl, J., Cunnington, R., Moser, E., Windischberger, C.: Slice-timing effects and their correction in functional MRI. Neuroimage **58**(2), 588–594 (2011)
37. Sorger, B., Dahmen, B., Reithler, J., Gosseries, O., Maudoux, A., Laureys, S., Goebel, R.: Another kind of bold response: answering multiple-choice questions via online decoded single-trial brain signals. Prog. Brain Res. **177**, 275–292 (2009)
38. Sorger, B., Reithler, J., Dahmen, B., Goebel, R.: A real-time fMRI-based spelling device immediately enabling robust motor-independent communication. Curr. Biol. **22**(14), 1333–1338 (2012)
39. Spiridon, M., Kanwisher, N.: How distributed is visual category information in human occipito-temporal cortex? An fMRI study. Neuron **35**(6), 1157–1165 (2002)
40. Subramanian, L., Hindle, J.V., Johnston, S., Roberts, M.V., Husain, M., Goebel, R., Linden, D.: Real-time functional magnetic resonance imaging neurofeedback for treatment of Parkinson's disease. J. Neurosci. **31**(45), 16309–16317 (2011)
41. Sulzer, J., Haller, S., Scharnowski, F., Weiskopf, N., Birbaumer, N., Blefari, M.L., Bruehl, A.B., Cohen, L.G., Gassert, R., Goebel, R., et al.: Real-time fMRI neurofeedback: progress and challenges. Neuroimage **76**, 386–399 (2013)
42. Weiskopf, N., Mathiak, K., Bock, S.W., Scharnowski, F., Veit, R., Grodd, W., Goebel, R., Birbaumer, N.: Principles of a brain-computer interface (BCI) based on real-time functional magnetic resonance imaging (fMRI). IEEE Trans. Biomed. Eng. **51**(6), 966–970 (2004)
43. Weiskopf, N., Scharnowski, F., Veit, R., Goebel, R., Birbaumer, N., Mathiak, K.: Self-regulation of local brain activity using real-time functional magnetic resonance imaging (fMRI). J. Physiol. Paris **98**(4), 357–373 (2004)
44. Weiskopf, N., Veit, R., Erb, M., Mathiak, K., Grodd, W., Goebel, R., Birbaumer, N.: Physiological self-regulation of regional brain activity using real-time functional magnetic resonance imaging (fMRI): methodology and exemplary data. Neuroimage **19**(3), 577–586 (2003)
45. Wells, W.M., Viola, P., Atsumi, H., Nakajima, S., Kikinis, R.: Multi-modal volume registration by maximization of mutual information. Med. Image Anal. **1**(1), 35–51 (1996)
46. Yoo, S.S., Fairneny, T., Chen, N.K., Choo, S.E., Panych, L.P., Park, H., Lee, S.Y., Jolesz, F.A.: Brain-computer interface using fMRI: spatial navigation by thoughts. NeuroReport **15**(10), 1591–1595 (2004)
47. Yoo, S.S., Jolesz, F.A.: Functional mri for neurofeedback: feasibility studyon a hand motor task. NeuroReport **13**(11), 1377–1381 (2002)
48. Yu-Feng, Z., Yong, H., Chao-Zhe, Z., Qing-Jiu, C., Man-Qiu, S., Meng, L., Li-Xia, T., Tian-Zi, J., Yu-Feng, W.: Altered baseline brain activity in children with adhd revealed by resting-state functional MRI. Brain Dev. **29**(2), 83–91 (2007)
49. Zang, Y., Jiang, T., Lu, Y., He, Y., Tian, L.: Regional homogeneity approach to fMRI data analysis. Neuroimage **22**(1), 394–400 (2004)
50. Zhang, J., Wang, J., Wu, Q., Kuang, W., Huang, X., He, Y., Gong, Q.: Disrupted brain connectivity networks in drug-naive, first-episode major depressive disorder. Biol. Psychiatry **70**(4), 334–342 (2011)
51. Zich, C., Debener, S., Kranczioch, C., Bleichner, M.G., Gutberlet, I., De Vos, M.: Real-time EEG feedback during simultaneous EEG-fMRI identifies the cortical signature of motor imagery. Neuroimage **114**, 438–447 (2015)

Computational Finance

Dynamic Bidding Strategy Based on Probabilistic Feedback in Display Advertising

Yuzhu Wu, Shumin Pan, Qianwen Zhang, and Jinkui Xie[✉]

Department of Computer Science and Technology, East China Normal University,
Shanghai 200062, China
cstxpxz@163.com, panshumin829@163.com, zqw1005@126.com,
jkxie@cs.ecnu.edu.cn

Abstract. Bidding strategy is an issue of fundamental importance to Demand Side Platform (DSP) in real-time bidding (RTB). Bidding strategies employed by the Demand Siders may have significant impacts on their own benefits. In this paper, we design a dynamic bidding strategy based on probabilistic feedback, called PFDBS, which is different from previous work that is mainly focused on fixed strategies or continuous feedback strategies. Our dynamic bidding strategy is more in accordance with environment of Internet advertising to solve the instability problem. If evaluated valid, we will retain the current strategy, otherwise, we present an approach to amend strategy combined with previous feedback. The experiments on real-world RTB dataset demonstrate that our method has the best performance on Key Performance Indicator (KPI) compared to other popular strategies, meanwhile, the consumption trend of overall budget is the most consistent with real market situation.

Keywords: Display advertising · Probabilistic feedback · Dynamic bidding strategy

1 Introduction

Recently, the online advertising has flourished and becomes the main source of revenue for many publishers. Unlike the sponsored ad, display advertising changes the pre-allocated style of advertising market to the per-impression manner [1]. As a new paradigm of display advertising, RTB regenerates the original advertising ecological chain, and enables selling and purchasing ad placement between advertisers and publishers programmatically [2].

The process of RTB is given in Fig. 1. A user visiting a web page will trigger an ad impression request. Ad exchange (Adx) will send this request to DSP along with features of user and page. Then DSP calculate a price for advertiser and sent back to Adx for auction. Typically, Adx will host a second-price auction to select the winner. The advertiser who sent the highest bidding price will win the auction and pay the second highest bidding price (called *payprice*). Then, the winner's ad will be sent to the webpage [3].

© Springer International Publishing AG 2017
D. Liu et al. (Eds.): ICONIP 2017, Part II, LNCS 10635, pp. 845–853, 2017.
https://doi.org/10.1007/978-3-319-70096-0_86

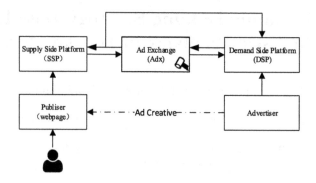

Fig. 1. RTB auction flow

DSP plays an important role on behalf of advertisers in the RTB. Calculating a bid is one of the most important problems for DSP which directly affects advertiser's KPI. KPI usually refers to CTR, CVR and so on. In the early stages, constant bidding and random bidding are widely used. In constant bidding, DSP bid a constant value for all request whereas arbitrarily choose a bid within a given range for the later. Both two strategies are irrelevant to CTR or CVR, which causes ample difficulty in optimising advertiser's KPI. Under charging model of cost-per-click (CPC) or cost-per-action (CPA) with limited budget of advertiser, most bidding strategies turn to rely on CTR (CVR) predictor [4]. Thus, high CTR (CVR) will cause high bidding price (e.g. $ecpc = ctr * cpc$). Zhang et al. analyze the relationship between bid and winning probability [5], and then propose a non-linear bidding strategy [6]. They continue to design a feedback control model by using proportion integration differentiation (PID) in Ref. [7]. In Ref. [8], Wu et al. focus on the *payprice* prediction by using censored model. In Ref. [9], they combine CTR prediction model to censored winning price model and therefore transform the bid strategy into a knapsack problem [10].

In this paper, we propose a model of dynamic bidding strategy based on probabilistic feedback. Our model, which we call PFDBS, mainly consists of three phases: (1) Basic Model: We establish a fundamental bidding model based on CTR. (2) Strategy Evaluation: We develop a deviation rate to evaluate the validation of current strategy. (3) Strategy Emendation: We give an approach to amend current strategy combined with previous feedback when necessary.

Organization. In Sect. 2, we introduce our PFDBS model, further formulate the deviation rate and the amendatory function. In Sect. 3, experiments with real world datasets are performed to assess the effectiveness of the proposed method. We finally conclude the paper in Sect. 4.

2 Modeling

2.1 Problem Definition

In [11], Andrei Broder defines that the core problem of computational advertising is finding the best match between a given user in a given context and a suitable ad. Every DSP tries to optimize the following return on investment (ROI) problem for each advertiser:

$$\max \frac{\sum revenue(a_i, u_i, c_i)}{\sum p_i}$$

where a, u, c, p refer to advertisement, user, context of webpage and cost respectively. For each request, DSP will receive a bid request which can be represented by a high dimensional feature vector $x = (x_1, x_2, \cdots, x_m)$, including the information of user, publisher and advertiser. In CTR-based bidding strategies, DSP will firstly estimate a CTR for the triple (a_i, u_i, c_i) by using machine learning (e.g. Logistic Regression)[12] and then calculate a bid according to CTR. We denote $b_1(i), b_2(i), \cdots, b_m(i)$ as the bids submitted by other DSPs, while $bid(i)$ as our DSP's at the ith auction. The cost and revenue for our advertiser at the ith auction is given by Eq. (1) according to the Vickrey auction:

$$cost_i = \begin{cases} b_1(i) & \text{if } bid(i) > b_1(i) \\ 0 & \text{if } bid(i) < b_1(i) \end{cases}, revenue_i = \begin{cases} ctr_i & \text{if } bid(i) > b_1(i) \\ 0 & \text{if } bid(i) < b_1(i) \end{cases} \quad (1)$$

Due to the limited budget of advertiser, the optimal ROI could be defined as follow:

$$\arg\max_{bid_i} \sum revenue_i$$
$$Subject\ to \sum cost_i \leq Budget \quad (2)$$

The Eq. (2) reveals that the excessive high bid at per auction will lead to the rapid budget consumption, while low bid will have little chance of impression. Both of current static and dynamic strategies have drawbacks.

(1) The parameters in static strategy are usually trained offline and will not be changed online. This is not fit for the changing bid situation.
(2) Current feedback control always changes the model according to the bid result which ignores the occasionalism.

Thus, in this paper we propose a dynamic bidding strategy based on probabilistic feedback (PFDBS). The details will be presented in next section.

2.2 Dynamic Bidding Strategy Based on Probabilistic Feedback

Deviation Rate. For every request, we should decide whether we need to change current strategy according to previous results of auction. We adopt p as the probability to change the model. The deviation rate $p(N)$ is defined in Eq. (3), N is the number of consecutive winning/failures.

$$p(N) = 1 - a^N, 0 \leq a \leq 1, \quad (3)$$

where $a = 0$ refers to continuous feedback model while $a = 1$ means static model. As Eq. (4), for each auction, the probability of adjustment is $p(N)$ while $1 - p(N)$ is the probability of maintaining strategy. $f(\cdot)$ is the amendatory function.

$$b_i(ctr) = \begin{cases} f(b_{i-1}(ctr)) & \text{if } random() < p(N) \\ b_{i-1}(ctr) & otherwise \end{cases} \tag{4}$$

Notice $p(N)$ is monotonically increasing and $\lim_{N \to \infty} p(N) = 1$, which means that if we always win/lose the auction, we should prefer to change current strategy.

Amendatory Function. Once we decide to change the model, we define an amendatory function $f(\cdot)$ in Eq. (5). According to the mechanism of auction, we could attain the *payprice* once we win the impression otherwise go for nothing.

$$f(\cdot) = \begin{cases} b_{i-1}(ctr) * \left(e^{-\frac{1}{|\Delta_{i-1}|} \sum_{\delta_i \in \Delta_i} \delta_j} \right), & if\ win \\ \lambda * b_{i-1}(ctr), & if\ lose \end{cases} \tag{5}$$

δ is the relative error between bid and *payprice*, $\Delta = \{\delta_1, \cdots, \delta_N\}$. λ is a constant greater than 1 which is used to drastically increase the bid to get the impression chance. If the bid calculated by current strategy is higher than market price, we should lower the strategy to save the budget. Since linear factor will cause zero or negative value, we choose exponential model as the negative signal. The whole bidding process under the limited budget is shown in Algorithm 1. After DSP submit a bid, we should update all parameters in each auction. Table 1 illustrates the details of update method.

Table 1. Parameters Update Function $paramUpdate(N, \Delta, flag, bid, payprice)$

	$flag_{i-1} = 1$	$flag_{i-1} = 0$
$bid_i \geq payprice_i$	$flag_i \leftarrow 1$ $N_i \leftarrow N_{i-1} + 1$ $\Delta_i \leftarrow \Delta_i \cup \{\delta_i\}$ $Budget \leftarrow Budget - payprice_i$	$flag_i \leftarrow 1$ $N_i \leftarrow 1$ $\Delta_i \leftarrow \delta_i$ $Budget \leftarrow Budget - payprice_i$
$bid_i < payprice_i$	$flag_i \leftarrow 0$ $N_i \leftarrow 1$ $\Delta_i \leftarrow \emptyset$	$flag_i \leftarrow 0$ $N_i \leftarrow N_{i-1} + 1$ $\Delta_i \leftarrow \emptyset$

Algorithm 1. Dynamic Bidding Strategy Based on Probabilistic Feedback

1: Initialize $N_0 \leftarrow 0, \Delta \leftarrow \emptyset, \beta_0 \leftarrow 1, flag_0 \leftarrow -1, Budget$
2: **while** $Budget > 0$ **do**
3:     $p \leftarrow random(0, 1)$
4:     **if** $p \leq 1 - a^{N_{i-1}}$ **then**
5:         **if** $flag_{i-1} = 1$ **then**
6:             $\beta_i \leftarrow \beta_{i-1} * \left(e^{-\frac{1}{|\Delta_{i-1}|} \sum_{\delta_j \in \Delta_{i-1}} \delta_j} \right)$
7:         **else**
8:             $\beta_i \leftarrow \beta_{i-1} * \lambda$
9:         **end if**
10:     **end if**
11:     $bid_i \leftarrow b(ctr, \beta_i)$
12:     $i \leftarrow i + 1$
13:     $paramUpdate(N_{i-1}, \Delta_{i-1}, flag_{i-1}, bid_i, payprice_i)$
14: **end while**

3   Experiments

Dataset. We use iPinYou dataset [13] for the experiments. Each data instance can be represented by $(\boldsymbol{x}, y)$, $\boldsymbol{x}$ is a feature vector while y is the label for click or not. We train a CTR model by using Logistic Regression (LR)[14]. For a new request, we calculate a bid based on predicted CTR.

Baseline and Evaluation. Four methods below were chosen to compare with our model. Table 2 lists the details. We design two situations for advertisers: under unlimited budget, we simulate N impression requests; under limited budget, we conduct the experiments until the budget is consumed. Finally, we analyze the impressions, clicks and $ecpc$ for every situation.

We run five strategies above on the prepared dataset. For every setting, we calculate the competitive ratio mentioned in [9] as below:

$$CR = \frac{eval_{method}}{eval_{baseline}} * 100\% \qquad (6)$$

Table 2. Bidding Strategies Description

Strategy	#Description
CBSH	Always bid with a high const price
CBSL	Always bid with a low const price
RBS	Bid with a const price in a given range
LBS	Linear bid mentioned in [4]
PFDBS	Proposed dynamic bidding strategy based on probabilistic feedback

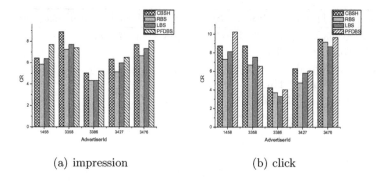

(a) impression   (b) click

Fig. 2. KPI comparison with unlimited budget

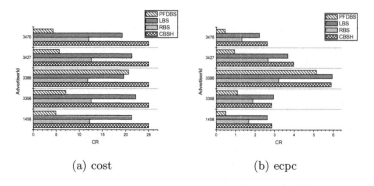

(a) cost   (b) ecpc

Fig. 3. cost comparison with unlimited budget

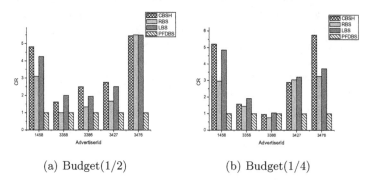

(a) Budget(1/2)   (b) Budget(1/4)

Fig. 4. ecpc comparison under different limited budget

Under the unlimited budget, we choose CBSL as the baseline while PFDBS under the limited budget.

Results with unlimited budget. Figure 2 shows the CR of impression and click for each advertisers during N auctions. The results indicate that CBSH receive highest KPI in most advertiser while the second is PFDBS. Although

CBSH is much higher than PFDBS, it suffer in the ecpc measures in Fig. 3. In total, we can conclude that PFDBS gets highest ROI $\left(\propto \frac{1}{ecpc} \right)$.

Results with limited budget. Figure 4 illustrates the CR of ecpc for each strategy under $(1/2)budget$ and $(1/4)budget$. Each ecpc of other strategies is several times to that of PFDBS. Thus, we can also conclude that PFDBS performs best under limited budget.

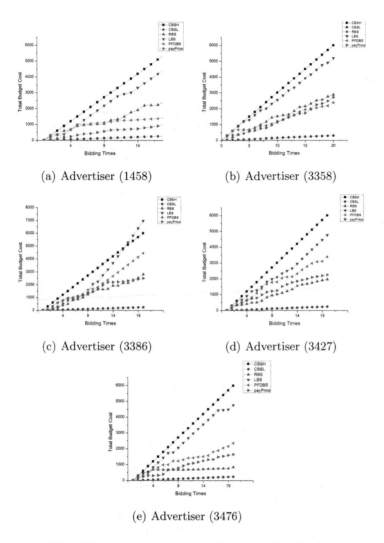

(a) Advertiser (1458)

(b) Advertiser (3358)

(c) Advertiser (3386)

(d) Advertiser (3427)

(e) Advertiser (3476)

Fig. 5. Trend of total consumption for each advertiser

Consumption Trend. In Fig. 5, we calculate the total consumption for every strategy compared with true market price. We could find that CBSH cost too quickly while the total cost of CBSL is too low to win the auction. The consumption of PFDBS is closest to the true cost.

All results reveal that PFDBS we proposed perform best among chosen bidding strategies. CBSH could get more KPI than PFDBS meanwhile it cost too much. CBSL has little chance to win the auction due to low bidding price. The performance of RBS is too unstable to be controlled. In addition, the PFDBS better accommodate Internet advertising market according to the analysis of the total consumption trend.

4   Conclusion

In this paper, we develop a dynamic bidding strategy based on probabilistic feedback, called PFDBS, to optimize the ROI. We first design an evaluation function to decide whether current strategy should be amended, further propose amendatory function to get better bidding price. The experiments demonstrate that our strategy perform best on KPI and ecpc compared to mainstream methods.

For further work, we are interested in integrating distribution of payprice into amendatory function to optimize the proposed strategy. Furthermore, we intend to explore CTR independent bidding models.

References

1. Wang, J., Yuan, S.: Real-time bidding: A new frontier of computational advertising research. In: 8th ACM International Conference on Web Search and Data Mining, pp. 415–416 (2015)
2. Google.: The arrival of real-time bidding and what it means for media buyers. Google (2011)
3. Yuan, Y., Wang, F.Y., Li, J.J., Qin, R.: A survey on real time bidding advertising. In: IEEE International Conference on Service Operations and Logistics, and Informatics, pp. 418–423 (2014)
4. Perlich, C., Dalessandro, B., Hook, R., Stitelman, O., Raeder, T., Provost, F.: Bid optimizing and inventory scoring in targeted online advertising. In: ACM SIGKDD International Conference on Knowledge Discovery and Data Mining, pp. 804–812 (2012)
5. Li, X., Guan, D.: Programmatic buying bidding strategies with win rate and winning price estimation in real time mobile advertising. In: Tseng, V.S., Ho, T.B., Zhou, Z.-H., Chen, A.L.P., Kao, H.-Y. (eds.) PAKDD 2014. LNCS (LNAI), vol. 8443, pp. 447–460. Springer, Cham (2014). doi:10.1007/978-3-319-06608-0_37
6. Zhang, W.N., Yuan, S., Wang, J.: Optimal real-time bidding for display advertising. In: ACM SIGKDD International Conference on Knowledge Discovery and Data Mining, pp. 1077–1086 (2014)
7. Zhang, W.N., Rong, Y.F., Wang, J., Zhu, T.C., Wang, X.F.: Feedback control of real-time display advertising. In: ACM International Conference on Web Search and Data Mining, pp. 407–416 (2016)

8. Wu, C.H., Yeh, M.Y., Chen, M.S.: Predicting winning price in real time bidding with censored data. In: The ACM SIGKDD International Conference, pp. 1305–1314 (2015)

9. Lin, C.C., Chuang, K.T., Wu, C.H., Chen, M.S.: Combining powers of two predictors in optimizing real-time bidding strategy under constrained budget. In: ACM International on Conference on Information and Knowledge Management, pp. 2143–2148 (2016)

10. Kellerer, H., Pferschy, U., Pisinger, D.: Introduction to NP-Completeness of knapsack problems. Knapsack problems, pp. 483–493. Springer, Heidelberg (2004)

11. Broder, A.: Computational advertising. In: 9th ACM-SIAM Symposium on Discrete Algorithms, pp. 992–992 (2008)

12. Bishop, C.M.: Pattern Recognition and Machine Learning. Springer, Heidelberg (2006)

13. Zhang, W.N., Yuan, S., Wang, J., Shen, X.H.: Real-time bidding benchmarking with ipinyou dataset. Comput. Sci. (2014)

14. Han, J.W., Kamber, M.: Data Mining: Concepts and Techniques. Morgan Kaufmann, San Francisco (2006)

Dempster-Shafer Fusion of Semi-supervised Learning Methods for Predicting Defaults in Social Lending

Aleum Kim[✉] and Sung-Bae Cho

Department of Computer Science, Yonsei University, Seoul 03722, South Korea
{aleum_kim, sbcho}@yonsei.ac.kr

Abstract. In social lending, it is hard to know whether borrowers will repay well or not. Most researchers use supervised learning for default prediction, but labeling data by hand is time-consuming. Moreover, labeling results of semi-supervised learning methods are not the same each other. In this paper, we propose a fusion method of label propagation and transductive SVM based on Dempster-Shafer theory for precisely labeling unlabeled data to improve the performance. We remove few unlabeled data with lower reliabilities in labeling results and fusion of the two results based on Dempster-Shafer theory. We have conducted experiments with supervised learning method trained with labeled unlabeled data. As a result, the proposed method produced the best accuracies, 6.15% higher than the result trained with labeled data only, and 1.3% higher than the conventional methods.

Keywords: Social lending · Semi-supervised learning · Label propagation · Transductive SVM · Dempster-Shafer fusion

1 Introduction

Social lending is a growing service providing the platform for getting a loan or investing on the loan between individuals. In the case of lenders, it is important to determine whether the borrowers will be in default or not. This problem is called "default prediction," or "risk evaluation". Default prediction in social lending is more important than traditional financial institutes, because lenders directly face credit risk [1].

Lending Club is the biggest social lending platform in U.S. that opened loan status with various information. Table 1 shows the statistics of loan status. These loans were started in 2015 and the paper is based on data download January 2017 [2]. 73.8% of data are unlabeled. A quarter of the entire data can be used for learning with supervised methods. Higher performance can be achieved by making unlabeled instances labeled.

Semi-supervised learning is training with small amount of labeled set and large amount of unlabeled set. The methods have labeling algorithm during training phase. Labeling results are different according to the methods. We propose a method of incorporating labeling results of two semi-supervised learning methods to increase the correct labeled instances.

© Springer International Publishing AG 2017
D. Liu et al. (Eds.): ICONIP 2017, Part II, LNCS 10635, pp. 854–862, 2017.
https://doi.org/10.1007/978-3-319-70096-0_87

Table 1. Values of class in the social lending dataset.

Value	Status	Type	Ratio
Current	In progress	Unlabeled	73.8%
Default			
In Grace Period			
Late (16–30 days)			
Late (31–120 days)			
Charged off	Complete	Labeled	26.2%
Fully Paid			

In this paper, we propose a fusion method of labeling results for predicting defaults in social lending. Label propagation and transductive SVM(TSVM) are used because of their independency. After training the algorithm, we remove the instances with lower class probabilities and the remained instances are fused by Dempster-Shafer theory. Finally, a decision tree model is trained with the train set added from the proposed method.

2   Related Works

2.1   Semi-supervised Learning

Semi-supervised learning constructs a better classifier using the data with a large amount of unlabeled data along with the labeled data. According to Zhu, semi-supervised learning methods can be divided into five categories [3]. There are generative model, self-training, co-training, some methods to avoid changes in the dense region, and graph-based methods. On the other hand, Triguero categorized generative models as semi-supervised clustering methods, self-training and co-training as self-labeled techniques [4]. In Chepelle's work, self-training and co-training are corporate into different categories such as wrapper methods and others are generative and discriminative model [5]. This paper focuses on semi-supervised learning based on discriminative model. As mentioned, it can be divided into a graph-based model and a semi-supervised SVM according to the approaches. As a result, we chose label propagation and TSVM in two completely different approaches to further enhance the effectiveness of Dempster-Shafer theory.

2.2   Default Prediction in Social Lending

Recently, social lending services are growing. Also, various research for default prediction are studied. Table 2 shows the latest research on default prediction in social lending.

Various machine learning techniques were conducted to assess credit risk in "Lending Club" and random forest achieved the best accuracy [6]. Byanjankar used loan data set of Bondora located in UK, but only labeled set was used [7]. Guo

Table 2. Previous research for default prediction in social lending

Year	Author	Method	Data source	Data size
2015	M. Malekipirbazari [6]	Random forest	Lending club	68,000
2015	A. Byanjankar [7]	Neural network	Bondora	16,037
2016	Y. Guo [8]	Logistic regression	Lending club	2,016,
			Prosper	4,128
2016	C.S.-Cinca [9]	Decision tree	Lending club	40,901
Proposed method		Decision tree	Lending club	**3,32,844**

developed an investment decision making method with credit risk assessment [8]. An approaches of Cinca is called profit scoring using an internal rate of return [9].

However, most studies only use supervised learning with labeled set. As social lending data has large amount of unlabeled, just using labeled data is not enough. Adding the unlabeled data will improve the accuracy even further. In this paper, the proposed method uses almost 330,000 data, 4 times larger than the conventional methods.

3   The Proposed Method

Figure 1 shows the overall process of the proposed method. The main idea is to Dempster-Shafer fusion of labeling results on label propagation and TSVM. Also, we consider class probabilities and remove data whose probabilities are lower than a specified threshold. Therefore, the predicted labels are more accurate and precise.

Practically, since various semi-supervised learning methods have been developed, the labeling results are not the same by methods. It can be solved by fusing labeling results to make labeling accurate and precise. Dempseter-Shafer fusion incorporates two probabilities to consider all available cases.

3.1   Label Propagation

Label propagation is a typical graph based semi-supervised learning, designed to maximize the consistency of predictions using graph Laplacian [10]. It considers the similarity between near data points and the proximity from labeled set to unlabeled set. The algorithm is suitable for abundant unlabeled set like social lending dataset. Before labeling unlabeled set, we train label propagation as shown in Fig. 2.

First, we initialize learning parameters, and make fully connected graph by each data as one node. The weight of the edge between two nodes is calculated by inverse Euclidean distance as follows.

$$w_{ij} = \exp\left(-\frac{\sum_{d=1}^{D}(x_i^d - x_j^d)^2}{\sigma^2}\right) \quad (1)$$

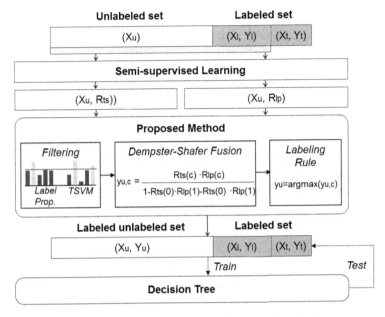

Fig. 1. The overall process of the proposed method

```
Input: transition matrix T   class probability Y

repeat
 Y = Y_-1 T
 Row-normalize Y
 Clamp Y of labeled data.
until Y converges.

Output: Y
```

Fig. 2. Learning algorithm of label propagation

where w_{ij} is the weight of the edge between nodes i and j, x^d is d-dimensional data and σ is value specified by the user. T is a probability transition matrix and is calculated by normalizing the row as follows.

$$T_{ij} = \frac{w_{ij}}{\sum_{k=1}^{l+u} w_{kj}} \tag{2}$$

where T_{ij} is transition matrix value from the ith node to the jth node and l, u are the size of the labeled and unlabeled sets. Y is a class probability matrix, calculated as follows.

$$y_{i,c} = \begin{cases} 1 & \text{if } i < l \text{ and } C_i = c \\ 0 & \text{if } i < l \text{ and } C_i \neq c \\ random & otherwise \end{cases} \quad (3)$$

where $y_{i,c}$ is a class probability value of class c for the ith data, C is a set of classes, and C_i is a class of the ith data.

3.2 Transductive SVM

TSVM is a SVM method that uses transductive inference [11]. It learns only the labeled data first, and gradually uses the unlabeled data to maximize the margins. Figure 3 shows the learning algorithm of TSVM. In this paper, we use Platt scaling to converse the distances between data and support vectors into reliability.

```
Input: labeled data Xₗ, unlabeled data Xᵤ, converging parame-
ters C, C*, numbers of unlabeled data to be assigned to posi-
tive class num₊.

Train SVM with Xₗ and classify Xᵤ.
The num₊ data with the highest value are assigned to the posi-
tive class and remaining data are assigned to negative class.
repeat
    Train SVM with Xₗ and Xᵤ. Then, classify Xᵤ.
    Calculate slack value ξ.
    repeat
        Exchange classes of two data.
        Train SVM with Xₗ and Xᵤ. Then, classify Xᵤ.
    until no different class data with slack value < 0.
until (C⁻ ≥ C*) and (C₊ ≥ C*)
Calculate distances D between each Xᵤ and support vector.

Output: the Platt scaled D.
```

Fig. 3. Learning algorithm of TSVM

3.3 Dempster-Shafer Fusion

In order to apply the Dempster-Shafer theory [12], Frame of Discernment (FOD) was set to 1 for successful repayment, and 0 for repayment failure. Belief (Bel) is the reliability of each model. The fusion rule as follows.

$$m_1 \oplus m_2(1) = \frac{m_1(1)m_2(1)}{1 - m_1(1)m_2(0) - m_1(0)m_2(1)} \quad (4)$$

M ($\{1,0\}$) = 0 because the data point must belong to one class. Finally, assign a label as follows.

$$L = \begin{cases} 1, & m_1 \oplus m_2(1) > m_1 \oplus m_2(0) \\ 0, & m_1 \oplus m_2(0) > m_1 \oplus m_2(1) \end{cases} \qquad (5)$$

4 Experiment and Result

4.1 Social Lending Dataset

In the experiment, we used the real social lending data set in the Lending Club. It contains various information about the loan, the borrower's demographies, and credit history information. The number of columns is 110. Loan information consists of loan status, interest rate, repayment period, etc. The Borrower's information includes career, homeownership, and so on. The borrower's credit information is the majority and consists of the number of defaults, the default period, and the number of normal accounts. Some properties have been added since January 1, 2015 because they were added or removed previously. Table 3 shows the distribution of class values and description.

Table 3. Class values and description

Value	Count	Description
Current	294,703	Loan is up to date on all outstanding payments
Charged off	27,501	Loan for which there is no longer a reasonable expectation of further payments
Default	22	Loan has not been current for 121 days or more
Fully Paid	82,850	Loan has been fully repaid
In Grace Period	4,087	Loan is past due but within the 15-day grace period
Late (16–30 days)	2,111	Loan has not been current for 16 to 30 days
Late (31–120 days)	9,829	Loan has not been current for 31 to 120 days

It is a binary classification problem divided into repayment success ("Fully Paid") as class 1, and failure ("Charged Off") as class 0. However, repayment in progress is almost 70% and this can be unlabeled data. Using supervised learning as in the previous study, only 30% of the data is available for the training model. We have conducted experiments using loans created at 2015 for training and 2016 for testing, and filtering threshold is 0.85. Table 4 describes the list of features.

4.2 Experiment of Results

We have conducted experiments to show the improvement of performance by using unlabeled data. Table 5 shows the confusion matrix of the proposed method of predicting class 1 more accurately than class 0. Table 6 shows the number of added instances to train set of decision tree. Figure 4 shows the accuracies and F1-score. Performances are improved in spite of fewer data than the conventional method.

Table 4. Features used in the experiment

Name	Description
DTI	A ratio calculated using monthly debt payments on the total debt obligations
Term	The number of payments on the loan
Total open	Total open to buy on revolving bankcards
Average balance	Average current balance of all accounts
Ratio of total high credit	Total high credit/credit limit
Mortgage account	Number of mortgage accounts
Bankcard utilization	Ratio of total current balance to high credit/credit limit
Bankcard percentage	Percentage of bankcard accounts >75% of limit
Total balance	Total current balance of all accounts
Annual Income	The self-reported annual income
Revolving utilization	Revolving line utilization rate
Home ownership mortgage	The home ownership status by mortgage
Home ownership rent	The home ownership status by rent
Ration of bankcard high credit	Total bankcard high credit/credit limit
Verification	Indicates if income was verified by LC, not
Loan amount	The amount of the loan applied for by the borrower
Installment	The monthly payment owed by the borrower

Table 5. Confusion matrix of proposed method

		Actual class		
		Fully paid	Charged off	Precision
Predicted class	Fully paid	24,546	3,674	86.9%
	Charged off	253	133	34.5%
	Recall	98.9%	3.5%	**86.28%**

Table 6. The number of labeled and unlabeled data in train set for decision tree

Model	Number of labeled data	Number of unlabeled data
Proposed method	110,351	222,493
Label propagation	110,351	310,752
TSVM	110,351	310,752
Simple Averaging	110,351	310,752
Labeled only	110,351	0

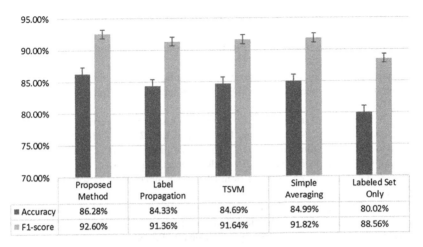

	Proposed Method	Label Propagation	TSVM	Simple Averaging	Labeled Set Only
■ Accuracy	86.28%	84.33%	84.69%	84.99%	80.02%
■ F1-score	92.60%	91.36%	91.64%	91.82%	88.56%

Fig. 4. Comparative results of the accuracy

5   Conclusion

In this paper, we have proposed a prediction method of default in social lending by increasing train set with Dempster-Shafer fusion of two labeling results. The experiments were based on the ratio of labeled and unlabeled instances. As the result, we confirm the feasibility of the proposed method in default prediction of social lending. We obtained comparative results, better than the model trained with labeled instances only and other existing methods. In the future, we need to validate the performance by comparing to various comparative methods. Also, we need to apply to state-of-art semi-supervised learning methods, and instead of decision tree we will use deep learning methods for the better performance.

Acknowledgements. This research was supported by the MSIT (Ministry of Science and ICT), Korea, under the ITRC (Information Technology Research Center) support program (IITP-2017-2015-0-00369) supervised by the IITP (Institute for Information & communications Technology Promotion).

References

1. Davis, K., Murphy, J.: Peer to Peer lending: structures, risks and regulation. Finsia J. Appl. Finan. **3**, 37–44 (2016)
2. Lending Club. https://www.lendingclub.com/info/download-data.action. Accessed 29 June 2017
3. Zhu, X.: Semi-Supervised Learning. Encyclopedia of Machine Learning. Springer, Heidelberg (2010)
4. Triguero, I., García, S., Herrera, F.: Self-labeled techniques for semi-supervised learning: taxonomy, software and empirical study. Knowl. Inf. Syst. **42**(2), 245–284 (2015)

5. Chapelle, O., Scholkopf, B., Zien, A.: Semi-Supervised Learning. The MIT Press, Cambridge (2006)
6. Malekipirbazari, M., Aksakalli, V.: Risk assessment in social lending via random forests. Expert Syst. Appl. **42**, 4621–4631 (2015)
7. Bayanjankar, A., Heikkilä, M., Mezei, J.: Predicting credit risk in peer-to-peer lending: a neural network approach. In: 2015 IEEE Symposium series on Computational Intelligence, pp. 719–725. IEEE (2015)
8. Guo, Y., Zhou, W., Luo, C., Liu, C., Xiong, H.: Instance-based credit risk assessment for investment decisions in P2P lending. Eur. J. Oper. Res. **249**(2), 417–426 (2016)
9. Serrano-Cinca, C., Gutiérrez-Nieto, B.: The use of profit scoring as an alternative to credit scoring systems in peer-to-peer (P2P) lending. Decis. Support Syst. **89**, 113–122 (2016)
10. Zhu, X., Ghahramani, Z.: Learning from labeled and unlabeled data with label propagation (2002)
11. Joachims, T.: Transductive inference for text classification using support vector machines. In: International Conference on Machine Learning, pp. 200–209. NIPS (1998)
12. Shafer, G.: A Mathematical Theory of Evidence. Princeton University Press, Princeton (1976)

Robust Portfolio Risk Minimization Using the Graphical Lasso

Tristan Millington$^{(\boxtimes)}$ and Mahesan Niranjan$^{(\boxtimes)}$

Department of Electronics and Computer Science, University of Southampton,
Highfield SO17 1BJ, Southampton, UK
{T.Millington,M.Niranjan}@Southampton.ac.uk

Abstract. We apply the statistical technique of *graphical lasso* for inverse covariance estimation of asset price returns in Markowitz portfolio optimisation. Graphical lasso induces sparsity in the inverse covariance matrix, thereby capturing conditional independences between different assets. We show empirical results that not only the resulting minimum risk portfolio is robust, in that the variation in expected returns is reduced when a fraction of the data is assumed missing, but also enables the construction of a financial network in which groups of assets belonging to the same financial sector are linked.

Keywords: Portfolio optimization · Graphical lasso · Financial network · Graphical model · Covariance estimation

1 Introduction

Portfolio optimisation and its variants have been of interest in empirical finance for decades, following the pioneering work of Markowitz [17]. This mean-variance optimisation problem defines a Pareto optimal frontier in the space of expected returns and the corresponding risks (variances) of a portfolio under the assumption that returns on the assets follow a multivariate Gaussian density. The formulation of such a model, under assumptions of no short selling, is given as follows:

$$
\begin{aligned}
& \underset{w}{\text{minimize}} && w^T \Sigma w \\
& \text{subject to} && \sum_{i=1}^{i=N} w_i = 1 \\
& && w_i \geq 0 \\
& && w^T m \geq \rho
\end{aligned}
\tag{1}
$$

where, w represents the portfolio weights $[w_1, w_2 \ldots w_N]^T$, m and Σ the parameters of the Gaussian distributed asset returns, and ρ, the expected returns. Solving the above quadratic programming problem at different values of ρ yields the well known efficient frontier.

© Springer International Publishing AG 2017
D. Liu et al. (Eds.): ICONIP 2017, Part II, LNCS 10635, pp. 863–872, 2017.
https://doi.org/10.1007/978-3-319-70096-0_88

In practice, however, m and Σ are not known and have to be estimated from data with the maximum likelihood estimates of

$$\widehat{m} = \frac{1}{T} \sum_{t=1}^{T} x_t \tag{2}$$

$$\widehat{\Sigma} = \frac{1}{T} \sum_{t=1}^{T} (x_t - m)(x_t - m)^T \tag{3}$$

being the common choice. Here, T is the time window of data and $x_t \in \mathcal{R}^N$ represents returns on the assets at time t.

In finance, these estimates from data are known to suffer robustness issues [4,14,18]. Financial data consists of occasional outliers to which maximum likelihood estimates are notoriously sensitive. Further, to estimate covariance matrices reliably we need a long enough window (T) of data, though due to non-stationarity in the markets, we may choose a small window. This (particularly when T and N are of similar values) can lead to the covariance matrix Σ being singular and non-invertible. The consequence of poor estimation of parameters is that the resulting portfolio can be unstable and produce poor out-of-sample performance, with extreme weights that are liable to have large changes over time [4]. In many cases these portfolios perform worse than a 1/N naive portfolio [8]. These issues are often addressed by regularisation, of which shrinkage estimation is a classic tool (e.g. [14]). Brodie et al. address this issue by regularisation using the l_1 (or lasso) penalty in an index tracking setting, deriving stable portfolios which are also sparse. Takeda et al. [19] use a combination of l_1 and l_2 regularisers to simultaneously induce sparsity and improve out-of-sample performance.

Estimation of covariance matrices with some desirable structure imposed on them falls under the field of structured matrix approximation (e.g. [7,16]). In the financial domain, Fan et al. [10] involve 3-factor model in the estimation of a covariance matrix. They find the factor model improves the estimation of the precision matrix, but affects errors in the estimation of the covariance matrix less. In this setting, Friedman et al. [11], introduced the graphical lasso (glasso) as a way of inducing structure into covariance matrices. Specifically, they argued that a sparse inverse covariance matrix of Gaussian distributed data captures conditional independences between the variables. From this algorithm, a well-conditioned covariance matrix and a sparse precision matrix are produced even when T is approaching N. From this sparse precision matrix, a network can be extracted, with a zero in the matrix indicating a conditional independence and a non-zero value indicating a relationship. We make use of the well-conditioned covariance matrix and the precision matrix in this paper.

To start, we assume the asset returns follow a multivariate Gaussian distribution. A multivariate Gaussian distribution can be written as

$$f(x, m, \Sigma) = \frac{1}{(2\pi)^{\frac{N}{2}} |\Sigma|^{\frac{1}{2}}} \exp(-\frac{1}{2}(x - m)^T \Sigma^{-1} (x - m)). \tag{4}$$

Suppose we have T measurements of N assets, denoted as $X = (\boldsymbol{x}_1 \ldots \boldsymbol{x}_N)^T$ where each $\boldsymbol{x}$ is a T dimensional vector. The log-likelihood this set of measurements belongs to a Gaussian distribution with Σ and $\boldsymbol{m}$ is

$$\log L(\boldsymbol{m}, \Sigma | X) = -\frac{TN}{2} \log(2\pi) - \frac{1}{2} \log |\Sigma| - \frac{1}{2} \sum_{t=1}^{T} (\boldsymbol{x}_t - \boldsymbol{m})^T \Sigma^{-1} (\boldsymbol{x}_t - \boldsymbol{m}). \quad (5)$$

Substituting the maximum likelihood covariance estimators from (2) and (3) and discarding the constant gives

$$\log L(\boldsymbol{m}, \Sigma | X) = \log |\Theta| - tr(\widehat{\Sigma}\Theta) \quad (6)$$

where $\Theta = \Sigma^{-1}$.

Input : Empirical Covariance Matrix $\widehat{\Sigma}$
            Convergence Tuning Parameter t
            Regularisation Parameter λ
Output: Covariance Matrix W
$W = \widehat{\Sigma} + \lambda I$;
while ave $(|W_{prev} - W|) > t$ ave$(|\text{offdiag}(\widehat{\Sigma})|)$ **do**
$\quad$ **for** $i=1\ldots p$ **do**
$\quad\quad$ // Partition the matrix into all but the ith row and column
$\quad\quad$ and the ith row and column without the ith value
$\quad\quad W_{11} \leftarrow W[1\ldots p \neq i][1\ldots p \neq i]$;
$\quad\quad w_{12} \leftarrow W[1\ldots p \neq i]$;
$\quad\quad s_{12} \leftarrow \widehat{\Sigma}[1\ldots p \neq i]$;
$\quad\quad$ // Run coordinate descent to calculate $\hat{\beta}$
$\quad\quad$ **while** norm$(\hat{\beta}_{prev} - \hat{\beta}) > t$ **do**
$\quad\quad\quad$ **for** $j=1\ldots p$ **do**
$\quad\quad\quad\quad \hat{\beta}_{prev} \leftarrow \hat{\beta}$;
$\quad\quad\quad\quad V \leftarrow W_{11}$;
$\quad\quad\quad\quad u \leftarrow s_{12}$;
$\quad\quad\quad\quad \hat{\beta}_j \leftarrow \frac{S_t(u_j - \sum_{k \neq j} V_{kj}\hat{\beta}_k, \lambda)}{V_{jj}}$;
$\quad\quad\quad$ **end**
$\quad\quad$ **end**
$\quad\quad W_{prev} \leftarrow W$;
$\quad\quad$ // Update W
$\quad\quad W[1\ldots p \neq i] \leftarrow W_{11}.\hat{\beta}$;
$\quad$ **end**
end

offdiag(M) = offdiagonal elements of matrix M
$S_t(x, t) = sign(x)(|x| - t)_+$
$|M|$ = absolute values of M
ave(M) = average of M
norm(M) = L_2 norm of M

Fig. 1. Pseudo-code for the Graphical Lasso

Following Banerjee *et al.* [2], we add a L_1 penalty term to impose sparsity on the precision matrix:

$$\log \det \Theta - tr(\widehat{\Sigma}\Theta) - \lambda \, ||\Theta||_1 \tag{7}$$

with λ as a regularising parameter.

Friedman *et al.* [11] propose the glasso to maximise this function using block coordinate gradient descent. Pseudo-code for the glasso algorithm is shown in Fig. 1.

We are not alone in looking for applications for the glasso. Goto *et al.* [12] use the glasso to construct a sparse precision matrix for portfolio hedging. Exploiting the sparsity allows for lower turnover in the portfolio hedging and gives a more predictable out-of-sample risk and return. Awoye [1] uses the glasso to estimate a covariance matrix for mean-variance portfolio optimisation, and compares its performance to existing covariance estimators with various constraints. Their portfolios designed using the glasso perform well when compared to other estimators, achieving a lower realised risk. We hope to exploit the lowered risk and increased robustness the glasso provides.

We are also not the first to construct networks on financial data. Mantegna [15] constructed a network from stock prices using a correlation matrix. Defining a distance metric using correlation coefficients, they construct a minimum spanning tree from the companies used to construct the Dow Jones Industrial Average. Companies in similar sectors are clustered in this minimum spanning tree. Boginski *et al.* [5] also use a correlation matrix to create a network. Using a threshold on the correlation coefficient to decide whether two companies are linked, they build a graph. They find the produced graph follows a power law rule when the threshold is set at a large enough value, and look at how varying the threshold changes the clusters in the graph. Huang *et al.* [13] follow a similar path, instead concentrating on the Chinese stock market. They use their network to classify the stocks and to test the stability of the market. We also wish to see how our constructed network can classify companies.

2   Methods and Data

In this work, instead of the general Markowitz frontier, we focus on the minimum variance portfolio, unconstrained by the expected return (*i.e.* one corner of the frontier curve). This allows us to negate the errors from mean estimation in constructing our portfolios.

$$\begin{aligned} \underset{w}{\text{minimize}} \quad & \boldsymbol{w}^T \Sigma \boldsymbol{w} \\ \text{subject to} \quad & \sum_{i=1}^{i=N} w_i = 1 \\ & w_i \geq 0 \end{aligned} \tag{8}$$

The covariance (Σ) is estimated using the empirical covariance and the glasso, with the convergence threshold (t) set to 0.001 and the regularisation parameter

(λ) varied with the dataset, due to the differences in the means and variances of the datasets (monthly returns will in general have larger absolute values than daily returns). We use an implementation of the glasso written using Cython [3], and CVXPY [9] to solve the optimisation problem.

Two datasets are used to test our methods, with different sizes and time periods. The first is taken from Center for Research in Security Prices (CRSP) database from the 30th November 1982 until the 31st December 1990. We use the monthly percentage returns. Any assets with incomplete data are removed, leaving us with 92 observations from 26 companies. The company sectors are shown in Table 1. We set λ to 0.01 for this dataset. Our second dataset is the S&P500 daily percentage returns from 2nd January 2003 until 25th January 2007. Again, assets with incomplete data are removed, leaving us with 1259 observations from 409 companies. We set λ to 0.0002 for this dataset. Both are split into 2 equally sized sets, a training set to calculate the optimal portfolio from and a test set to evaluate the out of sample performance.

Table 1. Number of companies in each sector from the CRSP database. The colouring and number represents the sector they belong to in Fig. 6

Sector	Number of Companies	Colour	Number
Agriculture	1	Brown	1
Communications	2	Cyan	2
Cyclical Consumer Goods & Services	5	Green	3
Energy	2	Red	4
Financials	2	Light Green	5
Industrials	1	Navy Blue	6
Insurance	2	Purple	7
Non-Cyclical Consumer Goods & Services	1	Grey	8
Technology	9	Yellow	9
Utilities	1	Orange	10

To test the robustness of the covariance estimation, we remove a number of samples randomly from the training data and calculate the mean and covariance from this corrupted data set. For the CRSP data we remove 4, and for the S&P500 data we remove 60, due to the much larger size of this dataset. We then solve the unconstrained risk minimization problem to get a set of portfolio weights. These weights are used to calculate a mean risk and return from the unseen data. This is run 25 times, although similar results are obtained when the number of runs is set to 10, 15 and 20. We can then compare how the corruption of the data affects the risks and returns of the portfolios produced on both seen and unseen data.

Following this we construct a network from the sparse precision matrix produced by the glasso. Focusing on the CRSP data due to the smaller number of companies, λ is set to 0.005. A link between companies implies their stocks are correlated in some way. Increasing the value of λ increases the sparsity of the precision matrix and will result in fewer links.

3   Results

In this section we test the portfolios constructed using the glasso covariance against those constructed using the empirical covariance and explore why they perform differently. Firstly we look at the CRSP data.

Figure 2 shows boxplots of the risk and return for the risk minimized portfolios using the CRSP data. We can see the portfolios produced using the glasso

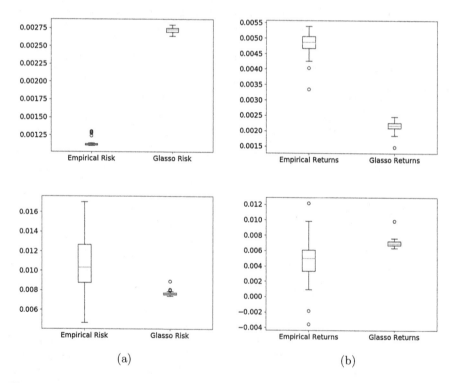

(a)   (b)

Fig. 2. Variation in risks (a) and returns (b) of portfolios on monthly returns of 26 companies using the empirical and glasso covariance. 4 samples are randomly removed each time (11.5% of the data) for 25 runs. The top row is the training set and the bottom row the test set. The portfolios produced using the glasso covariance have a slightly smaller variance and fewer outliers in their training risks and returns, and a much smaller variance in their test risks and returns.

covariance have a comparable or slightly smaller variance and fewer outliers in their risk and returns on the training set, and a much smaller variance in their test set than those produced with the empirical covariance.

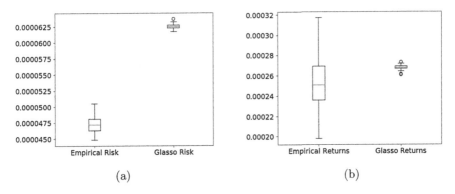

Fig. 3. Variation in risks (a) and returns (b) of portfolios on unseen daily returns of S&P500 comapanies. 60 samples (9.5% of the data) are removed each time. Again we can see the reduction in variance the glasso covariance provides

Figure 3 shows boxplots of the risks and returns for the S&P500 data. Again, we can see the significant reduction in variance of the risks and returns from using the glasso covariance. Due to room constraints, we do not show the training set boxplots, although these are similar to the results on the training set of CRSP data.

The results in Fig. 2 are generated using a λ of 0.01. What happens if we change our choice of λ? Fig. 4 shows the portfolio weights chosen as we vary lambda. As λ is increased, the portfolio weights become more evenly distributed throughout the companies. We would expect this to reduce the variance of risks and returns of the portfolios produced.

Now we explore relationships between the CRSP companies and how this affects our risk minimized portfolios. Figure 5 shows the generated network. Companies are tagged according to the sector the company belongs to. Sector colours and numbers are shown in Table 1. There is a general trend towards companies in the same sector being linked and unrelated companies being unlinked. Note in particular how 2 out of the 3 companies with no links are also the only members of their sector.

Relating this back to the optimal portfolios, we colour the nodes according to the weight put upon the company in Fig. 6. The darker the node, the larger the weight upon it. We can see that companies linked together have lower weights than those not linked. This should reduce the risk by diversifying the portfolio and avoiding companies who have correlated stocks.

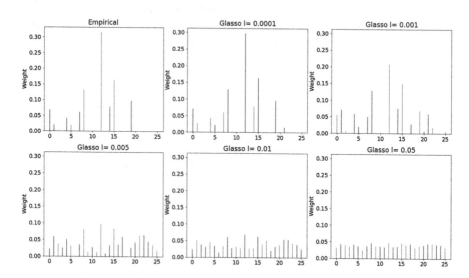

Fig. 4. Weights produced by the minimum risk unconstrained optimisation using empirical and glasso covariance. As we increase the regularization parameter for the graphical lasso, the weights tend to spread out to a 1/n portfolio.

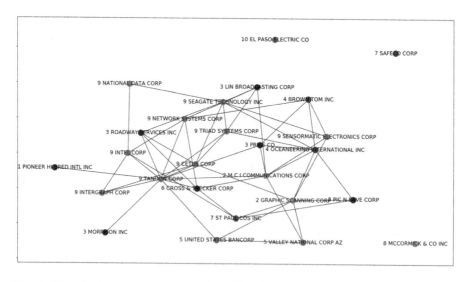

Fig. 5. Links between companies produced by the graphical lasso with λ set to 0.005. Companies are tagged according to the sector that they belong to - the number at the start of the label and the node colour indicate this (Colours and numbers are shown in Table 1). Note how companies in the same sectors are linked, particularly the cluster of technology companies.

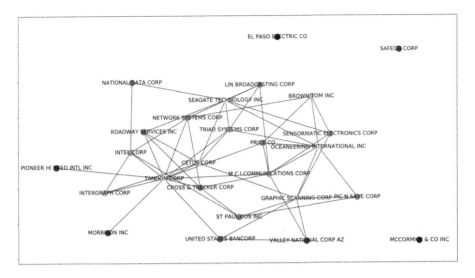

Fig. 6. Links between companies produced by the graphical lasso. The darker the node, the larger the weight on that company in the portfolio. The companies who are linked are lighter than those without links. This provides diversification away from correlated stocks and so should reduce the risk of the portfolio.

4   Conclusion

In this paper we have shown that using the graphical lasso to estimate covariance matrices can improve the robustness of portfolio optimization. The portfolios constructed using the graphical lasso have a lower variance of risks and returns than those constructed using the empirical covariance, particularly in their unseen data. We demonstrate this by removing data from the training set and comparing the risks and returns of the portfolios produced with both monthly and daily data. Finally we construct a network using the precision matrix estimated by the glasso to explore relationships between companies and how this affects the choice of assets to buy, with the minimum risk portfolios preferring to reduce their purchases of correlated stocks.

Acknowledgements. This work was partially funded by the Engineering and Physical Sciences Research Council, UK (EP/N014189: Joining the Dots, from Data to Insight).

References

1. Awoye, O.A.: Markowitz Minimum Variance Portfolio Optimization using New Machine Learning Methods. Ph.D. thesis, (UCL) University College London (2016)
2. Banerjee, O., El Ghaoui, L., d'Aspremont, A.: Model selection through sparse maximum likelihood estimation for multivariate gaussian or binary data. J. Mach. Learn. Res. **9**, 485–516 (2008)

3. Behnel, S., Bradshaw, R., Citro, C., Dalcin, L., Seljebotn, D., Smith, K.: Cython: the best of both worlds. Comput. Sci. Eng. **13**(2), 31–39 (2011)
4. Best, M.J., Grauer, R.R.: On the sensitivity of mean-variance-efficient portfolios to changes in asset means: some analytical and computational results. Rev. Finance Stud. **4**(2), 315–342 (1991)
5. Boginski, V., Butenko, S., Pardalos, P.M.: Statistical analysis of financial networks. Comput. Stat. Data Anal. **48**(2), 431–443 (2005)
6. Brodie, J., Daubechies, I., De Mol, C., Giannone, D., Loris, I.: Sparse and stable Markowitz portfolios. Proc. Natl. Acad. Sci. U.S.A. **106**(30), 12267–72 (2009)
7. Chu, M.T., Funderlic, R.E., Plemmons, R.J: Structured low rank approximation. Linear Algebra Appl. **366**, 157–172 (2003). special issue on Structured Matrices: Analysis, Algorithms and Applications
8. DeMiguel, V., Garlappi, L., Uppal, R.: Optimal versus naive diversification: how inefficient is the 1/n portfolio strategy? The Rev. Finance Stud. **22**(5), 1915–1953 (2007)
9. Diamond, S., Boyd, S.: CVXPY: a Python-embedded modeling language for convex optimization. J. Mach. Learn. Res. **17**(83), 1–5 (2016)
10. Fan, J., Fan, Y., Lv, J.: High dimensional covariance matrix estimation using a factor model. J. Econometrics **147**(1), 186–197 (2008). Econometric modelling in finance and risk management: An overview
11. Friedman, J., Hastie, T., Tibshirani, R.: Sparse inverse covariance estimation with the graphical lasso. Biostatistics **9**(3), 432–441 (2008)
12. Goto, S., Xu, Y.: Improving mean variance optimization through sparse hedging restrictions. J. Fin. Quant. Anal. **50**(6), 1415–1441 (2015)
13. Huang, W.Q., Zhuang, X.T., Yao, S.: A network analysis of the chinese stock market. Phys. A Stat. Mech. Appl. **388**(14), 2956–2964 (2009)
14. Ledoit, O., Wolf, M.: Honey, i shrunk the sample covariance matrix. J. Portfolio Mgmt. **30**(4), 110–119 (2004)
15. Mantegna, R.N.: Hierarchical structure in financial markets. Eur. Phys. J. B Condens. Matter Complex Syst. **11**(1), 193–197 (1999)
16. Markovsky, I., Niranjan, M.: Approximate low-rank factorization with structured factors. Comput. Stat. Data Anal. **54**(12), 3411–3420 (2010)
17. Markowitz, H.M.: Portfolio selection. J. Finance **7**(60), 77–91 (1952)
18. Qiu, H., Han, F., Liu, H., Caffo, B.: Robust portfolio optimization. In: Proceedings of the 28th International Conference on Neural Information Processing Systems, NIPS 2015, pp. 46–54. MIT Press, Cambridge (2015)
19. Takeda, A., Niranjan, M., Gotoh, J.Y., Kawahara, Y.: Simultaneous pursuit of out-of-sample performance and sparsity in index tracking portfolios. CMS **10**(1), 21–49 (2013)

Non-Negative Matrix Factorization with Exogenous Inputs for Modeling Financial Data

Steven Squires$^{(\boxtimes)}$, Luis Montesdeoca, Adam Prügel-Bennett,
and Mahesan Niranjan

Electronics and Computer Science, University of Southampton, Southampton, UK
{ses2g14,ljm1e14,apb,mn}@ecs.soton.ac.uk

Abstract. Non-negative matrix factorization (NMF) is an effective dimensionality reduction technique that extracts useful latent spaces from positive value data matrices. Constraining the factors to be positive values, and via additional regularizations, sparse representations, sometimes interpretable as part-based representations have been derived in a wide range of applications. Here we propose a model suitable for the analysis of multi-variate financial time series data in which the variation in data is explained by latent subspace factors and contributions from a set of observed macro-economic variables. The macro-economic variables being external inputs, the model is termed XNMF (eXogenous inputs NMF). We derive a multiplicative update algorithm to learn the factorization, empirically demonstrate that it converges to useful solutions on real data and prove that it is theoretically guaranteed to monotonically reduce the objective function. On share prices from the FTSE 100 index time series, we show that the proposed model is effective in clustering stocks in similar trading sectors together via the latent representations learned.

Keywords: Non-negative matrix factorisation · Computational finance · Dimensionality reduction

1 Introduction

Many modern problems in machine learning are posed in high dimensions, due to the ease with which we can now acquire and archive data. However, useful information we wish to extract about a problem domain might be expected to be characterised by fewer features. Hence dimensionality reduction is a useful tool in identifying the latent subspaces of interest. By working in a smaller subspace we hope to reduce the noise, compress the data and, potentially, enable classification or regression machines to generalise better. Non-negative matrix factorization (NMF) is an increasingly popular choice of linear dimensionality reduction in large part because it is often capable of producing a sparse and parts based representation of the data.

© Springer International Publishing AG 2017
D. Liu et al. (Eds.): ICONIP 2017, Part II, LNCS 10635, pp. 873–881, 2017.
https://doi.org/10.1007/978-3-319-70096-0_89

In standard NMF we consider an input matrix with m dimensions and n samples: $\mathbf{V} \in \mathbb{R}^{m \times n}$. The aim is to find a lower-dimensional representation of the data by factorizing $\mathbf{V}$ into two matrices $\mathbf{W}$ and $\mathbf{H}$ such that $\mathbf{V} \approx \mathbf{WH}$, where $\mathbf{W} \in \mathbb{R}^{m \times r}$ and $\mathbf{H} \in \mathbb{R}^{r \times n}$. Generally $r \ll m$ and $r \ll n$ so that NMF creates a new representation of the data in a significantly reduced subspace.

Financial systems are inherently complex, driven by the objectives of market players, along with monetary and fiscal policies of governments. Pure time series analysis has been applied extensively to asset returns [1–3], exchange rates [4] and derivatives [5,6]. NMF has been applied to financial data in several ways, such as identifying underlying trends in stock market data [7]. Also sparse-semi-NMF approaches to portfolio diversification have been used to minimise risk [8,9]. The appeal of NMF in this context is that returns on assets, expressed as ratios of their market prices, are positive. Factorizing multivariate asset return data into low rank factors can potentially discover low dimensional representations that are determined by sectors of assets that are likely to show similar responses. However, statistical signal analysis methods usually do not take into account exogenous information from macro-economic variables (referred to in this paper as macro-variables) that have significant contributions to market movements.

In this paper, we propose a matrix factorization method that includes known exogenous variables as additional components of subspace modelling. We expect such factorizations to potentially uncover sector-specific drivers from among a wide range of macro-variables available. Specifically, our model represents the variation in any asset as consisting of contributions from sector-specific components and selected macro-variables. Hence the main novel contributions in this paper are the specification of such a factorization model and a learning algorithm for it. We empirically demonstrate the effective performance of our approach on share price data from FTSE 100 companies and theoretically prove that the XNMF algorithm is guaranteed to monotonically reduce the objective function.

This paper is structured as follows: in Sect. 2 we present our model including the underlying mathematics and the proof of monotonic reduction of the objective function; in Sect. 3 we discuss the real and synthetic data we used; in Sect. 4 we display our results; and in Sect. 5 we conclude and summarize our results.

2 Model and Learning Algorithm

Our aim is to find a combined representation of the share price data using the share price itself with the addition of external macro-variables. We can utilise standard NMF methods to find representations such that $\mathbf{V} \approx \mathbf{W}_1\mathbf{H}_1$ and, separately, $\mathbf{V} \approx \mathbf{W}_2\mathbf{H}_2$ where $\mathbf{W}_1 \in \mathbb{R}^{m \times r_1}$, $\mathbf{H}_1 \in \mathbb{R}^{r_1 \times n}$ and $\mathbf{H}_2 \in \mathbb{R}^{r_2 \times n}$ are all matrices to be found. The macro-variables are recorded in $\mathbf{W}_2 \in \mathbb{R}^{m \times r_2}$ and are fixed quantities. Here m represents the number of time points, r_1 is a parameter to select, r_2 is the number of macro-variables and n is the number of stocks.

There are many approaches to perform NMF, a simple method is to utilise the multiplicative update technique of Lee and Seung [10] which gives updates for $\mathbf{W}$ and $\mathbf{H}$ of

$$\mathbf{W} \leftarrow \mathbf{W} \odot \frac{\left[\mathbf{VH}^T\right]}{\left[\mathbf{WHH}^T\right]}, \qquad \mathbf{H} \leftarrow \mathbf{H} \odot \frac{\left[\mathbf{W}^T\mathbf{V}\right]}{\left[\mathbf{W}^T\mathbf{WH}\right]} \qquad (1)$$

where $\odot$ is the Hadamard product and $\frac{[\,]}{[\,]}$ denotes element-wise division. These updates push the matrices towards a minimum of the objective function $||\mathbf{V} - \mathbf{WH}||^2_{\text{Fro}}$. In our combined representation we want to find matrices $\mathbf{W}_1$, $\mathbf{H}_1$ and $\mathbf{H}_2$ that satisfy $\mathbf{V} \approx \mathbf{W}_1\mathbf{H}_1 + \mathbf{W}_2\mathbf{H}_2$ which requires us to minimise

$$f = \frac{1}{2}||\mathbf{V} - \mathbf{W}_1\mathbf{H}_1 - \mathbf{W}_2\mathbf{H}_2||^2_{\text{Fro}}. \qquad (2)$$

As minimising Eq. (2) with respect to $\mathbf{W}_1$, $\mathbf{H}_1$ and $\mathbf{H}_2$ together is non-convex we hold two of the matrices constant whilst updating the third using multiplicative updates. Each individual problem is then convex, although the overall problem remains non-convex and there is no guarantee of reaching an optimal solution. Multiplicative updates are a type of scaled gradient descent therefore we need to find $\nabla_{\mathbf{W}_1}f$, $\nabla_{\mathbf{H}_1}f$ and $\nabla_{\mathbf{H}_2}f$. First we multiply out Eq. (2) and get:

$$\begin{aligned}
f =& \frac{1}{2}\text{tr}\left[(\mathbf{V} - \mathbf{W}_1\mathbf{H}_1 - \mathbf{W}_2\mathbf{H}_2)^T(\mathbf{V} - \mathbf{W}_1\mathbf{H}_1 - \mathbf{W}_2\mathbf{H}_2)\right] \\
=& \frac{1}{2}\text{tr}\Big[\mathbf{V}^T\mathbf{V} - \mathbf{V}^T\mathbf{W}_1\mathbf{H}_1 - \mathbf{V}^T\mathbf{W}_2\mathbf{H}_2- \\
& \mathbf{H}_1^T\mathbf{W}_1^T\mathbf{V} + \mathbf{H}_1^T\mathbf{W}_1^T\mathbf{W}_1\mathbf{H}_1 + \mathbf{H}_1^T\mathbf{W}_1^T\mathbf{W}_2\mathbf{H}_2- \\
& \mathbf{H}_2^T\mathbf{W}_2^T\mathbf{V} + \mathbf{H}_2^T\mathbf{W}_2^T\mathbf{W}_1\mathbf{H}_1 + \mathbf{H}_2^T\mathbf{W}_2^T\mathbf{W}_2\mathbf{H}_2\Big].
\end{aligned} \qquad (3)$$

We then differentiate Eq. 3 with respect to $\mathbf{W}_1$, $\mathbf{H}_1$ and $\mathbf{H}_2$ respectively to give three equations:

$$\nabla_{\mathbf{W}_1}f = (\mathbf{W}_1\mathbf{H}_1\mathbf{H}_1^T + \mathbf{W}_2\mathbf{H}_2\mathbf{H}_1^T - \mathbf{VH}_1^T), \qquad (4)$$

$$\nabla_{\mathbf{H}_1}f = (\mathbf{W}_1^T\mathbf{W}_1\mathbf{H}_1 + \mathbf{W}_1^T\mathbf{W}_2\mathbf{H}_2 - \mathbf{W}_1^T\mathbf{V}) \qquad (5)$$

and

$$\nabla_{\mathbf{H}_2}f = (\mathbf{W}_2^T\mathbf{W}_2\mathbf{H}_2 + \mathbf{W}_2^T\mathbf{W}_1\mathbf{H}_1 - \mathbf{W}_2^T\mathbf{V}). \qquad (6)$$

We apply multiplicative updates to $\mathbf{W}_1$, $\mathbf{H}_1$ and $\mathbf{H}_2$ by:

$$\mathbf{W}_1 \leftarrow \mathbf{W}_1 \odot \frac{\left[\mathbf{VH}_1^T\right]}{\left[\mathbf{W}_1\mathbf{H}_1\mathbf{H}_1^T + \mathbf{W}_2\mathbf{H}_2\mathbf{H}_1^T\right]}, \qquad (7)$$

$$\mathbf{H}_1 \leftarrow \mathbf{H}_1 \odot \frac{\left[\mathbf{W}_1^T \mathbf{V}\right]}{\left[\mathbf{W}_1^T \mathbf{W}_1 \mathbf{H}_1 + \mathbf{W}_1^T \mathbf{W}_2 \mathbf{H}_2\right]} \tag{8}$$

and

$$\mathbf{H}_2 \leftarrow \mathbf{H}_2 \odot \frac{\left[\mathbf{W}_2^T \mathbf{V}\right]}{\left[\mathbf{W}_2^T \mathbf{W}_2 \mathbf{H}_2 + \mathbf{W}_2^T \mathbf{W}_1 \mathbf{H}_1\right]} \tag{9}$$

where $\odot$ is the Hadamard product and $\frac{[]}{[]}$ indicates element-wise division. We will discuss how changes to $\mathbf{W}_1$ reduces the objective function noting that the same argument also applies to changes in $\mathbf{H}_1$ and $\mathbf{H}_2$. As we want to follow the gradient down towards a minimum, if $\nabla_{\mathbf{W}_1} f < 0$ then we want to increase $\mathbf{W}_1$. This is equivalent to $\mathbf{V}\mathbf{H}_1^T > \mathbf{W}_1\mathbf{H}_1\mathbf{H}_1^T + \mathbf{W}_2\mathbf{H}_2\mathbf{H}_1^T$, and, as shown in Eq. (7), $\mathbf{W}_1$ is increased. Conversely if $\nabla_{\mathbf{W}_1} f > 0$ then we need $\mathbf{W}_1$ to decrease, which the multiplicative update does because $\mathbf{W}_1\mathbf{H}_1\mathbf{H}_1^T + \mathbf{W}_2\mathbf{H}_2\mathbf{H}_1^T > \mathbf{V}\mathbf{H}_1^T$. The final eventuality, that $\nabla_{\mathbf{W}_1} f = 0$, implies we have found a minimum of $\mathbf{W}_1$ and so want to keep $\mathbf{W}_1$ the same. Our multiplicative update multiplies $\mathbf{W}_1$ by one, fulfilling our requirement. We should note that if $\nabla_{\mathbf{W}_1} f = 0$ we are not necessarily at a minimum of the objective function as the other two matrices may still change which might change the situation of $\mathbf{W}_1$ such that $\nabla_{\mathbf{W}_1} f$ is no longer zero.

While this argument shows that the updates move in the correct direction, that is no guarantee of a monotonic reduction of the objective function as we could overshoot the minimum. However, part of the value of multiplicative updates is that Lee and Seung proved that they do produce a monotonic reduction [11].

We prove that our algorithm monotonically reduces Eq. (2) by extending the proof of Lee and Seung [11] to cover the XNMF objective function using the same notation they did. Definition 1 and lemma 1 from their paper remain the same but we change the $K(h^t)$ diagonal matrix of lemma 2 to

$$K_{a,b}(h_{(1)}^t) = \delta_{a,b}(\mathbf{W}_1^T \mathbf{W}_1 \mathbf{h}_1^t + \mathbf{W}_1^T \mathbf{W}_2 \mathbf{h}_2)_a / h_{(1)a}^t \tag{10}$$

which changes only the $K(h_{(1)}^t)$ term of $G(\mathbf{h}_1, \mathbf{h}_1^t)$. We then prove that $G(\mathbf{h}_1, \mathbf{h}_1^t)$ is an auxiliary function of the altered $F(\mathbf{h}_1)$:

$$F(\mathbf{h}_1) = \frac{1}{2}(\mathbf{v} - \mathbf{W}_1\mathbf{h}_1 - \mathbf{W}_2\mathbf{h}_2)^T (\mathbf{v} - \mathbf{W}_1\mathbf{h}_1 - \mathbf{W}_2\mathbf{h}_2) \tag{11}$$

which requires the proof that $M_{a,b}(\mathbf{h}_1^t) = h_{(1)a}^t(K(\mathbf{h}_1^t) - \mathbf{W}_1^T\mathbf{W}_1)_{a,b}h_{(1)b}^t$ is positive semidefinite:

$$\boldsymbol{\nu}^T \mathbf{M} \boldsymbol{\nu}$$

$$= \sum_{a,b} \nu_a M_{a,b} \nu_b$$

$$= \sum_{a,b} \left[h_{(1)a}^t \left((\mathbf{W}_1^T\mathbf{W}_1\mathbf{h}_1^t + \mathbf{W}_1\mathbf{W}_2\mathbf{h}_2)_a / h_{(1)a}^t \right)_{a,b} h_{(1)b}^t \nu_a^2 - \nu_a h_{(1)a}^t (\mathbf{W}_1^T\mathbf{W}_1)_{a,b} h_{(1)b}^t \nu_b \right]$$

$$= \sum_{a,b} \left[(\mathbf{W}_1^T \mathbf{W}_1)_{a,b} h_{(1)a}^t h_{(1)b}^t \nu_a^2 - \nu_a h_{(1)a}^t (\mathbf{W}_1^T \mathbf{W}_1)_{a,b} h_{(1)b}^t \nu_b + (\mathbf{W}_1^T \mathbf{W}_2)_{a,b} h_{(2)b}^t h_{(1)a}^t \nu_a^2 \right]$$

$$= \sum_{a,b} \left[(\mathbf{W}_1^T \mathbf{W}_1)_{a,b} h_{(1)a}^t h_{(1)b}^t (\tfrac{1}{2}\nu_a^2 + \tfrac{1}{2}\nu_b^2 - \nu_a \nu_b) + (\mathbf{W}_1^T \mathbf{W}_2)_{a,b} h_{(2)b}^t h_{(1)a}^t \nu_a^2 \right]$$

$$= \sum_{a,b} \left[(\mathbf{W}_1^T \mathbf{W}_1)_{a,b} h_{(1)a}^t h_{(1)b}^t (\nu_a - \nu_b)^2 + (\mathbf{W}_1^T \mathbf{W}_2)_{a,b} h_{(2)b}^t h_{(1)a}^t \nu_a^2 \right]$$

$$\geq 0. \tag{12}$$

Our proof is then the same as Lee and Seung except, due to the different $K(h^t)$, we end with:

$$h_{(1)a}^{t+1} = h_{(1)a}^t \frac{(\mathbf{W}_1^T \mathbf{v})_a}{(\mathbf{W}_1^T \mathbf{W}_1 \mathbf{h}_1 + \mathbf{W}_1^T \mathbf{W}_2 \mathbf{h}_2)_a}. \tag{13}$$

which proves that our algorithm will monotonically reduce the objective function for $\mathbf{H}_1$. Equivalent proofs are trivially shown for $\mathbf{W}_1$ and $\mathbf{H}_2$.

3   Data

We demonstrate the effectiveness of our model and learning algorithm empirically using daily data from FTSE 100 companies taken over a twenty year period. To deal with non-stationarity that may exist over such a long period in time, we also split the data into four equal sections in time and show results on all four separately.

Table 1. Macro-variables used in this study

Macro-variable	Frequency	Macro-variable	Frequency
Gross domestic product	Quarterly	Unemployment	Monthly
Interest rate	Monthly	Inflation index rate	Monthly
Imports goods & services	Quarterly	Exports	Monthly
Oil imports	Monthly	Gross national income	Quarterly
M1 money supply	Monthly	Productivity	Quarterly
GBP/USD	Daily	Contribution to CPI	Monthly
Balance of payments	Monthly	Oil investment	Daily
Government gross reserve	Monthly		

In Table 1 we show the macro-variables used in this study. The choice of which macro-variables to use is somewhat arbitrary, there are many potential macro-variables, and they can be changed. To compensate for the differences in frequency between the share data (recorded on work days) and the macro-variable data we have linearly interpolated between all the macro-variable data so that the dimensionality (the number of time points) are equal.

4   Results

We first confirm empirically that our algorithm achieves the desired goal, the reduction in the error until it reaches a minimum. In Fig. 1(a) we show how the error changes with iteration for different values of r for the three different algorithms. We will use the same terminology throughout: NMF results are from the algorithm which minimised $||\mathbf{V} - \mathbf{W}_1\mathbf{H}_1||^2_{\text{Fro}}$, XNMF (exogenous inputs NMF) is for the minimisation of $||\mathbf{V} - \mathbf{W}_1\mathbf{H}_1 - \mathbf{W}_2\mathbf{H}_2||^2_{\text{Fro}}$ and EX (exogenous inputs alone) is for the minimisation of $||\mathbf{V} - \mathbf{W}_2\mathbf{H}_2||^2_{\text{Fro}}$. The blue dashed lines are for different values of r for NMF and the solid black lines for different values of r_1 for XNMF.

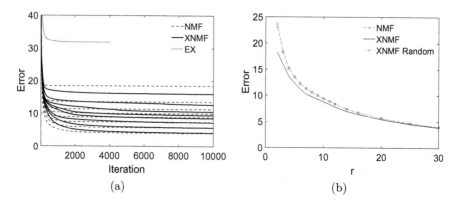

(a)   (b)

Fig. 1. (a) The extended multiplicative update algorithm reduces the error monotonically with iteration until a plateau is reached. The multiple blue dashed (NMF) and solid black (XNMF) lines are for different sizes of the subspace, r. Generally the XNMF algorithm requires more iterations to approach a minimum than the NMF algorithm, but reaches a lower final error. (b) The final errors for different sizes of the subspace, r, for NMF (blue dashed lines with crosses), XNMF (solid black line) and XNMF using a $\mathbf{W}_2$ with random values (red dotted with circles). At all values of r that were implemented XNMF produces smaller errors than NMF or the randomised XNMF. As r is increased the difference between the errors produced by the algorithms reduces as the capacity of the NMF model increases and begins to overfit the data. (Color figure online)

The EX algorithm (red dotted line) produces a poor approximation as it contains no information from the actual stocks themselves. The results of particular note are those of the XNMF algorithm which works as we expect it to, we see a fall in the objective function with iteration until it approaches a minimum where the error plateaus. The XNMF algorithm takes more iterations than the NMF algorithm to approach a minimum which might be expected as we have three matrices to optimise rather than two. In addition, the third matrix may make the objective function more non-convex than with just two matrices to optimise.

In Fig. 1(b) we show the final errors from performing normal NMF (blue dashed line with crosses) and XNMF (solid black line) for different sizes of the subspace, r. At low values of r the model does not have enough subspace dimensions (columns of $\mathbf{W}_1$) to effectively fit the data and so the errors are high. The additional macro-variables here make a significant difference to the quality of the fit. As r increases the benefit of the additional information decreases as the increased capacity of the $\mathbf{W}_1\mathbf{H}_1$ part of the model means that a good fit to the data is possible without any additional information. As r increases it is likely that the model is overfitting the data, so any use of NMF requires a sensible choice of r to be made [12]. We also include a version of XNMF (red dotted line with circles) called XNMF Random where the $\mathbf{W}_2$ matrix is composed of random numbers. The NMF and XNMF Random plots are hard to distinguish demonstrating that the XNMF method is extracting real information from the external data, and not just reducing the error by increasing the size of the parameter space.

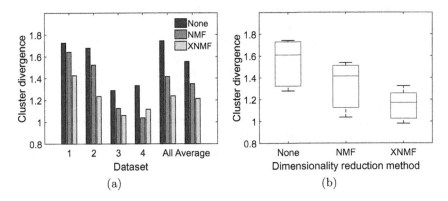

(a) (b)

Fig. 2. (a) A representation of how much clusters diverge with time. K-means clustering was applied to non-dimensionality reduced data (dark blue bars), dimensional reduction using NMF (light blue bars) and dimensional reduction using XNMF (yellow bars) for four times periods and for a combination of the four periods. The clusters produced from data with no dimensional reduction diverge the most, with application of NMF the divergence is reduced and with XNMF we see the smallest divergence, the clusters tend to hold together better through time. (b) Boxplots of the same results demonstrating the improvement of XNMF over NMF. (Color figure online)

A particular appeal of NMF is noise suppression, by reducing the noise we might expect to be able to extract more real features from the data. A key result demonstrated with gene expression data is that the reduction in noise achieved by matrix factorization leads to stable clustering and biologically relevant inference about genes [13,14]. In financial data we are often interested in how stocks and shares move together through time, a balanced portfolio would not contain lots of shares which are likely to fall in the same period. If we can effectively cluster the shares we can then build a more resilient portfolio.

We can cluster stock data into groups using a range of techniques including the popular K-means clustering. We are then interested in the quality of the clustering in the future, clusters that hold together better would be desirable. While NMF is not a clustering technique we can use the dimensionality reduction to create a new sub-space in which we apply clustering.

We performed K-means clustering on three versions of the data: (a) no dimensionality reduction; (b) dimensionality reduced using NMF; (c) dimensionality reduced using XNMF. A measure of the similarity of a cluster is the average distance to the cluster centre using the non-dimensionality reduced data. We are interested in the change in the average distance to the cluster centre as this gives us a measure of how similar the cluster is at different time points. In general, we would expect an increase in distance as clusters will tend to diverge with time. If we see a smaller increase using the dimensionality reduced versions, it shows that the NMF techniques are allowing us to produce clusters which generalise better.

In Fig. 2 we see the results of this forward prediction of clustering. First the data was split in half into a "training" set, the first half of the data in time, and a "testing" set, the second half of the data. The training data was then clustering into seven cluster centres using, respectively: the raw data, $\mathbf{V}$; $\mathbf{H}_1$ from NMF; and $\mathbf{H}_1$ from XNMF. We chose the size of the subspace, r, using a combination of domain knowledge about numbers of sectors in the data, and automatic techniques to assess subspace size [12]. The y-axis shows the ratio of the average distances from each data-point to its cluster centre between the testing data and the training data. A smaller value means the cluster stayed closer together. We see a clear trend, the raw data performs the worst whilst XNMF gives the best performance, and NMF gives a result in between the other two.

5   Conclusion

In this paper we introduce a matrix factorization model suitable for multi-variate financial time series that includes known exogenous macro-variables. We use real FTSE 100 stock data to show that the multiplicative update factorization algorithm of XNMF produces lower errors than standard NMF and that stock clusters formed with the addition of exogenous data stay tighter bound through time. We also prove theoretically that the algorithm is guaranteed to monotonically reduce the objective function.

References

1. Weigend, A.S., Huberman, B.A., Rumelhart, D.E.: Predicting the future: a connectionist approach. Int. J. Neural Syst. **1**(03), 193–209 (1990)
2. Tamiz, M., Hasham, R., Jones, D.F., Hesni, B., Fargher, E.K.: A two staged goal programming model for portfolio selection. In: Tamiz, M. (eds.) Multi-Objective Programming and Goal Programming. Lecture Notes in Economics and Mathematical Systems, vol. 432, pp. 286–299. Springer, Heidelberg (1996). doi:10.1007/978-3-642-87561-8_19

3. Omran, M.F.: Nonlinear dependence and conditional heteroscedasticity in stock returns: UK evidence. Appl. Econ. Lett. **4**(10), 647–650 (1997)
4. Babu, A., Reddy, S.: Exchange rate forecasting using arima, neural network and fuzzy neuron. J. Stock Forex Trading **3**(4), 1–5 (2015)
5. Niranjan, M.: Sequential tracking in pricing financial options using model based and neural network approaches. In: Advances in Neural Information Processing Systems, pp. 960–966 (1997)
6. Montesdeoca, L., Niranjan, M.: Extending the feature set of a data-driven artificial neural network model of pricing financial options. In: 2016 IEEE Symposium Series on Computational Intelligence (SSCI), pp. 1–6. IEEE (2016)
7. de Fréin, R., Drakakis, K., Rickard, S., Cichocki, A.: Analysis of financial data using non-negative matrix factorization. In: International Mathematical Forum, vol. 3, pp. 1853–1870. Journals of Hikari Ltd (2008)
8. de Fréin, R., Drakakis, K., Rickard, S.: Portfolio diversification using subspace factorizations. In: 42nd Annual Conference on Information Sciences and Systems, 2008, CISS 2008, pp. 1075–1080. IEEE (2008)
9. Wang, J.: Stock trend extraction via matrix factorization. In: Zhou, S., Zhang, S., Karypis, G. (eds.) ADMA 2012. LNCS, vol. 7713, pp. 516–526. Springer, Heidelberg (2012). doi:10.1007/978-3-642-35527-1_43
10. Lee, D.D., Seung, H.S.: Learning the parts of objects by non-negative matrix factorization. Nature **401**(6755), 788–791 (1999)
11. Lee, D.D., Seung, H.S.: Algorithms for non-negative matrix factorization. In: Advances in Neural Information Processing Systems, pp. 556–562 (2001)
12. Squires, S., Prügel-Bennett, A., Niranjan, M.: Rank selection in nonnegative matrix factorization using minimum description length. Neural Comput. **29**, 2164–2176 (2017)
13. Brunet, J.P., Tamayo, P., Golub, T.R., Mesirov, J.P.: Metagenes and molecular pattern discovery using matrix factorization. Proc. Nat. Acad. Sci. **101**(12), 4164–4169 (2004)
14. Devarajan, K.: Nonnegative matrix factorization: an analytical and interpretive tool in computational biology. PLoS Comput. Biol. **4**(7), e1000029 (2008)

Stacked Denoising Autoencoder Based Stock Market Trend Prediction via K-Nearest Neighbour Data Selection

Haonan Sun[1], Wenge Rong[2(✉)], Jiayi Zhang[1], Qiubin Liang[1], and Zhang Xiong[2]

[1] Sino-French Engineer School, Beihang University, Beijing, China
{shaonan,jiayizhang,qiubin_l}@buaa.edu.cn
[2] School of Computer Science and Engineering, Beihang University, Beijing, China
{w.rong,xiongz}@buaa.edu.cn

Abstract. In financial applications, stock-market trend prediction has long been a popular subject. In this research, we develop a new predictive model to improve the accuracy by enhancing the denoising process which includes a training set selection based on four K-nearest neighbour (KNN) classifiers to generate a more representative training set and a denoising autoencoder-based deep architecture as kernel predictor. Considering the good agreement between closing price trends and daily extreme price movements, we forecast extreme price movements as an indirect channel for realising accurate price-trend prediction. The experimental results demonstrate the effectiveness of the proposed method in terms of its accuracy compared with traditional machine-learning models in four principal Chinese stock indexes and nine leading individual stocks from nine different major industry sectors.

Keywords: K-nearest neighbour · Denoising autoencoder · Stock-trend prediction

1 Introduction

The ability to precisely forecast the direction of stock movements can assist investors to make economically sound decisions by minimizing investment risks and maximizing financial profits. Some articles divide trend predictions to multiple types. For example, Bara et al. [1] divided stock trends into five types, namely sharp decrease, decrease, normal, increase and sharp increase. However, most of articles are interested in binary classification [2–4] as binary classification task is fundamental for stock trend predictions and can more directly help investors find trading signals.

Both textual and numerical information can be involved to form dataset in binary classification task [5,6]. The efficient market hypothesis assumed that stock prices quickly adjust to new information as soon as possible [7]. Since stock price movement incorporates all visible and potential influences,

© Springer International Publishing AG 2017
D. Liu et al. (Eds.): ICONIP 2017, Part II, LNCS 10635, pp. 882–892, 2017.
https://doi.org/10.1007/978-3-319-70096-0_90

there is an interesting question regarding whether we should use only the technical indicators calculated with basic prices to increase the accuracy of stock-trend forecasting. Technical analysis for stock trend prediction has gained great achievements [8,9], but there still exists several challenges among which a notable one is how to treat with the dataset formed by the technical indicators. Kara et al. [10] directly used 10 normalised classic technical indicators as input for an artificial neural network (ANN). Patel et al. [11] changed technical indicators into 1 (oversold) or −1 (overbought) by their financial senses. When observing the dataset formed by technical indicators, we find out that even the same set of indicators could represent completely opposite labels which greatly affects the accuracy of trend predictions. To solve this problem, we constructed a KNN-based data selection process to generate a new training set, where a group of similarity value features corresponds to one label.

The challenge to conduct stock-market trend predictions lies that stock prices are complicated and dynamic time series streams including noise, uncertainty, volatility and hidden relationships [12]. As a consequence, another important task in such studies is to effectively learn elemental feature information from complex and heterogeneous time series streams. Many machine-learning-based models have been shown to be suitable for time-series forecasting, such as artificial neural network (ANN) [13] or support vector machine (SVM) [14]. By using non-linear activation functions and multiple connected layers architecture, the ANN model can abstract different features from initial indicators [15]. The objective of SVM is to find a hyper plane to maximize the margin of separation between positive and negative examples [11]. Compared to current shallow machine learning algorithms, deep-learning-based methods attempt to model high-level abstractions in data using multiple processing layers with complex structures, resulting in better representations from input examples [16]. In this study, a deep-learning method based on denoising autoencoder (DA) that extracts the robust features is proposed with respect to the complex stock series streams.

Previous researches usually directly forecast the closing price trends [5,11,17]. Different from other research, we attempted to first predict the direction of the next day's highest and lowest price movements in order to accurately determine the closing price trends because the direction in which values undergo extreme movements can also convey valuable information that may indicate the turning point of a stock's trend [18]. In addition, the lower volatility of daily extreme prices guarantees a higher accuracy [19] which makes using predicted extreme prices trends to indirectly predict closing trend possible.

The rest of this paper is organised as follows. In Sect. 2, we present the related works in the field of stock market prediction. In Sect. 3, we interpret explicitly the proposed model. Then, in Sect. 4, we analyse the experimental results, and in Sect. 5, we present our conclusion and discuss the direction of future work.

2   Related Work

In general, stock market prediction can be divided into two categories, i.e., fundamental analysis and technical analysis. The fundamental analysis is more interested in long-term predictions by analysing the intrinsic stock value [20]. The technical analysis methods mainly concentrate on short-term predictions by using historical trading data. They assume that the historical price variation would probably repeat itself and aim to predict stock market by seeking some existing patterns with various models [11].

Almost all machine-learning models have been employed in previous works. Ballings et al. [15] compared performance among seven different models, such as random forest, logistic regression (LG), SVM. The results indicated that random forest performed best. Qiu et al. [9] applied an optimised ANN model to predict the Japanese stock market index Nikkei225 with considerable accuracy. Yeh et al. [21] showed that SVM models with multiple kernels can have good performance for stock forecasting. There are also other methods such as fuzzy sets [22] and decision trees [23].

With the development of deep learning, the use of deep architectures has become another powerful solution to predict stock trends because of their superior predictive properties and robustness to over-fitting problems [24]. Akita et al. [25] demonstrated the performance of long short-term memory (LSTM) on real-world data provided by ten companies from the Tokyo Stock Exchange. Zeng et al. [26] proved that convolutional neural network (CNN) performs better than the traditional Bollinger bands. Rather et al. [27] merged two linear models and a non-linear model (recurrent neural network (RNN)) and confirmed that the hybrid prediction model outperformed the RNN. Different from the principles of these models, stacked denosing autoencoder (SDA) can extract the principal and robust components of the training set and easily form deep networks to improve the accuracy [28]. So we applied SDA in our denosing enhancement predictive model.

3   Methodology

In this study, the proposed stock-trend prediction model is composed of two distinct major steps (Fig. 1). First, we used a data preparation layer to form two training sets with different labels (train Label-High, train Label-Low) and four KNN-classifiers to eliminate noisy data in each training set. Secondly, we used two new training sets to train two SDA networks separately and a loop to search the best parameters. Best models with minimum cross-validation error are saved to predict the Label-Low and Label-High of the validation set and test set. By using the verification of the validation Label-Close, we can determine the relation between the predicted Label-Low, predicted Label-High and our target label. Afterwards, we can predict the Label-Close of the test set by using the predicted test Label-High, predicted test Label-Low and this relation.

3.1   Data Preparation

The original stock historical data is composed of four basic prices (open, highest, closing and lowest), with which we calculated 10 technical indicators [10] as

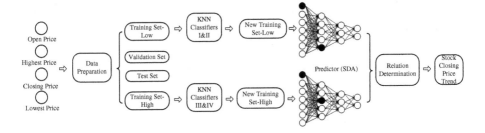

Fig. 1. Global prediction process

features of the dataset and three corresponding label sets defined by changes in the lowest, highest and closing prices. For example, the Label-Close is defined as up (1) if $C_{t+1} \geq C_t$ or down (0) if $C_{t+1} < C_t$ where C_t represents the closing price at time t (Eq. 1). Same method of definition is used to generate Label-High and Label-Low. Due to the difference of magnitude among the technical indicators, We also used the normalisation method to transform each technical indicator between 0 and 1 (Eq. 2). Then, we separated the entire dataset and three label sets into a training set, validation set and test set with percentages of 90%, 5% and 5% respectively. Finally, we formed two training sets whose labels are train Label-Low and train Label-High respectively.

$$Label\text{-}Close = \begin{cases} 1 \ \ if \ C_{t+1} \geq C_t \\ 0 \ \ if \ C_{t+1} < C_t \end{cases} \tag{1}$$

$$X_{normalised} = \frac{X - X_{min}}{X_{max} - X_{min}} \tag{2}$$

For each training set, we combined two KNN classifiers to pick out a purer training set. The first KNN classifier divided the training set into a RightDataSet and WrongDataSet by using a similarity metric such as the Euclidean distance to determine whether its label is coherent with the major label of its nearest k neighbours. The coherent ones were assigned into RightDataSet. We applied second KNN classifier to the first WrongDataSet to avoid the over-eliminating problem. The two RightDataSets are grouped as a new training set. We carried out the identical process for another training set. The algorithm of a KNN classifier is shown in Algorithm 1.

3.2 Stacked Denoising Autoencoder-Based Predictor

The SDA is a deep network formed by several denosing autoencoders (DAs) in series, where the output code of a DA serves as the input of the next DA. The training process composes two steps: pretraining and fine-tuning.

During the pretraining process (Fig. 2), each hidden layer of the SDA is trained successively as one DA. To train each DA layer, we first mapped the initial input x into $\tilde{x}$ by means of a binary masking noise mapping $\tilde{x} \sim q_D(\tilde{x}|x)$

Algorithm 1. A KNN Classifier.

Require: KNN Classifier Parameter k
Ensure: $RightDataSet, WrongDataSet$
1: init $RightDataSet = WrongDataSet = [\ ]$, $Distances = [\ ]$
2: **for all** $inX \in TrainingSet$ **do**
3:    $newTrainingSet \leftarrow (TrainingSet - inX)$
4:    **for** $inY \in newTrainingSet$ **do**
5:       $d(inX, inY) = \sqrt{\sum (inX_i - inY_i)^2}$, $Distances \leftarrow Distances + d(inX, inY)$
6:    **end for**
7:    $DistancesDescendSorted[: k] \leftarrow Distances$
8:    $inXPreLabel \leftarrow major\ \ label\ \ of\ \ DistancesDescendSorted[: k]$
9:    **if** $inXRealLabel = inXPreLabel$ **then**
10:       $RightDataSet \leftarrow (RightDataSet + inX)$
11:    **else**
12:       $WightDataSet \leftarrow (WightDataSet + inX)$
13:    **end if**
14: **end for**

---

which means turning x's elements to 0 with a binomial distribution. Whenever a training example x is presented, a different corrupted version $\tilde{x}$ of it is generated according to $q_D(\tilde{x}|x)$. The rest process is like the basic autoencoder including a coding function (Eq. 3) and a decoding function (Eq. 4). Compared with the original autoencoder, DAs still exhibit the same reconstruction loss between a clean input x and its reconstruction form z, but the reconstruction version z is acquired from a corrupted x. This forces the coding function f_θ and decoding function $g_{\theta'}$ to be sufficient to offset the effect of noise.

$$y = f_\theta(\tilde{x}) = s(W\tilde{x} + b) \tag{3}$$

$$z = g_{\theta'}(y) \tag{4}$$

Parameters θ and θ' are trained by stochastic gradient descent (SGD) to minimize the reconstruction error over a training set. With the sigmoid activation function and normalised dataset, we used the cross entropy loss as the reconstruction cost function (Eq. 5) [28]. All of the optimised hidden layer weights are used as the initial neural network weights for fine-tuning training.

$$Cost = L_H(x, z) = \sum_j [x_j \log(z_j) + (1 - x_j \log(1 - z_j))] \tag{5}$$

Fine-tuning is a supervised learning, and here, we added a logistic regression layer on the output code of the last hidden layer, after which we used a SGD to train the entire network as a multilayer perception (MLP) whose hidden layers' weights are shared with each DA. The cost function of fine-tuning is a cross-entropy function between the real label y and the predicted label $\tilde{y}$.

With the trained-prediction model, we could have the predicted Label-Low and Label-High of each validation set. The combination of results can form four

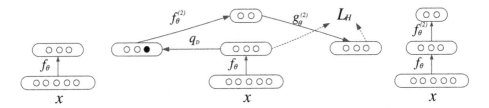

Fig. 2. Stacked DAs. After training a first-level DA, its learnt function f_θ is used on a clean input (left) to produce the input of the next layer. The next DA is trained in the same manner to learn a second-level encoder $f_\theta^{(2)}$. The procedure can be repeated in this way (right).

situations, namely [1,1], [0,1], [1,0] and [0,0]. Each situation corresponds to an up Label-Close (1) or a down Label-Close (0). We took the majority as the predicted Label-Close of this situation. In this manner, we obtained the relation of each situation to Label-Close. Afterwards, using the predicted test Label-Low and predicted test Label-High of the test set, we were able to predict the test Label-Close of the test set.

4   Experience and Results

4.1   DataSets and Evaluation Metrics

To prove the effectiveness of our proposed method, we considered four Chinese stock indices and nine individual stocks of nine industries (Table 1). The selection of the individual stocks is mainly based on market value, industry influence and trading activity. We downloaded all of the data using the tushare package of python. All datasets are sufficiently recent to prove that our method is useful and powerful for the current Chinese stock market. We use direction accuracy and F_β-Measure as our evaluation metrics which are defined in Eqs. 6 and 7.

$$Accuracy = \frac{TP + TN}{TP + FP + TN + FN} \tag{6}$$

$$F_\beta\text{-}Measure = \frac{(\beta^2 + 1)\, PR}{\beta^2 P + R} \tag{7}$$

TP, FP, TN and FN represent respectively the true positive, false positive, true negative and false negative. P means precision positive rate and R means recall positive rate as defined in [11]. As the forecast up trends usually indicate investors to buy stock, a higher precision rate can contribute to gather more profits and avoid risks, here we use $\beta = 0.5$ to assign more weight for precision rate.

Table 1. Details of four Chinese stock indexes

Code	Index name	Num of samples	Period
SH000001	Shanghai Composite Index	4218	1999/07/26-2016/12/23
SZ399001	Shenzhen Component Index	2948	2005/01/04-2017/02/23
SH000300	CSI 300 Index	2910	2005/01/04-2016/12/23
SZ399005	Small and Medium Enterprise Index	2104	2006/01/24-2017/02/23
Code	Stock name	Industry	Period
SH600030	CITIC Securities Com.	Securities	2006/01/04-2017/01/31
SH600221	Hainan Airlines	Transportation	2002/01/04-2016/12/23
SH600519	Kweichow Moutai Com.	Liquor making	2005/01/04-2017/01/31
SH600886	SDIC Huajing Power Holdings Com.	Energy	2005/01/04-2017/01/31
SH600887	Inner Mongolia Yili Industrial Group	Food & beverage	2006/01/04-2017/01/31
SH601668	CSCE Construction Corp.	Infrastructure	2009/07/29-2017/01/31
SZ000002	China Vanke Group	Real estate	2006/01/04-2017/01/31
SH600000	Shanghai Pudong Development Bank	Banking	2002/01/04-2016/12/23
SZ600690	Haier Group	Home appliances	2006/01/04-2017/01/31

4.2　Benchmark Models

The first set of comparison experiments was aimed at proving that the KNN-based data selection process could contribute to denoise the original training set. Here, we used two hidden layers SDA as kernel predictor and tested the performance with and without the data selection layer.

The second set of comparison experiments is to prove the effect of the denoising autoencoder on our prediction process. Here, we compared the performance between SVM with a RBF kernel, LG, one hidden layer ANN, one hidden layer SDA and two hidden layers SDA with our complete process in both the stock index and individual stock in China.

Our third set of comparison experiments is directly predicting closing price trend with normalised 10 technical indicators as input for an ANN (ANN-DC) [10] or 10 trend deterministic data with random forest as kernel predictor (TDD-RF-DC) [11].

4.3   Results and Discussion

In the presentation of experimental results, to prevent confusion, we use SDA-I as abbreviation for one hidden layer SDA and SDA-II for two hidden layers SDA. To prove the effect of the KNN-based denoising data selection process, we compared the performance of our proposed approach with and without the KNN-based data selection process. In addition, we also compared accuracy between using just one KNN classifer and two KNN classifiers for each training set. We used SDA-II as kernel predictor and as shown in Fig. 3, we find that the improvement is obviously positive with KNN-based data selection layer, in particular, performance with two KNN classifiers was better than one KNN classifier. So in the rest experiments, two KNN classifiers are applied for each training set.

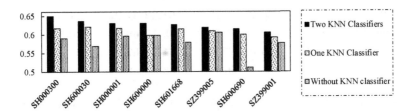

Fig. 3. Comparison between with and without KNN Classsifiers

Secondly, using our complete prediction approach with KNN-based data selection layer, we used SVM, ANN or LG as predictor to compare the performance of SDA family methods (SDA-I, SDA-II). The first advantage of using SDA family methods is the masking noise mapping which contributes to improve the robustness of the prediction models. Besides, the SDA family methods can easily form deep architecture to find out the potential relation between the technical indicators and the stock trends more efficiently. As shown in Table 2, we can see that the family of SDA methods has a better performance than traditional machine-learning methods (LG, SVM, ANN) both for the stock index and individual stock. The unit for all numbers in the results table is %. In particular, the difference between SDA-I and the one-hidden layer ANN lies only in the characteristics of the hidden layer, while the same approach with the SDA-I can realise a much better performance than ANN.

Table 2. Five models comparison results

Prediction models	SVM	LG	ANN	SDA-I	SDA-II
Stock index	61.59	61.9	61.6	**63.04**	62.82
Individual stock	57.09	58.52	60.38	61.9	**63.21**

Finally, Table 3 shows the comparison results with directly predicting closing price trends. ANN-DC means directly predicting closing price trends with normalised 10 technical indicators as input for an one-hidden layer ANN [10]. TDD-RF-DC means changing 10 technical indicators into 1 or −1 by their financial sense and using these trend deterministic data as input for a random forest predictor [11]. K-LH-SDA-I&II are our proposed approaches which are more effective compared with directly predicting closing price change.

Table 3. Stock index & individual stock comparison experiments

Method	ANN-DC		TDD-RF-DC		K-LH-SDA-I		K-LH-SDA-II	
Evaluation metric	Acc	F-Measure	Acc	F-Measure	Acc	F-Measure	Acc	F-Measure
SH000001	54.5	59.95	52.61	57.67	**63.51**	**66.39**	63.03	65.85
SZ399001	49.66	55.22	56.55	59.12	**61.22**	**61.22**	60.54	60.67
SH000300	51.72	57.25	50.34	53.17	**65.52**	**66.95**	64.83	66.12
SZ399005	50.48	56.03	56.19	57.76	**61.9**	**62.31**	**61.9**	**62.31**
Index average	51.59	57.11	53.92	56.93	**63.04**	**66.22**	62.58	63.74
SH600030	53.79	55.32	57.58	56.47	**63.64**	61.86	**63.64**	**62.01**
SH600221	55.43	60.85	57.71	61.95	60.57	64.15	**66.29**	**68.38**
SH600887	53.08	58.57	**63.08**	**64.84**	58.46	61.48	**63.08**	**64.84**
SH600519	50.35	55.90	54.55	55.41	**57.34**	**58.08**	**57.34**	57.89
SH600690	48.82	54.39	55.91	56.76	**61.42**	**60.56**	**61.42**	60.51
SH600886	54.74	60.19	61.31	64.37	65.69	67.37	**67.15**	**68.97**
SH601668	56.04	61.45	57.14	61.84	**67.74**	**69.11**	62.64	65.4
SZ000002	50	55.56	**64.29**	64.22	62.7	62.8	**64.29**	**64.64**
SH600000	54.55	60	56.25	60.28	60.23	63.18	**63.07**	**65.32**
Stock average	52.98	58.03	58.65	60.68	61.98	63.17	**63.21**	**64.22**

5   Conclusions and Future Work

In this paper, we proposed a model to forecast the stock market trends as defined by the changes of closing price. Our original motivation comes from the noisy characteristics of stock data. We develop a denoising enhancement predictive model by applying SDA-based deep architecture and a new KNN-based training data denosing process. Inspired by the importance of extreme values when predicting stock trends, we decided to forecast the highest and lowest price changes as an indirect way of predicting trends of closing price. We used three sets of experiments for comparison to prove the effectiveness of stock prediction performance of our denoising enhancement predictive approach. In addition, we offer the opportunity of using the highest and lowest prices to indirectly predicting closing price trends in Chinese stock market.

In future work, with the exception of noisy characteristics, stock data are also a type of time-series data, and it may be useful to involve the RNN or LSTM model throughout the entire process. Further, studies into the stock prediction focus on realising profits, so we can develop a trading strategy based on our method and use the profit as an evaluation metric.

Acknowledgement. This study was partially supported by the National Natural Science Foundation of China (No. 61332018).

References

1. Barak, S., Modarres, M.: Developing an approach to evaluate stocks by forecasting effective features with data mining methods. Expert Syst. Appl. **42**(3), 1325–1339 (2015)
2. Kamran, R.: Prediction of stock market performance by using machine learning techniques. In: Proceedings of 2017 International Conference on Innovations in Electrical Engineering and Computational Technologies (2017)
3. Sheelapriya, G., Murugesan, R.: Stock price trend prediction using Bayesian regularised radial basis function network model. Span. J. Finan. Account. **46**(2), 189–211 (2017)
4. Weng, B., Ahmed, M.A., Megahed, F.M.: Stock market one-day ahead movement prediction using disparate data sources. Expert Syst. Appl. **79**, 153–163 (2017)
5. Ding, X., Zhang, Y., Liu, T., Duan, J.: Deep learning for event-driven stock prediction. In: Proceedings of 24th International Joint Conference on Artificial Intelligence, pp. 2327–2333 (2015)
6. Liu, Y., Qin, Z., Li, P., Wan, T.: Stock volatility prediction using recurrent neural networks with sentiment analysis. In: Proceedings of 30th International Conference on Industrial Engineering and Other Applications of Applied Intelligent Systems, pp. 192–201 (2017)
7. Fama, E.F.: Efficient capital markets: a review of theory and empirical work. J. Finan. **25**(2), 383–417 (1970)
8. Patel, J., Shah, S., Thakkar, P., Kotecha, K.: Predicting stock market index using fusion of machine learning techniques. Expert Syst. Appl. **42**(4), 2162–2172 (2015)
9. Qiu, M., Yu, S.: Predicting the direction of stock market index movement using an optimized artificial neural network model. Plos One **11**(5), e0155133 (2016)
10. Kara, Y., Boyacioglu, M.A., Baykan, Ö.K.: Predicting direction of stock price index movement using artificial neural networks and support vector machines: the sample of the Istanbul stock exchange. Expert Syst. Appl. **38**(5), 5311–5319 (2011)
11. Patel, J., Shah, S., Thakkar, P., Kotecha, K.: Predicting stock and stock price index movement using trend deterministic data preparation and machine learning techniques. Expert Syst. Appl. **42**(1), 259–268 (2015)
12. Lin, Y., Guo, H., Hu, J.: An svm-based approach for stock market trend prediction. In: Proceedings of 2013 International Joint Conference on Neural Networks, pp. 1–7 (2013)
13. Weerachart, L., Nunnapus, B.: Stock price trend prediction using artificial neural network techniques: case study: Thailand stock exchange. In: Computer Science and Engineering Conference (2017)
14. Chen, Y., Hao, Y.: A feature weighted support vector machine and k-nearest neighbor algorithm for stock market indices prediction. Expert Syst. Appl. **80**, 340–355 (2017)

15. Ballings, M., den Poel, D.V., Hespeels, N., Gryp, R.: Evaluating multiple classifiers for stock price direction prediction. Expert Syst. Appl. **42**(20), 7046–7056 (2015)
16. Bengio, Y., Lamblin, P., Popovici, D., Larochelle, H.: Greedy layer-wise training of deep networks. In: Proceedings of 20th Annual Conference on Neural Information Processing Systems, pp. 153–160 (2006)
17. Shynkevich, Y., McGinnity, T.M., Coleman, S.A., Belatreche, A.: Forecasting movements of health-care stock prices based on different categories of news articles using multiple kernel learning. Decis. Support Syst. **85**, 74–83 (2016)
18. Laboissiere, L.A., Fernandes, R.A.S., Lage, G.G.: Maximum and minimum stock price forecasting of Brazilian power distribution companies based on artificial neural networks. Appl. Soft Comput. **35**, 66–74 (2015)
19. Gorenc Novak, M., Velušček, D.: Prediction of stock price movement based on daily high prices. Quant. Finan. **16**(5), 793–826 (2016)
20. Milosevic, N.: Equity forecast: Predicting long term stock price movement using machine learning (2016). arXiv preprint: arXiv:1603.00751
21. Yeh, C., Huang, C., Lee, S.: A multiple-kernel support vector regression approach for stock market price forecasting. Expert Syst. Appl. **38**(3), 2177–2186 (2011)
22. Chen, S., Manalu, G.M.T., Pan, J., Liu, H.: Fuzzy forecasting based on two-factors second-order fuzzy-trend logical relationship groups and particle swarm optimization techniques. IEEE Trans. Cybern. **43**(3), 1102–1117 (2013)
23. Sadegh, B.I., Mohammad, B.: Forecasting the direction of stock market index movement using three data mining techniques: the case of tehran stock exchange. Int. J. Eng. Res. Appl. **4**(6), 106–117 (2014)
24. Dixon, M.F., Klabjan, D., Bang, J.H.: Classification-based financial markets prediction using deep neural networks. In: Algorithmic Finance, pp. 1–20 (2016)
25. Akita, R., Yoshihara, A., Matsubara, T., Uehara, K.: Deep learning for stock prediction using numerical and textual information. In: Proceedings of 15th IEEE/ACIS International Conference on Computer and Information Science, pp. 1–6 (2016)
26. Zeng, Z., Xiao, H., Zhang, X.: Self CNN-based time series stream forecasting. Electron. Lett. **52**(22), 1857–1858 (2016)
27. Rather, A.M., Agarwal, A., Sastry, V.N.: Recurrent neural network and a hybrid model for prediction of stock returns. Expert Syst. Appl. **42**(6), 3234–3241 (2015)
28. Vincent, P., Larochelle, H., Lajoie, I., Bengio, Y., Manzagol, P.: Stacked denoising autoencoders: learning useful representations in a deep network with a local denoising criterion. J. Mach. Learn. Res. **11**, 3371–3408 (2010)

Ten-Quarter Projection for Spanish Central Government Debt via WASD Neuronet

Yunong Zhang[1(✉)], Zhongxian Xue[1], Mengling Xiao[1], Yingbiao Ling[1], and Chengxu Ye[2]

[1] School of Information Science and Technology, Sun Yat-sen University (SYSU),
Guangzhou 510006, China
{zhynong,isslyb}@mail.sysu.edu.cn
[2] School of Computer Science, Qinghai Normal University, Xining 810008, China
ycx@qhnu.edu.cn

Abstract. This paper makes a ten-quarter projection for Spanish central government debt (SCGD). Several Eurozone member states had been in debt crisis since 2008, including Spain. During the crisis, Spanish central government debt increased quickly. According to the data provided by the Bank of Spain, the SCGD reached to €969.5523 billion in December 2016, and debt-to-GDP ratio was more than 100% in 2016. It is important to conduct a projection for SCGD so that the government can make better fiscal policies and preparation for risks in future. In this paper, we use a 3-layer feed-forward neuronet to conduct a projection for SCGD. We use weights and structure determination (WASD) algorithm to build such a neuronet model and train the neuronet with Spanish central government debt data from December 1994 to December 2016. Finally, three different trends of SCGD are shown via experiments: quick increasing trend, increasing trend and decreasing trend.

Keywords: Central government debt · Debt crisis · Ten-quarter projection · WASD algorithm

1 Introduction

Government debt, also known as national debt and sovereign debt, is the debt owned by government. Central government debt, which is the most important part of general government debt, is the debt owned by central government.

Spain has a population of 46 million, which is the fourth largest economy in the Euro area (following Germany, France and Italy). Under the influence of the world financial crisis in 2007−2008, debt crisis broke out in several European countries including Spain [1–3]. That crisis had significant adverse economic effects and labour market effects, with unemployment rate in Spain reaching to 27% [4]. Spanish central government debt (SCGD) also increased quickly. Before the fourth quarter of 2007, SCGD was stable and increased very slowly. SCGD increased much quicker after the end of 2007. As the SCGD data provided by the Bank of Spain show, in the fourth quarter of 2007, SCGD was only €318.8691

© Springer International Publishing AG 2017
D. Liu et al. (Eds.): ICONIP 2017, Part II, LNCS 10635, pp. 893–902, 2017.
https://doi.org/10.1007/978-3-319-70096-0_91

billion; but, in the fourth quarter of 2016, SCGD reached to €969.5523 billion, more than three times as many as that of nine years ago. Spain entered the crisis period with a relatively modest public debt of 36.2% of GDP; but, in 2014, the debt-to-GDP ratio was more than 100%.

Nowadays, government debt has become the most pressing and difficult policy challenge that western governments have to face. Many scholars have researched Spain or European sovereign debt crisis. Klaus and Lucio pointed out that sovereign debt crisis is a complex problem, and internal devaluation policies imposed in Greece, Ireland, Italy, Portugal and Spain are ineffective [5]. Mario and Carsten examined the European sovereign debt crisis focussing on Spain, and presented empirical evidence indicating that German and Spanish government bond yields are cointegrated [4]. Trabelsi analyzed the recent development in the Eurozone, mainly the PIIGS (Portugal, Ireland, Italy, Greece and Spain) countries' financial crisis (including debt crisis) and the threats the Eurozone risks, and proposed some solutions for the crisis [6].

With the rapid growth of central government debt in Spain, predicting the trend of SCGD becomes important for government's policies making. In this paper, we introduce the weights and structure determination (WASD) neuronet to project the Spanish central government debt (SCGD). We have used this kind of neuronet to project the United States public debt [7], and obtained satisfactory projection results. We get the quarterly SCGD data from December 1994 to December 2016 provided by the Bank of Spain. The neuronet is trained and validated with these data; then, we conduct a ten-quarter projection of SCGD using such neuronet models.

2   Structure and Training of WASD Neuronet

In this section, we build a 3-layer feed-forward neuronet; then, we use weights and structure determination (WASD) algorithm to determine the neuronet's connecting weights and structure.

2.1   Neuronet Structure

A 3-layer feed-forward neuronet is built for SCGD projection, which is shown in Fig. 1. The neuronet includes input layer, hidden layer and output layer. In the hidden layer, there are N neurons activated by a group of Chebyshev polynomials $\phi_j(\cdot)$ (with $j = 1, 2, \cdots, N$) [8,9]. The input layer or the output layer each has one neuron, which is activated by linear identity function. We set the connecting weights from the input layer to the hidden layer to be 1, and the connecting weights from the hidden layer to the output layer to be w_j (with $j = 1, 2, \cdots, N$) which should be adjusted. Furthermore, the thresholds of all neurons are set to be 0. These settings mentioned above considerably decrease the complexity of neuronet and computation.

Then, we use WASD algorithm to determine the structure of neuronet. The weights and structure determination (WASD) algorithm can determine the connecting weights from the hidden layer to the output layer, and obtain the optimal

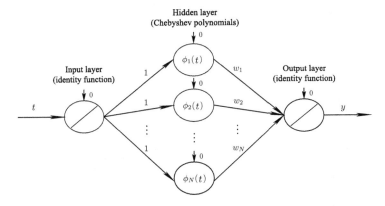

Fig. 1. Structure of 3-layer feed-forward WASD neuronet, which has input layer, hidden layer and output layer.

structure. For more details of the WASD algorithm, please refer to authors' previous works [10–14].

2.2 Normalization from [12/1994, 12/2016] to $[-1, \alpha]$

We get the SCGD data from the Bank of Spain, who officially provides the quarterly SCGD data from December 1994 to December 2016, so we can guarantee the accuracy of SCGD data. In this paper, originally and initially, the input of the neuronet is a date (e.g., 12/1994), the output is an SCGD datum in billion Euros (e.g., 209.3340). In order to make it convenient to normalize the input data, we change the format of date. We use the total number of months from 0 A.D. to the corresponding time as the input; for example, 23940 corresponds to 12/1994 because there are 23940 months from 0 A.D. to 12/1994, and 24204 corresponds to 12/2016. Therefore, the domain [12/1994, 12/2016] is converted to [23940, 24204]. Because the neurons in the hidden layer are activated by Chebyshev polynomials of class 1, the input domain should be $[-1, 1]$. Therefore, we normalized [23940, 24204] to $[-1, \alpha]$, with normalization factor $\alpha \in (-1, 0)$. Using the normalized data, we can train WASD neuronet.

2.3 WASD Neuronet Training and Validating

As mentioned in the previous subsection, the dates interval [12/1994, 12/2016] is normalized to interval $[-1, \alpha]$. The performance of neuronet is related to the normalization factor $\alpha \in (-1, 0)$. With different values of α, we obtain different projection performances. Specifically, we use $\{(t_i, \gamma_i)|_{i=1}^{Q}\}$ as the training set of sample pairs, where $t_i \in \mathbb{R}$ denotes the ith input, $\gamma_i \in \mathbb{R}$ denotes the ith target output, and Q denotes the total number of sample pairs in the training set. In this paper, there are totally 86 sample pairs corresponding to 86 quarters from

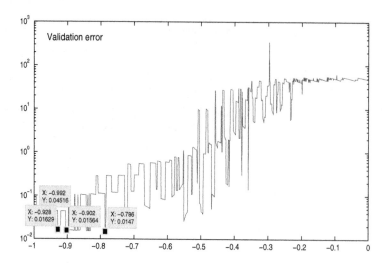

Fig. 2. Relationship between normalization factor α and validation error ϵ.

December 1994 to March 2016. We define the mean square error (MSE) [12] as follows:

$$E_N = \frac{1}{Q} \sum_{i=1}^{Q} \left(\gamma_i - \sum_{j=1}^{N} w_j \phi_j(t_i) \right)^2, \tag{1}$$

where E_N denotes the mean square error with the hidden layer's neurons number being N. By changing the number N of neurons in the hidden layer gradually, we obtain the relationship between N and MSE. As we know, the number of neurons in the hidden layer plays an important role in the neuronet's performance. Too many neurons in the hidden layer may cause over-fitting, while too few neurons cause under-fitting. Thus, we use the WASD algorithm to determine the optimal N by finding the corresponding N with the minimum MSE value. The optimal structure of neuronet can thus be determined.

Based on the well-trained neuronet models, we use additional 3 sample pairs to validate the neuronet models' projection performance. Note that sample pairs in interval $[12/1994, 03/2016]$ are used to train the neuronet (i.e., 86 sample pairs), while sample pairs in interval $[06/2016, 12/2016]$ are used to validate the performance (i.e., 3 sample pairs), which are also be normalized to the interval $[-1, \alpha]$. The validation error ϵ is defined as follows:

$$\epsilon = \frac{1}{M} \sum_{m=1}^{M} \left| \frac{y_m - \gamma_m}{\gamma_m} \right|, \tag{2}$$

where M denotes the number of validate sample pairs (i.e., $M = 3$ in this paper), y_m denotes the neuronet output with the mth sample input, and γ_m denotes the mth target output. We find again that different normalization factor α leads to different validation error ϵ. The relationship between them is shown in Fig. 2.

3 Projection Results

In the previous section, we train the neuronet successfully and validate the projection ability of the well-trained neuronet. We also obtain the relationship between the normalization factor and the validation error. As Fig. 2 shows, different values of α correspond to different validation errors. Smaller validation error means better projection result, or to say, more possible situation. We mark the global minimum point and several local minimum points in Fig. 2. Note that the global minimum point usually means the most possible situation, and the local minimum points also have relatively high possibilities. In this section, we choose the global minimum point and four local minimum points to analyze their projection results, and we list these points in Table 1.

Table 1. Validation errors of global minimum point and local minimum points

Value of α	−0.786	−0.839	−0.902	−0.928	−0.992
Validation error ϵ	0.0147	0.0153	0.0156	0.0163	0.0452

3.1 Projection Results via Global Minimum Point

Global minimum point here has normalization factor α corresponding to the minimum validation error in global range. As is shown in Fig. 2 and Table 1, $\alpha = -0.786$ corresponds to the global minimum point with the validation error $\epsilon = 0.0147$, which usually means the most possible situation. We conduct a ten-quarter projection from March 2017 to June 2019. The projection results with $\alpha = -0.786$ are shown in Fig. 3, and listed in Table 2. Specifically, in Fig. 3, the neuronet output data are very close to the real historical SCGD data before December 2016, which indicates the good performance of the neuronet. As the neuronet projects, SCGD has a quick increase in the ten quarters following the end of 2016, and the growth rate also increases. Moreover, Table 2 lists the detailed SCGD data in quarterly manner. In this table, we can see that SCGD exceeds €1000 billion for the first time in March 2017, and reach €3268.7426 billion in June 2019. The SCGD surges to a record high in June 2019, and triples within ten quarters.

We find that there was also a quick increase in the end of 2007. In 2012, Spain sank into debt crisis with a quick increase of SCGD. In December 2014, Spain's debt-to-GDP ratio exceeded 100%. Moreover, Spain's GDP has grown slowly in recent quarters, so this projection result shows an increase of SCGD and indicates that Spain may face a risk of debt crisis.

3.2 Projection Results via Local Minimum Points

Local minimum points have smaller validation errors than points around them. Similar to global minimum point, local minimum points are worth being discussed and analyzed. The validation errors of local minimum points may be a

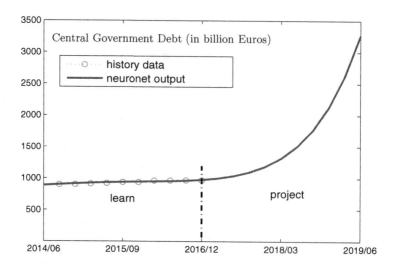

Fig. 3. Projection result of SCGD via WASD neuronet with global minimum point $\alpha = -0.786$.

Table 2. Projected data of SCGD corresponding to Fig. 3

Date (month/year)	03/2017	06/2017	09/2017	12/2017	03/2018
SCGD (billion Euros)	1000.9648	1038.8157	1098.1584	1187.9370	1319.6588
Date (month/year)	06/2018	09/2018	12/2018	03/2019	06/2019
SCGD (billion Euros)	1507.9560	1771.2369	2132.4639	2620.0196	3268.7426

little larger than that of global minimum point, which means that the situations of local minimum points also have high probabilities. So, we use four local minimum points $\alpha = -0.839, -0.902, -0.928$ and -0.992 to analyze their projection results. The projection results are shown in Fig. 4.

As Fig. 4(a) shows, SCGD increases in the next ten quarters, which is similar to global minimum point, but the growth rate corresponding to $\alpha = -0.839$ is smaller. After ten quarters, in June 2019, SCGD reaches to €1533.5036 billion. Besides, there is an increasing trend in Fig. 4(b) as well with $\alpha = -0.902$. In June 2019, SCGD reaches to €1563.7275 billion. This situation is quite similar to the situation in Fig. 4(a). Their growth rates are almost the same, and their SCGD data are very close. As for Fig. 4(c), there is also an increasing trend, but, compared with the previous situations, SCGD grows very slowly in Fig. 4(c). SCGD remains at a steady level in the first five quarters, and then increases to €1128.8017 billion in June 2019. However, the trend in Fig. 4(d) with $\alpha = -0.992$ is quite different from other trends. The SCGD decreases in the next ten quarters, and finally reaches to €417.2324 billion in June 2019.

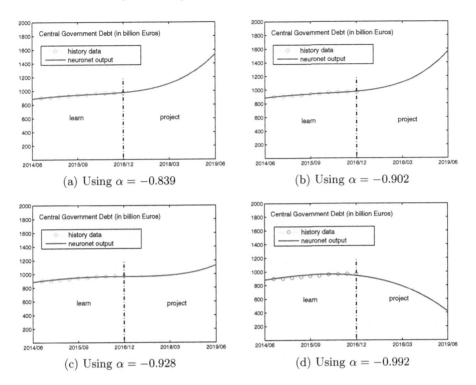

(a) Using $\alpha = -0.839$ (b) Using $\alpha = -0.902$

(c) Using $\alpha = -0.928$ (d) Using $\alpha = -0.992$

Fig. 4. Different projection results of SCGD via WASD neuronet using different local minimum point values of α.

3.3   Projection Results Analysis

We choose five normalization factor points including one global minimum point and four local minimum points, which have smaller validation error values than others. Noticeably, most of results except Fig. 4(d) project that the SCGD increases, and the trend of global minimum point increases quicker than other increasing trends, so we can divide all the five situations into three trends: quick increasing trend (with $\alpha = -0.786$), increasing trend (with $\alpha = -0.839, -0.902$ or -0.928) and decreasing trend (with $\alpha = -0.992$).

In the quick increasing trend, the SCGD data increases from €1000.9648 billion in March 2017 to €3268.7426 billion in June 2019. According to the historical SCGD data, we know that SCGD tripled in seven years and six months (from €315.4733 billion in March 2008 to €938.7676 billion in September 2015) mainly because of Spain's housing bubble, banking crisis and local government debt problem. Note that, in Fig. 5, we show the historical SCGD data from December 2003 to September 2010, which include the period of debt crisis (starting from December 2007) in 2008 and 2009. As shown in the figure, before the debt crisis broke out, there was a marked decrease in SCGD, and then there was a rapid increase. Compared with that situation, the quick increasing trend

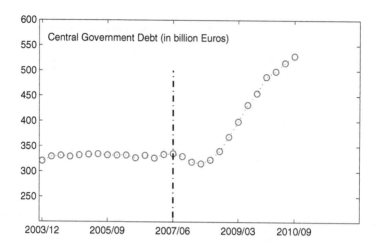

Fig. 5. Historical SCGD data from December 2003 to September 2010 including period of debt crisis (starting from December 2007) in 2008 and 2009.

predicted from now on does not have a decrease before the increase, which follows from the dissimilarity that the possibility of debt crisis is minor. Besides, in the increasing trend, the growth rate of SCGD is slower than the situation of quick increasing trend, especially in Fig. 4(c) with $\alpha = -0.928$. In Fig. 4(a) and Fig. 4(b), the growth rates of SCGD are similar to the recent years' (from March 2008 to December 2015) growth rate. As for trend in Fig. 4(c), we notice that, since March 2016, SCGD has increased more slower than before: SCGD was €962.0809 billion in March 2016, and €969.5523 billion in December 2016.

According to our analysis above, we could conclude that the increasing trend fits the current situation, which indicates that the SCGD will be increasing but under control. Finally, consider again the decreasing trend. From historical SCGD data, we find that SCGD decreased for many times; for example, SCGD decreased from €331.6199 billion in September 2006 to €326.3689 billion in December 2006; and, from June 2007 to March 2008, SCGD had a decrease for four consecutive quarters. Ten consecutive quarters' decrease has never happened in the mentioned history, and the trend may appear possibly because of polynomial characteristics, or indicating some emergencies ahead. In summary, more projection results show that SCGD follows the increasing trend. Besides, according to Spain's current economic situation and economic aid from the European Union, we incline to the increasing trend; or to say, we believe that SCGD may increase in the next ten quarters, but may not increase quickly. The other two trends also have possibilities: SCGD may increase quickly or decrease in next ten quarters. Spanish government should also prepare for these potential trends.

4   Conclusion

In this paper, we have conducted a ten-quarter projection for Spanish central government debt via a 3-layer feed-forward neuronet, with the WASD algorithm used for determining the connecting weights and structure of the neuronet. We have trained the neuronet with history SCGD data from December 1994 to March 2016. The projection results have been divided into three trends: quick increasing trend, increasing trend and decreasing trend. Projection results of the global minimum point have shown that the SCGD may increase quickly in the next ten quarters; results of three local minimum points have shown that the SCGD may increase gently; and results of one local minimum point have shown that the SCGD may decrease. Besides, according to our further analysis of the projection results, we may conclude from the dissimilarity that Spain would not have a debt crisis for the coming nearly 10 quarters. However, kindly note that all theories and models may be essentially approximate, erroneous, and even wrong. In addition to the above, based on this paper, we (including interested readers) may carry out more and further work such as comparing WASD method with other methods in SCGD projection and making accurate projection on the dates of future potential debt crisis.

Acknowledgments. This work is supported by the Foundation of Key Laboratory of Autonomous Systems and Networked Control, Ministry of Education, China (with number 2013A07), by the Natural Science Foundation of Qinghai (with number 2016-ZJ-739), and by the Students Innovation Training Program of Sun Yat-sen University (with number 201602118). Kindly note that all authors of the paper are jointly of the first authorship, with the following thoughts shared: (1) "A cold warning is also a kind reminder", (2) "My daughter at the age of 5 told me 'pen is dangerous' due to its sharp end, while one day I discovered Sun-zi's words telling 'war is dangerous' due to its unknown end", (3) "We, children, may just be the re-appearing of our ancestors' souls, to some extent", (4) "The more you think that they are going, the more they are actually or potentially coming", (5) "World (W) is always moving, while Mountain (M) often thinks about its stillness", (6) "As I sense, there are three levels of thinkers; i.e., (i) short thinkers (who think less while do more), (ii) long thinkers (who think much and long in a few directions), and (iii) far-and-deep thinkers (who think much, far and deep, in many directions)", and (7) "Nonlinear phenomena are often beyond thinking and imagining". Thanks a lot and best regards.

References

1. Lane, P.R.: The European sovereign debt crisis. J. Econ. Perspect. **26**, 49–67 (2012)
2. Missio, S., Watzka, S.: Financial contagion and the European debt crisis. In: CESifo Working Papers 3554, pp. 1–33 (2011)
3. Neal, L., Garcia-Iglesias, M.C.: The economy of Spain in the Euro-zone before and after the crisis of 2008. Q. Rev. Econ. Finan. **53**, 336–344 (2013)
4. Gruppe, M., Lange, C.: Spain and the European sovereign debt crisis. Eur. J. Polit. Econ. **34**, S3–S8 (2014)
5. Armingeon, K., Baccaro, L.: Political economy of the sovereign debt crisis: the limits of internal devaluation. Ind. Law J. **41**, 254–275 (2012)

6. Ali, T.M.: The impact of the sovereign debt crisis on the eurozone countries. Soc. Behav. Sci. **62**, 424–430 (2012)
7. Zhang, Y., Xiao, Z., Guo, D., Mao, M., Tan, H.: USPD doubling or declining in next decade estimated by WASD neuronet using data as of October 2013. Comput. Intell. Intell. Syst. **575**, 712–723 (2015)
8. Zhang, Y., Chen, Y., Jiang, X., Zeng, Q., Zou, A.: Weights-directly-determined and structure-adaptively-tuned neural network based on Chebyshev basis functions. Comput. Sci. **36**, 210–213 (2009)
9. Zhang, Y., Yin, Y., Guo, D., Yu, X., Xiao, L.: Cross-validation based weights and structure determination of Chebyshev-polynomial neural networks for pattern classification. Pattern Recogn. **47**, 3414–3428 (2014)
10. Zhang, Y., Wang, J., Zeng, Q., Qiu, H., Tan, H.: Near future prediction of European population through Chebyshev-activation WASD neuronet. In: International Conference on Intelligent Control & Information Processing, pp. 134–139. IEEE (2016)
11. Zhang, Y., Qu, L., Liu, J., Guo, D., Li, M.: Sine neural network (SNN) with double-stage weights and structure determination (DS-WASD). Soft Comput. **20**, 211–221 (2016)
12. Zhang, Y., Tan, N.: Weights direct determination of feedforward neural networks without iterative BP-training. In: International Conference on Communications, Circuits and Systems, pp. 59–63. IEEE (2010)
13. Zhang, Y., Liu, J., Guo, D., Ding, S., Tan, H.: Power-activated WASD neuronet based Russian population estimation, correction and prediction. In: International Conference on Computational Science and Engineering, pp. 1232–1236. IEEE (2014)
14. Zhang, Y., Guo, D., Luo, Z., Zhai, K., Tan, H.: CP-activated WASD neuronet approach to Asian population prediction with abundant experimental verification. Neurocomputing **198**, 48–57 (2016)

Data Augmentation Based Stock Trend Prediction Using Self-organising Map

Jiayi Zhang[1], Wenge Rong[2(✉)], Qiubin Liang[1], Haonan Sun[1], and Zhang Xiong[2]

[1] Sino-French Engineer School, Beihang University, Beijing, China
{jiayizhang,qiubin_l,shaonan}@buaa.edu.cn
[2] School of Computer Science and Engineering, Beihang University, Beijing, China
{w.rong,xiongz}@buaa.edu.cn

Abstract. Stock trend prediction has been of great interest for both investment benefits and research purposes. Unlike image processing or natural language processing, where the amount of data could easily reach a million order of magnitude, the application of artificial intelligent models is however limited in the domain of stock prediction because of insufficient amount of stock price data. This article seeks to ameliorate the stock prediction task from a different angle and provides a novel method to enlarge the training data by firstly clustering different stocks according to their retracement probability density function, and then combine all the day-wise information of the same stock cluster as enlarged training data, which is then fed into a recurrent neural network to make stock trend prediction. Experimental results show that this data augmentation technique suits for deep learning methods and notably improves the stock trend prediction task.

Keywords: Stock price predication · Self-organising map · Retracement

1 Introduction

For the past decades, stock prediction has been a popular topic in financial world, especially in emerging market because of their phenomenal economic growth. Meanwhile, this task is considered challenging due to the high volatility and complexity of stock markets [7]. With the astonishing advancement in artificial intelligence (AI) in recent years, researchers have successfully achieved better prediction performance by applying various AI models. Apart from typical machine learning models such as support vector machine (SVM) and random forest [26], Barak et al. [3] and Atsalakis et al. [2] present their forecasting models for stock markets on the basis of the ANFIS (Adaptive Neural Fuzzy Inference System), meanwhile ANN (artificial neural networks) based models are also widely applied for price trend prediction [4,19].

Regardless of all the great progress, what seems to prevent AI models from performing even better is the data insufficiency. Due to the background of stock

D. Liu et al. (Eds.): ICONIP 2017, Part II, LNCS 10635, pp. 903–912, 2017.
https://doi.org/10.1007/978-3-319-70096-0_92

market, a one-year-long stock price time series barely consists of 250 daily price information, let alone the newly listed stocks that has really limited amount of data. Hence, AI models could hopefully achieve better results if greater data volume is provided. In fact, the test error is more likely to be smaller with more training data (Vapnik's theroem [23]), suggesting a better generalisation ability.

One solution might be to perform clustering on stocks and increase the training data from other stocks that have similar temporal patterns. As for periodic pattern detection, various methods exist from basic works [20] to Gaussian based functions [11]. Besides, graphical dimension reduction techniques such as principal component analysis (PCA) [6,22] and self-organising map (SOM) [8,15,17] are especially preferred for their visual interpretability. The contribution of this paper is two-folders: (1)This is the first time to study stock-wise clustering for data augmentation purpose in the field of stock price prediction. (2)We aim to fill this gap by presenting an advanced SOM based clustering method with stock retracement chosen as a novel similarity criterion, after which GRU neural network is applied on the augmented data for price trend prediction.

The rest of this paper is organised as follows. Related works will be presented in Sect. 2. Section 3 will introduce the major steps that constitute the proposed methodology for stock trend prediction. The experimental study will be discussed in Sect. 4, while the last section serves as conclusion and future works.

2   Related Works

In order to deal with the lack of data, researchers have made an effort to extract predictive information from external world. Gálvez and Gravano [9] explored textual information in online message board as complementary features for stock price prediction, Jiang et al. [14] studied the announcement content of the stock during the suspension period that offered feasible suggestions for prediction task. Besides, Nader et al. [18] established a stock prediction system on the basis of social media with intelligent financial web-mining method. In this case, natural language processing techniques such as feature word extraction and text representation are required [18], and deep learning methods such as recurrent neural network [1,16] are also preferred to enhance the task performance.

On the other hand, starting from the price time series itself, researchers tend to extract more useful predictive information. Numerous feature selection methods are used for improving technical analysis on stock data. Tsai and Hsiao [22] compared PCA, decision tree and genetic algorithms, all of which are used for performing feature selection from technical indicators (TI), while Wei et al. [25] applied fuzzy inference system to extract rules from TI. Besides, Chandar et al. [4] performed wavelet transformation so as to preprocess the stock data.

Various day-wise temporal clustering methods are also applied in this field so that prediction systems could learn from clearer representative patterns. Hadavandi et al. [10] and Hsu [13] used self-organising map (SOM) to divide stock data into several sub-groups and the prediction is done by means of each cluster's test data. Fu et al. [8] took one step further and investigated the patterns learned by SOM from stock price time series and was able to show the discovered frequently appeared patterns. Similarly, Wei et al. also applied subtractive clustering to perform day-wise data clustering [25].

3   Methodology

In this research, the stock trend prediction process is composed of three major steps (as shown in Fig. 1). First, the retracement probability density function is chosen as similarity criterion and is computed for each stock in the data ensemble. Second, based on this similarity, un unsupervised stock-wise clustering is performed by using self-organising map (SOM) neural network. Third, one certain stock is chosen as prediction target and is split into training data and test data, where the former is enlarged by combining other stocks' information from the same cluster and is then fed into gated recurrent unit (GRU) neural network prediction model, which is finally evaluated on the original test set.

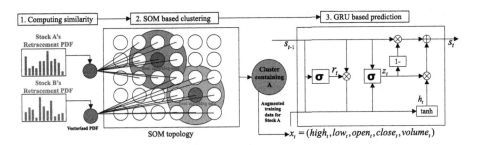

Fig. 1. The Overall Prediction Process

3.1   Similarity Criterion

Since increasing the training data from time dimension is simply not practical as mentioned before, it would be reasonable to consider space dimension: seek for "similar" stocks and take usage of their price time series. In this case, a wise criterion of similarity should be explored at first. Stocks are intuitively clustered into different sectors for they are engaged in similar industries, such as energy, online education sector and so on. This naive cluster, however, does not necessarily imply similar temporal behaviors of stock price time series.

Faced with trend prediction task, we found it reasonable to take stock price reversal phenomenon as the similarity criterion for stock-wise clustering. In this case, Wei and Huang [24] provides normalised retracement as a way of quantifying the stock price reversal phenomenon, which is proved to help discover an exotic long term pattern among stocks:

$$retrace(i) = \frac{P_{top}(i) - P_{min}(i+1)}{P_{top}(i) - P_{min}(i)}. \tag{1}$$

$P_{min}(i)$ is the i-th local minima of the stock price time series in a time interval, and $P_{top}(i)$ is the maximum price between two adjacent local minimum i and $i+1$. The retracement probability density function (PDF) is thus computed for each stock as the similarity criterion for the next clustering method (see Fig. 2 as an example).

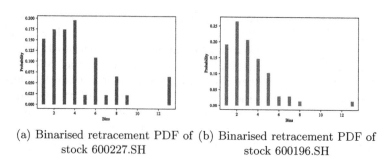

(a) Binarised retracement PDF of   (b) Binarised retracement PDF of
       stock 600227.SH   stock 600196.SH

Fig. 2. Retracement probability density function (PDF) of 2 example stocks, where all retracement values are binarised into 13 bins for each stock.

3.2 SOM Based Clustering

First introduced by Kohonen [15] as an unsupervised clustering and dimension reduction technique, self-organising map (SOM) has its advantage of stability and flexibility. Mangiameli et al. suggests that SOM achieves better performance in accuracy and robustness when dealing with chaotic data [17]. A typical SOM is composed of two layers: the input layer and Kohonen layer. The latter consists of a 2D lattice of "nodes", each of which is fully connected to the input layer and has a specific topological position (x, y coordinate in the lattice) with a vector of weights of the same dimension as the input vectors. The training process of SOM neural network is described as follows:

Step 1: Initialisation of weight vectors W_i, neighborhood functions $h_{i,j}$, neighborhood radius R_0, and learning rate L_0.

Step 2: Take stock retracement PDF as input vectors.

Step 3: Calculate the best matching unit (BMU), which is given by:

$$BMU = argmin_i(||X - W_i||) \qquad (2)$$

Step 4: For all nodes within the neighborhood of BMU, update weights W_i.

$$W_i(t + 1) = W_i(t) + L_t h_{i,BMU}(X - W_i) \qquad (3)$$

where t is the number of iteration, L_t is the learning rate for iteration t.

Step 5: Update learning rate L_t, neighborhood functions $h_{i,j}$, and radius R_t as follows:

$$R_t = R_0 \exp\frac{t}{\beta} \qquad (4)$$

where β denotes a time constant value.

Step 5: Repeat step 2-4 until stopping condition is reached.

Step 6: Return clustered stock based on their projection on Kohonen layer.

3.3 GRU Based Prediction

In this paper, recurrent neural network is applied for its appropriateness to address time series problems. Since basic RNN is rarely satisfying due to the vanishing gradient problem, long-short term memory (LSTM) architecture was first introduced in 1997 [12], and the gated recurrent unit (GRU), as a variation of LSTM, was recently proposed by Cho et al. [5] in 2014, both of which are able to capture dependencies of proper time scales. The latter gets especially popularised for its lighter architecture along with promising performance [21]. GRU neural networks are based on the following equations:

$$z_t = \sigma(U_z x_t + W_z s_{t-1}) \tag{5}$$

$$r_t = \sigma(U_r x_t + W_r s_{t-1}) \tag{6}$$

$$h_t = \tanh(U_h x_t + W_h(s_{t-1} * r_t)) \tag{7}$$

$$s_t = (1 - z_t) * s_{t-1} + z_t * h_t \tag{8}$$

$$y_t = W_y * s_t \tag{9}$$

where: $x_t \in R^n$ is the input at time t. $s_t \in R^m$ is the hidden state at time t. $y_t \in R^p$ is the output at time t. $r_t \in R^m$ corresponds to the reset gate that combines the current input with the previous memory. $z_t \in R^m$ corresponds to the update gate that decides how much of the previous memory to keep around.

In this study, one certain stock is chosen as prediction target, its training data is firstly augmented by combining other stocks data that are clustered together with target stock. At each time step, the input for GRU neural network is a 1-dimensinal vector containing stock's daily trading information for time t.

4 Experimental Results

4.1 Data Collection

Chinese stock market is known as emerging market, where many stocks have a shorter period of existence and hence price information is insufficient to guarantee the performance of intelligent models, which suits exactly our study case. In order to compare the proposed clustering method with the naive sector cluster, we chose 7 different sectors (1.CRM:Chemical raw material, 2.GA:General aviation, 3.MI:Medical instruments, 4.MP:Mobile payment, 5.NE:New energy, 6.OE:Online education, 7.RI:Railway infrastructure) in Shanghai stock exchange (SH) (see Table 1) containing 126 stocks, with complete daily trading information (including close, open, highest, lowest price and trading volume) starting from 15 August 2013 to 03 August 2016 (incomplete stocks are filtered).

Table 1. Data collection from SH Stock Exchange

Sector number	1	2	3	4	5	6	7
Sector name	CRM	GA	MI	MP	NE	OE	RI
Number of stocks	22	9	9	8	54	11	17

As the aforementioned criterion of clustering method, the probability distribution function (PDF) of retracement for each stock is then computed, where the PDF is represented using a d-dimensional vector. The most appropriate value of d is selected as 13 by comparing the silhouette analysis results.

4.2   Silhouette Analysis of SOM Based Clustering

As a method of interpretation and validation of consistency within clusters of data, the silhouette analysis is conducted in this study as follows. Note that a specified number of cluster, which equals to 7, is firstly assigned for SOM in order to make clear comparison with naive cluster approach with 7 sectors.

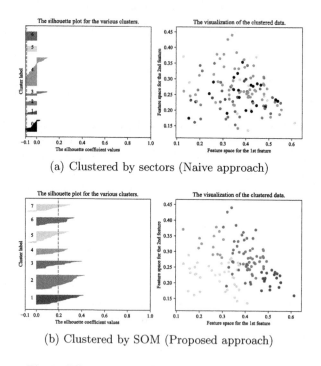

(a) Clustered by sectors (Naive approach)

(b) Clustered by SOM (Proposed approach)

Fig. 3. Silhouette analysis on stock-wise clustering

We see an average silhouette score (the dotted red line in left of Fig. 3(a)) inferior to 0 indicating that stocks of the same sector have poorly in common in terms of price reversals, which is also visually demonstrated by the clustered data on the right, while Fig. 3(b) clearly shows that SOM is effective enough to cluster similar stocks based on retracement PDF criterion, not only with a higher average silhouette score but with each cluster nearly equally sized as well.

4.3 Visualisation of Unsupervised SOM Based Clustering

We now perform unsupervised clustering as described in Sect. 3 and visualise the clustered stocks by mapping them onto the Kohonen layer as is shown in Fig. 4. There are 30×20 nodes so that most stocks could be well separated and not stacked together in one node. The colours of each node is generated using the first 3 features of its weight vector that is normalised into a $[0, 1]$ interval as RGB channels, while numbers correspond to the market code of stocks.

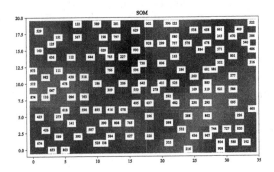

Fig. 4. SOM Clustering of 126 Stocks with coloured visualisation

Since each node of SOM learns to resemble stocks' PDF vector, it is reasonable to regard one colour block as a cluster. Hence, the author chose several stocks from different colour blocks as prediction target, where its data is firstly separated into training set and test set, and the training set is then enlarged by combining all other stock data from the same colour block.

4.4 Performing GRU Based Trend Prediction

Next day trend prediction is then made by GRU neural network, where an example learning curve is shown in Fig. 5. Daily trading information of the previous 5 days are used to predict the next day's close price trend.

First, it is clear that SOM based cluster method produced the smallest validation loss. Secondly, by observing the accuracy where minimum loss is reached, we see that our method gives the best accuracy of 0.591, while the naive approach gives 0.515, even worse than prediction on the original data set that gives 0.550. Similar analysis is done for several other stocks of different clusters and results are shown in Table 2.

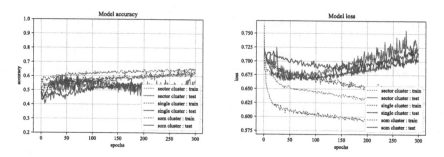

Fig. 5. Model accuracy and loss during training process for stock 601111.SH

Table 2. Prediction by GRU and SVM models

Stock code	Evaluation metric	Without data augmentation		With data augmentation			
				Naive approach		SOM approach	
		SVM	GRU	SVM	GRU	SVM	GRU
600316.SH	Accuracy	0.556	**0.573**	0.554	**0.554**	**0.614**	0.602
	F1 score	**0.620**	0.560	**0.649**	0.634	**0.684**	0.675
601111.SH	Accuracy	0.538	**0.555**	0.561	0.479	0.526	**0.591**
	F1 score	0.500	**0.536**	0.534	**0.548**	0.506	**0.612**
600804.SH	Accuracy	0.526	**0.538**	0.521	**0.591**	0.526	**0.624**
	F1 score	**0.497**	0.463	0.554	**0.646**	0.515	**0.663**

Another machine learning method SVM is introduced in order to make comparison with GRU neural network. The result shows that GRU neural network is not always better than SVM. However, the performances of both predictors are notably enhanced by the proposed approach. In contrast, the naive approach may result in worse prediction performance. Apart from improvement of accuracy, we could observe that the f1 score is especially enhanced. Since this score indicates in general the capability of detecting positive samples, namely the upward price trend in our case, our approach thus implies a better potential to make higher profits.

The result of SOM based prediction approach is somehow expected because we intend to cluster stocks with similar price reversal phenomenon so that by doing data augmentation, the model learns better temporal patterns. However, it is surprising that the naive approach, which simply combines stocks from the same sector, could also enhance the F1 score sometimes, although not as well as the proposed approach. One possible explanation could be that companies in the same sector do not have complete competitive relationships. Except for price reversal, there might be something else they have in common which enhanced the prediction by this naive data augmentation technique.

5 Conclusion and Future Work

In this paper, we show that the proposed data augmentation technique is useful for solving the problem of insufficient data that widely exists in stock market. The experimental result indicates that the proposed SOM based clustering method according to stock retracement PDF is able to enlarge the training data in a reasonable way. This technique suits for deep learning models such as RNN, and could notably improve the F1 score for price trend prediction, thus indicating a better ability to detect upward trend and make higher profits.

In future work, in order to enhance the prediction performance, it might be helpful to take preprocessing method and feature selection methods into consideration so as to filter noise and select more predictive information. Besides, doing technical analysis with additional index might also be of interest.

Acknowledgments. This work was partially supported by the National Natural Science Foundation of China (No. 61332018).

References

1. Akita, R., Yoshihara, A., Matsubara, T., Uehara, K.: Deep learning for stock prediction using numerical and textual information. In: Proceedings of the 15th IEEE/ACIS International Conference on Computer and Information Science, pp. 1–6 (2016)
2. Atsalakis, G.S., Protopapadakis, E.E., Valavanis, K.P.: Stock trend forecasting in turbulent market periods using neuro-fuzzy systems. Oper. Res. Int. J. **16**(2), 245–269 (2016)
3. Barak, S., Dahooie, J.H., Tichỳ, T.: Wrapper ANFIS-ICA method to do stock market timing and feature selection on the basis of japanese candlestick. Expert Syst. Appl. **42**(23), 9221–9235 (2015)
4. Chandar, S.K., Sumathi, M., Sivanandam, S.: Prediction of stock market price using hybrid of wavelet transform and artificial neural network. Indian J. Sci. Technol. **9**(8) (2016)
5. Cho, K., van Merrienboer, B., Gülçehre, Ç., Bahdanau, D., Bougares, F., Schwenk, H., Bengio, Y.: Learning phrase representations using RNN encoder-decoder for statistical machine translation. In: Proceedings of 2014 Conference on Empirical Methods in Natural Language Processing, pp. 1724–1734 (2014)
6. Dolson, M.: Discriminative nonlinear dimensionality reduction for improved classification. Int. J. Neural Syst. **5**(04), 313–333 (1994)
7. Engle, R.F.: The econometrics of ultra-high-frequency data. Econometrica **68**(1), 1–22 (2000)
8. Fu, T.c., Chung, F.l., Ng, V., Luk, R.: Pattern discovery from stock time series using self-organizing maps. In: Proceedings of Workshop Notes of KDD 2001 Workshop on Temporal Data Mining, pp. 26–29 (2001)
9. Gálvez, R.H., Gravano, A.: Assessing the usefulness of online message board mining in automatic stock prediction systems. J. Comput. Sci. **19**, 43–56 (2017)
10. Hadavandi, E., Shavandi, H., Ghanbari, A.: Integration of genetic fuzzy systems and artificial neural networks for stock price forecasting. Knowl.-Based Syst. **23**(8), 800–808 (2010)

11. Hartman, E.J., Keeler, J.D., Kowalski, J.M.: Layered neural networks with gaussian hidden units as universal approximations. Neural Comput. **2**(2), 210–215 (1990)
12. Hochreiter, S., Schmidhuber, J.: Long short-term memory. Neural Comput. **9**(8), 1735–1780 (1997)
13. Hsu, C.M.: A hybrid procedure for stock price prediction by integrating self-organizing map and genetic programming. Expert Syst. Appl. **38**(11), 14026–14036 (2011)
14. Jiang, Z., Chen, P., Pan, X.: Announcement based stock prediction. In: Proceedings of 2016 International Symposium on Computer, Consumer and Control, pp. 428–431 (2016)
15. Kohonen, T.: The self-organizing map. Neurocomputing **21**(1), 1–6 (1998)
16. Liu, Y., Qin, Z., Li, P., Wan, T.: Stock volatility prediction using recurrent neural networks with sentiment analysis. In: Proceedings of 30th International Conference on Industrial Engineering and Other Applications of Applied Intelligent Systems, pp. 192–201 (2017)
17. Mangiameli, P., Chen, S.K., West, D.: A comparison of som neural network and hierarchical clustering methods. Eur. J. Oper. Res. **93**(2), 402–417 (1996)
18. Nader, E., Badr, A., Fatah, A.: An intelligent framework using hybrid social media and market data, for stock prediction analysis. Int. J. Comput. Inf. Technol. **5**(3) (2016)
19. Patel, H., Parikh, S.: Comparative analysis of different statistical and neural network based forecasting tools for prediction of stock data. In: Proceedings of 2nd International Conference on Information and Communication Technology for Competitive Strategies, p. 126 (2016)
20. Rosenblatt, M., et al.: Remarks on some nonparametric estimates of a density function. Ann. Math. Stat. **27**(3), 832–837 (1956)
21. Tang, Y., Wu, Z., Meng, H.M., Xu, M., Cai, L.: Analysis on gated recurrent unit based question detection approach. In: Proceedings of 17th Annual Conference of the International Speech Communication Association, pp. 735–739 (2016)
22. Tsai, C.F., Hsiao, Y.C.: Combining multiple feature selection methods for stock prediction: Union, intersection, and multi-intersection approaches. Decis. Support Syst. **50**(1), 258–269 (2010)
23. Vapnik, V.: The Nature of Statistical Learning Theory. Springer, New York (2013)
24. Wei, J., Huang, J.: An exotic long-term pattern in stock price dynamics. PLoS ONE **7**(12), e51666 (2012)
25. Wei, L., Chen, T., Ho, T.: A hybrid model based on adaptive-network-based fuzzy inference system to forecast taiwan stock market. Expert Syst. Appl. **38**(11), 13625–13631 (2011)
26. Yang, J., Rao, R., Hong, P., Ding, P.: Ensemble model for stock price movement trend prediction on different investing periods. In: Proceedings of 12th International Conference on Computational Intelligence and Security, pp. 358–361 (2016)

Deep Candlestick Mining

Andrew D. Mann$^{(\boxtimes)}$ and Denise Gorse

Department of Computer Science, University College London,
London WC1E 6BT, UK
{A.Mann,D.Gorse}@cs.ucl.ac.uk

Abstract. A data mining process we name *Deep Candlestick Mining* (DCM) is developed using Randomised Decision Trees, Long Short Term Memory Recurrent Neural Networks and k-means++, and is shown to discover candlestick patterns significantly outperforming traditional ones. A test for the predictive ability of novel versus traditional candlestick patterns is devised using all significant candlestick patterns within the traditional or deep mined categories. The deep mined candlestick system demonstrates a remarkable ability to outperform the traditional system by 75.2% and 92.6% on the German Bund 10-year futures contract and EURUSD hourly data.

Keywords: Machine learning · LSTMs · RNNs · Decision trees · Clustering · Factor mining · OHLC Data · Candlestick patterns

1 Introduction

The ability to predict the movement of financial markets has been a longstanding aim of academics and industry practitioners, using a variety of techniques from technical analysis (TA) to machine learning (ML) and pattern recognition methodologies. Japanese candlesticks are one of the oldest forms of pattern recognition techniques used to attempt to predict markets. They were first proposed by Munehisa Homma around 1750 for charting the price behaviour of rice markets. Candlestick charts visualise an asset's price by aggregating period specific bars (e.g. 1 hour bars) consisting of open, high, low and close (OHLC) price levels, and frequently sequential patterns are used as a tool to predict future market direction. Many industry practitioners believe candlestick patterns are an effective predictive tool, though there is much debate in the academic world as to their effectiveness [1–3].

In this paper a process referred to as Deep Candlestick Mining (DCM) is proposed as a means to discover (rather than assess the value of, as in [4]) asset-specific predictive candlestick patterns using ML techniques (Randomised Decision Trees (RDT) [5], Long Short Term Memory Recurrent Neural Networks (LSTM RNNs) [6] and k-means++ [7]). DCM-based prediction is shown to substantially outperform the use of traditional candlestick patterns on hourly data for the German 10-year futures contract (FGBL) and EURUSD markets.

© Springer International Publishing AG 2017
D. Liu et al. (Eds.): ICONIP 2017, Part II, LNCS 10635, pp. 913–921, 2017.
https://doi.org/10.1007/978-3-319-70096-0_93

2   Background

2.1   Literature Review

There have been a number of past academic studies focusing on the power of candlestick patterns, reporting varying results. Most studies conclude there is little or no value in using candlestick patterns to predict future directional price movements as will be outlined below.

On the negative side, Marshall, Young and Rose (2005) [1] find that candlestick Open, High, Low, Close (OHLC) levels contain no useful information in the case of the Dow Jones Industrial Average. Further negative findings are reported by Horton (2009) [2] and by Fock, Klein, and Zwergel (2005) [3]. The latter applied candlestick charting techniques to both the DAX and the FGBL futures contract—interestingly this study presents positive findings on FGBL, but only by using the proposed deep mining process.

On the positive side significant directional prediction power is found in candlestick charting by Xie et al. (2012) [8] on US equity returns. Notably Lu (2014) [4] finds evidence of statistically significant candlestick patterns, three of which are novel, found using a simple "four-price-level" approach (although the rules were defined by Lu and not data mined as here). The results presented here show further evidence, through an exhaustive mining process, that novel candlestick patterns can be an effective tool to predict future directional price movement.

2.2   Machine Learning Models Used

Factor Importance Mining. The importance of a factor to its target is analysed using Randomised Decision Trees (RDT) [9]. To produce a ranked dictionary of factors (with most important at the top) the RDT uses the Gini impurity metric to measure the frequency of incorrect classification if a classification were to be randomly allocated; higher values indicate a greater correlation between the factor and its target.

Directional Prediction. A Long Short Term Memory Recurrent Neural Network (LSTM RNN) is used as the directional prediction model taking factors influenced from the factor importance mining step as input. The LSTM RNN is trained using RPROP [10], a first-order optimisation algorithm that uses only the sign of the partial derivative, ignoring magnitude, and acts independently on each weight. RPROP is beneficial in data-intensive applications as it provides a computationally cheap and fast-converging locally adaptive method for binary classification (here, into price movements predicted to be up or down).

Candlestick Mining. K-means++ is used to cluster the LSTM RNN test set factors. K-means++ is a data mining clustering algorithm which improves on k-means by providing an approximate solution to the NP-hard problem of selecting initial cluster centroids. We will later analyse these clusters to find out what directionally predicting OHLC patterns they represent.

2.3   Dataset Usage

Eleven years of hourly data are used, as shown in Fig. 1. The LSTM RNN is trained using five years of data. A dataset of two years is then used to assess the LSTM RNN's performance. This performance is then analysed and the factors used clustered to extract meaning—this is where the deep candlestick mining occurs. A further dataset of two years is used to select those candlestick patterns most effective in prediction. A final two years of data is used as an out of sample test set to assess the effectiveness of the developed candlestick prediction system.

[5 YEARS]	[2 YEARS]	[2 YEARS]	[2 YEARS]
LSTM RNN TRAIN SET	LSTM RNN TESTING & K-MEANS++ (CANDLESTICK MINING)	FILTER CANDLESTICKS FOR SIGNIFICANCE	TEST CANDLESTICK PREDICTION SYSTEM
[DATASET 1]	[DATASET 2]	[DATASET 3]	[DATASET 4]

Fig. 1. Dataset usage

2.4   Performance Metrics

Directional accuracy and Normalised Percentage Better than Random (NPBR) are used as evaluation metrics in this study. The former is simply the proportion of correct predictions whereas NPBR (also known as the Kappa Statistic [11]), as used by us previously [13], is more appropriate in trending markets, where there would be a tendency to overpredict the majority class. NPBR, which ranges from -100% to 100%, heavily penalises such overprediction and would assign a value of 0%—equivalent to random chance—to the case in which all instances were assigned to the majority class.

3   Methodology

3.1   OHLC Factor Mining

All possible combinations of ratios and differences of one hour OHLC data are calculated given L lags. Randomised Decision Trees are then used to rank the importance of each factor to a target (in this case the future close price directional change), deriving the importance value from the Gini metric. The top N factors are selected by inspection of the Gini metric curve. As can be seen in Fig. 2 the Gini metric curve noticeably flattens for FGBL beyond $N = 100$, though this is not the case for EURUSD. N should ideally be optimised for each asset when selecting a factor universe. However to keep a consistent approach in demonstrating the Deep Candlestick Mining process we chose to use a constant $N = 100$ here with no further optimization; the results presented below are therefore a general indication of the process's utility.

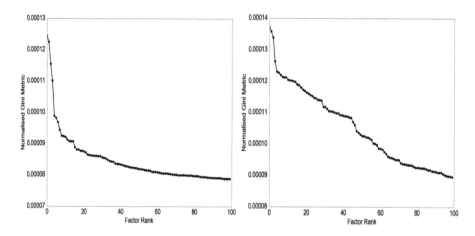

Fig. 2. Three-Lag importance mining curve: FGBL (left) and EURUSD (right)

Using the top N factor universe a further filtering is then applied focusing on correlation of factor-to-target (ft) and factor-to-factor (ff). Factors that pass the tests $|corr_{ft}| \leq c_1$ and $|corr_{ff}| \geq c_2$ make the optimal factor universe, with c_1 and c_2 being optimised on Dataset 1 (see Fig. 1).

3.2   Close-Price Directional Prediction

The optimal factors are then standardised and used as inputs to the LSTM RNN with targets of -1 (down) and $+1$ (up). The network architecture used 8 hidden LSTM units with a weight decay factor of 2%. Other architecture configurations were tested but results were found to be robust to reasonable variations of these quantities. It was decided not to optimise the network parameters to avoid the risk of overfitting. As with the decision in Sect. 3.1 to use a constant $N = 100$, results can therefore be viewed as a performance indicator where there is scope to improve the process.

3.3   Clustering

The LSTM RNN factors which were used to perform the directional prediction (Dataset 2) are now clustered using k-means++, where k is selected by maximising the Silhouette Coefficient [14]. An initial (parent) clustering revealed an interesting split in the data structure at $k = 2$, which was verified as real by plotting the magnitude of each factor dimension and verifying the clusters had very different structure. This clustering was then re-clustered into child clusters with the aim of revealing more interesting candlestick patterns. The optimal parent and child clustering configuration was found at $k = 2,6$ and $k = 2,9$ for FGBL and EURUSD respectfully. Other clustering techniques and k-selection criteria

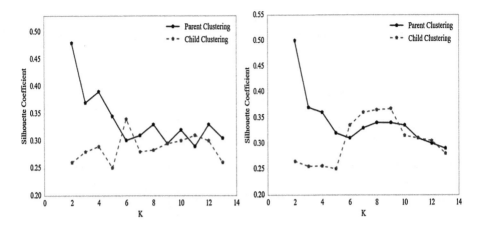

Fig. 3. Three-Lag silhouette coefficients: FGBL (left) and EURUSD (right)

could have been used; however the optimal selection of a clustering algorithm and associated selection criteria is outside the scope of this paper.

3.4   Candlestick Mining

For each cluster we look at: (1) the LSTM RNN's NPBR; (2) the direction the cluster represents. The latter is done by indexing each candidate in a cluster and computing an up-movement ratio (defined as proportion of up movements at $t+1$). It is important to confirm the LSTM RNN predicts the same direction the cluster is representing. If the LSTM RNN's NPBR is greater than 0%, the percentage of up movements deviates from 50% (indicating a directional bias) and the LSTM RNN's majority prediction direction agrees with the direction the cluster represents, then the cluster is valid. Clusters are then further validated by for each member identifying the OHLC patterns it corresponds to, in order to ensure the clustering did indeed group together patterns of similar shape; in all instances this was found to be the case. The mined candlestick patterns will be the centroids of the clusters. These patterns are essentially what the LSTM RNN would have 'seen' if it had been looking at OHLC data as a human might look at a candlestick chart when a prediction was made.

4   Results

4.1   Traditional Candlestick Patterns

To assess the power of the deep mined candlestick patterns against an appropriate baseline an assessment of 100 bull (predicting up) and bear (predicting down) traditional candlestick patterns (50 candlestick types)[1] were tested on FGBL and EURUSD hourly data (Dataset 3). Significance levels were calculated using a binomial distribution (as in [12]), where the null hypothesis was "candlesticks are no better than guessing," which translates to 50% directional accuracy. *Significant candlesticks* (see Table 1) are patterns with a directional predictive power significant at 10% or better.

Table 1. Significant traditional candlestick patterns

Candlestick pattern	Asset	Number of candlesticks	N	Accuracy	Type	Significance level
Advanced block	FGBL	3	83	54.21%	Bear	*
3 Outside	FGBL	3	74	54.05%	Bull	*
3 Inside	FGBL	3	20	55.00%	Bear	**
Harami	FGBL	2	104	52.88%	Bear	*
Harami	EURUSD	2	238	57.14%	Bull	*
Inverted hammer	EURUSD	1	76	55.26%	Bull	*
Matching low	EURUSD	2	221	55.20%	Bull	**
Advanced block	EURUSD	3	130	53.80%	Bear	*

(*: significant at 10%; **: significant at 5%; * * *: significant at 1%)

It should be noted from the above that only four patterns were significant at the 5% and 10% levels and no pattern was significant at the 1% level. Hence while there is some predictive ability in traditional candlestick patterns it appears not to be widespread, in line with the negative results of the majority of academic studies into candlestick charting.

4.2   Deep Mined Candlestick Patterns

Deep mined candlestick patterns are dataset-specific, being mined from the dataset the LSTM RNN predicted on. For FGBL eight candlesticks were found to be significant at 10% or better; for EURUSD this number was five. The significant patterns for both datasets are listed in Table 2.

Interestingly there were two significant candlestick patterns on EURUSD at the 1% level, while in contrast no patterns were found to be significant at this

---

[1] 2 Crows; 3 Black Crows; 3 Inside; 3 Line Strike; 3 Outside; 3 Stars in South; 3 White Soldiers; Abandoned Baby; Advance Block; Belt Hold; Break Away; Closing Marubozu; Conceal Baby Swell; Counter Attack; Dark Cloud Cover; Down Side Gap 3 Methods; Downside Gap 2 Crows; Engulfing; Evening Star; Gap Side White; Hammer; Hanging Man; Harami; High Wave; Hikkake; Hikkake Mod; Homing Pigeon; Identical 3 Crows; In Neck; Inverted Hammer; Ladder Bottom; Long Line; Marubozu; Mat Hold; Matching Low; Morning Star; Piercing; Rise Fall 3 Methods; Separating Lines; Shooting Star; Short Line; Spinning Top; Stalled Pattern; Stick Sandwich; Takuri; Tasuki Gap; Thrusting; Tri Star; Unique 3 River.

Table 2. Significant deep mined patterns

Candlestick pattern	Asset	Number of candlesticks	N	Accuracy	Type	Significance level
Pattern 0,2	FGBL	2	565	53.09%	Bull	*
Pattern 3,1	FGBL	2	83	61.44%	Bear	**
Pattern 1,0	FGBL	3	30	60.00%	Bull	*
Pattern 0,6	FGBL	3	92	59.78%	Bear	**
Pattern 5,6	FGBL	2	178	58.43%	Bear	**
Pattern 2,1	FGBL	2	563	55.06%	Bear	**
Pattern 5,2	FGBL	2	150	55.33%	Bear	*
Pattern 4,1	FGBL	2	408	53.19%	Bear	*
Pattern 1,1	EURUSD	4	312	58.01%	Bull	* * *
Pattern 1,3	EURUSD	4	47	57.44%	Bull	*
Pattern 1,7	EURUSD	4	156	58.33%	Bull	**
Pattern 1,0	EURUSD	3	73	62.64%	Bull	*
Pattern 1,6	EURUSD	2	470	57.02%	Bear	* * *

(*: significant at 10%; **: significant at 5%; * * *: significant at 1%)

level for traditional patterns. Moreover the significant deep mined candlesticks have an average accuracy of 57.04% and 57.7% on FGBL and EURUSD respectively, while the average accuracy for the significant traditional patterns was in comparison 54.04% on FGBL and 55.35% on EURUSD, showing the deep mined patterns outperformed the traditional patterns by 3% and 2.35% respectively.

Figures 4 and 5 show examples of novel patterns discovered by the deep candlestick mining (DCM) process. It is notable that clusters 0,2 and 2,1 in Fig. 4 (FGBL) look very similar to the bullish and bearish Engulfing candlestick pattern in reverse. Deep mined candlestick pattern 0,2 (leftmost) is in fact a traditional candlestick pattern called Bearish Harami which was identified as being significant when the traditional candlestick patterns were analysed. This is an important point as it shows the deep mining process can both find new candlestick patterns and identify significant traditional ones.

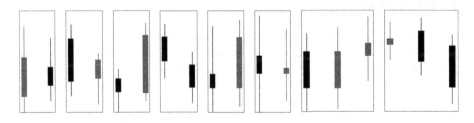

Fig. 4. FGBL candlestick patterns: 0,2; 2,1; 3,1; 4,1; 5,2; 5,6; 0,6; 1,0

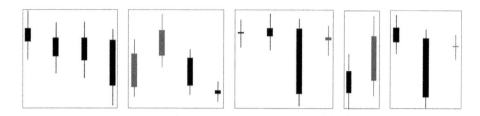

Fig. 5. EURUSD candlestick patterns: 1,1; 1,3; 1,7; 1,6; 1,0

Candlestick patterns for EURUSD (examples in Fig. 5) appear on average to require more lags to be significant, implying a greater level of information content is required to make correct predictions. For EURUSD there were no discovered correspondences between mined and significant traditional patterns.

4.3   Traditional Vs. Deep Mined Candlestick System

Often a practitioner will use multiple candlestick patterns for making decisions. A comparison in this spirit between traditional and deep mined candlesticks was carried out by using all the patterns available in either category. Dataset 4 was used to assess the predictive power of both systems, in terms of NPBR. As can be seen in Table 3 the DCM system outperformed the traditional system by 75.2% and 92.6% on FGBL and EURUSD respectively.

Table 3. Traditional prediction system vs. deep mined prediction system

Asset	Number of traditional patterns	Traditional NPBR	Number of deep mined patterns	Deep mined NPBR
FGBL	4	3.48%	8	6.10%
EURUSD	4	6.52%	5	12.56%

5   Discussion

The deep candlestick mining (DCM) process introduced here has been shown to be remarkably effective at discovering statistically significant OHLC patterns. This is not in conflict with the many academic studies which claim candlestick patterns have no, or limited, predictive power [1–3] because the patterns the DCM process discovers are largely novel (though for FGBL some interesting correspondences with traditional candlestick patterns were discovered). DCM-derived patterns outperformed the best-discovered traditional patterns by 75.2% and 92.6% on FGBL and EURUSD respectively in relation to their ability to forecast directional movement better than random. The DCM process has many parts that could be further optimised to produce potentially better results. It would be expected these optimisations would be both asset and time period granularity (daily, hourly, minute, etc.) dependent. The results here are therefore only an early indication of the promise of deep candlestick mining.

References

1. Marshall, B., Young, M., Rose, L.: Candlestick technical trading strategies: Can they create value for investors? J. Bank. Finance **30**, 2303–2323 (2005)
2. Horton, M.: Stars, crows, and doji: The use of candlesticks in stock selection. Q. Rev. Econ. Finance **49**, 283–294 (2009)
3. Fock, J., Klein, C., Zwergel, B.: Performance of candlestick analysis on intraday futures data. J. Deriv. **13**(1), 28–40 (2005)
4. Lu, T.: The profitability of candlestick charting in the Taiwan stock market. Pac.-Basin Financial J. **26**, 65–78 (2014)
5. Geurts, P., Ernst, D., Wehenkel, L.: Extremely randomized trees. Mach. Learn. **63**, 3–42 (2006)
6. Hochreiter, S., Schmidhuber, J.: Long short-term memory. Neural Comput. **9**(8), 1735–1780 (1997)
7. Arthur, D., Vassilvitskii, S.: k-means++: the advantages of careful seeding. In: 18th Annual ACM-SIAM Symposium on Discrete Algorithms, pp. 1027–1035. Society for Industrial and Applied Mathematics Philadelphia (2007)
8. Xie, H., Zhao, X., Wang, S.: A comprehensive look at the predictive information in Japanese candlesticks. In: International Conference on Computational Science (2012)
9. Breiman, L., Friedman, R.A., Olshen, R.A., Stone, C.G.: Classification and Regression Trees. Wadsworth, Pacific Grove, CA (1984)
10. Riedmiller, M., Braun, H.: A direct adaptive method for faster backpropagation learning: The RPROP algorithm. In: IEEE International Conference Neural Networks, pp. 586–591 (1993)
11. Smeeton, N.C.: Early history of the kappa statistic. Biometrics 41, 795. JSTOR 2531300 (1985)
12. Prado, A.H., Ferneda, E., Morais R.C.L., Luiz, B.J.A., Matsura, E.: On the effectiveness of candlestick chart analysis for the Brazilian stock market. In: 17th International Conference in Knowledge Based and Intelligent Information and Engineering Systems, vol. 22, pp. 1136–1145, Procedia Computer Science (2013)
13. Mann, A.D., Gorse, D.: A new methodology to exploit predictive power in (open, high, low, close) data. In: 26th International Conference on Artificial Neural Networks, Sardinia, September 2017. (in press)
14. Rousseeuw, J.P.: Silhouettes: A graphical aid to the interpretation and validation of cluster analysis. J. Comput. Appl. Math. **20**, 53–65 (1987)

Author Index

Printed in the United States
By Bookmasters